W9-CSA-272

THE PRESIDENTIAL ELECTION OF 2020

Joe Biden (Democrat) total electoral votes: 306

Donald Trump (Republican) total electoral votes: 232

Margin of victory:
<5%   5–10%   >10%

Margin of victory:
<5%   5–10%   >10%

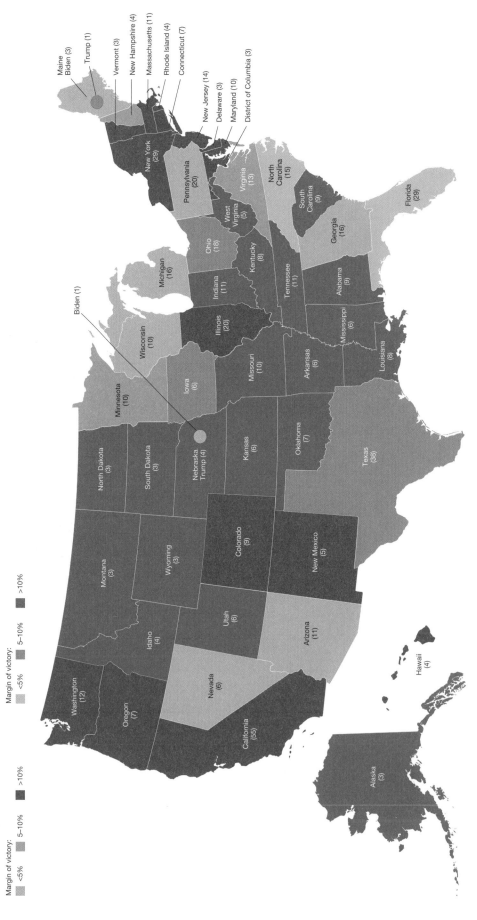

Source: "2020 Presidential Election Live Results," 270 to Win, www.270towin.com/2020-election-results-live/ (accessed 11/17/20).

CORE
★ *edition* ★
13

We the People

An Introduction to American Politics

CORE
★ *edition* ★
13

We the People

An Introduction to American Politics

★ **BENJAMIN GINSBERG**
THE JOHNS HOPKINS UNIVERSITY

★ **THEODORE J. LOWI**
LATE OF CORNELL UNIVERSITY

★ **MARGARET WEIR**
BROWN UNIVERSITY

★ **CAROLINE J. TOLBERT**
UNIVERSITY OF IOWA

★ **ANDREA L. CAMPBELL**
MASSACHUSETTS INSTITUTE OF TECHNOLOGY

W. W. NORTON & COMPANY
Independent Publishers Since 1923

W. W. Norton & Company has been independent since its founding in 1923, when William Warder Norton and Mary D. Herter Norton first published lectures delivered at the People's Institute, the adult education division of New York City's Cooper Union. The firm soon expanded its program beyond the Institute, publishing books by celebrated academics from America and abroad. By midcentury, the two major pillars of Norton's publishing program—trade books and college texts—were firmly established. In the 1950s, the Norton family transferred control of the company to its employees, and today—with a staff of five hundred and hundreds of trade, college, and professional titles published each year—W. W. Norton & Company stands as the largest and oldest publishing house owned wholly by its employees.

Copyright © 2021, 2019, 2017, 2015, 2013, 2011, 2009, 2007, 2005, 2003, 2001, 1999, 1997 by W. W. Norton & Company, Inc.

All rights reserved
Printed in Canada

Editor: Peter Lesser
Project Editor: Laura Dragonette
Associate Editor: Anna Olcott
Developmental Editor: John Elliott
Manuscript Editor: Sarah Johnson
Managing Editor, College: Marian Johnson
Managing Editor, College Digital Media: Kim Yi
Production Manager, College: Elizabeth Marotta
Media Editor: Spencer Richardson-Jones
Media Editorial Assistant: Lena Nowak-Laird
Media Project Editor: Marcus Van Harpen

Marketing Manager, Political Science: Ashley Sherwood
Art Director: Lissi Sigillo
Text Design: Jen Montgomery
Photo Editor: Thomas Persano
Photo Researcher: Donna Ranieri
Director of College Permissions: Megan Schindel
Permissions Consultant: Elizabeth Trammell
Information Graphics: Kiss Me I'm Polish LLC, New York
Composition: Graphic World, Inc.
Manufacturing: Transcontinental

Permission to use copyrighted material is included in the credits section of this book, which begins on page A73.

Library of Congress Cataloging-in-Publication Data

Names: Ginsberg, Benjamin, author. | Lowi, Theodore J., author. |
    Weir, Margaret, author. | Tolbert, Caroline J., author. | Campbell,
    Andrea Louise, 1966- author.
Title: We the people : an introduction to American politics / Benjamin
    Ginsberg, The Johns Hopkins University, Theodore J. Lowi, late of
    Cornell University, Margaret Weir, Brown University, Caroline J.
    Tolbert, University of Iowa, Andrea L. Campbell, Massachusetts Insitute
    of Technology.
Description: Thirteenth edition. | New York : W.W. Norton & Company, [2021] |
    Includes bibliographical references and index.
Identifiers: LCCN 2020051064 | ISBN 9780393427035 (hardcover)
Subjects: LCSH: United States—Politics and government—Textbooks.
Classification: LCC JK276.G55 2021 | DDC 320.473—dc23
LC record available at https://lccn.loc.gov/2020051064

ISBN: 978-0-393-42701-1

W. W. Norton & Company, Inc., 500 Fifth Avenue, New York, N.Y. 10110
www.wwnorton.com

W. W. Norton & Company Ltd., 15 Carlisle Street, London W1D 3BS

2 3 4 5 6 7 8 9 0

To:

Sandy, Cindy, and Alex Ginsberg

David, Jackie, Eveline, and Ed Dowling

Dave, Marcella, Logan, and Kennah Campbell

Contents

4 ★ Civil Liberties 98

PART II POLITICS

6 ★ Public Opinion 180

7 ★ The Media   226

10 ★ Campaigns and Elections 344

11 ★ Groups and Interests 394

PART III INSTITUTIONS

12 ★ Congress 428

13 ★ The Presidency   472

Appendix

Preface

· ·

The coronavirus pandemic and the racial injustice protests raging across the nation vividly display the relevance of government to the lives of ordinary Americans—even to those normally absorbed by school, work, and family. These profound events also reaffirm the commitment of this book to exploring the fundamental democratic question: Why should we be engaged with government and politics? Through the first 12 editions, we sought to answer this question by making the text directly relevant to the lives of the students who would be reading it. We tried to make politics interesting by demonstrating that students' concerns are at stake and that they therefore need to take a personal, even selfish, interest in the outcomes of government. With many students newly attentive and energized, we realize that they need guidance in how to become politically engaged. Beyond providing students with a core of political knowledge, we show them how they can apply that knowledge as participants in the political process. The (**NEW**) How To sections in Chapters 1, 3, 6, 7, 8, 10, 11, 12, and 14 help achieve that goal.

As events from the past several years have reminded us, "what government does" inevitably raises questions about political participation and political equality. The size and composition of the electorate, for example, affect who is elected to public office and what policy directions the government will pursue. Challenges to election administration, from the reliability of voting machines, to the ability of local officials to handle the many complications of running a voting operation during a global pandemic, became important in the 2020 election. Many questions arose about the integrity of the voting process, from fears of foreign attacks to concerns that there was not enough mail-in voting—or too much. Fierce debates about the policies of the Trump administration have heightened students' interest in politics. Other recent events have underscored how Americans from different backgrounds experience politics. Arguments about immigration became contentious as the nation once again debated the question of who is entitled to be an American and have a voice in determining what the government does. Debates about who benefited from pandemic relief legislation—and who slipped through the cracks—raised questions about which interests have effective voices in government policy. And charges that the police often use excessive violence against members of minority groups have raised questions about whether the government treats all Americans equally. Reflecting all of these trends, this new Thirteenth Edition shows more than any other book on the market (1) how students are connected to government, (2) why students should think critically about government and politics, and (3) how Americans from different backgrounds experience and shape politics.

To help us explore these themes, Professor Andrea Campbell has joined us as the most recent in a group of distinguished coauthors. Professor Campbell's scholarly work focuses on the ways in which government and politics affect the lives of ordinary citizens. Among her contributions are new chapter introductions that focus on stories of individuals and how government has affected them. Many Americans, particularly the young, can have difficulty seeing the role of government in their everyday lives. Indeed, that's a chief explanation of low voter participation among younger citizens. The new chapter openers profile various individuals and illustrate their interactions with government, from college students organizing a march against racial injustice in their hometown and attracting 15,000 people (Chapter 8), to a small business owner receiving relief payments during the coronavirus pandemic (Chapter 12), to a convict-turned-lawyer fighting to restore former felons' voting rights (Chapter 5). Several chapters highlight the racial injustice protests following the killing of George Floyd in May 2020, and many show how the pandemic affects ordinary Americans and their interactions with government.

Several other elements of the book also help show students why politics and government should matter to them. These include:

- **(NEW) How To guides** feature interviews with political experts to provide students with concrete advice about how to participate in politics. These guides offer easy-to-follow instructions about getting involved in politics in effective ways.

- **Who Are Americans? infographics**—many new and updated for the Thirteenth Edition—ask students to think critically about how Americans from different backgrounds experience politics. These sections use bold, engaging graphics to present a statistical snapshot of the nation related to each chapter's topic. Critical-thinking questions are included in each infographic.

- **Who Participates? infographics** show students how different groups of Americans participate in key aspects of politics and government, using engaging graphics and thought-provoking questions. The InQuizitive course includes accompanying exercises that encourage students to engage with these features.

- **America Side by Side boxes** in every chapter use data figures and tables to provide a comparative perspective. By comparing political institutions and behavior across countries, students gain a better understanding of how specific features of the American system shape politics.

- **Up-to-date coverage**, with more than 20 pages and numerous graphics on the 2020 elections, including a 12-page section devoted to analysis of these momentous elections in Chapter 10, as well as updated data, examples, and other information throughout the book.

- **For Critical Analysis questions** are incorporated throughout the text. For Critical Analysis questions in the margins of every chapter prompt students' own critical thinking about the material in the chapter, encouraging them to engage with the topic.

- **What Do You Think? chapter conclusions** ask students to relate the chapter content and the personal profiles that begin each chapter to fundamental questions about the American political system and to reflect on the significance of government to the lives of individuals.

- **(NEW) Weekly News Quiz feature** engages students with contemporary political news stories (in print, video, or podcast form) and the key concepts of the course. The Weekly News Quiz is supported by assessment and suggestions for classroom use.
- **This Thirteenth Edition is accompanied by InQuizitive**, Norton's award-winning formative, adaptive online quizzing program. The InQuizitive course for *We the People* guides students through questions organized around the text's chapter learning objectives to ensure mastery of the core information and to help with assessment. More information and a demonstration are available at digital.wwnorton.com/wethepeople13core.

We note with regret the passing of Theodore Lowi as well as Margaret Weir's decision to step down from the book. We miss them but continue to hear their voices and to benefit from their wisdom in the pages of our book. We also continue to hope that our book will itself be accepted as a form of enlightened political action. This Thirteenth Edition is another chance. It is an advancement toward our goal. We promise to keep trying.

Acknowledgments

· ·

We are pleased to acknowledge the many colleagues who had an active role in criticism and preparation of the manuscript. Our thanks go to:

Amy Acord, Lone Star College–CyFair

Janet Adamski, University of Mary Hardin-Baylor

Craig Albert, Augusta University

Maria J. Albo, University of North Georgia

Andrea Aleman, University of Texas at San Antonio

Stephen P. Amberg, University of Texas at San Antonio

Molly Andolina, DePaul University

Lydia Andrade, University of the Incarnate Word

Milan Andrejevich, Ivy Tech Community College

Greg Andrews, St. Petersburg College

Steve Anthony, Georgia State University

Brian Arbour, John Jay College, CUNY

Phillip Ardoin, Appalachian State University

Gregory Arey, Cape Fear Community College

Juan F. Arzola, College of the Sequoias

Joan Babcock, Northwest Vista College

Ellen Baik, University of Texas–Pan American

Ross K. Baker, Rutgers University

Thomas J. Baldino, Wilkes University

Evelyn Ballard, Houston Community College

Robert Ballinger, South Texas College

Alexa Bankert, University of Georgia

M. E. Banks, Virginia Commonwealth University

Mary Barnes-Tilley, Blinn College

Nathan Barrick, University of South Florida

Robert Bartels, Evangel University

Nancy Bednar, Antelope Valley College

Christina Bejarano, University of Kansas

Paul T. Bellinger, Jr., Stephen F. Austin State University

Annie Benifield, Lone Star College–Tomball

Donna Bennett, Trinity Valley Community College

Sarah Binder, Brookings Institution

David Birch, Lone Star College–Tomball

Daniel Birdsong, University of Dayton

Jeff Birdsong, Northeastern Oklahoma A&M College

Paul Blakelock, Lone Star College–Kingwood

Melanie J. Blumberg, California University of Pennsylvania

Louis Bolce, Baruch College

Matthew T. Bradley, Indiana University–Kokomo

Amy Brandon, El Paso Community College

Phil Branyon, University of North Georgia

Mark Brewer, University of Maine

Lynn Brink, Dallas College–North Lake

Gary Brown, Lone Star College–Montgomery

Sara Butler, College of the Desert

Joe Campbell, Johnson County Community College

Bill Carroll, Sam Houston State University

Jim Cauthen, John Jay College, CUNY

Ed Chervenak, University of New Orleans

Jeffrey W. Christiansen, Seminole State College

Gary Church, Dallas College–Mountain View

Mark Cichock, University of Texas at Arlington

Adrian Stefan Clark, Del Mar College

Dewey Clayton, University of Louisville

Jeff Colbert, Elon University

Cory Colby, Lone Star College–Tomball

Annie Cole, Los Angeles City College

John Coleman, University of Wisconsin–Madison

Darin Combs, Tulsa Community College

Greg Combs, University of Texas at Dallas

Sean Conroy, University of New Orleans

Amanda Cook Fesperman, Illinois Valley Community College

Paul Cooke, Lone Star College–CyFair

Cassandra Cookson, Lee College

Kevin Corder, Western Michigan University

McKinzie Craig, Marietta College

Brian Cravens, Blinn College

Christopher Cronin, Methodist University

John Crosby, California State University–Chico

Anthony Daniels, University of Toledo

Courtenay Daum, Colorado State University

Kevin Davis, North Central Texas College

Paul Davis, Truckee Meadows Community College

Terri Davis, Lamar University

Vida Davoudi, Lone Star College–Kingwood

Jennifer De Maio, California State University–Northridge

Louis DeSipio, University of California–Irvine

Robert DiClerico, West Virginia University

Corey Ditslear, University of North Texas

Peter Doas, University of Texas–Pan American

Kathy Dolan, University of Wisconsin–Milwaukee

John Domino, Sam Houston State University

Doug Dow, University of Texas at Dallas

Jeremy Duff, Midwestern State University

Jenna Duke, Lehigh Carbon Community College

Francisco Durand, University of Texas at San Antonio

Christopher D'Urso, Valencia College

Bruce R. Drury, Lamar University

Denise Dutton, University of Tulsa

Daphne Eastman, Odessa College

Carrie Eaves, Elon University

Sheryl Edwards, University of Michigan–Dearborn

Lauren Elliott-Dorans, Ohio University

Ryan Emenaker, College of the Redwoods

Heather Evans, Sam Houston State University

Andrew I. E. Ewoh, Texas Southern University

Hyacinth Ezeamii, Albany State University

Dennis Falcon, Cerritos College

William Feagin, Jr., Wharton County Junior College

Otto Feinstein, Wayne State University

Leslie Feldman, Hofstra University

Kathleen Ferraiolo, James Madison University

Del Fields, St. Petersburg College

Glen Findley, Odessa College

Bob Fitrakis, Columbus State Community College

Brian Fletcher, Truckee Meadows Community College

Paul M. Flor, El Camino College Compton Center

Elizabeth Flores, Del Mar College

Paul Foote, Eastern Kentucky University

Brandon Franke, Blinn College

Heather Frederick, Slippery Rock University

Adam Fuller, Youngstown State University

Frank Garrahan, Austin Community College

Steve Garrison, Midwestern State University

Michael Gattis, Gulf Coast State College

Jason Ghibesi, Ocean County College

Patrick Gilbert, Lone Star College–Tomball

Kathleen Gille, Office of Representative David Bonior

James Gimpel, University of Maryland at College Park

Jill Glaathar, Southwest Missouri State University

Randy Glean, Midwestern State University

Jimmy Gleason, Purdue University

Donna Godwin, Trinity Valley Community College

Christi Gramling, Charleston Southern University

Matthew Green, Catholic University of America

Steven Greene, North Carolina State University

Jeannie Grussendorf, Georgia State University

Matt Guardino, Providence College

Precious Hall, Truckee Meadows Community College

Sally Hansen, Daytona State College

Tiffany Harper, Collin College

Todd Hartman, Appalachian State University

Mary Jane Hatton, Hawaii Pacific University

M. Ahad Hayaud-Din, Brookhaven College

Virginia Haysley, Lone Star College–Tomball

David Head, John Tyler Community College

Barbara Headrick, Minnesota State University, Moorhead

David Helpap, University of Wisconsin–Green Bay

Rick Henderson, Texas State University–San Marcos

Shaun Herness, George Washington University

Rodney Hero, University of California–Berkeley

Richard Herrera, Arizona State University

Thaddaus Hill, Blinn College

Alexander Hogan, Lone Star College–CyFair

Justin Hoggard, Three Rivers Community College

Steven Holmes, Bakersfield College

Kevin Holton, South Texas College

Steven Horn, Everett Community College

Joseph Howard, University of Central Arkansas

Glen Hunt, Austin Community College

Teresa L. Hutchins, Georgia Highlands College

John Patrick Ifedi, Howard University

Cryshanna A. Jackson Leftwich, Youngstown State University

Robin Jacobson, University of Puget Sound

Amy Jasperson, Rhodes College

Mark Jendrysik, University of North Dakota

Krista Jenkins, Fairleigh Dickinson University

Loch Johnson, University of Georgia

Joseph Jozwiak, Texas A&M University–Corpus Christi

Carlos Juárez, Hawaii Pacific University

Mark Kann, University of Southern California

Demetra Kasimis, California State University–Long Beach

Eric T. Kasper, University of Wisconsin–Eau Claire

Robert Katzmann, Brookings Institution

Nancy Kinney, Washtenaw Community College

William Klein, St. Petersburg College

Casey Klofstad, University of Miami

Aaron Knight, Houston Community College

Kathleen Knight, University of Houston

Robin Kolodny, Temple University

Melinda Kovacs, Missouri Western State University

Nancy Kral, Lone Star College–Tomball

Douglas Kriner, Boston University

Thom Kuehls, Weber State University

Ashlyn Kuersten, Western Michigan University

Rick Kurtz, Central Michigan University

Paul Labedz, Valencia College

Elise Langan, John Jay College of Criminal Justice

Boyd Lanier, Lamar University

Jennifer L. Lawless, American University

Jeff Lazarus, Georgia State University

Jeffrey Lee, Blinn College

Alan Lehmann, Blinn College

Julie Lester, Middle Georgia State University

LaDella Levy, College of Southern Nevada

Steven Lichtman, Shippensburg University

Robert C. Lieberman, Columbia University

Timothy Lim, California State University–Los Angeles

Kara Lindaman, Winona State University

Mary Linder, Grayson College

Samuel Lingrosso, Los Angeles Valley College

Mark Logas, Valencia Community College

Fred Lokken, Truckee Meadows Community College

Timothy Lynch, University of Wisconsin–Milwaukee

William Lyons, University of Tennessee at Knoxville

Scott MacDougall, Diablo Valley College

Shari MacLachlan, Palm Beach State College

David Mann, College of Charleston

David A. Marcum, Laramie County Community College

Christopher Marshall, South Texas College

Guy Martin, Winston-Salem State University

Laura R. Winsky Mattei, State University of New York at Buffalo

Mandy May, College of Southern Maryland

Phil McCall, Portland State University

Kelly McDaniel, Three Rivers Community College

Larry McElvain, South Texas College

Corinna R. McKoy, Ventura College

Elizabeth McLane, Wharton County Junior College

Eddie L. Meaders, University of North Texas

Rob Mellen, Mississippi State University

Marilyn S. Mertens, Midwestern State University

Suzanne Mettler, Cornell University

Eric Miller, Blinn College

Michael Miller, Barnard College

Don D. Mirjanian, College of Southern Nevada

R. Shea Mize, Georgia Highlands College

Fred Monardi, College of Southern Nevada

Dana Morales, Montgomery College

Nicholas Morgan, Collin College

Vincent Moscardelli, University of Connecticut

Matthew Murray, Dutchess Community College

Christopher Muste, University of Montana

Jason Mycoff, University of Delaware

Carolyn Myers, Southwestern Illinois College–Belleville

Sugumaran Narayanan, Midwestern State University

Jalal Nejad, Northwest Vista College

Adam Newmark, Appalachian State University

Stephen Nicholson, University of California–Merced

Joseph Njoroge, Abraham Baldwin Agricultural College

Larry Norris, South Plains College

Anthony Nownes, University of Tennessee at Knoxville

Elizabeth Oldmixon, University of North Texas

Anthony O'Regan, Los Angeles Valley College

Harold "Trey" Orndorff III, Daytona State College

John Osterman, San Jacinto College–Central

Cissie Owen, Lamar University

Richard Pacelle, University of Tennessee at Knoxville

Randall Parish, University of North Georgia

Michelle Pautz, University of Dayton

Mark Peplowski, College of Southern Nevada

Maria Victoria Perez-Rios, John Jay College, CUNY

Robert L. Perry, University of Texas of the Permian Basin

Gerhard Peters, Citrus College

Michael Petri, Santa Ana College

Michael Pickering, Tulane University

Eric Plutzer, Pennsylvania State University

Sarah Poggione, Florida International University

Andrew Polsky, Hunter College, CUNY

Christopher Poulios, Nassau Community College

Michael A. Powell, Frederick Community College

Suzanne Preston, St. Petersburg College

Wayne Pryor, Brazosport College

David Putz, Lone Star College–Kingwood

Donald Ranish, Antelope Valley College

David Rankin, State University of New York at Fredonia

Grant Reeher, Syracuse University

Elizabeth A. Rexford, Wharton County Junior College

Richard Rich, Virginia Polytechnic

Glenn W. Richardson, Jr., Kutztown University of Pennsylvania

Sara Rinfret, University of Wisconsin–Green Bay

Andre Robinson, Pulaski Technical College

Jason Robles, Colorado State University

Paul Roesler, St. Charles Community College

J. Philip Rogers, San Antonio College

Susan Roomberg, University of Texas at San Antonio

Auksuole Rubavichute, Dallas College–Mountain View

Andrew Rudalevige, Bowdoin College

Ionas Aurelian Rus, University of Cincinnati–Blue Ash

Ryan Rynbrandt, Collin College

Robert Sahr, Oregon State University

Mario Salas, Northwest Vista College

Michael Sanchez, San Antonio College

Amanda Sanford, Louisiana Tech University

Elizabeth Saunders, Georgetown University

Mary Schander, Pasadena City College

Thomas Schmeling, Rhode Island College

Laura Schneider, Grand Valley State University

Ronnee Schreiber, San Diego State University

Ronald Schurin, University of Connecticut

Kathleen Searles, Louisiana State University

Jason Seitz, Georgia Perimeter College

Jennifer Seitz, Georgia Perimeter College

Allen K. Settle, California Polytechnic State University

Subash Shah, Winston-Salem State University

Greg Shaw, Illinois Wesleyan University

Kelly B. Shaw, Iowa State University

Mark Shomaker, Blinn College

John Sides, Vanderbilt University

Andrea Simpson, University of Richmond

Shannon Sinegal, University of New Orleans

Tracy Skopek, Stephen F. Austin State University

Roy Slater, St. Petersburg College

Captain Michael Slattery, Campbell University

Brian Smentkowski, Southeast Missouri State University

Daniel Smith, Northwest Missouri State University
Don Smith, University of North Texas
Michael Smith, Sam Houston State University
Matthew Snyder, Delgado Community College
Chris Soper, Pepperdine University
Thomas Sowers, Lamar University
Bartholomew Sparrow, University of Texas at Austin
Scott Spitzer, California State University–Fullerton
Laurie Sprankle, Community College of Allegheny County
Jim Startin, University of Texas at San Antonio
Robert Sterken, University of Texas at Tyler
Maryam T. Stevenson, University of Indianapolis
Debra St. John, Collin College
Dara Strolovitch, University of Minnesota
Barbara Suhay, Henry Ford Community College
Bobby Summers, Harper College
Steven Sylvester, Utah Valley University
Ryan Lee Teten, University of Louisiana at Lafayette
John Theis, Lone Star College–Kingwood
John Todd, University of North Texas
Dennis Toombs, San Jacinto College–North
Delaina Toothman, University of Maine
Linda Trautman, Ohio University–Lancaster
Elizabeth Trentanelli, Gulf Coast State College
David Trussell, Cisco College
Stacy Ulbig, Southwest Missouri State University
Ronald W. Vardy, University of Houston
Justin Vaughn, Boise State University
Linda Veazey, Midwestern State University
John Vento, Antelope Valley College
Kevin Wagner, Florida Atlantic University
Timothy Weaver, State University of New York at Albany
Aaron Weinschenk, University of Wisconsin–Green Bay
Eric Whitaker, Western Washington University
Clay Wiegand, Cisco College
Nelson Wikstrom, Virginia Commonwealth University
Clif Wilkinson, Georgia College
Donald Williams, Western New England University
Walter Wilson, University of Texas at San Antonio

Christina Wolbrecht, University of Notre Dame
Carolyn Wong, Stanford University
John Wood, Rose State College
Laura Wood, Tarrant County College
Robert Wood, University of North Dakota
Terri Wright, California State University–Fullerton
Peter Yacobucci, Buffalo State College
Kevan Yenerall, Clarion University
Michael Young, Trinity Valley Community College
Tyler Young, Collin College
Rogerio Zapata, South Texas College
Julian Zelizer, Princeton University

For this Thirteenth Edition:

Andrea Benjamin, University of Missouri–Columbia
David Birch, Lone Star College–Tomball
Melissa Buehler, Miami Dade College
Jeffrey W. Christiansen, Seminole State College
Andrew Clayton, McLennan Community College
Brian Cravens, Blinn College
Darin DeWitt, California State University–Long Beach
Maria Gabryszewska, Lone Star College–CyFair
Patrick Gilbert, Lone Star College
Virginia Haysley, Lone Star College–Tomball
Anika Jackson, Los Angeles City College
Anthony Jordan, Central Texas College
Milosz Kucharski, Lone Star College–CyFair
Paul Labedz, Valencia College
Prakash K. Mansinghani, Laredo College
Katie Marchetti, Dickinson College
Mandy May, College of Southern Maryland
Justin Moeller, West Texas A&M University
Patrick Novotny, Georgia Southern University
Jennifer Selin, University of Missouri
John Theis, Lone Star College–Kingwood
Herschel Thomas, University of Texas at Arlington
Austin Trantham, Jacksonville University
Corena White, Tarrant County College–Trinity River

We are also grateful to Daniel Fuerstman of State College of Florida Manatee-Sarasota, who contributed to the America Side by Side boxes.

Perhaps above all, we thank those at W. W. Norton. For the book's first five editions, editor Steve Dunn helped us shape it in countless ways. Ann Shin carried on the Norton tradition of splendid editorial work on the Sixth through Ninth Editions and on the Eleventh Edition. Lisa McKay contributed smart ideas and a keen editorial eye to the Tenth Edition. Peter Lesser brought intelligence, dedication, and keen insight to the development of the Twelfth and Thirteenth Editions. For our InQuizitive course, digital resources for learning management systems, and other instructor support, Spencer Richardson-Jones has been an energetic and visionary editor. Elizabeth Marotta, Lena Nowak-Laird, and Anna Olcott also kept the production of the Thirteenth Edition and its accompanying resources coherent and in focus. John Elliott helped streamline and sharpen our ideas. Sarah Johnson copyedited the manuscript, and our superb project editor Laura Dragonette and media project editor Marcus Van Harpen devoted countless hours to keeping on top of myriad details. We thank Donna Ranieri for finding new photos and our photo editor Thomas Persano for managing the image program. Finally, we thank the former head of Norton's college department, Roby Harrington, who provided guidance and support through these many editions.

Benjamin Ginsberg
Caroline J. Tolbert
Andrea L. Campbell

October 2020

CORE
edition
13

We the People

An Introduction to American Politics

American Political Culture

WHAT GOVERNMENT DOES AND WHY IT MATTERS When Kimberly Green-Yates, chief operating officer of a group of nursing homes in Oklahoma, heard about the coronavirus deaths in Washington State nursing homes in early 2020, she ordered a large supply of PPE, personal protective equipment such as masks and gloves, and locked it away. "The people we take care of are the most vulnerable. Without PPE, we can't keep them safe," she said. But Green-Yates worried; some of the equipment was used up during the flu season and it wasn't clear whether new equipment would be available. Her state's department of emergency management had requested additional supplies from the Strategic National Stockpile, which is managed by the federal Department of Health and Human Services for use during crises that overwhelm local resources. Usually such emergencies—think of hurricanes or chemical plant explosions—are geographically concentrated. But the nationwide coronavirus outbreak forced HHS to make decisions about how to allocate its stockpile around the country. It chose to allot medical masks, gloves, and gowns by a formula using outbreak severity and state population, rather than outbreak severity alone. That meant that Florida, population 21 million, received all

During the coronavirus pandemic in the spring of 2020, the Strategic National Stockpile was deployed to help get health care workers across the United States personal protective equipment. However, some states received more equipment for their health care workers than others, depending on the population and need of each state. Here, nurses in Florida don masks and face shields as they begin testing for the virus at a senior center.

of the 180,000 masks it requested, while Oklahoma, population 4 million, received only 10 percent of its 500,000-mask request.

Moreover, nearly all of the supplies in the national stockpile were expired. Most had been purchased in 2007 when extra funding for pandemic flu preparation had been included in the federal budget. But by 2020 they had "exceeded their shelf life," according to an HHS letter. "Public health emergency preparedness, which includes the Strategic National Stockpile, has been chronically underfunded for years," said Michael Lanza, spokesman for the New York City Health Department, which had

requested 2.2 million masks and received 78,000, all expired.[1]

Every day, government affects our lives and those of our family members, friends, and community. Sometimes those efforts are difficult to recognize, like when we eat a hamburger that because of government meat inspection doesn't make us sick. Sometimes government's activity is very visible, like when the governors of New York and Washington State, in response to the coronavirus pandemic, requested major disaster declarations, which the federal government approved, freeing government resources such as new medical stations for those states. And sometimes government's activity falls short, like the beleaguered Strategic National Stockpile, under-mining Americans' security and well-being.

In addition, Americans have a variety of different views about the appropri-ate role of government. Some saw the work-from-home orders put in place by some local and state governments in response to the coronavirus pandemic as threats to their liberty and a classic case of government overreach. Yet others thought such mandates came too late to ensure Americans' health and security. Moreover, the pandemic threatened to affect Americans very differently, as both the coronavirus's health effects and its economic implica-tions varied by age, gender, race, and class. Government's success in offset-ting the virus's health and economic effects varied across different groups as well.

Thus government affects us all in ways big and small. The purpose of this book is to show what government does, how, and why—and what you can do about it.

CHAPTER GOALS

★ **Differentiate between forms of government (pp. 5–9)**

★ **Describe the rights and responsibilities that citizens have in a democracy (pp. 9–11)**

★ **Describe the social composition of the American population and how it has changed over time (pp. 12–20)**

★ **Describe how cultural values of liberty, equality, and democracy influence the U.S. system of government (pp. 21–26)**

★ **Summarize Americans' attitudes toward government (pp. 26–30)**

Government

Differentiate between forms of government

Government is the term generally used to describe the formal institutions through which a territory and its people are ruled. A government may be as simple as a town meeting in which community members make policy and determine budgets together or as complex as the vast establishments found in many large countries today, with extensive procedures, laws, and bureaucracies. In the history of civilization, thousands of governments have been established. The hard part is establishing one that lasts.

government institutions and procedures through which a territory and its people are ruled

Even more difficult is developing a stable government that is true to the core American political values of liberty, equality, and democracy. Though in principle these three values are endorsed by most Americans, in practice each of them means different things to different people, and they often seem to conflict with one another. This is where politics comes in. Politics refers to conflicts and struggles over the leadership, structure, and policies of governments. As we will see in this chapter and throughout this book, much political conflict concerns policies and practices that seem to affirm one of the key American political values but may contradict another.

politics conflict over the leadership, structure, and policies of governments

IS GOVERNMENT NEEDED?

Thomas Jefferson famously observed that the best government was one that "governed least," and since the nation's founding, Americans have always viewed government with some suspicion and a desire that it play only a limited role in their lives. Generally speaking, a government is needed to provide those services, sometimes called "public goods," that citizens all need but probably cannot individually provide adequately for themselves. These might include defense against foreign aggression, maintenance of public order, a stable currency, enforcement of contractual obligations and property rights, and some measure of economic security. Government, with its powers to tax and regulate, is typically viewed as the best way to provide public goods. However, there is often disagreement about which public goods are essential and how they should be provided.

Much of what citizens have come to depend on and take for granted as part of their everyday environment is in fact created by government. Throughout the day, for example, a typical college student relies on a host of services and activities organized by national, state, and local government agencies. The extent of this dependence is illustrated in Table 1.1 on p. 6.

FORMS OF GOVERNMENT

Governments vary in their structure, their size, and the way they operate. Two questions are of special importance in determining how governments differ: Who governs? And how much government control is permitted?

Some nations are governed by a single individual—a king or dictator, for example. This system is called autocracy. Where a small group—perhaps landowners, military officers, or the wealthy—controls most of the governing decisions, that government is said to be an oligarchy. If citizens or the general adult population have the power to rule themselves, that government is a democracy.

autocracy a form of government in which a single individual—a king, queen, or dictator—rules

oligarchy a form of government in which a small group—landowners, military officers, or wealthy merchants—controls most of the governing decisions

democracy a system of rule that permits citizens to play a significant part in the governmental process, usually through the election of key public officials

GOVERNMENT 5

TABLE 1.1

The Presence of Government in the Daily Life of a Student at "State University"

TIME	SCHEDULE
7:00 A.M.	Wake up. Standard time set by the national government.
7:10 A.M.	Shower. Water courtesy of local government, and supplied by either a public entity or a regulated private company. Brush your teeth with toothpaste whose cavity-fighting claims have been verified by a federal agency. Dry your hair with an electric dryer manufactured according to federal government agency guidelines.
7:30 A.M.	Have a bowl of cereal with milk for breakfast. "Nutrition Facts" on food labels are a federal requirement, pasteurization of milk required by state law, freshness dating on milk based on state and federal standards, recycling the empty cereal box and milk carton enabled by state or local laws.
8:30 A.M.	Drive or take public transportation to campus. Airbags and seat belts required by federal and state laws. Roads and bridges paid for by state and local governments, speed and traffic laws set by state and local governments, public transportation subsidized by all levels of government.
8:45 A.M.	Arrive on campus of large public university. Buildings are 70 percent financed by state taxpayers.
9:00 A.M.	First class: Chemistry 101. Tuition partially paid by a federal loan (more than half the cost of university instruction is paid for by taxpayers), chemistry lab paid for with grants from the National Science Foundation (a federal agency) and smaller grants from corporations made possible by federal income tax deductions for charitable contributions.
Noon	Eat lunch. College cafeteria financed by state dormitory authority on land grant from federal Department of Agriculture.
12:47 P.M.	Felt an earthquake! Check the U.S. Geological Survey at www.usgs.gov to see that it was a 3.9 on the Richter scale.
2:00 P.M.	Second class: American Government 101 (your favorite class!). You may be taking this class because it is required by the state legislature or because it fulfills a university requirement.
4:00 P.M.	Third class: Computer Science 101. Free computers, software, and internet access courtesy of state subsidies plus grants and discounts from Apple and Microsoft, the costs of which are deducted from their corporate income taxes; internet built in part by federal government. Duplication of software prohibited by federal copyright laws.
6:00 P.M.	Eat dinner: hamburger and french fries. Meat inspected for bacteria by federal agencies.
7:00 P.M.	Work at part-time job at the campus library. Minimum wage set by federal, state, or local government; books and journals in library paid for by state taxpayers.
8:15 P.M.	Go online to check the status of your application for a federal student loan (FAFSA) on the Department of Education's website at studentaid.gov.
10:00 P.M.	Go home. Street lighting paid for by county and city governments, police patrols by city government.
10:15 P.M.	Watch TV. Networks regulated by federal government, cable public-access channels required by city law. Weather forecast provided to broadcasters by a federal agency.
10:45 P.M.	To complete your economics homework, visit the Bureau of Labor Statistics at www.bls.gov to look up unemployment levels since 1972.
Midnight	Put out the trash before going to bed. Trash collected by city sanitation department, financed by user charges.

Governments also vary considerably in terms of how they govern. In the United States and a number of other nations, constitutions and other laws limit what governments can do and how they go about it. Governments limited in this way are called liberal or **constitutional governments.**

In other nations, including some in Latin America, Asia, and Africa, the law imposes few real limits. The government is nevertheless kept in check by other political and social institutions that it cannot control—such as self-governing territories, an organized religion, business organizations, or labor unions. Such governments are generally called **authoritarian.**

In a third group of nations, including the Soviet Union under Joseph Stalin, Nazi Germany, and North Korea today, governments not only lack legal limits but also try to eliminate institutions that might challenge their authority. These governments typically attempt to control all of a nation's political, economic, and social life and, as a result, are called **totalitarian** (see Table 1.2).

Americans have the good fortune to live in a nation in which limits are placed on what governments can do and how they can do it. By one measure, 52 percent of the global population live in democracies, but only 14 percent enjoy true liberal democracy with free and fair elections, the rule of law, and constraints on the executive (president or prime minister); 38 percent live in more limited democracies.[2] Moreover constitutional, liberal democracies were unheard of before the modern era. Before about 1800, governments seldom sought—and rarely received—the support of their subjects.[3]

Beginning in the seventeenth century, in a handful of European nations, two important changes began to take place in the character and conduct of government. First, governments began to acknowledge formal limits on their power. Second, a small number of governments began to provide ordinary citizens with a formal voice in public affairs—through the vote. These ideas influenced the political climate in America. Support for limits on government and for

constitutional government a system of rule in which formal and effective limits are placed on the powers of the government

authoritarian government a system of rule in which the government recognizes no formal limits but may nevertheless be restrained by the power of other social institutions

totalitarian government a system of rule in which the government recognizes no formal limits on its power and seeks to absorb or eliminate other social institutions that might challenge it

America's Founders were influenced by the English thinker John Locke (1632–1704). Locke argued that governments need the consent of the people.

TABLE 1.2
Forms of Government

WHO GOVERNS	TYPE OF GOVERNMENT
One person	Autocracy
Small group (e.g., landowners, military officers, or wealthy merchants)	Oligarchy
Many people	Democracy

LIMITS ON GOVERNMENT	TYPE OF GOVERNMENT
Codified, legal substantive and procedural limits on what government can or cannot do	Constitutional
Few legal limits; some limits imposed by social groups	Authoritarian
No limits	Totalitarian

popular influence on it lay at the heart of the American Revolution, in which the slogan "No taxation without representation" was fiercely asserted (see Chapter 2).

LIMITING GOVERNMENT

On both sides of the Atlantic, a new commercial class emerged in the eighteenth century that was interested in changing governmental institutions to allow its political participation and to protect its economic interests—not just the aristocracy's. In defending its interests from government, the founding generation of the young United States established many of the principles that would come to define individual liberty for all citizens—freedom of speech, of assembly, and of conscience, as well as freedom from arbitrary search and seizure. It is important to note that the Founders generally did not favor democracy as we know it. Along with political institutions based on elected representatives, they supported property requirements and other restrictions for voting and for holding office so as to limit political participation to the White middle and upper classes. Yet once these institutions and the right to engage in politics were established, it was difficult to limit them to the economic elite.

ACCESS TO GOVERNMENT: THE EXPANSION OF PARTICIPATION

Pressure to expand voting rights came both from below (the excluded groups themselves agitating for the vote) and from above (by others who hoped to gain political advantage by expanding the franchise to groups they viewed as potential allies). After the Civil War, a chief reason that Republicans gave the vote to formerly enslaved people was to use their support to maintain Republican control in the defeated southern states. Similarly, in the early twentieth century, the Progressive movement advocated women's suffrage at least partly because they believed women were more likely than men to support the reforms Progressives favored around government corruption, education, and the family. The expansion of participation meant that more and more people had a legal right to take part in politics.

INFLUENCING THE GOVERNMENT THROUGH PARTICIPATION: POLITICS

As Harold Lasswell, a famous political scientist, once put it, politics is the struggle over "who gets what, when, how."[4] Although it can be found in any organization, in this book *politics* will refer only to conflicts over who the government's leadership is, how the government is organized, or what the government's policies are. Having a share or a say in these issues is called having **political power** or influence.

Participation in politics can take many forms, including voting, donating money, signing petitions, attending political meetings, tweeting and commenting online, sending emails to officials, lobbying legislators, working on a campaign, and participating in protest marches and even violent demonstrations. A system of government that gives citizens a regular opportunity to elect top government officials is usually called a **representative democracy**, or a **republic**. A system that permits citizens to vote directly on laws and policies is called a **direct democracy**.

John Stuart Mill (1806–73) presented a ringing defense of individual freedom in his famous treatise *On Liberty*. Mill's work influenced Americans' evolving ideas about the relationship between government and the individual.

political power influence over a government's leadership, organization, or policies

representative democracy (republic) a system of government in which the populace selects representatives, who play a significant role in governmental decision-making

direct democracy a system of rule that permits citizens to vote directly on laws and policies

At the national level, the United States is a representative democracy in which citizens select government officials but do not vote on legislation. Some states and cities, however, do provide for direct legislation through initiatives and referenda. These procedures allow citizens to collect petitions, or legislators to pass bills, requiring a direct popular vote on an issue. In 2020, 128 referenda appeared on state ballots, often dealing with hot-button issues, including measures in 6 states legalizing medical or recreational marijuana, in 12 states affecting taxes, in 2 states regarding abortion access and funding, and in 14 states regarding elections policies such as redistricting, voting requirements, and campaign finance.[5]

Groups and organized interests also participate in politics. Their political activities include providing funds for candidates, lobbying, and trying to influence public opinion. The pattern of struggles among interests is called group politics, or **pluralism.** Americans have always had mixed feelings about pluralist politics. On the one hand, the right of groups to support their views and compete for influence in the government is the essence of liberty. On the other hand, groups may sometimes exert too much influence, advancing their own interests at the expense of larger public interests. (We return to this problem in Chapter 11.)

pluralism the theory that all interests are and should be free to compete for influence in the government; the outcome of this competition is compromise and moderation

Sometimes, politics does not take place through formal channels at all but instead involves direct action. In addition to actions such as marches, demonstrations, and boycotts, direct action politics can also include violent activities or civil disobedience, both of which attempt to shock or force rulers into changing their behavior. In recent years in the United States, groups ranging from animal rights activists to right-to-life advocates to White supremacists to Black Lives Matter protesters have used direct action to underline their demands.

Citizenship: Participation, Knowledge, and Efficacy

Describe the rights and responsibilities that citizens have in a democracy

Citizenship in the United States comes with many rights but also with important responsibilities. Civil liberties and rights such as freedom of speech, freedom of worship, and trial by jury are found in the Constitution, particularly in the Bill of Rights, as Chapters 4 and 5 discuss. Citizens also have responsibilities, such as upholding the Constitution; obeying federal, state, and local laws; paying taxes; and serving on juries when called. Because political participation is the hallmark of the democratic form of government and the source of democracies' legitimacy, citizens also have a responsibility to be informed about issues and to participate in the democratic process.[6]

One key ingredient for political participation is **political knowledge** and information. Democracy functions best when citizens are informed and have the knowledge needed to participate in political debate. Indeed, our definition of **citizenship** derives from the ideal put forth by the ancient Greeks: *enlightened* political engagement.[7] Political knowledge means more than having a few opinions to post on Twitter or to guide your decisions in a voting booth. It is also important to know the rules and strategies that govern political institutions and the principles on which they are based, *and* to know them in ways that relate to your own interests. If your street

political knowledge information about the formal institutions of government, political actors, and political issues

citizenship informed and active membership in a political community

Politics sometimes involves direct action. People often hold public rallies or protests to draw attention to issues. These concerns can range from (left to right) government inaction on climate change, a woman's right to choose, immigration policies including border walls, and restrictions on the Second Amendment.

FOR CRITICAL ANALYSIS

Many studies seem to show that most Americans know very little about government and politics. Can we have democratic government without knowledgeable and aware citizens?

political efficacy the belief that one can influence government and politics

is blocked by snow, for example, you need to know that snow removal is a city or county responsibility and to be able to identify the agency that deals with the problem. Americans are fond of complaining that government is not responsive to their needs, but in some cases, they simply lack the information they need to present their problems to the appropriate officials.

Likewise, without political knowledge, citizens cannot be aware of their stakes in political disputes. For example, during the debate in 2017 about whether to repeal the health care reform enacted in 2010, one-third of Americans did not know that "Obamacare" and the "Affordable Care Act" are the same thing.[8] That meant that some of those enrolled in "Obamacare" did not realize their access to health insurance would be affected if the ACA were repealed. Citizens need knowledge in order to assess their interests and know when to act on them.

Surveys show that large majorities of Americans get political information online, although inequalities in internet access by income, education, race, and age remain. But while the internet has made it easier than ever to learn about politics, political knowledge in the United States remains spotty. Most Americans know little about current issues or debates, or even the basics of how government works. For example, in 2019 only 39 percent of those surveyed could identify all three branches of the federal government and only 53 percent knew the size of the majority in Congress needed to override a presidential veto (two-thirds). Just 55 percent correctly identified the party that controlled the House and 61 percent the Senate. On the other hand, 83 percent of Americans know that the Supreme Court has ruled that citizens have a constitutional right to own a handgun (see Table 1.3).

Another ingredient in participation is **political efficacy**, the belief that ordinary citizens can affect what government does. The feeling that you can't affect government decisions can lead to apathy, declining political participation, and withdrawal from political life. Americans' sense of political efficacy has declined over time. In 1960, only 25 percent felt shut out of government. In 2019, 71 percent of Americans said that elected officials don't care what people like them think.[9] Accompanying this sense that ordinary people are not heard is a growing belief that government is not run for the benefit of all. In 2019, 52 percent of the public disagreed with the idea that the "government is really run for the benefit of all the people."[10]

This widely felt loss of political efficacy is bad news for American democracy. Not every effort of ordinary citizens to influence government will succeed, but without the belief that such efforts can be effective, government decisions will be made by a smaller and smaller circle of powerful people. Fortunately, given the importance to American political ideals that all citizens be informed and able to act, individuals can build their own sense of political efficacy. Research shows that efficacy and participation are related: a feeling that one can make a difference leads to participation, and joining in can increase one's efficacy.

TABLE 1.3

What Americans Know about Government

RESPONDENTS WHO	PERCENTAGE
Could identify all three branches of government	39
Knew the Democratic Party controlled the House of Representatives	55
Knew the Republican Party controlled the Senate	61
Knew the size of the majority needed in Congress to override a presidential veto (two-thirds)	53
Knew the Supreme Court ruled that citizens have a constitutional right to own a handgun	83
Knew that a 5–4 Supreme Court ruling means the decision is law and needs to be followed	59
Knew that those in the country illegally have some rights under the U.S. Constitution	55

SOURCES: 2019 Annenberg Constitution Day Civics Survey, https://cdn.annenbergpublicpolicycenter.org /wp-content/uploads/2019/09/Annenberg_civics_2019_Appendix.pdf (accessed 1/19/20).

Who Are Americans?

Describe the social composition of the American population and how it has changed over time

While American democracy aims to give the people a voice in government, the meaning of "we the people" has changed over time. Who are Americans? Throughout American history, politicians, religious leaders, prominent scholars, and ordinary Americans have puzzled and fought over the answer to this fundamental question.

IMMIGRATION AND AMERICAN DIVERSITY

The U.S. population has grown from 3.9 million in 1790, the year of the first official census, to 330 million in 2020.[11] At the same time, it has become more diverse on nearly every dimension imaginable.[12] (See the Who Are Americans? feature on p. 15.)

In 1790, when the United States consisted of 13 states along the Eastern Seaboard, 81 percent of Americans traced their roots to Europe, mostly Britain and elsewhere in northern Europe; and nearly 20 percent were of African origin, the vast majority of whom were enslaved people.[13] Only 1.5 percent of the Black population were free. There were also an unknown number of Native Americans, the original inhabitants of the land, not counted by the census because the government did not consider them Americans. The first estimates of Native Americans and Latinos in the mid-1800s showed that each group made up less than 1 percent of the total population.[14]

Fast-forward to 1900. The country now stretched across the continent, and waves of immigrants, mainly from Europe, had boosted the population to 76 million. The population was still predominantly composed of people of European ancestry, but now included many from southern and eastern as well as northwestern Europe; the

Native American societies, with their own forms of government, existed for thousands of years before the first European settlers arrived. By the time this photo of Red Cloud and other Sioux warriors was taken, around 1870, Native Americans made up about 1 percent of the American population.

Debate Respectfully

APRIL LAWSON, the director of debates for Better Angels

Government by the people functions best when individuals discuss ideas, share their preferences, and talk about what government is doing. But political discussion and debate can be uncomfortable, particularly among people who disagree or when politics is polarized, as it is in the current era.

To learn how to engage others and to debate respectfully, we spoke with April Lawson, the director of debates for Better Angels, a national organization that works with individuals from across the political spectrum to "combat polarization and restore civil dialogue across America." She offers these tips for successful and civil political conversations:

1 **The most important thing is the presumption of good faith.** If someone says something you can't stand, know that the other person is trying, just like you are, to address hard questions. Assume that the other person is smart and that they are moral.

2 **Second, say what you actually believe.** Genuineness and sincerity are crucial. You could debate either by making a case no one could disagree with or by sharing what you really feel about the issue. The latter will make for a more productive exchange of ideas.

3 **How can you launch such a conversation and set the tone?** A good technique is to start with a question of genuine curiosity for the other person, which reassures them that you want to know what they believe. Another tip is to paraphrase what they have said before you respond, to make sure the other person feels heard.

4 **When you respond, it helps if you express some doubt or nuance in your own argument,** or mention that you agree with some aspect of the other person's position. You do not need to agree with everything they have said, but you can pick something reasonable the other person said and affirm, "You said X, which makes sense because of Y."

5 **Know that you may need to be the bigger person in the conversation.** In order to be an "ambassador of civility," you may need the patience to ask several genuine questions of curiosity before the other person believes that you are actually interested in what they have to say. And you need to control your own emotions and triggers, to manage your activation, since you know these rules for civil engagement, and they may not.

6 **Finally, realize that you have agency.** Prepare yourself for these tough conversations by telling yourself, "I will probably have feelings about this. But I can be patient and manage them." Remember, you're not trapped. You can take a break. You can change topics. Or you may want to have a conversational exit in mind. If it's Thanksgiving and you're speaking with your crazy uncle, you might pivot to the football game.

Debating respectfully requires coming to the table with a "posture of openness" and helping the other person feel heard. In America, at the talking point level, which is a surface level, we don't agree at all. But if you can go down even one level to political values, or even one more level to moral values, then there's a lot of common ground. With these conversations, we're not trying to change how you see the issue, we're trying to change how you see the other person.

Black population stood at 12 percent. Residents who traced their origin to Latin America or Asia each accounted for less than 1 percent of the population.[15] The large number of new immigrants was reflected in the high proportion of foreign-born people in the population; this figure reached its height at 14.7 percent in 1910.[16]

As growing numbers of immigrants from southern and eastern Europe crowded into American cities, anxiety mounted among those of British and other northwestern European ancestry, who feared their group could lose its long-dominant position in American society and politics. Much as today, politicians and scholars argued heatedly about whether the country could absorb such large numbers of immigrants. Concerns ranged from whether their political and social values were compatible with American democracy to whether they would learn English to what new diseases they might bring. Growing religious differences became a source of tension as well. The first European immigrants to the United States were overwhelmingly Protestant, many of them fleeing religious persecution. The many German and Irish Catholics who arrived in the mid-1800s began to shift the religious balance, which changed further in the early twentieth century as more Catholics from southern Europe and Jews from eastern Europe and Russia arrived. This new religious diversity challenged the Protestantism previously assumed in many aspects of American life.

After World War I, Congress responded to the fears swirling around immigrants with new laws that sharply limited how many could enter the country each year. It also established a new National Origins quota system, based on the nation's population in 1890, before the wave of immigrants from eastern and southern Europe arrived.[17] Supporters of these measures hoped to turn back the clock to an earlier America in which northern Europeans dominated. The new system set up a hierarchy of admissions: northern European countries received generous quotas for new immigrants, whereas eastern and southern European countries were granted very small quotas. By 1970, these guidelines had reduced the foreign-born population in the United States to an all-time low of 5 percent.

The use of ethnic and racial criteria to restrict the country's population and to draw boundaries around "American" identity began long before the National Origins quota system, however. Most people of African descent were not deemed citizens until 1868, when the Fourteenth Amendment to the Constitution granted citizenship to formerly enslaved people (see Chapter 2). Native Americans were not officially citizens until 1924. More broadly, efforts to limit nonwhite immigration

In the 1900s many immigrants entered the United States through New York's Ellis Island, where they were checked for disease before being admitted. Today, individuals hoping to immigrate to the United States often apply for a visa at the U.S. consulate in their home country before traveling to the United States, where the U.S. Customs and Border Protection checks their identity and legal status.

An Increasingly Diverse Nation

Since the Founding, the U.S. population has grown rapidly and people living in the United States have become increasingly diverse. Dramatic changes in population, demographics, and geography often drive changes in American government and politics.

Race

	1790*	1900*	2018**
	White 81%	White 88%	White 61%
	Black 19%	Black 12%	Black 13%
		Other 1%	Latino 18%
			Asian 6%
			Native American 1%
			Other 0.4%

= 1 million people

	1790*	1900*	2018**
TOTAL POPULATION	3,929,214	75,994,575	327,167,434

Geography

	1790	1900	2018

1790: Northeast 50%, South 50%

1900: Northeast 28%, Midwest 35%, South 32%, West 5%

2018: Northeast 17%, Midwest 21%, South 38%, West 23%

Age

	1900		2018
0–19	44%	0–19	25%
20–44	38%	20–44	33%
45–64	14%	45–64	26%
65 +	4%	65 +	16%

---

* The 1790 census does not accurately reflect the population because it only counted Blacks and Whites. It did not include Native Americans or other groups. The 1900 census did not count Latino Americans.

** Numbers may not add up to 100 percent due to rounding.

SOURCE: U.S. Census Bureau, American Community surveys, data.census.gov (accessed 5/23/19).

FOR CRITICAL ANALYSIS

1. The most recent census estimates show that the population of the South and the West continued to grow more rapidly than the Northeast and Midwest. What are some of the political implications of this trend?

2. Today, Americans over age 38 outnumber Americans under 38, and older adults are more likely to participate in the political process. What do you think this means for the kinds of issues and policies considered by the government?

and citizenship dated back to a 1790 law stating that only free Whites could become naturalized citizens, a ban not lifted until 1870. Even then, different restrictions applied to Asians: the Chinese Exclusion Act of 1882 outlawed the entry of Chinese laborers to the United States, a limit lifted only in 1943, when China became America's ally during World War II. Additional barriers enacted after World War I meant that virtually no Asians entered the country as immigrants until the 1940s.

With laws about citizenship linked to "Whiteness," questions arose about how to classify people of Latino origin. In 1930, for example, the census counted people of Mexican origin as nonwhite, but a decade later reversed this decision—after protests by those affected and by the Mexican government. Only in 1970 did the census officially begin counting persons of Hispanic origin, noting that they could be any race.[18] (Note that the census uses the term *Hispanic*, but we will generally use the terms *Latino* and *Latina* to refer to people of Spanish or Latin American descent.)

As this history suggests, debates have raged for more than two centuries about who can come to the United States, who can become a citizen, and who should be counted by the census and how.

TWENTY-FIRST-CENTURY AMERICANS

Race and Ethnicity Recent immigration patterns have profoundly shaped the nation's current racial and ethnic profile. The primary cause was Congress's decision in 1965 to lift the tight restrictions of the 1920s, allowing for much-expanded immigration from Asia and Latin America (see Figure 1.1). Census figures for 2018 show that Latinos, who can be of any race, constitute 18.3 percent of the total population, and Asians make up 5.6 percent. The Black, or African American, population is 12.7 percent of the total, while non-Latino Whites account for 60.2 percent—their lowest share ever. Moreover, 3.4 percent of the population now identifies itself as of "two or more races," a new category that the census added in 2000.[19] Although only a small share of the total, the multiracial category points toward the future possibility of a major shift in the American tradition of strict racial categorization. The blurring of labels poses challenges to a host of policies—many of them put in place to remedy past discrimination—that rely on racial counts of the population.

Large-scale immigration means that many more residents are foreign-born. In 2018, 13.7 percent of the population was born outside the United States, a figure comparable to that in 1900.[20] About half of the foreign-born population came from Latin America and the Caribbean—almost 1 in 10 from the Caribbean, just over one-third from Central America (including Mexico), and 1 in 15 from South America.[21] Those born in Asia made up 31 percent of foreign-born residents.[22] In sharp contrast to the immigration patterns of a century earlier, just 10.9 percent came from Europe.[23]

Estimates are that 12 million immigrants live in the country without legal authorization. The majority of these people are from Mexico and Central America.[24] This unauthorized population has become a flashpoint for controversy as states and cities have passed a variety of conflicting laws regarding their access to public services. Several decades ago, some states tried to exclude undocumented immigrants from public services such as education and emergency medical care, but the Supreme Court ensured access to K-12 education in its 1982 *Plyler v. Doe* ruling, and Congress guaranteed access to emergency medical care in a 1986

FIGURE 1.1

Immigration by Continent of Origin

Where did most immigrants come from at the start of the twentieth century? How does that compare with immigration in the twenty-first century?

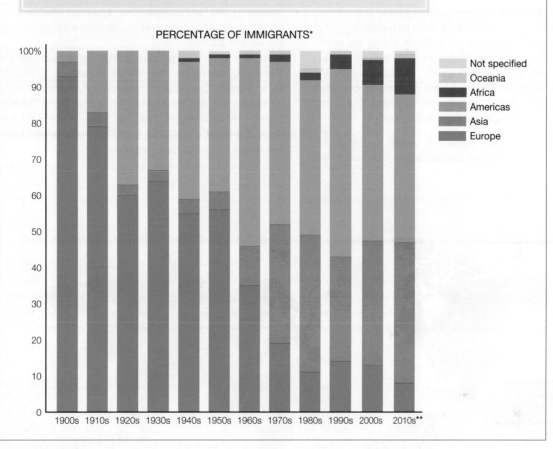

PERCENTAGE OF IMMIGRANTS*

Legend: Not specified, Oceania, Africa, Americas, Asia, Europe

*Less than 1 percent not shown.
**Through 2018.
Note: Figure shows those who have obtained "lawful permanent resident status" by continent of origin.
SOURCE: Department of Homeland Security, www.dhs.gov (accessed 1/19/20).

law.[25] Today, undocumented immigrants remain ineligible for most federal public benefits, but some states offer them driver's licenses or in-state tuition at public colleges and universities.[26]

Religion The new patterns of immigration have combined with differences in birth rates and underlying social changes to alter the religious affiliations of Americans. By 2019, only 35 percent of Americans identified themselves as Protestant, Catholics 22 percent, 10 percent Christian (nonspecific), 2 percent Jewish, 1 percent Mormon, and 6 percent "Other," which includes Muslim identifiers, who have grown to nearly 1 percent of the population. In one important shift, a growing number of people identify with no organized religion: 21 percent of the population in 2019.[27] These changes suggest an important shift in

Forms of Government

The question of whether a country is democratic or authoritarian is complex. Every year, countries are rated on a scale from "Full Democracies" to "Authoritarian" systems based on expert evaluations of electoral processes, political culture, respect for civil liberties, political participation, and other indicators. In 2016, for the first time, the United States was classified as a "Flawed Democracy" in response to declines in public confidence in governance and a rise in polarization.

1. Is there a geographic pattern to which countries are labeled "Full" or "Flawed Democracies" and which are labeled "Hybrid" or "Authoritarian" systems? What factors, historical, economic, geographic, or otherwise, might help explain this pattern?

2. What do you think separates a "Full Democracy" from a "Flawed Democracy"? The United States' categorization as a "Flawed Democracy" happened during the Obama administration and persisted during the Trump administration. What changes have you seen in the past five years that might explain this shift? How concerned should Americans be by this categorization?

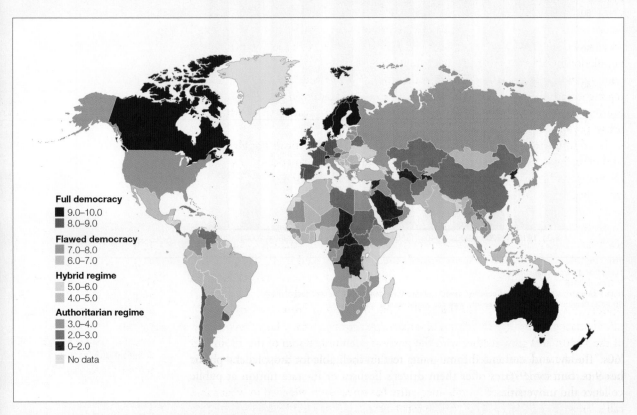

SOURCE: "Democracy Index 2019," The Economist Intelligence Unit.

American religious identity. Although many Americans think of the United States as a "Judeo-Christian" nation—and indeed it was 95 percent Protestant, Catholic, or Jewish as recently as 50 years ago—by 2019 this number had fallen to 70 percent of the adult population.[28]

Age As the American population has expanded and diversified, the country's age profile has shifted with it. In 1900 only 4 percent of the population was over age 65. As life expectancy increased, so did the number of older Americans: by 2018, 16 percent of the population was over 65. Over the same period, the percentage of children under the age of 18 fell, from 44 percent in 1900 to 25 percent in 2018.[29] As a group, Americans are still younger than the populations of many other industrialized countries, mainly because of the large number of immigrants. The share of the population aged 65 and over is 20 percent in the European Union and 27 percent in Japan.[30] But an aging population poses challenges to the United States as well. As the elderly population grows relative to those of working age, funding programs such as Social Security becomes more difficult.

Geography Over the nation's history, Americans have mostly moved from rural areas and small towns to large cities and suburbs. Before 1920 less than half the population lived in urban areas; today 82 percent of Americans do.[31] As a result, the national political system created when the population was still largely rural under-represents urban Americans. Providing each state with two senators, for example, overrepresents sparsely populated rural states and underrepresents those with large urban populations (see Chapter 2).

In addition to becoming more urban over time, the American population has shifted regionally. During the past 50 years especially, many Americans have left the Northeast and Midwest and moved to the South and Southwest, with congressional seats reapportioned to reflect the population shift.

Socioeconomic Status For much of U.S. history, most Americans were relatively poor working people, many of them farmers. A new, extremely wealthy elite emerged in the late 1800s, a period called "the gilded age," and by 1928 nearly one-quarter of the total annual national income went to the top 1 percent of earners; the top 10 percent took home 46 percent of the total. In the middle of the twentieth century, the distribution of income and wealth shifted away from the top. A large middle class grew after New Deal programs helped counteract the Great Depression of the 1930s, and grew further with the postwar economic boom of the 1950s and '60s. The share of national income going to the top 1 percent dropped sharply, to just 9 percent by 1976.

Since then, however, economic inequality has once again widened in what some call a "new gilded age."[32] By 2018 the top 1 percent earned 21.8 percent of annual income and the top 10 percent took home 50.5 percent of it.[33] At the same time, the incomes of the broad middle class have largely stagnated,[34] and the numbers of the poor and near poor have swelled to nearly one-third of the population.[35] (See Figure 1.2, which shows similar data for household income.)

Population and Politics The shifting contours of the American people have regularly raised challenging questions about politics and government. Population growth and shifts have spurred politically charged debates about how the population should

FOR CRITICAL ANALYSIS

What trend in America's changing population has had the biggest influence on politics? Increasing racial and ethnic diversity? Aging? Changing religious affiliation? Increasing urbanization? Increased economic inequality? Why?

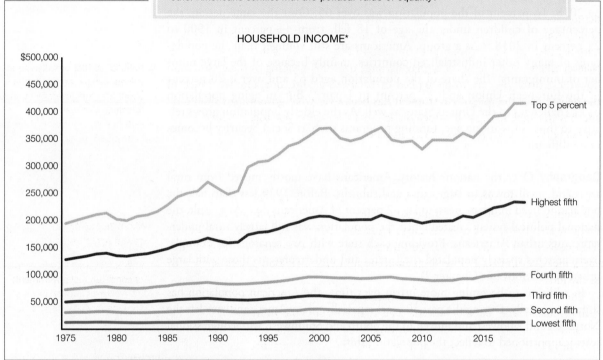

FIGURE 1.2

Income in the United States

The graph shows that while the income of most Americans has risen only slightly since 1975, the income of the richest Americans (the top 5 percent) has increased dramatically. What are some of the ways that this shift might matter for American politics? Does the growing economic gap between the richest groups and most other Americans conflict with the political value of equality?

HOUSEHOLD INCOME*

Top 5 percent

Highest fifth

Fourth fifth

Third fifth

Second fifth

Lowest fifth

*Dollar values are given in constant 2018 dollars, which are adjusted for inflation so that we can compare a person's income in 1975 with a person's income today.
SOURCE: U.S. Census Bureau, www.census.gov/data/tables/2019/demo/income-poverty/p60-266.html (accessed 1/19/20).

be apportioned among congressional districts and how those districts should be drawn. These conflicts have major implications for the balance of representation among different regions of the country and between urban and rural areas. The representation of various other demographic and political groups may also be affected, as substantial evidence shows that Americans are increasingly divided from one another geographically according to their education, income, marriage rates, and party voting.[36]

In addition, immigration and the cultural and religious changes that result spark passionate debate today, just as they did 100 years ago. The different languages and customs that immigrants bring trigger fears among some that the United States is changing in ways that undermine traditional or fundamental American values. The large number of unauthorized immigrants makes these anxieties even more acute. Yet a changing population has been one of the constants of American history. Indeed, each generation has confronted the many political challenges associated with answering the question anew, "Who are Americans?"

American Political Culture

Describe how cultural values of liberty, equality, and democracy influence the U.S. system of government

The essential documents of the American Founding—the Declaration of Independence and the Constitution—proclaimed a set of principles about the purposes of the new republic: liberty, equality, and democracy. (You can read these documents in the Appendix at the back of this book.) Americans actively embraced these principles and made them central to the national identity. Most Americans continue to affirm these values, which form our **political culture**, even though they may disagree over the meaning of these ideals and how these principles are to be applied or balanced against one another. Much of the debate over the role of government has been over what government should do and how far it should go to reduce the inequalities within our society and political system while still preserving essential liberties.

political culture broadly shared values, beliefs, and attitudes about how the government should function; American political culture emphasizes the values of liberty, equality, and democracy

LIBERTY

No ideal is more central to American values than liberty. The Declaration of Independence defined three "unalienable" rights: "Life, Liberty and the pursuit of Happiness." The Constitution likewise identified the need "to secure the Blessings of Liberty" as one of the key reasons for drawing up the document. For Americans, **liberty** means both personal freedom and economic freedom. Both are closely linked to the idea of **limited government**.

liberty freedom from governmental control

limited government a principle of constitutional government; a government whose powers are defined and limited by a constitution

The Constitution's first 10 amendments, known collectively as the Bill of Rights, delineate individual personal liberties and rights. In fact, the word *liberty* has come to mean many of the freedoms guaranteed in the Bill of Rights: freedom of speech and the press, the right to assemble freely, and the right to practice religious beliefs without interference from the government.

Over the course of American history, the scope of personal liberties has expanded as laws have become more tolerant and as individuals have successfully used the courts to challenge restrictions on their individual freedoms. Far fewer restrictions exist today on the press, political speech, and individual behavior than in the early years of the nation. Even so, conflicts emerge when personal liberties violate a community's accepted standards of behavior. For example, a number of cities have passed "sit-lie" ordinances, which limit the freedom of individuals to sit or lie down on sidewalks. Designed to limit the presence of the homeless and make city streets more attractive to pedestrians, the ordinances have also been denounced as restrictions on individual liberties.

Patrick Henry's famous "Give Me Liberty or Give Me Death" speech demanded freedom at any cost and has resonated with Americans throughout the nation's history.

The central historical conflict regarding liberty in the United States, the enslavement of Africans and their descendants, has cast a long shadow over all of American history. In fact, scholars today note that the American definition of freedom has been formed in relation to the concept of slavery. The rights to control one's labor and to be rewarded for it have been central elements of this definition precisely because these rights were denied to enslaved people.[37]

In addition to personal freedom related to one's labor, the American concept of economic freedom supports capitalism, free markets (including open competition and unrestricted movement of goods), and the protection of private property.[38] In the first century of the Republic, support for capitalism often meant support for the

laissez-faire capitalism an economic system in which the means of production and distribution are privately owned and operated for profit with minimal or no government interference

principle of *laissez-faire* (French for "allow to do"). **Laissez-faire capitalism** allowed the national government very little power to regulate commerce or restrict the use of private property. Today, however, federal and state governments impose many regulations to protect the public in such areas as health and safety, the environment, and the workplace. Government regulations to slow the spread of the coronavirus in 2020 included school closures, stay-at-home orders, and cancellations of entertainment and sporting events.

Not surprisingly, fierce disagreements often erupt over what the proper scope of government regulation should be. For example, one provision of the Affordable Care Act ("Obamacare") required that insurers pay for access to contraceptive care. The law's supporters argued that this provision simply ensured women's access to basic health care. Some businesses, however, denounced it as a violation of their fundamental liberty to run their businesses and use their property as they see fit. In 2014 a company called Hobby Lobby successfully challenged the provision, with the Supreme Court ruling that family-owned firms could be exempted from it on the basis of religious objections.[39]

Concerns about liberty have also arisen in relation to the government's efforts to combat terrorism and other threats to the nation's security. These concerns escalated in 2013 when Edward Snowden, a former National Security Agency (NSA) contractor, leaked top-secret documents from the NSA to the press. The NSA is the agency charged with monitoring electronic data flows—including radio, email, and cell phone calls—for foreign threats. The leaked documents revealed that the American government was listening in on the private communications of foreign governments, including many allies, such as Germany and Brazil. In addition, the NSA had access to Americans' Facebook, Google, Apple, and Yahoo! accounts, among many other electronic data sources, and for three years had been using these "metadata" to track connections among people, searching for suspicious ties.

This revelation set off a storm of controversy, since the NSA is not supposed to monitor Americans. The controversy reinforced the tech companies' commitment to guard their users' privacy from government. In 2016, Apple refused an FBI order to unlock the iPhone used by a terrorist who had killed 14 people in San Bernardino, California. Although the FBI dropped the case after it was able to open the phone without Apple's help, a new court order to Apple related to an iPhone used in a drug conspiracy case made it clear that the tension between privacy and security will continue.[40]

Can we find the proper balance between liberty and security? Between one person's liberty and another's? Because the threat of terrorism has no clear end point, doubts have grown about whether government powers that infringe on security-related liberties should be continued. And debates about religious liberties involve inherent conflicts that are likely to persist for decades to come.

EQUALITY

The Declaration of Independence declares as its first "self-evident" truth that "all men are created equal." As central as it is to the American political creed, however, equality has been an even less well-defined ideal than liberty, because people interpret it in such different ways. Few Americans have wholeheartedly embraced the ideal of full equality of results (that everyone deserves equal wealth and power), but most share the ideal of **equality of opportunity** (that everyone deserves a fair chance to go as far as his or her talents will allow). Yet it is hard to

FOR CRITICAL ANALYSIS

College students on spring break flocked to Florida beaches during the coronavirus pandemic. How do we balance their liberty against the health and security of the communities to which they returned?

equality of opportunity a widely shared American ideal that all people should have the freedom to use whatever talents and wealth they have to reach their fullest potential

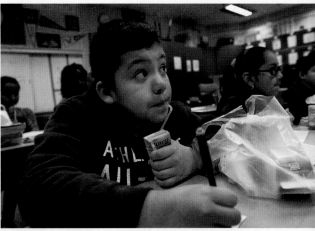

agree on what constitutes equality of opportunity. Furthermore, in contrast to liberty, which requires limits on the role of government, equality implies an *obligation* of the government to the people.[41] But how far does this obligation extend? Must a group's past inequalities be redressed to ensure equal opportunity in the present? Should legal, political, and economic inequalities all be given the same weight?

Americans do make clear distinctions between social or economic equality and **political equality**, the right of a community's members to participate in politics on equal terms. Beginning from a very restricted definition of political community, which originally included only White men who owned a certain amount of property, the United States has moved much closer to an ideal of political equality that can be summed up as "one person, one vote." Although considerable conflict remains over whether the political system makes it harder for some people to participate than others, and whether money plays too large a role in politics, most Americans agree that all citizens should have an equal right to participate and that government should enforce that right.

Many Americans see economic inequality as largely due to individual choices, virtues, or failures, and so they tend to be more skeptical of government action to reduce it (compared to government action to reduce political inequality). Even when severe economic hardships, like the Great Depression of the 1930s, affect many people, a large number of Americans have supported only a limited response by government.

Three kinds of controversies have arisen about government's role in addressing inequality. The first is determining what constitutes equality of access to public facilities, including both facilities operated by government and those operated privately but open to the public. In 1896 the Supreme Court ruled in *Plessy v. Ferguson* that providing "separate but equal" facilities for Blacks and Whites was constitutional,[42] a principle the Court overturned in 1954 in *Brown v. Board of Education* (see Chapter 5).[43] Today, new questions have been raised about what constitutes equal access to public facilities. Some argue, for example, that the unequal financing of public schools in different districts within a state violates the constitutional guarantee of "equal protection of the laws." To date, the federal courts have rejected such claims that the unequal economic effects of state and local government policies are a constitutional matter.[44]

A second debate concerns the government's role in ensuring equality of opportunity in private life, such as college admissions and corporate employment. Although

Americans struggle to define how equality of opportunity can be provided at the same time as individual liberty. One area of debate is in education. Does the fact that New York (left) spends on average $23,091 per student each year while Utah (right) spends on average $7,179 per student, mean that there is not an equality of opportunity for schoolchildren? *(Data from www.census.gov.)*

political equality the right to participate in politics equally, based on the principle of "one person, one vote"

The Fight for $15—a nationwide effort to increase the minimum wage to $15 an hour—first gained traction in 2013, increasing public awareness of income inequality in the United States. By 2020 many states had increased their minimum wage above the federal minimum wage, but few had reached the $15 threshold that workers had protested for.

Americans generally agree that discrimination in such areas should not be tolerated, they disagree over what should be done to ensure equality of opportunity in them (see Table 1.4).[45] Supporters of affirmative action programs, for example, claim that they are necessary to compensate for past discrimination in order to establish true equality of opportunity today. Opponents maintain that they amount to reverse discrimination and that a truly equal society should not acknowledge gender or racial differences. Some particularly pointed questions about public responsibility for private inequalities involve gender. The traditional view, still held by many today, takes for granted that women bear special responsibilities in the family and that the resulting challenges they face in the labor force are not matters for the government to address. In the past 40 years especially, this view has come under fire as advocates for women have argued that these inequalities *are* a topic of public concern.[46]

A third debate about equality concerns differences in income and wealth. As noted earlier, income inequality has seldom led to political controversy in the United States, which currently has the largest gaps in income and wealth between rich and poor citizens of any developed nation. This tolerance for inequality is reflected in America's tax code, which is more advantageous to wealthy taxpayers than that of almost any other Western nation.

Income inequality rose on the political agenda during the coronavirus pandemic of 2020, when the economic slowdown most affected lower-income workers without employee benefits, including those in the restaurant, retail, and gig economy sectors. As Congress deliberated economic stimulus measures and policy changes, perennial debates about the role of government reemerged. Would increased unemployment benefits breed dependence and undermine Americans' work ethic? Would a new, albeit temporary, federal paid-leave policy "crowd out" the existing paid-leave policies of larger corporations and substitute taxpayer-provided benefits? Such debates appear even under the toughest economic circumstances.[47]

DEMOCRACY

The essence of democracy is the participation of the people in choosing their rulers and the ability of the people to influence what those rulers do. The idea of placing power in the hands of the people is known as **popular sovereignty** and, together with political equality, makes politicians accountable to the people.

FOR CRITICAL ANALYSIS

Economic inequality among Americans has been widening since at least the 1970s. Many politicians and news commentators say that inequality is threatening the middle class. Is there any evidence that the American public is worried about the growth in inequality?

popular sovereignty a principle of democracy in which political authority rests ultimately in the hands of the people

TABLE 1.4

Equality and Public Opinion

Americans believe in some forms of equality more than others. How do these survey results reflect disagreement about what equality means in practice?

STATEMENT	PERCENTAGE WHO AGREE
It is very important that women have the same rights as men in our country.	97
It is very important that everyone has an equal opportunity to succeed.	82
It should be illegal for employers to fire people or refuse to hire people for being lesbian, gay, or bisexual.	90
It should be legal for gay and lesbian couples to get married.	61
There is too much economic inequality in the country these days.	61
Some amount of inequality is acceptable (among those who said there is too much economic inequality).	70
Our country has not gone far enough when it comes to giving Black people equal rights with Whites (according to Whites).	37
Our country has not gone far enough when it comes to giving Black people equal rights with Whites (according to Blacks).	78
The country hasn't gone far enough when it comes to gender equality (according to women).	64
The country hasn't gone far enough when it comes to gender equality (according to men).	49

SOURCE: Pew Research Center, www.pewresearch.org; Kaiser Family Foundation, kff.org. See endnote 45 for specific reports.

American democracy rests on the principle of **majority rule** with **minority rights**. Majority rule means that the wishes of the majority determine what government does. The House of Representatives—a large body elected directly by the people— was designed in particular to ensure majority rule. But the Founders feared that popular majorities could turn government into a "tyranny of the majority"; thus, concern for individual rights and liberties has been a part of American democracy from the beginning. The rights enumerated in the Bill of Rights and enforced through the courts provide an important check on the power of the majority.

Despite Americans' deep attachment to the *ideal* of democracy, many concerns can be raised about our *practice* of democracy. One concern is how the right to vote has been restricted, though that right has been expanded—slowly and fitfully—over the last two centuries. Property restrictions on the right to vote were eliminated by 1828. In 1870 the Fifteenth Amendment to the Constitution

majority rule, minority rights
the democratic principle that a government follows the preferences of the majority of voters but protects the interests of the minority

FOR CRITICAL ANALYSIS

In the United States, do citizens make the decisions of government, or do they merely influence them?

While levels of participation in politics are relatively low for young Americans, presidential primary campaigns often draw many young people to volunteer and to vote. What factors might energize young people to become involved in campaigns?

guaranteed the vote to nonwhite men, although in practice most of them were denied it for almost a century longer. In 1920 the Nineteenth Amendment guaranteed women the right to vote. And in 1965 the Voting Rights Act finally secured the right of African Americans to vote. The Twenty-Sixth Amendment, ratified in 1971 during the Vietnam War, gave 18- to 20-year-olds the right to vote.

More people securing the right to vote does not end concerns about democracy. The ways in which elections are carried out can significantly affect who can actually vote or get elected. During the first two decades of the twentieth century, states and cities enacted many reforms, including strict registration requirements and scheduling of elections, which made it harder to vote. The aim was to rid politics of corruption, but the consequence was to reduce participation. More recently, voter ID laws requiring government identification to register or to vote have been enacted for similar stated reasons and with similar consequences. Other institutional decisions affect which candidates stand the best chance of getting elected (see Chapter 10).

A further consideration about democracy concerns the relationship between economic power and political power. Although money has always played an important role in elections and governing in the United States, many argue that its pervasive influence in campaigns and lobbying activities today undermines democracy. With the decline of locally based political parties that depend on party loyalists to turn out the vote, and with the rise of political action committees, political consultants, expensive media campaigns, and court decisions reducing the government's regulatory power over campaign finance, money has become the central fact of life in American politics. It often determines who runs for office, it can exert a heavy influence on who wins, and some argue that it affects what politicians do once they are in office.[48]

Low turnout for elections and a pervasive sense of apathy and cynicism have characterized American politics for much of the past half-century. The widespread interest in the 2008 election and the near-record levels of voter turnout, which, at 61.6 percent, was the highest since 1968, reversed this trend.[49] Millions registered and voted for the first time in 2008, including near-record numbers of young people. After turnout sagged in 2012 and 2016, the hotly contested 2020 election drove turnout to the highest level in a century, with two-thirds of eligible Americans voting.[50]

What Americans Think about Government

> **Summarize Americans' attitudes toward government**

Since the United States was established as a nation, Americans have been reluctant to grant government too much power, and they have often been suspicious of politicians. But they have also turned to government for assistance in times of need and have strongly supported it in periods of war. In 1933 the power of the government began to expand to meet the crises created by the stock market crash of 1929, the massive business failures and unemployment of the Great Depression, and the threatened failure of the banking system.

Can Young People Make a Difference in Politics?

Young people are less likely to participate in politics than older people. Only 46 percent of young people (age 18–29) voted in the 2016 presidential election, compared to 71 percent of those over age 65. The 2018 election was historic, with the highest voter turnout for a midterm election in four decades, and youth voter turnout broke records in many states. Millennials are now the largest age cohort in the United States, and they made their voices heard in 2018.

Change in Voter Turnout, 2014–18

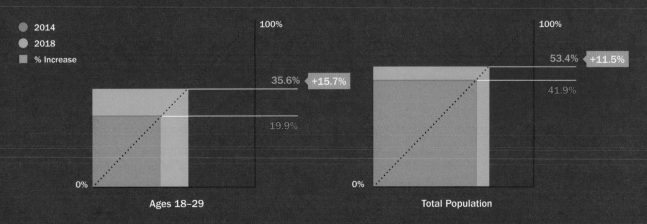

- 2014
- 2018
- % Increase

Ages 18–29
35.6% +15.7%
19.9%

Total Population
53.4% +11.5%
41.9%

Change in Voter Turnout by State, 2018

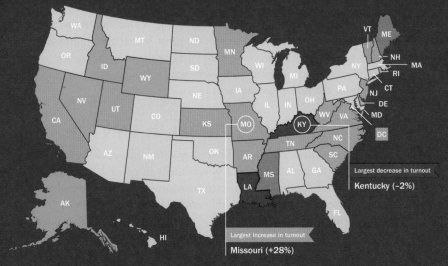

Percent difference in voter turnout

- + 20% and above
- + 15–19.9%
- + 10–14.9%
- + 5–9.9%
- + 0–4.9%
- % Decrease

Largest decrease in turnout
Kentucky (–2%)

Largest increase in turnout
Missouri (+28%)

FOR CRITICAL ANALYSIS

1. Which five states had the largest increase in youth voting in 2018? Which states saw youth turnout decline?

2. What factors do you think led to increased youth participation? Characteristics of the candidates running? The importance of key issues to young people? Something else?

SOURCE: William H. Frey, "Analysis of U.S. Census Bureau Current Population Survey Voting and Registration Supplement micro-files," www.brookings.edu; U.S. Census Bureau, "2018 Voting and Elections Supplement, Current Population Survey," www.census.gov (accessed 5/23/19).

Minds can achieve anything. We make sure they get to college.
At Federal Student Aid, we make it easier to get money for higher education.

HOW DO I PREPARE FOR COLLEGE?
Learn about exploring careers, choosing and applying to schools, and taking required tests. Use checklists to help get ready.

WHAT TYPES OF AID CAN I GET?
Read about the types of financial aid available from the government and other sources: grants, scholarships, loans, and work-study.

DO I QUALIFY FOR AID?
Most people are eligible for financial aid. Find out who gets aid, how to stay eligible, and how to get eligibility back if you've lost it.

HOW DO I APPLY FOR AID?
Learn how to submit your *Free Application for Federal Student Aid* (FAFSA®), how aid is calculated, and how you'll get your aid.

HOW DO I MANAGE MY LOANS?
Choose a repayment plan, pay on time, avoid default, and get help with problems.

The federal government maintains a large number of websites that provide useful information to citizens on such topics as loans for education, civil service job applications, the inflation rate, and how the weather will affect farming. These sites are just one way in which the government serves its citizens.

Congress passed legislation that brought the government into the businesses of home mortgages, farm mortgages, credit, and relief of personal financial distress. More recently, when the economy fell into a deep recession in 2008 and 2009, the federal government took action to stabilize the financial system, oversee the restructuring of the failing auto manufacturers, and provide hundreds of billions of dollars in economic stimulation. In 2020 federal funds helped fight the coronavirus pandemic, providing funds to businesses, state and local governments, and workers themselves.

Today the national government is enormous, with programs and policies reaching into every corner of American life. It oversees the nation's economy, it is the nation's largest employer, it controls the world's most formidable military, and it regulates a wide range of social and commercial activities. Americans use government services, benefits, and infrastructure every day, although they are simultaneously skeptical about the role of government in society.

CONSERVATIVE IN THEORY, LIBERAL IN PRACTICE

The Constitution lays out a system of limited government, and the majority of Americans, when asked about the role of government in general, give answers on the conservative side of the political spectrum. More Americans consider themselves politically conservative than liberal (37 versus 24 percent in 2019).[51] In 2019, 56 percent of Americans agreed with the statement that "the federal government has too much power," and 56 percent agreed that "government is almost always wasteful and inefficient."[52]

At the same time, however, when asked about specific government programs, majorities offer strong support. Strong majorities of Democrats and Republicans favor maintained or increased government spending on Social Security; high-ways, bridges, and roads; and economic assistance to needy people.[53] Thus many Americans prefer small government in the abstract, but very much like what government does in specific areas.[54]

TRUST IN GOVERNMENT

A key characteristic of contemporary political culture is low *trust* in government. In the early 1960s three-quarters of Americans said they trusted government most of the time or always. By 2020 only 20 percent did[55] (see Figure 1.3).

Trust spiked higher after the September 11 terrorist attacks, but fell to pre-attack levels within three years, and the trend has continued its downward path. Distrust of government greatly influenced the presidential primary elections in 2016, when a number of "outsider" candidates critical of government attracted wide support, including Donald Trump. Trust in government declined again during the early stages of the coronavirus pandemic, particularly trust in the federal government, which many Americans felt reacted more slowly to the crisis than their local and state governments.[56]

Does it matter if Americans trust their government? For the most part, the answer is yes. As we have seen, most Americans rely on government for a wide range of services and protections that they simply take for granted. But long-term distrust in government can result in opposition to the taxes necessary to support such programs and also make it difficult to attract talented workers to public service.[57] In addition, it may ultimately weaken the United States in defending its interests in the world economy and may jeopardize its national security.

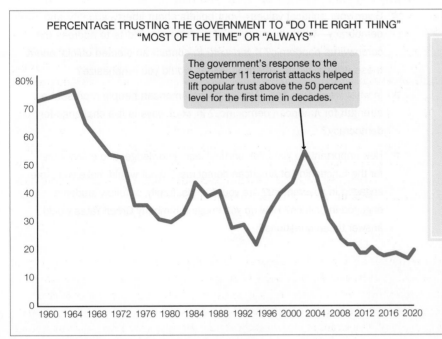

PERCENTAGE TRUSTING THE GOVERNMENT TO "DO THE RIGHT THING" "MOST OF THE TIME" OR "ALWAYS"

The government's response to the September 11 terrorist attacks helped lift popular trust above the 50 percent level for the first time in decades.

Note: The Pew data after 2004 represent a "three survey moving average."
SOURCE: The American National Election Studies, 1958–2004; Pew Research Center, www.people-press.org/2019 /04/11/public-trust-in-government-1958-2019 (accessed 1/19/20); Pew Research Center, "Americans' Views of Government: Low Trust, but Some Positive Performance Ratings," September 14, 2020, www.pewresearch.org/politics/2020/09/14 /americans-views-of-government-low-trust-but-some-positive-performance-ratings/ (accessed 10/12/20).

FOR CRITICAL ANALYSIS

What recent events have affected Americans' trust in government? What might it take to restore Americans' trust in the federal government?

FIGURE 1.3

Public Trust in Government, 1958–2020

Since the 1960s, general levels of public trust in government have declined. What factors might help to account for changes in the public's trust in government? Why has confidence in government dropped again since September 11, 2001?

Likewise, a weak government can do little to help citizens weather periods of tumultuous economic or technological change. Moreover, trust in government differs across groups: African Americans and Latinos express slightly more confidence in the federal government than do Whites (although even among the most supportive groups, considerably more than half trust the government only some of the time).[58] Declining trust is important because public confidence in government is vital for the health of a democracy.

American Political Culture: What Do You Think?

In this chapter we examined various components of American political culture. Nearly every American supports the political values of liberty, equality, and democracy. How we put them into practice, however, sparks many of the debates that shape American political life. In addition, we find that the make-up of the American people deeply influences American politics. Race, gender, and class divisions foster disagreement and debate and, as we will see throughout this book, influence how government and politics function.

At the start of this chapter, we introduced Kimberly Green-Yates, who was struggling to get protective medical equipment for the nursing homes she runs in Oklahoma. Given what you learned in this chapter about American political culture, take a closer look at the account of the coronavirus pandemic on pp. 2–4:

★ Given your political values—your beliefs about liberty, equality, and democracy—what do you think of government efforts to address the coronavirus pandemic? If you were to contact an elected official about these efforts, which American values would you emphasize?

★ In what ways does the diversity of the American people represent a strength for American democracy? In what ways is it a challenge for democracy?

★ How important do you think participation, knowledge, and efficacy are for the functioning of American democracy? What would make you more engaged in government? Are your friends, family, or fellow students engaged in politics? How do you imagine Kimberly Green-Yates would answer these questions?

★ STUDY GUIDE ★

Government

Differentiate between forms of government (pp. 5–9)

Government is needed to provide those services, sometimes called "public goods," that citizens all need but probably cannot individually provide adequately for themselves. Governments vary considerably in terms of who governs and how much government control is permitted. Many governments around the world (and most governments before the modern era) have accepted few limits on their behavior and provided citizens with limited opportunities to participate in public affairs. Today, numerous countries, including the United States, are constitutional democracies, in which laws limit what government can do and citizens enjoy personal and political freedom. America's democracy provides citizens with numerous opportunities to participate in politics, including the rights to elect officials, vote directly on laws in many states and localities, and take part in direct action politics.

Key Terms

government (p. 5)
politics (p. 5)
autocracy (p. 5)
oligarchy (p. 5)
democracy (p. 5)
constitutional government (p. 7)
authoritarian government (p. 7)
totalitarian government (p. 7)
political power (p. 8)
representative democracy (republic) (p. 8)
direct democracy (p. 8)
pluralism (p. 9)

Practice Quiz

1. Services that citizens need but are unlikely to provide for themselves, such as national defense, maintenance of public order, and a stable currency, are called
   a) laissez-faire goods.
   b) pluralist goods.
   c) provisional goods.
   d) public goods.
   e) private goods.

2. What is the basic difference between an autocracy and an oligarchy?
   a) the extent to which average citizens have a say in government affairs
   b) the means of collecting taxes and conscripting soldiers
   c) the number of people who control governing decisions
   d) the size and political influence of the military
   e) There are no differences between autocracies and oligarchies.

3. A government that is formally limited in terms of what it can do and how it can go about doing it is known as
   a) a totalitarian government.
   b) an authoritarian government.
   c) a constitutional government.
   d) an autocracy.
   e) an oligarchy.

4. A system of government that allows citizens to vote directly on laws and policies through initiatives and referenda is called
   a) a republic.
   b) representative democracy.
   c) direct democracy.
   d) pluralism.
   e) laissez-faire capitalism.

Citizenship: Participation, Knowledge, and Efficacy

Describe the rights and responsibilities that citizens have in a democracy (pp. 9–11)

Citizenship requires political knowledge. When citizens know about politics, they are better able to understand their own interests and to identify the best way to act on those interests. While the internet has made it easier to learn about and participate in politics, many Americans still do not know much about current issues or debates, or even the basics of how government works. Many Americans also have low levels of political efficacy; they do not believe that ordinary citizens can affect what government does. Political knowledge and participation in politics can help increase one's efficacy.

Key Terms

political knowledge (p. 9)

citizenship (p. 9)

political efficacy (p. 10)

Practice Quiz

5. How has the internet affected Americans' relationship with politics?
   a) Thanks to the internet, Americans' sense of political efficacy has increased in recent years.
   b) The internet has equalized access to political knowledge for people of different incomes, education levels, races, and ages.
   c) The internet now allows Americans to vote online.
   d) A large majority of Americans now gets political information from the internet.
   e) The internet has driven a decrease in rates of political participation among Americans.

6. *Political efficacy* is the belief that
   a) government is wasteful and corrupt.
   b) government operates efficiently.
   c) government has grown too large.
   d) government cannot be trusted.
   e) ordinary citizens can influence what government does.

Who Are Americans?

Describe the social composition of the American population and how it has changed over time (pp. 12–20)

The United States is defined, in part, by its ever-growing and changing population. During the last 200 years, America has become more racially, ethnically, geographically, and religiously diverse. Immigration has been an important reason for the country's shifting demographics, and it has frequently sparked intense debate about the nature of American identity and American democracy.

Practice Quiz

7. In 1900 residents who traced their origin to Latin America or Asia each accounted for
   a) less than 1 percent of the U.S. population.
   b) approximately 5 percent of the U.S. population.
   c) approximately 10 percent of the U.S. population.
   d) approximately 15 percent of the U.S. population.
   e) more than 20 percent of the U.S. population.

8. Which of the following statements best describes the history of income inequality in the United States?
   a) The top 1 percent has never earned more than 10 percent of the nation's annual income.
   b) The top 1 percent has never earned less than 10 percent of the nation's annual income.
   c) Income inequality has remained fairly constant since the late 1970s.
   d) Income inequality has increased considerably since the late 1970s.
   e) Income inequality has decreased considerably since the late 1970s.

American Political Culture

Describe how cultural values of liberty, equality, and democracy influence the U.S. system of government (pp. 21–26)

The foundational documents of the United States enshrined liberty, equality, and democracy as key components of the country's national identity. While Americans continue to affirm these ideals, questions about how to apply and balance these important elements of American political culture have motivated disagreements throughout the country's history.

Key Terms

political culture (p. 21)

liberty (p. 21)

limited government (p. 21)

laissez-faire capitalism (p. 22)

equality of opportunity (p. 22)

political equality (p. 23)

popular sovereignty (p. 24)

majority rule, minority rights (p. 25)

Practice Quiz

9. "Life, Liberty and the pursuit of Happiness" are three "inalienable" rights mentioned in
   a) the Constitution.
   b) the Declaration of Independence.
   c) the Bill of Rights.
   d) the Articles of Confederation.
   e) the Pledge of Allegiance.

10. Which of the following is *not* related to the American concept of liberty?
    a) freedom of speech
    b) economic freedom
    c) freedom of religion
    d) freedom of assembly
    e) All of the above are related to the American concept of liberty.

11. The principle of political equality can be best summed up as
    a) "equality of results."
    b) "equality of opportunity."
    c) "one person, one vote."
    d) "equality between the sexes."
    e) "leave everyone alone."

What Americans Think about Government

Summarize Americans' attitudes toward government (pp. 26–30)

While Americans have always been hesitant about granting government too much power, they have frequently relied on it during times of national crisis and have become increasingly dependent on it to provide important services. Over the last few decades, Americans' trust in government has declined significantly. Low levels of trust and efficacy may threaten American democracy by weakening the government and reducing the public's willingness to participate in political life.

Practice Quiz

12. What does it mean to say that Americans are "conservative in theory but liberal in practice"?
    a) The majority of Americans have no opinions about government in general or about the specific programs government implements.
    b) The majority of Americans prefer large government in the abstract and are very supportive of most specific government programs.
    c) The majority of Americans prefer large government in the abstract but are very opposed to most specific government programs.
    d) The majority of Americans prefer small government in the abstract but are very supportive of most specific government programs.
    e) The majority of Americans prefer small government in the abstract and are very opposed to most specific government programs.

13. Americans' trust in their government
    a) rose significantly between 1964 and 1980.
    b) increased immediately following September 11, 2001, but declined shortly thereafter.
    c) declined immediately after the September 11 attacks but has risen dramatically since 2004.
    d) reached its highest point ever in the fall of 2011.
    e) has remained the same over the last 50 years.

The Founding and the Constitution

WHAT GOVERNMENT DOES AND WHY IT MATTERS Sometimes a concrete way the U.S. Constitution affects average Americans comes vividly to life, highlighting the framers' views about the nature of government. Because they feared that centralizing governmental powers might endanger individual liberties, they divided executive, legislative, and judicial powers across separate institutions, each of which restrains the others. Power was further divided across two levels in the federal system, between the national and state governments.

This constitutional system dramatically shaped the life of Jim Obergefell, a real estate agent and IT consultant

in Cincinnati who in 1992 met and fell in love with John Arthur.[1] Although the couple wanted to marry, they could not. In 1996, Congress passed and President Bill Clinton signed the Defense of Marriage Act (DOMA), a federal law defining marriage as between one man and one woman. States could still permit same-sex marriage, but the marriages would not be recognized for federal purposes such as filing taxes or earning Social Security survivor benefits. The law also permitted states to refuse to recognize same-sex marriages performed in other states. Then in 2004 Ohio enacted its own DOMA, which prohibited same-sex marriage and refused to recognize those performed elsewhere.

From America's founding to today, debates over the role of the government in citizens' lives have persisted. After the historic decision to rule same-sex marriage a right guaranteed by the Constitution, Jim Obergefell holds a photo of his late husband on the steps of the Supreme Court to celebrate his bittersweet victory.

Thus Obergefell and Arthur were barred from marriage by the actions of two branches of the federal government—the executive and the legislative—and their state. The issue became more acute when Arthur was diagnosed with ALS, or Lou Gehrig's disease—a progressive debilitating disease. Obergefell served as Arthur's primary caregiver, and in 2013 the couple flew to Maryland, where same-sex marriage was permitted, and wed on the airport tarmac. Then they sued Ohio to have Obergefell be recognized as the surviving spouse on Arthur's imminent death certificate. "We decided to stand up for our marriage and to no longer accept being treated as second-class citizens,"[2] Obergefell explained. Arthur passed away three months later.

The case, *Obergefell v. Hodges*, made it to the Supreme Court, the top of the judicial branch of government, which in 2015 ruled that the due process and equal protection clauses of the Fourteenth Amendment to the Constitution guarantee to same-sex couples nationwide the fundamental right to marry.[3] Thus the Court secured a civil right that the executive and legislative branches and a number of states had denied.

The U.S. Constitution lays out the purposes of government: to promote justice, to maintain peace at home, to defend the nation from foreign foes, to provide for the "general welfare" of Americans, and, above all, to secure the "blessings of liberty" for them. It also spells out a plan for achieving these objectives, including institutions to exercise legislative, executive, and judicial powers and a division of powers among the federal government's branches and between the national and state governments. Jim Obergefell's quest to marry the love of his life intersected with all three branches and both levels of government.

His story also shows that although many Americans believe strongly in the values of liberty, equality, and democracy, the ways those values are defined and implemented by the institutions that the Constitution created lead to considerable controversy. The framers believed that a good constitution created a government with the capacity to act forcefully. But they also believed that government should be compelled to take a variety of interests and viewpoints into account when it formulates policies. Sometimes the deliberation and compromise encouraged by the constitutional arrangements of "separated institutions sharing powers" can result in policy making that is slow or even gridlocked.[4] Public policy is always a product of political bargaining. But so was the Constitution itself. As this chapter will show, the Constitution reflects high principle as well as political self-interest.

CHAPTER GOALS

★ Explain the conflicts and coalitions that led to the Declaration of Independence and the Articles of Confederation (pp. 37–40)

★ Describe the political context of the Constitutional Convention and the compromises achieved there (pp. 40–46)

★ Describe the principles of governance and the powers of the national government defined by the Constitution (pp. 46–53)

★ Differentiate between the Federalists' and Antifederalists' stances on the ratification of the Constitution (pp. 53–57)

★ Explain how, and how often, the Constitution has been changed (pp. 57–62)

The First Founding: Interests and Conflicts

> **Explain the conflicts and coalitions that led to the Declaration of Independence and the Articles of Confederation**

Competing ideals often reflect competing interests, and so it was in Revolutionary America. The American Revolution and the American Constitution were outgrowths of a struggle among economic and political forces within the colonies. Five sectors of society were important in colonial politics: (1) New England merchants; (2) southern planters; (3) "royalists"—holders of royal lands, offices, and patents (licenses to engage in a profession or business activity); (4) the "middling stratum" of shopkeepers, artisans, and town workers; and (5) small farmers.

Throughout the eighteenth century, these groups differed over issues of taxation, trade, and commerce. For the most part, however, the merchants, planters, and royalists—that is, the colonial elite—maintained a political alliance that held in check the more radical forces representing the other two groups. After 1760, however, by threatening the interests of the merchants and planters, British tax and trade policies split the elite, enhancing the radicals' political influence and setting off a chain of events that culminated in the American Revolution.[5]

BRITISH TAXES AND COLONIAL INTERESTS

During the first half of the eighteenth century, Britain ruled its American colonies with a light hand. British rule was hardly evident outside the largest towns, and colonists had found ways of evading most taxes levied in London. Beginning in

British colonists in America shipped many goods back to England, such as furs obtained by trading with Native Americans. The British government claimed that the colonists should pay more in taxes in light of the protection their shipments received from the British navy and the expenses Britain incurred defending the colonies.

the 1760s, however, debts and other financial problems forced the British government to search for new revenue sources. This search rather quickly led to the North American colonies.

The British government reasoned that much of its debt was due to defense of the colonies during the French and Indian War, which ended in 1763, and continuing protection that British land and naval forces were providing from Indian attacks and for colonial shipping. Thus, during the 1760s, Britain tried to impose new, though relatively modest, taxes on the colonists.

In the mid-eighteenth century, to raise revenue, governments relied mainly on tariffs, duties, and other taxes on commerce; and it was to such taxes, and to the Stamp Act, that the British turned during the 1760s.

The Stamp Act of 1765 imposed taxes on many printed items in the colonies, ranging from newspapers to playing cards to licenses for lawyers. Other new taxes included the Sugar Act of 1764, which taxed sugar and molasses as well as other commodities. These taxes most heavily affected the two groups in colonial society with the most extensive commercial interests and activities—the New England merchants and the southern planters. United under the slogan "No taxation without representation," these members of the elite broke with their royalist allies and turned to their former adversaries—the shopkeepers, small farmers, laborers, and artisans—for help in opposing the tax measures. With their assistance, the merchants and planters organized demonstrations and a boycott of British goods that ultimately forced the Crown to rescind most of its hated new taxes.

In contrast to their new allies, the merchants and planters were now anxious to end the unrest they had helped arouse. Indeed, most respectable Bostonians supported the actions of the British soldiers involved in the Boston Massacre—the 1770 killing of five colonists by British soldiers who were attempting to repel an angry mob gathered outside the Town House, the seat of the colonial government. In their subsequent trial, the soldiers were defended by John Adams, a pillar of Boston society and a future president of the United States. Adams asserted that the soldiers' actions were entirely justified, provoked by "a motley rabble of saucy boys, negroes and mulattoes, Irish teagues and outlandish Jack tars." All but two of the soldiers were acquitted.[6]

Despite the efforts of the British government and the colonial elite, however, it proved difficult to end the political strife. Under leadership that included Samuel Adams, a cousin of John Adams, the more radical forces continued to agitate for political and social change. They asserted that British power supported an unjust political and social structure within the colonies and began to advocate an end to British rule.[7]

POLITICAL STRIFE AND THE RADICALIZATION OF THE COLONISTS

The political strife within the colonies was the background for the events of 1773–74. With the Tea Act of 1773, the British government granted the politically powerful East India Company a monopoly on the export of tea from Britain, eliminating a lucrative trade for colonial merchants. To add to the injury, the company planned to sell the tea directly in the colonies instead of working through the colonial merchants. Tea was an extremely important commodity during the 1770s, and these British actions posed a serious threat to the New England merchants.

The British helped radicalize colonists through bad policy decisions in the years before the Revolution. For example, Britain gave the ailing East India Company a monopoly on the tea trade in the American colonies. Colonists feared that the monopoly would hurt colonial merchants' business and protested by throwing East India Company tea into Boston Harbor in 1773.

Together with their southern allies, the merchants once again called for support from the radicals, whose own grievances against the British and the colonial government included the Tea Act's continuation of a tax imposed in the 1760s on tea imported into the colonies. The most dramatic result was the Boston Tea Party. In three other colonies, antitax Americans blocked the unloading of taxed tea, resulting in its return to Britain. The royal governor of Massachusetts, however, refused to allow three shiploads of unsold tea to leave Boston Harbor. The radicals seized this opportunity: on the night of December 16, 1773, a group led by Samuel Adams, some of them "disguised" as Mohawk Indians, boarded the three vessels and threw all 342 chests of tea into the harbor.

This event played a decisive role in American history. Although the merchants had hoped to force the British to rescind the Tea Act, they did not seek independence from Britain. Through the Boston Tea Party, however, Adams and the other radicals hoped to provoke the British into actions that would alienate their colonial supporters and pave the way for a rebellion. Their plan succeeded, as Parliament enacted a number of harsh reprisals that included closing the port of Boston to commerce, changing the colonial government of Massachusetts, removing accused persons to Britain for trial, and, most important, restricting colonists' movement to the west—further alienating the southern planters, who depended on access to new western lands.

These acts of repression confirmed the worst criticisms of British rule and helped radicalize Americans. Thus, the Boston Tea Party set in motion a cycle of provocation and retaliation that in 1774 resulted in the convening of the First Continental Congress. An assembly of delegates from 12 colonies, the Congress called for a total boycott of British goods and, under the prodding of the radicals, began to consider the possibility of ending British rule. The eventual result was the Declaration of Independence.

FOR CRITICAL ANALYSIS

Conflicts over taxes did not end with the American Revolution. Why is tax policy almost always controversial? What differences and similarities are there between the debates over taxes in the 1760s and today?

THE DECLARATION OF INDEPENDENCE

In 1776, more than a year after open warfare had commenced in Massachusetts, the Second Continental Congress appointed a committee consisting of Thomas Jefferson of Virginia, Benjamin Franklin of Pennsylvania, Roger Sherman of

Connecticut, John Adams of Massachusetts, and Robert Livingston of New York to draft a statement of American independence from British rule. The Declaration of Independence, written by Jefferson and adopted by the Second Continental Congress, was an extraordinary document both philosophically and politically. Philosophically, it was remarkable for its assertion (heavily influenced by the works of the philosopher John Locke) that government could not deprive people of certain "unalienable rights" that include "Life, Liberty, and the pursuit of Happiness." In the world of 1776, in which some kings still claimed a God-given right to rule, this was a dramatic statement. Politically, the Declaration was remarkable because, despite the differences among the colonists along economic, regional, and philosophical lines, it focused on grievances, goals, and principles that might unify the various groups. The Declaration was an attempt to identify and put into words a history and set of principles to forge national unity.[8]

THE ARTICLES OF CONFEDERATION

Articles of Confederation America's first written constitution; served as the basis for America's national government until 1789

Having declared independence, the colonies needed to establish a government. In November 1777 the Continental Congress adopted the **Articles of Confederation**—the United States' first written constitution. Although not ratified by all the states until 1781, it functioned as the country's constitution until the final months of 1788.

The first goal of the Articles was to limit the powers of the central government; as provided under Article II, "each state retains its sovereignty, freedom, and independence." (These attributes define a **confederation**.) Given that there was no president or other presiding officer, the entire national government consisted of a Congress with very little power. Its members were little more than messengers from the state legislatures: their salaries were paid out of the state treasuries; they were subject to immediate recall by state authorities; and each state, regardless of its population, had only one vote. All 13 states had to agree to any amendments to the Articles of Confederation after it was ratified.

confederation a system of government in which states retain sovereign authority except for the powers expressly delegated to the national government

Congress was given the power to declare war and make peace, to make treaties and alliances, to issue currency or borrow money, and to regulate trade with the Native Americans. Any laws it passed, however, could be carried out only by state governments. It could also appoint the senior officers of the U.S. Army, but there was no such army because the nation's armed forces consisted only of the state militias. These extreme limits on the power of the national government made the Articles of Confederation hopelessly impractical.[9]

The Second Founding: From Compromise to Constitution

Describe the political context of the Constitutional Convention and the compromises achieved there

A series of developments following the armistice with the British in 1783 highlighted the shortcomings of the Articles of Confederation in holding the former colonies together as an independent and effective nation-state.

First, the United States had great difficulty conducting its foreign affairs successfully, as there was no national military and competition among the states for foreign commerce allowed the European powers to play them off against one another. At one point, John Adams, who had become a leader in the independence struggle after reversing his earlier pro-British sympathies, was sent to negotiate a new treaty with Britain, one that would cover disputes left over from the war. The British responded that since the United States under the Articles was unable to enforce existing treaties, it would negotiate with each of the 13 states separately. At the same time, the United States faced a threat from Spain, which still held vast territories in North and South America. Without a national military, the nation's borders were difficult to protect against this potentially hostile foreign power.

Second, the power that states retained under the Articles of Confederation began to alarm well-to-do Americans, in particular New England merchants and southern planters, when radical forces gained power in a number of state governments. As a result of the Revolution, one key segment of the colonial elite—the royal land, office, and patent holders—was stripped of its economic and political privileges. While the elite was weakened, the radicals had gained strength and now controlled states including Pennsylvania and Rhode Island, where they pursued policies that struck terror in the hearts of business and property owners throughout the country. In Rhode Island, for example, a legislature dominated by representatives of small farmers, artisans, and shopkeepers instituted economic policies that included drastic currency inflation. In Pennsylvania, the government redistributed land from large landowners to small farmers. The central government under the Articles was powerless to intervene.

The Congress of the Confederation did, however, agree on two laws that helped to shape American history: the Land Ordinance of 1785 and the Northwest Ordinance of 1787. The Land Ordinance established the principles of land surveying and ownership that governed America's westward expansion. Under the Northwest Ordinance, the individual states agreed to surrender their claims to incorporate land on their western frontiers, opening the way for the admission of new states to the Union.

Despite these legislative successes, the political and economic position of the new American states deteriorated during the 1780s. Europe's great powers— Britain, France, and Spain—adopted policies that excluded Americans from commerce, while political unrest at home further undermined trade and investment.

THE ANNAPOLIS CONVENTION

The continuation of international weakness and domestic economic turmoil led many Americans to consider whether their newly adopted form of government might not already require revision. In the fall of 1786, the Virginia legislature invited representatives of all the states to a convention in Annapolis, Maryland. Delegates from only five states actually attended, so nothing substantive could be accomplished. The only concrete result of the Annapolis Convention was a carefully worded resolution calling on the Congress to send commissioners to Philadelphia at a later time "to devise such further provisions as shall appear to them necessary to render the Constitution of the Federal Government adequate to the exigencies of the Union."[10] But the resolution did not necessarily imply any desire to do more than improve the Articles of Confederation.

SHAYS'S REBELLION

Daniel Shays's rebellion proved the Articles of Confederation were too weak to protect the fledgling nation.

It is quite possible that the Constitutional Convention of 1787 in Philadelphia would never have taken place at all except for Shays's Rebellion. In the winter following the Annapolis Convention, Daniel Shays, a former army captain, led a mob of debt-ridden farmers in an effort to prevent foreclosures on their land by keeping the county courts of western Massachusetts from sitting until after the next election. A militia organized by the state governor and funded by a group of prominent merchants dispersed the mob, but Shays and his followers then attempted to capture the federal arsenal at Springfield. Within a few days, the state government regained control and captured 14 of the rebels. Later that year, a newly elected Massachusetts legislature granted some of the farmers' demands.

George Washington summed up the effects of the incident on the leaders of the new nation: "I am mortified beyond expression that in the moment of our acknowledged independence we should by our conduct verify the predictions of our transatlantic foe, and render ourselves ridiculous and contemptible in the eyes of all Europe."[11] The Congress under the Confederation had shown itself unable to act decisively in a time of crisis, providing critics of the Articles with precisely the evidence they needed to push the Annapolis resolution through the Congress. Thus, the states were asked to send representatives to Philadelphia to discuss constitutional revision. Seventy-four delegates were chosen. Of these, 55 would actually attend the convention, representing every state except Rhode Island, and 39 would eventually sign the newly drafted Constitution.

THE CONSTITUTIONAL CONVENTION

The delegates who convened in Philadelphia in May 1787 had political strife, international embarrassment, national weakness, and local rebellion fixed in their minds. Recognizing that these issues were symptoms of fundamental flaws in the Articles of Confederation, the delegates soon abandoned the plan to revise the Articles and committed themselves to a second founding—a second, and ultimately successful, attempt to create a legitimate and effective national system of government. This effort would occupy the convention for the next five months.

A Marriage of Interest and Principle For years, scholars have disagreed about the motives of the Founders in Philadelphia. Among the most controversial views is the "economic interpretation" by the historian Charles Beard and his disciples,[12] in which the Founders were a group of securities speculators and property owners motivated only by money. From this perspective, the Constitution's lofty principles were little more than sophisticated masks behind which its sponsors aimed to enrich themselves.

Of course, the opposite view is that the framers of the Constitution *were* concerned with philosophical and ethical principles—that, indeed, they aimed to create a system of government consistent with the dominant philosophical and moral principles of the day, including limited government, separation of powers, and individual liberty. But in fact these two views belong together: the Founders' interests were reinforced by their principles. The convention that drafted the Constitution was chiefly organized by the New England merchants and southern planters. Although

The Constitutional Convention took place from May to September 1787 at Independence Hall in Philadelphia, where the Declaration of Independence had been signed 11 years prior. In order to keep their deliberations secret, the delegates voted to keep the hall's windows shut throughout the hot summer.

the delegates representing these groups did not all hope to profit personally from an increase in the value of their securities, as Beard would have it, they did hope to benefit in the broadest sense by breaking the power of their radical foes and establishing a system of government more compatible with their long-term economic and political interests. A new government, they believed, should be capable of promoting commerce and protecting property from radical state legislatures and populist forces hostile to the commercial and propertied classes.

The Great Compromise The proponents of a new government fired their opening shot on May 29, 1787, when Edmund Randolph of Virginia offered a resolution that proposed corrections and additions to the Articles of Confederation. The proposal, which showed the strong influence of James Madison, provided for virtually every aspect of a new government.

The portion of Randolph's motion that became most controversial was called the **Virginia Plan**. This plan provided for representation in the national legislature to be based on the population of each state or the proportion of each state's revenue contribution to the national government, or both. (Randolph also proposed a second chamber of the legislature, to be elected by the members of the first chamber.) Since the states varied enormously in population and wealth, the Virginia Plan was heavily biased in favor of the large states. The Virginia Plan also called for ratification of the Constitution by the people rather than the states. This form of ratification was intended to make it clear that the new government would be a national government and not a compact among the states.

While the convention was debating the Virginia Plan, opposition to it began to mount as more delegates arrived in Philadelphia. William Paterson of New Jersey introduced a resolution known as the **New Jersey Plan**. Its main proponents were delegates from the less populous states, including Delaware, New Jersey, Connecticut, and New York, who asserted that the more populous states—Virginia, Pennsylvania, North Carolina, Massachusetts, and Georgia—would dominate the new government if representation were determined by population. The smaller states argued that each state should be equally represented regardless of its population.

Virginia Plan a framework for the Constitution, introduced by Edmund Randolph, that called for representation in the national legislature based on the population of each state

New Jersey Plan a framework for the Constitution, introduced by William Paterson, that called for equal state representation in the national legislature regardless of population

Great Compromise the agreement reached at the Constitutional Convention of 1787 that gave each state an equal number of senators regardless of its population but linked representation in the House of Representatives to population

The issue of representation threatened to wreck the entire constitutional enterprise. As factions maneuvered and tempers flared, the Union, as Luther Martin of Maryland put it, was "on the verge of dissolution, scarcely held together by the strength of a hair."[13] Finally, the debate was settled by the Connecticut Compromise, also known as the **Great Compromise**. Under its terms, in one chamber of Congress—the House of Representatives—seats would be apportioned according to population, as delegates from the large states had wished. But in a second branch—the Senate—each state would have equal representation, as small states preferred.

This compromise was not easily achieved. Indeed, two vocal members of the small-state faction were so angered by their colleagues' concession to the large-state forces that they stormed out of the convention. In the end, however, most delegates preferred compromise to the breakup of the Union, and the plan was accepted.

The Question of Slavery: The Three-Fifths Compromise Many of the conflicts that emerged during the Constitutional Convention reflected the fundamental differences between the southern and northern states related to slavery. These disputes pitted the southern planters against the New England merchants at the convention and would almost destroy the Republic in later years. Even in the midst of debate about other issues, James Madison observed that "the great danger" lay in the opposition of "southern and northern interests."[14]

More than 90 percent of the country's enslaved people lived in five states—Georgia, Maryland, North Carolina, South Carolina, and Virginia—where they accounted for 30 percent of the total population. Were they to be counted as part of a state's population even though they were not citizens, thereby giving southern states increased representation in the House? If the Constitution was to incorporate the principle of the national government's supremacy over the states, decisions were required about slavery.

Despite the Founders' emphasis on liberty, the new Constitution allowed slavery, counting three-fifths of all enslaved people, in apportioning seats in the House of Representatives. In this 1792 painting, *Liberty Displaying the Arts and Sciences*, the books, instruments, and classical columns at the left contrast with the kneeling enslaved people at the right—illustrating the divide between America's rhetoric of liberty and equality and the reality of slavery.

Who Benefits from the Great Compromise? 1789 and Today

Representation in the First Congress

- ● Senators
- ■ Members of the House of Representatives
- — Population per Member of Congress

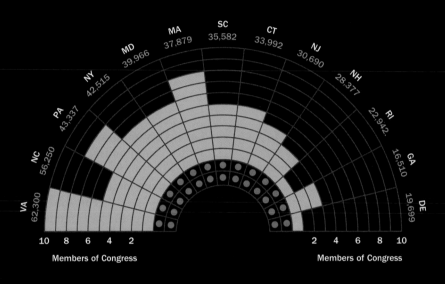

Members of Congress

Instead of allocating representatives in Congress only according to population, which would have privileged large-population states, the Great Compromise attempted to balance power between large and small states. Seats in the House are allocated by population but seats in the Senate are divided equally (each state represented by two senators). Even today, debates persist about how much influence small- and large-population states should have.

Representation in Congress, 2019

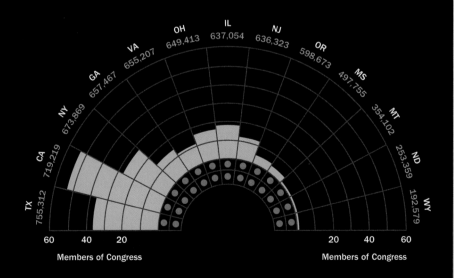

Members of Congress

FOR CRITICAL ANALYSIS

1. At the Constitutional Convention, large states supported a plan that would have made the whole Congress look like the House. Small states supported a plan that would have made the whole Congress look like the Senate. How would each group have benefited from its favored plan?

2. Because of rapid population growth over the past 200 years, people living in large-population states have much lower representation in Congress today than those living in small-population states. What are the advantages and disadvantages of equal representation by states?

SOURCE: U.S. House of Representatives, history.house.gov/; U.S. Census Bureau, "2018 American Community Survey 1-Year Estimates," www.census.gov (accessed 5/22/19).

Whatever they thought of slavery, most delegates from northern states opposed counting the population of enslaved people in the apportionment of congressional seats. James Wilson of Pennsylvania, for example, argued that if enslaved people were counted for this purpose, other forms of property should be as well. But southern delegates made it clear that they would never agree to the new government if the northerners refused to give in. Northerners and southerners eventually reached agreement through the **Three-Fifths Compromise**: congressional seats would be apportioned according to a "population" in which only three-fifths of enslaved people would be counted.

Slavery was the most difficult issue the framers faced, and it nearly destroyed the Union. Although some delegates saw it as an evil institution that made a mockery of the ideals expressed in the Constitution, morality was not what caused individual framers to support or oppose the Three-Fifths Compromise. Indeed, to keep the South in the Union, northerners even allowed the slave trade to continue. But in due course, the incompatible interests of the North and the South could no longer be reconciled, and a bloody civil war was the result.

The Constitution

Describe the principles of governance and the powers of the national government defined by the Constitution

The political significance of the Great Compromise and the Three-Fifths Compromise was to reinforce the unity of the merchant and planter forces aiming to create a new government. The Great Compromise reassured those in both groups who feared the new framework would reduce their own local or regional influence, and the Three-Fifths Compromise temporarily defused the rivalry between the groups. Their unity secured, members of the alliance moved to fashion a constitution consistent with their economic and political interests.

In particular, the framers wanted a new government that, first, would be strong enough to promote commerce and protect property from radical state legislatures such as Rhode Island's. This goal led to the constitutional provisions for national control over commerce and finance, for national judicial supremacy over state courts, and for a strong presidency. (See Table 2.1 for a comparison of the Articles of Confederation with the Constitution.)

Second, the framers wanted to prevent what they saw as the threat posed by the "excessive democracy" of both state and national governments under the Articles of Confederation. This desire led to such constitutional principles as a **bicameral**, or two-chambered, legislature; **checks and balances** among the branches of government; staggered terms in office; and indirect election (selection of the president by an electoral college and of senators by state legislatures, rather than directly by voters).

Third, lacking the power to force the states or the public to accept the new form of government, the framers wanted to identify principles that would help gain support for it. This goal became the basis of the constitutional provision for direct popular election of representatives and, later, of the addition of the **Bill of Rights** to the Constitution.

Finally, the framers wanted to ensure that the government they created did not pose an even greater threat to its citizens' liberties and property rights than did the

Three-Fifths Compromise the agreement reached at the Constitutional Convention of 1787 that stipulated that for purposes of the apportionment of congressional seats only three-fifths of enslaved people would be counted

bicameral having a legislative assembly composed of two chambers or houses; distinguished from *unicameral*

checks and balances mechanisms through which each branch of government is able to participate in and influence the activities of the other branches; major examples include the presidential veto power over congressional legislation, the power of the Senate to approve presidential appointments, and judicial review of congressional enactments

Bill of Rights the first 10 amendments to the U.S. Constitution, ratified in 1791; they ensure certain rights and liberties to the people

TABLE 2.1

Comparing the Articles of Confederation and the Constitution

MAJOR PROVISIONS	ARTICLES OF CONFEDERATION	CONSTITUTION
Executive branch	None	President of the United States
Judiciary	No federal court system. Judiciary exists only at state level.	Federal judiciary headed by Supreme Court
Legislature	Unicameral legislature with equal representation for each state. Delegates to the Congress of the Confederation were appointed by the states.	Bicameral legislature consisting of Senate and House of Representatives. Each state is represented by two senators, while apportionment in the House is based on each state's population. Senators are chosen by the state legislatures (changed to direct popular election in 1913) for six-year terms and members of the House by popular election for two-year terms.
Fiscal and economic powers	The national government is dependent upon the states to collect taxes. The states are free to coin their own money and print paper money. The states are free to sign commercial treaties with foreign governments.	Congress given the power to levy taxes, coin money, and regulate international and interstate commerce. States prohibited from coining money or entering into treaties with other nations.
Military	The national government is dependent upon state militias and cannot form an army during peacetime.	The national government is authorized to maintain an army and navy.
Legal supremacy	State constitutions and state law are supreme.	National Constitution and national law are supreme.
Constitutional amendment	Must be agreed upon by all states.	Must be agreed upon by three-fourths of the states.

radical state legislatures they despised. To prevent abuses of power, they incorporated principles such as the **separation of powers** and **federalism** into the Constitution. In Table 2.1, we assess the major provisions of the Constitution's seven articles to see how each relates to these objectives.

If the Declaration of Independence drew its philosophical inspiration from John Locke, the Constitution drew upon the thought of the French political philosopher Baron de La Brède et de Montesquieu (1689–1755). In Montesquieu's view, presented in his famous work *The Spirit of the Laws*, the powers of government must be divided to prevent any one group or institution from exercising tyrannical control over the nation. Montesquieu recommended placing the executive, legislative, and judicial powers in separate governmental bodies, claiming that such a three-part division had worked very well in the Roman Republic and in Britain. The delegates to the Constitutional Convention referred frequently to his writings in devising America's new governmental structure.

separation of powers the division of governmental power among several institutions that must cooperate in decision-making

federalism a system of government in which power is divided, by a constitution, between a central government and regional governments

Article I of the Constitution establishes the structure of Congress and lists certain specific powers of Congress. The language of the Constitution reflects the framers' desire to create government that was powerful enough to be effective but not so powerful that it would threaten individual liberty.

THE LEGISLATIVE BRANCH

In Article I, Sections 1–7, the Constitution provides for a Congress consisting of two chambers: a House of Representatives and a Senate. Members of the House of Representatives were given two-year terms in office and were to be elected directly by the people. Members of the Senate were to be appointed by the state legislatures (a provision changed in 1913 by the Seventeenth Amendment, which instituted direct election of senators) for six-year terms. These terms were staggered so that the appointments of one-third of the senators would expire every two years.

The Constitution assigned somewhat different tasks to the House and Senate. Though the enactment of a law requires the approval of both, the Senate alone is given the power to ratify treaties and approve presidential appointments. The House, on the other hand, is given the sole power to originate revenue bills.

The character of the legislative branch was related to the framers' major goals. The House was designed to be directly responsible to the people in order to encourage popular support for the new Constitution and thus enhance the power of the new government. At the same time, to guard against "excessive democracy," the power of the House was checked by that of the Senate, whose members were to be appointed by the states for long terms rather than elected directly by the people for short ones. The purpose of this provision, according to Alexander Hamilton, was to avoid "an unqualified complaisance to every sudden breeze of passion, or to every transient impulse which the people may receive."[15] Staggered terms in the Senate were intended to make that body even more resistant to popular pressure. Since only one-third of the senators would be selected at any given time, the institution would be protected from changes in public opinion transmitted by the state legislatures.

The issues of governmental power and popular consent are important throughout the Constitution. Section 8 of Article I specifically lists the powers of Congress, which include the authority to collect taxes, borrow money, regulate commerce, declare war, and maintain an army and navy. By granting Congress these powers, the framers indicated clearly that they intended the new government to be far more powerful than its predecessor under the Articles of Confederation. At the same time, by assigning its most important powers to Congress, they promoted popular acceptance of this critical change by reassuring citizens that their views would be fully represented whenever these powers were used.

As a further guarantee that the new government would pose no threat to the people, the Constitution implies that any powers not listed were not granted at all. This is what Chief Justice John Marshall named the doctrine of **expressed powers**: the Constitution grants only those powers specifically expressed in its text. But the framers intended to create an active and powerful government, so they also included the necessary and proper clause, sometimes known as the **elastic clause**, which declares that Congress can write laws needed to carry out its expressed powers. This clause indicates that the expressed powers could be broadly interpreted and were meant to be a source of strength to the national government, not a limitation on it. In response to the charge that they intended to give it too much power, the framers

expressed powers specific powers granted by the Constitution to Congress (Article I, Section 8) and to the president (Article II)

elastic clause the concluding paragraph of Article I, Section 8, of the Constitution (also known as the "necessary and proper clause"), which provides Congress with the authority to make all laws "necessary and proper" to carry out its enumerated powers

included language in the Tenth Amendment stipulating that powers not specifically granted by the Constitution to the federal government were reserved to the states or to the people. As we will see in Chapter 3, the resulting tension between the elastic clause and the Tenth Amendment has been at the heart of constitutional struggles between federal and state powers.

THE EXECUTIVE BRANCH

The Articles of Confederation had not provided for an executive branch. The president under the Articles was the official chosen by the Congress to preside over its sessions, not the chief executive of the national government. The framers viewed the absence of an executive as a source of weakness. Accordingly, the Constitution provides for the presidency in Article II. As Hamilton commented, the article aims toward "energy in the Executive."[16] It does so in an effort to overcome the natural tendency toward stalemate that was built into the separation of the legislature into two chambers and of governmental powers among the three branches. The Constitution affords the president a measure of independence from both the people and the other branches of government—particularly the Congress.

In line with the framers' goal of increased power to the national government, the president is granted the unconditional power to accept ambassadors from other countries—to "recognize" other governments—as well as the power to negotiate treaties, although their acceptance requires the approval of the Senate by a two-thirds vote. The president is also given the unconditional right to grant reprieves and pardons, except in cases of impeachment, and the powers to appoint major departmental personnel, to convene Congress in a special session, and to veto bills it passes. The veto power is important but not absolute, since Congress can override it by a two-thirds vote, reflecting the framers' concern with checks and balances.

The framers hoped to create a presidency that would make the federal government rather than the states the agency capable of timely and decisive action to deal with national issues and problems—hence the "energy" that Hamilton hoped to bring to the executive branch. At the same time, however, they tried to help the presidency withstand excessively democratic pressures by creating a system of indirect rather than direct election through an electoral college.

THE JUDICIAL BRANCH

In establishing the judicial branch in Article III, the Constitution reflects the framers' preoccupations with nationalizing governmental power and checking radical democratic impulses while preventing the new national government itself from interfering with liberty and property.

Article III created a court intended to be literally the supreme judicial authority of the United States, not merely the highest court of the national government. The most important expression of this intention is granting the Supreme Court the power to resolve any conflicts between federal and state laws. In particular, it can determine whether a power is exclusive to the national government, exclusive to the states, or shared between the two.

In addition, the Supreme Court is assigned jurisdiction over controversies between citizens of different states. The long-term significance of this provision was that as the country developed a national economy, it came to rely increasingly on the federal judiciary, rather than state courts, to resolve disputes.

Federal judges are given lifetime appointments to protect them from political or public pressure and from interference by the other branches. The judiciary is not totally free of political considerations or the other branches, however, for the president appoints the judges and the Senate must approve the appointments. Congress also has the power to create inferior (lower) courts, change the jurisdiction of the federal courts (the geographic area or types of cases they have authority over), add or subtract federal judges, and even change the size of the Supreme Court.

The Constitution does not explicitly mention **judicial review**—the power of a court to determine whether the actions of the Congress or the executive are consistent with law and the Constitution. The Supreme Court eventually assumed the power of judicial review. Its assumption of this power, as we shall see in Chapter 15, was based not on the Constitution itself but on the politics of later decades and the membership of the Court.

judicial review the power of the courts to review actions of the legislative and executive branches and, if necessary, declare them invalid or unconstitutional; the Supreme Court asserted this power in *Marbury v. Madison* (1803)

NATIONAL UNITY AND POWER

The Constitution addressed the framers' concern with national unity and power in the comity clause of Article IV, which provides for reciprocity among all states and their citizens. That is, each state is prohibited from discriminating against the citizens of or goods from other states in favor of its own citizens or goods, with the Supreme Court charged with deciding cases where such discrimination is alleged. The Constitution thus restricts the power of the states so as to give the national government enough power to ensure a free-flowing national economy.

The framers' concern with national supremacy was also expressed in Article VI, whose "**supremacy clause**" provides that national laws and treaties "shall be the supreme Law of the Land." This means that laws made under the "Authority of the United States" are superior to those adopted by any state or other subdivision and that the states must respect all treaties made under that authority. The supremacy clause also binds all state and local as well as federal officials to take an oath to support the national Constitution. Therefore, they must enforce national law over state law if the two conflict.

supremacy clause Article VI of the Constitution, which states that laws passed by the national government and all treaties are the supreme law of the land and superior to all laws adopted by any state or any subdivision

AMENDING AND RATIFYING THE CONSTITUTION

The Constitution establishes procedures for its own amendment in Article V. The requirements are so difficult that, as we shall see below, the amending process has succeeded only 17 times since 1791, when the first 10 amendments were adopted. The rules for ratification, or adoption, of the Constitution are set forth in Article VII. Of the 13 states, 9 would have to ratify it in order for it to go into effect. Even if all the states did not ratify the Constitution, it would take effect for those that did once the threshold of 9 had been crossed.

CONSTITUTIONAL LIMITS ON THE NATIONAL GOVERNMENT'S POWER

Although the framers wanted a powerful national government, they also wanted to guard against possible misuse of that power. Thus they incorporated two key principles into the Constitution—federalism and the separation of powers. A third set of limitations, the Bill of Rights, was added to the Constitution in the form of

10 amendments proposed by the first Congress and ratified by the states. Most of the framers had thought a Bill of Rights unnecessary but accepted the idea during the ratification debates after the new Constitution was submitted to the states for approval.

The Separation of Powers No principle of politics was more widely shared at the time of the 1787 Founding than the principle that power must be used to balance power. Although the principle of the separation of powers is not explicitly stated in the Constitution, the entire structure of the national government was built precisely on Article I, the legislature; Article II, the executive; and Article III, the judiciary (see Figure 2.1).

The method adopted to maintain that separation became known by the popular label "checks and balances" (see Figure 2.2). Each branch is given not only its own powers but also some power over the other two branches. Among the most familiar checks and balances are the president's veto power over Congress and Congress's power over the president through its control of appointments to high executive posts and to the judiciary. Congress also has power over the president with its control of appropriations (the spending of government money) and the requirement that the Senate ratify treaties. The judiciary has the power of judicial review over the other two branches.

Another important principle of the separation of powers is giving each branch a distinctly different constituency. Theorists such as Montesquieu called this arrangement a "mixed regime," with the president chosen, indirectly, by electors; the House, by popular vote; the Senate (originally), by state legislatures; and the judiciary, by presidential appointment. By these means, the occupants of each branch would tend to develop very different outlooks on how to govern, different definitions of the public interest, and different alliances with private interests.

FOR CRITICAL ANALYSIS

How does the separation of powers limit the national government's power? What are the consequences for the ability of the federal government to govern?

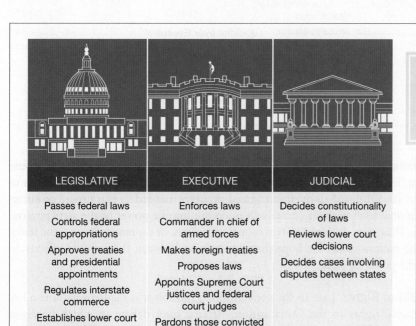

LEGISLATIVE	EXECUTIVE	JUDICIAL
Passes federal laws	Enforces laws	Decides constitutionality of laws
Controls federal appropriations	Commander in chief of armed forces	Reviews lower court decisions
Approves treaties and presidential appointments	Makes foreign treaties	Decides cases involving disputes between states
Regulates interstate commerce	Proposes laws	
Establishes lower court system	Appoints Supreme Court justices and federal court judges	
	Pardons those convicted in federal court	

FIGURE 2.1

The Separation of Powers

FIGURE 2.2

Checks and Balances

Executive over Legislative

Can veto acts of Congress

Can call Congress into a special session

Carries out, and thereby interprets, laws passed by Congress

Vice president casts tie-breaking vote in the Senate

LEGISLATIVE

Legislative over Judicial

Can change size of federal court system and the number of Supreme Court justices

Can propose constitutional amendments

Can reject Supreme Court nominees

Can impeach and remove federal judges

Legislative over Executive

Can override presidential veto

Can impeach and remove president

Can reject president's appointments and refuse to ratify treaties

Can conduct investigations into president's actions

Can refuse to pass laws or to provide funding that president requests

Judicial over Legislative

Can declare laws unconstitutional

Chief justice presides over Senate during hearing to impeach the president

JUDICIAL

Executive over Judicial

Nominates Supreme Court justices

Nominates federal judges

Can pardon those convicted in federal court

Can refuse to enforce Court decisions

Judicial over Executive

Can declare executive actions unconstitutional

Power to issue warrants

Chief justice presides over impeachment of president

EXECUTIVE

Federalism Compared with the decentralizing principle of the Articles of Confederation, federalism was a step toward greater concentration of power. The delegates to the Constitutional Convention agreed that they needed to place more power at the national level without completely undermining the power of the state governments. Thus, they devised a system of two sovereigns, or supreme powers—the states and the nation—with the hope that competition between them would effectively limit the power of each.

The Bill of Rights Late in the convention, a motion was made to include a list of citizens' rights in the Constitution. After a brief debate in which hardly a word was said in its favor and only one speech was made against it, the motion was almost unanimously turned down. Most delegates sincerely believed that since the federal government was already limited to its expressed powers, further protection of citizens was not needed. These delegates argued that it was states that should adopt bills of rights because their greater powers needed greater limitations. But almost immediately after the Constitution was ratified, a movement arose to adopt a national bill of rights. This is why the Bill of Rights, adopted in 1791, comprises the first 10 amendments to the Constitution rather than being part of the body of it. (We will have more to say about the Bill of Rights in Chapter 4.)

The Fight for Ratification

Differentiate between the Federalists' and Antifederalists' stances on the ratification of the Constitution

The first hurdle faced by the proposed Constitution was ratification by state conventions of delegates elected by White, property-owning male voters. This struggle for ratification included 13 separate campaigns, each influenced by local as well as national considerations.

Two sides faced off in all the states, calling themselves **Federalists** and **Antifederalists** (see Table 2.2). The Federalists (who more accurately could have called themselves "Nationalists") supported the Constitution and preferred a strong national government. The Antifederalists opposed the Constitution and preferred a more decentralized federal system; they took their name by default, in reaction to their better-organized opponents. The Federalists were united in their support of the Constitution, whereas the Antifederalists were divided over possible alternatives.

During the struggle over ratification of the Constitution, Americans argued about great political issues and principles. How much power should the national government have? What safeguards would most likely prevent the abuse of power? What institutional arrangements could best ensure adequate

Federalists those who favored a strong national government and supported the Constitution proposed at the American Constitutional Convention of 1787

Antifederalists those who favored strong state governments and a weak national government and who were opponents of the Constitution proposed at the American Constitutional Convention of 1787

TABLE 2.2

Federalists versus Antifederalists

	FEDERALISTS	ANTIFEDERALISTS
Who were they?	Property owners, creditors, merchants	Small farmers, frontiersmen, debtors, shopkeepers, some state government officials
What did they believe?	Believed that elites were most fit to govern; feared "excessive democracy"	Believed that government should be closer to the people; feared concentration of power in hands of the elites
What system of government did they favor?	Favored strong national government; believed in "filtration" so that only elites would obtain governmental power	Favored retention of power by state governments and protection of individual rights
Who were their leaders?	Alexander Hamilton, James Madison, George Washington	Patrick Henry, George Mason, Elbridge Gerry, George Clinton

representation for all citizens? Was tyranny of the many to be feared more than tyranny of the few?

FEDERALISTS VERSUS ANTIFEDERALISTS

Thousands of essays, speeches, pamphlets, and letters were presented for and against ratification of the proposed Constitution. The best-known pieces in support were the 85 articles published in New York City newspapers by Alexander Hamilton, James Madison, and John Jay. These *Federalist Papers*, as they are collectively known today, defended the principles of the Constitution and sought to dispel fears of a strong national government. Meanwhile, the Antifederalists, including Patrick Henry and Richard Henry Lee, argued in their speeches and writings that the new Constitution betrayed the Revolution and was a step toward monarchy.

Representation One major area of contention between the two sides was the nature of political representation. The Antifederalists asserted that representatives must be "a true picture of the people . . . [possessing] the knowledge of their circumstances and their wants."[17] This could be achieved, they argued, only in small republics such as each of the existing states, whose people were relatively similar to one another. In their view, the size and diverse population of the entire nation made a truly representative form of government impossible.

Federalists, for their part, saw no reason that representatives should be precisely like those they represented. In their view, one of the great advantages of representative government over direct democracy was precisely the possibility that the people would choose individuals with experience and talent greater than their own to represent them. In Madison's words, rather than mirroring society, representatives must be "[those] who possess [the] most wisdom to discern, and [the] most virtue to pursue, the common good of the society."[18]

Tyranny A second important issue dividing Federalists and Antifederalists was the threat of tyranny—unjust rule by the group in power. The two sides, however, had different views of the most likely source of tyranny, and thus they had different ideas about how to keep it from emerging.

Federalist Papers a series of essays written by Alexander Hamilton, James Madison, and John Jay supporting ratification of the Constitution

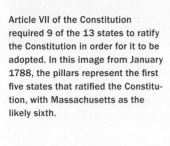

FOR CRITICAL ANALYSIS

The Antifederalists worried that the size and diversity of the United States made democratic government impossible. In what ways might a large heterogeneous population limit democracy? How might it enhance democracy?

tyranny oppressive government that employs cruel and unjust use of power and authority

Article VII of the Constitution required 9 of the 13 states to ratify the Constitution in order for it to be adopted. In this image from January 1788, the pillars represent the first five states that ratified the Constitution, with Massachusetts as the likely sixth.

Democratic Systems

Executive authority is vested in different positions in different countries. In parliamentary systems the prime minister is both the chief executive and the head of the legislature. In presidential systems, such as in the United States, the executive and legislative branches are separate. Some countries use a semi-presidential system in which there is a president who heads the executive branch and has limited authority, and a prime minister who heads the legislative branch. Parliamentary systems can be more efficient, as the prime minister can wield a lot of authority, but only if his or her party has a sizable and stable majority in Parliament. Presidential and semi-presidential systems can lead to more gridlock, as there are multiple seats of power.

1. Does one system seem more common than another? Why might one country have a parliamentary system while its neighbor has a presidential system?

2. What do you think would be the advantages to having executive and legislative authority vested in the same individual? What are the advantages to a system such as that of the United States, where powers are separated in independent branches? Do you think the advantages of one system over another are different today than they were 250 years ago at the founding of the United States?

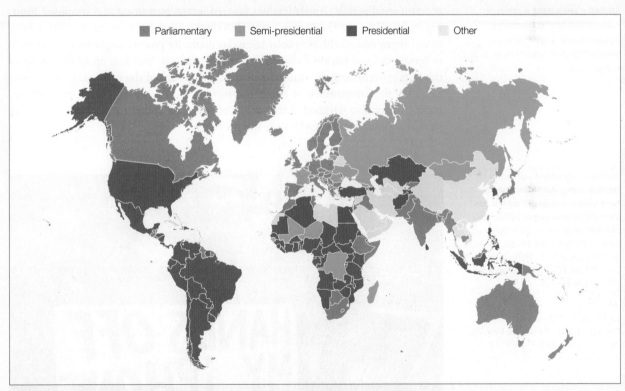

SOURCE: CIA World Factbook, https://www.cia.gov/library/publications/the-world-factbook/fields/299.html (accessed 12/5/2019).

For the Antifederalists, the great danger was the tendency of republican governments to become gradually more and more "aristocratic," with members of the small group in authority using their positions to gain more and more power over other citizens. In essence, Antifederalists feared, the few would tyrannize the many. For this reason, they sharply criticized those features of the Constitution that created governmental institutions without direct responsibility to the people—such as the Senate, the presidency, and particularly the federal judiciary, with its lifetime appointments.

The Federalists, on the other hand, viewed the danger particularly associated with republican governments not as aristocracy but as tyranny over the few by the many. They feared that a popular majority, "united and actuated by some common impulse of passion, or of interest, adverse to the rights of other citizens," would "trample on the rules of justice."[19] From their perspective, those features of the Constitution that the Antifederalists attacked as potential sources of tyranny actually offered the best hope of preventing it. They saw the nation's size and diversity as further protection because these made it harder to unite a tyrannical majority.

Governmental Power A third major difference between Federalists and Antifederalists concerned the fundamentally important question of how to place limits on governmental action. Antifederalists favored **limited government** and proposed limiting and spelling out the powers granted to the national government in relation both to the states and to the people at large. To them, its powers ought to be "confined to certain defined national objects"[20] so that it did not "swallow up all the power of the state governments."[21] Antifederalists bitterly attacked the supremacy and elastic clauses of the Constitution as dangerous surrenders of power to the national government.[22] They also demanded that a bill of rights be added to the Constitution to limit the government's power over the people.

limited government a principle of constitutional government; a government whose powers are defined and limited by a constitution

Debates over how much power the national government should have continue today. After the San Bernardino shooting in 2015, the FBI demanded Apple unlock the perpetrator's iPhone for details into his criminal activity. Here, a group protests the FBI's infringement on the right to privacy.

In reply, Federalists such as Hamilton acknowledged the possibility that every power could be abused. They argued, however, that the risk was worth taking in order to give the government the powers needed to achieve essential national goals. In addition, the risk of abuse would be minimized by the various checks and controls on power incorporated into the Constitution. As Madison put it, "the power surrendered by the people is first divided between two distinct governments (state and national), and then the portion allotted to each subdivided among distinct and separate departments. Hence, a double security arises to the rights of the people. The different governments will control each other, at the same time that each will be controlled by itself."[23] The Federalists' concern with avoiding unwarranted limits on governmental power led them to oppose a bill of rights as unnecessary.

"The very idea of power included a possibility of doing harm," said the Federalist John Rutledge during the South Carolina ratification debates. "If the gentleman would show the power that could do no harm," Rutledge continued, "he would at once discover it to be a power that could do no good."[24] This aspect of the debate between Federalists and Antifederalists, perhaps more than any other, continues to reverberate through American politics. Should the nation limit the federal government's power to tax and spend? Should Congress limit federal agencies' authority to issue new regulations? Should the government create new rights for minorities, the disabled, and others? Though the details have changed, these are the same questions that have been debated since the Founding.

FOR CRITICAL ANALYSIS

Do you agree with Rutledge that a power that can do no harm can also do no good? How can a system of government maximize the ability of government to do good while minimizing the possibility of harm?

REFLECTIONS ON THE FOUNDING

The final product of the Constitutional Convention was a victory for the Federalists. While Antifederalist criticisms did force the addition of a bill of rights, overall it was the Federalist vision of America that triumphed. The Constitution adopted in 1789 created the framework for a powerful national government that for more than 200 years has defended the nation's interests, promoted its commerce, and maintained national unity. In one notable instance, the government fought and won a bloody war to prevent the nation from breaking apart. And at the same time, the system of checks and balances has functioned reasonably well, as the Federalists predicted, to prevent the government from tyrannizing its citizens. The national unity created under the Constitution also gradually helped America become a great world power—as many of the framers had hoped.

Although they were defeated in 1788, the Antifederalists present us with an important picture of an America that might have been. Would Americans today be worse off if they were governed by a confederacy of small republics linked by a national administration with severely limited powers? Were the Antifederalists correct in predicting that a government given great power in the hope that it might do good would, through "insensible progress," inevitably turn to evil purposes?

The Citizen's Role and the Changing Constitution

Explain how, and how often, the Constitution has been changed

Although the Constitution has endured for more than two centuries, it has not gone unchanged. Citizens are assigned an indirect but

FIGURE 2.3

Four Ways the Constitution Can be Amended

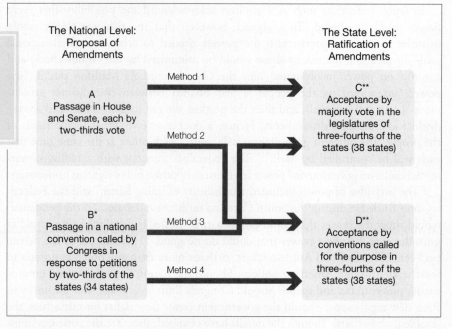

The National Level:
Proposal of
Amendments

A
Passage in House
and Senate, each by
two-thirds vote

B*
Passage in a national
convention called by
Congress in
response to petitions
by two-thirds of the
states (34 states)

Method 1

Method 2

Method 3

Method 4

The State Level:
Ratification of
Amendments

C*
Acceptance by
majority vote in the
legislatures of
three-fourths of the
states (38 states)

D*
Acceptance by
conventions called
for the purpose in
three-fourths of the
states (38 states)

*This method of proposal has never been employed. Thus, amendment routes 3 and 4 have never been attempted.
**For each amendment proposal, Congress has the power to choose the method of ratification, the time limit for consideration by the states, and other conditions of ratification. The movement to repeal Prohibition in the Twenty-First Amendment was the only occasion in which route 2 was used successfully.

FOR CRITICAL ANALYSIS

What are the U.S. Constitution's greatest strengths? What are its most pronounced weaknesses? If you were revising the Constitution today, what would you change? Why?

amendment a change added to a bill, law, or constitution

important role in this process of change. Figure 2.3 outlines the ways in which the Constitution can be amended, all of which involve citizens through the election of members of Congress and state legislatures or, hypothetically, through the election of delegates to national and state constitutional conventions. Amending the Constitution may be difficult, but it is ultimately controlled by institutions elected by the people. Of course, the federal courts, whose judges are not elected but are appointed by the president with the consent of the Senate, also interpret the Constitution and adapt it to changing circumstances. Many voters are aware that their presidential ballots may also help to shape the character of the Supreme Court and other federal courts.

AMENDMENTS: MANY ARE CALLED; FEW ARE CHOSEN

The inevitable need for change was recognized by the framers of the Constitution, and provisions for **amendment** were incorporated into Article V. Four methods of amendment are described:

1. Passage in House and Senate by two-thirds vote, then ratification by majority vote of the legislatures of three-fourths (now 38) of the states; in nine cases Congress mandated a time limit for state ratification

2. Passage in House and Senate by two-thirds vote, then ratification by conventions called for the purpose in three-fourths of the states

3. Passage in a national convention called for by Congress in response to petitions by two-thirds of the states, then ratification by majority vote of the legislatures of three-fourths of the states

4. Passage in a national convention (as in method 3), then ratification by conventions called for the purpose in three-fourths of the states

Who Gained the Right to Vote through Amendments?

The right to vote is seen as a cornerstone of American democracy, but not all Americans have had that right. Three constitutional amendments, ratified over roughly a 100-year span, have had a profound effect on who can vote in U.S. elections.

Adult Citizens Eligible to Vote in National Elections*

27.9%	31.7%	92.6%	99.9%
1789	**1869**	**1920**	**1971**
The Founding:	15th Amendment	19th Amendment	26th Amendment
White men of property, age 21+	All men, age 21+	All men and women, age 21+	All men and women, age 18+

Proportion of 2018 Electorate by Amendment

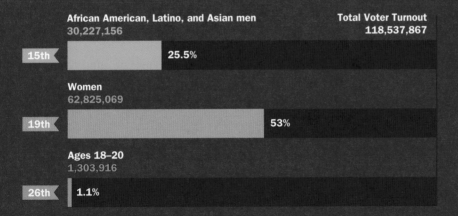

African American, Latino, and Asian men
30,227,156

Total Voter Turnout
118,537,867

15th — 25.5%

Women
62,825,069

19th — 53%

Ages 18–20
1,303,916

26th — 1.1%

* Percentages are of the adult (18+) population. These figures are approximate for 1789 and 1869. The voting rights of convicted felons are restricted in some states, and of noncitizens in all states.

SOURCE: Data from U.S. House of Representatives, U.S. Census Bureau, Pew Research Center, United States Election Project, and Catalist Data (accessed 6/12/19).

FOR CRITICAL ANALYSIS

1. Which amendment had the greatest effect in increasing the percentage of the population allowed to vote?

2. Roughly how many voters today would have been denied the chance to vote if not for the ratification of the Twenty-Sixth Amendment? Do you think the voting age should be decreased even further?

The Equal Rights Amendment (ERA) is an example of an amendment that almost succeeded, and gained new traction in 2020 when Virginia became the 38th state to ratify the amendment. The proposed amendment guaranteed equality under the law for women and made gender discrimination illegal.

FOR CRITICAL ANALYSIS

It is very difficult to amend the Constitution. Should the amendment process be made easier? Would the American system of government be more democratic if the Constitution could be revised more easily?

Since no amendment has ever been proposed by national convention, however, methods 3 and 4 have never been employed. And method 2 has been employed only once (the Twenty-First Amendment, which repealed the Eighteenth Amendment, or Prohibition). Method 1 has been used for all the others.

The Constitution has proved extremely difficult to amend. Since 1789, more than 11,000 amendments have been formally introduced in Congress. Of these, Congress officially proposed only 29, and 27 of these were eventually ratified by the states. Two of these—Prohibition and its repeal—cancel each other out, so for all practical purposes, only 25 amendments have been added to the Constitution since 1791.

The Equal Rights Amendment (ERA), proposed in 1972 to outlaw gender-based discrimination, was not ratified by the states within the prescribed time limit of seven years. However, in January 2020, after the limit expired, Virginia became the 38th state to ratify the proposal. In the meantime, five states had decided to rescind their ratifications. The federal courts will be asked to decide whether the ERA has been properly ratified.

WHICH WERE CHOSEN? AN ANALYSIS OF THE 27

There is more to the amending difficulties than the politics of campaigning and voting. Most amendment efforts have failed because they simply attempted to use the Constitution instead of ordinary legislation to deal with a specific public problem. The 25 successful amendments, on the other hand, are concerned with the structure or composition of government (see Table 2.3). This pattern is consistent with the dictionary, which defines *constitution* as the makeup or composition of something. And it is consistent with the concept of a constitution as "higher law," whose purpose is to establish a framework within which the processes of governing and making ordinary law can take place.

Even those who would have preferred more changes to the Constitution must admit the great wisdom in this principle. A constitution ought to make laws and policies possible, but not determine what they ought to be. For example, property

Amendments to the Constitution

AMENDMENT	PURPOSE	YEAR PROPOSED	YEAR ADOPTED
I	Congress is not to make any law establishing a religion or abridging free exercise of religion, speech, press, assembly, or petitioning the government for redress of grievances.	1789	1791
II, III, IV	No branch of government may infringe on the right of people to keep arms (II), is not arbitrarily to occupy homes for a militia (III), and is not to engage in the search or seizure of evidence without a court warrant swearing to belief in the probable existence of a crime (IV).	1789	1791
V, VI, VII, VIII	The courts* are not to hold trials for serious offenses without provision for a grand jury (V), a petit (trial) jury (VII), a speedy trial (VI), presentation of charges (VI), confrontation of hostile witnesses (VI), immunity from testimony against oneself (V), and immunity from more than one trial for the same offense (V). Neither bail nor punishment can be excessive (VIII), and no property can be taken without just compensation (V).	1789	1791
IX, X	All rights and powers not enumerated are reserved to the states or the people.	1789	1791
XI	Limited jurisdiction of federal courts over suits involving the states.	1794	1795
XII	Provided separate ballot for vice president in the electoral college.	1803	1804
XIII	Eliminated slavery and eliminated the right of states to treat persons as property.	1865	1865
XIV	Asserted the principle of national citizenship and prohibited the states from infringing upon the rights of citizens of the nation, no matter that they happened to live in that state. Also prohibited states from denying voting rights to male citizens over the age of 21.**	1866	1868
XV	Extended voting rights to all races.	1869	1870
XVI	Established national power to tax incomes.	1909	1913
XVII†	Provided for direct election of senators. This diminished the power of the state legislatures and underscored the idea of a direct connection between Americans and the government of the United States.	1912	1913
XIX	Extended voting rights to women.	1919	1920
XX	Eliminated "lame-duck" session of Congress.	1932	1933
XXII	Limited presidential term.	1947	1951
XXIII	Extended voting rights to residents of the District of Columbia.	1960	1961
XXIV	Extended voting rights to all classes by abolition of poll taxes.	1962	1964
XXV	Provided presidential succession in case of disability.	1965	1967
XXVI	Extended voting rights to citizens aged 18 and over.	1971	1971††
XXVII	Limited Congress's power to raise its own salary.	1789	1992

*These amendments also impose limits on the law-enforcement powers of federal, state, and local executive branches.

**In defining *citizenship*, the Fourteenth Amendment actually provided the constitutional basis for expanding the electorate to include all races, women, and residents of the District of Columbia. Only the "18-year-olds' amendment" should have been necessary, since it changed the definition of citizenship. The fact that additional amendments were required following the Fourteenth suggests that voting is not considered an inherent right of U.S. citizenship. Instead, it is viewed as a privilege.

†The Eighteenth Amendment, ratified in 1919, outlawed the sale and transportation of liquor. It was repealed by the Twenty-First Amendment, ratified in 1933.

††The Twenty-Sixth Amendment holds the record for speed of adoption. It was proposed on March 23, 1971, and adopted on July 5, 1971.

is one of the most fundamental and well-established rights in the United States not because it is recognized as such in the Constitution, but because legislatures and courts, working within an agreed-upon constitutional framework, have made it a crime for anyone, including the government, to trespass or to take away property without compensation. A constitution is good if it leads to good legislation, courts that protect citizens' liberties and rights, and appropriate police behavior. Its principles can be a citizen's dependable defense against the abuse of power.

Ordinary citizens, including students, can influence America's constitution. Take the case of the Twenty-Seventh Amendment, which declares that no congressional pay increase can take effect until the next Congress is elected. This amendment was proposed in 1789 along with the 10 that became the Bill of Rights; it was ratified by several states, but never the three-fourths needed to be added to the Constitution.

In 1982, however, a University of Texas undergraduate, Gregory Watson, wrote a term paper proposing a campaign to complete the ratification process. His professor gave it a C, calling the proposal unrealistic. Watson was undeterred and launched a student-led campaign. In 1992 the Twenty-Seventh Amendment was added to the Constitution, more than two centuries after it was proposed.

THE SUPREME COURT AND CONSTITUTIONAL CHANGE

Although the process of amendment outlined in Article V has seldom been used successfully, another form of constitutional revision is constantly at work: interpretation by the Supreme Court as it reviews cases. In some instances, the Court may give concrete definition to abstract constitutional principles.

For example, the Constitution's Fifth Amendment asserts in general terms that individuals accused of crimes are entitled to procedural rights. The Supreme Court, in a series of decisions, established principles giving effect to those rights. Every viewer of television crime programs knows that arrested individuals must be informed of their rights to remain silent and to have an attorney. These so-called Miranda warnings are the result of a 1966 Supreme Court decision about the Fifth Amendment.

In some instances, the Supreme Court does more than interpret or flesh out constitutional provisions: it seems to modify or supplement the text itself. For example, in decisions in 1965 and 1973 on birth control and abortion, respectively, the Court said that Americans were constitutionally entitled to a right of privacy. The Constitution does not explicitly mention this right, but the Court found it implied in the Fourteenth Amendment and several provisions in the Bill of Rights.

As we examine in more depth later in the book, much of the Supreme Court's power is itself based on constitutional interpretation rather than on the text of the document. In particular, although the Constitution nowhere mentions the power of judicial review, the Court asserted in a number of its early cases that the Constitution gave it this power, and this interpretation has prevailed. Advocates of "strict construction" of the Constitution denounce many court rulings as constitutional amendment by the judiciary and demand that judges' interpretations adhere closely to the words of the document's text. Proponents of the "living Constitution," on the other hand, assert that the Constitution's principles need to be adjusted to new problems and times and that the judiciary is the branch of government best qualified to do so.

Despite the Constitution's promises, a blight marred America's founding—the institution of slavery. The new nation's population included several hundred thousand enslaved Black persons—individuals who had been transported to America from Africa and their native-born descendants. Indeed, as Thomas Jefferson sat writing the Declaration of Independence, boldly declaring that all men are created equal, he was reportedly attended by an enslaved teenage boy who happened to be his wife's half brother. The Civil War brought an end to slavery, but in the decades following the War and Reconstruction, African Americans were subject to persecution and vilification. As a result of two centuries of resistance and protest from enslaved Africans and their descendants, America was gradually forced to recognize and act in accordance with its declared principles. Black struggles, moreover, paved the way for other groups, including women, LGBTQ people, immigrants, and others, to assert their own rights. In this way, the descendants of enslaved people helped to build American democracy.

The Constitution: What Do You Think?

Jim Obergefell's fight to secure marriage equality for same-sex couples illustrates the ways in which the Constitution's structure shapes politics to this day. The framers placed individual liberty ahead of all other political values. They feared that democracy could degenerate into a tyranny of the majority. They feared that economic or social equality would inspire the have-nots to interfere with the liberty of the haves. As a result, they designed many of the Constitution's key provisions, such as separated powers, internal checks and balances, and federalism, to safeguard liberty, and designed others, such as indirect election of senators and the president and the appointment of judges for life, to limit democracy and the threat of majority tyranny.

By championing liberty, however, the framers virtually guaranteed that democracy and even a measure of equality would eventually come to the United States. Liberty promotes political activity and participation, encouraging people and groups to fight for their rights and interests. In so doing, they may achieve greater equality, as did Jim Obergefell (featured at the beginning of this chapter).

★ What do you think about the values of liberty, equality, and democracy? Which is most important to you? Which do you think is most important to Jim Obergefell? How might your life be different if you lived in a country with different commitments to these values?

★ Advocates arguing for a particular policy position often invoke cherished values such as liberty, equality, and democracy to support their positions. What kinds of arguments could both supporters and opponents of same-sex marriage make using these three values?

★ Are there policy areas where you were frustrated by the slow policy-making process created by the separation of powers and the system of checks and balances? Or policy areas where you were relieved that changes that you opposed were slowed or halted? How do you think Jim Obergefell would answer these questions?

★ STUDY GUIDE ★

The First Founding: Interests and Conflicts

Explain the conflicts and coalitions that led to the Declaration of Independence and the Articles of Confederation (pp. 37–40)

Parliament's imposition of taxes, trade policies, and acts of political repression during the 1760s and 1770s radicalized many colonists to push for independence from British rule. The Declaration of Independence helped forge a sense of national unity among diverse groups in colonial society by identifying a set of grievances, goals, and principles that most colonists shared. The first written constitution of the United States, the Articles of Confederation, placed strong limits on the powers of the national government and left most power in the hands of the states.

Key Terms

Articles of Confederation (p. 40)

confederation (p. 40)

Practice Quiz

1. The British attempted to raise revenue in the North American colonies by
   a) imposing income taxes.
   b) imposing tariffs, duties, and other taxes on commerce.
   c) expropriating and selling Native American lands.
   d) levying licensing fees for the mining of natural resources.
   e) requesting voluntary donations.

2. In their fight against British taxes, such as the Stamp Act and the Sugar Act of 1764, New England merchants and southern planters allied with which of the following groups?
   a) shopkeepers, small farmers, laborers, and artisans
   b) shopkeepers only
   c) laborers only
   d) artisans only
   e) shopkeepers and laborers only

3. The first governing document in the United States was
   a) the Declaration of Independence.
   b) the Articles of Confederation.
   c) the Constitution.
   d) the Bill of Rights.
   e) the Virginia Plan.

4. Who was responsible for carrying out laws passed by the national government under the Articles of Confederation?
   a) the presidency
   b) the Congress
   c) the state governments
   d) the federal bureaucracy
   e) the federal judiciary

The Second Founding: From Compromise to Constitution

Describe the political context of the Constitutional Convention and the compromises achieved there (pp. 40–46)

International weakness, domestic economic problems, and the national government's inability to act decisively in response to Shays's Rebellion led to a Constitutional Convention to replace the Articles of Confederation. The convention's delegates were deeply divided on the issues of legislative representation and slavery. The Great Compromise and the Three-Fifths Compromise

temporarily reconciled these divisions and allowed the Founders to move forward with a new constitutional framework for the United States.

Key Terms

Virginia Plan (p. 43)

New Jersey Plan (p. 43)

Great Compromise (p. 44)

Three-Fifths Compromise (p. 46)

Practice Quiz

5. Which of the following was *not* a reason that the Articles of Confederation seemed inadequate?
   a) It did not provide for a national military.
   b) It did not allow the federal government to enforce treaties.
   c) It resulted in persistent economic turmoil among states.
   d) It permitted radical forces to take power in state legislatures.
   e) The Congress of the Confederation strictly controlled state governments.

6. Which event led directly to the Constitutional Convention by providing evidence that the government created under the Articles of Confederation was unable to act decisively in times of national crisis?
   a) the Boston Tea Party
   b) the Boston Massacre
   c) Shays's Rebellion
   d) the Annapolis Convention
   e) the War of 1812

7. The draft constitution that was introduced at the start of the Constitutional Convention by Edmund Randolph showed the strong influence of
   a) William Patterson.
   b) Benjamin Franklin.
   c) James Madison.
   d) George Clinton.
   e) Thomas Jefferson.

8. Which proposal argued that states should be represented in the national legislature according to their size and wealth?
   a) the New Jersey Plan
   b) the Maryland Plan
   c) the Rhode Island Plan
   d) the Virginia Plan
   e) the Connecticut Plan

9. The agreement reached at the Constitutional Convention that determined how enslaved people would be counted for the purposes of taxation and congressional representation was called the
   a) Connecticut Compromise.
   b) Three-Fifths Compromise.
   c) Great Compromise.
   d) Virginia Plan.
   e) New Jersey Plan.

The Constitution

Describe the principles of governance and the powers of the national government defined by the Constitution (pp. 46–53)

The framers wanted to create a stronger national government than the one that existed under the Articles of Confederation. In particular, they aspired to draft a constitution that would promote commerce, protect citizens' liberty and property rights, and secure popular support while avoiding the perils of "excessive democracy." The framers granted the national government supremacy over state governments in Article VI, but at the same time placed significant constraints on it through the separation of powers, federalism, and the Bill of Rights.

Key Terms

bicameral (p. 46)
checks and balances (p. 46)
Bill of Rights (p. 46)
separation of powers (p. 47)
federalism (p. 47)
expressed powers (p. 48)
elastic clause (p. 48)
judicial review (p. 50)
supremacy clause (p. 50)

Practice Quiz

10. Which of the following mechanisms was instituted in the Congress to guard against "excessive democracy"?
  a) bicameralism
  b) staggered terms in office
  c) checks and balances
  d) selection of senators by state legislatures
  e) all of the above

11. Which of the following best describes the Supreme Court as understood by the Founders?
  a) the principal check on presidential power
  b) the arbiter of disputes within the Congress
  c) the body that would choose the president
  d) a figurehead commission of elders
  e) the highest court of both the national government and the states

12. The ability of the president to veto a bill passed by Congress is a good example of
  a) federalism.
  b) the system of checks and balances.
  c) the supremacy clause.
  d) civil liberties.
  e) bicameralism.

The Fight for Ratification

> **Differentiate between the Federalists' and Antifeder-alists' stances on the ratification of the Constitution (pp. 53–57)**

Before the Constitution could go into effect, it had to be ratified by 9 of the 13 states. In the debate over ratification, the Federalists supported the Constitution, and the Antifederalists opposed it. The two groups disagreed on three major issues: the nature of political representation, the threat of tyranny, and the question of how to place limits on government action.

Key Terms

Federalists (p. 53)
Antifederalists (p. 53)
Federalist Papers (p. 54)
tyranny (p. 54)
limited government (p. 56)

Practice Quiz

13. During the debate over ratification, the Federalists were
  a) those who opposed the new Constitution because it created a stronger national government than existed under the Articles of Confederation.
  b) those who opposed the new constitution because it created a weaker national government than existed under the Articles of Confederation.
  c) those who opposed the new constitution because it did not end slavery.
  d) those who supported the new constitution because it created a stronger national government than existed under the Articles of Confederation.
  e) those who supported the new constitution because it ended slavery.

14. Which feature(s) of the Constitution did Antifederalists fear would lead to the emergence of tyranny?
  a) the Three-Fifths Compromise
  b) the provisions that created government institutions without direct responsibility to the people
  c) the provisions that lent power to a popular majority of citizens
  d) the checks that the Constitution placed on the legislative branch of government
  e) the supremacy clause

The Citizen's Role and the Changing Constitution

Explain how, and how often, the Constitution has been changed (pp. 57–62)

The amendment process outlined in Article V of the Constitution creates significant hurdles to changing the document that have rarely been cleared in American history. Attempts to solve specific public problems through the constitutional amendments have been particularly unsuccessful at winning sufficient levels of support. The Supreme Court, however, has provided new meaning and new substance to the Constitution on countless occasions through its decisions on important cases.

Key Term

amendment (p. 58)

Practice Quiz

15. Which of the following best describes the process of amending the Constitution?
    a) It is difficult and has rarely been used successfully to address specific public problems.
    b) It is difficult and has frequently been used successfully to address specific public problems.
    c) It is easy but has rarely been used successfully to address specific public problems.
    d) It is easy and has frequently been used successfully to address specific public problems.
    e) It is easy, but it has never been used for any purpose.

★ chapter ★
03

Federalism

As the coronavirus pandemic swept through the nation in early 2020, people looked to government for answers. But who had the responsibility, and the power, to help—the states, the federal government, or both? And how could they work together to provide the testing and support needed to battle the virus's spread?

Early on, federal and state officials assured Americans that they could get tested to see if they had contracted the virus. During a March 2020 visit to the Centers for Disease Control and Prevention in Atlanta, President Trump said, "Anybody that wants a test can get a test. That's what the bottom line is."[1]

But how was that promise being fulfilled by the state and local workers who needed to provide testing and care? Bill Whitmar, director of the Missouri state public-health laboratory, worried that statements such as Trump's resulted in far more people requesting testing than local medical communities could handle, creating supply shortages. "When that happens, then the supply chain on the front end—which is the swabs, the viral transport media, the collection tubes—started to evaporate from suppliers." He said that before promising widespread testing, "you have to look at your supply chain and analyze it closely. Not just make a promise, but look at your

In March of 2020, President Trump visited the Centers for Disease Control and Prevention (CDC) in Atlanta, Georgia, to discuss the availability of coronavirus testing in the United States. While there, he asserted there were plenty of tests in the country for anyone who wanted one, though this quickly proved false. To increase testing capabilities, the Food and Drug Administration (FDA) offered emergency power to the states to authorize private labs to process coronavirus tests, like the San Diego facility pictured here.

ability to provide a test for everybody. If you think you can, you may be surprised."

Under pressure from states, the federal government tried to address the testing shortfall. President Trump signed a memorandum allowing state public-health laboratories to authorize other labs in their states to develop and run coronavirus tests, a regulatory power normally reserved for the Food and Drug Administration (FDA), a federal agency. Although granting this power to the states was intended to expand much-needed testing capacity, state lab directors worried about their new authority. Joanne Bartkus, director of the Minnesota state public-health laboratory, said, "There is pressure to get these tests out: from the public, from the laboratories, from the politicians. It is a challenge to do that in a scientific and equitable way when you have no expertise in authorizing other labs to do testing." When other lab directors saw the headline on the FDA memo, "States Are Now in Charge of Testing," they "thought it was a hoax," she added. "It's almost like the FDA has thrown in the towel and said, 'Hey, you know, do whatever.'"[2]

The struggle over coronavirus-testing authority engages some of the oldest questions in American government: What is the responsibility of the federal government, and what is the responsibility of the states? Throughout American history, politicians and citizens have wrestled with questions about how responsibilities should be allocated across the nation's different levels of government. Some responsibilities, such as international relations, clearly lie with the federal government. Others, such as divorce laws, are controlled by state governments. In fact, most of the rules and regulations that Americans face in their daily lives are set by state and local governments. In response to the coronavirus pandemic, President Trump could only issue guidelines suggesting social distancing; it was mayors and governors who had the legal authority to ban large gatherings and issue work-from-home orders.

The fact that some mayors and governors did so while others did not raises another question of federalism: When should there be uniformity across the states, and within states, and when is it better to let states and localities adopt their own policies based on the needs and desires of their own populations? Which approach serves the common good? Does the answer vary across issue areas?

Given overlapping responsibilities and policy variation across subnational units like cities and states, the American form of federalism inevitably brings conflict. The debate about "who should do what" remains one of the most important discussions in American politics.

CHAPTER GOALS

★ Describe how the Constitution structures the relationships among the national, state, and local governments (pp. 71–76)

★ Explain how the relationship between the federal and state governments has evolved over time (pp. 76–84)

★ Analyze what difference federalism makes for politics and government (pp. 84–93)

Federalism in the Constitution

> **Describe how the Constitution structures the relationships among the national, state, and local governments**

The Constitution has profoundly influenced American life through its **federalism**, the division of powers and functions between a national government and lower levels of government, such as regions or states.

Federalism stands in contrast to a **unitary system**, in which lower levels of government have little independent power and primarily just implement decisions made by the central government. In France, for example, the central government was once so involved in the smallest details of local government that the minister of education boasted that by looking at his watch he could tell what all French schoolchildren were learning at that moment, because the central government set the school curriculum.

The United States was the first nation to adopt federalism as its governing framework. By granting just a few "expressed powers" to the national government and reserving all the rest to the states, the original Constitution recognized two authorities: state governments and the federal government. Table 3.1 indicates which level of government has responsibility for some of the actions that affect Americans' everyday lives.

While federalism was adopted to solve some practical governing problems that arose under the Articles of Confederation, as Chapter 2 noted, it has its own important implications for government and politics. Compared to unitary systems, with a single governing authority, federal systems with their multiple levels of government offer a number of possible advantages. Federalism offers the possibility of national unity for diverse countries. The nations most likely to have federal arrangements are those with diverse ethnic, language, or regional groupings, such as Switzerland and Canada and certainly the United States. The multiple governments at the national, state, and local levels present many opportunities for citizens to express their preferences, offering to maximize democratic participation. Because states and even localities have their own taxing, spending, and policy-making powers (especially in the United States), policy experimentation and innovation is another possibility, as is the tailoring of policy to local preferences. And competition among states and localities to attract individuals and businesses may maximize the efficiency of government services.[3]

The question is how well federalism delivers on these possibilities, a question particularly important in the United States. No two federal systems are exactly the same—they vary greatly in how power is shared—but in the American version of federalism state and local governments have even more policy-making responsibilities than in most federal systems. The result is particularly wide variation in policies and a centuries-long tug-of-war between the national and state governments, and between state and local governments. The federal structure's division of labor across the levels of government makes **intergovernmental relations**—the processes by which those levels of government negotiate and compromise over policy responsibility—one of the most characteristic aspects of American government.

THE POWERS OF THE NATIONAL GOVERNMENT

As we saw in Chapter 2, the **expressed powers** granted to the national government are found in Article I, Section 8, of the Constitution. These 17 powers include the power to collect taxes, coin money, declare war, and regulate commerce. Article I, Section 8,

---

federalism a system of government in which power is divided, by a constitution, between a central government and regional governments

unitary system a centralized government system in which lower levels of government have little power independent of the national government

intergovernmental relations the processes by which the three levels of American government (national, state, local) negotiate and compromise over policy responsibility

expressed powers specific powers granted by the Constitution to Congress (Article I, Section 8) and to the president (Article II)

TABLE 3.1

The Presence of Federal, State, and Local Government in the Daily Life of a Student at "State University"

TIME	SCHEDULE	LEVEL OF GOVERNMENT
7:00 A.M.	Wake up. Standard time set by the national government.	Federal and state
7:10 A.M.	Shower. Water courtesy of local government, either a public entity or a regulated private company.	Local
7:18 A.M.	Brush your teeth with toothpaste whose cavity-fighting claims have been verified by a federal agency.	Federal
7:30 A.M.	Have a bowl of cereal with milk for breakfast. "Nutrition Facts" on food labels are a federal requirement, pasteurization of milk required by state law, freshness dating on milk based on state and federal standards.	Federal and state
7:57 A.M.	Recycle the empty cereal box and milk carton.	State or local
8:30 A.M.	Drive or take public transportation to campus. Airbags and seat belts required by federal and state laws. Roads and bridges paid for by state and local governments, speed and traffic laws set by state and local governments, public transportation subsidized by all levels of government.	Federal, state, and local
8:45 A.M.	Arrive on campus of large public university. Buildings are 70 percent financed by state taxpayers.	State
9:00 A.M.	First class: Chemistry 101. Tuition partially paid by a federal loan (more than half the cost of university instruction is paid for by taxpayers), chemistry lab paid for with grants from the National Science Foundation (a federal agency) and smaller grants from business corporations made possible by federal income tax deductions for charitable contributions.	Federal
2:00 P.M.	Second class: American Government 101 (your favorite class!). You may be taking this class because it is required by the state legislature or because it fulfills a university requirement.	State
4:00 P.M.	Third class: Computer Science 101. Free computers, software, and internet access courtesy of state subsidies plus grants and discounts from Apple and Microsoft, the costs of which are deducted from their corporate income taxes; internet built in part by federal government. Duplication of software prohibited by federal copyright laws.	Federal and state
6:00 P.M.	Eat dinner: hamburger and french fries. Meat inspected for bacteria by federal agencies.	Federal
7:00 P.M.	Work at part-time job at the campus library. Minimum wage set by federal government; some states and cities set a higher minimum. Books and journals in library paid for by state taxpayers.	Federal, state, and local
8:15 P.M.	Go online to check the status of your application for a federal student loan (FAFSA) on the Department of Education's website at https://studentaid.ed.gov.	Federal
10:00 P.M.	Go home. Street lighting paid for by county and city governments, police patrols by city government.	Local
10:15 P.M.	Watch Netflix. Broadband internet service regulated by federal government. Check app for tomorrow's weather. Weather forecast provided by a federal agency.	Federal
10:45 P.M.	To complete your economics homework, visit the Bureau of Labor Statistics at www.bls.gov to look up unemployment levels since 1972.	Federal
Midnight	Put out the trash before going to bed. Trash collected by city sanitation department, financed by "user charges."	Local

also contains another important source of power for the national government: the **implied powers** that enable Congress "to make all Laws which shall be necessary and proper for carrying into Execution the foregoing Powers." Not until several decades after the Founding did the Supreme Court allow Congress to exercise the power implied in this **necessary and proper clause**. But as we shall see later in this chapter, this power allowed the national government to expand considerably— if slowly—the scope of its authority. In addition to these expressed and implied powers, the Constitution affirmed the power of the national government in the supremacy clause (Article VI), which made all national laws and treaties "the supreme Law of the Land."

THE POWERS OF STATE GOVERNMENT

One way in which the framers preserved a strong role for the states in the federal system was through the Tenth Amendment to the Constitution, which says that the powers the Constitution does not delegate to the national government or prohibit to the states are "reserved to the States respectively, or to the people." The Antifederalists, who feared that a strong central government would encroach on individual liberty, repeatedly pressed for such a "**reserved powers** amendment." Federalists agreed to it because they did not think it would do much harm.

The most fundamental power that the states retain is that of coercion—the power to develop and enforce criminal codes, to administer health and safety rules, and to regulate the family through marriage and divorce laws. The Founders saw differing state approaches to these issues as appropriate because they relate closely to differences in state and local values. States also have the power to regulate individuals' livelihoods; if you're a doctor or a lawyer or a plumber or a barber, you must be licensed by the state. Even more fundamentally, the states have the power to define private property—which exists only because state laws against trespass define who is and is not entitled to use it. Owning a car isn't worth much unless government makes it a crime for someone else to drive your car without your consent.

A state's authority to regulate these fundamental matters of the health, safety, welfare, and morals of its citizens is much greater than the powers of the national government and is commonly referred to as the **police power**. Policing is what states do—they coerce you in the name of the community and, for example, order you to self-isolate during the coronavirus pandemic, in the interest of maintaining public order and safety. And this was exactly the type of power that the Founders intended the states, not the federal government, to exercise.

States also retain and share with the national government **concurrent powers** to regulate commerce and the economy—for example, they can charter banks, grant or deny charters for corporations, grant or deny licenses to engage in a business or practice a trade, regulate the quality of products or the conditions of labor, and levy taxes. Wherever there is a direct conflict of laws between the federal and state levels, the issue will most likely be resolved in favor of national supremacy.

STATES' OBLIGATIONS TO ONE ANOTHER

The Constitution also creates obligations among the states, spelled out in Article IV. By requiring the states to recognize or uphold governmental actions and decisions in other states, the framers aimed to make the states less like independent countries and more like components of a unified nation. Article IV, Section 1, calls for

implied powers powers derived from the necessary and proper clause of Article I, Section 8, of the Constitution; such powers are not specifically expressed but are implied through the expansive interpretation of delegated powers

necessary and proper clause Article I, Section 8, of the Constitution, which provides Congress with the authority to make all laws "necessary and proper" to carry out its expressed powers

reserved powers powers, derived from the Tenth Amendment to the Constitution, that are not specifically delegated to the national government or denied to the states

police power power reserved to the state government to regulate the health, safety, and morals of its citizens

concurrent powers authority possessed by *both* state and national governments, such as the power to levy taxes

Previously a state-level policy, same-sex marriage was declared a fundamental right nationwide by the Supreme Court in 2015. The decision prompted a brief backlash from clerks in some states, such as Kim Davis from Kentucky, pictured here, who refused to issue marriage licenses to same-sex couples.

full faith and credit clause
provision from Article IV, Section 1, of the Constitution requiring that the states normally honor the public acts and judicial decisions that take place in another state

"Full Faith and Credit" among states, meaning that each state is normally expected to honor the "Public Acts, Records, and Judicial Proceedings" that take place in any other state. So, for example, if a restraining order is placed on a stalker in one state, other states are required to enforce that order as if they had issued it.

Nevertheless, some courts have found exceptions to the **full faith and credit clause:** if one state's law is against the "strong public policy" of another state, that state may not be obligated to recognize it.[4] The history of interracial marriage policy shows how much leeway states have had about recognizing marriages performed in other states. In 1952, 30 states prohibited interracial marriage, and many of these also refused to recognize such marriages performed in other states.[5] For example, in the 1967 Supreme Court case of *Loving v. Virginia*, which successfully challenged state bans on interracial marriage, Mildred and Richard Loving, a Black woman and a White man, were married in the District of Columbia. However, when they returned to their home state of Virginia, it refused to recognize them as a married couple.[6]

Until recently, same-sex marriage was in a similar position to interracial marriage half a century ago. Thirty-five states had passed "Defense of Marriage Acts," defining marriage as a union between one man and one woman, or had adopted constitutional amendments to this effect. In 1996 Congress passed a federal Defense of Marriage Act, which declared that states were not required to recognize a same-sex marriage from another state and that the federal government did not recognize same-sex marriage even if it was legal under state law.

In 2015, however, the Supreme Court ruled that the Fourteenth Amendment guaranteed a fundamental right to same-sex marriage. The case, *Obergefell v. Hodges*, combined four lawsuits by same-sex couples challenging their home states' refusals to grant same-sex marriage licenses or recognize same-sex marriages performed out of state.[7] The Court's 5–4 decision meant that all states must now offer marriage licenses to two people of the same sex and recognize same-sex marriages licensed by other states. In one stroke, same-sex marriage turned from a state-level policy choice to a nationally recognized right.

Who Participates in Local Elections Compared to National Elections?

Local politics is critically important to the lives of Americans, but participation in local politics is low. While over 50 percent of eligible Americans voted in the 2018 national elections, voter turnout in municipal elections, which are often conducted in off-off years (when there is no national election), can be in the single digits. Who does participate at the local level? And why don't more people participate in the politics closest to home?

Percent of U.S. Adults Who Say They ...

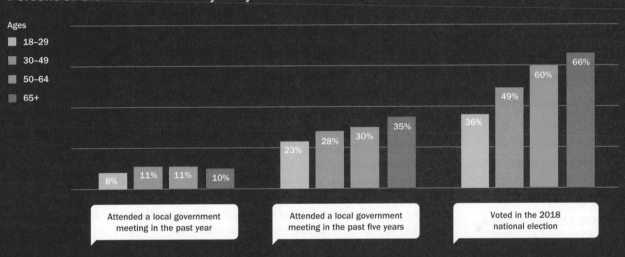

Ages
- 18–29
- 30–49
- 50–64
- 65+

Attended a local government meeting in the past year: 8%, 11%, 11%, 10%

Attended a local government meeting in the past five years: 23%, 28%, 30%, 35%

Voted in the 2018 national election: 36%, 49%, 60%, 66%

Turnout in Most Recent Municipal Election
Percentage of voting-age population in selected cities*

- Chicago 33%
- Seattle 43%
- Washington, D.C. 38%
- Detroit 27%
- Denver 24%
- Houston 22%
- San Antonio 10%
- New York City 7%

* The voting-eligible population excludes noncitizens and people who are institutionalized or not allowed to vote in some states because they are ex-felons. The voting-age population includes everyone over 18.

SOURCE: Data from U.S. Vote Foundation and Pew Research Center (accessed 11/18/19).

FOR CRITICAL ANALYSIS

1. Why don't more people attend local government meetings and participate in local elections? Is this a problem for democracy? Why or why not?

2. Many local elections are off-cycle (held in odd-numbered years when no national elections take place). Should local elections be moved so they overlap with national elections? Why or why not?

TABLE 3.2

90,126 Governments in the United States

TYPE	NUMBER
National	1
State	50
County	3,031
Municipal	19,495
Townships	16,253
School districts	12,754
Other special districts	38,542

SOURCE: U.S. Census Bureau, 2017 Census of Governments, Table 2, www.census.gov/data/tables/2017/econ/gus/2017-governments.html (accessed 1/21/20).

privileges and immunities clause provision, from Article IV, Section 2, of the Constitution, that a state cannot discriminate against someone from another state or give its own residents special privileges

home rule power delegated by the state to a local unit of government to manage its own affairs

Article IV, Section 2, known as the "comity clause," also seeks to promote national unity, by providing that citizens enjoying the "**privileges and immunities**" of one state should be entitled to similar treatment in other states. What this has come to mean is that a state cannot discriminate against someone from another state or give special privileges to its own residents. For example, in the 1970s, the Supreme Court struck down as unconstitutional an Alaska law that gave Alaska residents preference over nonresidents for jobs on the state's oil and gas pipelines.[8] The comity clause also regulates criminal justice among the states by requiring states to return fugitives to the states from which they have fled. Thus, in 1952, when an escaped prisoner sued to avoid being returned to Alabama on the grounds that he was being subjected to "cruel and unusual punishment" there, the Supreme Court ruled that he must be returned according to Article IV, Section 2.[9]

LOCAL GOVERNMENT AND THE CONSTITUTION

Local government occupies a peculiar but very important place in the American system (see Table 3.2). It has no status in the U.S. Constitution. Instead, state constitutions define local government structures and responsibilities. Thus local governments are subject to ultimate control by the states.

This imbalance of power means that state governments could legally dissolve local governments or force multiple local governments to consolidate into one. Most states have amended their constitutions to give their larger cities **home rule**—a guarantee of noninterference in various areas of local affairs.[10] In recent years, however, as discussed below, some local governments have passed laws making policy on matters from minimum wage to public broadband, only to have state legislatures preempt, or remove, that authority.

National and State Power over Time

> **Explain how the relationship between the federal and state governments has evolved over time**

The most fundamental impact of federalism on the way the United States is governed comes not from any particular provision of the Constitution but from the framework itself, which has determined which level of government does what and, in that way, how the country has developed politically. As we shall see, important aspects of federalism have changed, but the framework has survived two centuries and a devastating civil war.

At the time of the Founding, the states far surpassed the federal government in their power to influence the lives of ordinary Americans. In the system of shared powers, they played a much more active role in economic and social regulation than the federal government, which tended toward a hands-off approach. Although Supreme Court decisions gradually expanded its authority in this area, not until the New Deal response to the Great Depression in the 1930s did the national government gain vast new powers. Since then, even as this trend toward centralization has continued, the states have asserted themselves at certain times and in certain policy

Make Your Voice Heard at a Local Meeting

DOMINGO MOREL, cofounder of the Rhode Island Latino Policy Institute and assistant professor at Rutgers University–Newark

How can you change policy in your community? There are over 90,000 local governments in the United States, including school boards, city councils, county boards, and special districts for public transportation, utilities, libraries, parks, police, fire, water, and more. Domingo shared his advice for making your voice heard in local government:

1 Figure out which governmental entity has jurisdiction over your issue and get on its agenda. Most school boards, city councils, and other local government entities have an online sign-up to speak at their meetings.

2 Do research on your issue. Local governments often do not have staffs to do research. Many local officeholders have day jobs. You can be an effective advocate and partner by supplying the research they can't do. Young people would be surprised to learn how far that can get them.

3 Prepare your statement. Your time will be limited, so lay out your issue concern and suggested solution succinctly. The most effective statements don't just articulate an argument but also attach a personal narrative about why this issue is important and convey that to the people who are in power.

4 Follow up. Email the members of the board or council. Broadcast your issue concern and proposals on social media. Monitor the agenda and attend subsequent meetings. Build relationships with local officials.

5 Consider that collective action may be even more powerful. I recall a mother who attended Newark school board meetings for four months, urging, without success, that Muslim holidays be added to the school calendar. In the fifth month she said, "Today I brought my community. Can all of the Muslims in attendance please stand up?" Seeing an auditorium full, the school board changed the policy. I advise bringing

friends, finding out what groups may already work on your concerns, or creating your own group if needed (see How to Start an Advocacy Group on p. 403).

6 Work across the generations. Seek the advice of elders and community leaders who worked on such issues in the past. In turn, recruit younger people to keep the effort going, giving them information so they don't have to start over. It's not easy getting engaged, it's not easy to go out there and be an activist on the individual or collective level, but once you get to that place, it's important to ensure you're recruiting others.

7 Work the federal system. Many issues are addressed at multiple levels of government. Strategize about the best level for addressing your particular concern. And if you make no headway at one level, target another. Federalism brings its challenges but also has its advantages.

areas, sometimes aided by the courts. But at other moments a crisis shifts power toward the national government again, as during the September 11, 2001, terror attacks and the fiscal crisis that began in 2008. During the coronavirus pandemic, the federal government issued policies on travel from abroad and awarded contracts to pharmaceutical firms developing treatments and vaccines, while state and local governments were responsible for shutdown orders and mask mandates. Federalism creates a complex, flexible form of government whose workings shift over time.

RESTRAINING NATIONAL POWER WITH DUAL FEDERALISM

dual federalism the system of government that prevailed in the United States from 1789 to 1937 in which most fundamental governmental powers were shared between the federal and state governments

Historically, the **dual federalism** fundamental to the American system of government has meant that states have done most of the fundamental governing. We call this state-centered federalism the "traditional system" because it prevailed for much of American history. Under this system, the national government was quite small and very narrowly specialized in the functions it performed. For evidence, look at Table 3.3, which lists the major types of public policies by which Americans were governed for the first century and a half under the Constitution.

What do the functions of the national government reveal? First, virtually all of them were aimed at assisting commerce, such as building roads or protecting domestic industries with tariffs on imported goods. Second, virtually none of them directly

TABLE 3.3

The Federal System: Specialization of Governmental Functions in the Traditional System, 1789–1937

NATIONAL GOVERNMENT POLICIES (DOMESTIC)	STATE GOVERNMENT POLICIES	LOCAL GOVERNMENT POLICIES
Internal improvements	Property laws (including slavery)	Adaptation of state laws to local conditions
Subsidies	Estate and inheritance laws	Public works
Tariffs	Commerce laws	Contracts for public works
Public land disposal	Banking and credit laws	Licensing of public accommodation
Patents	Corporate laws	Zoning and other land-use regulation
Currency	Insurance laws	Basic public services
	Family laws	
	Morality laws	
	Public health laws	
	Education laws	
	General penal laws	
	Eminent domain laws	
	Construction codes	
	Land-use laws	
	Water and mineral laws	
	Criminal procedure laws	
	Electoral and political party laws	
	Local government laws	
	Civil service laws	
	Occupations and professions laws	

coerced citizens. The emphasis was on promotion and encouragement—providing land or capital needed for economic development.

State legislatures were also actively involved in economic regulation during the nineteenth century. American capitalism took its form from state property and trespass laws and from state laws and court decisions regarding contracts, markets, credit, banking, incorporation, and insurance. Until the Thirteenth Amendment abolished slavery, property law extended to slavery, with the fugitive slave clause of the Constitution (Article IV, Section 2) requiring even "free states" without slavery to return freedom-seeking enslaved people to the states from which they had escaped.

By allowing states to do most of the governing, the Constitution saved the national government from many policy decisions that might have proved too divisive for a large and very young country. And the state and regional variation in policy allowed by the federal framework continues to facilitate governance in this vast and diverse nation.

THE SLOW GROWTH OF THE NATIONAL GOVERNMENT'S POWER

As the nation grew, disputes arose about the powers of the federal government versus the powers of the states. In the first several decades after the Founding, the Supreme Court decided several critical cases that expanded federal powers, removed barriers to trade across the states, and laid the groundwork for a national economy. These early decisions to expand federal power rested on a pro-national interpretation of Article I, Section 8, of the Constitution. That article enumerates the powers of Congress, including the power to tax, raise an army, declare war, establish post offices, and "regulate commerce with foreign nations, and among the several States and with the Indian tribes." Though its scope initially was unclear, this **commerce clause** would later form the basis for expanding federal government control over the economy.

The Court's early decisions began to define national power by favoring federal control over the economy when there was a conflict between the states and the federal government. The first and most important such case was *McCulloch v. Maryland* (1819), which involved the question of whether Congress could charter a national bank—an explicit grant of power nowhere to be found in Article I, Section 8.[11] Chief Justice John Marshall answered that this power could be "implied" from other powers expressly delegated to Congress, such as the power to regulate commerce. His decision rested on the necessary and proper clause of Article I, Section 8, which gave Congress the power to enact laws "necessary and proper" for carrying out its delegated powers.

Marshall also concluded in *McCulloch* that any state law conflicting with a federal law is invalid since the Constitution states that "the Laws of the United States . . . shall be the supreme Law of the Land." Both aspects of his ruling thus created the potential for an unprecedented increase in national government power, yet Congress did not immediately pursue such an expansion.

Another major case, *Gibbons v. Ogden* (1824), reinforced this nationalistic interpretation of the Constitution. The issue was whether New York State could grant a monopoly to Robert Fulton's steamboat company to operate an exclusive service between New York and New Jersey. In arguing that the state lacked the power to do so, Chief Justice Marshall had to define what Article I, Section 8, meant by "commerce among the several states." He insisted that the definition was "comprehensive," extending to "every species of commercial intercourse." However, this

commerce clause Article I, Section 8, of the Constitution, which delegates to Congress the power "to regulate commerce with foreign nations, and among the several States and with the Indian tribes"; this clause was interpreted by the Supreme Court in favor of national power over the economy

In 1916 the national government passed the Keating-Owen Child Labor Act, which excluded from interstate commerce all goods manufactured by children under age 14. The act was ruled unconstitutional by the Supreme Court, and the regulation of child labor remained in the hands of state governments until the 1930s.

comprehensiveness was limited "to that commerce which concerns more states than one."

Gibbons is important because it established the supremacy of the national government in all matters affecting what later came to be called "interstate commerce."[12] But the precise meaning of that term would remain uncertain over the next few decades. Backed by the implied-powers decision in *McCulloch* and by the broad definition of "interstate commerce" in *Gibbons*, Article I, Section 8, was a source of power for the national government as long as Congress aimed to encourage commerce through subsidies, services, and land grants.

Later in the nineteenth century, though, any effort of the national government to *regulate* commerce in such areas as fraud, product quality, child labor, or working conditions or hours was declared unconstitutional by the Supreme Court. The Court said that with such legislation the federal government was entering workplaces—local areas—and attempting to regulate goods that had not yet passed into interstate commerce. To enter local workplaces was to exercise police power—a power reserved to the states.

No one questioned the power of the national government to regulate businesses that by their nature crossed state lines, such as railroads, gas pipelines, and waterway transportation. But well into the twentieth century the Supreme Court used the concept of interstate commerce as a barrier against most efforts by Congress to regulate local conditions. Thus, federalism, as interpreted by the Supreme Court for 70 years after the Civil War, enabled business to have its cake and eat it, too: entrepreneurs enjoyed the benefits of national policies promoting commerce and were shielded by the courts from policies regulating commerce by protecting consumers and workers.[13]

This barrier fell after 1937, however, when the Supreme Court issued a series of decisions that laid the groundwork for a much stronger federal government. Most significant was the Court's dramatic expansion of the commerce clause. By throwing out the old distinction between interstate and intrastate commerce, the Court converted the clause from a source of limitations to a source of power for the national government. The Court upheld acts of Congress that protected the rights of employees to organize and engage in collective bargaining, regulated the amount of farmland in cultivation, extended low-interest credit to small businesses and farmers, and restricted the activities of corporations dealing in the stock market.[14]

The Court also upheld many other laws that contributed to the construction of the modern safety net of social programs created in response to the Great Depression. With these rulings, the Court decisively signaled that the era of dual federalism was over. In the future, Congress would have very broad powers to regulate activity in the states.

THE NEW DEAL: NEW ROLES FOR GOVERNMENT

The economic crisis of the Great Depression and the nature of the government response signaled a new era of federalism in the United States. Before this national economic catastrophe, it was states and localities that took responsibility for assisting the poor, usually channeling aid through private charity. But the extent of the depression quickly exhausted their capacities. By 1932, 25 percent of the workforce was unemployed, and many people had lost their homes and settled into camps called "Hoovervilles," after President Herbert Hoover. Elected in 1928, the year before the depression hit, Hoover steadfastly maintained that the federal government could do little to alleviate the misery caused by the depression. It was a matter for state and local governments, he said.

Yet demands mounted for the federal government to take action. In Congress, some Democrats proposed that the federal government finance public works to aid the economy and put people back to work. Other members of Congress introduced legislation to provide federal grants to the states to assist them in their relief efforts. Most of these measures failed to win congressional approval or were vetoed by President Hoover.

When Franklin Delano Roosevelt took office in 1933, he energetically threw the federal government into the fight against the depression through a number of proposals known collectively as the New Deal. He proposed a variety of temporary relief and work programs, most of them to be financed by the federal government but administered by the states. In addition to these temporary measures, Roosevelt presided over the creation of several important federal programs designed to provide future economic security for Americans. The New Deal signaled the rise of a more active national government.

The New Deal expanded the scope of the federal government. One of the largest and most effective New Deal programs, the Works Progress Administration (WPA) employed millions of Americans in projects such as constructing highways, bridges, and public parks.

FROM LAYER CAKE TO MARBLE CAKE: COOPERATIVE FEDERALISM AND THE USE OF CATEGORICAL GRANTS

For the most part, the new national programs that the Roosevelt administration developed did not directly take power away from the states. Instead, the national government typically offered states **grants-in-aid**, money provided on the condition that it be spent for a particular purpose defined by Congress. The New Deal expanded the range of grants-in-aid into social programs, providing grants to the states for financial assistance to poor children. Congress added more grant programs after World War II to help states fund activities such as providing school lunches and building highways. Sometimes state or local governments were required to match the national contribution dollar for dollar, but in programs such as the development of the interstate highway system, the congressional grants provided 90 percent of the cost.

grants-in-aid programs through which Congress provides money to state and local governments on the condition that the funds be employed for purposes defined by the federal government

categorical grants congressional grants given to states and localities on the condition that expenditures be limited to a problem or group specified by law

cooperative federalism a type of federalism existing since the New Deal era in which grants-in-aid have been used strategically to encourage states and localities (without commanding them) to pursue nationally defined goals; also known as *intergovernmental cooperation*

These types of federal grants-in-aid are called **categorical grants**, because the national government determines the purposes, or categories, for which the money can be used. For the most part, the categorical grants created before the 1960s simply helped the states perform their traditional functions.[15] During that decade, however, the number of categorical grants increased dramatically,[16] and new ones announced national purposes much more strongly than had earlier grants. One of the most important—and expensive—was the federal Medicaid program, which provides grants to pay for medical care for the poor, the disabled, and many nursing home residents. Over time the value of categorical grants has risen dramatically, increasing from $54.8 billion in 1960 to an estimated $598.2 billion in 2021 (see Figure 3.1).

The growth of categorical grants created a new kind of federalism. If the traditional system of two authorities—the federal government and the states—performing highly different functions could be called dual federalism, historians of federalism suggest that the system since the New Deal could be called **cooperative federalism**.

FIGURE 3.1

Federal Grants-in-Aid,* 1960–2021

Spending on federal grants-in-aid to the states and local governments has grown dramatically since 1990. These increases reflect the growing public expectations about what government should do. What has been the most important cause of the steady increase in these grants?

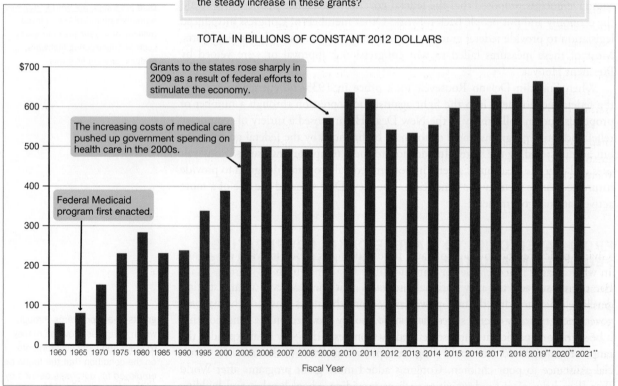

TOTAL IN BILLIONS OF CONSTANT 2012 DOLLARS

Grants to the states rose sharply in 2009 as a result of federal efforts to stimulate the economy.

The increasing costs of medical care pushed up government spending on health care in the 2000s.

Federal Medicaid program first enacted.

Fiscal Year

*Excludes outlays for national defense, international affairs, and net interest. Data in constant (fiscal year 2012) dollars.
**Estimate.
SOURCE: Office of Management and Budget, U.S. Budget for Fiscal Year 2020, "Historical Tables: Table 12.1," www.whitehouse.gov/omb/historical-tables/ (accessed 1/21/20).

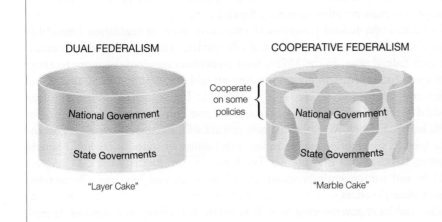

DUAL FEDERALISM

National Government

State Governments

"Layer Cake"

Cooperate on some policies

COOPERATIVE FEDERALISM

National Government

State Governments

"Marble Cake"

FIGURE 3.2

Dual versus Cooperative Federalism

In layer-cake (dual) federalism, the responsibilities of the national government and state governments are clearly separated. In marble-cake (cooperative) federalism, national policies, state policies, and local policies overlap in many areas.

The political scientist Morton Grodzins characterized this as a move from "layer cake federalism" to "marble cake federalism,"[17] in which intergovernmental cooperation and sharing have blurred a once-clear distinguishing line, making it difficult to say where the national government ends and the state and local governments begin (see Figure 3.2).

As important as the states were in this new system of grants, some new federal grants, particularly during the War on Poverty of the 1960s, bypassed the states and instead sent money directly to local governments and even to local nonprofit organizations. One of the reasons for this shift was the way African American citizens were treated in the South. As the civil rights movement gained momentum, the southern defense of segregation on the grounds of states' rights helped create the impression in Washington that the states could not be trusted to carry out national purposes.

Yet other new programs of the 1960s, such as Medicaid, relied on state governments for their implementation. In addition, as the national government expanded existing state-run programs, states had to take on more responsibilities, which gave them a critical role in the federal system.

REGULATED FEDERALISM AND THE RISE OF NATIONAL STANDARDS

Giving policy responsibilities to states raises questions about to what extent and in what areas it is acceptable for states to differ from one another. Supreme Court decisions have provided important answers to many of these questions, typically pushing for greater uniformity across the states. But in other policy areas, national government has created greater uniformity by offering incentives or imposing rules.

Federal grants, as we have seen, are one such tool: Congress provides an incentive by giving money to state and local governments if they agree to spend it for the purposes Congress specifies. But as Congress in the 1970s began to enact legislation in new areas, such as environmental policy, it resorted to another tool: regulations on states and localities. In what some political scientists call **regulated federalism**,[18] the national government began to set standards of conduct or to require the states to set standards that met national guidelines. As a result, state and local policies in

regulated federalism a form of federalism in which Congress imposes legislation on states and localities, requiring them to meet national standards

environmental protection, social services, and education are more uniform from coast to coast than are other nationally funded policies.

Sometimes the federal government takes over areas of regulation from state or local governments when their standards are less strict or otherwise inconsistent with federal ones. In the 1970s, such **preemptions** required the states to abide by tougher federal rules in areas including air and water pollution, occupational health and safety, and access for the disabled. The regulated industries often opposed preemptions because they increased the cost of doing business. After 1994, however, when Republicans took control of Congress, the federal government used its preemption power to limit the ability of states to tax and regulate industry. For example, the Internet Tax Freedom Act, first enacted by Congress in 1998 and subsequently renewed, prohibits states and localities from taxing internet access services.

State and local governments as well as individuals often challenge federal preemptions. For example, in 2001, Attorney General John Ashcroft declared that Oregon's law permitting doctor-assisted suicide was illegal under federal drug regulations. Ashcroft's rule was challenged by the state, a physician, a pharmacist, and several terminally ill state residents, and in 2006 the Supreme Court ruled that the attorney general did not have the authority to prohibit the Oregon law.[19]

The Trump administration took actions much like the congressional Republicans of 1994. California has long had more stringent vehicle emissions and mileage targets than the federal government, but the administration moved to prohibit any state from setting standards different from federal ones. In 2019, California and 22 other states sued to keep their ability to set stricter regulations in place.[20]

The Politics of Federalism Today

Analyze what difference federalism makes for politics and government

Debates about the appropriate role for each level of government—national, state, and local—have continued into the contemporary era. Both court decisions and policy responsibilities continue to shift, increasing intergovernmental tensions. The significant role for the states in particular raises important questions. Do some divisions of responsibility among the levels work better than others? Might states be sources of experimentation and innovation, the "laboratories of democracy," as Supreme Court Justice Louis Brandeis suggested?[21] Which responsibilities are states capable of managing and financing? Does interstate competition enhance efficiency? What about the political implications of federalism? Who prefers national rather than state control? And do multiple levels of government in fact promote citizen engagement?

STATES' RIGHTS

The Tenth Amendment, which reserves to the states the powers the Constitution does not specifically delegate to the national government, has been used over time by various groups, for various purposes, to bolster the role of the states in the federal system. For much of the nineteenth century, when federal power remained limited, the Tenth Amendment was used to argue in favor of **states' rights**. The extreme version of this position, known as nullification, claimed that the states did not

---

preemption the principle that allows the national government to override state or local actions in certain policy areas; in foreign policy, the willingness to strike first in order to prevent an enemy attack

FOR CRITICAL ANALYSIS

When is federal preemption of local laws desirable? Is preemption justified for some issues more than for others?

FOR CRITICAL ANALYSIS

How have Supreme Court decisions affected the balance of power between the federal government and the states? Has the Supreme Court favored the federal government or the states?

states' rights the principle that the states should oppose the increasing authority of the national government; this principle was most popular in the period before the Civil War

Federal and Unitary Systems

Worldwide, unitary systems of government are much more common than federal systems. Geographically they may appear to be roughly even on this map, but that is because larger countries such as the United States and Russia often use federal systems. In fact, fewer than 15 percent of the world's countries use federal systems. Each type of system brings its own strengths and drawbacks: unitary systems can be more efficient, but federal systems can allow for more regional autonomy and policy innovation.

1. What explains why a country might use a federal or a unitary system? Why would a country with a large amount of territory to govern, such as Canada or Brazil, prefer a federal arrangement? Are there any geographic or regional patterns that you see? What might lead to countries on a continent being more likely to have similar government arrangements?

2. What are some of the other advantages to having a unitary system? In what ways might a federal system be more responsive? If you were designing your own country, which would you prefer and why?

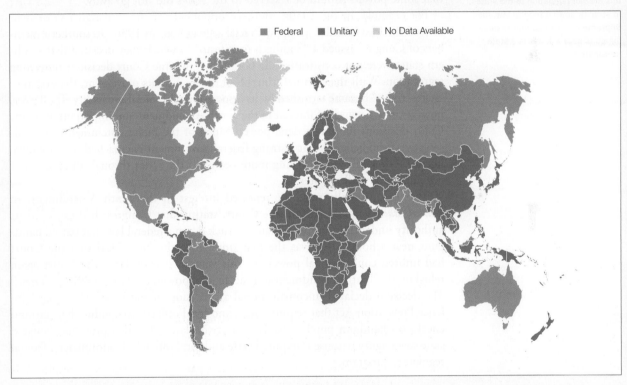

■ Federal ■ Unitary ■ No Data Available

SOURCE: CIA World Factbook, cia.gov (accessed 3/31/2020).

In 1995 the Supreme Court ruled that the Gun-Free School Zones Act was an unconstitutional application of the commerce clause, leaving this area of regulation to the states. In striking down a federal law, the Supreme Court ruled that regulating guns near schools is a state prerogative.

have to obey federal laws that they believed exceeded the national government's constitutional authority.

Prior to the Civil War, sharp differences between the North and the South over tariffs and slavery gave rise to nullification arguments that were most fully articulated by John C. Calhoun, vice president under Andrew Jackson and later a senator from South Carolina. (Calhoun was a slaveowner and White supremacist, and his political positions were often informed by his support of the expansion of the institution of slavery.) Such arguments were voiced less often after the Civil War. But the Supreme Court continued to use the Tenth Amendment to strike down laws that it thought exceeded national power, including the Civil Rights Act passed in 1875, which would have eliminated discrimination against African Americans in public accommodations and transportation.

By the late 1930s, although the Supreme Court had struck down some national regulations limiting the power of large corporations and promoting the health and welfare of citizens, overall its decisions expanded federal power—so much so that the Tenth Amendment appeared irrelevant. Yet the idea that some powers should be reserved to the states did not go away.

For example, in the 1950s, southern opponents of the civil rights movement revived the idea in order to support racial segregation. In 1956, 96 southern members of Congress issued a "Southern manifesto" in which they declared that southern states were not constitutionally bound by Supreme Court decisions outlawing segregation. With the eventual triumph of the civil rights movement, the slogan of "states' rights" became tarnished by its association with racial inequality. The 1990s, however, saw a revival of interest in the Tenth Amendment and important Supreme Court decisions limiting federal power. Much of the interest stemmed from conservatives who believed that a strong federal government encroached on individual liberties. They favored returning more power to the states through the process of devolution, as we'll see later.[22]

Two key cases illustrate the renewed interest in the Tenth Amendment. In *United States v. Lopez* (1995), the Court, stating that Congress had exceeded its authority under the commerce clause, struck down a federal law that barred handguns near schools. This was the first time since the New Deal that the Court had limited congressional powers in this way. Two years later, the Court again relied on the Tenth Amendment to limit federal power, in *Printz v. United States.*[23] The decision declared unconstitutional a provision of the Brady Handgun Violence Prevention Act that required state and local officials to conduct background checks on handgun purchasers. The Court declared that this provision violated state sovereignty because it required state and local officials to administer a federal regulatory program.

DEVOLUTION

devolution a policy to remove a program from one level of government by delegating it or passing it down to a lower level of government, such as from the national government to the state and local governments

Since the 1970s, as states have become more capable of administering large-scale programs, the idea of **devolution**—transferring responsibility for policy from the federal government to states and localities—has become popular. Its proponents maintain that states are potential innovators and experimenters, whose good ideas might spread horizontally to other states and even vertically to the federal government. Devolution's supporters also assert that governments closer to the people can better tailor policies to local needs than can the federal government in "far-off"

Washington, D.C. Political conservatives have been the chief proponents of such views, but as we will see later, views about federalism sometimes depend on which party controls which levels of government.

An important tool of devolution is the **block grant**, federal funding that states have considerable leeway in spending. President Nixon led the first push for block grants in the early 1970s as part of his **New Federalism** initiative, when programs in the areas of job training, community development, and social services were consolidated into three large block grants. These grants imposed some conditions on how the money should be spent, but not the narrow regulations contained in categorical grants. In addition, Congress provided an important new form of federal assistance to state and local governments, called **general revenue sharing**, which had no strings attached; recipients could spend the money as they wished.

In his version of the New Federalism in the 1980s, President Reagan also looked to block grants to reduce the national government's control and return power to the states. But unlike Nixon, he used them to cut federal spending as well. The 12 new block grants enacted between 1981 and 1990 cut federal spending in those areas by 12 percent.[24] Reagan's view was that states could spend their own funds to make up the difference if they chose to do so.

The Republican Congress elected in 1994 attempted to take the devolution strategy even further through more block grants and spending cuts in federal programs. Their biggest success was the 1996 welfare reform law, which delegated to states important new responsibilities. Most of the other major proposed block grants or spending reductions, however, failed to pass Congress or were vetoed by President Clinton.[25] While Congressional Republicans failed to turn the Medicaid program into a block program in 2017 due to opposition among the public and among governors concerned that such a change would result in future funding cuts, in 2020 the Trump administration gave states the option to convert part of their Medicaid funding into a block grant.[26]

Those who argue for state policy control note that states have often been important sources of policy innovations that have diffused to other states or to the federal government. For example, Minnesota first created charter schools in 1991; now 44 states and the District of Columbia permit them.[27] Policy ideas tend to diffuse geographically to neighboring states or ideologically to states with similar political environments. **Diffusion** can also proceed through the layers of the federal system. In 1990, San Luis Obispo, California, became the first city to ban smoking in bars and restaurants. The state of California followed with a statewide ban on smoking in enclosed workplaces in 1995, and the federal government banned smoking on commercial flights in 1998. The Massachusetts health care reform of 2006 became the template for the federal Affordable Care Act of 2010 ("Obamacare").

On the other hand, proponents of national-level policy point to the fiscal burden of policy responsibility. Forty-nine states are required to have their proposed budgets balance; most are also prohibited from carrying deficits into the next fiscal year.[28] States often complain about **unfunded mandates**—requirements on states imposed by the national government without accompanying funding. For example, a 1973 law prohibiting discrimination against the disabled in programs that were partly funded by the federal government required state and local governments to make public transit accessible. But the legislation provided no funding for the wheelchair lifts and elevators that would be necessary, leaving states to cover the

block grants federal grants-in-aid that allow states considerable discretion in how the funds are spent

New Federalism attempts by Presidents Nixon and Reagan to return power to the states through block grants

general revenue sharing the process by which one unit of government yields a portion of its tax income to another unit of government, according to an established formula; revenue sharing typically involves the national government providing money to state governments

diffusion the process by which policy decisions in one political jurisdiction are influenced by choices made in another jurisdiction

unfunded mandate a law or regulation requiring a state or local government to perform certain actions without providing funding for fulfilling the requirement

The federal government frequently passes laws that impose mandates on the states, such as the 1990 Americans with Disabilities Act, which protects against discrimination based on disability. States were required to pay for changes to meet federal standards for accessibility in public transportation and public facilities.

redistributive programs economic policies designed to transfer income through taxing and spending, with the goal of benefiting the poor

FOR CRITICAL ANALYSIS

Should states be required to implement unfunded mandates? How much of the funding should the federal government provide for policies or standards that it sets?

multibillion-dollar cost.[29] A 1995 law meant to reduce unfunded mandates on states solved the problem only partially, and many state and local government officials advocate that its coverage be broadened.[30]

Additional concerns with state responsibility are variation in policy outcomes and questions of who benefits or suffers from government action or inaction. For example, many political scientists and economists maintain that state and local governments should not be in charge of **redistributive programs**—those intended primarily to benefit the poor. They argue that since state and local governments have to compete with one another for residents and businesses, they lack any incentive to spend money on needy people in their areas. Instead, they want to keep taxes low and spend money on things that promote economic development.[31] This situation encourages states to engage in a "race to the bottom": if one state cuts assistance to the poor, neighboring states will make similar or deeper cuts both to reduce spending and to discourage poor people from moving to their states. As one New York legislator put it, "The concern we have is that unless we make our welfare system and our tax and regulatory system competitive with the states around us, we will have too many disincentives for business to move here."[32]

In 1996, when Congress enacted major welfare reform, it followed a different logic. By changing welfare from a combined federal–state program into a block grant, Congress gave the states more responsibility for programs that serve the poor. Supporters of the change hoped to reduce welfare spending and argued that states could experiment with many different approaches to find those that best met the needs of their citizens.

As states altered their welfare programs in the wake of the new law, they did indeed design diverse approaches. For example, Minnesota adopted an incentive-based approach that offers extra assistance to families that take low-wage jobs, while six other states imposed very strict time limits on receiving benefits, allowing welfare recipients less than the five-year lifetime limit in the federal legislation (the limit is shortest in Arizona: 12 months).[33] As of 2018, cash welfare benefits per month for a family of three are $714 in California, $462 in Colorado, and $290 in Texas.[34] After the passage of the law, welfare rolls declined dramatically—on average, by more than half from their peak in 1994. In 12 states the decline was 70 percent or higher. Politicians have cited these statistics to claim that the poor have benefited from greater state control of welfare, yet most studies have found that the majority of those leaving welfare remain in poverty.

The devolution of policy responsibilities to the state level can result in great variation across the states in eligibility and benefit levels in redistributive programs beyond welfare, differences driven by differences in wealth and political environment.[35] For example, the same person can be eligible for Medicaid in one state but not in another, or for different benefits depending on where they live. Under federal Medicaid rules, dental and vision services are required for children but optional for adults. In most states Medicaid does not cover eyeglasses for adults, but in Texas it does. Utah provides adults with eyeglasses only if they are pregnant, while Tennessee provides them only after cataract surgery. Most adults on Medicaid do not have dental coverage; for several years during the Great Recession, adults in Massachusetts could get cavities filled, but only in the front 12 teeth, not in the molars, because the state budget was tight.[36] The massive work disruptions during the coronavirus pandemic illustrated differences across states in the availability of paid leave and eligibility for unemployment insurance.

Because the division of responsibility in the federal system has important implications for who benefits, few conflicts over state-versus-national control will ever be settled once and for all. New evidence about the costs and benefits of different arrangements provides fuel for ongoing debates. Likewise, changes in partisan control of the presidency and Congress usually means that new leaders seek to alter federal arrangements for the benefit of the groups they represent.

FEDERAL–STATE TENSIONS IN THREE ISSUE AREAS

Some of the most significant political issues in recent years have involved federal–state conflicts. One source of controversy concerns whether states and localities have to enforce federal immigration laws. For example, the Secure Communities program, launched in 2008 and expanded under President Obama, required state and local authorities to check the fingerprints of people being booked into jail against a Department of Homeland Security database. The program led to a record number of deportations in 2009 and 2010 and then to several states and localities pulling out of it on the grounds that too many of the undocumented immigrants being detained had not committed a crime. The Obama administration softened its deportation policy in 2011 and ended the Secure Communities program in 2014, replacing it in 2015 with one containing a more limited deportation policy.[37]

Having campaigned on promises for more rigorous immigration enforcement, President Trump signed an executive order days after his inauguration restarting Secure Communities and expanding the types of immigrants considered a priority for deportation, from those convicted of felonies or multiple misdemeanors (as under Obama) to those accused or convicted of minor crimes as well.[38] In response, a growing number of cities, counties, and states declared themselves "sanctuaries" that limit their cooperation with federal enforcement of immigration law. Trump pledged to withhold federal grants from these jurisdictions, but a federal judge's ruling blocked him from doing so.[39] In 2019, a federal appeals court ruled that the Trump administration did have authority to withhold Community Oriented Policing Services (COPS) grants from sanctuary cities and instead focus such grants on

FOR CRITICAL ANALYSIS

Why were Obama and Trump administration actions on immigration controversial? How have federal courts' decisions about immigration enforcement reflected the principles of federalism?

In August 2019 officers from Immigration and Customs Enforcement (ICE) detained around 680 undocumented workers at food processing plants in Jackson, Mississippi. How does federal immigration policy affect individual communities?

FIGURE 3.3

Marijuana Laws across the States

While buying, selling, and possessing marijuana remain federal crimes, states have adopted policies that conflict with federal laws. Should this be allowed?

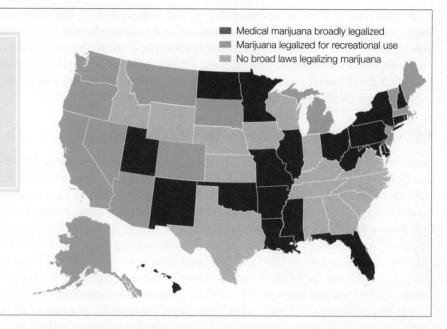

- Medical marijuana broadly legalized
- Marijuana legalized for recreational use
- No broad laws legalizing marijuana

SOURCE: National Organization for the Reform of Marijuana Laws, https://norml.org/laws (accessed 11/7/18); "33 Legal Medical Marijuana States and DC," https://medicalmarijuana.procon.org/view.resource.php?resourceID=000881 (accessed 11/7/18); Marijuana Policy Project, 2020 Ballot Initiatives, www.mpp.org/policy/ballot-initiatives (accessed 11/5/20).

CREDIT: State Marijuana Laws in 2018 Map, originally published by Governing.com, March 30, 2018. Reprinted by permission of Governing.

locations that agreed to give the federal Immigration and Customs Enforcement (ICE) agency access to jail records and immigrants in custody.[40]

With regard to marijuana policy, federal authority has also been upheld by the courts. In 2005, the Supreme Court upheld the right of Congress to ban medical marijuana, even though 11 states had legalized its use. Overturning a lower-court ruling in a case involving marijuana grown for noncommercial purposes in a single state, the Court found that the commerce clause gave the federal government the power to regulate use of all marijuana. Nonetheless, by 2020, 35 states and the District of Columbia had legalized medical marijuana (see Figure 3.3). Amid this legal confusion, a medical marijuana industry began to flourish, and a number of states went further by legalizing recreational marijuana. The mismatch between federal and state laws has precipitated federal raids on marijuana dispensaries and growers, even if their states have legalized the practice.[41]

As with immigration and marijuana, several other court decisions in the 2000s upheld federal authority: rulings upholding the federal Family and Medical Leave Act and the Americans with Disabilities Act asserted federal authority against state claims of immunity from the acts. But then, in its 2012 ruling on the Affordable Care Act, *National Federation of Independent Business v. Sebelius*, the Supreme Court struck a significant blow to federal power over the states. The Court ruled that the federal government could not cut off Medicaid funding to states that did not expand their Medicaid programs to cover more low-income residents; doing so would violate the Tenth Amendment. This ruling represented a sharp departure from the past, and has far-reaching potential to change the federal government's power to impose conditions on the states when it supplies funds.[42] The decision will surely invite challenges to federal power in other areas, possibly including education programs, the drinking age, and environmental regulations.

Who Benefits from Federal Spending?

Federal Grants to State and Local Governments, 2017

Health $407 billion				Income security $107 billion	Transportation $65 billion	Education $62 billion	Other $34 billion

Although Americans often think they pay a lot in federal taxes, they receive much in return in the form of federal money for state and local programs. Federal outlays for grants to state and local governments have grown from $54.8 billion in 1960 to $675 billion in 2017.

Fiscal Transfers between the States and the Federal Government, 2018

Federal spending per tax dollar

- $1.50+
- $1.01–1.50
- —————————— $1.00
- $0.80–1.00
- < $0.80

Every U.S. state contributes to the federal government through the federal taxes paid by the state's citizens, and every state receives money from federal spending. Federal spending is a broad category that includes the grants described above as well as spending on military bases and federal procurement. Not every state receives the same amount from the federal government, however. The map above shows how much federal spending each state received for each dollar paid in federal taxes in 2018.

FOR CRITICAL ANALYSIS

1. Which states receive significantly more in federal government expenditures than their citizens pay in federal taxes? Which states pay more federal taxes than they receive in government spending?

2. Fiscal federalism involves the federal government influencing public policy in the states using federal government dollars. What are some explanations for those differences? Why would states pay more in federal taxes than they receive in government spending?

SOURCE: Data from Laura Schultz and Michelle Cummings, "Giving or Getting? New York's Balance of Payments with the Federal Government," 2019 Report, January 8, 2019, and Congressional Research Service, "Federal Grants to State and Local Governments: A Historical Perspective on Contemporary Issues," May 22, 2019, https://fas.org/sgp/crs/misc/R40638.pdf (accessed 11/18/2019).

Despite the Charlotte City Council's ordinance prohibiting sex discrimination in public facilities, state preemption allowed for the North Carolina legislature to pass the "Charlotte bathroom bill," which undid the provisions originally set out by the city council. In Texas, the city of Denton prohibited fracking within city limits, but the Texas legislature passed a law preempting the local statute and allowing fracking.

STATE–LOCAL TENSIONS

Another notable development in the recent politics of federalism has been the willingness of state governments to preempt local policy. Just as states sometimes seize the policy initiative from the federal government, so too have cities made policy in areas where states have not or where policy preferences in the city differ from those in the state at large. In recent years some cities have set higher minimum wages than are in effect elsewhere in the state, required employers to provide paid sick leave, regulated the "sharing economy" of car- and home-sharing (such as Uber and Airbnb), prohibited gender-based discrimination in public facilities such as bathrooms, and attempted to establish public broadband services.

In each of these areas, however, some state legislatures have responded with laws preempting (limiting or prohibiting) municipal law or authority. As of 2019, 25 states preempt local minimum-wage ordinances, 23 prohibit local paid-leave ordinances, 44 limit local authority to regulate ride-sharing, and 10 ban local regulation of e-cigarettes. Michigan bans cities from banning plastic bags; Texas bans them from banning fracking. Twenty states prohibit localities from establishing municipal broadband service, and three—most famously North Carolina—preempt local antidiscrimination ordinances.[43]

In February 2016, the city council in Charlotte, North Carolina's largest city, passed an ordinance prohibiting sex discrimination in public facilities. The following month the North Carolina legislature passed HB2, the Public Facilities Privacy and Security Act. The "Charlotte bathroom bill," as it came to be known, eliminated local authority to regulate access to public facilities and required people to use the bathroom of their gender as designated at birth. Opponents attacked the law as a violation of transgender rights, and the state lost nearly $400 million in investment as plans for new jobs and for events such as the 2017 NBA all-star game, NCAA basketball championship games, and business conferences were canceled.[44]

POLITICAL RAMIFICATIONS OF FEDERALISM

American federalism has significant effects on policy outcomes. Because of the policy variation made possible by the authority of state and local governments, where you live determines how old you have to be to get a license to drive or get married, how much you pay for public college tuition, what you have to do to get a license to work as a barber or accountant or athletic trainer, and whether you would get unemployment benefits if you were out of work and, if so, how much. But federalism has important effects on American politics as well.

First, political preferences arising from federalism are not set in stone. Although conservatives typically support a smaller federal government or a return of power to the states, once in power, they find at times they need a strong federal government to respond to public demands. Also, federal power can be used to advance conservative policy goals.

For President George W. Bush, for example, the importance of a strong federal government became apparent after the terrorist attacks in 2001. Aware that the American public was looking to Washington for protection, Bush worked with Congress to pass the USA PATRIOT Act, which greatly increased the surveillance powers of the federal government. A year later he created the enormous new federal Department of Homeland Security. Bush also increased federal control and spending in policy areas far removed from security. The 2001 No Child Left Behind Act (NCLB) introduced unprecedented federal intervention in public education, traditionally a state and local responsibility, through detailed new requirements for states' testing of students and treatment of failing schools.

Democratic presidents, too, have sometimes made decisions about national–state responsibilities that defy the usual ideological expectations. As president, Obama released the states from the federal NCLB mandates, and in 2015 he sponsored a new law called Every Student Succeeds that returned power to the states to evaluate schools—a move that might have been expected more from a conservative president. Thus the preferences of conservatives and liberals, Republicans and Democrats about federal versus state versus local policy making are more fluid and situational than we might expect, and vary by issue area, policy goal, and party control of different levels of government.

A second important political implication of federalism concerns individuals' democratic participation and the accountability of government to the people. The multiple layers of government provide many opportunities for ordinary citizens to vote, contact elected officials, and engage in "venue shopping"—seeking policy change at a different level of government if stymied at first. But federalism can also discourage individuals' political participation. The overlapping policy responsibilities created by federalism make it difficult for individuals to figure out which government is responsible for the problem that concerns them, and they may give up. Federalism can also complicate accountability—it is difficult for individuals to demand answers from government if they can't determine which government is in charge.[45] For example, different levels of government were responsible for different types of policy responses to the coronavirus pandemic, complicating citizens' efforts to voice their approval or disagreement with government action.

Federalism: What Do You Think?

As described in the opening of this chapter, turning federal authority over to the states for certifying laboratories for coronavirus testing, and allowing some states and localities to issue stay-at-home orders while others do not, highlights the tensions inherent in a federal system of government. The United States' history of federalism shows that Americans generally accept the idea that states should have the freedom

FOR CRITICAL ANALYSIS

The role of the national government has changed significantly from the Founding era to the present. Do you think the framers of the Constitution would be pleased with the current balance of power between the national government and the state governments?

to enact policies that best serve their residents, within the bounds set by Congress and the courts. But variation across the states may not be desirable in some policy areas. These are perennial questions in American government.

★ Is the federal government endangering people by allowing states to certify coronavirus-testing labs? Or would it have harmed people by requiring all certifications to go through the FDA?

★ Are some of the issues on which the states differ matters of fundamental rights that should be uniform across the country? Or is it important to preserve state choice on most matters?

★ Is it fair that a transgender person in California can legally change the sex on their birth certificate, but a transgender person in Tennessee cannot? Is it reasonable that a gun owner can openly carry a handgun in Georgia but not in Florida? Why or why not?

★ How might your life be different if you lived in a different state? Imagine being a student in a state with very different state-college tuition levels. Or a state with a very different minimum-wage level. For example, in 2020 the minimum wage is $7.25 per hour in Texas and $12.00 in Arizona.[46]

★ How do you think government response to the coronavirus pandemic would be the same or different in a unitary system in which the national government had all the power, compared to a federal system in which national, state, and local governments shared power?

STUDY GUIDE

Federalism in the Constitution

Describe how the Constitution structures the relationships among the national, state, and local governments (pp. 71–76)

The system of federalism embedded in the Constitution has had important implications for American government and politics. Federalism promotes unity among diverse groups within the United States, maximizes opportunities for democratic participation, and secures an important role for the states in the creation of innovative, locally tailored public policies. The Constitution outlines the scope of federal power through the necessary and proper clause, the supremacy clause, and the specific powers granted to Congress in Article I, Section 8. It preserves state power through the Tenth Amendment, which grants all powers not delegated to the federal government to the states; states also retain and share certain powers with the national government. In addition, the Constitution creates obliga-tions among the states. It does not, however, have anything to say about local government.

Key Terms

federalism (p. 71)

unitary system (p. 71)

intergovernmental relations (p. 71)

expressed powers (p. 71)

implied powers (p. 73)

necessary and proper clause (p. 73)

reserved powers (p. 73)

police power (p. 73)

concurrent powers (p. 73)

full faith and credit clause (p. 74)

privileges and immunities clause (p. 76)

home rule (p. 76)

Practice Quiz

1. Which term describes the division of powers and functions between the national government and lower levels of government?
   a) home rule
   b) separation of powers
   c) federalism
   d) checks and balances
   e) unitary system

2. Which amendment to the Constitution states that the powers the Constitution does not delegate to the national government or prohibit to the states are "reserved to the states"?
   a) First Amendment
   b) Fifth Amendment
   c) Tenth Amendment
   d) Fourteenth Amendment
   e) Twenty-Sixth Amendment

3. A state government's authority to regulate the health, safety, welfare, and morals of its citizens is frequently referred to as
   a) the reserved power.
   b) the police power.
   c) the expressed power.
   d) the concurrent power.
   e) the implied power.

4. Which constitutional clause requires that states normally honor the public acts and judicial decisions of other states?
   a) privileges and immunities clause
   b) necessary and proper clause
   c) interstate commerce clause
   d) preemption clause
   e) full faith and credit clause

5. Most states have amended their constitutions to guarantee that their larger cities will have the authority to manage local affairs without interference from state government. This power is called
   a) home rule.
   b) devolution.
   c) preemption.
   d) states' rights.
   e) New Federalism.

National and State Power over Time

Explain how the relationship between the federal and state governments has evolved over time (pp. 76–84)

The relative power of the states and the federal government has changed significantly over time. Historically, the United States operated under a system of dual federalism, in which the national government was small, reluctant to directly coerce citizens, and focused primarily on assisting commerce; most of the fundamental governing during this period was done by the states. In the 1930s, the Supreme Court increased the power of the federal government through its expansive interpretation of the commerce clause, and the national New Deal policies implemented during the Great Depression expanded the government's scope even further. The New Deal ushered in a system of cooperative federalism characterized by grants-in-aid, which the federal government offered to states to encourage them to pursue national goals. In the 1970s, as Congress began to enact legislation that required states to meet national guidelines in previously unregulated areas, the national government grew even more under a system often referred to as regulated federalism.

Key Terms

dual federalism (p. 78)

commerce clause (p. 79)

grants-in-aid (p. 81)

categorical grants (p. 82)

cooperative federalism (p. 82)

regulated federalism (p. 83)

preemption (p. 84)

Practice Quiz

6. The relationship between the states and the national government during the majority of American history (from 1789 to 1937) can best be described as
   a) unitary government.
   b) New Federalism.
   c) dual federalism.
   d) cooperative federalism.
   e) regulated federalism.

7. In which case did the Supreme Court create the potential for increased national power by ruling that Congress could, based on the necessary and proper clause, exercise powers "implied" by its delegated powers?
   a) *United States v. Lopez*
   b) *Printz v. United States*
   c) *Loving v. Virginia*
   d) *McCulloch v. Maryland*
   e) *Gibbons v. Ogden*

8. In 1937 the Supreme Court laid the groundwork for a stronger federal government by issuing a number of decisions that
   a) dramatically narrowed the definition of the commerce clause.
   b) dramatically expanded the definition of the commerce clause.
   c) struck down the supremacy clause.
   d) struck down the privileges and immunities clause.
   e) struck down the full faith and credit clause.

9. The value of categorical grants
   a) increased from $51.5 billion in 1960 to approximately $115 billion in 2019.
   b) increased from $51.5 billion in 1960 to approximately $630 billion in 2019.
   c) decreased from $31 billion in 1960 to approximately $2 billion in 2019.
   d) decreased from $667 billion in 1960 to approximately $2 billion in 2019.
   e) remained the same between 1960 and 2019.

10. The principle that allows the federal government to take over areas of regulation from states or local governments is called
    a) regulated federalism.
    b) preemption.
    c) devolution.
    d) "layer cake" federalism.
    e) exemption.

The Politics of Federalism Today

Questions about the appropriate role for each level of government have persisted and provoked political conflict throughout the history of the United States. While the national government has continued to expand since the 1930s, attempts to enhance state authority have endured from the states' rights arguments of the nineteenth century through the block grants and revenue-sharing programs of more recent years. Sometimes, states seek to go their own way regardless of federal law, and other times, the federal government has succeeded in advancing its policy agenda through the states. It is often up to the courts to decide who gets the final say. Many of today's important public policy issues, such as immigration policy, marijuana policy, and health care, are debated and addressed through the United States' unique system of federalism. Lawmakers' preferences about federal versus state and local policy making are often fluid and situational, varying by issue area and party control of different levels of government.

Key Terms

states' rights (p. 84)

devolution (p. 87)

block grants (p. 87)

New Federalism (p. 87)

general revenue sharing (p. 87)

diffusion (p. 87)

unfunded mandate (p. 87)

redistributive programs (p. 88)

Practice Quiz

11. The process of transferring responsibility for policy from the national level to the state level is known as
    a) devolution.
    b) diffusion.
    c) incorporation.
    d) home rule.
    e) preemption.

12. To what does the term *New Federalism* refer?
    a) the era of federalism initiated by President Roosevelt during the late 1930s
    b) the national government's regulation of state action through grants-in-aid
    c) the type of federalism that uses categorical grants to influence state action
    d) efforts to return more policy-making discretion to the states through the use of block grants
    e) the recent emergence of local governments as important political actors

13. When state and local governments conform to requirements imposed by the national government but do not receive funding for the expenditures required to fulfill them, they are complying with
    a) states' rights.
    b) block grants.
    c) general revenue sharing.
    d) unfunded mandates.
    e) redistributive programs.

14. The Supreme Court's decision in *National Federation of Independent Business v. Sebelius* was significant because
    a) it affirmed the federal government's absolute power to impose conditions on state governments attempting to receive federal funding.
    b) it limited the federal government's power to impose conditions on state governments attempting to receive federal funding.
    c) it struck down the individual mandate of the Affordable Care Act.
    d) it eliminated the federal government's ability to provide subsidies for health insurance coverage.
    e) it invalidated the testing requirements imposed by the No Child Left Behind Act.

15. The preferences of conservatives and liberals when it comes to federal versus state and local policy making can best be described as
    a) invariable: conservatives always advocate for more state power and liberals always advocate for more federal power.
    b) invariable: conservatives always advocate for more federal power and liberals always advocate for more state power.
    c) always in agreement: conservatives and liberals agree on which policy areas should be handled by the states and which should be handled by the federal government.
    d) irrelevant: both conservatives and liberals always defer to the courts to decide questions of federal and state power.
    e) fluid and situational: preferences of both conservatives and liberals vary by issue area, policy goal, and party control of different levels of government.

★ *chapter* ★

04

Civil Liberties

WHAT GOVERNMENT DOES AND WHY IT MATTERS In Portland in 2006, Simon Tam founded what *Oregon Music News* called the first and only all Asian American dance-rock band, or "Chinatown Dance Rock," as the band prefers. The various members of the band are of Chinese, Taiwanese, Vietnamese, and Filipino descent. In addition to playing at anime conventions and cultural festivals, they are known for their activity battling Asian stereotypes and supporting young Asian people.[1]

They are also known for a First Amendment case over the band's name, the Slants. The name had three sources. "We can share our personal experiences about what it's like being people of color—our own slant on life, if you will," Tam said. "It's also a musical reference. There are slant guitar chords that we use in our music." The legal case grew out of the third source: a "reclaiming" and repurposing of an old ethnic slur about Asian people. When the band members were growing up, Tam explained, "having slanted eyes was always considered a negative thing. Kids would pull their eyes back in a slant-eyed gesture to make fun of us. . . . I wanted to change it to something that was powerful, something that was considered beautiful or a point of pride instead."

The First Amendment protects Americans from government infringement on their right to free speech. In the case of the Slants, they used the First Amendment as grounds to re-appropriate a term deemed offensive for themselves and their cultures.

The U.S. Patent and Trademark Office had a different view. Tam's application for a trademark on the band's name was rejected as a violation of the "disparagement clause" of the Lanham Act of 1946, which prohibits trademarks that disparage a racial or ethnic group. The denial stated that although the "applicant, or even the entire band, may be willing to take on the disparaging term as a band name, in what may be considered an attempt . . . to wrest 'ownership' of the term," that "does not mean that all [Asian Americans] share the applicant's view." The case ultimately went to the Supreme Court, which in 2017 ruled unanimously that the disparagement clause violated the First Amendment's guarantee of free speech. The band could keep the name.

But in a further twist, the band's victory inadvertently undermined legal challenges to the name of the Washington Redskins football team. A group of Native Americans who found the "Redskins" name offensive had filed a petition to revoke the team's trademark, citing the Lanham Act's disparagement clause. Once the Court declared the clause unconstitutional, they lost the legal basis for their argument, so the team was able to keep the name. Thus the Slants' success in reclaiming what had been a term offensive to their group meant that one offensive to another group remains in use. The Slants' free speech was protected to their joy, but so was the Redskins' free speech to the disappointment of many Native Americans (in 2020, amid protests over racial justice, the Redskins changed their name to the Washington Football Team).

Free speech, along with the freedoms of assembly, religion, and privacy, is among the civil liberties contained in the Bill of Rights and elsewhere in the Constitution. Thomas Jefferson said that a bill of rights "is what people are entitled to against every government on earth." Note the wording: *against government*. Civil liberties are *protections from* improper government action.

Today in the United States, we often take for granted the liberties contained in the Constitution. But these freedoms raise difficult questions. Do the cases of the Slants and the Redskins strike you as different or the same? Under what circumstances can the government restrict Americans' liberties, especially in the realms of speech, assembly, and privacy? Do freedoms for some people, such as free speech, threaten other people? How should conflicting views be reconciled, or can they? And how should we think about possible trade-offs, as between the right of privacy from surveillance and the need for national security? Can freedom of assembly and even free exercise of religion be restricted by state governments that seek to slow the spread of a contagious disease?

CHAPTER GOALS

★ Outline the founding debate about civil liberties and explain how civil liberties apply to the federal government and the states (pp. 101–6)

★ Explain how the Supreme Court has interpreted freedom of religion through the establishment and free exercise clauses (pp. 106–9)

★ Explain how the Supreme Court has interpreted freedom of speech, assembly, petition, and the press (pp. 109–19)

★ Explain how the Supreme Court has interpreted the right to bear arms (pp. 119–22)

★ Explain how the Supreme Court has interpreted the right to due process (pp. 122–28)

★ Describe how the Supreme Court has identified and interpreted the right to privacy (pp. 128–33)

Civil Liberties and the Constitution

> **Outline the founding debate about civil liberties and explain how civil liberties apply to the federal government and the states**

Civil liberties are related to but different from civil rights, which we will discuss in Chapter 5. Instead of being protections from government power, civil rights are obligations of government power—what government must do to guarantee that citizens are treated equally. The foundations of civil liberties and civil rights are to be found in the state and federal constitutions, which guarantee freedom of speech, freedom of the press, freedom of assembly, and so forth. The federal Constitution's Bill of Rights includes both liberties and rights.

However, the evolution and expansion of civil liberties in the United States is mainly a story of judicial action to overturn state and federal government policies, ones that placed limits on these liberties. Thus, this chapter often focuses on court cases that restricted government power. Civil rights, on the other hand, were shaped as much or more by actions of Congress and state legislatures as by decisions of courts overturning policies. Thus, in Chapter 5 we will consider such pieces of federal legislation as the Voting Rights Act and the 1964 Civil Rights Act.

Why might federal and state government actions threaten civil liberties? The fundamental reason is the clash between two forces: the basic duty of governments to protect the public's health, safety, and general welfare from such dangers as crime, environmental hazards, and terrorism versus the freedom of citizens to go about their business without governmental interference. Most Americans wish to be protected against criminals, but few would say there should be no restraint on police conduct. Most want to be protected against terrorist plots, but few approve of unrestricted government surveillance and intrusions into their own communications. How do we balance safety and freedom?

A BRIEF HISTORY OF THE BILL OF RIGHTS

When the first Congress under the newly ratified Constitution met in 1789, the most important item of business was the consideration of a proposal to add a bill of rights to the Constitution. Such a proposal had been turned down with little debate in the waning days of the Philadelphia Constitutional Convention in 1787 because, as the Federalists, led by Alexander Hamilton, later argued, it was "not only unnecessary in the proposed Constitution but would even be dangerous."[2]

First, according to Hamilton, a bill of rights would be irrelevant to a national government that was given only delegated powers in the first place. To put restraints on "powers which are not granted" could provide a pretext for governments to claim such powers: "For why declare that things shall not be done which there is no power to do?"[3] Second, to Hamilton and the Federalists the Constitution as originally written amounted to a bill of rights (see Table 4.1). For example, Article I, Section 9, included the right of **habeas corpus**, which prohibits the government from depriving a person of liberty without an open trial before a judge. Many of the framers, moreover, saw the very structure of the Constitution, including checks and balances, as protective of citizens' liberties.

habeas corpus a court order demanding that an individual in custody be brought into court and shown the cause for detention

TABLE 4.1

Rights in the Original Constitution (Not in the Bill of Rights)

CLAUSE	RIGHT ESTABLISHED
Article I, Section 9	Guarantee of habeas corpus
Article I, Section 9	Prohibition of bills of attainder
Article I, Section 9	Prohibition of ex post facto laws
Article I, Section 9	Prohibition against acceptance of titles of nobility, etc., from any foreign state
Article III	Guarantee of trial by jury in state where crime was committed
Article III	Treason defined and limited to the life of the person convicted, not to the person's heirs

Despite the power of Hamilton's arguments, when the Constitution was submitted to the states for ratification, Antifederalists, most of whom had not been delegates in Philadelphia, picked up on the argument of Thomas Jefferson (also not a delegate) that the lack of a bill of rights was a major imperfection. The Federalists realized that to gain ratification they would have to add a bill of rights, including a confirmation (in what would become the Tenth Amendment) that all powers not expressly delegated to the national government or explicitly prohibited to the states were reserved to the states.[4]

The House of Representatives approved 17 amendments; of these, the Senate accepted 12. Ten of the amendments were ratified by the necessary three-fourths of the states on December 15, 1791; from the start, these 10 were called the **Bill of Rights** (see Table 4.2).[5] The protections against improper government action contained in the Constitution and the Bill of Rights represent important **civil liberties**.

Bill of Rights the first 10 amendments to the U.S. Constitution, ratified in 1791; they ensure certain rights and liberties to the people

civil liberties areas of personal freedom constitutionally protected from government interference

NATIONALIZING THE BILL OF RIGHTS

The First Amendment provides that "Congress shall make no law. . . ." But this is the only amendment in the Bill of Rights that addresses itself exclusively to the national government. For example, the Second Amendment provides that "the right of the people to keep and bear Arms, shall not be infringed." And the Fifth Amendment says, among other things, that "no person shall . . . be twice put in jeopardy of life or limb" for the same crime. Thus a fundamental question inevitably arises: Do the provisions of the Bill of Rights other than the First Amendment put limits only on the national government, or do they limit the state governments as well?

The Supreme Court first answered this question in 1833 by ruling that the Bill of Rights limited only the national government.[6] This meant that the actions of state governments were restricted only by their own constitutions as interpreted by their

TABLE 4.2

The Bill of Rights

Amendment I	Congress cannot make any law establishing a religion or abridging freedoms of religious exercise, speech, the press, assembly, or petition.
Amendments II, III, IV	No branch of government may infringe upon the right of the people to keep arms (II), cannot arbitrarily take houses for militia (III), and cannot search for or seize evidence without a court warrant swearing to the probable existence of a crime (IV).
Amendments V, VI, VII, VIII	The courts cannot hold trials for serious offenses without provision for a grand jury (V), a trial jury (VII), a speedy trial (VI), presentation of charges and confrontation by the accused of hostile witnesses (VI), and immunity from testimony against oneself and immunity from trial more than once for the same offense (V). Furthermore, neither bail nor punishment can be excessive (VIII), and no property can be taken without "just compensation" (V).
Amendments IX, X: Limits on the national government	Any rights not enumerated are reserved to the state or the people (X), and the enumeration of certain rights in the Constitution should not be interpreted to mean that those are the only rights the people have (IX).

own courts. But the question arose again in 1868 with the adoption of the Fourteenth Amendment, which reads:

> No State shall make or enforce any law which shall abridge the privileges or immunities of citizens of the United States; nor shall any State deprive any person of life, liberty, or property, without due process of law; nor deny to any person within its jurisdiction the equal protection of the laws.

This language sounds like an effort to extend the entire Bill of Rights to all citizens, in whatever state they might reside.[7] Yet this was not the Supreme Court's interpretation for nearly 100 years. Within 5 years of ratification of the Fourteenth Amendment, the Court was making decisions as though the amendment had never been adopted.[8]

In 1897, the Supreme Court did hold that the amendment's due process clause prohibited states from taking property for a public use without just compensation, a form of deprivation of property that is specifically prohibited in the Fifth Amendment.[9] But even though in both amendments "due process" is required for the taking of life and liberty as well as property, only the provision protecting property was "incorporated" into the Fourteenth Amendment as a limitation on state power.

Civil liberties did not expand through the Fourteenth Amendment again until 1925, when the Supreme Court held that freedom of speech is "among the fundamental personal rights and 'liberties' protected by the due process clause of the Fourteenth Amendment from impairment by the states."[10] In 1931 the Court added freedom of the press to that "fundamental" list; in 1939 it added freedom of assembly.[11] Until the 1960s, that was as far as the Court was willing to go. Indeed, in the 1937 case of *Palko v. Connecticut*, the Court affirmed the states' existing power to determine their own laws on a number of fundamental civil liberties issues. In that case, a Connecticut court had found Frank Palko guilty of second-degree murder and sentenced him to life in prison. Unhappy with the verdict, Connecticut appealed it to the state's highest court, won the appeal, and succeeded in getting Palko convicted of first-degree murder in a new trial. Palko appealed to the Supreme Court on what seemed an open-and-shut case of double jeopardy, which is prohibited by the Fifth Amendment.

The majority of the Court, however, decided that protection against double jeopardy was *not* one of the provisions of the Bill of Rights incorporated into the Fourteenth Amendment as a restriction on the powers of the states. Not until more than 30 years later did the Court reverse this ruling. Because Palko was tried in Connecticut rather than a state whose constitution protected against double jeopardy, he was eventually executed for the crime.

The *Palko* case established the principle of **selective incorporation**, by which each provision of the Bill of Rights was to be considered separately as a possible limit on the states through the Fourteenth Amendment. To make clear that "selective incorporation" should be narrowly interpreted, Justice Benjamin Cardozo, writing for an 8–1 majority, asserted that some rights, although important, do not represent a "principle of justice so rooted in the traditions and conscience of our people as to be ranked as fundamental."[12] *Palko* left states with most of the powers they had possessed even before the Fourteenth Amendment, such as the power to engage in searches and seizures without a warrant, to deprive accused persons of trial by jury, and to prosecute accused persons more than once for the same crime.[13] Few states chose to use these powers, but some did.

So, until 1961 (see Table 4.3), only the First Amendment and one clause of the Fifth Amendment had been clearly incorporated into the Fourteenth Amendment as binding on the states as well as on the national government.[14] After that, however, one by one, almost all the other provisions of the Bill of Rights were applied to the

selective incorporation the process by which different protections in the Bill of Rights were incorporated into the Fourteenth Amendment, thus guaranteeing citizens protection from state as well as national governments

TABLE 4.3

Incorporation of the Bill of Rights into the Fourteenth Amendment

SELECTED PROVISIONS AND AMENDMENTS	KEY CASE
Eminent domain (V)	*Chicago, Burlington, and Quincy R.R. v. Chicago* (1897) required the city of Chicago to compensate a railroad company for seizing its property for the purpose of widening a city road.
Freedom of speech (I)	*Gitlow v. New York* (1925) upheld Gitlow's conviction for "criminal anarchy" for publishing a left-wing manifesto. The Court held that the First Amendment allowed the states to suppress speech directly advocating the overthrow of the government.
Freedom of press (I)	*Near v. Minnesota* (1931) overturned Minnesota's permanent injunction against those who created a "public nuisance" by publishing, selling, or distributing a "malicious, scandalous and defamatory newspaper, magazine or other periodical" as an infringement on freedom of the press.
Free exercise of religion (I)	In *Hamilton v. Regents of the University of California* (1934), students filed suit to protest mandatory military training at the University of California on religious grounds. The Court upheld the right of California to mandate that its students receive military training as permissible under the First Amendment's free exercise of religion clause.

Incorporation of the Bill of Rights into the Fourteenth Amendment—cont'd

SELECTED PROVISIONS AND AMENDMENTS	KEY CASE
Freedom of assembly (I) and freedom to petition the government for redress of grievances (I)	*DeJonge v. Oregon* (1937) overturned DeJonge's conviction for addressing a meeting of the Communist Party as an infringement on freedom of assembly.
Free exercise of religion (I)	*Cantwell v. Connecticut* (1940) said state governments may not prohibit the dissemination or expression of religious views.
Nonestablishment of state religion (I)	In *Everson v. Board of Education* (1947) the Court, applying the establishment clause, found that using taxpayer money to bus students to private religious schools did not constitute establishing a religion because busing was a "separate" function from the school's religious purpose.
Freedom from warrantless search and seizure (IV) ("exclusionary rule")	In *Mapp v. Ohio* (1961) the Court overturned the conviction of Dollree Mapp for possession of obscene materials because the evidence was obtained in violation of the Fourth Amendment's requirement of a warrant for conducting a search.
Freedom from cruel and unusual punishment (VIII)	*Robinson v. California* (1962) overturned a California law imposing a 90-day jail sentence on persons found guilty of "addiction to the use of narcotics" as cruel and unusual punishment for what amounted to illness.
Right to counsel in any criminal trial (VI)	In *Gideon v. Wainwright* (1963) the Supreme Court held that the right to counsel in the Sixth Amendment applied to the states. Gideon had requested a lawyer at his trial for a felony crime but was denied under Florida law, but because of the Supreme Court ruling, Gideon got a new trial with counsel.
Right against self-incrimination and forced confessions (V)	In *Malloy v. Hogan* (1964) the Supreme Court held that the Fifth Amendment secures defendants against self-incrimination. Malloy had been imprisoned for contempt after refusing to answer questions about gambling activities on grounds it might implicate him. After the Supreme Court ruling, Malloy could not be forced to testify.
Right to remain silent (V)	In *Escobedo v. Illinois* (1964) the Court held that Escobedo's Sixth Amendment rights to counsel and to the right to remain silent were violated after police denied repeated requests by Escobedo to see his lawyer during interrogation. Escobedo had incriminated himself in a murder.
Right to counsel and to remain silent (V)	In *Miranda v. Arizona* (1966) the Court held that defendants in police custody must be informed of their rights. Miranda had been questioned by police and signed a statement of confession without being informed of his right to counsel and protection from self-incrimination.
Right against double jeopardy (V)	In *Benton v. Maryland* (1969) the Supreme Court held "double jeopardy" as impermissible under the Fifth Amendment. Benton had been tried twice for the same crime of larceny.
Right to bear arms (II)	In *McDonald v. Chicago* (2010) the Supreme Court struck down a Chicago firearms ordinance making it extremely difficult to own a gun within city limits as violating the Second Amendment.
Excessive fines prohibited (VIII)	In *Timbs v. Indiana* (2019) the Court held unanimously that the Eighth Amendment's prohibition against excessive fines applied to the states as well as the federal government.
Jury trial (VI)	*Ramos v. Louisiana* (2020) held that a jury must give its unanimous consent to a guilty verdict in a state criminal trial. Most states had already adopted this requirement.

states. Table 4.3 shows the progress of this revolution in the interpretation of the Constitution. Today, only the Third and Seventh amendments remain unincorporated, though it should be noted that almost every state voluntarily complies with the Seventh Amendment's requirement of jury trials.

Before we leave the topic, it is worth mentioning that one element of the Fourteenth Amendment is being called into question today: the idea that all persons "born or naturalized" in the United States are citizens. Some politicians and public figures, most notably President Donald Trump, have called for an end to "birthright citizenship" and argued that the U.S.-born children of undocumented immigrants should not be considered U.S. citizens. Ending birthright citizenship would probably require a constitutional amendment, so it seems unlikely to occur.

The First Amendment and Freedom of Religion

★ *Congress shall make no law respecting an establishment of religion, or prohibiting the free exercise thereof; or abridging the freedom of speech, or of the press; or the right of the people peaceably to assemble, and to petition the Government for a redress of grievances.*
—from the First Amendment

> **Explain how the Supreme Court has interpreted freedom of religion through the establishment and free exercise clauses**

The Bill of Rights begins by guaranteeing freedom of religion, and the First Amendment provides for that freedom in two distinct clauses: "Congress shall make no law [1] respecting an establishment of religion, or [2] prohibiting the free exercise thereof." The first clause is called the "establishment clause," and the second is called the "free exercise clause."

establishment clause the First Amendment clause that says "Congress shall make no law respecting an establishment of religion"; this constitutional provision means that a "wall of separation" exists between church and state

SEPARATION BETWEEN CHURCH AND STATE

The **establishment clause** and the idea of "no law" regarding the establishment of religion could be interpreted in several ways. One interpretation, which probably reflects the views of many of the First Amendment's authors, is simply that the national government is prohibited from establishing an official church. Official "established" churches, such as the Church of England, were common in Europe in the eighteenth century as well as in some of the 13 colonies and were viewed by many Americans as inconsistent with a republican form of government. Indeed, many American colonists had fled Europe to escape persecution for having rejected established churches.

A second possible interpretation is that the government may provide assistance to religious institutions or ideas as long as it does not take sides or show favoritism among them. The United States accommodates religious beliefs in a variety of ways, from the reference to God on currency to the prayer that begins every session of Congress. These forms of religious establishment have always been upheld by the courts.

The third view regarding religious establishment, the most commonly held today, favors a "wall of separation"—Jefferson's formulation—between church and state. For two centuries, Jefferson's words have powerfully influenced Americans' understanding of the proper relationship between government and religion. Despite the seeming absoluteness of the phrase, however, there is ample room to disagree on how high the "wall of separation" should be.

One area of conflict over the appropriate boundary is public education. For example, the Court has consistently struck down such practices in public schools as

The First Amendment affects everyday life in a multitude of ways. Because of the amendment's ban on state-sanctioned religion, the Supreme Court ruled in 2000 that school-sponsored prayer in public schools is illegal. Requiring pregame prayer at public schools violates the establishment clause of the First Amendment.

Bible reading,[15] prayer,[16] a moment of silence for meditation, and pregame public prayer at sporting events.[17] In each of these cases, the Court reasoned that organized religious activities, even when apparently nondenominational, strongly suggest the school is sponsoring them and therefore violate the prohibition against establishment of religion.

For decades, the Supreme Court has faced cases involving government financial support for religious schools. In its 1971 decision in *Lemon v. Kurtzman*, it attempted to specify some criteria to guide its future decisions, and those of lower courts, about when the Constitution permits such support. Collectively, these criteria came to be called the **Lemon test**. The Court held that government aid to religious schools would be constitutional if (1) it had a secular purpose, (2) its effect was neither to advance nor to inhibit religion, and (3) it did not entangle government and religious institutions in each other's affairs.[18]

Although these restrictions make the *Lemon* test hard to pass, imaginative authorities have found ways to do so, and the Supreme Court has demonstrated a willingness to let them. For example, in the 2017 case of *Trinity Lutheran Church v. Comer*, the Supreme Court upheld the right of a religious school to benefit from a state-funded playground-resurfacing program (582 U.S. __ [2017]). The Court reasoned that excluding religious schools from this program would actually represent discrimination against them because of their religious character.

Another area of ongoing dispute over the meaning of the establishment clause is in public displays of religious symbols, such as city-sponsored nativity scenes. In *Van Orden v. Perry*, the Court decided that a display of the Ten Commandments outside the Texas state capitol did not violate the Constitution.[19] However, in *McCreary County v. American Civil Liberties Union of Kentucky*, the Court determined that a display of the Ten Commandments inside two Kentucky courthouses was unconstitutional.[20] Justice Stephen Breyer, the deciding vote in both cases, said that the display in *Van Orden* had a secular purpose, whereas the displays in *McCreary* had a purely religious purpose. The key difference is that the Texas display had been exhibited in a park for 40 years with other monuments related to the development

Lemon test a rule articulated in *Lemon v. Kurtzman* that government action toward religion is permissible if it is secular in purpose, neither promotes nor inhibits the practice of religion, and does not lead to "excessive entanglement" with religion

FOR CRITICAL ANALYSIS

Despite the establishment clause, the United States still uses the motto "In God We Trust" and calls itself "one nation, under God." Do you think its reference to God is a violation of the separation of church and state?

In 2001, Alabama Supreme Court Chief Justice Roy Moore had a large granite statue of the Ten Commandments installed in the Alabama Supreme Court building. Despite a court injunction requiring Justice Moore to remove the statue, citing a violation of the establishment clause, the statue remained until the building manager was compelled to remove it.

free exercise clause the First Amendment clause that protects a citizen's right to believe and practice whatever religion he or she chooses

of American law, whereas the Kentucky display was erected much more recently and initially by itself, suggesting to some justices that its posting had a religious purpose. Clearly, the issue of government-sponsored displays of religious symbols has not been settled.

FREE EXERCISE OF RELIGION

The **free exercise clause** protects the right to believe and to practice whatever religion one chooses (and also protects the right to be a nonbeliever). The precedent-setting case involving free exercise is *West Virginia State Board of Education v. Barnette* (1943), which involved the children in a family of Jehovah's Witnesses who refused to salute and pledge allegiance to the American flag in their school on the grounds that their religious faith did not permit it. Three years earlier, the Court had upheld such a requirement and had permitted schools to expel students for refusing to salute the flag. But the entry of the United States into a war to defend democracy in 1941, coupled with the ugly treatment to which the Jehovah's Witnesses children had been subjected, persuaded the Court to reverse itself and to endorse the free exercise of religion even when it may be offensive to the beliefs of the majority.[21]

More recently, the principle of free exercise has been bolstered by legislation prohibiting religious discrimination by public and private entities in a variety of realms, including the treatment of prison inmates, hiring, and health care. Two cases illustrating this point are *Holt v. Hobbs*[22] and *Burwell v. Hobby Lobby Stores.*[23]

The *Holt* case involved a prisoner in an Arkansas jail, Gregory Holt, who asserted that his Muslim beliefs required him to grow a beard. The Court held that an Arkansas prison policy prohibiting beards violated a federal statute designed to protect the ability of prisoners to worship as they pleased.

The *Hobby Lobby* case involved the owners of a chain of craft stores who claimed that a section of the Affordable Care Act (ACA, or Obamacare) requiring employers to provide their female employees with free contraceptive coverage violated the owners' religious beliefs as protected by the Religious Freedom Restoration Act (RFRA). This law, enacted in 1993, requires the government to prove a "compelling interest" for requiring individuals to obey a law that violates their religious beliefs. The Supreme Court ruled in favor of Hobby Lobby. Despite these cases, free exercise of religion continues to have limits, though those limits are contested. During the COVID-19 pandemic in 2020, a Louisiana minister was cited on a misdemeanor

Does religious freedom lead to discrimination on the basis of religion? Here, senior counsel for Hobby Lobby stores speaks to supporters after the Supreme Court ruled that businesses were not required to provide free contraceptive coverage if they find it in violation of their religious beliefs.

charge for ignoring the state's ban on gatherings of more than 50 people. He said he was being persecuted for his religion in violation of the Constitution. However, the power of the state to protect the public's health probably takes precedence over the minister's right to hold religious services.

The First Amendment and Freedom of Speech and of the Press

> **Explain how the Supreme Court has interpreted freedom of speech, assembly, petition, and the press**

Freedom of speech and freedom of the press have a special place in American political thought. Democracy depends on the ability of individuals to talk to one another and to disseminate information. It is difficult to conceive how democratic politics could function without free and open debate.

Such debate, moreover, is seen as an essential way to evaluate competing ideas. As Justice Oliver Wendell Holmes said in 1919, "The best test of truth is the power of the thought to get itself accepted in the competition of the market. . . . That at any rate is the theory of our Constitution."[24] What is sometimes called the "marketplace of ideas" receives a good deal of protection from the courts. In 1938 the Supreme Court held that any legislation restricting speech "is to be subjected to a more exacting judicial scrutiny . . . than are most other types of legislation."[25]

This higher standard, which came to be called "strict scrutiny," places a heavy burden of proof on the government if it seeks to restrict speech. Americans are assumed to have the right to voice their ideas publicly unless a compelling reason can be identified to prevent them. But strict scrutiny does not mean that speech can never be regulated. Over the past 200 years, the courts have scrutinized many different forms of speech and constructed different principles and guidelines for each.

★ *Congress shall make no law . . . abridging the freedom of speech, or of the press.*
—from the First Amendment

According to the courts, although virtually all speech is protected by the Constitution, some forms are entitled to a greater degree of protection than others.

POLITICAL SPEECH

Political speech was the form of greatest concern to the framers of the Constitution, even though some found it the most difficult one to tolerate. Within seven years of the ratification of the Bill of Rights in 1791, Congress adopted the infamous Alien and Sedition Acts (long since repealed), which, among other things, made it a crime to say or publish anything that might tend to defame or bring into disrepute the government of the United States.

The first modern free speech case arose immediately after World War I and involved persons convicted under the federal Espionage Act of 1917 for opposing U.S. involvement in the war. The Supreme Court upheld the Espionage Act and refused to protect the speech rights of the defendants on the grounds that their activities—appeals to draftees to resist the draft—constituted a **"clear and present danger"** to national security.[26] This is the first and most famous "test" for when government intervention or censorship can be permitted, though it has since been discarded.

Since the 1920s, political speech has been consistently protected by the courts even when judges acknowledged that the speech was "insulting" or "outrageous." In the 1969 case *Brandenburg v. Ohio*, the Supreme Court ruled that as long as speech falls short of actually inciting action, it cannot be prohibited, even if it is hostile to or subversive of the government and its policies. This decision came in the case of a Ku Klux Klan leader, Charles Brandenburg, who had been arrested and convicted of advocating "revengent" action against the president, the Congress, and the Supreme Court, among others, if they continued "to suppress the [W]hite, Caucasian race."

Although Brandenburg was not carrying a weapon, some of the members of his audience were. Nevertheless, the Supreme Court reversed the state courts and freed Brandenburg, while also declaring Ohio's Criminal Syndicalism Act unconstitutional because it did not distinguish "mere advocacy" of issues or opinions from "incitement to imminent lawless action."[27] It would be difficult to go much further in protecting freedom of speech.

Another political speech issue that has recently received much attention is monetary contributions to political campaigns. Campaign finance reform laws of the early 1970s, arising out of the Watergate scandal, aimed to put severe limits on campaign spending. In the 1976 case *Buckley v. Valeo*, however, the Supreme Court declared important provisions of these laws unconstitutional on the basis of a new principle that spending by or on behalf of candidates is a form of speech protected by the First Amendment.[28] (For more details, see Chapter 10.)

The issue came up again in 2003 with passage of an even stricter campaign finance law, the Bipartisan Campaign Reform Act (BCRA). Initially, the Supreme Court upheld the BCRA, but in 2007, the Court reversed itself in *Federal Election Commission v. Wisconsin Right to Life*, declaring that political advocacy groups' last-minute issue ads that had been prohibited by the BCRA were protected speech so long as they focused mainly on issues and were not simply appeals to vote for or against a specific candidate.[29]

Likewise, in the 2010 case of *Citizens United v. Federal Election Commission*, the Court struck down the BCRA's ban on corporate funding of advertisements supporting or opposing particular candidates[30] on the grounds that this spending is

"clear and present danger" test
test used to determine whether speech is protected or unprotected, based on its capacity to present a "clear and present danger" to society

During the 2008 presidential primaries, the conservative organization Citizens United released a documentary criticizing Hillary Clinton. A lower court found that ads for the film violated the BCRA's ban on corporate funding of ads for or against a particular candidate. In 2010 the Court declared the BCRA ban unconstitutional under the First Amendment.

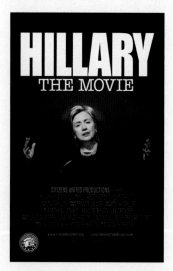

Global Freedom of the Press

While freedom of the press is a cornerstone of American civil liberties, it is neither as firmly enshrined in law nor as respected as a matter of practice in other countries. This map looks specifically at how "free and independent" the media is in each country.

1. Where is the press most free and independent? Where is it less so? Are there regions of the world that are better at respecting freedom of the press than others? How does the United States fare in comparison to other countries on this measure?

2. Why might a government want to impose constraints on media operating in its borders? On the other hand, what do governments gain by allowing, or even encouraging, the functioning of a free and independent press?

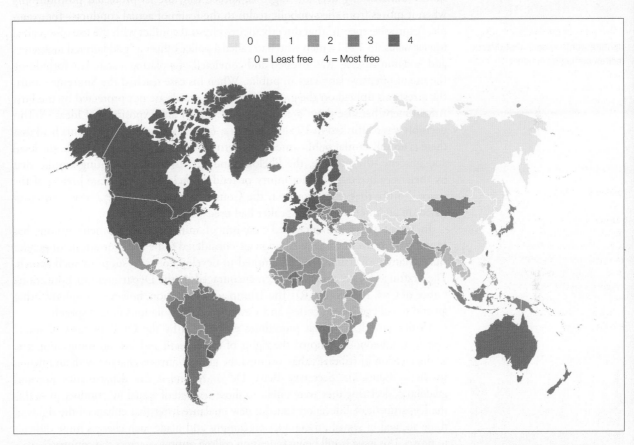

0   1   2   3   4

0 = Least free   4 = Most free

SOURCE: Sarah Repucci, "Freedom and the Media: A Downward Spiral," Freedom House, 2019, https://freedomhouse.org/report/freedom-media/freedom-media-2019 (accessed 2/24/2020).

political speech that the Constitution prohibits the government from regulating. In 2014 the Court again expanded its protection of campaign expenditures under the First Amendment by overturning limits on the total amount an individual may contribute.[31] As a result of this decision, several wealthy donors contributed more than $10 million each to presidential candidates in 2016.

Republicans hailed the recent decisions deregulating campaign spending, while Democrats denounced them. President Obama called *Citizens United* "a major victory for big oil, Wall Street banks, health insurance companies, and the other powerful interests that marshal their power every day in Washington to drown out the voices of everyday Americans."[32]

FIGHTING WORDS AND HATE SPEECH

As the *Brandenburg* decision suggests, speech can lose its protected position only when it moves from the symbolic realm to the realm of actual conduct—for example, "expressive speech" that directly incites physical conflict with the use of so-called **fighting words**. In 1942 a man who had called a police officer a "goddamned racketeer" and "a damn Fascist" was arrested and convicted of violating a state law forbidding the use of offensive language in public. When his case reached the Supreme Court, the arrest was upheld on the grounds that such words are not protected by the First Amendment because they "are no essential part of any exposition of ideas."[33] This decision was reaffirmed in 1951 in *Dennis v. United States*, when the Court held that there is no substantial public interest in permitting certain kinds of speech: the lewd and obscene, the profane, the libelous, and the insulting—"fighting words" that by their very utterance inflict injury or tend to incite an immediate breach of the peace.[34] Since that time, however, the Court has reversed almost every conviction based on arguments that the speaker had used "fighting words."

In recent years, the increased activism of minority and women's groups has prompted a movement against language considered to be racial or ethnic or gender slurs. Many universities have attempted to develop codes to suppress such speech. The drafting of such codes had been encouraged by the Department of Education's Office of Civil Rights (OCR). The Trump administration, however, sought to bring an end to college speech codes, and viewed them as violations of free speech.

Critics also charged that procedures encouraged by the OCR in cases of sexual assault or misconduct ignored the rights of the accused and led, on some campuses, to the creation of tribunals that assumed the guilt of anyone charged with an offense. In 2017, Education Secretary Betsy DeVos rescinded the department's previous guidelines, declaring they were unfair to those accused of sexual misconduct. In 2019, the Department of Education issued a new guidance letter that enhanced the rights of those accused of sexual misconduct on campus and made such charges more difficult to prove. This issue is still being fought on college campuses across the country.[35]

Similar issues have arisen in large corporations, both public and private, with many successful complaints and lawsuits alleging that the words of employers or supervisors created a "hostile or abusive working environment." The Supreme Court has held that such an environment can result from "sexual harassment," defined as "unwelcome sexual advances, requests for sexual favors, and other verbal or physical conduct of a sexual nature."[36] A fundamental free speech issue is involved in these regulations of hostile speech.

Many local governments have adopted ordinances banning hate speech—forms of expression intended to assert hatred toward one or another group of people, be

fighting words speech that directly incites damaging conduct

they African Americans, Jews, Muslims, or others. Such ordinances seldom pass constitutional muster. The leading Supreme Court case in this realm is the 1992 decision in *R.A.V. v. City of St. Paul*,[37] where a White teenager was arrested for burning a cross on the lawn of a Black family in violation of a municipal ordinance that banned cross burning. The Court ruled that such an ordinance must be *content neutral*—that is, it must not prohibit actions directed at some groups but not others. The statute in question prohibited only cross burning, which is typically directed at African Americans. Since a statute banning all forms of hateful expression would be deemed overly broad, the *R.A.V.* standard suggests that virtually all hate speech is constitutionally protected.

These cases have all involved action by the federal or state governments, but what about private action to prohibit various forms of speech? Today, the ability to post messages on social media platforms like Facebook is critically important to those who want to disseminate their ideas. In 2019, Facebook announced a change in its terms-of-service agreement designed to prevent users from posting hateful commentary and claims. The ban seemed especially, though not exclusively, aimed at a group of right-wing activists. Facebook is, of course, a private organization so the constitutional restrictions on the government's actions may not apply. However, social media platforms are now some of the most important public forums in America. Their actions have an enormous impact upon free speech. Should they be free to regulate speech as they see fit? This question is one likely to generate intense debate and may one day end up in front of the Supreme Court.

The issue of hate speech has also arisen on a number of college campuses, where some students and faculty have demanded that certain public figures (usually conservative and far-right ones) be banned from speaking, on the grounds that they promote hatred. Student protesters have forced the cancellation of speeches by conservatives like Ann Coulter and Milo Yiannopoulos, disrupted talks by such prominent conservative scholars as Charles Murray, and unsuccessfully tried to prevent White nationalist Richard Spencer from speaking. There seems little doubt that the right of all these individuals to speak is protected by the Constitution. The conflict

FOR CRITICAL ANALYSIS

Is there speech that should be banned because it does not contribute to the exchange of ideas? How do we determine what speech should be protected because it contributes to this exchange and what speech does not?

Are social media companies responsible for the proliferation of offensive and hateful speech on their sites? Here, Facebook CEO Mark Zuckerberg testifies before Congress on Facebook's role in allowing hateful content on the site.

In 2017, students at the University of California, Berkeley, held protests ahead of a scheduled campus appearance by Milo Yiannopoulos, a conservative commentator, that led to the cancellation of the event. This prompted a larger discussion of censorship and free speech on college campuses, and Yiannopoulos was allowed to speak at the school surrounded by a large police presence, pictured here.

arises when that right comes up against university policies to emphasize safety—a consideration that not so long ago led to bans on left-wing speakers. Perhaps people of all political persuasions should think about the words of Supreme Court Justice Oliver Wendell Holmes, who said, "If there is any principle of the Constitution that more imperatively calls for attachment than any other, it is the principle of free thought—not free thought for those who agree with us but freedom for the thought that we hate."[38]

STUDENT SPEECH

One category of speech with only limited protection is that of students in public high schools. In 1986 the Supreme Court backed away from a broad protection of student free speech rights by upholding the punishment of a high school student for making a sexually suggestive speech. The Court opinion held that such speech interfered with the school's goal of teaching students the limits of socially acceptable behavior.[39] Two years later the Court restricted students' freedom of speech and the press even further, defining their speech and journalism in school as part of their education and not protected with the same standard as adult speech in a public forum.[40]

A later case, *Morse v. Frederick*,[41] dealt with the policies of Juneau-Douglas High School in Juneau, Alaska. In 2002 the Olympic torch relay had passed through Juneau on its way to Salt Lake City for the opening of the Winter Olympics. As the torch passed Juneau-Douglas High, a senior, Joseph Frederick, unfurled a banner reading "BONG HITS 4 JESUS." The school's principal promptly suspended Frederick, who then brought suit for reinstatement, alleging that his free speech rights had been violated. Like most of America's public schools, Juneau-Douglas High prohibits assemblies or expressions on school grounds that advocate illegal drug use. In the Supreme Court's majority decision in 2007, Chief Justice John Roberts said that the First Amendment did not require schools to permit students to advocate illegal drug use.

COMMERCIAL SPEECH

Commercial speech, such as newspaper or television advertisements, was initially considered to be entirely outside the protection of the First Amendment and is still subject to limited regulation. For example, the prohibition of false and misleading advertising by the Federal Trade Commission is an old and well-established power of the federal government. The Supreme Court has upheld city ordinances prohibiting the posting of all commercial signs on publicly owned property (as long as the ban is total so that there is no hint of selective censorship).[42]

However, commercial speech has become more and more protected under the First Amendment. For example, in 1975 the Supreme Court struck down a state law making it a misdemeanor to sell or circulate newspapers encouraging abortions; the Court ruled that the statute infringed both on constitutionally protected speech and on readers' right to make informed choices.[43]

SYMBOLIC SPEECH, SPEECH PLUS, AND THE RIGHTS OF ASSEMBLY AND PETITION

Because the First Amendment treats the freedoms of religion and political speech as equal to those of assembly and petition, the Supreme Court has always largely protected an individual's right to "symbolic speech": peaceful actions designed to send a political message. One example is the burning of the American flag as a protest. In 1984, at a rally during the Republican National Convention in Dallas, Texas, a protester burned an American flag, thereby violating a Texas statute that prohibited desecration of a venerated object. In a 5–4 decision, the Supreme Court declared the law unconstitutional on the grounds that flag burning was expressive conduct protected by the First Amendment.[44] Since 1995 the House of Representatives has seven times passed a resolution for a constitutional amendment to ban this form of expressive conduct, but each time the Senate has failed to go along.[45]

The Supreme Court has ruled that high school students' speech can be restricted. In a 2007 case involving a student who displayed the banner above, the Court found that the school principal had not violated the student's right to free speech by suspending him.

Should the First Amendment's protection of free speech apply even when that speech is seen as offensive? In 2011 the Supreme Court ruled 8–1 that members of the Westboro Baptist Church had a right to picket soldiers' funerals to demonstrate what they take as a sign of God's disapproval of homosexuality.

"speech plus" speech accompanied by conduct such as sit-ins, picketing, and demonstrations; protection of this form of speech under the First Amendment is conditional, and restrictions imposed by state or local authorities are acceptable if properly balanced by considerations of public order

prior restraint an effort by a governmental agency to block the publication of material it deems libelous or harmful in some other way; censorship; in the United States, the courts forbid prior restraint except under the most extraordinary circumstances

In the 2011 case of *Snyder v. Phelps*, the Court gave protection to another form of symbolic speech. Members of the Westboro Baptist Church in Topeka, Kansas, had frequently demonstrated at military funerals, claiming that the deaths of the soldiers were a sign that God disapproved of the acceptance of homosexuality in the United States. The father of a soldier killed in Iraq brought suit against the church and its pastor, claiming that the demonstrators had caused him and his family severe emotional distress. The Supreme Court ruled, however, that the First Amendment protected free speech in a public place against such suits.[46]

Closer to the original intent of the assembly and petition clause is the category of **"speech plus"**—combining speech with physical activity such as picketing, distributing leaflets, and other forms of peaceful demonstration or assembly. In the 1939 case of *Hague v. Committee for Industrial Organization*, the Supreme Court declared that the government may not prohibit speech-related activities such as demonstrations or leafleting in public areas traditionally used for that purpose, though it may impose rules to protect the public safety at such events so long as they do not discriminate against particular viewpoints.[47] Such "public forum" assemblies have since been consistently protected by courts; state and local laws regulating such activities are closely scrutinized and frequently overturned.

But the same kind of assembly on private property is quite another matter and can in many circumstances be regulated. For example, the directors of a shopping center can lawfully prohibit an assembly protesting a war or supporting a ban on abortion. Even in public areas, assemblies or demonstrations can be restricted under some circumstances, especially when they jeopardize the health, safety, or rights of others. This condition was the basis of the Supreme Court's decision to uphold a lower-court order that restricted access by abortion protesters to the entrances of abortion clinics.[48]

FREEDOM OF THE PRESS

With the exception of the broadcast media, which are subject to federal regulation, the press is protected against **prior restraint**. That is, beginning with the landmark 1931 case of *Near v. Minnesota*, the Supreme Court has held that, except under

Should individuals be prosecuted for leaking classified information to the press? Chelsea Manning and Edward Snowden were charged for the crime of leaking classified information related to government surveillance.

the most extraordinary circumstances, the First Amendment prohibits government agencies from preventing newspapers or magazines from publishing whatever they wish.[49] Indeed, in the 1971 case *New York Times Co. v. United States* (the so-called Pentagon Papers case), the Supreme Court ruled that the government could not block publication of secret Defense Department documents furnished to the *New York Times* by an opponent of the Vietnam War who had obtained the documents illegally.[50]

Another press freedom issue that the courts have often been asked to decide is whether journalists can be compelled to reveal their sources of information. Journalists assert that if they cannot ensure their sources' confidentiality, the flow of information will be reduced and press freedom effectively curtailed. Government agencies, however, argue that names of news sources may be relevant to criminal or even national security investigations. More than 30 states have "shield laws" that protect journalistic sources to varying degrees. There is, however, no federal shield law and no special constitutional protection for journalists. The Supreme Court has held that the press has no constitutional right to withhold information in court.[51]

In addition to prosecuting journalists for refusing to reveal their sources, the government may seek to prosecute individuals who leak information to the press. During the Obama presidency, seven individuals were charged or prosecuted for disclosing classified information. They included Pfc. Chelsea Manning, an army intelligence analyst sent to prison for providing classified documents to WikiLeaks, which published many of the documents; and Edward Snowden, an employee of the National Security Agency (NSA) who fled the country to escape arrest after revealing the details of NSA domestic spying operations. Manning was released from prison in 2017.

Libel and Slander Some speech is not protected at all. If a written statement is made in "reckless disregard of the truth" and is considered damaging to the victim because it is "malicious, scandalous, and defamatory," it can be punished as **libel**. If such a statement is made orally, it can be punished as **slander**.

Most libel suits today involve freedom of the press, but American courts have narrowed the meaning of libel to the point that it is extremely difficult

libel a written statement made in "reckless disregard of the truth" that is considered damaging to a victim because it is "malicious, scandalous, and defamatory"

slander an oral statement made in "reckless disregard of the truth" that is considered damaging to the victim because it is "malicious, scandalous, and defamatory" for politicians or other public figures (as opposed to private individuals), to win a libel suit against a newspaper. In the important 1964 case of *New York Times Co. v. Sullivan*, the Supreme Court held that to be found libelous, a story about a public official not only had to be untrue but also had to result from "actual malice" or "reckless disregard" for the truth.[52] In other words, the newspaper had to print false and damaging material deliberately. Because in practice this charge is nearly impossible to prove, essentially the print media have become able to publish anything they want about a public figure. President Trump asserted that stricter libel laws were needed to prevent what he called "fake news," though no action was taken and no policies changed.

With the emergence of the internet as a communications medium, the courts have had to decide how traditional libel law applies to online content. In 1995 the New York courts held that an online bulletin board could be held responsible for the libelous content of material posted by a third party. To protect internet service providers, Congress subsequently enacted legislation absolving them of responsibility for third-party posts. The federal courts have generally upheld this law.[53]

Obscenity and Pornography If libel and slander cases can be difficult because of the problem of determining both whether statements are true and whether they are malicious and damaging, cases involving pornography and obscenity can be even trickier. Not until 1957 did the Supreme Court try to define obscenity, and its definition may have caused more confusion than it cleared up. In writing the Court's opinion, Justice William Brennan defined obscenity as speech or writing that appeals to the "prurient interest"—that is, whose purpose is to excite lust, as this appears "to the average person, applying contemporary community standards." Even so, Brennan added, the work should be judged obscene only when it is "utterly without redeeming social importance."[54] In 1964, Justice Potter Stewart confessed that, although he found pornography impossible to define, "I know it when I see it."[55] The vague and impractical standards that had been developed meant ultimately that almost nothing could be banned on the grounds that it was pornographic and obscene.

In recent years, the battle against obscene speech has targeted online pornography, whose opponents argue that it should be banned because of the easy access children have to the internet. The first major effort to regulate the content of the internet occurred in 1996, when Congress passed the Telecommunications Act. Attached to it was an amendment, called the Communications Decency Act (CDA), designed to regulate the online transmission of obscene material. In the 1997 case of *Reno v. American Civil Liberties Union*, the Supreme Court struck down the CDA, ruling that it suppressed speech that "adults have a constitutional right to receive" and that governments may not limit the adult population to messages fit for children. Supreme Court Justice John Paul Stevens described the internet as the "town crier" of the modern age and said it was entitled to the greatest degree of First Amendment protection possible.[56] In 2008, however, the Court upheld the PROTECT Act, which outlawed efforts to sell child pornography via the internet.[57]

In 2000 the Court extended the highest degree of First Amendment protection to cable (not broadcast) television. In *United States v. Playboy Entertainment Group*, it struck down a portion of the 1996 Telecommunications Act that required cable

TV companies to limit the availability of sexually explicit programming to late-night hours. The decision noted that the law already enabled parents to restrict access to sexually explicit cable channels through blocking devices. Moreover, such programming could come into the home only if parents purchased such channels in the first place.[58]

Closely related to the issue of obscenity is the question of whether governments can prohibit broadcasts or publications considered excessively violent. Here, too, the Court has generally upheld freedom of speech. For example, in the 2011 case of *Brown v. Entertainment Merchants Association*, the Court struck down a California law banning the sale of violent video games to children.[59]

The Second Amendment and the Right to Bear Arms

> **Explain how the Supreme Court has interpreted the right to bear arms**

Some argue that the purpose of the Second Amendment was the maintenance of militias. *Militia* was understood at the time of the Founding to be a military or police resource for state governments to maintain local public order. Others have argued that the Second Amendment also establishes an individual right to bear arms.

The judicial record of Second Amendment cases is far sparser than that of First Amendment cases, and localities across the country have very different gun-ownership standards, the result of a patchwork of state and local laws. For instance, in Wyoming, there is no ban on owning any type of gun, there is no waiting period to purchase a firearm, and individuals are not required to obtain a permit for carrying a concealed weapon. In California, in contrast, the possession of assault weapons is banned, there is a 10-day waiting period to purchase a firearm, and a permit is required to carry a concealed weapon. Figure 4.1 shows the background check requirements to purchase a firearm across the country.

★ *A well regulated Militia, being necessary to the security of a free State, the right of the people to keep and bear Arms, shall not be infringed.*
—from the Second Amendment

A string of mass shootings in the United States, including one at a Walmart in El Paso, Texas, in which 22 people were killed and 24 injured, have prompted calls for legislation to limit the availability of guns.

FIGURE 4.1

Gun Rights by State

Although state gun laws must conform to the Second Amendment as interpreted by the U.S. Supreme Court, laws concerning gun sales and ownership vary widely from state to state. It is much more difficult to buy a gun in, say, New York or California than in Texas or Kentucky. While federal law requires background checks when purchasing a firearm from a licensed seller, only 21 states require them from unlicensed sellers as well. Should all states require unlicensed firearm sellers to perform background checks? Why or why not?

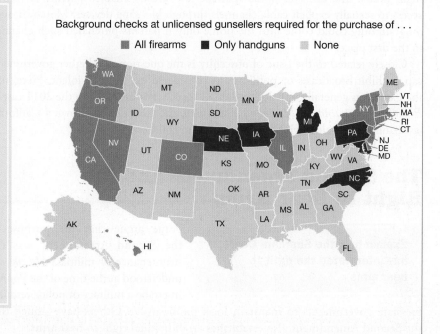

Background checks at unlicensed gunsellers required for the purchase of . . .

■ All firearms   ■ Only handguns   □ None

SOURCE: Background Checks, Gun Law Navigator, www.everytownresearch.org/ (accessed 6/12/18).

The Supreme Court's silence on the meaning of the Second Amendment ended in 2008 with the first of two rulings in favor of expansive rights of gun ownership by individuals. In *District of Columbia v. Heller*, at issue was a strict Washington, D.C., law that banned handguns. In a 5–4 decision, the Court ruled that the Second Amendment provides a constitutional right to keep a loaded handgun at home for self-defense, a view that had long been subject to debate. And in the majority opinion, Justice Antonin Scalia stated that the decision was not intended to cast doubt on all laws limiting firearm possession, such as by felons or the mentally ill.[60] In his dissenting opinion, Justice Stevens asserted that the Second Amendment protects the rights of individuals to bear arms only as part of a militia force, not in an individual capacity.

The District of Columbia is an entity of the federal government, and the Court did not indicate that its ruling applied to state firearms laws. However, in the 2010 case of *McDonald v. Chicago*, the Supreme Court applied the Second Amendment to the states, its first new incorporation decision in 40 years. The ruling effectively overturned a Chicago ordinance that made it extremely difficult to own a gun within city limits.[61]

Despite these rulings, the debate over gun control continues to loom large in American politics. The issue of gun laws has been kept firmly on the national agenda by a recent series of tragic shootings (including the killings of 50 people at a nightclub in Orlando, Florida; 59 individuals at a concert in Las Vegas, Nevada; 27 worshippers at a church in Sutherland Springs, Texas; 17 students and staff members at a high school in Parkland, Florida; 11 worshippers at a synagogue in Pittsburgh, Pennsylvania, and 22 people at a Walmart in El Paso, Texas). Proponents of gun control point to these shootings as evidence of the need to restrict the availability of firearms; opponents say they

The Right to Bear Arms

The Second Amendment of the U.S. Constitution reads: "A well-regulated Militia, being necessary to the security of a free State, the right of the people to keep and bear Arms, shall not be infringed." For decades, Americans have debated gun rights. Who owns guns in the United States, and where is gun ownership restricted?

Gun Ownership, 2017

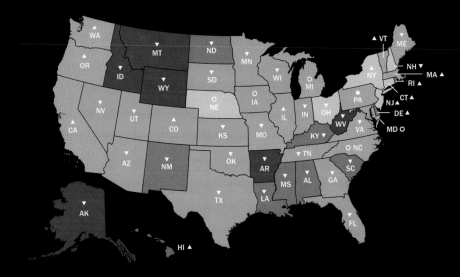

Percentage of Adult Population That Owns a Gun

- ● <10%
- ● 10–19.9%
- ● 20–29.9%
- ● 30–39.9%
- ● 40–49.9%
- ● 50%+

Background Check Required

- ▲ Yes
- ▼ No
- ○ Handgun only

Firearm Mortality Rate, 2017

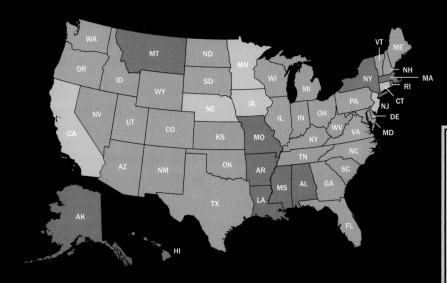

Percentage of Deaths Caused by Firearms

- ● <5%
- ● 5–9.9%
- ● 10–14.9%
- ● 15–19.9%
- ● 20%+

FOR CRITICAL ANALYSIS

1. Compare the data on gun laws and gun deaths per state. Do states with higher rates of gun deaths have more or less restrictive gun laws?

2. Why do you think state laws regulating gun ownership vary dramatically across the states?

SOURCES: Data from Bindu Kalesan, Marcos D. Villarreal, Katherine M. Keyes, and Sandro Galea, "Gun Ownership and Social Gun Culture," Injury Prevention, Centers for Disease Control and Prevention, and *The Washington Post*

demonstrate that Americans are not safe and should be free to carry arms for self-protection.

Interestingly, after each mass shooting, opposition to gun control has increased, perhaps suggesting that many Americans equate gun ownership with personal safety. In 2016, President Obama issued several executive orders designed to expand background checks for gun purchasers and licensing requirements for firearms dealers. In 2017, however, most of these orders were rescinded by President Trump.

Rights of the Criminally Accused

Explain how the Supreme Court has interpreted the right to due process

Except in the case of the First Amendment, most of the battle to apply the Bill of Rights to the states has been fought over the various protections it grants to individuals accused or suspected of a crime or testifying in court as a witness to a crime (Table 4.4). The Fourth, Fifth, Sixth, and Eighth amendments, taken together, are the essence of the **due process of law**, even though these precise words for this fundamental concept do not appear until the end of the Fifth Amendment.

due process of law the right of every individual against arbitrary action by national or state governments

The procedural safeguards that we discuss below may seem remote to most law-abiding citizens, but they help define the limits of government action against the personal liberty of every citizen. Many Americans believe that "legal technicalities" are responsible for setting many criminals free. In fact, few convictions are actually lost because of excluded evidence.

But one of America's traditional and most strongly held judicial values is that "it is far worse to convict an innocent man than to let a guilty man go free."[62] In civil suits, verdicts rest on "the preponderance of the evidence"; but in criminal cases, guilt has to be proven "beyond a reasonable doubt"—a far higher standard.

THE FOURTH AMENDMENT AND SEARCHES AND SEIZURES

★ *The right of the people to be secure in their persons, houses, papers, and effects, against unreasonable searches and seizures, shall not be violated, and no Warrants shall issue, but upon probable cause, supported by Oath or affirmation, and particularly describing the place to be searched, and the persons or things to be seized.*
—from the Fourth Amendment

The purpose of the Fourth Amendment is to guarantee the security of citizens against unreasonable (i.e., improper) searches and seizures. In 1990 the Supreme Court summarized its understanding of the Fourth Amendment: "A search compromises the individual interest in privacy; a seizure deprives the individual of dominion over his or her person or property."[63] But how are we to define what is reasonable and what is unreasonable?

The 1961 case of *Mapp v. Ohio* illustrates one of the most important principles to have grown out of the Fourth Amendment—the **exclusionary rule**, which prohibits evidence obtained during an illegal search from being introduced in a trial. Acting on a tip that Dollree (Dolly) Mapp was harboring a suspect in a bombing incident, several policemen forcibly entered Mapp's house, claiming they had a search warrant. They did not find the suspect but, in an old trunk in the basement, did find some materials they declared to be obscene. Although no warrant was ever produced, the evidence that had been seized was admitted by a court, and Mapp was convicted of possessing obscene materials.

exclusionary rule the ability of courts to exclude evidence obtained in violation of the Fourth Amendment

The Supreme Court's opinion in the case affirmed the exclusionary rule: under the Fourth Amendment (applied to the states through the Fourteenth Amendment), "all evidence obtained by searches and seizures in violation of the Constitution . . . is inadmissible."[64] This means that even people who are clearly guilty of the crime of which they are accused cannot be convicted if the only evidence for their conviction was obtained illegally.

In recent years, however, the Supreme Court has softened the application of the exclusionary rule, allowing federal courts to use their discretion about it depending on the "nature and quality of the intrusion."[65] In 2006, in the case of *United States v. Grubbs*, the Court ruled that the police could conduct searches using "anticipatory warrants"— warrants issued when the police know that incriminating material is not yet present at a particular location but have reason to believe that it will eventually arrive.[66] The warrants are held until the police are ready to conduct their search. In some instances, such as during an arrest, the authorities can conduct searches without obtaining any warrants at all.

The Fourth Amendment is also at issue in the controversy over mandatory drug testing. In 1989 the Supreme Court upheld the U.S. Customs Service's drug-testing program for its employees[67] and drug and alcohol tests for railroad workers if they were involved in serious accidents.[68] Since then, more than 40 federal agencies have initiated mandatory employee drug tests, giving rise to controversy about the general practice of "suspicionless testing" of employees. A 1995 case, in which the Court upheld a public school district's policy requiring all students participating in interscholastic sports to submit to random drug tests, surely contributed to the efforts of federal, state, and local agencies to initiate random and suspicionless drug and alcohol testing.[69]

TABLE 4.4
The Rights of the Accused from Arrest to Trial
No improper searches and seizures (Fourth Amendment)
No arrest without probable cause (Fourth Amendment)
Right to remain silent (Fifth Amendment)
No self-incrimination during arrest or trial (Fifth Amendment)
Right to be informed of charges (Sixth Amendment)
Right to counsel (Sixth Amendment)
No excessive bail (Eighth Amendment)
Right to grand jury (Fifth Amendment)
Right to open trial before a judge (Article I, Section 9)
Right to speedy and public trial before an impartial jury (Sixth Amendment)
Evidence obtained by illegal search not admissible during trial (Fourth Amendment)
Right to confront witnesses (Sixth Amendment)
No double jeopardy (Fifth Amendment)
No cruel and unusual punishment (Eighth Amendment)

The most recent cases suggest, however, that the Court is beginning to consider limits on the war against drugs. In a decisive 8–1 decision in 1997, the Court applied the Fourth Amendment as a shield against "state action that diminishes personal privacy" in cases that do not involve high-risk or safety-sensitive tasks.[70] And in 2013, the Court held that the use of a drug-sniffing dog on the front porch of a home constituted a search that violated the Fourth Amendment in the absence of consent or a warrant.[71]

Changes in technology have also had an impact on Fourth Amendment jurisprudence. In the 2012 case of *United States v. Jones*, the Court held that prosecutors violated a defendant's rights when they attached a Global Positioning System (GPS) device to his Jeep and monitored his movements for 28 days.[72] On the other hand, in *Maryland v. King*, the Court upheld DNA testing of arrestees without the need for individualized suspicion. Writing for the majority, Justice Anthony Kennedy characterized DNA testing as an administrative tool for identifying the arrestee and thus legally indistinguishable from photographing and

Under what circumstances can the police search an individual's car? The Fourth Amendment protects against "unreasonable searches and seizures," but the Supreme Court has had to interpret what is unreasonable.

grand jury jury that determines whether sufficient evidence is available to justify a trial; grand juries do not rule on the accused's guilt or innocence

★ *No person shall be held to answer for a capital, or otherwise infamous crime, unless on a presentment or indictment of a Grand Jury, except in cases arising in the land or naval forces, or in the Militia, when in actual service in time of War or public danger; nor shall any person be subject for the same offence to be twice put in jeopardy of life or limb; nor shall be compelled in any criminal case to be a witness against himself, nor be deprived of life, liberty, or property, without due process of law; nor shall private property be taken for public use, without just compensation.*
—from the Fifth Amendment

fingerprinting.[73] In the 2014 case of *Riley v. California*, the Court held that the police were constitutionally prohibited from seizing a cell phone and searching its digital contents during an arrest.

As new technologies develop, the Court will continue to face the question of what constitutes a reasonable search.[74] In 2016 the FBI sought to compel the Apple corporation to unlock the cell phone used by Syed Farook, who, along with his wife, had allegedly killed 14 people in a terrorist attack in San Bernardino, California. Apple asserted that creating new software to enable the FBI to unlock the phone would allow the agency to invade the privacy of millions of iPhone users. The case became moot when the FBI was able to unlock the phone without Apple's help.

Fourth Amendment issues have also been raised by aggressive police tactics, particularly the one known as "stop and frisk," in which an individual acting "suspiciously" is confronted, questioned, and searched for weapons. In the 1968 case of *Terry v. Ohio*, the Supreme Court held that if an officer had "probable cause" to believe the individual was armed, such a search was permitted.[75] In recent years, some police departments, most notably the New York City police, made stop and frisk a routine practice, searching thousands of individuals and arguing that doing so reduced crime rates.

In 2013, however, a federal judge ordered an end to stop and frisk in New York on the grounds that it amounted to a form of racial profiling. After taking office in 2014, Mayor Bill de Blasio dropped the city's appeal of the order and announced an end to aggressive stop-and-frisk tactics. Critics charged that the policy change would lead to an increase in New York crime rates, but this has not occurred.

THE FIFTH AMENDMENT

Grand Juries The first clause of the Fifth Amendment, the right to a **grand jury** to determine whether a trial is warranted, is considered "the oldest institution known to the Constitution."[76] A grand jury is a body of citizens that must agree that a prosecutor has sufficient evidence to bring criminal charges against a suspect.

Although grand juries do play an important role in federal criminal cases, the provision for them is the one important civil liberties provision of the Bill of Rights that was not incorporated into the Fourteenth Amendment and applied to state criminal prosecutions. Thus, some states operate without grand juries. In such states, the prosecutor simply files a "bill of information" affirming that sufficient evidence is available to justify a trial. For the accused person to be held in custody, the prosecutor must persuade a judge that the evidence shows "probable cause" to justify further action.

Double Jeopardy "Nor shall any person be subject for the same offence to be twice put in jeopardy of life or limb" is the constitutional protection from **double jeopardy**, or being tried more than once for the same crime. The protection from double jeopardy was at the heart of the *Palko* case in 1937, which, as we saw earlier in this chapter, also established the principle of selective incorporation of the Bill of Rights. However, in the 1969 case of *Benton v. Maryland*, the Supreme Court expressly overruled *Palko* and declared that the double jeopardy clause did, in fact, apply to the states.[77] In this case, the state of Maryland wanted to try a defendant, John Benton, for larceny, even though he had previously been acquitted by a jury. Maryland's constitution did not prohibit double jeopardy, and at the second trial Benton was convicted. The Supreme Court, however, ruled that the second trial violated Benton's rights under the U.S. Constitution. Double jeopardy now joined those rights "incorporated" via the Fourteenth Amendment.

double jeopardy the Fifth Amendment right providing that a person cannot be tried twice for the same crime

Self-Incrimination Perhaps the most significant liberty found in the Fifth Amendment is the guarantee that no citizen "shall be compelled in any criminal case to be a witness against himself." The most famous case concerning self-incrimination is one of such importance that Chief Justice Earl Warren assessed its results as going "to the very root of our concepts of American criminal jurisprudence."[78]

In 1963, Ernesto Miranda was convicted and sentenced to between 20 and 30 years in prison for the kidnapping and rape of a woman in Arizona. The woman had identified him in a police lineup, and after two hours of questioning, Miranda

DEFENDANT		LOCATION	

SPECIFIC WARNING REGARDING INTERROGATIONS

1. YOU HAVE THE RIGHT TO REMAIN SILENT.

2. ANYTHING YOU SAY CAN AND WILL BE USED AGAINST YOU IN A COURT OF LAW.

3. YOU HAVE THE RIGHT TO TALK TO A LAWYER AND HAVE HIM PRESENT WITH YOU WHILE YOU ARE BEING QUESTIONED.

4. IF YOU CANNOT AFFORD TO HIRE A LAWYER ONE WILL BE APPOINTED TO REPRESENT YOU BEFORE ANY QUESTIONING, IF YOU WISH ONE.

SIGNATURE OF DEFENDANT		DATE
WITNESS		TIME

☐ REFUSED SIGNATURE   SAN FRANCISCO POLICE DEPARTMENT   PR.9.1.4

The case of Ernesto Miranda resulted in the creation of Miranda rights, which must be read to those arrested to make them aware of their constitutional rights.

confessed and subsequently signed a statement that his confession had been made voluntarily, without threats or promises of immunity. The statement was admitted into evidence and served as the basis for Miranda's conviction.

After his conviction, Miranda argued that his confession had not been truly voluntary and that he had not been informed of his right to remain silent or his right to consult an attorney. In 1966, the Supreme Court agreed and overturned the conviction, one of the most intensely and widely criticized decisions in the Court's history. *Miranda v. Arizona* produced the rules the police must follow before questioning an arrested criminal suspect, and the reading of a person's "Miranda rights" became a standard scene in every police station and on virtually every television and film dramatization of police action.

Miranda advanced the civil liberties of accused persons not only by expanding the Fifth Amendment's protection against coerced confessions and self-incrimination but also by confirming the right to counsel, as discussed below. Although the Supreme Court later considerably loosened the *Miranda* restrictions, the **Miranda rule** still stands as a protection against police abuses.

THE SIXTH AMENDMENT AND THE RIGHT TO COUNSEL

Some provisions of the Sixth Amendment, such as the right to a speedy trial and the right to confront witnesses before an impartial jury, are not very controversial. The "right to counsel" provision, however, like the exclusionary rule of the Fourth Amendment and the self-incrimination clause of the Fifth Amendment, is notable for sometimes freeing defendants who seem to be clearly guilty as charged.

Gideon v. Wainwright (1963) is the perfect case study because it involved a disreputable person who had been in and out of jails for most of his 51 years. Clarence Earl Gideon received a five-year sentence for breaking into and entering a poolroom in Panama City, Florida. He was too poor to afford a lawyer, and Florida law provided court-appointed counsel only for crimes carrying the death penalty. While serving time, however, Gideon became a fairly well-qualified "jailhouse lawyer," made his own appeal on a handwritten petition, and eventually won the landmark ruling on the right to counsel in all felony cases.[79]

The right to counsel has been expanded during the past few decades, even as the courts have become more conservative. For example, although at first judges required local lawyers to represent poor defendants, now most states and cities employ public defenders; these professional defense lawyers typically provide much better representation. In addition, the right to counsel extends beyond trials for serious crimes to any trial, with or without a jury, that holds the possibility of imprisonment. Finally, defendants have the right to appeal a conviction on the grounds that the counsel provided by the state was deficient. For example, in 2003 the Supreme Court overturned the death sentence of a Maryland death-row inmate, holding that the defense lawyer had failed to inform the jury fully of the defendant's history of "horrendous childhood abuse."[80]

THE EIGHTH AMENDMENT AND CRUEL AND UNUSUAL PUNISHMENT

Virtually all the debate over Eighth Amendment issues focuses on the last clause of the amendment, because what is considered "cruel and unusual" varies from culture to culture and from generation to generation. In 1972 the Supreme Court

Miranda rule the requirement, articulated by the Supreme Court in *Miranda v. Arizona*, that persons under arrest must be informed prior to police interrogation of their rights to remain silent and to have the benefit of legal counsel

★ *In all criminal prosecutions, the accused shall enjoy the right to a speedy and public trial, by an impartial jury of the State and district wherein the crime shall have been committed, which district shall have been previously ascertained by law, and to be informed of the nature and cause of the accusation; to be confronted with the witnesses against him; to have compulsory process for obtaining witnesses in his favor, and to have the Assistance of Counsel for his defence.*
—from the Sixth Amendment

★ *Excessive bail shall not be required, nor excessive fines imposed, nor cruel and unusual punishment inflicted.*
—from the Eighth Amendment

overturned several state death penalty laws, not because they were cruel and unusual but because they were being applied unevenly—that is, African Americans were much more likely than Whites to be sentenced to death, the poor more likely than the rich, and men more likely than women.[81] Very soon after that decision, a majority of states revised their capital punishment provisions to meet the Court's standards, and the Court reaffirmed that the death penalty could be used if certain standards were met.[82] Since 1976, the Court has consistently upheld state laws providing for capital punishment, although it also continues to review death penalty appeals each year.

Between 1976 and October 2020, states executed 1,524 people. Most of those executions occurred in southern states, with Texas leading the way at 570. As of October 2020, 28 states had statutes providing for capital punishment for specified offenses, a policy supported by a majority of Americans, according to polls.[83] On the other hand, 22 states bar the death penalty, and since the end of the 1990s, both the number of death sentences and the number of executions have declined annually.[84] In 2019, 22 people were executed in the United States, a slight decrease over the 25 executed in 2018.

Despite the seeming popularity of the death penalty, the debate over it has become, if anything, more intense. Many death penalty supporters argue that it deters other would-be criminals. Although research studies usually fail to demonstrate any direct deterrent effect, this failure may be due to the lengthy delays—typically years and even decades—between convictions and executions. A system that eliminated undue delays might enhance deterrence. And deterring even one murder or other heinous crime, proponents argue, is ample justification for such laws.

Death penalty opponents are quick to counter that the death penalty has not been proved to deter crime, either in the United States or abroad. In fact, America is the only Western nation that still executes criminals. If the government is to serve as an example of proper behavior, say foes of capital punishment, it has no business sanctioning killing when incarceration will similarly protect society.

Furthermore, execution is time-consuming and expensive—more expensive than life imprisonment—precisely because the government must make every effort to ensure that it is not executing an innocent person. Curtailing legal appeals would make the possibility of a mistake too great. Race is also a factor in death penalty cases: people of color are disproportionately more likely than Whites charged with identical crimes to be given the ultimate punishment. And although most Americans do support the death penalty, people also support life imprisonment without the possibility of parole as an alternative.

The Supreme Court has long struggled to establish principles to govern executions under the Eighth Amendment. In recent years, the Court has declared that death was too harsh a penalty for the crime of rape of a child,[85] prohibited the execution of a defendant with an IQ under 70 and of a youthful defendant, and invalidated a death sentence for an African American defendant after the prosecutor improperly excluded African Americans from the jury.[86] In 2015, however, the Court upheld lethal injection as a mode of execution despite arguments that this form of execution was likely to cause considerable pain.[87]

The question of cruel and unusual punishment goes beyond the death penalty. Federal courts have on occasion held that overcrowding and other dangerous conditions within prisons, such as inadequate food, medical care, and sanitation, may violate the Eighth Amendment, as may prison workers' threats against and beatings of inmates.[88] The Court has also been concerned with punishments given out to the mentally disabled and to juveniles. In a recent case, the Court held that life

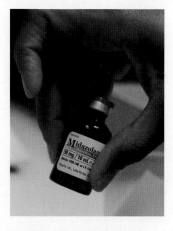

Opponents of the death penalty argue that it constitutes cruel and unusual punishment. In recent years the use of lethal-injection drugs, including Midazolam, has come under scrutiny after some troubling executions where the process was drawn out and painful. In 2015 the Supreme Court upheld the use of lethal injection.

imprisonment without parole for a juvenile, even one convicted of murder, constituted cruel and unusual punishment.[89]

The Eighth Amendment also prohibits excessive fines. In the 2019 case of *Timbs v. Indiana* (586 U.S. ___ [2019]), the Supreme Court ruled that this prohibition applied to the states. In the *Timbs* case, the state confiscated Timbs's car after he was convicted of drug possession. The car was worth much more than the maximum possible fine Timbs could have received. Lower Indiana courts acknowledged that Timbs was being forced to pay a fine in excess of the statutory fine for his offense. The Indiana Supreme Court agreed that the fine may have been excessive but said this did not matter because the Eighth Amendment had never been applied to the states. The U.S. Supreme Court reversed that decision and added excessive fines to the list of constitutional provisions the states were obligated to recognize.

The Right to Privacy

right to privacy the right to be left alone, which has been interpreted by the Supreme Court to entail individual access to birth control and abortions

> **Describe how the Supreme Court has identified and interpreted the right to privacy**

A **right to privacy** was not specifically mentioned in the Bill of Rights. In a 1928 case, however, Supreme Court Justice Louis Brandeis argued in a dissent that the Fourth Amendment's provision for "the right of the people to be secure in their persons, houses, papers, and effects, against unreasonable searches and seizures" should be extended to a more general principle of "privacy in the home."[90]

Justice Brandeis knew that the Constitution's framers regarded privacy as an important component of political freedom. Citizens' ability to exercise political power requires that they have considerable protection from the state's scrutiny. Those intent on expressing anything but support for the groups in power need privacy to plan, organize, and mobilize. The efforts of people out of power can certainly be compromised if the government becomes privy to their plans. For example, the Nixon administration wanted to undermine Democratic campaign plans in 1972 and engaged in surveillance activities.

Known political dissidents, moreover, always face some risk of official reprisal. Accordingly, at least some citizens may refrain from acting upon their political beliefs for fear that they will draw attention to themselves and become targets for tax audits and other government efforts to find evidence of criminality or other misconduct that can be used against them. This is a realistic concern given the fact that recently, so-called Tea Party groups and other conservative organizations found themselves the recipients of special scrutiny from the IRS. Privacy for political activities is, like the secret ballot, an important element of political freedom.

The relationship between privacy and freedom of political expression is at the heart of the Fourth Amendment, in its prohibition of unreasonable searches. While many currently see the Fourth Amendment as related to evidence in criminal cases, the framers were aware that government intrusions into private homes were often aimed at identifying papers, manuscripts, and books that might show plans to encourage political discontent.[91] As Justice Brennan wrote for a unanimous court in the 1961 case of *Marcus v. Search Warrant*, "The Bill of Rights was fashioned against the background of knowledge that unrestricted power of search and seizure could also be an instrument for stifling liberty of expression."[92] In her dissent in a recent case, Justice Ruth Bader Ginsburg called attention to this original purpose and meaning of the Fourth Amendment as an instrument for protecting liberty of political expression.[93] In an era when the government can listen to every phone call, read electronic communications, and even collect the DNA of millions of Americans from their efforts to trace their ancestry, the Fourth Amendment takes on new importance.

EMINENT DOMAIN

One important element of privacy is the possession of private property—property belonging to individuals for their own peaceful enjoyment. The privacy of private property, however, is conditioned by the needs of the public at large. What if the government believes that the construction of a public road or irrigation project or other public project requires that a private home be torn down to make way for the public good? Where does privacy end and the public good begin? The power of any government to take private property for public use is called **eminent domain**.

The Fifth Amendment, through the "takings clause," regulates that power by requiring that the government show a public purpose and provide fair payment for the taking of someone's property. This provision is now observed by all governments within the United States, but it has not always been.

The first modern Supreme Court case about eminent domain involved a mom-and-pop grocery store in the District of Columbia. In carrying out a vast urban redevelopment program, the city government took the property as one of a large number of privately owned lots to be cleared for new housing and business construction. The owner of the grocery store took the government to court on the grounds that it was an unconstitutional use of eminent domain to take property from one private owner and eventually to turn that property back, in altered form, to another private owner.

In 1945 the store owner lost the case. The Supreme Court's argument was a curious but very important one: the "public interest" can mean virtually anything a legislature says it means. In other words, since the overall slum-clearance-and-redevelopment project was in the public interest, according to the appropriate government agency, the eventual transfers of property were justified.[94] This principle was reaffirmed in the 2005 case of *Kelo v. City of New London*, where the Court held that the city could seize land from one private owner and transfer it to another as part of a redevelopment plan.[95] The question of what constitutes a "taking" took a new twist in 2020. Dare County, North Carolina, prohibited nonresidents from entering the county to prevent the spread of the coronavirus. Several nonresident property owners were blocked from using their vacation homes and threatened to sue the county government for intruding upon their property rights without offering compensation.

BIRTH CONTROL

The sphere of privacy as a constitutional principle was formally recognized in 1965, when the Court ruled that a Connecticut law forbidding the use of contraceptives violated the right of marital privacy. For providing information, instruction, and medical advice about contraception to married couples, Estelle Griswold, the executive director of the Planned Parenthood League of Connecticut, and an associate were found guilty as accessories to the crime of contraceptive use and fined $100 each. The Supreme Court declared the Connecticut law unconstitutional because it violated "a right of privacy older than the Bill of Rights."[96] Justice William O. Douglas, who wrote the majority opinion in the *Griswold* case, argued that this right of privacy is also grounded in the Constitution because it fits into a "zone of privacy" created by a combination of the Third, Fourth, and Fifth amendments.

eminent domain the right of government to take private property for public use

FOR CRITICAL ANALYSIS

Read the Third, Fourth, Fifth, and Ninth amendments in the appendix at the end of this book. In your opinion, do American citizens have a constitutional right to privacy?

A concurring opinion, written by Justice Arthur Goldberg, attempted to strengthen Douglas's argument by adding that "the concept of liberty . . . embraces the right of marital privacy though that right is not mentioned explicitly in the Constitution [and] is supported by numerous decisions of this Court . . . and *by the language and history of the Ninth Amendment* [emphasis added]."[97] The Ninth Amendment provides that "the enumeration in the Constitution, of certain rights, shall not be construed to deny or disparage others retained by the people." According to Justice Goldberg, this language means that just because the Constitution does not specifically mention a particular right to privacy does not mean that the people do not retain that right.

ABORTION

The right to privacy was confirmed and extended in 1973 in a revolutionary Supreme Court decision: *Roe v. Wade*, which established a woman's right to seek an abortion. The decision prohibited states from making abortion a criminal act prior to the point in pregnancy at which the fetus becomes viable, which in 1973 was the 27th week.[98]

In extending privacy rights to include the rights of women to control their own bodies, the Court was following both historical and recent precedents. The states did not begin regulating abortion until the 1840s, when 6 of the 26 states existing at the time outlawed the practice. By the twentieth century, many states began to ease their abortion restrictions well before the 1973 *Roe* decision.

By extending the umbrella of privacy, this sweeping ruling dramatically changed abortion practices in America. In addition, it galvanized and nationalized the abortion debate. Groups opposed to abortion, such as the National Right to Life Committee, organized to fight the liberal new standard, while abortion rights groups have fought to maintain that protection.

While the Supreme Court has continued to affirm a woman's right to seek an abortion, it has increasingly limited that right. In *Webster v. Reproductive Health Services* (1989), the Court narrowly upheld (by a 5–4 majority) the constitutionality of restrictions on the use of public medical facilities for abortion.[99] And in the 1992

One of the most important cases related to the right to privacy was *Roe v. Wade*, which established a woman's right to seek an abortion. However, the decision has remained highly controversial, with opponents arguing that the Constitution does not guarantee this right.

Abortion and the Right to Privacy

Do Americans have a right to obtain an abortion? In its 1973 landmark case *Roe v. Wade*, the Supreme Court established a right to privacy enshrined in the Bill of Rights that included a person's right to receive an abortion. President Trump's appointment of two antiabortion justices has fueled opposition to *Roe*, and in 2019 nine states passed laws that effectively ban abortions statewide. These bans are not yet in effect and will likely face extended legal challenges, where the Supreme Court may ultimately decide whether Americans have this form of a right to privacy.

Access to Abortion, 2019

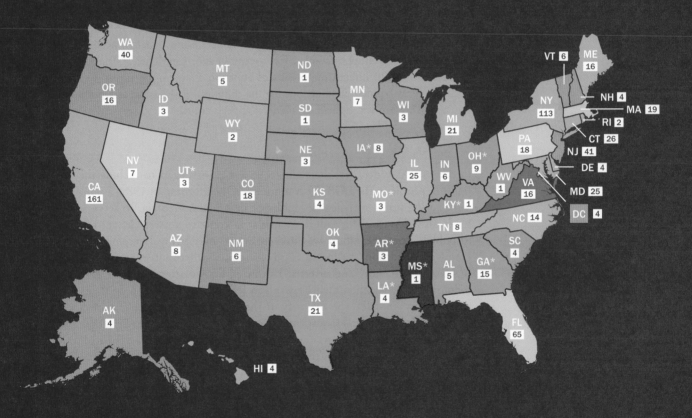

Abortion prohibited after...

● 15 Weeks ● 18 Weeks ● 22 Weeks ● 24 Weeks ● 25 Weeks ● Viability ● None

Number of clinics, 2017

* Several states, including Alabama, Georgia, Kentucky, Louisiana, Mississippi, and Missouri, have recently passed laws effectively banning abortion that have not yet gone into effect.

SOURCE: Data from R. K. Jones, E. Witwer, and J. Jerman, *Abortion Incidence and Service Availability in the United States, 2017* (New York: Guttmacher Institute, 2019), www.guttmacher.org/report/abortion-incidence-service-availability-us-2017 (accessed 11/18/19).

FOR CRITICAL ANALYSIS

1. Compare each state's restrictions on abortions and the number of facilities in that state that provide abortions. Which state offers the most access to abortion, and which the least?

2. Should civil liberties like the right to privacy vary from state to state?

case of *Planned Parenthood of Southeastern Pennsylvania v. Casey*, another 5–4 majority upheld *Roe* but narrowed its scope, defining the right to an abortion as a "limited or qualified" right subject to regulation by the states as long as the regulation does not constitute an "undue burden."[100] In the 2006 case of *Ayotte v. Planned Parenthood of Northern New England*, the Court held that a law requiring parental notification before a minor could obtain an abortion was not an undue burden.[101] And in the 2007 *Gonzales v. Carhart* decision, the Court effectively upheld the federal partial-birth abortion ban, which outlaws a particular type of abortion procedure.[102]

In recent years a number of states have also imposed new restrictions, including lowering the viability standard to 20 weeks (Texas), 12 weeks (Arkansas), and 6 weeks (North Dakota). In 2019, Georgia and several other states adopted "heartbeat" bills, prohibiting abortion if a physician could detect a fetal heartbeat, usually at about 6 weeks. Some women might not even be aware they are pregnant at this point. In June 2020, the Supreme Court struck down an effort by Louisiana to restrict abortion rights. A state law required that abortion providers have admitting privileges in a nearby hospital if they were to be allowed to perform abortions. In a 5–4 decision the Court ruled that this law, like a similar Texas statute that had been previously overturned, was an impermissible effort to restrict abortion rights.[103] The coronavirus pandemic of 2020 offered opponents of abortion a new opportunity to limit the practice. Texas banned all abortions for the duration of the crisis as a public-health measure. This ban was upheld by a federal appeals court.

SEXUAL ORIENTATION

In the last three decades, the right to be left alone began to include the privacy rights of people in the LGBTQ community. One morning in 1982, a police officer came to the home of Michael Hardwick in Atlanta, Georgia, to serve a warrant for Hardwick's arrest for failure to appear in court to answer charges of drinking in public. After the officer was invited by an unknowing housemate to look in Hardwick's bedroom, he found Hardwick and another man engaging in "consensual sexual behavior" and arrested Hardwick for violating Georgia's laws against sodomy. Hardwick then filed a lawsuit in federal court challenging the law's constitutionality. In 1986 the majority of the Court ruled against Hardwick on the grounds that "the federal Constitution confers [no] fundamental right upon homosexuals to engage in sodomy" and that therefore there was no basis to invalidate "the laws of the many states that still make such conduct illegal and have done so for a very long time."[104]

Seventeen years later, to almost everyone's surprise, in *Lawrence v. Texas* (2003) the Court overturned *Bowers v. Hardwick* with a dramatic pronouncement that gay people are "entitled to respect for their private lives"[105] as a matter of constitutional due process and that "the State cannot demean their existence or control their destiny by making their private sexual conduct a crime." In explicitly encompassing lesbians and gay men within the umbrella of privacy, the Court maintained that "in our tradition the State is not omnipresent in the home. And there are other spheres of our lives and existence outside the home, where the State should not be a dominant presence."[106]

In 2015 the Court took another important step in the protection of gay rights by declaring that state bans on same-sex marriage were unconstitutional because they violated the Fourteenth Amendment's equal protection and due process clauses.[107] See Chapter 5 for more on same-sex marriage. In 2020, LGBTQ and transgender individuals won a significant victory in the Supreme Court. In a 6–3 decision written by Justice Neil Gorsuch, the Court ruled that the 1964 Civil Rights Act prohibited employment discrimination based on sexual orientation, just as it prohibited employment discrimination based on race and gender.[108] The fact that the decision was authored by one of the Court's most conservative justices suggests that LGBTQ and transgender individuals have won an increased measure of acceptance in the United States.

Civil Liberties: What Do You Think?

The prominent place of civil liberties is one of the hallmarks of American government. The freedoms enshrined in the Constitution and its amendments help define the relationship between government and citizens by limiting what government can do to individuals. But these freedoms also come with trade-offs, as the Slants and Native Americans experienced in the debate over legal protections from ethnicity- or race-based disparagement.

★ Have you had experiences where someone else's exercise of freedom interfered with yours? How do you think members of the Slants thought about the trade-offs between their freedom to choose their band name and the implications for others, such as the Native American critics of the Redskins football team's name?

★ What do you think about questions concerning the right to bear arms, the use of the death penalty, and religious freedom? What are your rights to act upon your beliefs? What are the rights of people who disagree with you? How do you think the Slants would react to critics of their First Amendment claims?

★ How have new technologies affected the government's ability to monitor its citizens? What are your expectations of privacy in your email conversations, your plane tickets, your reading habits?

STUDY GUIDE

Civil Liberties and the Constitution

Outline the founding debate about civil liberties and explain how civil liberties apply to the federal government and the states (pp. 101–6)

The framers did not originally include a bill of rights in the U.S. Constitution because Federalists believed it would be "unnecessary" and potentially "dangerous." However, in order to secure Antifederalists' support for the document during the ratification process, the Federalists conceded to adding one, and the first 10 amendments came to compose the Bill of Rights. Until 1897, the Bill of Rights was interpreted to limit only the actions of the federal government. Since then, most of its important provisions have been incorporated one by one into the Fourteenth Amendment and applied to the states.

Key Terms
habeas corpus (p. 101)

Bill of Rights (p. 102)

civil liberties (p. 102)

selective incorporation (p. 104)

Practice Quiz

1. From 1791 until the end of the nineteenth century, the Bill of Rights was interpreted to put limits on
   a) the national government only.
   b) the state governments only.
   c) both the national and state governments.
   d) neither the national nor state governments.
   e) political parties and interest groups.

2. Which of the following rights was included in the original Constitution?
   a) the right to freedom of speech
   b) the right to bear arms
   c) the right of habeas corpus
   d) the right to peaceful assembly
   e) None of these rights was included in the original Constitution.

3. The process by which some of the liberties in the Bill of Rights were applied to the states is known as
   a) preemption.
   b) selective incorporation.
   c) habeas corpus.
   d) ratification.
   e) establishment.

4. Which of the following provisions of the Bill of Rights was the first to be incorporated and applied to the states?
   a) the right to counsel in any criminal trial
   b) the right against self-incrimination
   c) freedom from unnecessary searches and seizures
   d) freedom to petition the government for redress of grievances
   e) protection against the taking of private property for a public use without just compensation

The First Amendment and Freedom of Religion

Explain how the Supreme Court has interpreted freedom of religion through the establishment and free exercise clauses (pp. 106–9)

Two parts of the First Amendment concern religious freedom: the establishment clause and the free exercise clause. Though the establishment clause implies a "wall of separation" between church and state, there is ample room for debate on how to define the relationship between government and religion in practice. The free exercise clause protects the right to believe and practice the religion of one's choice; in recent years, this protection has been bolstered by legislation prohibiting religious discrimination in a variety of public and private realms.

Key Terms
establishment clause (p. 106)

Lemon test (p. 107)

free exercise clause (p. 108)

5. The Supreme Court's ruling in *Lemon v. Kurtzman*, which led to the *Lemon* test, concerned the issue of
   a) school desegregation.
   b) government financial aid to religious schools.
   c) cruel and unusual punishment.
   d) obscenity.
   e) prayer in public schools.

6. Which piece of recent legislation was challenged in the Supreme Court on the grounds that some of its provisions violated the free exercise clause?
   a) the Affordable Care Act
   b) the Religious Freedom Restoration Act
   c) the Espionage Act
   d) the Bipartisan Campaign Reform Act
   e) the Higher Education Act

The First Amendment and Freedom of Speech and of the Press

Explain how the Supreme Court has interpreted freedom of speech, assembly, petition, and the press (pp. 109–19)

Given the importance of freedom of speech and of the press to the functioning of democracy, Americans are assumed to have the right to voice their ideas publicly unless there is a compelling reason to prevent them. According to the courts, although virtually all speech is protected by the Constitution, some forms are entitled to a greater degree of protection than others. The courts have consistently protected political speech and symbolic speech, but they have ruled that the government may place certain limits on campaign spending, some kinds of hostile speech, commercial speech, libel, and slander.

Key Terms

"clear and present danger" test (p. 110)

fighting words (p. 112)

"speech plus" (p. 116)

prior restraint (p. 116)

libel (p. 117)

slander (p. 117)

Practice Quiz

7. The judicial standard that places a heavy burden of proof on the government when it seeks to restrict speech is called
   a) judicial restraint.
   b) judicial activism.
   c) habeas corpus.
   d) prior restraint.
   e) strict scrutiny.

8. The standard articulated by the Supreme Court in *R.A.V. v. City of St. Paul* suggests that
   a) virtually no "hate speech" is constitutionally protected by the First Amendment.
   b) virtually all "hate speech" is constitutionally protected by the First Amendment.
   c) "hate speech" is not constitutionally protected by the First Amendment when it is directed at religious groups.
   d) "hate speech" is not constitutionally protected by the First Amendment when it is directed at racial or ethnic minority groups.
   e) "hate speech" is not constitutionally protected by the First Amendment when it is expressed on college campuses.

9. Which of the following describes a written statement made in "reckless disregard of the truth" that is considered damaging to a victim because it is "malicious, scandalous, and defamatory"?
   a) slander
   b) libel
   c) speech plus
   d) fighting words
   e) expressive speech

The Second Amendment and the Right to Bear Arms

Explain how the Supreme Court has interpreted the right to bear arms (pp. 119–22)

Some argue that the Second Amendment granted Americans the right "to keep and bear Arms" for the sole purpose of maintaining militias, while others claim that the amendment also establishes an individual right to bear arms. In the 2008 case *District of Columbia v. Heller*, the Supreme Court ruled in favor of the latter interpretation. And in the 2010 case *McDonald v. Chicago*, the Court incorporated the right to bear arms to state governments.

Practice Quiz

10. In *District of Columbia v. Heller*, the Supreme Court ruled that
    a) states can require citizens to own firearms.
    b) federal grants can be used to support the formation of state militias.
    c) felons cannot be prevented from purchasing assault rifles.
    d) the Second Amendment provides a constitutional right to keep a loaded handgun at home for self-defense.
    e) the Second Amendment applies only to the federal government and not to states.

Rights of the Criminally Accused

Explain how the Supreme Court has interpreted the right to due process (pp. 122–28)

The Fourth, Fifth, Sixth, and Eighth amendments are the essence of the Constitution's protections for due process of the law. The Fourth Amendment protects individuals from unreasonable searches and seizures. The Fifth Amendment provides individuals with the right to a grand jury, protection from double jeopardy, and a guarantee against self-incrimination. The Sixth Amendment provides the right to legal counsel, the right to a speedy trial, and the right to confront witnesses before an impartial jury. The Eighth Amendment protects individuals against cruel and unusual punishment.

Key Terms

due process of law (p. 122)

exclusionary rule (p. 122)

grand jury (p. 124)

double jeopardy (p. 125)

Miranda rule (p. 126)

Practice Quiz

11. In *Mapp v. Ohio*, the Supreme Court ruled that
    a) evidence obtained from an illegal search could not be introduced in a trial.
    b) the government must provide legal counsel for defendants who are too poor to provide it for themselves.
    c) persons under arrest must be informed prior to police interrogation of their rights to remain silent and to have the benefits of legal counsel.
    d) the government has the right to take private property for public use if just compensation is provided.
    e) a person cannot be tried twice for the same crime.

12. Which of the following is considered "the oldest institution known to the Constitution"?
    a) the Third Amendment's freedom from forced quartering of soldiers during peacetime
    b) the Fourth Amendment's freedom from warrantless search and seizure
    c) the Fifth Amendment's right to remain silent
    d) the Fifth Amendment's right against self-incrimination and forced confessions
    e) the Fifth Amendment's right to a grand jury to determine whether a trial is warranted

13. Which landmark ruling deals with the Sixth Amendment's guarantee of the right to counsel?
    a) *Roe v. Wade*
    b) *Mapp v. Ohio*
    c) *Gideon v. Wainwright*
    d) *McDonald v. Chicago*
    e) *Miranda v. Arizona*

The Right to Privacy

Describe how the Supreme Court has identified and interpreted the right to privacy (pp. 128–33)

The right to privacy is never specifically mentioned in the Constitution, but Supreme Court justices have argued that a relationship between privacy and freedom of political expression lies at the heart of the Fourth Amendment's prohibition of unreasonable searches. The Constitution's restrictions on government repossession of private property also involve citizens' privacy rights. In 1965, the Supreme Court grounded the right to privacy in the Constitution, arguing that it fits into a "zone of privacy" created by the Third, Fourth, Fifth, and Ninth amendments. The right to privacy has since been used to strike down laws limiting access to birth control, outlawing abortion, and criminalizing same-sex sexual activity.

Key Terms

right to privacy (p. 128)

eminent domain (p. 129)

Practice Quiz

14. In which case was a right to privacy related to the use of birth control first formally recognized by the Supreme Court?
    a) *Griswold v. Connecticut*
    b) *Roe v. Wade*
    c) *Lemon v. Kurtzman*
    d) *Planned Parenthood v. Casey*
    e) *Miranda v. Arizona*

15. In which case did the Supreme Court rule that state governments no longer had the authority to make private sexual conduct a crime?
    a) *Riley v. California*
    b) *Webster v. Reproductive Health Services*
    c) *Gonzales v. Carhart*
    d) *Lawrence v. Texas*
    e) *Bowers v. Hardwick*

★ *chapter* ★

05

Civil Rights

WHAT GOVERNMENT DOES AND WHY IT MATTERS In August 2005, Desmond Meade stood by a railroad track in South Florida, contemplating suicide. Out of prison but homeless and unemployed, he had difficulty getting a job due to his felony record, nor could he vote in Florida, where since 1868 the state's constitution had banned felons from voting. "I didn't see any light at the end of the tunnel. I didn't have any hope or any self-esteem and I was ready to end my life."[1] It was then that Meade vowed to change course. He first attended community college and then earned a law degree from Florida International University.

Despite his degrees, his civil rights remained limited. He still couldn't vote, even when his wife was running for the state legislature.[2] Nor was he able to practice law, as the state's bar association prevented him from sitting for the bar exam. But he put his legal training to use to fight the ban on voting. As president of the Florida Rights Restoration Coalition (FRRC), he lobbied policy makers across the state and gathered more than 750,000 signatures to place an initiative on the November 2018 ballot to restore former felons' voting rights.

Amendment 4 passed with more than 64 percent of the vote. On January 8, 2019, Meade walked into

In 2018, Amendment 4, a ballot initiative to restore voting rights to former felons, passed in Florida thanks to the efforts of the Florida Rights Restoration Coalition and its executive director, Desmond Meade, pictured here.

the Orange County Supervisors of Elections office to register to vote. "The impact of Amendment 4 will be felt for decades to come and I believe that we have not yet even begun to see the impact that it will have," he said. "I don't care about how people vote. What I care about is that they do register to vote if they are eligible and that they get as informed as they possibly can and that they go and vote."[3] He framed his voter registration card and hung it in his office above his law degree.

But Meade's fight isn't over yet. In spring 2019 the Florida legislature passed and Governor Ron DeSantis signed a bill undercutting the amendment. The new law requires felons to pay back all of their court fees and fines before being eligible to vote, threatening to continue the disenfranchisement of hundreds of thousands of former felons.[4] Voting rights groups filed lawsuits, calling the new law a modern-day "poll tax," but in September 2020 a federal appeals court upheld the law.[5] In the face of this requirement, Meade's FRRC organization started a fund to help what it calls "returning citizens" pay off their financial penalties, although disenfranchisement continued because of the state's inability to inform many such citizens of how much they owed.

As we saw in the previous chapter, in the Bill of Rights, civil liberties are phrased as negatives—what government must *not* do. Civil rights, on the other hand, are positives—what the government *must* do to guarantee equal citizenship and protect citizens from discrimination. Civil liberties protect Americans from various forms of governmental abuse. Civil rights regulate *who* can participate in the political process and *how* they can participate: for example, who can vote, who can hold office, who can serve on juries, and when and how citizens can petition the government to take action. Civil rights also define how people are treated in employment, education, and other aspects of American society.

As in the case of civil liberties, Americans agree with the basic principle of civil rights but quarrel frequently over their application. The question of who has the constitutional right to do what underlies some of the major controversies of American history, such as the twentieth-century African American struggle for equal rights known as the civil rights movement. Many of its goals that once aroused bitter opposition are now widely accepted. But even today the question of what is meant by "equal rights" is hardly settled. To what extent can states require racial preferences in college admissions? What rights do undocumented immigrants possess? Do transgender individuals have the right to choose a public restroom on the basis of their gender identification rather than their physical characteristics? And can felons returning to society vote?

As we saw in Chapter 4, the evolution of civil liberties in the United States mainly, though not exclusively, involved the actions of the federal courts. Liberties are limits on government action, and the courts are the institution best situated to tell Congress, the president, and state governments what they may not do. Civil rights, though, involve the government's obligation to act, and the evolution of civil rights has required much more action on the part of Congress and the president.

CHAPTER GOALS

★ Outline the legal developments and social movements that affected civil rights (pp. 141–58)

★ Explain how the courts have evaluated recent civil rights concerns (pp. 158–73)

★ Explain the key Supreme Court decisions on affirmative action (pp. 173–76)

The Struggle for Civil Rights

Outline the legal developments and social movements that affected civil rights

In the United States the history of slavery and legalized racial **discrimination** against African Americans coexists uneasily with a strong tradition of individual liberty. With the adoption of the Fourteenth Amendment in 1868, **civil rights** became part of the Constitution, guaranteed to each citizen through "equal protection of the laws." This **equal protection clause** launched a century of political movements and legal efforts to press for racial equality.

For African Americans, the central fact of political life for most of American history has been a denial of full citizenship rights. By accepting the institution of slavery, the Founders embraced a system fundamentally at odds with the "Blessings of Liberty" promised in the Constitution. Their decision set the stage for two centuries of African American struggles to achieve full citizenship.

For women, electoral politics was a decidedly masculine world. Until 1920, not only were most women barred from voting in national elections, but electoral politics was closely tied to such male social institutions as lodges, bars, and clubs. Yet the exclusion of women from this political world did not prevent them from engaging in public life. Instead, women carved out a "separate sphere" emphasizing female responsibility for moral issues, and they became important voices in social reform well before they won the right to vote.[6] Prior to the Civil War, for example, women played leading roles in the abolitionist movement.

discrimination the use of any unreasonable and unjust criterion of exclusion

civil rights obligation imposed on government to take positive action to protect citizens from any illegal action of government agencies and of other private citizens

equal protection clause provision of the Fourteenth Amendment guaranteeing citizens "the equal protection of the laws." This clause has been the basis for the civil rights of African Americans, women, and other groups

SLAVERY AND THE ABOLITIONIST MOVEMENT

No issue in the nation's history so deeply divided Americans as that of slavery. The importation and subjugation of Africans kidnapped from their native lands was a practice virtually as old as European colonial settlement: the first enslaved people brought to what became the United States arrived in Jamestown, Virginia, in 1619, a year before

Slavery tore the nation apart and ultimately led to the Civil War. The abolition movement organized in the North and pushed to end slavery. Harriet Tubman (far left in photograph) was an abolitionist and formerly enslaved person who helped many enslaved people escape bondage through a system of safe houses called the "Underground Railroad."

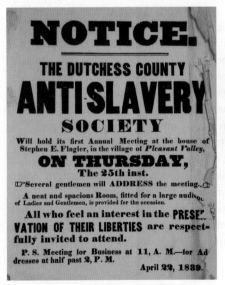

the Plymouth colony was established in Massachusetts. White southerners built their agricultural economy (especially cotton production) on a large slave-labor force. By 1840 nearly half of the populations of Alabama and Louisiana consisted of enslaved Black people. Even so, only about one-quarter of southern White families were slaveowners.

Though a violent and cruel system, slavery became so vital to the economy of the South that efforts to restrict or abolish it met with fierce resistance. Enslaved people periodically revolted against their inhumane treatment but such revolts were always brutally suppressed by state militia forces and local law-enforcement agencies. Although abolitionist sentiment could be traced back to the prerevolutionary era, an abolitionist movement grew among northerners in the 1830s. Soon two political parties emerged from the movement: the staunchly antislavery Liberty Party and the more moderate Free Soil Party, which aimed primarily to restrict slavery from spreading into new western territories. Some opponents of slavery took matters into their own hands, aiding in the escape of freedom-seeking enslaved people along the Underground Railroad. In the South, similarly strong, if opposing, feelings led mobs to break into post offices to destroy antislavery literature.

In 1857 the Supreme Court inflamed this tense atmosphere with its infamous decision in *Dred Scott v. Sanford*. Dred Scott was an enslaved person who sued for his freedom because his owner had taken him to Illinois and the territory of Wisconsin, both of which prohibited slavery. The Court, however, ruled that enslaved people—indeed, all Blacks—were not citizens of the United States and that Scott was his master's permanent property, regardless of his having been taken to a free state or territory.[7] This decision split the country deeply and helped to precipitate the Civil War. From the ashes of that conflict came the Thirteenth, Fourteenth, and Fifteenth amendments, which would redefine civil rights from that time on.

THE WOMEN'S RIGHTS MOVEMENT

Through the nineteenth century, American women were denied rights that most take for granted today. In most American states, women did not have the right to vote, and the doctrine of "coverture," applied by many state courts in the nineteenth century, gave the husband control over his wife's property. Lacking political and property rights, women in the United States were effectively second-class citizens.

Less than 10 years before the Dred Scott decision, the quiet upstate New York town of Seneca Falls played host to what would later come to be known as the starting point of the modern women's movement. Organized by Elizabeth Cady Stanton and Lucretia Mott, the 1848 Seneca Falls Convention drew 300 delegates to formulate plans for advancing the political and social rights of women. The centerpiece of the convention was adoption of a Declaration of Sentiments and Resolutions patterned after the Declaration of Independence; it declared, "We hold these truths to be self-evident: that all men and women are created equal" and "The history of mankind is a history of repeated injuries and usurpations on the part of man toward woman, having in direct object the establishment of an absolute tyranny over her." The most controversial provision of the declaration, nearly rejected as too radical, was the call for the right to vote for women.

Although most of the delegates were women, about 40 men participated, including the renowned abolitionist Frederick Douglass. Stanton and Mott had themselves attended the World Anti-Slavery Convention in London in 1840 but had been denied delegate seats because of their sex. This rebuke helped precipitate the 1848 convention in Seneca Falls.

The convention and its participants were subjected to widespread ridicule, but similar conventions were organized in other states. And in the same year as the Seneca Falls Convention, New York State passed the Married Women's Property Act in order to affirm the right of married women to own property.

THE CIVIL WAR AMENDMENTS TO THE CONSTITUTION

African American hopes for achieving full citizenship seemed fulfilled when three constitutional amendments were adopted soon after the Civil War: the **Thirteenth Amendment** abolished slavery, the **Fourteenth Amendment** guaranteed equal protection and due process under the law, and the **Fifteenth Amendment** guaranteed voting rights for Blacks. Protected by the federal troops occupying the former Confederate states to enforce their "Reconstruction," or reintegration into the Union, African American men in the South (where the overwhelming majority of them lived) began exercising their political rights. Between 1869 and 1877, Blacks were elected to many political offices: two Black senators were elected from Mississippi, and a total of 14 African Americans were elected to the House of Representatives. African Americans also held many state-level political offices. As voters and public officials, Black citizens found a home in the Republican Party, which had sponsored the three constitutional amendments guaranteeing their rights and continued to reach out to them to build Republican strength in the South.[8]

This political equality was short-lived, however. The national government withdrew its troops from the South and turned its back on African Americans in 1877, when Reconstruction ended. In the Compromise of 1877, southern Democrats agreed to allow the Republican candidate, Rutherford B. Hayes, to become president after the disputed 1876 election. In exchange, northern Republicans dropped their support for the civil rights and political participation of African Americans.

After that, southern states erected a "Jim Crow" system of social, political, and economic inequality that made a mockery of the promises in the Constitution. The first **Jim Crow laws** were adopted in the 1870s, in each southern state, to criminalize intermarriage of the races and to segregate railroad travel. These were promptly followed by laws segregating all public accommodations, and within 10 years all southern states had adopted laws segregating public schools.

Even after formerly enslaved men won the right to vote, most politicians in both parties still rejected appeals for women's suffrage. At the state level, a referendum in 1867 to give women the vote in Kansas failed. Frustration over such setbacks intensified suffrage activism. In 1872, Susan B. Anthony and several other women were arrested in Rochester, New York, for illegally registering and voting in that year's national election. (The men who allowed them to do so were also indicted. Anthony paid their expenses and eventually won presidential pardons for them.)

At Anthony's trial, Judge Ward Hunt ordered the jury to find her guilty without deliberation. Yet Anthony was allowed to address the court, saying, "Your denial of my citizen's right to vote is the denial of my right of consent as one of the governed, the denial of my right of representation as one of the taxed, the denial of my right to

---

THE FIRST CONVENTION

EVER CALLED TO DISCUSS THE

Civil and Political Rights of Women,

SENECA FALLS, N. Y., JULY 19, 20, 1848.

———

WOMAN'S RIGHTS CONVENTION.

———

A Convention to discuss the social, civil, and religious condition and rights of woman will be held in the Wesleyan Chapel, at Seneca Falls, N. Y., on Wednesday and Thursday, the 19th and 20th of July current; commencing at 10 o'clock A. M. During the first day the meeting will be exclusively for women, who are earnestly invited to attend. The public generally are invited to be present on the second day, when Lucretia Mott, of Philadelphia, and other ladies and gentlemen, will address the Convention.*

———

* This call was published in the *Seneca County Courier*, July 14, 1848, without any signatures. The movers of this Convention, who drafted the call, the declaration and resolutions were Elizabeth Cady Stanton, Lucretia Mott, Martha C. Wright, Mary Ann McClintock, and Jane C. Hunt.

Many see the Seneca Falls Convention of 1848 as the starting point of the modern women's rights movement. Its Declaration of Sentiments proclaiming equality for women is one of the movement's most important documents.

Thirteenth Amendment one of three Civil War amendments; it abolished slavery

Fourteenth Amendment one of three Civil War amendments; it guaranteed equal protection and due process

Fifteenth Amendment one of three Civil War amendments; it guaranteed voting rights for African American men

Jim Crow laws laws enacted by southern states following Reconstruction that discriminated against African Americans

a trial of my peers as an offender against the law."[9] Hunt assessed Anthony a fine of $100 but did not sentence her to jail. She refused to pay the fine.

CIVIL RIGHTS AND THE SUPREME COURT: "SEPARATE BUT EQUAL"

Resistance to equality for African Americans in the South led Congress to adopt the Civil Rights Act of 1875, which attempted to protect Blacks from discrimination in hotels, theaters, and other public accommodations. But the Supreme Court declared it unconstitutional on the grounds that it applied to *private* businesses, whereas the Fourteenth Amendment, according to the Court's interpretation, was intended to protect against discrimination only by *public* officials of state and local governments.

In the infamous case of *Plessy v. Ferguson* (1896), the Court went still further by upholding a Louisiana law that *required* segregation of the races on trolleys and other public transit (and, by implication, in all public facilities, including schools). Homer Plessy, a man defined as "one-eighth Black," sat in a trolley car reserved for Whites and was found guilty of violating a law providing for "equal but separate accommodations" on trains; it levied a $25 fine on any White passenger who sat in a car reserved for Blacks and on any Black passenger who sat in a car reserved for Whites. The Supreme Court held that the Fourteenth Amendment's equal protection clause was not violated by racial restrictions as long as the facilities were equal. Although "the object of the Amendment was undoubtedly to enforce the absolute equality of the two races before the law," the Court said, "it could not have intended to abolish distinctions based on color, or to enforce social, as distinguished from political, equality, or a commingling of the two races upon terms unsatisfactory to either."[10]

In effect, *Plessy v. Ferguson* legally authorized Whites' use of race to exclude nonwhites and established the **"separate but equal" rule** that prevailed through the

"separate but equal" rule doctrine that public accommodations could be segregated by race but still be considered equal

The 1896 Supreme Court case of *Plessy v. Ferguson* upheld legal segregation and created the "separate but equal" rule, which fostered national segregation. Overt discrimination in public accommodations was common.

mid-twentieth century. As long as some accommodation for Blacks existed, judges in this period generally accepted the pretense that it was equal to that for Whites.

ORGANIZING FOR EQUALITY

The creation of a Jim Crow system in the southern states and the lack of a legal basis for "equal protection of the laws" prompted the beginning of a long process in which African Americans built organizations and devised strategies for asserting their constitutional rights.

The National Association for the Advancement of Colored People One such strategy aimed to win political rights through political pressure and litigation. This approach was championed by the National Association for the Advancement of Colored People (NAACP), established in 1909 by a group of Black and White reformers. Because the northern Black vote was so small in the early 1900s, the NAACP relied primarily on the courts to press for Black political rights. After the 1920s it built a large membership base, with some strength in the South, which would be critical when the civil rights movement gained momentum in the 1950s.

Women's Organizations and the Right to Suffrage The 1886 unveiling in New York Harbor of the Statue of Liberty, depicting liberty as a woman, prompted women's rights advocates to call it "the greatest hypocrisy of the nineteenth century," in that "not one single woman throughout the length and breadth of the Land is as yet in possession of political Liberty."[11] The climactic movement toward women's suffrage had been formally launched in 1878 with the introduction of a proposed constitutional amendment in Congress.

Parallel efforts were made in the states, many of which granted women the right to vote before the national government did. Western states with less entrenched political systems opened politics to women earliest. When Wyoming became a state in 1890, it was the first to grant full suffrage to women. Colorado, Utah, and Idaho all followed suit in the next several years.

Meanwhile, suffrage organizations grew—the National American Woman Suffrage Association (NAWSA), formed in 1890, claimed 2 million members by 1917 and staged mass meetings, parades, petitions, and protests. NAWSA organized

FOR CRITICAL ANALYSIS
What were the consequences of the "separate but equal" policy for southern society and for Blacks' civil rights?

Women fought for decades for the right to vote. The Nineteenth Amendment, ratified in 1920 over the opposition of President Wilson, guaranteed that right. Pictured here on the right are women voting for the first time after the passage of the amendment.

state-by-state efforts to win the right for women to vote. Members of a more militant group, the National Woman's Party, picketed and got arrested in front of the White House to protest President Wilson's opposition to the proposed constitutional amendment. When the Nineteenth Amendment was ratified in 1920, all American women were finally guaranteed the right to vote.

LITIGATING FOR EQUALITY AFTER WORLD WAR II

Reports of discrimination against Black military personnel during World War II, as well as Nazi racial atrocities, moved President Harry S. Truman to finally bring racial discrimination to the nation's attention. In 1946, Truman created the President's Commission on Civil Rights. In its 1948 report, *To Secure These Rights*, the commission severely criticized America's system of racial segregation and suggested ways in which the problem of segregation might be resolved.

Even before the war, the Supreme Court had begun to enforce more strictly the requirement of equal facilities in the "separate but equal" rule. In 1938, for example, the Court rejected Missouri's policy of paying the tuition of Black students at out-of-state law schools rather than admitting them to the University of Missouri Law School.[12] After the war, in 1950, the Court rejected Texas's claim that its new "law school for Negroes" provided education equal to that of the all-White University of Texas Law School, a ruling that opened the question of whether any segregated facilities could be truly equal.[13]

The most important civil rights decision during this period, however, was probably *Shelley v. Kraemer*. In this case, the Court in 1948 outlawed "restrictive covenants" widely used in sales contracts for homes, clauses requiring the buyer never to sell the home to a non-Caucasian, non-Christian, and so on. The Court ruled that such covenants could not be judicially enforced since the Fourteenth Amendment prohibits any organ of the state, including the courts, from denying equal protection of its laws.[14]

None of these three cases directly challenged "separate but equal" or racial discrimination. They did, however, strongly encourage Black leaders to believe that they had the opportunity and legal arguments to change the legal principles used to justify segregation. In 1948 the NAACP's Legal Defense and Educational Fund, which previously had concentrated on winning small victories within the existing framework, upgraded its approach by simultaneously filing suits against "separate but equal" education in different federal district courts and for each level of schooling.

After success in most of these suits, the NAACP lawyers decided the time was ripe to confront the "separate but equal" rule head-on. Their choice to do so was the African American lawyer Thurgood Marshall, who had been fighting, and often winning, equalization suits since the early 1930s. Marshall was pessimistic about whether the Supreme Court was ready to overturn segregation itself and the constitutional principle sustaining it. But the unwillingness of Congress after the 1948 election to consider legislation against job discrimination seems to have convinced him that the courts were the only hope.

Oliver Brown, the father of three girls, lived in a racially mixed neighborhood of Topeka, Kansas. Every school day, his daughter Linda took the school bus to the Monroe Elementary School, for Black children, about a mile away. In September 1950, Linda's father took her to the all-White Sumner School, closer to their home, and tried to enroll her in the third grade, in defiance of state law and local segregation rules. When they were refused, Brown went to the NAACP, and soon thereafter, the case *Brown v. Board of Education* was born.

In the course of its progress through the federal courts, *Brown* was combined with other cases challenging the constitutionality of school segregation in Delaware, South Carolina, Virginia, and the District of Columbia. In 1954, the Supreme Court responded to these cases in one of the most important decisions in its history:

> Does segregation of children in public schools solely on the basis of race, even though the physical facilities and other "tangible" factors may be equal, deprive the children of the minority group of equal educational opportunities? We believe that it does. . . . We conclude that in the field of public education the doctrine of "separate but equal" has no place. Separate educational facilities are inherently unequal.[15]

The *Brown* decision not only altered the constitutional framework by indicating that racial discrimination violated the Constitution; it also signaled more clearly the Court's determination to use the **strict scrutiny** test in cases related to discrimination. That is, the burden of proof would fall on the government to show that the law in question *was* constitutional—not on the challengers to show the law's *un*constitutionality.[16]

CIVIL RIGHTS AFTER *BROWN V. BOARD OF EDUCATION*

Although strict scrutiny would give an advantage to those attacking racial discrimination, the *Brown* decision was merely a small opening move. First, most states refused to obey it until sued, and many ingenious schemes were created to delay obedience (such as paying the tuition for White students to attend newly created "private" academies). Second, even as southern school boards began to eliminate their legally enforced (**de jure**) school segregation, extensive actual (**de facto**) school

Brown v. Board of Education the 1954 Supreme Court decision that struck down the "separate but equal" doctrine as fundamentally unequal; this case eliminated state power to use race as a criterion of discrimination in law and provided the national government with the power to intervene by exercising strict regulatory policies against discriminatory actions

strict scrutiny a test used by the Supreme Court in racial discrimination cases and other cases involving civil liberties and civil rights that places the burden of proof on the government rather than on the challengers to show that the law in question is constitutional

de jure literally, "by law"; refers to legally enforced practices, such as school segregation in the South before the 1960s

de facto literally, "by fact"; refers to practices that occur even when there is no legal enforcement, such as school segregation in much of the United States today

"Massive resistance" among White southerners attempted to Block the desegregation efforts of the national government. For example, at Little Rock Central High School in 1957, an angry mob of White students prevented Black students from entering the school.

FOR CRITICAL ANALYSIS

Describe the changes in American society between the *Plessy v. Ferguson* and the *Brown v. Board of Education* decisions. How have changes in civil rights policy since the *Brown* case impacted society?

segregation remained, in the North as well as in the South, as a consequence of racially segregated housing. Third, discrimination in employment, public accommodations, juries, voting, and other areas of political, social, and economic activity was not directly affected by *Brown*.

School Desegregation, Phase One Although the District of Columbia and some school districts in the border states almost immediately began desegregation, state governments in the South responded with a carefully planned delaying tactic commonly called "massive resistance." Southern politicians stood shoulder to shoulder to declare that the Supreme Court's decisions had no effect. Southern state legislatures passed laws ordering school districts to maintain segregated schools and state superintendents to cut off state funding to districts that did not. Some southern states centralized public school authority under the governor or the state board of education and gave these officials the power to close the schools and provide alternative private schooling wherever local school boards began desegregation.

Most of these "massive resistance" plans were struck down by federal courts as unconstitutional.[17] But southern resistance was not confined to legislation. Perhaps the most serious incident occurred in Arkansas in 1957, when Governor Orval Faubus mobilized the Arkansas National Guard to intercede against enforcement of a federal court order to integrate Little Rock Central High School. In response, President Dwight Eisenhower deployed U.S. troops and placed Little Rock under martial law. The Supreme Court considered the Little Rock confrontation so historically important that its opinion upholding the court order was not only agreed to unanimously but also, uniquely in the Court's history, signed personally by every justice.[18]

The end of massive resistance, however, became simply the beginning of still another southern strategy to delay desegregation. "Pupil placement" laws avoided any mention of race but authorized school districts to assign each student to a school based on various academic, personal, and psychological considerations. This strategy put the burden on nonwhite children and their parents to request individual transfers to all-White schools, making it almost impossible for a single court order to cover a whole district, let alone a whole state.[19]

Social Protest after *Brown* Ten years after *Brown*, therefore, fewer than 1 percent of Black school-age children in the Deep South were attending schools with Whites,[20] making it fairly obvious that the goal of "equal protection" required not just court decisions but also positive, or affirmative, action by Congress and administrative agencies. And given massive southern resistance and only lukewarm northern support for racial integration, progress clearly also required intense, well-organized support. Figure 5.1 shows the increase in the number of civil rights demonstrations for voting rights and public accommodations during the years following *Brown*.

The number of organized demonstrations began to mount slowly but surely after *Brown v. Board of Education*. Only a year later, African Americans in Montgomery, Alabama, challenged the city's segregated bus system with a yearlong boycott that began with the arrest of Rosa Parks, who refused to give up her seat to a White man. Parks eventually became a civil rights icon, as did one of the ministers leading the boycott, Martin Luther King, Jr. A year of private carpools and walking ended with

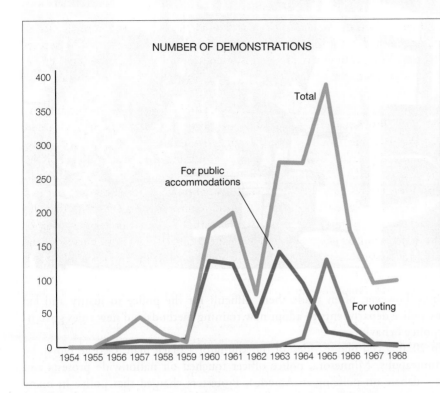

NUMBER OF DEMONSTRATIONS

Total

For public accommodations

For voting

1954 1955 1956 1957 1958 1959 1960 1961 1962 1963 1964 1965 1966 1967 1968

Note: The data are drawn from a search of the *New York Times* index for all references to civil rights demonstrations.
SOURCE: Jonathan D. Casper, *The Politics of Civil Liberties* (New York: Harper and Row, 1972), 90.

FIGURE 5.1
. . . .
Peaceful Civil Rights Demonstrations, 1954–68

Peaceful demonstrations were an important part of the civil rights movement. Why did the number of demonstrations grow after 1955? Why do you think the focus shifted from public accommodations to voting rights after 1964?

Montgomery's bus system desegregated, but only after the Supreme Court ruled the system unconstitutional.

By the 1960s the Southern Christian Leadership Conference, the Student Non-violent Coordinating Committee, and the many other organizations that made up the civil rights movement had built networks capable of launching large-scale direct-action campaigns against southern segregationists. The movement stretched across the South and used the media to attract nationwide attention and support. Images of protesters being beaten, attacked by police dogs, and set upon with fire hoses did much to win broad sympathy for the cause of Black civil rights and to discredit state and local governments in the South. In the massive March on Washington in 1963, the Reverend Martin Luther King, Jr., staked out the movement's moral claims in his famous "I Have a Dream" speech. Steadily, the movement created intense pressure for a reluctant federal government to take more assertive steps to defend Black civil rights.

Protests against discriminatory treatment of African Americans did not end in the 1960s. In recent years, a variety of protests coalesced under the banner Black Lives Matter to focus attention on allegations of police misconduct toward African Americans. The movement took off in Ferguson, Missouri, after the shooting of an unarmed Black man by a White police officer and spread across the nation, often via social media, which presented live photos and videos taken by cell phone cameras. African Americans had long asserted that they were often victims of racial profiling and more likely than Whites to be harassed, physically harmed, or arrested by the police. Police departments had often replied that Blacks were more likely than Whites to commit crimes. Visual evidence of

The struggle for African American civil rights has spanned decades. Among the key moments are Rosa Parks and the Montgomery Bus Boycott (1955–56), sit-ins at segregated lunch counters throughout the South, the March on Washington and Martin Luther King, Jr.'s famous "I Have a Dream" speech (1963), and the Black Lives Matter movement that persists today.

killings, however, often made them difficult for the police to justify and led many police departments to adopt new training methods and new rules governing police behavior.

In 2020, a cell phone video of the killing of a Black man, George Floyd, by a Minneapolis, Minnesota, police officer touched off nationwide protests and a new debate on policing in America. Protesters charged that police in many cities commonly treated African Americans with disrespect and brutality. In New York, Seattle, Minneapolis, and elsewhere protesters demanded that police departments be "defunded" and replaced with alternative public safety institutions focused on fighting poverty and defusing conflict. Critics charged that the idea of eliminating the police was utopian and would simply lead to more crime and violence. Most Americans agreed that police departments should receive better training, that officers with records of abuse should be promptly fired, and that new approaches to public safety, including expanded social services in poor and minority communities, should be found.

THE CIVIL RIGHTS ACTS

In enforcing civil rights, the courts, legislatures, and administrative agencies all play important roles: the legislatures need constitutional authority to act, and the courts need legislative and administrative assistance to implement judicial orders. Consequently, even as the U.S. Congress finally became involved in school desegregation (and other areas of "equal protection"), the courts continued to exercise their powers, not only by issuing orders against resistant school districts but also by extending and reinterpreting aspects of the equal protection clause to support legislative and administrative actions (see Table 5.1).

Three civil rights acts were passed in the years immediately following the 1954 Supreme Court decision in *Brown v. Board of Education*. Most important was the Civil Rights Act of 1964, which attacked discrimination in public accommodations, segregation in the schools, and, at long last, discrimination by employers in hiring, promoting, and laying off employees. Discrimination against women was also included, extending important provisions of the 1963 civil rights act.

The ban on discrimination in some businesses was made possible because over the previous 20 years, the federal courts had come to agree that the clause in the Constitution empowering Congress to regulate interstate commerce also allowed it to regulate commercial activity broadly defined. And this time, when southern business owners challenged the law, the Supreme Court upheld it.

Public Accommodations After the 1964 Civil Rights Act was passed, public accommodations quickly removed some of the most blatant forms of racial discrimination, such as signs labeling "colored" and "White" restrooms, water fountains, waiting rooms, and seating arrangements. In addition, the federal government filed more than 400 antidiscrimination suits in federal courts against hotels, restaurants, taverns, gas stations, and other establishments.

Many aspects of legalized racial segregation—such as separate Bibles to swear in Black and White witnesses in the courtroom—seem like ancient history today. But the issue of racial discrimination in public settings is by no means over. In 2014, for example, an African American customer at a Vancouver, Washington, restaurant noticed that he was being asked to pay for his food before it was served while White customers were not. The case was settled out of court for an undisclosed amount.[21] But some forms of such discrimination, such as taxi drivers' refusing to pick up Black passengers,[22] are difficult to prove or prevent through laws.

School Desegregation, Phase Two The 1964 Civil Rights Act also declared discrimination by state governments and their agencies (such as school boards) illegal and created administrative agencies to help the courts implement laws against it. Title IV of the act, for example, authorized the Justice Department to implement federal court orders for school desegregation without waiting for individual parents to bring complaints. Title VI of the act vastly strengthened the role of the executive branch and the credibility of court orders by providing that federal grants-in-aid for education must be withheld from any school system practicing racial segregation.

Title VI became the most effective weapon for desegregating schools outside the South, because segregation in northern school districts was subtler and more

TABLE 5.1

Cause and Effect in the Civil Rights Movement

Political action and government action worked in tandem to produce dramatic changes in American civil rights policies.

JUDICIAL AND LEGAL ACTION	POLITICAL ACTION
1954 *Brown v. Board of Education*	**1955** Montgomery, Alabama, bus boycott
1956 Federal courts order school integration; of special note is one ordering that Autherine Lucy be admitted to the University of Alabama, with Governor Wallace officially protesting	
1957 Civil Rights Act creating Civil Rights Commission; President Eisenhower sends 101st Airborne Division paratroops to Little Rock, Arkansas, to enforce integration of Central High School	**1957** Southern Christian Leadership Conference formed, with Martin Luther King, Jr., as president
1960 First substantive Civil Rights Act, primarily voting rights	**1960** Student Nonviolent Coordinating Committee formed to organize protests, sit-ins, freedom rides
1961 Interstate Commerce Commission orders desegregation on all buses and trains and in terminals; President Kennedy (JFK) favors executive action over civil rights legislation	
1963 JFK shifts, supports strong civil rights law; JFK's assassination; President Johnson asserts strong support for civil rights	**1963** Nonviolent demonstrations in Birmingham, Alabama, lead to King's arrest and his "Letter from Birmingham Jail"; March on Washington
1964 Congress passes historic Civil Rights Act covering voting, employment, public accommodations, education	
1965 Voting Rights Act	**1965** King announces drive to register 3 million Blacks in the South
1966 War on Poverty in full swing	**Late 1960s** Movement diverges: part toward litigation, part toward community action programs, part toward war protest, part toward more militant "Black Power" actions

FOR CRITICAL ANALYSIS

Brown v. Board of Education led to the end of de jure segregation. However, de facto segregation remains in many areas, including housing and schooling. Should there be legal or social efforts to address de facto segregation?

difficult to address. In the South, the problem was segregation by law coupled with open resistance to the national government's efforts to change the situation. In contrast, outside the South, the instruments of segregation were more subtle. These included such practices as "redlining," through which banks declined to offer mortgages in Black neighborhoods; school district boundaries seemingly neutral but actually conforming to segregated neighborhood patterns; and restrictive covenants written into private real estate deeds designed to prevent the sale of homes to nonwhite buyers. These practices often resulted in de facto segregation without a clear legal or "de jure" basis. To address this problem, the 1964 Civil Rights Act gave (1) the president, through the Justice Department's Office for Civil Rights, the power to withhold federal education grants[23] and (2) the attorney general of the United States the power to initiate suits (rather than having to await complaints) wherever there was a "pattern or practice" of discrimination.[24]

In the following decade, the Justice Department made a particular effort to desegregate America's public schools. It sued more than 500 school districts while other federal administrative agencies sued 600 districts, threatening to suspend federal aid to them unless real desegregation steps were taken. One step that had the potential to reduce segregation in the schools was busing children across existing school district boundaries to ensure that Black and White children would attend school together.

In 1971 the Supreme Court held that state-imposed desegregation could be brought about by busing children across school districts.[25] Under certain circumstances, the Court said, even racial quotas could be used as the "starting point in shaping a remedy to correct past constitutional violations," and pairing or grouping schools and reorganizing attendance zones would also be acceptable. Three years later, however, this principle was severely restricted when the Court determined that only districts found guilty of deliberate and de jure racial segregation would have to desegregate their schools,[26] effectively exempting most northern states and cities from busing.

The prospects for further school integration diminished with a 1991 Supreme Court decision holding that lower federal courts could end supervision of local school districts that could show "good faith" compliance with court orders to desegregate and evidence that "vestiges of past discrimination" had been eliminated "to the extent practicable."[27] It was not necessarily easy for a district to prove that the new standard had been met, but this was the first time since *Brown* and the 1964 Civil Rights Act that the Court had opened the door at all to retreat.

In a 2007 ruling, the Court limited school-integration measures still further.[28] By making race one factor in assigning students to schools, the cities of Seattle, Washington, and Louisville, Kentucky, had hoped to achieve greater racial balance across their school systems. The Court ruled, however, that these plans were unconstitutional because there was no compelling government interest in using race as a criterion in assigning students to schools. Many observers described the decision as the end of the *Brown* era because it attacked one of the few government strategies that might have promoted racial integration in America's public schools. According to many studies, school segregation, mainly based upon residential patterns, continues to be a persistent feature of American life.

Outlawing Discrimination in Employment Despite the agonizingly slow progress of school desegregation, some progress was made in other areas of civil rights during the 1960s and '70s. Voting rights were established and fairly quickly began to revolutionize southern politics. Service on juries was no longer denied to minorities. But progress in the right to participate in politics and government dramatized the relative lack of progress in the economic domain, where battles over civil rights were increasingly being fought.

The federal courts and the Justice Department entered this area through Title VII of the Civil Rights Act of 1964, which outlawed job discrimination by all private and public employers, including governmental agencies (such as fire and police departments) that employed more than 15 workers. Title VII makes it unlawful to discriminate in employment on the basis of color, religion, sex, or national origin, as well as race.

Title VII delegated some of the powers to enforce fair-employment practices to the Justice Department's Civil Rights Division and others to a new agency created in the 1964 act, the Equal Employment Opportunity Commission (EEOC).

By executive order, these agencies had the power to revoke or prohibit federal contracts for goods and services with any private company that could not guarantee that its rules for hiring, promotion, and firing were nondiscriminatory. And in 1972, President Nixon and a Democratic Congress cooperated to strengthen the EEOC by giving it authority to initiate suits rather than wait for grievances.

But one problem with Title VII was that the accusing party (the plaintiff) had to show that deliberate discrimination was the cause of the failure to get a job or a training opportunity. The courts have since allowed plaintiffs to make their case if they can show that an employer's hiring practices had the *effect* of exclusion. A leading case in 1971 involved a "class action" by several Black employees in North Carolina attempting to show with statistical evidence that the Duke Power Company had restricted Blacks to the least desirable manual-labor jobs by adding a high school education and passage of aptitude tests as qualifications for higher jobs. The Supreme Court held that although the statistical evidence did not prove intentional discrimination and the requirements were race-neutral in appearance, their effects were sufficient to shift the legal burden to the employer to show that they were a "business necessity" with "a demonstrable relationship to successful performance."[29] The ruling in this case was subsequently applied to other hiring, promotion, and training programs.[30]

Voting Rights In the 1965 Voting Rights Act, Congress significantly strengthened voting rights protections by barring literacy and other tests as a condition for voting in six southern states,[31] by setting criminal penalties for interference with efforts to vote, and by providing for the replacement of local registrars with federally appointed ones in counties designated by the attorney general as significantly resistant to registering eligible Blacks to vote. The right to vote was further strengthened in 1964 with ratification of the Twenty-Fourth Amendment, which abolished the poll tax, and in 1975 with legislation permanently outlawing literacy tests in all 50 states and mandating bilingual ballots or oral assistance for Spanish, Chinese, Japanese, and Korean speakers and for Native Americans and Alaska natives.

In the long run, the laws extending and protecting voting rights could prove to be the most effective of all the great civil rights legislation because the progress in Black political participation produced by these acts has altered the shape of American politics. In 1965, in the seven states of the Old Confederacy covered by the Voting Rights Act, 29.3 percent of the eligible Black residents were registered to vote, compared with 73.4 percent of the White residents (see Table 5.2). By 1972 the racial gap in registration was only 11.2 points. And today, more African Americans hold public office in the states of the Deep South than in the North.

Several provisions of the 1965 act were scheduled to expire in 2007, but Congress renewed the act for another 25 years in 2006 after the U.S. Commission on Civil Rights charged that Black voters still faced extensive discrimination at the polls. At the commission's hearings on the disputed 2000 presidential election in Florida, Black voters testified about being turned away from the polls and wrongly purged from the voting rolls and about the unreliable voting technology in their neighborhoods.[32]

More recently, Texas was accused of **gerrymandering** congressional districts so as to discriminate against Latino voters. Due to population growth, most of it among Latinos, Texas gained four new congressional seats after the 2010 census. The heavily Republican state legislature redrew the state's map of congressional districts to ensure that three of the new ones would almost certainly elect Republicans. However, a

gerrymandering the apportionment of voters in districts in such a way as to give unfair advantage to one racial or ethnic group or political party

TABLE 5.2

Registration by Race and State in Southern States Covered by the Voting Rights Act (VRA)

The VRA had a direct impact on the rate of Black voter registration in the southern states, as measured by the gap between White and Black voters in each state. Further insights can be gained by examining changes in White registration rates before and after passage of the VRA and by comparing the gaps between White and Black registration. Why do you think registration rates for Whites increased significantly in some states and dropped in others? What impact could the increase in Black registration have had on public policy?

	BEFORE THE ACT*			AFTER THE ACT* 1971–72		
	WHITE	BLACK	GAP**	WHITE	BLACK	GAP
Alabama	69.2%	19.3%	**49.9%**	80.7%	57.1%	**23.6%**
Georgia	62.6	27.4	**35.2**	70.6	67.8	**2.8**
Louisiana	80.5	31.6	**48.9**	80.0	59.1	**20.9**
Mississippi	69.9	6.7	**63.2**	71.6	62.2	**9.4**
North Carolina	96.8	46.8	**50.0**	62.2	46.3	**15.9**
South Carolina	75.7	37.3	**38.4**	51.2	48.0	**3.2**
Virginia	61.1	38.3	**22.8**	61.2	54.0	**7.2**
TOTAL	73.4	29.3	**44.1**	67.8	56.6	**11.2**

*Available registration data as of March 1965 and 1971–72.
**The gap is the percentage-point difference between White and Black registration rates.
SOURCE: U.S. Commission on Civil Rights, *Political Participation* (1968), Appendix VII: Voter Education Project, attachment to press release, October 3, 1972.

coalition of minority groups and the Justice Department charged that the map failed to create a sufficient number of majority-minority districts. After extensive legal wrangling, the new redistricting plan included three majority-minority districts.[33]

The 1965 Voting Rights Act had also required some state and local governments with a history of voting discrimination to obtain prior federal approval, or preclearance, for any changes to their voting laws or practices. In the 2013 case *Shelby County v. Holder*, however, the Supreme Court overturned the formula for determining which governments needed preclearance, saying it was based on data more than 40 years old.[34]

A more recent controversy over voting rights concerns so-called voter ID laws. Most states have enacted legislation requiring voters to show identification before they cast a ballot, and some require a specific form with a photograph. Republicans generally support such laws, arguing that they deter voter fraud. Democrats generally oppose them, saying they are designed to discourage poor and minority voters, who are less likely than others to possess such IDs. Each party, of course, sees an advantage in its position. ID laws tend to hurt the Democrats and help the GOP. Cases challenging voter ID laws on equal protection grounds have met mixed success. In 2008 the Supreme Court upheld the constitutionality of Indiana's law, affirming the state's "valid interest" in improving election procedures and deterring fraud.[35] On the other hand, in 2013 the Court struck down an Arizona law requiring proof of U.S. citizenship in order to register to vote. Voter ID laws have been struck down or modified by courts in several states, and the Supreme Court will likely be asked to offer a definitive ruling on the matter in the near future.

In the 2020 primary and general elections, many states sought to expand voting by mail procedures to bolster turnout and to guard against the spread of coronavirus in voting lines. Democrats have generally lauded this effort while Republicans have viewed mail-in voting with some suspicion. Historically, Republicans have benefited from mail balloting since they appeal to older voters who prefer to avoid a trip to the polling station, but the GOP fears that expansion of mail-in voting would make it easier for Democratic campaign workers to mobilize young and minority voters who generally support the Democrats but often do not go to the polls.

Housing The Civil Rights Act of 1964 did not address housing, but in 1968 Congress passed another law specifically to prohibit housing discrimination. Called the Fair Housing Act, it eventually covered the sale or rental of nearly all the nation's housing. Housing was among the most controversial discrimination issues because of entrenched patterns of residential segregation across the country. Besides the lingering effects of restrictive covenants, local authorities had deliberately segregated public housing, and federal guidelines had allowed discrimination in Federal Housing Administration mortgage lending, effectively preventing Blacks from joining the movement to the suburbs in the 1950s and '60s.

At first, however, the Fair Housing Act had little effect because its enforcement mechanisms were so weak. Individuals had to file suit and prove that they had been discriminated against, but housing discrimination is often subtle and difficult to document. Although local fair-housing groups emerged to assist in suits, the procedures for proving discrimination remained quite challenging until Congress passed the Fair Housing Amendments Act in 1988. This law put more teeth in the enforcement mechanisms and allowed the Department of Housing and Urban Development (HUD) to initiate legal action in cases of discrimination.[36]

Efforts to prohibit discrimination in lending have met some success. Several laws passed in the 1970s required banks to report information about their mortgage-lending patterns, making it more difficult for them to engage in **redlining**, the practice of refusing to lend to buyers in entire neighborhoods. The 1977 Community Reinvestment Act required banks to lend in neighborhoods in which they do business. Through vigorous use of this act, many neighborhood organizations have reached agreements with banks that have resulted in significantly increased investment in poor neighborhoods.

Even so, racial discrimination in home mortgage lending remains a significant issue. In 2007 the issue of predatory lending—offering loans well above market rates, often with complex provisions that borrowers do not understand—attracted nationwide attention as the number of home foreclosures skyrocketed. In 2009 civil rights organizations, several states, and some cities filed charges against banks and other lenders claiming they had illegally discriminated against African American and Latino home buyers. These buyers, the suits charged, had been offered mortgages with higher interest rates than had Whites with similar income levels. By 2012 some of these lawsuits had resulted in the largest financial settlements ever issued for lending discrimination.

Marriage The Civil Rights Act of 1964 was also silent on interracial marriage, which 16 states continued to outlaw in 1967. In that year, the Supreme Court ruled in *Loving v. Virginia* that such state laws were unconstitutional. The case concerned

redlining a practice in which banks refuse to make loans to people living in certain geographic locations

a Virginia couple, a White man and a Black woman, who married in Washington, D.C., where such unions were legal. When they moved back to Virginia, they were charged with violating the state's law against interracial marriage. The Lovings moved back to Washington and challenged the Virginia law. In striking such laws down, the Court declared marriage "one of the 'basic civil rights of man,' fundamental to our very existence and survival."[37]

Mass Incarceration Some have argued that mass incarceration and the disenfranchisement of former convicts is a key civil rights issue. More than 2.2 million Americans are currently incarcerated, most in state prisons and local jails. African Americans account for about one-third of these inmates, though making up only about 12 percent of the U.S. population. About 20 percent of prison inmates, including many African Americans, are minor drug offenders who received harsh mandatory sentences stemming from the "war on drugs" begun in the 1970s and 1980s. Another 20 percent of inmates are awaiting trial and too poor to post bail. African Americans make up a substantial percentage of this group as well. The result is that large numbers of African Americans, mainly but not exclusively men, are in prison awaiting trial or for relatively minor drug offenses.

The Supreme Court ruled in 1967 that state laws banning interracial marriage were unconstitutional. The case *Loving v. Virginia* was invoked numerous times in the Court's decision almost 50 years later that declared marriage a fundamental right for same-sex couples.

The years-long incarceration of hundreds of thousands of African American men contributes to reduced supervision of teenagers and increased social disruption in the Black community. Moreover, when they leave prison, these individuals have few, if any, legitimate employment opportunities and instead make use of the criminal skills honed during prison life. In these ways, mass incarceration has produced, more than solved, social problems. Citing these issues, before he left office in 2016 President Obama issued pardons and commutations to several hundred drug offenders. Mass incarceration will be a major problem until America finds other ways to address drug abuse and crime.

Former prison inmates often lose their voting rights. Since many are poor and members of minority groups, the Democratic Party has pushed for restoration of

The prosecution of minor drug offenses, among other crimes, has led to a growing prison population in the United States. Mass incarceration has led to overcrowded prisons with poor conditions, like this prison in Lancaster, California, which houses twice the number of inmates the facility intended to hold.

voting rights to former inmates. For the same reason, the GOP has resisted the effort. As we saw with the story of Desmond Meade at the beginning of the chapter, Florida has recently restored voting rights to felons released from prison and several other states may follow suit.

Extending Civil Rights

Explain how the courts have evaluated recent civil rights concerns

Title VII of the 1964 Civil Rights Act prohibited discrimination not only against African Americans but against other groups as well, prohibiting discrimination based upon such characteristics as gender, religion, and national origin. Eventually other groups also sought protection under Title VII, asserting that the law implied that discrimination based upon such factors as age or sexual orientation was also prohibited.

LEVELS OF SCRUTINY UNDER THE EQUAL PROTECTION CLAUSE

Before we examine the civil rights movements of the past 60 years, it is useful to describe how the courts have analyzed laws in cases where an individual or group has claimed discrimination. Recall that civil rights are the rules governing who may participate in the political process and regulating the ways in which the government may or may not treat citizens. The equal protection clause of the Fourteenth Amendment does not require that everyone be treated equally. State and federal laws often create classifications allowing some, but not other, individuals to engage in activities or receive benefits. States, for example, allow only those with certain qualifications to engage in various occupations (such as medical professions) and set a minimum age for driving automobiles, voting, and consuming alcohol.

Courts generally recognize the need for such systems of classification. Other systems, however, such as those based on race, gender, or religion, raise serious constitutional questions. When dealing with challenges to state-imposed systems of classification, the courts use a three-tiered approach, placing a greater burden of proof on the government to defend some types of systems than it does to defend others. The three tiers are often called "levels of scrutiny."

First Level The first and lowest level of scrutiny is applied by the courts to most state and federal regulatory schemes, such as motor vehicle and occupational licensing, as well as to laws setting a minimum age for the purchase of alcohol and cigarettes. Here, the courts will generally apply the "rational basis test." Under this level of scrutiny, the burden of proof is on the plaintiff to show that there is no rational basis whatsoever for the government's rules. Doing so is extremely difficult, and few plaintiffs succeed.

intermediate scrutiny a test used by the Supreme Court in gender discrimination cases that places the burden of proof partially on the government and partially on the challengers to show that the law in question is unconstitutional

Second Level The next level of judicial scrutiny of state action is **intermediate scrutiny**. Here, there is a greater burden on the government to show that its classification scheme not only is rational but also serves an important interest or purpose. Courts generally apply intermediate scrutiny to laws that treat men and women differently or discriminate against the inheritance and property rights of illegitimate children. In recent years, federal courts have generally applied intermediate scrutiny in cases involving sexual orientation. For example, in the 2013 case

Have Women Achieved Equal Rights?

Title VII of the 1964 Civil Rights Act prohibits gender discrimination, and the Supreme Court has consistently upheld the principle that women should have the same rights as men. Since 1960 the United States has made great strides toward gender equality in some areas but, as the data show, still has a long way to go in other areas.

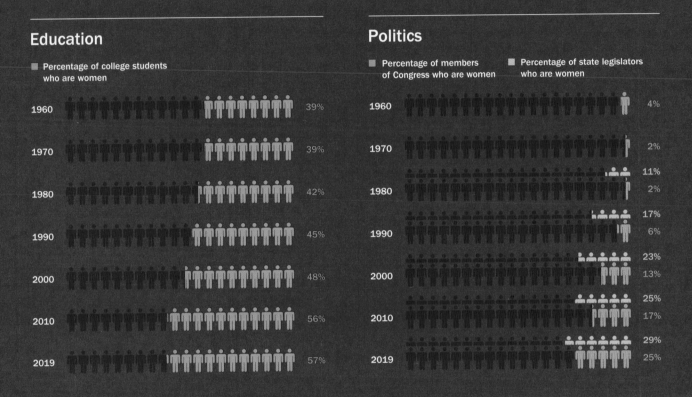

Education

■ Percentage of college students who are women

Year	%
1960	39%
1970	39%
1980	42%
1990	45%
2000	48%
2010	56%
2019	57%

Politics

■ Percentage of members of Congress who are women   ■ Percentage of state legislators who are women

Year	Congress	State legislators
1960		4%
1970		2%
1980	11%	2%
1990	17%	6%
2000	23%	13%
2010	25%	17%
2019	29%	25%

Median Weekly Earnings by Race and Gender

White women earned 80 percent as much as their male counterparts, compared with 91.8 percent for Black women, 78.3 percent for Asian women, and 86.7 percent for Latina women.

White		African American		Latino		Asian American	
Men	Women	Men	Women	Men	Women	Men	Women
$1,033	$826	$772	$709	$728	$631	$1,299	$1,017

SOURCE: Data from the Bureau of Labor Statistics, Congressional Research Service, and National Conference of State Legislatures (accessed 9/25/19).

FOR CRITICAL ANALYSIS

1. How much does each of these factors—education, political office, and income—say about gender equality in the United States?

2. While most Americans support the principle of equal opportunity for all groups, there is disagreement over how much the government should do to ensure equal outcomes. Discuss the difference between equal opportunity and equal outcomes in the context of women's rights.

of *Windsor v. United States* the Second Circuit Courts of Appeals used intermediate scrutiny in finding that the federal Defense of Marriage Act, which applied the terms *marriage* and *spouse* only to heterosexual unions, was unconstitutional.[38] The Supreme Court affirmed the decision but did not indicate which level of scrutiny it had applied.

Third Level The highest level of scrutiny employed by the courts, "strict scrutiny," places the burden of proof on the government to show that discrimination serves a "compelling interest," that the law is "narrowly tailored to achieve that goal," and that the government has used the "least restrictive means" for achieving it. Strict scrutiny generally applies to laws that discriminate on the basis of race, religion, or national origin, which are termed *suspect classifications*. It also applies to laws that interfere with the exercise of fundamental rights, such as access to the courts or the right to vote. When a federal court employs strict scrutiny, the government is seldom able to meet its burden of proof. All race-based classifications are automatically subject to strict scrutiny.[39]

In 2013 the Supreme Court also applied strict scrutiny to a case involving a claim of "reverse discrimination." In the case of *Fisher v. University of Texas*, a White plaintiff charged that she had been rejected for admission to the university in favor of less qualified minority applicants.[40] The Supreme Court instructed a lower federal court to reconsider the case and apply strict scrutiny to the admissions process. The court of appeals still rejected Fisher's claim, however, and in 2016 the Supreme Court upheld the university's procedures.[41]

WOMEN AND GENDER DISCRIMINATION

In many ways Title VII fostered the growth of the women's movement in the 1960s and '70s. The first major campaign of the National Organization for Women (NOW) involved picketing the EEOC for its refusal to ban sex-segregated job advertisements. NOW also sued the *New York Times* for continuing to publish such ads after the passage of Title VII. Another organization, the Women's Equity Action League (WEAL), pursued legal action on a wide range of issues, suing law schools and medical schools for discriminatory admission policies, for example.

Building on their success in these efforts, feminist activists proposed an "Equal Rights Amendment" (ERA) to the Constitution, stating simply that "equality of rights under the law shall not be denied or abridged by the United States or by any State on account of sex." Supporters believed that such a sweeping guarantee was necessary to end discrimination against women and make gender roles more equal. Opponents, however, charged that it would introduce disruptive changes (such as unisex restrooms) that most Americans did not want. The amendment easily passed Congress in 1972 and won quick approval in many state legislatures, but it fell 3 states short of the 38 needed to ratify it by the 1982 deadline.[42] In the years since 1982, more states ratified the ERA, seeming to push it over the 38-state barrier. However, in the meantime, several states rescinded their earlier approvals and there seems to be no legal basis for overturning the seven-year deadline originally specified by Congress.

Despite the failure of the ERA, beginning in the 1970s the conservative Supreme Court under Chief Justice Warren Burger helped establish gender discrimination as a major and highly visible civil rights issue. While refusing to treat it as the equivalent of racial discrimination,[43] the Court did make it easier for plaintiffs to file and win gender-discrimination suits by applying an "intermediate" level of scrutiny in these cases, as described earlier.[44]

In recent years, laws and court decisions designed to deal with discrimination against women have been used to press for equal rights for transgender people, especially in employment. For example, in 2015 President Obama issued an executive order prohibiting federal contractors from discriminating against workers based on their sexual orientation or gender identity, and the EEOC filed its first-ever lawsuits to protect transgender workers under Title VII.

Controversy arose after some states passed laws requiring transgender individuals to use public bathrooms that correspond to the gender designated on their birth certificates. In 2016, North Carolina enacted such a law, leading to boycotts and protests, with several corporations announcing plans to reduce their operations in the state. When the Department of Justice warned North Carolina that the law violated the Civil Rights Act, the state sued the federal government over the issue. In 2017, the law was repealed under pressure from the business community.

More recently, President Trump banned transgender individuals from joining the military, though those already in the armed forces would generally be allowed to continue.

Equality in Education Title IX of the 1972 Education Act outlawed gender discrimination in education but led to few lawsuits until the Supreme Court's 1992 ruling, in *Franklin v. Gwinnett County Public Schools*, that monetary damages could be awarded for gender discrimination.[45] In the two years after the *Franklin* case, complaints to the Education Department's Office for Civil Rights about unequal treatment of women's athletic programs nearly tripled. In several high-profile legal cases, prominent universities were ordered to create more women's sports programs, prompting many other schools to follow suit to avoid potential litigation.[46]

In 1997 the Supreme Court refused to hear a petition by Brown University challenging a lower-court order that the university establish strict sex equity in its athletic programs. The decision meant a school's varsity athletic positions for men and women must reflect its overall enrollment numbers.[47] Though the ruling has had a major impact on college athletic programs, advocates for gender equality note that gender barriers continue in important fields such as science, technology, engineering, and math, which female students are much less likely to enter.[48]

Sexual Harassment Largely through interpretation of Title VII of the 1964 Civil Rights Act, during the late 1970s courts began to find sexual harassment to be a form of sex discrimination. In 1986 the Supreme Court recognized two forms of sexual harassment. One is "quid pro quo" harassment, an explicit or strongly implied threat that submission is a condition of continued employment. The second is harassment that creates offensive or intimidating working conditions amounting to a "hostile environment."[49]

Employers and many employees have complained that "hostile environment" sexual harassment is too vague. When can an employee bring charges? When is the employer legally responsible? In 1986 and 1993 cases, the Court said that conduct may meet the legal definition of sexual harassment even if the employee did not suffer tangible economic or job-related losses or tangible psychological costs because of it.[50] In two 1998 cases, the Court further strengthened the law when it said that whether or not harassment causes economic harm to the employee, the employer

FOR CRITICAL ANALYSIS

Has Title IX created equality in men's and women's college athletic programs? Should there be public efforts to encourage more female students to enter well-paid fields such as science and technology, or is that mainly a matter of individual choice?

Gains for women in the area of civil rights have come, but slowly. Title IX of the 1972 Education Act has helped promote gender equality in education and helped increase women's participation in college sports, though women continue to be underrepresented in science, technology, engineering, and math. In 2009, President Obama signed the Lilly Ledbetter Fair Pay Act to help combat pay discrimination. After serving in the military for decades, women were finally allowed to serve in combat in 2013. Despite these steps forward, gender inequity persists in American life.

is financially liable if someone with authority over the employee committed it—a supervisor, for example. But the Court also said that an employer may defend itself by showing that it had a sexual harassment prevention and grievance policy in effect.[51]

In 2011 the Department of Education's Office of Civil Rights (OCR) issued a "Dear Colleague" letter to the more than 7,000 colleges and universities receiving federal money, advising them, under the authority of Title IX, to adopt strict procedures to deal with charges of sexual assault and harassment on campus. OCR told colleges to shift the burden of proof from the accuser toward the accused in such cases, to allow accusers to appeal not-guilty findings (contrary to the Fifth Amendment's ban on double jeopardy) and to refrain from allowing accused persons to cross-examine their accusers (contrary to the Sixth Amendment). These procedures have led on many campuses to a flurry of charges of false accusations and unfair proceedings.[52] In 2018, Education Secretary Betsy DeVos rescinded the Obama-era guidelines and announced new rules that strengthened protections for those accused of sexual misconduct on college campuses.

At one time, women victimized by sexual harassment and sexual violence were often reluctant to come forward because they feared they would be stigmatized or even blamed for what had taken place. Over the past several years, what came to be called the #MeToo movement has encouraged women to speak out publicly and demand justice for sexual crimes committed against them. As a result of #MeToo, a number of prominent men, such as television star Bill Cosby and film producer Harvey Weinstein, were accused and convicted of sexual misconduct.

In 2018, more than 150 women athletes sued Michigan State University, charging that school officials had ignored years of sexual abuse on the part of sports-medicine doctor Larry Nassar. The university settled most of these suits by paying an estimated $500 million in damages. Other suits are still pending. Nassar himself was found guilty of a number of acts of criminal sexual conduct and sentenced to 40 to 175 years in state prison. The potential for substantial monetary damages has made universities and public schools take the problem of sexual harassment by school officials much more seriously than in the past.

Equality in Employment Women have also pressed for civil rights in employment. In particular, they have fought against pay discrimination—paying a male employee

more than a female employee of equal qualifications in the same job. After the Equal Pay Act of 1963 made such discrimination illegal, women's pay slowly moved toward the level of men's pay, although it remains about 20 percent less.

In 2007 this movement received a setback in the Supreme Court. The case, *Ledbetter v. Goodyear Tire and Rubber Co.*, involved a female supervisor named Lilly Ledbetter, who learned late in her career that she was being paid up to 40 percent less than male supervisors, including those with less seniority. Ledbetter filed a grievance with the EEOC, charging sex discrimination.[53] But the Supreme Court denied her claim because the law says workers must file their grievance within 180 days after the discrimination occurs.

Many observers found the ruling unfair because workers often do not know about pay differentials until well after that point. Justice Ruth Bader Ginsburg, the only female member of the Court at the time, marked her disagreement by reading her dissent aloud, a rare occurrence. In January 2009 the Lilly Ledbetter Fair Pay Act became the first bill that President Obama signed into law. The act gave workers expanded rights to sue in cases when they learn of discriminatory treatment well after it has started.[54]

LATINOS

The labels *Latino* and *Hispanic* encompass a wide range of groups with diverse national origins, cultural identities, and experiences. As a result, civil rights issues for them have varied considerably by group and by place.

For example, the early political experiences of Mexican Americans were shaped by race and by region. In 1848, under the Treaty of Guadalupe Hidalgo, Mexico ceded to the United States territory that now comprises Arizona, California, New Mexico, and parts of Colorado, Nevada, and Utah, as well as extended the Texas border to the Rio Grande. Although the treaty guaranteed full civil rights to the residents of these territories, Mexican Americans in fact experienced ongoing discrimination. Even after the courts in 1898 reconfirmed their formal political rights, including the right to vote, they were prevented from voting through various means in many places, especially in Texas.[55] They also had to attend separate schools in Texas and much of southern California, and in many neighborhoods restrictive covenants banned them from buying or renting houses.

Global Economic Gender Equality

There are many measures one could use when trying to determine whether there is parity between the genders in a country. Participation in the labor force, wage equality, and representation in the managerial and technical professions are used to measure economic equality: countries at the top of the list are ones where women are most likely to have the same participation and opportunities as men, regardless of the level of income or skill-level of the employment.

1. Does the United States's position, 19th out of 149 countries, surprise you? What do you think accounts for the country ranking in the top 25? What might explain why 18 other countries ranked higher? Cameroon ranks 8th while its neighbor, Nigeria, ranks 79th. What kinds of factors could explain why geographically close countries might differ on this kind of ranking?

2. The measurement used here prioritizes gender equality over attempting to measure the quality of the opportunities that women have. What do you think are the benefits to this approach? What might be gained if we looked instead at a ranking of countries by women's economic opportunities rather than their economic equality?

COUNTRY	RANK	INDEX RATING	COUNTRY	RANK	INDEX RATING
Lao PDR	1	0.915	Philippines	14	0.801
Barbados	2	0.871	Slovenia	15	0.795
Bahamas	3	0.863	Iceland	16	0.793
Benin	4	0.850	Finland	17	0.786
Burundi	5	0.839	Moldova	18	0.785
Belarus	6	0.838	**United States**	**19**	**0.782**
Guinea	7	0.820	Mongolia	20	0.780
Cameroon	8	0.816	Lithuania	21	0.765
Sweden	9	0.808	Thailand	22	0.763
Latvia	10	0.807	New Zealand	23	0.761
Norway	11	0.806	Singapore	24	0.761
Namibia	12	0.804	Ghana	25	0.753
Botswana	13	0.802			

SOURCE: World Economic Forum, "Economic Participation and Opportunity Subindex," *Global Gender Gap Report 2018*, http://www3.weforum.org/docs/WEF_GGGR_2018.pdf (accessed 7/26/2019).

The earliest Mexican American civil rights organizations included the League of United Latin American Citizens (LULAC), founded in 1929, and the GI Forum, created in 1948. LULAC pursued a legal strategy like the NAACP's to eliminate the segregation of Mexican American students. Its victory in the 1946–47 *Mendez v. Westminster* case overturned school segregation in Orange County, California.[56] In 1954, LULAC attorneys achieved a major victory in the case of *Hernandez v. Texas* (347 U.S. 475 [1954]). In this case the Supreme Court affirmed that Mexican Americans and all other nationality groups were entitled to equal protection under the Fourteenth Amendment. The decision was an important extension of constitutional protections.

In the 1960s a new kind of Mexican American political movement was born. By the late 1950s the first Mexican American had been elected to Congress, and four others followed in the 1960s. A central inspiration for political mobilization emerged from the United Farm Workers union and its charismatic leader, César Chávez. In an era of unprecedented prosperity, California's farmworkers, mainly Mexican migrants, remained poorly paid and lacked basic rights for fair treatment on the job. Using novel tactics such as a national grape boycott, the union drew Americans' attention to the injustices that confronted Mexican migrants and Mexican Americans in the fields. Chávez, whose hunger strikes and inspirational speeches kept the movement in the public eye, came to symbolize the quest for Mexican American civil rights more broadly.[57]

The fields were not the only focus of conflict. In the late 1960s, Mexican American students inspired by the Black civil rights movement launched boycotts of high school classes in East Los Angeles, Denver, and San Antonio, demanding bilingual education, an end to discrimination, and more cultural recognition. They were soon joined by students in colleges and universities across California.

Since that time, Latino political strategy has developed along two tracks. One is a traditional ethnic-group path of voter registration and voting along ethnic lines. This path was blazed by La Raza Unida, an organization that worked to register Mexican American voters in Texas and a number of other states. The other is a legal strategy using the various civil rights laws designed to ensure fair access to the political system. The Mexican American Legal Defense and Educational Fund (MALDEF), founded in 1968, has played a key role in designing and pursuing the latter strategy.

Immigrants and Civil Rights Since the 1960s, rights for Latinos have been intertwined with immigrant rights. For much of American history, legal immigrants were treated much the same as citizens. But continuing immigration and growing economic insecurity have led many voters to support drawing a sharper line between immigrants and citizens.

The Supreme Court has ruled that unauthorized immigrants are eligible for education and emergency medical care but can be denied other government benefits. In the 1990s, a movement in California tried to deny unauthorized immigrants all services except emergency medical care in an attempt to pressure them to leave the country and to discourage others from entering. Although the effort ultimately failed, unauthorized immigration has remained a hot-button political issue.

One priority for Latino advocacy groups has been the status of undocumented immigrants who were brought to the United States as young children and have no real ties to the nation in which they were born. The Development, Relief, and Education Act for Alien Minors, known as the DREAM Act, was introduced in Congress in 2001 with the aim of allowing such individuals to become permanent legal residents

Immigration is one of today's most controversial issues. Supporters of immigration advocate for the rights of undocumented people and believe they should have a path to American citizenship. Supporters of stricter immigration policies believe restrictions on immigration, including the construction of a wall at the U.S.–Mexico border, will protect jobs for American citizens. In 2018 and 2019, the Trump administration instituted a controversial policy at the border, separating undocumented immigrant families when placed in immigrant detention centers.

through military service or college attendance. It has been defeated every year since, however, on the grounds that it would encourage illegal immigration.

Absent legislation, the Department of Homeland Security instituted its own policy, Deferred Action for Childhood Arrivals (DACA), instructing immigration officials to take no action to deport law-abiding individuals who entered the United States illegally as children. In 2014, President Obama issued executive memoranda granting quasi-legal status and work permits to some 5 million people who entered the United States illegally as children or who have children who are American citizens. In 2017, President Trump announced that DACA would be discontinued. Trump's action was blocked by a lower federal court decision. In 2020, the Supreme Court ruled that the Trump administration did not follow the proper procedure for dismantling DACA, and therefore could not end the program. Though this decision does not ensure the program's future, it was touted as a win for immigrant rights.

Another ongoing issue is federal cooperation with local and state law-enforcement agencies to enforce federal immigration laws. Programs initiated by the Department of Homeland Security in the final years of the George W. Bush administration led to immigrant "sweeps" that sometimes rounded up many Latinos who were legal immigrants or even American citizens. A broad coalition of civil rights organizations opposed the program for engaging in racial profiling, and the congressional Hispanic Caucus called on the next president to end it. Yet the Obama administration's Secure Communities program, which initially sought to focus on major drug offenders, violent criminals, and those already in prison, also came under fire for illegally detaining citizens and legal immigrants and was terminated in 2014. Several cities and a handful of states declared themselves "sanctuaries" and declined to cooperate with federal immigration agents. The administration responded by threatening to cut off federal funding from local governments that failed to help federal authorities.

In 2017, President Trump ordered stricter immigration enforcement and began to expand the ranks of Immigration and Customs Enforcement (ICE) agents. Many thousands of immigrants who had not committed serious crimes were slated for deportation, and immigration enforcement at the border was increased. Often, children

and parents who crossed the border were separated and sent to different facilities. This policy contributed to a humanitarian crisis at America's southern border. In 2019, President Trump declared that he would impose severe tariffs on goods produced in Mexico if Mexican authorities did not make strong efforts to block immigrants from seeking to cross into the United States. After negotiations, Mexico dispatched 6,000 troops to try to prevent migrants from crossing into the United States.

Finally, as we saw in Chapter 3, while some local governments declared themselves to be sanctuaries, a number of states, including Arizona, Utah, South Carolina, Indiana, Georgia, and Alabama, passed very strict immigration laws within the past few years. Arizona's 2010 law provided the inspiration for these far-reaching state measures. It required immigrants to carry identity documents with them at all times, made it a crime for an undocumented immigrant to apply for a job, gave the police greater powers to stop anyone they suspected of being an unauthorized immigrant, and required them to check the immigration status of any person they detained if they suspected that person was an unauthorized immigrant.

Civil rights groups contested these laws in court, as did the Justice Department, on the grounds that the federal government rather than the states was responsible for making immigration law. The Supreme Court's 2012 decision on the Arizona law was a partial victory for the federal government, as the Court struck down the provisions that immigrants must carry identity papers, that undocumented immigrants could not apply for jobs, and that police could stop persons they suspected of being undocumented immigrants. But it let stand the provision that required local police to check the immigration status of an individual detained for other reasons if they had grounds to suspect that the person was in the country illegally.

Immigration was a very divisive topic during the 2016 presidential election. During the campaign for the Republican nomination, Donald Trump asserted that he would build a wall along the U.S. border with Mexico, institute a temporary ban on Muslims seeking to travel to the United States, and end the Obama administration's program to accept several thousand Syrian refugees every year. When Trump took office, he lost little time in seeking to implement these campaign promises, though not all came to fruition.

FOR CRITICAL ANALYSIS

Why are immigration and the rights of immigrants so controversial?

Immigration remains a highly divisive topic in the United States. In 2018, the Immigration and Customs Enforcement (ICE) staged a raid in Brooklyn, New York, to arrest a number of undocumented immigrants, despite New York City's status as a sanctuary city.

After his inauguration in January 2017, Trump issued executive orders barring entry into the United States for travelers from six predominantly Muslim countries and blocking for 120 days the admission of all refugees seeking admission to the United States. Critics charged Trump, who had frequently stated his concerns that Muslim immigrants might include terrorists, with religious discrimination, and in particular with violating the 1965 Immigration Act, which states that individuals seeking to enter the United States should not experience discrimination on account of their "race, sex, nationality, place of birth or place of residence." Other immigration laws seem to give the president broad discretion in the matter, however, and in a 5–4 decision, the Supreme Court upheld the ban.[58]

ASIAN AMERICANS

Like *Latino*, the label *Asian American* encompasses a wide range of people from very different national backgrounds who came to the United States, or whose ancestors came, at different points in history. As a consequence, Asian Americans have had very diverse experiences.

The early Asian experience in the United States was shaped by a series of naturalization laws dating back to 1790, the first of which declared that only White immigrants were eligible for citizenship. Chinese immigrants began arriving in California in the 1850s, drawn by the gold rush, but met with intense antagonism. In 1870, Congress declared Chinese immigrants ineligible for citizenship; in 1882 the first Chinese Exclusion Act suspended the entry of Chinese laborers.

At the time of the Exclusion Act, most Chinese people in the United States were single male laborers, with few women and children. The few Chinese children in San Francisco were denied entry to the public schools until parents of those who were American-born pressed legal action, and even then they had to attend a separate Chinese school. American-born Chinese children could not be denied citizenship,

Who Are America's Immigrants?

America has always called itself a nation of immigrants, but immigration has consistently been a controversial issue. In 1900, 1.3 million of New York City's 3.4 million people were foreign born. The immigrants at that time came mostly from mainland Europe, the UK, and Ireland. Who are today's immigrants?

Rate of Foreign-Born Residents by State, 2017

Percentage Key

- <5%
- 5.0–9.9%
- 10–14.9%
- 15–19.9%
- 20%+

What kind of education do immigrants get?

Bachelor's degree
17.8%

Postgraduate degree
13.4%

Where do immigrants come from?

Mexico	11.2M
China	2.9M
India	2.6M
Philippines	2M
El Salvador	1.4M

What is the legal status of immigrants?

- 45%
- 27%
- 5%
- 23%

- Naturalized citizens
- Lawful permanent residents
- Temporary lawful
- Unauthorized

Do immigrants help the economy?

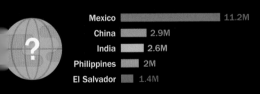

25% of new businesses are started by immigrants

20% of Fortune 500 CEOs are immigrants

10% of Americans work for a private company owned by an immigrant

FOR CRITICAL ANALYSIS

1. What states or regions have the highest percentage of foreign-born people? Why might immigrants live in some regions of the country and not others?

2. Do the data in this graphic confirm or contradict what you have heard about immigrants in America? Do you think immigration to the United States should be easier or more restrictive? What other information would be helpful in making your decision?

SOURCES: Jynnah Radford, "Key Findings about U.S. Immigrants," Pew Research Center, June 17, 2019; Jynnah Radford and Luis Noe-Bustamante, "Facts on U.S. Immigrants, 2017: Statistical Portrait of the Foreign-Born Population in the United States," Pew Research Center, June 3, 2019; U.S. Census Bureau, "American Community Survey," November 2018; Sari Pekkala Kerr and William R. Kerr, "2018 Immigrant Entrepreneurship in America: Evidence from the Survey of Business Owners 2007 & 2012," National Bureau of Economic Research,

During World War II, many Japanese Americans were forced into unsanitary internment camps on the grounds of "military necessity" after the Japanese government launched an attack on Pearl Harbor. Internees faced great losses both during and in the aftermath of internment.

however; in 1898, the Supreme Court ruled in *United States v. Wong Kim Ark* that anyone born in the United States was entitled to full citizenship.[59] Still, new Chinese immigrants were barred from the United States until 1943. After China had become a key World War II ally, Congress repealed the Chinese Exclusion Act and permitted Chinese immigrants to become citizens.

The earliest Japanese immigrants, who came to California in the 1880s, at the height of the anti-Chinese movement, faced similar discrimination. Early in the twentieth century, California and several other western states passed laws denying them the right to own property. The denial of their civil rights culminated in President Franklin Roosevelt's decision to forcibly remove people of Japanese descent from their homes and confine them in internment camps during World War II, after the Japanese government launched its attack on Pearl Harbor.

Suspected of disloyalty, 120,000 people of Japanese descent, including 90,000 American citizens, were forced to move to 10 internment camps located mostly in western states and characterized by overcrowding, insufficient food, and primitive sanitary facilities. The Supreme Court ruled that the internment was constitutional on the grounds of military necessity.[60] Although in 1944 Roosevelt closed the camps and ended internment, many of the internees would never recover from the property losses and health problems they had suffered from it. Not until the Civil Liberties Act of 1988 did the federal government formally acknowledge this denial of civil rights as a "grave injustice" that had been "motivated largely by racial prejudice, wartime hysteria, and a failure of political leadership."[61]

Asian immigration increased rapidly after the 1965 Immigration Act, which lifted discriminatory quotas. Nevertheless, limited English proficiency barred many new Asian American (as well as Latino) immigrants from full participation in American life. Two developments in the 1970s, however, established civil rights for language minorities. In 1974 the Supreme Court ruled in *Lau v. Nichols*, a suit filed on behalf of Chinese students in San Francisco, that school districts have to provide instruction that students whose English is limited can understand.[62] And as we saw earlier, the 1970 amendments to the Voting Rights Act permanently outlawed literacy tests for voting and mandated bilingual ballots or oral assistance for speakers of Chinese, Japanese, Korean, Spanish, or Native American or Alaskan languages.

NATIVE AMERICANS

Although the political status of Native Americans was left unclear in the Constitution, in the early 1800s the courts had defined each Indian tribe as a nation and thus declared Native Americans to be noncitizens of the United States. In fact, in the 1823 case of *Johnson v. McIntosh*, the Supreme Court declared that Native Americans did not actually own the land upon which they lived (21 U.S. 543 [1823]). The 1830 Indian Removal Act forced many Native Americans to give up their lands east of the Mississippi River and forcibly removed them to tribal "reservations" on less desirable lands west of the Mississippi.

In 1924, congressional legislation granted citizenship to all persons born in the United States, including Native Americans. Though Native Americans were now citizens, it was not clear whether the government viewed them as individuals or as members of tribes. Several pieces of legislation enacted in the nineteenth century, including the 1887 Dawes Act, sought to break up the various tribes by encouraging individuals to leave their tribal groups and strike out on their own. The 1934 Wheeler-Howard Law, however, renewed tribal rights and tribal self-government, though individuals were still free to leave their tribal lands.

Despite the problems associated with tribal reservations, strengthening of tribal sovereignty gave Native Americans a ready-made instrument through which to achieve a measure of political influence. In the 1960s, Native Americans used the tribes as vehicles for protest and litigation to improve their situation. The federal government responded with the Indian Self-Determination and Education Assistance Act, which began to give Native Americans more control over their own land.[63]

As a language minority, Native Americans also benefited from the 1975 amendments to the Voting Rights Act and the *Lau* decision, which established their right to be taught in their own languages. In boarding schools run by the federal Bureau of Indian Affairs, Native Americans had been forbidden to speak their own languages until reforms began in the 1930s.

In addition to these language-related issues, sovereign status is another basis on which Native Americans have expanded their rights. Most significant in economic terms was a 1987 Supreme Court decision that freed Native American tribes from most state regulations prohibiting gambling. The establishment of casino gambling on tribal lands has brought a substantial flow of new income to desperately poor reservations.

Many Native Americans continue to live on reservations. Some reservations are poorly governed and, according to critics, mismanaged by the Federal Bureau of Indian Affairs, which exercises supervisory responsibility over the reservations. On some reservations, rates of poverty, alcoholism, and unemployment are far above the national average, leading to concern that the current reservation system does far more harm than good.[64] However, in many cases, tribes have been a vehicle for fostering cultural heritage and asserting political influence.

DISABLED AMERICANS

The concept of rights for disabled people began to emerge in the 1970s out of a little-noticed provision of the 1973 Rehabilitation Act, which outlawed discrimination against individuals on the basis of disabilities. As it did with many other groups, the law itself helped give rise to the movement demanding rights.[65] Inspired by the NAACP's use of a legal defense fund, the disability movement founded the Disability Rights Education and Defense Fund to press its legal claims.

The movement achieved its greatest success with the passage of the Americans with Disabilities Act (ADA) of 1990, which guarantees disabled people access to public spaces and prohibits discrimination in employment, housing, and health care. The impact of the law has been far-reaching, as businesses and public facilities have installed ramps, elevators, and other devices to meet its requirements.[66]

LGBTQ AMERICANS

Over the last 50 years, the lesbian, gay, bisexual, transgender, and queer (LGBTQ) movement has become one of the largest civil rights movements in contemporary America. For most of American history, any sexual orientation other than heterosexuality was considered "deviant," and many states criminalized sexual acts considered "unnatural." Gay people were usually afraid to reveal their sexual orientation for fear of the consequences, including being fired from their jobs, and the police in many cities raided bars and other establishments where they gathered. While their political participation was not formally restricted, they faced the likelihood of discrimination and even prosecution.[67]

The contemporary gay rights movement began in earnest in the 1960s. In 1962, Illinois became the first state to repeal its sodomy laws. The movement drew national attention in 1969 after patrons at the Stonewall Inn, a gay bar in New York City, rioted when police attempted to raid the establishment. The first march for gay rights was held in New York the following year to mark the anniversary of the Stonewall riots, and gay pride parades now take place in dozens of cities across the country.

Gay rights became a national political issue in 1993 when President Bill Clinton was pressed to fulfill a campaign pledge to allow gay people to serve openly in the military. The issue set off a huge controversy in the first months of Clinton's presidency, since the military leadership and many members of Congress strongly opposed the change. The compromise "Don't Ask, Don't Tell" policy that resulted allowed gay men and lesbians to serve in the military as long as they did not publicly reveal their sexual orientation or engage in homosexual activity. Multiple court challenges to the policy failed, but in 2010 President Obama signed an executive order repealing it and allowing openly gay service members.

No Supreme Court ruling or national legislation explicitly protected gay men and lesbians from discrimination until 1996. After losing the first gay rights case decided by the Court, *Bowers v. Hardwick*, as discussed in Chapter 4, the gay rights movement looked for other suitable cases to test the constitutionality of discrimination, much as the African American civil rights movement had done in the late 1940s and 1950s. Test cases challenged local ordinances restricting the right to marry and allowing discrimination in employment, adoption, and parental rights.

In 1996 the Supreme Court, in *Romer v. Evans*, explicitly extended civil rights protections to gay men and lesbians by declaring unconstitutional a 1992

In 2015 the Supreme Court legalized same-sex marriage nationwide with its decision in *Obergefell v. Hodges*. Supporters outside the Supreme Court and across the country celebrated the landmark decision.

amendment to the Colorado state constitution that prohibited local governments from passing ordinances to protect gay rights.[68] Then in 2003, in *Lawrence v. Texas*, the Court overturned *Bowers* and extended the right to privacy to sexual minorities. However, gay men and lesbians still lacked full civil rights, including the right to marry. In 1993, Hawaii's supreme court had declared the state's ban on same-sex marriage discriminatory, raising the possibility that such marriages could become legal and leading Congress to pass the Defense of Marriage Act.

But almost 20 years later, in 2015, the Supreme Court's decision in *Obergefell v. Hodges* guaranteed same-sex couples the right to marry in all states and required states to recognize same-sex marriages performed in other jurisdictions (see Chapter 2).[69] Some local officials briefly refused to issue marriage licenses to same-sex couples, but opposition soon melted away.[70] Gay rights advocates had won a significant victory of a different kind in 2009, when new legislation extended the definition of hate crimes to include crimes motivated by hatred of gay and transgender people. Congressional legislation to ban discrimination in the workplace based on sexual orientation and (in later versions) gender identity also came close to passage in 2013, when it passed the Senate by a large majority. The House did not take up the bill, however, so it has not become law.

Like other minorities fighting for civil rights, the LGBTQ community has organized politically to support such measures. The Human Rights Campaign is the primary national political organization focused on gay rights; it provides campaign financing and volunteers for candidates endorsed by the group. The movement has also formed legal rights organizations, including the Lambda Legal Defense and Education Fund.

FOR CRITICAL ANALYSIS

Political conflicts over gay rights have been carried out in the courts, in state legislatures, in Congress, and in elections. What are some of the decisions that have been reached in each of these different decision-making arenas? Where should decisions about gay rights be made?

Affirmative Action

Explain the key Supreme Court decisions on affirmative action

Beginning in the 1960s, the relatively narrow goal of equalizing educational and economic opportunity by eliminating discriminatory barriers evolved into the broader goal of **affirmative action**, policies designed to compensate for disadvantages due to past discrimination and to encourage greater diversity. Such policies take race or some other status into account in order to provide

affirmative action government policies or programs that seek to redress past injustices against specified groups by making special efforts to provide members of those groups with access to educational and employment opportunities

greater opportunities to historically disadvantaged groups. In 1965, President Lyndon Johnson issued executive orders promoting minority employment in the federal civil service and in companies doing business with the government. But affirmative action did not become a prominent goal of the national government until the 1970s.

Affirmative action also took the form of efforts by the Department of Health, Education, and Welfare to shift the focus of "desegregation" efforts to "integration."[71] HEW agencies, sometimes using court orders, required school districts to present plans for busing children across district lines, for closing certain schools, and for redistributing faculties as well as students. These efforts, enforced by threats of ending federal grants-in-aid, dramatically increased the number of children attending integrated classes.

THE SUPREME COURT AND THE BURDEN OF PROOF

Efforts by the executive, legislative, and judicial branches to shape the meaning of affirmative action today tend to center on one key issue: What is the appropriate level of judicial scrutiny in affirmative action cases? That is, on whom should the burden of proof be placed: the person or organization seeking to show that discrimination has not occurred, or the individual attempting to show that discrimination has occurred?

The reason this question is difficult is that the cases in which the Court strictly scrutinized and struck down racially discriminatory laws—cases like *Brown* and *Loving*—all involved historically disadvantaged racial minority groups. The Court struck down those laws partly because it concluded they were motivated by racial hostility—which is not a valid government purpose—and partly because it concluded that the disadvantaged groups were effectively unable to use the political process to challenge laws that harmed them.

The new laws, however, did not fit this pattern. Instead of being motivated by racial hostility, they were enacted with the objective of assisting victims of past injustice. And instead of harming minority groups, they disadvantaged members of the dominant majority racial group. Yet critics argued that discriminating against *any* individual because of the person's race violated the equal protection clause.

This question was addressed directly by the Supreme Court in 1978 in the case of Allan Bakke (see Table 5.3). Bakke, a White male, brought suit against the medical school of the University of California at Davis on the grounds that, in denying him admission, the school had discriminated against him on the basis of his race. That year, the school had reserved 16 of 100 admission slots for minority applicants. Bakke argued that his grades and test scores ranked him well above many students who were accepted and that he had been rejected because he was White, whereas those others accepted were Black or Latino.

Although the Court ruled in Bakke's favor and ordered him admitted to the medical school, it stopped short of declaring affirmative action unconstitutional. It accepted the school's argument that achieving "a diverse student body" was a "compelling public purpose" but found that the method of a rigid quota of admission slots assigned on the basis of race violated the Fourteenth Amendment's equal protection clause. Thus, the Court permitted universities (and presumably other schools, training programs, and hiring authorities) to continue to consider minority status but limited the use of quotas to situations in which (1) previous discrimination had been shown and (2) the quotas served more as a guideline than as a precisely defined ratio.[72]

For nearly a decade after *Bakke*, the Court was tentative and permissive about efforts by universities, corporations, and governments to experiment with affirmative action programs.[73] But in 1995 another of its rulings further weakened affirmative action. This decision stated that race-based policies, such as preferences given by the government to minority contractors, must survive strict scrutiny, placing the burden on the government to show that they serve a compelling government interest and address identifiable past discrimination.[74]

The status of affirmative action remained uncertain in 2003, when the Supreme Court decided two cases involving suits against the University of Michigan. The first alleged that by automatically adding 20 points (out of a maximum of 150) to the ratings of African American, Latino, and Native American applicants, the university's undergraduate admissions office discriminated unconstitutionally against White students. The Court agreed, saying that the admissions policy amounted to a quota because it lacked the necessary "individualized consideration" and instead used a "mechanical one," based too much on the extra minority points.[75]

In the second case, *Grutter v. Bollinger*, Michigan's law school was sued on the grounds that its admissions policy discriminated against White applicants with equal or superior grades and scores on law board exams. A 5–4 majority of the Supreme

TABLE 5.3

Supreme Court Rulings on Affirmative Action

CASE	COURT RULING
Regents of the University of California v. Bakke, 438 U.S. 265 (1978)	Affirmative action upheld, but quotas and separate admission for minorities rejected; burden of proof on defendant
Wards Cove Packing Co., Inc. v. Atonio, 490 U.S. 642 (1989)	All affirmative action programs put in doubt: burden of proof shifted from defendant to plaintiff (victim), then burden of proof shifted back to employers (defendants)
St. Mary's Honor Center v. Hicks, 509 U.S. 502 (1993)	Required victim to prove discrimination was intentional
Adarand Constructors, Inc. v. Peña, 515 U.S. 200 (1995)	All race-conscious policies must survive "strict scrutiny," with burden of proof on government to show the program serves "compelling interest" to redress past discrimination
Hopwood v. Texas, 78 F.3d 932 (5th Cir., 1996)	Race can *never* be used as a factor in admission, even to promote diversity (Supreme Court refusal to review limited application to the Fifth Circuit—Texas, Louisiana, Mississippi)
Gratz v. Bollinger, 539 U.S. 244 (2003)	Rejection of a "mechanical" point system favoring minority applicants to University of Michigan as tantamount to a quota; *Bakke* reaffirmed
Grutter v. Bollinger, 539 U.S. 306 (2003)	Upheld race-conscious admission to Michigan Law School, passing strict scrutiny with diversity as a "compelling" state interest, as long as admission was "highly individualized" and not "mechanical," as in *Gratz*
Fisher v. University of Texas, 570 U.S. 297 (2013)	Held that strict scrutiny should be applied to college admissions policies that used race as a factor even if the intent was to favor Black applicants

Court sided with the law school; applying strict scrutiny to the policy, they found that it was tailored to a compelling state interest in diversity because it gave a "highly individualized, holistic review of each applicant's file" in which race counted but was not used in a "mechanical" way.[76] The Court's ruling that diversity in education is a compelling state interest and that racial categories can be used to serve that interest put affirmative action on stronger constitutional ground. The Court reaffirmed the *Grutter* decision in 2013 in *Fisher v. University of Texas*; then, as noted earlier, it rejected a White student's suit challenging the use of race as one factor among many in admissions decisions.

Civil Rights: What Do You Think?

The civil rights revolution, which began with African Americans, has broadened to include women and Latinos and to address such matters as sexual orientation, gender identification, and immigration status. As our nation becomes more and more diverse, equal protection of the laws will become more and more important if we are to succeed and prosper. The tumultuous history of civil rights in America demonstrates that exclusion is a recipe for national calamity. It also demonstrates that struggles for civil rights often take a long time, beginning with political action by a small group of committed individuals such as Desmond Meade and often ending with legislation and legal decisions from the highest court in the country.

★ Knowing what you know now, do you support the kinds of actions Desmond Meade (disussed at the start of the chapter) took in trying to secure civil rights for himself and others? Do you feel that civil rights are absolute, or are there situations in which you think curtailing them is justified?

★ Have you—or people you know—experienced civil rights violations? What was the issue, and was there a remedy?

★ How does a country based on the democratic principle of majority rule ensure that the civil rights of minorities are protected? What can and should be done to remedy past wrongs that have current consequences, such as when discrimination has resulted in a racial or ethnic minority becoming an economic underclass? How do you think Desmond Meade would answer that question?

★ What civil rights battles now appear on the country's horizon? In 2017 the Department of Justice declared that it was planning to investigate discrimination against Whites. Some said it was high time for such an investigation, while others lamented what they saw as a step backward for the nation. What do you think?

★ STUDY GUIDE ★

The Struggle for Civil Rights

Outline the legal developments and social movements that affected civil rights (pp. 141–58)

Discrimination against individuals on the basis of their race and gender was legal throughout much of American history. With the adoption of the Fourteenth Amendment and its equal protection clause in 1868, civil rights became part of the Constitution. However, civil rights were not automatically honored for all citizens. The civil rights that Americans enjoy today are largely the product of powerful African American and women's rights movements that lasted for more than a century after the passage of the Fourteenth Amendment. However, a gap still exists between Americans' belief in equality and the reality of life in the United States.

Key Terms

discrimination (p. 141)

civil rights (p. 141)

equal protection clause (p. 141)

Thirteenth Amendment (p. 143)

Fourteenth Amendment (p. 143)

Fifteenth Amendment (p. 143)

Jim Crow laws (p. 143)

"separate but equal" rule (p. 144)

Brown v. Board of Education (p. 147)

strict scrutiny (p. 147)

de jure (p. 147)

de facto (p. 147)

gerrymandering (p. 154)

redlining (p. 156)

Practice Quiz

1. When did civil rights first become part of the Constitution?
   a) in 1789 at the Founding
   b) with the adoption of the Fourteenth Amendment in 1868
   c) in 2008 when Barack Obama was elected president
   d) with the adoption of the Nineteenth Amendment in 1920
   e) in the 1954 *Brown v. Board of Education* decision

2. Which of the following could be described as a Jim Crow law?
   a) a law forcing Black people and White people to ride in separate train cars
   b) a law criminalizing interracial marriage
   c) a law requiring Black students and White students to attend different schools
   d) a law segregating all public accommodations, such as hotels, restaurants, and theaters
   e) All of the above are examples of Jim Crow laws.

3. Which Supreme Court case established the "separate but equal" rule?
   a) *Plessy v. Ferguson*
   b) *Grutter v. Bollinger*
   c) *Brown v. Board of Education*
   d) *Regents of the University of California v. Bakke*
   e) *Loving v. Virginia*

4. Which of the following organizations mobilized a legal defense fund to file lawsuits challenging segregation?
   a) the Association of American Trial Lawyers
   b) the National Association of Evangelicals
   c) the National Association for the Advancement of Colored People
   d) the Student Nonviolent Coordinating Committee
   e) the Southern Christian Leadership Council

5. *Massive resistance* refers to efforts by southern states to
   a) build public housing for poor Black citizens.
   b) defy federal mandates to desegregate public schools.
   c) give women the right to have an abortion.
   d) bus Black students to White schools.
   e) stage large-scale protests against Jim Crow laws.

6. Which of the following outlawed discrimination by employers in hiring, promoting, and laying off their employees?
   a) the Fourteenth Amendment
   b) the Fifteenth Amendment
   c) *Brown v. Board of Education*
   d) the 1964 Civil Rights Act
   e) *Regents of the University of California v. Bakke*

7. The Voting Rights Act of 1965 significantly extended and protected voting rights by
   a) barring literacy tests as a condition for voting in six southern states.
   b) requiring all voters to register two weeks before any federal election.
   c) eliminating all federal-level registration requirements.
   d) allowing voters to sue election officials for monetary damages in civil court.
   e) requiring that all voters show a valid government-issued photo ID.

Extending Civil Rights

Within the last 60 years, minority groups in American society—including coalitions defined by gender, ethnicity, national origin, disabilities, and sexual orientation—have continued to push for full recognition of their civil rights, building on the mid-century gains of African Americans and women. For many of these groups, government policies played an important role in giving rise to movements that demanded equal treatment.

Key Term

intermediate scrutiny (p. 158)

Practice Quiz

8. The judicial test that places the burden of proof on government to show that a race-based policy serves a "compelling interest," is "narrowly tailored," and uses the "least restrictive means" for achieving its goal is called
   a) strict scrutiny.
   b) intermediate scrutiny.
   c) limited scrutiny.
   d) de facto segregation.
   e) de jure segregation.

9. Which of the following declared that "equality of rights under the law shall not be denied or abridged by the United States or by any State on account of sex"?
   a) the Lilly Ledbetter Fair Pay Act
   b) Title IV of the 1964 Civil Rights Act
   c) the DREAM Act
   d) the Equal Rights Amendment
   e) *Obergefell v. Hodges*

10. The Supreme Court's decision in *Hernandez v. Texas* was significant because it
    a) affirmed all nationality groups were entitled to equal protection under the Fourteenth Amendment.
    b) determined that anyone born in the United States was entitled to full citizenship.
    c) allowed school districts to achieve racial integration through busing.
    d) held that public accommodations could be segregated by race but still be equal.
    e) eliminated the government's power to use race as a criterion for discrimination in law.

11. In *United States v. Wong Kim Ark*, the Supreme Court ruled that
    a) school districts must provide bilingual education for students whose English is limited.
    b) the internment of Japanese Americans during World War II was constitutional on the grounds of military necessity.
    c) the 1882 Chinese Exclusion Act was an unconstitutional form of racial discrimination.
    d) anyone born in the United States was entitled to full citizenship.
    e) Chinese immigrants were ineligible for citizenship in the United States.

12. Which two Supreme Court decisions reached opposite conclusions about the constitutionality of laws that discriminate against gay men and lesbians?
    a) *Bowers v. Hardwick* and *Lawrence v. Texas*
    b) *Lau v. Nichols* and *Korematsu v. United States*
    c) *Romer v. Evans* and *Obergefell v. Hodges*
    d) *Grutter v. Bollinger* and *Gratz v. Bollinger*
    e) *Lawrence v. Texas* and *Texas v. Johnson*

Affirmative Action

Explain the key Supreme Court decisions on affirmative action (pp. 173–76)

Affirmative action policies take race or some other status into account in order to provide greater educational and employment opportunities to historically disadvantaged groups. The Supreme Court has ruled that affirmative action programs are constitutional if the government can show evidence that the programs serve a compelling government interest and are narrowly tailored to address identifiable past discrimination.

Key Term

affirmative action (p. 173)

Practice Quiz

13. When did affirmative action become a prominent goal of the national government?
    a) the 1870s
    b) the 1920s
    c) the 1950s
    d) the 1970s
    e) the 1990s

14. In *Regents of the University of California v. Bakke*, the Supreme Court ruled that
    a) race can never be considered as a factor in university admissions, even to promote diversity.
    b) achieving "a diverse student body" was a "compelling public purpose," and the method of a rigid quota of admission slots assigned on the basis of race was consistent with the Fourteenth Amendment's equal protection clause.
    c) achieving "a diverse student body" was a "compelling public purpose," but the method of a rigid quota of admission slots assigned on the basis of race violated the Fourteenth Amendment's equal protection clause.
    d) achieving "a diverse student body" was a "compelling public purpose," but affirmative action policies can be used only to give preferences to African Americans.
    e) achieving "a diverse student body" was a "compelling public purpose," but affirmative action policies can be used only to give preferences to Asian Americans.

15. In which case did the Supreme Court rule that race may be considered in college admissions decisions as part of a "highly individualized, holistic review of each applicant's file"?
    a) *Ledbetter v. Goodyear Tire and Rubber Co.*
    b) *Mendez v. Westminster*
    c) *Brown v. Board of Education*
    d) *Grutter v. Bollinger*
    e) *Fisher v. University of Texas*

Public Opinion

WHAT GOVERNMENT DOES AND WHY IT MATTERS Americans, even those who have had similarly vivid, harrowing experiences, hold strongly different opinions on many important issues. In 1991, Suzanna Hupp was eating lunch in a Texas restaurant when a man drove his truck through the window and began shooting. The gunman killed 23 people, including her parents. Hupp had often carried a handgun in her purse, but had recently taken it out because at the time Texas did not allow carrying a concealed handgun, and she was afraid she would lose her license as a chiropractor if caught.

"Could I have hit the guy? He was fifteen feet from me. . . . Could I have missed? Yeah, it's possible. But the one thing nobody can argue with is that it would have changed the odds," Hupp maintains. She has since become a strong proponent of gun rights. "One of my bugaboos is gun laws. Anytime we list a place where you can't carry guns, to me, that's like a shopping list for a madman. . . . If you think about nearly every one of these mass shootings, they have occurred at places where guns weren't allowed. That's frustrating to me, particularly when you talk about schools. Where do these madmen go? They go to schools and slaughter people."[1]

Suzanna Hupp (left) and Justin Gruber (right) were both present during episodes of gun violence. These events pushed Hupp to advocate for more gun rights, and Gruber to speak out for more restrictive gun laws. How do political opinions form? And how do government officials respond to shifts in public opinion?

Fifteen-year-old Justin Gruber also survived a mass shooting, in his case at the Marjory Stoneman Douglas High School in Parkland, Florida, in 2018. The incident left 17 students and teachers dead but led Gruber and many of his schoolmates to the opposite view from Suzanna Hupp's: support for stronger gun control measures such as assault weapon bans and increased age limits for purchase. Objecting to one suggestion raised after the shooting, Gruber said that arming teachers is a "terrible idea." "Adding guns to solve a gun problem will increase the possible negative outcomes," he said. "Teachers shouldn't have to be trained to carry weapons. They are supposed to mold the minds of the next generation."[2] Some students formed a group, Never Again MSD, known by the hashtag #NeverAgain, to advocate for tighter gun control.

After mass shootings, public support for stronger gun control measures tends to increase. The percentage of Americans telling the Gallup Organization that they wanted stricter laws covering the sale of firearms increased 5 points after the 2017 mass shooting in Las Vegas and 7 more points after the Parkland shooting five months later, to 67 percent overall.[3] At the same time, gun sales typically increase after mass shootings as gun supporters fear tighter controls (although this pattern was more muted under President Trump than it was under President Obama).[4] Soon after an incident, however, public outcry tends to fade, and elected officials seem to take no action. In these cases, are politicians following public opinion, or are they ignoring it?

The "consent of the governed," which is demanded in the Declaration of Independence, is critical for the functioning of a democracy. We expect government to pay attention to the people. But whose opinion gets represented in public policy, particularly on issues, such as gun rights and gun control, where there are strong divides within the public? How influential is public opinion relative to other political forces, such as organized interest groups? How well informed are people, and by what channels can individuals make their voices heard? As we will see in this chapter, research shows that public opinion does indeed have a significant impact on public policy. But scholars continue to debate whether the public is sufficiently informed about politics, as well as whether elected officials represent the interests of all Americans or only some.

CHAPTER GOALS

★ Describe Americans' core political values and ideologies (pp. 183–88)

★ Describe the major forces that shape public opinion (pp. 189–201)

★ Explain how Americans' level of political knowledge affects public opinion and democracy (pp. 201–7)

★ Explain the relationship between public opinion and government policy (pp. 207–10)

★ Explain how surveys and big data can accurately measure public opinion (pp. 210–20)

Defining Public Opinion

Describe Americans' core political values and ideologies

The term **public opinion** refers to the attitudes that people have about policy issues, political events, and elected officials. It is useful to distinguish between values and beliefs, on the one hand, and attitudes and opinions, on the other. **Values (or beliefs)** make up a person's basic orientation to politics and include guiding principles. Values are not limited to the political arena; they include deep-rooted morals, ethics, aspirations, and ideals that shape an individual's perceptions of society, government, and the economy. **Liberty** (freedom), democracy, and **equality of opportunity**, for example, are basic political values held by most Americans.

Another useful term for understanding public opinion is *ideology*. **Political ideology** refers to a set of beliefs and values that form a general philosophy about government. For example, many Americans believe that governmental solutions to problems are inherently inferior to solutions offered by the private sector and free markets. Such a philosophy may predispose them to view specific government programs negatively even before they know much about them.

Attitudes (or opinions) are views about particular issues, persons, or events. An individual may have an attitude toward American trade policy toward China or Mexico or an opinion about President Trump or House Speaker Nancy Pelosi. The attitude may have emerged from a broad belief about free trade, the role of government in the economy, or the political ideology of conservatism or liberalism, but the opinion itself is very specific. Some attitudes may be short-lived and can change based on changing circumstances or new information; others may change over a few years, and still others may not change over a lifetime.

When we think of public opinion, we often think in terms of differences of opinion. The media are fond of reporting political differences between Republicans and Democrats, rural and urban residents, Blacks and Whites, women and men, the young and the old, and so on. Certainly, differences in opinion on many issues are often associated with partisanship or with social and demographic characteristics such as race and ethnicity, gender, income, education, age, religion, and region. For example, people with varying incomes differ in their views on many important economic and social programs, including government health care. In general, the poor, who are the chief beneficiaries of these programs, support them more strongly than do those who are wealthier and pay more of the taxes that fund the programs.

public opinion citizens' attitudes about political issues, leaders, institutions, and events

values (or beliefs) basic principles that shape a person's opinions about political issues and events

liberty freedom from governmental control

equality of opportunity a widely shared American ideal that all people should have the freedom to use whatever talents and wealth they have to reach their fullest potential

political ideology a cohesive set of beliefs that forms a general philosophy about the role of government

attitude (or opinion) a specific preference on a particular issue

POLITICAL VALUES

Despite their differences, most Americans share a common set of values, including a belief in the principles, if not always the actual practice, of liberty, equality, and democracy. The United States was founded on the principle of individual liberty, or freedom, and Americans have always voiced strong support for that principle and usually also for the idea that governmental interference with individuals' lives and property should be kept to a minimum. Liberty is, after all, closely tied to the European settlement of what became the United States—the Puritans and many other groups fled to America to escape persecution in Europe for their religious beliefs—and it remains as important in contemporary politics as it was during the Founding era, when the colonists fought for their freedom from Britain during the Revolutionary War.

Americans have stronger views about the importance of liberty and freedom of expression than do citizens in other democratic countries. One example is the growing concern about privacy and security of personal information online in an era of digital commerce and social media. Seventy-six percent of Americans believe major technology companies and their products and services don't "do enough to protect the personal data of their users" and 75 percent say "they often fail to anticipate how their products and services will impact society." A minority of Americans think big technology companies can be trusted to do the right thing just about always (3 percent) or most of the time (25 percent), while half think they should be regulated more than they are now.[5] Nevertheless, support for freedom of speech, a free internet, and a free press is higher in the United States than in most other countries: 71 percent of Americans believe it is very important that "people can say what they want without state or government censorship," compared to a global average of 56 percent.[6]

Similarly, equality of opportunity has always been an important value in American society. Most Americans believe that all individuals should be allowed to seek personal and economic success. Moreover, most believe that such success should be the result of individual effort and ability, rather than family connections or other forms of special privilege. Quality public education and a college degree are among the most important mechanisms for obtaining equality of opportunity in that they allow individuals, regardless of personal or family wealth, a chance to get ahead. Most people believe a college degree helps a young person succeed in the world, and college graduates themselves say their degree helped them develop the skills they needed for the workplace.[7] Education is one of the most important pathways to a high-paying job, but rising tuition limits access to a college degree for many people. Among the reasons Americans give to be concerned about higher education is that tuition costs are too high, a view shared by 77 percent of Republicans and 90 percent of Democrats.[8]

Most Americans also believe in democracy and the rule of law. They believe that all citizens should have the opportunity to take part in the nation's elections and policy-making processes.[9] (See Chapter 8 for a discussion of rules affecting voting in elections.) Figure 6.1 shows there is consensus among Americans on fundamental democratic values: for instance, nearly 90 percent believe free and fair elections are essential to U.S. democracy, while 83 percent say checks and balances of power among the president, the Congress, and the courts are also very important. Eighty percent believe people should be able to criticize the government, including engaging in nonviolent protest, and 74 percent believe democracy requires protecting the rights of people with unpopular views. The value of free and fair elections is challenged when foreign governments interfere in U.S. elections through the hacking of voter-registration files, or when a political candidate questions the legitimacy of election results, such as by stating mail-in ballots lead to fraud (when there is very little evidence of this).[10] But there are emerging partisan divisions, even over core values. For example, only 53 percent of Republicans say people being free to peacefully protest is very important for the country compared to 83 percent of Democrats.[11]

Obviously, the political values that Americans espouse have not always been put into practice. For 200 years, Americans proclaimed the principles of equality of opportunity and individual liberty while denying them in practice to generations of African Americans. Ultimately, however, slavery and, later, segregation were defeated in the arena of public opinion because these practices differed so sharply from the fundamental principles accepted by most Americans.

FOR CRITICAL ANALYSIS

The news often focuses on issues on which public opinion is sharply divided, but in fact there are many issues on which Americans largely agree. What issues do you think have strong consensus among Americans?

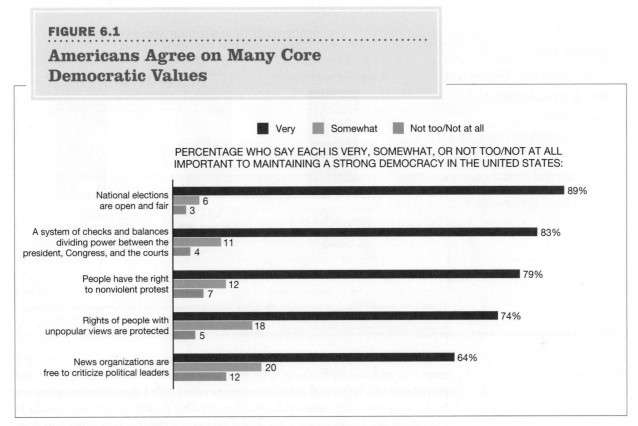

FIGURE 6.1
....
Americans Agree on Many Core Democratic Values

■ Very   ■ Somewhat   ■ Not too/Not at all

PERCENTAGE WHO SAY EACH IS VERY, SOMEWHAT, OR NOT TOO/NOT AT ALL IMPORTANT TO MAINTAINING A STRONG DEMOCRACY IN THE UNITED STATES:

National elections are open and fair — 89% / 6 / 3

A system of checks and balances dividing power between the president, Congress, and the courts — 83% / 11 / 4

People have the right to nonviolent protest — 79% / 12 / 7

Rights of people with unpopular views are protected — 74% / 18 / 5

News organizations are free to criticize political leaders — 64% / 20 / 12

SOURCE: Pew Research Center, "Broad Public Agreement on Importance of Many Aspects of a Strong Democracy," March 2, 2017, www.people-press.org (accessed 1/23/18).

Even when there is broad agreement over principles, practical *interpretations* of principles can differ. Fundamental commitment to equality of opportunity has led to divisions over affirmative action programs for college admissions, government contracts, or government jobs, with both proponents and opponents citing this principle as the justification for their position (see Figure 6.2). Proponents of these programs see them as necessary to ensure equality of opportunity, whereas opponents believe that affirmative action is a form of preferential treatment that violates basic American values (see Chapter 5).[12]

POLITICAL IDEOLOGY

Americans share many fundamental political values, but the application of these values to specific policies and political candidates varies. As noted earlier, a set of underlying ideas and beliefs through which people understand and interpret politics is called a *political ideology*. In the United States the definitions of the two most common political ideologies—liberalism and conservatism—have changed over time. To some extent, contemporary liberalism and conservatism can be seen as differences in emphasis with regard to the fundamental American political values of liberty and equality.

Liberalism In classical political theory, a liberal was someone who favored individual entrepreneurship and was suspicious of government and its ability to manage

FIGURE 6.2

Americans' Support for Fundamental Values

Americans support equality of opportunity, liberty, and democracy in principle; but do they always support these values in practice? What limits, if any, do you think Americans favor when it comes to equality, liberty, and democracy?

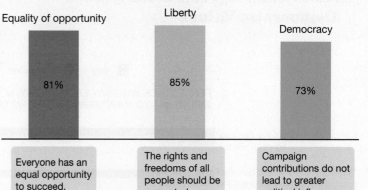

PERCENTAGE OF AMERICANS WHO SAY IT IS IMPORTANT FOR THE COUNTRY THAT

Equality of opportunity — 81% — Everyone has an equal opportunity to succeed.

Liberty — 85% — The rights and freedoms of all people should be respected.

Democracy — 73% — Campaign contributions do not lead to greater political influence.

SOURCES: Pew Research Center, "In Views of U.S. Democracy, Widening Partisan Divides Over Freedom to Peacefully Protest," September 2, 2020, www.pewresearch.org/politics/2020/09/02/in-views-of-u-s-democracy-widening-partisan-divides-over-freedom-to-peacefully-protest/ (accessed 10/18/20).

economic and social affairs—a definition akin to that of today's libertarian. The proponents of a larger and more active government called themselves progressives. In the early twentieth century, however, many liberals and progressives united in support of "social liberalism," the belief that government action (laws and policies) are often needed to preserve individual liberty and promote equality. Today's liberals are social liberals rather than classical liberals. Many conservatives today are classical liberals.

In contemporary politics, being a **liberal** has come to mean supporting government policies to create a fairer economic system and opportunity for upward mobility, including more progressive taxation (taxing those with more income or wealth more heavily); the expansion of federal social service and health care programs; government spending on education, on infrastructure, and on science and technology, including measures to fight climate change; efforts to protect people of color and women from discrimination; and vigorous protection of the environment. Liberals generally support reproductive rights for women and LGBTQ rights, and are concerned with protecting the rights of refugees, immigrants, and people accused of crimes. While they are in favor of legalizing marijuana, they seek more regulation of guns and assault weapons that have been linked to increased violence. In international affairs, liberals tend to support foreign aid to poor nations; arms control; free trade; and international organizations that promote peace, such as the United Nations and the European Union; and to oppose U.S. military interventions in other countries.

Conservatism By contrast, **conservatives** believe that a large government poses a threat to the freedom of individual citizens, small businesses, free markets, and democracy. Ironically, today's conservatives support the views of classical liberalism: they generally oppose the expansion of governmental activity, believing that solutions to many social and economic problems can and should be developed in

liberal today this term refers to those who generally support social and political reform, governmental intervention in the economy, more economic equality, expansion of federal social services, and greater concern for consumers and the environment

conservative today this term refers to those who generally support the social and economic status quo and are suspicious of efforts to introduce new political formulas and economic arrangements; conservatives believe that a large and powerful government poses a threat to citizens' freedom

the private sector or by local communities or religious organizations. Conservatives support cutting taxes and reducing government spending and generally oppose government regulation of business. While liberals tend to be pragmatic and policy oriented, conservatives tend to be more ideological.[13]

In social policy, conservatives generally support traditional family arrangements and oppose legalized abortion and same-sex marriage. They often oppose environmental protections that interfere with private business. Many conservatives prefer stricter criminal justice laws and oppose recreational drug legalization. On issues such as immigration, international trade, and the fairness of the U.S. economic system, conservatives today are deeply divided. For example, business-oriented conservatives often support a legal path to citizenship for immigrants, but social conservatives want to lower legal and illegal immigration and build a wall between the United States and Mexico. In international affairs, conservatism has come to mean support for military intervention abroad and the maintenance of American military power. Conservatives are also deeply divided on foreign trade. Business-oriented conservatives favor free trade while social conservatives prefer tariffs that reduce trade with foreign countries.

Libertarianism Other political ideologies also influence American politics. **Libertarians** argue that government interferes with freedom of expression, free markets, and society, and thus should be involved as little as possible in both the economy and society. They oppose business- and environmental-regulation measures and support legalization of drugs and abortion. In 2016, Republican senator and libertarian Rand Paul ran for president based on his opposition to foreign wars and his commitment to civil liberties and smaller government.

libertarian someone who emphasizes freedom and believes in voluntary association with small government

Socialism and the Green Party While libertarians believe in less government across the board, **socialists** argue that more government is necessary to promote justice and to reduce economic and social inequality. In 2016 and 2020, Senator

socialist someone who generally believes in social ownership, strong government, free markets, and a reduction in economic inequality

---

BOX 6.1

Profile of a Liberal: Representative Barbara Lee (D-Calif.)

★ Supports stricter environmental protections to address climate change

★ Favors health coverage for all Americans

★ Advocates increased funding for education, and in some cases student loan forgiveness

★ Supports equal rights for LGBTQ Americans

★ Supports abortion rights and birth control

★ Supports an increase in the minimum wage and workers' rights

★ Supports more equitable tax policy that benefits middle-class Americans by raising taxes on very wealthy people and corporations

★ Supports investment in alternative energy, including solar, wind, geothermal, electric cars, biofuels, etc.

Bernie Sanders, who calls himself a "democratic socialist," gained widespread support from progressive or liberal Democrats, especially Millennials, in the party's presidential primaries. Like Social Democratic politicians in Europe, Sanders and House member Alexandria Ocasio-Cortez support free markets and private enterprise but want government to ensure more equality of opportunity through such means as free public college, single-payer health care, higher taxes on the wealthy, and protection of workers' rights and unions. MoveOn.org, an online organization with millions of members, advocates policies consistent with democratic socialism, as did 2016 Green Party presidential candidate Jill Stein and 2020 presidential candidate Tom Steyer.

Americans' Ideologies Today Although many Americans hold at least some libertarian or socialist views, most describe themselves as either liberals, conservatives, or moderates. Figure 6.3 shows that the percentages of Americans calling themselves moderates, liberals, or conservatives have remained relatively constant for the past 15 years, though liberals have recently been gaining. Gallup surveys indicate that as of 2019, 37 percent of Americans considered themselves conservatives, 35 percent moderates, and 24 percent liberals. Among people aged 18 to 29, 26 percent identified as conservative, while 30 percent identified as liberals and 40 percent as moderates.[14] Some moderates tend to hold middle-ground opinions on issues across the board, while others are economically liberal but socially conservative or vice versa.

Within each ideological group, individuals' beliefs vary. Many conservatives support government social programs to provide assistance to the poor and needy, while many liberals hold fiscally conservative opinions, like seeking to reduce the size of the national debt. Today many liberals favor free trade and oppose tariffs on China and Mexico (a traditionally conservative position), while President Trump and many conservatives favor tariffs to protect U.S.-made goods, opposing free trade (a traditionally liberal position). The real political world is far too complex to be seen simply in terms of a struggle between liberals and conservatives.

BOX 6.2

Profile of a Conservative: Senator Chuck Grassley (R-Iowa)

★ Wants to reduce the size of the federal government and regulation on businesses

★ Supports capital punishment for certain crimes

★ Opposes restrictions on the right to bear arms (gun control)

★ Supports using traditional energy sources (oil and gas) and opposes climate change action that reduces manufacturing jobs

★ Opposes many affirmative action programs and is antiabortion

★ Favors tax cuts

★ Favors reducing immigration

★ Favors government programs to support farmers, miners, businesses

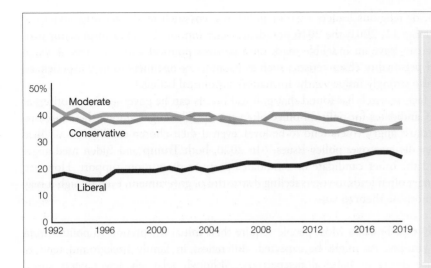

SOURCE: Lydia Saad, "The U.S. Remained Center-Right, Ideologically, in 2019," Gallup, January 9, 2020, https://news.gallup.com/poll/275792/remained-center-right-ideologically-2019.aspx (accessed 10/18/2020).

FIGURE 6.3

American Ideology

While slightly more Americans identify themselves as "conservatives" than "liberals," the majority identify as independent; overall a majority of Americans hold more liberal opinions on policy issues. During the period shown in this figure, however, Americans have had Democratic and Republican presidents. What might account for this apparent discrepancy? What role do moderates play in the electorate? How stable is Americans' ideology over time?

How We Form Political Opinions

> **Describe the major forces that shape public opinion**

As noted before, broad ideologies do not necessarily determine every political opinion a person holds. How are political opinions formed? When and how do political opinions change?

POLITICAL SOCIALIZATION

People's attitudes about political issues and elected officials tend to be shaped by their underlying political beliefs and values. For example, someone who dislikes government regulation of the economy would probably be predisposed to oppose the development of new health care programs. Similarly, someone who values environmental protection is probably likely to support the creation of a new national park, a ban on fracking, or tighter regulations on auto emissions. The processes through which these underlying political beliefs and values are formed are collectively called **political socialization.**

Probably no nation, and certainly no democracy, could survive if its citizens did not share some fundamental beliefs. In contemporary America, the **agents of socialization** that promote differences in political opinions include family and friends, membership in social groups, religion, party affiliation, economic factors like income, and political environment such as the media. Other agents, such as public education, promote similarities in Americans' political opinions.

Of course, no list of the agents of socialization can fully explain an individual's basic political beliefs. In addition to the factors that are important for everyone, experiences and influences that are unique to each individual play a role in shaping political orientation. These may include an important mentor, such as a teacher,

political socialization the induction of individuals into the political culture; learning the underlying beliefs and values on which the political system is based

agents of socialization social institutions, including families and schools, that help to shape individuals' basic political beliefs and values

coach, or religious leader; a major political event such as the terrorist attacks of September 11, 2001, the 2016 presidential election, or the 2020 coronavirus pandemic can leave an indelible mark on a person's political consciousness. A deep-seated personality characteristic, such as paranoia or openness to new experiences, may also strongly influence the formation of political beliefs.

In fact, research has found that political beliefs can be governed by emotions as well. Candidates for political office often try to stoke anger among their supporters because angry voters tend to be loyal, even if their chosen candidate is disliked or they disagree over policy issues.[15] In 2020, both Trump and Biden used anger toward the other candidate or candidate's party to draw more support. However, this anger often leads to voters feeling distrustful of government, even though it may help motivate them to vote.

Family and Friends Most people acquire their initial orientation to politics from their families. As might be expected, differences in family background tend to produce divergent political perspectives. Although relatively few parents spend significant time directly teaching their children about politics, political conversations occur in many households, and children tend to absorb the political views of parents and other caregivers, often without realizing it. Studies find, for example, that party preferences are initially acquired at home, even in households that don't explicitly talk about politics. Children raised in households in which both primary caregivers are Democrats or Republicans tend to become Democrats or Republicans, respectively.[16] Of course, not all children absorb their parents' political views. Two of the four children of Republican president Ronald Reagan, for instance, rejected their father's conservative values and became active on behalf of Democratic candidates.

In addition to family members, friends, coworkers, and neighbors are an important source of political orientation for nearly everyone. Political scientist Betsy Sinclair argues that individuals are "social citizens" whose political opinions and behavior are significantly influenced by their social networks.[17] When members of a social network express a particular opinion, Sinclair finds, others notice and conform, particularly if their conformity is likely to be highly visible. The conclusion is that political behavior is surprisingly subject to social pressures.

The family is one of the largest influences on a person's political views. Children raised in conservative or liberal families usually, but not always, hold those same views later in life.

Online social networks such as Facebook, Snapchat, Instagram, and Twitter may increase the role of peers in shaping public opinion. For example, the widely shared Facebook meme of an equal sign against a red background in 2013 communicated support for gay rights at the same time that the U.S. Supreme Court was deciding two court cases affecting gay and lesbian marriage rights. This social media discussion, along with the growing number of people who had friends and family that were gay, was associated with upticks in public support for same-sex marriage nationally. Public opinion on this issue changed rapidly over a decade. In 2018, 67 percent of Americans believed marriages between same-sex couples should be recognized by law, an increase of over 30 percent from 2005, when only 36 percent of Americans felt this way.[18] Similarly, the #MeToo movement that emerged in 2017 to highlight and combat sexual harassment used social media to organize both online and offline. Social media raise attention to salient problems and policy issues that help shape what people think.

Debates over the nation's gun laws have intensified following recent mass shootings. In 2019, mass shootings in El Paso, Texas, and Dayton, Ohio, brought renewed attention to gun violence in the

United States. Mass shootings have increased support for stricter gun laws. Today 57 percent of U.S. adults say gun laws should be more strict; 44 percent of Americans strongly favor and another 18 percent somewhat favor banning assault-style weapons. But there are big differences in opinion based on party. Nearly 80 percent of Democrats say gun laws should be stricter, while only 28 percent of Republicans do. Despite deep partisan divisions on guns, we also see some cross-party agreement. Ninety percent of Republicans and Democrats say people with mental illnesses should be prevented from buying guns, and more than 80 percent of both parties say people on federal no-fly or watch lists should be barred from purchasing firearms. And strong majorities of both Democrats (91 percent) and Republicans (79 percent) favor background checks for private gun sales and sales at gun shows.[19]

By sharing their personal stories with the #MeToo hashtag, women and men were able to network and organize (online and offline) to draw attention to what they saw as pervasive sexual harassment in American life.

Education Governments use public education to try to teach all children a common set of civic values; it is mainly in school that Americans acquire their basic beliefs in liberty, equality, and democracy. At the same time, however, differences in formal education are strongly associated with differences in political opinions. In particular, those who attend college are often exposed to ways of thinking that will distinguish them from their friends and neighbors who do not attend. Education is one of the most important factors in predicting who engages in civic and political activities, such as regularly following the news, voting, and participating in politics, as well as in predicting how much an individual will earn over a lifetime—itself another important factor in political beliefs.[20]

SOCIAL GROUPS AND PUBLIC OPINION

The social groups to which individuals belong are another important source of political values. Social groups include those that individuals haven't chosen (national, gender, and racial groups, for example) and those they have (political parties, labor unions, the military, and religious, environmental, educational, and occupational groups). Membership in a particular group can give individuals experiences and perspectives that shape their view of political and social life.

After the killing of George Floyd, Black Lives Matter protests erupted around the country, with participants of different ages, races, and backgrounds showing solidarity with the movement.

Race Race plays an important role in shaping political attitudes and opinions, among people of color and Whites. The experiences of African Americans, Whites, and Asian Americans, for example, can differ significantly. African Americans have been victims of persecution and discrimination throughout American history, and while many Asian Americans are relatively recent immigrants to the United States, they too can face discrimination. African Americans and Whites also have different occupational opportunities and often live in separate communities and attend separate schools. Such differences tend to produce distinctive political views. Many Black Americans perceive other Blacks as members of a group with a common identity and a shared political interest in overcoming persistent racial and economic inequality. Political scientists refer to this phenomenon as "linked fate": African Americans see their fate as linked to that of other African Americans.[21] This linked fate acts as a sort of filter through which Black Americans evaluate information and determine their own opinions and policy preferences.

That Black and White Americans have different views is reflected in public perception of fair treatment across racial groups in the United States. Figure 6.4 shows that 84 percent of African Americans believe that Blacks in their community are treated less fairly than Whites in dealing with the police, compared to 63 percent of Whites. In a striking difference, 74 percent of Blacks but only 38 percent of Whites believe Blacks are treated unfairly in applying for a loan or home mortgage, while 82 percent of Blacks but just 44 percent of Whites believe Blacks are treated less fairly in hiring, pay, and promotions. Blacks are over 20 percentage points more likely to believe that Blacks face racial discrimination in voting in elections compared to Whites.[22]

Even with highly charged issues of race, events and circumstances can cause opinions to change. In 2009, 80 percent of African Americans said Blacks and other minorities did not get equal treatment under the law; the number of Whites giving this response was just 40 percent.[23] In the past few years, however, widely publicized incidents of excessive use of police force against African Americans and resulting protests by the Black Lives Matter movement have begun to cause a shift in public opinion on this issue (see Figure 6.4). Nationwide protests condemning police brutality erupted in May and June of 2020 when George Floyd, an unarmed African

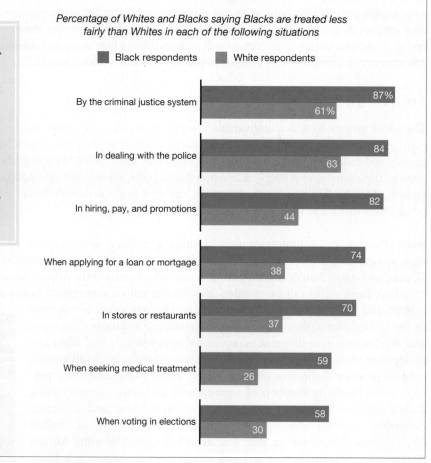

FIGURE 6.4

Perception of Fair Treatment across Racial Groups

In the United States, racial groups may not perceive race relations in precisely the same way. According to the data in this figure, are Blacks or Whites more likely to think that race relations are good? What factors help to account for these differences in perception?

Percentage of Whites and Blacks saying Blacks are treated less fairly than Whites in each of the following situations

■ Black respondents   ■ White respondents

Situation	Black respondents	White respondents
By the criminal justice system	87%	61%
In dealing with the police	84	63
In hiring, pay, and promotions	82	44
When applying for a loan or mortgage	74	38
In stores or restaurants	70	37
When seeking medical treatment	59	26
When voting in elections	58	30

SOURCE: Juliana Menasce Horowitz, Anna Brown, and Kiana Cox, "Race in America, 2019," Pew Research Center, www.pewresearch.org (accessed 7/15/20).

Who Talks about Politics?

If you turn on the TV or look at your social media feed, you might feel that everyone is expressing political opinions on an almost constant basis. Who expresses their opinions most often? And how do they do it?

Who Expresses Their Political Opinions?

Percentage of U.S. adults who say they express opinions about politics by discussing politics and government with others a few times a week or more

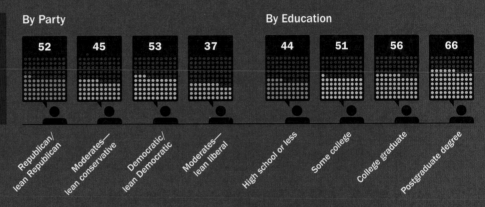

By Party

52	45	53	37
Republican/ lean Republican	Moderates— lean conservative	Democratic/ lean Democratic	Moderates— lean liberal

By Education

44	51	56	66
High school or less	Some college	College graduate	Postgraduate degree

How Do Americans Express Their Political Opinions?

Percentage of U.S. adults who say they have done the following activities on social media in the last year

By Party
- Republican
- Democratic

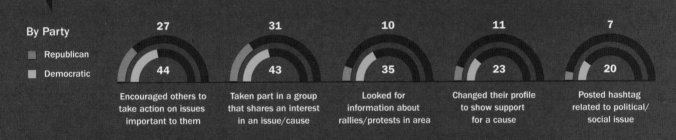

27	31	10	11	7
44	43	35	23	20
Encouraged others to take action on issues important to them	Taken part in a group that shares an interest in an issue/cause	Looked for information about rallies/protests in area	Changed their profile to show support for a cause	Posted hashtag related to political/ social issue

Percentage of U.S. adults who say they have done each of the following in the last year

By Education
- High school or less
- Some college
- College graduate
- Postgraduate degree

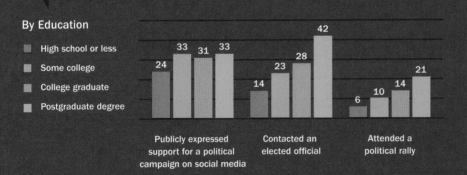

Publicly expressed support for a political campaign on social media: 24, 33, 31, 33

Contacted an elected official: 14, 23, 28, 42

Attended a political rally: 6, 10, 14, 21

FOR CRITICAL ANALYSIS

1. Who is more likely to talk about politics and express a political opinion online or at an event—those with less education or more?

2. Why do you think Democrats are more likely than Republicans to use social media to express their political opinions?

SOURCE: Data from Pew Research Center (accessed 11/18/19).

American man, was arrested and killed by police. The Black Lives Matter protests saw millions of people marching and demonstrating in the nation's cities to draw attention to the racial disparities not only in police treatment, but in American society at large. Two-thirds of U.S. adults supported the movement, with 38 percent saying they strongly supported it, though there was a 40 percent difference in strong support for the protests when comparing Whites to African Americans.[24] However, increased public support for the movement and the persistence of its organizers has galvanized police reforms across the country. As of October 2020, 653 police reform bills in 39 states had been introduced in state legislatures or passed.[25] Iowa, for example, restricted chokeholds and prevented the rehiring of officers fired for misconduct, while New York and New Jersey criminalized the use of chokeholds.

Ethnicity Ethnicity also affects political attitudes, separately from race. Latinos, who make up 17 percent of the total population, are the fastest-growing minority in the United States. While most Latinos and Latinas are racially White, their shared ethnic and, to a large extent, linguistic background contributes to a group consciousness that shapes opinions. The U.S. Latino population is diverse, comprising individuals of Mexican, Cuban, Central American, South American, and Caribbean descent whose backgrounds and circumstances are often quite different.[26] In spite of the differences, however, the Latino population has a growing sense of "linked fate."

There are 11.2 million first-generation immigrants from Mexico living in the United States today. Nationwide, foreign-born citizens account for 13.6 percent of the U.S. population, and Census estimates that about 23 percent are undocumented immigrants. Unsurprisingly, immigration is one of the most important policy issues among Latinos, with significant majorities of Latinos concerned about restrictive immigration policies and the threat of deportation to themselves, a family member, or a friend.[27] In 2019, three in four Americans supported a path to citizenship for immigrants, but 55 percent of Latinos, regardless of legal status, still worried a lot or some about deportation.[28]

President Trump pushed for new immigration enforcement policies that expanded the pool of unauthorized immigrants who could be deported because of previous criminal charges, including misdemeanor offenses from unpaid parking tickets. There have also been raids of communities and businesses looking for undocumented immigrants.

The opinions of women and men diverge greatly on some, but by no means all, political issues. One of the biggest gender gaps appears around gun control. Many more women than men favor more restrictions on gun ownership.

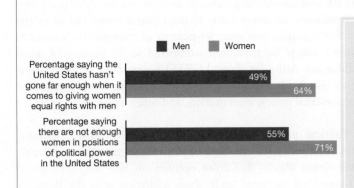

Percentage saying the United States hasn't gone far enough when it comes to giving women equal rights with men
- Men: 49%
- Women: 64%

Percentage saying there are not enough women in positions of political power in the United States
- Men: 55%
- Women: 71%

FIGURE 6.5

Differences in Public Opinion by Gender

Data reveal significant differences in men's and women's opinions about the political world. What might explain the differences between men and women on equal rights for women? What might explain the differences in how men and women view women's roles in political power in the United States?

SOURCE: Amanda Barroso, "Key Takeaway on Americans' Views On Gender Equality a Century After U.S. Women Gained the Right to Vote," Pew Research Center, August 13, 2020, www.pewresearch.org/fact-tank/2020/08/13/key-takeaways -on-americans-views-on-gender-equality-a-century-after-u-s-women-gained-the-right-to-vote/ (accessed 10/20/20).

Likely as a result of these actions, a 2017 Pew survey found that 47 percent of Hispanic adults, regardless of their immigration status, say they worry "a lot" or "some" that they themselves, a family member, or a close friend could be deported.[29]

While immigration has been at the forefront of a national political debate, a majority of Americans have positive views about immigrants. Just one in four Americans believe legal immigration to the United States should decrease.[30] Sixty-two percent say immigrants strengthen the country "because of their hard work and talents," while 28 percent say immigrants burden the country by taking jobs, housing, and health care.

With respect to ideology, Latinos typically support government programs to reduce inequality and create jobs, including public funding for education, health, and welfare. While Latinos tend to be fairly religious Christians, surveys find their religious beliefs do not dictate their political decisions—they are thus less likely than non-Hispanic Whites to vote for conservative politicians because of social issues.[31]

Gender Men and women have important differences of opinion as well. Reflecting differences in social roles and occupational patterns, women tend to oppose military intervention more than men do and are more likely than men to favor gun control and government social programs. Perhaps because of these differences on issues, women are more likely than men to vote for Democratic candidates. In the 2020 presidential election, men were much more likely to favor Republican Donald Trump and women to favor Democrat Joe Biden. This tendency of men's and women's voting to differ is known as the **gender gap**.

In 2020, a majority of Americans believed the United States hasn't gone far enough when it comes to giving women equal rights with men. However, there were significant differences by gender—64 percent of women agreed with the statement, compared to 49 percent of men. Women are also more likely than men to believe there are major obstacles to gender equality, specifically in women's positions of political power.[32] (See Figure 6.5).

Religion Religious affiliation, frequency of church attendance, and the belief that religion and prayer are important in one's life are important predictors of opinion on a wide range of issues. White evangelical Protestants and weekly church-goers are much more likely than average citizens to hold conservative views and be

gender gap a distinctive pattern of voting behavior reflecting the differences in views between women and men

Republican, while those without any religious affiliation, who now make up almost 25 percent of the population, are more likely to hold liberal views and favor the Democratic Party.[33] For example, just over 30 percent of evangelical Protestants believe abortion should always be permitted, compared to 75 percent of those without religious affiliation. Attitudes about LGBTQ rights show similarly sharp differences.[34] Religion also helps explain opinions on teaching evolution in the public schools, environmental policy, immigration, and other issues.

Party Affiliation Political party membership is one of the most important factors affecting political attitudes. We can think of partisanship as red (Republican)- or blue (Democratic)-tinted glasses that color opinion on how we "see" a vast array of issues. Self-identified partisans (individuals affiliating with the Republican or Democratic Party) tend to rely on party leaders and the media for cues on the appropriate positions to take on major political issues.[35]

In recent years, party polarization has become a defining feature of Congress, many state legislatures, and the mass public. As a result, the leadership of the Republican Party has become increasingly conservative, whereas that of the Democratic Party has become more liberal, a shift reflected in public opinion. Geographic sorting—with liberals choosing to live in neighborhoods, cities, counties, and states that are more liberal, while conservatives move to areas whose populations hold more conservative views—also contributes to mass polarization. Large cities, such as New York City, Chicago, and Los Angeles, have predominantly Democratic populations, while Republicans are more numerous in rural and suburban areas.

According to recent studies, opinion differences between Democratic and Republican partisans are greater today than during any other period for which data are available. Across a wide range of issues—including immigration, energy, income inequality, infrastructure, job creation, climate change, environment, national defense, budget deficits, taxes, terrorism, trade, race relations, the coronavirus pandemic, and much more—Democrats and Republicans strongly disagree (see Figure 6.6). Partisans even hold opinion differences on current events and their effects. For example, while Republicans and Democrats generally agreed that anger over George Floyd's death caused nationwide protests, only 45 percent of Republicans believe the protests reflect longstanding concerns about racial inequality for Blacks, compared to 84 percent of Democrats.[36]

Some have called partisanship today a "mega-identity." In her book *Uncivil Agreement*, political scientist Lilliana Mason argues that Americans' political identities are now strongly tied to social identities, such as race or religion, while opinions on policy issues are becoming less important. Results show that the more social connections people have to their party (African Americans who are also liberal Democrats, or evangelical Christians who are also conservative Republicans), the more emotionally invested they are in the party's success (winning at all costs) and the more negatively they feel about members of the opposing party. The increasing alignment among partisan, ideological, racial, and religious identities results in social polarization. This social polarization divides American society along partisan lines, separating neighbors and family members and reducing tolerance.

Though the rift between "red" and "blue" America seems deeper than ever, political scientist Morris Fiorina and his colleagues argue that most Americans hold moderate opinions.[37] While political elites and members of Congress may be highly polarized, they say, there is general agreement among most Americans even on those issues thought to be most divisive.

FOR CRITICAL ANALYSIS

Political scientists have observed "geographic sorting" in the United States, where liberals live in areas with other liberals and conservatives live in areas with other conservatives. Is the area where you live strongly liberal, strongly conservative, or evenly mixed? What are the political consequences of geographic sorting?

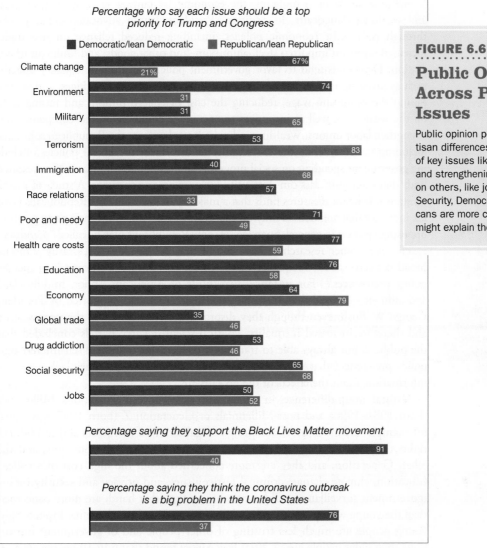

Percentage who say each issue should be a top priority for Trump and Congress

Democratic/lean Democratic ■ **Republican/lean Republican** ■

Issue	Democratic/lean Democratic	Republican/lean Republican
Climate change	67%	21%
Environment	74	31
Military	31	65
Terrorism	53	83
Immigration	40	68
Race relations	57	33
Poor and needy	71	49
Health care costs	77	59
Education	76	58
Economy	64	79
Global trade	35	46
Drug addiction	53	46
Social security	65	68
Jobs	50	52

Percentage saying they support the Black Lives Matter movement

91	40

Percentage saying they think the coronavirus outbreak is a big problem in the United States

76	37

FIGURE 6.6

Public Opinion Across Policy Issues

Public opinion polls show wide partisan differences on the importance of key issues like the environment and strengthening the military, while on others, like jobs and Social Security, Democrats and Republicans are more closely aligned. What might explain these differences?

SOURCE: "Public's 2019 Priorities: Economy, Health Care, Education, and Security All Near Top of List," Pew Research Center, January 24, 2019, https://www.people-press.org/2019/01/24/publics-2019-priorities-economy-health-care -education-and-security-all-near-top-of-list/; Kim Parker, Juliana Menasce Horowitz, and Monica Anderson, "Amid Protests, Majorities Across Racial and Ethnic Groups Express Support for the Black LIves Matter Movement," Pew Research Center, June 12, 2020, www.pewresearch.org; Amina Munn, "As the U.S. Copes with Multiple Crises, Partisans Disagree Sharply on Severity of Problems Facing the Nation," Pew Research Center, July 14, 2020, www.pewresearch.org (accessed 7/16/20).

Economic Class and Group Self-Interest Another way that membership in groups can affect political beliefs is through economic class and self-interest. On many issues, for example, the interests of the rich and the poor differ significantly. Inevitably, these differences in interests will produce differences in policy preferences.

The framers of the Constitution thought that the inherent gulf between the rich and the poor would always be the most important source of conflict in political life. Today, 61 percent of Americans say there is too much income inequality in the United States, including 41 percent of Republicans and 78 percent of Democrats, and existing inequality has been magnified by the economic crisis from the coronavirus pandemic. But while there might be agreement on the problem, there are huge disagreements about the solution.

Republicans favor stimulating the economy by cutting taxes on corporations and wealthier Americans. In addition, President Trump advocated creating jobs through isolationist economic policies, including reduced reliance on free trade; increased tariffs on imported steel, aluminum, and other goods; and limits on immigration. Democrats tend to favor government policies to promote equality directly, such as investing in alternative energy and infrastructure (roads, bridges, and so on), raising the minimum wage, reducing the cost of college tuition, and raising taxes on the wealthy, as well as incentives to encourage employee-owned companies and strengthen labor unions. Wealthier individuals tend to favor the Republican solutions, including tax cuts, while the less wealthy tend to favor the liberal policies, including government spending on social programs and economic stimulus.[38] New research finds that economic class can shift attitudes, even among partisans. A study of voting on statewide ballot measures finds that a majority of lower-income Republicans favor tax increases that are focused only on the wealthy, defecting from their party position opposing taxation in general. Such low-income Republicans may be called "populists."

FOR CRITICAL ANALYSIS

An individual's family, social networks, group membership, party affiliation, education, self-interest, and political environment can influence his or her political perspectives. What influences in your life have affected your political opinions and beliefs?

However, other researchers have found that people don't necessarily translate broad concerns about inequality or their own economic self-interest into specific policy preferences.[39] For instance, two-thirds of Americans—poor, middle class, and affluent—favored the 2001 and 2003 federal tax cuts supported by President George W. Bush, even though they disproportionately benefited the very wealthy and therefore increased inequality. Political scientist Larry Bartels concluded that the public is not always able to translate a concern for economic self-interest into policy preferences that would benefit average citizens, because they lack necessary information about the effects of the tax cuts.[40]

Natural group differences in interest also exist between generations. Millennials (born 1981–1996) and post-Millennials or Generation Z (born 1997 and later), for example, are much more accepting of legalization of marijuana and of LGBTQ rights than are older age cohorts such as Generation X, Baby Boomers, and the Silent Generation, and they are more concerned about the high cost of a college education, climate change, criminal justice issues, and privacy and security online (government surveillance). Older citizens, on the other hand, are more concerned than the young with protecting Social Security and Medicare benefits. Interestingly, young people are much less trusting of other people and of government institutions than older people are. A 2019 Pew survey found that 6 in 10 people aged 30 and younger say most people "can't be trusted." Young people also have lower trust in Congress and the presidency, and are less likely than older adults to say they have a great deal or fair amount of confidence in religious leaders, police officers, and business leaders.[41] In addition to age, some of these differences are rooted in where individuals learn about politics; the young are significantly more likely to get their news online and are less likely to watch television news (see Chapter 7).

Nevertheless, group membership can never fully explain a person's political views. An individual's unique personality and life experiences may produce political views very different from those of a group to which he or she belongs. Some Latinos are conservative Republicans, and some wealthy businesspeople are liberal Democrats. Group membership encourages particular outlooks, but it does not guarantee them.

POLITICAL LEADERS

All governments try to influence, manipulate, or manage their citizens' beliefs. But the extent to which public opinion is actually affected by government public

Confidence in Democratic Institutions

Legislatures, political parties, and the press are three institutions that play an important role in making democracy work. While these institutions are important to all democracies, we do notice that Americans tend to be much less confident in these institutions than are citizens in other democracies.

1. Are one of the three institutions more or less popular than the others across the globe? Are you surprised by any of the numbers on this chart? Why might some countries

have a citizenry that has more trust in the press while in others the legislature scores higher?

2. Why are the U.S. scores so low? What does it mean for politics when a large percentage of a population loses confidence in the institutions that keep its democracy functioning?

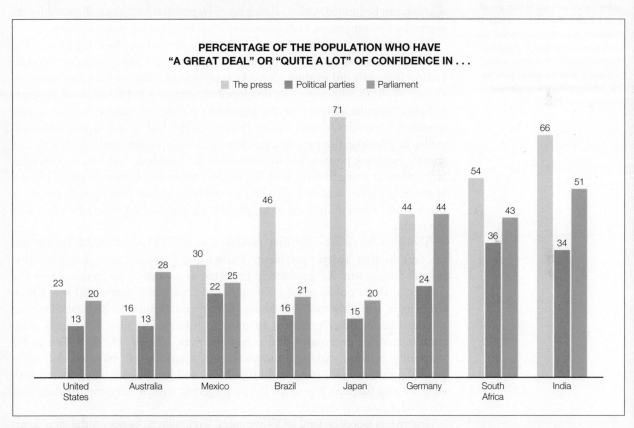

PERCENTAGE OF THE POPULATION WHO HAVE "A GREAT DEAL" OR "QUITE A LOT" OF CONFIDENCE IN . . .

The press · Political parties · Parliament

	The press	Political parties	Parliament
United States	23	13	20
Australia	16	13	28
Mexico	30	22	25
Brazil	46	16	21
Japan	71	15	20
Germany	44	24	44
South Africa	54	36	43
India	66	34	51

Source: R. Inglehart et al., eds., "World Values Survey: Round Six—Country-Pooled Datafile Version," 2014, www.worldvaluessurvey.org (accessed 8/12/19).

Donald J. Trump ✓
@realDonaldTrump

I am SUBSTANTIALLY LOWERING MEDICARE PREMIUMS. Have instituted Favored Nations Clause and Rebates on Drug Companies. Never been done before. Drug companies are hitting me with Fake Ads, just like sleepy Joe. Be careful! Drug prices will be reduced massively, and soon.

8:03 AM · Sep 17, 2020 · Twitter for iPhone

Presidents have used a variety of methods over the years to help shape public opinion in support of their policies. President Franklin D. Roosevelt held "fireside chats," or radio broadcasts that highlighted his policy goals. President Trump frequently tweeted about policies and other politicians to connect with citizens.

relations can be limited. Often, claims made by political leaders are disputed by the media, by interest groups, and, increasingly, by the opposing political party.

These challenges haven't stopped modern presidents from focusing a great deal of attention on shaping public opinion to support their policy agendas. Franklin Delano Roosevelt did so through his famous "fireside chat" radio broadcasts. The George W. Bush administration developed an extensive public-relations program to bolster popular support for the president's policies, including the war against terrorism.[42] Barack Obama's White House was the first to use digital and social media to promote the president's policy agenda, especially national health care reform. Facebook posts served to personalize the president, and Obama was especially adept at using Twitter, with 70 million followers on that network. His use of multiple Twitter accounts allowed him to communicate directly with people to shape public opinion in favor of his policies without having to be interviewed by the media.

Though Obama was the first president to use Twitter, Donald Trump was the nation's first Twitter president. Twitter and Facebook were key tools that helped Trump win the presidency in 2016; as president he continued to use Twitter to shape public opinion, though not always in a purposeful way. Often tweeting in the early morning hours, Trump communicated his sentiments on politics like no other president in modern history, although his tweets often contradicted his own staff—and sometimes even himself. He used Twitter for proposing policies, making announcements, attacking his enemies, defending himself, promoting his party and his policies, and just plain venting. Laced with emotion and frequent typos, his tweets projected authenticity, even if they were not always factually correct.

Trump was especially fond of Twitter rants, with multiple tweets on the same topic. For example, facing mounting criticism and a federal investigation into whether his campaign coordinated with the Russians to sway the 2016 election, he tweeted in June 2017, "I am being investigated for firing the FBI Director by the man who told me to fire the FBI Director! Witch Hunt"[43] and "You are witnessing the single greatest WITCH HUNT in American political history - led by some very bad and conflicted people! #MAGA" ("Make America Great Again"—Trump's campaign slogan).[44] New scholarship argues that political leaders like Trump prefer social media to traditional media since they can control the content and keep it unfiltered by the mainstream press.[45]

FOR CRITICAL ANALYSIS

Does it matter what news sources an individual reads? How can the news influence public attitudes on issues of public policy?

THE MASS MEDIA

The media are among the most powerful forces operating in the **marketplace of ideas.** As we shall see in Chapter 7, the mass media are not simply neutral messengers for ideas developed by others, but instead are opinion makers that have an enormous impact on popular attitudes. For example, since the publication of the Pentagon Papers by the *New York Times* and the exposure of the Watergate scandal led by the *Washington Post* in the 1970s, the national news media have relentlessly investigated personal and official wrongdoing by politicians and public officials. Media revelation of corruption in government has contributed to the cynicism and distrust of government that prevail in much of the general public.

At the same time, the ways in which media coverage interprets or "frames" specific events can have a major impact on popular responses to and opinions about these events.[46] Given the critical importance of media framing to the way the public perceives the news, President George W. Bush went to great lengths to persuade broadcasters to follow his administration's lead in their coverage of both terrorism and America's response to it in the months following the September 11, 2001, attacks. The media went along, supporting the administration's military campaigns in Afghanistan and Iraq, as well as its domestic antiterrorist effort. Even supposedly liberal newspapers such as the *New York Times* published articles supportive of the invasion of Iraq in 2003. After months of presidential messages and media coverage focused on the threat of terrorism, by the time of the invasion public support for it had reached over 70 percent, according to Gallup polls.[47] By 2008 54 percent of Americans thought using military force in Iraq was a mistake, as the war dragged on and media framing of the conflict changed.[48] More than 15 years later, in 2018, one in two Americans thought the Iraq war was a mistake.[49]

marketplace of ideas the public forum in which beliefs and ideas are exchanged and compete

Political Knowledge and Changes in Public Opinion

> **Explain how Americans' level of political knowledge affects public opinion and democracy**

The underlying factors that shape individuals' political opinions remain relatively constant through time: one's level of education, for example, is generally set by early adulthood. However, individuals also encounter new information from political leaders and the media throughout their lives. What role does political knowledge and information play in forming opinions? What causes people's opinions to change?

STABILITY AND CHANGE OF PUBLIC OPINION

One of the most important studies of how public opinion is formed is by political scientist John Zaller,[50] who argues that individuals learn about politics by converting information from the news, elected officials, and other sources into opinions. His model of opinion formation works in three stages. In the "receive" stage, an individual receives information from a number of different sources. In the "accept" stage, the individual assesses this information through the lens of her previously held political views and accepts only those messages that fit with these beliefs, meaning that some information will be rejected. Finally, in the "sample" stage, the individual selects some of the accepted information—often the most recent—and forms an opinion from it.

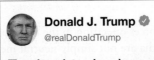

Donald J. Trump ✓
@realDonaldTrump

Follow ⌄

Excited to be heading home to see the House pass a GREAT Tax Bill with the middle class getting big TAX CUTS!

#MakeAmericaGreatAgain🇺🇸

6:21 PM - 13 Nov 2017

After political opinions form, they remain relatively stable. The most knowledgeable people are generally able to discern whether new information fits or contradicts their previously held beliefs. Do you think the people in this protest (left) would change their opinions about tax cuts after seeing President Trump's tweet (right)?

So, according to this theory, if you receive information from various sources about a new White House policy to prevent California from setting stricter auto-emission standards than the federal standards, you will then assess the different messages based on what you already believe about environmental policy. If you believe environmental regulations are generally bad, you will likely reject messages suggesting this policy change is bad and accept only those suggesting it is good. Alternatively, if you are generally concerned with climate change, you will accept news saying this policy change over emissions is bad for the environment, air quality, and states' rights.

The decision to accept or reject information is based on political knowledge. When asked about his opinion on a topic, the individual selects the most relevant or most recently acquired and accepted information from his "bucket" of information (the third stage above). Citizens with more political knowledge can differentiate between information that fits and information that does not fit with their beliefs—and then correctly accept or reject it.

For less-informed citizens, the media and political leaders may play a larger role in influencing public opinion. These individuals are more susceptible than more-informed individuals to fake news or disinformation, partisan news, and political propaganda from political elites. This reliance on politicians and the media, Zaller concludes, means that the public's opinions are often unstable and unreliable because these sources provide competing, changing information. As a result, public opinion is often a reflection of whatever recent campaign message (or media story) an individual has stored in her short-term memory. As we will see in Chapter 7, this effect is called *priming*.

Another way of understanding how individuals form political opinions is the online-processing model.[51] According to this model, an individual keeps a running tally of information and uses that tally to form an opinion on a policy issue or to decide which candidate to vote for. However, by the time the individual actually votes or voices the opinion, she may have forgotten some of the older information included in her decision-making process. This effect leads to the misconception that voters are uninformed, when in fact their opinion is informed but they have not retained all of the facts used to form that opinion.

Online processing implies a large role for political elites and the media but does not necessarily suggest that public preferences are unstable or not worthwhile. If public opinion is easily manipulated, the democratic process, which relies on citizens to play a significant part in the government, will be at risk. But other research has shown that individuals are quite stable in their policy attitudes.[52]

To take a closer look at whether and how public opinion changes, see Figure 6.7. The Pew Research Center tracks public opinion over time with annual surveys asking identical questions. Some opinions are relatively stable: support for abortion, for example, has remained virtually unchanged over the past decade, with over half of Americans saying it should be legal in all or most cases. Similarly, opinions on protecting the environment have been remarkably stable. In contrast, opinion on same-sex marriage has changed dramatically over the past two decades, with approval of it increasing by 25 percentage points.

The shift in public opinion on same-sex marriage has occurred partly in response to government policy—a response political scientists call "policy feedback." In 2009, Iowa became just the third U.S. state to allow same-sex marriages when the

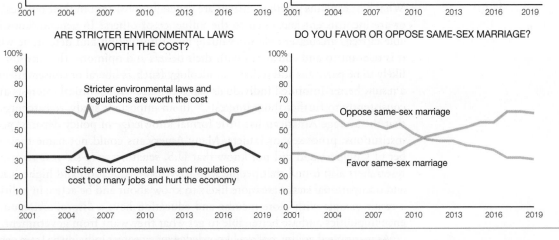

FIGURE 6.7
. . . .
Stability and Change in Public Opinion

Public opinion on some issues has stayed stable in the last two decades, while opinion on other issues has shifted. What might explain why opinion on gun control and same-sex marriage has changed, while opinion on abortion and protecting the environment has stayed relatively constant?

DO YOU THINK ABORTION SHOULD BE LEGAL IN ALL OR MOST CASES?

Legal in all/most cases

Illegal in all/most cases

WHAT DO YOU THINK IS MORE IMPORTANT, TO CONTROL GUN OWNERSHIP OR PROTECT THE RIGHT TO OWN GUNS?

Control gun ownership

Protect the right to own guns

ARE STRICTER ENVIRONMENTAL LAWS WORTH THE COST?

Stricter environmental laws and regulations are worth the cost

Stricter environmental laws and regulations cost too many jobs and hurt the economy

DO YOU FAVOR OR OPPOSE SAME-SEX MARRIAGE?

Oppose same-sex marriage

Favor same-sex marriage

SOURCES: Pew Research Center, "Public Opinion on Abortion," August 29, 2019, www.pewforum.org/fact-sheet/public-opinion-on-abortion/; Katherine Schaeffer, "Share of Americans Who Favor Stricter Gun Laws Has Increased Since 2017," Pew Research Center, www.pewresearch.org/fact-tank/2019/10/16/share-of-americans-who-favor-stricter-gun-laws-has-increased-since-2017/; Pew Research Center, "Attitudes on Same-Sex Marriage," May 14, 2019, www.pewforum.org/fact-sheet/changing-attitudes-on-gay-marriage/; Cary Funk, Brian Kennedy "How Americans See Climate Change and the Environment in 7 Charts," April 21, 2020, www.pewresearch.org/fact-tank/2020/04/21/how-americans-see-climate-change-and-the-environment-in-7-charts/ft_2020-04-21_earthday_03/ (accessed 10/19/20).

state Supreme Court issued a unanimous decision in the case *Varnum v. Brien*.[53] Although the decision was unpopular at the time, a survey of Iowans conducted immediately before and after it showed that it had led to large changes in public opinion in favor of same-sex marriage, with certain groups—Democrats, educated, young, and nonreligious people and those who had gay/lesbian family members or friends—the most likely to have changed their opinion.[54] In 2015 the U.S. Supreme Court ruled in favor of legalizing same-sex marriage in all 50 states. Favorable public opinion may have helped pave the way for national policy change.[55]

Public opinion on the environment also shows evidence of significant change. Surveys reveal most Americans favor protecting the environment consistent with the terms of the Paris Agreement; President Trump in 2017 withdrew the United States from that international treaty, which aims to prevent climate change by reducing reliance on fossil fuels such as coal, oil, and gas and developing alternative energy sources such as wind and solar. Compared with a decade ago, more Americans today say protecting the environment and dealing with global climate change should be top priorities for the president and Congress. Only 30 percent of Americans said dealing with climate change should be a top priority in 2008, compared to 44 percent in 2019. Over the same time period, support for protecting the environment rose from 40 percent to 56 percent.[56] Two-thirds of U.S. adults said the "government is not doing enough to reduce the effects of global climate change." Most Americans favor developing alternative energy sources, including more solar panel farms (89 percent) and wind turbine farms (85 percent),[57] which are large increases from the previous decade.

Though there is growing agreement on protecting the environment, partisan differences about these issues persist. Roughly 90 percent of liberal Democrats believe the federal government is not doing enough to protect key aspects of the environment such as air and water quality, compared with just 26 percent of conservative Republicans who say the same. About half of conservative Republicans argue that policies to protect the environment can hurt the economy and jobs.[58]

POLITICAL KNOWLEDGE

What best explains whether citizens are generally consistent in their political views or are inconsistent and open to the influence of others? In general, knowledgeable citizens are better able to evaluate new information and determine whether it is relevant to and consistent with their beliefs and opinions; they are also more likely to be partisans and to have an ideology (such as liberal or conservative).[59] As a result, better-informed individuals can recognize their political interests and act consistently to further those interests.[60] In an important study, researchers found that the average American has little formal knowledge of policy debates, political institutions, processes, or leaders. Many Americans could not name their member of Congress and did not know that U.S. senators serve six-year terms.[61] The researchers also found that people who have more education and higher incomes and occupational status are more likely to know about and be active in politics. As a result, people with more income and education have a disproportionate influence in politics and are better able to get what they want from government.

As mentioned before, political knowledge may protect individuals from exposure to misinformation that can distort public opinion. While social media have created new platforms for organizing and voter mobilizing, discussing politics, and creating networks (see Chapter 7), they have also been associated with increased misinformation. Fake news on Facebook—with its billion users globally—was extensive in the

2016 election. In 2020, YouTube (owned by Google) became a primary platform for misinformation campaigns.

Russian "bot" accounts on Twitter were the source of many of the fake stories in 2016. Both Google and Facebook implemented new protocols to block content from deceptive outlets, and Twitter, Reddit, and Instagram deleted millions of fake accounts in response. During the 2020 presidential election and its aftermath, misinformation was spread largely by Americans and elected officials, including President Trump. In the days after the election, Twitter labeled 37 percent of Trump's tweets as false or misleading. Misinformation spread by elected officials and online news has encouraged more Americans to seek websites such as PolitiFact .com, FactCheck.org, and Snopes.com to verify the content of political information.

Shortcuts and Cues Because being informed politically requires a substantial investment of time and energy for reading the daily news, most Americans try to get political information and make political decisions "on the cheap" by using shortcuts. As noted previously, researchers have found that individuals rely on cues from sources they trust—party elites, interest groups, and media outlets—to help them form their attitudes.[62] Today, tweets from trusted elected officials are an increasingly important source of information. Other "inexpensive" ways to become informed involve taking cues from trusted friends, social networks and social media, relatives, colleagues, and sometimes religious leaders.

Political scientists Richard Lau and David Redlawsk have found that by using informational shortcuts, average citizens can form political opinions that are, in most instances, consistent with their underlying preferences. They call this consistency "voting correctly."[63] Even individuals with low levels of political knowledge, Lau and Redlawsk find, can make relatively informed political choices by relying on these cues.[64] From this perspective, low levels of knowledge about politics, or instability of opinions, may not be a serious problem as long as individuals can receive reliable shortcuts from opinion leaders.

The public's reliance on elite cues has taken on new significance, though, in today's era of party polarization. As elected officials have become increasingly polarized, political

People use cues from political elites and other trusted sources as a shortcut to forming opinions. Someone might not know the details about voting rights and the For the People Act, but if they were a liberal or Democrat, they might hear former Representative John Lewis (D-Ga.), an activist during the civil rights movement, speaking on behalf of the bill and then feel they, too, supported it.

scientists have found stark evidence that this new environment changes how citizens form opinions and make decisions. Notably, polarization means that party endorsements of an issue or candidate have a larger impact on public opinion than they used to.

For example, if Republican leaders in Congress support a plan to impose higher taxes (tariffs) on foreign goods, people who identify as Republicans are more likely to support the plan regardless of its possible negative economic effects or the party's and conservatives' traditional support for free trade and opposition to tariffs. At the same time, party polarization decreases reliance on other sources, as people increasingly filter the news, relying on sources that put forth news, opinion, and information that conform to what they already believe. Party polarization may thus reduce overall levels of political knowledge.[65]

Skim and Scan Another factor affecting political knowledge is the *form* in which people consume news and information. The transformation of media in the digital era has had a profound effect on the way the news is reported and how citizens learn about politics. Today more than three in four Americans read the news online or seek political information there.[66] Recent research also indicates a trend in journalism toward shorter articles and flashier headlines, and Twitter limits text to 280 characters. Americans today are likely to read the news by skimming and scanning multiple headlines online, in bits and bytes, rather than by reading long news articles.[67]

Has the shift to digital media created a more informed public, considering the broader diversity of information sources and more personalized communication of the news via social media, or a less informed one, because of a tendency to favor skimming and scanning over in-depth reading? As noted earlier, some research indicates that most people use simple cues and shortcuts to process political information. If so, skimming and scanning might provide a reasonable way to be informed without extensive time or effort.

Costs to Democracy Low levels of political knowledge pose problems for democratic governments. Those who lack political knowledge cannot effectively defend their political interests, rights, and freedoms and can easily become losers in political struggles and government policy. The presence of large numbers of politically

More and more people are getting their news online, which seems to have altered reading habits. News articles have become shorter, and people are spending more time scanning headlines and less reading in-depth coverage.

ignorant citizens means that power can more easily be manipulated by political elites, the media, foreign governments, and wealthy special interests that seek to shape public opinion. If knowledge is power, then a lack of knowledge can contribute to growing political and economic inequality.

Take one of the most important areas of government policy: taxation. Although the United States has one of the largest gaps between the rich and the poor of any nation in the world, over the past several decades the rate of taxation on its wealthiest citizens has been substantially reduced.[68] In 2001, President George W. Bush signed into law a bill providing a substantial tax break mainly benefiting the top 1 percent of the nation's wage earners. Political scientist Larry Bartels has shown that the 2001 tax cuts were favored by millions of middle- and lower-middle-class citizens who did not stand to benefit from them, and that 40 percent of Americans had no opinion at all about the cuts.

The explanation for this odd state of affairs appears to be a lack of political knowledge. Millions of people who were unlikely to benefit from the cuts thought they would. Since most Americans think they pay too much in taxes, they favored the policy, even if the wealthy benefited much more than the middle class. (See the Who Are Americans? feature for public opinion on income inequality.)

In 2017, President Trump and the Republican-controlled Congress adopted even larger tax cuts for the affluent and dramatically reduced corporate taxes. This time, however, polls showed a majority of Americans opposed the cuts. Had political knowledge around taxes increased, or did the opposition reflect the low approval ratings for Trump and Congress at the time? The public response to the coronavirus outbreak in 2020 shows that lack of political knowledge can sometimes have dire consequences. Early in the outbreak, lack of knowledge of the seriousness of the pandemic hindered public health efforts encouraging social distancing and wearing face masks to prevent the spread of the disease. In turn, the public health crisis may deepen existing economic inequalities in the United States. Middle-class and lower-income Americans have taken the brunt of the economic fallout from the coronavirus outbreak in terms of lost jobs and reductions in salary. Half of lower-income Americans report household job or wage loss due to the coronavirus pandemic.[69]

Public Opinion and Government Policy

> **Explain the relationship between public opinion and government policy**

Given generally low levels of political knowledge among voters and the changing nature of public opinion, it's little wonder that politicians are sometimes unwilling to act solely on the basis of public opinion. But one could argue that consulting public opinion is a duty of elected officials in a democracy. Is government policy responsive to public opinion?

GOVERNMENT RESPONSIVENESS TO PUBLIC OPINION

Studies generally find that elected officials are influenced by the preferences of the public. Political scientists Benjamin Page and Robert Shapiro explored the relationship between broad changes in opinion toward various political issues and the policy outcomes that most closely correspond to the issues.[70] They found that shifts in public opinion on particular issues do in fact tend to lead to changes in public

HERE'S THE LATEST POLL ON YOUR PERFORMANCE AS DAD. YOUR APPROVAL RATING IS PRETTY LOW, I'M AFRAID.

THAT'S BECAUSE THERE'S NOT NECESSARILY ANY CONNECTION BETWEEN WHAT'S GOOD AND WHAT'S POPULAR. I DO WHAT'S RIGHT, NOT WHAT GETS APPROVAL.

YOU'LL NEVER KEEP THE JOB WITH *THAT* ATTITUDE.

IF SOMEONE ELSE OFFERS TO DO IT, LET ME KNOW.

© 1994 Watterson/Dist. by Universal Press Syndicate 2-10

To what extent do political leaders listen to the opinions of their constituents? To what extent should they listen? Is Calvin's father right that leaders should do what they believe is right, not what the public wants?

policy. This is especially true when there are wide swings in opinion on particularly high-profile issues that are relatively simple, such as requiring all Americans to have health insurance, and government aid for those unable to afford it. Other studies have found similar evidence. At the state level, states where conservative opinions predominate tend to adopt more conservative laws and states with more liberal public opinion adopt more liberal policies.[71]

However, there is reason to believe that the relationship between government policy and public opinion is more dynamic, with policy responding to opinion but also mass opinions shifting based on new government policies.[72] Recent studies have found government policy to have an effect on opinion in various areas, such as environmental protection, health care, welfare reform, the death penalty, and smoking bans. For example, in states that adopted smoking bans, public opinion then shifted to become more critical of cigarette smoking than in states without such bans.[73] This phenomenon is called policy feedback.

Scholars have suggested a number of possible mechanisms to explain policy feedback. New policies may expose the public to new ideas, causing opinion to change. Or experience with a successful or unsuccessful policy may give the public new information that may also modify opinions. A policy might act as a "signal" of a moral or ethical view (such as a smoking ban acting as a "signal" that smoking should be stigmatized).

Of course, sometimes public opinion and policy do not align, as illustrated by the prior discussion of environmental policy and the Paris Agreement; similarly, while a majority (53 percent) of Americans oppose building the wall between the United States and Mexico, it is being built. Sometimes public officials act on their own preferences if they believe doing so will benefit government, the private sector (businesses), or society, and lawmakers typically do use their own judgment when making policy choices.[74] When elected officials pursue policies not aligned with public opinion, it is often because they view particular groups of the electorate as more important than others. Groups or individuals that regularly vote for or contribute financially to a candidate have their interests more closely represented than the general public does.[75]

DOES EVERYONE'S OPINION COUNT EQUALLY?

In a democracy, where each person has one vote, it is assumed that elected representatives will implement the policies favored by the majority of the people, and in a general sense this happens in the United States. But when policy issues are more complicated (such as taxation or foreign policy regarding trade and tariffs), the

What Shapes Public Opinion on Income Inequality?

> In your opinion, which generally has more to do with . . .

An individual's party identification, gender, and income may influence his or her opinions on specific issues. A recent study showed there are significant differences of opinion about the government's role in reducing the income gap between men and women and across income groups, but the most pronounced differences are between Democrats and Republicans.

SOURCES: Data from Pew Research Center (accessed 11/19/17).

Why a person is rich

 Worked harder   Had advantages in life

Overall
45%   43%

By gender
49%   39%
Men

41%   47%
Women

By party
66%   21%
Republicans

29%   60%
Democrats

By education
47%   41%
High school or less

42%   47%
College grad

By income
39%   49%
Family income <$30K

46%   44%
Family income $30K–$74,999

51%   37%
Family income $75K+

Why a person is poor

 Lack of effort   Circumstances beyond control

Overall

34%   53%

By gender
42%   46%
Men

26%   60%
Women

By party
56%   32%
Republicans

19%   71%
Democrats

By education
38%   49%
High school or less

28%   59%
College grad

By income
31%   56%
Family income <$30K

38%   51%
Family income $30K–$74,999

33%   57%
Family income $75K+

FOR CRITICAL ANALYSIS

1. Do the findings in this study show that opinions are shaped by economic self-interest? Why or why not?

2. Which of these groups is most likely to support government action to address inequality? Are the other groups not concerned about inequality? Use the data to explain your answers.

Charles Koch, one of the wealthiest people in the world, is a major donor to Republican candidates and causes. Some say that the opinions of wealthier individuals have more influence on politicians and government policy, though this has been difficult to prove unequivocally.

public is likely to have less of a voice. Further, citizens who are more affluent and more educated have a disproportionate influence over politics and public policy decisions. Likewise, elected officials respond more strongly to voters than nonvoters, and to Whites than people of color.

How do more affluent and educated citizens manage to exert outsize influence over policy makers? One way is obvious: they vote at higher rates, and they are more likely to contribute money to political campaigns. As we will discuss in Chapter 8, voters and individuals making political contributions tend to be more affluent and educated than nonvoters and noncontributors. And a recent comparative study of the roll-call votes of U.S. senators demonstrated that they are indeed responsive to the policy preferences of voters but not to those of nonvoters.[76]

In regard to income group, research has found that both Republican and Democratic senators are less likely to respond to the opinions of low-income constituents than higher-income ones.[77] Senate votes on such varied issues as the minimum wage, civil rights, and abortion are all more likely to reflect the opinions of the rich. Their influence may explain government policies such as failure to increase the federal minimum wage and the 2017 tax reform that significantly reduced corporate taxes and reduced taxes paid by the wealthiest citizens, policies that contribute to growing income inequality.[78]

Research by political scientist Martin Gilens also suggests that those with higher incomes are more likely to have their policy preferences represented by actual policies.[79] He considered public-opinion surveys on a wide variety of policy issues conducted over 20 years and compared the responses of upper- and lower-income groups with related federal policy outcomes. Gilens found a relationship between what the public wants and what the government actually does, with a strong bias toward the status quo. But when Americans with different income levels are inconsistent in their policy preferences as a group (both rich and poor people are Democrats and Republicans), actual policies strongly reflect the preferences of the most affluent and show little or no relationship to the preferences of poor or middle-income Americans. Better educated and informed individuals have more consistent preferences across a wide range of policy areas to articulate and transmit to elected officials and that can also explain why some groups are better represented, beyond income.[80] Most members of Congress are affluent and educated themselves, which may bias them to favor information from individuals and businesses with interests similar to their own, or from groups that helped them gain public office. Although every American citizen has an equal right to voice opinions in the political arena, some voices receive a very attentive listening, while others are hardly heard at all.[81]

Measuring Public Opinion

> Explain how surveys and big data can accurately measure public opinion

Public officials and political campaigns make extensive use of data analytics and **public-opinion polls** to help them decide whether to run for office, what policies to support, how to vote on important legislation, and what types of appeals to make in their campaigns. Understanding how public opinion is measured can help us evaluate claims and arguments made by politicians and political commentators.

public-opinion polls scientific instruments for measuring public opinion

MEASURING PUBLIC OPINION FROM SURVEYS

It is not feasible to interview all 330 million-plus residents of the United States on their opinions of who should be the next president or how the government should improve the economy and create jobs. Instead, pollsters take a **sample** of the population and use it to make inferences (predictions and educated guesses) about the preferences of the population as a whole. For a political survey to be an accurate representation of the population, it must meet certain requirements, including an appropriate sampling method (choosing respondents randomly), a sufficiently large sample size, and the avoidance of selection bias.[82] Random sample surveys are used extensively in business and marketing as well as politics; they ensure that the samples are accurate and reliable predictions of the underlying population.

Websites such as RealClearPolitics.com list the results of most political surveys released each day; during elections, this can be dozens of different surveys daily. Every week, the opinions of Americans regarding candidates and public policies are measured, as are opinions on a vast array of products (toothpaste), entertainment (movies), and even college political science textbooks!

Representative Samples One way to obtain a representative sample is what statisticians call a **simple random sample (or probability sample)**. To take such a sample, one would need a complete list of all the people in the United States, and individuals would be randomly selected from that list. Imagine that everyone's name was entered into a lottery, with names then drawn blindly from an enormous box. If everyone had an equal chance of selection, the result would be a random sample.

Since there is no complete list of all Americans, pollsters use census data, lists of telephone numbers, or national commercial voter-roll files (which include all U.S. adults—registered and nonregistered), to draw samples of people to interview. State voter-registration files are often used in political surveys designed to predict public opinion or election results. If respondents are chosen randomly and everyone has an equal chance of being selected, then the results can be used to predict behavior for the overall population. If randomization is not used or some people are excluded from the chance to be selected, then the sample will be biased and cannot be used to generalize to the population accurately. The timing of surveys is important; surveys conducted two months before an election may produce very different results from those the week before an election, because public opinion may have changed during this time as one candidate gains momentum over the other.

Another method of drawing a random sample is a technique called **random digit dialing**. A computer random-number generator is used to produce a list of 10-digit telephone numbers. Given that 95 percent of Americans have telephones (cell phones or landlines), this technique usually results in a random national sample because almost every citizen has a chance of being selected for the survey. Telephone and text message surveys are fairly accurate, cost-effective, and flexible in the type of questions that can be asked; but many people refuse to answer political ones, and response rates—the percentage of those called who actually answer the survey—have been falling steadily, now averaging less than 10 percent.[83]

Sample Size A sample must be large enough to provide an accurate representation of the population. Surprisingly, the size of the population being measured doesn't matter, only the size of the sample. A survey of 1,000 people is almost as effective

sample a small group selected by researchers to represent the most important characteristics of an entire population

simple random sample (or probability sample) a method used by pollsters to select a representative sample in which every individual in the population has an equal probability of being selected as a respondent

random digit dialing a polling method in which respondents are selected at random from a list of 10-digit telephone numbers, with every effort made to avoid bias in the construction of the sample

Evaluate a Poll

NEIL NEWHOUSE, partner and cofounder of Public Opinion Strategies, a leading Republican polling firm

One of the main ways in which elected officials, other policy makers, the media, and members of the public know what Americans think about government, politics, and policy is the public-opinion poll. How can you know which poll results are credible and worthy of your attention?

We spoke to Neil Newhouse, partner and cofounder of Public Opinion Strategies, a leading Republican polling firm. He gave us these tips for evaluating surveys:

1 Who did they interview? Did the pollsters interview adults? Registered voters? Likely voters? Different topics require different interviewees. If you are interested in which candidate is ahead in an electoral contest, for example, you want a poll of likely voters, because they're who are going to make that decision. A poll of adults would be misleading since only a subset of adults turn out to vote.

2 How did they interview their subjects? Surveys should strive for a random sample of the target population, meaning all members of the target population had an equal chance of being interviewed. Polls where people opt in to be interviewed do not have random samples and will be misleading. A phone call into a radio station is not a poll.

3 How many did they interview? A random sample allows pollsters to draw accurate conclusions about the attitudes of the underlying population. Surveying just 800 people nationwide can provide an estimate of an attitude such as presidential approval. It's just like the doctor's office. The doctor takes a sample of your blood rather than draining your entire body.

4 What confidence do we have in the results? Pollsters typically report a "point estimate," for example "43 percent of likely voters approve of the president's performance." Random sampling also allows calculation of the "confidence interval," how confident we are in the results; larger samples provide more certainty. A confidence interval of plus or minus 3 points means true

presidential approval is probably between 40 and 46 percent. A smaller sample might have a confidence interval of plus or minus 5 points, meaning the true answer is probably between 38 and 48 percent.

5 Over what length of time? The ideal poll is a "snapshot in time," conducted over three to five days, particularly for outcomes like election preferences. The problem with polls done over four or five weeks is that people's opinions change.

6 What survey mode was used? Was it a live phone call, an automated call ("press 1 for candidate Smith, 2 for candidate Jones"), or on the internet? Each survey mode has a bias. Online polls result in more male and younger respondents. Landline phone surveys yield more older individuals, while cell phone surveys yield more young people. Often it is better to have a live phone call than an automated call, but a live interviewer can introduce bias as well. For example, Donald Trump's support before the 2016 presidential election was 3 percentage points higher in automated polls than in live phone polls, since some people were reluctant to tell pollsters that they were planning to vote for him.

7 In what order were questions asked, and with what question wording? To assess trends, it is best to ask the same questions in the same order over time so that you can compare apples to apples. Question wording also matters; quality polls use appropriate wording that doesn't go begging for an answer.

8 **Who conducted the poll?** Look for a name brand, a pollster that surveys on an ongoing basis, not just occasionally. If you never heard of the outfit or it seems obscure, it may not be the most reliable source of poll data.

Go to the aggregators, such as RealClearPolitics.com or FiveThirtyEight.com. They have made some judgments about quality and only include credible polls. And even if some lower-quality polls are included, you can see many poll results at once and triangulate the overall picture.

FiveThirtyEight's Pollster Ratings

Based on the historical accuracy and methodology of each firm's polls.

Read more   Download the data   See the latest polls

Ratings	Definitions

Search for a pollster

POLLSTER	METHOD	LIVE CALLER WITH CELLPHONES	NCPP/ AAPOR/ ROPER	POLLS ANALYZED	SIMPLE AVERAGE ERROR	RACES CALLED CORRECTLY	ADVANCED +/-	PREDICTIVE +/-	538 GRADE	BANNED BY 538	MEAN-REVERTED BIAS
SurveyUSA	IVR/ online/ live	O	O	790	4.6	90%	-1.1	-0.8	A		D+0.1
Rasmussen Reports/ Pulse Opinion Research	IVR/ online			716	5.3	78%	+0.3	+0.8	C+		R+1.5
Zogby Interactive/JZ Analytics	Online			464	5.6	78%	+0.5	+1.0	C		R+0.8
Mason-Dixon Polling & Research Inc.	Live	O		428	5.2	86%	-0.5	-0.2	B+		R+0.7
Public Policy Polling	IVR/ online/ text			418	5.0	80%	-0.3	+0.2	B		D+0.3
YouGov	Online			395	5.0	89%	-0.1	+0.4	B-		D+0.4
Research 2000	Live*			278	5.5	88%	-0.1	+0.4	F		D+1.4

Not all pollsters are created equal. Here, FiveThirtyEight, an online source that rates and aggregates polls, grades pollsters on a scale from A to F based on how reliable the pollster gathers data and assesses it.

for measuring the opinions of all Texans (29.5 million residents) as the opinions of all Americans (over 330 million residents).

Flipping a coin shows how sample sizes work. After tossing a coin 10 times, the number of heads may not be close to 5. After 100 tosses of the coin, though, the number of heads should be close to 50 and, after 1,000 tosses, very close to 500. In fact, after 1,000 tosses, there is a 95 percent chance that the percentage of heads will be somewhere between 46.9 and 53.1.

This 3.1 percent variation from 50 percent is called the **sampling error (or margin of error)**: the chance that a sample used does not accurately represent the population from which it is drawn. In this case, 3.1 percent is the amount of uncertainty we can expect with a typical 1,000-person survey. If we conduct a national survey and find candidate A leads candidate B 52 to 47 percent with a margin of error of 3 percent, it means the likely support for candidate A is anywhere from 55 to 49 percent and the likely support for candidate B is anywhere from 50 to 44 percent. Thus, in this scenario, the margin of error tells us that despite seeming to trail by 5 percent, B could actually be leading the election (50 to 49 percent)!

Normally, samples of 1,000 people are considered sufficient for accurately measuring public opinion through the use of surveys. Larger sample sizes can yield even more accurate predictions, but there is a trade-off in terms of cost since it is more expensive to survey more people. Why is a sample size of only 1,000 generally accepted as adequately representative of much larger populations?

The answer is the "diminishing returns" of sampling more and more people. The sampling error from a sample of 500 people is 4.4 percent. With 1,000 respondents it drops to 3.1 percent, but with 1,500 only to 2.5 percent. That is, smaller and smaller gains in accuracy have to be weighed against the increasing costs of polling more people. The consensus among statisticians and pollsters is that the optimal trade-off point—the "gold standard"—is 1,000. But today many surveys conducted online include sometimes hundreds of thousands of respondents, making their predictions potentially even more accurate. But if the sample is biased or does not reflect the electorate, even very large surveys can be wrong.

Survey Design and Question Wording Even with a good sample design, surveys may fail to reflect the true distribution of opinion within a target population. One frequent source of measurement error is the wording of survey questions. The words used in a question can have an enormous impact on the answers it elicits. The reliability of survey results can be adversely affected by poor question wording (such as giving respondents only yes-or-no choices when many of them favor a third or middle-ground option), the ordering of questions (such as earlier questions encouraging certain responses to later ones), ambiguous questions, awkward questions, or questions with built-in biases (questions that prime answers in some way or another).

Differences in the wording of a question can convey vastly different meanings to respondents and thus produce quite different response patterns (see Box 6.3). For example, for many years the University of Chicago's National Opinion Research Center has asked respondents whether they think the federal government is spending too much, too little, or about the right amount of money on "assistance for the poor." Answering the question posed this way, about two-thirds of all respondents seem to believe that the government is spending too little. However, the same survey also asks whether the government spends too much, too little, or about the right amount for welfare. When the word *welfare* is substituted for "assistance for the poor," about half of all respondents indicate that too much is being spent.[84]

sampling error (or margin of error) polling error that arises based on the small size of the sample

BOX 6.3
....
It Depends on How You Ask

THE SITUATION
The public's desire for tax cuts can be hard to measure. In 2000, pollsters asked what should be done with the nation's budget surplus and got different results depending on the specifics of the question.

THE QUESTION
President [Bill] Clinton has proposed setting aside approximately two-thirds of an expected budget surplus to fix the Social Security system. What do you think the leaders in Washington should do with the remainder of the surplus?

VARIATION 1
Should the money be used for a tax cut, or should it be used to fund new government programs?

VARIATION 2
Should the money be used for a tax cut, or should it be spent on programs for education, the environment, health care, crime fighting, and military defense?

SOURCE: Pew Research Center, reported in the *New York Times*, January 30, 2000, WK 3.

Online Surveys Today, pollsters are increasingly turning to the use of online surveys, often using similar techniques to those of telephone surveys. Online surveys can be more efficient, less costly, and more accurate than standard phone surveys, and they include much larger samples of young people and yield more accurate results within age cohorts. But many surveys you will find online do not use probability random sampling and thus are not representative of the American population. Instead, they reflect the opinions of those willing to take a quiz online.

Knowledge Networks and YouGov are leaders in internet polling using sampling methods in which respondents complete surveys online instead of being interviewed on the phone. YouGov has a large population of respondents (hundreds of thousands of individuals) identified using random sampling, so the sample is representative of the American population. Individuals without internet access are given free subscriptions to internet service providers or complete the surveys using the TV. If a client commissions a survey, YouGov randomly draws a sample of, say, 1,000 people from its population of online respondents. Because respondents receive free internet access in return for completing a number of surveys, they are more likely to actually do so. YouGov has been more accurate than other polling firms in predicting the outcomes of recent presidential elections.[85]

Other polling companies use different methods for conducting internet surveys, often by using statistical weights to make the surveys generally representative of the American population.[86] An example is the Cooperative Congressional Election Study, which has very large samples, more than 50,000 people, and rolling panel survey designs, where the same respondents are interviewed repeatedly over months. In the future, internet surveys may be more representative of the American population than traditional telephone surveys and may replace them entirely, especially given falling response rates for telephone surveys. Many surveys are now hybrid, sometimes using telephone for the first contact and online methods for a follow-up survey. Pollsters now often provide incentives, such as a $25 gift card, to respondents who complete a survey. Short text message surveys are now being used by political campaigns that hope to see higher response rates.

Critics of internet surveys contend that the samples may be biased by not including enough respondents from groups that are more likely to be offline, especially non-English speakers, Latinos, the elderly, and the poor. Online surveys may also include a higher share of politically minded respondents than the general population does. Proponents contend that minorities and the poor are increasingly online, even via mobile access, and that the samples are representative of the American population. Because online surveys from sites such as YouGov have proved to be more accurate in forecasting elections than many telephone surveys relying on cell phones and landlines, online surveys are likely here to stay.[87]

With more than 60 years' experience studying American public opinion, the American National Election Studies (ANES) is considered the gold standard for political survey research because of its accuracy, survey design, and question wording. The ANES traditionally has conducted surveys using face-to-face interviews, but because these are very costly, the ANES increasingly conducts online surveys as well.

Telephone and online surveys increasingly include experimental techniques within the survey design, in which one group of respondents are given a treatment, or unique question wording, and their responses are compared with those of a control group of respondents who do not receive the treatment. Experiments are one of the most rigorous methods for detecting causal relationships. During Obama's 2012 presidential campaign, for example, mobilizers found that if they asked individuals to list everything in their daily schedule and state the time of day they planned to vote within that schedule, the individual was more likely to actually vote, as compared to individuals who were simply asked to vote for the candidate.

In another survey experiment, individuals in one group were exposed to a perspective arguing that affirmative action is necessary to correct past discrimination, while those in a second group received a perspective arguing that affirmative action gives African Americans special treatment. Not surprisingly, those in the first group showed greater support for affirmative action than did those in the second. By using a treatment and control-group design, these kind of experiments provide researchers an important way to understand how public opinion changes in response to political elites and the mass media.

WHEN POLLS ARE WRONG

The history of polling and political data analytics over the past century contains many instances of getting it wrong and learning valuable lessons in the process. Opinion polls are best understood as best guesses of a political outcome but not as predictions of fact. The 2016 election provides a recent example. The vast majority of national public-opinion polls leading up to the election predicted that Hillary Clinton would win enough Electoral College votes to win the presidency, but in fact she lost. The failure of opinion polls was repeated in 2020, when they predicted Biden would win the presidency on average by 8.4 percentage points, but he ended up only winning by roughly 4 percent. In some states, like Wisconsin, the polls were off by nearly 10 percentage points.

Social Desirability Effects Survey results can sometimes be inaccurate because the surveys include questions about sensitive issues for which individuals do not wish to share their true preferences. For example, respondents tend to overreport

their voting in elections and the frequency of their church attendance because these activities are considered socially appropriate. Political scientists call this the **social desirability effect**: respondents report what they expect the interviewer wishes to hear or what they think is socially acceptable, rather than what they actually believe or know to be true.[88] On other topics, such as their income or alcohol and drug use, respondents may feel self-conscious and choose not to answer the questions.

Questions that ask directly about race or gender are particularly problematic. Social desirability makes it difficult to learn voters' true opinions about some subjects because respondents hide their preferences from the interviewer for fear of social retribution (against what might be deemed "politically incorrect" opinions). For example, researchers have found that respondents in surveys didn't want to admit that they opposed school integration or would not vote for a Black candidate and, therefore, abstained from answering questions about these topics. However, surveys using experiments can be designed to tap respondents' latent or hidden feelings about sensitive issues without directly asking them to express their opinions.

Selection Bias Some polls prove to be inaccurate because of **selection bias**—when the sample chosen is not representative of the population being studied. Recently, selection bias came into play in preelection polls in the 2012 presidential election, when Gallup significantly overestimated Latino support for the Republican candidate, Mitt Romney, suggesting a close race between him and the Democratic candidate, Barack Obama. The Gallup numbers were incorrect because of selection bias.[89]

As discussed, in the 2016 presidential election, although most polls predicted the direction of the popular vote correctly in Hillary Clinton's favor, they failed to predict the size of the vote margin and the election outcome (see Figure 6.8). Possible explanations for the polling inaccuracies included the use of "likely voter models," which left out some groups that ended up voting at higher-than-usual rates, such as rural, non-college-educated, blue-collar voters, who supported Trump in large numbers. In 2020, while the polls accurately predicted the winner of the election, their samples once again did not include enough White non-college-educated voters and Trump supporters.

In 2016, an *LA Times*/USC survey accurately predicted a Trump win, relying on a different methodology than the others. It used rolling panel surveys, where the same individuals were interviewed repeatedly over time. This method detected a

Though public opinion is important, it is not always easy to interpret, and polls often fail to predict how Americans will vote. In 1948, election-night polls showed Thomas Dewey defeating Harry S. Truman for the presidency, which caused the *Chicago Daily Tribune* to print a banner incorrectly announcing Dewey's win. In 2016, polls considerably favored Hillary Clinton over Donald Trump, causing many to doubt the possibility of Trump winning the election.

social desirability effect the effect that results when respondents in a survey report what they expect the interviewer wishes to hear rather than what they believe

selection bias polling error that arises when the sample is not representative of the population being studied, which creates errors in overrepresenting or underrepresenting some opinions

FOR CRITICAL ANALYSIS

Is it important that public-opinion polls be accurate? How might polls fail to be accurate? What are the consequences if polls are systematically inaccurate?

FIGURE 6.8
. . . .

Accuracy of Final Preelection Polls, 2016

A large number of news organizations conducted polls to predict the outcome of the 2016 election. For how many of these polls was the actual result within their margin of error, assuming a sample size of 1,000 and a margin of error of plus or minus 3.1 percent? What might explain why some respected organizations, like Pew and Politico, were so far off the mark?

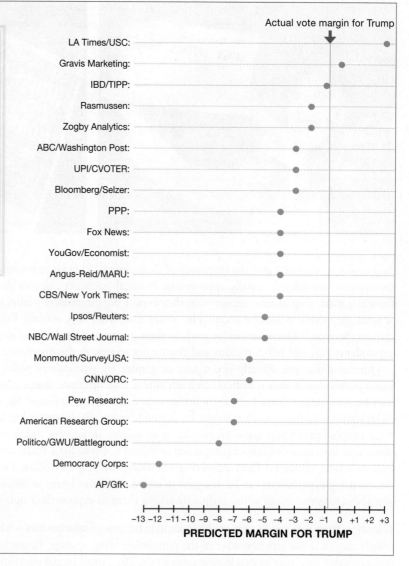

SOURCES: All poll data, except *LA Times*/USC, from HuffPost Pollster, www.elections.huffingtonpost.com/pollster (accessed 11/10/16). Poll results are from the most recent polls prior to election day in the database. *LA Times*/USC data from www.cesrusc.org/election/ (accessed 11/11/16). Popular vote margin data from "CNN 2016 Election Results," www.cnn.com/election/results (accessed 11/11/16).

late surge in support for Trump. Panel surveys are now used increasingly for public-opinion polling. They have a stronger internal research design, where the researcher can measure opinion change for the same sample of individuals. Campaigns and researchers increasingly recognize that measuring change over time is an important component to accurately measuring public opinion.

In recent years, the issue of selection bias has been complicated by the growing number of individuals who refuse to answer pollsters' questions or who use voice mail or caller ID to screen unwanted callers. And certain demographic groups—young people, Latinos, and those who frequently move—are less likely to be found in national commercial voter-roll files that include information on most U.S. adults. Today most pollsters and political campaigns use these voter files from all 50 states to develop their samples.[90] This would be no problem if the views of those who responded to surveys and were included in samples simply mirrored the views of those who refused or those who were omitted, but some studies suggest that the views of respondents and non-respondents can differ, especially along lines of social class and age.

Push Polling **Push polls** are not scientific polls and are not intended to measure public opinion accurately. Instead, they involve asking respondents a loaded question designed to produce a particular response about a political candidate or issue and to simultaneously shape respondents' perception of that candidate or issue. One of the most notorious uses of push polling occurred in the 2000 South Carolina Republican presidential primary, in which George W. Bush defeated John McCain. Callers working for Bush supporters asked conservative White voters if they would be more or less likely to vote for McCain if they knew he had fathered an illegitimate Black child, a false statement.

push poll a polling technique in which the questions are designed to shape the respondent's opinion

The Bandwagon Effect Public-opinion polls can influence political realities and elections. In fact, sometimes polling can even create its own reality. The so-called **bandwagon effect** occurs when polling results convince people to support a candidate identified as the probable victor.

bandwagon effect a shift in electoral support to the candidate whom public-opinion polls report as the front-runner

This effect is especially likely in the presidential nomination process, where multiple candidates are often vying to be a party's nominee. Researchers found that the change in the amount of national media coverage received by a candidate before and after the Iowa caucuses, the first nominating event, was a major predictor of how well the candidate would do in the New Hampshire primary (the second nominating event) and in later presidential primaries nationwide.[91] A candidate who has "momentum"—that is, one leading or rising in the polls—usually also finds it considerably easier to raise campaign funds than a candidate whose poll standing is poor. In 2020, Biden may have benefited from the national and statewide polls showing a wide advantage for the Democrats in a bandwagon effect.

BIG DATA, POLLING AGGREGATORS, AND MEASURING PUBLIC OPINION

Political data analytics, data mining, and social media have opened new ways to measure public opinion. Opinions on some of the most fundamental questions about politics are now being measured not with surveys but with data mining of actual behavior online, including Google searches. *Big data* refers to sets of data so large and complex that they require advanced analytics, rather than traditional methods, to yield insights.

Journalist Sasha Issenberg has shown how mining of big data played a critical role in Obama's presidential election campaigns. By analyzing Netflix movie-rental queues, for example, campaign consultants were able to measure concern for global warming based on the titles a person put into her queue, even if she did not actually end up watching the film. Opinions about a wide range of policy issues could be determined from the aggregate preferences of millions of movie viewers.[92]

Twitter has introduced another way to measure public opinion and agenda setting using text analysis. One study analyzed the number of Twitter followers for the 2016 presidential candidates and tracked changes over time, as well as tracking mentions of any of the candidates within millions of tweets.[93] Today a candidate's lead in positive Twitter coverage may be more important to winning the

White House than a lead in traditional public-opinion polls. Coding large amounts of Twitter data can also be valuable for measuring phenomena that are difficult or impossible to measure with standard telephone surveys, such as the use of racial slurs.

Researchers are also now using Google search data to measure Americans' opinions. An example is public response in Flint, Michigan, and the surrounding communities when the city's water supply was contaminated by lead. The incident exposed roughly 100,000 residents to harmful contaminants, requiring them to drink filtered or bottled water. Residents used online search engines as a way to follow the news and understand the health problems from drinking contaminated water.

Pew Research Center analyzed 18 months of Google search data to track public interest in the crisis. The study covered events including advisories to boil water to kill bacteria, reports of elevated lead levels in children's blood and tap-water samples, bottled-water distribution, emergency warnings, and criminal charges. Based on 2,700 different search terms, the data revealed that residents of Flint were searching for information about their water long before the government recognized the contamination or the media drew national attention to it.[94]

Beyond Twitter, Facebook, Instagram, and Google, big data is playing a role in other ways in election forecasting, predictive analytics, and the measuring of public opinion. For example, polling aggregators, which combine results from multiple polls, can be used to forecast election results or track public opinion more accurately. Blogger and sport statistician Nate Silver became an overnight sensation in 2008 by aggregating thousands of polls conducted in each of the 50 states to predict the winner of the presidential election state by state more accurately than any single polling organization—a feat he repeated in 2012. (He was incorrect, like many others, though, in predicting the winner in the tumultuous 2016 general election.[95])

Silver and FiveThirtyEight.com also use statistics to average thousands of polls over time to create a more accurate estimate of presidential approval than any single poll can. The polls they draw from are weighted based on their sample size, methodological rigor, and past accuracy—polls that historically have been more accurate count more.[96]

The Democratic Party and the Republican Party now use national commercial voter files of 240 million Americans, including a wide range of data from individuals' voting history and party registration, social media use, consumer purchasing patterns, and so on. Using big data and data mining, researchers can predict factors that make a person more likely to vote and, if she votes, predict whom she might vote for. Data mining has been used for years in business, marketing, and economics but is growing in importance in campaigns, elections, and policy. The study of politics has been in the forefront of this big-data revolution, with sophisticated analyses of massive amounts of data, including text scraping—or drawing text data from websites or the news media to analyze statistically in terms of the frequency of word or phrase usage, or sentiment expressed. These are just a few examples of how very large sets of data—containing millions and millions of data points—are changing how we measure public opinion in the digital age.

Public Opinion and Democracy: What Do You Think?

In theory, public opinion plays a major role in American politics. After all, a central purpose of democratic government, with its participatory procedures and representative institutions, is to ensure that political leaders will heed the public will.

★ It is not always clear what the public will is. How do you think Suzanna Hupp and Justin Gruber, featured at the start of this chapter, would characterize public preferences regarding gun policy?

★ Whose preferences should prevail when attitudes differ among groups? Or when they differ between the public and elites? Or between the affluent and the poor?

★ What are the methods elected politicians use to understand what the public wants? And what do they do when they hear conflicting messages?

★ The media are an important source of political information for the public, and the amount and diversity of that information has only grown as politics has migrated online. Do you think the greater availability of information increases the accuracy of public opinion?

★ STUDY GUIDE ★

Defining Public Opinion

Describe Americans' core political values and ideologies (pp. 183–88)

Public opinion refers to the attitudes that people have about policy issues, political events, and elected officials. Despite their differences of opinion on many issues, most Americans share a common set of values, including a belief in the principles of liberty, equality of opportunity, and democracy. In terms of political ideology, most Americans describe themselves as liberals, conservatives, or moderates, though a good number subscribe to other ideologies, such as libertarianism or socialism. Contemporary liberalism and conservatism differ in the degrees to which they emphasize the values of liberty and equality.

Key Terms

public opinion (p. 183)

values (or beliefs) (p. 183)

liberty (p. 183)

equality of opportunity (p. 183)

political ideology (p. 183)

attitude (or opinion) (p. 183)

liberal (p. 186)

conservative (p. 186)

libertarian (p. 187)

socialist (p. 187)

Practice Quiz

1. The term *public opinion* is used to describe
   a) the speeches and writings made by a president during his or her term in office.
   b) political punditry and analysis broadcast on cable news channels.
   c) the beliefs and attitudes that people have about policy issues, political events, and elected officials.
   d) decisions of the Supreme Court.
   e) any political statement that is made by a citizen outside of his or her home.

2. Today, the term _____ refers to someone who generally opposes the expansion of governmental activity and believes that private businesses, local communities, and religious organizations are in a better position to address social and economic problems.
   a) libertarian
   b) liberal
   c) conservative
   d) democrat
   e) moderate

3. *Socialism* refers to a political ideology that
   a) emphasizes the importance of strong government in reducing economic and social inequality.
   b) emphasizes freedom and voluntary association with small government.
   c) argues for the need to place strict limitations on voting rights and civil liberties.
   d) argues that a single ruler should have total control over every aspect of people's lives.
   e) argues that governments are inherently repressive and should be abolished entirely.

How We Form Political Opinions

Describe the major forces that shape public opinion (pp. 189–201)

A number of agents of political socialization—including family and friends; education; membership in racial, ethnic, religious, and other kinds of social groups; party affiliation; self-interest; and the political environment created by current politicians and the mass media—influence the formation of people's underlying political beliefs and values.

Key Terms

political socialization (p. 189)

agents of socialization (p. 189)

gender gap (p. 195)

marketplace of ideas (p. 201)

Practice Quiz

4. The process by which Americans form political beliefs and values is called
a) brainwashing.
b) propaganda.
c) indoctrination.
d) political socialization.
e) political development.

5. The fact that women tend to oppose military intervention more than men do is an example of
a) the rally around the flag effect.
b) partisan polarization.
c) the peace paradox.
d) the bandwagon effect.
e) the gender gap.

6. Which type of social-group affiliation has been called a "mega-identity" that is strongly tied to other social identities?
a) race
b) gender
c) religion
d) party affiliation
e) economic class

Political Knowledge and Changes in Public Opinion

Explain how Americans' level of political knowledge affects public opinion and democracy (pp. 201–7)

As people encounter new political knowledge and information, their opinions may (or may not) be influenced. Whether new knowledge affects people's opinions depends in large part on their existing political views; people are more inclined to accept information that aligns with what they already know and believe about politics. Public opinion is relatively stable over time. When change occurs, it happens slowly and steadily, usually in one direction. Many people acquire political information and make political decisions by relying on cues from political elites, trusted acquaintances, and media outlets and by skimming and scanning superficial online news. However, low levels of political knowledge can prevent individuals from effectively defending their political interests, rights, and freedoms.

Practice Quiz

7. Which of the following statements about political knowledge is *not* accurate?
a) In general, citizens with high levels of political knowledge are more likely to be partisans (Democrats or Republicans).
b) In general, citizens with high levels of political knowledge are more likely to have an ideology (such as liberal or conservative).
c) In general, citizens with high levels of political knowledge are better able to evaluate new information and determine whether it is consistent with their beliefs and opinions.

d) In general, citizens with high levels of political knowledge are less likely to belong to political organizations and to be active in politics.
e) In general, citizens with high levels of political knowledge are better able to recognize their political interests and act consistently to further those interests.

8. The three stages of John Zaller's model of opinion formation are
a) "skim," "scan," and "sample."
b) "skim," "scan," and "accept."
c) "skim," "receive," and "accept."
d) "scan," "receive," and "accept."
e) "receive," "accept," and "sample."

9. Average citizens who rely on informational cues to form political opinions often
a) end up making political choices that are consistent with their underlying preferences.
b) end up making political choices that are not consistent with their underlying preferences.
c) end up rejecting the political opinions of their trusted friends and colleagues.
d) spend much more time gathering political information than the average person does.
e) begin to question their party affiliation and may ultimately change it.

Public Opinion and Government Policy

Explain the relationship between public opinion and government policy (pp. 207–10)

Research has generally shown that elected officials are influenced by the preferences of the public, and there is evidence for a correlation between what government does and what people want. Research has also shown, however, that more-affluent and more-educated citizens have disproportionately large influence over policy decisions.

Practice Quiz

10. Which statement best describes citizens' influence over politics and public policy decisions in the United States?
    a) All citizens exert an equal influence over politics and public policy decisions in the United States.
    b) Citizens who are less affluent and less educated have a disproportionately large influence over politics and public policy decisions in the United States.
    c) Citizens who are more affluent and more educated have a disproportionately large influence over politics and public policy decisions in the United States.
    d) Less affluent and less educated citizens exert an influence over politics and public policy decisions only when the Democratic Party controls the U.S. Congress.
    e) Less affluent and less educated citizens exert an influence over politics and public policy decisions only when the Republican Party controls the U.S. Congress.

11. What is policy feedback?
    a) the process of submitting public comments on a proposed new policy
    b) the tendency of lawmakers to focus only on one policy area for the length of a congressional term
    c) the way in which government policy can work to shift public opinion
    d) the effect that public policies have on citizens' voting decisions
    e) the influence that interest groups and wealthy Americans have on policy formation

Measuring Public Opinion

Explain how surveys and big data can accurately measure public opinion (pp. 210–20)

Surveys can provide a very accurate description of public opinion on an issue if they employ an appropriate sampling method and include a sufficient sample size. In addition to the characteristics of the sample, the ordering and wording of the questions pollsters choose to ask, selection bias, and social desirability effects can also affect the reliability of survey results. Today, political data analytics, data mining, and social media have opened new ways to measure public opinion.

Key Terms

public-opinion polls (p. 210)

sample (p. 211)

simple random sample (or probability sample) (p. 211)

random digit dialing (p. 211)

sampling error (or margin of error) (p. 214)

social desirability effect (p. 217)

selection bias (p. 217)

push poll (p. 219)

bandwagon effect (p. 219)

Practice Quiz

12. The small group that pollsters use to make inferences about the opinions of the whole population is called
    a) a control group.
    b) a sample.
    c) a micropopulation.
    d) respondents.
    e) median voters.

13. A *push poll* is a poll in which
    a) the questions are designed to shape the respondent's opinion rather than measure the respondent's opinion.
    b) the questions are designed to measure the respondent's opinion rather than shape the respondent's opinion.
    c) the questions are designed to reduce measurement error.
    d) the sample is chosen to include only undecided or independent voters.
    e) the sample is not representative of the population it is drawn from.

14. A familiar polling problem is the *bandwagon effect*, which occurs when
    a) the same results are used over and over again.
    b) polling results influence people to support the candidate marked as the probable victor in a campaign.
    c) polling results influence people to support the candidate who is trailing in a campaign.
    d) background noise makes it difficult for a pollster and a respondent to communicate with each other.
    e) a large number of people refuse to answer a pollster's questions.

15. Which of the following is a big-data strategy that political analysts use to measure public opinion today?
    a) analysis of Google search data
    b) analysis of the language that people use on Twitter
    c) aggregation of results from multiple polls
    d) analysis of national commercial voter files
    e) All of the above are common big-data strategies.

The Media

WHAT GOVERNMENT DOES AND WHY IT MATTERS The sharing of information, whether via traditional or digital media, is an essential component of American democracy. So central is information to citizen participation that the Constitution's First Amendment guarantees freedom of the press, and most Americans believe that a free press is an essential condition for both liberty and democratic politics. The media's effects on politics are widespread. The media help set the agenda of topics that Americans think about and discuss, and they shape public opinion on political issues and politicians.

As the media have evolved, questions about their role in government and politics have grown ever more complex. According to the Pew Research Center, 20 percent of adult Americans say they "often" get their news from social media and 33 percent from news websites (compared to 49 percent for television, 26 percent for radio, and 16 percent for print newspapers).[1] But it is increasingly difficult to tell real news from fake news, and the numbers of those who put out fake stories and those who try to debunk them are growing.

For more than two decades, Christopher Blair of Maine worked in construction, but it was tough

Christopher Blair turned to political satire after losing work in construction during the Great Recession. His posts now contribute to the growing presence of "fake news" on the internet—false news stories that are meant to inflame political divides. What effect does fake news have on how Americans perceive politics?

on his body and the jobs dried up during the Great Recession that began in 2007.[2] He had a way with words, though, and turned to political blogging as a creative outlet. The problem was that blogging didn't pay much. That changed a few years later when he realized that he could use Google's advertising platform to make money from the clicks on his sites. A new website he created on Facebook during the 2016 presidential campaign did particularly well.

Blair launched scores of stories that were entirely made up—the very definition of fake news. He made up stories that would outrage political conservatives, such as "BREAKING: Clinton Foundation Ship Seized at Port of Baltimore Carrying Drugs, Guns and Sex Slaves" or "BREAKING: New Orleans Saints Stranded on Runway in London after Pilot Takes a Knee and Walks Off." He meant it all as satire. Blair is a liberal Democrat who made up the headlines to lure in susceptible conservatives. Each story would close with his kicker, that it was all made up to fool his readers: "Please don't use our page in conjunction with Google or the news, it will only serve to confuse you further." His goal was to "trick conservative Americans into sharing false news, in the hope of showing what he [called] their 'stupidity.'"[3] He would then trace and expose some of the more extreme fans who posted to the comment section beneath his fake articles, including Ku Klux Klan members, he claimed.

The only problem? His articles were widely shared, liked, and copied at other fake news sites. In fact, when a Belgian computer expert named Maarten Schenk began tracking and debunking stories that were trending on Facebook and other websites, he found that he could trace much of the content—which was often just cut and pasted from other fake news sites—back to one source: Christopher Blair.

So while Blair's goal had been to satirize and expose extremists, taken out of context his stories helped fuel the fake news explosion. And they even contributed to how media companies planned on handling what they deemed to be questionable content. In spring 2018, Congress held hearings about the spread of misinformation on social media, grilling Facebook CEO Mark Zuckerberg, among others. In response to the scrutiny, Facebook changed its algorithms in July 2018 to try to lessen "spam, clickbait, fake news and data misuse." That meant less traffic coming Christopher Blair's way.

The tussle over online content—from Christopher Blair's attempts to troll conservative readers to Congress's hearings on online content to Facebook's policy changes—underlines how important media of all types are to democracy. The fights would not be so fierce if the stakes were not so high. As the nature of the media and the associated issues evolve, a full understanding of America's dynamic media landscape may be more important than ever.

CHAPTER GOALS

★ **Describe the key roles the media play in American political life (pp. 229–34)**

★ **Describe how different types of media cover politics (pp. 234–49)**

★ **Analyze the ways the media can influence public opinion and politics (pp. 250–55)**

★ **Explain how politicians and others try to shape the news (pp. 256–57)**

★ **Describe the evolution of rules that govern broadcast media (pp. 258–59)**

The Media in American Democracy

Describe the key roles the media play in American political life

Freedom of the press is protected under the First Amendment along with the most cherished individual rights in American democracy, including freedom of speech and religion. Political speech is especially protected. In the United States, individuals, groups, private organizations, and companies have the right to publish newspapers, magazines, and digital media without government censorship and with few government restrictions. In many authoritarian countries there is no freedom of the press, and the government controls the news and political information through state-sponsored media.

Why would the Founders care so much about the rights of the media to report the news without interference from government? Under British rule, before the American Revolution, freedom of speech and the press did not exist in the American colonies. Criticizing the British king was a crime punishable, in some cases, by death.

When the colonists won their independence, they wanted to be able to express their political opinions freely without fear of retaliation. The first of 10 amendments to the U.S. Constitution adopted during the Founding period states, "Congress shall make no law respecting an establishment of religion, or prohibiting the free exercise thereof; or abridging the freedom of speech, or of the press; or the right of the people peaceably to assemble, and to petition the Government for a redress of grievances." Despite attacks from both Republicans and Democrats who claim that major media outlets are biased, most Americans believe freedom of the press is very important for maintaining a strong democracy, and that "news organizations are free to criticize political leaders" (see Figure 6.1 in Chapter 6).

The **media** serve three important roles in American democracy: informing the public about current political issues and events; providing a forum for candidates, politicians, and the public to debate policies and issues; and acting as a watchdog on the actions of politicians and government. Part of the media's role of informing the public involves providing a variety of perspectives and fact-checking sources to provide unbiased coverage of current events. The media serve as a type of public square where citizens become informed about their government, political leaders, societal problems, and possible solutions—a forum where information necessary for democracy is exchanged.

The information presented by the media about politics and current events, government policy, candidates, and political parties allows citizens to make informed decisions in elections and to form knowledgeable opinions about policy issues. American philosopher John Dewey believed the media served to educate the public. A strong democracy, he said, was based not only on voting rights, but also on ensuring that public opinion on current issues is based on communication among citizens, experts, and elected officials. This communication ensures that elected officials adopt policies consistent, for the most part, with the preferences of the citizens and serves as a counterweight to communication among elites, the wealthy, and corporations.

In other words, the mass media help level the playing field between political elites and "the people," giving citizens a more potent voice in society. Without the news media, citizens would not know about the actions of political leaders, corporations,

media print and digital forms of communication, including television, newspapers, radio, and the internet, intended to convey information to large audiences

Internet Freedom

Digital communications are central to how the media function in the twenty-first century and how citizens stay informed about their government. Not every country allows for a free and largely uncensored internet, though. Every year selected countries are assessed on issues related to internet access, freedom of expression, and privacy, and placed on a scale from *free* to *not free*.

1. Which regions of the world appear to have more free access to information and privacy while viewing the internet? What

factors might make a government more or less likely either to want to restrict access to information on the internet or to monitor its citizens' use of the internet? How might a country benefit from offering freer access to the internet?

2. Compare this map to the map in America Side by Side in Chapter 1 on types of governments. Do any patterns emerge? If so, why might there be a relationship between type of government and internet censorship?

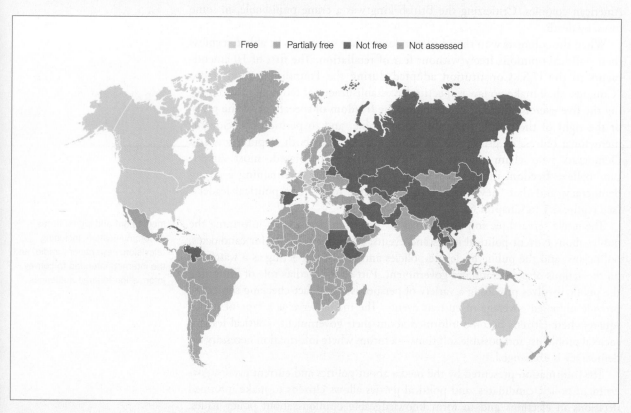

Legend: Free, Partially free, Not free, Not assessed

SOURCE: "Freedom on the Net: 2018," Freedom House, https://freedomhouse.org/sites/default/files/2020-02/10192018_FOTN_2018_Final_Booklet.pdf (accessed 8/1/2019).

or foreign governments and would be powerless to challenge them in the face of corruption. Journalists (people trained to report the news) give ordinary citizens information, and this information is ultimately power.

Finally, the media serve as a watchdog for the public, scrutinizing the actions of elected officials on behalf of citizens—most of whom cannot closely follow the actions of politicians and government. Like an alarm system for a home, the media notify the public of government actions that may harm them. The media inform the public about what policy issues are at stake in terms of changes in laws and regulations. They reveal which individuals and groups are exerting power in politics and what their goals and strategies are, and shed light on the different arguments they are using (such as those for and against a national mask mandate during the coronavirus pandemic, escalating the trade war with China, or a law to create free public college). The media often expose ties between financial interests and political leaders and policy making, or scandalous behavior. By reporting the news in the public interest, the media continuously monitor the actions of public officials and strive to protect the public from government overreach and corruption by serving as a check on political power.

Informing the public, creating a forum for debate, and keeping a watchful eye on government leaders are critical components of democracy. And they seem like a lot to ask of the media. Do the media meet these goals?

The media's role as a watchdog includes investigating political scandals. In February 2019, a conservative website accused Virginia Governor Ralph Northam of appearing in a medical school yearbook photo in blackface. After initially denying the allegations, the governor eventually admitted to the incident and apologized to the public.

JOURNALISM

Most journalists are trained in schools of journalism and mass communication. They are guided by standards in reporting the news in the public interest, known as the principles of journalism. Above all, they seek to report the truth, by fact-checking, verifying sources as legitimate and credible, and engaging in investigative journalism.

The traditional news media aim to balance coverage of current events by providing objective and factual reporting of current events that avoids including personal views of reporters or editors. Objective journalism includes being as accurate as possible, relying on original sources whenever possible, being transparent about sources, and presenting multiple viewpoints. While complete objectivity—reporting the news without bias—is impossible because all individuals have biases that influence how they understand and describe events, it remains a journalistic ideal.

THE PROFIT MOTIVE

The media are sometimes referred to as the fourth branch of government, providing a check on the power of government and political leaders. But who checks or controls the media? In the United States the media are not part of government and not subject to checks and balances like Congress, the presidency, and the courts. Instead most media in the United States are privately owned for-profit companies, like Verizon, Comcast, the New York Times Company, Amazon, Fox Corporation, or Apple.

Public broadcasting refers to television, radio, and digital media that receive partial funding from license fees and government subsidies. In most other democratic countries public broadcasting plays a major role in informing the public about politics and current events. In contrast, public broadcasting in the United States—such as National Public Radio (NPR) or the Public Broadcasting Service (PBS)—plays a relatively small role in the nation's media system. Public broadcasting in the United States has just 2 percent of market share, compared to 35 percent in France, 40 percent in Germany, and 65 percent in Denmark.[4] According to evidence from cross-national surveys, U.S. citizens have lower levels of political knowledge than those in European democracies, who consume more public broadcasting.[5]

Public media in Europe usually come with greater restrictions than in the United States. Swiss law, for example, prohibits political campaign ads on radio and TV programs; they are allowed only in newspapers. In France, the media are prohibited from covering news about candidates for public office the last few days before the election. American media face many fewer government regulations.

U.S. media companies earn most of their revenue from advertising, although revenue from subscriptions has been increasing. They are, therefore, motivated by what audiences want, because higher ratings generate more advertising revenue. Because of the need to reach wide audiences to sell advertisements, the U.S. media are more focused on "soft news," such as entertainment, sports, and celebrity news, than are European media, which provide more "hard news" coverage of politics and government. This may help explain why political knowledge is higher in some European countries than in the United States.[6]

And when it comes to political news, American media tend to focus increasingly on more dramatic, highly conflictual events and issues. Sensational stories of scandals, corruption, or candidates' attacks often generate more interest—and thus revenue—than the stories of everyday governing and details of public policy.

Because of the U.S. media's profit motive, they tend to focus on highly conflictual political events like impeachment, candidate debates, and scandals, and less on the subtle details of changes in public policy.

Nonetheless, objectivity is still the goal, and standard practice is that news, opinion, and ads should be separate and distinct; that is why the opinions of editors are reserved for opinion pages.

The profit motive of the news industry may have contributed to Donald Trump's unexpected victory in the 2016 election. Due to the novelty of a television celebrity running for president without previous political experience, Trump's campaign was a financial boon for the media industry. His candidacy received double the media coverage of his Democratic opponent, Hillary Clinton. The former head of CBS, Les Moonves, said the Trump phenomenon "may not be good for America, but it's damn good for CBS."[7] Throughout the election and Trump's first year in office, the cable news channels profited from higher ratings because of the public's fascination with Trump; CNN, for example, earned about $100 million more in television and advertising revenue than expected in 2016.[8] Newspapers and digital news outlets found that if the word *Trump* was mentioned in a headline, it was more likely to be read and shared online.

MASS MEDIA OWNERSHIP

One noteworthy feature of the traditional media in the United States is the concentration of their ownership. A small number of giant global corporations control a wide swath of media, including television networks, movie studios, record companies, cable channels and local cable providers, book publishers, magazines, newspapers, and online and digital media outlets.[9] **Media monopolies**, such as AT&T, Disney, Comcast, and Fox Corporation, have prompted questions about whether enough competition exists among traditional media to produce a truly diverse set of views on political matters (see Figure 7.1).[10] As major newspapers, television stations, and radio networks fall into fewer hands, the risk increases that politicians and citizens who express less popular viewpoints will have difficulty finding a public forum.

media monopoly the ownership and control of the media by a few large corporations

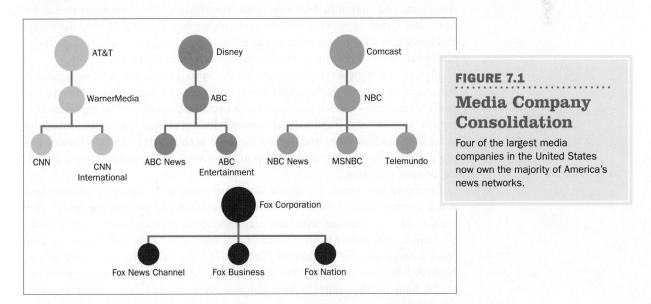

Source: Andrea Murphy, Hank Tucker, Marley Coyne, and Halah Touryalai, "The World's Largest Public Companies," *Forbes*, May 13, 2020, https://www.forbes.com/global2000/#6e8f52f0335d; and company websites (accessed 6/4/2020).

FIGURE 7.1

Media Company Consolidation

Four of the largest media companies in the United States now own the majority of America's news networks.

Despite the appearance of substantial diversity overall, the number of traditional news-gathering sources operating nationally is actually quite small—several wire services, four broadcast networks, a few elite print newspapers, and a smattering of other sources, such as a few large local papers and several small, independent radio networks. More than three-fourths of the daily print newspapers in the United States are owned by large media conglomerates such as the Hearst Communications, McClatchy, and Gannett corporations. Much of the national news that is published by local newspapers is provided by one wire service, the Associated Press. More than 500 of the nation's 1,022 commercial television stations are affiliated with one of just four networks and carry that network's evening news programs.

The trend in concentration of traditional media ownership occurred in large part due to the relaxation of government regulations in the 1980s and '90s. The 1996 Telecommunications Act opened the way for additional consolidation; a wave of mergers has further reduced the field of independent media across the country (more on this below). But as more digital-only news sources come online, these trends toward concentration in media ownership may change.

FOR CRITICAL ANALYSIS

In recent years, a number of major media corporations have acquired numerous newspapers, television stations, and radio properties. Is media concentration a serious problem? Why or why not?

The Media Today

Describe how different types of media cover politics

The past three decades have resulted in a massive transformation of the U.S. news media, as competition from free digital sources has put pressure on traditional subscription-based news sources. Whether offline or online, today 47 percent of Americans prefer watching the news (television or streaming video) compared to reading it (34 percent) or listening to it on the radio (19 percent).[11] Of adults who prefer to read the news, 63 percent read the news online and 54 percent of U.S. adults regularly read news from social media.[12] Less than 20 years ago, most Americans said that after television, print newspapers were their main source for news, and under 20 percent read the news online (see Figure 7.2).[13] As the media and news have migrated online, so has revenue generated from advertising. Today nearly half of all ad revenue in the United States is from digital advertising.[14]

Despite the digital transformation of the news media, much of what makes the media important in American politics remains the same. Major newspapers and TV networks—even if their content is increasingly delivered in digital form—remain popular and important sources of news. Political leaders are successful in making headline news and setting the news agenda. And journalists trained in professional schools create and develop much of what we consume as news, including original reporting.

But more and more, the media are online companies facing an environment where anyone with access to an internet connection can publish the news.[15] The number of organizations that have credibility and large audiences is still small; the leading newspapers in the United States, such as the *New York Times*, the *Wall Street Journal*, and the *Washington Post*, receive some of the highest traffic online. Nevertheless, the digital transformation of the media has created a reorganization of the industry that impacts how the news is made and how consumers learn about politics.

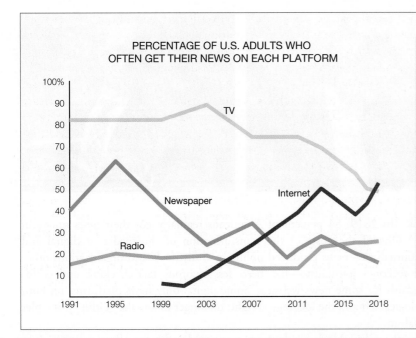

PERCENTAGE OF U.S. ADULTS WHO
OFTEN GET THEIR NEWS ON EACH PLATFORM

SOURCE: Elisa Shearer, "Social Media Outpaces Print Newspapers in the U.S. as a News Source," Pew Research Center, December 10, 2018, pewresearch.org (accessed 7/21/20).

FIGURE 7.2

Use of Online News Continues to Grow

The media landscape for news has seen remarkable shifts in a short period of time. Twenty years ago, more than 80 percent of Americans watched news on television and more than half read news in a newspaper. Today, fewer than half of Americans watch television news, while over one-third read the news online or in print. Since 2000, which media sources have gained rather than lost their audiences?

The news media are increasingly influenced by big technology companies. Before the internet, private, for-profit media companies largely controlled making the news, including original reporting, writing and production, packaging and delivery (think rolled newspapers delivered to your front porch), and the selection of editors. In recent years, however, big technology companies like Apple, Amazon, Alphabet (owner of Google and YouTube), Microsoft, and Facebook (owner of Instagram and WhatsApp) have become major players in the business of journalism, creating media technology companies. This has changed many aspects of the production, packaging, and delivery of the news. Using advanced technology and market research, for example, they push specific news alerts to specific people based on those individuals' interests and preferences, often through social media. Editors choose stories and titles based on consumer interests. And it seems to be working. In 2018, half of all digital ad revenue for display ads went to just two tech companies: Facebook (40 percent) and Google (12 percent).[16]

The interdependence between technology and media companies continues to grow. In one of the latest trends, technology companies and their CEOs have been developing or buying major news media companies, such as eBay founder Pierre Omidyar creating the Intercept or Amazon CEO Jeff Bezos purchasing the *Washington Post*. Both the Intercept and the *Washington Post* have a reputation for forceful investigative journalism and original reporting. Facebook editors control trending topics in the news on the global platform, a key editorial role in what makes the headline news.

Beyond making some news outlets profitable again, these high-tech collaborations are changing how Americans learn about current events in the United States and globally.[17] This is evident in the growing number of Americans who read or watch the news using social network platforms such as YouTube, Twitter, or

Two trends in media have been the consolidation of media outlets into large conglomerates and the growing influence of technology on media. Founded by Rupert Murdoch (left), News Corp is a media conglomerate that has owned the *Wall Street Journal*, among other news outlets. As of 2019, Fox Corporation, of which Murdoch is the current chairman, owns NewsCorp, along with Fox News Channel. Amazon's Jeff Bezos (right), since acquiring the *Washington Post*, has deepened the paper's focus on investigative journalism, which has made the *Post* profitable again.

Facebook. (In 2019, 54 percent of Americans regularly got their news on social media.)[18] One of the costs of the transformation of the media to digital and citizen journalism—news produced online by individuals and organizations other than professional journalists—has been less rigorous fact-checking and editorial standards for some news websites. Some digital-only news platforms, on both the ideological left and the ideological right, no longer follow the guiding principles of journalism.

Facebook's CEO Mark Zuckerberg came under fire for allowing politicians to lie in 2020 political campaign ads, highlighting how corporate decisions can shape the news and politics. While Facebook cracked down on made-up news flooding its platforms after the 2016 election, with fact-checking software to stop everyday users from sharing viral misinformation, politicians are exempt. If a political candidate or public official is expressing an opinion on issues, the company decided that is protected speech, and the ad will not be removed. According to Zuckerberg, "People worry, and I worry deeply, too, about an erosion of truth. . . . At the same time, I don't think people want to live in a world where you can only say things that tech companies decide are 100 percent true."[19] While Facebook doesn't want to police political speech, others contend media companies have a responsibility to regulate content. Zuckerberg is, after all, a digital publisher. Fully 98.5 percent of Facebook's revenue comes from advertising, and publishers always have discretion and editorial control over the ads they run.[20]

In contrast, Twitter announced that all political ads would be banned from its platform beginning in 2019. On all Google platforms and on YouTube, political advertisers are able to target only broad categories of individuals—by gender, age, or zip code—and cannot use more specific information such as voting records or political leaning. Advertisers will no longer be able to target political ads based on users' interests learned from browsing or search history. The new rules put more pressure on other social media platforms to act, as the tech/media industry faces growing public criticism of how user data is used for paid political campaign ads. To avoid misinformation about the 2020 election results, Facebook banned all political or issue ads after the polls closed on election day.

Despite more concentrated ownership of all types of media outlets, the American news media remain among the world's freest and most diverse. Americans get their news from (1) newspapers and magazines; (2) broadcast media (radio and television); and increasingly, (3) digital media. Each of these three sources—newspapers, broadcast, and digital—has distinctive characteristics.

NEWSPAPERS

Newspapers are the oldest medium for the dissemination of the news, though today most Americans read digital rather than print versions. The leading newspapers have an especially influential audience because they help set the political agenda for the nation. Their audience of political elites and the mass public relies on the detailed coverage provided by professional journalists to inform their views about public matters and politics. In March 2019, for example, the *Washington Post* recorded 86.6 million unique visitors (or about one-third of U.S. adults).[21]

Beginning in the late nineteenth century, the emergence of newspapers (and later of radio and television networks) as mass-audience businesses operated primarily for profit significantly shaped politics in the United States. In fact, the development of standardized reporting and writing practices emphasizing objectivity in political news coverage was motivated largely by financial factors. The owners of large newspaper companies determined that the best way to make a profit was to appeal to as broad an audience as possible, which meant not alienating potential readers who held either liberal or conservative views. This goal, in turn, required training and "disciplining" reporters to produce a standardized, seemingly neutral news product. Today, in contrast, native digital news—that is, journalism in those media outlets that originated online—is less likely to emphasize neutrality than is journalism from older, predigital outlets.

This approach proved successful in attracting readers, and for a long time most cities and towns in the country had their own newspaper, and sometimes more than one. However, for most traditional newspapers, recent decades have been financially challenging. Competition from broadcast media and new online content sources has resulted in declines in advertising revenue and circulation levels, thus undermining the traditional business model of newspapers.[22] From 2008 to 2019, employment of newspaper journalists dropped 51 percent, from about 71,000 workers to 35,000.[23] Estimates indicate daily newspaper print circulation has declined by 50 percent over the past two decades.[24] Over the same time period, employment in digital-native newsrooms more than doubled.

In the last four years, however, some major U.S. newspapers reported a sharp increase in digital subscriptions.[25] The *New York Times* added more than 500,000 digital subscriptions in 2016—a 47 percent increase from the previous year—while the *Wall Street Journal* and the *Chicago Tribune* also increased. Digital ad revenue continues to explode, accounting for 35 percent of all revenue to newspapers.

The *Washington Post* may be a model for making the news media profitable. While revenues for most newspapers have continued to decline or remain constant (see Figure 7.3), the *Post* experienced double-digit revenue growth over multiple years. Along with providing a viable financial model, it has emerged as a leader in investigative reporting, data analytics, and marketing. New owner (and Amazon CEO) Jeff Bezos rebuilt the *Post* into a media technology company, producing over 1,200 articles, graphics, or videos per day, including staff-produced articles and wire stories written by others. The *Post* editorial staff produces about 500 stories per day, compared to 250 for the *New York Times*. The paper has an exploding digital readership and dynamic digital content. It distributes news content using social media and offers discounts to Amazon Prime members, and the *Post* app is preinstalled on Amazon's Fire tablets. The *Post* also tracks how different headlines and story framings affect readership of each story.

For most newspapers and magazines today, non-ad revenue comes mainly from digital subscriptions rather than print circulation. The *Washington Post*, the *New*

FIGURE 7.3
....
Advertising Revenue

Media is a business, not a branch of government, so media rely on subscription and advertising money to fund their services. As print newspapers' readership declined, their advertising revenue fell sharply. Some of this money shifted to online advertising, including ads for mobile devices.

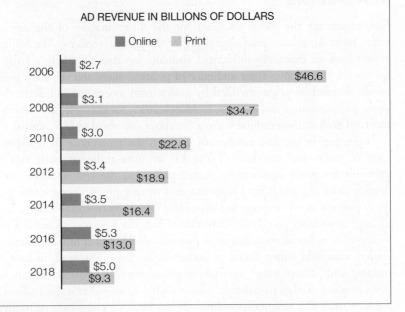

AD REVENUE IN BILLIONS OF DOLLARS

Online   Print

Year	Online	Print
2006	$2.7	$46.6
2008	$3.1	$34.7
2010	$3.0	$22.8
2012	$3.4	$18.9
2014	$3.5	$16.4
2016	$5.3	$13.0
2018	$5.0	$9.3

SOURCE: Newspaper Association of America (2003–2013), Pew Research Center, "Newspapers Fact Sheet," July 9, 2019, pewresearch.org (accessed 8/10/20).

York Times, and *The Economist* were among the first to charge customers for reading their content online. These "paywalls" allow a certain number of free visits before requiring users to pay and appears to be a viable business model, expanding nationwide for some smaller or mid-sized local, regional, and even big-city papers. Traditional newspapers face their greatest competition from digital-only news outlets, such as The Hill, Politico, Bloomberg News, Business Insider, Vox, Vice, the Drudge Report, the National Review, and a host of others without paywalls. And the pace of technological change in the news media shows no signs of slowing down.[26]

TELEVISION

Despite the rise of digital media, television news (local, national network, and cable) still commands much larger audiences than other kinds of news sources. Most Americans have a television, and tens of millions of people watch national and local news programs every day, though younger people are the least likely to get news from television, preferring to get news online. The major broadcasting television companies are NBC, CBS, ABC, Fox, and AT&T WarnerMedia (CNN).

Television news serves the important function of alerting viewers to issues and events—headline news—via brief quotes and short characterizations of the day's events. It generally covers relatively few topics, however, and provides little depth of coverage. Print and digital media, as (mostly) written text, can provide more detailed and complete information and context. Furthermore, **broadcast media** do very little of their own reporting, instead relying on leading newspapers or digital media to set their news agenda. Because they are aware of the character of television news coverage, politicians and others often seek to manipulate the news by providing sound bites that will dominate this coverage.

broadcast media television, radio, or other media that transmit audio and/or video content to the public

Twenty-four-hour cable news stations such as MSNBC, CNN, and Fox News offer more detail and commentary than the half-hour evening news shows on ABC, NBC, and CBS. But even these channels, especially during their prime-time broadcasts, are more focused on headlines and sound bites than newspapers are. In 2018, both viewership and revenue for the top three cable television news channels increased significantly, with viewership rising 8 percent and revenue growing over the previous year. Media monopolies (see Figure 7.1) also affect television. For example, Sinclair Broadcast Group (SBG) is an American telecommunications conglomerate. The family-owned company is the second largest television station operator in the United States (after Nexstar Media Group), owning or operating 193 stations across the country, covering 100 media markets and 40 percent of American households.

Before Twitter became a leading platform for politicians to directly express their opinions unmediated by journalists, politicians used to consider local broadcast news a friendlier venue than the national news. National reporters are often inclined to criticize and question, whereas local reporters are more likely to accept the pronouncements of national leaders at face value. Local TV continues to be a major source of news, especially for older Americans, African Americans, and people with lower formal education.[27] However, its importance is declining overall, especially among younger people (see Figure 7.4).[28] Generally, however, Americans' reliance on television as a news source does not appear to be going away.[29]

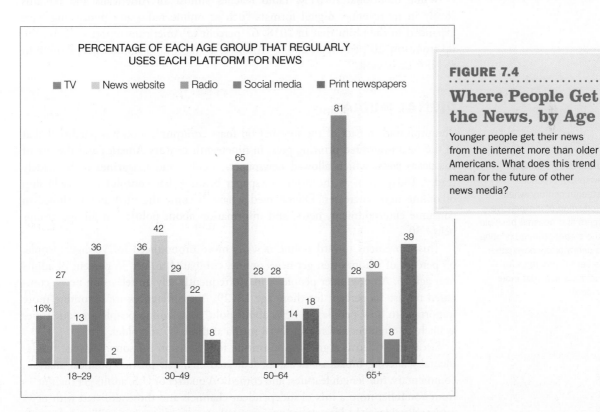

PERCENTAGE OF EACH AGE GROUP THAT REGULARLY USES EACH PLATFORM FOR NEWS

■ TV   ■ News website   ■ Radio   ■ Social media   ■ Print newspapers

18–29: 16%, 27, 13, 36, 2
30–49: 36, 42, 29, 22, 8
50–64: 65, 28, 28, 14, 18
65+: 81, 28, 30, 8, 39

FIGURE 7.4

Where People Get the News, by Age

Younger people get their news from the internet more than older Americans. What does this trend mean for the future of other news media?

Source: Elisa Shearer, "Social Media Outpaces Print Newspapers in the U.S. as a News Source," Pew Research Center, December 10, 2018, pewresearch.org (accessed 7/21/20).

Comedy Comedy talk shows with political content, such as *The Daily Show* and *The Late Show*, attract millions of television viewers. These shows use humor and sarcasm to discuss serious topics and provide social criticism, covering almost every major political event and issue. Pew surveys have shown that they are important sources of political news, especially for young people and liberals, and that frequent viewers are well informed about politics.[30] It is also likely, though, that people who watch comedy news are already better informed in the first place.

RADIO

Radio has seen significant growth as a news source in recent years with the increasing popularity of online radio and podcasting. Listening to radio news while commuting is a primary way many Americans become informed about politics. Nationwide, one in five Americans prefers to get the news by listening to it on radio or from podcasts.[31]

In the 1990s, talk radio became an important source of political commentary as well as entertainment. Conservative radio hosts such as Rush Limbaugh and Sean Hannity have huge audiences and have helped to mobilize support for conservative political causes and candidates. In the political center or center left, National Public Radio (NPR) is a major source for in-depth political reporting. While public broadcasting, as noted earlier, has a much smaller share of the total media market in the United States than in many other countries, NPR remains a popular way for people to learn about politics each day.

While traditional AM/FM radio reaches almost all Americans and remains steady in its revenue, digital formats such as online radio and podcasting have expanded to the point that in 2018, 67 percent of Americans reported tuning in, up from just 20 percent in 2007.[32] And, on average, 28.5 million people tune in to NPR each week.[33]

DIGITAL MEDIA

The profound impact of the internet on mass communication has paralleled that of the steam-powered printing press in nineteenth-century America and the rise of the **penny press**, which allowed newspapers, books, and magazines to be widely read.[34] Today, even as the print newspaper business has consolidated, readership of online news increases. Digital media have become the medium of choice to consume entertainment, news, and information about politics for all age groups below 50.

This movement toward online news is more pronounced for younger people, 63 percent of whom often get news online, compared to just 36 percent of adults over age 65. Among older people, 8 in 10 frequently rely on television news, compared to just 16 percent for those age 18–29. Age differences are becoming more important in how people get news about politics, as young people are four times as likely to often get news from social media as those 65 and older.

Streaming video is a growing substitute for television for some viewers, fundamentally altering broadcast news, as dedicated channels provide political analysis, commentary, full-length features, and comedy. A quarter of U.S. adults get their news from YouTube, from a mix of independent channels and those affiliated with news outlets. Presidential addresses are now regularly streamed live, and millions of people tune in to hear the president in this format.[35] As large gatherings were prohibited

penny press cheap, tabloid-style newspaper produced in the nineteenth century, when mass production of inexpensive newspapers first became possible due to the steam-powered printing press; a penny press newspaper cost one cent compared with other papers, which cost more than five cents

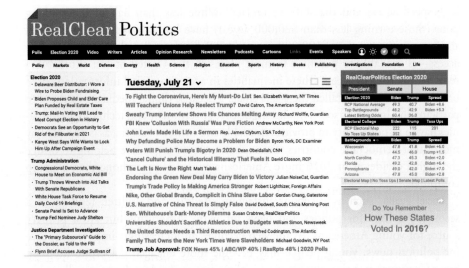

RealClearPolitics is a news aggregator that compiles stories from sources across the political spectrum on various topics in American politics.

during the coronavirus pandemic in 2020, many political candidates streamed town halls and campaign speeches through live video to reach potential voters. (See the Who Are Americans? feature on p. 253 for more information on where Americans get their news.)

News aggregators such as Google News, Reddit, and RealClearPolitics generally compile and repackage stories that were created by other sources, and then deliver them online to consumers in convenient formats. They serve as a platform that allows users to share and comment on the news. The content producers include digital-only news organizations, mainstream media, social movement organizations, and ordinary users as well as political groups, governments, candidates, nonprofit organizations, corporations, and professional media organizations. Aggregators deliver thousands of news stories each day, as well as the latest public-opinion polls and their own synthesis of the headline news.

Social media sites are particularly convenient for obtaining breaking news 24 hours a day, and formats for doing so are becoming more diverse and interactive. About 70 percent of Reddit, Twitter, and Facebook users get news on those sites,[36] and using social media for political information is evident across all demographic groups.

The rise of digital media has changed the way that people get information and share it, affecting everything from political activism to campaigning, voter mobilization, and public opinion. Online media are more diverse than traditional ones, representing a wider range of political views. They have also created a more participatory press, one in which citizens and nonprofit organizations now play a prominent role and journalists regularly interact with readers via social media, especially Twitter. Readers can now share (and retweet) news articles, post comments online, upload videos, and participate in a community, providing feedback on almost all online news articles.

The internet has the potential to benefit society by making political participation easier through greater access to political information and news.[37] However, regular and effective use of it requires high-speed access and digital literacy, the skills to evaluate and use information online.[38] Individuals without such access or skills may become increasingly uninformed and excluded from the world of politics.

The term *digital citizenship* refers to the ability to participate in society and politics online. In 2019 73 percent of Americans were **digital citizens**, having home

news aggregator an application or feed that collects web content such as news headlines, blogs, podcasts, online videos, and more in one location for easy viewing

digital citizen a daily internet user with broadband (high-speed) home internet access and the technology and literacy skills to go online for employment, news, politics, entertainment, commerce, and other activities

high-speed access and the skills to use it.[39] While less than half of the working poor (those earning less than $20,000 a year) have home broadband, 9 in 10 of those earning more than $100,000 a year do.[40] While broadband—wired or mobile access—is available to purchase in most places in the United States, affordability remains a barrier to access. These inequalities in access to digital information based on income are what is called the **digital divide**.[41] Because digital media are essential to participation in today's society, some argue that government and technology companies have a responsibility to provide affordable and universal access, as is provided by most other democratic countries. Smartphones, some argue, are helping to bridge the digital divide; as of 2016 more Americans owned a smartphone than a laptop computer.[42]

Social media, such as Facebook/Instagram, Reddit, and Twitter, tend to be a secondary source for politics and news for many Americans but are a primary source for young Americans. As the web becomes an increasingly important source for political news, young people may become more engaged.[43] Despite the high rate of exposure to political news via social media, young Americans overall are less engaged in politics than their older counterparts, though this may be changing. For example, among people 18–29 years old, voter turnout increased from 20 percent in 2014 to 36 percent in 2018, the largest percentage point increase for any group.[44]

In fact, use of social media for news is growing across all demographic groups, including older people, both women and men, and groups defined by race, education, and income. Figure 7.5 shows the breakdown of each social media site's users across gender, age, education level, and race. As of 2019, 72 percent of

digital divide the gap in access to the internet among demographic groups based on education, income, age, geographic location, and race/ethnicity

social media web- and mobile-based technologies that are used to turn communication into interactive dialogue among organizations, communities, and individuals; social media technologies take on many different forms, including text, blogs, podcasts, photographs, streaming video, Facebook, and Twitter

FIGURE 7.5

Social Media Users by Age, Race, Gender, and Education Level

People of different genders, ages, education levels, and races tend to use different social media sites to get news. What do you think causes this variation?

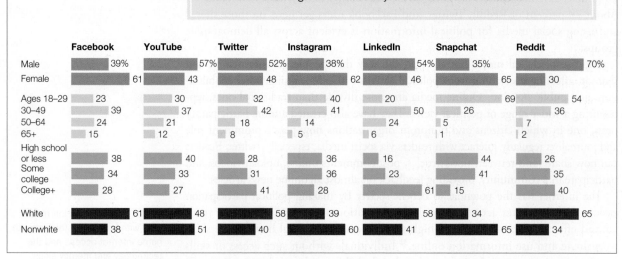

Source: Elisa Shearer and Elizabeth Grieco, "Americans Are Wary of the Role Social Media Sites Play in Delivering the News," Pew Research Center, October 2, 2019 (accessed 6/4/2020).

Americans use social media, as well as 90 percent of young people (age 18–29). Roughly 73 percent of Americans use YouTube, 69 percent use Facebook, 37 percent Instagram, and 22 percent Twitter, all of which feature political news.[45] With then-president Trump tweeting multiple times per day, and congressional leaders and other politicians using Twitter and Facebook, social media sites have become a news source in their own right, as well as forums to share news published in other media.

Besides becoming a key way to produce and consume the news, social media have also increased filtering of the news. Political scientists Jason Gainous and Kevin Wagner use the metaphor of social media as the new dinner table, in that discussions of politics and current events occur within digital social networks of friends and family. Their research shows that people prefer to consume news consistent with their preexisting beliefs, because discussing news that contradicts those beliefs can make people feel uncomfortable. Digital social networks tend to be homogeneous, with people holding similar perspectives, a tendency that has contributed to growing party polarization in politics.[46]

Further, social media provide a platform for citizens to engage directly with political candidates and elected officials, who have been quick to adopt Facebook and Twitter as means of communicating with their supporters and filtering the daily news for them. Gainous and Wagner, in their book *Tweeting to Power*, argue that social media change "the political calculus in the United States by filtering who controls information, who consumes information, and how that information is distributed."[47] Because users pick their own networks and can avoid disagreeable ideas and information they might be exposed to in traditional media, politicians are able to directly make news without the moderating influence of journalists and other media organizations, who tend to present multiple sides of an issues.

Organizations on the ideological right, such as the Tea Party, and on the left, such as MoveOn.org, have also taken advantage of this power to filter the news for their audiences, giving users an ideologically conservative or liberal position. Whether driven by filtered media or in response to it, Gainous and Wagner found, people who are more active politically online hold stronger partisan opinions. Using social media for reading the news, therefore, may increase differences in opinions about politics and may make politics more conflictual.

As discussed in Chapter 6, Obama was the first American president to use social media extensively in his campaign and during his administration. But Trump was the nation's first "Twitter President," communicating his opinions directly to the people, unmediated by the media or even his White House press staff. With over 80 million Twitter followers worldwide, Trump had an enormous audience. His unconventional political strategy involved using tweets and emotional speeches at live, televised rallies to communicate directly with the American people and set the media agenda (discussed later in this chapter), while attacking the credibility of other sources that provide information countering his statements.

On any given day, the president tweeted multiple times, often calling out his opponents in the famous celebrity take-down mode that he perfected during his years as a reality TV host. Among his core supporters, the truth was what Trump said it was on Twitter or in speeches before rally crowds. However, fact-checking websites such as PolitiFact found that 70 percent of Trump's statements were false or misleading and another 15 percent were only half true.[48]

Donald J. Trump ✓
@realDonaldTrump

Obamacare will be replaced with a MUCH better, and FAR cheaper, alternative if it is terminated in the Supreme Court. Would be a big WIN for the USA!

10:09 AM · Sep 27, 2020 · Twitter for iPhone

Joe Biden ✓
@JoeBiden

President Trump can claim he wants to protect people with pre-existing conditions all he wants — but the fact is he's fighting tooth and nail to take their protections away.

4:00 PM · Sep 28, 2020 · TweetDeck

Both presidential candidates used Twitter in the 2020 election to filter the news and set the media's agenda. While President Trump suggested a new health care plan for Americans, Joe Biden underscored the protections already provided by the Affordable Care Act.

While Trump used Twitter to his advantage to filter the news for his supporters during the 2016 election and then set the media's agenda during his administration, his strategy of going public all the time may backfire. A Gallup survey found that 72 percent of Americans said Trump's tweets do not send the right message to other world leaders, and 71 percent say Twitter is a "risky way for a president to communicate," leading to misunderstandings.[49] During the first wave of the coronavirus pandemic, Trump's daily press briefings included promoting scientifically unproven remedies, such as consuming hydroxychloroquine to prevent contracting the virus. These recommendations were refuted by scientists, and the administration frequently offered clarifying statements contradicting Trump's suggestions.

Social media use for news makes citizens more informed and engaged in politics, and more likely to participate. On the down side, it may make citizens more vulnerable to misinformation and conspiracy theories, especially from a candidate or organization that is their only source of news. (We discuss "fake news" later in this chapter.)

CITIZEN JOURNALISM

Digital news is creating a new generation of whistle-blowers, enhancing the media's traditional role as a watchdog against government corruption. **Citizen journalism** includes news reporting and political commentary by ordinary citizens and even crisis coverage from eyewitnesses on the scene, thus involving a wider range of voices in gathering news and interpreting political events. Cameras on cell phones give millions of Americans the capacity to photograph or record events, thus providing eyewitness accounts. At the same time, social media permit users to upload videos that can be viewed by hundreds of thousands of subscribers or relayed by the mainstream media for even wider dissemination.

In 2017, for example, a global firestorm erupted over United Airlines' treatment of a passenger, an older Asian man, who was violently dragged off a boarded plane for refusing to voluntarily give up his seat. Filmed by other passengers using smartphones and uploaded to social media, video footage of the incident was viewed by millions of people. In response, the CEO of United apologized and the airline changed its policies; this event also led to a congressional investigation of regulations

citizen journalism news reported and distributed by citizens, rather than by professional journalists and for-profit news organizations

As we have seen with recent dramatic events like the Black Lives Matter protest in Louisville, Kentucky, in September 2020, social media and citizen journalism are transforming the news. Groups can mobilize and push out their messages quickly using social media, and citizen journalists can use mobile technology to capture and disseminate news without the filter of mainstream media outlets.

on U.S. airlines.[50] The United example illustrates how social media and grassroots politics can fuel policy change, not just candidate campaigns.

Citizen journalism supplements the work of professional journalists in many important ways. For one, new opinion leaders and voices have platforms to react to mainstream media, often improving the quality and accuracy of information reported. In recent years, for example, social media users have uncovered major factual errors in mainstream media reports and forced networks and newspapers to issue corrections. Furthermore, because individuals and some online news outlets do not have strict editorial boards, they can post a story within minutes. This ability to scoop the mainstream media means digital media can frame stories about political candidates, for example, before those stories break in the mainstream media.[51]

By sharply lowering the technological and financial barriers that previously prevented all but a few individuals from reaching mass audiences, news created by ordinary people can be effective in political action. On the other hand, the freewheeling nature of social media often means that there is less of the traditional quality control provided by professional journalists and traditional institutional media. Because they do not face the burden of fact-checking required for the mainstream media or some digital-only news outlets, even well-meaning users can post false information.

BENEFITS OF ONLINE NEWS

The reasons Americans appear to prefer online news include (1) the convenience, (2) the up-to-the-minute currency of information, (3) the depth of information available, (4) the diversity of viewpoints, and (5) the low cost.[52]

Information online is always easily available for those with access to the internet on a computer or through mobile devices. Pew surveys show that nearly half of those who access online news and political information cite its convenience.[53] In addition, one of the fundamental changes ushered in by online news is the speed with which local, national, and international events are covered. Social media have accelerated even further the speed with which news travels around the globe. For example, when President Trump announced on Twitter that he and First Lady Melania Trump had contracted COVID-19 in early October 2020, the news spread rapidly through social media and traditional media.

Online news can provide more information than the sound bites that dominate television and radio news. By blending more detailed and substantive treatment of topics with the emotive visual appeal of videos, digital media share the distinctive qualities of both print media (providing knowledge) and television (arousing interest and engagement).[54] Despite the multimedia capacities of digital media, most websites still rely heavily upon written text. Thus political "web surfing," which is based on reading, makes it easier for people to recall the information they encounter and, in turn, to acquire political knowledge.[55]

Importantly, online information sources are much more diverse than those found in the traditional media, and this diversity may lead to an increase in political knowledge and interest.[56] By making foreign media such as the British Broadcasting Company (BBC), the UK's *The Guardian*, and Al Jazeera television as easily available as mainstream American outlets, for example, digital media have made the physical proximity of media less important and created a more global news environment.

CONCERNS ABOUT ONLINE NEWS

While online news holds significant promise for improving access to the political information citizens need, the shift toward online media has also given rise to several major concerns. These include the quality of online news content, the increased presence of false information, and the negative effects of these factors on knowledge and tolerance.

Quality As already noted, the growing diversity of digital news sources has led to substantial variation in the quality of available information. Multiple perspectives create a livelier marketplace of ideas, but hate speech, unsubstantiated rumors, and factual errors can overwhelm thoughtful, original, and factually based voices, especially in anonymous online forums. This can influence public opinion, and it poses challenges for democratic government if people are misinformed.

Fake News and Misinformation Political candidates and leaders are particularly susceptible to online attacks because negative stories about them can easily "go viral,"

Without traditional media's commitment to fact-checking, digital media sometimes spread inaccurate information and rumors. In 2008, the false claim that President Obama was not a natural-born citizen spread rapidly online and remained a top story even after Obama released his official long-form birth certificate.

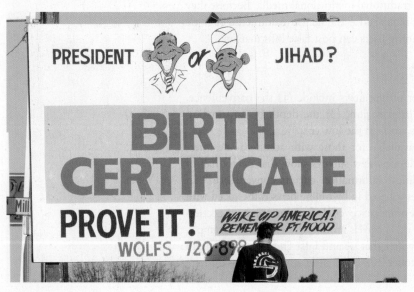

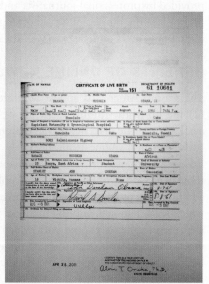

Evaluate a News Source

BILL ADAIR, the founder of the Pulitzer Prize–winning website PolitiFact and the Knight Professor of the Practice of Journalism and Public Policy at Duke University

Every day we read news stories that we seek out, that friends and family send us, or that appear in our social media feed. How can we figure out which stories are credible and worthy of our attention?

Bill shared the techniques that fact checkers use to assess the content of stories in newspapers, on Facebook, and in other media sources. Here are Bill's five tips for evaluating news sources:

1 **The most important step is to evaluate the web address.** Established news sources will typically have a web address that ends in ".com," such as nbcnews.com or washingtonpost.com. Much good journalistic content is available at .org and .net addresses, but be suspicious and dig deeper when you see an ending other than .com. Of course all .coms are not reliable news sources—this is just step one.

2 **Check the labeling of the article to assess the type of content.** Is the article labeled as news or opinion or analysis? A lot of time we hear bad things about bias: "Bias! Bias is always bad!" But we read opinion because it is biased. But the best opinion publishers will label the content as opinion, so you want to look for that label. The important point is to realize what you are reading: Is it a factual news article, or an opinion piece with a point of view?

3 **Check the attribution in the article—the sources cited.** Are there links to credible sources (government publications, research from prominent universities, and so on)? Do the links provide information that backs up the points in the article?

4 **Read the publication's "About" page (and be skeptical if it's missing).** Is the publisher a for-profit company or a nonprofit? If it is a nonprofit, does it list its funding sources? Is it transparent about any political leaning? If there is advertising, is it high quality ("Test Drive the Ford F-150 Today") or clickbait ("13 Potatoes That Look Like Channing Tatum")? Is the publisher transparent about its staff? Are they journalists? Or is it a business and the content essentially an infomercial?

5 **Figure out who's producing this content.** Is it written by the publication's staff or brought in from another source? If the content is copied or purchased from elsewhere, you need to check out that source as well.

All of these are clues that a smart reader can use to assess the credibility of what the reader is consuming. I also encourage people to engage with multiple points of view. One thing I recommend students do is try to get out of their filtered bubble by reading every day one person or post or publication that they disagree with. I think that's really important.

This is a story from PolitiFact, showing a debunked Facebook post claiming the Coronavirus Aid, Relief, and Economic Security Act gives members of Congress a pay increase.

Facebook posts

stated on March 20, 2020 in a text post:

Says the Coronavirus Aid, Relief, and Economic Security Act gives members of Congress a pay increase.

CONGRESS   FACEBOOK FACT-CHECKS   CORONAVIRUS   ℞ FACEBOOK POSTS

fake news false stories intended to be read as factual news that are circulated to benefit one candidate or party over another or to generate ad revenue

spreading quickly without fact-checking. **Fake news**—false stories circulated to benefit one candidate or party over another or just to generate ad revenue—is an increasing problem. In the 2016 presidential election, for example, circulation of the top 10 fake news stories on Facebook was more widespread than the top real news stories about the election. A study published by Stanford University found that fake news stories on social media about the election disproportionately favored Trump (the most widely publicized was the false story that the pope had endorsed him[57]). The Republican Senate Intelligence Committee and Special Counsel Robert Mueller both released reports that the Russian government was involved in generating many of the fake news stories to discredit Clinton and her campaign.[58]

Encountering misinformation online is a common problem. Four in ten Americans (38 percent) say they often come across made-up news and information, and another 51 percent say they sometimes do. In response, people have changed their news and technology habits. Seventy-eight percent of Americans say they now regularly check the facts in news stories themselves, 63 percent have stopped getting news from a particular outlet, and 43 percent have reduced their overall news intake on social media.[59] (A number of websites, such as FactCheck.org, Snopes.com, and PolitiFact.com, are devoted exclusively to checking the truthfulness of political claims in both traditional and online media.)

One example of fake news in the 2020 election surrounded the claim, which many people incorrectly believed, that Biden had voiced support for defunding the police, one of the reforms advocated for by the Black Lives Matter movement to end racial inequality in policing. Trump repeatedly made this claim about his opponent, and it was restated on conservative news channels. Sixty-six percent of Republicans who frequently relied on Fox News or talk radio for political news believed that Biden supported defunding the police, versus 27 percent of people who used other news sources.

Despite frequent attacks on the mainstream media as fake news by conservatives and President Trump, only about a third of Americans blame journalists, the media, or a foreign government for the proliferation of fake news. Sixty percent of people say political leaders and their campaigns create a lot of made-up news, and about half say the same thing of political activist groups.[60] Two-thirds of Americans say that made-up news that is designed to mislead and video that is altered or made up causes "a great deal of confusion" about the basic facts of current events and politics. Nearly 8 in 10 Americans favor restrictions on this kind of content online.[61]

Effects on Tolerance and Knowledge Perhaps the greatest concern about politics in the digital age is that the very diversity of online news may actually *lower* tolerance for social, religious, and political diversity, leading to more partisan polarization and societal conflict. Fully 85 percent of Americans believe that the tone and nature of political debate in the United States has become more negative in recent years—as well as less respectful, less fact based, and less focused on policy issues.[62] Digital media often do not abide by traditional media's principle of objective journalism. Instead, the specialization of information online and on cable television means that liberals and conservatives alike can self-select media that are consistent with their existing beliefs and avoid exposure to information that might challenge these.[63] The natural tendency to select news that conforms with our own beliefs is strengthened by the way search engines cater to our individual preferences. This "filter bubble," or "self-selection bias," screens out information that might broaden our worldview.[64]

In addition, exposure to highly partisan news (for example, Fox News for conservatives, MSNBC for liberals) or to news on social media may actually lower political

FOR CRITICAL ANALYSIS

Does digital news coverage differ from traditional print and television media? What impact do digital media have on American politics?

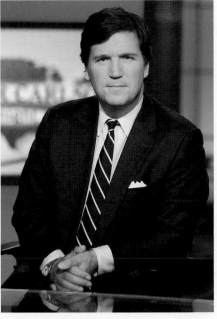

Though the media generally attempt to remain unbiased, a number of media figures and outlets are distinctly left- or right-leaning, such as Rachel Maddow of MSNBC and Tucker Carlson of Fox News. Consumers are increasingly turning to partisan media, reflecting a tendency to self-select information that already conforms with their beliefs, making it more difficult to evaluate information objectively.

knowledge. Despite the dramatic rise in available political news and in diversity of the media over the last few decades, average levels of political knowledge in the population have not increased, due to individuals "customizing" the political information they receive and therefore, as discussed earlier, being less likely to encounter new information that challenges their partisan viewpoints.[65] If the new digital media are to create a more informed democratic process, citizens must have "information literacy," the ability to find and evaluate information.[66] Greater access to information online makes education and critical thinking among citizens more important than ever before.

DO AMERICANS TRUST THE MEDIA TODAY?

According to Pew, just one in five American adults has a lot of trust in "information from national news organizations," 49 percent have some trust, and 29 percent have not much/none at all.[67] (During the coronavirus pandemic, however, public trust in media seemed to rise, as most people believed the media was providing needed information.[68]) There are large partisan differences in trust of the news media when it comes to its watchdog role and perceived fairness in political coverage; Democrats, for example, are 23 percentage points more likely than Republicans to think information from national news organizations is very trustworthy. Distrust in the mainstream media increased with the Trump presidency. In response to negative coverage of his campaign and administration, Trump waged an unprecedented war on the American media, frequently referring to major newspapers and broadcast media as "fake news" to discredit them (though these mainstream sources are generally not producing fabricated news). In a tweet shortly after his inauguration, he even called the press "the enemy of the American people." In response, the late Republican senator John McCain publicly criticized Trump, warning that "when you look at history, the first thing that dictators do is shut down the press. And I'm not saying that President Trump is trying to be a dictator. I'm just saying we need to learn the lessons of history."[69]

Media Influence

Analyze the ways the media can influence public opinion and politics

The content and character of news programming—what the media choose to present and how they present it—can have far-reaching political consequences. The media can shape and modify, if not fully form, the public's perception of events, issues, and institutions. Media coverage can rally support for, or intensify opposition to, national policies on important matters such as health care, the economy, wars, or impeachment proceedings of a president. And as discussed earlier, it can greatly enhance or fatally damage the careers of political leaders.

At the same time, the media are influenced by the individuals or groups who are subjects of the news. The president in particular has the power to set the news agenda through speeches, actions, and tweets. All politicians, for that matter, seek to shape their media images by cultivating good relations with reporters and by leaking news and staging news events.

In American political history, the media have played a central role in many major events. For example, in the civil rights movement of the 1950s and '60s, television images showing peaceful demonstrators attacked by club-swinging police helped to generate sympathy among northern Whites for the civil rights struggle and greatly increased the pressure on Congress to bring an end to segregation.[70] The media were also instrumental in compelling the Nixon administration to negotiate an end to American involvement in the Vietnam War by portraying the war as misguided and unwinnable.[71]

Conservatives have long charged that the liberal biases of journalists, and now media technology companies, result in distorted news coverage.[72] Though some professional journalists do lean Democratic, they generally defend their professionalism, insisting that their personal political leanings do not affect the way they perform their jobs.[73] Those who decry "the liberal media" seldom acknowledge the political leanings of media owners. Rupert Murdoch, for example, chairman of the Fox Corporation, is a politically active conservative. Sheldon Adelson is another media mogul with a clear conservative partisan and ideological agenda.

Many news sources are perceived as distinctly left- or right-leaning, and, as discussed earlier, people have a tendency to select ones that conform with their own ideology. Table 7.1 shows where different ideological groups get political news. With the exception of Fox News, there is not much credible evidence for the idea that any particular mainstream news source is, as a whole, explicitly ideologically biased in one direction or another, at least in terms of its news coverage. Most have been found to be centrist.[74] Of course, many people perceive particular news stories to be biased. This perception may be what drives ideological self-selection of news sources.

FOR CRITICAL ANALYSIS

To what extent, do you think, are the media biased? As more news sources have become available, has this led to more or less bias in the media?

HOW THE MEDIA INFLUENCE POLITICS

Traditional and digital media influence American politics in a number of important ways.[75] The power of all media collectively, offline and online, lies in their ability to shape what issues Americans think about (agenda setting and selection bias) and what opinions Americans hold about those issues (framing and priming).

agenda setting the power of the media to bring public attention to particular issues and problems

Agenda Setting The first source of media power in politics is **agenda setting**, or gatekeeping: designating some issues, events, or people as important, and others not.

Who Sees Fake News . . .
and Who Does Something about It?

More and more Americans are getting their news via social media. Social media can be an effective and efficient way to share news and information, but it can also be used to spread fake news and misinformation. Who tends to encounter fake news, and what do those people do about it?

Who Sees, and Shares, Fake News?

Percentage of U.S. adults who . . .

■ Highly politically aware*
■ Less politically aware

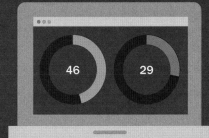

Often come across made-up
news and information

46   29

Shared news and information they
knew at the time was made up

5   14

Shared news and information they
later found out was made up

46   51

What Do People Do about Fake News?

Percentage of U.S. adults who say the issue of made-up news and information has led them to . . .

■ Highly politically aware*
■ Less politically aware

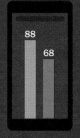
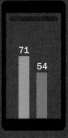
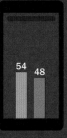

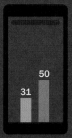

Check facts of a news story themselves	Stop getting news from a specific outlet	Change the way they use social media	Report or flag a story they think is made up	Reduce the amount of news they get overall
88 / 68	71 / 54	54 / 48	34 / 28	31 / 50

* Political awareness is measured by answers to three political knowledge questions and one question about how closely respondents follow what is going on in government and public affairs.

SOURCE: Amy Mitchell et al, "Many Americans Say Made-Up News Is a Critical Problem That Needs to Be Fixed," Pew Research Center, June 5, 2019.

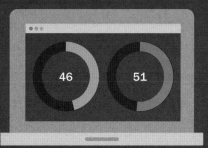

FOR CRITICAL ANALYSIS

1. When they encounter fake news, what do highly politically aware people do compared to those who are less politically aware? Are there differences between the two groups in who spreads made-up news?

2. Young people are more likely to read news online than other age groups and are thus more likely to be exposed to misinformation online. What effect does this exposure have on young people's motivation to engage with politics?

TABLE 7.1

Ideology of Media Consumers

SOURCE	REPUBLICAN/ LEAN REPUBLICAN	DEMOCRATIC/ LEAN DEMOCRATIC	REFUSED/NO LEAN
Fox News	93%	6%	1%
ABC News	44	53	3
CBS News	41	55	4
NBC News	38	57	5
CNN	17	79	4
NPR	12	87	2
New York Times	7	91	1

gatekeeping a process by which information and news are filtered to the public by the media; for example, a reporter choosing which sources to include in a story

The mass media act as a **gatekeeper** with the power to bring public attention to particular issues and problems. Groups or politicians that wish to generate support for policy proposals must secure media coverage. If the media are persuaded that an idea is newsworthy, such as climate change, then they may declare it an "issue" that must be confronted or a "problem" to be solved, thus helping it clear the first hurdle in the policy-making process.

Some stories—such as those about wars, natural disasters, presidential impeachment, major health crises, and terrorist attacks—have such overwhelming significance that the main concern of political leaders is not whether a story will receive attention but whether they themselves will figure prominently and positively in media accounts. At the same time, many important issues don't often appear on the media's agenda, such as solar and wind power as alternative energy sources, homelessness, impacts of artificial intelligence on low-skill jobs, or election reform. When policy issues are not on the media's agenda they receive relatively little attention from politicians.

Media attention plays a central role in whether or not officials act on a policy issue, but how issues make the news in the first place has remained a puzzle. Political scientist Amber Boydstun has shown that the media have two "modes": an "alarm mode" for breaking stories and a "patrol mode" for covering them in greater depth.[76] The incentive to reach a wider audience (and generate ad revenue) often sets off the "alarm mode" around a story, after which news outlets go into "patrol mode" to monitor what effect (if any) the story has on government policy—until the next big story alarm goes off. This pattern results in skewed coverage of political issues, with a few issues receiving the majority of media attention while others receive none at all. Today, Twitter often sets off the alarm mode by breaking news and causing it to go viral, setting the agenda for mainstream news. News from an anonymous government whistle-blower of possible misconduct by President Trump in 2019 put the media in fire-alarm mode. The media then went into patrol mode, covering the impeachment story in depth on a daily basis.

Where Do Americans Get Their News?

Percentage of each voter group who got news about politics and government in the previous week from ...

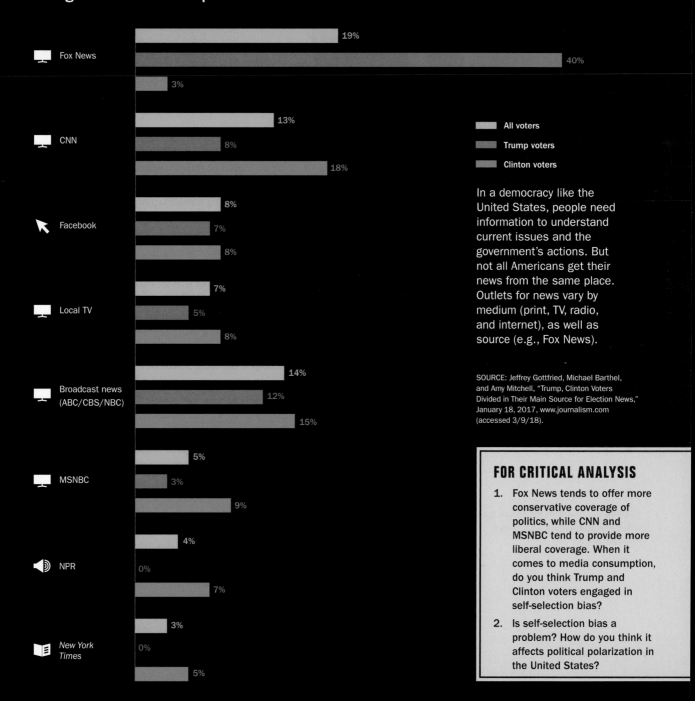

Fox News
- All voters: 19%
- Trump voters: 40%
- Clinton voters: 3%

CNN
- All voters: 13%
- Trump voters: 8%
- Clinton voters: 18%

Facebook
- All voters: 8%
- Trump voters: 7%
- Clinton voters: 8%

Local TV
- All voters: 7%
- Trump voters: 5%
- Clinton voters: 8%

Broadcast news (ABC/CBS/NBC)
- All voters: 14%
- Trump voters: 12%
- Clinton voters: 15%

MSNBC
- All voters: 5%
- Trump voters: 3%
- Clinton voters: 9%

NPR
- All voters: 4%
- Trump voters: 0%
- Clinton voters: 7%

New York Times
- All voters: 3%
- Trump voters: 0%
- Clinton voters: 5%

Legend:
- All voters
- Trump voters
- Clinton voters

In a democracy like the United States, people need information to understand current issues and the government's actions. But not all Americans get their news from the same place. Outlets for news vary by medium (print, TV, radio, and internet), as well as source (e.g., Fox News).

SOURCE: Jeffrey Gottfried, Michael Barthel, and Amy Mitchell, "Trump, Clinton Voters Divided in Their Main Source for Election News," January 18, 2017, www.journalism.com (accessed 3/9/18).

FOR CRITICAL ANALYSIS

1. Fox News tends to offer more conservative coverage of politics, while CNN and MSNBC tend to provide more liberal coverage. When it comes to media consumption, do you think Trump and Clinton voters engaged in self-selection bias?

2. Is self-selection bias a problem? How do you think it affects political polarization in the United States?

During the 1960s, civil rights protesters learned a variety of techniques designed to elicit sympathetic media coverage. Television images of police brutality in Alabama led directly to the enactment of the 1965 Civil Rights Act.

Political candidates also need the media's agenda-setting role to win elections. Candidates who receive positive news coverage gain momentum: they pick up political endorsements, attract campaign contributions, and win more support from voters.[77] In the 2020 Democratic primaries for president, Joe Biden exceeded the media's expectations with his win in South Carolina and strong support among African Americans. Biden's victory earned him increased press attention and led him to win the Democratic nomination.[78]

Because most large media outlets are for-profit businesses looking for the largest possible audiences, they naturally tend to focus on stories with dramatic or entertainment value, such as crimes and scandals—especially those involving prominent people—and national emergencies. They also focus on who is ahead in elections (what is known as the horse race), instead of the policy issues. The age-old journalistic instinct and public appetite for sensational stories often trump the media's responsibility to inform the public about what really matters.

What the mainstream media decide to report on or highlight and what they ignore or downplay have important implications. For example, the Bush tax cuts of 2001 and 2003, extended under Obama in 2010, dramatically increased the federal budget deficit and widened the income gap between the super-rich and most other Americans. But the media provided little coverage of these measures, the result being that 40 percent of Americans had no opinion on whether they favored the 2001 cuts.[79]

framing the power of the media to influence how events and issues are interpreted

Framing Framing is the power of the media to influence how events, issues, and people's actions are interpreted and understood. Each issue or event has many different possible frames, each with a slightly different spin in describing the problem and possible solutions. Framing includes the media's power to include or exclude information. Frames, which political leaders and groups also help to develop, shape the meaning that individuals perceive from words or phrases, photographs, or video.[80]

In the lead-up to the 2016 election, for example, the mainstream media covered with zeal the controversy around Hillary Clinton's use of a private email server during her tenure as secretary of state, with special focus on the risk of jeopardizing government secrets. The issue dominated the media agenda, especially in the 10 days before the election, when FBI director James Comey reopened the investigation into Clinton's email server. Clinton was framed by the media as possibly going to jail for her illegal use of a private email server (Trump even nicknamed her "crooked Hillary"). Clinton herself credits media coverage of the FBI investigation for changing public opinion and allowing Trump to win the 2016 presidential election.

Because few citizens read legislation, the public relies on media coverage in forming opinions about policy and politics. This means that arguments made by elected officials and other political actors—and the way the media use these frames in presenting the news—are critical in how the public interprets events and policy. For example, the Obama administration labeled its health care initiative the Patient Protection and Affordable Care Act, thus framing the proposal as a matter of responsibility and good economic sense. Early press coverage framed the bill as "health care reform." Sensing that Americans generally approve of the idea of "reform," Republican opponents of the legislation chose different language. The law's provisions for limiting excessive medical testing were labeled as "health care rationing," for example, and proposed committees to advise patients about end-of-life care were called "death panels." Later this law became known as simply "Obamacare."

Priming Another important way the media can shape political events is by **priming**, which involves calling attention to some issues, and not others, when evaluating political officials.[81] Priming is the power the media have to alter how voters make choices. While agenda setting is about gatekeeping and what issues the media are covering (such as presidential impeachment or the coronavirus pandemic), framing and priming involve the media filtering the news and providing cues to the public for how to interpret issues or events.

Media priming occurs when an issue becomes more important in evaluating political candidates. This occurred when a dozen statewide ballot measures prohibiting same-sex marriage received extensive media coverage in the lead-up to the 2004 presidential election. Four in 10 Americans said the issue of same-sex marriage was very important in their vote for president (compared to 8 in 10 who cited terrorism prevention), but the people who cited marriage were more likely to vote to re-elect President George W. Bush. Media attention to the ballot measures primed voters to think about traditional moral values and favorably evaluate the Republican candidate.[82]

Priming involves the public judging a politician according to the media's attention to one issue rather than others. In the lead-up to the 2020 election, the coronavirus pandemic was in the national media spotlight. The continuing public health crisis coupled with the economic crisis became the most important lens through which the public evaluated the presidential candidates, benefiting Biden and hurting Trump.

Parties, candidates, and groups also engage in priming. They use the media to try to strategically link policy issues to how citizens evaluate candidates. In the case of political candidates, the media's focus on which candidate "has momentum" and "is winning the horse race" can prime the public to evaluate the candidates based on their likelihood of winning the election rather than on their positions on policy issues. As with agenda setting and framing, news media are not alone in priming; elected officials, interest groups, and other political players compete over all three in hopes of influencing public opinion.

priming the process of making some criteria more important than others when evaluating a politician, problem, or issue

FOR CRITICAL ANALYSIS

How do the media distort political reality? What are the consequences for American democracy when the electorate is informed through such a filter?

News Coverage

Explain how politicians and others try to shape the news

News coverage, or the content of the news, comes from numerous sources. Governments, politicians, corporations, interest groups, non-profit organizations, and others produce press releases and hold press conferences to draw attention to issues and tell their side of the story. Journalists also gain information through investigative journalism and media leaks.

MEDIA LEAKS

Leaks, the disclosure of confidential government information to the news media, may originate from a variety of sources. These include "whistle-blowers," lower-level officials who hope to publicize what they view as their bosses' or the government's improper activities. In 1971, for example, Daniel Ellsberg, a minor Defense Department staffer, sought to discredit official justifications for America's military involvement in Vietnam by leaking top-secret documents to the press. The Pentagon Papers—the Defense Department's own secret history of the war—were published by the *New York Times* and the *Washington Post* after the U.S. Supreme Court ruled that the government could not block their release.[83] The Pentagon's credibility was severely damaged, hastening the erosion of public support for the war. Most leaks, though, originate not with low-level whistle-blowers but rather with senior government officials, prominent politicians, and political activists.

Digital media has taken the cat-and-mouse game of leaks to a new level. WikiLeaks, an international organization dedicated to publishing classified information, posts leaked government documents to its website and uses an anonymous system so that leakers cannot be identified. In recent years, WikiLeaks has released thousands of secret government documents involving corruption, war crimes in Afghanistan and Iraq, torture at U.S. military detention camps, and stolen emails from the Democratic National Committee in the 2016 election.

The mass media exposed possible misconduct by President Trump in a July 25, 2019, phone call between U.S. President Trump and Ukrainian President Volodymyr Zelensky. A government whistle-blower alleged that Trump had pressured the Ukrainian president to open a corruption investigation against 2020 Democratic presidential candidate and former vice president Joe Biden—threatening to withhold $400 million in U.S. military aid if Zelensky didn't comply. The *Wall Street Journal* was one of the first to report that the military aid to Ukraine was deliberately held up by the Trump administration in the weeks before the phone call. While Trump denied any bribery, the House of Representatives opened an impeachment inquiry of the president. The House voted to impeach Trump on December 18, 2019, with two articles of impeachment on charges of abuse of power and obstruction of Congress, though Trump was acquitted by the Republican-controlled Senate on both counts on February 5, 2020.

ADVERSARIAL JOURNALISM

The political power of the news media vis-à-vis the government has greatly increased in recent years through the growing prominence of **adversarial journalism**,

adversarial journalism a model of reporting in which the journalist's role involves adopting a stance of opposition and a combative style in order to expose perceived wrongdoings

The United States charged Julian Assange, founder of WikiLeaks, for breaching national security by publishing classified documents.

a form of reporting in which the media adopt a skeptical or even hostile posture toward the government and public officials.

On the presidential level, the growth of adversarial journalism represented a reversal of the relationship between presidents and the media that had developed through much of the twentieth century. By communicating directly to the electorate through newspapers and magazines, Theodore Roosevelt and Woodrow Wilson established political constituencies for themselves, independent of party organizations, and thereby strengthened their own power relative to that of Congress. President Franklin Delano Roosevelt used the radio, most notably in his famous fireside chats, to reach out to voters throughout the nation and to make himself the center of American political life. Subsequent presidents all tried to use the media to enhance their popularity, and friendly relationships with journalists became a key strategy of presidential administrations.

The Vietnam War shattered this relationship between the press and the presidency. During the early stages of U.S. involvement, American officials in Vietnam who disapproved of the way the war was being conducted leaked to reporters information critical of administrative policy. Publication of this material infuriated the White House, which pressured publishers to block its release, but the national broadcast media and especially the two leading national newspapers, the *Washington Post* and the *New York Times*, refused to do so. As the war dragged on, adverse media coverage fanned antiwar sentiment among the public and in Congress. In turn, these shifts in opinion emboldened journalists and publishers to continue to present news reports critical of the war.

The media were also central figures in the Watergate affair, the cluster of scandals that ultimately forced President Nixon to resign from office in 1974. A series of investigations by the *Washington Post*, the *New York Times*, and the television networks uncovered various crimes of which Nixon was guilty, leading to threats of impeachment and his subsequent resignation. Gradually, a generation of journalists developed a commitment to adversarial journalism.

Adversarial journalism intensified during Trump's administration as the president became embroiled in a federal investigation into possible collusion between Russia and Trump's 2016 campaign for president. The national news media, led by the *New York Times* and the *Washington Post*, revealed how Russia used a sophisticated cyber campaign to interfere in the 2016 election; they also closely followed the federal investigation led by Robert Mueller into whether anyone close to Trump participated in the Russian interference.

Without rigorous investigative and adversarial journalism, citizens would not have the means (and information) necessary to hold their elected representatives accountable. It is easy to criticize the media for their aggressive tactics of investigation, publicity, and exposure, but without them, important questions about the conduct of American foreign and domestic policy, police violence, drone attacks, election interference by foreign governments, political corruption, and civil liberty violations may not ever be raised. Adversarial journalism, with reporting that is skeptical of government and public officials, is a critical part of what makes democratic governments work.

The famous photograph of the aftermath of a napalm attack was one of many media images that shaped the American public's views on the Vietnam War. Media accounts critical of the war helped to turn public opinion against it and hastened the withdrawal of American troops.

FOR CRITICAL ANALYSIS

Richard Nixon, Bill Clinton, Donald Trump, and many other presidents have criticized the media. Why are many politicians hostile to media? Do you share their views?

Regulation of the Media

Describe the evolution of rules that govern broadcast media

In many countries, such as China, the government exercises strict control over traditional media content. In others, the government owns some of the country's broadcast media (for example, the BBC in Britain) but does not tell the media what to say.

In the United States, the print and online media are essentially free from government interference. Broadcast radio and television, on the other hand, are regulated by the Federal Communications Commission (FCC), an agency established in 1934. Radio and TV stations must have FCC licenses, which must be renewed every five years. Through regulations prohibiting obscenity, indecency, and profanity, the FCC has sought to prohibit radio and television stations from airing explicit sexual and excretory references between 6 a.m. and 10 p.m., the hours when the audience is most likely to include children. Generally speaking, FCC regulation applies only to the over-the-air broadcast media and not to cable television, the internet, or satellite radio.

In 1996, Congress passed the Telecommunications Act, a broad effort to end most regulations of business practices and mergers, allowing the formation of media tech giants and media conglomerates. The legislation loosened restrictions on media ownership and allowed telephone companies, cable television providers, and broadcasters to compete with one another to provide telecommunication services. Following the passage of this act, mergers between telephone and cable companies and different entertainment media produced a greater concentration of

The debate over net neutrality highlights fundamental questions about democracy. If the media are intended to be a marketplace of ideas, what should the government do to regulate that marketplace? Should any single entity be allowed to exert more influence or control, or should everyone be allowed to participate equally?

media ownership than had been possible since regulation of the industry began in 1934. In radio, for example, a 40-station ownership cap was lifted, leading to an unprecedented consolidation. ClearChannel Communications (rebranded as iHeartMedia in 2014) grew from 40 to 1,200 stations.

Although the government's ability to regulate the content of the internet is limited, the FCC has used its licensing power to impose several regulations that can affect the political content of radio and TV broadcasts. The first of these is the **equal time rule**, under which broadcasters must provide to candidates for the same political office equal opportunities to communicate their messages to the public. Under the terms of the Telecommunications Act, during the 45 days before an election, broadcasters are required to make time available to candidates at the lowest rate charged for that time slot. The second regulation affecting the content of broadcasts is the **right of rebuttal**, which requires that individuals be given the opportunity to respond to personal attacks.

For many years, a third important federal regulation was the *fairness doctrine*. Under this rule, broadcasters that aired programs on controversial issues were required to provide time for opposing views. In addition, the fairness doctrine included a requirement that TV and radio stations cover controversial issues of public and social importance in their communities. In 1985, however, the FCC stopped enforcing the fairness doctrine on the grounds that there were so many radio and television stations—to say nothing of newspapers and newsmagazines—that in all likelihood many different viewpoints were already being presented without each station being required to try to present all sides of every argument. In 1987 the FCC officially revoked the fairness doctrine. Critics of this decision charge that in many media markets the number of competing viewpoints is actually quite small.

The rise of online media challenges traditional thinking about regulation of the media, as it is more difficult—some say impossible—to regulate political content online (Facebook, Twitter, and Google are grappling with this today). In 2011 the United Nations declared that access to the internet is a human right.[84] While this declaration came in response to threats by authoritarian governments against internet access, it demonstrates the significance of information technology in modern life.[85]

equal time rule the requirement that broadcasters provide candidates for the same political office equal opportunities to communicate their messages to the public

right of rebuttal a Federal Communications Commission regulation giving individuals the right to have the opportunity to respond to personal attacks made on a radio or television broadcast

The Media and Democracy: What Do You Think?

The freedom of the press is essential to democratic government. Ordinary citizens depend on the media to investigate wrongdoing, publicize and explain governmental policy, evaluate politicians, and bring to light matters that might otherwise be known to only a handful of governmental insiders. In short, without free and active media, democratic government would be virtually impossible. Citizens would have few means through which to know or assess the government's actions—other than the claims or pronouncements of the government itself. Moreover, without active (indeed, aggressive) media, citizens would be hard-pressed to make informed choices among competing candidates at the polls. But the rise of digital media has fundamentally changed

how political information is gathered and distributed. News today is participatory and involves citizens as well as professional journalists. New platforms raise new questions about who should decide what content is disseminated.

★ Knowing what you know now, what do you think of investigations into online content and the debates over the responsibilities and liabilities of digital media companies such as Facebook and Twitter? Should they monitor and edit content and users? Should they be legally responsible for content that users post? What would Christopher Blair, featured at the beginning of this chapter, say?

★ How widely do your friends and family seek out information? Do they tend to rely on a small number of sources, or reach out more broadly? What about your media habits?

★ What media sources do you see playing the role of "watchdog" over government and politics? What kinds of stories do they publish? Do you see these sources as biased or unbiased?

STUDY GUIDE

The Media in American Democracy

> **Describe the key roles the media play in American political life (pp. 229–34)**

The First Amendment guarantees the right to publish newspapers, magazines, and digital media without government censorship and with few restrictions. The media serve three important roles in American democracy: they inform the public about current political developments, provide a forum for debating political issues, and act as a watchdog on the actions of politicians and government. Trained journalists seek to report the news in the public interest—that is, factually, objectively, and transparently. The American media landscape is unusual when considered alongside that of other democracies in that public broadcasting plays a relatively small role, and a few giant profit-motivated corporations control a wide swath of American media.

Key Terms
media (p. 229)
media monopoly (p. 233)

Practice Quiz

1. Public broadcasting outlets that receive partial funding through license fees and government subsidies
   a) are prohibited by the Constitution from operating in the United States.
   b) account for less than 5 percent of media market share in the United States.
   c) account for nearly one-third of media market share in the United States.
   d) account for approximately half of media market share in the United States.
   e) account for more than two-thirds of media market share in the United States.

2. More than three-fourths of the daily print newspapers in the United States are owned by
   a) large media conglomerates.
   b) the national government.
   c) small local companies.
   d) private individuals.
   e) the employees who run them.

The Media Today

> **Describe how different types of media cover politics (pp. 234–49)**

The rise of the internet over the last three decades has produced a massive transformation in the U.S. news media. While newspapers, television, and radio outlets are still important sources of news, large percentages of Americans now choose to get their news through digital versions of print media, streaming video, podcasts, online-only news platforms, or social media. The convenience, currency, depth, diversity, and low cost of online news have led many Americans to prefer it to more traditional sources. However, the shift toward online media has also raised concerns about the quality of news content, the increased circulation of false information, and the negative effects of these factors on political knowledge and tolerance.

Key Terms
broadcast media (p. 238)
penny press (p. 240)
news aggregator (p. 241)
digital citizen (p. 241)
digital divide (p. 242)
social media (p. 242)
citizen journalism (p. 244)
fake news (p. 248)

Practice Quiz

3. Digital citizenship requires
   a) a subscription to one or more online newspapers.
   b) high-speed internet access and the skills to use and evaluate online information.
   c) a social media account.
   d) maintaining a political blog.
   e) registering one's computer with the government.

4. In addition to becoming a key way to disseminate and access the news, social media have also
   a) eclipsed television as the news source that commands the largest audience.
   b) made it more difficult for citizen journalists to share their stories.
   c) increased filtering of the news, such that users are more likely to consume information that aligns with their preexisting beliefs.

d) decreased filtering of the news, such that consumers are more likely to encounter and learn from opposing viewpoints.

e) made it more difficult to directly engage with political candidates and elected officials.

5. Which of the following is *not* a reason that many Americans appear to prefer online news?
a) the convenience of getting news online
b) the up-to-the-minute currency of the information available online
c) the depth of the information available online
d) the diversity of global online sources
e) the accuracy and objectivity of online news compared to traditional media outlets

6. Which of the following best describes Americans' level of trust in the media today?
a) Nearly 90 percent of all Americans express high levels of trust in national news organizations.
b) Just 10 percent of all Americans express high levels of trust in national news organizations.
c) Republicans are more likely than Democrats to think that information from national news organizations is very trustworthy.
d) Democrats are more likely than Republicans to think that information from national news organizations is very trustworthy.
e) Republicans and Democrats are equally likely to think that information from national news organizations is very trustworthy.

Media Influence

> **Analyze the ways the media can influence public opinion and politics (pp. 250–55)**

The content and character of news programming can have far-reaching political consequences. In recent American political history, the media have played a central role in shaping public opinion and policy related to numerous major events, such as the civil rights movement of the 1950s and '60s and the Vietnam War. The power of the media lies in their ability to direct the public's attention to certain issues and not others (agenda setting), influence how people interpret and understand political events (framing), and provide cues to the public about which issues should guide their political decision making (priming).

Key Terms

agenda setting (p. 250)

gatekeeping (p. 252)

framing (p. 254)

priming (p. 255)

Practice Quiz

7. Which of the following best describes the level of ideological bias in the news media overall?
a) Most sources exhibit a clear liberal bias.
b) Most sources exhibit a clear conservative bias.
c) Most sources have been found to be centrist.
d) Sources with conservative owners are likely to be conservative, and those with liberal owners are likely to be liberal.
e) Sources tend to change from right-leaning to left-leaning, or vice versa, depending on which party has more power in government at the time.

8. The media's power to determine which issues become a part of political discussion is known as
a) framing.
b) priming.
c) agenda setting.
d) ideological bias.
e) citizen journalism.

9. The fact that Democrats discussed the Patient Protection and Affordable Care Act as a matter of compassionate responsibility and good economic sense while Republicans discussed it as a matter of "health care rationing" is an example of
a) framing.
b) priming.
c) agenda setting.
d) ideological bias.
e) citizen journalism.

News Coverage

Explain how politicians and others try to shape the news (pp. 256–57)

Governments, politicians, corporations, interest groups, and nonprofit organizations all attempt to shape the content of the news. While journalists often gain information through official channels, they also hold government accountable by reporting on leaked information and using the tactics of adversarial journalism. Leaks, which are confidential pieces of information disclosed to members of the media, have driven press coverage on issues ranging from foreign policy to government corruption. Adversarial journalism, a form of reporting in which the media adopt a skeptical or even hostile posture toward public officials, has increased the political power of the press in recent years.

Key Terms

adversarial journalism (p. 256)

Practice Quiz

10. Most leaks originate with
    a) low-level government whistle-blowers.
    b) senior government officials, prominent politicians, and political activists.
    c) members of the public who witness misbehavior.
    d) ambassadors from foreign countries.
    e) members of the media.

11. Which organization has used the internet to anonymously release thousands of secret U.S. government documents relating to corruption, war crimes, and election administration in recent years?
    a) the Federal Communications Commission
    b) WikiLeaks
    c) the National Security Agency
    d) the Project for Excellence in Journalism
    e) the Freedom of Information Agency

12. *Adversarial journalism* refers to
    a) the recent shift in American society away from general-purpose sources of information toward narrowly focused niche sources.
    b) an era in American history when political parties provided all of the financing for newspapers.
    c) a form of reporting in which the media adopt a skeptical or even hostile posture toward the opinions and behaviors of their audience.
    d) a form of reporting in which the media adopt an accepting and friendly posture toward the government and public officials.
    e) a form of reporting in which the media adopt a skeptical or even hostile posture toward the government and public officials.

13. Which event shattered the once-friendly relationship between the press and the presidency?
    a) September 11, 2001
    b) the Vietnam War
    c) Watergate
    d) World War II
    e) the Monica Lewinsky affair

Regulation of the Media

Describe the evolution of rules that govern broadcast media (pp. 258–59)

Although American print and online media are essentially free from government interference, broadcast radio and television are regulated by the Federal Communications Commission (FCC). The FCC has used its licensing power to impose several regulations, such as the equal time rule and the right of rebuttal, that affect the political content of radio and television broadcasts.

Key Terms

equal time rule (p. 259)

right of rebuttal (p. 259)

Practice Quiz

14. In general, FCC regulations apply only to
    a) cable television.
    b) internet websites.
    c) over-the-air broadcast media.
    d) satellite radio.
    e) newspapers and magazines.

15. The now-defunct rule that required broadcasters to provide time for opposing views when they aired programs on controversial issues was called
    a) the equal time rule.
    b) the free speech doctrine.
    c) the fairness doctrine.
    d) the right of rebuttal.
    e) the response rule.

Political Participation and Voting

WHAT GOVERNMENT DOES AND WHY IT MATTERS In 2020 protests against racial injustice broke out across the country on a scale not seen in the United States in 50 years. The immediate cause was the killing of George Floyd, an unarmed 46-year-old African American man, by a Minneapolis police officer. Floyd's encounter with the police was caught on a widely shared video that showed one officer with his knee on Floyd's neck as Floyd begged for his life and ultimately died. Protests spread from there to over 140 cities in the first week after Floyd's death alone. Those participating in the marches and protests invoked the names of others who had been killed by police or in police custody—Michael Brown, Trayvon Martin, Eric Garner, Sandra Bland, Philando Castile, Tamir Rice, Breonna Taylor, and Freddie Gray, among others—as well as larger issues of systemic racism in the criminal justice system and in the economy. That the coronavirus pandemic and ensuing economic crisis had affected minority communities disproportionately—with death rates and unemployment rates far higher among African Americans and Latinos than among Whites—added to the protesters' grievances.

Xavier Brown, a freshman at Howard University, and Akil Riley, a freshman at the University of California at Los Angeles, organized a march in their

Protesters in Oakland, Minneapolis, and around the world took to the streets following the killing of George Floyd. The coordinated protests were some of the largest seen since the civil rights movement in the 1960s. Many protests were organized by students and young people hoping to foment positive change in their communities.

hometown of Oakland that drew 15,000 people. "We were just trying to inspire other youth that anyone can organize, anyone can protest, so to begin a revolution in your own way," said Brown. Riley said that he had been harassed by police after being pulled over and that a cousin had been wrongly sent to jail. At other protests he had been hit with tear gas by police who "looked ready to hurt somebody. . . . As a Black man who's affected by this, the real root of it was just pain at the end of the day," Riley said.[1]

Nevada Littlewolf, a veteran of many protests including the Standing Rock demonstrations against the Dakota Access pipeline project in 2016, joined the protests in Minneapolis. Littlewolf, who is Anishinaabe Ojibwe, said, "Our community knows what that violence feels like. . . . What we have to do is we have to stand together because none of this is going to stop." She lives two miles from where George Floyd was killed and noted the trauma of "seeing a community member murdered at the hands of people who are supposed to protect us and serve us" as well as the destruction in the neighborhood: "It's hard, sad, and hurts to see our neighborhood burned down and destroyed, but if this is what it takes to get justice, this is what it takes. The majority of damage was caused by outsiders, not community members.

I don't blame community members who are in pain. We need change. We need justice."[2]

Americans can participate in democracy through dramatic acts such as protesting as well as through more conventional means such as voting, donating to campaigns, and contacting lawmakers. Through participation, individuals make their voices heard and their preferences known, a crucial element in making government accountable to the people. As we will see in this chapter, who participates and how they participate matter a great deal—in elections and in influencing government policy.

CHAPTER GOALS

★ Describe the major forms of participation in politics (pp. 267–79)

★ Describe the patterns of participation among major demographic groups (pp. 279–88)

★ Explain the factors that influence voter turnout (pp. 289–92)

★ Explain the effect of electoral laws on voting (pp. 292–98)

Forms of Political Participation

Political participation refers to a wide range of activities in politics. Participation in politics includes not only voting in elections but also attending campaign events, rallies, and fundraisers; contributing money to campaigns, candidates, and parties; contacting elected officials; working on behalf of candidates and campaigns, such as canvassing voters; displaying campaign signs; and signing political petitions. Protests, demonstrations, and strikes, too, are age-old forms of participatory politics. Participation also includes publicly expressing support for or opposition to candidates or campaigns on social media (Facebook, Twitter, Instagram, and others); and organizing campaign events. The expansive world of digital politics includes not only the exchange of information but also new forms of fundraising and voter mobilization.

RIOTS AND PROTESTS

If there is any natural or spontaneous form of popular political participation, it is not the election but the protest or riot. In fact, for much of American history, fewer Americans exercised their right to vote than participated in urban riots and rural uprisings, as voting for a long time was limited to White, male, land-owning citizens.

The vast majority of Americans today reject rioting or other violence for political ends, but peaceful **protest** is protected by the First Amendment and generally recognized as a legitimate and important form of political activity. During the height of the civil rights movement in the 1960s, hundreds of thousands of Americans took part in peaceful protests to demand social and political rights for African Americans. Peaceful marches and demonstrations have since been employed by a host of groups across the ideological spectrum.

> **protest** participation that involves assembling crowds to confront a government or other official organization

People participate in public protests to attract media attention, raise public awareness, and send a message to politicians about the policies they want. Even before the protests following George Floyd's death in May 2020, growing concern over excessive use of police force against African Americans had led to hundreds of protests across the nation in recent years, including by NFL players, coaches, and owners kneeling with locked arms during the playing of the national anthem in silent protest of racial inequality. The Black Lives Matter movement and NFL protests prompted national discussion and political action around racial inequity in the criminal justice system and reform, including revamped training programs and calls to equip police officers with body cameras, although critics argued that continued instances of excessive force, such as George Floyd's death in police custody, showed continued need for reform.[3]

Some protests can lead to violence, though the overwhelming majority of them are peaceful. In August 2017, clashes erupted in Charlottesville, Virginia, between White nationalists rallying against the city's decision to remove a statue of Confederate general Robert E. Lee from a park and counterprotesters. Thirty people were injured and one counterprotester was killed by a White nationalist who drove his car into the crowd. Many participants in the protests after George Floyd's death in 2020 were injured as well. Some have claimed protesters escalated violence, while others point to the forceful police response to the protests.

One advantage of protest is visibility: through media attention, protesters can raise awareness, attract like-minded individuals, and put pressure on politicians. That was the goal of (left to right) the Women's March, NFL players kneeling during the national anthem to protest police brutality, White nationalists in Charlottesville, Virginia, protesting the removal of a Confederate statue, and the Black Lives Matter protests in 2020.

POLITICAL PARTICIPATION IN ELECTIONS

Political participation refers to a wide range of activities designed to influence government, politics, and public policy. For most people, voting in elections is the most common form of participation in politics. When asked what makes a good citizen, the top reason mentioned by three in four Americans is voting. For reference, the next most common traits were paying taxes (70 percent), always following the law (69 percent), serving on a jury if called (61 percent), and respecting the opinions of others who disagree (61 percent).[4]

By such activities as contacting political officials, attending campaign events and rallies, or volunteering to work on a campaign, citizens can communicate much more detailed information to public officials than they can by voting, thus making these other political activities often more satisfying.[5] These forms of political action generally require more time, effort, and/or money than voting. As a result, the percentage of the population that participates in ways other than voting is relatively low (see Figure 8.1).

Voting For most Americans, voting is the single most important political act. The right to vote gives ordinary Americans an equal voice in politics, since each vote within the same district or state has the same value. Voting is especially important because it selects the officials who make the laws that the American people must follow.

During early periods of American history, the right to vote, called **suffrage**, was usually restricted to White males over the age of 21. Many states further limited voting to those who owned property or paid more than a specified amount of annual tax. Until the early 1900s, state legislatures elected U.S. senators, and there were no direct elections for members of the Electoral College (who in turn elect the president). As a result, elections for the U.S. House as well as for state legislatures and local offices were how eligible citizens could participate in government. Voter turnout as a percentage of the adult U.S. population during this period was relatively low.

suffrage the right to vote; also called *franchise*

During the nineteenth and early twentieth centuries, states often further restricted voting rights, initially through poll taxes (fees charged to vote) and literacy tests (reading tests) designed to limit immigrant voting in northern cities. These strategies were later imported into the southern states to prevent African Americans and poor Whites from voting during the Jim Crow era—the period after the Civil War when African Americans were legally granted the right to vote and before the

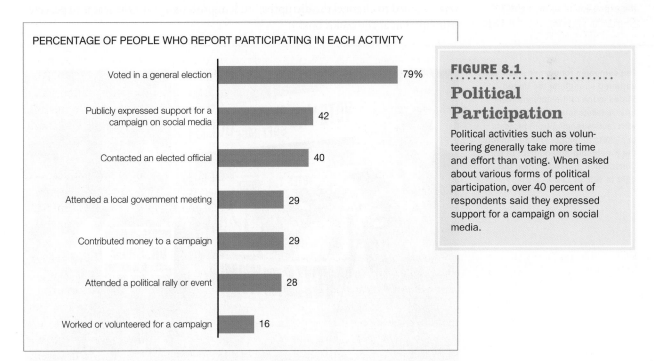

PERCENTAGE OF PEOPLE WHO REPORT PARTICIPATING IN EACH ACTIVITY

Activity	Percentage
Voted in a general election	79%
Publicly expressed support for a campaign on social media	42
Contacted an elected official	40
Attended a local government meeting	29
Contributed money to a campaign	29
Attended a political rally or event	28
Worked or volunteered for a campaign	16

FIGURE 8.1

Political Participation

Political activities such as volunteering generally take more time and effort than voting. When asked about various forms of political participation, over 40 percent of respondents said they expressed support for a campaign on social media.

SOURCE: Based on a sample made up primarily of registered voters; "Political Engagement, Knowledge, and the Midterms," Pew Research Center, April 26, 2018, www.people-press.org/2018/04/26/10-political-engagement-knowledge-and-the-midterms/ (accessed 10/12/18).

passage of the 1965 Voting Rights Act (see Chapter 5). Before the 1960s civil rights movement, voting rights often varied greatly from state to state, with many southern states using an array of laws to prevent participation in politics, including all-White primaries and requiring that voters own property in order to be able to vote.[6]

Given the variation in voting rights across states, over the past two centuries of American history many federal statutes, court decisions, and constitutional amendments have been designed to override state voting laws and expand suffrage.[7] In the South, voting rights for African American men were established in 1870 by the Fifteenth Amendment, which prohibited states from denying the right to vote on the basis of race. After the states of the former Confederacy effectively got around the amendment by such means as poll taxes and literacy tests, as discussed above, voting rights for African Americans became a central goal of the civil rights movement in the 1950s and '60s. African Americans won the right to vote with the enactment of the 1965 Voting Rights Act, which authorized the federal government to register voters in states that had discriminated against minority citizens and to challenge state voting rules and practices that systematically disenfranchise minority voters. The result was giving southern Blacks the right to vote in the United States.

Women nationwide won the right to vote in 1920 through the adoption of the Nineteenth Amendment. The women's suffrage movement had held rallies, demonstrations, and protest marches for more than half a century before achieving this goal. Before the Nineteenth Amendment, numerous states and territories adopted women's suffrage, paving the way for women to earn the right to vote nationally.

The most recent expansion of the right to vote, the Twenty-Sixth Amendment, lowered the voting age from 21 to 18. Ratified during the Vietnam War, in 1971, it was intended to channel the disruptive student protests against the war into peaceful participation at the ballot box.

FOR CRITICAL ANALYSIS

Describe the expansion of suffrage in the United States since the Founding. Why might the government have denied participation to so many for so long? What forces influenced the expansion of voting rights?

The campaign for women's suffrage gathered strength in the United States in the mid-eighteenth century. Activists fought for decades—with tactics ranging from protests to pickets to hunger strikes—before the Nineteenth Amendment to the Constitution granted women the right to vote in 1920.

Current Trends in Voter Turnout Today, voting rights are granted to all American citizens age 18 and above, although some states bar voting by those who have committed a felony or are mentally impaired. America's overall rate of voting participation, or **turnout**, remains relatively low, however: the United States ranked 32nd in voter turnout among developed countries in 2016. Just over 66 percent of citizens eligible to vote did so in the 2020 presidential election. This is still lower than voting rates in the most recent national elections in other democracies: 87 percent in Belgium, 86 percent in Sweden, and 71 percent in France. Turnout in state and local elections, especially those that do not coincide with national contests, is typically much lower.[8]

Not only does the United States have relatively low rates of participation in elections; compared with Americans who vote, those who do not are more likely to lack a college education and to have a lower income. The fact that education and income track so closely with voter turnout is unique to the United States among Western democracies. Low voter turnout coupled with unequal participation rates can result in the election of candidates who do not reflect the interests of most citizens, government policies that benefit wealthy voters over the middle and lower classes, and lower trust in government.

In 1996, participation reached a modern low when only 52 percent of eligible voters went to the polls. Since then, however, turnout has improved due to highly contested presidential elections and major efforts to get out the vote. In 2008, turnout reached 62 percent when Barack Obama's campaign mobilized many new voters. The 2016 presidential election turnout was 59 percent, but broke a record in terms of votes cast at 137 million.[9] Turnout in 2020 was the highest since 1900 at over 66 percent, and broke the record for most ballots cast at nearly 159 million.[10]

PARTICIPATION IN THE HISTORIC 2018 MIDTERMS

Midterm elections, with only congressional elections at the national level, tend to have much lower voter turnout. Comparing turnout in midterm versus presidential elections is like comparing college and professional football—they are governed by different rules (legislative districts versus electoral college), different players (types of candidates), strategies (statewide/districtwide versus national campaigns) and fans (voters). Turnout in midterm elections is usually 20 points lower than in presidential elections. It is also usually heavily skewed in favor of demographic groups that vote regularly—older, educated, affluent, partisans, and Whites.

In the 2014 midterm elections, only 36 percent of eligible citizens voted. In 2018, just four years later, turnout rose 17 points to 53 percent, a record for midterm elections since 1966 (see Figure 8.2).[11] The composition of the 2018 electorate resembled recent presidential electorates more than that of midterm elections, with younger voters, voters of color, and political independents a substantially larger share of the electorate than in traditional congressional elections.

Beyond voting, other forms of **traditional political participation** were also common in 2018. In that year, 30 percent of Americans contacted an elected official and 19 percent contributed money to a campaign, while 15 percent attended a local government meeting, campaign event, or rally. Half of Democratic voters reported having participated in at least one of the four campaign-related

turnout the percentage of eligible individuals who actually vote

traditional political participation activities designed to influence government, including voting, campaign contributions, and face-to-face activities such as volunteering for a campaign or working on behalf of a candidate or political organization

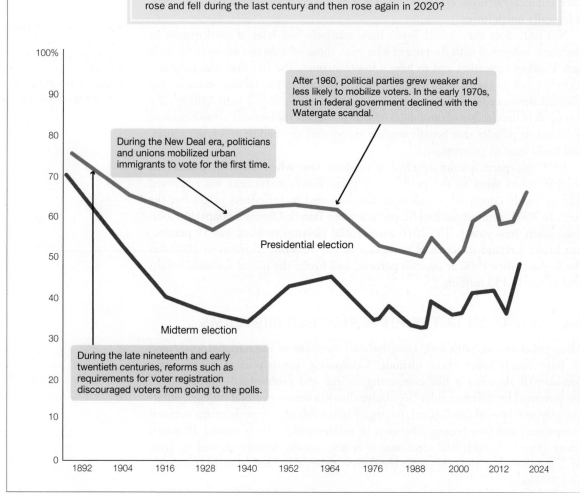

FIGURE 8.2
Voter Turnout* in Presidential and Midterm Elections, 1892–2020

Since the 1890s, participation in elections has declined substantially, with the exception of the 2020 presidential election. One pattern is consistent across time: more Americans tend to vote in presidential election years than in years when only congressional and local elections are held. What are some of the reasons that participation rose and fell during the last century and then rose again in 2020?

After 1960, political parties grew weaker and less likely to mobilize voters. In the early 1970s, trust in federal government declined with the Watergate scandal.

During the New Deal era, politicians and unions mobilized urban immigrants to vote for the first time.

Presidential election

Midterm election

During the late nineteenth and early twentieth centuries, reforms such as requirements for voter registration discouraged voters from going to the polls.

*Percentage of voting-eligible population
SOURCES: Erik Austin and Jerome Clubb, *Political Facts of the United States since 1789* (New York: Columbia University Press, 1986); United States Election Project, www.electproject.org (accessed 11/14/16); "2018 November General Election Turnout Rates," United States Election Project, November 12, 2020, www.electproject.org/2020g (accessed 11/12/20).

activities mentioned above, compared with 40 percent of Republican voters. In sum, 2018 mattered for political participation not only because overall turnout was similar to turnout for a presidential election but because the electorate more closely matched the overall population in terms of age, race and ethnicity, and socioeconomic status.

ONLINE POLITICAL PARTICIPATION

The internet gives citizens greater access to information about candidates and campaigns and a greater role in politics than ever before. While building on traditional forms of participation, digital politics makes many of those activities easier, more immediate, and more personalized. The internet, particularly social media, offers an active, two-way form of communication, rather than the more passive, one-way communication involved in reading newspapers, watching television, or listening to the radio. It allows for person-to-person communication as well as broadcast capability, where information can be widely shared.

Digital political participation includes a wide range of activities: discussing issues and candidates or mobilizing supporters through social media, email, and text messaging; reading online news stories and commenting on them; viewing YouTube videos and campaign ads; contributing money to candidates, parties, and groups; contacting political leaders and following them on Twitter; running campaign ads on social networking sites; organizing petition drives; and organizing face-to-face neighborhood meetings online. With 67 percent of Americans reading the news using social media, digital participation is the most common way average Americans participate in politics outside of voting.[12]

Why are digital media so effective for mobilization and political participation? Online mobilization works through emotional appeals, immediacy, personal networks, and social pressure. The work of political scientist Meredith Rolfe reveals that one's social network plays a much stronger role in political participation than do individual factors such as income and education. When members of a social network indicate they have voted in an election or contributed to a candidate, for example, that can motivate others in their network to do the same.[13]

Social media in particular can efficiently coordinate the actions of millions of people required for political campaigns and winning elections. One in three social media users has encouraged others to vote, and roughly the same percentage have shared their own thoughts on politics or government online.[14] Social media make possible tiny acts of political participation—sharing, following a candidate or organization, liking a post, commenting—that can scale up to dramatic changes, leading to real-world political protests, voter-mobilization drives, and the election of candidates and parties to government.[15] Such acts give those who are uninterested in or rarely engaged by politics an easy way of getting involved, which can then encourage them to do more.

Politicians, too, make much use of social media. Every serious presidential candidate has a Twitter account, Facebook, Instagram, and YouTube channel. These outlets have thousands or in some cases millions of followers, who receive daily updates from the candidates and campaigns. These fans, in turn, use social media to signal to their friends which candidates they support, making politics a seamless part of everyday online discussion. Digital political campaigns are much less expensive for candidates than running television ads.

Unlike traditional social movements that gain momentum more slowly, digital politics can create punctuated bursts of collective action. For example, during the 2016 presidential primaries, Bernie Sanders's supporters relied heavily on Reddit to organize rallies and rock concerts on his behalf. After Donald Trump won the 2016 election despite losing the popular vote by nearly 3 million votes, over 700,000 people signed an online petition to eliminate the electoral college and elect the president based on actual votes cast.

digital political participation activities designed to influence politics using the internet, including visiting a candidate's website, organizing events online, and signing an online petition

Some have dismissed political activity on social media as *clicktivism*—forms of participation that require little effort and may not convert to offline acts of participation in politics. Others argue that so-called clicktivism is the building block for sustained participation in politics. Donald Trump's extensive use of Twitter is evidence that audience-building on social media matters for political leadership and winning votes. A survey analysis of 65,000 registered voters found that frequent social media users were more likely to vote for Trump than for any other candidate in 2016.[16] The clicks of millions of Americans can and do add up.

Online Politics Blends with Offline Participation The discussion above suggests a number of mechanisms by which social networks and small acts of political participation online lead to voting and offline engagement in politics. Digital politics encourages both information-gathering and interaction among users and elected officials by combining the content of traditional media with interpersonal communication, and this combination promotes interest in politics and increases participation. Research finds reading digital news, commenting on posts, and using email or social media for politics increase the likelihood not only of voting but also of contributing to political campaigns, volunteering on behalf of candidates, and even contacting elected officials. Online participation also makes people more likely to discuss politics with friends or family, develop an interest in politics in general, and become informed about politics.[17]

The ease of making monetary contributions online, for example, has increased the number of small individual donations. The percentage of people who donate directly to candidates has doubled since 1992. Barack Obama was the first candidate to capitalize on online fundraising, raising much of the money needed to win the 2008 presidential election from small (less than $100) individual online donations. In fact, that election ushered in the modern era of digital politics, as Obama's campaign developed comprehensive online strategies to mobilize supporters, and citizens made unprecedented use of digital media to learn about candidates and to participate in campaigns.[18] In an election year estimated to cost nearly $14 billion, money from small donors made up 22 percent of 2020 fundraising, up from 15 percent in 2016.[19] Contributions from individuals made up about 38 percent of Biden's total fundraising and 45 percent of Trump's.[20]

Twitter has become an especially important tool for voter mobilization, as the percentage of Americans following elected officials on Twitter continues to grow. Individuals like following political figures on social media because it makes them feel more emotionally connected to the candidates.[21] Social media also allow users to avoid exposure to information that challenges their preexisting views—it's easier to follow people online whom you agree with. Elected officials and organizations on the ideological left and right have taken advantage of this dynamic to filter the news and current events. Recent research finds that people who use social media for politics frequently hold stronger opinions and are more polarized by party than those who do not.[22] In this way social media may contribute to party polarization (see Chapter 9). But research finds that frequent Twitter users are also more interested in politics and more likely to participate in politics.[23]

Studies have suggested a number of possible reasons that digital politics may foster participation. First, information and political news are available 24 hours a day and access is often free. Digital politics may also engage individuals who

Voter Turnout in Comparison

There are many factors that influence whether an individual decides to vote or not. Governments can take several steps to try to increase voter turnout. These include making registration automatic upon reaching voting age, scheduling elections on weekends or a national holiday, conducting elections by mail-in ballot, or even making voting compulsory with the potential for being fined if one does not have a valid excuse.

1. Which of the government policies seem to have the greatest effect on voter turnout? How does each of these policies make voting easier? Why might even countries with compulsory voting fail to achieve high turnout? How difficult might it be to enforce such a law?

2. What are the downsides to each of these policies? How can a country balance the desire for electoral participation against the desire to protect the right of its citizens to choose to abstain from politics? Which of these policies do you think would be most likely to improve voter turnout in the United States?

COUNTRY	TURNOUT AS PERCENT OF VOTING-AGE POPULATION	COMPULSORY VOTING	WEEKEND OR HOLIDAY VOTING	AUTOMATIC OR COMPULSORY REGISTRATION
Australia	81%	Yes	Yes	Yes
Brazil	78	Yes	Yes	Yes
Germany	71		Yes	Yes
India	65		Yes	Yes
South Africa	61		Yes	
Japan	60		Yes	Yes
United Kingdom	60			Yes
Canada	57			
Mexico	56	Yes	Yes	Yes
Tunisia	54			
United States	45			
Switzerland	39		Yes	Yes

SOURCES: International Institute for Democracy and Electoral Assistance (IDEA) Voter Turnout Database, www.idea.int/data-tools/data/voter-turnout; and ACE Electoral Knowledge Network, http://aceproject.org/epic-en/CDTable?view=country&question=VR008 (accessed 8/8/2019).

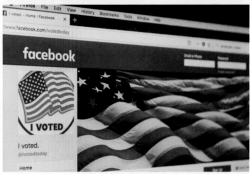

Like the traditional "I Voted" stickers, political messages shared on social media may remind and encourage others to participate too. In recent elections, Facebook users could click an "I Voted" button to announce that they had cast a ballot.

otherwise would not be involved in politics. The internet creates a form of "accidental mobilization" for those who are greeted by political content on social media—sometimes politics finds the individual, rather than the other way around.[24] It is common for candidates to place political ads on social media sites and in Google searches, prompting the individuals exposed to these ads, who may be online for entirely separate reasons, to learn about politics.

Donald Trump took advantage of online political ads in the 2016 campaign unlike any other modern candidate, spending millions of dollars on them.[25] In 2020, Trump invested heavily in campaign ads on YouTube, a platform used by one in four Americans to get news. YouTube has been called Trump's "secret weapon" (much like Facebook in 2016) to gain a below-the-radar advantage that wasn't apparent until after the election.

Further, digital media have unique characteristics that enhance participation. Streaming video online combines the qualities of print media that promote knowledge and in-depth reporting with the immediate and visual aspects of television that generate interest, engagement, and emotion.[26] Emotional responses to candidates or issues generated by online media have been shown to trigger interest and engagement in politics.

Finally, as we have discussed, online politics makes it easier for people to participate simply because it requires less effort. By its very nature, digital politics occurs in ways that are less location-dependent than traditional politics: *community* takes on a very different meaning in an online social network compared with, say, a voter's actual neighborhood polling place. The internet facilitates participation that is potentially broad but loosely connected, low in intensity, and sporadic. Thus, digital politics may tend to attract individuals with only moderate political interest.[27]

For all these reasons, digital media may foster a new kind of community-building that has contributed to a reversal of the decline in political participation since the 1960s. Some analysts have explained low voter turnout in the United States over the last half century by citing reduced trust in government, unresponsive elected officials, and a diminishing stock of what Robert Putnam, author of *Bowling Alone*, calls social capital—community networks that motivate political participation.[28] By making political news, discussion, communication, and mobilization easier, the internet, and especially social media, may help Americans grow a new kind of digital social capital, one based on shared political experiences online.

Expressive Politics Political scientist Russell Dalton has argued that participation in politics is becoming more expressive than ever before, largely aided by social media.[29] Today, individuals turn to social media to express their opinions on issues or candidates in many ways. This trend was exemplified by the response to the 2015 Supreme Court ruling that made same-sex marriage legal in all 50 states.

In the wake of the decision, digital politics created a media firestorm as responses to the decision took over the internet. With remarkable immediacy, both traditional and social media converged to celebrate or denounce the news that marriage for same-sex couples was the new law of the land. Social media enabled citizens to share their opinions in uniquely expressive ways. For example, the #LoveWins hashtag was used almost 5.5 million times in 24 hours, including by celebrities and President Obama, and there were 10 million tweets about the decision in less than 12 hours.[30] And millions of people, too, used Facebook's tool to add a rainbow-colored background to their profile pictures or shared news stories and memes using rainbow images to show their support for marriage rights.[31]

#LoveWins

News about the Supreme Court's 2015 decision to legalize same-sex marriage spread rapidly, in part through viral activity on social media. Sites such as Twitter provided users with a highly visible platform to show support.

Are There Drawbacks to Digital Participation? While social media can be effective in political mobilization, at the same time they create echo chambers where individuals with similar views communicate to the exclusion of others, leading to increased polarization—and eventually hyper-partisanship. As mentioned earlier, people tend to surround themselves with news from like-minded sources. In such environments, they may uncritically believe news from outlets they trust while dismissing or ignoring information from sources they dislike. Social media algorithms can also contribute to echo chambers and lead to biased views that get more extreme over time, creating a world of "fictional narratives" or "alternative facts" where individuals cannot agree on basic principles.

Indeed, considerable evidence shows that social media have intensified political conflict, social and cultural divisions, and intolerance based on race, ethnicity, gender, and religion. Anonymous social media discussion boards can unintentionally create forums for racism and hate speech, terrorist appeals, and sexual harassment—forums that have mobilized far-right groups, including White nationalists. Consequently, members of some groups—such as women and minorities—may opt out of participating in discussion of politics, in what has been called the "disruption of the public square."[32] Critics also see social media as contributing more generally to a lack of civility in political discussion, or what is often called a "coarsening of public discourse."[33]

THE DARK SIDE OF DIGITAL POLITICS: RUSSIAN INTERFERENCE AND VOTER SUPPRESSION

Free and fair elections are the foundation for democracies. But democratic elections may be increasingly vulnerable to manipulation by foreign governments and political extremists because of open networks—individuals from any country can participate—and unregulated political advertising on social media. In the 2016 presidential election, Donald Trump's campaign benefited from a Russian campaign that used social media to discredit his opponent Hillary Clinton. Intelligence agencies confirmed Russia interfered in the election, which was intended to mobilize Trump supporters to vote, discourage Clinton supporters, promote third-party candidates to Bernie Sanders's supporters, and sow discord in the American public.

The first strategy focused on mobilizing voters to cast a ballot for Donald Trump. One notable ad featured a kneeling soldier and stated that the Constitution should be amended to take control of the army from Clinton should she be elected president. A similar ad had the false caption "69 percent of veterans favor Trump" (in reality, roughly 52 percent of veterans voted for Trump compared to 48 percent for Clinton). As Senator Chris Coons (D-Del.) said, "This ad is nothing short of the Russian government directly interfering in our elections, lying to American citizens, duping folks who believe they are joining and supporting a group that is about veterans and based in Texas, when in fact it is paid for in rubles [Russian currency] by Russians."[34]

A second category of Russian propaganda worked to suppress votes for Clinton. These ads were targeted in sophisticated ways toward particular demographic groups in swing states such as Wisconsin, Michigan, and Pennsylvania (three states Trump narrowly won over Clinton) and also nationwide. Fake news stories in the two weeks leading up to the election focused on Clinton's health and mental stability. The most troubling Russian propaganda ads encouraged people to cast a vote for Clinton by texting or tweeting their ballot, both of which are invalid forms of voting in the United States.

Finally, Russia's campaign on social media also tried more generally to divide the public over controversial issues such as race, immigration, abortion, gay rights, and gun ownership. Fake Facebook accounts linked to Russia included, for example, Infidels against Islam, Fed-Up with Illegals, and Stop Killing White People.

The scope of Russian interference in the 2016 election was far greater than initially understood. Thousands of false political ads paid for by Russian operatives appeared on Facebook and other social media platforms, with many of them focused on voter suppression. These ads are estimated to have reached 126 million people on Facebook alone. (To put this number in perspective, there were only 135 million votes cast in the 2016 election.) The information was shared hundreds of millions of times. Russian propaganda on Instagram during the election reached another 20 million people. Twitter found nearly 3,000 accounts controlled by Russian operatives and 36,000 more bot accounts that tweeted 1.4 million times during the election. A recent study found that one in five tweets about the election was from a bot account; the majority promoted stories damaging to Clinton.[35]

Russian interference has exposed the outsize role played by social media platforms in American politics—and the fact that these companies don't always follow the same rules as government institutions. Unlike political ads in older media (radio, television, newspapers, and magazines), those on Google and social media sites are not regulated. A foreign government was able to take advantage of the United States' digital communication and media system to interfere in the election. In response, Congress has enacted economic sanctions on Russia and is considering new regulations for media companies.[36] The technology companies have also taken steps to crack down on fake accounts. In 2019, Facebook removed 5.4 billion fake accounts from its main platform, but millions likely remain, especially in the form of memes and streaming video that are harder to detect. Although foreign interference was muted in 2020, misinformation is widespread, despite social media companies' efforts to take it down or prevent it from spreading.[37]

SUMMING UP DIGITAL PARTICIPATION

As we have seen, digital participation in politics has both benefits and costs. It has the potential to foster innovation, free expression, social connection, and political knowledge and participation. But it may also foster misinformation, intolerance, a lack of civility, breaches of privacy, and even demobilization. In 2020, 64 percent of Americans believed social media have a mostly negative effect on the way things are going in this country today.[38]

Another possible drawback of technology in politics is the digital divide—defined as the gap between those with and those without home internet or mobile access. Growing inequalities online mirror existing societal inequalities based on race and economic class and threaten to widen the resulting gaps in who is informed about politics and who participates. Today, 27 percent of Americans don't have home broadband, and those without access tend to be poorer, less educated, older, and rural.[39] As the world of politics moves online, the digital divide creates new inequalities.

Perhaps the most transformative aspect of digital media, however, is how they affect candidates and parties. Political candidates find campaigning online particularly attractive because it is cost-efficient and can reach a wide audience of prospective voters. Running for office can be enormously expensive, but social media may help level the playing field by reducing candidate reliance on money from corporations, other interest groups, and wealthy individuals.

Digital politics thus holds the promise of reinvigorating a more grassroots and participatory democracy. In 2016, Bernie Sanders largely rejected Super PAC funding for his campaign and relied heavily on digital media. But in 2020, both Joe Biden and Donald Trump heavily relied on Super PACs with extensive paid campaign ads on social media and television.

Who Votes?

> **Describe the patterns of participation among major demographic groups**

Just as in any other activity in life, an individual is likely to vote in an election only if the benefits outweigh the costs.[40] One benefit associated with voting is the favorable policies that might result from having one's preferred candidate or party in office, which the potential voter weighs against the slim likelihood of one's vote actually influencing the outcome of the election. Another benefit of voting is the sense of pride gained from fulfilling one's civic duty. The costs related to voting include the time and resources needed to become informed and to cast a ballot, factors that may help explain why the poor and the less educated are less likely to vote and to participate in politics in other ways.

To understand who votes, it helps to understand why some Americans don't vote. The U.S. Census Bureau indicates the top reason for not voting in the 2018 election, cited by one in four nonvoters, was "too busy," followed by "not interested/ my vote doesn't matter," "illness or disability (own or family)," and "didn't like the candidates or campaign issues." As we can see, even personal health can be a factor, with the healthier more likely to vote.[41]

The factors that help us explain voting in elections can be grouped into three general categories: (1) a person's social and demographic characteristics and attitudes about politics; (2) the political environment in which elections take place, such as how strongly campaigns seek to mobilize voters and whether an election is contested by two candidates; and (3) the state electoral laws that shape the electoral process.

SOCIOECONOMIC STATUS

One of the most important and consistent findings from surveys about participation is that Americans with higher levels of education, more income, and higher-level occupations—collectively, what social scientists call higher **socioeconomic status**—

socioeconomic status status in society based on level of education, income, and occupational prestige

participate much more in politics than do those with less education and less income.[42] Education is the single most important factor in predicting not only whether an individual will vote but also whether she will participate in most other ways, such as encouraging other people to vote or support an issue and donating to a candidate or cause.[43] Just 52 percent of those with only a high school diploma voted in the 2016 presidential election, compared with 74 percent of college graduates.[44] In the 2018 midterm election 66 percent of college graduates and 74 percent of people with an advanced degree voted, compared to just 42 percent of those with a high school degree and 27 percent of those with less than a high school degree.[45]

Unsurprisingly, income is another important factor when it comes to making contributions, as well as voting. Among people age 45–64, for example, the 2016 census found that 83 percent of individuals earning over $150,000 a year voted compared to 43 percent of those earning less than $20,000 per year.[46] Individuals with higher socioeconomic status (income, education and occupational status) also tend to have higher levels of interest in politics.[47] The Who Participates? feature on p. 283 shows the differences in voter turnout linked to education level, employment status, ethnic and racial groups, and age.

The Who Participates? feature on p. 283

AGE

Older people have much higher rates of participation than do young people, in part because they are more likely to own homes and pay property taxes, which makes them more aware of the importance of government.

The pattern of older people voting more was evident in 2016, with citizens 65 years and older reporting the highest turnout (71 percent), followed by those age 45–66 (67 percent), age 30–44 (58 percent), and age 18–29 (46 percent), according to the Census. In midterm elections without a presidential race, youth turnout has historically been extremely low, but it is growing rapidly. Among the youngest age cohort, voter turnout went from 20 percent in 2014 to 36 percent in 2018, the largest percentage point increase for any age group. In 2020, youth turnout increased from 36 percent to between 53–56 percent.

Millennials (ages 24–39) are now the largest age cohort in the United States. In 2020, 59–60 percent supported Democrat Joe Biden compared to just 29–36 percent for Republican Donald Trump.[48]

Two primary reasons young people don't vote are that they lack an interest in politics or have not been mobilized to participate. Studies have found that if young people do vote, they tend to maintain this habit throughout their lifetime. Another reason younger people vote less is because they are less likely to be contacted by political campaigns;[49] candidates often target older voters because campaigns rely on state voter rolls—people who have voted in previous elections.[50] But this pattern may be changing as more organizations channel energy and resources into getting younger people to vote. NextGen America, for example, which supports candidates who favor addressing climate change, developing alternative

Why are upper-income Americans, and those with more education, more likely to be voters than lower-income Americans?

FOR CRITICAL ANALYSIS

Why are upper-income Americans, and those with more education, more likely to be voters than lower-income Americans?

Even though much time and effort is spent mobilizing young voters, people who actually vote tend to be older than the average American.

energy sources, and reversing economic inequality, helped register 1 million voters in the 2016 election and over 120,000 in the 2020 election.

Since the early 1990s, several other campaigns have sought to increase the participation of young voters. Rock the Vote, which enlists musicians and actors to urge young people to vote, has spawned other initiatives, including Rap the Vote and Rock the Vote a lo Latino. The Obama campaign made young voters central to its electoral strategy in 2008 and 2012 and won a significantly higher percentage of the youth vote than Obama's Republican opponents.[51] Rather than focusing primarily on television ads, which target older voters, the campaign posted videos on YouTube and used social media to reach out to young people.

In 2016 and 2020, Bernie Sanders was also effective in inspiring youth participation in politics. Although Sanders failed to secure his party's nomination, polls consistently showed that over 80 percent of people age 18–29 preferred him to his opponents. Sanders called for a political revolution and focused on ending a corrupt campaign-finance system, combating economic inequality, and providing free college tuition. Young people were drawn to the candidate's reputation for honesty and authenticity.

Low voter turnout by young people has implications for the policies addressed by government at the local, state, and federal levels. For example, young people share older Americans' concerns about the economy and national security, but they tend to be more concerned than older people about economic inequality and student debt, and express support for stronger environmental laws, higher funding for public education and colleges, and more tolerance for personal freedoms.[52] The distinctive attitudes of today's young people suggest that higher levels of political participation by this group could significantly alter government policy and politics.

RACE AND ETHNICITY

Increased demographic diversity is rapidly changing U.S. politics. Members of racial and ethnic groups are more likely to vote Democratic, while White non-Hispanics are more likely to vote Republican. The 2016 and 2020 electorates were the country's most racially and ethnically diverse ever; combined, African Americans, Latinos, Asian Americans, and other racial or ethnic minorities accounted for 33 percent of all registered voters in 2018, while the share of White non-Hispanic registered voters declined from 76 percent in 2000 to 67 percent by 2018. Latino voters now make up a larger share of the electorate in every state, but their double-digit gains are notable in Nevada, California, and Texas.

In 2018, when Democrats won control of the U.S. House, young voters, voters of color, and Hispanics were a substantially larger share of the electorate than in past midterms. White non-college-educated voters were a smaller share. Understanding patterns of political participation for different racial and ethnic groups is critical, as their turnout often decides which party wins control of government.

African Americans As we saw in Chapter 5, during much of the twentieth century, the widespread use of the poll tax, literacy tests, and other measures deprived African Americans in the South of the right to vote and meant that they had few avenues for participating in politics. Through a combination of protest, legal action, and political pressure, however, the victories of the civil rights movement made Blacks full citizens and stimulated a tremendous growth in voter turnout. The

FOR CRITICAL ANALYSIS

When the Twenty-Sixth Amendment changed the voting age from 21 to 18 in 1971, observers expected that the youth vote would add a significant new voice to American politics. Why has the youth vote turned out to be less important than was hoped? What changes would engage more young people in the political system?

movement drew on a network rooted in Black churches, the National Association for the Advancement of Colored People (NAACP), and historically Black colleges and universities. Because they tended to vote largely as a cohesive bloc, African American voters began to wield considerable political power, and the number of African American elected officials grew significantly. Today, however, state laws requiring government voter identification have created new impediments that tend to have a disproportionate impact on minority voters in some states, as discussed below.

Being represented by a member of one's racial and/or ethnic group—what is called descriptive representation—appears to have positive effects on participation levels. African Americans are more likely to vote when residing in states with more Black representation in the state legislature.[53] African Americans represented by a Black member of Congress are more likely to vote in elections and to have a sense of efficacy—the belief that the government is responsive to them—and higher levels of political knowledge.[54]

With Barack Obama running in 2008 as the first Black major-party candidate for president, African American interest in the election surged. The gap in turnout rates between White non-Hispanics and Blacks fell from 7 percentage points in 2004 to 1 percentage point in 2008 as many African Americans voted for the first time.[55] In 2012, Blacks were more likely to vote than Whites.[56] Exit polls indicated that 95 percent of African Americans who voted cast ballots for Obama.

In 2018 51 percent of Blacks voted in the midterm election, an increase of 11 percentage points from 2014. In addition, African American turnout was high in local elections in 2019, resulting in the election of Democratic governors in Kentucky and Louisiana, two states Trump won by over 20 percentage points in 2016. Black voters were critical in Joe Biden's initial victory in the 2020 South Carolina primary, eventually sealing his nomination for president for the Democratic Party. Black voters made up 11 percent of the national electorate in the 2020 presidential election, and nearly 9 in 10 of them supported Biden. In the battleground state of Georgia, over 30 percent of the population is African American, and voted for a Democrat for president in 2020 for the first time since 1992.[57]

Racial segregation remains a fact of life in the United States, along with Black urban poverty.[58] These conditions, often called *concentrated poverty*, pose barriers to African American political participation. As the previous section on socioeconomic status described, participation (for Blacks as well as Whites) is highly correlated with more income, higher education, and higher-level occupations. Nevertheless, African Americans are somewhat more likely to vote than Whites of similar socioeconomic status.[59]

This may be *because* African Americans are a minority group. Political scientist Michael Dawson argues that African Americans who feel a shared sense of collective identity, a concept called *linked fate*, are more likely to vote and participate politically. Dawson uses this concept to measure the degree to which African Americans believe that their own personal self-interest is linked to the interests of their race.[60] He finds that the experiences of African Americans with race and racial discrimination in the United States, including a history of slavery, lead them to unify their personal interests in seeking candidates and policies that benefit their racial group. Black civic, community, religious, and political organizations are also important in increasing political participation for this group.

Whites A majority of people who vote in U.S. elections are White non-Hispanics (just under 7 in 10 voters in 2020). This group has tended to vote Republican;

Who Votes for President?

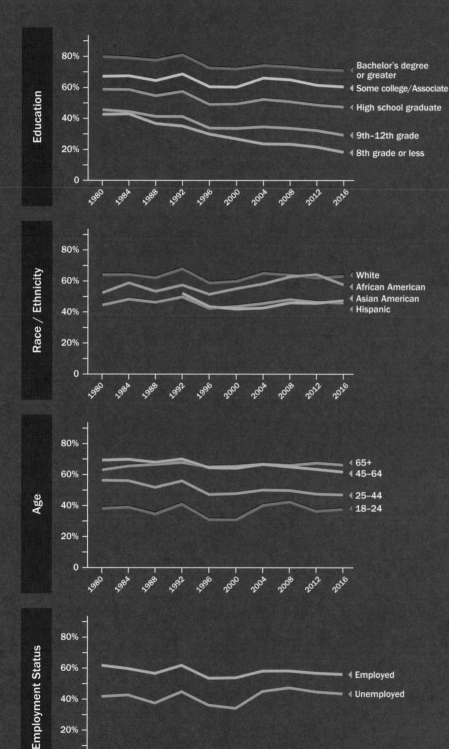

Education

- Bachelor's degree or greater
- Some college/Associate
- High school graduate
- 9th–12th grade
- 8th grade or less

Race / Ethnicity

- White
- African American
- Asian American
- Hispanic

Age

- 65+
- 45–64
- 25–44
- 18–24

Employment Status

- Employed
- Unemployed

Though the right to vote is almost universal for citizens age 18 and older, voting rates have varied substantially by race and ethnicity, education, employment status, and age.

SOURCE: U.S. Census Bureau, "Current Population Survey, Voting and Registration Supplement," www.census.gov.

FOR CRITICAL ANALYSIS

1. Why do you think people with higher levels of education vote at higher rates?

2. Older people vote at higher rates than younger people. How do you think this affects what issues politicians emphasize in their campaigns? How does this affect what kinds of policies government implements?

In the 2020 election, Joe Biden was able to win by building a large, diverse coalition of African Americans, Latinos, Muslim Americans, young people, and many other groups.

59 percent voted for Mitt Romney in 2012 and 57 percent for Trump in 2016. Stated another way, among Whites, just 39 percent voted for the Democratic presidential candidate in 2012 and 37 percent four years later.[61] But there are big differences among Whites based on education levels. A majority of Whites with a college degree support Democratic candidates and turn out at higher rates, while Whites without a college degree support Republicans and are less likely to vote.

In 2016, Donald Trump helped mobilize less educated and lower-income Whites with a populist campaign promising to "Make America Great Again" and bring back manufacturing jobs. He organized nationwide campaign rallies with high turnout, while his Twitter account provided daily updates and he invested heavily in Facebook political campaign ads. In 2020 Biden won back many blue-collar workers, with Biden and Trump almost evenly split among non-college-educated voters. Biden won 20 percent more White non-college-educated men in 2020 than Hillary Clinton had in 2016.

In-group identification is generally less prevalent among White Americans than it is for other racial groups. In-group identity tends to arise from actual or perceived discrimination and economic hardship. The fact that Whites have always been a numerical majority in the United States, with disproportionate political, economic, and social resources, has hampered the development of White ethnic identity.

In the face of rapid demographic change and losses of manufacturing jobs, some Whites feel threatened, especially economically. Half of all Whites, but just 2 in 10 African Americans, believe life is worse for people like them in America than it was 50 years ago. Whites' perceptions of discrimination against their own racial group are increasing. Approximately 6 in 10 White Americans and roughly two-thirds of non-college-educated Whites said that "discrimination against Whites is as big a problem today as discrimination against Blacks and other minorities"—an increase of 50 percent from five years earlier.[62]

Political scientists John Sides, Lynn Vavreck, and Michael Tesler found Trump's presidential campaign focused on amplifying perceived threats posed to Whites from nonwhites, which activated White consciousness.[63] White consciousness strongly predicted support for Donald Trump in the 2016 presidential primaries—much more so than it did for Mitt Romney in 2012.

Latinos and Latinas While 95 percent of Hispanics identify racially as White, they are a separate ethnic identity, connected to a shared linguistic heritage. For many years, political analysts called the Hispanic vote "the sleeping giant" because Latinos and Latinas, while accounting for a large portion of the U.S. population, as a group had relatively low levels of political participation. For instance, 48 percent of Latinos and Latinas voted in the 2016 presidential election, compared with 65 percent of non-Hispanic Whites and just under 60 percent of African Americans.[64] Compared with Whites and African Americans, more Latinos and Latinas are recent immigrants to this country and thus have fewer opportunities, such as access to a quality education. Therefore, they are more likely to lack resources for participation in politics, such as money, time, and language skills.[65]

Today, politicians, political parties, and scholars view Latinos, the largest and fastest-growing minority in the United States, as a political group of critical importance. Latinos and Latinas make up 18 percent of the population, or 60 million people, and represent 1 in 10 voters. In large states such as California and Texas, they are approaching 50 percent of the population, and in battleground states like Florida and Arizona, they are nearly a quarter of all voters.[66] Although voter registration and turnout are lower among Hispanics than among White non-Hispanics, these rates have been increasing. President Trump's anti-immigration policies, which affect many Latinos, increased voter turnout in the 2018 elections by 50 percent compared to the 2014 elections.[67]

Uncertain partisan attachment also magnifies the importance of the Latino vote. While historically those in some states and from some countries have traditionally voted Republican (such as Cubans in Florida), and as Catholics many are religious, Latinos and Latinas have tended to favor the Democrats in national elections, particularly due to Republican opposition to immigration. Today 62 percent of Latinos and Latinas affiliate with the Democratic Party, compared to 27 percent for the Republicans.[68] In addition to favoring an easier path to citizenship for immigrants, Latinos also increasingly favor more liberal economic policies, national health care, and more funding for public education.

In 2016, Latinos strongly favored Clinton over Trump, who made ending illegal immigration a major theme of his campaign and as president also sought to cut back legal immigration. The issue of immigration has continued to widen the partisan divide between minorities and White non-Hispanics. While 55 percent of White non-Hispanics voted for Republicans in 2018, 69 percent of Latinos voted Democratic.[69] In the 2018 election, voter turnout increased by 13 percentage points, a 50 percent increase from four years ealier. In the 2020 elections, 63–65 percent of Latinos supported the Democratic Party for president and 29–32 percent supported the Republican Party.[70]

Like African Americans, Latinos are more likely to vote when residing in states with higher representation of their group in the state legislature, or in a congressional district with a Latino member.[71] As the Latino population continues to grow, this group may influence more strongly who wins and who loses in U.S. elections.

Asian Americans Asian Americans are a smaller group than Whites, Latinos, or African Americans, making up roughly 6 percent of the population, or 21 million citizens. In particular states, such as California, home to 33 percent of the nation's Asian American population, the group has become an important political presence. Asian Americans have education and income levels closer to those of Whites than of Latinos and Latinas or African Americans, but they are less likely to participate in politics than Whites or African Americans[72] and have voter turnout rates similar to Hispanics.[73]

No one national group dominates among the Asian American population, and this diversity has impeded the development of group-based political power.

FOR CRITICAL ANALYSIS

How significant a factor was the Latino vote in the 2020 election? Why does the percentage of eligible Latinos who vote still lag behind that of other groups?

Asian Americans often have different political concerns from one another, stemming from their different national backgrounds and experiences in the United States. Historically, these groups have united most effectively around common issues of ethnic discrimination or anti-Asian violence, federal immigration policies, and discriminatory mortgage-loan practices.

The Asian American voter turnout rate increased to 49.3 percent in 2016, up from just under 47 percent in 2012 and surpassing Latinos and Latinas for the first time since 1996. Voter turnout increased by 13 percentage points for Asian Americans in 2018, a 49 percent increase compared to their turnout four years earlier. Although a majority of Asian Americans voted Republican in the early 1990s, in the 2000s they have been voting increasingly Democratic, and 61 percent voted for Joe Biden in 2020.[74] In 2020, presidential candidate Andrew Yang was among the most successful Asian Americans ever to run for president and mobilized many young people to volunteer for and vote for him before ultimately dropping out after the New Hampshire Primary.[75]

GENDER

Women register to vote at rates similar to men but are more likely to vote. In the high-turnout 2018 midterm election, 55 percent of women voted compared with 52 percent of men, a 3 percentage point gap. The ongoing significance of gender issues in American politics is best exemplified by the **gender gap**—a distinctive pattern of male and female voting decisions—in electoral politics. Women tend to vote in higher numbers for Democratic candidates, whereas Republicans win more male votes. Though the gender gap generally runs around 10 percentage points in presidential elections, the 2016 presidential election saw the first female major-party candidate, and a significantly larger gender gap: surveys showed that 54 percent of women supported Clinton compared to 41 percent of men, a 13-point difference.[76] In 2020, this gap increased to 15 points. Looking at women as a whole, women prefer Democrats, but among White non-Hispanic women with lower education and income, support for Trump in 2016 and 2020 was high. In presidential elections from 1952 to 2020, White women supported a Democratic candidate for president only twice.

Behind these voting patterns are differing assessments of key policy issues. Women are more likely than men to oppose military activities, especially war, and to support gun control and social spending for health care, mental health, public education, and child care.

One key development in gender politics in recent decades is the growing number of women in elective office (see Figure 8.3), an increasingly significant form of sociological representation. A record number of women ran for office in 2020, and at least 141 will serve in the 117th Congress; one-third are women of color. The numbers mark a new all-time high for the number of women in Congress. One hundred two women won House seats and at least 13 women won Senate seats, in addition to the 10 female senators who were not up for re-election this year.

Recent research has shown that one key to increasing the number of women in political office is to encourage more women to run. Although women candidates are just as likely as men to win an election, women are less likely to run for office, even if they are equally qualified. Because women are less likely than men to hold office, they are also less likely to benefit from the advantage of incumbency.[77] Several organizations are devoted to encouraging more women to run for office and supporting them financially. In addition to the bipartisan National Women's Political

gender gap a distinctive pattern of voting behavior reflecting the differences in views between women and men

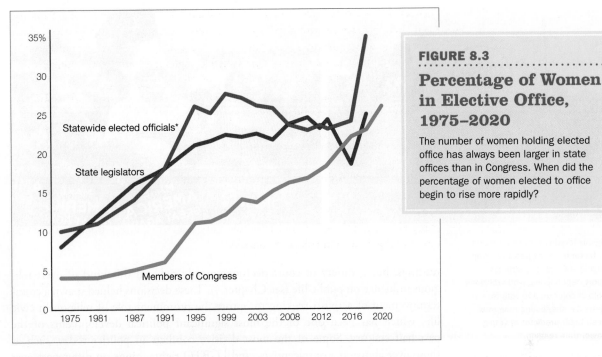

*Governors, attorneys general, etc.
Note: Data for statewide elected officials and state legislators are through 2018.
SOURCES: Cynthia Costello, Shari Miles, and Anne J. Stone, eds., *The American Woman, 2001–2002* (New York: W. W. Norton, 2002), 328; and Center for American Women and Politics, www.cawp.rutgers.edu (accessed 11/15/20).

Caucus, the Women's Campaign Fund and EMILY's List provide prochoice Democratic women with early campaign financing, which is critical to establishing electoral momentum.

Why does the gender of public officials matter? Although women in public office by no means take uniform positions on policy issues, surveys show that, on the whole, female legislators are more supportive than their male counterparts of women's rights and of spending on education and health care and are also more attentive to children's and family issues. Nevertheless, partisanship matters more than gender in terms of representation of women's issues, especially in the current highly partisan political environment in Congress.[78]

RELIGION

For many Americans, religious groups provide an infrastructure for political participation. African American churches, for example, were instrumental in the civil rights movement, and African American religious leaders continue to play important roles in national and local politics. Jews have also been active as a group in politics, but less through religious bodies than through a variety of social action agencies, including the American Jewish Congress and the Anti-Defamation League. In much of the United States, churches are an important social institution where many people learn civic skills that encourage and prepare them to participate in the political world.

For most of American history, religious language, symbols, and values have been woven deeply into the fabric of public life. Until the mid-twentieth century, for example, public school students generally began the day with prayers or Bible

Religious identity remains a significant factor in voting patterns. White evangelical Christians strongly support Republicans, while religious people of color tend to vote for Democrats, suggesting race may be a stronger predictor of voting behavior than religion.

readings, but a variety of court decisions greatly reduced this kind of overt religious influence on public life (see Chapter 4). These decisions helped spawn a countermovement of activists seeking to restore the prominent role of religion in civic life, which has been one of the most significant political developments of the past half century. Some of the most divisive conflicts in politics today, such as those over abortion, contraceptives, and LGBTQ rights, hinge on differences over religious beliefs.

One of the most significant drivers of this new politics was the mobilization of White evangelical Protestants into a cohesive political force. The Moral Majority, the first broad-based political organization of evangelical Christians, quickly rose to prominence in the late 1970s, aligning with the Republican Party and eventually backing Ronald Reagan for president in the 1980 election. Over the next few years, evangelicals strengthened their movement by registering voters and mobilizing them. Their success was evident in the 1984 election, when 8 in 10 evangelical Christian voters cast their ballots for Reagan. President George W. Bush was also closely aligned with religious conservatives, who played an important role in electing him. In 2016 and 2020, most White evangelical Christians supported Trump in the general election.

The close alliance of White evangelicals with the Republican Party, however, has contributed to the growing number of Americans who do not identify with any religion. Today more than one in four Americans is religiously unaffiliated (secular), and members of this group vote heavily Democratic. Secularism can play a role similar to religiosity in terms of political orientations and being active politically.[79]

Despite the influences of race and ethnicity, gender, age, religion, and socioeconomic status, these factors alone do not explain voter turnout or other forms of political participation. Our incomplete understanding of what motivates participation is evident when we compare voting across countries. If more economic resources make people more likely to vote, why does the United States, one of the wealthiest countries in the world, have only moderate voting rates? And Americans have become more educated over the past century, with more people finishing high school and attending college. Given the well-documented links between educational attainment and voting, why has participation declined during this period?[80] These puzzles mean that we need to look beyond the demographic characteristics of individuals and to the larger political environment in which participation occurs.

Political Environment and Voter Mobilization

Explain the factors that influence voter turnout

Whether or not people feel engaged or are recruited to participate in politics depends on their political environment—that is, their social setting, their friends and family, where they live, what organizations they belong to. For example, during presidential elections, residents of battleground states (states with roughly equal numbers of Democrats and Republicans) are exposed to a torrent of campaign ads, candidate visits, and grassroots mobilization efforts. These individuals are more knowledgeable about presidential elections, are more interested in the campaign, and have a higher probability of voting than residents of states that are "safe" for either the Republican Party, such as Alabama or Utah, or the Democratic Party, such as New York or California.

MOBILIZATION

A critical aspect of political environments is whether people are mobilized—by candidate campaigns and political parties. People become much more likely to participate when someone—especially someone they know—asks them to get involved. A recent study of the decline in political participation in the United States found that half of the drop-off could be accounted for by reduced **mobilization** efforts before 2004.[81] This decline has been largely reversed by nationwide political campaigns for president and Congress over the last decade.

A series of experiments conducted by political scientists Donald Green and Alan Gerber demonstrate the importance of personal contact for mobilizing voters. Evaluating the results of several get-out-the-vote drives shows that face-to-face interaction with a canvasser greatly increased the chances that the person contacted would go to the polls, boosting overall voter turnout by almost 10 percent. The impact of direct mail was much smaller, increasing turnout by just 0.5 percent[82] "Robocalls" (prerecorded phone calls) had no measurable effect on turnout, while in-person telephone calls were found to have a modest positive effect.

As means of mobilization, social media networks can mimic face-to-face communication. In a study involving 61 million users of Facebook, political scientists found that election appeals from Facebook friends were responsible for increasing turnout by 340,000 people (who otherwise would not have voted). Users' closest connections ("friends" on the network) had the most influence in getting them to vote.[83]

For much of American history, political parties and social movements relied on personal contact to mobilize voters. As we will see in Chapter 9, during the nineteenth century, party machines employed hundreds of thousands of workers to bring voters to the polls. The result was a very high turnout rate, typically more than 90 percent of eligible voters.[84] But party machines began to decline in strength at the beginning of the twentieth century. By the late twentieth century, political parties had become essentially fundraising and advertising organizations rather than mobilizers of people. Without party workers to encourage them to go to the polls, many eligible voters will not participate.

Since 2000, however, competitive presidential elections have once again motivated both parties to build strong grassroots organizations to reach voters and

mobilization the process by which large numbers of people are organized for a political activity

FOR CRITICAL ANALYSIS

Why do efforts toward direct mobilization seem to be more successful than television advertising in promoting voter turnout? How is the internet becoming an important tool for increasing political participation?

People are more likely to turn out to vote if someone asks them face-to-face. Direct mail and impersonal phone calls are less likely to have an effect on turnout.

turn them out on Election Day. In 2004, Republicans were more successful in this effort, training more than 1.4 million volunteers to make calls, go door to door to register voters, write letters in favor of President Bush, create pro-Bush blogs, and phone local radio call-in shows.

In 2008, Barack Obama's campaign made mobilization a centerpiece of its strategy, organizing a base of volunteers to go door to door seeking support for their candidate. Many of Obama's crucial primary victories relied on direct voter mobilization. The campaign then created a nationwide organization, opening more than 700 field offices. Obama campaigned in all 50 states, rather than focusing solely on battleground states as his predecessors had done. By mobilizing support in places where Democrats had not seriously contended in the past, the Obama campaign expanded the party's electoral map. For the first time in decades, turnout rates were comparable to those in 1960.

In the 2016 and 2020 elections, political campaigns shifted to social media as a primary way to mobilize voters and directly provide their supporters with election updates. In 2016, three in ten Americans received digital messages about the elections, with far more people turning to the candidates' social media posts rather than to their websites or emails.[85] The 2020 elections also witnessed a huge campaign to mail voters forms to request an absentee ballot.

ELECTORAL COMPETITION

To be motivated to vote, individuals must be interested in the election and knowledgeable about the candidates. Campaigns must spend money to mobilize voters and educate them on the issues. Another important factor is whether the election is competitive, that is, whether at least two parties (and their candidates) are actively contesting it.[86] Political scientist Todd Donovan uses a sports analogy to explain the importance of competitive elections in mobilizing turnout: if a game is a foregone conclusion, people are less likely to watch it, or cheer as vigorously for their team. If a game is close, it captures our attention and we watch, usually until the end.

When candidates and political parties spend more effort and money to compete for an elected office, more information becomes available to voters in the form of media ads, news coverage, door-to-door campaigns, online campaigns, and more. In this way, competition reduces the effort necessary for individuals to become informed, leading to higher turnout. Conversely, if elections are uncompetitive (the winner beats the loser by more than 5 percentage points) or uncontested (only one name appears on the ballot), they generate little political information. Without active campaigns, individuals have few opportunities to become interested in an election and may not vote.[87]

In many congressional, statewide, and local races, a candidate (often the incumbent) runs unopposed or is expected to win by such a large margin that the challenger's chances are virtually nil. When legislative districts are drawn to favor one political party over another—what is termed *gerrymandering* (see Chapter 10)—election outcomes are thus often highly lopsided. Most members of Congress win by landslides. Because competitive elections, and the campaign spending and mobilization efforts that go along with them, play a key role in turnout,[88] lack of competition in many congressional, state, and local races may be one reason for the lower levels of turnout in those elections since the 1960s.

Unique rules for presidential elections in the United States create variation in electoral competition across the 50 states. To win, a U.S. presidential candidate must receive a majority of the votes in the electoral college, where each state is given a set number of votes based on the size of its congressional delegation. (The electoral college is covered in more detail in Chapter 10.) In "battleground" states such as Florida, Michigan, Wisconsin, and Pennsylvania, there is close competition between the parties. Most Americans, however, live in non-battleground states (also called "safe" states) such as California, New York, Alabama, and Oklahoma, where one of the major parties is generally assured of victory in presidential elections.

Hence, presidential elections are often decided by a relatively small number of voters in the dozen or so battleground states. (For example, if Hillary Clinton had

Voters often turn out in higher numbers when there are controversial initiatives on the ballot. In 2016 groups for and against Proposition 64 in California, which would legalize recreational marijuana, spent millions of dollars on media and mobilization campaigns.

won just 110,000 more votes across Michigan, Pennsylvania, and Wisconsin, she would have won the 2016 election.) Every four years, residents of these battleground states get smothered with attention from candidate campaigns and media, while residents of safe states barely get noticed. One study found that voter turnout is higher in battleground states than in non-battleground states and that these states see higher-than-average turnout among poor and younger voters.[89]

BALLOT MEASURES

Beyond candidate races, ballot measures (initiatives and referenda) have been found to increase voter turnout, especially in lower-turnout midterm elections.[90] Elections in which citizens vote directly on controversial policy questions such as the minimum wage, immigration, or taxation have also been found to increase political awareness, political interest, and contributions to interest groups.[91] In many states, ballot-measure campaigns are important for mobilizing voters and can have spillover effects on candidate races.[92]

Initiatives often involve high campaign spending by proponents and opponents of the proposed laws, which generates mass media coverage. The *Los Angeles Times* estimated that $200 million was spent in California alone in 2020 on controversial ballot measures including the exemption of ride-hailing and delivery drivers from a state law requiring them to be considered as employees.[93] But simply being asked to vote on issues—significant or otherwise—can increase participation. This has been called the "educative effects" of direct democracy, as voters are forced to make a yes-or-no choice on the policy issue.[94]

Only 24 of the 50 states have the initiative process that lets citizens draft legislation, circulate petitions, and place the issue on the ballot for a popular vote. This is another reason that what state one lives in can matter for how likely one is to participate in politics.

State Electoral Laws and Participation

| Explain the effect of electoral laws on voting |

As stipulated by the Constitution, the states, not the federal government, control voter registration and voting itself. This creates wide variation in the laws governing elections and voting, which affect participation in politics.[95] Voter turnout in presidential elections in the last decade ranges from a high of nearly 80 percent of eligible voters in Minnesota to a low of 55 percent in Oklahoma. State electoral laws can make voting easier or can impede voting.

REGISTRATION REQUIREMENTS

One of the most common reasons people in the United States give for not voting is that they are not registered. Young people especially are less likely to register to vote than are older Americans, in part because they tend to change residences more often.[96] Other groups with lower registration rates include people with lower incomes and education, who also tend to change residences more frequently. Once individuals become interested in the election and learn about the candidates, it may be too late for them to register. Registration requirements thus not only reduce the number of people who vote but also tend to create an electorate that is, on average, better educated, more affluent, older, and whiter than the citizenry as a whole.

In most democratic countries, residents are automatically registered to vote in elections at adult age. In most U.S. states except North Dakota, which doesn't require voter registration, individuals who are eligible to vote must take the initiative to register with the state election board before they are actually allowed to vote—sometimes 30 days beforehand.

In 1993, Congress passed the National Voter Registration Act (NVRA). It required most states to provide citizens with an opportunity to register to vote when applying for or renewing a driver's license at a department of motor vehicles (DMV) or other designated state agency. Because of the requirement for DMVs to participate in voter registration, the NVRA is often referred to as "motor-voter."[97]

Oregon instituted automatic voter registration (AVR) in 2016, and this process has since spread across the states in what is called the "Oregon model." As of 2020, 19 states and the District of Columbia have approved AVR. AVR makes voter registration "opt-out" instead of "opt-in." Eligible citizens who interact with government agencies such as the DMV are automatically registered to vote or have their existing registration information updated, unless they decline. Any individual can opt out; voter registration is not compulsory. AVR also allows government agencies to transfer voter-registration information electronically to election officials instead of using paper registration forms. These reforms can increase voter registration, fix errors in voter rolls, and save state governments money.

Oregon used automatic voter registration (AVR) in the 2016 election, along with Georgia and Connecticut, and 10 states used it in 2018. A study of the voter rolls found that 2.2 million people who previously were not eligible to vote were automatically registered and thus became eligible. Oregon went from 73 percent of eligible voters registered in 2014 to 90 percent in 2018. Roughly 6 million people had their registrations automatically updated with new addresses or other information; when names and addresses don't match, people can be denied the chance to vote on election day.[98]

Automatically registering residents to vote is related to another state election reform, **same-day registration**. As of 2020, in an effort to boost voter turnout, 17 states plus Washington, D.C., had enacted same-day registration laws, which means that people can both register and vote when they go to the polls on Election Day. Not only is voter turnout in these states higher than the national average, but younger and less educated voters are also more likely to participate.[99] Research shows that same-day registration is the most effective law to boost turnout.[100]

Registering to vote requires resources (time, money, and information) necessary to develop civic skills for political engagement. This includes knowing how to register, how and where to vote, and whom to vote for. Election reforms such as AVR and same-day registration are designed to address some of these challenges.

same-day registration the option in some states to register on the day of the election, at the polling place, rather than in advance of the election

VOTER IDENTIFICATION REQUIREMENTS

Another barrier to voting is the requirement that voters provide proof of identity. Recent adoption of voter ID laws in many states has reduced turnout rates, especially for racial minorities, the elderly, and people with low income or disabilities—all of whom disproportionately lack government ID. Thirty-six states have some identification requirements (35 of which are in force in 2020) to cast a ballot at the polls, and 7 of them have strict laws that require a government-issued photo.[101]

Register . . . and Vote

MAGGIE BUSH, Programs and Outreach Director for the League of Women Voters of the United States

The League of Women Voters emerged from the fight for women's suffrage in the early twentieth century. Its primary goal today is to help Americans of all descriptions understand and navigate the voting process. Maggie Bush, Programs and Outreach Director for the League of Women Voters of the United States, says, "In most elections, only 50 percent of 18-year-olds are registered to vote, which means that older voters are making decisions that affect all of us. We need to be part of the process. Elections are how we determine how safe our streets are, what kind of health care we have, how community college decisions are made and resources allocated. The first step to participating in these democratic decisions is voting." Here are Maggie's tips for registering to vote and going to the polls:

Registering to Vote

1 How do I know how to register? Consult a website such as Vote411.org, run by the League of Women Voters. Registration procedures and rules vary from state to state. From your state's site at Vote411.org, you can register online (in over 30 states) or print and fill out a paper form. Note that the registration deadline can be up to 30 days prior to the election.

2 What information do I need to provide? On the voter-registration form, you will provide your name and address and will certify that you are eligible—that you are a U.S. citizen and of the appropriate age. The voting age is 18, but some states allow preregistration or primary-election voting at younger ages. You may also need an identification number such as a driver's license, state ID, or the last four digits of your Social Security number, depending on your state.

3 Which address should I use? It is up to the student where they want to vote. You can use your school address or be registered and vote absentee from your home address if it differs.

4 Am I required to register with a political party? In most states, you will be asked to declare an affiliation with a political party or to remain an independent or unaffiliated voter. In many states, if you do not specify a party, you will not be able to vote in primary elections, which parties use to choose their candidates for general elections. Some states have "open primaries," which do not require voters to have a party affiliation.

After you submit your registration electronically or by mail to your local election official, they will follow up, usually by mail, to confirm that you are eligible to vote in the next election. If your address changes—even if you switch apartments in the same building—you need to update your registration. You can update at Vote411.org.

Voting

5 **Where can you vote?** At Vote411.org you can enter your address of residency to find your polling place, its hours of operation, and any early voting options. Many states offer early voting in the evenings and on weekends in the weeks before elections to facilitate voting by busy people such as students.

6 **What's on the ballot?** You can check Vote411.org to see a list of candidates and ballot initiatives for your location. When you go to vote you can take a sample ballot or notes on your phone or on paper with your selections, though some states prohibit taking a selfie with your ballot.

7 **What will happen at the polling place?** You will check in with a poll worker, who will locate your name on the registration list and may check your identification, depending on state rules. You will then be directed to a voting machine or given a paper ballot. Voters have the right to privacy while they vote and the right to accommodations for disabilities. After you vote, you submit your ballot electronically or insert it into a ballot box.

8 **What happens if you have a problem voting?** The first step is to ask a poll worker on-site for help. Another resource is the 866-OUR-VOTE hotline run by volunteers with a legal support staff to make sure people's votes are being counted properly.

That's it. At many polling places you will receive an "I Voted" sticker so you can proudly display your democratic participation.

Voter Registration Application

Before completing this form, review the General, Application, and State specific instructions.

This space for office use only.

Are you a citizen of the United States of America?
Will you be 18 years old on or before election day?
If you checked "No" in response to either of these questions, do not complete form.
(Please see state-specific instructions for rules regarding eligibility to register prior to age 18.)

1	Last Name	First Name		Middle Name(s)
2	Home Address	Apt. or Lot #	City/Town	State
3	Address Where You Get Your Mail If Different From Above		City/Town	State
4	Date of Birth ___ ___ ___ Month Day Year	5 Telephone Number (optional)	6 ID Number – (See item 6 in the instructions f...
7	Choice of Party (see item 7 in the instructions foy your State)	8 Race or Ethnic Group (see item 8 in the instructions for your State)	

...state's instructions and I swear/affirm that:
...state and

Please sign full na...

On the other end of the spectrum, in 14 states and the District of Columbia no ID is required to vote at the ballot box.

Some reports estimate that these laws reduce turnout by 2 to 3 percentage points, which can amount to millions of people who are prevented from voting nationwide. A recent study found that more stringent forms of these laws lower voter turnout and especially participation by racial and ethnic minorities relative to non-Hispanic Whites.[102]

Estimates indicate that millions of U.S. citizens do not have government-issued photo identification, including 1 in 5 African Americans. Government identification can be difficult to obtain even if the ID itself is free, because citizens must present a birth certificate to apply for it and applying for a replacement birth certificate costs money. In addition, travel to places where IDs are issued, such as a department of motor vehicles office, can be difficult for elderly and disabled people and residents of rural areas.

Photo identification laws can be a partisan issue. Republicans argue that such laws protect against voter fraud and ensure that the vote is fair. Opponents, mainly Democrats, counter that there have been almost no significant instances of voter fraud in the modern era and that these laws suppress the vote of segments of the population most likely to vote for Democrats and least likely to have photo ID—racial minorities and the poor.[103] Studies have shown that illegal voting by impersonating someone else is very rare in the United States.

VOTING RIGHTS OF FELONS

A barrier to voting that has grown more important in recent years is restrictions on the voting rights of people convicted of a felony. Forty-eight states and the District of Columbia prohibit prison inmates serving a felony sentence from voting. In most states, felons lose their right to vote while incarcerated and during probation or parole, but voting rights are restored automatically after parole or probation is complete. In 9 states, felons lose their voting rights forever for some crimes. On the other end of the spectrum, felons never lose their right to vote in Maine and Vermont.

With the sharp rise in incarceration rates over the past three decades, restrictions on voting for felons have had a significant impact. By one estimate, 5.3 million people (2.4 percent of the voting-age population) have lost their voting rights as a result. Felon voting restrictions disproportionately affect minorities because 59 percent of the prison population is African American or Latino, though these groups make up only 30 percent of the population.[104] One in eight Black men cannot vote because of a criminal record.[105] Concern over the impact of disenfranchising felons, which has been especially frequent in the South, has led to campaigns to restore their voting rights.[106] In 2018 Florida voters passed Amendment 4, a ballot initiative that restored voting rights to 1.4 million people with felony convictions after they complete all terms of their parole or probation (see Chapter 5).

VOTING REFORMS

Election reform efforts over the past century have focused on making voter registration and voting more accessible and convenient. In 1998, Oregon became the first state to create a system for voting exclusively by mail, thus eliminating polling places altogether. Voters there fill in their ballot at home and place it in the mail or

FOR CRITICAL ANALYSIS

Why is voter turnout so low in the United States? What are the consequences of low voter turnout?

Which States Make Voting Easier?

States have increasingly passed laws to make voting easier, such as early voting, which allows voters to cast a ballot before Election Day; "no-excuse" absentee voting, which permits voters to request an absentee ballot without providing justification; all-mail voting, whereby voters fill in their ballot at home and mail it, eliminating polling places altogether; and same-day and automatic voter registration. At the same time, many states have passed voter-identification requirements, which make voting harder for some people. The maps show these laws by state as of the 2018 election.

Voting Policies by State, 2018

Voting Key

- Early voting (in person)
- Home voting (mail or no-excuse absentee voting ballot)
- Same-day registration
- Photo ID requirement*

* Some states requiring a photo ID to vote allow voters to cast a provisional ballot, or show a non-photo voter-registration card.

** North Dakota does not register voters.

SOURCES: "Absentee and Early Voting," National Conference of State Legislatures, April 3, 2019, www.ncsl.org/research /elections-and-campaigns/absentee-and -early-voting.aspx; Kate Rabinowitz and Kevin Uhrmacher, "How Easy Is It to Vote in Your State?" *Washington Post*, September 19, 2018, www.washingtonpost.com/graphics/2018 /politics/voter-access/; Jordan Misra, "Behind the 2018 Midterm Elections: Current Population Survey," U.S. Census Bureau, April 23, 2019.

Voter-Roll-Purge Rates per State**

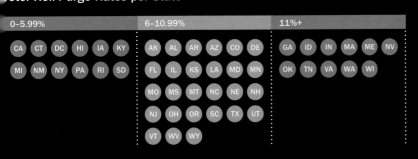

0–5.99%	6–10.99%	11%+
CA CT DC HI IA KY	AK AL AR AZ CO DE	GA ID IN MA ME NV
MI NM NY PA RI SD	FL IL KS LA MD MN	OK TN VA WA WI
	MO MS MT NC NE NH	
	NJ OH OR SC TX UT	
	VT WV WY	

Average Wait Times to Vote**

0–5 minutes

CO	DE	HI	IA	ME	MA
MT	NH	OR	SD	VT	WA

6–10 minutes

AK	AZ	CA	CT	FL	ID	IL	KS	KY
MI	MN	MS	NE	NV	NJ	NM	NY	ND
OH	RI	TN	UT	VA	WV	WI	WY	

11–15 minutes

AL	AR	LA	MO	NC	PA	TX

16 minutes +

DC	GA	IN	MD	OK	SC

FOR CRITICAL ANALYSIS

1. Which one law of those shown above do you think is the most important for making voting easier and updating the U.S. election system?

2. Why do you think state voting laws vary so much? Would you be in favor of a national law that would make voting more accessible?

Convenience voting, such as early voting and voting by mail, removes the need to stand in a potentially long line to cast a vote and may result in increased voter turnout.

permanent absentee ballots the option in some states to have a ballot sent automatically to your home for each election, rather than having to request an absentee ballot each time

early voting the option in some states to cast a vote at a polling place or by mail before the election

in drop boxes throughout the state. As of 2020, in Washington State, Colorado, California, New Jersey, and many other states, many citizens cast votes using **permanent absentee ballots**, which are mailed.

In 2018, 24 states had home voting, defined as either all-mail voting or no-excuse absentee voting, where a ballot is mailed to the person's home and the person completes the ballot and mails it back. No-excuse absentee voting means any voter can request an absentee/vote-by-mail ballot without providing a justification. Not only can voting by mail increase turnout, but it also saves the government money by not having to staff polling stations throughout the state.

In the wake of the coronavirus pandemic, the issue of voting by mail became critically important and hotly debated. Numerous states (Republican- and Democratic-controlled governments) mailed forms to all registered voters allowing them to request an absentee mail ballot for the 2020 presidential primary and general election. This change makes no-excuse absentee voting or all-mail voting available to 83 percent of eligible citizens, and record mail-in ballot voting was expected. President Trump strongly opposed the expansion of voting by mail and expressed concern over voter fraud. However, fact-checkers say there is no evidence that mail-in ballots are linked to voter fraud.

Another reform that has been adopted by many states is **early voting**, which allows registered voters to cast a ballot at their regular polling place during a designated period before Election Day. Almost two-thirds of votes cast in the 2020 election were cast early, either in person or via mail. As of 2020, 40 states allow early voting (Delaware will allow early voting beginning in 2022).[107] Six states—Connecticut, Kentucky, Mississippi, Missouri, New Hampshire, and South Carolina—do not offer pre–Election Day in-person voting options. Early voting and mail-in voting is rapidly updating and modernizing how Americans vote, with record-breaking turnout in 2020.

The effects of early voting laws on turnout and the demographic composition of who votes are not yet clear.[108] One study from Oregon finds that early voting tends to advantage upper-class and older citizens, who are more likely to vote anyway. But others contend that early voting increases turnout among disadvantaged demographic groups, including African Americans and other minorities.[109]

Political Participation: What Do You Think?

The American political community has expanded over the course of history, with new groups winning and asserting political rights. But for much of the twentieth century, the electoral system in the United States failed to mobilize an active citizenry, giving rise to an uneven pattern of political participation that gives some people more voice in politics than others. Since 2000 a series of highly competitive presidential elections has spurred political campaigns to pay more attention to drawing greater numbers of voters into the political process; even so, many Americans still do not participate in politics. Unequal participation has consequences: one important study found that elected officials respond more to the preferences of voters than nonvoters, confirming long-held assumptions that affluent, more educated, and older citizens have more voice in politics and public policy.[110]

★ What would it take to increase political engagement among citizens of all backgrounds? What do you think Xavier Brown, Akil Riley, and Nevada Littlewolf–all protesters featured at the start of the chapter–would say?

★ What if every state adopted automatic voter registration? Would this increase turnout for young voters, who are the most mobile and are now the largest age cohort?

★ What barriers to participation do you observe among your friends and family? What reforms would help?

★ STUDY GUIDE ★

Forms of Political Participation

Describe the major forms of participation in politics (pp. 267–79)

Political participation refers to a wide range of activities designed to influence government, politics, and policy. It includes not just voting in elections but also engaging in protest; attending campaign events; and donating to, volunteering for, or advocating for candidates in any number of ways, whether in person or online. Voting is the most common form of participation in politics, but America's overall rate of voter turnout is relatively low. Digital media have become an effective tool for fostering mobilization and political participation, as they engage individuals who may not otherwise be involved and they make traditional forms of participation easier, more immediate, and more personalized. However, digital media may also contribute to the circulation of misinformation and the intensification of ideological polarization.

Key Terms

protest (p. 267)

suffrage (p. 268)

turnout (p. 271)

traditional political participation (p. 271)

digital political participation (p. 273)

Practice Quiz

1. Which group won voting rights most recently?
   a) 18- to 20-year-olds
   b) Asian Americans
   c) White property owners
   d) women
   e) African Americans

2. Which of the following most accurately describes the relationship between online participation and offline participation?
   a) Participating in political activity online decreases the likelihood that someone will vote or otherwise participate in politics offline.
   b) Participating in political activity online increases the likelihood that someone will vote or otherwise participate in politics offline.
   c) Americans usually participate in politics either online or offline, but rarely both.
   d) Only people who habitually participate in politics offline will participate in politics online.
   e) Rates of online participation are decreasing as rates of offline participation are increasing among Americans.

3. Which of the following is a drawback to digital participation?
   a) Digital participation is less expressive than offline participation.
   b) Digital participation impedes community-building.
   c) Digital participation usually requires more time and effort than offline participation.
   d) Digital participation can unintentionally create forums for hate speech.
   e) Digital participation is open only to members of the country that is holding elections at a given time.

4. The *digital divide* refers to
   a) the fact that some citizens watch television news and some do not.
   b) the differences between the stories that newspapers publish on their websites and those in their print editions.
   c) the fact that few politicians maintain websites once they are elected to office.
   d) the gap between those citizens with and those without internet access.
   e) the difference in levels of political knowledge between people who learn about politics online and those who learn about politics through traditional media.

Who Votes?

Describe the patterns of participation among major demographic groups (pp. 279–88)

Socioeconomic status, age, race and ethnicity, gender, and religious affiliation are associated with different levels and types of political participation. Generally speaking, Whites, older people, women, and those with higher levels of education and income vote most dependably. Recent elections have seen upward trends in turnout for African Americans, Latinos and Latinas, and young people, all of whom are more likely to support Democratic candidates.

Key Terms

socioeconomic status (p. 279)

gender gap (p. 286)

Practice Quiz

5. Which of the following statements about young people's political attitudes is most accurate?
   a) Young people are less supportive of strong environmental laws than older people.
   b) Young people are less concerned about economic inequality than older people.
   c) Young people express less tolerance for personal freedoms than older people.
   d) Young people are less concerned about national security than older people.
   e) Young people are more supportive of funding for public education and colleges than older people.

6. When it comes to voting, African Americans
   a) almost never vote.
   b) consistently support the Republican Party in elections.
   c) vote at much higher rates than Whites.
   d) have never voted as a cohesive bloc.
   e) who feel a shared sense of collective identity are more likely to vote.

7. Which of the following statements about Latinos and Latinas is *not* accurate?
   a) Latinos have tended to favor Democratic candidates in recent national elections.
   b) In some large states, such as California and Texas, Latinos are approaching 50 percent of the population.
   c) Latinos have tended to favor Republican candidates in recent national elections.
   d) Latinos make up approximately 18 percent of the U.S. population.
   e) Hispanic registration and turnout rates have been lower than those of White non-Hispanics in recent elections.

8. One reason that there are fewer women than men in elected office is that
   a) there is a limit set by the Constitution on the number of women who can serve in the House of Representatives.
   b) fewer women are eligible to run for office under the rules created by state and local governments.
   c) women are less likely to vote in elections than men.
   d) women are less likely to run for office than men.
   e) women are less likely to win elections than men.

Political Environment and Voter Mobilization

Explain the factors that influence voter turnout (pp. 289–92)

Three general factors in the political environment influence whether individuals vote or not: mobilization efforts, electoral competition, and the presence or absence of state-level ballot initiatives. People who are mobilized by candidate campaigns and political parties are more likely to vote than people who are not reached by mobilization efforts. In competitive elections, turnout is higher because individuals have more opportunities to become interested in and informed about the races as candidates campaign to get their message out. People also make the effort to vote when ballot measures address issues that are important to them.

Key Term

mobilization (p. 289)

Practice Quiz

9. Which of the following techniques is considered most effective in mobilizing voters?
   a) direct mailings
   b) "robocalls"
   c) phone calls made by volunteers
   d) face-to-face contact
   e) television advertisements

10. Which of the following best describes how the unique rules for presidential elections affect voter turnout?
    a) All primary and caucus contests are highly competitive, so primary-election turnout is typically high across all states.
    b) Primary-election voter turnout is typically higher in states that hold these elections later than most other states, when the race for the nomination is at its most competitive.
    c) General-election voter turnout is usually higher in non-battleground states, where political parties do the most work mobilizing voters.
    d) General-election voter turnout is usually higher in battleground states, where campaigns do the most work mobilizing voters.
    e) The rules of the electoral college ensure that levels of general-election voter turnout are roughly the same across all states.

11. How many states currently have an initiative process that lets citizens draft legislation, circulate petitions, and place measures on the ballot for a popular vote?
    a) 0
    b) 12
    c) 24
    d) 36
    e) 50

State Electoral Laws and Participation

Explain the effect of electoral laws on voting (pp. 292–98)

As stipulated by the Constitution, states retain control of voter registration and voting. In practice, there is wide variation in the laws governing elections and voting from state to state. Registration requirements and other barriers, such as ID requirements and restrictions on the voting rights of people convicted of a felony, are estimated to reduce participation. States have experimented with reforms, such as automatic registration, same-day registration, home voting, and early voting, to make it easier to vote.

Key Terms

same-day registration (p. 293)

permanent absentee ballots (p. 298)

early voting (p. 298)

Practice Quiz

12. Voter-registration requirements and processes are determined and controlled by
    a) local governments.
    b) the federal government.
    c) the U.S. Constitution.
    d) the states.
    e) an independent organization.

13. Which of the following factors is *not* currently an obstacle to voting in the United States?
    a) registration requirements
    b) motor-voter laws
    c) the restriction of voting rights for people who have committed a felony
    d) voter identification laws
    e) All of these are obstacles to voting in the United States.

14. States that allow for same-day registration
    a) have lower overall voter turnout rates than the national average.
    b) have the same overall voter turnout rates as the national average.
    c) have higher rates of overall voter turnout than the national average.
    d) have overall turnout rates that are very close to 100 percent.
    e) have lower rates of voter turnout among younger and less educated voters than states that do not allow for same-day registration.

15. Laws that restrict the voting rights of people convicted of a felony disproportionately affect
    a) women.
    b) turnout in northern states.
    c) religious minorities.
    d) racial minorities.
    e) immigrants.

Political Parties

WHAT GOVERNMENT DOES AND WHY IT MATTERS Political parties play a variety of important roles in American democracy. They mobilize people to participate in the political arena and to vote. They convey information about what policies candidates support. And they are broader than interest groups, which generally seek narrow policy objectives. Political parties are capable of mobilizing many more voters to win control of government.

For all their important mobilizing and information-conveying functions, parties, like other aspects of government and politics, can seem far from ordinary people. But ordinary people can have a big impact on political parties. Early in 2009, before the term *Tea Party* had been coined, Keli Carender was a conservative blogger in Seattle. She became concerned that the stimulus bill that Congress was considering to address the financial crisis and ensuing recession was simply more of "big government" trampling on her "freedom and liberty." After calls and emails to her congressional representative were ignored, she organized a "Porkulus Protest" in Seattle without support from any national organization. "I just got fed up and planned it....I had 120 people show up, which is amazing for the bluest of blue cities I live in, and on only four days' notice!! This was due to me

Individuals can have profound effects on political parties. Keli Carender took her belief in limited government and her anger over excessive government spending and started the Tea Party movement, which has strongly influenced the direction of the Republican Party.

spending the entire four days calling and emailing every person, think tank, policy center, university professors (that were sympathetic), etc. in town, and not stopping until the day came." She also contacted conservative author Michelle Malkin, who publicized the rally on her blog. At a second rally later that month, twice as many people showed up, in part because Carender had collected email addresses at the first rally. Her advice to other would-be organizers: "Number one: just get it done. Do you need a permit? Find out and then just get it. Do you want a guest speaker? Get on the phone and call anyone you can think of and get them there. You will need

to alert the media, so just get that done.... Let people help you. Almost immediately I had two women email me and say, what can I do? And boom, I had two other organizers to start helping me with the next event."[1]

Carender's protests were among the first events in what became known as the Tea Party movement, which gained steam when CNBC business analyst Rick Santelli called for a "tea party" protest of the Obama administration's plans for addressing the Great Recession. This conservative populist movement not only challenged Democratic policies but also the Republican Party establishment. As political candidates associated with the Tea Party ran for office starting in the 2010 midterm elections, they sometimes won Republican Party endorsement but often ran against the mainstream party. Indeed, as a nontraditional Republican candidate, Donald Trump courted Tea Party supporters during his presidential campaign in 2016.

As we will see in this chapter, parties play an important role in American democracy, mobilizing voters and organizing their choices. Revolts against the political parties by rank-and-file members occur very rarely in American history. But sometimes, parties are shaken up by grassroots activity like Keli Carender's. Her story, and others like it, shows that individuals can make a difference, not just in political parties but also in the broader political arena. The key is to "just get it done."

CHAPTER GOALS

★ Explain how political parties form and change (pp. 307–10)

★ Describe political party organizations and the roles they play in elections (pp. 310–17)

★ Explain how parties organize government and influence policy making (pp. 317–20)

★ Identify the reasons for and sources of party identification and increased party polarization (pp. 320–30)

★ Describe the history of U.S. party systems and the influence of third parties (pp. 330–39)

What Are Political Parties?

Political parties, like interest groups (see Chapter 11), are organizations that seek influence over government. They can generally be distinguished from interest groups on the basis of their mission. A party seeks to control the government by nominating candidates, electing them to public office, and winning elections. As we will see in Chapter 11, interest groups do not seek to control the operation of government or win elections, but rather try to influence government policies, often through lobbying elected officials and contributing to campaigns.

political parties organized groups that attempt to influence the government by electing their members to important government offices

Although the Founders did not envision the rise of political parties, these quickly became a core feature of the American political system. Parties and **partisanship** organize the political world and simplify complex policy debates for citizens and elected officials. Parties also play central roles in mobilizing citizens to vote, informing the public about government policies, and ensuring that the public voice is heard in policy debates.

partisanship identification with or support of a particular party or cause

Political parties have been the chief points of contact between government officials, on the one side, and individual citizens and interest groups, on the other. Through organized political parties, citizens and groups can influence government policies. As political scientist Walter Dean Burnham wrote, political parties "generate . . . collective power on behalf of the many [who are] individually powerless against the relatively few who are individually or organizationally powerful."[2] It may be difficult for ordinary citizens to have any real influence on government when they act as individuals, that is, but they can do so when they act collectively. Political parties also seek to organize and influence important groups in society to win elections and gain political power. For example, the Republican Party has pulled together religious and pro-business conservatives into one coalition.

In a landmark book written over a half century ago, political scientist E. E. Schattschneider advocated for a political system run by parties instead of interest groups. Schattschneider argued that for a democracy to give all citizens equal representation in making decisions about government, there must be responsible political parties that provide real choices to the electorate. Because they are competing to win elections, he believed, parties motivate more people to participate than interest groups can. While interest groups benefit from focusing on specific policy issues, competitive parties have incentives to broaden the scope of political conflict by focusing on a wide range of issues, from the economy to health care to foreign policy, in order to win elections by activating citizens who otherwise would not vote.

This strategy of seeking to engage more of the public has been evident in the extremely competitive presidential elections since 2000, with widespread voter-mobilization campaigns on the part of the Democratic and Republican parties. Voter turnout in 2008, 2012, 2016, and 2020 was at the highest levels since 1960, largely because of party-organized get-out-the-vote drives.

Political parties, Schattschneider believed, must act "responsibly" by continually informing the people of current policies that are in their best interests. And once in power, they must enact laws that represent their members' interests. In this idealized view, competitive and responsible parties can help increase voter turnout, creating more equal representation for those in lower socioeconomic classes.

While both major parties often claim to be looking out for working people, studies have shown that both Democrats and Republicans in Congress respond more to the interests of affluent and middle-class Americans.

Some political scientists argue that Schattschneider's vision is far from reality. Those critics say that though we have large, powerful, and active political parties, they are controlled more by interest groups, especially big business, and by wealthy campaign donors than by the public. Political scientist Larry Bartels found that on economic issues both the Democratic and the Republican parties are more responsive to the preferences of the upper classes (and sometimes the middle class) and ignore those of the lower class. Bartels calls this "unequal democracy."[3] Stagnating wages for the middle class and rising income inequality in the United States help explain why many voters have grown increasingly frustrated by both major parties; in the 2016 presidential election, many supported populist candidates, such as Donald Trump and Bernie Sanders, who called for drastic changes in the political system.[4]

Many people believe that the problem with parties and political leaders today is that they are too divided along liberal and conservative lines (what is called party polarization), whereas the majority of Americans hold moderate opinions and values; thus, Congress, the president, and the parties do a poor job of representing citizens.[5] Others argue that our election system needs reform so that there are more than two major parties to better represent citizens' views.[6]

As long as political parties have existed, they have been criticized for introducing self-interested, partisan concerns into public debates and national policy. Yet parties are extremely important to the functioning of a democracy. As we will see, parties can increase participation in politics, provide a central cue for citizens to cast informed votes, and organize the business of legislatures and governing.[7]

HOW DO POLITICAL PARTIES FORM AND CHANGE?

Historically, parties form in one of two ways. The first occurs when political conflicts lead officials and competing factions within government to mobilize popular support. This is precisely what happened during the early years of the American Republic. Competition in Congress between northeastern merchants and southern farmers led each group to attempt to organize its supporters. The result was the foundation of America's first national parties: the Federalists, whose strength was greatest in New England, and the Jeffersonians or Antifederalists, whose primary base was in the South.

The second way that parties form takes place when a group outside of government organizes popular support to win governmental power. For example, during the 1850s a group of state civic and community leaders (ministers, educators, artists and authors, business leaders, and politicians) who opposed slavery, especially the expansion of slavery into U.S. territories such as Oklahoma, built what became the Republican Party by constructing party organizations and mobilizing popular support in the Northeast and West.

America's two major parties, the Democrats and the Republicans, both trace their roots back over 150 years and have undergone significant changes over time in their policy positions and their membership. These changes have been prompted by issues and events (such as war, economic crisis, the civil rights movement, immigration) and by demographic and social change in the United States. Today growing differences in the demographic profiles of Republicans and Democrats suggest more change in the party system is underway. The success of "outsider" populist candidates within both major parties in the 2016 presidential campaign may also signal increasing change to the party system (see discussion in this chapter on the history of party systems and party realignments).

THE UNITED STATES' TWO-PARTY SYSTEM

Over the past 200 years, Americans' conception of political parties has changed considerably. In the early Republic, parties were seen as threats to the social order and to the stability of the new democratic government and were referred to as "factions." In the *Federalist Papers*, both Alexander Hamilton and James Madison condemned factions that pursued narrow self-interest over the well-being of the nation as a whole.[8] In his 1796 Farewell Address, President George Washington warned his countrymen to shun partisan politics. Nonetheless, a **two-party system** emerged quickly. Beginning with the Federalists and the Jeffersonian Republicans in the late 1780s, two major parties have dominated national politics, although which two parties has changed with the times and issues. (See Party Systems, which follows later in this chapter.)

Most other democratic countries use a proportional representation system for elections to their national legislature or parliament, in which some or all seats are allocated to political parties based on their share of the total votes cast in the election (if a party wins 40 percent of the votes in an election, it controls 40 percent of the seats in the legislature). In contrast, in most elections the United States uses geographic single-member districts combined with winner-take-all (or "first-past-the-post") elections. For example, in a U.S. House district election, the candidate who wins the most votes (the plurality) wins the seat, no matter if that candidate won 40 percent, 51 percent, or 80 percent of the overall vote. That is why the system is winner take all: unlike in proportional representation, no runners-up gain seats in government (see Chapter 10 as well). Other countries require the winning candidate to win a majority (50 percent plus one), not just a simple plurality. In the United States, proportional voting rules and runoff elections to ensure the winning candidate has a majority are uncommon, especially above the local level, and are absent at the national level.

two-party system a political system in which only two parties have a realistic opportunity to compete effectively for control

FOR CRITICAL ANALYSIS

What rules governing the American electoral process promote a two-party system? How might different rules impact the party system?

Election rules largely determine how many political parties there are in a country. Plurality voting rules in the United States create its two-party–dominant system, and third parties have won few seats in Congress or state legislatures and have never won the presidency. **Duverger's law** holds that plurality voting rules with single-member districts (just one candidate wins each legislative seat, as we see in the United States) will result in a two-party system. Why? Under U.S. election rules, voters have an incentive not to vote for small- or third-party candidates for fear of "wasting" their vote, because only one party's candidate (usually the Republican or Democrat) can win the election for each office. Proportional representation systems used in many other countries tend to result in multiple parties in government, and some suggest that system would decrease polarization in the United States.

Duverger's law a law that holds that plurality rule elections where the winner has the most votes, but not necessarily a majority within single-member geographic districts, tend to result in a two-party system, whereas proportional representation tends to result in a multi-party system

WHAT POLITICAL PARTIES DO

Without political parties, democracy as we know it would be difficult to achieve. In the United States, citizens take for granted that the people elect leaders to public office, that there will be competition among candidates, that citizens will be able to learn about candidates and policy issues from campaigns and cast their ballots in fair elections, and that once in office, political leaders will work together to make policy and govern. Each of these tasks is complex, however, and would be all the more so if political parties did not exist. Parties mobilize people to vote, offer choices to voters in elections, and provide officeholders with organization for running government. As political scientist John Aldrich argues in *Why Parties?*, parties solve three fundamental problems of democracy: how to regulate the number of people seeking public office, how to mobilize voters, and how to achieve and maintain the majorities needed to pass legislation once in office.[9]

Parties and Elections

> **Describe political party organizations and the roles they play in elections**

Parties have always been central to the electoral process, recruiting candidates, coordinating campaigns, mobilizing voters, and raising money. Parties succeed when they win elections; thus, we begin with parties and elections.

RECRUITING CANDIDATES

One of the most important party activities is the recruitment of candidates to run for office. As Schattschneider argued, "responsible parties" recruit candidates who are loyal to the party's philosophy and policy agenda, with the goal of controlling government and adopting laws that are consistent with the party's platform. Each election year, candidates run for thousands of state and local offices and congressional seats. For "open" seats, where they do not have an incumbent running for re-election, party leaders attempt to identify strong candidates and encourage them to run.

An ideal candidate has experience holding public office and the capacity to raise enough money to mount a serious campaign, especially if that candidate will face an incumbent or a well-funded opponent in the general election. Party leaders are usually not willing to provide financial backing to candidates unable to raise substantial funds on their own. For a U.S. House seat, this can mean several hundred thousand dollars; for a Senate seat, a serious candidate must be able to raise several million dollars. Presidential candidates raise hundreds of millions of dollars.

Often, party leaders have difficulty finding strong candidates and persuading them to run. Candidate recruitment is problematic in an era when politicians must assume that their personal lives will be intensely scrutinized on social media, in the press, and in negative campaign ads run by their opponents.[10] Other barriers to recruiting quality candidates include the extremely high cost of campaigns, the extensive time required for fundraising, and widespread gerrymandering (see Chapter 10) that gives challengers only a slim chance of success against incumbents.

PARTY PRIMARY ELECTIONS

Nomination is the process by which a party selects a single candidate to run for each elective office. A party wants only one candidate representing it on the general-election ballot so the party's vote is not split, allowing the other party's candidate to win. The nomination process varies from state to state and office to office, but it usually involves a **primary election** or **caucus** among multiple candidates from the same party.

Scholars have found that although the nomination process appears democratic, in that average citizens have a say, party elites play an outsize role in selecting the candidates who will compete to be the next president of the United States or member of Congress.[11] This is in part because of very low turnout in primary elections, where generally only the most active members of the party vote. In 2016, however, Republican insiders lost control over their party's presidential nominating process; reality TV star and billionaire Donald Trump, with no previous experience in public office, won the nomination despite many leaders of the party emphatically speaking out against him. Only a handful of Republican members of Congress endorsed Trump for president.

nomination the process by which political parties select their candidates for election to public office

primary elections elections held to select a party's candidate for the general election

caucus (political) a normally closed political party business meeting of citizens or lawmakers to select candidates, elect officers, plan strategy, or make decisions regarding legislative matters

In 2020, Massachusetts representative Joe Kennedy III (right) challenged incumbent senator Ed Markey (left) in the Democratic primary for his seat in the U.S. Senate. Senator Ed Markey, a progressive Democrat, won the primary over Kennedy's more moderate views.

GENERAL ELECTION AND MOBILIZING VOTERS

The general-election campaign is a time of intense partisanship, when popular support for the parties is high. All the paraphernalia of party committees—from signs, bumper stickers, drink Koozies, and buttons to social media slogans, hashtags, and YouTube ads—are on display, and party members are activated into local party workforces.

One of the earliest activities of party workers is voter registration. To ensure that potential voters are registered, parties and candidate campaigns, along with nonprofit organizations, send mail and email notices, make phone calls, organize registration drives on college campuses or, in 2020, via mail, and knock on doors.

The next step is turning out the vote. Convincing voters to actually show up to cast a ballot on Election Day is one of the hardest tasks the parties face; it involves getting individuals to go to the polls, stand in line, and vote for the party's candidates on the ballot. If voting by mail—as one in three Americans now does—each voter must fill out the ballot and return it (see Chapter 8).

Voter mobilization, once an art, has now become a science. In typical election years, campaigns organize mobilization drives involving field offices with hundreds of thousands of volunteers and party workers contacting millions of voters. In recent years, the two major parties and their partners have developed extensive databases of over 240 million potential adult voters, combining state voter-registration files, demographic data from the U.S. Census, and commercial data (individual buying patterns, credit history, social media activity), which allow the parties to more accurately seek out voters, financial contributions, and volunteers. Using these databases, modern political campaigns can often predict who you will vote for, and they are extremely effective at turning out the voters most likely to vote for their candidates. One way campaigns use these data is through **micro-targeting**, which involves tailoring campaign messages to individuals in small, specialized groups (such as suburban mothers or fans of NASCAR) and emphasizing specific, often heated issues, rather than a one-size-fits-all campaign message.

micro-targeting the tailoring of messages by political campaigns to individuals in small homogeneous groups based on their group interests to support a candidate or policy issue

Research by political scientists and campaign organizations has shown that face-to-face, in-person contacts are much more effective than mailings, robocalls, or TV advertising in mobilizing voters. Here, Beth Van Duyne, the Republican candidate for Texas's 24th congressional district in the 2020 elections, meets with voters at a local cafe.

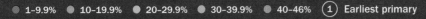

Who Votes in Primaries and Caucuses?

Turnout in 2020 Primaries

Percentage of voting-eligible population

● 1–9.9%   ● 10–19.9%   ● 20–29.9%   ● 30–39.9%   ● 40–46%   (1) Earliest primary

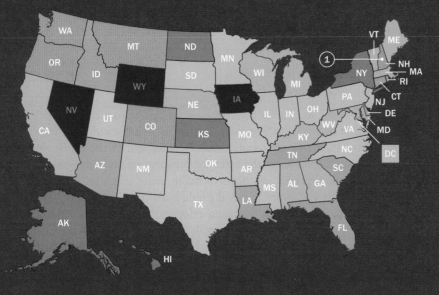

During presidential primary elections, early primaries and caucuses have important impacts on who the parties' nominees will be. Despite this impact, voter turnout in primary elections remains low, even in states with early contests like Iowa and New Hampshire. In recent years, many states have turned away from caucuses, which require voters to attend events in person, and instituted primaries instead in an attempt to increase voter turnout.

SOURCE: Michael P. McDonald, "2020 Presidential Nomination Contest Turnout Rates," United States Election Project, September 15, 2020, www.electproject.org/ (accessed 9/15/20).

NOTES:
Alaska, Hawaii, Kansas, South Carolina, Virginia: Data are for the Democratic primary only.
Nevada: Data are for the Democratic caucus only. No Republican caucus was held.
North Dakota: Data are for the Democratic primary only. The Republican presidential candidate was decided via convention.
Wyoming: Data are for the Democratic caucus only. The Republican presidential candidate was decided via convention.
Since there was no significant Republican challenger in the 2020 primary contests, data reflects mostly Democratic turnout measured over the total voting-eligible population, which skews the turnout rates lower than they really are. In states with caucuses or closed primaries, only registered party members can vote.

Turnout in 2020 Caucuses

Percentage of voting-eligible population

● 1–9.9%   (1) Earliest caucus

FOR CRITICAL ANALYSIS

1. Are participation rates higher, lower, or about the same for primaries versus caucuses? Why?

2. Determine which states have the highest voter turnout and look into voting laws in those states. Do these states' laws impact their high voter turnout?

The massive voter databases and targeted campaign messages have revolutionized how parties and candidates conduct voter-mobilization drives. In 2008 the Obama campaign learned that face-to-face and other in-person contacts are much more effective than mailings or robocalls at getting out the vote.[12] YouTube was especially important in turning out voters for both candidates in 2020.[13] The lessons of 2008 were improved on in 2012, 2016, and 2020 as both parties built more accurate databases to use when developing their messages and turning out the vote.

PARTY ORGANIZATIONS

party organization the formal structure of a political party, including its leadership, election committees, active members, and paid staff

In the United States **party organizations**, usually called committees, exist at virtually every level of government (see Figure 9.1). State law and party rules dictate how such committees are created. Usually, committee members are elected at local party business meetings, called caucuses, or as part of primary elections. The best-known examples of these committees are at the national level: the Democratic National Committee (DNC) and the Republican National Committee (RNC).

NATIONAL COMMITTEES

Each national political party is headed by the chairperson of the national committee. The DNC and RNC are gatekeepers for their respective parties, influencing which candidates have a chance to win the primaries by giving candidates money for their campaigns. They also try to minimize disputes within the party, work to enhance its media image, and set the rules for primary elections and caucuses. Sometimes the rules that parties set down actually cause disputes. The RNC was criticized for holding too many televised presidential debates in 2016, which some think helped Trump (a former television celebrity) win his party's nomination. In 2020, the DNC used performance in polls as a key criterion for candidates to qualify for the nationally televised presidential debates, which some candidates and campaigns objected to.

Money for campaigns is critical to winning elections. The DNC and RNC have each established Super PACs (see Chapter 10) as critical fundraising organizations.

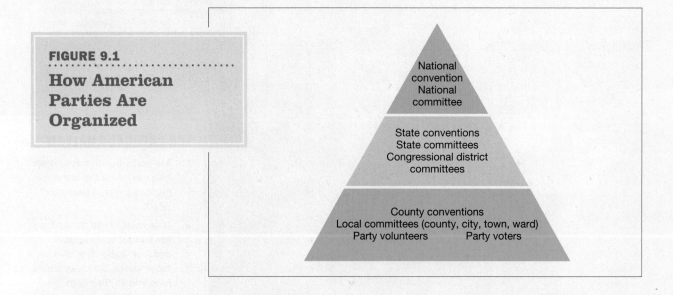

FIGURE 9.1

How American Parties Are Organized

National convention
National committee

State conventions
State committees
Congressional district committees

County conventions
Local committees (county, city, town, ward)
Party volunteers   Party voters

These Super PACs promote and publicize political issues, including by airing campaign ads. As nonprofit political advocacy groups, they can claim tax-exempt status under Section 527 of the Internal Revenue Code.

Super PACs can raise and spend unlimited amounts of money as long as their activities are not coordinated with those of formal party organizations or candidates and their activities aim to increase voter turnout for their party's candidates. Many Super PACs are directed by former Republican or Democratic party officials and run "shadow" campaigns during elections alongside the party's official campaign.[14] Because they can run expensive ads for and against candidates, Super PACs can have outsize influence in elections. While Super PACs are required to report the identity of their donors, they may accept money from "dark money" nonprofits, which are not required to report their donors. So Super PACs can, in effect, use secret money. Because wealthy individual, corporate, and even foreign donors can mask their identity through donations to Super PACs, these are often criticized as a form of political corruption.

NATIONAL CONVENTION

The national committees (DNC and RNC) organize each party's **national convention**, which is held every four years and attended by delegates from each of the 50 states. The convention has three formal tasks, the most important of which is to nominate the party's presidential and vice-presidential candidates. Before World War II, selecting the party's presidential nominee occupied most of the time at the convention, often requiring days of negotiation and compromise and multiple ballots. More recently, however, presidential candidates have been chosen by winning enough delegates in state primary elections and caucuses to win the nomination on the first ballot. Today, the convention serves more as a media event to promote the party's candidates, not as a forum to decide which presidential candidate will represent the party.

The convention's other two formal tasks, determining the party's rules and setting its **platform**, are also important. Party rules can determine the influence of competing groups within the party, which may affect the party's chances for electoral success. In 1972, for example, the Democratic National Convention adopted a new set of rules favored by the party's liberal wing. State delegations to the convention were

national convention convened by the Republican National Committee or the Democratic National Committee to nominate official candidates for president and vice president in the upcoming election, establish party rules, and adopt the party's platform

platform a party document, written at a national convention, that contains party philosophy, principles, and positions on issues

Today, the parties use their national conventions to provide more entertainment than substantive policy in order to attract media attention and promote their candidate. In 2020, the Democratic National Convention was held virtually, and the Republican National Convention was held from the White House.

required to include women and members of minority groups in rough proportion to those groups' representation among the party's membership in that state.

The convention also approves the party platform, or statement of policy positions. The parties' presidential candidates often develop their own campaign themes, moving beyond their party's platform. A platform should be seen less as a public pledge than as an internal party document: a contract in which the various party factions state their terms for supporting the party's nominees.

CONGRESSIONAL, STATE, AND LOCAL CAMPAIGN COMMITTEES

Each party also has House and Senate campaign committees, and each of these four congressional campaign committees is made up of members of the House or Senate who are expected to raise a certain sum of money, the achievement of which allows them to move up in the chamber's power structure. Congressional committees direct funds to competitive House and Senate races each election. They compete with presidential fundraising committees for dollars from the biggest donors, who are often corporations, millionaires, and billionaires. The Democrats and the Republicans also each have a central committee in each state and traditionally have county committees and, in some instances, state senate district committees, judicial district committees, and, in larger cities, citywide party committees and local assembly district "ward" committees.

During the nineteenth and early twentieth centuries, many cities and counties and even a few states had such well-organized parties that they were called **party machines**, whose leaders were called "bosses." The famous old party machines of New York, Chicago, and Boston relied on "precinct captains"; these were usually leaders in neighborhood party "clubhouses," which were important social centers and places for distributing favors (or bribes) to constituents.[15] Traditional party machines depended heavily on **patronage**, the power to appoint supporters to government jobs. With thousands of jobs to dispense, such as police officer, firefighter, or garbage collector, bosses were able to recruit armies of voters to support their party and voter turnout was very high. The party machines even distributed free turkeys on Thanksgiving in exchange for support on Election Day.

The Progressive movement in the early 1900s was motivated by the corruption and abuses of power of these party machines and their bosses. Progressive reformers changed the rules of politics to reduce the power of parties and to give voters more voice in deciding who was elected to public office. A few of the many reforms to weaken the machines included the direct election of U.S. senators; the replacement of single-party ballots that voters had to publicly cast with the secret ballot and the long ballot, where the names of candidates running for both parties were listed; primary elections where voters, not party officials, picked candidates; and voter registration, which reduced turnout and prevented party officials from casting false ballots for their candidates.

Few political machines are left today. With civil service based on the merit system, party leaders no longer control many government jobs. Nevertheless, state and local party organizations still play an important role in recruiting candidates and registering

party machines strong party organizations in late nineteenth- and early twentieth-century American cities; these machines were led by often corrupt "bosses" who controlled party nominations and patronage

patronage the resources available to higher officials, usually opportunities to make partisan appointments to offices and to confer grants, licenses, or special favors to supporters

Political parties used to be ruled by powerful local "bosses," who handed out jobs and favors in exchange for loyalty on Election Day. The cartoon shows "fat cat" New York boss Richard Croker controlling the Democratic Party organization (the donkey) with his pit bulls.

voters, and under current federal law they can spend unlimited amounts of money on "party-building" activities such as voter-registration and get-out-the-vote drives. National party organizations, which have enormous fundraising abilities, transfer millions of dollars to state and local party organizations.[16]

Parties in Government

Explain how parties organize government and influence policy making

When the bumps, bruises, and dust of the campaign and election have settled, does it matter which party has won? Yes. The party with the majority of seats in the House, Senate, or in the seat of the presidency controls party leadership positions and sets the policy-making agenda.

policy entrepreneur an individual who identifies a problem as a political issue and brings a policy proposal into the political agenda

PARTIES AND POLICY

For decades, one of the most familiar complaints about American politics was that the two major parties tried to be all things to all people and were therefore indistinguishable from each other. But since the 1980s fundamental differences have emerged between the positions of Democratic and Republican party also leaders on a number of key issues.

For example, the national leadership of the Republican Party supports reducing spending on social and health care programs, cutting taxes on corporations and the wealthy, protecting rights of gun owners, reducing immigration to the United States, maintaining or increasing military spending, preserving traditional family structures, and opposing abortion. The Republican Party also opposes government regulation of businesses, including environmental laws.

The Democratic Party, on the other hand, supports expanded funding for public education and social services, a national health insurance system, investing in alternative energy sources to address climate change, higher taxes on the wealthy and corporations to reduce economic inequality, restrictions on gun ownership, and consumer protection programs. Democrats also support legalized abortion and support protecting the rights of racial, ethnic, religious, and sexual minorities and undocumented immigrants.

Partisan conflict has intensified in recent years. Americans believe there are stronger conflicts in U.S. society today between Democrats and Republicans than between Blacks and White non-Hispanics, the rich and the poor, and other social groups (see Figure 9.2). In 2020, 91 percent of Americans said conflicts between Democrats and Republicans are either strong or very strong.[17]

Party leaders, like their counterparts in the business world, often play the role of **policy entrepreneurs** by developing issues and programs they hope will add new groups to their party's

Beginning in the 1980s the Republican Party, led by Ronald Reagan, sought to expand its base by focusing on social issues that mattered to conservative religious voters. Ted Cruz (R-Tex.) announced his 2016 presidential campaign at Liberty University.

FIGURE 9.2
. . . .

Partisan Divisions Have Increased

When asked about 10 aspects of political values, Americans' difference of opinion was stronger between political parties than it was between Whites and African Americans, men and women, those that do and don't attend church regularly, old and young, and highly and less educated.

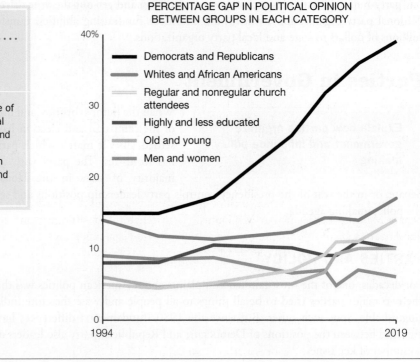

PERCENTAGE GAP IN POLITICAL OPINION
BETWEEN GROUPS IN EACH CATEGORY

— Democrats and Republicans
— Whites and African Americans
— Regular and nonregular church attendees
— Highly and less educated
— Old and young
— Men and women

SOURCE: Pew Research Center, "In a Politically Polarized Era, Sharp Divides in Both Partisan Coalitions," December 17, 2019, www.pewresearch.org/politics/2019/12/17/in-a-politically-polarized-era-sharp-divides-in-both-partisan-coalitions/ (accessed 8/10/20).

constituent base while eroding the base of the opposition. During the 1980s, under the leadership of Ronald Reagan, the Republicans used social issues, including support for school prayer and opposition to abortion and affirmative action, to gain the support of White southerners. This effort was successful at increasing Republican strength in the once solidly Democratic South. In the 2016 presidential election, Donald Trump proposed to build a wall between the southern U.S. border and Mexico to prevent illegal immigration, appealing to White working-class citizens who see immigrants as an economic or cultural threat.

FACTIONS WITHIN THE PARTIES

While party polarization, or the depth of divisions between Republicans and Democrats, is at an all-time high (see later in this chapter), the divisions *within* each party may be nearly as important. Parties are coalitions of people and groups who agree on a broad common approach to issues but also represent many diverse interests competing for power and influence. For leaders in Congress and state legislatures, keeping these different groups working toward shared goals can be difficult.

The Republican Party today, for example, is divided in at least four major ways. Pro-business conservatives or traditional Republicans, such as Nebraska senator Benjamin Sasse, are a generally affluent group that favors small government and lower corporate taxes along with global free trade. Far-right or alt-right conservatives, such as President Trump, are opposed to immigration and global free trade and to institutions like the United Nations. They favor tariffs on imports to the United States in order to protect American-made products and tend to be social conservatives, often with lower levels of education. Social and religious conservatives, such as Texas senator Ted Cruz, are primarily driven by their values on cultural and moral issues, such as opposition to abortion and gay marriage. Finally, libertarians, such as Kentucky senator Rand Paul, believe in small government, less government regulation, and more individual freedoms, and they oppose foreign wars. These divisions have presented severe challenges for governing. For example, far-right conservatives like Donald Trump see very strict immigration policies as protecting American workers, while pro-business conservatives see immigration as important to maintain a healthy economy. These differences make it difficult to find common ground.

During his presidency, Donald Trump has waged a war against virtually everyone, through his use of Twitter, including many leaders within his party, such as Senate Majority Leader Mitch McConnell, Utah senator Mitt Romney, and the late Arizona senator John McCain.[18] Nonetheless, Republican members of Congress have generally rallied around the president even if they have personally been subject to his wrath on Twitter. Despite serious divisions, parties can often unify behind shared goals.

In 2020, Democrats in Congress staunchly opposed President Trump and his policies, but differences between the moderate and progressive wings of the party threatened to undermine Democratic Party unity. The super-progressives like members of "The Squad"—Representatives Alexandria Ocasio-Cortez (N.Y.), Ayanna Pressley (Mass.), Rashida Tlaib (Mich.), and Ilhan Omar (Minn.)—seek European Union–type policies to create universal national health care and eliminate private health insurance. Traditional Democrats support traditional liberal government policies, but seek more incremental rather than dramatic change. Such divisions may have contributed to the Democrats losing the White House and Congress in 2016, as many Sanders supporters refused to vote for Clinton in the general election and 10 percent voted for Trump. Democrats strongly favor expanded social safety nets, reducing student-loan debt, and addressing climate change.

Representatives Alexandria Ocasio-Cortez (D-N.Y.), Ayanna Pressley (D-Mass.), Rashida Tlaib (D-Mich.) and Ilhan Omar (D-Minn.) are often the faces of the super-progressive wing of the Democratic party. They advocate for Medicare for all, a Green New Deal, and many other progessive reforms.

PARTIES IN CONGRESS

majority party the party that holds the majority of legislative seats in either the House or the Senate

minority party the party that holds the minority of legislative seats in either the House or the Senate

Parties form the basic organization for running Congress. The Speaker of the House is a party office. All the members of the House take part in the election of the Speaker, but the actual selection is made by the **majority party**—the party that holds a majority of seats in the House. (The other party is known as the **minority party**.) When the majority party caucus presents a nominee for Speaker to the entire House, its choice is usually ratified in a straight vote along party lines.

Today, party leaders in both the U.S. House (Nancy Pelosi) and the Senate (Mitch McConnell) yield more power, and there is more party unity when important votes are held on policy issues. As Congress has become more ideologically extreme, members have given more power to their party leaders, who have changed the rules in Congress so that the majority party can control the legislative process more easily, further intensifying polarization. The ability to debate legislation on the floor of the House has been restricted, and individual members have less personal choice about how to vote. (See Chapter 12.)

A high-profile example of party-line voting was Trump's impeachment. The House impeachment inquiry of President Trump found that he had asked a foreign government (Ukraine) to interfere in the 2020 presidential election to help his re-election campaign in exchange for millions in military funding, and then obstructed Congress by telling his White House staff to ignore subpoenas for documents and testimony. When the House voted to impeach the president on December 18, 2019, on charges of abuse of power and obstruction of Congress, 228 Democrats voted for Articles I and II, with just 2 Democrats voting no on the first and 3 voting no on the second. Republicans in the House universally opposed the articles of impeachment, with 195 members voting no and not a single member voting yea. One of the two Democrats opposing impeachment switched his affiliation to the Republican Party after the vote. The other, who has been in Congress for three decades, has a mostly Republican constituency. Party polarization means that party-line voting in Congress is now common.

Beyond party leadership, the committee system of both houses of Congress is also a product of the two-party system; the majority party in each chamber selects the chairs for that chamber's committees, thus providing strong influence over the policy agenda. Membership of each committee is divided between the parties roughly according to the percentage of total seats each holds (though there are some variations). As we shall see in Chapter 12, the assignment of individual members to committees is a party decision. Granting a member permission to transfer to another committee is also a party decision, as is advancement up the committee ladder toward serving as chair.

FOR CRITICAL ANALYSIS

How do parties attract the popular support they need to win elections?

Party Identification

Identify the reasons for and sources of party identification and increased party polarization

One reason why parties are so important is that individuals tend to develop an identification with one of them at a young age. **Party identification** has been likened to wearing blue- or red-tinted glasses: they color voters' understanding of politics in general and are the most important cue in how to vote in elections. Party identification can create information bubbles and filters, where citizens follow news media or

party identification an individual voter's psychological ties to one party or another

Comparing Party Systems

While the American political system is dominated by two political parties, many countries have more than two parties. The number varies depending on the electoral rules in place. Here we compare the United States, which uses winner-take-all electoral rules, with the Netherlands, which uses a proportional representation system, and Mexico, which uses a mix of both systems in determining seats in its lower house.

1. Which system do you think would do a better job of reflecting the will of the voters? Do you see any evidence for your answer in the data?
2. We can see that 3 percent of Americans voted for third parties in Congressional elections but all the seats in the House are held by Democrats and Republicans. Why do you think third parties in America find it so difficult to win seats in the legislature?

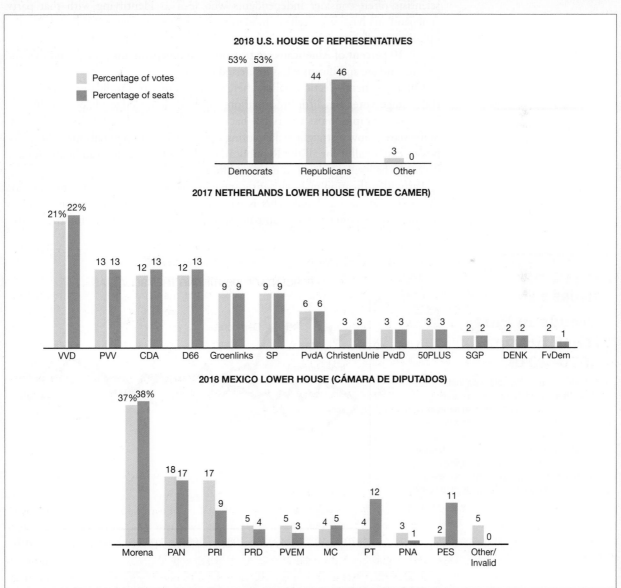

SOURCES: U.S. Clerk of the House of Representatives, https://history.house.gov/Institution/Election-Statistics /Election-Statistics/; www.kiesraad.nl; www.electionguide.org/elections/id/3064/; and https://computos2018 .ine.mx/#/diputaciones/nacional/1/3/1/1 (accessed 8/8/2019).

candidates on social media that are of the same partisan leaning. The vast majority of Republicans vote for Republican candidates, and the vast majority of Democrats vote for Democrats.

Although it is partly an emotional attachment, party identification also has a rational component. Voters generally form attachments to the party that reflects their views and interests. Once those attachments are formed, usually in youth, they are likely to persist and even be handed down to children, unless some very strong factors convince individuals that their party is no longer serving their interests.[19]

Yet 34 percent of Americans describe themselves as independents, while 33 percent call themselves Democrats and 29 percent Republicans. The number of people identifying as Democrats has outnumbered Republican identifiers for a long time, but independents are growing, especially among young people (see Figure 9.3). However, most independents lean toward one of the major parties, and political scientists often consider independents who lean as identifying with that party. Independents have been called "hidden partisans" because even if they hold policy opinions similar to partisans they don't tend to voice these opinions publicly.[20] Just 7–10 percent of Americans are true political independents—they tend to avoid politics and are significantly less interested in politics.[21]

On any general-election ballot, there are a number of candidates about whom the average voter has little information. Without knowledge of local or judicial races, for example, most voters fall back on their party identification or leaning. Some states allow a straight-ticket voting option, where individuals may check one box to cast a ballot for all the Republican or all the Democratic candidates up and down the ballot, from local to national offices.

Party identification gives citizens a stake in election outcomes that goes beyond the particular race at hand. This is why strong party identifiers are more likely to vote, to be contacted by campaigns, and to become activists for their party.

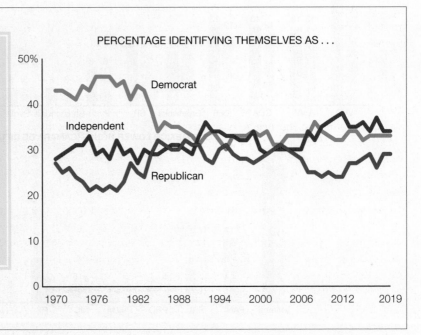

FIGURE 9.3

Trends in Party Identification, 1970–2019

Over time, the Democrats have lost strength as more Americans identified themselves as Republicans and independents. Since 2004, however, the number of Democrats has held steady and the number of Republicans has declined, while the number of Americans identifying as independent of either party has increased to an all-time high. Why do you think this is?

PERCENTAGE IDENTIFYING THEMSELVES AS . . .

SOURCE: Pew Research Center, "Democratic Edge in Party Identification Narrows Slightly," June 2, 2020, https://www.pewresearch.org/politics/2020/06/02/democratic-edge-in-party-identification-narrows-slightly/ (accessed 8/7/20).

Party activists are those who not only vote but also contribute their time, money, and effort to party affairs, organizations, and elections, thus giving them an outsize role in the party. They also tend to be more ideologically extreme than the average person in the party. No party could succeed without the thousands of volunteers who undertake the tasks needed to keep the organization going.

party activists partisans who contribute time, energy, and effort to support their party and its candidates

WHO ARE REPUBLICANS AND DEMOCRATS?

The Democratic and Republican parties are currently the only truly national parties that draw substantial support in every region of the country. Each party draws support from different social groups, defined by race and ethnicity, gender, religion, ideology, region, and age.[22] Today's divide between the parties reflects an unprecedented alignment of many different divides—racial and ethnic, religious, ideological, and geographic—and social and cultural group identities are becoming more important in defining partisanship.[23]

The Democratic Party at the national level seeks to unite organized labor, the poor, the working class, middle-class professionals, people with college degrees, nonwhite racial and ethnic groups, the young, the nonreligious, and civilian government workers. The Republicans, by contrast, appeal to business, non-Hispanic Whites, those without college degrees, the very wealthy, the elderly, military families, and religious conservatives. Women are more likely to affiliate with the Democrats than the Republicans. Rural areas tend to vote for Republicans, while urban areas are dominated by Democrats. The suburbs are a swing region, more evenly divided between Republicans and Democrats. Suburbs in larger metro areas swung Democrat in the 2018 and 2020 elections, but those in smaller metros often remained Republican.

Race and Ethnicity The United States' growing racial and ethnic diversity is reflected both in changing partisanship among racial and ethnic groups and growing divisions between the two major parties in their racial and ethnic makeup. One group whose partisan allegiance remains largely unchanged is African Americans, approximately 90 percent of whom describe themselves as Democrats and support Democratic candidates in national, state, and local elections. In 2020, between 87–89 percent of African Americans voted for Democrat Joe Biden for president.[24] In contrast, a small majority of non-Hispanic Whites regularly vote Republican; in 2018, 53 percent of non-Hispanic Whites overall and 56 percent of non-Hispanic Whites without a college degree supported Republican House candidates.[25]

Latinos and Latinas now make up over 18 percent of the population and as voters are less monolithic than African Americans. Cuban Americans, for example, generally vote Republican, whereas Mexican Americans have favored Democrats. Overall, however, a strong Democratic shift occurred in 2008, when 67 percent of Latinos supported Obama. This trend has continued, with 63–65 percent voting for Democrats in 2020.[26] Latino party affiliation is particularly important because it has the potential to alter the electoral map and change traditionally "red" states to "blue" states.[27] However, in 2020, Trump showed increasing strength among Latinos, winning nearly a third of this group's votes nationwide.

Asian Americans were also politically divided until recent years and now solidly favor Democratic candidates. In 2018, 77 percent voted for Democratic House candidates, and in 2020 nearly two-thirds voted for Joe Biden. Like Latinos, they are extremely diverse (see Chapter 8), reflecting cultural differences and political influences from their home countries.

Members of racial and ethnic minority groups tend to favor Democratic candidates. In 2020, Joe Biden gained strong support from Latinos, African Americans, and Asian Americans.

The affiliation of African Americans and Latinos with the Democratic Party can be traced to the party's historical policy positions. In the twentieth century, the Democrats were the party of the civil rights movement, desegregation, and affirmative action policies, which solidified African American support. Today Democrats tend to be more supportive than Republicans of policies that favor an easier path to citizenship for immigrants and reducing racial inequity in the criminal justice system. Immigration issues are critically important for many Latino and Asian voters, especially in states like California, where a third of the population are legal immigrants. President Trump's anti-immigrant and anti-minority policies and the Republican Party's hard line against immigration have increased perceptions that the party is racially divisive and anti-immigrant.

Gender Women are more likely to support Democrats than Republicans, and men are more likely to support Republicans. This difference, known as the **gender gap**, reflects the fact that women tend to prioritize health care, education, and social services, issues emphasized by the Democratic Party, while men tend to prioritize budgetary and economic issues and national security, issues emphasized by the Republican Party. There are also more women lawmakers in the Democratic party. The gender gap in voting has hovered at 10 percent since 1992 but is now wider than at any point over the past two decades. In 2020, the gender gap was approximately 15 percent, with women favoring Democrat Joe Biden (57 percent) to Republican Donald Trump (42 percent). Men favored Trump over Biden 53 to 45 percent.

gender gap a distinctive pattern of voting behavior reflecting the differences in views between women and men

Religion Religious beliefs and preferences also affect partisanship. White Protestants are more likely to identify with the Republican Party. White evangelical Protestants, in particular, have been drawn to the Republicans' conservative stances on social issues, such as opposition to same-sex marriage and abortion. Jews are among the Democratic Party's most loyal constituent groups, with nearly 90 percent of Jewish Americans describing themselves as Democrats. Those unaffiliated with a

religion—a growing segment of the population, at roughly 25 percent—strongly favor the Democratic Party.[28] Sixty-eight percent of people unaffiliated with a religion supported Democrats in 2018.[29]

Class Rising income inequality has led to economic populism in the United States. The patterns of class voting that emerged from the New Deal of the 1930s were simple: upper-income Americans were considerably more likely to be Republican, whereas lower-income Americans were far more likely to identify with the Democrats, and this pattern still generally holds, driven by differences between the two parties on economic issues.[30] In general, Republicans support reductions in taxes, in regulation of business, and in spending on social services—positions that often reflect the interests of the wealthy. Democrats favor increasing government spending and raising taxes on the wealthy—positions consistent with the interests of less affluent Americans.

But beginning in the 1970s, many White working-class voters turned to the Republican Party, and today a majority of White workers without a college degree vote Republican, while working-class minorities tend to vote Democratic. In the 2016 election, non-college-educated voters favored Trump over Clinton by 8 percentage points (52 to 44 percent), but in 2020, that gap narrowed to 2 percent as Democrats gained ground among this group. College-educated voters continued to support Democrats in 2020, favoring Biden over Trump 55 to 43 percent (see Figure 9.4).

Ideology Ideology and party identification are very closely linked. Most individuals who describe themselves as conservatives identify with the Republican Party, whereas most who call themselves liberals support the Democrats. This division has increased in recent years as the two parties have taken very different positions on social and economic issues.

The Pew Research Center finds that 61 percent of Americans are "ideological" and identify strongly with one of the two major parties. For the rest, partisan and ideological identification is not so clear-cut: 30 percent of Americans hold

FIGURE 9.4

Education and Party Affiliation

Recently, people with higher levels of education have affiliated with the Democratic Party more and more, while those with lower levels of education have identified with the Republican Party. Do you think this trend will continue? How will this affect party platforms, long term?

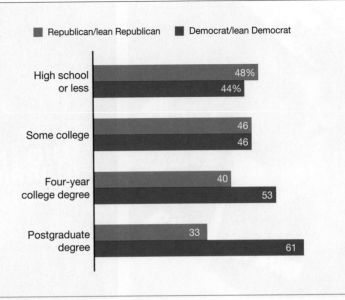

■ Republican/lean Republican   ■ Democrat/lean Democrat

High school or less: 48% / 44%
Some college: 46 / 46
Four-year college degree: 40 / 53
Postgraduate degree: 33 / 61

SOURCE: Pew Research Center, "In Changing U.S. Electorate, Race and Education Remain Stark Dividing Lines," June 2, 2020, www.pewresearch.org/politics/2020/06/02/in-changing-u-s-electorate-race-and-education-remain-stark-dividing-lines/ (accessed 10/20/20).

policy preferences that are a mix of liberal and conservative. Finally, 9 percent of Americans are less politically engaged and non-ideological although they tend to vote Democrat. This group is older and a majority are nonwhite.[31]

Region Since the 2000 election, maps showing the regional distribution of the vote have given rise to the idea of America being divided between "blue" and "red" states and areas. Democrats, represented as blue, tend to be clustered on the coasts, in the upper Midwest, across the northern states, and in urban areas nationwide. Republicans, represented as red, tend to be concentrated in the Mountain West, the Great Plains, and the South, and in suburbs and rural areas.[32]

Some states that used to be solidly red or blue are now turning "purple" as Republicans and Democrats battle to win elections. In the 2020 presidential election, the most competitive states included the perennial Florida, Texas, North Carolina, Arizona, and Georgia where Republicans used to dominate, and Midwestern states such as Wisconsin, Michigan, Iowa, Ohio, and Pennsylvania, which had gone Democrat in past elections since the early 1990s, but were carried by Trump in 2016 (see Figure 9.5).

Age Today young people are much more likely to be Democrats and the oldest voters are likely to be Republicans. Individuals from the same age cohort are likely to have experienced a similar set of events during the period when their party loyalties were formed. Millennials, for example, who came of age during the Great Recession and growing economic inequality, reacted sharply against the Republican Party as a result. In the 2020 elections, support for Republicans among the elderly decreased in part because older voters were concerned about the coronavirus pandemic.

There has been a striking uptick in the percentage of young people who identify as independent, which may be a reflection of increasing frustration with government. Nonetheless, in 2020, between 59–60 percent of people ages 18 to 29 voted for

FOR CRITICAL ANALYSIS

What are the major components of each party's political coalition? What factors tie these groups to their respective parties?

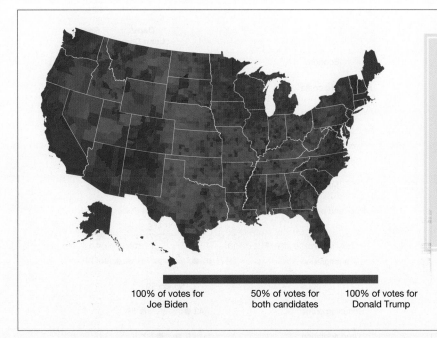

FIGURE 9.5

Presidential Vote by County, 2020

In 2020, Republicans dominated in most counties in the center of the country while Democrats won many of the most populous counties. Overall, the United States is becoming much more "purple," demonstrating that in most counties across the country, each party received roughly half the votes cast.

100% of votes for
Joe Biden

50% of votes for
both candidates

100% of votes for
Donald Trump

SOURCES: Provided by Robert J. Vanderbei, Princeton University, "2020 Presidential Election, Purple America," https://vanderbei.princeton.edu/JAVA/election2020/ (accessed 11/12/20).

Joe Biden, compared to just 36 percent for Donald Trump.[33] As a group, young people have distinct policy preferences that overlap with the Democratic Party, including support for LGBTQ rights, legalization of marijuana, protection of the environment, and greater economic equality.

PARTY POLARIZATION IN SOCIETY

Since Trump's election in 2016, divides between people who affiliate with the Republican and Democratic parties have been growing. Negative feelings among partisans toward members of the opposing party have intensified too. A recent survey asked respondents to rate individuals or groups on a scale from 0 to 100, with 0 being very cold, 100 very warm, and 50 neutral. A cold rating is a number below 50. Overall about 8 in 10 Democrats and Republicans give the opposite party a cold rating. The share of Republicans who give Democrats a cold rating grew 14 percentage points from 2016 to 2019, and Democrats' negative views of Republicans grew at a similar rate.[34]

Political divisions have moved beyond disagreements about policy and become more personal, though Democrats and Republicans remain far apart on many policy issues (see Figure 9.6). A majority of Republicans (63 percent) believe Democrats are more unpatriotic compared to other Americans. Just 23 percent of Democrats say the same about Republicans. Five in ten Republicans say Democrats are more immoral compared to other Americans; a similar number of Democrats say the same about Republicans. And three in four Democrats say Republicans are more "closed-minded" than other Americans.[35] Party polarization is so intense that a nationally representative survey finds that 20 percent of Republicans and 15 percent of Democrats say the country would be better off if large numbers of the other party died.[36]

FIGURE 9.6

Partisan Divisions on Key Issues

Is there a difference between the two parties? Surveys show those who identify with each political party differ widely in their views on important issues. This figure shows the percent who said each issue should be a top priority for Trump and Congress in 2019.

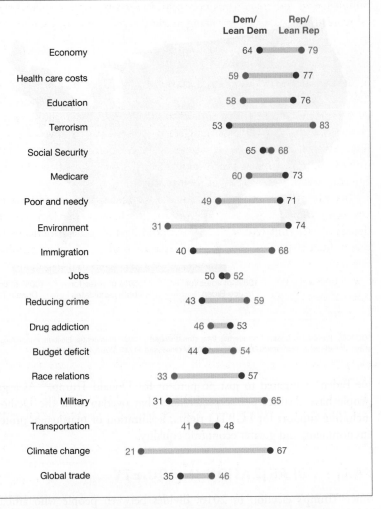

	Dem/ Lean Dem	Rep/ Lean Rep
Economy	64	79
Health care costs	59	77
Education	58	76
Terrorism	53	83
Social Security	65	68
Medicare	60	73
Poor and needy	49	71
Environment	31	74
Immigration	40	68
Jobs	50	52
Reducing crime	43	59
Drug addiction	46	53
Budget deficit	44	54
Race relations	33	57
Military	31	65
Transportation	41	48
Climate change	21	67
Global trade	35	46

Source: Pew Research Center, "Public's 2019 Priorities: Economy, Health Care, Education and Security All Near Top of List," January 24, 2019, https://www.people-press.org/2019/01/24/publics-2019-priorities-economy-health-care-education-and-security-all-near-top-of-list/ (accessed 6/5/2020).

Democracies, where ordinary people have power by voting in elections, require debate, discussion, and compromise to elect lawmakers, make laws, and solve problems. Today large majorities (85 percent) of the public say the tone and nature of political discussion in the United States has become more negative and less respectful, three-quarters (76 percent) say it has become less fact based, and 60 percent say it has become less focused on policy issues. A majority (55 percent) say Trump has changed the tone of political debate for the worse, while just 24 percent say he has changed it for the better. Most Americans (78 percent) say elected officials should stop using aggressive or heated language to talk about certain people or groups, because it makes violence against those people or groups more likely.[37]

Yet on many basic policy issues there is a fair amount of agreement. Significant majorities of Americans want to expand national health care, want to rebuild the nation's economy following the pandemic, favor a tax on millionaires and billionaires to address growing economic inequality, support increased environmental regulations, and favor legalizing marijuana and banning assault weapons.

PARTY POLARIZATION IN CONGRESS

A distinguishing feature of the contemporary party system is **party polarization**. The vast and growing gap between Democrats and Republicans has become a defining feature of American politics today, with Democrats holding strongly liberal positions and Republicans holding strongly conservative views. We see particularly high levels of polarization in Congress, where polarization is measured by party unity in roll-call votes. Over 90 percent of the time, members of Congress vote in agreement with the majority of their party.[38]

The extent of party polarization in Congress was exemplified by party-line voting in 2017 for the most significant overhaul of the U.S. tax code in three decades.[39] The bill reduced taxes temporarily for some Americans but provided major financial gains to affluent taxpayers and provided a massive tax cut to corporations. Through concessions, threats, and extended negotiations, Republican leaders secured votes of support from every Republican member of the House but 12, and every Senate Republican but 1. Democrats in the House and Senate unanimously opposed the bill.

While members of Congress are generally strong conservatives or strong liberals, most Americans are actually moderates in their opinions on major issues.[40] Party polarization in Congress may result from how members of the House are elected. Every 10 years, in states with more than one House member, congressional district boundaries are redrawn so that each district has roughly the same population. These districts are increasingly drawn to be "safe" for one political party or another so that a district has a clear majority of either Republicans or Democrats. With most lawmakers now elected from safe districts, incumbents have little chance of losing in the next election; on average, they win 70 percent of the vote to challengers' 30 percent.[41] Facing little competition during general elections, those elected to Congress can be strong partisans. Today lawmakers face the greatest risk during their own party's primary elections, which can have the effect of moving candidates more to the party's ideological extremes in order to win in the primary.

Others argue that party polarization has occurred not because of how congressional districts are drawn but because individuals segregate themselves by choosing to live in liberal or conservative geographic areas or consume only liberal or conservative news and social media. This tendency is known as self-sorting. No matter what the cause of increased geographical separation between Democrats and Republicans, however, lawmakers in safe districts have less incentive to compromise; thus, such districts add to the polarization of the parties.

SOCIAL GROUP IDENTITIES AND POLITICAL DIVIDES

Political scientist Lilliana Mason argues that party polarization in the U.S. electorate is more about allegiance to social groups defined by race and ethnicity, religion, age cohort, or geography than about difference in opinion about public policy. In her book *Uncivil Agreement* she argues that the political divide in the United States is only partially based on genuine policy disagreements and is rooted more in divergent cultural and social identities. These cultural identities now overlap more with partisan identities, moving Americans further apart over the

party polarization the division between the two major parties on most policy issues, with members of each party unified around their party's positions with little crossover

FOR CRITICAL ANALYSIS

What are the principal issues dividing the two major parties today? What are the chief areas of agreement between the two parties?

past 50 years. In Mason's words, partisanship has become a "mega-identity." It means rooting for your team or party at all costs.

Mason illustrates contemporary party polarization with a 1954 social experiment in which 22 fifth-grade boys were unknowingly split into two separate teams—named the Eagles and the Rattlers—at separate campsites at a state park. Over a couple of weeks, the teams bonded with their teammates and, upon learning about the existence of the other team, began devising demeaning stereotypes about them—viewing them as both outsiders *and* intruders. When the Eagles and the Rattlers first interacted with each other in a baseball game, it resulted in insults. The relations between the teams eroded until the experiment was finally ended after the boys started acting violently toward each other. The results of the experiment were telling: "By the end of the second week, 22 highly similar boys who had met only two weeks before had formed two nearly warring tribes, with only the gentle nudge of isolation and competition to encourage them."[42] The Who Are Americans? feature indicates the relationship between party identification and a number of social identities.

The social experiment illustrates the power of in-group bias that develops, independent of reality—there was no real reason for the campers to hate each other, but they did. Similarly, Democrats and Republicans have growing negative feelings toward each other, even though they agree on many basic policy issues. Since democracy requires unity to some degree, this serious division can undermine American democracy and the nation's unity.

Party Systems

> **Describe the history of U.S. party systems and the influence of third parties**

Despite the deep divides we see between the parties today, the groups supporting them, the parties themselves, and the parties' policy goals are not chiseled in stone. History shows that parties can change significantly as they respond to important events and are influenced by charismatic leaders.

Historians often refer to the set of parties that are important at any given time as a nation's party system. The United States has usually had a two-party system, meaning that only two parties have a serious chance to win national elections. But they have not been the same two parties (see Figure 9.7), and, as we shall see, minor parties often put forward candidates.

The term *party system*, however, refers to more than just the number of parties competing for power. It also includes the organization of the parties, the dominant form of campaigning, the main issues that divide the parties, the balance of power between and within party coalitions, and the parties' social bases. Seen from this broader perspective, the character of a nation's party system can change even if the number of parties remains the same and even when the same two parties seem to be competing for power. Today's American party system is very different from the one of 100 years ago, but the Democrats and Republicans continue to be the major competing forces. Over the course of American history, changes in political alignments have produced six distinct party systems.

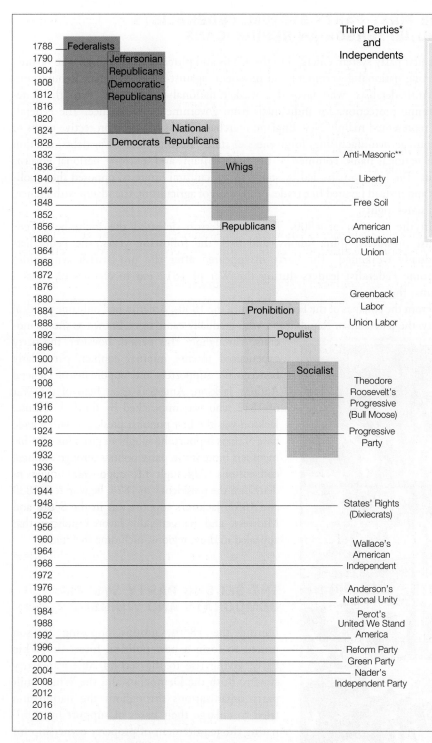

Third Parties* and Independents

Year				Third Parties and Independents
1788	Federalists			
1790		Jeffersonian		
1804		Republicans		
1808		(Democratic-		
1812		Republicans)		
1816				
1820				
1824			National	
1828	Democrats	Republicans		
1832				Anti-Masonic**
1836		Whigs		
1840				Liberty
1844				
1848				Free Soil
1852				
1856		Republicans		American
1860				Constitutional
1864				Union
1868				
1872				
1876				
1880				Greenback
1884		Prohibition		Labor
1888				Union Labor
1892		Populist		
1896				
1900				
1904		Socialist		
1908				Theodore
1912				Roosevelt's
1916				Progressive
1920				(Bull Moose)
1924				Progressive
1928				Party
1932				
1936				
1940				
1944				
1948				States' Rights
1952				(Dixiecrats)
1956				
1960				Wallace's
1964				American
1968				Independent
1972				
1976				Anderson's
1980				National Unity
1984				Perot's
1988				United We Stand
1992				America
1996				Reform Party
2000				Green Party
2004				Nader's
2008				Independent Party
2012				
2016				
2018				

FIGURE 9.7
· ·

How the Party System Evolved

During the nineteenth century, the Democrats and Republicans emerged as the two dominant parties in American politics. As the American party system evolved, many third parties emerged, but few of them remained in existence for very long.

*Or, in some cases, fourth parties; most of these parties lasted through only one term.

**The Anti-Masonics had the distinction of being not only the first third party but also the first party to hold a national nominating convention and the first to announce a party platform.

THE FIRST PARTY SYSTEM: FEDERALISTS AND JEFFERSONIAN REPUBLICANS

The first party system emerged in the 1790s and pitted the Federalists, who favored a strong national government and president, against the Jeffersonian Republicans, or Antifederalists, who favored a weaker national government, with the states retaining protections for individuals from government interference. The Federalists represented mainly New England merchants and supported protective tariffs to encourage manufacturing, forgiveness of states' Revolutionary War debts, creation of a national bank, commercial ties with Britain, and a strong national government. The Jeffersonians, led by southern agricultural interests, opposed these policies and instead favored free trade, promotion of agriculture, friendship with France, and states' rights.

In the election of 1800, Thomas Jefferson defeated the incumbent Federalist president, John Adams, and over the following years, the Federalists gradually weakened. The party disappeared after the pro-British sympathies of some Federalist leaders during the War of 1812 led to charges of treason against the party.

From the collapse of the Federalists until the 1830s, America had only one political party, the Jeffersonian Republicans, who gradually came to be known as the Democrats. Throughout this period, however, the party experienced intense internal conflict, particularly between the supporters and opponents of General Andrew Jackson, America's great hero of the War of 1812 who was impeached by the U.S. House. Jackson was the first populist president with a wide base of mass support; he sought to give rank-and-file members more say in party politics through national conventions. Although his opponents united to deny him the presidency in 1824, he won it in 1828 and 1832. Jackson's support was in the South and Midwest, and he generally favored policies that appealed to those regions, including free trade.

In the 1830s the Whig Party emerged as the Democrats' main rival. This drawing depicts a Whig rally and parade during the 1840 election.

THE SECOND PARTY SYSTEM: DEMOCRATS AND WHIGS

During the 1830s, groups opposing Jackson united to form a new political force, the Whig Party, giving rise to the second American party system. Both the Democrats and the Whigs built party organizations throughout the nation and tried to enlarge their bases of support by eliminating the requirement of property ownership for voting. Support for the Whigs was stronger in the Northeast than in the South and West and among merchants than among small farmers. Hence, in some measure, the Whigs were the successors of the Federalists.

Who Identifies with Which Party?

Party identification varies by income, race, and gender. For example, as these statistics from 2016 show, Americans with higher incomes are more supportive of the Republican Party than are Americans with lower incomes. Women are significantly more likely than men to identify with the Democratic Party, whereas more men identify as independents.

Gender

	Republican	Independent	Democratic
Men	31%	40%	28%
Women	27%	34%	39%

Age

	Republican	Independent	Democratic
18–29	24%	41%	35%
30–49	25%	41%	34%
50–64	32%	34%	34%
65+	29%	37%	34%

Race

	Republican	Independent	Democratic
White	35%	37%	28%
Black	4%	23%	73%
Hispanic	16%	39%	46%
Asian	27%	39%	34%

Education

	Republican	Independent	Democratic
Postgraduate	24%	33%	44%
College graduate	35%	34%	31%
Some college	30%	39%	31%
High school diploma or less	26%	39%	35%

Income

	Republican	Independent	Democratic
< $20K	20%	40%	40%
$20–$40K	23%	39%	38%
$40K–$75K	31%	37%	32%
>$75K	34%	35%	32%

Republican Party

Democratic Party

★

Independent

NOTES: Percentages do not add to 100 because the category "Other/don't know" is omitted. ANES does not include rural/urban/suburban data.

SOURCE: American National Election Study 2016 time series, www.electionstudies.org (accessed 11/4/17).

FOR CRITICAL ANALYSIS

1. How do younger Americans differ from older Americans in their party identification? What is the best predictor of party identification?

2. Do you think of yourself as a Democrat, Republican, or independent? Are other Americans of your gender, age, race, and income level likely to share your references?

Yet conflict between the two parties revolved more around personalities than policies. The Whigs were a diverse group united more by opposition to the Democrats than by policies. In 1840 they won their first presidential election under the leadership of General William Henry Harrison. The Whig campaign carefully avoided issues—since the party could agree on almost none—and emphasized the personal qualities and heroism of the candidate. They also invested heavily in campaign rallies and entertainment to win the hearts, if not exactly the minds, of the voters.

During the late 1840s and early 1850s, conflicts over slavery produced sharp divisions within both the Whig and the Democratic parties. By 1856 the Whig Party had all but disintegrated under the strain, and many Whig politicians and voters, along with antislavery Democrats, joined the new Republican Party, which pledged to ban slavery from the western territories. In 1860 the Republicans nominated Abraham Lincoln for the presidency. Lincoln's victory in a four-way candidate race with less than 40 percent of the popular vote strengthened southern calls for secession from the Union and, soon thereafter, led to civil war.

THE CIVIL WAR PARTY SYSTEM

During the war, President Lincoln depended heavily on Republican governors and state legislatures to raise troops, provide funding, and maintain popular support for a long and bloody conflict. The secession of the South had stripped the Democratic Party of many supporters, but the Democrats remained politically competitive throughout the war and nearly won the 1864 presidential election. With the defeat of the Confederacy in 1865, Republicans granted the right to vote to formerly enslaved people, thus creating a large pro-Republican voting bloc. Voting rights for Blacks failed, however, because of violent resistance by southern Whites via the Ku Klux Klan.

After the war, the former Confederate states regained full control of their internal affairs and party politics. Throughout the South, African Americans were deprived of political rights, including the right to vote, despite post–Civil War constitutional guarantees to the contrary. From the end of the Civil War to the 1890s, the Republican Party remained the party of the North, with strong business and middle-class support, while the Democrats were the party of the South and of farmers, and benefited from the support of northern working-class and immigrant groups.

THE SYSTEM OF 1896: POPULISM AND REPUBLICAN RESPONSES

During the 1890s, profound and rapid social and economic changes led to the emergence of a variety of protest third parties, including the Populist Party, which won support in the South and West. The Populists appealed mainly to small farmers but also attracted western miners and urban workers. In the 1892 elections, the Populist Party

Following the Civil War, the Republican Party remained dominant in the North. This poster supporting Republican Benjamin Harrison in the 1888 election promises protective tariffs and other policies that appealed to the industrial states in the North.

carried four states in the presidential race and elected governors in eight. In 1896 the Populists effectively merged with the Democrats, who nominated William Jennings Bryan for the presidency. The Republicans nominated the conservative senator William McKinley.

In the ensuing campaign, northern and midwestern business interests made an all-out effort to defeat what they saw as a radical threat from the Populist–Democratic alliance, and the Republicans won a resounding victory, advocating for low taxes and high tariffs on imports. They carried the more heavily populated North and confined the Democrats to their smaller bases of support in the South and far West. For the next 36 years, the Republicans remained the nation's majority party, winning seven of nine presidential elections and majorities in both houses of Congress in 15 of 18 contests.[43] The Republicans favored government regulation, an expansion of voting rights, and the creation of the national bureaucracy to professionalize the work of government.

THE NEW DEAL PARTY SYSTEM: GOVERNMENT HELPS THE WORKING CLASS

Soon after Republican Herbert Hoover won the 1928 presidential election, the nation's economy collapsed. The Great Depression stemmed from a variety of causes, including high tariffs on imports, but from the perspective of the majority of voters, the Republican Party did not do enough to promote economic recovery and relief when up to a fourth of American workers were without jobs and millions were actually starving.[44] In 1932, Americans elected Democrat Franklin Delano Roosevelt (FDR) as president and a solidly Democratic Congress. Roosevelt developed a program for economic recovery that he dubbed the New Deal. The New Deal increased the size of the national government substantially, as it took responsibility for economic management and social welfare to an extent unprecedented in American history. For the first time, government took an active role in the individual lives of Americans, providing unemployment benefits, jobs, food, and more.

Roosevelt expanded the political base of the Democratic Party. He rebuilt and revitalized the party around unionized workers, upper-middle-class intellectuals and professionals, southern White farmers, Jews, Catholics, and northern African Americans—the so-called New Deal coalition that made the Democrats the nation's majority party for the next 36 years. Groping for a response, Republicans often wound up supporting popular New Deal programs such as Social Security. Even the relatively conservative administration of Dwight D. Eisenhower in the 1950s left the principal New Deal programs intact.

The New Deal coalition was severely strained during the 1960s by conflicts over civil rights and the Vietnam War. The movement for equal rights for African Americans initially divided northern Democrats, who supported it, from White southern Democrats, who defended racial segregation. As the movement launched a northern campaign aimed at equal access to jobs, education, quality public schools, and housing, northern Democrats also split, often along income lines. The Vietnam War further divided the Democrats, with upper-income Democrats strongly opposing President Lyndon Johnson's decision to greatly expand the numbers of U.S. troops fighting in Southeast Asia. These divisions provided an opportunity for the Republican Party, which recaptured the White House in 1968 under the leadership of Richard Nixon.

Richard Nixon's "southern strategy" helped broaden the Republican Party's base in the late 1960s and the 1970s by appealing to White southerners. Here, Nixon meets supporters in Georgia in 1968.

THE CONTEMPORARY AMERICAN PARTY SYSTEM

The Republican Party widened its appeal in the second half of the twentieth century. In 1964, Barry Goldwater's presidential campaign made the case for substantially lower taxation and spending, less government regulation of the economy, and the elimination of many federal social programs. Though Goldwater was defeated by Lyndon Johnson, his ideas remained major themes for the Republican Party.

Nixon appealed to southern Whites by sending subtle signals of support for their resistance to racial equality, sparking the shift that gave Republicans a strong position in all the states of the former Confederacy. The shift of White voters in the South from Democrats to Republicans in national elections was also spurred by Democratic presidents who supported the civil rights movement, including Presidents John F. Kennedy and Johnson.

During the 1980s, under President Ronald Reagan, Republicans added two additional important groups to their coalition. The first was religious conservatives, who were opposed to abortion and felt the Democrats were not protecting traditional family and religious values. The second was working-class Whites, who were drawn to Reagan's tough approach to foreign policy and opposition to affirmative action. Many Republicans consider Reagan's tenure in office as a "golden era" that saw deregulation of many industries (airlines, railroads, mail), a reduction of government intervention in the economy, and robust economic growth.

Meanwhile the Democratic Party maintained its support among a majority of unionized workers, the poor and working class, upper-middle-class professionals, and racial and ethnic minorities. The 1965 Voting Rights Act greatly increased Black voter participation in the South and helped the Democratic Party retain some southern congressional seats. The Democrats appealed to Americans concerned with economic fairness and inequality, women's rights, the environment, and other progressive social causes.

In 2000, George W. Bush united the Republican Party behind a program of tax cuts, education reform, military strength, and family values. However, Republicans fared poorly in the 2008 elections, held during the worst financial crisis since the 1930s (replaced by the economic crisis in 2020). Democrat Barack Obama, the nation's first African American president, was elected in 2008 and re-elected in 2012. He united racial and ethnic minorities, youth, and other liberals with older White moderates in a powerful national coalition, winning large popular majorities in the 2008 and 2012 elections. Obama helped the nation recover from global economic recession; reformed national health care and the financial sector; and promoted clean energy and environmental protections, labor policies, and LGBTQ rights. However, he became deeply unpopular with Republicans, who objected to what they saw as overreach by the federal government. Republicans captured both houses of Congress in 2014, and in 2016 they also won the presidency in a tight race.

During the Obama administration the Tea Party movement emerged and became a powerful conservative force in the Republican Party.[45] A number of high-profile Tea Party candidates were elected in the 2010 midterm elections after defeating several incumbents and other officially endorsed Republican candidates in primaries. In total, the Tea Party succeeded in electing about 32 percent of its candidates in 2010—a strong showing for a newly organized group—and its ideological influence in elections has continued. In reaction to the surprising election of Donald Trump and his conservative agenda, Democrats organized effectively to recruit strong candidates, increase voter turnout, and win back control of Congress in 2018 in a historic victory.

THIRD PARTIES

Although the United States has a political system dominated by two parties, it has always had more than two parties. Typically, **third parties** in the United States have represented social and economic interests that for one reason or another were not expressed by the two major parties.[46] The Populists, centered in the rural areas of the West and Midwest, and the Progressives, representing the urban middle class, are important examples in the late nineteenth and early twentieth centuries. The most successful recent third-party presidential candidate, H. Ross Perot, who ran in 1992 as an independent and in 1996 as the Reform Party's nominee, won the votes of almost one in five Americans in 1992.

Because third parties almost always lose at the national level, they exist mainly as protest movements against the two major parties or to promote specific policies. Third parties can be sources of new ideas, and they can profoundly affect elections, taking votes from one of the major parties and enabling the other to win. In the extremely close 2000 presidential election, for example, third-party candidate Ralph Nader won just 3 percent of the popular vote, but that split the Democratic vote enough to swing the election in favor of Republican George W. Bush. Leaders in both major parties fear third-party challenges in presidential elections. In the 2016 election, neither major-party candidate won a majority of the popular vote because third parties took 5 percent of it. Table 9.1 lists the top candidates in the presidential election of 2016, including the top third-party and independent candidates. Third-party candidates fared better in 2016 than in the previous three presidential elections, though the 2020 election had low third-party voting compared to 2016, and Joe Biden won a majority of the popular vote.

Third-party and independent candidacies also arise at the state and local levels. The Libertarian and Green parties in particular run candidates in many state and local elections. Independent candidates won Senate races in Maine and Vermont in 2012 and were re-elected in 2018.

third parties parties that organize to compete against the two major American political parties

Third-party candidates rarely win elections, but they can influence campaigns. In 2016, Jill Stein (left) and Gary Johnson and his vice-presidential running mate William Weld (right) ran as alternatives to the Democratic and Republican candidates. Enough votes went to Johnson and Stein that they denied Clinton and Trump from winning a majority.

TABLE 9.1

Parties and Candidates in 2016

CANDIDATE	PARTY	VOTE TOTAL	PERCENTAGE OF VOTES	ELECTORAL COLLEGE VOTES*
Hillary Clinton	Democratic	65,147,421	48%	227
Donald Trump	Republican	62,634,907	46%	304
Gary Johnson	Libertarian	4,454,855	3%	0
Jill Stein	Green	1,426,922	1%	0
Other candidates		1,047,140	0.8%	0

*As was their right, seven members of the electoral college voted for other candidates despite Trump or Clinton carrying the state.

SOURCE: U.S. Election Atlas, "2016 Presidential General Election Results," www.uselectionatlas.org/RESULTS/national.php?year=2016&minper=0&f=0&off=0&elect=0 (accessed 12/1/16).

Obstacles Facing Third Parties Third parties face overwhelming obstacles to electing their candidates in the United States. Most people assume that only candidates nominated by the two major parties have any chance of winning an election. As noted above, voters who would prefer a third-party candidate may feel compelled to vote for the major-party candidate they regard as the "lesser of two evils," to avoid wasting their votes.

The biggest barriers to third-party candidates are plurality voting rules, the single-member district system for allocating seats in Congress and most state legislatures, and the electoral college system of electing the president. In many other nations, several individuals are elected to represent each legislative district—a system more favorable to third-party candidates. Some American states do have such multiple-member districts for their legislature, but the vast majority do not. Plurality voting rules (winner receives the most votes of other candidates, but not necessarily a majority), discussed earlier in this chapter, also discourage minor parties in the United States.[47] In the proportional system used in many other countries, parties can win seats in government with only 15–20 percent of the popular vote; if the party wins 15 percent of the popular vote it gets 15 percent of the seats in Parliament.

The Influence of Third Parties Although the Republican Party was the only American third party to make itself into a major one (by replacing the Whigs), others have enjoyed an influence far beyond their electoral size. They have done so because large parts of their platform were adopted by one or both of the major parties, which wanted to appeal to the voters mobilized by the new party and thus expand their own electoral strength. The Democratic Party, for example, became stronger when it adopted most of the Progressive Party reforms in the early twentieth century. Many Socialists felt that President Franklin Roosevelt's New Deal had adopted most of their party's platform, including unemployment compensation and laws guaranteeing workers the right to organize into unions. This kind of influence explains the short lives of most third parties. Their causes are usually eliminated when the major parties adopt their policies and draw their supporters into the mainstream.

Election Reform and Third Parties In part because third parties have become increasingly common in American politics despite election rules favoring a two-party system, one-third of all winning presidential candidates since the Civil War have been elected with a plurality (more votes than any other candidate) but not a majority of the national popular vote.[48] Many people believe that two parties are not sufficient to represent the varied interests of America's 330 million people and that additional parties would make public officials more responsive to the public, and reduce party polarization.[49] Forms of proportional representation, multiple-member districts, or instant runoff (or ranked choice) voting would increase the probability of success of third parties in American politics. Another major impediment for third parties is state laws setting criteria to get on the ballot, such as registration fees or requirements that a certain number of voters sign a petition for the third-party or independent candidate. Those who favor a stronger role for third parties argue that states should make it easier to get on the ballot. Supporters of the two-party system, on the other hand, contend that it creates stability in governing.

Ranked Choice Voting An example of an election reform that may reduce party polarization and result in more centrist candidates, while also increasing opportunities for third parties, is ranked choice voting (RCV). RCV is a form of instant runoff voting that guarantees that the winner of an election has support from a majority of those voting, rather than just a plurality. Developed by an American in 1870, the ballot design is used in countries around the world, including Ireland, New Zealand, and Australia. It is also used in a growing number of American states and cities and in some states for congressional elections and 2020 presidential primaries. The idea is to give voters more choice. Rather than casting a single vote for one's preferred candidate, a voter ranks multiple candidates (usually three) from most preferred (first choice) to least preferred (third choice). If a candidate wins a majority of first-choice votes, that candidate is declared the winner, and second- and third-choice votes are not counted. But if no candidate receives a majority, the candidate with the fewest first-choice votes is eliminated, and those voters' ballots are redistributed to their second-choice candidates. The ballots are recounted; if any candidate now has a majority, a winner is declared. The process is repeated until one candidate has a majority.

Ranked choice voting eliminates the possibility that votes for a third-party candidate will be wasted, and research suggests that it leads to more civility in campaigns and to cooperation among candidates who seek to be a voter's second choice if they cannot be a first choice.[50] There is evidence that ranked choice voting could lead to the emergence of more parties and would thus reduce party polarization, as candidates would have an incentive to moderate their positions and appeal to voters for second- and third-place votes. Successful local experiments in election reform may open the doors to more use of this process at the state or even national level.

Political Parties: What Do You Think?

Parties provide an important opportunity for citizen participation in American government. They help to crystallize a world of possible government actions into a set of distinct choices. In so doing, they make it easier for ordinary citizens to understand politics, evaluate candidates, and make their own choices. They are also important to the health of the democracy. The presence of an opposition party is an important check on those in power. And competition among the political parties gives citizens an incentive to vote and politicians an incentive to get them to vote.[51]

★ How have changes from the advent of primary elections decades ago to the more recent digital revolution altered party politics? What would Keli Carender, featured at the start of the chapter, say about the possibilities for citizen influence?

★ Is party polarization likely to remain high in the near future? Is this a problem? What rules or processes, if any, could reduce party polarization?

★ Is the two-party system ideal for American politics, or would electoral reforms encourage more parties to form and, hence, more choice for voters?

★ STUDY GUIDE ★

What Are Political Parties?

> **Explain how political parties form and change (pp. 307–10)**

A political party is an organization that seeks to influence the government by nominating and successfully electing party members to public office. Although some people believe that today's parties are too polarized to adequately represent all Americans, parties are extremely important to the functioning of a democracy because they can increase participation in politics, provide a central cue for citizens to cast informed votes, and organize the business of legislatures and governing. While the particular parties have changed over time, the United States has had a two-party system since the 1780s. Today, America's two major parties are the Democrats and the Republicans.

Key Terms

political parties (p. 307)

partisanship (p. 307)

two-party system (p. 309)

Duverger's law (p. 310)

Practice Quiz

1. A political party is different from an interest group in that a political party
   a) seeks to control the government by nominating candidates and electing its members to office.
   b) is constitutionally exempt from taxation.
   c) is entirely nonprofit.
   d) has a much larger membership.
   e) has a much smaller membership.

2. The congressional election system in the United States is called "first past the post" because
   a) candidates must win both a primary election and a general election before taking office.
   b) seats in the House of Representatives and Senate are allocated to political parties based on their share of the total votes cast in the election.
   c) the candidate with the most votes wins even if she did not win a majority of the total.
   d) a candidate can win an election only if he wins a majority of the total vote.
   e) more Americans now vote by mail than at their local polling places.

3. Duverger's law holds that plurality voting rules with single-member districts will result in
   a) ideologically polarized parties.
   b) a system that favors small parties.
   c) a one-party system.
   d) a two-party system.
   e) a system that favors populist candidates.

Parties and Elections

> **Describe political party organizations and the roles they play in elections (pp. 310–17)**

Because parties succeed when they win elections, parties have a large role in recruiting candidates, coordinating campaigns, mobilizing voters, and raising money. Party organizations exist at virtually every level of government in the United States, and they play an important role in structuring electoral competition. At the national level, for example, party organizations give candidates money for their campaigns and assemble national conventions to formalize the parties' nominations for president and vice president. Similarly, at the state and local levels, party organizations play an important role in recruiting candidates, registering voters, and funding candidate campaigns and "party-building" activities.

Key Terms

nomination (p. 311)

primary elections (p. 311)

caucus (political) (p. 311)

micro-targeting (p. 312)

party organization (p. 314)

national convention (p. 315)

platform (p. 315)

party machines (p. 316)

patronage (p. 316)

Practice Quiz

4. The practice of tailoring campaign messages to individuals in small, specialized groups is referred to as
   a) indexing.
   b) micro-targeting.
   c) winnowing.
   d) external mobilization.
   e) internal mobilization.

5. Which of the following is *not* confirmed at a party's national convention?
   a) the party's candidate for president
   b) the party's candidate for vice president
   c) the party's platform or statement of policy positions
   d) the congressional committees to which party representatives will be assigned
   e) the rules governing party procedures

6. Super PACs
   a) were outlawed by the 2002 Bipartisan Campaign Reform Act.
   b) are ineligible for tax-exempt status under Section 527 of the Internal Revenue Code.
   c) are campaign fundraising organizations legally affiliated with the Democratic National Committee only.
   d) are prohibited from running advertisements during election campaigns.
   e) can raise and spend unlimited amounts of money as long as their activities are not coordinated with those of formal party organizations or the candidates.

7. The strength of traditional party machines depended most heavily on
   a) patronage.
   b) primary elections.
   c) progressive reforms.
   d) support from national committees.
   e) merit-based civil service.

Parties in Government

Explain how parties organize government and influence policy making (pp. 317–20)

Political parties can make significant changes to public policy, and the sharp ideological divisions between Democrats and Republicans on key issues mean that election outcomes are directly related to the kinds of laws that government enacts. While divisions between parties are important, the divisions within parties are significant as well; party leaders must always work to keep the different factions within their parties focused on shared goals. Many of the most important organizational features and characteristics of Congress, such as the role of the House Speaker, the prevalence of party-line voting, and the strength of the committee system, also depend on the party system.

Key Terms

policy entrepreneur (p. 317)

majority party (p. 320)

minority party (p. 320)

Practice Quiz

8. By developing issues and programs that will expand their party's base of support, party leaders can act as
   a) whips.
   b) convention delegates.
   c) patrons.
   d) policy entrepreneurs.
   e) party activists.

9. Which of the following best describes the role of factions within the major parties?
   a) Factions do not exist; party members largely agree about all issues in a party's platform.
   b) Parties are usually divided into no more than two factions: one liberal and one conservative.
   c) Factions exist within parties because parties are coalitions of people who represent many diverse interests.
   d) Factions are relevant only during elections; they are not relevant among officials who have already been elected.
   e) Factions nearly always result in major parties being split up into smaller parties.

10. Which of the following features of the House of Representatives is determined by a vote of the whole membership?
    a) the assignments of individual members to particular committees
    b) advancement up the committee ladder
    c) the ability of individual members to transfer from one committee to another
    d) the use of the seniority system for determining committee chairs
    e) selection of the Speaker of the House

Party Identification

Identify the reasons for and sources of party identification and increased party polarization (pp. 320–30)

Party identification refers to the attachments people have to one of the political parties. Although it is partly an emotional attachment, party identification also has a rational component; voters generally form attachments to the party that reflects their views and interests. In contemporary American politics, a wide variety of group characteristics, including race and ethnicity, gender, religion, ideology, region, and age, are associated with an individual's party identification. Party loyalties in the United States have become polarized and occasionally hostile. Political divisions are no longer just about policy disagreements; increasingly, they reflect in-group biases and social group identities, accompanied by negative feelings toward members of the other party.

Key Terms

party identification (p. 320)

party activists (p. 323)

gender gap (p. 324)

party polarization (p. 329)

Practice Quiz

11. Which of the following social groups usually votes for Republicans?
    a) women
    b) nonwhite racial and ethnic groups
    c) people with college degrees
    d) organized labor
    e) the very wealthy

12. How are electoral districts related to party polarization?
    a) Most lawmakers come from highly contested districts, so they must campaign on hard-line liberal or conservative issues to attract voters.
    b) Most lawmakers come from districts with clear majorities of Democratic or Republican constituents, so those elected to Congress can be strong partisans.
    c) Levels of party polarization tend to decrease every 10 years, once districts are redrawn.
    d) Ranked choice–voting rules in certain electoral districts tend to favor strong partisans.
    e) Districts that are uneven in population size tend to produce strong partisans; larger-population districts vote Democratic, and smaller-population districts vote Republican.

Party Systems

Describe the history of U.S. party systems and the influence of third parties (pp. 330–39)

Party system refers to the organization of parties within a country, the dominant form of campaigning, the main issues that divide the parties, the balance of power between and within party coalitions, and the parties' social bases. Over the course of American history, changes in political forces and alignments have produced six distinct party systems. One distinguishing feature of the contemporary American party system is party polarization between Democrats and Republicans; Democrats are strongly liberal and Republicans are strongly conservative. Although third parties have occasionally (though profoundly) influenced election outcomes and placed new ideas on the political agenda, numerous structural factors limit their success.

Key Terms

third parties (p. 337)

Practice Quiz

13. Which party was formed in the 1830s in opposition to Andrew Jackson's presidency?
    a) American Independent
    b) Federalist
    c) Jeffersonian Republican
    d) Democratic
    e) Whig

14. The so-called New Deal coalition was severely strained
    a) during the 1860s by conflicts over slavery and southern secession.
    b) during the 1890s by conflicts over the gold standard.
    c) during the 1930s by conflicts over the Great Depression and America's involvement in World War II.
    d) during the 1960s by conflicts over civil rights and the Vietnam War.
    e) during the 1990s by conflicts over abortion and affirmative action.

15. Why might voters who prefer a third-party candidate vote for the major-party candidate whom they regard as the "lesser of two evils"?
    a) They want to avoid "wasting" their vote on a candidate who they know is not likely to win.
    b) Third-party votes are not counted in presidential elections.
    c) Voting for the major-party candidate is a key component of ranked choice voting.
    d) They want their vote to act as a "spoiler" that helps split the vote for the other major-party candidate.
    e) They want to avoid voting a straight ticket.

★ *chapter* ★

10

Campaigns and Elections

WHAT GOVERNMENT DOES AND WHY IT MATTERS Elections are the core of any democracy. In a democratic system like the United States, citizens self-govern by choosing among candidates and electing leaders to represent them in government. The rules of elections affect who runs, how they run, who votes, and who wins.

As you will see in this chapter, one concern with elections in America is that running for office and donating to campaigns is concentrated among the affluent and well connected. Voters in the city of Seattle decided to try an experiment to open up politics to more participants. In 2015 they approved

a ballot initiative creating the Seattle Democracy Voucher Program. The city sends residents four $25 vouchers that they can donate to candidates running for city council. The program is funded by an increase in the local property tax.

The Democracy Voucher Program has succeeded in encouraging new types of candidates. Pat Murakami, an IT professional, had lived in Seattle for 40 years and had served on various school- and community-related associations, but decided to run for city council only because of the vouchers. "I never would have attempted to run" without them, she said. In 2017 they made up 90 percent of her funding, and

In 2019, Seattle city council candidate Shaun Scott was able to use the Seattle Democracy Voucher Program to help publicly fund his campaign. Though he ultimately lost the election, these programs aim to enable candidates of all economic statuses and backgrounds to run successful campaigns for public office.

she managed to win the primary election. Although she lost the general election, she was heartened enough to run again in 2019. "I would have been a complete non-contender without the program," she said.[1] Other new candidates from a variety of backgrounds have been inspired by the program as well. Teresa Mosqueda, a first-time candidate in 2017, was a renter paying off student loans.[2] Shaun Scott, a 2019 candidate, described himself on Twitter as a "Black working-class Millennial candidate with a net worth of approximately $10,000. If it weren't for the democracy voucher program, running for office would be a pipe dream."[3]

The program appears to have boosted voter interest and turnout as well. A University of Washington study found that residents who had voted in fewer than half of local elections before 2017 were four times more likely to vote in 2017 if they had used their vouchers. But the program is not without its hiccups. In the first year, some people thought the vouchers were junk mail. The city ran a commercial with a talking dog to remind people what they were: "That's my human. She's looking for Democracy Vouchers. But she's not going to find them because I ate them." In its early years, the program had high administrative costs as well. But it survived a court challenge, with the Washington State Supreme Court affirming that the program does not violate First Amendment rights, as the plaintiffs, who objected to the property tax increase, alleged.[4] (Many observers expect the case to go to the U.S. Supreme Court.)

Seattle is not alone in attempting to increase electoral participation. Since 2015, city and county governments around the country have enacted at least eight public campaign-finance programs, and many states have enacted same-day voter-registration laws. Of the 10 states with the highest average voting rates, 7 offer same-day registration.[5]

In this chapter, we will learn about how elections work in the United States and how electoral rules and other considerations influence campaign strategy and turnout. We will see how election laws, the candidates' campaigns, and voters' choices determined the outcome of the 2020 presidential and congressional elections, and thus determined who represents the American people in government.

CHAPTER GOALS

★ Describe the major rules and types of elections in the United States (pp. 347–60)

★ Explain strategies campaigns use to win elections (pp. 360–69)

★ Identify the rules that govern campaign fundraising and spending (pp. 369–72)

★ Identify the major factors that influence voters' decisions (pp. 373–75)

★ Analyze the strategies, issues, and outcomes of the 2020 elections (pp. 375–89)

Elections in America

In the United States, elections usually occur on fixed dates. Presidential elections take place every four years and congressional elections every two years, both on the first Tuesday after the first Monday in November. Congressional elections that do not coincide with a presidential election are called **midterm elections**. Localities and states can choose when to hold their elections. Most Americans have the opportunity to vote in several elections each year. Voting in elections is the most common form of participation in American politics, and elections are central to democratic government.

THE BASIC RULES OF THE GAME FOR U.S. ELECTIONS

In the American federal system, the responsibility for running elections is decentralized, resting largely with state and local governments. Elections are administered by state, county, and city election boards, which are responsible for establishing and staffing polling places, processing mail-in ballots, and verifying the eligibility of voters. State laws influence who may vote, how they vote, and where they vote. For example, states decide whether to require photo identification to vote and whether to allow residents to vote by mail, to vote in person before Election Day, and to register to vote and then vote on the same day. Sixteen states have approved automatic voter registration (AVR), making voter registration "opt-out" instead of "opt-in." Eligible citizens who interact with government agencies (e.g., the department of motor vehicles), are registered to vote or have their existing registration information updated, unless they decline.

Election season begins with **primary elections**, which in most states are held to select each party's candidates for the **general election**. (A few states have "top two primaries," in which candidates from all parties run against one another and

midterm elections congressional elections that do not coincide with a presidential election; also called *off-year elections*

primary elections elections held to select a party's candidate for the general election

general election a regularly scheduled election involving most districts in the nation or state, in which voters select officeholders; in the United States, general elections for national office and most state and local offices are held on the first Tuesday after the first Monday in November in even-numbered years (every four years for presidential elections)

Elections are the most important way that Americans participate in politics. Some of the rules of elections have changed over time. (Left) African Americans vote for the first time in Wilcox County, Alabama, after the passage of the Voting Rights Act in 1965. (Right) An 18-year-old woman registers to vote in Illinois after the Twenty-Sixth Amendment in 1971 lowered the nationwide voting age from 21 to 18.

then the two who get the most votes face each other in the general election.) Used for offices at the national, state, and often local levels, primary elections are thus usually races where Democrats compete against Democrats and Republicans against Republicans.

The United States is one of the few nations to hold primary elections. In most countries, nominations of candidates are controlled completely by party officials, as they once were in the United States. Primary elections were introduced at the turn of the twentieth century by Progressive Era reformers who hoped to weaken the power of party leaders by enabling voters to pick candidates directly (see Chapter 9). In states with **closed primaries**, only registered members of a political party may vote in a primary election to select that party's candidates, and independents do not get to participate. States with **open primaries** allow all registered voters, including independents, to choose which party's primary they will participate in.

WHAT IT TAKES TO WIN—WINNER TAKE ALL

On the surface, the basic idea of how an election works may seem simple: voters select their preferred candidate on the ballot, votes are counted, and the candidate with the most votes wins the election. But while we take this system for granted in the United States, there are actually three different ways that winners are determined in countries using democratic elections.

In some countries, a candidate must receive an absolute majority (50 percent plus one) of all the votes cast to win the election. This type of electoral system is called a **majority system**. Majority systems usually include a provision for a **runoff election** between the two top finishers because if several candidates are competing, there is little chance that one will win a majority in the first round. (Ranked choice voting, as used in the state of Maine, is a form of instant runoff election that guarantees that the winner has a majority of the votes. See Chapter 9.)

In some other countries, including the United States in most elections, the candidate who receives the most votes wins the election regardless of whether he or she has a majority of votes cast (50 percent plus one). A candidate receiving even 30 percent of the vote can win if no other candidate receives more. This type of electoral system is called a **plurality system**, and its rules are commonly referred to as single-district "winner take all." In the 2016 Republican primaries, for example, Donald Trump was frequently referred to by the media as the winner, but in most states he won only around 35 percent of the vote because there were three or more candidates in the race. (Trump also did not win a majority of the popular vote in the general election.)

For legislative elections, most democratic countries use a third type of electoral system, called **proportional representation**. Under proportional rules, each political party is awarded legislative seats in rough proportion to the overall percentage of votes that it wins. For example, a party that wins 30 percent of the total national vote will receive roughly 30 percent of the seats in the national legislature.

Proportional representation benefits smaller parties such as the Green Party, Libertarian Party, or far-right populist parties, because it usually allows a party to win legislative seats with fewer votes than would be required under a majority or plurality system. A party that wins 10 percent of the national vote might win 10 percent of the seats. In the United States, by contrast, a party that wins 10 percent of the vote would probably win no seats in Congress. Because they give small parties little chance of success, plurality and majority systems tend to reduce the number

closed primary a primary election in which voters can participate in the nomination of candidates but only of the party in which they are enrolled for a period of time prior to primary day

open primary a primary election in which the voter can wait until the day of the primary to choose which party to enroll in to select candidates for the general election

majority system a type of electoral system in which, to win a seat in the parliament or other representative body, a candidate must receive a majority of all the votes cast in the relevant district

runoff election a "second-round" election in which voters choose between the top two candidates from the first round

plurality system a type of electoral system in which, to win a seat in the parliament or other representative body, a candidate need only receive the most votes in the election, not necessarily a majority of the votes cast

proportional representation a multiple-member district system that allows each political party representation in proportion to its percentage of the total vote

of political parties that can hold power. This is one of the reasons that the United States has only two significant parties (see Chapter 9 for more on the two-party system in the United States).

THE BALLOT

Before the 1890s voters cast ballots according to political parties. Each party printed its own ballots, which listed only its own candidates for each office, and employed party workers to distribute them at the polls. Because voters had to choose which party's ballot to use, it was very difficult for a voter to cast anything other than a **straight-ticket vote**, selecting candidates from the same party for all offices on the ballot.

The introduction of a neutral and secret ballot at the turn of the twentieth century was a significant change in election rules. The new ballot—called the Australian ballot or long-form ballot—was prepared and administered by the government rather than the political parties. Each ballot was identical and included the names of all candidates (from all parties) running for each office. This reform made it possible for voters to make their choices on the merits of the individual candidates rather than the overall party and also to have their choices be private (not known to party leaders). They also cast their ballot in secret, instead of using a public ballot where others could know how an individual voted.

This change gave rise to frequent split-ticket voting, where voters may, for example, vote for a Democrat for senator and a Republican for governor. Today, however, split-ticket voting in national elections is far less common than it was in the 1970s and '80s; most people now cast straight-ticket ballots or at least vote for the same party's candidates for Congress and president.[6]

In the United States, it is the state and county governments, not the federal government, that run elections and create ballots. Some counties still use paper ballots, but most now use computerized electronic voting systems. The controversial 2000 presidential election led to a closer look at different ballot forms and voting systems used across the 3,000 U.S. counties. In 2000 the margin of victory for Republican George W. Bush over Democrat Al Gore in Florida was so small that the state ordered a recount. Careful examination of the results revealed that the punch card voting machines and "butterfly ballot" used in Florida had led to many voting and counting errors.

straight-ticket voting selecting candidates from the same political party for all offices on the ballot

Ballots have changed dramatically over the years. In 2000 the configuration of the "butterfly" ballot (left) caused confusion in a key county in the swing state of Florida. This contested election led to the passage of the Help America Vote Act, which required states to upgrade their voting procedures. Many increased their use of computerized voting machines (right).

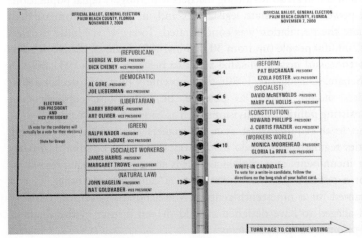

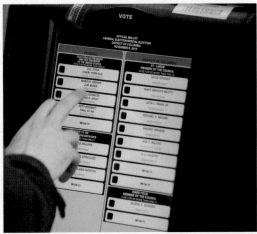

In the wake of this election, Congress adopted the Help America Vote Act (HAVA) in 2003, requiring the states to use computerized voter-registration databases. Critics of HAVA feared that such systems might be vulnerable to unauthorized use, or hacking. In 2016, 21 states experienced intrusion by Russian hackers into their computerized election systems, although to date there is no evidence that ballots were changed. In Illinois, for example, hackers viewed 300,000 active Illinois voter-registration records (including names, addresses, birth dates, and voting history) but were unable to modify the data.[7] In the past, computerized voting machines generally worked well and significantly updated America's election system, but all computerized systems have vulnerabilities. Protecting state and county election systems from hackers is a new priority for reform.

LEGISLATIVE ELECTIONS AND ELECTORAL DISTRICTS

The boundaries for some elected offices are straightforward: all eligible U.S. citizens 18 years or older may vote for president; all eligible residents of a state may vote for that state's governor and two U.S. senators. Other legislators, such as members of the U.S. House of Representatives and state lawmakers, are elected from geographic districts whose boundaries are drawn by state governments—either legislatures or independent commissions or state courts. The boundaries for congressional and state legislative districts are redrawn every 10 years to reflect population changes, as determined by the U.S. census. The process of redrawing district boundaries is called **redistricting**. The geographic shape of legislative district boundaries is influenced by several factors, including population size and existing government boundaries such as counties, as well as the partisanship of the people who live in the districts.

Federal court decisions have played a major role in how legislative districts are drawn. In the 1962 landmark case *Baker v. Carr*, the Supreme Court ruled that federal courts can intervene on this issue. In a series of decisions in 1963 and 1964, the Court held that within each state, districts for Congress and the state legislature must include roughly equal populations so as to accord with the principle of "one person, one vote."[8] Prior to these decisions, many state legislative districts were simply county boundaries, with each county electing one representative regardless of its population. This meant that rural areas had far more elected officials than urban areas. Requiring districts with roughly equal populations shifted political power, both in state legislatures and in Congress, from rural to urban areas, where the population was concentrated. Today, U.S. House districts average roughly 700,000 people (up from 30,000 in 1800). State legislative districts vary from a few thousand people in some states to nearly a million (931,000) in the California Senate. During the 1980s the Supreme Court also declared that legislative districts should, insofar as possible, be contiguous, compact, and consistent with existing political subdivisions such as counties or townships.[9]

Despite these legal requirements, state lawmakers responsible for drawing district boundaries regularly seek to do it in a way that favors one political party over another, or incumbents over challengers. This strategy of drawing legislative districts to favor a political party or incumbents is called **gerrymandering**. Gerrymandering is named for a nineteenth-century Massachusetts governor, Elbridge Gerry, who was alleged to have designed an odd-shaped district in the shape of a salamander to promote his party's interests.[10]

redistricting the process of redrawing election districts and redistributing legislative representatives; this happens every 10 years, to reflect shifts in population or in response to legal challenges in existing districts

gerrymandering the apportionment of voters in districts in such a way as to give unfair advantage to one racial or ethnic group or political party

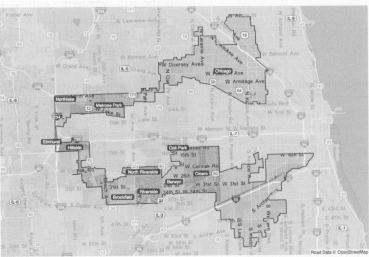

The original gerrymander was a districting plan attributed to the Massachusetts governor Elbridge Gerry (1744–1814) that had the shape of a salamander. This practice continues today across the country, as seen here in the odd shape of Illinois's 4th Congressional District, which was drawn to create a majority Latino district.

The principle behind gerrymandering is simple: distributing a party's voters differently across geographically defined districts can produce different electoral results. For example, by dispersing the party's voters across multiple districts, gerrymandering can dilute their voting power and prevent the party from electing a representative in any district. This technique is known as "cracking." Alternatively, by concentrating the party's voters in as few districts as possible, gerrymandering can try to ensure that the party cannot elect representatives in other districts, a technique called "packing."

Gerrymandering has created many "safe" districts in Congress and state legislatures where incumbents rarely face a serious challenger in the primaries or general election. This pattern helps to explain why members of Congress are so often re-elected in landslides. In 2018, 93 percent of House members won re-election.[11] A lack of serious challengers to incumbents raises the risk that legislators will become so secure in their positions that they no longer represent the broad public interest but instead make laws that benefit narrow special interests or only members of their political party. To address this problem and the increasing partisan divisions that may result, some states use nonpartisan redistricting boards or commissions for whom the partisan distribution of voters is not considered in drawing district boundaries.

As it has become more open and extreme in recent years, **partisan gerrymandering** has become increasingly controversial, with critics charging that it goes against the principle of "one person, one vote." Its defenders argue that the process of legislative districting is by nature political and that there is no agreed-upon standard for too much partisan tilt in these decisions. The controversy has found its way into the courts. Legislative districts drawn by the Republican state legislature in Pennsylvania, for example, were ruled unconstitutional in 2018 because of gerrymandering. The U.S. Supreme Court took up the matter in *Gill v. Whitford*, in which Democratic voters of a Wisconsin district sued to overturn the allegedly gerrymandered state district map.[12] In June 2018 the Court unanimously agreed to send the case back to the district court, delaying Supreme Court action on partisan gerrymandering. While the Court has ruled that extreme partisan gerrymandering can be unconstitutional, it has not yet agreed on how to measure and define it.

partisan gerrymandering occurs when politicians from one party intentionally manipulate the boundaries for legislative election districts to disadvantage their political opponents' chance of winning an election and advantage their own political party

FOR CRITICAL ANALYSIS

How do district boundaries affect elections for the U.S. House and state legislatures? Should districts be drawn based on partisan considerations or on other criteria?

In the late twentieth century, the federal government often supported the creation of congressional districts made up primarily of minority group members, a practice intended to increase the number of African Americans and Latinos elected to public office in accordance with the 1965 Voting Rights Act. Beginning with the 1993 case of *Shaw v. Reno*, however, the Supreme Court has generally opposed efforts to force states to create such **majority-minority districts**.[13] The Court has asserted that districting based exclusively on race or ethnicity is unlawful. However, most majority-minority districts occur naturally in states and geographic areas with large minority populations. Most African Americans in Congress, for example, are elected from districts with a majority of African American voters.

PRESIDENTIAL ELECTIONS

Presidential elections follow unique rules because the president and vice president are the only public officials elected by all American voters (though they are technically elected by the electoral college). Moreover, presidential candidates from the two major parties are officially nominated at the parties' national conventions, following a series of state-by-state primary elections and caucuses to select delegates to the conventions. While primary elections are also used to select candidates in congressional and other types of elections, the national convention delegate system for nominating candidates is unique to presidential elections.

Nominating Presidential Candidates: Primaries and Caucuses Before the presidential election every four years, the major parties start the process of selecting their presidential candidates by holding primary elections and caucuses. Most states hold primaries, but some use caucuses.

Caucuses are party business meetings. At the lowest level, precinct caucuses are meetings of registered voters of the same party within a local geographic area. Each state has thousands of precinct caucuses, whose purpose is to elect delegates supporting particular candidates to county caucuses. The county caucuses in turn elect delegates to represent their preferences at district caucuses, and the district caucuses elect delegates to the state party convention, where delegates to the national convention are chosen. Delegates to the national conventions choose the party's presidential candidate. If members of a Democratic precinct caucus prefer Bernie Sanders for president, for example, the delegates representing that precinct at the county, district, and state caucuses would continue to cast votes for Sanders. Compared with primary elections, caucuses give party leaders and activists a larger role in selecting candidates for public office. (In 2020 many fewer states held caucuses because of rule changes by the Democratic Party that required states to give voters the option of absentee voting, which is easier to do in a primary election than an in-person caucus.)

The Iowa caucuses and the New Hampshire primary are especially famous, Iowa being the first state to vote in the presidential nomination every four years and New Hampshire being the second. The Nevada caucus is the third and the South Carolina primary the fourth. Campaigns in these early, small-population states make heavy use of **retail politics**, where candidates spend a great deal of time in the state meeting with voters face-to-face, such as at rallies and town halls. There's an advantage to presidential nominations beginning in smaller-population states because candidates don't have to have millions of dollars to run national TV ads.

majority-minority district an electoral district, such as a congressional district, in which the majority of the constituents belong to racial or ethnic minorities

retail politics a style of campaigning where candidates connect to voters face-to-face at intimate gatherings, rallies, town halls, and local events

Campaigning for early primaries and caucuses typically involves grassroots politics, with candidates attempting to connect directly with citizens. Here, 2020 presidential candidate Pete Buttigieg speaks to potential voters at a panadería in Denison, Iowa.

Like general elections, early primaries and caucuses tend to be highly contested, with high levels of national media coverage, candidate campaign ads, and intensive voter-mobilization drives. For primaries and caucuses in later, larger-population states, campaigns typically have raised enough money to rely on national campaign ads to reach voters, and retail politics is less common.

The primaries and caucuses traditionally begin in January or February of a presidential election year and end in June, with state elections roughly every two weeks. Iowa and New Hampshire's disproportionate role in picking presidential candidates is due to their being the first states to cast votes. In fact, the presidential nomination process today has become "front-loaded," with states vying to increase their political influence by holding their primaries or caucuses earlier in the year. Early voting states are important because they can help candidates gain momentum by securing national media attention, campaign contributions, and higher ratings in public-opinion polls. Candidates who perform well in Iowa, New Hampshire, Nevada, or South Carolina send signals to voters in later voting states that they are viable (can win the nomination) and electable (can win the general election). A candidate who fares poorly in these early voting states may be written off as a loser and drop out of the race.

In 2016, Donald Trump and Bernie Sanders beat expectations by both placing second in the Iowa caucuses and first in the New Hampshire primary. These early successes helped solidify Trump's campaign for the Republican nomination and indicated that Sanders would be a viable rival of Hillary Clinton throughout the Democratic nominating process. One study found that the change in media coverage that candidates receive between the periods before and after the Iowa caucuses predicts how large a share of the vote they will receive in the New Hampshire primary and in later primaries nationwide.[14] This study suggests that it is not winning the Iowa caucuses that matters but doing better than expected by the national media. For example, if Barack Obama had not won the Iowa caucuses in 2008, unexpectedly beating presumed Democratic front-runner Hillary Clinton, most commentators believe he would not have gone on to capture the Democratic nomination. Similarly, Republican candidate Donald Trump fared much better than political elites and the media expected by placing second in the Iowa caucuses and first in the New Hampshire primary in 2016. In an era of social media, media coverage of early nominating events is even greater than before and may further increase the importance of states holding early primaries and caucuses.[15]

In the 2020 Democratic primary, Pete Buttigieg and Bernie Sanders tied for first place in the Iowa caucuses, while Sanders went on to win the New Hampshire primary. Historically, winning Iowa and New Hampshire would have helped deliver the Democratic nomination to the winner of those states. But other early voting states can also be critical to candidate fortunes. Despite a poor showing in the Iowa caucuses and New Hampshire primary, Joe Biden went on to the win the South Carolina primary with strong support from African American voters. After the South Carolina primary, many prominent Democratic challengers endorsed Biden. Facing the COVID-19 public health crisis, with most of the nation living under stay-at-home orders that closed schools and businesses, Biden's last opponent, Bernie Sanders, dropped out of the race in April, leaving Biden as the 2020 Democratic presidential candidate.

The result of each state's primary election or caucuses determines how its **delegates** will vote at their party's national convention. As noted in Chapter 9, the Democratic Party requires that state presidential primaries allocate delegates on the basis of proportional representation; Democratic candidates win delegates in rough proportion to their percentage of the primary vote. The Republican Party does not require proportional representation, but many state Republican parties do now use it. A few still use the winner-take-all system, by which the candidate with the most votes wins all the party's delegates in that state. When the primaries and caucuses are concluded, it is usually clear which candidates have won their parties' nominations.

Nominating Presidential Candidates: Party Conventions For more than 50 years after America's Founding, presidential nominations were controlled by each party's congressional caucus—all the party's members in the House and the Senate. Critics referred to this process as "King Caucus" and charged that it did not fairly represent the views of party members throughout the nation. Thus, the King Caucus process was replaced by the system of national party conventions. As it developed over the next century, the convention became the decisive institution in the presidential nominating processes of the two major parties.

Composed of delegates from each state who pledge loyalty to different presidential candidates, the convention was a deliberative body in which party elites argued, negotiated, and eventually chose a single candidate to support. The size of a state's delegation depended on the state's population, and each delegate was allowed one vote for the purpose of nominating the party's presidential and vice-presidential candidates. Between the 1830s and World War II, delegates to the national conventions were selected by a state's party leaders. These individuals were public officials, political activists, and party notables from all regions of the state, representing most major party factions.

Over time, reformers came to view the convention as a symbol of rule by party elites and the affluent. Around the turn of the twentieth century, many states adopted direct primary elections to choose convention delegates, enabling average citizens to have a voice in picking their president. As we saw earlier in this chapter, today the nomination is determined in a series of primary elections and caucuses held in all the states and U.S. territories prior to the party's national convention. These elections determine how each state's convention delegates

FOR CRITICAL ANALYSIS

Is it fair that two relatively small states (in terms of population) such as Iowa and New Hampshire should have such outsize influence in picking presidents?

delegate a representative who votes according to the preferences of his or her constituency

Although the party's nominees for the president and vice president are officially announced at the party conventions, they are actually selected much earlier through caucuses and primary elections.

will vote. Candidates usually arrive at the convention knowing who has enough delegate support in hand to assure a victory in the first round of balloting. If one candidate does not win a majority in the first round, a second ballot is issued, and delegates can choose to vote for a different candidate.

In addition to delegates chosen in primaries and caucuses and bound to the voting results there, the Democratic Party also designates a number of party leaders as so-called superdelegates, who can vote as they wish. At the 2016 Democratic National Convention, most superdelegates backed Hillary Clinton, giving her a significant advantage over her opponent and independent Bernie Sanders, despite Sanders's strong support among voters. The Republican Party does not use superdelegates, and their use is increasingly controversial among Democrats. In 2020 Democrats reduced the power of superdelegates so they vote only if no candidate wins a majority of regular delegates in the first round of convention voting.

Even though the party convention usually does not control presidential nominations, it still has a number of important tasks. The convention makes the rules concerning delegate selection and future presidential primary elections. In 1972, for example, the Democratic Party adopted rules requiring convention delegates to be broadly representative of the party's membership in terms of race and gender. Another important task for the convention is the drafting of a **party platform**, a statement of principles and pledges around which the delegates can unite.

party platform a party document, written at a national convention, that contains party philosophy, principles, and policy positions

Most important, the convention allows the party to showcase its candidates in anticipation of the general election. Before a large national audience, with television cameras rolling, the presidential and vice-presidential nominees deliver acceptance speeches that begin their formal general-election campaign and provide them an opportunity to make a positive impression on voters.

Picking Presidents: The Electoral College As noted earlier, the presidential election differs from other elections in an important way: voters do *not* directly elect the president. Long ago, countries would often use indirect elections in which voters chose the members of an intermediate group (i.e., a nominating committee) who

Selecting an Executive

The United States is somewhat distinct from other democracies on two dimensions. First, the United States has a combined head of state and head of government in the person of the president. Second, the United States indirectly elects this head of state through the electoral college. While there are other democracies that do each of these things, the United States is unique in that it does both.

1. Some countries have presidents or monarchs in ceremonial head-of-state roles while the day-to-day governing is run by a prime minister as head of government. Why might a country want to have a separate head of government and head of state? What benefits do you think might come from having the two roles united in the same person?

2. Why do we describe America's electoral college system as an indirect selection method? As you can see, several other democracies also indirectly select their head of state. What kinds of systems do you think they might use?

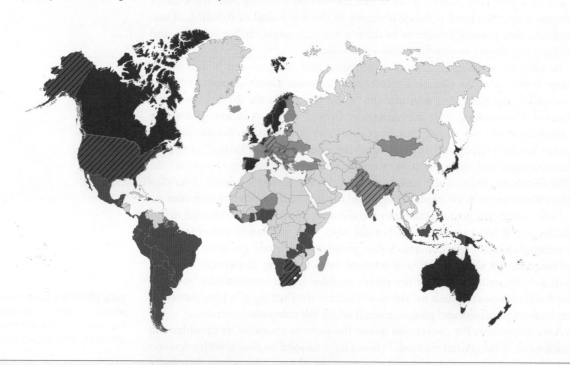

- ■ Combined head of state and head of government, elected directly
- ■ Separate head of state and head of government, elected directly
- ■ Separately elected head of government and hereditary monarch
- ■ Combined head of state and head of government, elected indirectly
- ▨ Separate head of state and head of government, elected indirectly
- ■ Nondemocratic countries

SOURCE: "U.S. among Few Democracies That Indirectly Elect Combined Head of State/Government," Pew Research Center, www.pewresearch.org/fact-tank/2016/11/22/among-democracies-u-s-stands-out-in-how-it-chooses-its-head-of-state/ft_16-11-21_headsofstate_map/ (accessed 2/21/20).

would, in turn, actually select public officials. The last vestige of this procedure in the United States is the **electoral college**, the group of electors who formally select the president and vice president. No other country in the world uses an electoral college to pick its president.

electoral college the presidential electors from each state who meet after the general election to cast ballots for president and vice president

When Americans vote for president, then, they are technically not voting directly for candidates, even though they mark ballots as such; they are instead choosing among slates of electors selected by each party in the state and pledged, if elected, to support that party's presidential candidate. Electors are allocated to each state based on the size of its congressional delegation (senators plus House members). North Dakota, for example, has 3 votes in the electoral college (based on its 2 senators plus 1 representative), while California has 55 (2 senators plus 53 representatives). Each elector in North Dakota (a state with roughly 770,000 people) represents roughly 253,000 people in 2019, while each elector in California (39.5 million people) represents 718,000. Because of this, the electoral college is biased against large-population states and overrepresents small-population states. Under the electoral college, one vote in California is worth about one third of a vote in North Dakota.

The president of the United States is the winner of the electoral college—the candidate who wins at least 270 of the college's 538 votes—and not necessarily the candidate with the most popular votes, or votes from the people. This is in part because the electoral college and most elections in the United States are governed by plurality, winner-take-all rules. With only two exceptions, each state awards *all* of its electors to the candidate who receives the most votes in the state.[16] Thus, in 2020, Biden received all 16 of Georgia's electoral votes, though he won only 49 percent of the votes in the state.

Since electoral votes are won on a state-by-state basis, it is mathematically possible for a candidate who receives the most popular votes nationwide to fail to carry enough states for their electoral votes to add up to a majority. This has happened four times. In 1876, Rutherford B. Hayes won the electoral college despite receiving fewer popular votes than Samuel Tilden, and in 1888 Benjamin Harrison defeated Grover Cleveland in the same way. The third instance was the 2000 election, discussed earlier, when the Supreme Court's decision in *Bush v. Gore* handed George W. Bush Florida's electoral votes and the presidency, even though Al Gore won 500,000 more popular votes. And the fourth instance was in 2016 when Hillary Clinton won almost 3 million more votes than Donald Trump, but Trump won the majority in the electoral college.

Given the two recent cases where the popular vote winner has lost the election, calls for eliminating the electoral college and using a national popular vote for president have become widespread. Public-opinion polls continue to show that most Americans prefer a direct election for the president.[17] Eliminating the electoral college entirely, however, would require a constitutional amendment, which would be extremely difficult to pass.

Reform of the system is possible, since the Constitution allows states to choose the method of selecting their electors. One example of a recent reform attempt is the National Popular Vote Interstate Compact. Under this plan, each state's electoral college votes would go to the candidate who won the national popular vote, whether or not the candidate won a plurality of votes in that specific state. Under the National Popular Interstate Compact plan, if Joe Biden won more votes nationally than Trump, Arizona's electors would go to Biden even if

FIGURE 10.1

Electing the President: Steps in the Process

Formation of an Exploratory Committee
Formed 18 to 24 months before the election, this committee begins fundraising and bringing the candidate's name to the attention of the media and influential groups.

Fundraising
Presidential candidates must develop fundraising strategies, hire expert fundraisers, and quickly build a substantial "war chest" early on to show they are serious contenders.

Campaigning
Months before the primaries, candidates begin meetings with local leaders, public appearances, ad campaigns, and other strategies.

Primaries and Caucuses
Candidates need to do well in early contests such as Iowa and New Hampshire in order to build momentum and win their party's nomination. Party debates give candidates an opportunity to impress large television audiences.

The Convention
The Democratic and Republican parties hold national conventions in September prior to the November general election. The parties' nominees for president and vice president are officially announced.

The General Election Campaign
In the months leading up to the November election, candidates focus on battleground or swing states as they aim to win at least 270 votes in the electoral college. They run television ads and use new media to reach voters. They must continue to raise money throughout this process.

The Debates
In October, the major-party candidates engage in several televised debates along with one vice-presidential debate.

The General Election
On the Tuesday following the first Monday in November, voters in each state cast ballots. In most states, the candidate who wins the most votes in the state wins all of the state's votes in the electoral college.

The Electoral College
The electors meet in their state capitals in December, and their votes are officially counted in January.

The Inauguration
The president is officially inaugurated on January 20.

Trump won that state. States would enter a compact with other states making the same change, which would go into effect when it was approved by enough states to make up a majority in the electoral college (270 electoral votes). This reform would effectively bypass the electoral college without the need for a constitutional amendment. As of 2020, 15 states plus Washington, D.C., have enacted the bill into law, representing 196 electoral votes, or 73 percent of the 270 votes needed for the compact to take effect.

Another drawback of the electoral college system is that even presidents who win the most popular votes as well as the electoral college often lack majority support. Including the four U.S. presidents who lost the popular vote, roughly one-third of American presidents since the Civil War have been elected with only a plurality (less than 50 percent) rather than a majority of it.[18] Notably, Abraham Lincoln won just 40 percent of the popular vote in a four-way election in 1860, and Bill Clinton was elected with just 43 percent in 1992.[19] When a third-party candidate receives a significant percentage of votes and is more closely aligned ideologically with the losing major-party candidate than with the winning one, then a majority of voters may not support the winner. Few democracies in the world elect a president who does not win a majority of the popular vote.

DIRECT-DEMOCRACY ELECTIONS

Besides elections for president, Congress, and state offices, 24 states also provide for the initiative process. **Ballot initiatives** allow citizens to circulate petitions to place policy changes or proposed laws on the ballot for a popular vote, without prior approval by the state's legislature or governor. If a ballot initiative receives majority support, it becomes law (in Florida, a two-thirds vote—a supermajority—is required for initiatives to change the state constitution).

ballot initiative a proposed law or policy change that is placed on the ballot by citizens or interest groups for a popular vote

Ballot initiatives frequently deal with controversial policy issues that elected officials are reluctant to address. At the turn of the twentieth century, they were used to grant women the right to vote, prevent child labor, limit the workday to eight hours, and allow voters to elect U.S. senators directly (rather than having them chosen by state legislatures). In recent years, voters in several states have used them to raise or lower taxes, pass term limits for elected officials, prohibit social services for undocumented immigrants, raise taxes on the wealthy, create non-partisan redistricting, legalize marijuana, and much more. An initiative in Maine in 2016 created a new system of voting for gubernatorial and congressional elections called "ranked choice voting," discussed in Chapter 9, in which voters rank three candidates in order of preference rather than choosing only one.

While only half the states allow ballot initiatives, all 50 states provide for legislative **referendums**, in which the state legislature refers certain laws to the voters for a popular vote. Referendum votes are also required for changes to state constitutions.

referendum the practice of referring a proposed law passed by a legislature to the vote of the electorate for approval or rejection

The initiative and the referendum, both referred to as *ballot measures*, are examples of direct democracy. They allow voters to make laws directly without intervention by government officials or political parties. Like laws and policies made by legislatures and executives, however, ballot-measure results are subject to judicial review. If a court finds that a measure approved by voters violates the state or national constitution, it can overturn the result. This happened in 2012 when the federal courts overturned California's Proposition 8, which banned same-sex marriage.

Ballot initiatives not only change policy but also appear to affect political engagement, participation, and behavior. One study found that states with initiatives on the ballot tend to have higher voter turnout over time. Citizens living in these states report more interest in politics and are more likely to discuss politics. Why is this so? The opportunity to directly make policy and change laws may have an "educative" effect on voters.[20] When they have more opportunities to act politically, citizens may learn to participate more and come to believe their participation has meaning.

Elections with policy choices as well as candidates on the ballot also provide more information to voters. Ballot measures about controversial issues generate their own campaigns, with attention and advertising in television, newspaper, and digital media and voter-mobilization drives by volunteers.[21] In fact, these campaigns often involve high spending by both sides and advertising that can rival that of congressional and presidential candidates within a state.

Ballot measures are increasingly common: more initiatives and referenda have appeared on state ballots over the last 30 years than at any time since the Progressive Era at the turn of the twentieth century, when the initiative was first adopted. In 2020, 128 of them appeared on the ballot in 32 states.[22] These included measures for legalizing marijuana in four states and ranked choice voting in Massachusetts.

In addition to their effects on state policy and on voter turnout, ballot measures can help shape both the national agenda and evaluations of candidates.[23] In 2006, coordinated ballot measures raising the minimum wage in multiple states may have influenced voters to focus on the economy, priming them to cast ballots for Democrats in Congress and Democratic governors. Placing issues on the ballot as part of an effort to influence candidate elections is an important strategy for campaigns attempting to shape the political agenda.

Finally, 18 states provide for **recall** elections, which allow voters to remove governors and other state officials from office before their terms end. In California, for example, if 12 percent of those who voted in the last general election sign petitions demanding a recall election, the state board of elections must schedule one. In 2003, California governor Gray Davis became only the second governor in American history to be recalled, and the actor Arnold Schwarzenegger was elected in his place. In 2012, in contrast, Wisconsin governor Scott Walker won a recall election, keeping his position. Federal officials, such as the president and members of Congress, are not subject to recall.

Election Campaigns

> **Explain strategies campaigns use to win elections**

Because of the complexity of the campaign process and the amount of money that candidates must raise, presidential campaigns often begin almost two years before the November election; and congressional campaigns, a year in advance. The **campaign** for any office consists of a number of steps. Candidates often form an exploratory committee consisting of supporters who will help them raise funds and bring their names to the attention of the media, potential donors, and voters. Money from corporations and individuals is an important component of U.S. elections, since public funding is limited. **Incumbents** have an advantage in these areas over the candidates challenging them. They usually are already well known

recall a procedure to allow voters to remove state officials from office before their terms expire by circulating petitions to call a vote

campaign an effort by political candidates and their supporters to win the backing of donors, political activists, and voters in their quest for political office

incumbent a candidate running for re-election to a position that he or she already holds

and have little difficulty attracting supporters and contributors—unless, of course, they have been subject to damaging publicity while in office.

CAMPAIGN CONSULTANTS

A formal organization and professional campaign managers are critical for campaign success. For a local campaign, candidates generally need hundreds of volunteers and a few paid professionals. State-level campaigns call for thousands of volunteers, and presidential campaigns require tens of thousands of volunteers and hundreds of paid staff nationwide. Virtually all serious contenders for national and statewide office retain the services of professional campaign consultants, including a campaign manager, media consultants, pollsters and a data analytics team, financial advisers, a press spokesperson, and staff directors to coordinate the activities of volunteer and paid workers. Consultants offer candidates the expertise necessary to craft campaign messages, conduct opinion polls, produce television and social media ads, organize direct-mail campaigns, open field offices, and make use of information about their constituents from digital voter files, text messaging, email, political donations, and more. Most consultants who direct campaigns specialize in politics, advertising, strategic communication, public relations, and computing. They may work with commercial clients in addition to politicians.

FUNDRAISING

Candidates generally begin raising funds long before they face an election, and many politicians spend more time on it than on any other campaign activity. For Democratic members of Congress, the party leadership recommends spending 40 to 50 percent of their working hours on fundraising.[24] Serious fundraising efforts involve appealing to both small and large donors. To have a reasonable chance of winning a seat in the House of Representatives, a candidate may need to raise more than $1 million; in 2014 candidates in the most competitive House races spent $10 million or more. In 2018 candidates in the most competitive House races spent

Candidates for national office rely on campaign advisers to guide their campaigns and direct volunteers. Here, Donald Trump's campaign manager, Bill Stepien, observes as Trump speaks with the press on Air Force One.

$20 million or more, a huge increase over just four years.[25] In the 2020 congressional races, candidates spent a record $7.2 billion, an increase from $5.9 billion in 2018.

Once elected to office, members of Congress find it much easier to raise funds and are thus able to outspend their challengers (see Figure 10.2).[26] Incumbents outraise their opponents by significant amounts because most donations from businesses, interest groups, and PACs go to incumbents. These donors seek a voice in government from their investment; thus, they want to invest in the candidate most likely to win, and incumbents win most of the time. Members of the majority party in the House and Senate are particularly attractive to donors who want access to those in power.[27]

FIGURE 10.2

Average Congressional Campaign Expenditures, 1984–2020

The average amount spent by House and Senate incumbents to secure re-election has risen sharply in recent years, whereas spending by challengers has remained more stable. What would you expect to see as a consequence of this trend? Is legislation needed to level the playing field?

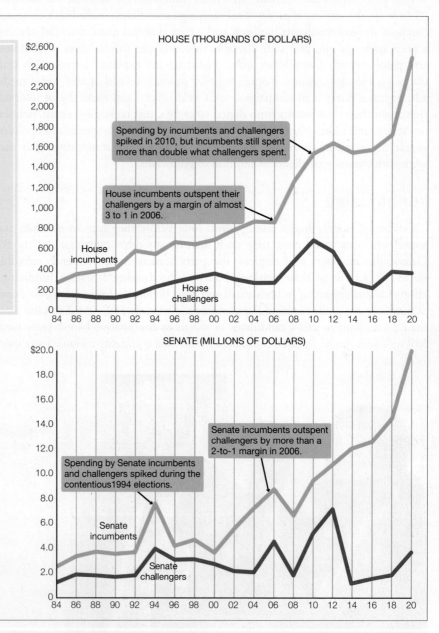

Spending by incumbents and challengers spiked in 2010, but incumbents still spent more than double what challengers spent.

House incumbents outspent their challengers by a margin of almost 3 to 1 in 2006.

Senate incumbents outspent challengers by more than a 2-to-1 margin in 2006.

Spending by Senate incumbents and challengers spiked during the contentious 1994 elections.

SOURCES: Norman J. Orstein, Thomas E. Mann, and Michael J. Malbin, eds., *Vital Statistics on Congress, 2001–2002* (Washington, DC: American Enterprise Institute, 2002), 87, 93; and OpenSecrets.org, "Incumbent Advantage," www.opensecrets.org/overview/incumbs.php (accessed 11/19/20).

Who Participates in Political Campaigns and Elections?

Percentage of U.S. adults who say they have done each of the following in the past five years:

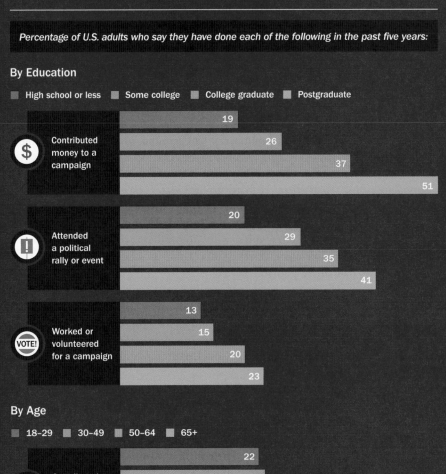

By Education

■ High school or less   ■ Some college   ■ College graduate   ■ Postgraduate

$ Contributed money to a campaign
- 19
- 26
- 37
- 51

! Attended a political rally or event
- 20
- 29
- 35
- 41

VOTE! Worked or volunteered for a campaign
- 13
- 15
- 20
- 23

The first step in participating in politics is getting informed about the candidates and the issues. Beyond this basic first step, people can display bumper stickers supporting a candidate, work or volunteer on behalf of a campaign, attend a rally or campaign event, and contribute financially to candidate campaigns. Participation in politics often increases with higher levels of educational attainment and sometimes age.

SOURCE: Michael Dimock, "An Update on Our Research into Trust, Facts and Democracy," Pew Research Center, June 5, 2019; "Political Engagement, Knowledge and the Midterms," Pew Research Center, April 26, 2018.

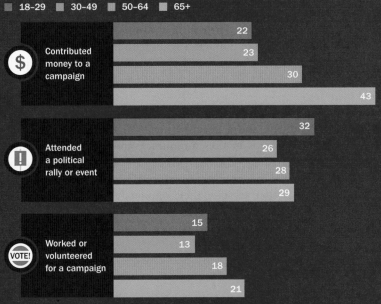

By Age

■ 18–29   ■ 30–49   ■ 50–64   ■ 65+

$ Contributed money to a campaign
- 22
- 23
- 30
- 43

! Attended a political rally or event
- 32
- 26
- 28
- 29

VOTE! Worked or volunteered for a campaign
- 15
- 13
- 18
- 21

FOR CRITICAL ANALYSIS

1. Common ways that people participate in political campaigns include attending a campaign event or rally, donating money to campaigns (even small amounts), and volunteering for a campaign. What are the differences in campaign participation based on formal education?

2. What are the differences in campaign participation based on age? Are young people particularly more likely to engage in certain activities for campaigns over others?

CAMPAIGN STRATEGY

grassroots campaigns political campaigns that operate at the local level, often using face-to-face communication to generate interest and momentum by citizens

For candidates who win the nomination, the last hurdle is the general election. There are essentially two types of general-election campaigns in the United States today: **grassroots campaigns** and mass media campaigns. Grassroots campaigns, which include local and many congressional elections, are organizationally driven and labor intensive. Candidates make many public appearances—some involving celebrity supporters—and recruit many volunteers to knock on doors, hand out leaflets, and organize rallies and other public events. Such extensive grassroots outreach and mobilization is designed to make candidates more visible than their opponent. Statewide campaigns, some congressional races, and the presidential election are mass media campaigns: media driven and money intensive. Barack Obama's campaigns in 2008 and 2012 were notable in combining both types of campaigns.

All campaigns must decide on a strategy: What will their main message be? How will they allocate their resources (to television, social media, face-to-face mobilization)? Which voters will they target? The electoral college is one election rule that influences the campaign strategy of presidential candidates by forcing them to campaign heavily in a small number of battleground, or swing, states—those whose populations are divided roughly evenly between Democrats and Republicans—while often ignoring the rest of the country. In 2016, 94 percent of the presidential campaign events occurred in 12 battleground states, especially the populous ones of Florida, Ohio, Pennsylvania, and Virginia.[28] Residents of battleground states are smothered with attention from the candidates and media as presidential candidates vie for those states' votes, while the millions of residents of states considered safe for Republicans (West Virginia, Utah) or Democrats (New York, Illinois, California) are often ignored.

The Media Contemporary political campaigns rely on a number of communication tools to reach the voters they want to target for support, including television, radio, social media/digital advertising, massive computerized databases, and micro-targeting. Digital media are especially important in mobilizing people to vote (see Chapter 7).

Extensive use of the broadcast media, television in particular, is central to modern political campaigns. Most presidential and many congressional candidates spend millions of dollars for *paid media* time in the form of television and radio ads, many of which consist of 15-, 30-, or 60-second spots. The most expensive commercials air during the Super Bowl. The cost of a 30-second commercial during the game rose from $2.2 million in 2000 to $5.6 million in 2020. Presidential candidates in the 2020 election spent more than $21 million on ad buys for Super Bowl Sunday, with President Donald Trump and Mike Bloomberg spending more than $10 million each.[29]

Television ads are used to establish candidate name recognition, create a favorable image of the candidate and a negative image of the opponent, link the candidate with desirable groups in the community, and communicate the candidate's stands on selected issues. Often in the later stages of a campaign, candidates and the political advocacy groups that support them (see below) will "go negative," airing ads that criticize their opponents' policy positions, qualifications, or character. For example, President Lyndon Johnson's 1964 "daisy" ad suggested that Johnson's opponent, Barry Goldwater, would lead the United States into nuclear war.

Volunteer on a Campaign

SAM LOZIER, a Democratic campaign operative

One of the best ways to see firsthand how American government and politics work is to volunteer on a campaign. In the United States there are tens of thousands of elected officials, most of whom run election campaigns to attract voter attention. And most of those campaigns need volunteers to help with the many tasks associated with getting the candidate's name, ideas, and policy goals in front of voters.

We spoke with Sam Lozier, who has done everything from running field organizing efforts (such as door-knocking campaigns) to running digital campaigns. Sam notes that while presidential campaigns dominate news coverage and often spark the most interest among prospective volunteers, what he wants "as an organizer" is for "people to focus on small races, the small races taking place where you live, where you can have more impact as a volunteer." He shared his tips about the best ways to get involved:

1 How do you learn about local races? I recommend starting with the website of the county party organization and looking for events. Usually there is some function within driving distance, which you can check out as a way to get started. If the county party does not have a website, try the state party website, which will tell you who your legislator is by zip code.

2 What can volunteers do? The most important thing is direct voter contact. This includes making phone calls, knocking on doors, dropping leaflets, preparing mailers, and now, using apps like Hustle that allow for peer-to-peer texting to spread a campaign's message. Because many states allow early voting, helping people with their absentee ballot requests is important as well, since many voters have difficulty getting to the polls or taking the time to vote on election day.

3 What is the time commitment? It's up to you and the tasks you volunteer for. If you commit to knock on doors or make phone calls, you should count on one or two hours, three times per week. The easiest lift is using Hustle on your phone. You can send Hustle texts while you're studying, so it's not much time commitment at all.

4 What's it like to reach out to voters? You have to have pretty thick skin. You're going to get rejected. You're going to get pushback. Coming up with a script to handle those situations is important. If you're working with a county party or a campaign, they have people to help you

through those situations. I grew to love it. I figured out how to do it with some moderate success, liked it, and saw the importance of it.

5 Can volunteering lead to other positions? Certainly, depending on performance and knowledge. Sometimes volunteering can lead to a paid position on the campaign or in government, if the candidate is elected. The step in between is a fellowship—getting credit hours for working for an elected official, like an internship.

Volunteering is a great way to see how campaigns and elections work, an important component of American democracy. It's also an exciting and high-energy way to meet lots of other people of all ages and to learn about your community.

While voters often complain about the prevalence of negative campaigning, it can be an effective strategy. Donald Trump often used his large campaign rallies to admonish other politicians, including his Democratic opponent Joe Biden.

Though voters consistently say they reject so-called negative campaigning, political scientist John Geer found that negative ads can benefit voters more than positive ones in some cases.[30] Negative ads are more likely to address important policy differences and provide supporting evidence, Geer found, while positive ads tend to focus on candidates' personal characteristics. Interestingly, when negative ads are misleading or even patently false, they are effective in that voters remember more from them than from positive ads, possibly because they are designed to elicit emotional responses, such as fear, anxiety, or anger.

In addition to ads sponsored by the candidates, a growing percentage of campaign ads are sponsored by the political parties and by political advocacy groups. The 2010 *Citizens United* Supreme Court decision (discussed later in this chapter) allowed corporations, unions, and interest groups to form Super PACs that can spend unlimited amounts to advocate for or against candidates, as long as the Super PACs are "independent" of the candidate's campaign. When viewers see attack ads against a candidate, they can have difficulty determining who sponsored the ads because the sponsoring Super PAC has a generic name—Citizens for America, for example. The effect of unlimited spending on television advertising remains unclear.

Candidates also benefit from *free media*, where the cost of advertising is borne by the television and print media themselves when they cover the candidates' statements and activities as news. In the 2016 Republican presidential primaries, Donald Trump benefited from much free media coverage, largely due to his many controversial statements and tweets.[31] Critics claimed that the media's tendency to focus on Trump, rather than provide balanced coverage of all candidates, occurred because he drew the biggest audience.

Digital media have become another major weapon in modern political campaigns as more Americans turn to the internet, and social media in particular, for news. Today, every campaign for presidential, congressional, and major state offices develops a social media strategy for fundraising, mobilizing supporters, and getting out the vote. (See Chapters 7 and 8 for a fuller discussion of political candidates' digital strategy.) One reason digital media are so effective at organizing presidential campaigns is cost: social media enable inexpensive organization of volunteers and offer more opportunities for free advertising, such as on Twitter and YouTube. In addition, political videos may be more effective than television ads because viewers make a conscious choice to watch them, instead of having their television program interrupted by an unwanted ad.

Debates Public debates were a critical part of the democratic process of ancient Greece, where they were both a form of public entertainment and the principal means of what today would be called "voter education." Many successful American politicians, such as Abraham Lincoln and Barack Obama, came to prominence largely because of their skill as debaters. Today, both presidential and vice-presidential candidates hold debates, as do candidates for statewide and even local offices. Debates give voters the opportunity to see how the candidates fare in direct, face-to-face exchanges outside the "campaign bubble" of stage-managed public appearances and carefully scripted speeches. Candidates who can think on their feet may be seen as demonstrating the kind of on-the-spot decision-making that is more like actual governing than anything else they do in a campaign.

Televised presidential debates began with the famous 1960 Kennedy–Nixon clash. John F. Kennedy's strong performance in the debate and the perception of many voters that the youthfully vigorous Kennedy "looked presidential" were major factors in his victory over the much better-known Richard Nixon. Indeed, candidates can make or break their campaigns with the strength of their debate performances, including high-profile gaffes and even unconscious gestures and the nuances of facial expressions, but not always.

Presidential debates usually involve relatively civilized disagreement about substantive policy issues. For the most part, this characterized the multiple nationally televised primary debates for the 2020 Democratic Party with an unusually large field of candidates. In contrast, the Republican primary debates in 2016 included fierce arguments, harsh character attacks, and personal insults, many of which stemmed from the bombastic style of Donald Trump and his opponents' occasional attempts to match it. When Trump faced off against Democrat Hillary Clinton in the general election, the antagonistic tone continued, and their first televised debate set a record as the most watched in U.S. history (84 million viewers, not counting streaming online).[32] In contrast, the

Since John F. Kennedy and Richard Nixon debated on live television in 1960 (left), presidential debates have been one of the most closely watched events in election campaigns. The presidential debates in 2020 were highly conflictual, and drew in many viewers.

largest audience for the 2020 Democratic primary debate was 20 million viewers in the February debate.

Micro-Targeting and Polling The media and televised debates allow candidates to communicate their policy goals and promises to a broad range of voters. While this method is efficient, it is also a blunt instrument; different voters care about different issues, after all. The idea behind micro-targeting is to send different campaign ads or messages to different demographic groups of voters and potential voters. Suburban "soccer moms," for instance, would be targeted with ads different from those targeting rural "cowboy dads" (see Chapter 9).

Republican president George W. Bush is credited with successfully using micro-targeting in the 2000 and 2004 elections. His campaign focused on wedge issues—issues where a voter's preferences diverge from those of his political party. By targeting Democratic voters with messages focusing on Bush's opposition to same-sex marriage, the campaign hoped to convince socially conservative Democrats to cast a ballot for Bush rather than for his opponent.[33]

Micro-targeting became more sophisticated during the 2008 presidential campaign as Democrats built an extensive organization to contact and turn out voters. The Obama campaign made use of an unprecedented volume of survey data, conducting thousands of interviews each week to gauge voters' preferences. Statistical algorithms looked for patterns in the data the campaign had assembled for voters based on massive state voter-registration files, consumer data, and past campaign contacts. The campaign used this mountain of information to generate different, carefully targeted messages for different demographic, regional, and ideological groups to persuade them to turn out and vote for Obama.[34] Because of micro-targeting, millions of Americans heard from the campaign about issues that mattered the most to them. It was the first time "big data" had been used to win a presidential election. Most serious candidates are now following Obama's lead.

In 2020, campaigns limited their door-knocking efforts in light of the coronavirus pandemic. In the highly competitive state of Pennsylvania, though, both campaigns cautiously deployed volunteers to help mobilize voters.

Almost all campaigns for national and statewide offices make extensive use of random sample public-opinion polling of likely voters (see Chapter 6). These polls provide the campaign with information about which issues are the most important and about the candidates' strengths and weaknesses, and measure voter responses to the campaign.

Once campaigns have identified their target audiences, they reach out to them for fundraising and voter mobilization. Personal contact has been found to be the most effective at mobilizing voters to turn out but requires field offices and volunteers. In 2020, campaigns used text messages along with phone calls, mailings (from glossy color ones to handwritten letters and postcards), social media, and, to a limited extent, door-knocking (face-to-face contact) to reach potential voters.

"People power" remains critical in modern political campaigns, since research suggests that direct mail and robocalls are less effective than face-to-face and in-person phone contacts.[35] Candidates continue to use the services of tens of thousands of volunteers, especially for get-out-the-vote drives. Still, even the recruitment of volunteers has become a job for electronic technology. Employing a technique called "instant organization," paid staff use phone banks to contact not only potential voters in computer-targeted areas but also potential campaign workers there.

Money and Politics

Identify the rules that govern campaign fundraising and spending

Modern campaigns require a great deal of money. In the nineteenth century, labor-intensive campaigns allowed parties whose chief support came from poorer Americans to use their numerical superiority as a partial counterweight to the institutional and economic resources of the opposition. As many as 2.5 million individuals worked on political campaigns during the 1880s.[36] The money-intensive campaign of the modern era, by contrast, has given a major boost to candidates whose supporters are able to furnish the large sums now needed to compete effectively, or who are billionaires themselves.[37]

Candidates with the most campaign dollars often, but don't always, win. In 2008 and 2012, Barack Obama raised more than his Republican opponents. In 2016, though Hillary Clinton spent more than her opponent, Donald Trump, she did not win in the electoral college. Nonetheless, the 2016 election shattered previous records. The total cost of the 2020 elections (congressional and presidential) was an unprecedented $14 billion, making it the most expensive election in history and twice as expensive as the 2016 presidential election. In 2020, roughly half was spent on the congressional races and half on the presidential election.[38]

WHY IS CAMPAIGN SPENDING SO HIGH IN THE UNITED STATES?

The United States is rare among democracies in allowing candidates to spend unlimited sums of money on their campaigns with no time restrictions on the spending. In most democratic countries, publicly financed campaigns are the norm;

In the last two decades, courts have ruled that campaign contributions are a form of speech and, for the most part, cannot be restricted. However, many people worry that these decisions reinforce the influence of the very affluent in American politics at the expense of everyone else.

in such a system, the government provides candidates or parties a set amount to spend. In the United States, candidates may raise ever-increasing amounts of money from individuals, corporations, and interest groups, a system that has long sparked concerns about the potential for corruption. Although a number of federal laws have tried to limit and regulate contributions to political campaigns, key Supreme Court decisions over a 40-year period have dismantled most of these restrictions.

The first, *Buckley v. Valeo* (1976), struck down several provisions of the Federal Election Campaign Act of 1974, including limits on candidate spending, candidates' use of personal funds, and independent expenditures (money spent to influence an election by an organization that is not allowed to coordinate with a candidate's official campaign). The decision introduced the idea that money (in this case, campaign contributions) counts as "speech" under the First Amendment and so candidates could spend unlimited amounts of their own money on their own campaign. However, the Court left intact the provision of the law that sets limits on individuals' campaign contributions.[39]

In 2010 the Supreme Court ruled in *Citizens United v. Federal Election Commission* that restrictions on independent expenditures by corporations, nonprofits, unions, and other groups in support of political candidates also violated the First Amendment.[40] With this decision, the United States entered a new era of campaign finance, in which corporations and interest groups can spend unlimited sums. Another 2010 Court decision, *SpeechNow v. FEC*, allowed wealthy individuals and organizations to form committees called Super PACs as a way of engaging in unlimited independent expenditures.[41] These decisions resulted in a significant increase in campaign spending in the 2010 midterm election and unprecedented spending in the 2012 and 2016 presidential elections.

FOR CRITICAL ANALYSIS

What purpose do limits on monetary contributions to political campaigns serve? Should there be limits? How do monetary contributions affect the outcomes of elections?

As the Court struggles to balance permitting free speech with preventing political corruption, the sum of these three decisions tips the scale in favor of speech. However, concerns that unlimited spending by individuals, corporations, and other organizations could worsen existing corruption in American politics is bolstered by a number of new studies finding that members of Congress make decisions that represent the interests of wealthy donors, not average voters.[42]

SOURCES OF CAMPAIGN FUNDS

Although restrictions remain on how campaign money is raised and spent, there is today a great deal of latitude on where money comes from and what it is used for. Campaigns have at least six potential sources of funds.

Individual Donors Politicians spend a great deal of time asking people for money via direct mail, email, text, phone, and face-to-face meetings. Individuals may donate as much as $2,800 per candidate per election, $5,000 per federal PAC per calendar year, $35,500 per national party committee per calendar year, and $10,000 to state and local committees per calendar year. (There is no limit to the number of candidates or PACs that an individual can give to, however—a result of the Supreme Court's decision in *McCutcheon et al. v. Federal Election Commission*.[43]) Bernie Sanders's 2016 presidential campaign raised an unprecedented $231 million in individual contributions, 58 percent of which was made up of small contributions under $200.[44]

Political Action Committees Political action committees (PACs) are organizations established by corporations, labor unions, or interest or advocacy groups to channel money into political campaigns. Nearly two-thirds of all PACs represent corporations, trade associations, and other business and professional groups. Under the terms of the 1971 Federal Election Campaign Act, PACs are permitted to make larger contributions to any given candidate than individuals are allowed to make. Moreover, related PACs often coordinate their contributions, increasing the amount of money a candidate actually receives from the same interest group. More than 4,600 PACs are registered with the Federal Election Commission, which oversees campaign finance practices in the United States. Many congressional and party leaders have established PACs, known as "leadership PACs," to provide funding for their political allies.

Soft Money Before 2002 most campaign donations took the form of "soft money," unregulated contributions to the national parties that were officially intended for party building and voter-registration-and-mobilization efforts rather than for particular campaigns. Federal campaign finance legislation crafted by Senators John McCain and Russell Feingold and enacted in 2002 aimed to ban soft money by prohibiting the national parties from receiving contributions from corporations, unions, or individuals and preventing them from directing such funds to their affiliated state parties. However, it did not reduce money in politics. Under federal rules, a national political party may make unlimited "independent expenditures" advocating support for its own presidential candidate or defeat for an opposing party's candidate as long as these expenditures are not coordinated with the candidate's own campaign.

political action committee (PAC)
a private group that raises and distributes funds for use in election campaigns

527 committee (Super PAC) a nonprofit independent political action committee that may raise unlimited sums of money from corporations, unions, and individuals but is not permitted to contribute to or coordinate directly with parties or candidates

501(c)(4) committees (dark money) politically active nonprofits; under federal law, these nonprofits can spend unlimited amounts on political campaigns and not disclose their donors as long as their activities are not coordinated with the candidate campaigns and political activities are not their primary purpose

Outside Spending/Independent Expenditures: Super PACs and Dark Money

527 committees (i.e., Super PACs) and **501(c)(4) committees (i.e., dark money)** are forms of independent expenditures that are not covered by the spending restrictions imposed in 2002 by the Bipartisan Campaign Reform Act, but now raise much of the money used for political campaigns. These groups are named for the sections of the tax code under which they are organized. They can raise and spend unlimited amounts of money for political campaigns.

A 527 is a group established specifically for the purpose of political advocacy and is required to report its sources of funding to the IRS. A 501(c)(4) is a nonprofit group that also engages in campaign advocacy but may not spend more than half its revenue for political purposes. Unlike a 527, a 501(c)(4) is not required to disclose where it gets its funds or exactly what it does with them—as a result, its funding has earned the name "dark money." Indeed, it has become a common practice for wealthy and corporate donors, as well as foreigners, to route campaign contributions through 501(c)(4)s to avoid the legal limits on contributions through other channels.

Outside spending by 527s and 501(c)(4)s played an unprecedented role in the 2012, 2016, and 2020 presidential races and 2018 midterm elections, as these groups ran extensive television and digital ads. Super PACs on both sides relied on very large contributions. Outside spending more than doubled in the 2020 election compared to 2016 and 2018. A growing concern is that elections in the United States can be bought with big money from corporations and wealthy donors, who will then hold significant influence when that candidate is elected.

Public Funding The Federal Election Campaign Act also provides for public funding of presidential campaigns, as discussed earlier. Candidates running in the major-party presidential primaries become eligible for public funds by raising at least $5,000 in individual contributions of $250 or less in each of 20 states. Candidates who reach this threshold may apply for federal funds to match, on a dollar-for-dollar basis, all contributions of $250 or less. But by accepting matching funds they agree to spend no more than $48.07 million in their presidential primary campaigns, including with their personal funds and funds from private donors.

Under current law, no presidential candidate is required to accept public funding. Candidates who do not are not subject to any spending limits. In 2008, John McCain accepted public funding for the general-election campaign, receiving $84 million, but Barack Obama declined, choosing to rely on his own fundraising prowess. Obama was ultimately able to outspend McCain by a wide margin. Neither major-party candidate has accepted public financing since 2008, and most believe the 2008 race marked the last time a candidate would take federal money.

Unlimited Spending by Candidates of Their Own Money On the basis of the *Buckley v. Valeo* decision, the right of individuals to spend their *own* money to campaign for office is a constitutionally protected matter of free speech and is not subject to limitation.[45] Thus, extremely wealthy candidates often contribute millions of dollars to their own campaign. Donald Trump, for example, spent millions of his own money on his 2016 campaign, as did Ross Perot in 1992 and 1996. Tom Steyer and Mike Bloomberg spent millions of dollars of their own money in the 2020 Democratic presidential primary.

How Voters Decide

Identify the major factors that influence voters' decisions

Even if well-funded groups and powerful individuals influence the electoral process, it is the millions of individual voter decisions that ultimately determine election outcomes. Three factors influence voters' choices: partisan loyalty, issues and policy preferences, and candidate characteristics.

PARTISAN LOYALTY

Most voters feel a certain sense of identification or kinship with the Democratic or Republican Party, predisposing them to favor their party's candidates and oppose those of the other party (see Figure 10.3). Partisanship is the most reliable indicator of which candidates people will vote for, from presidential elections to local elections. While issues and candidate personalities get more national attention in presidential elections compared to down-ballot elections, they often have very little impact on how partisans vote.

Once formed, voters' partisan loyalties seldom change unless some crisis causes them to reexamine their loyalties. During such a crisis, millions of voters can change their party ties. For example, at the beginning of the New Deal era, between 1932 and 1936, millions of former Republicans traumatized by the Great Depression transferred their allegiance to President Franklin Roosevelt and the Democrats.

ISSUES AND POLICY PREFERENCES

Policy preferences are a second factor influencing voters' choices. Voters may cast their ballots for the candidate whose position on health care, climate change, funding college education, or economic issues they believe to be closest to their

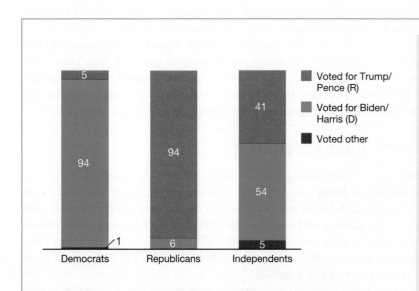

Voted for Trump/Pence (R)

Voted for Biden/Harris (D)

Voted other

FIGURE 10.3

The Effect of Party Identification on the Vote, 2020

In 2020 around 94 percent of Democrats and Republicans supported their party's presidential candidate. Should candidates devote their resources to mobilizing members of their party to turn out and vote, to converting voters who identify with the opposition, or to winning more support among independents? What factors might make it difficult for candidates to simultaneously pursue all three courses of action?

own, or the one they believe has the best experience in foreign policy. Though candidates for the presidency or Congress are often judged on the basis of their economic policies or promises, other issues vary in importance depending on the election. In 2008, for example, Obama made ending the war in Iraq and providing national health care for all Americans his core issues. In 2016, Donald Trump made curbing immigration and building a wall along the U.S.–Mexico border a key issue.

If candidates express and publicize very different positions on important policy issues, voters are more likely to be able to identify and act on whatever policy preferences they may have. Their ability to make choices on this basis is diminished, however, if they are uninformed or misinformed about the issues and candidates. Political scientists call choices that focus on future events or campaign promises **prospective voting**, whereas those based on past performance are called **retrospective voting**. Retrospective economic voting, in which voters evaluate candidates based on the strength of the economy, has been found to be more important than prospective voting.

Candidates try to define the issues of an election in terms that will benefit them. Incumbents running during a period of prosperity will seek to take credit for the economy's strength and define the election as revolving around their record of success. This strategy encourages voters to make retrospective judgments. By contrast, a challenger running during a period of economic uncertainty will tell voters it is time for a change and ask them to make prospective judgments. In 2016, Donald Trump focused on change and "making America great again."

The Economy The best-laid plans of politicians often go awry, however, and election outcomes are affected by a variety of forces that candidates cannot control. Among the most important of these is the condition of the economy at the time of the election. If voters are satisfied with their economic conditions, they tend to support the party in power, while concern about the economy tends to favor the opposition. For example, the 2008 financial crisis gave Barack Obama and the Democrats a significant advantage in that year's election.

Over the past quarter-century, the Consumer Confidence Index, calculated by the Conference Board, a business research group, has been a fairly accurate predictor of presidential election outcomes. The index is based on surveys asking voters how optimistic they are about the future of the economy. A generally rosy view, indicated by an index score over 100, bodes well for the party in power. A score under 100, indicating a pessimistic outlook, suggests that incumbents should worry about their own job prospects (see Figure 10.4). In recent presidential elections, personal economic conditions were an important factor in explaining voter decisions.

CANDIDATE CHARACTERISTICS

Candidates' personal attributes are a third factor influencing voters' decisions, with the more important being race, ethnicity, religion, gender, geography, and socioeconomic background. Voters may be proud to see someone similar to themselves in a position of leadership and may presume that such candidates are likely to have perspectives close to their own. This is why politicians often seek to "balance the ticket," by making certain that their party's slate of candidates includes members of as many important groups as possible.

Just as candidates' personal characteristics may attract some voters, they may repel others. Some voters are prejudiced against candidates from certain ethnic,

prospective voting voting based on the imagined future performance of a candidate or political party

retrospective voting voting based on the past performance of a candidate or political party

FOR CRITICAL ANALYSIS

Do American political campaigns help voters make a decision? Or do they produce more confusion than enlightenment?

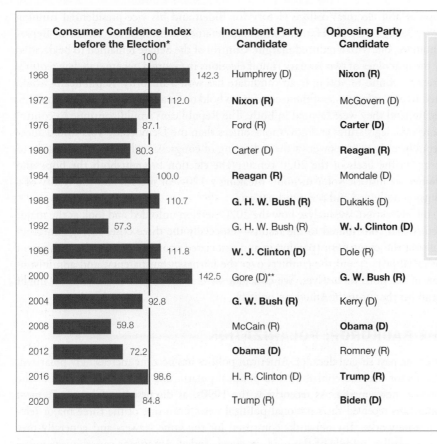

Consumer Confidence Index before the Election*

Year	Index	Incumbent Party Candidate	Opposing Party Candidate
1968	142.3	Humphrey (D)	**Nixon (R)**
1972	112.0	**Nixon (R)**	McGovern (D)
1976	87.1	Ford (R)	**Carter (D)**
1980	80.3	Carter (D)	**Reagan (R)**
1984	100.0	**Reagan (R)**	Mondale (D)
1988	110.7	**G. H. W. Bush (R)**	Dukakis (D)
1992	57.3	G. H. W. Bush (R)	**W. J. Clinton (D)**
1996	111.8	**W. J. Clinton (D)**	Dole (R)
2000	142.5	Gore (D)**	**G. W. Bush (R)**
2004	92.8	**G. W. Bush (R)**	Kerry (D)
2008	59.8	McCain (R)	**Obama (D)**
2012	72.2	**Obama (D)**	Romney (R)
2016	98.6	H. R. Clinton (D)	**Trump (R)**
2020	84.8	Trump (R)	**Biden (D)**

FIGURE 10.4

Consumer Confidence and Presidential Elections

Since 1968 the Consumer Confidence Index has been a fairly reliable predictor of incumbents' political fortunes. Was the result of the 2020 election consistent with this trend? What issues other than the economy influenced the 2020 election?

*Survey was bimonthly prior to 1977 so figures for 1968, 1972, and 1976 are for October and they are for September from 1983 on.

**Gore and Clinton won the popular vote, but Bush and Trump were elected by the electoral college.

Note: A score above 100 means most people are optimistic about the economy. A score below 100 means most people are pessimistic about the economy. The candidate who won the election appears in bold.

SOURCE: The Conference Board, www.conference-board.org/data/consumerdata.cfm (accessed 11/18/20).

racial, religious, or gendered groups. The fact that the 2008 Democratic presidential candidate was African American, the 2016 Democratic candidate a woman, and the 2020 Democratic vice-presidential candidate a Black and South Asian woman indicates the increasing diversity of candidates for public office.

Voters also pay attention to candidates' personality characteristics, such as "authenticity," "decisiveness," and "honesty." In recent years, "integrity" has become a key election issue. In the 2020 presidential election many Americans questioned the trustworthiness of both Joe Biden and Donald Trump. Nonetheless, Trump supporters saw their candidate as unafraid to speak his mind, while Biden supporters felt he could unite the country and had good judgment.

The 2020 Elections: A Tale of Three Crises

Analyze the strategies, issues, and outcomes of the 2020 elections

In 2020, Democratic former vice president Joseph Biden faced incumbent Republican President Donald Trump in one of the most divisive and bitter presidential elections in American history. The end result was a solid

FOR CRITICAL ANALYSIS

What factors influence voters' choices? What factors matter most to you when you decide how to cast your ballot?

popular and electoral college victory for Biden and his vice-presidential running mate, Senator Kamala Harris. Democrats retained control of the House of Representatives, but with a reduced margin. Control of the Senate remained to be decided by the outcomes of two January runoff elections in Georgia, where state law requires a second round of voting if no candidate has won a majority. Republicans would need to win at least one of these contests to hold on to a majority of seats in the U.S. Senate, and they were favored in both. The Republicans would continue to control more state legislatures and governors' offices than the Democrats. This would allow Republicans greater power in the redrawing of congressional district boundaries to come on the heels of the 2020 census. The election brought both the hope and promise of historic voter turnout, breaking a 120-year record, and the reality of a continued divided and polarized nation.

In this section, we analyze how the 2020 election unfolded and look at the major factors that contributed to the results—especially the three crises facing American politics: the coronavirus pandemic and associated economic crisis, the movement for racial justice, and the conflicts over the fairness, transparency, and administration of elections themselves. We conclude by considering what the election might mean for the future of American politics.

THE BACKDROP: POLARIZATION

Over the past several decades, American politics has become increasingly polarized. One factor that has contributed to political polarization is the organization of the national news media. As recently as the 1990s, as discussed in Chapter 7, most Americans received their national political news from one of the three major television networks. The networks competed for the same viewers and generally presented similar, middle-of-the-road coverage. Today, Americans can choose among numerous news sources that compete by appealing to the sentiments of ideological subgroups rather than reaching for the political center. Thus, some media outlets, like MSNBC, appeal to liberals by castigating conservatives; while other outlets, like

The 2020 elections demonstrated in several ways how polarized the United States has become, culminating with both sides demanding that all legal votes be counted. Trump supporters hoped this would diminish Biden's lead, and Biden supporters hoped it would buoy his winning margins.

FOX or OAN, reach out to conservatives by criticizing liberal politicians. As Americans understand political events through these partisan and ideological lenses, their preexisting partisan views and ideological predispositions are strengthened.

Partly as a result, over the past 50 years, America's two major political parties have experienced an ideological realignment that has made both parties more ideologically homogeneous and less willing to compromise or seek common ground. The Democratic Party is the political home of those who view themselves as ideologically liberal, while the Republican Party is the party of conservatives. There are, to be sure, some differences of political perspective within each party. The perspectives in the Democratic camp range from traditional social-welfare liberalism, which traces its roots to the New Deal, to left-liberal progressivism, which envisions a substantially expanded role for the federal government, including a "Green New Deal" of environmental programs, single-payer national health insurance, and reparations to African Americans for slavery and racial injustice. The Republican camp ranges from business conservatives, who favor reducing government regulation and taxes, to social conservatives, who oppose abortion and same-sex marriage, to Trump conservatives, who favor reducing international trade and immigration to the United States.

Party activists have also become highly polarized.[46] Many local party organizations responsible for organizing voter mobilization on both sides have been taken over by ideological activists inclined to demonize the opposition.[47] More than a few party activists view presidential elections as contests between good and evil, democracy and authoritarianism, and they communicate this perspective to the general public as they work to mobilize supporters via social media and the generally partisan mass media outlets. Democratic politicians and activists declare that Republicans are racist, sexist, homophobic, and ignorant. Republican activists tell their voters that the Democrats are hostile to working American families and indifferent to the nation's values and traditions. More than half of Republicans and Democrats have developed highly negative views of the other party's supporters.[48]

Polarization has been sharpened even more by the nationalization and centralization of American political struggles. The growth of presidential power (see Chapter 13) has greatly increased the intensity of political battles in the United States. To put it simply, as the presidency has become more important, Americans have become more concerned with the results of presidential contests. The number of people who believe it really matters who wins the presidency has been rising steadily for the past two decades, as have the number who say they have thought a lot about presidential elections and those who say they follow the news about presidential candidates.[49] These changes were occurring before the arrival of Donald Trump.

Trump undoubtedly did much to step up the level of anger in the public forum with his often intemperate rhetoric. Trump's opponents responded in kind. Beginning in 2016, Trump sought to mobilize angry White working-class voters from the political periphery. To appeal to disaffected groups, Trump mocked established elites and excoriated what he termed the "fake" elite media. Trump also trafficked in racism and White nationalism, particularly suggesting in his tweets and at his rallies that Latino immigrants were criminals and Middle Eastern immigrants terrorists who represented threats to America. Using executive orders, Trump sought to limit immigration from both groups.

Political acrimony had already come to a head during the third year of the Trump presidency when the majority of congressional Democrats, particularly those in the party's powerful progressive wing, decided that because of what they claimed

After President Trump delivered his State of the Union speech in February 2020, Speaker of the House Nancy Pelosi tore her copy of the speech in half for all to see. Many saw the action as representative of the bitterness of politics in the Trump era.

was abuse of power and obstruction of Congress, Donald Trump must be removed from office. The House of Representatives impeached Trump for allegedly asking the leader of Ukraine to investigate Trump's political opponents in exchange for U.S. military aid to Ukraine, and for obstructing the inquiry by telling White House officials to ignore subpoenas from Congress for documents and testimony.

House Speaker Nancy Pelosi initially said she opposed impeachment but, instead, wanted to see Trump defeated in 2020 and then sent to prison. Eventually, though, with members fearing 2020 primary challenges from angry progressives, Pelosi gave in to the pressure within her party and allowed the impeachment process to move forward. Speaker Pelosi made her feelings about Trump clear when, in full view of the television cameras, she tore in half her copy of the president's 2020 State of the Union address when he finished speaking. Trump, for his part, showed nothing but contempt for his enemies in Congress, labeling the impeachment a "witch hunt," and castigating the Democrats for making a case "loaded with lies and misrepresentations." The Republican-controlled Senate declined to convict Trump on the charges brought by the Democratic-controlled House. Acquittal, however, did little to soften the president's feelings about his Democratic foes in the Congress.

Trump also succeeded in appointing large numbers of conservative judges to the federal courts, including three Supreme Court justices, to fill vacancies that arose during his term. In the final months before the election, the death of liberal Supreme Court Justice Ruth Bader Ginsburg ignited a partisan battle over the vacancy left by her passing. Democrats requested that Republicans honor the precedent Republicans set in 2016 when they would not hold hearings for Obama's nomination to the Court because it was an election year, but Republicans saw an opportunity to establish a long-lasting conservative majority on the Court. In a record 27 days, the Republican-controlled Senate confirmed Justice Amy Coney Barrett, a staunch religious conservative, establishing a six-member conservative majority on the Court. Every Democrat and only one Republican voted against her nomination. Many Democrats declared that they would support "court packing" plans to expand the size of the federal courts, including the Supreme Court, to make room for the appointment of liberal judges.

THE CAMPAIGN

2020 Presidential Primaries Against this backdrop of intense partisan rancor, the two parties prepared for the 2020 presidential race. On the Republican side, the incumbent president, Donald Trump, was certain to be renominated and busied himself attacking the Democratic candidates. On the Democratic side more than 20 candidates sought the nomination. These included former vice president Joe Biden, who represented the party's traditional moderate liberal wing; Senators Bernie Sanders and Elizabeth Warren, who spoke for the party's progressive wing; and a variety of others, who spoke for disparate party factions or mainly for themselves. Biden struggled in three of the early state nominating contests. In the February 3 Iowa caucuses, he came in fourth, and he then lost the New Hampshire primary and Nevada caucus to Sanders. The South Carolina primary was the turning point for the Biden campaign. With strong support from African American voters, Biden scored a huge victory in South Carolina, which caused several of his opponents to drop out of the race and endorse the former vice president. With a growing coalition behind him, Biden dominated the so-called Super Tuesday March 3 primaries. In mid-April, and facing the coronavirus pandemic,

While Biden's campaign for the Democratic nomination struggled in the first three primaries and caucuses, his resounding win in the South Carolina primary, largely from the overwhelming support of Black voters, secured his path forward to win the nomination.

Biden's strongest opponent, Vermont Democratic-Socialist Senator Bernie Sanders, withdrew from the race, and the party nominated Biden. Trump retained Vice President Mike Pence as his running mate, while Biden named California Democratic Senator Kamala Harris as his vice-presidential running mate. Harris became both the first Black woman and the first South Asian woman on a major-party presidential ticket.

The candidates focused on issues that had long divided the Democratic and Republican parties. The Trump campaign praised the president's record of tax cuts, deregulation, opposition to immigration, suspicion of international organizations and agreements, and increased military spending financed by further cuts in social spending, particularly on health care. The Biden campaign called for new taxes on the wealthy, stronger environmental and financial regulations, liberalization of immigration rules, increases in social spending, a return to an internationalist foreign policy, and a return to "normalcy" and civility in American politics after what it called "the chaos, the tweets, the anger, the hate, the failure" of the Trump administration.[50] Though many of the issues in the campaign indicated a traditional Democratic–Republican divide, the 2020 general election played out amid crises that dominated American political life: the coronavirus pandemic and the movement for racial justice.

The Coronavirus Pandemic Beginning in the spring of 2020, Americans began to fall ill with COVID-19. This deadly disease was caused by a coronavirus that originated in Wuhan, China, and touched off a pandemic that ultimately killed several million people around the world, including more than 250,000 Americans. The Trump administration reacted to the emergency in fits and starts but did partially seal the nation's borders. The administration also launched "Operation Warp Speed," an effort to press pharmaceutical companies and medical equipment companies to ramp up research and production for a vaccine to combat the virus. State governors used their own emergency powers to close schools, businesses, factories, and houses of worship and to ban large gatherings. These public-health measures caused social and economic upheaval and threw millions of people out of work. The administration, with the support of Congress, developed an enormous economic stimulus package that was designed to ease the nation's economic pain. President Trump claimed that his quick actions had slowed the spread of the virus and prevented economic collapse. He frequently pointed to a rebounding stock market to indicate that the economy was strong despite the pandemic. Democrats charged that the president had been too slow to act and had not done enough to lead the nation through the pandemic. Trump frequently attacked scientists and public-health professionals, and sometimes promoted dubious drugs as potential cures for COVID-19. Democrats pointed out that the president had failed even to lead by example, usually declining to require social distancing at his numerous campaign rallies or even to wear a face mask himself in public places. Trump's refusal to wear a mask became a political statement, with many of the president's supporters also refusing to wear masks in public. Joe Biden, by contrast, did not hold large public rallies and observed COVID-19 precautions. The significance of this difference became manifest when the president contracted COVID-19 in October 2020, briefly throwing the presidential campaign into turmoil. After a short hospitalization, though, Trump recovered and resumed campaigning. Wearing a face mask became an outward symbol of the party polarization of the nation, with Democratic leaders and partisans regularly wearing them but Republicans sometimes not.

Racial Strife and Mass Protests The second crisis affecting the campaign began in the summer of 2020 when the killing of an unarmed Black man, George Floyd, by Minneapolis, Minnesota, police sparked nationwide Black Lives Matter protests. Protests were intensified by police killings of three other African Americans: Rayshard Brooks in Atlanta, Georgia; Daniel Prude in Rochester, New York; and Breonna Taylor in Louisville, Kentucky. Major protests broke out in New York; Chicago; Portland; Kenosha, Wisconsin; Minneapolis; and other cities. While the protests were mostly peaceful, there were significant incidents of violent clashes with the police and counterprotesters and reports of looting, vandalism, and arson.

In each killing, police said they were acting properly, while protesters called their actions murderous. Democrats charged that the killings and subsequent disturbances revealed the systemic racism in criminal justice and society that had plagued America since its founding. President Trump supported police actions, accused protesters of causing widespread violence, charged that Democratic governors and mayors were not doing enough to protect public safety, and dispatched federal forces to several cities to help quell disturbances. Democrats said the president's actions only added fuel to the fire and hoped that these events would demonstrate to Americans the importance of going to the polls and voting for Joe Biden. Republicans, on the other hand, hoped that suburbanites would be frightened by the protests and would respond to Republicans' promise to restore law and order.

The State of the Polls before the Election Leading up to the election, national and statewide polls predicted that Biden had a 90 percent chance of becoming president, and that Democrats had a 98 percent chance of winning the House and an 80 percent chance of winning a majority in the Senate.[51] Even though pollsters called the presidential race correctly in 2020, the national polls vastly underestimated support for President Trump and congressional Republicans, as they had in 2016. While Biden still delivered a decisive win in the popular vote, by roughly a 4 percent margin, and also won the electoral college, the national polling average had Biden up 8.4 percent before the election, demonstrating a gap between polling methods and voters' actual preferences.[52] While the cause of the polling error is uncertain, a few factors may have contributed. First of all, most polls undercounted White non-college-educated people in general, who form a large part of Trump's base. Second of all, as more and more people refuse to answer survey questions asked by pollsters, survey samples shrink, which may lead to a response pool that does not represent the electorate accurately (see more on polling errors in Chapter 6).

THE RESULTS

As mentioned above, Joe Biden defeated Donald Trump in the presidential race, Democrats retained control in the House of Representatives, and Republicans were likely to retain control in the Senate, pending the results of two runoff elections in Georgia in January.

President The 2020 presidential election witnessed historic voter turnout, with nearly 159 million votes cast (66.4 percent of eligible voters, up from 60 percent in 2016).[53] It was the highest voter turnout in the United States since 1900. In some states—Minnesota, Maine, Colorado, and Iowa—nearly 8 in 10 eligible adults voted.

In order to make voting safer during the coronavirus pandemic, all but six states made it easier to vote by mail and vote early in person. As a result, the 2020 election saw nearly two-thirds of all votes cast early—a record 101 million—roughly one-third of which were in person and two-thirds by mail. With so many people voting by mail for the first time, fears of rejected mail ballots ran high, but rejection rates were lower than predicted and generally voting by mail went more smoothly than expected.

Nationwide, Democrats were much more likely to vote by mail, and Republicans in person, as President Trump vocally claimed mail voting would lead to fraud. (In Pennsylvania, where the candidates spent a disproportionate amount of time campaigning, Democrats returned nearly three times as many mail-in ballots as Republicans.[54]) This partisan divide created a new dynamic in the vote-counting process. On election night, in many states it seemed as though President Trump had a strong lead. But this was dubbed a "red mirage"—the illusion of Republican strength—because as mail-in votes began to be counted, Biden gained ground—the country saw a "blue shift"—and ultimately overtook Trump in the key states that led Trump to victory in 2016. This unique and time-consuming process was new to many Americans and led many Republicans, including President Trump, to claim that, at best, there were widespread voting irregularities, and at worst, that Biden and the Democrats had stolen the election. (See below.)

Biden beat Trump with razor-thin victories in just six of the swing states—a mix of traditional battleground states in the upper Midwest (Wisconsin, Michigan, and Pennsylvania) and untraditional battleground states in the Southwest (Arizona and Nevada) and Southeast (Georgia). Trump won the presidency in 2016 by a narrow margin of just under 40,000 votes in Pennsylvania, Michigan, and Wisconsin combined. In 2020, those three swing states flipped back to the Democrats by just over 220,000 votes. Biden's narrowest victories came in Arizona (just over 10,000 votes), Georgia (about 13,000), and Wisconsin (20,000). Other traditional swing states moved decisively toward the Republicans, including Ohio, Iowa, and Florida (see Figure 10.5). Late in the game, Texas was added to the list of battleground states because of the growing strength of the youth and Latino vote, but Trump held on with a solid 6-point vote margin.

Congress While Democrats won the presidency, in Congress, Republicans won back nearly a dozen seats in the House that they had lost in 2018 (though Democrats retained control) and Republicans were likely to hold on to the U.S. Senate.

House Democrats lost seats where voters feared too-aggressive progressivism from the party's left wing. Moderate Democrats voiced concern that the progressive wing of the Democratic Party hurt the party with policy proposals such as single-payer health insurance, the Green New Deal, and defunding the police, which are unpopular.[55] Republicans promised to rebuild the economy damaged by the coronavirus pandemic, opposed a national lockdown to prevent the virus's spread, and emphasized restoring law and order to protect families and communities. A record 35 Republican women were elected to Congress, which breaks the previous record of 30 and is a sharp increase over the 13 Republican women elected to the House of Representatives in 2018 (including Democrats, a record 141 women will serve in Congress in 2021).

Most incumbent Republican U.S. senators were re-elected despite the massive campaign mounted by Democrats to "Flip the Senate" blue. The vote margin for Senate races closely mirrored the statewide votes for president, with high rates of party-line voting. The three senators who lost re-election were outliers in terms of the partisan

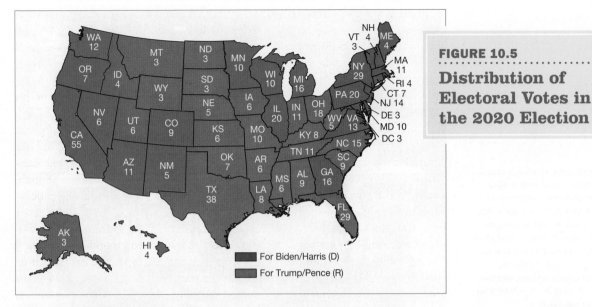

FIGURE 10.5
....

Distribution of Electoral Votes in the 2020 Election

Note: Maine and Nebraska allocate electoral college votes by congressional district. Donald Trump won one of Maine's four electoral votes, and Joe Biden won one of Nebraska's five electoral votes.
SOURCE: "Presidential Election Results: Biden Wins," *New York Times*, www.nytimes.com/interactive/2020/11/03/us/elections/results-president.html?action=click&module=Spotlight&pgtype=Homepage (accessed 11/19/20).

composition of their respective states. Republicans Cory Gardner (Colo.) and Martha McSally (Ariz.) lost re-election, but their states also supported Biden for president. Democratic Senator Doug Jones (Ala.), after winning in a special election, lost as Alabama strongly supported Trump. Even so-called vulnerable Republicans such as Maine's Susan Collins and Iowa's Joni Ernst won by wide margins. Additionally, Republicans maintained control of every state legislature where they had a majority going into 2020 and flipped the Maine state legislature. The election was a reality check for Democrats that the electorate is moderate and desires practical policy solutions rather than radical change.

THE AFTERMATH

In addition to the coronavirus pandemic and related economic crisis and the movement for racial justice, the 2020 campaign was affected by a third crisis, the validity of the vote count. Republicans charged that the growing use of mail-in ballots in 2020 had opened the way for systematic electoral fraud. President Trump refused to promise to accept the legitimacy of the outcome if he thought it had been obtained fraudulently. In the days before the election, Republicans mounted legal challenges to early votes cast in counties they believed to be overwhelmingly Democratic in potential swing states like Pennsylvania, Florida, and Texas. These challenges were generally unsuccessful. For example, a Republican effort to disqualify more than 100,000 votes cast via drive-through voting in presumptively Democratic precincts of Harris County, Texas, failed when a federal judge allowed the votes to be counted, though agreeing that the procedure had not been specifically authorized by Texas law.

After nearly all the votes had been tallied and it appeared that Biden won, Trump mounted court challenges to the outcome in several states carried by Biden, including Nevada and Pennsylvania. While these challenges seemed to have little foundation, President Trump and his supporters vowed to continue the fight.

In every election, election workers in each state and county meticulously process and count mail-in ballots. Some states are permitted to begin counting before Election Day, but some must wait until after the polls close on Election Day to begin. In 2020, due to the high volume of mail-in ballots, election workers counted mail-in ballots for days after the election.

Thousands of Trump supporters participated in "Stop the Steal" rallies throughout the nation, and groups quickly formed on social media and attracted hundreds of thousands of followers. This development seemed to indicate that America's bitter political divisions would not dissipate quickly.

ANALYZING THE 2020 ELECTIONS

The winner of this nail-biting election was not known until four days after November 3, the time it took for mail ballots to be counted. The election captivated the nation, even drawing media attention away from the coronavirus pandemic, which had dominated headlines for the previous eight months. It took a week for the magnitude of Biden's victory to sink in—the exceptional mobilization of young and diverse voters, a continuation of the Democrats' advance in the suburbs, plus Biden's success in winning back a sufficient share of blue-collar, non-college-educated voters.

It was not a win for the progressive wing of the Democratic Party, nor a win for Trump and the conservative Republicans, but a win for moderates and the hope for a return to normalcy in the White House. After the 2020 election, the nation remained closely and bitterly divided, with the Senate nearly tied, the House nearly tied, and deep partisan polarization ingrained.

Two key shifts in the electorate were at play in 2020, compared to 2016. First, exit polls nationwide and in key battleground states report that ideological moderates supported Biden by nearly two to one, and 54 percent of independents supported Biden, compared to 41 percent for Trump.[56] Second, among first-time voters, Biden won nearly 65 percent of the vote, showing the strength and depth of the Democrats' ground game. Biden won by convincing moderates and independents to support the Democratic ticket and mobilizing a large number of new voters.

The rural/urban split was even more evident in 2020 than in the past, with Trump winning most rural areas nationwide, even in the bluest of states, and Biden winning

Who Runs for Office?

While the United States has over 90,000 local governments, with hundreds of thousands of elected positions, only 2 percent of Americans have run for office. Who runs for office in the United States? How does this compare to the makeup of the U.S. population?

Gender

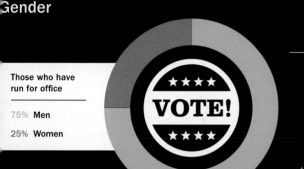

Those who have run for office

75% Men

25% Women

U.S. population

49% Men   51% Women

Race/Ethnicity

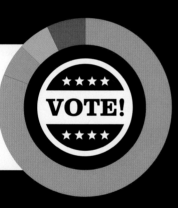

Those who have run for office

82% White

6% Latino

5% Black

7% Other

U.S. population

60% White   18% Latino

13% Black   9% Other

SOURCES: Seth Motel, "Who Runs for Office? A Profile of the 2%," Pew Research Center, September 3, 2014, www.pewresearch.org; U.S. Census Bureau, "2019 Quickfacts," www.census.gov (accessed 9/15/20).

Education

Those who have run for office

19% High school or less

36% Some college

29% College graduate

16% Postgraduate

U.S. population

38% High school or less

16% Some college

33% College graduate

13% Postgraduate

FOR CRITICAL ANALYSIS

1. Historically, those who have run for office (and hold office) have been predominantly White, college-educated men. How does this affect representation in the United States at all levels of government?

2. Which groups run for office the least? What kinds of barriers do these groups face when deciding to run for office?

most large cities and urban areas, even in the reddest of states. Biden won two-thirds of the votes from people living in urban areas, while Trump won 57 percent from those living in small cities or rural areas.[57]

Despite these shifts, 2020 was largely a continuation of the past. The election proved the nation was still deeply, and closely, divided between Republicans and Democrats. Biden won a record-breaking 80 million votes, the most votes for president ever received, and Trump won over 74 million votes, the second-most votes ever received. In 2016 Trump won the electoral college with 306 electoral votes and just 46 percent of the popular vote, and in 2020 Biden won 306 electoral votes, though he won over 51 percent of the popular vote.

What the Exit Polls Said Exit polls conducted by Edison Research and reported in the *New York Times* provide a preliminary estimate of the demographic breakdown in support of the candidates based on interviews with 15,590 voters, weighted or adjusted to match the actual vote count. While the exit polls offer an indication of how groups voted, they are not precise enough to distinguish between, say, 53 and 50 percent support for a certain group, because of sampling error (see Chapter 6).

- Historic voter turnout meant many new voters came to the polls. Young people (ages 18–29) cast more ballots in this election than in any other in the modern era, with nearly two-thirds supporting Biden over Trump. While an estimated 46 percent of eligible young voters cast a ballot in 2016, similar to 2012, estimates indicate that more than half of young people (53–56 percent) voted in 2020.[58] Looking closely at one of the key swing states reveals how important the youth vote was for Biden's victory. In Pennsylvania young voters broke for Biden 58 percent to 39 percent—representing a 154,000-vote margin. The overall vote margin for Pennsylvania was much closer than that. Without high youth voter turnout, Biden may not have won Pennsylvania, and thus the election.

Youth turnout increased significantly in the 2020 elections, as did early voting and mail-in voting. Here, a young person votes early in Allentown, Pennsylvania, contributing one ballot to many that were counted after the polls closed on Election Day.

- Women were much more likely to favor Biden compared to men (57–42 percent) in what is known as the gender gap, while men preferred Trump (53–45 percent), as they did in 2016.

- Biden won suburban voters by 10 percentage points. Trump had won a majority of suburban voters in 2016.

- While nearly 95 percent of Democrats supported Biden and 95 percent of Republicans Trump, 54 percent of independents broke for Biden compared to 41 percent for Trump, while nearly two-thirds of ideological moderates supported Biden.

- Similar to previous elections, more than two-thirds of Black Americans, Latinos, and Asian Americans favored Democrat Joe Biden, but Trump gained ground among Latinos and Asian Americans, winning 32 percent and 34 percent of each group, respectively. Trump's appeal to the Latino community was broader than just to Cubans in Florida, spreading to some Mexican American communities in Texas. Native Americans, though a small percentage of the electorate, cast 60–90 percent of their votes for Biden in key swing states like Arizona and Wisconsin where Biden won by very small margins.

- Age group differences continued to matter, with nearly two in three young people (18–29) supporting the Democrats and older people (65 and older) more evenly split between the two candidates. Four years earlier, Trump had won the oldest age group by nearly two-thirds. Trump's handling of the coronavirus pandemic likely eroded support for him among the elderly.

- Biden and Trump almost evenly split non-college-educated voters, which was a significant increase for Democrats over 2016. Trump won this group by 2 percentage points in 2020 (50–48), down from 8 points in 2016. Biden won nearly 13 percentage points more votes among the college educated.

- In another surprising departure from 2016, Trump's support among White born-again Christians dropped from nearly 90 percent four years earlier to 76 percent in 2020.

- Reflecting patterns from previous elections, Biden won strong majorities among lower- and middle-income groups while Trump won among families earning more than $100,000 a year. Nearly 8 in 10 voters who said they were financially worse off today supported Biden, as did 2 in 3 who said their finances were about the same.

The Impact of COVID-19 and the Economy In historical terms, it is rare for a sitting president to lose re-election. Only nine previous presidents who ran for re-election failed to win a second term.[59] But during economic crises, incumbents are much more likely to lose because the president is held accountable for the nation's economic well-being. President Jimmy Carter lost in 1980 facing an energy crisis and a recession. Herbert Hoover lost in 1932 after presiding over the worst economic downturn in U.S. history—the 1929 Great Depression, when the stock market crashed (losing 82 percent of its value) and 25 percent of the workforce was unemployed. During the economic panic of 1837–38, Martin Van Buren lost re-election when hundreds of banks and businesses failed. In light of this, perhaps it is less surprising that Trump was not re-elected in the midst of the coronavirus pandemic and the resulting economic uncertainty.

The coronavirus pandemic and resulting economic crisis colored the 2020 elections, and as the polls closed on November 3, many Americans were facing unemployment and food insecurity as well as rising COVID-19 cases in their state. In many communities across the nation, Americans lined up at food banks and unemployment offices.

The magnitude of the economic crisis caused by the 2020 coronavirus pandemic and government shutdowns of nonessential businesses cannot be overestimated. At the height of the pandemic in April 2020, the Bureau of Labor Statistics reported 14.7 percent of the population was unemployed. By the election, unemployment had decreased, but was still double pre-pandemic levels. (These numbers also significantly underestimate those without work, because people who stop looking for employment are not counted in the workforce.) Eight months after the pandemic began, the census's Household Pulse Survey reported that 40 percent of Americans were living in a household where at least one adult had lost employment income, and 24 percent expected someone in their household to experience a loss of employment in the next month. One in 10 were living in a household where there was sometimes or often not enough to eat in the previous week and nearly 3 in 10 households said it had been somewhat or very difficult to pay household expenses and basic necessities. The economic fallout from the pandemic hit lower-income people the hardest. Small businesses, the workhorses of the economy, also suffered tremendously, as 75 percent of them reported experiencing large or moderate negative effects from the pandemic. As a result, exit polls indicated the economy was the most important issue influencing how people voted. In separate questions asking what was the most important issue facing the country overall, the coronavirus and the economy were the top two.

CONCLUSION: THE 2020 ELECTION AND AMERICA'S FUTURE

In the 2020 election, each party made a massive push to mobilize voters, and it worked. Nearly 67 percent of those eligible to vote went to the polls, almost 10 percentage points higher than in 2016 and the highest turnout level seen in the United States since 1900. The historic turnout in 2020 showed that when the stakes are high, America can achieve a robust level of political participation, a healthy sign for democracy. Giving cause for concern, however, were multiple warning signs, including deep partisan rancor, an increased belief in political conspiracy theories, and efforts to undermine the election results.

Ultimately, led by Joe Biden, the Democrats prevailed in the presidential race by assembling a diverse electoral coalition and winning large majorities among African Americans, Latinos, and young people, especially college graduates. The Republicans carried a sizable majority of the White vote (though slightly less than in 2016) but may have done slightly better with African American and Latino voters (especially men) than they did in 2016.

The Democrats seem best positioned to govern a nation that is rapidly becoming more diverse and better educated. If it is to remain competitive, the Republican Party must find a way to reach beyond its core White, male constituencies. But some results give Republicans hope. For most of his term, President Trump seemed determined to alienate Latinos through his rhetoric on immigration, but in the closing months of the race Trump campaigned vigorously for Latino votes and increased Republicans' Latino vote percentage over 2016, suggesting that Republicans can compete in a more diverse America. Closely contested, intensely fought elections are likely to persist.

Joe Biden and Kamala Harris won the 2020 presidential election over Donald Trump and Mike Pence with 306 electoral votes to 232. While their win was decisive and historic, the future of the United States remained uncertain due to the coronavirus pandemic, economic insecurity, and a highly polarized population.

The future will, of course, depend upon the programs and policies of the Biden era and President Biden's ability to heal a fractured and polarized nation. The Great Seal of the United States features the motto *E pluribus unum*, a Latin phrase that means "out of many, one." The motto offers the hope that, though diverse, America can be one nation. At the moment, many Americans, including former president Trump, believe the 2020 election was stolen. Ideological polarization seems unabated. Control of the government will likely be divided. And yet, Americans are generally a hopeful people. The fact that record numbers of Americans went to the polls in 2020 is a sign of their continuing belief in America and in democracy and their hope for a better future.

Campaigns and Elections: What Do You Think?

As politicians ponder the questions discussed in this chapter, individual Americans must think about what the 2020 election might mean for them.

★ Will the new administration's economic policies create more jobs or leave Americans with less secure economic futures? What could divided government mean for America's recovery from the pandemic? Will a new administration's national security policies make us more or less safe?

★ Will moneyed interests continue to play a large role in the election process? Will campaign spending increase to the point that the citizens of tomorrow enact reform for public financing or free media for all qualified candidates? What new laws may be needed to make the rules of the game fair? What do you think Pat Murakami, Teresa Mosqueda, and Shaun Scott, the first-time candidates featured at the beginning of the chapter, would say?

★ How might you be involved in campaigns and elections in the future? Do you feel that your voice is heard? What changes would increase electoral participation among young people?

STUDY GUIDE

Elections in America

Describe the major rules and types of elections in the United States (pp. 347–60)

The responsibility for administering elections rests mainly with state, county, and city election boards. Most Americans have the opportunity to vote in several elections each year; the United States is one of the few nations to hold primary elections in addition to a general election. Most elections use the Australian ballot and operate under a plurality, rather than majority or proportional representation, system. Members of the House of Representatives are directly elected by voters in their geographic districts, which are redrawn every 10 years to reflect population changes. Candidates for president are nominated at the major parties' national conventions after a series of state-by-state caucuses and primaries, and the president is ultimately elected indirectly by the electoral college.

Key Terms

midterm elections (p. 347)

primary elections (p. 347)

general election (p. 347)

closed primary (p. 348)

open primary (p. 348)

majority system (p. 348)

runoff election (p. 348)

plurality system (p. 348)

proportional representation (p. 348)

straight-ticket voting (p. 349)

redistricting (p. 350)

gerrymandering (p. 350)

partisan gerrymandering (p. 351)

majority-minority district (p. 352)

retail politics (p. 352)

delegate (p. 354)

party platform (p. 355)

electoral college (p. 357)

ballot initiative (p. 359)

referendum (p. 359)

recall (p. 360)

Practice Quiz

1. An open primary is a primary election in which
   a) one's vote is made public.
   b) only registered members of the party may vote.
   c) all registered voters, including independents, are able to choose which party primary they will participate in.
   d) only two candidates are allowed to run.
   e) voting is conducted by mail.

2. To win under the plurality system used in most American elections, a candidate must receive
   a) more than 50 percent of the popular vote.
   b) more than 50 percent in the runoff election.
   c) more than two-thirds of the popular vote.
   d) more than 75 percent of the popular vote.
   e) more votes than any of the other candidates, regardless of the percentage.

3. If a person votes for candidates from more than one party for different offices in the same election, she is said to be engaging in
   a) retrospective voting.
   b) two-way voting.
   c) prospective voting.
   d) straight-ticket voting.
   e) split-ticket voting.

4. If a state has 10 members in the U.S. House of Representatives, how many votes in the electoral college does that state have?
   a) 2
   b) 10
   c) 12
   d) 20
   e) The number of votes cannot be determined from this information.

Election Campaigns

Explain strategies campaigns use to win elections (pp. 360–69)

In order to successfully run for office, candidates must create formal campaign organizations that employ both professional consultants—including campaign managers, media consultants, pollsters, and others—and hundreds if not thousands of volunteers and paid staff. Candidates must start raising money well before they face an election, a task that is easier for incumbents than it is for challengers. Campaigns must decide on a message and come up with a strategy for communicating that message to the voters they want to reach through the media, televised debates, and micro-targeting.

Key Terms

campaign (p. 360)

incumbent (p. 360)

grassroots campaigns (p. 364)

Practice Quiz

5. An incumbent is a candidate who
   a) does not currently hold office.
   b) has the support of both major parties.
   c) already holds the office he or she is running for.
   d) has won his or her party's primary election.
   e) has been nominated at the party convention.

6. The two main types of general-election campaigns in the United States today are
   a) grassroots campaigns and self-funded campaigns.
   b) grassroots campaigns and mass media campaigns.
   c) mass media campaigns and self-funded campaigns.
   d) grassroots campaigns and primary campaigns.
   e) self-funded campaigns and primary campaigns.

Money and Politics

Identify the rules that govern campaign fundraising and spending (pp. 369–72)

Modern political campaigns in the United States are enormously expensive, and candidates with the most money often win. Despite legislative efforts to regulate contributions, several key Supreme Court cases since the mid-1970s have removed many restrictions on campaign finance. Candidates can finance their campaigns with money from individual donors, political action committees, the national political parties, and their own bank accounts. Certain groups, such as 527 committees and 501(c)(4) committees, can raise and spend unlimited amounts of money for political campaigns. The Federal Election Campaign Act also provides for public funding of presidential campaigns.

Key Terms

political action committee (PAC) (p. 371)

527 committee (Super PAC) (p. 372)

501(c)(4) committees (dark money) (p. 372)

Practice Quiz

7. In *Buckley v. Valeo*, the Supreme Court ruled that
   a) PAC donations to campaigns are constitutionally protected.
   b) it is unconstitutional for candidates to spend their own money to campaign for office.
   c) the right of individuals to spend their own money to campaign for office is constitutionally protected.
   d) there is no limit to the number of candidates to whom an individual can contribute.
   e) the Bipartisan Campaign Reform Act is unconstitutional.

8. The main difference between a 527 committee and a 501(c)(4) committee is that
   a) a 527 is not legally required to disclose where it gets its money, while a 501(c)(4) is legally required to do so.
   b) a 501(c)(4) is not legally required to disclose where it gets its money, while a 527 is legally required to do so.
   c) a 527 can contribute to only one campaign, while a 501(c)(4) can contribute to many.
   d) a 501(c)(4) can contribute to only one campaign, while a 527 can contribute to many.
   e) a 527 can legally coordinate its spending with a candidate's campaign, while a 501(c)(4) cannot.

9. Public funding of presidential campaigns was
   a) outlawed by the Federal Election Campaign Act.
   b) declared unconstitutional by the Supreme Court in *McCutcheon et al. v. Federal Election Commission*.
   c) accepted by both major-party presidential candidates in 2020.
   d) rejected by all four major-party presidential candidates in 2016 and 2020.
   e) limited to only $25 million in 2008, 2012, 2016, and 2020.

How Voters Decide

Three factors influence voters' choices: partisan loyalty, issues and policy preferences, and candidate characteristics. Voters' partisan attachments do not change frequently, and these attachments often predispose voters to favor their preferred party's candidates. Voters may consider how candidates' positions on important policy issues align with their own preferences when deciding which candidate to choose. Finally, a candidate's race, ethnicity, religion, gender, geography, and socioeconomic background may also affect voters' decisions on Election Day.

Key Terms

prospective voting (p. 374)

retrospective voting (p. 374)

Practice Quiz

10. When a voter decides which candidate to vote for based on imagined future events or campaign promises, the voter is engaged in
    a) prospective voting.
    b) retrospective voting.
    c) introspective voting.
    d) straight-ticket voting.
    e) split-ticket voting.

11. The Consumer Confidence Index
    a) measures how business leaders rate the federal government's regulation of the economy during election years.
    b) was a federal government program designed to increase economic growth during the Reagan administration.
    c) has been an inaccurate predictor of presidential outcomes.
    d) has been a fairly accurate predictor of presidential outcomes.
    e) is based on government reports of objective economic indicators.

The 2020 Elections

. . . .

Analyze the strategies, issues, and outcomes of the 2020 elections (pp. 375–89)

After an embittered election, Joe Biden was elected president in 2020 over Donald Trump. Three crises characterized the election: the pandemic and the economic fallout it caused, racial strife, and controversy over the ballot count. With the backdrop of extreme party polarization fostered by the media environment and Trump's divisive presidency, these issues colored the campaigns and the election results. Record turnout was achieved, along with a record number of early votes cast. Democrats were able to mobilize voters and won 306 electoral votes to Trump's 232, including swing states Clinton had lost in 2016. While Democrats lost some seats in the House of Representatives, they kept their majority, and the Senate majority rested on the results of two Georgia senate runoff elections.

Practice Quiz

12. Joe Biden was able to win his party's nomination because of his decisive win in which state's primary?
    a) Georgia
    b) South Carolina
    c) Alaska
    d) Iowa
    e) Nevada

13. Which of the following states flipped from Republican to Democratic in the 2020 election?
    a) Arizona, Georgia, and Pennsylvania
    b) California, New York, and Massachusetts
    c) Texas, Alabama, and Kentucky
    d) West Virginia, Missouri, and Kansas
    e) Oregon, Washington, and Delaware

14. Which of the following statements is *false* about the 2020 elections?
    a) More people voted on Election Day than in previous years.
    b) Youth turnout increased significantly.
    c) A record number of Republican women won seats in Congress.
    d) Joe Biden won the popular vote.
    e) Voter turnout was its highest since 1900.

15. In 2020, Trump and the Republicans received a majority of votes from
    a) Whites and Asian Americans.
    b) Whites, Latinos, and women.
    c) Whites and men.
    d) African Americans and more affluent voters.
    e) Latinos and young voters.

★ *chapter* ★

11

Groups and Interests

WHAT GOVERNMENT DOES AND WHY IT MATTERS As the economy stalled in early 2020, with widespread business shutdowns and mass layoffs because of the coronavirus pandemic, one group was hard at work: lobbyists for corporations and business associations who sought a piece of the $2 trillion stimulus bill Congress was negotiating. Many of these lobbying efforts paid off. In the legislation, signed by President Trump in late March 2020, prominent economic sectors secured relief: loans for the airline industry (promoted by Airlines for America), emergency aid for agriculture (pushed by the American Farm Bureau Federation), a public health emergency fund for hospitals and other health-care providers (desired by the American Hospital Association, among others), and assistance for small businesses (endorsed by the National Federation of Independent Business).[1] Some more surprising sectors won provisions as well: casinos, which had been barred from relief after Hurricane Katrina, were allowed to apply for Small Business Administration or Treasury Department loans, depending on their size; and sunscreen manufacturers won streamlined Food and Drug Administration (FDA) review of new ingredients and safety labels.[2]

Business interests are not the only entities that lobby the federal government. State and local governments do as well, and they won budgetary aid in the stimulus bill for local schools and colleges, transit systems, and even harbor dredging. At the

During the coronavirus pandemic of 2020, many special interests rushed to lobby Congress and the president to receive emergency aid from the stimulus bill. Here, airline executives speak with President Donald Trump and the coronavirus task force to discuss relief for airlines.

behest of small states, a provision was added that asserted no state would get less than $1.5 billion.[3]

The stimulus bill was unusual in that it included aid for those who are not organized, such as ordinary citizens, who won direct government checks to bolster their household budgets ($1,200 per adult and $500 per child under age 17 for those with incomes below a cutoff). Workers normally excluded from the unemployment insurance system—the self-employed, independent contractors, and gig economy workers such as Uber and Lyft drivers—became eligible, and unemployment benefits were temporarily increased. Homeowners with a federally backed mortgage, such as an FHA loan, gained increased protection from foreclosure. Student loan borrowers

were allowed to suspend payments without penalty for several months.[4]

Although the stimulus included provisions for the unorganized (who do not belong to organized groups or enjoy representation by lobbyists and who are normally unable to exert much influence on government), some people were left out, including college students and dependent elders. The stimulus payments to households excluded those who are dependents on someone else's tax returns but are not under 17, leaving Travis Miller of Iowa to wonder why he would get a $500 payment for his 16-year-old son but not for his 18-year-old daughter: "It doesn't make or break our household as far as money goes. To me, it's more of a principle thing. If we are going to give money out to people in general, why are we not giving it out to all people?" Similarly, Jeff Cunningham of Pittsburgh has three children between 18 and 22 who are in school and working part-time but who also will not qualify for payments because they are still dependents on his tax returns. "I think that they should get the 1,200 bucks," he said, "they could certainly use it." Fern Maklin, a 71-year-old who is ineligible because she lives with her daughter and son-in-law in Florida, says, "That [$500] could be a month's worth of food," adding, "The stress and the anxiety, we try to keep it low key, but it's there."[5]

As the lobbying activity around the pandemic relief legislation shows, some interests in society are organized while others are not. Economic interests tend to be organized. Some Americans belong to organized groups, ranging from local civic associations to huge nationwide organizations such as the National Rifle Association (NRA), whose chief cause is promoting gun rights, and Common Cause, a public interest group that advocates for such issues as limits on campaign spending. Indeed, Alexis de Tocqueville, the French author of a famous nineteenth-century book about American democracy, once wrote that America was "a nation of joiners."[6] This defining characteristic of American political life has not changed since Tocqueville made his observation. Americans are much more likely to join political and social organizations than are people in other countries, and America has more organized interest groups than other nations.

Many believe this unique tendency has a positive impact on democracy. However, many worry that despite the array of interest groups in American politics, not all interests—like those of young people—are represented equally, and the results of competition among various interests are not always consistent with the common good. Yet others worry that the power and money wielded by interest groups can dominate Congress, the president, and the political process—such as elections—at the expense of average citizens and the public welfare.

CHAPTER GOALS

★ Describe the major types of interest groups and whom they represent (pp. 397–402)

★ Analyze why interest groups form and how they attract and activate members (pp. 404–7)

★ Explain how interest groups try to influence government and policy (pp. 408–19)

★ Identify the influence interest groups have on government and policy (pp. 419–24)

Defining Interest Groups

Describe the major types of interest groups and whom they represent

An **interest group** is an organized group of people or institutions that lobbies government to change public policy. This definition includes membership organizations of ordinary individuals as well as business organizations and trade associations, labor unions, university associations, professional groups for particular occupations, and even government groups such as the National League of Cities or National Governors Association that lobby other levels of government. Individuals and other entities form groups to increase the chance that their views will be heard and their interests treated favorably by the government.

Interest groups are sometimes referred to negatively as "lobbies," "special interests," or "pressure groups," or discussed positively as "advocacy organizations" or, in some cases, "citizen groups." They are also sometimes confused with political action committees (PACs), which are groups that raise and distribute money for use in election campaigns (see Chapter 10). Many interest groups do create PACs in their name to be the money-giving arm of the interest group. For example, the NRA Political Victory Fund donates money to political candidates and officeholders on behalf of the NRA, which represents the interests of gun owners.

Interest groups are also different from political parties. Both link individuals and groups to government, but political parties are broad coalitions while interest groups are typically more specific. Parties organize to nominate candidates and to win elected office and interest groups do not, although interest groups are increasingly engaged in political campaigns and seek to help candidates favorable to their policy goals win elections. In other words, parties tend to concern themselves with the *personnel* of government, while interest groups tend to focus on the *policies* of government.

interest group individuals who organize to influence the government's programs and policies

FOR CRITICAL ANALYSIS

How do interest groups and parties differ? In general, which do you think organizes more people, a political party or interest groups? Why?

Although public school teachers are a minority of the total population, the unions that represent them are an influential interest group in many states because they are highly informed and act as a group in support of issues related to their profession, including teachers' salaries.

Global Interest Group Membership

AMERICA SIDE by SIDE

Interest groups play important roles in shaping and sustaining democracies. The level of interest group membership, and the kinds of groups that individuals join, are shaped by the unique historical experiences and institutional frameworks of each country.

1. Looking over the chart, are there any countries or categories that surprise you as being higher or lower than expected? What might explain why some countries have more people who report being members of advocacy and public interest groups while others are higher in professional association memberships?

2. Does the United States fall where you would have expected it to compared to other countries? What factors do you think explain why the United States has higher overall membership rates in interest groups than other countries?

Percent of survey respondents who self-identify as active members of . . .

COUNTRY	ADVOCACY AND PUBLIC INTEREST GROUPS	LABOR UNIONS	PROFESSIONAL ASSOCIATIONS
Australia	7%	9%	14%
Brazil	3	8	6
Germany	2	4	3
India	8	6	6
Japan	2	2	4
South Africa	12	9	7
United States	9	7	12

SOURCE: R. Inglehard et al., eds., "World Values Survey: Round Six–Country-Pooled Datafile Version," 2014, www.worldvaluessurvey.org (accessed 8/8/2019).

Interest groups serve important functions in American democracy, interacting with nearly all of the players in the governmental system. Millions of Americans are members of one or more citizen interest groups, at least to the extent of paying dues, attending an occasional meeting, following a group on social media, reading its newsletter or website, or being on its email list. Organized groups use these means to educate their members on policy issues and mobilize them for elections. Interest groups of businesses, professionals, governments, and other entities similarly conduct research and provide information to the members about relevant policy matters. Both types of groups furnish information to and lobby members of Congress during the lawmaking process. They provide information to the executive branch and participate in administrative rule making and the design of regulations. They also monitor government programs and regulations to ensure these do not adversely affect their members. Additionally, they use the judicial system to engage in litigation. Through these means, organized interest groups represent their members' interests and help promote democratic politics. But as we will see, not all interests are represented equally in society, nor are all organized groups equally successful.

TYPES OF INTEREST GROUPS

Corporate Groups and Trade Associations One predominant set of interest groups is those with a direct economic interest in governmental policy: businesses. Corporations commonly form trade associations with other businesses in their economic sector, such as the American Beverage Association or the American Fuel and Petrochemical Manufacturers. They may join broader groups as well, such as the U.S. Chamber of Commerce, which represents many types of businesses, and the National Federation of Independent Business, which represents small businesses. Until the 1970s, such groups were the primary form of corporate representation in Washington. But as government regulation increased in the 1970s, many individual firms began hiring their own lobbyists to try to persuade government officials and influence policy outcomes.[7] (See more on lobbying in What Do Interest Groups Do? on p. 408.)

Groups working on behalf of businesses and industry far outweigh citizen groups and unions in terms of the number of registered lobbyists in Washington, D.C., and state capitals, and in terms of their financial resources to influence government and elections. Corporations and trade associations constitute nearly half of all entries in the *Washington Representatives* directory, the "phone book" of organizations with a lobbying presence in the nation's capital.[8] Their financial resources are even more disproportionate. Data from the Center for Responsive Politics show that in 2018, labor organizations spent $48 million on lobbying, and "ideology/single issue" groups—CRP's label for citizen groups—spent $148 million. But those amounts are eclipsed by lobbying expenditures by businesses and business and trade associations. The health sector alone spent $567 million.[9] Altogether, corporations, trade associations, and business associations spend $34 on lobbying to every $1 spent by citizen groups and labor unions combined.[10]

Which industries, associations, and businesses spend the most money on lobbying activities? The left side of Table 11.1 lists the top spenders from 1998 to 2019 by industry. At the top of the list is the pharmaceutical industry, which has spent more than $4 billion lobbying lawmakers in an effort to maintain high prices and patent protection for their products, followed by the insurance, electric utility, electronics manufacturing, and oil and gas industries. When it comes to specific businesses and business or trade associations, the top spender is the U.S. Chamber of Commerce, which alone spent over $1.5 billion during this period, followed by national associations representing realtors, physicians, and hospitals.[11]

Labor Groups Labor organizations are also active in lobbying government. Unions such as the United Auto Workers, the United Mine Workers, and

TABLE 11.1

Top Spending on Lobbying by Industry and by Specific Business or Association, 1998–2019

INDUSTRY	TOTAL (BILLIONS $)	BUSINESSES AND BUSINESS OR TRADE ASSOCIATIONS	TOTAL (MILLIONS $)
Pharmaceuticals and health products	$4.2	U.S. Chamber of Commerce	$1,547
Insurance	$2.9	National Assn. of Realtors	$568
Electric utilities	$2.5	American Medical Assn.	$405
Electronics manufacturing and equipment	$2.4	American Hospital Assn.	$385
Oil and gas	$2.2	Pharmaceutical Research & Manufacturers of America	$381
Miscellaneous manufacturing and distributing	$1.8	General Electric	$362
Hospitals and nursing homes	$1.7	Blue Cross Blue Shield	$360
Education	$1.7	Business Roundtable	$291
Securities and investment	$1.6	AARP	$286
Real estate	$1.6	Boeing	$282
Telecom services	$1.6	Northrop Grumman	$281
Health professionals	$1.5	Lockheed Martin	$262
Civil servants and public officials	$1.5	ExxonMobil	$260
Air transport	$1.5	AT&T	$256
Health services and HMOs	$1.2	Verizon	$251
Automotive	$1.2	National Assn. of Broadcasters	$236
Defense Aerospace	$1.1	Edison Electric Institute	$229
Miscellaneous issues	$1.1	Southern Company	$229
Television, movies, and music	$1.1	Comcast	$204

SOURCES: Center for Responsive Politics, "Lobbying Database: Top Industries," www.opensecrets.org/lobby/top.php?showYear=a&indexType=i; and "Lobbying Database: Top Spenders," www.opensecrets.org/lobby/top.php?indexType=s&showYear=a (accessed 9/10/19).

the Teamsters lobby on behalf of organized labor in the private sector, while the American Federation of State, County and Municipal Employees (AFSCME) and the American Federation of Teachers are examples of public-sector unions that represent members who work in government and public education. Some labor unions, such as the Service Employees International Union (SEIU), organize workers in both the private and public sectors. In addition to their individual activities, unions may join together in a confederation, which also lobbies; the AFL-CIO is the largest such confederation in the United States.

Unions constitute less than 1 percent of the organized interests in Washington.[12] Despite declining membership, especially in the private sector, where union membership fell from 35 percent in the 1950s to 6.4 percent in 2018,[13] and despite having fewer resources than business groups, labor unions continue to exercise influence in Washington and state capitals. Union members vote at high rates and often work on campaigns.[14] Members of Congress cannot ignore labor's power at the polls. For example, in 2018 Democrat Conor Lamb won a special election for a congressional seat in Pennsylvania, a state that Donald Trump had won just two years earlier, in part because of strong union support.[15]

Professional Associations Professional associations represent the interests of individuals who work in specific occupations (as opposed to trade associations, which are composed of business firms in a given sector), and constitute 5.4 percent of the organized groups in Washington.[16] Physicians, lawyers, accountants, real estate agents, dentists, and even college faculty have professional associations. Many individuals may not think of themselves as participants in the interest group system, but nonetheless have professional associations working on their behalf. Some professional lobbies such as the American Bar Association, the American Medical Association, and the National Realtors Association have been particularly successful at furthering their members' interests in Congress. Professional associations are active at the state level as well, in part because states are responsible for licensing many occupations from physicians to beauticians.

Citizen Groups Citizen groups are open to ordinary citizens, and represent a wide variety of interests, with groups organized on issues from the environment to abortion, to gun policy, to disability rights. The largest citizen group is AARP (formerly the American Association for Retired People), which has around 40 million members—anyone age 50 and older can join— and represents the interests of older Americans. Other citizen groups include the National Rifle Association, the Sierra Club, and Mothers Against Drunk Driving (MADD). The wide variety of citizen groups makes for some confusing terminology. Some citizen groups are referred to as "**public interest groups**" if they purport to lobby for the general good rather than their own economic interests, although this term has been abandoned by many scholars.[17] Some citizen groups are also referred to as "ideological groups," organized in support of a particular political or philosophical perspective. Examples include the Christian Coalition, the National Taxpayers Union, and NARAL Pro-Choice America.

public interest groups groups that claim they serve the general good rather than only their own particular interests

Wealthy corporate interest groups usually find it easier to gain attention from elected officials than do other types of groups. Here, former Maine governor Paul LePage speaks at a news conference to discuss a report from the Pharmaceutical Research and Manufacturers of America (PhRMA), an interest group representing biopharmaceutical companies and researchers.

Citizen groups make up only 14 percent of the groups with lobbying offices in Washington.[18] However, a survey of lobbyists and government officials regarding 98 randomly selected policy issues found that citizen groups were more likely than any other type to be mentioned as being influential in the debate.[19] Though vastly outspent by corporate groups, citizen groups testify at hearings and are cited in the media with great frequency.[20] Corporate groups also try to form coalitions with citizen groups. The corporate interests bring resources to the table, while the citizen groups bring increased legitimacy and credibility to the cause.[21]

Government Groups In the American federal system, governments lobby each other, as policy responsibility, funding, and regulatory power are often shared across the national, state, and local levels. A wide variety of subnational governments seek representation in Washington, D.C., with organizations including the National League of Cities, the National Conference of State Legislatures, the National Governors Association, and so on. For example, the National Governors Association may lobby the federal government for more highway funding for the states, while the National League of Cities provides research and lobbying assistance for cities appealing to state and federal government regarding crime prevention, economic development, and other issues. The "intergovernmental lobby," as it is sometimes called, constitutes 12 percent of organized groups in Washington, D.C.[22]

Think Tanks Think tanks conduct research and promote policy alternatives in an effort to influence government policy. Examples include the American Enterprise Institute, the Heritage Foundation, Human Rights Watch, and the Center for American Progress. They typically employ researchers and fellows who generate studies and reports advocating certain policy solutions. Many have an explicit ideological stance and generate research in keeping with that perspective.

WHY ARE INTEREST GROUPS SO COMMON IN THE UNITED STATES?

The strong presence of interest groups is one of the unique aspects of American government, politics, and society. Interest groups are more numerous and diverse in the United States than in other countries.[23] One reason for the difference is simply the size and scope of America's society and economy: the United States is a continent-sized nation with the largest economy in the world, and the third-largest population, with people of every imaginable background. This size and diversity creates a lot of interests wanting to advance their well-being. Those interests can all have a voice due to a second feature of American government and politics: the constitutionally guaranteed freedoms of speech and assembly, which facilitate group formation. A third reason for the multitude of organized interests in the United States is the American federal system and constitutional design, which divides political power across multiple levels of government (national, state, and local) and across three branches (executive, legislative, and judicial). This multifaceted system provides many points where organized interests can try to exert influence over public policy. The combination of these elements makes the United States what political scientist Anthony Nownes calls a unique "interest group incubator."[24]

FOR CRITICAL ANALYSIS

Why do you think politicians more often cite citizen groups—rather than corporate interest groups—as being influential in policy debates?

Start an Advocacy Group

SHANNON WATTS, the founder of Moms Demand Action for Gun Sense in America

Do you ever think, "Hey, that's not right. Somebody should do something about that"? That somebody could be you. Shannon Watts was a stay-at-home mom of five who "wasn't political at all" when the shooting at Sandy Hook Elementary School in Newtown, Connecticut, occurred in December 2012. She decided to mobilize "mothers and others" around gun safety, and her grassroots network now has chapters in all 50 states. Here is Shannon's advice for starting an advocacy group:

1 **Figure out what you're passionate about and get educated about the issue.** Don't be afraid to call people for their wisdom. You don't have to take every piece of advice—some people may even advise you not to start an organization. But seek out any input and issue information that will help.

2 **Decide on the scope and the goal and the objective that you are trying to accomplish.** Are you trying to create change in your neighborhood, your community, your state, your region, even nationwide? What policy change do you seek?

3 **Think about the people you need around you.** Start with your personal networks to find volunteers willing to help out. Seek help from experts for website development or pro bono legal work or other organizing help. Recruit in person, online—use every mode that works. (Shannon notes that she started with just 75 Facebook friends.) I was able to tap into the power of perfect strangers because of social media.

4 **Figure out your group's branding: the group's look and feel, including name, logo, font, and colors.** A successful brand brings people together, empowers them, and bonds them. Our organization (Moms Demand Action) uses the color red, which makes the mom members feel like they have superhero capes.

5 **Keep going even when you face defeats.** Regroup, learn from the loss, and take advantage of the positives that emerge even from setbacks. It's important to emphasize to your volunteers that you may have created new relationships with lawmakers; you may have made relationships with the media; you may have grown your organization.

6 **Realize that change typically comes in small steps.** I think young people are particularly frustrated with incrementalism, but that's how our democracy is set up. Change doesn't happen overnight. I always say, incrementalism is what leads to revolution.

Each generation and each segment of the population has very specific levers of power that are available to them and they have to figure out what those are. Our members' special power is motherhood and love for their children. What's your group's special power?

Why Do Interest Groups Form?

> **Analyze why interest groups form and how they attract and activate members**

collective goods benefits sought by groups that are broadly available and cannot be denied to nonmembers

free riders those who enjoy the benefits of collective goods but did not participate in acquiring or providing them

informational benefits special newsletters, periodicals, training programs, conferences, and other information provided to members of groups to entice others to join

material benefits special goods, services, or money provided to members of groups to entice others to join

solidary benefits selective benefits of group membership that emphasize friendship, networking, and consciousness-raising

purposive benefits selective benefits of group membership that emphasize the purpose and accomplishments of the group

Suppose there is a community where polluted air threatens the health of thousands or even millions of residents. Each resident wants to breathe clean air. But no single individual has an incentive to join an environmental group—and pay membership dues or volunteer—as the group works to reduce pollution. Why join the group and spend your precious time and money on this when you are going to benefit from the **collective good** of reduced pollution anyway? Each of the inactive residents would be a **free rider** on the efforts of the residents who joined the group and worked to reduce pollution. The collective action problem is that if all individuals follow the same logic, then no one would join environmental groups, and pollution would continue.

The challenge for interest groups is that they would be more influential if more concerned individuals were active members—if there were fewer free riders. To overcome the free-rider problem, groups offer "selective benefits" available only to group members. These benefits can be informational, material, solidary, purposive, or a combination of these. A community association, for example, can offer its members a sense of belonging (solidary benefit), involvement in community decision-making (purposive benefit), an email newsletter (informational benefit), and a community swimming pool or reduced rates on homeowners' insurance (material benefits). Table 11.2 gives some examples of the range of benefits in each of these categories.

Informational benefits, the most widespread and important category of selective benefits, are provided through online communication such as email, conferences, training programs, and newsletters and other periodicals sent automatically to those who have paid membership dues.

Material benefits include anything that can be measured monetarily, such as gifts like tote bags and mugs; discounts on travel (provided by AARP), gun club memberships (offered by the National Rifle Association), and other purchases; and, perhaps most valuable of all, health and retirement insurance (offered by many professional associations).

Solidary benefits include the friendship and networking opportunities that membership provides as well as the satisfaction of working toward a common goal with like-minded individuals. The Sierra Club, for example, offers "Sierra Singles" programming by which single people can participate in hikes, picnics, and cultural outings with others interested in environmental issues and meet new friends and perhaps a life partner at the same time.[25] Some women's organizations claim that active participation conveys to each member an enhanced sense of her own value and a stronger ability to advance individual as well as collective rights. Members of associations based on ethnicity, race, or religion also derive solidary benefits from interacting with individuals they perceive as sharing their own backgrounds, values, and perspectives.

A fourth type of benefit involves the appeal of the purpose of an interest group. An example of these **purposive benefits** is businesses joining trade associations to further their economic interests. Similarly, individuals join consumer, environmental,

TABLE 11.2
Selective Benefits of Interest Group Membership

CATEGORY	BENEFITS
Informational benefits	Conferences
	Professional contacts
	Publications
	Coordination among organizations
	Research
	Legal help
	Professional codes
	Collective bargaining
Material benefits	Travel packages
	Insurance
	Discounts on consumer goods
Solidary benefits	Friendship
	Networking opportunities
Purposive benefits	Advocacy
	Representation before government
	Participation in public affairs

SOURCE: Adapted from Jack Walker, Jr., *Mobilizing Interest Groups in America: Patrons, Professions, and Social Movements* (Ann Arbor: University of Michigan Press, 1991), 86.

or other civic groups to pursue goals important to them. Many of the most successful interest groups of the past 30 years have been organized largely around shared ideological goals, including government reform, civil rights, economic equality, "family values," and even opposition to government itself.

The dilemma for interest groups is that as the size of the group increases, its potential political influence increases, but so does the free-rider problem. Large citizen groups face a particularly acute free-rider problem, hence the reliance on selective benefits. A related problem is that as group size grows, it becomes more difficult to coordinate actions among members and to monitor members' activities. Coordination and accountability are easier to achieve in smaller groups (consider the incentives to be active that you would face as a member of a national organization with millions of members compared to a neighborhood association with a couple of dozen members). Many business associations have relatively few members compared to citizen groups, but they can be quite influential not

FOR CRITICAL ANALYSIS

Where do you experience the "free-rider" problem in your life? What do you or other group members do to overcome it?

only because of their monetary resources but also because their lobbying and other activities are well coordinated.

WHAT INTERESTS ARE NOT REPRESENTED?

pluralism the theory that all interests are and should be free to compete for influence in the government; the outcome of this competition is compromise and moderation

Pluralism, the theory that all interests are and should be free to compete for influence in the government, was long the dominant view of the U.S. political system. However, critics point out that not all interests are equally represented in debates over government and policy. Some of them speak with loud voices (major corporations, for example), while others can barely make themselves heard (the homeless). Pluralism does not guarantee political equality. Indeed, important research indicates that, through group politics, economic elites have considerably more influence than mass-based forces in the American political process.[26] This version of pluralism is called elite pluralism and more accurately describes American politics.

As the political scientist E. E. Schattschneider put it, "The flaw in the pluralist heaven is that the heavenly chorus sings with a strong upper-class accent."[27] His point was that interest group politics is heavily skewed in favor of corporate, business, and upper-class groups, leaving those with lower socioeconomic status less able to participate in and influence government. The central reason for this skew is that people with higher incomes, more education, and managerial or professional occupations are much more likely to become members of groups than are those who occupy the lower rungs on the socioeconomic ladder.[28] Well-educated, upper-income business and professional people are more likely to have the time, money, and skills needed to play a role in a group or contribute financially to it. Moreover, for these people, group membership may provide personal contacts and access to information that can help advance their careers, as well as travel perks, discounted insurance, and other financial benefits. At the same time, corporations and other businesses usually have ample resources to form or participate in groups that seek to advance their interests.

Though interest groups are prevalent in America, certain people do not have a strong voice in government. These include the unemployed, the homeless, and students. Often these groups have little financial backing to help them organize.

The result is that although many interest groups do have a working- or lower-class membership—labor organizations, for example—the vast majority of groups and their members are drawn from the middle and upper-middle classes. Thus, when interest groups play a large role in policy making, many policy issues critical to working- and middle-class people—quality public education, efficient transportation, affordable housing, safe neighborhoods—may be ignored by government, while issues of importance to the upper class and to business receive priority.

In recent years, for example, while ordinary Americans have favored raising taxes on corporations and upper-income groups, these groups have preferred lower taxes and have funded the election campaigns of lawmakers who shared their interest in major tax reform. In December 2017, President Trump signed the Tax Cuts and Jobs Act, which reduced the corporate tax rate from 35 to 21 percent and reduced the top individual tax rate from nearly 40 to 37 percent, a significant tax cut for corporations and the wealthiest Americans, even though among ordinary Americans there was more opposition to the tax cut than support, both before and after it became law.[29] The $448 billion in lost revenue will increase the federal government's budget deficit and may increase pressure to cut government spending, including programs that benefit primarily lower- and middle-class Americans.[30]

As long as there is freedom, it is possible that any interest shared by a lot of people can develop through "voluntary association" into a genuine interest group that can make demands. The political scientist David Truman referred to these interests as "potential interest groups."[31] Two such "potential" groups are the homeless and the poor. Although both groups have strong interests in policy outcomes, such as job programs and affordable housing, they lack organization through which to push for government policy to address these concerns.[32] And one reason they lack organization is that they lack the resources—money, time, and skills—that organization requires, illustrating the barriers to interest formation and the pluralist vision.

What Do Interest Groups Do?

Explain how interest groups try to influence government and policy

Interest groups work to improve the likelihood that their policy interests will be heard and treated favorably by the government. The quest for political influence or power takes many forms. "Insider strategies" include gaining access to key decision makers, lobbying, and litigating cases in courts. "Outsider strategies" include using electoral politics and going public. These strategies do not exhaust all the possibilities, but they paint a broad picture of ways that groups use their resources in the competition for influence (see Figure 11.1).

Many groups employ a mix of insider and outsider strategies. For example, environmental groups such as the Sierra Club lobby members of Congress and key congressional staff members, participate in bureaucratic rule making by offering comments and suggestions to agencies on new environmental rules, and bring lawsuits under various environmental acts such as the Endangered Species Act, which authorizes groups and citizens to come to court if they believe the act is

FIGURE 11.1

How Interest Groups Influence Congress

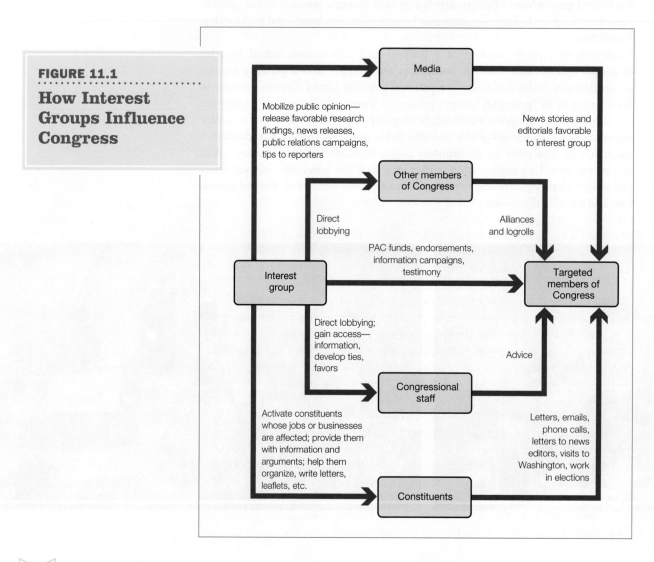

being violated. At the same time, the Sierra Club attempts to influence public opinion through media campaigns and to influence electoral politics by supporting candidates who it believes share its environmental views and by opposing candidates it views as foes of environmentalism. While most groups win sometimes and lose sometimes when advocating for their policy goals, in general, groups that are well organized and have resources are more effective.

DIRECT LOBBYING

Lobbying is an attempt by a group to influence the policy process through persuasion of government officials. Most Americans tend to believe that interest groups exert their influence through direct contact with members of Congress, but lobbying encompasses a broad range of activities that groups engage in with all sorts of government officials and the public as a whole.

The 1946 Federal Regulation of Lobbying Act defines a lobbyist as "any person who shall engage himself for pay or any consideration for the purpose of attempting to influence the passage or defeat of any legislation of the Congress of the United States." Some lobbyists are directly employed by a particular interest group or a specific business corporation, while others work for lobbying firms that can be hired by any group seeking representation and lobbying services. The 1995 Lobbying Disclosure Act—strengthened by the 2007 Honest Leadership and Open Government Act—requires all organizations employing lobbyists to register with Congress and to disclose whom they represent, whom they lobby, what they are looking for, and how much they are paid.

Approximately 11,000 lobbyists are currently registered, down from a high of over 14,000 in 2007.[33] The large decline in the number of registered lobbyists has several causes.[34] The Great Recession that started in 2007 reduced the possibilities for new government initiatives and therefore lobbying, as did the 2011 ban on congressional earmarks (setting aside funds for a particular project in a lawmaker's district, which had been a major focus of lobbying). Recent presidential administrations also adopted rules that diminished lobbying registrations: President Obama did not allow recently registered federal lobbyists to serve in his administration, while President Trump signed an executive order early in his presidency requiring political appointees to sign a pledge prohibiting them from lobbying the agencies they had worked in for five years after they left government. Critics allege that these rules and requirements merely reduce the number of official lobbying registrations while the true amount of lobbying remains undiminished, and that the disclosure laws have significant loopholes.[35] For example, the 2007 lobbying law does not require those spending less than 20 percent of their time lobbying to register. Nor does it require those who engage in policy advocacy but who are termed "strategic policy consultants" or "historical advisors" rather than "lobbyists" to disclose their lobbying activities. Some watchdogs believe the true amount of lobbying is twice what is reported.[36]

Lobbyists attempt to influence the policy process in a variety of ways,[37] the most important being providing information to lawmakers, administrators, and committee staff about their interests and the legislation and regulations that they seek to promote, amend, or defeat. In addition, they often testify on behalf of their clients at congressional committee and agency hearings, talk to reporters, place ads in newspapers, and organize letter-writing, phone-call, email, and social media campaigns. Many lobbying efforts occur in private meetings with lawmakers and

lobbying a strategy by which organized interests seek to influence the passage of legislation by exerting direct pressure on government officials

campaign leaders. Lobbyists also play an important role in fundraising, helping to direct clients' contributions to certain members of Congress and presidential candidates.

Lobbying Congress Traditionally, the term *lobbyist* referred to those seeking to influence the passage of legislation in Congress. The First Amendment provides for the right to "petition the Government for a redress of grievances." As early as the 1870s, *lobbying* became the common term for petitioning: since petitioning cannot take place on the floor of the House or Senate, petitioners must confront members of Congress in the lobbies of the two chambers.

Congress is a common focus of lobbyists' attention because there are so many points of access. Congress divides its workload by using committees and subcommittees (see Chapter 12), and between the House and the Senate there are 535 members and thousands of staffers. As they work to create legislation, all of these people are in search of information, information that lobbyists are eager to supply. Thus, lobbying Congress consists of two main activities, meeting with legislators and their staffs and testifying at legislative hearings. The information provided by interest groups can be analytical (for example, research the group has conducted that supports its preferred policy alternative), political (for example, data on the policy position of potential allies or on the state of public opinion), or even procedural (many lobbyists are former lawmakers and may have suggestions about how to move a piece of legislation through the many steps required for a bill to become a law).[38]

Over time, Congress has cut funding for its own research and support staff; the combined staffs of the Congressional Research Service, Government Accountability Office, and Congressional Budget Office fell by 45 percent between 1975 and 2015.[39] Also, the total number of congressional staff working directly for representatives and senators in Washington has fallen since the late 1970s, as lawmakers have sent more staff to home districts and states to help constituents. These D.C. staff members are stretched thin and work across many issue areas at the same time that public policy has become more complex.[40] Lobbyists, who typically target legislative allies, have incentives to fill the information and expertise void.

Lobbying the President So many individuals and groups clamor for the president's time and attention that only the most skilled and best-connected members of the lobbying community can hope to influence presidential decisions. Typically, a

Like many of their colleagues, John Boehner (R-Ohio, left) and Mary Landrieu (D-La., right) worked as lobbyists after leaving Congress. Members of Congress have knowledge and contacts that make them particularly attractive to lobbying firms.

president's key political advisers and fundraisers will include individuals with ties to the lobbying industry who can help their friends gain access to the White House. During the four years after President Donald Trump's January 2017 inauguration, more than 200 advocacy groups, companies, and foreign governments sought contact by booking events at Mar-a-Lago, his resort in Florida, and at various Trump golf courses and hotels. For example, the CEO of T-Mobile stayed at the Trump International Hotel in Washington, D.C., as his company sought federal government approval for a merger with Sprint.[41]

Lobbying the Executive Branch Even when an interest group is successful at getting its bill passed by Congress and signed by the president, full implementation of that law is not guaranteed. Often a group and its allies do not pack up and go home as soon as the president turns the new law they lobbied for over to the appropriate agency for enforcement. Indeed, Congress often leaves many details up to executive branch agencies, and participation in their rule-making process is a key activity for many interest groups. Just like lawmakers and their staffs, executive branch bureaucrats engaged in rule making are in need of information and expertise, which lobbyists readily provide.

In some respects, interest group access to the executive branch is facilitated by federal law. The Administrative Procedure Act, first enacted in 1946 and frequently amended, requires most federal agencies to provide notice and an opportunity for comment before implementing proposed new rules and regulations. This "notice and comment rule making" is designed to allow interest groups an opportunity to make their views known and to participate in the implementation of federal legislation that affects them. In 1990, Congress enacted the Negotiated Rulemaking Act to encourage agencies to negotiate directly and openly with affected interests when developing new regulations. These two pieces of legislation have played an important role in opening the bureaucratic process to interest group influence. Today, few federal agencies would consider attempting to implement a new rule without consulting affected interests, known in Washington as "stakeholders."[42]

Business owners are often able to gain special access to elected officials. Here, President Trump holds a roundtable discussion with small business owners from across the country.

iron triangle the stable,
cooperative relationship that
often develops among a
congressional committee, an
administrative agency, and one or
more supportive interest groups;
not all of these relationships are
triangular, but the iron triangle is
the most typical

How Interest Groups Make Policy; Iron Triangles and Issue Networks Many
government policies are the product of a so-called **iron triangle**, which has one angle
in an executive branch program (bureaucratic agency), another angle in a Senate
or House committee or subcommittee, and a third angle in some highly stable and
well-organized interest group. In policy areas such as agriculture, energy, or veterans'
affairs, interest groups, government agencies, and congressional committees routinely
work together for mutual benefit. The interest group provides campaign contributions for members of Congress, lobbies for larger budgets for the agency, and provides
policy expertise to lawmakers. The agency, in turn, provides government contracts for
the interest group and constituency services for friendly members of Congress. The
congressional committee or subcommittee, meanwhile, supports the agency's budgetary requests and the programs the interest group favors. Together the three angles in
an iron triangle create a mutually supportive relationship that can last a long time,
especially if a committee member has considerable seniority in Congress. Figure 11.2

FIGURE 11.2
. . . .
The Iron Triangle in the Defense Sector
Defense contractors are powerful actors in shaping defense policy; they act in concert
with defense committees and subcommittees in Congress and executive agencies
concerned with defense.

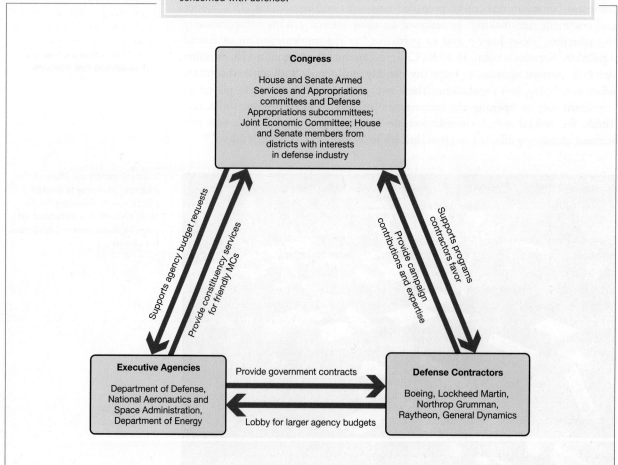

illustrates an important iron triangle in recent American political history: that of the defense industry.

Policy development in a number of important areas, such as the environment, taxes, and immigration, is controlled not by highly structured and unified iron triangles but by broader **issue networks**. These consist of like-minded politicians, consultants, activists, and interest groups who care about the issue in question. Issue networks are more fluid than iron triangles, coming together when an issue is on the agenda and then dissolving again until the next round of policy making. The two concepts can coexist: some issue networks have iron triangles at their core. For example, there are iron triangles at the center of many areas of energy policy, but sometimes a high-profile proposal, such as a new interstate pipeline, activates a broader issue network including landowners, environmentalists, state officials, and so on.

issue network a loose network of elected leaders, public officials, activists, and interest groups drawn together by a specific policy issue

USING THE COURTS

Interest groups sometimes turn to litigation when they lack access or feel they have insufficient influence to change a policy. A group can use the courts to affect public policy in at least three ways: (1) by bringing suit directly on behalf of the group itself, (2) by financing suits brought by individuals, or (3) by filing a companion brief as an *amicus curiae* (literally "friend of the court") to an existing court case (see Chapter 15 for a discussion of amicus briefs).

Among the best-known examples of using the courts for political influence is the litigation by the National Association for the Advancement of Colored People (NAACP) that led to *Brown v. Board of Education of Topeka, Kansas*, in which the U.S. Supreme Court held that legal segregation of public schools was unconstitutional.[43] Later, extensive litigation accompanied the women's rights movement in the 1960s and the movement for rights for gays and lesbians in the 1990s. In 2015 the case of *Obergefell v. Hodges* illustrated the success of this litigation strategy as the Supreme Court declared that the Fourteenth Amendment prohibited states from refusing to issue marriage licenses to same-sex couples.[44]

Since 1973, conservative groups have made extensive use of the courts to diminish the scope of the privacy doctrine initially defined by the Supreme Court in the case of *Roe v. Wade*, which took away a state's power to ban abortions. They obtained rulings, for example, that prohibit the use of federal funds to pay for voluntary abortions. And in 1989 right-to-life groups were able to use the case of *Webster v. Reproductive Health Services* to restore the right of states to place restrictions on abortion, thus undermining the *Roe v. Wade* decision (see Chapter 4).[45] The *Webster* case brought more than 300 interest groups on both sides of the abortion issue to the Supreme Court's door.

On the other side of the political spectrum, the American Civil Liberties Union (ACLU) regularly uses litigation to challenge state and federal laws that restrict the rights of individuals and groups. This includes recent successful challenges to laws ending affirmative action in the states.

Litigation involving large businesses is frequent in such areas as taxation, antitrust actions, interstate transportation, patents, and product quality and standardization. Often a business is brought to litigation against its will by other businesses or by government agencies. But many

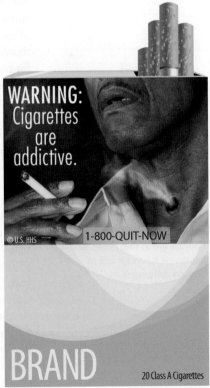

When the FDA required cigarette packages to carry new warning labels (such as the one below), a coalition of tobacco companies sued the government, claiming the labels violated First Amendment rights. The companies won their suit. In response, anticigarette groups such as the Campaign for Tobacco-Free Kids are urging the FDA to develop new warnings.

individual businesses bring suit themselves to influence government policy, and business groups also frequently use the courts because of the number of government programs applied to them. Major corporations and trade associations pay tremendous amounts of money each year in fees to the most prestigious Washington law firms. Much of this money is used to keep the best and most experienced lawyers prepared to represent the corporations in court or before administrative agencies when necessary.

INFLUENCING ELECTORAL POLITICS

In addition to attempting to influence members of Congress and other government officials, interest groups seek to use the electoral process to elect their preferred legislators in the first place and to ensure that those elected owe the groups a debt of gratitude for their support. Although groups invest more resources overall in lobbying than in electoral politics—for example, corporations spend 13 times as much on lobbying as on PAC contributions[46]—campaign contributions and activism can nevertheless be important tools for organized interests. The NRA, for example, dramatically increased its spending in the 2016 election, supporting Donald Trump and Republican Senate candidates. The group spent less in 2020, but still far more than gun control groups.[47]

Political Action Committees and Super PACs By far the most common electoral strategy employed by interest groups is giving financial support to political parties or specific candidates running for office. Because such support could potentially cross the threshold into outright bribery, Congress has occasionally attempted to regulate this strategy, but with limited success. The Federal Election Campaign Act of 1971 (and its amendments) requires that each candidate or campaign committee itemize the full name and address, occupation, and principal business of each person who contributes more than $200. These provisions create an open record of which organizations and individuals fund the campaigns of candidates for public office.

The Watergate scandal was triggered by the illegal entry in 1972 of a group of agents employed by President Nixon's re-election committee into the office of the Democratic National Committee in Washington, D.C. An investigation quickly revealed numerous violations of campaign finance laws, involving millions of dollars in unregistered cash contributions from corporate executives to the re-election committee. Reaction to Watergate produced further legislation on campaign finance in 1974 and 1976, but the effect was to restrict individual giving rather than interest group campaign activity.

In the 2019–20 election cycle, individuals could contribute no more than $2,800 to any candidate for federal office in any primary or general election. A **political action committee (PAC)** representing an interest group, however, could contribute $5,000, provided it contributed to at least five different federal candidates each year. (Campaign finance regulations are discussed in more detail in Chapter 10.) Corporations, unions, and other interest groups form PACs to participate in electoral politics, an option made available by law in the early 1970s.

The flurry of reform legislation in the 1970s attempted to reduce the influence that interest groups have over elections, but the effect has been almost the exact opposite. Electoral spending by interest groups has been increasing dramatically. Given the enormous costs of running political campaigns, most politicians are

political action committee (PAC)
a private group that raises and distributes funds for use in election campaigns

Who Is Represented by PACs?

n the 2018 election cycle, political action committees (PACs) spent a grand total of $3.1 billion to elect and defeat political candidates, including donating $500 million directly to federal candidates. PACs representing ideological or single issue groups spent the most, followed closely by the finance, insurance, and real estate sector. For many sectors, the amount donated to Republican candidates exceeded that donated to Democratic candidates.

PAC Contributions to Federal Candidates, 2018

■ Democratic candidates   ■ Republican candidates

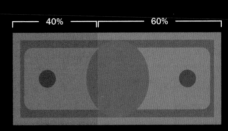

48% — 52%

Ideological/single issue
$95.1M

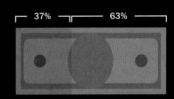

40% — 60%

Finance, insurance, and real estate
$89.3M

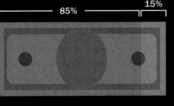

85% — 15%

Labor
$59M

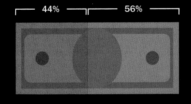

44% — 56%

Health
$54.7M

37% — 63%

Miscellaneous business
$42.6M

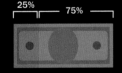

25% — 75%

Energy/natural resources
$31.6M

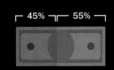

45% — 55%

Communications/electronics
$28.6M

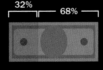

32% — 68%

Agribusiness
$28.1M

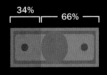

34% — 66%

Transportation
$27.8M

40% — 60%

Defense
$18.1M

27% — 73%

Construction
$16.6M

54% — 46%

Lawyers/lobbyists
$13.8M

FOR CRITICAL ANALYSIS

1. Business PACs are among the biggest spenders. What effect might this have on which candidates get elected and what policies they pass?

2. Why do you think PACs are more likely to donate to Republican candidates than to Democratic candidates?

OURCE: Center for Responsive Politics, www.opensecrets.org/pacs/ (accessed 6/11/20).

eager to receive contributions and at least willing to give a friendly hearing to the needs and interests of contributors. While most politicians do not "sell out" to the interests that fund their campaigns, there is evidence that interest groups' campaign contributions do influence the overall pattern of political behavior in Congress and in the state legislatures, and that lawmakers represent affluent individuals and groups more than the middle class.[48] (See the Who Are Americans? feature on p. 415 for one depiction of who is represented by PACs.)

Concern about PACs grew through the 1980s and '90s, creating a call for reform of federal election laws. Proposals to abolish or restrict PACs were introduced in Congress on many occasions, with perhaps the most celebrated being the "McCain-Feingold bill" in 1996. But when McCain-Feingold was passed as the Bipartisan Campaign Reform Act in 2002, it placed limits on issue advertising immediately before elections but did not restrict PACs in any significant way.

One consequence of this reform was the creation of new organizations to fund candidates: **527 committees (Super PACs)**. Unlike PACs, Super PACs cannot donate to candidates or parties directly, but they can spend unlimited sums to influence an election in favor of a candidate or party as long as their activity (for example, campaign ads or mobilization efforts) is not coordinated with the candidate's campaign or the party. Such expenditures are viewed as "issue advocacy" and are protected by the First Amendment. Because there are no limits on the amount of money Super PACs may raise from corporations, unions, and other interest groups, they have become more important than PACs and have had the effect of strengthening interest groups. The flow of money from interest groups into politics and campaigns through Super PACs was dramatically increased by the Supreme Court's landmark decision *Citizens United v. Federal Election Commission* (2010), which removed the restrictions on independent corporate and union political spending imposed under the Bipartisan Campaign Reform Act.[49]

PACs played a major role in both the 2016 and 2020 elections. In 2016, PACs provided 5 percent of the $451 million that presidential candidate Donald Trump raised and 24 percent of the $846 million that Hillary Clinton raised.[50] In congressional elections, PACs also played a strong role, especially for incumbents. In the House, PACs provided nearly half the funds raised by incumbents, compared to just 15 percent for challengers; in the Senate the figures were 25 percent for incumbents and 6 percent for challengers.[51] The 2020 election cycle was the most expensive ever, more than double the spending for presidential and congressional races just four years earlier. Super PACs provided almost two-thirds of all outside spending (spending by groups and individuals independent of candidates).[52]

Campaign Activism Financial support is not the only way that organized groups seek influence through electoral politics. Sometimes activism can be even more important than campaign contributions. Organized groups can endorse candidates, create voter guides comparing candidates on the issues the group cares about, and mount get-out-the-vote drives to mobilize their supporters to turn out at election time. For example, in the Republican capture of both houses of Congress in 1994, Christian Coalition activists played a role in many races, including those in which Republican candidates were not strongly identified with the religious right. In many congressional districts, Christian Coalition efforts were augmented by grassroots campaigns launched by the NRA, which had been outraged by Democratic support

527 committee (Super PAC) a nonprofit independent political action committee that may raise unlimited sums of money from corporations, unions, and individuals but is not permitted to contribute to or coordinate directly with parties or candidates

for gun control legislation. In 2020, massive efforts by nonprofit groups such as the Texas Organizing Project (for Democrats) and Engage Texas (for Republicans) registered millions of new voters. Nationwide such efforts spurred turnout to record levels.[53]

Ballot Initiatives Another political tactic that interest groups use is sponsorship of ballot initiatives at the state level. The initiative, available in half the states, allows proposed laws for which a certain number of citizens have signed petitions to be placed on the general-election ballot and submitted directly to the voters, bypassing the state legislature and the governor.

The initiative was originally promoted by late-nineteenth-century Populists and Progressives as a mechanism that would allow the people to govern directly—an antidote to interest group influence in the legislative process. Ironically, however, some studies have suggested that many initiative campaigns today are actually sponsored by interest groups trying to get around legislative opposition to their goals. In recent years, for example, initiative campaigns have been sponsored by the insurance industry, the automobile industry, trial lawyers associations, and tobacco companies.[54]

The amount of money spent by organized interests on elections has increased dramatically in the last decade. This cartoon raises the concern that influence in government is for sale and only the extremely wealthy can buy it.

The success of business groups in promoting initiatives to limit taxes in the 1970s and '80s led liberal activists to develop their own issue campaigns. Liberal activists established the Ballot Initiative Strategy Center to provide national coordination for these efforts, which led to successful statewide ballot measures to raise the minimum wage, protect the environment in Colorado, and increase taxes for corporations and high-income wage earners in Oregon and California. Over the past two decades, both conservative and liberal groups have had success with initiatives.

Overall, ballot measures sponsored by business are much more likely to be rejected by voters than initiatives sponsored by citizen groups. In an important study, political scientist Elisabeth Gerber finds that citizen groups and unions are more effective at sponsoring ballot measures, whereas businesses, trade associations, and professional associations are more effective at lobbying state legislatures. The implication is that mechanisms of direct democracy, like the initiative process, favor citizen interests while lobbying favors economic interests.[55]

MOBILIZING PUBLIC OPINION AND POLITICAL ACTIVITY

Going public is a strategy to mobilize the widest and most favorable public opinion for an issue or societal problem, and is a favored strategy of citizen groups, membership groups, and online advocacy groups. It is a form of lobbying aimed not at policy makers but rather at members of the public. Ordinary citizens play important roles in American policy making, such as choosing elected officials, voting on ballot initiatives, and contacting government officials. Interest groups try to capitalize on this not only by mobilizing people to vote, as mentioned above, but also by trying to shape public opinion itself and mobilizing individuals to engage in nonelectoral political activities, such as contacting elected officials and even protesting.

Influencing Public Opinion A quick scan of websites, newspapers, and television will provide numerous examples of expensive and well-designed ads by

Throughout American history, groups have staged mass protests to bring greater attention to their causes. These have included (left to right) the Selma to Montgomery march for civil rights, organized by Martin Luther King, Jr., and others in 1965; Tea Party rallies for lower taxes and smaller government, which erupted in 2009; the Occupy Wall Street movement of 2011, which protested income inequality; and the Black Lives Matter movement, which began in 2013 in response to the killing of Trayvon Martin by George Zimmerman.

institutional advertising
advertising designed to create a positive image of an organization

grassroots mobilization a lobbying campaign in which a group mobilizes its membership to contact government officials in support of the group's position

the major oil and gas companies, automobile and steel companies, other large corporations, and trade associations—various forms of **institutional advertising**. These advertisements do not promote the firms' products but rather try to shape public opinion in one of two ways. Some attempt to show how much these organizations are doing for the country. Their purpose is to create and maintain a positive association between an organization and the community at large in the hope of drawing on these favorable feelings as needed for specific political campaigns later on. Other ads engage in "values lobbying"—shaping individuals' opinions about a given issue area. A good example is the advertisements that ExxonMobil has been running for many decades with the company's thoughts and views about energy policy.[56] The idea is to encourage the public to adopt these views as well, as opposed to the views of other interest groups such as environmental organizations.

Grassroots Mobilization In addition to shaping public opinion, interest groups also try to influence individuals' political behavior. One important form of going public is **grassroots mobilization**, in which an interest group mobilizes its members throughout the country to write, call, or email their elected representatives in support of the group's position. Among the most effective users of the grassroots effort in contemporary American politics is the religious right. Networks of evangelical churches have the capacity to generate hundreds of thousands of letters, phone calls, and emails to Congress and the White House. Similarly, the NRA maintains a powerful grassroots lobbying effort, spending more on mobilization of its 5 million dues-paying members through voter guides and ads than on campaign contributions.[57]

The NRA was itself seriously challenged by a grassroots campaign when, in the aftermath of a mass shooting at a high school in Parkland, Florida, in 2018, students there used social media to mobilize Americans across the nation in support of stronger gun laws. Largely as a result of the students' efforts, and those of supporters they attracted, several states enacted tougher gun laws. Grassroots campaigns have been so effective in recent years that a number of Washington consulting firms have begun to specialize in this area.[58]

Protests and Demonstrations Sometimes groups encourage nonconventional forms of political participation such as protests because they lack the resources, the contacts, or the experience to use other political strategies. The sponsorship of boycotts, sit-ins, mass rallies, and marches by civil rights organizations such as the Southern Christian Leadership Conference, led by Martin Luther King, Jr., during the 1950s and '60s, is one of the most significant and successful cases of going public to create a more favorable climate of opinion by calling attention to abuses. The success of these events inspired similar efforts by women's groups, environmental groups, and gay rights groups.

Such "outsider" strategies can be quite effective. The 2010 Republican takeover of the House of Representatives began with the spontaneous self-organization of the Tea Party movement in 2009 as an angry response to the Obama administration's health care initiatives. In 2011 the Occupy Wall Street movement gave voice to those outraged by economic inequality across America and around the world. In 2013 the Black Lives Matter movement took off after the shooting of an unarmed Black teenager (Trayvon Martin) by a member of the local neighborhood watch and quickly spread across the nation. Shootings of Black people by police and vigilantes across the country—including the police killing of George Floyd in 2020—have led to major demonstrations protesting institutionalized racism and calling for the elimination of racial inequality in the criminal justice system.

FOR CRITICAL ANALYSIS

What do you think are the most effective interest group strategies? Why?

How Influential Are Interest Groups?

Identify the influence interest groups have on government and policy

Americans' ambivalence about interest groups is most apparent when we consider their influence over public policy. Membership in citizen interest groups is an important form of political participation for ordinary Americans. Interest groups are an essential channel for exercising voice in the policy-making process, and in this way they enhance democratic governance. At the same time, critics have concerns about the influence of "special interests." Do some organized groups have too much power, and do they succeed in shaping public policy in a way that is in their interest but perhaps not in the interest of the broader public? Here we examine the factors that make interest groups effective, evaluate attempts to measure their influence over government and public policy, and discuss efforts to regulate interest groups so they do not have undue influence.

FACTORS IN INTEREST GROUP EFFECTIVENESS

Although interest groups are many and varied, most successful groups share certain key organizational components, including strong leadership, an effective strategy, an appropriate structure, and resources such as staff, members, and money.

Strong and charismatic leaders are crucial to interest group success. They can help convince organizations and individuals to join the interest group. They can devise packages of selective benefits that help overcome the free-rider dilemma discussed earlier. They can spearhead recruitment campaigns for members and media campaigns to spread the group's message. And they can engage in lobbying and the other activities of group influence.

Strong leaders will also think hard about strategy and structure. Which level or branch of government should the group try to influence? Should it partner with other groups with similar goals? What kind of structure will maximize influence? Should the group be based in Washington, D.C., with members around the country who merely send in their dues? Or should the group have a federated structure, with state and local chapters that mimic the design of the government? Some studies show that a federated structure can be both more engaging for members, because they can more easily meet fellow members, and more influential, because the group has a presence at all levels of government.[59] The Chamber of Commerce, for example, has a federated structure, with local and state chapters in addition to the Washington, D.C., office.

Resources are also a factor in group effectiveness. The sheer number of members can be a resource that leaders cite in their interactions with government officials. The fact that AARP has 40 million members—about half the U.S. population aged

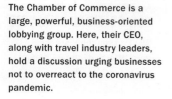

The Chamber of Commerce is a large, powerful, business-oriented lobbying group. Here, their CEO, along with travel industry leaders, hold a discussion urging businesses not to overreact to the coronavirus pandemic.

50 and over—can make lawmakers hesitate to adopt policies that older Americans view as harmful to their interests.[60] The type of members matters as well. Among citizen interest groups, the groups that achieve greater prominence and voice tend to be those whose members and underlying constituency have more "civic and political capacity"—more education and income, better interpersonal networks, and greater political interest.[61]

Staff members are another type of group resource—their numbers and their talent for recruiting members, publicizing the group's activities through media, conducting research, monitoring government activity, and lobbying. And money is perhaps the ultimate resource. Money is necessary for group maintenance. It funds membership drives and it is necessary for conducting media campaigns aimed both at the public and at policy makers. Having more money means a group can hire more and better-connected lobbyists who can access more government decision makers. Money helps interest groups engage in all of their activities, but studies show that more money doesn't always lead to more interest group success. Contributing PAC money to a candidate's campaign, for example, may help an interest group access the politician after the election. But as interest group scholar Lee Drutman points out, "access is only the first step," and there are many other ways—like providing valuable information and analysis—that can earn a group influence over policy making.[62]

Corporate and professional groups typically enjoy organizational and resource advantages over citizen interest groups, but there are exceptions.[63] In the late 1960s, the United Farm Workers (UFW) mobilized thousands of members in California—mostly low-paid immigrants—to reach collective bargaining agreements with growers and to achieve legislation protecting farmworker rights. Despite the group's low level of resources, they achieved policy victories, in part because of the vision and effectiveness of the UFW founder, César Chávez.[64]

MEASURING INTEREST GROUP INFLUENCE

How influential are interest groups? Some people are concerned that interest groups are *too* effective—that their lobbying is too convincing or that their campaign contributions can buy lawmakers' votes on legislation. Indeed, some scholars characterize American politics as less about electoral politics than about "organized combat" among high-resource interest groups fighting over issues far from ordinary Americans' concerns.[65] For analysts, the dilemma is trying to measure the effectiveness of interest groups. We are pretty sure they have an influence on government and policy, but how much? And how do we know?

As noted earlier, the most important way lobbyists win influence is by providing information about policies affecting their clients to busy members of Congress and the bureaucracy. Although interest groups do not necessarily buy roll-call votes, they do "buy time" with lawmakers to promote their preferred policy solutions.[66] Those groups with demonstrated technical expertise have been shown to have more access to lawmakers.[67] Similarly, executive branch officials engaged in rule making are most responsive to the side of an issue that participates the most.[68]

The groups with the most expertise and that participate the most tend to be corporate and professional groups. Although citizen groups are important players in policy making, corporate and professional groups have several advantages.[69] First, they are much more likely to be mobilized on issues than are ordinary citizens and to mold the government's agenda. Even organized citizen groups are spread more thinly than many corporate or professional groups, which can monitor and develop deep expertise in a core set of issues. Second, because corporate and professional groups typically have more resources than citizen groups, they can afford to watch all of their relevant policy areas over extended periods of time. They may not win on all issues, but they get many chances. Third, corporate and professional groups often work on issues that are out of the public eye and attract little media coverage. Such interests may prevail because the other side simply is not activated. Finally, in many instances, corporate and professional groups are defending the status quo, which scholars find is the biggest factor in success.[70] The American political system has many points at which a policy or rule change can be blocked; defending existing policy is easier than changing policy. And corporate and professional interests are advantaged to the degree to which the status quo reflects the victories of these more deeply resourced interests from past rounds of policy making.

REGULATING LOBBYING

The role that lobbyists play in policy making raises concerns, and periodically Congress tries to address abuses. Sometimes the actions of lobbyists are outside of the law. In 2005 a prominent Washington lobbyist, Jack Abramoff, was indicted on numerous charges of fraud and violations of federal lobbying laws. During the investigation of his activities, it was revealed that Abramoff had collected tens of millions of dollars from several American Indian tribes that operated lucrative gambling casinos. Much of this money found its way into the campaign war chests of Abramoff's friends in Congress, including former House majority leader Tom DeLay (R-Tex.). In exchange for these campaign funds, key Republican members of Congress helped Abramoff's clients shut down rival casino operators. Thus, through a well-connected lobbyist, money had effectively purchased access and influence. Abramoff and several of his associates pleaded guilty to federal bribery and fraud charges, and Abramoff was sentenced to more than five years in prison.

Because lobbyists are so influential in Washington, D.C., Congress has tried periodically to limit their role by adopting stricter guidelines. For example, businesses may no longer deduct lobbying costs as a business expense. Trade associations must report to members the proportion of their dues that goes toward lobbying, and that proportion may not be reported as a business expense. Congress also passed legislation limiting the size of gifts its members could accept from interest groups, and members cannot accept honoraria for speeches.[71]

The Abramoff affair prompted the most important new regulation, an amendment to the 1995 Lobbying Disclosure Act (LDA), which broadened the definition of the organizations and individuals that must register to lobby. The 2007 Honest Leadership and Open Government Act expanded on the LDA by increasing the frequency with which lobbying reports must be filed. It also prohibited lobbyists from paying for most meals, trips, parties, and gifts for members of Congress. Lobbyists were also required to disclose the amounts and sources of small campaign contributions they collected from clients and "bundled" into large contributions. And interest groups were required to disclose the funds they used to rally voters to support or oppose legislative proposals.

The effectiveness of these rules is unclear. According to the *Washington Post*, within a few weeks of the 2007 law, lobbyists had learned how to circumvent many of the new rules, and lobbying firms were as busy as ever.[72] Moreover, critics say such rules fail to get at the real problems. Scholars find that there is not much overt corruption of the Abramoff sort. Instead, they argue, the chief difficulties with

FOR CRITICAL ANALYSIS

Some people claim that regulation of lobbying activity is ineffective and irrelevant. Do you agree or disagree? Would you support more or fewer restrictions on lobbying?

How Much Do Major Groups Spend?

Major industries and companies spend billions of dollars every year lobbying the U.S. government on a variety of policy areas. In 2018, lobbyists spent $3.46 billion lobbying Congress and federal agencies.

Lobbying Expenditures, 2018 (top spenders)

 = $1,000,000

$94,800,000
U.S. Chamber of Commerce

$72,808,648
National Association of Realtors

$31,520,000
Open Society
Policy Center

$27,989,250
Pharmaceutical Research
& Manufacturers of America

$23,937,842
American Hospital
Association

$23,884,221
Blue Cross
Blue Shield

$23,160,000
Business
Roundtable

$21,770,000
Alphabet Inc.

$20,427,000
American Medical
Association

$18,529,000
AT&T

$15,120,000
Boeing

$15,072,000
Comcast

$14,400,000
Amazon.com

$14,390,000
Northrop Grumman

$14,170,000
National Association
of Broadcasters

$13,240,000
The Internet & Television
Association (NCTA)

SOURCE: Center for Responsive Politics,
www.opensecrets.org/lobby/ (accessed 6/11/20).

$13,205,502
Lockheed Martin

$12,620,000
Facebook

$12,310,000
Bayer AG

$12,300,000
Southern Company

FOR CRITICAL ANALYSIS

1. What effect does lobbying have on the policy-making process?

2. Is there a relationship between the interests that are represented in Congress and the groups that spend millions lobbying Congress members?

interest groups are the resource and informational inequalities, both among groups and between organized groups and policy makers; the fact that corporate groups spend far more than citizen interest groups on lobbying; and the fact that lobbyists can focus on specific policies while congressional staff and agency bureaucrats have such broad responsibilities and are so outmatched in terms of information.[73] Solutions to these inequalities are difficult to achieve.

Interest Groups: What Do You Think?

We would like to think that government policies are products of legislators representing the public interest. But in truth few programs and policies ever reach the public agenda without the vigorous efforts of important interest groups. In realms including economic policy, social policy, and international trade policy, the activity of interest groups is of critical importance. As we saw at the start of this chapter, interest groups have strong incentives to try to influence policy outcomes—and often they succeed.

★ James Madison wrote that "liberty is to faction as air is to fire."[74] By this he meant that the organization and proliferation of interests are inevitable in a free society. In what ways do organized interests enhance liberty? In what ways do they limit it?

★ If there were no organized interests, would the government pay more attention to ordinary voters? Does group politics foster or impede democracy?

★ Would young people be better or worse off if there were no interest groups in the United States? What do you think the college-age children of Travis Miller or Jeff Cunningham would say?

★ What do you think of competition among different interests—is it free, open, and vigorous, or are some types of interests more likely to organize? What are the implications for government and politics?

★ STUDY GUIDE ★

Defining Interest Groups

Describe the major types of interest groups and whom they represent (pp. 397–402)

An interest group is an organized group of people or institutions that lobbies government to change public policy. Interest groups serve several important functions in American democracy, from educating group members on policy issues to monitoring government programs. Common types include corporate groups and trade associations, labor groups, professional associations, citizen groups, government groups, and think tanks. Interest groups are numerous and diverse in the United States because of the country's large size and scope, citizens' guaranteed freedoms of speech and assembly, and the multitude of opportunities for interest groups to influence public policy across different levels of government.

Key Terms

interest group (p. 397)

public interest groups (p. 401)

Practice Quiz

1. Which of the following best describes how interest groups are different from political parties?
   a) Interest groups represent broad coalitions of people, while political parties represent smaller, more specific groups of people.
   b) Interest groups organize to nominate candidates and to win elected office, while political parties do not.

c) Interest groups tend to focus on the personnel of government, while political parties tend to focus on the policies of government.
   d) Interest groups tend to focus on the policies of government, while political parties tend to focus on the personnel of government.
   e) Political parties are one type of interest group.

2. Which category of interest group tends to spend the most money, collectively, on lobbying?
   a) labor organizations
   b) citizen groups
   c) businesses and business and trade organizations
   d) think tanks
   e) political parties

3. The Sierra Club, the National Rifle Association, and the National Taxpayers Union are all examples of
   a) membership associations.
   b) citizen groups.
   c) professional associations.
   d) ideological groups.
   e) public-sector groups.

Why Do Interest Groups Form?

Analyze why interest groups form and how they attract and activate members (pp. 404–7)

In order to overcome the free-rider problem and encourage more citizens to become active members, interest groups offer selective benefits available only to group members. These benefits can be informational, material, solidary, purposive, or a combination. Well-educated, upper-income, professional people are more likely to have the time, money, and skills to participate in interest groups. As a result, interest group politics tends to skew in favor of corporate, business, and upper-class groups, leaving those with lower socioeconomic status less able to participate in and influence government.

Key Terms

collective goods (p. 404)

free riders (p. 404)

informational benefits (p. 404)

material benefits (p. 404)

solidary benefits (p. 404)

purposive benefits (p. 404)

pluralism (p. 406)

Practice Quiz

4. Friendship and networking are examples of
   a) purposive benefits.
   b) informational benefits.
   c) solidary benefits.
   d) material benefits.
   e) collective goods.

5. Discounts and health insurance are examples of
   a) purposive benefits.
   b) informational benefits.
   c) solidary benefits.
   d) material benefits.
   e) collective goods.

6. Which of the following is a challenge that large interest groups face?
   a) As the size of a group increases, its political influence decreases.
   b) As the size of a group increases, it becomes more difficult to coordinate actions among members.
   c) As the size of a group increases, it is less likely that government will listen to and respond to its concerns.
   d) As the size of a group increases, the free-rider problem decreases.
   e) As the size of a group increases, the number of benefits it can offer decreases.

7. What is a "potential interest group"?
   a) an interest group whose lobbyists are not registered with Congress
   b) a group of people who all support the same candidate for Congress
   c) a group of people who focus on grassroots mobilization but not direct lobbying
   d) a group of people who share strong interests in policy outcomes but lack organization
   e) an interest group that doesn't have an associated Super PAC

What Do Interest Groups Do?

Explain how interest groups try to influence government and policy (pp. 408–19)

Interest groups work to improve the likelihood that their policy interests will be heard and treated favorably by the government. Their quest for political influence may take many different forms. In addition to directly lobbying members of Congress and the executive branch, interest groups may push their policy objectives through litigation, spend money to influence elections in favor of their preferred candidates or ballot initiatives, and work to mobilize Americans in support of their desired policies.

Key Terms

lobbying (p. 409)
iron triangle (p. 412)
issue network (p. 413)
political action committee (PAC) (p. 414)
527 committee (Super PAC) (p. 416)
institutional advertising (p. 418)
grassroots mobilization (p. 418)

Practice Quiz

8. Which of the following best describes the federal government's laws regarding lobbying?
   a) Federal law allows lobbying but only on issues related to taxation.
   b) Federal law allows lobbying but only if the lobbyists receive no monetary compensation for their lobbying.
   c) Federal law strictly prohibits any form of lobbying.
   d) Federal law requires all organizations employing lobbyists to register with Congress and to disclose whom they represent, whom they lobby, what they are looking for, and how much they are paid.
   e) There are no laws regulating lobbying because the federal government has never passed any legislation on the legality of the activity.

9. A loose network of like-minded politicians, consultants, activists, and interest groups drawn together by a public policy issue is referred to as
   a) an issue network.
   b) a public interest group.
   c) a political action committee.
   d) pluralism.
   e) an iron triangle.

10. Which of the following is a way that interest groups use the courts to influence public policy?
    a) supplying judges with solidary benefits
    b) joining an issue network
    c) creating an iron triangle
    d) forming a political action committee
    e) filing amicus curiae briefs

11. Which of the following are examples of "going public"?
    a) free riding, pluralism, and issue networking
    b) donating money to political parties, endorsing candidates, and sponsoring ballot initiatives
    c) institutional advertising, grassroots mobilization, and sponsoring protests and demonstrations
    d) providing informational benefits, providing solidary benefits, and providing material benefits
    e) filing an amicus brief, bringing a lawsuit, and financing those who are filing a lawsuit

12. Which of the following is *not* an activity in which interest groups frequently engage?
    a) starting their own political party
    b) litigation
    c) sponsoring ballot initiatives at the state level
    d) lobbying
    e) contributing to campaigns

13. One of the major differences between PACs and Super PACs is that
    a) a PAC has a maximum contribution limit of $500 per candidate in each election cycle while a Super PAC has a maximum contribution limit of $1,000.
    b) a PAC has a maximum contribution limit of $1,000 per candidate in each election cycle while a Super PAC has a maximum contribution limit of $5,000.
    c) a PAC has a maximum contribution limit of $5,000 per candidate in each election cycle while a Super PAC has a maximum contribution limit of $10,000.
    d) a PAC has a maximum contribution limit of $5,000 per candidate in each election cycle while a Super PAC cannot donate to candidates directly.
    e) a Super PAC has a maximum contribution limit of $5,000 per candidate in each election cycle while a PAC cannot donate to candidates directly.

How Influential Are Interest Groups?

Identify the influence interest groups have on government and policy (pp. 419–24)

While critics of interest groups express concerns about the influence of "special interests," interest groups are an essential channel for exercising voice in influencing the policy process. Most successful groups share certain key organizational components, including strong leadership, an effective strategy, an appropriate structure, and resources such as staff, members, and money. Corporate and professional groups tend to have the most success in influencing legislators because they have deep expertise in their core issues, they have more resources than other kinds of groups, their issues are usually out of the public eye, and they often advocate for keeping the status quo. Though Congress has instituted regulations on the lobbying process, their effectiveness is unclear.

Practice Quiz

14. Among citizen interest groups, the groups that achieve greater prominence are those whose members
    a) are diverse in terms of gender, race, and socioeconomic status.
    b) have high levels of civic and political capacity.
    c) have direct connections to members of Congress.
    d) contribute relatively high membership dues.
    e) are mostly college students.

15. Groups with _____ have been shown to have more access to lawmakers.
    a) a history of supporting successful candidates for office
    b) large constituencies who have an interest in hot-button policy issues
    c) the most money
    d) headquarters in Washington, D.C.
    e) demonstrated technical expertise

12

Congress

WHAT GOVERNMENT DOES AND WHY IT MATTERS As the nation's chief legislative body, Congress affects Americans every day with its decisions. In early 2020, business owner Glynis Donnelly kept paying her eight part-time employees out of her savings even as the coronavirus pandemic brought sales at her Tampa, Florida, jewelry store to a standstill. "It may not be the most business-smart thing to do," she said, "but I know my employees very well, and I know that they need me as much as I need them." To help small business owners like Donnelly, Congress passed a coronavirus economic stimulus bill in March 2020 that included forgivable loans: if a business with fewer than 500 employees used such a loan to keep its workers on payroll, the amount borrowed would later be forgiven, with the company paying back only the interest. Donnelly planned to apply for the program right away.[1]

Congressional *inaction* affects Americans as well. In Huntington, West Virginia, Police Chief Hank Dial's police force was so overwhelmed by the number of fentanyl-contaminated heroin overdoses in the summer of 2016, with people dying at eight times the national rate, that he called the federal government for help. Dozens of FBI, Drug Enforcement Agency, and Alcohol, Tobacco and Firearms agents joined his drug

The members of Congress—100 senators and 435 representatives—represent the voices of the people across America. Yet some observers worry that Congress does not represent all voices equally. From small business owners to police departments, congressional action and inaction can have major consequences.

unit raiding drug dens and arresting dealers. But for all the arrests, the big problem remained: the seemingly endless supply of opioids—especially deadly fentanyl—continuing to stream into his city from abroad. What was Congress doing to stem the fentanyl tide? For years, nothing. Senator Kelly Ayotte, then Republican of New Hampshire, introduced legislation in 2015 to increase prison sentences for fentanyl distribution as deaths surged in her state. Senator Rob Portman, Republican of Ohio, raised the alarm, as did Senator Edward Markey, Democrat of Massachusetts, both from states that, like New Hampshire, had been especially hard hit by fentanyl deaths. And yet congressional inaction continued, because of the stigma of the issue, because many lawmakers outside the hardest-hit areas did not think the issue would help them win re-election, because "if Congress had acted sooner and stopped the epidemic before tens of thousands of Americans died, it would have been difficult to publicly claim victory over a theoretical problem," as Mary Bono, a former Republican congresswoman of California, said. Finally, in October 2018, Congress passed a major opioids bill, but only after 72,000 drug-overdose deaths in 2017 alone— more than the number of people who died in the Vietnam War.[2]

Congress has vast authority over many aspects of American life. Laws related to federal spending, taxing, regulation, and judicial appointments all pass through Congress. While the debates over these laws may seem hard to follow because they are often complex and technical or because heated, partisan struggles distract from the substance of the issue, it is important for the American people to learn about what Congress is doing. As the examples of the coronavirus stimulus and opioid bills indicate, actions taken—or not taken—in Congress affect the everyday experiences we take for granted. With its power to spend and tax, Congress also affects what choices people have and what opportunities they can expect in life.

With so much information about Congress available on the internet, it is not hard to get beyond the heated rhetoric and simplistic headlines and ask your own questions about a proposed law. How will it affect my life and the lives of people I care about? What is the impact on my country? Making laws is a complex and often messy process. Even so, it is vital for citizens to monitor what Congress does, because the laws it passes are so central to their lives.

CHAPTER GOALS

★ Describe who serves in Congress and how they represent their constituents (pp. 431–44)

★ Describe the factors that structure congressional business (pp. 444–50)

★ Describe the regular order and new order processes of how a bill becomes a law (pp. 450–59)

★ Identify the factors that influence which bills Congress passes (pp. 459–64)

★ Describe the powers that Congress uses to influence other branches of government (pp. 464–67)

Congress: Representing the American People

Describe who serves in Congress and how they represent their constituents

Congress is the most important representative institution in American government. Each member's primary responsibility in theory is to the people in his or her district or state—his or her **constituency**—not to the congressional leadership, a party, or even Congress itself. Yet the task of representation is not simple. Views about what constitutes fair and effective representation differ, and different constituents may have very different expectations of their representatives. Members of Congress must consider these diverse views and expectations as they represent their constituencies.

constituency the residents in the area from which an official is elected

HOUSE AND SENATE: DIFFERENCES IN REPRESENTATION

The framers of the Constitution provided for a **bicameral** legislature—that is, a legislative body consisting of two chambers. As we saw in Chapter 2, the framers intended each of these chambers, the House of Representatives and the Senate, to serve a different constituency. Members of the Senate, appointed by state legislatures for six-year terms, were to represent the states while members of the House were to represent the people of the United States. (Today, members of both the House and the Senate are elected directly by the people.) The 435 members of the House are elected from districts apportioned according to population; the 100 members of the Senate are elected in a statewide vote, with two senators from each state. Senators continue to have much longer terms in office and usually represent much larger and more diverse constituencies than do their counterparts in the House (see Table 12.1).

bicameral having a legislative assembly composed of two chambers or houses, distinguished from *unicameral*

The House and Senate play different roles in the legislative process. Traditionally, the Senate is the more deliberative of the two bodies—the forum in which any and all ideas that senators raise can receive a thorough public airing. The House is the more centralized and organized of the two bodies. In part, this difference stems from the different rules governing the two bodies. These rules give House leaders more control over the legislative process and allow House members to specialize in certain legislative areas. The rules of the much smaller Senate give its leadership less power and discourage specialization.

Other factors, both formal and informal, also contribute to differences between the two chambers. Differences in the length of terms and the requirements for holding office, specified by the Constitution, generate differences in

TABLE 12.1

Differences between the House and the Senate

	HOUSE	SENATE
Minimum age of member	25 years	30 years
U.S. citizenship	At least 7 years	At least 9 years
Length of term	2 years	6 years
Number representing each state	1–53 per state (depends on population)	2 per state
Constituency	Local	Statewide

For its first 128 years, Congress was a decidedly masculine world. In 1917, Jeanette Rankin (R-Mont.; pictured back row, far right) became the first woman to serve in the House or Senate. As of 2019, a total of 366 women had served as U.S. representatives or senators, while 11,982 men had served.

delegate a representative who votes according to the preferences of his or her constituency

trustee a representative who votes based on what he or she thinks is best for his or her constituency

FOR CRITICAL ANALYSIS

Why is descriptive representation important? If congressional representatives have racial, religious, or educational backgrounds similar to those of their constituents, are they better representatives? Why or why not?

how members of each body serve their constituencies and exercise their powers of office. For the House, the relatively small size and uniform nature of their constituencies and the need to seek re-election every two years make members more attuned to the immediate legislative needs of local interest groups. The result is that the constituents they most effectively and frequently serve are well-organized local interests with specific legislative agendas—for instance, used-car dealers seeking relief from regulation, labor unions seeking more favorable legislation, or farmers looking for higher subsidies. Senators, on the other hand, serve larger and more diverse constituencies and seek re-election every six years. As a result, they are somewhat more insulated from the pressures of individual, narrow, and immediate interests.

TRUSTEE VERSUS DELEGATE REPRESENTATION

For the Founders, Congress was the national institution that best embodied the ideals of representative democracy. But what is the role of a representative? A member of Congress can interpret her job as representative in two different ways: as a **delegate**, acting on the express preferences of her constituents, or as a **trustee**, more loosely tied to constituents and empowered to make the decisions she thinks best.

The delegate role requires representatives to stay in constant touch with constituents; it also requires constituents to follow each policy issue very closely. But most constituents do not do this; instead, they focus only on issues of particular interest to them. Many people are too busy to become well informed even on issues they care about. Thus, the delegate form of representation runs the risk that the voices of only a few active and informed constituents get heard. Although it seems more democratic at first glance, it may actually open Congress up to even more influence by special interests.

When congressional members act as trustees, on the other hand, they may not pay sufficient attention to the wishes of their constituents. In this scenario, the only way the public can exercise influence is by voting every two years for representatives and every six years for senators. In fact, most members of Congress take this electoral check very seriously. They try to anticipate the wishes of their constituents even when they don't know exactly what those wishes are, because they know that unpopular decisions can be used against them in the coming election.

DESCRIPTIVE VERSUS SUBSTANTIVE REPRESENTATION

We have become so accustomed to the idea of representative government that we tend to forget what a peculiar concept representation really is. A representative claims to act or speak for some other person or group. But how can one person be trusted to speak for another? How do we know that those who call themselves our representatives are actually speaking on our behalf, rather than simply pursuing their own interests?[3]

There are two circumstances under which one person might reasonably be trusted to speak for another. The first occurs if the two individuals are so similar in background, character, interests, and perspectives that anything said by one would very likely reflect the views of the other as well. This principle is at the heart of what is sometimes called **descriptive representation**—the sort that takes place when representatives have the same racial, gender, ethnic, religious, or educational backgrounds as their constituents. If demographic, or sociological similarity helps to promote good representation, then the sociological composition of a representative assembly like Congress should mirror the composition of society.

The second circumstance under which one person might be trusted to speak for another occurs if the representative is in some way formally accountable to those he is supposed to represent. If representatives can somehow be punished for failing to speak properly for their constituents, then they have an incentive to provide good representation even if their own personal backgrounds, views, and interests differ from the backgrounds of those they represent. This principle is called **substantive representation**—the sort of representation that takes place when constituents have the power to hire and fire their representatives. Both descriptive and substantive representation play a role in the relationship between members of Congress and their constituencies.

The Social Composition of the U.S. Congress The extent to which the U.S. Congress is representative of the American people in a sociological sense can be seen by examining social characteristics of the House and Senate today (see the Who Are Americans? feature on p. 435). African Americans, Latinos, and Asian Americans have increased their congressional representation in the past two decades (see Figure 12.1), but the representation of people of color in Congress is still not comparable to their increasing proportions in the general population. After

descriptive representation a type of representation in which representatives have the same racial, gender, ethnic, religious, or educational backgrounds as their constituents; it is based on the principle that if two individuals are similar in background, character, interests, and perspectives, then one can correctly represent the other's views

substantive representation a type of representation in which a representative is held accountable to a constituency if he or she fails to represent that constituency properly; this is incentive for the representative to provide good representation when his or her personal background, views, and interests differ from those of his or her constituency

To more effectively promote a legislative agenda addressing issues that disproportionately affect racial and ethnic minority groups, members of Congress from those groups have formed caucuses. Here, Rep. Chuy Garcia (D-Ill.) speaks with fellow members of the Congressional Hispanic Caucus in support of DACA (Deferred Action for Childhood Arrivals).

FIGURE 12.1
· ·

Diversity in Congress, 1971–2020

Congress has become much more socially diverse since the 1970s. After a gradual increase from 1971 to 1990, the number of female and African American members grew quickly during the first half of the 1990s. Do you think these numbers will rise in the future? Why or why not?

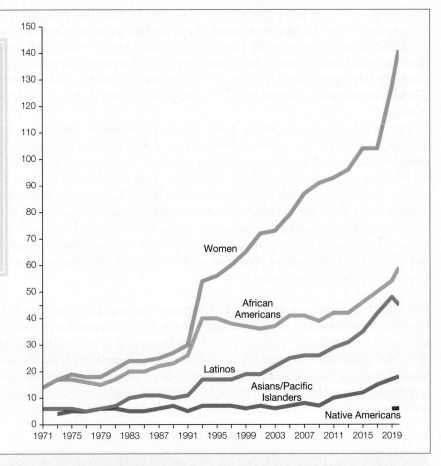

Note: As of mid-November 2020, several races that impact these statistics had still not been called.

SOURCES: Vital Statistics, "Demographics of Members of Congress," Tables 1-16, 1-17, 1-18, 1-19, www.brookings .edu/multi-chapter-report/vital-statistics-on-congress/; Jennifer E. Manning, *Membership of the 116th Congress: A Profile* (Washington, DC: Congressional Research Service, March 31, 2020), https://fas.org/sgp/crs/misc/R45583.pdf (accessed 4/8/20; authors' updates).

the 2020 elections, Congress was 11 percent African American, 8 percent Latino, and 3 percent Asian American. By contrast, the American population was 13.4 percent African American, 18.1 percent Latino, and 5.8 percent Asian American.[4]

Similarly, the number of women in Congress continues to trail far behind their proportion of the population. In 2006, Nancy Pelosi (D-Calif.) became the first female Speaker of the House. Following the 2020 elections, the 117th Congress (2021–23) included 117 women in the House and 24 women in the Senate, a total all-time high. Since many important contemporary issues cut along racial and gender lines, pressure for reform in the representative process is likely to continue until all groups are proportionally represented.

The occupational backgrounds of members of Congress have always been a matter of interest because many issues split along lines relevant to occupations and industries. The legal profession is the most common career of members prior to their election, and public service or politics is also a frequent background. In addition, many members have important ties to business and industry.[5] Moreover, members of Congress are much more highly educated than most Americans. More than 9 in 10 have college degrees, and more than one-third have law degrees.[6]

Who Are the Members of Congress?

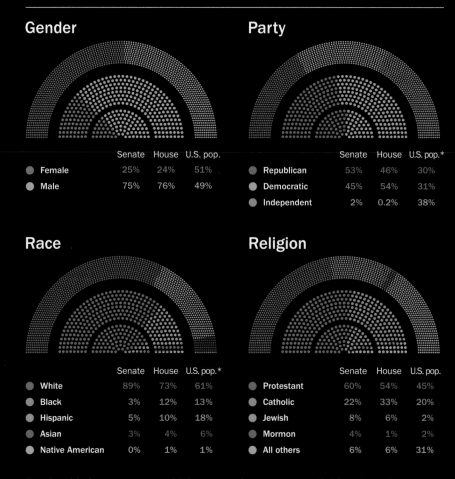

Gender

	Senate	House	U.S. pop.
Female	25%	24%	51%
Male	75%	76%	49%

Party

	Senate	House	U.S. pop.*
Republican	53%	46%	30%
Democratic	45%	54%	31%
Independent	2%	0.2%	38%

Key

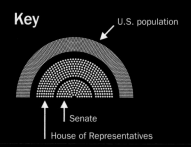

U.S. population

Senate

House of Representatives

Although the number of women, African Americans, and Latinos in Congress has increased in recent decades, Congress is still much less diverse than the American population. Members of Congress are predominantly male, White, and Protestant, and a large percentage hold a law degree. These data compare the 116th Congress, which took office in 2019, with the U.S. population as a whole.

Race

	Senate	House	U.S. pop.*
White	89%	73%	61%
Black	3%	12%	13%
Hispanic	5%	10%	18%
Asian	3%	4%	6%
Native American	0%	1%	1%

Religion

	Senate	House	U.S. pop.
Protestant	60%	54%	45%
Catholic	22%	33%	20%
Jewish	8%	6%	2%
Mormon	4%	1%	2%
All others	6%	6%	31%

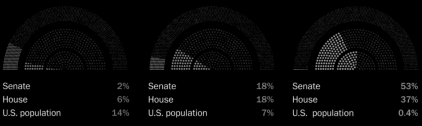

Foreign birth

Senate	2%
House	6%
U.S. population	14%

Military service

Senate	18%
House	18%
U.S. population	7%

Holds a law degree

Senate	53%
House	37%
U.S. population	0.4%

Average age

Senate 62.9   House 57.6   U.S. population 38

* Data may not add up to 100 percent due to rounding.

SOURCES: Jennifer E. Manning, "Membership of the 116th Congress: A Profile," *Congressional Research Service*, https://fas.org; U.S. Census Bureau, "Data Profile of the United States of America," https://census.gov; Daniel Cox and Robert P. Jones, "America's Changing Religious Identity," Public Religion Research Institute, www.prri.org; "Legal Profession Statistics," American Bar Association, www.americanbar.org.

FOR CRITICAL ANALYSIS

1. Does it matter whether the backgrounds of members of Congress reflect the population as a whole? Can members represent their constituents effectively if they do not come from similar backgrounds?

2. Visit www.house.gov and www.senate.gov to identify your representatives in Congress and visit their web pages. How similar are their backgrounds to yours?

On many dimensions, Congress is not a reflection of the U.S. population. Can Congress legislate fairly or take account of a diversity of views and interests if it is not a sociologically representative assembly? Representatives, as we shall see shortly, can serve as the agents of their constituents even if they do not precisely mirror their sociological attributes. Yet sociological representation is a matter of some importance. At the least, the social composition of a representative assembly is important for symbolic purposes: to demonstrate to groups in the population that the government takes them seriously. If Congress is not representative symbolically, then its own authority, and indeed that of the entire government, is reduced.[7]

Representatives as Agents A good deal of evidence indicates that whether or not members of Congress share their constituents' sociological characteristics, they *do* work very hard to speak for their constituents' views and to serve their constituents' interests. The idea of representative as agent is similar to the relationship of lawyer and client. True, the relationship between the House member and an average of 710,767 "clients" in the district, or the senator and millions of "clients" in the state, is very different from that of the lawyer and client. But the criteria of performance are comparable. One expects at the very least that each representative will constantly seek to discover the interests of the constituency and take those interests into account as she governs. Whether members of Congress always represent the interests of their constituents is another matter, as we will see later in this chapter.[8]

The internet has made communication between constituents and congressional offices constant and congressional offices have struggled to find effective ways to respond in a timely manner.[9] At the same time, members of Congress use the internet to communicate with constituents in new ways. They create websites describing their achievements, establish a presence on social networking sites, and issue e-newsletters that alert constituents to current issues. Many use blogs and other forms of social media to establish a more informal style of communication with constituents.

The seriousness with which members of Congress attempt to behave as representatives can be seen in the amount of time and resources members spend on constituency service (called "casework"). One measure is the percentage of House and Senate staff assigned to district and state offices as opposed to offices in

Representative Alexandria Ocasio-Cortez (D-N.Y.), since being elected to office in 2018, has used social media effectively to communicate with her constituents and explain the details of the lawmaking process. Here, she posts on Twitter explaining her position opposing the military's use of recruitment advertisement on the popular platform Twitch.

Women's Legislative Representation

While the percentage of women in the U.S. House of Representatives has increased over time, reaching an all-time high in 2018, the United States still lags behind much of the rest of the world in this area.

1. Which parts of the world have the highest proportion of women in their legislatures? What do you think may account for certain areas having higher levels of elected women officeholders than others? Are there areas of the world where the percentage of women in the legislature surprises you?

2. How much should a legislature reflect the demographic makeup of its citizens? Should a country create legal requirements, or change its electoral rules, to encourage the election of underrepresented groups?

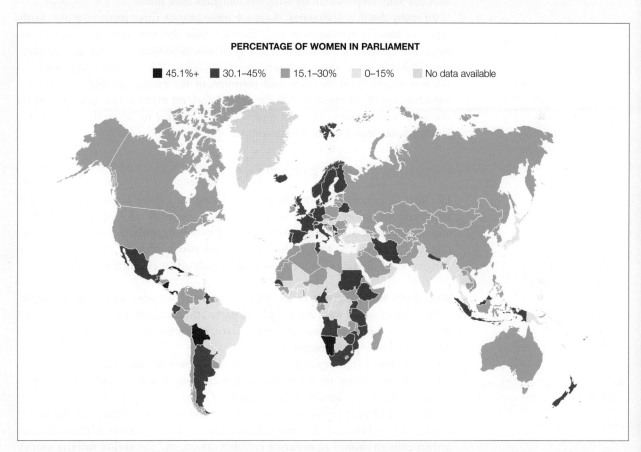

PERCENTAGE OF WOMEN IN PARLIAMENT

■ 45.1%+   ■ 30.1–45%   ■ 15.1–30%   ■ 0–15%   ■ No data available

SOURCE: Inter-Parliamentary Union (IPU), "Women in National Parliaments," April 1, 2018, http://archive.ipu.org (accessed 5/18/18).

Washington. In 1972, 22.5 percent of House members' personal staff were located in district offices; by 2016 the number had grown to 47.3 percent. For the Senate, the staff in state offices grew from 12.5 percent in 1972 to 43.2 percent in 2016.[10] The service that these offices provide is not merely a matter of handling correspondence. It includes talking to constituents; providing them with minor services; presenting special bills for them; attempting to influence decisions by regulatory commissions on their behalf; helping them apply for federal benefits such as Social Security and Small Business Administration loans; and assisting them with immigration cases.

For example, during his fight for re-election in 2014, Senate Minority Leader Mitch McConnell (R-Ky.) ran a campaign ad featuring Noelle Hunter, a Kentucky resident whose ex-husband had abducted their daughter and taken her to Africa. According to Hunter, McConnell "took up my cause personally" and worked with the State Department to bring her daughter back home.[11]

In many districts and states, there are often two or three issues that are clearly top priorities for constituents and, therefore, for the representatives. For example, representatives from districts that grow wheat, cotton, or tobacco will likely give legislation on these subjects great attention. In oil-rich states such as Oklahoma and Texas, senators and members of the House are likely to be leading advocates of oil interests. On the other hand, on many issues, constituents do not have very strong views, and representatives are free to act as they think best. Foreign policy issues often fall into this category.

CONGRESSIONAL ELECTIONS

Elections have an enormous impact on Congress. Three factors are especially important in understanding who serves as a member of Congress. The first concerns who decides to run for office and which candidates have an edge over others. The second is that of incumbency advantage. Finally, the way in which congressional district lines are drawn can greatly affect electoral outcomes.

Who Runs for Congress In the past, decisions about who would run for a particular elected office were made by local party officials. A person who had a record of service to the party, who was owed a favor, or whose "turn" had come up might be nominated by party leaders.

Today, few party organizations have the power to slate candidates in this way. Instead, parties try to ensure that their congressional candidates are well qualified. Even so, the decision to run for Congress is a personal one, and one of the most important factors determining who runs for office is an individual candidate's ambition.[12] A potential candidate may also assess whether he can attract enough money to mount a credible campaign. The ability to raise money depends on connections with other politicians, interest groups, and national party organizations.

Features distinctive to each congressional district also affect the field of candidates. For example, the way the congressional district overlaps with state legislative boundaries may affect a candidate's decision to run. A state legislator considering running for Congress is more likely to assess her prospects favorably if her state district coincides with the congressional district (because the voters will already know her).

Incumbency Incumbency plays a very important role in the American electoral system and in the kind of representation citizens get in Washington. Once in office, members of Congress gain access to an array of tools they can use to stack the deck in favor of their re-election. Their success in doing so is evident in the high rates of re-election for congressional incumbents (see Figure 12.2). It is also evident in what is called "sophomore surge"—the tendency for first-term incumbents to win a higher percentage of the vote when seeking subsequent terms in office. As of mid-November 2020, roughly 90 percent of House and Senate incumbents seeking re-election had been successful, with most winning by comfortable margins.[13] The electoral success of incumbents does not mean that Congress is immutable, though—over the course of a decade, it is likely that nearly half the members of Congress will be replaced by new individuals.[14]

Incumbents have a number of political advantages. To begin with, members of Congress and their staffs are in a position to provide many individual services to constituents—the casework described on the previous page. Also, under a law enacted in 1789, members of Congress may send mail free of charge to their constituents informing them of governmental business and public affairs. Currently, members receive an average of $100,000 in free postage for mailings to voters in their own states or districts. Most senators and representatives send regular newsletters to all constituent households highlighting the many efforts and initiatives the incumbent has undertaken on behalf of the community.

Members of Congress lose no opportunity to garner local publicity and advertise their efforts on the constituency's behalf. Events that are ignored by the national media may nevertheless be of considerable significance to local voters. Senators and representatives seek to associate themselves with these events and send out press releases highlighting their involvement. For example, a press release issued by the office of Congressman Eric Swalwell of California's 15th

incumbency holding the political office for which one is running

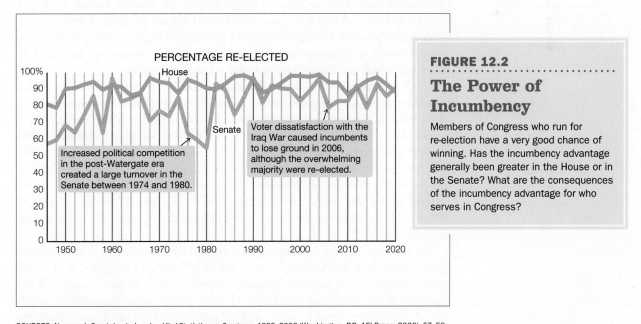

PERCENTAGE RE-ELECTED

Increased political competition in the post-Watergate era created a large turnover in the Senate between 1974 and 1980.

Voter dissatisfaction with the Iraq War caused incumbents to lose ground in 2006, although the overwhelming majority were re-elected.

FIGURE 12.2

The Power of Incumbency

Members of Congress who run for re-election have a very good chance of winning. Has the incumbency advantage generally been greater in the House or in the Senate? What are the consequences of the incumbency advantage for who serves in Congress?

SOURCES: Norman J. Ornstein et al., eds., *Vital Statistics on Congress, 1999–2000* (Washington, DC: AEI Press, 2000), 57–58; "Reelection Rates over the Years," www.opensecrets.org; and authors' update.

District honored the managers and employees of a new sanitation facility in his district. In fact, at the ribbon-cutting ceremony for the new plant, a staffer from Swalwell's office presented the facility's general manager with a "Certificate of Special Congressional Recognition," for the facility's "commitment and dedication to renewable energy."[15] Thousands of these certificates, suitable for framing, are awarded by members of Congress every year. Generally, the recipients are grateful and the event is covered by the local media and vigorously tweeted about by all concerned.

Unlike challengers, who can offer only promises, incumbents have a chance to promote legislation favored by important groups and interests in their districts. If the constituency includes a major industry, representatives will almost always promote legislation that will please the workers and managers of that industry. The late senator Henry M. Jackson of Washington took pleasure in being known as the Senator from Boeing (a large aerospace manufacturer based in Seattle).

Incumbents make it their business to support the interests of local companies and labor unions and of the district or state more generally when it comes to federal projects and contracts. Such efforts are known as **pork barreling** and are seen by incumbents as tangible evidence of achievements for which they can claim credit and as crucial to their re-election chances.[16] The late senator Robert Byrd of West Virginia, longtime chair of the Senate Appropriations Committee, was sometimes called the King of Pork, for his skill at steering federal projects to his state. During Byrd's tenure in office several billion dollars in federal funds for highways, dams, and government facilities flowed into West Virginia.

Often, representatives find it useful to strongly support essentially symbolic legislation that will please constituency groups. For example, representatives from New York and Florida, states with large numbers of Jewish voters, have no problem voting in favor of symbolic resolutions calling for recognition of Jerusalem as Israel's capital. Similarly, members with large numbers of African American constituents were eager to support recognition of Dr. Martin Luther King, Jr.'s birthday as a national holiday. These symbolic gestures are one form of what is sometimes called "position taking."[17] Generally, position taking is a more effective tactic when it comes to pleasing ordinary voters. Organized interests are less likely to focus on symbols and more likely to look for tangible benefits.

Another important electoral advantage generally possessed by incumbents is superior access to campaign funds. Incumbents are usually far more able than challengers to raise money. For most senators and representatives, fundraising is a year-round activity. Incumbents hope not only to outspend challengers but to deter prospective challengers from even undertaking the race knowing they probably face an insurmountable fundraising disadvantage. Incumbents also fear the possibility that outside interests will target their own race. In recent years, national liberal and conservative "Super PACs" have raised tens of millions of dollars to attempt to sway the congressional balance of power, as well as presidential contests.

The electoral success of congressional incumbents is often cast in a negative light as though it was undeserved or a result of improper activities. It is worth noting, however, that incumbents are re-elected, at least in part, because of the vigorous efforts they make on behalf of their constituents. Incumbents undertake constituency casework, try to make certain that the flow of funds from the federal pork barrel favors their own districts, and work to identify legislative responses to the constituents' concerns.

pork barrel (or pork)
appropriations made by legislative bodies for local projects that are often not needed but that are created so that local representatives can win re-election in their home districts

Who Elects Congress?

2018 Voters as Compared with U.S. Population

During non-presidential election years, congressional elections are the highest-profile races on the ballot. While members of the House of Representatives are re-elected every two years, Senators are re-elected every six years.

← U.S. population

↑ Electorate

*Numbers may not add up to 100 percent due to rounding.

SOURCES: CNN House Exit Polls, www.cnn.com/election/2018/exit-polls (accessed 11/12/18); U.S. Census Bureau, 2014 American Community Survey, www.census.gov/programs-surveys/acs /data.html (accessed 10/22/15).

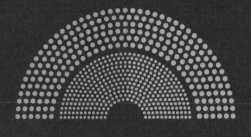

Gender	U.S. pop.	Electorate
● Women	51%	52%
● Men	49%	48%

Age	U.S. pop.	Electorate
● 18–29	22%	13%
● 30–44	25%	22%
● 45–64	34%	39%
● 65+	19%	26%

Race	U.S. pop.	Electorate
● White	62%	72%
● Black	13%	11%
● Latino	17%	11%
● Asian	5%	3%
● Other	3%	3%

FOR CRITICAL ANALYSIS

1. What kinds of voters tend to vote in midterm elections? Should the electorate closely match the U.S. population?

2. Though the 2018 midterm elections saw historic turnout, turnout rates tend to be low in midterm elections. Why do you think that is?

Income	U.S. pop.	Electorate*
● Under $30k	52%	17%
● $30–$50k	20%	21%
● $50–$100k	20%	29%
● $100–$200k	6%	25%
● Over $200k	2%	9%

Apportionment and Redistricting The drawing of congressional district lines also has a major impact upon election outcomes. Districting, of course, affects only the House of Representatives. (Senators are chosen from states and these boundaries do not change.) At least every 10 years, and sometimes more frequently, state legislatures redistrict, or redraw the borders of their state's districts. Decennial redistricting is required by the Constitution to reflect population changes in accordance with the federal census.

Because the number of House seats has been fixed at 435 since 1929, the census results mean that every 10 years some states gain or lose seats. **Apportionment**, the distribution of seats among the states, is a zero-sum process: for one state to gain a seat, another must lose one. So some states with population growth over the previous decade gain additional seats; some with a population decline or lower growth lose seats.

Over the past several decades, the shift of the American population to the South and the West has greatly increased the size of the congressional delegations from those regions. This trend will likely continue after the 2020 census (see Figure 12.3). Texas is likely to gain three seats (after gaining four after 2010), and Florida will likely gain two. States in the Northeast and "Rust Belt" are likely to lose seats. Proportionally, Latino voters are nearly three times as numerous in states that gained seats compared with states that lost seats, suggesting that the growth of the Latino population is a major factor in the American political landscape.[18]

In most states, **redistricting** is controlled by the legislature and is a highly political process to create an advantage for the party with a majority in the legislature. For example, redistricting can put two incumbents of the opposing party into the same district, ensuring that one of them will lose, while creating an open seat that favors the redistricting party. Redistricting can also give an advantage to one

apportionment the process, occurring after every decennial census, that allocates congressional seats among the 50 states

redistricting the process of redrawing election districts and redistributing legislative representatives; this happens every 10 years to reflect shifts in population or in response to legal challenges to existing districts

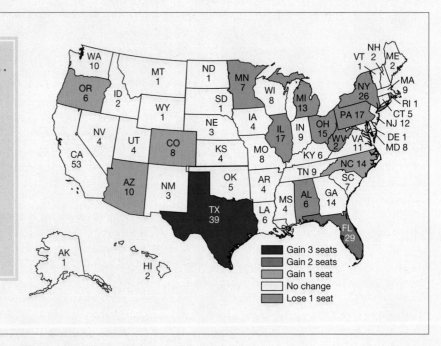

FIGURE 12.3

Projected Congressional Reapportionment, 2020

States in the South and the West will likely be the big winners in the reapportionment of House seats following the 2020 census. The old manufacturing states in the Midwest and Mid-Atlantic regions will be the biggest losers. Is this shift likely to favor Democrats or Republicans?

SOURCE: Rebecca Tippett, "2020 Congressional Reapportionment: An Update," December 21, 2017, Carolina Population Center, University of North Carolina, www.demography.cpc.unc.edu (accessed 6/8/18).

Redrawing legislative districts is a difficult task because it has implications for who will be elected. Here, the attorney for Arizona's Independent Redistricting Commission discusses a possible layout with a city council member from Casa Grande. Arizona gained one congressional seat following the 2010 census.

party by clustering voters with some ideological or sociological characteristics in a single district or by separating those voters into two or more districts. The manipulation of electoral districts to serve the interests of a particular group is known as **gerrymandering** (see Chapter 10).

Some analysts claim that Republicans have benefited from partisan gerrymandering since the 2010 redistricting cycle, because they controlled the majority of state legislatures at the time. To support this argument, they point to the recent congressional elections in which the Republican Party generally has won a higher percentage of House seats than its percent of the popular vote. But other analysts argue that districting that favors Republicans may reflect the natural clustering of Democrats in urban areas, not deliberate bias.[19]

Even so, concern about partisan gerrymandering has led some states to take redistricting power away from state legislatures and give it to independent bipartisan commissions that try to develop congressional district maps that do not give an unfair advantage to either party. Currently, seven states—California, Arizona, Hawaii, Idaho, New Jersey, Washington, and Montana—require district lines to be drawn by commissions.[20] In 2015 a legal challenge to the use of commissions failed when the Supreme Court upheld the legality of relying on commissions to draw congressional district lines.[21]

The federal courts have often sought to intervene in cases involving partisan gerrymandering. In 2019, however, the Supreme Court heard a North Carolina case in which the GOP state official who led the state's redistricting efforts had stated publicly that the congressional map had been drawn to give Republicans more of the state's congressional seats. The Court declared, in *Rucho v. Common Cause* (2019), nevertheless, that gerrymandering was a "political question" beyond the reach of the federal judiciary.[22] The Court's decision left the possibility open that state courts might continue to intervene in gerrymandering cases. The decision, moreover, applied only to partisan gerrymandering, not to claims of racial gerrymandering.

gerrymandering the apportionment of voters in districts in such a way as to give unfair advantage to one racial or ethnic group or political party

FOR CRITICAL ANALYSIS

How does redistricting alter the balance of power in Congress? Why do political parties care so much about the redistricting process?

As we saw in Chapter 10, since the passage of the Voting Rights Act of 1965, race has become a major, and controversial, consideration in drawing voting districts. These amendments, which encouraged the creation of districts in which people of color have decisive majorities, have greatly increased the number of representatives of color in Congress. After the 1990 redistricting cycle, the number of predominantly minority districts doubled, rising from 26 to 52. Among the most fervent supporters of creating these districts were White Republicans, who used the opportunity to create more districts dominated by White Republican voters. Some analysts argue that this pattern grants people of color greater descriptive representation but makes it more difficult for them to win substantive policy goals.[23]

In the case of *Miller v. Johnson* (1995), the Supreme Court limited racial redistricting by ruling that race could not be the "predominant" factor in creating electoral districts,[24] but the distinction between being "predominant" and being one factor among many is hazy. This became evident in a Texas case that resulted from a redrawing of the state's congressional district boundaries after the 2010 census. The state had gained four congressional seats mainly because of growth in the Latino population, which tends to support the Democrats. The Republican-dominated state legislature, nevertheless, managed to redraw the state's district lines in a way that increased the number of districts friendly to the GOP. After several years of litigation, the state's legislative map was, for the most part, upheld by the Supreme Court, which found that race had not been a predominant factor in the drawing of district lines.[25]

The Organization of Congress

> **Describe the factors that structure congressional business**

To exercise its power to make laws, Congress must first bring about something close to an organizational miracle. The building blocks of congressional organization include the political parties, the committee system, congressional staff, the caucuses, and the parliamentary rules of the House and Senate. Each of these factors plays a key role in the organization of Congress and in the process through which Congress formulates and enacts laws.

PARTY LEADERSHIP IN THE HOUSE

Political parties are not mentioned in the Constitution but, soon after the nation's founding, a party system developed in the Congress (see Chapter 9). Much of the actual work of Congress is controlled by the parties, which write most of the rules of congressional procedure and select the leaders who direct the flow of congressional business. Without party leadership and party organization, Congress could not function as a lawmaking body.

Every two years, at the beginning of a new Congress, the members of each party gather to elect their House leaders. House Republicans call their gathering the **conference**. House Democrats call theirs the **caucus**. The elected leader of the majority party is later proposed to the whole House and is automatically elected to the position of **Speaker of the House**, with voting along straight party lines. The House majority conference or caucus then also elects a **majority leader**. The minority party goes through the same process and selects a **minority leader**. Each

conference a gathering of House Republicans every two years to elect their House leaders; Democrats call their gathering the "caucus"

caucus (political) a normally closed political party business meeting of citizens or lawmakers to select candidates, elect officers, plan strategy, or make decisions regarding legislative matters

Speaker of the House the chief presiding officer of the House of Representatives; the Speaker is the most important party and House leader and can influence the legislative agenda, the fate of individual pieces of legislation, and members' positions within the House

majority leader the elected leader of the majority party in the House of Representatives or in the Senate; in the House, the majority leader is subordinate in the party hierarchy to the Speaker of the House

minority leader the elected leader of the minority party in the House or Senate

party also elects a **whip** to line up party members on important votes and to relay voting information to the leaders.

Next in order of importance for each party after the Speaker and majority or minority leader is what Democrats call the Steering and Policy Committee (Republicans have a separate steering committee and a separate policy committee). These committees' tasks are to assign new legislators to committees and to deal with the requests of incumbent members for transfers from one committee to another. At one time, party leaders strictly controlled committee assignments, using them to enforce party discipline. Today, in principle, representatives receive the assignments they want. But often too many individuals seek assignments to the most important committees, which gives the leadership an opportunity to curry favor with their members when it resolves conflicting requests.

Generally, representatives seek assignments that will allow them to influence decisions of special importance to their districts. Representatives from farm districts, for example, often request seats on the Agriculture Committee.[26] Seats on powerful committees such as Ways and Means, which is responsible for tax legislation, and Appropriations are especially popular.

PARTY LEADERSHIP IN THE SENATE

Within the Senate, the majority party usually designates a member with the greatest seniority to serve as president pro tempore, a position of primarily ceremonial leadership. Real power is in the hands of the majority leader and minority leader, who together control the Senate's calendar, or agenda for legislation. The structure of majority party leadership in the House and the Senate is shown in Figures 12.4 and 12.5.

THE COMMITTEE SYSTEM

The committee system is a prominent feature of Congress. At each stage of the legislative process, Congress makes use of committees and subcommittees to sort through alternatives, secure information, and write legislation. There are several

whip a party member in the House or Senate responsible for coordinating the party's legislative strategy, building support for key issues, and counting votes

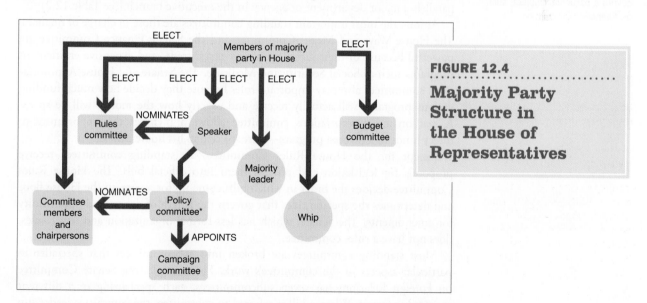

FIGURE 12.4

Majority Party Structure in the House of Representatives

*Includes Speaker, majority leader, chief and deputy whips, caucus chair, chairs of five major committees, members elected by regional caucuses, members elected by recently elected representatives, and at-large members appointed by the Speaker.

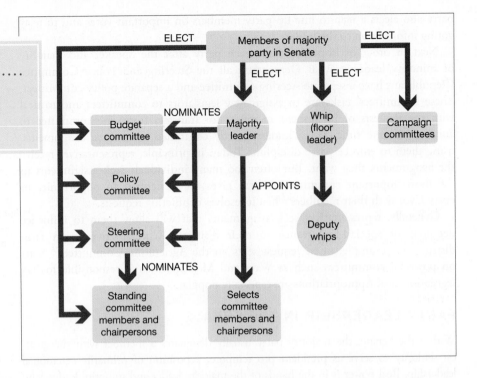

FIGURE 12.5
....
**Majority Party
Structure in the
Senate**

Majority Party Structure in the Senate

Members of majority party in Senate

ELECT — ELECT — ELECT — ELECT

NOMINATES

Budget committee

Policy committee

Steering committee

Majority leader

Whip (floor leader)

Campaign committees

APPOINTS

Deputy whips

NOMINATES

Standing committee members and chairpersons

Selects committee members and chairpersons

different kinds of congressional committees: standing committees, select committees, joint committees, and conference committees.

Standing Committees The most important arenas of congressional policy making are **standing committees**. These committees remain in existence from one session of Congress to the next; they have the power to propose and write legislation. The jurisdiction of each one covers a particular subject matter, which in most cases parallels a major department or agency in the executive branch (see Table 12.2).

Among the most important standing committees are those in charge of finances. The House Ways and Means Committee and the Senate Finance Committee are powerful because of their jurisdiction over taxes, trade, and expensive entitlement programs such as Social Security and Medicare. The Senate and House Appropriations committees also play important roles because they decide how much funding various programs will actually receive and exactly how the money will be spent. A seat on an appropriations committee allows a member the opportunity to direct funds to a favored program—perhaps one in his home district.

Except for the House Rules Committee, all standing committees receive proposals for legislation and process them into official bills. The House Rules Committee decides the order in which bills come up for a vote on the House floor and determines the specific rules that govern the length of debate and opportunity for amendments. The Senate, which has less formal organization and fewer rules, does not have a rules committee.

Most standing committees are broken into subcommittees that specialize in particular aspects of the committee's work. For example, the Senate Committee on Foreign Relations has seven subcommittees, each specializing in a different geographic region. When a bill is referred to committee, the committee leadership will determine which subcommittee is most appropriate for the matter in question.

standing committee a permanent committee with the power to propose and write legislation that covers a particular subject, such as finance or agriculture

TABLE 12.2

Permanent Committees of Congress

HOUSE COMMITTEES		
Agriculture	Financial Services	Oversight and Government Reform
Appropriations	Foreign Affairs	Rules
Armed Services	Homeland Security	Science, Space, and Technology
Budget	House Administration	Small Business
Education and the Workforce	Intelligence	Transportation and Infrastructure
Energy and Commerce	Judiciary	Veterans' Affairs
Ethics	Natural Resources	Ways and Means
SENATE COMMITTEES		
Agriculture, Nutrition, and Forestry	Energy and Natural Resources	Intelligence
Appropriations	Environment and Public Works	Judiciary
Armed Services	Finance	Rules and Administration
Banking, Housing, and Urban Affairs	Foreign Relations	Small Business and Entrepreneurship
Budget	Health, Education, Labor, and Pensions	Veterans' Affairs
Commerce, Science, and Transportation	Homeland Security and Governmental Affairs	

Subcommittee jurisdictions are poorly defined and committee chairs have considerable discretion in assigning bills. Much of the hard work of deliberating, holding hearings, and "marking up," as the process of amending and rewriting a bill is called, takes place in the subcommittees, though further markup may occur in the full committee after the amended bill leaves the subcommittee.

One important power of the standing committees is the power to conduct hearings and launch investigations. There are two types of legislative hearings. In the most common variety of oversight hearing, Congress listens to testimony, quizzes executive branch officials, and hears complaints from members of the public in order to better fulfill its legislative responsibilities. A second type of hearing, called an investigative hearing or ethics probe, has no immediate legislative intent, though it may eventually result in legislation. The chief purpose of such a hearing is to look into allegations of misconduct on the part of one or more public officials, possibly culminating in a recommendation that the officials in question be dismissed or even subjected to criminal prosecutions. These are discussed in the following pages.

In 2019, Special Counsel Robert Mueller testified before the House permanent select committee on intelligence. Mueller was appointed as special counsel in May 2017 to investigate Russian interference in the 2016 election and any potential connections to the Trump campaign, and he reported his findings to the committee in July 2019.

select committees (usually) temporary legislative committees set up to highlight or investigate a particular issue or address an issue not within the jurisdiction of existing committees

Select Committees Select committees are usually not permanent and usually do not have the power to present legislation to the full Congress. (The House and Senate Select Intelligence committees are exceptions.) These committees hold hearings and serve as focal points for the issues they are charged with considering. Congressional leaders form select committees when they want to take up issues that fall outside the jurisdictions of existing committees, to highlight an issue, or to investigate a particular problem.

For example, the Senate set up the Senate Watergate Committee in 1973 to investigate the Watergate break-in and cover-up. More recently, the House Select Committee on Benghazi was established to investigate the 2012 attack on the U.S. embassy in Benghazi, Libya. In 2015 the committee held hearings to investigate Hillary Clinton's use of a private email server during her tenure as secretary of state.

joint committees legislative committees formed of members of both the House and Senate

Joint Committees Joint committees involve members from both the Senate and the House. There are four such committees—economic, taxation, library, and printing; they are permanent, but do not have the power to present legislation. The Joint Economic Committee and the Joint Taxation Committee have often played important roles in collecting information and holding hearings on economic and financial issues.

conference committees joint committees created to work out a compromise on House and Senate versions of a piece of legislation

Conference Committees Finally, conference committees are temporary committees whose members are appointed by the Speaker of the House and the presiding officer of the Senate. These committees are charged with reaching a compromise on legislation once it has been passed by the House and the Senate. Conference committees can play an important role in determining the laws that are actually passed because they must reconcile any differences in the legislation passed by the House and Senate. Today, however, House and Senate leaders often prefer to bypass conference committees in favor of a process known as "ping-ponging," in which the leaders of the two chambers send a bill back and forth until agreement is achieved.

Politics and the Organization of Committees Within each committee, leadership has usually been based on **seniority**, determined by years of continuous service on that particular committee. In general, each committee is chaired by the most senior member of the majority party. But the principle of seniority is not absolute. When the Republicans took over the House in 1995, they disregarded it in the selection of key committee chairs. House Speaker Newt Gingrich defended the new practice, saying, "You've got to carry the moral responsibility of fielding the team that can win or you cheat the whole conference."[27]

seniority the ranking given to an individual on the basis of length of continuous service on a committee in Congress

Since then, Republicans have continued to depart from the seniority principle, often choosing committee chairs on the basis of loyalty to the party leadership's legislative priorities or the member's fundraising abilities rather than seniority. In 2007, Democrats returned to the seniority principle for choosing committee chairs but altered traditional practices in other ways by offering freshman Democrats choice committee assignments to increase their chances of re-election.[28]

Over the years, Congress has reformed its organizational structure and operating procedures. Most changes have been made to improve efficiency, but some reforms have also been a response to political considerations. For example, the Republican leadership of the 104th Congress (1995–97), seeking to concentrate its authority, reduced the number of subcommittees and limited the time committee chairs could serve to three terms. They made good on this limit in 2001, when they replaced 13 committee chairs.

As a consequence of these changes, committees no longer have as central a role as they once held in policy making. Furthermore, sharp partisan divisions have made it difficult for committees to deliberate and bring bipartisan expertise to bear on policy making as in the past. Today they typically do not deliberate for very long or call witnesses, and it has become more common in recent years for party-driven legislation to go directly to the floor, bypassing committees altogether.[29] Nonetheless, committees continue to play a role in the legislative process, especially on issues that are not sharply partisan.[30]

THE STAFF SYSTEM

The congressional institution third in importance to the leadership structure and the committee system is the staff system. Every member of Congress employs many staff members (the total is set by law), whose tasks include handling constituent requests and, to a large extent, dealing with legislative details and the activities of administrative agencies. Staffers often bear the primary responsibility for formulating and drafting proposals, organizing hearings, dealing with administrative agencies, and negotiating with lobbyists. Indeed, legislators typically deal with one another through staff, rather than through direct personal contact. Representatives and senators together employ roughly 11,500 staffers in their Washington and home offices—about half in each.

In addition, Congress employs more than 2,000 committee staffers.[31] These make up the permanent staff that stays attached to every House and Senate committee regardless of turnover in Congress and that is responsible for organizing and administering the committee's work, including doing research, scheduling, organizing hearings, and drafting legislation. Committee staffers can play key roles in the legislative process.

Not only does Congress employ personal and committee staff, but it has also established **staff agencies** designed to provide the legislative branch with resources and expertise independent of the executive branch. These agencies include the Congressional Research Service, which performs research for legislators who wish to know the facts and competing arguments relevant to policy proposals or other legislative business; the Government Accountability Office, through which Congress can investigate the financial and administrative affairs of any government agency or program; and the Congressional Budget Office, which assesses the economic implications and likely costs of proposed federal programs.

staff agencies legislative support agencies responsible for policy analysis

INFORMAL ORGANIZATION: THE CAUCUSES

In addition to the official organization of Congress, an unofficial organizational structure also exists: the caucuses. **Caucuses** are groups of senators or representatives who share certain opinions, interests, or social characteristics. A large number of them represent particular economic or policy interests, such as the Travel and Tourism Caucus, the Steel Caucus, and Concerned Senators for the Arts. Legislators who share common backgrounds have organized caucuses such as the Congressional Black Caucus, the Congressional Caucus for Women's Issues, and the Congressional Hispanic Caucus.

caucuses (congressional) associations of members of Congress based on party, interest, or social group, such as gender or race

Rules of Lawmaking: How a Bill Becomes a Law

> **Describe the regular order and new order processes of how a bill becomes a law**

The institutional structure of Congress is a key factor in shaping the legislative process. A second and equally important set of factors is the rules of congressional procedure, which govern everything from the introduction of a **bill** through its submission to the president for signing (see Figure 12.6). Not only do these regulations influence the fate of every bill, but they also help determine the distribution of power in Congress.

bill a proposed law that has been sponsored by a member of Congress and submitted to the clerk of the House or Senate

We will begin the story of how a bill becomes a law with what is called "regular order." This is the set of procedures Congress claims to follow and often does. As we will see in the following pages, however, many important bills do not follow regular order but, instead, follow a less formal and more leadership-driven process that we will call the "new order."

COMMITTEE DELIBERATION

The first step in getting a law passed is drafting legislation. Members of Congress, the White House, and federal agencies all take roles in developing and drafting initial legislation. Bills can originate in the House or the Senate, but only the House can introduce "money bills," those that spend or raise revenues. The framers inserted this provision in the Constitution because they believed that the chamber closest to the people should exercise greater authority over taxing and spending.

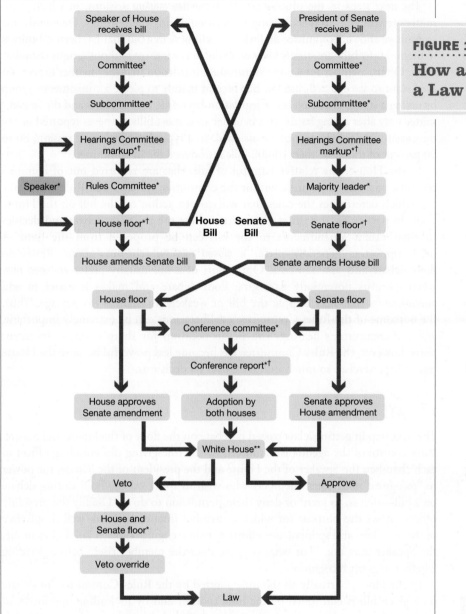

FIGURE 12.6

How a Bill Becomes a Law

Speaker of House receives bill

President of Senate receives bill

Committee*

Subcommittee*

Hearings Committee markup*†

Rules Committee*

Speaker*

House floor*†

House Bill

Senate Bill

Committee*

Subcommittee*

Hearings Committee markup*†

Majority leader*

Senate floor*†

House amends Senate bill

Senate amends House bill

House floor

Senate floor

Conference committee*

Conference report*†

House approves Senate amendment

Adoption by both houses

Senate approves House amendment

White House**

Veto

Approve

House and Senate floor*

Veto override

Law

*Points at which a bill can be amended.
**If the president neither signs nor vetoes a bill within 10 days, it automatically becomes law.
†Points at which a bill can die by vote.

After it is drafted, the bill is officially submitted by a senator or representative to the clerk of the House or Senate and referred to the appropriate committee for deliberation. During the course of its deliberations, the committee typically refers the bill to one of its subcommittees, which may hold hearings, listen to expert testimony, and amend the proposed legislation before referring it to the full committee for consideration. The full committee may then accept the recommendation of the subcommittee or hold its own hearings and prepare its own amendments.

committee markup the session in which a congressional committee rewrites legislation to incorporate changes discussed during hearings on a bill

closed rule a provision by the House Rules Committee limiting or prohibiting the introduction of amendments during debate

open rule a provision by the House Rules Committee that permits floor debate and the addition of new amendments to a bill

filibuster a tactic used by members of the Senate to prevent action on legislation they oppose by continuously holding the floor and speaking until the majority backs down; once given the floor, senators have unlimited time to speak, and it requires a vote of three-fifths of the Senate to end a filibuster

Once a senator is granted the floor, Senate rules permit him or her to speak for as long as he or she wishes. Although "talking filibusters" are rare today, in May 2015 Senator Rand Paul (R-Ky.) spoke continuously for 10½ hours, challenging the legality of government surveillance in his opposition to renew the Patriot Act.

The next steps in the process are the **committee markup** sessions, in which committees rewrite bills to reflect changes discussed during the hearings. Frequently, the committee and subcommittee do little or nothing with a bill that has been submitted to them. Many bills are simply allowed to die in committee without serious consideration. Often, members of Congress introduce legislation that they neither expect nor even want to see enacted into law but present mainly to please a constituency group by taking a stand. Other pieces of legislation have ardent supporters and die in committee only after a long battle. But in either case, most bills are never reported out of the committees to which they are assigned. In a typical congressional session, 80 to 90 percent of the more than 10,000 bills introduced die in committee.[32]

In the House, the relative handful of bills that are reported out of committee must pass one last hurdle within the committee system—the Rules Committee, which determines the rules that will govern action on the bill on the House floor. In particular, the Rules Committee allots the time for debate and decides to what extent amendments to the bill can be proposed from the floor. A bill's supporters generally prefer a **closed rule**, which puts severe limits on floor debate and amendments. Opponents of a bill usually prefer an **open rule**, which permits potentially damaging floor debate and makes it easier to add amendments that may cripple the bill or weaken its chances for passage. Thus, the outcome of the Rules Committee's deliberations can be extremely important, and the committee's hearings can be an occasion for sharp conflict. In recent years, however, the Rules Committee has become less powerful because the House leadership exercises so much influence over its decisions.

DEBATE

The next step in getting a law passed is debate on the floor of the House and Senate. Party control of the agenda is reinforced by the rule giving the presiding officer of each chamber, the Speaker of the House and the president of the Senate, the power to "recognize" individual members who wish to speak on the floor during debate on a bill—that is, to grant or deny them permission to do so. Usually the presiding officer knows the purpose for which a member intends to speak well in advance of the occasion, and spontaneous efforts to gain recognition often fail. For example, the Speaker may ask, "For what purpose does the member rise?" before deciding whether to grant recognition.

In the House, virtually all the time allotted by the Rules Committee for debate on a given bill is controlled by the bill's sponsor and by its leading opponent. In almost every case, these two people are the chair and the ranking minority member of the committee that processed the bill—or those they designate. These two participants are, by rule and tradition, granted the power to allocate most of the debate time in small amounts to members seeking to speak for or against the measure.

Filibuster In the Senate, the leadership has much less control over floor debate. Indeed, the Senate is unique among the world's legislative bodies for its commitment to unlimited debate. Once given the floor, a senator may speak as long as she wishes. On a number of memorable occasions, senators have used this opportunity to prevent action on legislation that they opposed. Through this tactic, called the **filibuster**, small minorities or even one individual in the Senate can force the majority to give in. The threat of a filibuster ensures that, in crafting legislation, the majority takes into account the viewpoint of the political minority.

Filibusters can be ended by a Senate vote to cut off debate, called **cloture**. From 1917 to 1975, it took two-thirds of the Senate, or 67 votes, to end a filibuster. In 1975 the Senate reduced the requirement to three-fifths of the Senate, or 60 votes.

In 2013 the Democratic Senate leader Harry Reid (Nev.) mobilized his party to alter the filibuster rules for the first time in many decades. Frustrated by the repeated failure of the Senate to vote on many of President Obama's nominees to executive and judicial positions, Reid imposed what senators had come to call "the nuclear option": nominees for positions in the executive branch and the federal courts—except the Supreme Court—could no longer be filibustered and could be approved by a simple majority vote. Republicans denounced the change, but after winning control of both houses of Congress and the White House in 2016 they expanded it to include Supreme Court justices as well. Thus they were able to secure the appointment of Justices Neil Gorsuch, Brett Kavanaugh, and Amy Coney Barrett, who would undoubtedly have been blocked by Senate Democrats under the old rules. Legislation is still subject to filibuster, though some Republicans, along with President Trump, have declared that it is time to bring an end to the filibuster altogether.

Amendments and Holds The filibuster is not the only technique used to block Senate debate. Under Senate rules, members have virtually unlimited ability to propose amendments to a pending bill. Each amendment must be voted on before the bill can come to a final vote, and the introduction of new amendments can be stopped only by unanimous consent of the Senate. These rules permit a determined minority to filibuster by amendment, indefinitely delaying the passage of a bill.

Senators can also place "holds" on bills to delay debate when they fear that more openly opposing the bills will be unpopular. Before 2007, holds were kept secret; the senators placing them did not have to take public responsibility for their action. Since 2007 senators who impose a hold have been required to identify themselves in the *Congressional Record* after six days and to state the reasons for the hold.[33] Nevertheless, senators continue to impose holds on legislation and especially on presidential appointees. In 2013, for example, Senator Lindsey Graham (R-S.C.) threatened to use holds on all of President Obama's nominees unless the administration made survivors of the 2012 terrorist attack on the U.S. mission in Benghazi, Libya, available to Congress for questioning.[34]

Voting Once a bill is debated on the floor of the House and the Senate, the leaders schedule it for a vote on the floor of each chamber. Leaders do not bring legislation to the floor unless they are fairly certain it is going to pass. On rare occasions, however, the last moments of the floor vote can be very dramatic as each party's leadership puts its whip organization into action to make sure that wavering members vote with the party. Historically, members of Congress must be present to vote. In 2020, however, House rules were changed to allow proxy voting so that most members could remain home during the COVID-19 pandemic. Senate rules continue to require senators to be present to vote.

In 2015 the House of Representatives failed to pass a spending bill to fund the Department of Homeland Security hours before the agency was to run out of money and begin to shut down. Despite having a majority in the chamber and a preliminary vote that suggested that the bill would pass easily, House Republican leaders failed to prevent their party's most conservative members from suddenly abandoning the bill over objections that it failed to block President Obama's executive actions

cloture a rule or process in a legislative body aimed at ending debate on a given bill; in the U.S. Senate, 60 senators (three-fifths) must agree in order to impose a time limit and end debate

FOR CRITICAL ANALYSIS

Two of Congress's chief responsibilities are representation and lawmaking. How do these responsibilities support and reinforce each other? How might they also conflict with each other?

on immigration. As the deadline approached, the House agreed on a one-week extension to keep the department open.[35] Leaders later secured sufficient support to enact longer-term funding. The importance of being able to attract wavering members with "pork" for their districts is one reason President Trump urged Congress in 2018 to restore earmarks, which have been banned since 2011.

CONFERENCE COMMITTEE: RECONCILING HOUSE AND SENATE VERSIONS OF LEGISLATION

Getting a bill out of committee and through both houses of Congress is no guarantee that the bill will be enacted into law; it must be considered by a conference committee. Frequently, bills that begin with similar provisions in both chambers emerge with little resemblance to each other. Alternatively, a bill may be passed in its original form by one chamber but undergo substantial revision in the other. In such cases, a conference committee composed of the senior members of the committees or subcommittees that initiated the bill may be required to iron out differences between the two now dissimilar pieces of legislation. Sometimes members or leaders will let objectionable provisions pass on the floor, knowing that they will get the chance to make changes in conference. Usually, conference committees meet behind closed doors; agreement requires a majority of each of the two delegations.

When a bill comes out of conference, it faces one more hurdle. Before it can be sent to the president for signing, the conference committee's version of the bill must be approved on the floor of each chamber. Usually such approval is given quickly. Occasionally, however, a bill's opponents use this as one last opportunity to defeat a piece of legislation.

PRESIDENTIAL ACTION

The final step in passing a law is presidential approval. Once adopted by the House and Senate, a bill goes to the president, who may choose to sign the bill into law or to veto it. If the president does neither within 10 days while Congress is in session, the bill automatically becomes law. The **veto** is the president's constitutional power to reject a piece of legislation. To veto a bill, the president returns it unsigned within 10 days to the house of Congress in which it originated. If Congress adjourns during the 10-day period and the president has taken no action, the bill is also considered to be vetoed. This latter method is known as the **pocket veto**.

The possibility of a presidential veto affects how willing members of Congress are to push for a piece of legislation at a particular time; if they think it is likely to be vetoed, they might shelve it until later. There is also the possibility that a veto may be overridden by a two-thirds vote in both the House and the Senate. A veto override is rare and delivers a stinging blow to the executive branch. Presidents will often back down from a veto threat if they believe that Congress will override the veto.

IS REGULAR ORDER STILL REGULAR? THE RISE OF THE NEW ORDER IN CONGRESS

The foregoing discussion summarizes regular order in Congress. Regular order guarantees that a bill's journey to become a law will be long and arduous. Indeed, the process can be maddeningly slow for a bill's proponents. Most bills are not enacted into law and even those that do become law are seldom enacted during the first

veto the president's constitutional power to turn down acts of Congress; a presidential veto may be overridden by a two-thirds vote of each house of Congress

pocket veto a presidential veto that is automatically triggered if the president does not act on a given piece of legislation passed during the final 10 days of a legislative session or even second congressional session in which they are considered. Regular order, however, ensures a deliberative process in which many voices are heard and both the majority and minority parties play a role. In short, regular order exemplifies deliberative democracy at its best. For better or worse, however, there is no longer anything regular about regular order. In modern times, regular order is usually, albeit not always, abandoned in favor of procedures designed to move bills along more quickly, or with fewer layers of review, trading deliberation for what the framers of the Constitution dismissed as "promptitude."

Today, instead of regular order, bills tend to follow a set of paths that collectively might be called the "new order." Regular order enhanced the power of committees and subcommittees. The new order generally reflects the contemporary strengthening of partisanship and the power of party leaders, in particular the Speaker of the House and the Senate majority leader, but also leaves room for individual action by the members of Congress. One thing the new order does not emphasize is deliberation. The new order allows party leaders to push the president's agenda if the president is of their own party or to do battle with the president if the president is of the opposite party. This is primarily why Congress is prone to deadlock today—an era of high levels of partisan division and frequently divided control of government. Some in Congress call for a return to regular order, but it is not clear how realistic that is.[36] As we shall see below, the forces that led to the new order were set in motion by institutional reforms of the 1970s and other factors that are not likely to be reversed.[37]

"FOLLOW-THE-LEADER" LAWMAKING

The most important element of the new order is what we can call "follow-the-leader" lawmaking. This is when party leaders rather than committees control the legislative process. These leaders use various tactics to achieve their legislative goals and move legislation more quickly than regular order would allow.

Closed Rules The first element of follow-the-leader lawmaking is the frequent use of closed rules to prevent rank-and-file members—and the minority party—from amending legislation approved by the leadership. Closed rules, which some critics call "gag rules," prohibit most floor amendments and often limit debate to a short period of time. Debate on a complex measure may be limited to one hour—hardly enough time to begin to read, much less debate, a bill that may be more than 1,000 pages long.

For many years, tax bills have been considered under closed rules because most members have agreed that tax provisions are too complex and the provisions too intertwined to be amended from the floor.[38] What once was limited mainly to tax bills has now become what Walter Oleszek calls the "new normal."[39] Whether Congress is controlled by the Democrats or the Republicans, party leaders use closed rules and strict time limits on debate to enhance their own power, compel the rank and file to follow the leader, and restrict the influence of the other party on legislation.

Multiple Referral A second element of follow-the-leader lawmaking is **multiple referral**. In the House multiple referral was introduced by a rule change in 1975 and has since become commonplace. Used more often in the House than the Senate, multiple referral means that bills are sent to several committees rather than just one for consideration and markup.

multiple referral the practice of referring a bill to more than one committee for consideration

Though Speaker of the House Nancy Pelosi and Senate Majority Leader Mitch McConnell frequently disagree, they must often coordinate conferences and bill markup in order to pass legislation.

There are three types of multiple referrals: joint, sequential, and split. Joint referral means that the leadership assigns the same bill to more than one committee. Sequential referral means that the leadership assigns a bill to a second committee if it does not like the actions of the first committee. Split referral means that different sections of a bill will be assigned to different committees.

Multiple referral might seem to allow more participation in the deliberative process, and sometimes it does. At the same time, however, multiple referral works to expand the power of party leaders and reduce the power of committees by preventing any one committee from blocking a piece of legislation.

Ping-ponging A third element of follow-the-leader lawmaking is the declining use of the conference committee. Conference committees can expand the number of voices heard in discussions of a piece of legislation. However, the effort to create a conference committee, particularly in the case of a controversial bill, gives the Senate minority, in particular, many opportunities to block enactment of the bill. Under Senate rules, the minority party has opportunities to filibuster several steps in the process, to propose amendments, and to move to instruct its conferees to insist upon provisions known to be unacceptable to the House. The House minority also has procedural weapons with which it might derail a conference. As mentioned earlier, to deal with these problems, House and Senate leaders have developed procedures for "ping-ponging" amendments back and forth between the relevant House and Senate committees to reconcile differences between bills or major measures without convening a conference committee at all.

House Speaker Nancy Pelosi (D-Calif.) made extensive use of the "ping-pong" procedure in the 111th Congress (2009–11). In general, the ping-pong approach to legislating strengthens the House and Senate leadership and further marginalizes the role of the minority parties.[40]

Catching the Omnibus: The New Order Budget Process A key element of follow-the-leader lawmaking is the use of the omnibus budget bill. The U.S.

Congress is one of the only legislatures in the world to have the primary role in its government's budgetary process. This "power of the purse" derives directly from Article I, Section 8, of the Constitution, which asserts that Congress "shall have the Power to lay and collect Taxes, Duties, Imposts, and Excises [and] To borrow Money on the credit of the United States." According to Article I, Section 9, moreover, "no Money shall be drawn from the Treasury, but in Consequence of Appropriations made by Law." The Constitution also specifies that revenue measures must originate in the House so that taxation is levied by the body closest to the people. By tradition, **appropriations** bills also originate in the House.

While giving Congress the power of the purse, the Constitution does not prescribe the procedures to be used for actually drafting the government's budget. Over the years Congress has enacted legislation specifying budgetary procedures and has developed a "regular order" for appropriations bills. Every federal program requires both an authorization and an appropriation. Authorization bills, which might cover multiple years, must be passed by Congress to grant the actual legal authority for government agencies to spend budget money. Appropriations bills are the funding mechanisms that specify how much money will be given to different government agencies and programs. If a program is authorized but no money is appropriated, the program cannot be implemented. In principle, authorizing bills set policies and appropriations bills pay for them. In practice, the line is sometimes not so clear. Appropriations committees sometimes attach limitation riders to the appropriations bill, prohibiting funds from being spent for particular purposes. Republicans, for example, have sought to use limitation riders to prevent federal dollars from being spent on abortions.

Section 300 of the 1974 Congressional Budget and Impoundment Control Act (Public Law no. 93-344) gives the timetable for the budget process. It follows four basic steps:

- Each year, before the first Monday in February, the president is required to submit a budget request to Congress based on agency budget proposals reviewed by the Office of Management and Budget (OMB) and OMB's preparation of the president's budget;

- The House and Senate Committees on the Budget each prepare and pass budget resolutions, with the House initiating the process; the 12 House and Senate Appropriations subcommittees "mark up" the appropriations bills to determine the exact funding levels for all discretionary funding;

- The House and the Senate debate and vote on the appropriations bills and reconcile the differences from each of the 12 subcommittees involved (following the so-called Byrd rule, named for the late senator Robert Byrd of West Virginia, reconciliation provisions may not deviate from the goals established by each chamber in its budget bill);

- The president signs each of the 12 appropriations bills and the budget becomes law.[41]

If this blueprint is not followed, continuing resolutions must be passed to keep the government operating, or nonessential federal agencies will be forced to close their doors, as happened in 2013 and briefly in 2019.

As is true for much of the rest of contemporary congressional policy making, the "regular order" of the budget process is not typically followed in Congress. Partisan division and struggles between Congress and the White House have made

appropriations the amounts of money approved by Congress in statutes (bills) that each unit or agency of government can spend

In the winter of 2018, President Trump and Congress were unable to reach an agreement on the budget and unable to pass a continuing resolution to keep the government funded temporarily, leading to a shutdown of the federal government in 2019. This included the closure of the National Park Service, which operates many of the parks in Washington, D.C., and around the country.

omnibus appropriations bill a bill that deals with a number of unrelated topics

it difficult to secure the enactment of the 12 separate appropriations bills reported by the 12 House and Senate appropriations committees. In 2016, for example, congressional Republicans and Democrats agreed in January to cooperate in passing the 12 regular spending bills. By mid-year, though, failed appropriations bills had "piled up in the Senate like a multicar crash on the highway."[42] Similar problems in 2019 led to a brief government shutdown. Republicans were especially outraged that Senate Democrats filibustered the defense appropriations bill. Republicans said Democrats were willing to compromise national security for partisan reasons. Democrats said it was the GOP that demonstrated indifference to the nation's real security needs. Given the parties' stark disagreements over spending priorities, regular order seems generally unlikely to prevail. Indeed, since 1999, the "regular" budget process has failed to produce a budget as often as it has succeeded.

Departing from regular order, Congress has come to rely on the **omnibus appropriations bill** crafted by party leaders. The omnibus bill combines all or many of the smaller appropriations bills into a single package that can be passed with one vote in each house of Congress. The omnibus allows party leaders to establish their own spending priorities and to offer opportunities—seats on the omnibus— to individuals or groups of legislators to add their own favored programs to ensure their support for the overall bill.

For the most part, the legislative minority is excluded from the process, though in some instances the support of minority party members can be garnered by giving their interests seats on the omnibus. In 2015, for example, Democratic senator Dianne Feinstein agreed to support the GOP's omnibus spending bill after the Republican leadership agreed to include several of her pet projects, including a cyber-security bill that would have been unlikely to pass on its own. In 2019, President Trump signed an omnibus spending bill containing provisions aimed at securing the support of enough Democrats to ensure the bill's passage. This included increased funding for the Department of Education and expansion of some Medicaid programs. Generally, some members of the Senate minority must be given seats on the omnibus to reduce the threat of filibusters.

In sum, the omnibus bill is the budgetary component of the new order. Generally constructed by the House and Senate leadership, omnibus bills discourage deliberation because of their sheer size. Members may have only a couple of days to digest a bill that can be 2,000 pages long and include many complex funding provisions. Rather than read, members seek to make sure that their own favored programs are included in the omnibus spending bill. Like harried commuters throughout the nation's capital, members must run to "catch the omnibus." The idea of deliberation is lost in the rush.

Taken together, closed rules, multiple referrals, ping-ponging, and omnibus bills are designed to strengthen party leaders in Congress, reduce the power of the committees and subcommittees, and compel members to follow the leader. Though there have been pleas from current and former members of Congress to return to regular order, it appears unlikely that party leaders will be willing to give up control over the legislative process.

Congressional Decision-Making

> **Identify the factors that influence which bills Congress passes**

What determines the kinds of legislation that Congress ultimately produces? According to the simplest theories of representation, members of Congress respond to the views of their constituents. In fact, the process of creating a legislative agenda, drawing up a list of possible measures, and deciding among them is a very complex one, in which a variety of influences from inside and outside government play important roles. External influences include a legislator's constituency and various interest groups. Influences from inside government include party leadership, congressional colleagues, and the president.

CONSTITUENCY

Because members of Congress, for the most part, want to be re-elected, we would expect the views of their constituents to be a primary influence on the decisions that they make. In fact, most constituents pay little attention to politics and often do not even know what policies their representatives support. Nonetheless, members of Congress spend a lot of time worrying about what their constituents think because they realize that the choices they make may be used as ammunition by an opposing candidate in a future election.[43]

For example, in 2017, despite lobbying by President Trump, the House Republican leadership could not muster enough votes to pass a measure that would have repealed Obamacare. Some Republicans from swing districts—those where voters are closely divided between the parties—feared upsetting constituents who favored Obamacare, while more conservative Republicans thought the bill did not go far enough in dismantling government-sponsored health insurance.

INTEREST GROUPS

Interest groups are another important influence on congressional policies. Members of Congress pay close attention to interest groups for a number of reasons: they can mobilize constituents, serve as watchdogs on congressional action, and supply candidates with money.

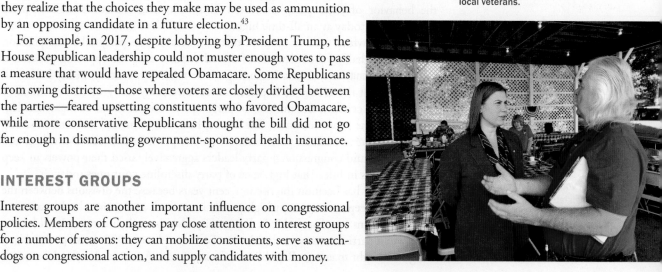

Representatives spend a lot of time meeting with constituents in their districts to explain how they have helped their district and learn what issues their constituents care about. Such meetings are often informal events at local restaurants or fairs, or town halls where constituents can ask questions. Here, Rep. Elissa Slotkin (D-Mich.) speaks with a constituent at an event for local veterans.

Many interest groups also use legislative "scorecards" that rate how members of Congress vote on issues of importance to that group, often posting them on their websites for members and the public to see. A high or low rating by an important interest group may provide a potent weapon in the next election. Interest groups can increase their influence over a particular piece of legislation by signaling their intention to include it in their scoring. Among the most influential groups that use scorecards are the National Federation of Independent Business, the American Federation of Labor and Congress of Industrial Organizations (AFL-CIO), National Right to Life, the League of Conservation Voters, and the National Rifle Association.

Interest groups also have substantial influence in setting the legislative agenda and, working with members and staffers of congressional committees, in helping to craft specific language in legislation. Today, sophisticated lobbyists representing such groups win influence by providing information about policies, as well as campaign contributions, to busy members of Congress (see Chapter 11). The $1.1 trillion end-of-year spending bill passed at the end of 2014 included an amendment exempting many financial transactions from federal regulation under the Dodd-Frank Act. The amendment language was taken from a bill originally written by Citigroup lobbyists, with 70 of 85 lines of the bill directly copying Citigroup's language.[44] After further lobbying by the banking industry, legislation enacted in 2018 loosened a number of other Dodd-Frank rules and exempted regional banks from a number of remaining rules.

Close financial ties between members of Congress and interest group lobbyists often raise concerns that interest groups get favored treatment in exchange for political donations. Interest groups are influential in Congress, but the character of their influence is often misunderstood. Interest groups seldom "buy" votes, in the sense of pressuring members of Congress to radically change their positions on issues. Their main effect is to encourage members already inclined to agree with them to work harder on behalf of the group's goals. Lobbyists for the coal industry, for example, are not likely to sway the votes of environmentally minded members of Congress, however hard they try. Instead, such lobbyists work to make certain that members already friendly to energy interests vigorously pursue pro-industry energy policies.

PARTY

In both the House and Senate, party leaders have a good deal of influence over the behavior of their party members. This influence, sometimes called "party discipline," is today at an all-time high.

A vote in which half or more of the members of one party take one position while at least half of the members of the other party take the opposing position is called a **party unity vote**. At the beginning of the twentieth century, nearly half of all **roll-call votes** in the House of Representatives were party unity votes. For much of the twentieth century, the number of party unity votes declined as bipartisan legislation became more common. The 1990s, however, witnessed a return to strong party discipline as partisan polarization drew sharper lines between Democrats and Republicans, and congressional party leaders aggressively used their powers to keep their members in line. That high level of party discipline continues today.

Party unity has been on the rise in recent years because the divisions between the parties have deepened on many high-profile issues such as abortion, health care, and financial reform (see Figure 12.7). Party unity also rises when congressional leaders try to put a partisan stamp on legislation. For example, in 1995 then-Speaker Newt Gingrich sought to enact a Republican "Contract with America" that few Democrats

FOR CRITICAL ANALYSIS

How does congressional ethics legislation address concerns about corruption? Why is it important that lawmakers identify the earmarks they add to legislation?

party unity vote a roll-call vote in the House or Senate in which at least 50 percent of the members of one party take a particular position and are opposed by at least 50 percent of the members of the other party

roll-call vote a vote in which each legislator's yes or no vote is recorded as the clerk calls the names of the members alphabetically

Contact Your Member of Congress

NATHAN BARKER, Legislative Correspondent for a Republican member of the House of Representatives

Let's say you feel strongly about an issue, and you want to contact those in power who can make a difference. One important way is to reach out to your member of Congress. Nathan Barker says, "I love my job. I love being able to connect people, connect the constituent and the member each and every day because this republic of ours wouldn't work without it." Here are his tips for contacting legislators in the most effective way:

1 It's important to do some research first. You can convey your opinion about a general issue area, but it's even better to refer to a specific piece of legislation by title or the House H.R. number or the Senate S. number. At Congress.gov you can search by key word or member name and follow bills through the process. Also make sure you're contacting about a federal issue, not a state legislative bill.

2 Identify which office to contact about your issue. If you want to voice your opinion about an issue or a piece of legislation, contact your representative or senator's Washington, D.C., office, as that's where the experts on policy issues are. If you need casework assistance—help with a federal agency, for example—contact the member's local office.

3 Should you write, email, or call? If you want a response, a letter or email is best (keep in mind that a response may take a couple of weeks due to volume). If you simply want to register your opinion, a phone call is good. Leave a voice mail with your full name, your city or town, your subject, and a short message, and staff will log your call.

4 Always contact your own representative or senator. They very much want to hear from their constituents. Contacting officials from other districts or states, who have no obligation to respond, or every single Republican or Democrat, or those in leadership,

is not an effective use of your time. Better to contact your own member and urge them to speak with leadership or other members of the congressional delegation about your issue.

5 Always state your name, your location, your background, and your opinion or call for action. There is no single script to follow. Saying "I'm a veteran" or "I'm a teacher" provides a helpful frame of reference. It's important to be specific and succinct ("I'm a student worried about student loans, and I support bill H.R. ____ for ____ reason"). If you're calling about a specific piece of legislation, better to call and voice support or opposition *before* it comes up for a vote. And feel free to contact them again. The status quo is always shifting, and new bills are constantly coming up.

To follow up, sign up for legislators' newsletters to keep informed about their activities, legislation under consideration, and upcoming events such as town hall meetings or coffee meetups. Most have Facebook and Twitter accounts as well. You may even be able to set up a one-on-one meeting, especially with a House member. It helps to be persistent but also kind and respectful in interacting with the office—hard-working staff members really appreciate that—as well as being informed about your issue.

There is nothing that should stop a student in college from contacting a member about an issue they find important. If you're passionate about an issue, just do it.

FIGURE 12.7
• •

Party Unity Votes in Congress

Party unity votes are roll-call votes in which a majority of one party lines up against a majority of the other party. Party unity votes increase when the parties are polarized and when the party leadership can enforce discipline. Why did the percentage of party unity votes decline in the 1970s? Why has it risen in recent years?

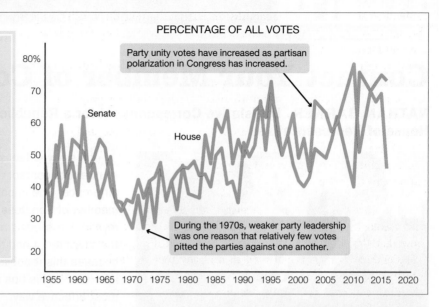

PERCENTAGE OF ALL VOTES

Party unity votes have increased as partisan polarization in Congress has increased.

Senate

House

During the 1970s, weaker party leadership was one reason that relatively few votes pitted the parties against one another.

SOURCES: CQ Roll Call's Vote Studies, http://media.cq.com/votestudies (accessed 6/9/14); Eliza Newlin Carney, "Standing Together against Any Action," *CQ Weekly*, March 16, 2015; and "2015 Vote Studies: Party Unity Remained Strong," *CQ Weekly*, February 8, 2016; Brookings, *Vital Statistics on Congress*, "Table 8-3: Party Unity Votes in Congress, 1953–2016," May 21, 2018, www.brookings.edu/multi-chapter-report/vital-statistics-on-congress/ (accessed 11/9/18).

supported. The result was more party unity in the House than in any year since 1954. Since then, increasing polarization has resulted in very high party unity scores. Initial results for the 116th Congress indicate that party unity scores will increase, particularly in the House.

Typically, party unity is greater in the House than in the Senate. House rules grant greater procedural control of business to the majority party leaders, which gives them more influence over House members.

To some extent, party unity is based on ideology and background. Republican members of the House are more likely to have been elected by rural or suburban districts and Democrats by urban ones; in both houses, Democrats are more liberal on economic and social questions than their Republican colleagues.

WHEN CONGRESS HAS TROUBLE DECIDING

The 116th Congress (2019–20) was the least productive in modern history, enacting only 163 pieces of legislation. The previous record was held by the 112th Congress (2011–13), which had enacted 284 laws.[45] A small number of the bills that were passed by the 116th Congress were, however, quite important. These included a major measure to protect public land and a significant set of changes to Medicaid. Perhaps the most important legislative success of the 116th Congress was the enactment of a multibillion dollar stimulus package to help cushion the economic effects of the coronavirus pandemic. Congress's legislative efforts were plagued by partisan polarization and divided government. Congress's attention, moreover, was often focused on major nonlegislative matters such as the 2019 Mueller probe into Russian efforts to influence the 2016 election, and the monthslong struggle over President Trump's impeachment (2019–20).

In 2018, the 115th Congress enacted a major government spending bill, but the spending authority given to the government under that bill was due to lapse on

FOR CRITICAL ANALYSIS

Why has it become so difficult for members of Congress to compromise? How is American democracy harmed when Congress is unable to agree on major pieces of legislation?

September 30, 2020.[46] After months of partisan battles, the 116th Congress was able only to enact a stopgap bill that would extend funding for federal agencies through December 11, 2020.[47]

Many critics of Congress charge that America's legislative body is too slow and cumbersome to deal with crises. Yet, when faced with emergencies, Congress can act quickly. For example, Congress enacted major funding programs in 2020 in response to the coronavirus pandemic and resulting financial collapse. Some pundits became impatient as Congress debated, but argument, debate, and partisanship are part of democracy. Self-government is never smooth, but it can be effective. As of mid-November 2020, however, Congress had not passed a second stimulus bill in response to the pandemic.

Congressional Polarization Congress's sometime inability to decide reflects the deep ideological distance between the two parties. Efforts to measure this distance show that Republicans and Democrats have been diverging sharply since the mid-1970s and are now more polarized than at any time in the last century. Democrats have become more liberal and Republicans have become more conservative on issues related to the economy and the role of government.[48] But as Figure 12.8 shows, the Republican Party has experienced the greater shift, becoming sharply more conservative.

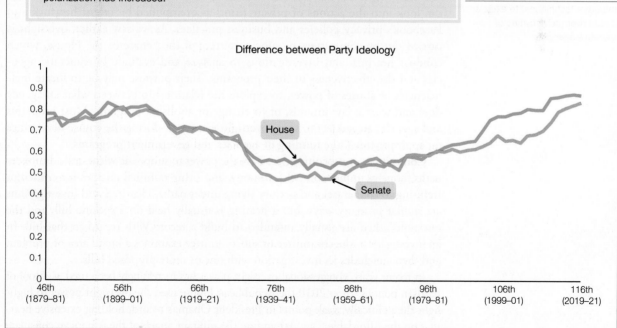

FIGURE 12.8

Polarization in Congress

In recent decades Democrats and Republicans in Congress have been increasingly polarized as Democrats have become more liberal and Republicans more conservative. The graph below shows the difference between each party's average ideology in each chamber of Congress over time. As the graph shows, the parties' average ideologies in both chambers were less polarized in the 1940s and '50s, while in recent years, polarization has increased.

Difference between Party Ideology

House

Senate

SOURCE: Voteview, http://voteview.com/dwnl.htm (accessed 10/6/20).

FOR CRITICAL ANALYSIS

How does polarization
contribute to congressional
gridlock? How has the use
of congressional procedures
made it more difficult to enact
legislation in recent years?

Moreover, because congressional districts are increasingly unified in their ideology—due in part to gerrymandering but mainly to natural clustering of the population—most members of Congress are in safe seats. Their constituents will not punish them for failing to compromise. In addition, organizations on the right, such as the National Rifle Association (NRA), often punish Republican members of Congress who do support compromises, by recruiting and financing alternative candidates to challenge members who vote against the organization's positions.[49]

Congressional polarization is here to stay so long as voters elect representatives with sharply different views about what government should and shouldn't do. Until there is more agreement about the role of government and the best way to manage the budgetary challenges that face the country, congressional standoffs on major legislation will remain a regular feature of American politics.

Beyond Legislation: Other Congressional Powers

> Describe the powers that Congress uses to influence other branches of government

In addition to the power to make the law, Congress has a number of other ways to influence the process of government. The Constitution gives the Senate the power to approve treaties and appointments. And Congress has a number of other powers through which it can help administer laws.

OVERSIGHT

oversight the effort by Congress, through hearings, investigations, and other techniques, to exercise control over the activities of executive agencies

Oversight, as applied to Congress, usually refers to the effort to oversee or to supervise how the executive branch carries out legislation. Sometimes, committees can look into the actions of private firms, as exemplified by recent hearings into Facebook's privacy policies and business practices. As we saw earlier, oversight is carried out by committees or subcommittees of the Senate or the House, which conduct hearings and investigations to analyze and evaluate bureaucratic agencies and the effectiveness of their programs. Their purpose may be to locate inefficiencies or abuses of power, to explore the relationship between what an agency does and what a law intends, or to change or abolish a program. Most programs and agencies are subject to some oversight every year during the course of hearings on appropriations, the funding of agencies and government programs.

Committees or subcommittees have the power to subpoena witnesses, administer oaths, cross-examine, compel testimony, and bring criminal charges for contempt (refusing to cooperate) and perjury (lying under oath). Hearings and investigations are similar in many ways, but a hearing is usually held on a specific bill, and the questions asked are usually intended to build a record with regard to that bill. In an investigation, the committee or subcommittee examines a broad area or problem and then concludes its investigation with one or more proposed bills.

In recent years, congressional oversight power has increasingly been used as a tool of partisan politics. After 2010 the Republican House used the oversight power to highlight the politically weak points in President Obama's record, holding extensive hearings on the Affordable Care Act and on the militant attack of the American consulate in Benghazi, Libya, that resulted in American deaths.[50] First convened in 2014, the

Select Committee on Benghazi became enmeshed in partisan contention after Hillary Clinton, secretary of state during the attacks, announced that she would run for president. In 2015, as revelations emerged that Clinton had used a private email server during her tenure as secretary of state, the committee began to investigate whether appropriate procedures had been followed and whether national security had been compromised.[51] When the FBI undertook an investigation into the matter in 2016, FBI director James Comey recommended no criminal charges against Clinton but also questioned her judgment and called her actions "extremely careless."

Almost as soon as Donald Trump took office in 2017, Democrats called for investigations into allegations that his campaign had colluded with Russian operatives to help Trump win the 2016 election. House and Senate committees, chaired by Republicans, failed to find evidence of presidential wrongdoing. Democrats, however, demanded the appointment of a special counsel after President Trump's firing of FBI director James Comey. Over the course of the investigation, the special counsel, Robert Mueller, indicted several close Trump aides for improper contacts with Russian officials. In 2018, four former Trump aides—George Papadopoulos, Paul Manafort, Rick Gates, and Michael Flynn—pleaded guilty to a variety of crimes related to the investigation. However, in 2019, Mueller's final report indicated no conclusive evidence of collusion between the Trump campaign and the Russians. Congressional Democrats were not convinced. In 2020, House Democrats threatened further investigations of the president while House Republicans launched their own investigations of Justice Department and FBI officials who had pursued investigations of Trump aides.

ADVICE AND CONSENT: SPECIAL SENATE POWERS

The Constitution says the president has the power to make treaties and to appoint top executive officers, ambassadors, and federal judges—but only "with the Advice and Consent of the Senate" (Article II, Section 2). For treaties, two-thirds of senators present must consent; for appointments, a simple majority is required.

The power to approve or reject presidential requests includes the power to set conditions. In fact, the Senate only occasionally exercises its power to reject treaties and appointments, and despite recent debate surrounding judicial nominees, during the past century only a small number of them have been rejected by the Senate or withdrawn by the president to avoid rejection, whereas hundreds have been approved. However, the recent increase in use of the filibuster to block judicial nominees led the Democratic Senate to bar the filibuster in deliberations about judicial and executive branch appointments.

Most presidents make every effort to take potential Senate opposition into account in treaty negotiations with foreign powers. Instead of treaties, presidents

The Constitution provides the Senate with the power to confirm executive branch appointments such as Supreme Court nominee Amy Coney Barrett (left). Congress also has the power to call cabinet officials to testify on behalf of their departments on certain policy issues. Secretary of Health and Human Services Alex Azar (right) speaks to congressional subcommittees on the topic of coronavirus and the 2021 budget.

executive agreement an agreement, made between the president and another country, that has the force of a treaty but does not require the Senate's "advice and consent"

frequently resort to **executive agreements** that do not need Senate approval. The Supreme Court has held that such agreements are equivalent to treaties.[52] In the past, presidents sometimes concluded secret agreements without informing Congress of the agreements' contents or even their existence. For example, American involvement in the Vietnam War grew in part out of a series of secret arrangements made between American presidents and the South Vietnamese during the 1950s and '60s. Congress did not even learn of the existence of these agreements until 1969.

In 1972, Congress passed the Case Act, which requires that the president inform Congress of any executive agreement within 60 days of its having been reached and provides Congress with the opportunity to cancel agreements it opposes. In addition, Congress can limit the president's ability to conduct foreign policy through executive agreement by refusing to appropriate the funds needed to implement an agreement. In this way, for example, Congress can modify or even cancel executive agreements to provide American economic or military assistance to foreign governments.

IMPEACHMENT

impeachment the formal charge by the House of Representatives that a government official has committed "Treason, Bribery, or other high Crimes and Misdemeanors"

The Constitution also grants Congress the power of **impeachment**, which means formally charging a federal official with "Treason, Bribery, or other high Crimes and Misdemeanors"; if the official is found guilty, he is removed from office. Impeachment is thus like a criminal indictment in which the House of Representatives acts like a grand jury, voting (by simple majority) on whether the accused ought to be impeached. If the House votes to impeach, the Senate then acts like a trial jury, voting on whether to convict and remove the official (which requires a two-thirds majority of the Senate).

The impeachment power is a considerable one; in particular, the power of Congress to remove the president is a safeguard against the executive tyranny so greatly feared by the framers of the Constitution. The House has initiated impeachment proceedings more than 60 times in U.S. history. Fewer than 20 officials were ultimately impeached, however, and only 8—all federal judges— were convicted by the Senate and removed from office.[53]

Controversy over Congress's impeachment power has arisen over the grounds for impeachment, especially the meaning of "high Crimes and Misdemeanors." A strict reading of the Constitution suggests that the only impeachable offense is an actual crime. But a more common working definition is that "an impeachable offense is whatever the majority of the House of Representatives considers it to be at a given moment in history."[54] In other words, impeachment, especially impeachment of a president, is a political decision.

The political nature of impeachment was very clear in the three instances of presidential impeachment that have occurred in American history. In the first, in 1867, President Andrew Johnson, a southern Democrat who had battled a congressional Republican majority over Reconstruction, was impeached by the House but saved from conviction by one vote in the Senate. In 1998 the House impeached President Bill Clinton on charges of lying under oath and obstructing justice during the investigation into his sexual affair with the White House intern Monica Lewinsky. The vote was highly partisan, with only five Democrats voting for impeachment on each charge. In the Senate, where a two-thirds majority was needed for conviction, only 45 senators voted to convict on the charge of lying and 50 on the charge of obstructing justice. As in the House, the vote was highly partisan, with all Democrats and only five Republicans supporting the president's ultimate acquittal.

FOR CRITICAL ANALYSIS

Under what circumstances should Congress exercise its power of impeachment? Why has impeachment been used so rarely in U.S. history?

In 2019, House Democrats voted to impeach President Trump on charges that he had sought to pressure the Ukrainian government to investigate Joe Biden and Biden's son, Hunter, for their business activities in the Ukraine. Democrats asserted that Trump had threatened to cut military aid to Ukraine if they did not help him undermine a major political foe. Despite a leaked phone call that seemed to support the allegation, Trump denied the charge and averred that the Democrats and liberal media were conspiring against him. After a short Senate trial, Trump was acquitted, with all but one GOP senator (Mitt Romney) choosing to support the president. Most Republican voters agreed that the charges against the president did not merit his removal from office.

The House possesses the power to impeach federal officials. In American history, 17 federal officials have been impeached, including three presidents. Andrew Johnson was impeached in 1868 for improperly removing the Secretary of War. In 1998 the House impeached President Bill Clinton for lying under oath about his affair with White House intern Monica Lewinsky. In 2019–20, the House impeached Donald Trump for abuse of power and obstruction of Congress after aid to Ukraine was allegedly withheld, though he was acquitted in February 2020.

Congress: What Do You Think?

Much of this chapter has described the major institutional components of Congress and has shown how they work as Congress makes policy. But what do these institutional features mean for how Congress represents the American public?

★ Does the organization of Congress promote the equal representation of all Americans? Or are there institutional features of Congress that allow some interests more access and influence than others? What can we learn from a stimulus bill that passes Congress and an opioids bill that almost fails? What might Huntington, West Virginia, police chief Hank Dial say?

★ What areas of public policy might suffer if Congress continues its inability to decide?

★ What types of institutional changes would make Congress work better? Some suggest the appointment of citizen commissions to draw district lines in order to elect more moderate candidates and make compromise in Congress easier. Others argue for eliminating the filibuster in the Senate to reduce gridlock. What do you think the effects would be?

★ Will continued partisan gridlock hurt Congress as an institution?

STUDY GUIDE

Congress: Representing the American People

Describe who serves in Congress and how they represent their constituents (pp. 431–44)

A member of Congress's primary responsibility is to the people in his or her district or state. Senators usually represent much larger and more diverse constituencies than do their counterparts in the House. Because of differences in their constituencies and the rules governing each body, House members are generally more attuned to the immediate legislative needs of groups in their districts than senators are. While the number of African Americans, women, Latinos, and Asian Americans in Congress has increased over the last two decades, these groups are still not proportionally represented relative to their proportions in the general population. Regardless of whether members of Congress share their constituents' sociological characteristics, however, representatives do work hard to speak for their constituents' views and to serve their constituents' interests. Generally speaking, three factors are especially important in understanding who serves as a member of Congress: who decides to run, incumbency, and the way congressional districts are drawn.

Key Terms

constituency (p. 431)

bicameral (p. 431)

delegate (p. 432)

trustee (p. 432)

descriptive representation (p. 433)

substantive representation (p. 433)

incumbency (p. 439)

pork barrel (or pork) (p. 440)

apportionment (p. 442)

redistricting (p. 442)

gerrymandering (p. 443)

Practice Quiz

1. Which of the following is a way in which the House and the Senate are different?
   a) The House is a more deliberative legislative body than the Senate.
   b) The House is more centralized and organized than the Senate.
   c) Senators serve smaller and more homogeneous constituencies than members of the House.
   d) Senators are often more attuned to the legislative needs of local interest groups than members of the House.
   e) There are no important differences between the House and the Senate.

2. Which type of representation is based on the idea that constituents have the power to hire and fire their representatives?
   a) descriptive representation
   b) substantive representation
   c) philosophical representation
   d) ideological representation
   e) economic representation

3. Which of the following statements best describes the social composition of the U.S. Congress?
   a) The majority of representatives do not have university degrees.
   b) Men and women are equally represented in Congress.
   c) Most members of Congress do not affiliate with any specific religion.
   d) The legal profession is the dominant career of most members of Congress prior to their election.
   e) The number of African American, Latino, and Asian American representatives has decreased over the last 20 years.

4. The Supreme Court has ruled that
   a) only the House of Representatives has the constitutional authority to redraw congressional district lines.
   b) race can be the predominant factor in drawing congressional districts.
   c) race cannot be the predominant factor in drawing congressional districts.
   d) states cannot use unelected, nonpartisan committees to draw congressional districts.
   e) only the Senate has the constitutional authority to redraw congressional district lines.

The Organization of Congress

Describe the factors that structure congressional business (pp. 444–50)

The building blocks of congressional organization include the political parties and party leaders, the formal committee system, congressional staff, and informal caucuses. The committee system, with committee membership largely determined by party leadership, is particularly important because Congress uses committees and subcommittees to sort through alternatives, secure information, and write legislation.

Key Terms

conference (p. 444)

caucus (political) (p. 444)

Speaker of the House (p. 444)

majority leader (p. 444)

minority leader (p. 444)

whip (p. 445)

standing committee (p. 446)

select committees (p. 448)

joint committees (p. 448)

conference committees (p. 448)

seniority (p. 449)

staff agencies (p. 450)

caucuses (congressional) (p. 450)

Practice Quiz

5. Which of the following types of committees includes members of both the House and the Senate?
   a) standing committee
   b) select committee
   c) joint committee
   d) rules committee
   e) No committees include both House members and senators.

6. A series of reforms instituted by Congress in the 1990s, including reducing the number of subcommittees and limiting the time committee chairs can serve to three terms, had the effect of
   a) reducing the power of committees.
   b) increasing the power of committees.
   c) eliminating the incumbency advantage in congressional elections.
   d) ending the filibuster.
   e) expanding the number of joint committees in Congress.

Rules of Lawmaking: How a Bill Becomes a Law

Describe the regular order and new order processes of how a bill becomes a law (pp. 450–59)

The rules of congressional procedure govern everything from the introduction of a bill to its submission to the president for signing. Traditionally, bills have followed a "regular order" of congressional procedures on their way to becoming law: bills originate in committees, legislators debate them on the floor of both the House and the Senate, differences between House and Senate bills may be reconciled in a conference committee, and presidents sign (or decline to sign) the final versions. Today, however, congressional party leaders may move important bills along following a set of "new order" paths that deemphasize deliberation, involving closed rules, multiple referrals, ping-ponging, and omnibus bills.

Key Terms

bill (p. 450)

committee markup (p. 452)

closed rule (p. 452)

open rule (p. 452)

filibuster (p. 452)

cloture (p. 453)

veto (p. 454)

pocket veto (p. 454)

multiple referral (p. 455)

appropriations (p. 457)

omnibus appropriations bill (p. 458)

Practice Quiz

7. What is the difference between a closed rule and an open rule in the House?
   a) A closed rule puts severe limits on floor debate and amendments, whereas an open rule permits floor debate and makes amendments easier.
   b) An open rule puts severe limits on floor debate and amendments, whereas a closed rule permits floor debate and makes amendments easier.
   c) A closed rule allows journalists and members of the public to listen to debates about a bill, whereas an open rule prevents journalists and members of the public from listening to debates about the bill.

d) An open rule allows journalists and members of the public to listen to debates about a bill, whereas a closed rule prevents journalists and members of the public from listening to debates about the bill.

e) A closed rule prevents the federal judiciary from declaring a bill unconstitutional once passed, whereas an open rule allows the federal judiciary to declare a bill unconstitutional.

8. Which of the following statements about the filibuster is most accurate?
   a) The filibuster was first used in 1975.
   b) The votes of 67 senators are currently required to end a filibuster.
   c) The filibuster was used far more frequently in the 1930s and 1940s than it has been in the last two decades.
   d) Nominees for positions in the executive branch and the federal courts cannot currently be filibustered.
   e) Filibusters were declared unconstitutional by the Supreme Court in 2013.

9. In which type of multiple referral do party leaders assign different sections of the same bill to different committees?
   a) joint referral
   b) split referral
   c) sequential referral
   d) priority referral
   e) specialized referral

10. Which of the following best describes omnibus appropriations legislation?
    a) 12 separate bills that, taken together, set funding levels for all federal programs for one year
    b) one bill that sets funding levels for all federal programs for one year
    c) one bill that sets funding levels for federal transportation programs and state transportation grants for one year
    d) any legislation related to spending that comes about as a result of a conference committee
    e) any spending bill that is veto-proof, meaning that it has the support of two-thirds of all House members and senators

Congressional Decision-Making

Identify the factors that influence which bills Congress passes (pp. 459–64)

A variety of influences from inside and outside government play a role in congressional decision-making. External influences include the policy preferences of the legislator's constituency and the lobbying of various interest groups. Within Congress, leaders maintain strong party discipline, and most roll-call votes now fall along party lines. The growing polarization of Democrats and Republicans along congressional-district lines has led to the election of more partisan members in recent years. The resulting polarization in Congress has significantly hindered its legislative productivity.

Key Terms

party unity vote (p. 460)

roll-call vote (p. 460)

Practice Quiz

11. Members of Congress take their constituents' views into account because
    a) the Supreme Court can invalidate laws passed without the public's majority support.
    b) interest groups are forbidden from lobbying during legislative votes.
    c) most constituents pay close attention to what's going on in Congress at all times.
    d) they worry that their voting record will be scrutinized at election time.
    e) they can be impeached if they go against their constituents' policy preferences.

12. Which of the following is *not* a way that interest groups can influence Congress?
    a) They create and distribute "scorecards" that rate how members of Congress vote on issues of importance to the group.
    b) They work with members and staffers of congressional committees to craft specific language in legislation.
    c) They encourage members of Congress who already agree with them to work harder on behalf of the group's goals.
    d) They serve as watchdogs on congressional action.
    e) They can submit large numbers of individual contributions to a member of Congress's campaign in a single, anonymous bundle.

Beyond Legislation: Other Congressional Powers

> **Describe the powers that Congress uses to influence other branches of government (pp. 464–67)**

Congress has a number of other powers beyond lawmaking. Using hearings, investigations, and other techniques, Congress exercises oversight power over the agencies of the executive branch. Per the Constitution, the president can make treaties and appoint top executive officers, ambassadors, and federal judges only "with the Advice and Consent of the Senate." The Constitution also grants Congress the power to impeach the president and other executive officials.

Key Terms

oversight (p. 464)

executive agreement (p. 466)

impeachment (p. 466)

Practice Quiz

13. When Congress conducts an investigation to explore the relationship between what a law intended and what an executive agency has done, it is engaged in
    a) oversight.
    b) advice and consent.
    c) appropriations.
    d) executive agreement.
    e) direct patronage.

14. Instead of treaties, presidents frequently resort to executive agreements, which
    a) require the Senate's advice and consent.
    b) do not require the Senate's advice and consent.
    c) remain secret from Congress for the duration of the agreement.
    d) allow the president to settle impeachment charges without involving the Senate.
    e) require a majority vote of approval in both the House and Senate.

15. Which of the following statements about impeachment is *not* true?
    a) The president is the only official who can be impeached by Congress.
    b) Impeachment means to charge a government official with "Treason, Bribery, or other high Crimes and Misdemeanors."
    c) The House of Representatives decides by simple majority vote whether the accused ought to be impeached.
    d) The Senate decides whether to convict and remove the person from office.
    e) There have been only three instances of presidential impeachment in American history.

The Presidency

WHAT GOVERNMENT DOES AND WHY IT MATTERS Presidents inevitably face tough challenges during their time in office. Donald Trump's presidency was no exception, as the coronavirus pandemic of 2020 strained the nation's health care system, killing thousands, and forced millions out of work. Indeed, Trump declared himself a "wartime president," an apt title given the magnitude of the pandemic's devastating effects on the nation's social and economic fabric.

An earlier wartime period had produced the Defense Production Act (DPA), enacted in 1950 during the Korean War. The DPA allows a presidential administration to secure or ramp up production of needed equipment from private businesses by increasing vendor capacity through loans, directing distribution of a company's product, or, most commonly, forcing vendors to prioritize the government's order over orders from other clients. In March 2020, President Trump invoked the DPA for a nonmilitary purpose: to compel auto manufacturer GM to produce much-needed ventilators for hospitals.

Some observers urged the president not to stop there, but to use the DPA to force production of additional medical equipment in short supply, such as masks, eye protection, and other types of personal protective equipment (PPE). Dr. Craig Spencer, director of global health in emergency medicine at

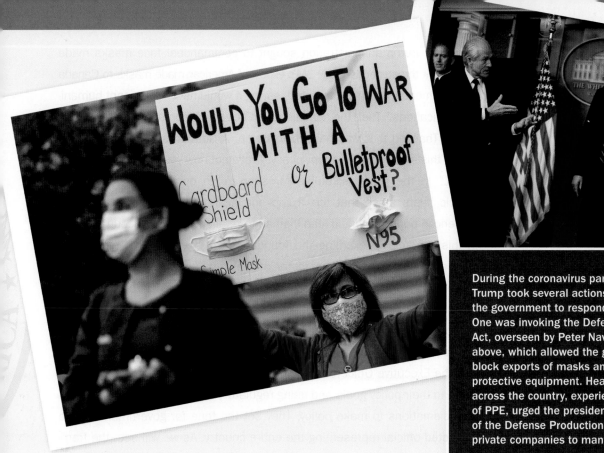

During the coronavirus pandemic, President Trump took several actions to mobilize the government to respond to the virus. One was invoking the Defense Production Act, overseen by Peter Navarro, pictured above, which allowed the government to block exports of masks and other personal protective equipment. Health care workers across the country, experiencing a shortage of PPE, urged the president to use the power of the Defense Production Act to force private companies to manufacture PPE.

New York-Presbyterian/Columbia University Medical Center, made such a plea, saying that supplies were running out at his hospital and others in New York, a virus hot spot. "If we don't take decisive and aggressive action now, many more of my colleagues will be infected."[1] A number of governors and members of Congress as well as the American Medical Association called for the further use of the DPA as well.

Through March 2020, President Trump declined to invoke the DPA further. "We're a country not based on nationalizing our businesses," Trump said. Some parts of the business community had urged him not to invoke the DPA, worrying that it would introduce government bureaucracy at the precise time when streamlined processes were acutely important. "The Defense Production Act isn't a magic wand," said Neil Bradley, chief policy officer at the U.S. Chamber of Commerce. "It can't produce highly specialized manufacturing equipment overnight. It can't convert a refrigerator factory into a ventilator factory." But the law does allow federal agencies to skip the normal bidding and contracting process and sign contracts with companies quickly. Congressional Democrats contemplated passing a law that would force President Trump to use his DPA powers more broadly.[2]

Then in April 2020, President Trump changed course, invoking the DPA, but not in a way his earlier critics anticipated. Under DPA Policy Coordinator Peter

Navarro, the Trump administration sought to commandeer face masks made by 3M. First it threatened to block 3M's export of American-made masks to Canada and Latin America, which 3M resisted, saying it would have "significant humanitarian implications." Then the administration seized a shipment of masks made by 3M in Thailand that was headed to Berlin. A German spokesperson said, "We view this as an act of modern piracy. That's not how you treat trans-Atlantic partners." In the global scramble for supplies to combat the coronavirus pandemic, fears arose that the Trump administration's attempts to protect the American populace would lead instead to retaliation by other countries.[3]

In this chapter, we examine the foundations of the American presidency and assess the origins and character of presidential power. Presidents are empowered by democratic political processes and, increasingly, by their ability to control and expand the institutional resources of the office. They sit atop the executive branch, a large bureaucracy of departments and agencies. They influence policy with their appointments to the Cabinet, the White House staff, and to the Executive Office of the President, choosing officials who are sympathetic to their policy goals and using regulatory review and executive orders and proclamations to make policy. They set the tone for government as the sole elected official representing the entire country. As we will see, the framers thought a powerful and energetic president would make America's government more effective but knew that presidential power needed to be subject to constraints to prevent it from becoming a threat to citizens' liberties. The checks and balances in the constitutional design not only constrain each branch's powers but also ensure that those powers are shared. The branches must work together, and sometimes one branch can try to compel another to act, as the Defense Production Act example shows.

CHAPTER GOALS

★ Identify the expressed, implied, delegated, and inherent powers of the presidency (pp. 475–88)

★ Describe the institutional resources presidents have to help them exercise their powers (pp. 489–93)

★ Explain how modern presidents have become even more powerful (pp. 493–503)

The Constitutional Powers of the Presidency

> Identify the expressed, implied, delegated, and inherent powers of the presidency

The presidency was established by Article II of the Constitution, which begins by asserting that "the executive power shall be vested in a President of the United States of America." This language is known as the Constitution's "vesting clause." The president's executive power is underscored in Section 3 of Article II, the "take care clause," which confers upon the president the duty to "take care that the laws be faithfully executed." The president's oath of office at the end of Section 1, moreover, obligates—and thus empowers—the chief executive to "preserve, protect and defend the Constitution of the United States."

This language seems to require the president to take action, without specifying any limits to that action, if constitutional government is threatened. President Abraham Lincoln cited his oath of office as justification for suspending the writ of habeas corpus, which protects against arbitrary government detention of individuals, in 1861. He declared that his oath would be broken if the government were overthrown and that suspension of habeas corpus was necessary to prevent that calamity from taking place.

By vesting the executive power in the president, Article II also implies that the president serves as America's head of state and is therefore entitled to special deference and respect. At the time of the Constitution's adoption, most European chief executives and heads of state were monarchs. While presidents are not monarchs, as the holders of executive power they might appear to be entitled to the respect due a king or emperor. See Table 13.1 for the qualifications for president laid out in the Constitution.

On the basis of Article II, presidents make use of three types of powers available to their office: expressed powers, implied powers, and delegated powers. A fourth

TABLE 13.1

Constitutional Qualifications of the President

According to Article II of the Constitution, to be president a person must fulfill the following requirements:

Citizenship	"Natural-born citizen" (Includes individuals who were born abroad to U.S. citizens; an individual born a noncitizen who acquires citizenship through "naturalization" is not eligible.)
Age	35+
Residency	14+ years living in the United States
Term Limit (according to 26th Amendment)	Presidential terms last 4 years; cannot be elected to presidency more than twice.

Abraham Lincoln, like many other presidents, cited the presidential oath of office as providing the president the authority to take all the necessary actions to protect the nation.

type of power claimed by presidents does not appear in Article II. This is called the inherent power of the office.

EXPRESSED POWERS

expressed powers specific powers granted by the Constitution to Congress (Article I, Section 8) and to the president (Article II)

The **expressed powers** of the presidency are those specifically established by the language of the Constitution. These fall into several categories:

1. *Military.* Article II, Section 2, provides for the power as "Commander in Chief of the Army and Navy of the United States, and of the Militia of the several States, when called in to the actual Service of the United States."

2. *Judicial.* Article II, Section 2, also provides the power to "grant Reprieves and Pardons for Offences against the United States, except in Cases of Impeachment."

3. *Diplomatic.* Article II, Section 2, further provides the power "by and with the Advice and Consent of the Senate to make Treaties." Article II, Section 3, provides the power to "receive Ambassadors and other public Ministers."

4. *Executive.* Article II, Section 3, authorizes the president to see to it that all the laws are faithfully executed; Section 2 gives the power to appoint, remove, and supervise all executive officers and to appoint all federal judges.

5. *Legislative.* Article I, Section 7, and Article II, Section 3, give the president the power to participate authoritatively in the legislative process.

commander in chief the role of the president as commander of the national military and the state National Guard units (when called into service)

Military Power The president's military powers are among the most important ones of the office. The position of **commander in chief** makes the president the highest military authority in the United States, with control of the entire defense establishment. The president is also head of the nation's intelligence network, which includes not only the Central Intelligence Agency (CIA) but also the National Security

Council (NSC), the National Security Agency (NSA), the Federal Bureau of Investigation (FBI), and a host of less well-known but very powerful international and domestic security agencies.

The president's military powers extend into the domestic sphere. Article IV, Section 4, provides that the "United States shall [protect] every State . . . against . . . Invasion . . . and . . . domestic Violence." Congress has made this an explicit presidential power through statutes directing the president as commander in chief to discharge these obligations.[4] The Constitution restrains the president's use of domestic force, however, by providing that a state legislature (or governor when the legislature is not in session) must request federal troops before the president can send them into the state to provide public order.

Yet the use of domestic force remains largely a matter of the president's discretion. Presidents are not obligated to deploy national troops merely because the state legislature or governor makes such a request. More important, the president may deploy troops without a specific request from the state legislature or governor if the president considers them necessary to keep order, maintain an essential national service during an emergency, enforce a federal judicial order, or protect federally guaranteed civil rights.[5]

A historic example of the unilateral use of presidential emergency power when a state did not request or even want it is the decision by President Dwight D. Eisenhower in 1957 to send troops into Little Rock, Arkansas, against the wishes of the Arkansas government, to enforce court orders to integrate Little Rock's Central High School. The state's governor, Orval Faubus, had posted the Arkansas National Guard at the school entrance to prevent the court-ordered admission of nine Black students. After an effort to negotiate with Governor Faubus failed, President Eisenhower reluctantly sent 1,000 paratroopers from the U.S. Army's 101st Airborne Division to Little Rock; they stood watch while the Black students took their places in the previously all-White classrooms.

In 2020, Trump considered issuing orders to mobilize as many as 10,000 federal troops to help quell protests that broke out in the wake of the killing of George Floyd, an African American man, by a Minneapolis police officer. Military officials balked at Trump's proposed use of troops and Trump did not issue the order. The president did, however, dispatch federal law enforcement agents to Portland, Oregon, and several other cities to guard federal property and help local police. These agents were withdrawn after local officials declared that they were not needed.

One of the president's responsibilities is the maintenance of public order in times of crisis. In 1951, President Eisenhower used this to justify sending the troops to Little Rock to enforce racial integration of public schools (left). During the coronavirus crisis of 2020, President Trump sent the USNS *Mercy*, a navy hospital ship, to Los Angeles to treat patients suffering from COVID-19 as hospitals became overwhelmed (right).

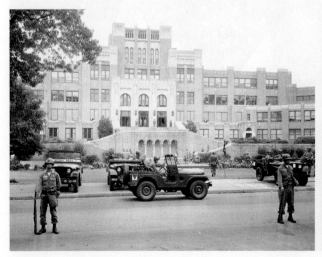

In most instances of domestic disorder, whether from human or natural causes, presidents tend to exercise unilateral power by declaring a "state of emergency." President Trump did so in response to three hurricanes in 2017, thereby making available federal grants, insurance, and direct aid. In 2019, President Trump ordered federal troops to America's southern border after declaring that illegal immigration constituted a national emergency. President Trump also declared states of emergency in all fifty states to free federal funds for use in 2020 during the coronavirus pandemic.

Judicial Power The presidential power to grant reprieves, pardons, and amnesty involves power over all individuals who may be a threat to the security of the United States. Presidents may use this power on behalf of a particular individual, as did Gerald Ford when he pardoned Richard Nixon in 1974 "for all offenses against the United States which he . . . has committed or may have committed." Or they may use it on a large scale, as did President Andrew Johnson in 1868, when he gave full amnesty to all southerners who had participated in the Civil War.

Presidents' use of the pardon power can be very controversial. President Trump was criticized for pardoning former Arizona sheriff Joe Arpaio after Arpaio was found guilty of criminal contempt for ignoring a court order that directed his office to halt illegal racial-profiling practices. The pardon was criticized because Trump did not first consult with the Justice Department's office of pardons and because the pardon was issued before Arpaio had been sentenced.

Diplomatic Power The president is America's chief representative in dealings with other nations, having the power to make treaties for the United States (with the advice and consent of the Senate) as well as the power to "recognize" the governments of other countries. Diplomatic recognition means that the United States acknowledges a government's legitimacy—that is, its claim to be the legal and rightful government of the country.

In recent years, presidents have expanded the practice of using executive agreements instead of treaties to establish contracts with other countries.[6] An

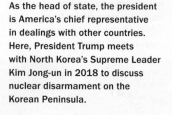

As the head of state, the president is America's chief representative in dealings with other countries. Here, President Trump meets with North Korea's Supreme Leader Kim Jong-un in 2018 to discuss nuclear disarmament on the Korean Peninsula.

executive agreement is exactly like a treaty except that it does not require approval by two-thirds of the Senate. The courts have held that executive agreements have the force of law, as though they were formal treaties.

There are actually two types of executive agreements. For an *executive–congressional agreement*, the president submits the proposed arrangement to Congress for a simple majority vote in both houses, usually easier to win than the two-thirds approval of the Senate. The United States' 2015 accord with Iran is a recent example of an executive–congressional agreement.

A *sole executive agreement*, on the other hand, is simply an understanding between the president and a foreign state and is not submitted to Congress for approval. In the past, sole executive agreements were used to flesh out commitments already made in treaties or to arrange for matters well below the level of policy. Since the 1930s, however, presidents have entered into sole executive agreements on important issues when they were uncertain about their prospects for securing congressional approval. For example, the General Agreement on Tariffs and Trade (GATT), one of the cornerstones of U.S. international economic policy in the post–World War II era, was based on an executive agreement.

Executive Power The Constitution focuses executive power and legal responsibility on the president. The most important constitutional basis of the president's power as chief executive is found in Article II, Section 3, which stipulates that the president must see that all the laws are faithfully executed, and Section 2, which provides that the president will appoint and supervise all executive officers and appoint all federal judges (with Senate approval). The power to appoint the principal executive officers and to require each of them to report to the president on subjects relating to the duties of their departments makes the president the true chief executive officer (CEO) of the nation.

Another component of the president's power as chief executive is **executive privilege**, the claim that confidential communications between a president and close advisers should not be revealed without presidential consent. Presidents have made this claim ever since George Washington refused a request from the House of Representatives to deliver documents concerning negotiations of an important treaty. Washington refused (successfully) on the grounds that, first, the House was not constitutionally part of the treaty-making process and, second, diplomatic negotiations required secrecy.

Although many presidents have claimed executive privilege, the concept was not tested in the courts until the "Watergate" affair of the early 1970s, when President Richard Nixon refused congressional demands that he turn over secret White House tapes that congressional investigators suspected would establish his involvement in illegal activities. In *United States v. Nixon* (1974), the Supreme Court ordered Nixon to turn over the tapes.[7] The president complied with the order and was eventually forced to resign from office as a result.

Although *United States v. Nixon* is often seen as a blow to presidential power, the Court's ruling actually recognized for the first time the legal validity of executive privilege, though holding that it did not apply in this particular instance. Subsequent presidents have cited the case in support of their claims of executive privilege. The Obama administration invoked executive privilege once, in response to congressional demands for records from Attorney

executive agreement an agreement, made between the president and another country, that has the force of a treaty but does not require the Senate's "advice and consent"

executive privilege the claim that confidential communications between a president and close advisers should not be revealed without the consent of the president

The Supreme Court's decision in *United States v. Nixon* is often seen as a blow to presidential power because Nixon was required to turn over secret tapes related to the Watergate scandal, despite his claims of executive privilege. Here, Nixon points to transcripts of the tapes that he is turning over to House impeachment investigators.

General Eric Holder relating to Operation Fast and Furious, an arms-trafficking sting operation that went awry, with federal agents losing track of hundreds of guns they had sold to suspected gun smugglers. In 2019, President Trump asserted executive privilege to block the release of portions of the Mueller Report on Russian meddling in the 2016 election and to prevent the release of certain documents relating to the Census Bureau's deliberations over the proposed addition of a citizenship question to the 2020 census. Trump's use of executive privilege to withhold information from Congress became the basis for one of the articles of impeachment drafted by the House to impeach the president in 2019. Trump was acquitted by the Senate.

Legislative Power—Agenda Setting Two constitutional provisions are the primary sources of the president's power in the legislative process. The first of these is the portion of Article II, Section 3, providing that the president "shall from time to time give to the Congress Information of the State of the Union, and recommend to their Consideration such Measures as he shall judge necessary and expedient." Delivering a "State of the Union" address may at first appear to be little more than the president's obligation to make recommendations for Congress's consideration. But in the twentieth century, as political and social conditions began to favor an increasingly prominent presidential role, each president, especially since Franklin Roosevelt, has increasingly relied on this provision. In doing so, the president became the primary initiator of proposals for legislative action in Congress and the most important single participant in legislative decision-making, as well as the principal source for public awareness of national issues.[8]

With some important exceptions, Congress depends on the president to set the agenda of public policy. For example, under the terms of the 1921 Budget and Accounting Act, the president is required to submit a budget to Congress. This gives presidents the power of being able to set the terms of debate about budgetary matters. Presidents also often set the country's policy agenda, beyond the budget. For example, during the weeks immediately following the September 11, 2001, terrorist attacks, President George W. Bush took many presidential initiatives to Congress, and each was given almost unanimous support. President Obama made health care his chief domestic priority and negotiated with divided congressional

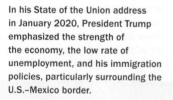

In his State of the Union address in January 2020, President Trump emphasized the strength of the economy, the low rate of unemployment, and his immigration policies, particularly surrounding the U.S.–Mexico border.

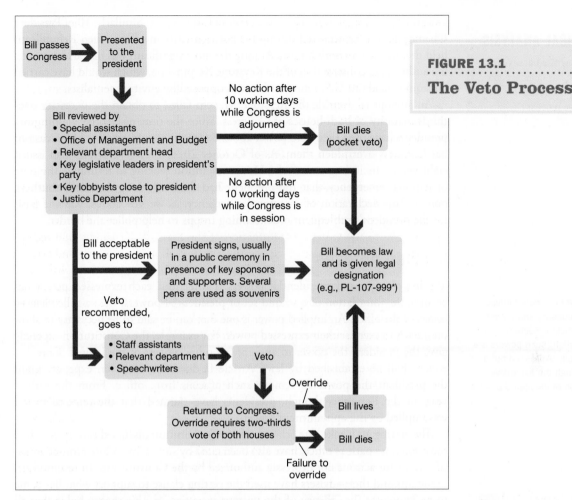

FIGURE 13.1
·······························
The Veto Process

Bill passes Congress → **Presented to the president**

Bill reviewed by
• Special assistants
• Office of Management and Budget
• Relevant department head
• Key legislative leaders in president's party
• Key lobbyists close to president
• Justice Department

No action after 10 working days while Congress is adjourned → **Bill dies (pocket veto)**

No action after 10 working days while Congress is in session →

Bill acceptable to the president → **President signs, usually in a public ceremony in presence of key sponsors and supporters. Several pens are used as souvenirs** → **Bill becomes law and is given legal designation (e.g., PL-107-999*)**

Veto recommended, goes to → • Staff assistants • Relevant department • Speechwriters → **Veto** → **Returned to Congress. Override requires two-thirds vote of both houses** → Override → **Bill lives** / Failure to override → **Bill dies**

*PL—public law; 107—number of Congress (107th was 2001–02); 999—number of the law.

Democrats to bring about the enactment of the Affordable Care Act, informally known as "Obamacare." President Trump tried to lead Congress to eliminate Obamacare but was unable to muster a majority of the fractious Republicans behind this central element of his agenda. However, Congress did enact Trump's proposals for a sweeping tax reform bill and a budget that substantially lifted spending on military and domestic programs.

Legislative Power—the Veto The second of the president's constitutionally authorized legislative powers is the **veto** power to reject acts of Congress (see Figure 13.1), which is provided in Article I, Section 7.[9] This power effectively makes the president the most important single legislative leader,[10] since no vetoed bill can become law unless both the House and Senate override the veto by a two-thirds vote. In the case of a **pocket veto**, as explained in Chapter 12, Congress does not even have the opportunity to override the veto and instead must pass the bill again in its next session.

Use of the veto varies according to the political situation each president confronts. During his last two years in office, when Democrats had control of both houses of Congress, Republican president George W. Bush vetoed 10 bills, including legislation designed to prohibit the use of harsh interrogation tactics, saying it "would take

FOR CRITICAL ANALYSIS

How might the anticipation of a veto affect the behavior of Congress? And how might the anticipation of a congressional override affect the president's behavior?

veto the president's constitutional power to turn down acts of Congress; a presidential veto may be overridden by a two-thirds vote of each house of Congress

pocket veto a presidential veto that is automatically triggered if the president does not act on a given piece of legislation passed during the final 10 days of a legislative session

FOR CRITICAL ANALYSIS

Although Congress passes laws, the president has influence too. What is the president's role in the legislative process?

away one of the most valuable tools in the war on terror."[11] Similarly, 10 of President Obama's 12 vetoes occurred during his last two years in office, when Republicans held the majority in both houses. Among the most significant was his 2015 veto of a bill authorizing construction of the Keystone XL pipeline, which would have carried oil from Canada to U.S. refineries but was opposed by environmentalists.

An attempt to override the Keystone XL veto failed to obtain the necessary two-thirds majority of both houses of Congress. Since the time of George Washington, presidents have used their veto power about 2,600 times, and on only 111 occasions has Congress overridden them. As of October 2020, President Trump had issued eight vetoes, including a veto of a House resolution seeking to terminate the state of national emergency that the president had declared along America's southern border. This declaration of a national emergency, as we saw above, was the basis for the president's subsequent order sending troops to help police the border.

IMPLIED POWERS

implied powers powers derived from the necessary and proper clause of Article I, Section 8, of the Constitution; such powers are not specifically expressed but are implied through the expansive interpretation of delegated powers

The list of expressed presidential powers is brief, but each expressed power has become the foundation of a second set of presidential powers, the so-called **implied powers** of the office. An implied power is one that can be said to be necessary to allow presidents to exercise their expressed power. For example, the Constitution expressly gives the president the power to appoint "all other officers of the United States . . . which shall be established by law." Article II does not, however, expressly grant the president the power to remove such officials from office. From the earliest years of the Republic, though, presidents have claimed that the removal power was implied by the appointment power.

The vesting and "take care" clauses of the Constitution discussed earlier, as well as the president's oath of office, have also been cited by successive White Houses as justifications for actions not expressly authorized by the Constitution. In recent years, presidents and their advisers have used the vesting clause to support what has come to be known as the "theory of the unitary executive."[12] This theory holds that all executive power within the national government belongs to the president except as explicitly limited by the Constitution.[13] Thus, all the officials of the executive branch must take their orders from the president. Moreover, according to this view, Congress has little authority over the executive branch and the president is a sovereign or supreme authority subject only to specific restraints, such as Congress's control of revenues, its impeachment power, and its power to override presidential vetoes.

Some proponents of unitary executive theory also maintain that presidents have their own power to interpret the Constitution as it applies to the executive branch and do not necessarily have to defer to the judiciary. This claim was advanced by President George W. Bush when he signed a defense appropriation bill that included language he had opposed about the treatment of terrorist suspects—the so-called anti-torture provision introduced by Senator John McCain. In his signing statement, Bush declared that he would construe the portion of the act relating to the treatment of detainees "in a manner consistent with the constitutional authority of the President to supervise the unitary executive branch and as Commander in Chief and consistent with the constitutional limitations on the judicial power."[14] The president was claiming, in other words, that particularly in the military realm, he possessed the authority to execute acts of Congress according to his own understanding of the law and the nation's interests. He also seemed to be claiming that the authority of the courts to interfere with his actions was limited.

Unitary executive theory particularly holds that the president controls all policy making by the executive branch and that Congress wields only limited, if any, direct power over executive agencies. This idea has been the basis for such presidential programs as "regulatory review," discussed below, which has been used by every president since Ronald Reagan to guide rule making by the various federal agencies. Sometimes presidents have used this process to write authoritative rules when they could not persuade Congress to enact laws they wanted.[15]

Critics of unitary executive theory, however, argue that the principle of constitutional checks and balances provides Congress with powers over executive agencies through what has come to be called "congressional oversight" of the executive branch. Article I of the Constitution gives Congress a number of powers, including the power to appropriate funds, to raise and support armies and navies, to regulate interstate commerce, and to impeach officials of the executive branch. Article I also gives Congress the authority "to make all laws which shall be necessary and proper for carrying into execution the foregoing powers."

Congressional oversight, which includes hearings, investigations, studies, and reports, is arguably implied by this language. If Congress is to carry out its constitutional responsibilities, it must be able to obtain information about the activities of executive branch agencies and officials. Thus, the stage is set for conflict between the implied powers of Congress and those of the president.

DELEGATED POWERS

Many of the powers exercised by the president and the executive branch are not found in the Constitution but are **delegated powers**, the products of congressional statutes and resolutions. Over the past century, Congress has voluntarily delegated a great deal of its own legislative authority to the executive branch. To some extent, this delegation of power has been an almost inescapable consequence of the expansion of government activity in the United States since the New Deal.

In the nineteenth century there were relatively well-defined congressional guidelines for administering federal programs. During much of the century, the federal government had relatively few domestic responsibilities, and Congress could pay close attention to details. Given the vast range of the federal government's responsibilities today, however, Congress cannot possibly execute all federal laws and administer all of the thousands of federal programs. Inevitably, it must turn more and more to the hundreds of departments and agencies in the executive branch or, when necessary, create new agencies to implement its goals. Thus, for example, in 2002, to strengthen protection against terrorist attacks, it established the Department of Homeland Security, with broad powers in the realms of law enforcement, public health, and immigration.

As they implement congressional legislation, federal agencies collectively develop thousands of rules and regulations and issue thousands of orders and findings every year. Agencies interpret Congress's intent, publish rules aimed at implementing that intent, and issue orders to individuals, firms, and organizations to compel them to conform to the law. Such administrative rules have the effect of law; the courts treat them like congressional statutes.

When it establishes a program, Congress sometimes grants the agency implementing it only limited discretionary authority, providing very specific guidelines and standards that must be followed by the program's administrators. Take the Internal Revenue Service (IRS), for example. Most Americans view the IRS as a powerful

delegated powers constitutional powers that are assigned to one governmental agency but are exercised by another agency with the express permission of the first

The influence of the president and the executive branch is widespread, as the executive is responsible for the implementation of many laws that Congress passes. For example, after Congress passed the Affordable Care Act, it was up to the executive branch to orchestrate the health insurance enrollment process for millions of Americans.

inherent powers powers claimed by a president that are not expressed in the Constitution but are inferred from it

agency with broad and often arbitrary control over their lives. In fact, congressional tax legislation is very specific and detailed, leaving little to the discretion of IRS administrators.[16] The agency certainly develops numerous rules and procedures to enhance tax collection. It is Congress, however, that establishes the structure of the liabilities, exemptions, and deductions that determine each taxpayer's burdens and responsibilities.

In most instances, though, congressional legislation is not very detailed. At least since the New Deal, Congress has tended to draft legislation that defines a broad goal but offers few clear standards or guidelines for how that goal is to be achieved. The 1972 Consumer Product Safety Act, for example, authorizes the Consumer Product Safety Commission to reduce "unreasonable" risks of injury from household products but offers no suggestions about what constitutes reasonable and unreasonable risks or how the latter are to be reduced.[17] As a result, the executive branch, under the president's direction, has wide discretion to make rules that impact American citizens and businesses.

A recent, and typical, example of the executive branch's role is the 2010 Affordable Care Act. After the law passed, several members of Congress admitted that they did not fully understand how it would work and were depending upon the Department of Health and Human Services, the agency with primary administrative responsibility for it, to explain it to them.

INHERENT POWERS

Presidents have also claimed a set of powers not specified in the Constitution but said to stem from the rights, duties, and obligations of the presidency. These are referred to as **inherent powers** and are most often asserted by presidents in time of war or national emergency. President Lincoln relied upon a claim of inherent power to raise an army after the fall of Fort Sumter. Similarly, Presidents Roosevelt (World War II), Truman (Korean War), and both Presidents Bush (Persian Gulf and Middle East wars) claimed inherent powers to defend the nation.

Since the Korean War, presidents have used their claim of inherent powers along with their constitutional power as commander in chief to bypass the constitutional provision giving Congress the power to declare war. Congress declared war after the Japanese attack on Pearl Harbor on December 7, 1941. Since that time, American forces have been sent to fight foreign wars on more than 100 occasions, but not once was Congress asked for a declaration of war. In 1973, Congress passed the War Powers Resolution, designed to restore its role in military policy. Presidents, however, have regarded the resolution as an improper limitation on their inherent powers and have studiously ignored its provisions.

The difference between inherent and implied powers is often subtle, and the two are frequently jointly claimed in support of presidential action. Implied powers can be traced to the powers expressed in the actual language of the Constitution.[18] Inherent powers, on the other hand, derive from national sovereignty. Under international law and custom, sovereign states possess a number of inherent rights and powers, the most important being the rights to engage in relations with other nations, to defend themselves against attacks from other states, and to curb internal violence and unrest. Since the Constitution explicitly makes the president commander in chief of the armed forces and gives him or her the power to

Who Are America's Presidents?

American presidents have all been men. Until the election of Barack Obama in 2008, they had all been White. As the data show, a majority of presidents have come from the eastern United States, with Virginia producing the most American presidents, especially in the nation's first decades.

Gender

++++++++++++++++++++++++
++++++++++++++++++++++

Male 45   Female 0

Race

White **44**   African American **1**

Age

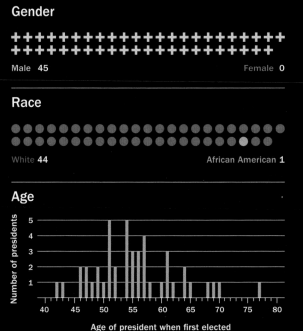

Number of presidents

Age of president when first elected

Party*

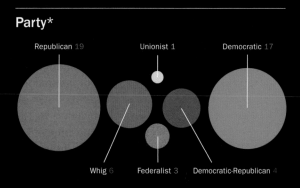

Republican 19   Unionist 1   Democratic 17

Whig 6   Federalist 3   Democratic-Republican 4

Top Occupations**

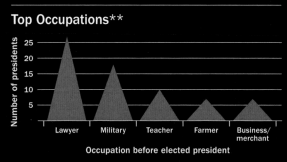

Number of presidents

Lawyer   Military   Teacher   Farmer   Business/merchant

Occupation before elected president

Region†

Presidents

○ 0
● 1
● 2
● 4
● 5
● 7
● 8

NOTE: Grover Cleveland served as America's 22nd and 24th presidents. He is counted only once in the demographic data here, thus the total number of people who have served as U.S. president is 44.

*Some presidents switched parties during their political careers, thus the numbers sum to more than 44.

**This chart reflects the top nonpolitical careers of U.S. presidents. (All presidents except George Washington and Donald Trump had previous political and/or public service experience.) Presidents may have had more than one occupation, and some occupations do not appear on this list, thus the numbers do not sum to 44.

† Andrew Jackson was born in the Waxhaw area, on the North Carolina–South Carolina border.

SOURCES: Roper Center, www.ropercenter.uconn.edu/elections/common/pop_vote.html; David Leip, http://uselectionatlas.org/RESULTS/; the American Presidency Project, www.presidency.ucsb.edu/showelection.php?year=1840; Miller Center, University of Virginia, http://millercenter.org/president (accessed 3/17/14).

FOR CRITICAL ANALYSIS

1. Why do you think all presidents have been men and all but one have been White? Do you think this is likely to change in coming years?

2. Why do you think so many presidents have come from the South and the East? What electoral or historical factors may have produced this trend?

negotiate treaties with other nations and to see to it that the laws are faithfully executed, it might be said to imply that it is the president who has the inherent power to act to defend the nation, to conduct its foreign relations, and to safeguard law and order.

Most presidents believe that they and only they are constitutionally authorized to manage the nation's relations with foreign states. If challenged, presidents and their aides will cite John Marshall's 1800 speech to the House of Representatives, in which the future chief justice called the president "the sole organ of the nation in its external relations, and its sole representative with foreign nations."[19] According to constitutional scholar Louis Fisher, Marshall meant that the president was the sole organ in implementing, not making, foreign policy.[20] Yet the Supreme Court took the more expansive view in its 1936 *Curtiss-Wright* decision, which cites Marshall in support of the idea that the president possesses broad inherent power in the making of foreign policy.[21]

A number of presidents have claimed that the presidency also possessed inherent powers in conducting military affairs and dealing with domestic emergencies—powers that were not necessarily spelled out in the Constitution or authorized by law.[22] In 1861, during the Civil War, President Lincoln suspended habeas corpus, imposed martial law in a number of areas, called out the state militias, withdrew funds from the Treasury, and ordered a naval blockade of southern ports, all without congressional authorization.

No president has acted so frequently on the basis of inherent powers as President George W. Bush. He claimed that they authorized him to create military commissions; designate U.S. citizens as enemy combatants; engage in "extraordinary renditions" of captured suspects, who would be moved to unknown facilities in unnamed countries for interrogation; and order the National Security Agency (NSA) to monitor phone conversations between the United States and other nations.[23] When challenged, some but not all of these actions were overturned by the courts. We will examine these decisions in some detail in Chapter 15.

Bush's successor, President Obama, continued to rely on the concept of inherent power in ordering drone strikes against suspected terrorists and ordering American air strikes in Libya. Testifying before Congress in 2014, Attorney General Eric Holder defended the president's unilateral actions, saying, "Given what the president's responsibility is in running the executive branch, I think there is an inherent power there for him to act in the way that he has."[24]

In 2017, President Trump's order banning travelers from several Muslim countries was based mainly on a claim that the president had the inherent power to bar any class of immigrants he thought to be a threat to the United States. In its 2018 decision in the case of *Trump v. Hawaii* overruling lower-court decisions that had sought to block Trump's travel ban, the Supreme Court said that the president was entitled to deference in judging whether a particular group of immigrants represented a threat to the United States. In 2020, President Trump asserted that he had the inherent power to determine whether businesses could reopen or must remain closed in the face of the coronavirus threat.

Congress has tried to place some limits on powers that presidents claim to be inherent. For example, although presidents believe they have the inherent power to deal with emergencies, Congress has passed legislation to restrict and guide the use of this power. Under the 1976 National Emergencies Act, the president is authorized to declare a national emergency in the event of major threats to America's

Comparing Executive Authority

The American president is the face of the federal government. While the role has become much more powerful since the founding, the president is actually quite weak compared to his or her peer executives in other countries. While most countries have constitutions that outline the powers of the executive, such as the power to dissolve the legislature, or the power to initiate legislation, in practice, executives often claim powers beyond what is explicitly granted to them. The figure below shows the countries with the most and least powerful executives.

1. What are the benefits of having a strong executive in a country? Do you think the office of the president in the American system has too much power? Not enough? Does seeing the data in this graphic change your opinion?
2. What might be an argument for giving an executive the ability to dissolve the legislature or declare a state of emergency? How do you put checks on such a strong executive while still granting them some powers?

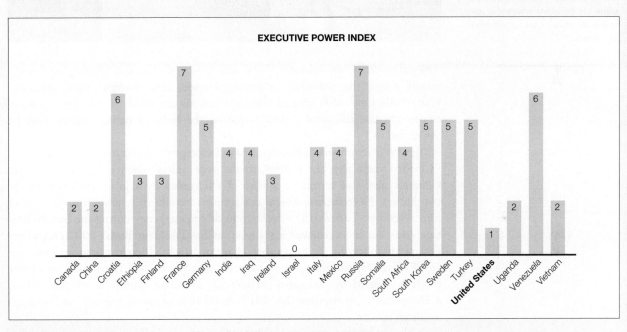

EXECUTIVE POWER INDEX

SOURCE: Comparative Constitutions Project, http://comparativeconstitutionsproject.org/ccp-rankings/ (accessed 8/12/19).

Governors must ask the federal government for help in an emergency, as Governor Greg Abbott did in the face of Hurricane Harvey. However, some say decisions whether or not to provide support are largely driven by politics.

national security or economy.[25] An emergency declaration relating to foreign threats allows the president to embargo trade, seize foreign assets, and prohibit transactions with whatever foreign nations are involved. During a state of emergency, constitutional rights, including the right of habeas corpus, may be suspended.

The 1976 act provided, however, that an emergency declaration does not remain in force indefinitely but expires in one year unless renewed by the president. Congress may also terminate a state of emergency by a joint resolution of the two houses. Nevertheless, several declarations have been renewed for quite some time. President Carter's 1979 declaration of an emergency during the Iranian hostage crisis has been renewed every year, as has President Bush's 2001 emergency declaration following the September 11 terror attacks. These declarations have provided a basis for various trade embargoes, asset freezes, and restrictions on money transfers ordered by successive presidents.[26] President Trump, as we saw, vetoed a House effort to overturn his 2019 declaration of an emergency on America's southern border.

A closely related area in which Congress has tried to regulate matters that presidents tend to view as involving their own inherent power is the nation's response to natural disasters. Under the 1988 Stafford Act, the governor of a state affected by a flood, hurricane, earthquake, fire, or other calamity must ask the Federal Emergency Management Agency (FEMA) for a determination that the scope of the disaster is beyond the abilities of state and local authorities to handle. The president may then declare a disaster and make the state eligible for federal funds and relief. The purpose of the Stafford Act was to ensure that presidential disaster declarations were governed by objective criteria defined in law. In recent years, however, critics have charged that presidential determinations and funding authorizations seemed, nevertheless, to be driven by political motivations.[27] In 2020, President Trump invoked the Stafford Act to make $50 billion available to state and local governments to help them respond to the coronavirus pandemic.

The Presidency as an Institution

Describe the institutional resources presidents have to help them exercise their powers

Since the ratification of the Constitution, the president has been joined by thousands of officials and staffers who work for, assist, or advise the chief executive (see Figure 13.2). Collectively, these individuals could be said to make up the institutional presidency and to give the president a capacity for action that no single individual could duplicate. The first component of the institutional presidency is the president's Cabinet.

THE CABINET

In the American system of government, the **Cabinet** is the traditional but informal designation for the heads of all the major federal government departments. The Cabinet has no constitutional status. Unlike in Great Britain and many other parliamentary countries, where the cabinet *is* the government, the American Cabinet is not a formal organized body. It meets but makes no decisions as a group.

Cabinet the secretaries, or chief administrators, of the major departments of the federal government; Cabinet secretaries are appointed by the president with the consent of the Senate

---

FIGURE 13.2

The Institutional Presidency

THE WHITE HOUSE STAFF

Includes:
- Chief of Staff
- Press Secretary
- Senior Advisers
- Special Assistants

INDEPENDENT AGENCIES AND GOVERNMENT CORPORATIONS

Includes:
- Central Intelligence Agency
- Environmental Protection Agency
- Federal Labor Relations Authority
- General Services Administration

THE PRESIDENT

THE CABINET

- Department of Agriculture
- Department of Commerce
- Department of Defense
- Department of Education
- Department of Energy
- Department of Health and Human Services
- Department of Homeland Security
- Department of Housing and Urban Development
- Department of the Interior
- Department of Justice
- Department of Labor
- Department of State
- Department of Transportation
- Department of the Treasury
- Department of Veterans Affairs

EXECUTIVE OFFICE OF THE PRESIDENT

- Council of Economic Advisers
- Council on Environmental Quality
- National Security Council
- Office of Administration
- Office of Management and Budget
- Office of National Drug Control Policy
- Office of Science and Technology Policy
- Office of the United States Trade Representative
- President's Intelligence Advisory Board and Intelligence Oversight Board
- White House Military Office
- White House Office

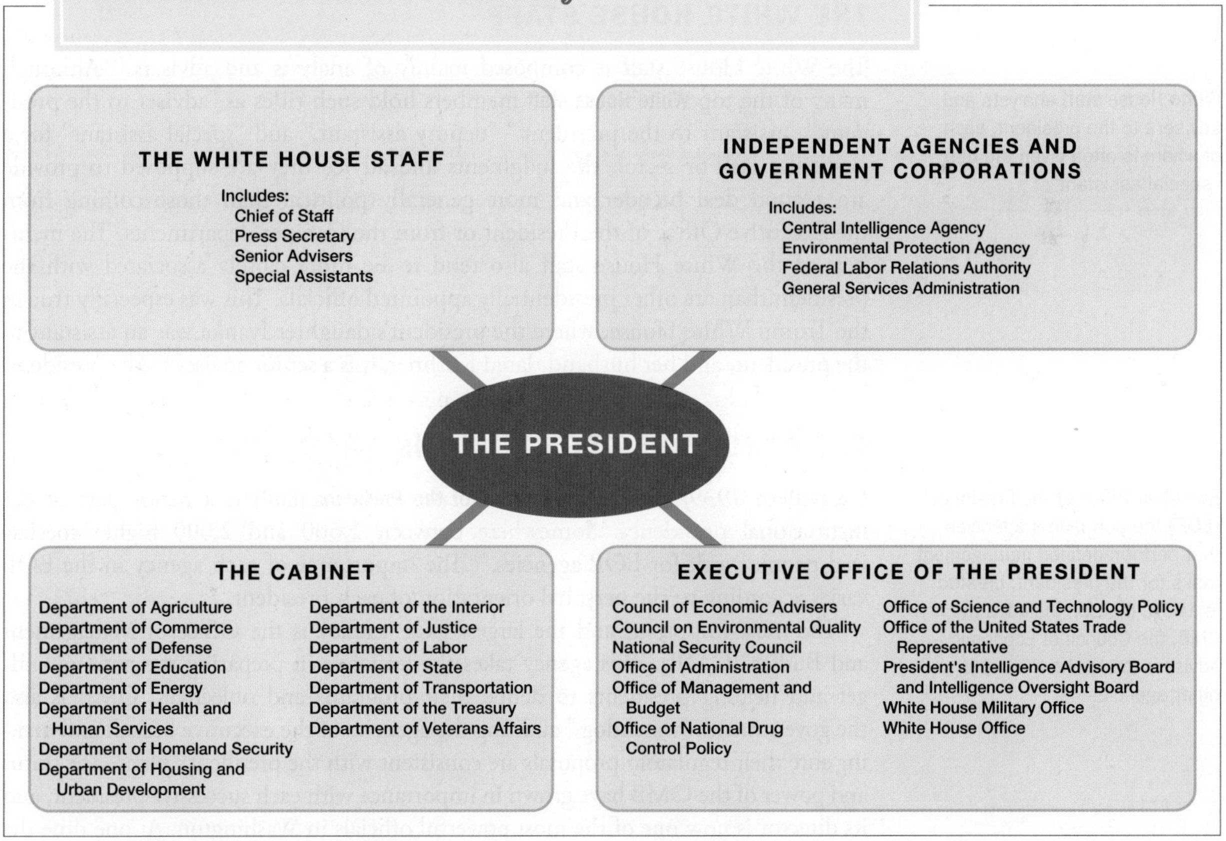

Each appointment to it must be approved by the Senate, but Cabinet members are not responsible to the Senate or to Congress at large. However, Cabinet secretaries and their deputies frequently testify before congressional committees to justify budgets and policy objectives, or to explain policies or recent major events or issues.

Each of the 15 government departments is led by a secretary, who is a member of the president's Cabinet. Reporting to the secretary is a deputy secretary, while individual offices and activities are led by undersecretaries and assistant secretaries. Government departments range in size from the Department of Education, which employs only about 4,200 people, to the Department of Defense (DoD), which oversees some 700,000 civilian employees and 1.3 million military personnel and is also responsible for maintaining the military readiness of 1.1 million reserve and National Guard troops.

In addition to the Cabinet agencies, the executive branch also includes a number of "independent" agencies reporting to the president. Like Cabinet secretaries, the chief executives of the independent agencies are appointed by the president and usually require senatorial confirmation. Congress engages in oversight of these agencies as it does the Cabinet departments. The major independent agencies, such as the Social Security Administration, are usually headed by a senior official with a title like commissioner, administrator, or director, who is in turn supported by deputies and assistant deputies. The independent agencies also vary in size. The Social Security Administration employs about 60,000 individuals, while some of the smaller agencies are staffed by only a few dozen.

THE WHITE HOUSE STAFF

White House staff analysts and advisers to the president, each of whom is often given the title "special assistant"

The White House staff is composed mainly of analysts and advisers.[28] Although many of the top **White House staff** members hold such titles as "adviser to the president," "assistant to the president," "deputy assistant," and "special assistant" for a particular task or sector, the judgments and advice they are supposed to provide are a good deal broader and more generally political than those coming from the Executive Office of the President or from the Cabinet departments. The members of the White House staff also tend to be more closely associated with the president than are other presidentially appointed officials. This was especially true in the Trump White House, where the president's daughter Ivanka was an assistant to the president, and her husband, Jared Kushner, was a senior adviser to the president.

THE EXECUTIVE OFFICE OF THE PRESIDENT

Executive Office of the President (EOP) the permanent agencies that perform defined management tasks for the president; created in 1939, the EOP includes the OMB, the Council of Economic Advisers (CEA), the NSC, and other agencies

Created in 1939, the **Executive Office of the President (EOP)** is a major part of the institutional presidency. Somewhere between 1,500 and 2,000 highly specialized people work for EOP agencies.[29] The importance of each agency in the EOP varies according to the personal orientation of each president.

The most important and the largest EOP agency is the Office of Management and Budget (OMB). This agency takes the lead role in preparing the nation's budget and helping presidents to define their programs and objectives. OMB is also the government's "watchdog," auditing the agencies of the executive branch and making sure their regulatory proposals are consistent with the president's plans. The status and power of the OMB have grown in importance with each successive president, and its director is now one of the most powerful officials in Washington. At one time the process of budgeting was a "bottom-up" one, with expenditure and program requests passing from the lowest bureaus through the departments to "clearance" in the OMB and thence to Congress, where each agency could be called in to explain what its "original request" was before the OMB revised it. Now the budgeting process is "top-down": the OMB sets the terms of discourse for agencies as well as for Congress.

Another prominent EOP agency is the Council of Economic Advisers (CEA), whose staff constantly analyzes the economy and economic trends in order to help the president anticipate events rather than reacting to them after the fact. The Council on Environmental Quality was designed to do for environmental issues what the CEA does for economic issues.

The **National Security Council (NSC)** is composed of designated Cabinet officials who meet regularly with the president to give advice on national security. The staff of the NSC assimilates and analyzes data from all intelligence-gathering agencies (such as the CIA and NSA). In some administrations, the head of the NSC, the president's national security adviser, has played a more important role in foreign and military policy than the Cabinet secretaries in these domains. Henry Kissinger, President Nixon's national security adviser, was such an individual. Some national security advisers have been disappointments to the presidents who chose them. For example, General Michael Flynn, President Trump's first national security adviser, was forced to resign amid charges of improper relations with Russian officials. In 2019, President Trump fired Flynn's successor, John Bolton, because Bolton disagreed with several of Trump's foreign policy judgments.

THE VICE PRESIDENCY

The vice presidency is a constitutional peculiarity, even though the office was created along with the presidency by the Constitution. The vice president exists for two purposes only: to succeed the president in case of death, resignation, or incapacity, and to preside over the Senate, casting a tie-breaking vote when necessary.[30]

The main value of the vice president as a political resource for the president is electoral. Sometimes, presidential candidates choose running mates who they

National Security Council (NSC) a presidential foreign policy advisory council composed of the president, the vice president, the secretary of state, the secretary of defense, and other officials invited by the president

Kamala Harris served as a U.S. senator from California and was the first woman and person of color ever elected to the vice presidency. She helped improve Biden's appeal with younger voters and nonwhite voters.

feel can win the support of at least one state that may not otherwise support the ticket. Presidents often choose a vice-presidential nominee who provides some regional, gender, ideological, or ethnic balance as well.

In 2020, Joe Biden chose Senator Kamala Harris of California as his running mate. Harris was an articulate former prosecutor who could be counted upon to do well in debates and on the campaign trail. Harris, the daughter of a Black father and South Asian mother, also reflected the diversity of the Democratic coalition. From her seat on the Senate Judiciary Committee, Harris had been a vocal and visible opponent of Trump judicial nominees and a proponent of Trump's impeachment.

During the course of American history, eight vice presidents have had to replace presidents who died in office, and one, Gerald Ford, became president when his predecessor resigned. Until the ratification of the Twenty-Fifth Amendment in 1965, the succession of the vice president to the presidency was a tradition, launched by John Tyler when he assumed the presidency after William Henry Harrison's death, rather than a constitutional or statutory provision. The Twenty-Fifth Amendment codified this tradition by providing that the vice president would assume the presidency in the event of the chief executive's death or incapacity and setting forth the procedures that would be followed. The amendment also provides that if the vice presidency becomes vacant, the president is to nominate an individual who must be confirmed by a majority vote of both houses of Congress. Thus, in 1973 when Vice President Spiro Agnew was forced to resign, President Nixon nominated Gerald Ford, who was confirmed. In 1974, when Nixon was forced to resign as a result of the Watergate scandal, Ford became president.

In the event that both the president and vice president are killed, the Presidential Succession Act of 1947 establishes an order of succession, beginning with the Speaker of the House and continuing with the president pro tempore of the Senate and the Cabinet secretaries.

THE PRESIDENT'S PARTY

Presidents have another tool: their own political party. Most presidents have sought to use their own party to implement their legislative agenda. For example, in 2009–10, President Obama relied on congressional Democrats to pass the Affordable Care Act ("Obamacare") in the face of virtually unanimous Republican opposition. For his part, President Trump counted on Republican senators to ratify his judicial nominations despite solid Democratic opposition. All but one Republican senator voted to acquit President Trump in his impeachment trial before the Senate in 2020, thus blocking the president's removal from office. The president does not control his party; party members have considerable autonomy. President Trump was unable to rally enough Republican legislators to repeal Obamacare, although he was able to bring about the enactment of tax reform. Consequently, although the party is valuable, it has not been a fully reliable presidential tool.

Moreover, in America's system of separated powers, the president's party may be in the minority in Congress and unable to do much to advance the president's agenda. When the 2018 elections gave Democrats control of the House of Representatives, very few of Trump's policy initiatives could be enacted even though the GOP supported him.

THE FIRST SPOUSE

The president serves as both America's chief executive and its head of state—the equivalent of Great Britain's prime minister and monarch rolled into one, simultaneously leading the government and representing the nation at official ceremonies and functions. Because they are generally associated exclusively with the head-of-state aspect of the presidency, presidential spouses are usually not subject to the same sort of media scrutiny or partisan attack as that aimed at the president. Historically, most first ladies have limited their activities to the ceremonial portion of the presidency: greeting foreign dignitaries, visiting other countries, and attending important national ceremonies. Some take up causes and advocate for them—in 2018, Melania Trump launched the "Be Best" public awareness campaign. This effort focused on well-being for youth and especially advocated against cyberbullying and drug use by young people.[31]

Some first spouses, however, have had considerable influence over policy. Franklin Roosevelt's wife, Eleanor, was widely popular but also widely criticized for her active role in many elements of her husband's presidency. During the 1992 campaign, Bill Clinton often implied that his wife would be active in the administration; he joked that voters would get "two for the price of one." And indeed, after the election, Hillary Clinton took a leading role in many policy areas, most notably heading the administration's health care reform effort. She also became the first presidential spouse to seek public office on her own, winning a seat in the U.S. Senate in 2000 and then running for president in 2008 and 2016, having served in between as President Obama's secretary of state. Jill Biden, wife of President Joe Biden, is a community college professor and has long been her husband's closest political adviser. It is assumed that she will continue to advise the president and to advocate for causes she had long supported like expansion of educational opportunities.

First spouses often take on specific causes once in the White House. First Lady Melania Trump launched her initiative "Be Best," which aimed to promote the well-being of children and address issues such as online safety and opioid abuse.

The Growth of Presidential Power

> **Explain how modern presidents have become even more powerful**

During the nineteenth century, Congress was America's dominant institution of government, and its members sometimes treated the president with disdain. Today, however, no one would assert that the presidency is unimportant. Presidents seek to dominate the policy-making process and claim the power to lead the nation in time of war. The expansion of presidential power over the course of the past century has come about not by accident but as the result of an ongoing effort by successive presidents to enlarge the powers of the office. Generally, presidents can expand their power in two primary ways: by "going public"[32] and by taking steps to reduce their dependence on Congress and give themselves a more independent governing and policy-making capability.

GOING PUBLIC

In the nineteenth century, it was considered inappropriate for presidents to engage in personal campaigning on their own behalf or in support of programs and policies. In the twentieth century, though, popular mobilization became a favored weapon in the political arsenals of most presidents. The first to make systematic use of appeals to the public were Theodore Roosevelt and Woodrow Wilson, but the

Over the last century, presidents and candidates have made more and more use of direct appeals to the American people. President Franklin Roosevelt made effective use of radio to build public support for his programs.

president who used them most effectively was Franklin Delano Roosevelt. In particular, he made effective use of a relatively new medium, the radio, to reach millions of Americans. In his famous "fireside chats," the president's voice could be heard in almost every living room in the country, discussing programs and policies and generally assuring Americans that Franklin Delano Roosevelt was aware of their difficulties and working diligently toward solutions.

Roosevelt was also an innovator in what now might be called press relations. When he entered the White House, he faced a press mainly controlled by conservative members of the business establishment.[33] To bypass these generally hostile editors and publishers, the president worked to cultivate the reporters who covered the White House. FDR made himself available for biweekly press conferences, where he offered candid answers to reporters' questions and made important policy announcements that would provide the reporters with significant stories for their papers.[34]

Every president since FDR has sought to craft a public-relations strategy that would emphasize his strengths and maximize his popular appeal. For John F. Kennedy, who was handsome and quick witted, the televised press conference was an excellent public-relations vehicle. Both Bill Clinton and Barack Obama held televised town hall meetings—carefully staged events that let these presidents appear to consult with rank-and-file citizens about their goals and policies without having to face the sorts of pointed questions preferred by reporters.

An innovation introduced by Clinton and continued by his successors was to make the White House Communications Office an important institution within the EOP. The Communications Office became responsible not only for responding to reporters' queries but also for developing and implementing a coordinated communications strategy—promoting the president's policy goals, developing responses to

FOR CRITICAL ANALYSIS

What are the advantages and disadvantages of presidents governing via digital media? How do these pros and cons compare with "going public" in the age of television?

adverse news stories, and making certain that a favorable image of the president would, insofar as possible, dominate the news.

Going Public Online President Obama was the first chief executive to make full use of another new communication medium—the internet. Drawing on the interactive tools of the web, Obama's 2008 and 2012 campaigns changed the way politicians organize supporters, advertise to voters, defend against attacks, and communicate with their constituents.[35]

In the 2016 presidential campaign, candidates Hillary Clinton and especially Donald Trump made particular use of Twitter to communicate with millions of voters, bypassing traditional media. Trump usually tweeted many times a day, often making outrageous claims that guaranteed that he would dominate media coverage as reporters rushed to analyze and criticize his assertions. While Trump may have pioneered the social media campaign, by 2020 the Democrats followed suit and both campaigns made extensive use of social media including YouTube, Twitter, Facebook, and Instagram. In August 2020, the major social media platforms announced a partnership to guard against misinformation and foreign efforts to use American social media to influence the outcome of the election.

The internet has changed not only the way modern presidents campaign but also how they govern. Circumventing television and other older media, it allows them to broadcast their policy ideas directly to citizens. Whitehouse.gov keeps the president's constituents abreast of his or her policy agenda with a weekly streaming video address by the president, press briefings, speeches and remarks, a daily blog, photos of the president, the White House schedule, and other information.

In the Trump administration, every presidential **legislative initiative** and policy proposal was preceded by a flurry of tweets repeated by the broadcast and print media. And Trump's language seemed tailored to the Twitter age. For example, calling North Korean leader Kim Jong-un "Little Rocket Man" in his tweets allowed Trump to boil down his contempt and harsh posture toward North Korea into a tweet-sized threat to use force.

The Limits of Going Public Some presidents have been able to make effective use of popular appeals to overcome congressional opposition. Popular support, though, has not been a firm foundation for presidential power. President George W. Bush maintained an approval rating of over 70 percent for more than a year following the September 11 terrorist attacks. By the end of 2005, however, Bush's approval rating had dropped to 39 percent as a result of the growing unpopularity of the Iraq War, the administration's handling of hurricane relief, and a number of White House scandals.

Between the time President Obama took office in January 2009 and May 2016, his public approval ranged from a high of 76 percent in January 2009 to a low of 36 percent in the fall of 2014.[36] By the end of his term in 2016, Obama's popularity had recovered somewhat to about 56 percent. Declines in popular approval during a president's term in office are nearly inevitable and follow a predictable pattern.[37] Both before and after they are elected, presidents generate popular support

Donald J. Trump @
@realDonaldTrump

The Ballots being returned to States cannot be accurately counted. Many things are already going very wrong!

(!) Learn how voting by mail is safe and secure

To combat misinformation from politicians and foreign influence, social media platforms began flagging posts that contained misleading information. During the 2020 election and the coronavirus pandemic, President Trump's tweets were often labeled by Twitter as containing misinformation, with links to reliable sources of information.

legislative initiative the president's inherent power to bring a legislative agenda before Congress by promising to undertake important programs that will contribute directly to the well-being of large numbers of Americans. Almost without exception, presidential performance falls short of promises and popular expectations, leading to a decline in public support and the ensuing weakening of presidential influence.[38] It is a rare American president, such as Bill Clinton, who exits the White House more popular than when he went in. Donald Trump's approval rating had risen to 45 percent by June 2018, after hitting a low of 35 percent in 2017; as of October 2020, Trump's approval rating stood at 46 percent, with 52 percent disapproving of the president's performance.[39]

THE ADMINISTRATIVE STRATEGY

Contemporary presidents have increased the administrative capabilities of their office in three ways. First, they have enhanced the reach and power of the EOP. Second, they have increased White House control over the federal bureaucracy. Third, they have expanded the role of executive orders and other instruments of direct presidential governance. Taken together, these three components of what might be called the White House "administrative strategy" have given presidents a capacity to achieve their programmatic and policy goals even when they are unable to secure congressional approval. Indeed, some recent presidents have been able to accomplish a great deal with remarkably little congressional, partisan, or even public support.

The Growth of the EOP The EOP has grown from six administrative assistants in 1939 to several hundred employees working directly for the president in the White House office today, along with some 2,500 individuals staffing the several divisions of the Executive Office. The creation and growth of the White House staff have given the president enormous capacity to gather information, plan programs and strategies, communicate with constituencies, and exercise supervision over the executive branch. The staff multiplies the president's eyes, ears, and arms, becoming a critical instrument of presidential power.[40]

In particular, the Office of Management and Budget serves as a potential instrument of presidential control over federal spending and hence as a mechanism through which the White House has greatly expanded its power. The OMB has the capacity to analyze and approve all legislative proposals, not only budgetary requests, emanating from all federal agencies before being submitted to Congress. This procedure, now a matter of routine, greatly enhances the president's control over the entire executive branch. All legislation originating in the White House and all executive orders also go through the OMB.[41] Thus, through one White House agency, the president has the means to exert major influence over the flow of money and the shape and content of national legislation.

Regulatory Review A second instrument that presidents have used to increase their power and reach is an agency within OMB called the Office of Information and Regulatory Affairs (OIRA), which supervises the process of regulatory review. Whenever Congress enacts a law, implementing it requires the promulgation of hundreds of rules by the agency charged with administering the law and giving effect to what Congress intended. For example, if Congress wishes to improve air quality, it must delegate to an agency—say, the Environmental Protection Agency (EPA)—the power to establish numerous regulations governing actions by businesses, individuals, and government agencies (including the EPA itself) that may affect the atmosphere.

The agency rule-making process is itself governed by a number of statutory requirements concerning public notice (the most important being publication in the *Federal Register*), hearings, and appeals. But once completed and published in the massive *Code of Federal Regulations*, administrative rules have the effect of law and will be enforced by the federal courts. Beginning with little fanfare during the Nixon administration, recent presidents gradually have tried to take control of the rule-making process and to use it in effect to make laws without the interference of the legislature.

For example, during the course of his presidency, Clinton issued 107 directives ordering agency administrators to propose specific rules, such as one ordering the Food and Drug Administration (FDA) to develop rules designed to restrict the marketing of tobacco products to children.[42] Presidents George W. Bush and Barack Obama continued this practice, and the Obama administration also launched a "look back" program to eliminate several hundred existing rules it deemed obsolete.[43] In his final two years in office, Obama sought new regulations governing power plant emissions, overtime pay for workers, the educational practices of career (for-profit) colleges, and a host of other matters.

President Trump moved aggressively to reverse these and other Obama directives by issuing new rules or repealing existing ones. Trump's actions reduced or eliminated regulations related to the environment, banking, and workplace safety and removed protections for transgender workers, among others. Most notably, during the four years of his presidency, Trump eliminated or began the process of rescinding 95 environmental regulations.[44] In June 2020, the Trump administration eliminated Obama-era regulations prohibiting health care facilities from discriminating against transgender patients. Within a few days, however, the Supreme Court ruled (see Chapter 15) that existing civil rights laws protected gay and transgender individuals in the workplace. This decision cast doubt on the legality of discrimination against transgender patients. The administration also proposed new rules that

In 2020, President Trump signed an executive order to prevent hoarding and price gouging after the coronavirus pandemic sparked a climate of panic in its early days, causing many to hoard groceries and cleaning supplies and prices to surge on sought-after items like hand sanitizer.

would rewrite the nation's asylum rules, blocking asylum in most new cases and likely foreclosing asylum to the more than 300,000 individuals whose cases have already been filed.

Governing by Decree: Executive Orders and Memoranda A third mechanism through which contemporary presidents have sought to enhance their power to govern unilaterally is the use of executive orders and other forms of presidential decrees.

An **executive order** is a direct presidential directive to the bureaucracy to undertake some action, bypassing Congress and the legislative process. Executive orders have a long history in the United States and have been the means for imposing a number of important policies, including the purchase of the Louisiana Territory, the annexation of Texas, the emancipation of enslaved people, the wartime internment of Japanese Americans, the desegregation of the military, the initiation of affirmative action, and the creation of federal agencies, including the Environmental Protection Agency, the Food and Drug Administration, and the Peace Corps.[45] Historically, executive orders were most often used during times of war or national emergency. In recent years, though, executive orders have become routine instruments of presidential governance rather than emergency wartime measures (Figure 13.3).

President George W. Bush issued more than 300 executive orders, many relating to the war on terrorism but others pertaining to domestic policy matters, such as his ban on the use of federal funds to support international family-planning groups and his prohibition of the use of embryonic stem cells in federally funded research projects. President Obama issued executive orders halting the deportation of undocumented immigrants who had come to the United States as children, prohibiting federal agencies and contractors from discriminating against transgender employees, and declaring more than 700,000 square miles of the central Pacific Ocean off-limits to fishing. In addition to his orders on immigration, by the first three months of 2020, President Trump had issued more than 150 executive orders on such matters as the COVID-19 pandemic, other health care issues, regulatory reform, cybersecurity, freedom of speech at colleges and universities, and the imposition of new sanctions on Iran. Trump's orders included several that rescinded some of former president Obama's orders; for example, he invalidated several environmental protections and limits on gun purchases. During the same month, in the wake of two weeks of protests over police violence, President Trump issued an executive order placing limits on police use of force. Critics charged that the order was too little, too late.

When presidents issue executive orders, in principle they do so using the powers granted to them by the Constitution or delegated to them by Congress, and they generally must state the constitutional or statutory basis for their actions. For example, when President Lyndon Johnson ordered U.S. government contractors to initiate programs of affirmative action in hiring, he said the order was designed to implement the 1964 Civil Rights Act, which prohibited employment discrimination. Where the courts have found no constitutional or statutory basis for a presidential order, they have invalidated it. Such cases, however, are rare. Generally, the judiciary has accepted executive orders as the law of the land.

Additional forms of presidential decree include administrative orders, national security findings and directives, presidential memoranda, and presidential proclamations.[46] Like executive orders, they establish policy and have the force of law, and presidents often use them interchangeably. Generally speaking, though, administrative

executive order a rule or regulation issued by the president that has the effect and formal status of legislation

FIGURE 13.3
Presidential Executive Orders*

Executive orders are a tool presidents have for influencing policy. Their use has varied considerably over time. Each bar in the graph shows the average number of executive orders each president issued per year in office. Which presidents issued the most executive orders? What events in U.S. history were occurring when those presidents were in office?

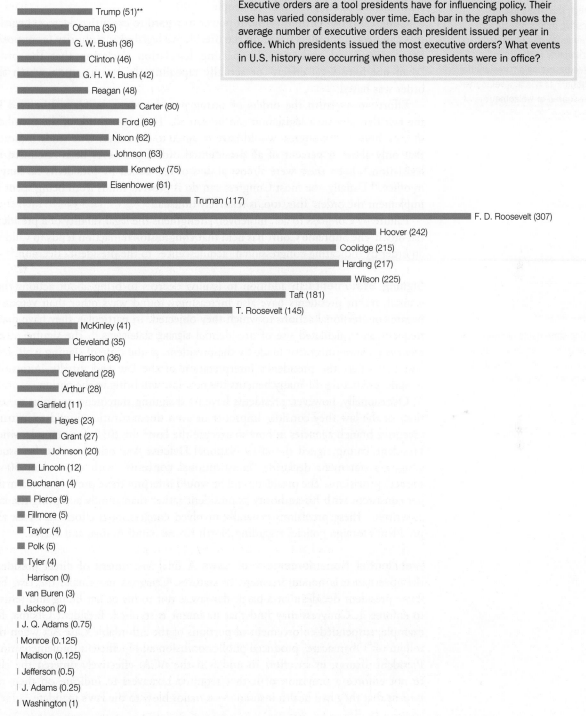

Trump (51)**
Obama (35)
G. W. Bush (36)
Clinton (46)
G. H. W. Bush (42)
Reagan (48)
Carter (80)
Ford (69)
Nixon (62)
Johnson (63)
Kennedy (75)
Eisenhower (61)
Truman (117)
F. D. Roosevelt (307)
Hoover (242)
Coolidge (215)
Harding (217)
Wilson (225)
Taft (181)
T. Roosevelt (145)
McKinley (41)
Cleveland (35)
Harrison (36)
Cleveland (28)
Arthur (28)
Garfield (11)
Hayes (23)
Grant (27)
Johnson (20)
Lincoln (12)
Buchanan (4)
Pierce (9)
Fillmore (5)
Taylor (4)
Polk (5)
Tyler (4)
Harrison (0)
van Buren (3)
Jackson (2)
J. Q. Adams (0.75)
Monroe (0.125)
Madison (0.125)
Jefferson (0.5)
J. Adams (0.25)
Washington (1)

*Does not include memoranda or other forms of executive action.
**As of October 2020.
SOURCE: The American Presidency Project, "Executive Orders," August 26, 2020, www.presidency.ucsb.edu (accessed 10/6/20).

FOR CRITICAL ANALYSIS

In recent years, presidents have expanded their power through increased use of executive orders, executive agreements, and other unilateral instruments. Is the United States becoming a "presidential republic"? Is this a development to be feared or welcomed?

orders apply to matters of administrative procedure and organization; directives seem most often associated with national or homeland security; memoranda are used to clarify or modify presidential positions and orders; and proclamations are usually used to emphasize an especially important decree, such as Lincoln's proclamation emancipating all enslaved people.

Congress is not entirely without power in regard to executive decrees. Legislators can overturn orders based on the president's legislative authority (as opposed to constitutional authority) by passing legislation declaring that the order "shall not have legal effect," or actually repealing the statute upon which the order was based.

Efforts to overturn the orders of sitting presidents are, however, hindered by the fact that any such legislation can be vetoed. Thus, two-thirds of the members of both houses of Congress would have to agree to the move. One study indicates that only about 4 percent of all presidential orders have ever been rescinded by legislation.[47] Even these were almost always orders issued by presidents no longer in office.[48] Usually, the most Congress can do is prevent funds from being spent to implement the order. This, too, is relatively unusual.[49]

Failure by Congress to act, moreover, strengthens the legal validity of a presidential order. The Supreme Court has held that congressional inaction tends to validate an order by indicating congressional "acquiescence" to the president's decision.[50]

Signing Statements In addition to issuing decrees to bring about actions they wanted, recent presidents have also increasingly found ways other than vetoes to negate congressional actions to which they objected. In particular, they have made frequent and calculated use of presidential **signing statements**.[51] The signing statement is an announcement made by the president, at the time of signing a bill into law, that offers the president's interpretation of the law and usually innocuous remarks predicting the many benefits the new law will bring to the nation.

Occasionally, however, presidents have used signing statements to point to sections of the law they consider improper or even unconstitutional, and to instruct executive branch agencies in how to execute the law.[52] In 2018, for example, when President Trump signed the 2019 National Defense Authorization Act, he issued a signing statement declaring "constitutional concerns" with more than 50 of the act's provisions. The president said he would interpret these provisions in a manner consistent with his authority as president rather than simply accepting the law as written. These provisions generally involved congressional efforts to check the president's foreign policies regarding North Korea, Saudi Arabia, and Russia.[53]

Presidential Nonenforcement of Laws A final instrument of direct presidential governance is nonenforcement of statutes. Congress may make the law, but if the president decides that a particular law is not to his or her liking and refuses to enforce it, Congress may find that its intent is stymied. President Obama, for example, suspended enforcement of portions of the Affordable Care Act when the rollout of "Obamacare" produced public confusion and inefficient implementation. President Trump, in an effort to undercut the ACA, effectively ordered the IRS to not enforce a provision of it that required taxpayers to indicate on their tax returns that they had health insurance—a major blow to the law's mandate.

The Advantages of the Administrative Strategy Through the course of American history, popular appeals have played important roles in presidential efforts to

signing statements announcements made by the president when signing bills into law, often presenting the president's interpretation of the law

Who Supports the President's Agenda?

Percentage Who Approved of the President before Election Day 2012 and 2020*

■ Donald J. Trump, 2020
■ Barack Obama, 2012

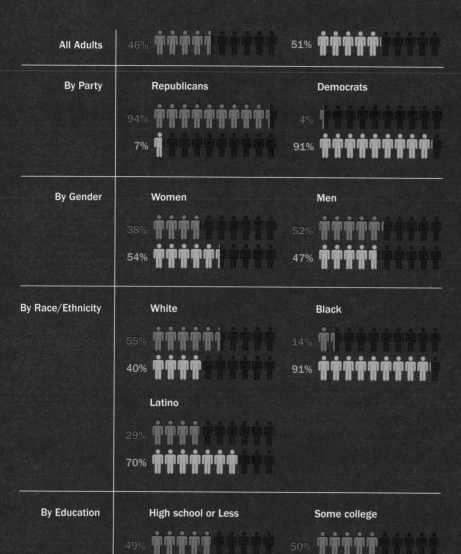

All Adults	46%	51%

By Party

Republicans		Democrats	
94%		4%	
7%		91%	

By Gender

Women		Men	
38%		52%	
54%		47%	

By Race/Ethnicity

White		Black	
55%		14%	
40%		91%	

Latino	
29%	
70%	

By Education

High school or Less		Some college	
49%		50%	
52%		50%	

College graduate		Postgraduate	
35%		28%	
46%		55%	

Many factors contribute to why a person supports a certain president—from their support of policies he or she has enacted, to their gender, to which region of the country they live in. Recently, however, party identification has been the most influential feature of a candidate that voters consider. As polarization in the country has increased, fewer Democrats have approved of Republican presidents, and vice versa.

* Based on data collected the week of the presidential elections in 2012 and 2020.

SOURCE: Gallup, "Presidential Job Approval Center," gallup.com (accessed 10/27/20).

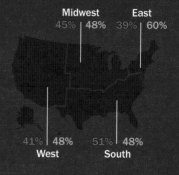

Midwest	East
45% | 48%	39% | 60%

West	South
41% | 48%	51% | 48%

FOR CRITICAL ANALYSIS

1. Should the president aim to gain votes from both parties, or just his or her own? Why?

2. What are some of the differences between those who supported Barack Obama and those who supported Donald Trump? What are the similarities?

overcome political opposition, and continue to be an instrument of presidential power. Yet, as we have seen, in the modern era presidents have not always been able to rely upon support from their own parties, and the effects of popular appeals have often proved fleeting. The limitations of these alternatives have encouraged presidents to expand the administrative powers of the office and their own capacity for unilateral action as means of achieving their policy goals. In recent decades, the expansion of the Executive Office of the President, the development of regulatory review, and the use of executive orders and signing statements have allowed presidents to achieve significant policy results despite congressional opposition to their legislative agendas.

In principle, perhaps, Congress could respond more vigorously to unilateral policy making by the president than it has. Certainly, a Congress willing to impeach a president should have the strength to overturn presidential administrative directives. But the president has significant advantages in such struggles. In battles over presidential directives and orders, Congress is on the defensive, reacting to presidential initiatives. When the president issues a decree, Congress must respond through the cumbersome and time-consuming lawmaking process, overcome internal divisions, and enact legislation that the president may ultimately veto. Moreover, as the political scientist Terry Moe has argued, its members are likely to be more sensitive to the substance of a president's actions and its short-term effects on their constituents than to the more general long-term implications of presidential power for the vitality of Congress as an institution.[54]

THE LIMITS OF PRESIDENTIAL POWER: CHECKS AND BALANCES

While the framers of the Constitution wanted an energetic executive, they were also concerned that executive power could be abused and might stifle citizens' liberties. To guard against this possibility, the framers contrived a number of checks on executive power. The president's term is limited to four years, though with the

Congress serves as an important check on presidential power, from holding oversight committee hearings on the actions of the executive branch to controlling which legislation hits the president's desk. However, this means Congress and the president are often at odds.

possibility of re-election. Congress is empowered to impeach and remove the president, to reject presidential appointments and refuse to ratify treaties, to refuse to enact laws requested by the president, to deny funding for the president's programs, and to override presidential vetoes of congressional actions.

The framers viewed the threat of impeachment as an important check upon executive power. The Constitution provides that a president may be impeached for "high Crimes and Misdemeanors." Such charges are to be brought by the House and tried in the Senate, with the chief justice presiding and a two-thirds vote needed for conviction.

During the course of American history, only three presidents, Andrew Johnson, Bill Clinton, and Donald Trump have been impeached, and none have been convicted. Johnson's impeachment was triggered by his veto of the Tenure in Office Act; and Clinton's by charges of sexual improprieties and lying under oath about them. Trump was impeached for attempting to compel a foreign nation (Ukraine) to investigate Trump's political opponents and for lying to the Congress. A fourth president, Richard Nixon, would almost certainly have been impeached for his misdeeds in the Watergate affair, but Nixon chose to resign to avoid the impeachment process.

Although the requirement that the Senate consent to presidential appointments was seen by the framers as another important check on executive power, in recent years severe partisan disagreements often have led presidents to resort to—and the Senate to resist—"recess appointments." These are authorized by Article II, Section 2, which states, "The President shall have power to fill up all Vacancies that may happen during the Recess of the Senate, by granting Commissions which shall expire at the End of their next Session."

Until recent years, recess appointments were made only when the Senate was between sessions or when a regular session of the Senate was adjourned for holidays or other lengthy periods. However, presidents have sometimes sought to make recess appointments even when the Senate was only briefly recessed. The Senate has responded with a strategy also sometimes used to prevent pocket vetoes. During periods when the Senate is recessed, one senator is assigned the task of calling the chamber to order for a few moments every day for a pro forma session so that the president cannot claim the Senate was actually in recess. Presidents have viewed this procedure as nothing more than a subterfuge, since the Senate is incapable of actually conducting business during these periods. The Supreme Court, however, has supported the Senate's strategy.[55]

And, of course, under the Constitution, only the Congress has the power to enact legislation, levy taxes, or appropriate funds. Indeed, so many were the constitutional checks on executive power that some delegates to the Constitutional Convention feared that the executive would be too weak and the potential energy of executive power lost. As we can see, however, from the many actions of presidents in recent years, presidential power has grown significantly beyond the framers' vision.

Presidential Power: What Do You Think?

The framers of the Constitution created a system of government in which Congress and the executive branch were to share power. At least since the New Deal, however, the powers of Congress have waned, whereas those of the presidency have expanded dramatically. There is no doubt that Congress continues to be able to confront presidents and even, on occasion, hand the White House a sharp rebuff. Still, in the larger view, presidents' occasional defeats, however dramatic, have to be seen as temporary setbacks in a gradual but decisive shift toward increased presidential power.

A powerful presidency, a weak Congress, and a partially apathetic electorate make for a dangerous mix. Who we vote into the office of the president matters. Presidential power, to be sure, can be a force for good. To cite one example from the not-so-distant past, it was President Lyndon Johnson, more than Congress or the judiciary, who faced the task of smashing America's racial segregation system. Yet, as the framers knew, unchecked power—whether executive or legislative—is always dangerous. The framers of the Constitution believed that liberty required checks and balances. Conversely, sometimes presidential *inaction* can be a concern, as President Trump's reluctance to use the Defense Production Act during the coronavirus pandemic demonstrates.

★ Presidential strength works both ways. The growth of executive power means that policies and individual favors can more easily become the law of the land, because Congress works slowly while the president can work quickly. But what if the president fails to act? What would Craig Spencer and Governor Pritzker have to say about presidential power? How have the checks and balances between branches in the Constitution changed in practice over the decades?

★ Are there some issue areas—or certain conditions—in which presidential rather than congressional policy making is necessary?

★ Have you been affected by a presidential decision? Do you think the policy outcome would have been different if Congress had been more involved?

STUDY GUIDE

The Constitutional Powers of the Presidency

> ### Identify the expressed, implied, delegated, and inherent powers of the presidency (pp. 475–88)

Presidents make use of four kinds of powers: expressed, implied, delegated, and inherent. The president's expressed powers, as defined by Article II of the Constitution, include military, judicial, diplomatic, executive, and legislative powers. The expressed powers have become the foundation for a set of implied powers, which are considered necessary in order to carry out the expressed powers. The president's delegated powers are not found in the Constitution but are instead the products of congressional statutes and resolutions. The president's inherent powers stem from the rights, duties, and obligations of the presidency, and presidents most often assert these powers during times of war and national crisis.

Key Terms

expressed powers (p. 476)

commander in chief (p. 476)

executive agreement (p. 479)

executive privilege (p. 479)

veto (p. 481)

pocket veto (p. 481)

implied powers (p. 482)

delegated powers (p. 483)

inherent powers (p. 484)

Practice Quiz

1. Which of the following does *not* require the Senate's approval?
   a) a sole executive agreement
   b) a treaty
   c) an appointment of an ambassador
   d) a Supreme Court nomination
   e) an appointment of an executive officer

2. What did the Supreme Court rule in *United States v. Nixon*?
   a) Nixon had to turn his secret White House tapes over to congressional investigators because presidents do not have the power of executive privilege.
   b) Nixon did not have to turn his secret White House tapes over to congressional investigators because, in general, presidents have the power of executive privilege.
   c) Nixon had to turn his secret White House tapes over to congressional investigators but, in general, presidents have the power of executive privilege.
   d) Nixon did not have to turn his secret White House tapes over to congressional investigators but, in general, presidents do not have the power of executive privilege.
   e) All presidents are immune from criminal investigations and cannot, therefore, be tried in any court of law.

3. What are the requirements for overriding a presidential veto?
   a) 50 percent plus one vote in both houses of Congress
   b) two-thirds vote in both houses of Congress
   c) two-thirds vote in the Senate only
   d) three-fourths vote in both houses of Congress
   e) A presidential veto cannot be overridden by Congress.

4. The president's power to remove executive appointees is an example of
   a) an expressed power.
   b) an implied power.
   c) a delegated power.
   d) an inherent power.
   e) a legislative power.

5. The "theory of the unitary executive" argues that
   a) Congress controls all policy making by the executive branch and the president wields only limited power over executive agencies.
   b) the president controls all policy making by the executive branch and Congress wields only limited power over executive agencies.
   c) all executive agencies are independent from the influence of both the president and Congress.
   d) presidents should be limited to serving only a single term in office.
   e) the presidency should be replaced by a three-person executive council.

6. Over the past century, Congress has _____ the executive branch.
   a) relinquished its powers of advice and consent to
   b) taken control of the war-making powers originally given to
   c) delegated a great deal of its own legislative authority to
   d) passed laws affirming the inherent powers of
   e) become much more powerful with respect to

7. President George W. Bush justified his orders authorizing the National Security Agency to monitor phone conversations between the United States and other nations on the basis of
    a) the president's expressed powers to deal with national emergencies.
    b) the president's inherent powers to deal with national emergencies.
    c) the president's delegated powers to deal with national emergencies.
    d) the president's implied powers to deal with national emergencies.
    e) the president's imperial powers to deal with national emergencies.

8. Which of the following statements about presidential declarations of national emergency is *not* accurate?
    a) Presidents can declare a state of national emergency only in response to foreign threats and with the approval of Congress.
    b) Once the president has declared a state of national emergency, constitutional rights, including the right of habeas corpus, may be temporarily suspended.
    c) A declaration of national emergency in response to foreign threats allows the president to embargo trade, seize foreign assets, and prohibit transactions with whatever foreign nations are involved.
    d) Declarations of national emergency expire one year after they are issued unless they are renewed by the president.
    e) Congress may, by a joint resolution of the two houses, terminate a declaration of national emergency.

The Presidency as an Institution

Describe the institutional resources presidents have to help them exercise their powers (pp. 489–93)

The institutional presidency is made up of the Cabinet, the White House staff, the Executive Office of the President, the vice president, and the first spouse. The president's party also works to advance the president's agenda in Congress. Through their advice and assistance, these thousands of individuals give the president a capacity for action that no single individual could duplicate. When coupled with the president's formal powers, the institutional presidency makes the chief executive an important player in the country's policy-making process.

Key Terms

Cabinet (p. 489)

White House staff (p. 490)

Executive Office of the President (EOP) (p. 490)

National Security Council (NSC) (p. 491)

Practice Quiz

9. The EOP agency responsible for preparing the nation's budget and helping presidents to define their programs and objectives is called
    a) the Office of Management and Budget.
    b) the National Security Council.
    c) the Council of Economic Advisers.
    d) the Congressional Budget Office.
    e) the Bureau of Economic Analysis.

10. Approximately how many people work for agencies within the Executive Office of the President?
    a) 25 to 50
    b) 700 to 1,000
    c) 1,500 to 2,000
    d) 4,500 to 5,000
    e) 25,000 to 30,000

11. Which of the following statements about vice presidents is *not* true?
    a) The vice president succeeds the president in case of death, resignation, or incapacity.
    b) The vice president casts the tie-breaking vote in the Senate when necessary.
    c) The vice president serves as an honorary member of the Supreme Court.
    d) Eight vice presidents have had to replace American presidents who died in office.
    e) Presidential candidates often select a vice-presidential running mate who is likely to bring the support of a state that would not otherwise support the ticket.

The Growth of Presidential Power

Explain how modern presidents have become even more powerful (pp. 493–503)

Although Congress was America's dominant institution of government throughout the nineteenth century, presidential power has since expanded greatly, thanks to the efforts of modern presidents. Contemporary presidents commonly turn to popular mobilization and executive administration in their pursuit of policy change. Presidents have increased the administrative capabilities of their office by enhancing the reach and power of the Executive Office of the President, increasing White House control of the federal bureaucracy, and expanding the role of executive orders and other instruments of direct presidential governance.

Key Terms

legislative initiative (p. 495)

executive order (p. 498)

signing statements (p. 500)

Practice Quiz

12. What are two primary ways that presidents can expand their power?
    a) avoiding "going public" and increasing their dependence on Congress
    b) "going public" and reducing their dependence on Congress
    c) "going public" and increasing their dependence on Congress
    d) avoiding "going public" and reducing their dependence on Congress
    e) weakening national partisan institutions and reducing their dependence on Congress

13. Which of the following is an advantage of using the internet as part of a president's "going public" strategy?
    a) Using the internet allows presidents to collect campaign funds by putting their content behind a paywall.
    b) Using social media platforms like Twitter usually ensures that a president's approval rating will remain high throughout the entire presidency.
    c) The rise of the internet and social media platforms has made the White House Communications Office obsolete.
    d) Using the internet allows presidents to circumvent television and older media to broadcast their policy ideas directly to citizens.
    e) Before the internet, presidents could not go public at all; the internet enables them to do so.

14. The Environmental Protection Agency and the Food and Drug Administration were created through the use of
    a) a pocket veto.
    b) an executive–congressional agreement.
    c) a sole executive agreement.
    d) an executive order.
    e) executive privilege.

15. An announcement made by the president at the time of signing a bill into law that offers his or her interpretation of the law is called
    a) a signing statement.
    b) a line-item veto.
    c) an executive order.
    d) legislative initiative.
    e) regulatory review.

The Bureaucracy

WHAT GOVERNMENT DOES AND WHY IT MATTERS In late January 2020, Dr. Helen Y. Chu, an infectious disease expert in Seattle, heard that the first confirmed case in the United States of a new coronavirus had been detected in her area. She realized that she had a way to verify whether the virus was spreading in the community—she could repurpose nasal samples she had already collected for a flu study of the region. But to do so, she needed approval from state and federal officials. They denied her requests, both because her lab did not have permission from the research subjects and because her lab was not certified for clinical work.

She argued that these strictures should be lifted in an emergency. Officials were unmoved. Her lab performed tests for the virus anyway and discovered that it had infected not just those who had traveled to impacted countries like China, but also people with no recent travel history. Community transmission of the disease—what every public health expert fears—had already started. "It must have been here this entire time," she thought. "It's just everywhere already." Nonetheless, in early March state regulators ordered her lab to stop testing.

In the meantime, the Centers for Disease Control and Prevention (CDC) had sent virus test kits to

In early 2020, Dr. Helen Chu attempted to test a sample of nasal swabs for coronavirus after collecting them for a separate study on influenza. The FDA refused to certify her lab to do so, but in testing the samples, she found community spread of the virus as the CDC sent out faulty test kits to labs across the country.

public health labs around the country, but they didn't work. Labs started doing their own tests, but the FDA was slow to approve them and insisted that the labs first get an Emergency Use Authorization from the agency. When working test kits were finally available, there were not enough of them for widespread testing. Only patients who had traveled outside the country or who were already sick were tested. Throughout February and early March it seemed like there were relatively few cases in the United States, but that was because so few people were being tested. In fact, the coronavirus was spreading rapidly throughout this time period. "We just twiddled our thumbs as the coronavirus waltzed in," said Harvard epidemiologist William Hanage. Without data from testing, mayors and governors were reluctant to issue lockdown orders, which were the best public health intervention in the absence of a vaccine but which also had severe economic effects. And without data, hospitals could not prepare properly. Meanwhile, the nation's Strategic National Stockpile—reserves of medical equipment and other disaster relief goods— had not been replenished after the 2009 swine-flu epidemic because of budget cuts. States and localities would end up bidding against one another in a mad scramble to secure supplies on the open market.[1]

The coronavirus testing and supply missteps are a dramatic, tragic example of bureaucratic failure. Americans depend on public bureaucracies to provide services they use both every day and in emergencies. On a typical day, a college student might check the weather forecast, drive on an interstate highway, mail the rent check, drink from a public water fountain, attend a class, go online, and meet a relative at the airport. Each of these activities is possible because of the work of a government bureaucracy: the National Weather Service, the U.S. Department of Transportation, the U.S. Postal Service, the Environmental Protection Agency, the student loan programs of the U.S. Department of Education, the Advanced Research Projects Agency (which developed the internet in the 1960s), and the Federal Aviation Administration. Without the ongoing work of these agencies, many of these common activities would be impossible, unreliable, or more expensive. When bureaucracies work well, we barely notice.

But when they fail, the results can be truly alarming, like the botched virus testing, or the September 11, 2001, terror attacks, widely viewed as a failure of the national security bureaucracy.[2] Such failures play into Americans' ambivalence about the role of government. Some disasters prompt politicians to promise that they will slash the bureaucracy, especially at the federal level. Yet others result in an increase in the bureaucracy, like the creation of the federal Department of Homeland Security after September 11. Each instance raises a number of questions: should the bureaucracy be smaller or larger? How can it become more efficient and effective? How can the bureaucracy be made more responsive to the needs of the American people?

CHAPTER GOALS

★ Describe the characteristics and roles of bureaucrats and bureaucracies (pp. 511–21)

★ Explain civil service hiring, political appointments, and the use of federal contracting (pp. 521–27)

★ Explain how the president, Congress, and the judiciary try to manage the bureaucracy (pp. 527–37)

What Is the Federal Bureaucracy?

> **Describe the characteristics and roles of bureaucrats and bureaucracies**

Although Congress, the president, and the courts may garner more attention as they make policy, the **bureaucracy** plays a crucial role in administering policy on the ground. Bureaucrats carry out the everyday work of government, implementing the policies that Congress and the president have passed and that the court system may have weighed in on. The teachers you had in elementary school, the Social Security officer who approved your grandmother's retirement pension, the air traffic controller who guided the plane on your last vacation, the engineers who designed the roads that carried you to class, and the inspector who approved the meat in this morning's breakfast sausage are all bureaucrats.

bureaucracy the complex structure of offices, tasks, rules, and principles of organization that is employed by all large-scale institutions to coordinate the work of their personnel

At its best, bureaucracy ensures fair, accountable administration performed by expert professionals. To provide services, government bureaucracies employ specialists such as meteorologists, doctors, and scientists. To do their jobs effectively, these specialists require resources and tools (ranging from paper to complex computer software). They must coordinate their work with others (for example, traffic engineers must communicate with construction engineers). And they must effectively reach out to the public (for example, people must be made aware of health warnings). Bureaucracy is a means of coordinating the many different parts that must work together for the government to provide useful services.

When bureaucracy runs well, it can be virtually invisible. When it fails, the results can be spectacularly public (and even tragic), as when Hurricane Katrina breached levies built by the Army Corps of Engineers in 2005 and the Federal Emergency Management Agency reacted ineffectually, or when the Department of Veterans Affairs was criticized in 2014 for long waiting lists for veterans seeking medical care and was even blamed for veteran deaths in Phoenix.[3] Or when FDA and CDC missteps delayed coronavirus testing as the pandemic swept across the nation. How bureaucrats carry out their responsibilities shapes individuals' experiences of government in profound ways.

WHAT BUREAUCRATS DO

Bureaucrats execute and implement laws. They determine who is eligible for Medicare, for example, or study whether a new medicine is safe and effective. They deliver mail, tell national park campers that they can build a fire *here* but not *there*, calculate how long it would take a spacecraft to reach the edge of the solar system. They gather data and conduct research. Some, like customs officials, are "street-level bureaucrats" who regularly interact with the public. Yet others, like researchers at the National Institutes of Health, work in specialized facilities with other experts. As they carry out their responsibilities, implementing and enforcing laws, making rules, and innovating, they exercise discretion and help define how public policy gets expressed.

Bureaucrats Implement Laws Congress is responsible for making the laws, but the federal bureaucracy is responsible for putting laws into effect (and sometimes state bureaucracies as well, since some policies are delegated to the states—see Chapter 3). In most cases legislation sets only the broad parameters for government action. Bureaucracies are responsible for filling in the blanks by

implementation the efforts
of departments and agencies
to translate laws into specific
bureaucratic rules and actions

determining how the laws should be implemented. This requires bureaucracies to draw up detailed rules that guide the process of **implementation** and to play a key role in enforcing the laws. For example, during the coronavirus pandemic, while Congress appropriated funds for direct payments to individuals and for economic relief for small businesses, these programs were implemented by the Internal Revenue Service (part of the Treasury Department) and the Small Business Administration, an independent agency of the federal government. Congress also increased Unemployment Insurance benefits and broadened eligibility, but had to rely on the state-level bureaucracies that run the program, which were overwhelmed by the enormous rise in jobless claims. Administrative capacity is an important factor in bureaucracies' ability to implement laws effectively.

Bureaucrats Make Rules One of the most important activities that government agencies do is issue rules that provide more detailed and specific indications of what a given congressional policy will actually mean. For example, the Clean Air Act empowers the Environmental Protection Agency (EPA) to assess whether current or projected levels of air pollutants pose a threat to public health, determine whether motor vehicle emissions are contributing to such pollution, and create rules designed to regulate these emissions. During the coronavirus pandemic, the Department of Labor's Occupational Safety and Health Administration (OSHA) and the Centers for Disease Control and Prevention (CDC) jointly released guidance for meatpacking plants to increase employees' protection from the coronavirus, after infections soared at several facilities.[4]

The regulatory process is defined by the Administrative Procedure Act of 1946, which sets forth the steps by which rules are created and adopted. Once Congress passes a new law, the relevant agency studies the legislation and proposes a set of rules to guide implementation. These proposed rules are submitted to the White House Office of Management and Budget (OMB) for review. If OMB approves, the proposed rule is published in the *Federal Register*, a daily publication of the federal government, which anyone from ordinary citizens to interest group lobbyists can read and where they can leave comments, which are also published. After reviewing public comments and making changes, the agency proposes a final rule, which goes back to OMB for clearance, upon which it is published in the *Federal Register*. The agency's rules have the force of law.

During the 1970s and '80s, the length of time required to develop an administrative rule from a proposal to publication in the *Federal Register* grew from an average of 15 months to an average of 35 to 40 months. Was this due to inefficiency? No. Most of the increased time is attributable to new procedures requiring more public notice, more public hearings in Washington and elsewhere, more cost-benefit analysis, and to stronger legal obligations to prepare "environmental impact statements" demonstrating that the proposed rule will not have an unacceptably large negative impact on the human or physical environment.[5] Thus, a great deal of what is popularly decried as the lower efficiency of public agencies can be attributed to the political, judicial, legal, and public-opinion restraints and extraordinarily high expectations imposed on public bureaucrats. If a private company such as Apple were required to open up all its decision processes and management practices to full view by the media, its competitors, and all interested citizens, Apple—despite its profit motive and the pressure of competition—would likely appear far less efficient, perhaps no more efficient than public bureaucracies.

An example of bureaucratic rules that affect Americans both positively and negatively are the regulations set forth by the Environmental Protection Agency (EPA). When President Obama extended the EPA's authority to regulate greenhouse gas emissions in 2014, many people applauded the benefits to the environment, but at the same time, thousands lost jobs because of the new rules.

Although bureaucratic rule making has the force of law, it can be more fragile than government by congressional legislation.[6] If Congress passes a new law, changing it usually requires another congressional action, while rules made by the bureaucracy in one administration can be easily reversed by the next. For example, during the Obama administration, the EPA imposed new emission standards for automobiles that raised the average fuel economy for new vehicles to 35.5 miles per gallon starting in 2016, a standard later boosted to 54.4 miles per gallon by 2025.[7] But under President Trump the EPA both rolled back the Obama-era rules and ended California's special status under the 1970 Clean Air Act that allows it to set its own vehicle pollution standards, although both moves prompted court battles.[8]

Bureaucrats Enforce Laws In addition to rule making, bureaucracies play an essential role in enforcing the laws, thus exercising considerable power over private actors. In 2015 the EPA charged Volkswagen with cheating on emissions tests of its diesel vehicles. For over seven years, the company had installed software that showed emissions at legal levels during testing conditions, but once the cars were on the road emissions were actually 10 to 40 percent higher. After the EPA threatened to bar the company from selling some of its 2016 cars in the United States, Volkswagen admitted that it had cheated and agreed to a $15.8 billion settlement that required it to buy back the faulty vehicles and compensate owners and to fund several clean-air programs.[9]

Bureaucrats Innovate A good case study of the important role agencies can play is the story of how ordinary federal bureaucrats created the internet. It's true: what became the internet was developed largely by the U.S. Department of Defense, and defense considerations still shape the basic structure of the internet. In 1957, immediately following the profound American embarrassment over the Soviet Union's launching of *Sputnik*, the first satellite to orbit the Earth, Congress authorized the establishment of the Advanced Research Projects Agency (ARPA)

The National Aeronautics and Space Administration (NASA), an independent agency of the federal government, was established by President Eisenhower in 1958. Its mission is "To reach for new heights and reveal the unknown so that what we do and learn will benefit all humankind." Here, NASA public affairs officer Dwayne Brown announces the presence of water on Mars.

to develop, among other things, a means of maintaining communications in the event of a strategic attack on the existing telecommunications network (the telephone system). Since the telephone network was highly centralized and therefore could have been completely disabled by a single attack, ARPA developed a decentralized, highly redundant network with an improved probability of functioning after an attack. The full design, called ARPANET, took almost a decade to create. By 1971 around 20 universities were connected to the ARPANET. The forerunner to the internet was born.[10]

Key Characteristics of Bureaucracies Many governments around the world, including the federal and state governments in the United States, use bureaucracies to implement and enforce laws and to make rules because they have particular attributes and possess certain tools that enable them to carry out the government's work. They are institutions designed with policy implementation in mind.

In the United States, bureaucracies are typically defined by mission statements, which lay out each agency's role and responsibilities. For example, the mission of the Department of Health and Human Services (HHS) is to "enhance the health and well-being of all Americans, by providing for effective health and human services and by fostering sound, sustained advances in the sciences underlying medicine, public health, and social services." Mission statements constitute both a resource for agencies, because they lay out an agency's authority, and a basis for accountability, as members of Congress, interest groups, and the public can assess whether an agency is fulfilling its mission.

Another key characteristic is expertise. Bureaucracies are populated by policy-specific experts who are deeply knowledgeable about the issue areas they oversee. Expertise is one of the main resources and distinguishing characteristics of the federal bureaucracy. There is policy expertise in other branches as well, for example members of Congress and their staffs who develop expertise, particularly if they serve on certain committees and work on specific issues through multiple terms of office. But bureaucrats often have specialized training, such as advanced degrees, and may spend their careers working on a given set of issues, developing deep knowledge.

What Do People Think of Federal Agencies?

Agency	Approval by Party		Overall Performance Rating*		

By Party
- ● Democrat
- ● Republican

Performance Rating
- ● Excellent/good
- ● Only fair
- ● Poor

U.S. Postal Service — 76% / 69% — 74% 18% 8%

U.S. Secret Service — 66% / 74% — 69% 19% 8%

Centers for Disease Control and Prevention (CDC) — 61% / 71% — 64% 22% 12%

Central Intelligence Agency (CIA) — 61% / 59% — 60% 25% 12%

NASA — 60% / 61% — 60% 26% 5%

FBI — 66% / 46% — 57% 23% 19%

Department of Homeland Security — 42% / 65% — 55% 26% 17%

Federal Emergency Management Agency (FEMA) — 38% / 64% — 52% 29% 16%

Internal Revenue Service (IRS) — 52% / 53% — 50% 30% 19%

Federal Reserve Board — 45% / 51% — 48% 34% 13%

Food and Drug Administration (FDA) — 37% / 52% — 44% 33% 22%

Environmental Protection Agency (EPA) — 38% / 54% — 43% 30% 26%

Veterans Affairs (VA) — 35% / 45% — 39% 31% 28%

Despite the stereotype of being staffed by apathetic employees mired in red tape, federal government agencies provide important services, and most get positive ratings from the people using them. When is the last time you interacted with a federal government agency? What was your experience?

*"No opinion" category has been omitted and numbers may not add up to 100 percent.

SOURCE: Gallup, "Postal Service Still Americans' Favorite Federal Agency" https://news.gallup.com (accessed 6/11/20).

FOR CRITICAL ANALYSIS

1. What factors might explain why some federal agencies receive higher evaluations than others? In particular, why might the EPA and the VA be rated so low? Why would the Postal Service, the CDC, and the Secret Service be rated so high?

2. What might explain the differences (or similarities) between Democrats' and Republicans' ratings of federal agencies?

Bureaucracies are also characterized by hierarchical structures with clear lines of authority and standardized procedures governed by rules. These structures are intended to foster equal treatment of citizens. In the United States, the bureaucracy is supposed to be insulated from politics as well. The long length of employment of many career civil servants—whose service may persist through many presidencies and congressional terms—is one form of protection. There are also merit systems in place for hiring and promotion, meant to maximize the political neutrality of the bureaucracy regardless of which party controls the presidency or the chambers of Congress. In addition, the nonpartisan nature of the bureaucracy is underscored by the 1939 Hatch Act and its amendments, which prevent federal employees from engaging in certain types of political activities, such as wearing political buttons while on duty or using their official authority to interfere with an election. The bureaucratic means of carrying out policy, characterized by expertise and analysis, adherence to rules, and hierarchy, can be frustratingly slow; hence citizen complaints about "red tape." But these procedures also represent a safeguard from politics and favoritism.

FOR CRITICAL ANALYSIS

Would it be possible to run a large national government without a bureaucracy? What do bureaucracies do that other elements of a government, such as a legislature or a court system, do not do?

The Decision to Delegate As federal bureaucrats implement and enforce laws, as they innovate and make rules, they shape the nation's public policy. We might wonder why Congress writes laws but then delegates such significant policy-making responsibility to the bureaucracy. One reason is that bureaucracies employ people who have much more specialized expertise in specific policy areas than do members of Congress. Decisions about how to achieve many policy goals—from managing the national parks to regulating air quality to ensuring a sound economy—rest on the judgment of specialized experts. A second reason that Congress needs bureaucracy is that updating legislation can take many years, and bureaucratic flexibility can ensure that laws are administered in ways that take new conditions into account more quickly. Finally, members of Congress often prefer to delegate politically difficult decision-making to bureaucrats, thus avoiding having to deal with controversial issues that might anger constituents or interest groups and threaten their chances for re-election. For example, when Congress wrote the Affordable Care Act, it required health insurance plans to cover "essential health benefits" but did not define what those benefits are. Instead, lawmakers provided some general guidelines and instructed the bureaucracy—the Department of Health and Human Services—to specify which benefits must be covered. In this way Congress avoided controversial decisions that could potentially anger consumers and health care providers.[11]

While advantageous for Congress, delegation comes with risks. In delegating, Congress gives agencies discretion to use their expertise as they implement laws and create rules. But such discretion can lead to the **principal-agent problem**, which occurs when one entity (the principal) gives decision-making authority to another (the agent), but the agent makes decisions that are different from what the principal may have wanted. For example, Congress might delegate aspects of air quality standards to the Environmental Protection Agency, but the EPA may write rules that are stricter than Congress would have written had it had the time and expertise to make the legislation more detailed. Congress delegated implementation of the Paycheck Protection Program, the small business pandemic relief program, to the Small Business Administration, which in turn used banks as the intermediaries to which businesses applied for funds. Problems arose in spring 2020 when numerous small businesses were unable to secure loans before the funds ran

principal-agent problem a conflict in priorities between an actor and the representative authorized to act on the actor's behalf

out because many banks only accepted applications from their existing business customers, met the needs of larger businesses first, or quickly hit their program lending limits. Amid great outcry, Congress responded by passing a second round of small business relief with tighter rules and pressuring larger, publicly traded companies like Shake Shack and Auto Nation to return the program funds they had received.[12] Later we will consider the tools that Congress uses to overcome the principal-agent problem and try to control the bureaucracy.

HOW THE BUREAUCRACY IS ORGANIZED

Currently there are 15 **executive departments** in the federal government. The first 4 were established in 1789 under President George Washington: State, Treasury, Defense, and Justice. Others were added over time: Interior, Agriculture, Commerce, Labor, Health and Human Services, Housing and Urban Development, Transportation, Energy, Education, Veterans Affairs, and most recently, in 2002, Homeland Security. These 15 executive departments employ over 80 percent of the federal civilian workforce, with Defense, Veterans Affairs, and Homeland Security having the most employees.[13] The rest work in agencies in the Executive Office of the President (for example, the Council of Economic Advisers or the Office of the United States Trade Representative) or in agencies outside of the executive departments (for example, the Central Intelligence Agency or the National Aeronautics and Space Administration [NASA]). At the top of each department is an official who is called the secretary of the department (though the head of the Justice Department is the attorney general). The executive department secretaries, along with the vice president and attorney general, make up the president's "Cabinet." Presidents can also confer Cabinet-level status on additional agencies. For example, since its creation by executive order by President Nixon in 1970, the EPA has often had Cabinet status.

Beyond the executive departments, the federal bureaucracy also consists of independent agencies that are not part of executive departments but that have

executive departments the 15 departments in the executive branch headed by Cabinet secretaries and constituting the majority of the federal bureaucracy

The president regularly meets with the Cabinet to discuss the affairs of each department or agency. Here, President Trump delivers remarks before beginning a Cabinet meeting.

independent authority to implement policy and design regulations in their particular area. Some are called administrations, including NASA, the Small Business Administration, and the Social Security Administration. There are also **independent regulatory commissions** such as the Federal Trade Commission (FTC), Federal Communications Commission (FCC), and Securities and Exchange Commission (SEC). These commissions are typically run by a small number of commissioners appointed by the president for fixed terms. And there are **government corporations**, which receive federal funding and are subject to federal control but function like private businesses in charging for a service, such as transporting railroad passengers (Amtrak) or delivering the mail (United States Postal Service).

For simplicity we will call all of these bureaucratic entities "agencies." As Figure 14.1 shows, the federal bureaucracy handles a vast number of important functions, as a few examples illustrate. Some agencies work to promote national

independent regulatory commission a government agency outside the executive department usually headed by commissioners

government corporation a government agency that performs a market-oriented public service and raises revenues to fund its activities

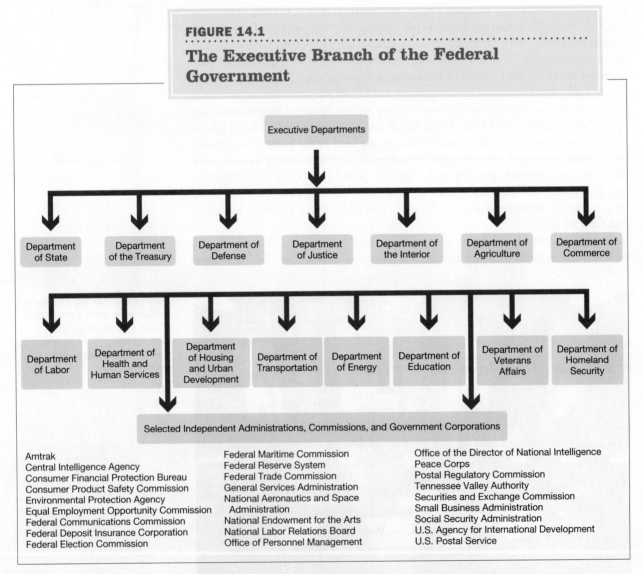

FIGURE 14.1

The Executive Branch of the Federal Government

SOURCE: Based on GPO Access: Guide to the U.S. Government, http://bensguide.gpo.gov/files/gov_chart.pdf (accessed 9/22/12).

Bureaucracy in Comparison

As the third-largest country by area, with over 330 million residents, the United States has a sizable bureaucracy to run government programs and services. As a percentage of the labor force, however, the number of government employees in the United States is not especially high compared to other nations. We can also see differences in whether most government employees work at the national level or the subnational (state and local) level in each country.

1. What factors might lead a country like Norway or Japan to have a significantly larger or smaller government workforce

as a percentage of its population? Would you expect these percentages to be going up or down over time? How might you expect them to change during times of economic growth versus during recessions?

2. What might explain the differences in how some countries have most of their government employment at the national level whereas others focus their employment at the subnational level? How does America's federal structure influence its bureaucratic hiring?

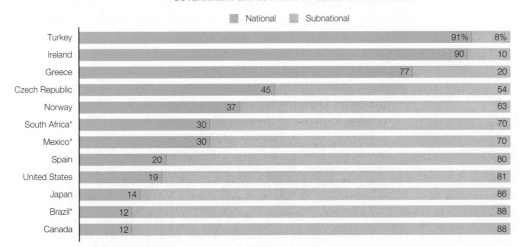

TOTAL GOVERNMENT EMPLOYMENT AS A PERCENTAGE OF THE LABOR FORCE MARKET

Country	Percentage
Norway	30%
Canada	18
Greece	18
South Africa*	17
Czech Republic	16
Spain	16
United States	16
Ireland	15
Turkey*	12
Brazil*	12
Mexico*	12
Japan	8

NOTE: Includes national and sub-national government employees.
*Brazil, Mexico, South Africa, and Turkey data are from 2014.

GOVERNMENT EMPLOYMENT BY LEVEL OF GOVERNMENT

■ National ■ Subnational

Country	National	Subnational
Turkey	91%	8%
Ireland	90	10
Greece	77	20
Czech Republic	45	54
Norway	37	63
South Africa*	30	70
Mexico*	30	70
Spain	20	80
United States	19	81
Japan	14	86
Brazil*	12	88
Canada	12	88

*Brazil, Mexico, and South Africa data are from 2013.

SOURCE: OECD, "Public Employment and Pay," Government at a Glance, 2017, www.stats.oecd.org (accessed 4/16/18).

security, such as the State Department, whose primary mission is diplomacy, sending foreign-service officers and ambassadors to other countries where they work to promote American perspectives and interests in the world; and the Defense Department, one of the largest bureaucracies in the world. Headquartered at the Pentagon, across the Potomac River from Washington, D.C., the Department of Defense includes the Office of the Secretary of Defense, which provides civilian oversight of the military; the Joint Chiefs of Staff, which includes the five military service chiefs; the six regional Unified Combatant Commands, which execute military operations in different parts of the world; and a number of additional agencies that supply and service the military.

While the State and Defense Departments confront threats from outside the nation, the Department of Homeland Security has responsibility for maintaining domestic security, and was created after the September 11, 2001, terrorist attacks to reorganize existing agencies and expand their mission from fighting crime to preventing terrorism as well. The antiterrorism mandate requires the DHS to integrate information from intelligence agencies and law enforcement to protect the nation. That alone is a broad mandate, but the DHS is also responsible for securing the nation's borders; administering and enforcing its immigration laws; addressing cybersecurity and energy security issues; running the Secret Service, which protects federal officials; administering disaster relief through FEMA; and any number of other responsibilities, from running the national flood insurance program to coordinating national health security response to infectious-disease outbreaks and natural disasters with the Department of Health and Human Services.[14] Little wonder that the Government Accountability Office—an agency that works for Congress as a "watchdog" over executive branch functions, as we will see below—has issued hundreds of recommendations for managerial improvements over the DHS's two-decade history.[15] The myriad responsibilities of this one agency give a sense of how complex the federal bureaucracy is.

Yet other federal agencies work to maintain a strong economy. The Treasury Department collects taxes through the Internal Revenue Service (IRS), manages the national debt, prints currency, and performs economic policy analysis. The Federal Reserve System (called the Fed) is the nation's key monetary agency (see Chapter 16 on economic policy) and is headed by the Federal Reserve Board. The Fed has authority over the interest rates and lending activities of the nation's most important banks. It was established by Congress in 1913 as a clearinghouse for adjusting the supply of money and credit to the needs of commerce and industry in different parts of the country. Many other agencies work to strengthen other parts of the economy, for example the Agriculture Department, which disseminates information on effective farming practices; the Transportation Department, which promotes economic growth by overseeing the nation's highway and air traffic systems; and the Commerce Department, whose Small Business Administration provides loans and technical assistance to small businesses across the country.

Another set of agencies promotes citizen well-being. The Department of Health and Human Services (HHS) includes the National Institutes of Health, which conducts cutting-edge biomedical research, the Food and Drug Administration (FDA), which monitors the safety and efficacy of human and veterinary drugs, cosmetics, and the nation's food supply, the Centers for Disease Control and Prevention (CDC), which protects public health and safety, and the Medicaid and Medicare programs, which provide health insurance to low-income and elderly Americans. The Department of Agriculture's Food and Nutrition Service administers the federal school-lunch program and Supplemental Nutrition

Assistance Program (SNAP, formerly known as food stamps). The Interior Department's National Park Service maintains natural areas for the public to enjoy. Yet other agencies, such as the Food and Drug Administration (FDA, within HHS); the Occupational Safety and Health Administration, within the Labor Department; and the Consumer Product Safety Commission, an independent regulatory commission, make rules to protect the public's health and welfare.

Location and Structure Matter Beyond giving a sense of the scope of federal bureaucratic activity, this partial listing of agencies and their responsibilities conveys a second point: the location within the government and the design of specific functions often reflect politicians' attempts to shape agency behavior and jurisdiction. Most agencies are created by Congress, which decides whether to locate them within the executive branch or outside of it. The president has greater control over organizations contained within executive departments, whereas independent agencies, such as the Securities and Exchange Commission (SEC), which oversees the security industry, including the nation's stock exchanges, have more freedom from both the president and Congress.

In creating agencies, Congress also decides whether they will be headed by one person (who reports to the president, if the agency is in the executive branch) or by a multiperson board. A board structure allows for bipartisan leadership. For example, no more than three of the SEC's five commissioners can be from the same political party. Boards may also have members with staggered terms of office, which reduces the power of any one president to name the entire agency leadership. Other structural features can increase independence as well, for example the fact that the president appoints SEC commissioners but cannot fire them. Independent agencies and regulatory commissions are meant to be relatively insulated from politics, hence their location outside of the executive departments, but escaping politics entirely is impossible. Since presidents appoint agency heads or commissioners, they may do so on the basis of party loyalty. Also, the budgets of most such agencies are proposed by the president and approved by Congress, and agencies must therefore be responsive to congressional oversight.

Finally, the location of agencies is not just a matter of control by the president and Congress but also can have policy consequences. For example, the location of the Occupational Safety and Health Administration in the Department of Labor rather than the Department of Health, Education, and Welfare (now HHS) meant that regulations on workplace hazards initially focused on mechanical hazards rather than biological ones.[16] The structure and design of bureaucratic agencies has implications both for control over their activities and for policy outputs.

Who Are Bureaucrats?

Explain civil service hiring, political appointments, and the use of federal contracting

The vast majority of bureaucrats are members of the "civil service" and work under the **merit system** created by the Pendleton Civil Service Reform Act of 1883. With this act, the federal government attempted to imitate business by requiring bureaucratic personnel to be qualified for the jobs to which they were hired. The goal was to end the "spoils system" that dominated federal hiring during the 1800s and awarded government jobs based on political connections and support for the political party

merit system a product of civil service reform, in which appointees to positions in public bureaucracies must objectively be deemed qualified for those positions

in office. The Pendleton Act replaced such patronage with a system of competitive examinations through which the very best candidates were to be hired for every job.

As a further safeguard against political interference, merit-system employees were given legal protection against being fired without a show of cause. Reasonable people may disagree about the value of such job security and how far it should extend in the civil service, but the objective of this job protection, cleansing bureaucracy of political interference while upgrading performance, cannot be disputed. The 1883 civil service reform was updated by the Civil Service Reform Act of 1978, which set up new processes to ensure that the recruitment and promotion of civil servants remained merit based rather than political. The 1978 act created the Merit Systems Protection Board to defend competitive and merit-based recruitment and promotion of civil servants from efforts to make these personnel policies more political. The Federal Labor Relations Authority was set up to administer collective bargaining and to address individual personnel grievances. A third new agency, the Office of Personnel Management, was created to manage the recruiting, testing, and training of federal employees, as well as their retirement system.[17]

political appointees the presidentially appointed layer of the bureaucracy on top of the civil service

At the higher levels of government agencies are several thousand **political appointees**, who fill posts as Cabinet secretaries and assistant secretaries and who are not part of the civil service. Of the 4,000-some political appointees, just over 1,000 require Senate confirmation. Many political appointees have ties to the president or the president's party—they may have worked on the president's campaign, for example—and serve to advance the president's agenda through agency action. Presidents also often use Cabinet secretary nominations—the handful of appointed positions at the very top of the bureaucracy, which are the most visible to the public—to make political statements or to send messages about their style of management or expectations for government. For example, President Obama, the nation's first Black president, nominated seven women and ten people of color to his first Cabinet. Both President George W. Bush (the first president with an MBA) and President Trump came from business backgrounds and nominated many business leaders to their Cabinets.

Senior Executive Service (SES) the top, presidentially appointed management rank for career civil servants

In addition to political appointees, in many agencies there are top executives who are members of the **Senior Executive Service (SES)**, a top management rank for career civil servants and sometimes individuals from outside of government. The SES was created by the 1978 civil service reform and intended to foster "public management" as a profession. For career bureaucrats, moving to the SES means losing their civil service protections, but it also provides an opportunity to pursue a top position. The SES also provides the president with an additional layer of high-level managers to select beyond the political appointees.

Appointing individuals to these 4,000 positions at the top of the bureaucracy is an enormous task. Newly elected presidents have a "transition team" that assists in the many tasks that must take place as the reins of government are handed from one president to the next. The appointments team, typically among the largest in the transition organization, begins working even before the election and continues through the inauguration; once the new administration is in place, appointments are handled by the White House Presidential Personnel Office. Often the goal has been to get Cabinet positions ready to announce between Thanksgiving and Christmas after the November general election, since those candidates need to prepare for Senate confirmation hearings, which begin in January. The Partnership for Public Service, a nonpartisan organization promoting effective government whose Center for Presidential Transition has worked with many incoming administrations,

Who Are Bureaucrats?

Bureaucrats are often stereotyped as being more concerned with procedure and forms than with helping people. But the reality is that the millions of executive branch employees that work in agencies in D.C. and around the country are essential to keeping America running smoothly. Bureaucrats manage everything from national security and veterans' services to providing help for needy families and ensuring that Americans have clean and safe drinking water. But who are bureaucrats? How is the bureaucracy similar to the American population? How is it different?

Executive Branch Employees, 2017

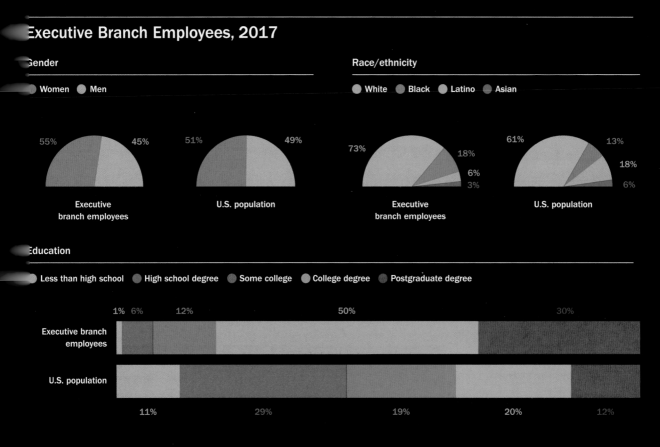

Gender

Women • Men

- Executive branch employees: 55% / 45%
- U.S. population: 51% / 49%

Race/ethnicity

White • Black • Latino • Asian

- Executive branch employees: 73% / 18% / 6% / 3%
- U.S. population: 61% / 13% / 18% / 6%

Education

Less than high school • High school degree • Some college • College degree • Postgraduate degree

- Executive branch employees: 1% / 6% / 12% / 50% / 30%
- U.S. population: 11% / 29% / 19% / 20% / 12%

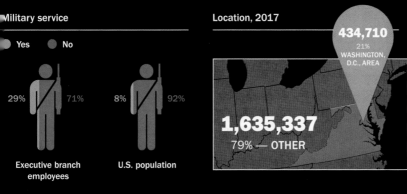

Military service

Yes • No

- Executive branch employees: 29% / 71%
- U.S. population: 8% / 92%

Location, 2017

434,710 — 21% WASHINGTON, D.C., AREA

1,635,337 — 79% — OTHER

FOR CRITICAL ANALYSIS

1. How do the demographics of the United States compare to the demographics of the bureaucracy? What do you think explains the differences?

2. With 2 million people working for the executive branch, mostly outside of the Washington, D.C., area, how can Congress and the president be sure that these employees are serving the public's interests?

NOTE: Numbers may not add up to 100 percent due to rounding. The category of "other" has been omitted.
SOURCES: American Community Survey 5-Year Estimates, www.factfinder.census.gov (accessed 6/15/18); Gallup, https://news.gallup.com (accessed 7/16/20).

including President Trump's, says that in order to enact the president's agenda, it is ideal to have the rest of the senior leadership in place by the August recess, about 200 days into the presidency, although not all presidential administrations have been able to achieve that goal.[18]

Compared to those in past administrations, appointments to senior leadership positions in the Trump administration have stood out for several reasons. Many of the political appointment slots in the bureaucracy remained unfilled well into President Trump's term. He also had a large number of agency leaders in "acting" positions. The Federal Vacancies Reform Act of 1998 (FVRA) allows a president to name officials to top posts on a temporary basis while awaiting Senate confirmation of permanent personnel. President Trump used the FVRA provisions in a more permanent manner and, as of summer 2019, two years into his presidency, had acting leaders as secretary of Defense, secretary of the Department of Homeland Security, UN ambassador, Immigration and Customs Enforcement (ICE) director, Federal Emergency Management Administration (FEMA) director, and Federal Aviation Administration (FAA) administrator, among others. "I sort of like 'acting,'" he said in January 2019. "It gives me more flexibility." Critics say that the seemingly permanent use of "acting" heads undermines congressional oversight of the executive branch by skirting the Senate confirmation process.[19]

Today's federal bureaucrats are distributed around the country—nearly four out of five federal employees work outside of Washington, D.C. Compared to private-sector workers, members of the full-time civilian federal workforce are more educated—more hold college and advanced degrees—and more likely to hold occupations in science, engineering, diplomacy, and other professional fields.[20] As the Who Are Americans? feature indicates, federal workers are more diverse than the private workforce in terms of race and ethnicity. Nearly one-third of them are veterans.

The size of the federal service has been a subject of political contention for decades. Particularly in the post–Watergate era of low trust in government, politicians from both parties, from Reagan to Clinton, have asserted that the federal government

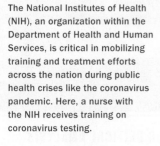

The National Institutes of Health (NIH), an organization within the Department of Health and Human Services, is critical in mobilizing training and treatment efforts across the nation during public health crises like the coronavirus pandemic. Here, a nurse with the NIH receives training on coronavirus testing.

is too big. Bill Clinton's vice president, Al Gore, headed a National Performance Review during the 1990s, which sought to reduce paperwork, improve communications across agencies, streamline government purchasing procedures, and cut the federal workforce; by 2000 the number of federal jobs had fallen by more than 400,000.[21] While President Barack Obama struck a different note in his first inaugural address, saying, "The question we ask today is not whether our government is too big or too small, but whether it works."[22] President Trump's first budget proposed major decreases in federal departments outside of Defense and Homeland Security. Under President Trump, some agencies were reorganized or had positions relocated, such as the relocation of two USDA research groups from Washington, D.C., to Kansas City, Missouri, which reduced the federal workforce when over half of the researchers declined to move.[23]

Despite fears of bureaucratic growth getting out of hand—or perhaps because of such fears—the federal service has shrunk in size both absolutely and relative to the total population. The number of civilian federal employees has fallen from a postwar peak of just over 3.0 million in the late 1980s to 2.8 million in 2019, while the number of military personnel has fallen from 3.6 million to 1.29 million over the same period.[24] As a percentage of the total workforce, federal employment has declined since the 1950s, as Figure 14.2 indicates.

FOR CRITICAL ANALYSIS

How has the size of the federal service changed over the past six decades? How are calls for smaller government related to the size of the federal service?

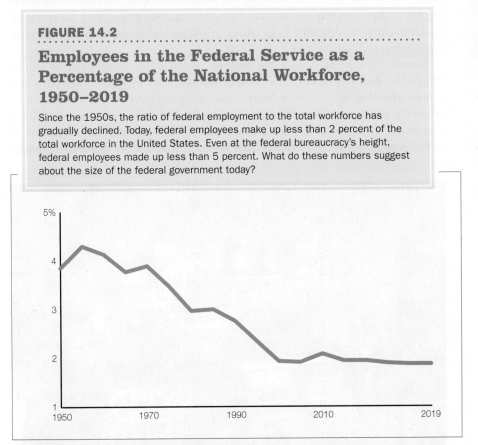

FIGURE 14.2

Employees in the Federal Service as a Percentage of the National Workforce, 1950–2019

Since the 1950s, the ratio of federal employment to the total workforce has gradually declined. Today, federal employees make up less than 2 percent of the total workforce in the United States. Even at the federal bureaucracy's height, federal employees made up less than 5 percent. What do these numbers suggest about the size of the federal government today?

SOURCES: Office of Personnel Management, "Executive Branch Civilian Employment Since 1940," www.opm.gov (accessed 4/24/20); United States Postal Service, "Number of Postal Employees Since 1926," https://about.usps.com/who-we-are /postal-history/employees-since-1926.pdf (accessed 4/24/20).

While the federal bureaucracy has decreased in size, both state and local government employment and government contracting have grown. State and local civil service employment has increased from about 6.5 percent of the country's workforce in 1950 to 13 percent in 2020.[25] Federal employment, in contrast, exceeded 6 percent of the workforce only during World War II, and almost all of that temporary growth was military.

The number of federal contractors has also grown, and exceeds the number of federal employees, as Figure 14.3 shows. Private contractors of all types provide an enormous range of goods and services, from nonprofit firms that run Head Start day-care centers, to military contractors that build fighter jets, to universities that conduct government-funded basic science research. **Privatization** downsizes the government in that the workers providing the service are no longer counted as part of the government bureaucracy—and pointing to a small federal government has appealed to both Republican and Democratic elected officials over the past several decades. Contracting may or may not lead to reduced costs, depending on the performance of the contractors and the competitiveness of the bidding process to begin with: while close to 60 percent of all competitive contracts were awarded competitively in 2015, fewer than half were between 2000 and 2011. And while contracting reduces the size of the federal workforce, it also requires a new role for government, as managerial expertise is needed to write contracts and oversee the private companies carrying out government work.[26] Critics of contracting worry that oversight and accountability are insufficient and that the emphasis on contracting has detracted from efforts to recruit and retain talented employees in the career civil service itself.[27]

Because contracting is such big business, it has become the focus of reform efforts. For example, in 2013 the national security leaks by Edward Snowden and a mass shooting at a U.S. military base—both by government contractors—prompted Congress to pass legislation calling for a review of contractors' security clearances.[28] In 2016 the Obama Department of Justice decided to end the use of private prisons for federal inmates after an audit found more safety and security

privatization the process by which a formerly public service becomes a service provided by a private company but paid for by the government

FOR CRITICAL ANALYSIS

Private firms play a significant role in providing government services, including both internal and external security. What are the advantages and disadvantages of relying on private firms to provide essential services? Can government provide adequate oversight of these private companies?

One strategy to carry out the tasks of government is privatization. The U.S. military and Department of Defense contract many services to companies such as Booz Allen Hamilton, which provides systems for personnel management, program support, and assessment, among other services.

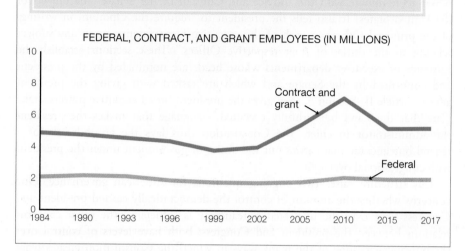

FIGURE 14.3

Outsourcing the Government

The number of contractors employed by the federal government has increased, especially since September 11, 2001. Does contracting out government jobs save money, or does it create problems of oversight and accountability? Or both?

FEDERAL, CONTRACT, AND GRANT EMPLOYEES (IN MILLIONS)

Contract and grant

Federal

1984　1990　1993　1996　1999　2002　2005　2010　2015　2017

Note: Federal employment full-time equivalents; excludes Post Office employees (503,000 in 2017).
SOURCE: Paul Light, *The Government-Industrial Complex* (New York: Oxford University Press, 2019), Table 2.1.

problems than in government-run facilities.[29] And federal contracts can become the focus of other administration goals: in 2015 President Obama signed an executive order compelling contractors to pay a $10.10 minimum wage ($10.80 as of 2020) and to provide paid sick leave for their employees.[30] Those regulations continue to stand, but in 2017, President Trump signed legislation rolling back several other Obama contracting regulations, including a rule barring companies from receiving a federal contract if they had violated labor, wage, or workplace-safety rules.[31]

Managing the Bureaucracy

Explain how the president, Congress, and the judiciary try to manage the bureaucracy

By their very nature, bureaucracies pose challenges to democratic governance. Although they provide the expertise needed to implement the public will, they can also become entrenched organizations that serve their own interests. As political scientist William Howell has noted, "Bureaucrats enjoy substantial discretion by virtue of their expertise about policy matters, their networks of relationships with interest groups and politicians, and the fact that much of their labor takes place well beyond the watchful eyes of elected officials."[32] The challenge is to take advantage of the bureaucracy's strengths while making it more accountable to the demands of democratic politics and representative government. Because the bureaucracy is unelected but plays such an important role in conducting policy, it is crucial that democratically elected officials such as the president and Congress exercise some control over agency policy making.

The word *bureaucracy* does not appear in the Constitution, but the bureaucracy has constitutional roots nonetheless. Several provisions imply the existence of executive departments as well as the control that elected officials—chiefly the president and Congress—have over them. Article II, Section 2, gives the president the power to nominate with the "Advice and Consent of the Senate" the officers of the United States. It also tells the president to "require the Opinion, in writing, of the principal Officer in each of the executive Departments, upon any subject relating to the duties of their respective Offices." These sections establish the existence of executive departments whose heads are nominated by the president and confirmed by the Senate and which are tasked with giving the president advice. Article II, Section 3, then gives the president broad executive powers: "take Care that the Laws be faithfully executed," language that makes the president the administrator in chief. The Constitution thus lays the groundwork for a federal bureaucracy that carries out the duties of government under the president with congressional oversight.

This structure raises two ongoing questions for American governance. One concerns whether the amount of control the democratically elected president and Congress have over the unelected bureaucracy is sufficient. The other concerns relations between the president and Congress: both have levers of control over the bureaucracy—one of the many ways in which the Constitution creates what Richard Neustadt termed "separated institutions sharing powers"[33]—and this framework ensures that the president and Congress will disagree at times about bureaucratic action. Much of the controversy that we observe in federal government is a result of the push-and-pull between the president and Congress that the constitutional framework makes inevitable.

THE PRESIDENT AS CHIEF EXECUTIVE

The Constitution charges the president with seeing that the laws are faithfully executed. The president heads the federal government, which is the largest employer in the country and the largest purchaser of goods and services in the world.[34] As the CEO of this enormous organization, the president may have goals associated with both management (striving for efficiency) and control (shaping policy outcomes). Presidents have several tools at their disposal.

One major tool of bureaucratic control that presidents possess is appointment power over the top layer of the executive branch—the political appointees atop the career civil service. Presidents have an incentive to appoint officials who are loyal to them and who they believe are likely to pursue their policy agendas. And many such appointments require Senate approval, as the Constitution gives both the president and the Congress mechanisms for controlling the bureaucracy. The Senate rarely rejects nominees; more commonly, if it is clear that Senate support is weak, a president will withdraw a nominee before the confirmation vote. For example, Andrew Puzder, the CEO of the parent company of Hardee's and Carl's Jr., withdrew his nomination to be President Trump's secretary of labor after liberals criticized his treatment of fast-food workers and conservatives criticized his employment of an undocumented immigrant as his housekeeper.[35] Over time, the number of appointed positions has grown, increasing presidential influence over many agencies. The increased penetration of political appointees into more

After the federal budget is approved, it must be printed. Here, acting director of the Office of Management and Budget Russ Vought presses "start" on the printer.

agencies is one indicator of increased power of the president over Congress throughout the last few decades.[36]

Another instrument of presidential control over the bureaucracy is the Executive Office of the President (EOP). The EOP was established during the presidency of Franklin Roosevelt, when the rapid growth of the national government led a Committee on Administrative Management to note in 1937, "The president needs help." The EOP includes key staffs reporting directly to the president on budgetary, military, and economic policies, such as the National Security Council and the Council of Economic Advisers. The EOP is usually considered the component of the bureaucracy most responsive to the presidency because it has the highest share of political appointees and because Congress gives the president greater control over its structure.[37]

One of the most important EOP agencies is the **Office of Management and Budget (OMB)**, which Roosevelt moved from the Treasury Department to the EOP, giving him more direct control over the federal budget and federal regulations. All federal rules go through OMB, as previously noted. OMB also collects the budgets for all government agencies, allowing presidents to emphasize their own priorities and policy goals in the federal budget submitted annually to Congress. The centralization of these regulatory and budgetary functions is another indicator of increased presidential power relative to Congress.

Presidents also try to influence where agencies are located. They may wish to place agencies within the executive departments, which maximizes presidential control over agency leadership, budgets, and policy direction (in contrast, interest groups, and members of Congress trying to be responsive to interest groups to maximize their re-election chances, may wish agencies to be independent so as to minimize presidential control).[38] Presidents can also choose to elevate an agency to Cabinet status, which means that the head of the agency joins the secretaries of the 15 executive departments in the president's Cabinet, a way for the president to signal the importance of that issue area.

In addition to making political appointments at the top of the bureaucracy, presidents may also appoint "policy czars" with responsibilities for addressing a

Office of Management and Budget (OMB) the agency in the Executive Office of the President with control over the federal budget and regulations

specific policy need, often working across agencies. President Roosevelt was the first to appoint policy czars; Presidents Bush and Obama each had dozens in their administrations. President Trump has not tended to use czars, having a leaner presidential staff, although he did appoint a coronavirus pandemic task force in late January 2020, headed first by Health and Human Services Secretary Alex Azar and later by Vice President Mike Pence.[39] Presidents often appoint czars to signal responsiveness to some acute policy problem. There have been multiple illicit-drug czars, several AIDS czars, a car czar (who managed the auto industry bailout during the Great Recession), an Ebola czar who managed the response to an outbreak in 2014, an Asian carp czar, cybersecurity czars, and so on. These advisers are more firmly under presidential control, as they report directly to the president and do not require Senate confirmation. Critics worry about the effectiveness of czars, as they do not have authority over budgets or personnel and have to rely on the formal departments and agencies to act.[40]

Although the president is ostensibly in charge of the federal bureaucracy and has the tools of control just discussed, influence over the bureaucracy remains a challenge. Even though presidents nominate their own department secretaries, and try to select like-minded individuals, sometimes those officials pursue their own agendas, or become advocates for the agency itself rather than the president's agenda. Sometimes presidential appointees turn out to be poor managers, and their agency is unable to execute its duties optimally.[41] Interest groups also have ongoing relationships with agencies and may try to shape agency agendas, interfering with presidential preferences (some critics say, for example, that the pharmaceutical industry has too much influence over its regulatory agency, the Food and Drug Administration).[42] And the president is in competition with Congress for control of the bureaucracy: while Congress wants to see the laws it writes executed effectively, it also tries to make bureaucratic action more transparent and to diminish presidential control. One reason that bureaucratic action may seem inefficient is that the bureaucracy answers to many players, not just the president.

CONGRESSIONAL CONTROL

The Constitution gives Congress several tools of control over the bureaucracy as it interprets and implements laws the Congress has passed. Most important, Congress approves agencies' funding, as most require annual budget appropriations to operate. At hearings on appropriations, members of Congress can evaluate agency performance and may reduce funding if they are not satisfied. Agencies wish to avoid this fate and so take congressional opinion—and by extension public opinion—into account as they implement programs. As we have seen, an additional way in which the Constitution grants power to both Congress and the president over the bureaucracy is the requirement that the Senate approve presidential nominations to the top levels of the executive agencies.

Like the president, Congress can change the location of agencies or their structure, creating new ones or reorganizing policy responsibilities across existing agencies in an effort to shape agency behavior or to reduce presidential control. For example, Congress may choose to place a regulatory body or commission outside of the 15 executive departments. Or it can designate a multimember board rather than a single person to head an agency, which limits presidential control by allowing for a partisan balance requirement (members have to come from both parties,

Apply for a Federal Job

ANTHONY MARUCCI, the director of communications at the Office of Personnel Management

The federal government employs a couple of million people, mostly outside of Washington, D.C. Now that you see the wide variety of responsibilities the federal government carries out, perhaps you would like to apply your skills and knowledge to an issue that you care about and that the federal government tackles. Anthony Marucci gave us these tips to getting a job in the federal government:

1 **Where can I look for a job in the federal government?** Look at USAJobs (www.usajobs.gov), the official federal government portal. You can also look at the "employment" or "careers" section of any government agency website.

2 **Can I find a job in the federal government outside of Washington, D.C.?** Yes. You should set up a profile on USAJobs, where you can add work preferences such as desired work location. This and other preferences you include on your profile will refine and improve your results when searching for jobs on USAJobs.

3 **How can I tell if I'm qualified?** Read the entire job announcement and focus on the "critical information" in three key sections: Duties and Qualifications, How to Apply, and How You Will Be Evaluated. You will be able to see the level and amount of experience, education, and training needed.

4 **What should I include on my résumé?** Show how your skills and experiences meet the qualifications and requirements listed in the job announcement in order to be considered. List your experiences, beginning with the most recent, and include dates, hours, level of experience, and examples of your activities and accomplishments. The best examples use numbers to highlight your accomplishments, such as "Managed a student organization budget of more than $7,000" or "Wrote 25 news releases in a three-week period under daily deadlines." Also, provide greater detail for experiences that are relevant to the job for which you are applying. And be sure to use the key terms in the job listing: if the qualifications section says you need experience with MS Project you need to use the words "MS Project" in your résumé. You should customize your résumé for each job to which you apply.

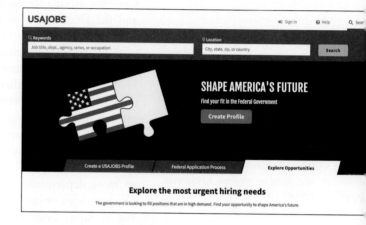

5 **Will I have to take a civil service exam?** Federal government hiring in the civil service positions in the executive branch, with some exceptions, must be done through a competitive process. This typically means an evaluation of the individual's education and experience, and/or an evaluation of other attributes necessary for successful performance in the position to be filled. In some cases the process may also consist of a written test.

6 **Can I apply for more than one position?** Yes, you can apply for multiple jobs at USAJobs, but note that you must apply for each under the specific job announcement. One key thing to remember (and this is likely true for any job to which you apply): hiring agencies often receive dozens or even hundreds of résumés for certain positions, so you want to look at your résumé and ask, "Can a hiring manager see my main credentials within 10 to 15 seconds? Does critical information jump off the page? Do I effectively sell myself on the top quarter of the first page?" Working for the federal government can be rewarding. As with pursuing any job, it can take time. So if you do apply, be patient and persistent. Best of luck!

not just the president's), or staggered terms of office (so that a president cannot replace all board members at once). Fixed terms of office, especially long ones, also diminish presidential control (members of the Board of Governors of the Fed serve 14-year terms, for example, far longer than a president). And one of the most important ways Congress can check presidential control of the bureaucracy is by limiting the president's ability to *remove* agency officials. In many instances the congressional statutes creating or reorganizing agencies do not allow presidents to remove officials except "for cause," such as neglect of duty or wrongdoing, not merely for policy disagreements.

Congress can also make political or policy statements with its organizational choices. For example, in 1988 Congress created the Department of Veterans Affairs, elevating the Veterans Administration into the 15th executive department. Likewise, Congress first created the Department of Health, Education, and Welfare in 1953. Then, 25 years later, during the Carter administration, the Democrat-led Congress divided the agency into the Department of Health and Human Services and the Department of Education to underscore the federal role in education, a move that many Republicans, who wished education to remain the province of state and local governments, opposed. When Congress placed the Transportation Security Administration, in charge of airport security, in the Department of Homeland Security rather than the Department of Transportation, it signaled that domestic security concerns were to be a more central aspect of the administration's mission than facilitating transportation, as those who have stood in interminable TSA lines at airports can attest.[43]

Congress can also hold the bureaucracy accountable through **oversight**. Congressional committees and subcommittees have jurisdictions roughly parallel to one or more departments and agencies in the executive branch, and members of Congress who sit on these committees can develop expertise in these policy areas. For example, both the House and Senate have Agriculture Committees and subcommittees that oversee the Department of Agriculture.

The most visible indication of Congress's oversight efforts is the use of public hearings, before which bureaucrats and other witnesses are summoned to discuss and defend agency budgets and past decisions. Congress can also pass laws requiring agencies to submit regular reports on their activities and can create advisory committees to make recommendations to agencies and to help Congress oversee them. For example, the Food and Drug Administration (FDA) has several dozen advisory committees consisting of physicians, scientists, statisticians, pharmaceutical industry representatives, and members of the public, including an FDA Patient Representative, which provide independent advice on scientific and policy questions concerning the safety and effectiveness of new medical and drug therapies.[44]

In recent years, there appears to be less **"police patrol" oversight**—regular or even anticipatory hearings on agency operations—and more **"fire alarm" oversight** prompted by media attention or advocacy group complaints. For example, consumer outrage prompted the 2016 inquiry by the House Oversight and Government Reform Committee into a 500 percent price hike on EpiPens, used to treat severe allergic reactions.[45] One dilemma for Congress is that overseeing the bureaucracy as it implements the laws Congress wrote takes time away from Congress's activities making new laws.

As a result, Congress has created additional sources of oversight. The Inspector General Act of 1978 established **inspectors general (IGs)**, which are nonpartisan,

oversight the effort by Congress, through hearings, investigations, and other techniques, to exercise control over the activities of executive agencies

"police patrol" oversight regular or even preemptive congressional hearings on bureaucratic agency operations

"fire alarm" oversight episodic, as-needed congressional hearings on bureaucratic agency operations, usually prompted by media attention or advocacy group complaints

inspectors general (IGs) independent audit organizations located in most federal agencies

EpiPens are lifesaving tools for those who suffer from allergies to various foods or animals. After the cost of EpiPens surged, EpiPen CEO Heather Bresch was called to testify before Congress to report on the soaring prices.

independent organizations now located in most agencies, which investigate agency activities on Congress's behalf. IGs audit agency operations to uncover cases of waste, fraud, or misconduct. They alert agency heads of any severe problems, and the agency head must then send the IG's report, along with comments and corrective plans, to Congress. Inspectors general of the Cabinet-level agencies are appointed by the president and approved by the Senate, another example of shared control over the bureaucracy; in other federal agencies, the agency head appoints the IG. In both cases, agency heads cannot interfere with IG audits or investigations. On several occasions, President Trump exerted control over inspectors general. For example, during the coronavirus pandemic, he replaced a deputy inspector general in HHS whose report revealed extensive supply shortages at hospitals, and he blocked a Defense Department inspector general from heading a new Pandemic Response Accountability Committee to oversee the government's coronavirus relief spending. Critics alleged that while the president did have the authority to remove these officials, he did so in an effort to avoid transparency and Congressional oversight.[46]

Another source of oversight involves the three large agencies Congress created for itself to research the executive branch: the Government Accountability Office (GAO), the Congressional Research Service, and the Congressional Budget Office. These organizations provide information independent from what Congress gets from the executive branch through hearings and other communications.[47] The GAO is the nation's "supreme audit institution," providing Congress with information about how tax dollars are spent and how the government could be made more efficient.[48] The Congressional Research Service (CRS), part of the Library of Congress, provides expert analysis to congressional committees and members of Congress on policy issues. The CRS responds to inquiries from individual congresspeople; creates tailored memos, briefings, and consultations; runs seminars and workshops; and provides congressional testimony.[49] And the Congressional Budget Office provides independent analyses of budgetary and economic issues to assist Congress in its budget process, for example estimating the cost of proposed legislation.[50]

PRESIDENTIAL–CONGRESSIONAL STRUGGLE FOR BUREAUCRATIC CONTROL: A CASE STUDY

A look at the birth of a new agency, the Consumer Financial Protection Bureau (CFPB), helps illustrate the struggle between the president and Congress over the bureaucracy. The financial crisis that began in 2007 had its roots in the collapse of the housing market. Many borrowers had taken on home mortgages that were difficult to understand and unaffordable, and when they could no longer pay, they lost their homes to foreclosure, which in turn caused their neighbors' home values to fall. Critics of this system believed there were insufficient consumer protections in place and proposed creating the CFPB. This new agency would address consumer complaints and regulate banks, credit unions, payday lenders, debt collectors, and other firms that provide consumer financial products and services such as mortgages, credit cards, student loans, and so on. In July 2010, Congress passed and President Obama signed the Dodd-Frank Wall Street Reform and Consumer Protection Act, which imposed new banking regulations in the aftermath of the financial crisis and which also created the CFPB.[51]

President Obama and congressional Republicans disagreed about the structure, funding, and location of the CFPB. The disagreements were partly partisan— Democrats were more concerned with the adequacy of consumer protections, Republicans were more concerned with government overregulation—but also institutional. The 2010 legislation made the CFPB an independent agency located inside the Federal Reserve System, with automatic funding based on a fixed percentage of the Fed's operating expenses and with a single director appointed by the president with the consent of the Senate. Critics, including many congressional Republicans, argued that the CFPB's funding should be annually appropriated by Congress instead, obviously increasing Congress's influence over the agency, and that it should be headed by a multimember board rather than a single person, diminishing any president's influence over the agency's leadership. Proponents argued that the automatic funding and the location inside the Fed, which is already an independent institution, were necessary to give the CFPB independence from political forces and the muscle it needed to help consumers confronting powerful financial institutions. They felt Senate consent for the director was a sufficient check on the president's influence.

Disagreements over the CFPB's design have continued ever since. The idea for the agency came from Massachusetts senator and 2020 Democratic presidential candidate Elizabeth Warren, back when she was a law professor studying bankruptcy. President Obama had planned to appoint her the first head of the agency but, in the face of Republican opposition, selected former Ohio attorney general and Ohio treasurer Richard Cordray instead. But that nomination was held up as well by Senate Republicans, who continued to urge a multimember board structure. (Cordray became head in a recess appointment.) Later, President Trump appointed the head of the Office of Management and Budget, Mick Mulvaney, as the acting head of the agency. As a congressman, Mulvaney had proposed legislation eliminating the CFPB. After some members of the CFPB's consumer advisory board criticized him in June 2018, Mulvaney had the entire 25-member board removed.

Controversy continued in a suit brought by the Selia law firm of California, which challenged the CFPB's power to investigate its debt relief services, arguing that the agency director's insulation from presidential control was unconstitutional. In 2020,

FOR CRITICAL ANALYSIS

Through elected officials (the president and Congress), the public can achieve some control over the bureaucracy. What are the relative advantages and disadvantages of presidential and congressional control of the bureaucracy?

The Consumer Financial Protection Bureau is an agency created by President Obama under the Department of the Treasury. Here, President Obama, with Timothy Geithner, Treasury secretary at the time, nominates Elizabeth Warren as its head (although congressional Republicans later blocked the nomination).

the Supreme Court agreed in part, declaring the CFPB itself constitutional but also increasing the president's influence and decreasing Congress's by ruling that the president has the power to fire the CFPB director at will, not just for cause. Supporters of the CFPB worried that the ruling would further politicize the agency since the head would now serve at the pleasure of a president, like a cabinet member.[52]

JUDICIAL OVERSIGHT

The role of elected officials in overseeing the bureaucracy—the president heading the executive branch, Congress evaluating its performance and controlling its funding—is an important pathway by which the public can hold the bureaucracy accountable. The third branch of government serves an important role as well. The bureaucracy's decisions are subject to judicial review; the *Marbury v. Madison* decision in 1803 posited that the Supreme Court has final authority to judge the constitutionality of executive actions, whether taken by the president or the bureaucracy. The courts settle disputes between Congress and executive agencies about the interpretations of laws. The courts also monitor the implementation of laws by creating an arena in which individuals or groups who are negatively affected by a regulation or program can bring lawsuits.

WHISTLEBLOWING

Sometimes a form of control comes from within bureaucratic agencies themselves. **Whistleblowers** are federal employees who report wrongdoing within agencies. Congress passed the Whistleblower Protection Act in 1989 to protect those reporting mismanagement or corruption from punishment by their colleagues or superiors. In August 2019 a whistleblower from the U.S. intelligence community filed a complaint about a phone call between President Trump and the president of Ukraine in which the whistleblower feared that the president was "using the power of his office to solicit interference from a foreign country in the 2020 U.S. election," including "pressuring a foreign country to investigate one of the president's main domestic

whistleblowers federal employees who report wrongdoing in federal agencies

political rivals," Joe Biden and his son Hunter Biden.[53] The whistleblower complaint prompted an impeachment investigation by the House Democrats that began in fall 2019.

CITIZEN OVERSIGHT

The Freedom of Information Act of 1966 (FOIA) provides ordinary citizens and journalists the right to request records from any federal agency. Congress's intent in passing the law was to increase bureaucratic transparency and to create another mechanism of executive branch oversight.[54] Agencies must comply with the requests unless they fall under one of nine exemptions, which concern issues such as personal privacy, national security, or law enforcement, or unless disclosure of the information is prohibited by another federal law. Agencies are required by law to produce records within 20 days, but frequently there are backlogs. Agencies can also decide to disclose portions rather than entire records.

FOIA requests can sometimes prompt congressional oversight and investigation when agency misbehavior is revealed. At the end of the Obama administration, in early 2017, a *USA Today* story revealed that the Centers for Disease Control and Prevention (CDC), an agency within the Department of Health and Human Services that conducts research and provides information to protect people from health threats, had tried to keep secret a series of accidents from 2013 to 2015 involving dangerous pathogens such as anthrax and Ebola. The article was based on heavily redacted lab incident reports that a reporter had obtained through a FOIA request. After the article was published, the House Committee on Energy and Commerce sent a letter to the director of the CDC stating that "the details in the article seem to indicate that most, if not all, of these incidents were not disclosed to the Committee," and demanding that the CDC turn over the unredacted reports.[55]

THE DIFFICULTIES OF BUREAUCRATIC CONTROL

Controlling the bureaucracy is difficult. On the one hand, having a federal branch populated by experts who implement laws and issue regulations in an impartial, uniform manner, with minimal political interference, is necessary to make the government operate as efficiently and responsibly as possible. On the other hand, bureaucrats may pursue their own goals rather than those of the president, who oversees the bureaucracy, or Congress, which writes the laws the bureaucracy implements. The tools of control are imperfect.

In addition, there are sometimes outright bureaucratic failures. In 2014 a waiting-list scandal rocked the Veterans Health Administration, the organization within the Veterans Administration that provides health care to military veterans. Some VHA hospitals that had not met the target of providing appointments for veterans within 14 days had created unofficial lists to make their waiting times look better. A VA audit and FBI investigation found that over 120,000 veterans were left waiting or never got appointments. In response, Veterans Administration Secretary Eric Shinseki resigned, and Congress passed and President Obama signed legislation that added funding, allowed some veterans to get private health care at government expense, and gave the VA secretary increased authority to fire poorly performing managers.[56]

Bureaucracies can also be subject to **regulatory capture**. This occurs when an agency, rather than acting in the public interest, becomes too favorable toward the organized interests or corporations it is supposed to be regulating. Critics point to the two

regulatory capture a form of government failure in which regulatory agencies become too sympathetic to interests or businesses they are supposed to regulate

737 Max airliner crashes in 2018 and 2019, which killed nearly 400 people, as a classic example of regulatory capture, in which the Federal Aviation Administration allowed the Boeing Corporation to handle key aspects of safety assessments needed to get the new airliner model approved for commercial service. The FAA approved Boeing's safety analysis, which was later revealed to have critical lapses.[57]

Due to failure or capture, or a desire for more control or better performance, bureaucratic reorganization is a recurring phenomenon in American government. Many presidents have proposed or enacted broad-based reorganization schemes to enhance their control or to increase bureaucratic efficiency. More specific reforms have often been enacted in response to bureaucratic failures. The September 11, 2001, terrorist attacks not only prompted the creation of the Department of Homeland Security in 2002, as we have seen, but also the creation of the Office of the Director of National Intelligence (DNI) in 2004. With that reform, the DNI became the head of the intelligence community, a role previously played by the director of the CIA. Similarly, both the savings-and-loan crisis of the 1980s and the financial crisis of 2007–09 prompted reorganized or new entities regulating the financial industry. And the Deepwater Horizon Gulf oil spill prompted reorganization in the Department of the Interior. Sometimes reorganization schemes aim at the elimination of agencies and programs, but typically the functions are absorbed by some other part of the bureaucracy, as Congress can be reluctant to "give up" a program or responsibility once established.[58]

Bureaucracy: What Do You Think?

Americans' views about the federal government bureaucracy present something of a paradox. On the one hand, the public expresses dislike for "big government," exemplified by bureaucracy. From this perspective, the federal government is too large, inherently wasteful, and at odds with individual freedom. On the other hand, Americans support many government programs and have high expectations for government. One consequence of these divergent views can be that bureaucracies try to maximize one benefit for citizens but in doing so undermine others. As we saw in the chapter opener, the FDA put up bureaucratic hurdles for public health labs trying to develop their own tests for the coronavirus, after the CDC's tests failed. In ordinary times, such processes are intended to ensure patient safety. But in a public health emergency, they endangered the lives of Americans as the virus spread unabated.

★ Some argue that Americans' liberties are threatened when the bureaucracy grows too large, while others contend that a bureaucracy with too few resources is the real threat. What do you think Helen Chu, featured at the start of the chapter, would say?

★ Are there ways in which you have benefitted from bureaucratic action, or been harmed by it? What types of bureaucratic activity are most noticeable to you, and what types are most hidden?

★ What kinds of reforms would make the bureaucracy more accountable to the public?

★ STUDY GUIDE ★

What Is the Federal Bureaucracy?

Bureaucracy is defined as the complex structure of offices, tasks, rules, and principles of organization that private and public organizations use to coordinate the work of their personnel. Bureaucrats in the federal government implement and enforce laws, create rules and regulations, and develop innovative programs. As institutions designed with policy implementation in mind, bureaucracies are also mission oriented, staffed with policy-specific experts, and characterized by hierarchy. The federal executive branch is composed of executive departments and independent agencies, the latter of which include administrations, independent regulatory commissions, and government corporations.

Key Terms

bureaucracy (p. 511)

implementation (p. 512)

principal-agent problem (p. 516)

executive departments (p. 517)

independent regulatory commission (p. 518)

government corporation (p. 518)

Practice Quiz

1. Which of the following statements about Congress and the bureaucracy is *not* true?
   a) Bureaucracies employ people who have much more specialized expertise in specific policy areas than do members of Congress.
   b) Members of Congress often prefer to delegate politically difficult decision-making to bureaucrats.
   c) While Congress is responsible for making laws, the bureaucracy is responsible for putting laws into effect.
   d) Congress banned rule making by the federal bureaucracy in 1995.
   e) Congress relies heavily on bureaucratic flexibility in implementing laws because updating legislation can take many years and bureaucrats can ensure that laws are administered in ways that take new conditions into account.

2. Which of the following is an example of a government corporation?
   a) National Aeronautics and Space Administration
   b) Amtrak
   c) Federal Bureau of Investigation
   d) Environmental Protection Agency
   e) Department of Justice

3. If Congress wants to create an agency with independent, bipartisan leadership, it will likely
   a) locate the agency within the executive branch.
   b) refrain from exercising its oversight powers on the agency.
   c) install a multiperson board at the head of the agency.
   d) provide for the election, rather than the appointment, of the agency's leadership.
   e) allow the president to decide how the agency should be organized.

Who Are Bureaucrats?

> **Explain civil service hiring, political appointments, and the use of federal contracting (pp. 521–27)**

The bureaucracy is made up of both political appointees and civil servants. The majority of bureaucrats—civil servants—are hired according to a merit system that is meant to safeguard the bureaucracy against political interference. Appointees to positions at the top of the bureaucracy often have ties to the president or the president's party. Though the size of the bureaucracy is perennially a subject of political contention, federal employment has shrunk since the 1950s. Increasingly, private contractors, rather than federal bureaucrats, have a hand in providing government goods and services.

Key Terms

merit system (p. 521)

political appointees (p. 522)

Senior Executive Service (SES) (p. 522)

privatization (p. 526)

Practice Quiz

4. The Pendleton Civil Service Reform Act of 1883 required that bureaucratic personnel
   a) pledge an oath of loyalty to the United States.
   b) register as independents rather than as members of an organized political party.
   c) be qualified for the job to which they were appointed.
   d) serve for no more than 10 years.
   e) serve for no fewer than 10 years.

5. Federal bureaucrats are
   a) more likely to work in Washington, D.C., than anywhere else in the country.
   b) less likely to be female than private-sector workers.
   c) more racially and ethnically diverse than the private-sector workforce.
   d) less educated than the private-sector workforce.
   e) less likely to hold occupations in science, engineering, diplomacy, and other professional fields than the private-sector workforce.

6. Which president's administration instituted the National Performance Review?
   a) Richard Nixon
   b) Lyndon Johnson
   c) Jimmy Carter
   d) Bill Clinton
   e) George W. Bush

7. Which of the following best describes the size of the federal service?
   a) The size of the federal service has grown exponentially over the last 35 years.
   b) The military workforce is greater in size than the civilian federal workforce.
   c) As a percentage of the total workforce, federal employment has declined since 1950.
   d) The federal service has employed at least 15 percent of the American workforce every year since 1950.
   e) The federal service was eliminated during the 1990s in order to hire more state government employees.

8. The number of federal contractors _____ the number of federal employees.
   a) exceeds
   b) is slightly less than
   c) is significantly less than
   d) is roughly the same as
   e) is projected to soon overtake

Managing the Bureaucracy

Explain how the president, Congress, and the judiciary try to manage the bureaucracy (pp. 527–37)

Although federal bureaucratic agencies provide the expertise needed to implement the public will, they can also become entrenched organizations that serve their own interests. To ensure that the bureaucracy remains accountable, elected officials such as the president and Congress exercise some control over agency policy making. Presidents have several powerful tools at their disposal, including high-level appointment power, the Executive Office of the President, and influence over agencies' locations. Congress also exerts influence over bureaucratic behavior, by approving agency funding, changing the location or structure of agencies, and engaging in vigorous oversight. The federal courts play an important role in monitoring and interpreting bureaucratic actions. Ordinary citizens and bureaucrats themselves may also shed light on bureaucratic misconduct.

Key Terms

Office of Management and Budget (OMB) (p. 529)

oversight (p. 532)

"police patrol" oversight (p. 532)

"fire alarm" oversight (p. 532)

inspectors general (IGs) (p. 532)

whistleblowers (p. 535)

regulatory capture (p. 536)

Practice Quiz

9. The concept of *oversight* refers to the effort made by
   a) Congress to make executive agencies accountable for their actions.
   b) the president to make executive agencies accountable for their actions.
   c) the president to make Congress accountable for its actions.
   d) the courts to make executive agencies accountable for their actions.
   e) the states to make the executive branch accountable for its actions.

10. "Police patrol" oversight refers to
   a) hearings conducted by the FBI to investigate lawbreaking by members of Congress.
   b) any congressional hearings related to state or local law-enforcement agencies.
   c) episodic, as-needed congressional hearings on bureaucratic agency operations, usually prompted by media attention or advocacy group complaints.
   d) regular or even anticipatory congressional hearings on agency operations.
   e) any congressional hearings related to federal law-enforcement agencies.

11. Which of the following agencies were created to give Congress independent information about matters related to the executive branch?
   a) Government Accountability Office, Congressional Research Service, Congressional Budget Office
   b) Department of Justice, Department of the Interior, Department of the Treasury
   c) Congressional Oversight Organization, Bureau of Government Performance, National Performance Review Association
   d) Office of Management and Budget, Council of Economic Advisers, Oversight and Government Reform
   e) Government Accountability Office, National Performance Review, Troubled Asset Relief Program

12. Which act provides ordinary citizens and journalists the right to request records from any federal agency?
   a) Hatch Act of 1939
   b) Administrative Procedure Act of 1946
   c) Freedom of Information Act of 1966
   d) Civil Service Reform Act of 1978
   e) Whistleblower Protection Act of 1989

13. What is regulatory capture?
   a) when Congress uses its oversight powers to block agencies from creating regulations
   b) when an executive department assumes control over an agency that is outside of its traditional jurisdiction
   c) when regulations get stuck in the notice-and-comment stage for over a year
   d) when Congress refuses to confirm the president's nominees to high-level bureaucratic offices
   e) when an agency becomes too favorable toward the organized interests or corporations it is supposed to be regulating

The Federal Courts

WHAT GOVERNMENT DOES AND WHY IT MATTERS Mark Janus worked for the Illinois Department of Healthcare and Family Services as a child-support specialist. He is not a member of the union representing many public-sector workers in the state, the American Federation of State, County, and Municipal Employees (AFSCME). Nonetheless, he is required to pay a "fair-share" fee to the union on the grounds that nonmembers benefit from the union's bargaining activities over issues such as pay and benefits. Nonmembers do not have to contribute to the union's political activities, such as endorsements of political candidates.[1]

Janus argues, however, that *all* activity that public-sector unions engage in is inherently political. In particular, he disagrees with the union's bargaining for increased benefits when Illinois was facing a budget crisis due in part to mismanagement of the state pension program. "The union's fight is not my fight," he says. "For years it supported politicians who put the state into its current budget and pension crises. . . . That's not public service." He believes that being forced to pay a fee that supports the union's activities violates his First Amendment rights.

His case went to the Supreme Court, which heard oral arguments in 2018. Janus's lawsuit challenged

Although the Supreme Court is often viewed as the least political of the three branches, its rulings touch on major political issues that affect Americans in many ways. Here, Mark Janus (left) celebrates with supporters after winning his Supreme Court case, which could have a profound effect on how unions operate.

a 1977 case, *Abood v. Detroit Board of Education*, in which the Court allowed state and local governments to require public employees to pay union fees, a practice in 22 states. The Court almost overturned *Abood* in 2015 in a case in which a California teacher sued the local teachers' union over such fees. But after Justice Antonin Scalia died in 2016, the Court split 4–4 in the California case.[2]

President Barack Obama nominated Merrick Garland to replace Scalia, but the Republican-controlled Senate took no action on the nomination in the hope, which was fulfilled, of a Republican victory in the 2016 presidential election. After taking

office in 2017, President Donald Trump nominated conservative appeals court judge Neil Gorsuch to the vacant seat. With the Gorsuch appointment, conservatives once again enjoyed a 5–4 Supreme Court majority. Perhaps not surprisingly, the Gorsuch appointment resulted in a conservative decision in *Janus v. AFSCME*, and Janus's First Amendment rights would be upheld. But union supporters say the decision will have devastating effects on public-sector unions' ability to protect workers.

For both Democrats and Republicans, the importance of the Supreme Court's 5–4 decision underscored the significance of Supreme Court appointments. Had

Garland rather than Gorsuch been seated on the Court, the mandatory-dues requirement would likely have been upheld. With the *Janus* decision in mind, Democrats and Republicans intensified their efforts to win subsequent battles over judicial appointments. After Justice Anthony Kennedy announced his retirement from the Court in July 2018, Trump nominated Brett Kavanaugh, another conservative judge, to take his place. After a divisive political battle, Kavanaugh was confirmed by the Senate and joined the Court in October. In September 2020, Justice Ruth Bader Ginsburg passed away, and Trump nominated conservative judge Amy Coney Barrett to the Court days before the 2020 presidential election.

Every year, approximately 25 million cases are tried in American courts. Cases can arise from disputes between citizens, from efforts by government agencies to punish wrongdoing, from citizens' efforts to prove that government action—or inaction—has infringed on their rights, and from efforts by interest groups to promote their agendas. Many critics of the U.S. legal system assert that Americans have become too litigious, too ready to use the courts for all purposes. But the heavy use that Americans make of the courts is also an indication of the extent of conflict in American society. And given the existence of social conflict, it is far better that Americans seek to settle their differences through the courts than resort to violence or otherwise take matters into their own hands.

The framers of the Constitution called the Supreme Court the "least dangerous branch" of American government. Today, though, it is not unusual to hear the Court described as an all-powerful "imperial judiciary." But before we can understand this transformation and its consequences, we must look in some detail at America's judicial process.

CHAPTER GOALS

★ Identify the general types of cases and types of courts in America's legal system (pp. 545–49)

★ Describe the different levels of federal courts and the process of appointing federal judges (pp. 549–55)

★ Explain the Supreme Court's judicial review of national law (pp. 555–61)

★ Describe the process by which cases are considered and decided by the Supreme Court (pp. 561–69)

★ Describe the factors that influence court decisions (pp. 569–74)

The Legal System

Identify the general types of cases and types of courts in America's legal system

Originally, a "court" was the place where a sovereign ruled—where the king or queen governed. Settling disputes between one's subjects was part of governing. In modern democracies, courts made up of judges and juries have taken over the power to settle conflicts, which they do by hearing the facts on both sides of a case and applying the relevant law or constitutional principle to the facts to decide which side has the stronger argument. Courts have been given the authority to settle disputes not only between citizens but also between citizens and the government itself, where judges and juries must maintain the same impartiality as they do in disputes involving two citizens. This is the essence of the "rule of law": that "the state" and its officials must be judged by the same laws as the citizenry.

CASES AND THE LAW

Court cases in the United States proceed under two broad categories of law: criminal law and civil law, each with many subdivisions.

Cases of **criminal law** are those in which the government charges an individual with violating a statute enacted to protect public health, safety, morals, or welfare. In criminal cases, the government is always the **plaintiff** (the party that brings charges) and alleges that a criminal violation has been committed by a named **defendant**. Most criminal cases arise in state and municipal courts and involve matters ranging from traffic offenses to robbery and murder. However, a large and growing body of federal criminal law deals with matters ranging from tax evasion and mail fraud to acts of terrorism and the sale of narcotics. Defendants found guilty of criminal violations may be fined or sent to jail or prison.

Cases of **civil law** involve disputes among individuals, groups, corporations, and other private entities or between such litigants and the government, in which no

criminal law the branch of law that regulates the conduct of individuals, defines crimes, and specifies punishment for proscribed conduct

plaintiff the individual or organization that brings a complaint in court

defendant the one against whom a complaint is brought in a criminal or civil case

civil law the branch of law that deals with disputes that do not involve criminal penalties

In criminal cases, the government charges an individual with violating a statute protecting health, safety, morals, or welfare. Most such cases arise in state and municipal courts. Here, an Illinois county court hears testimony in a murder case.

criminal violation is charged. Unlike in criminal cases, the losers in civil cases cannot be fined or incarcerated, although they may be required to pay monetary damages to the winners.

The two most common types of civil cases involve contracts and torts. In a typical contract case, an individual or corporation charges that it has suffered because of another's violation of an agreement between the two. For example, the Smith Manufacturing Corporation may charge that Jones Distributors failed to honor an agreement to deliver raw materials at a specified time, causing Smith to lose business. Smith asks the court to order Jones to compensate it for the damage it allegedly suffered. In a typical tort case, one individual charges that he has been injured by another's negligence or bad conduct. Medical malpractice suits are one example of tort cases.

Another important area of civil law is administrative law, which involves disputes over the jurisdiction, procedures, or authority of administrative agencies. A plaintiff may assert, for example, that an agency did not follow proper procedures when issuing new rules and regulations. A court will then examine the agency's conduct in light of the Administrative Procedure Act, the legislation that governs agency rule making.

precedent a prior case whose principles are used by judges as the basis for their decision in a present case

In deciding cases, courts apply statutes (laws) and legal **precedents** (prior decisions). State and federal statutes, for example, often govern the conditions under which contracts are and are not legally binding. Jones Distributors might argue that it was not obliged to fulfill its contract with the Smith Manufacturing Corporation because actions by Smith, such as the failure to make promised payments, constituted fraud under state law. Precedents established in previous cases also guide courts' decisions in new cases. Attorneys for a physician being sued for malpractice might search for prior instances in which courts ruled that actions similar to those of their client did not constitute negligence. Such precedents are applied using the legal principle of stare decisis, a Latin phrase meaning "let the decision stand."

If a case involves the actions of the federal government or a state government, a court may also be asked to examine whether the government's conduct was consistent with the Constitution. In a criminal case, for example, defendants might assert that their constitutional rights were violated when the police searched their property. Similarly, in a civil case involving federal or state restrictions on land development, plaintiffs might assert that government actions violated the Fifth Amendment's prohibition against taking private property without just compensation. Thus, both civil and criminal cases may raise questions of constitutional law.

TYPES OF COURTS

trial court the first court to hear a criminal or civil case

court of appeals a court that hears appeals of trial court decisions

supreme court the highest court in a particular state or in the United States; this court primarily serves an appellate function

In the United States, systems of courts have been established both by the federal government and by the governments of the individual states. Both systems have several levels, as shown in Figure 15.1. More than 97 percent of all court cases in the United States are heard in state courts. The overwhelming majority of criminal cases, for example, involve violations of state laws prohibiting such actions as murder, robbery, fraud, theft, and assault. If such a case is brought to trial, it will be heard at a state **trial court**, in front of a judge and sometimes a jury, who will determine whether the defendant violated state law. If the defendant is convicted, she may appeal the conviction to a higher court, such as a state **court of appeals**, and from there to a court of last resort, usually called the state's **supreme court**. The government is not entitled to appeal if the defendant is found not guilty.

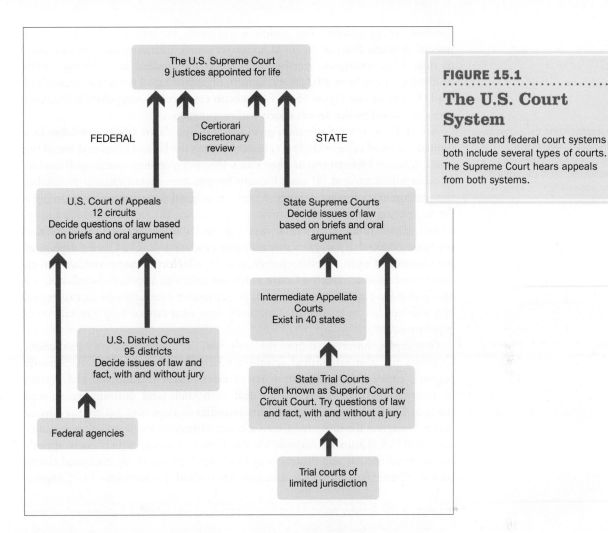

FIGURE 15.1
....

The U.S. Court System

The state and federal court systems both include several types of courts. The Supreme Court hears appeals from both systems.

The party filing an appeal, known as an *appellant*, usually must show that the trial court made a legal error in deciding the case. Appeals courts do not hear witnesses or examine additional evidence and will consider new facts only under unusual circumstances. Thus, for example, a physician who loses a malpractice case might appeal on the basis that the trial court misapplied the relevant law or incorrectly instructed the jury. It should be noted that in both criminal and civil matters most cases are settled before trial through negotiated agreements between the parties. In criminal cases these agreements are called **plea bargains.**

Cases are heard in the federal courts if they involve federal laws, treaties with other nations, or the U.S. Constitution; these areas are the official **jurisdiction** of the federal courts. In addition, any case in which the U.S. government is a party is heard in the federal courts. If, for example, an individual is charged with violating a federal criminal statute, such as evading the payment of income taxes, charges are brought before a federal judge by a federal prosecutor. Civil cases involving the citizens of more than one state and in which more than $75,000 is at stake may be heard in either the federal or the state courts, usually depending on the preference of the plaintiff.

But even if a matter belongs in federal court, which federal court should exercise jurisdiction over the case? For the most part, Congress has assigned jurisdictions on

plea bargain a negotiated agreement in a criminal case in which a defendant agrees to plead guilty in return for the state's agreement to reduce the severity of the criminal charge or prison sentence the defendant is facing

jurisdiction the sphere of a court's power and authority

the basis of geography. The nation is currently, by statute, divided into 94 judicial districts. Each of the 94 U.S. district courts, including one court for each of three U.S. territories, exercises jurisdiction over federal cases arising within its district. The judicial districts are, in turn, organized into 11 regional circuits and the D.C. circuit (see Figure 15.2). Each circuit court exercises appellate jurisdiction over cases heard by the district courts within its region.

Article III of the Constitution gives the Supreme Court **original jurisdiction** in a limited variety of cases, including (1) cases between the United States and one of the states, (2) cases between two or more states, (3) cases involving foreign ambassadors or other ministers, and (4) cases brought by one state against citizens of another state or against a foreign country. Courts of original jurisdiction are responsible for discovering the facts in a controversy and creating the record on which a judgment is based. In all other federal cases, Article III assigns original jurisdiction to the lower courts that Congress was authorized to establish. The Constitution gives the Supreme Court appellate jurisdiction in all federal cases, and almost all cases heard by the Supreme Court today are under its appellate jurisdiction. In courts that have appellate jurisdiction, judges receive cases after the factual record is established by the trial court. Ordinarily, new facts cannot be presented before appellate courts.

Geography, however, is not the only basis for federal court jurisdiction. Congress has also established several specialized courts that have nationwide original jurisdiction in certain types of cases. These include the U.S. Court of International Trade, created to deal with trade and customs issues; and the U.S. Court of Federal Claims, which handles damage suits against the United States. Congress has also established a court with nationwide appellate jurisdiction, the U.S. Court of Appeals for the Federal Circuit, which hears appeals involving patent law and those arising from the decisions of the trade and claims courts. Other federal courts assigned specialized jurisdictions by Congress

original jurisdiction the authority to initially consider a case; distinguished from appellate jurisdiction, which is the authority to hear appeals from a lower court's decision

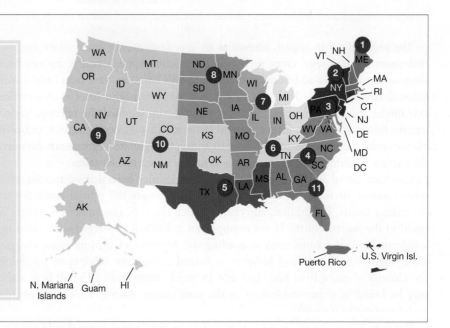

FIGURE 15.2

Federal Appellate Court Circuits

The 94 federal district courts are organized into 12 regional circuits: the 11 shown here, plus the District of Columbia, which has its own circuit. Each circuit court hears appeals from lower federal courts within the circuit. A thirteenth federal circuit court, the U.S. Court of Appeals for the Federal Circuit, hears appeals from a number of specialized courts, such as the U.S. Court of Federal Claims.

SOURCE: "Federal Court Finder," www.uscourts.gov/court_locator.aspx (accessed 7/27/10).

include the U.S. Court of Appeals for Veterans Claims, which exercises exclusive jurisdiction over cases involving veterans' claims; and the U.S. Court of Military Appeals, which deals with questions of law arising from trials by court-martial.

With the exception of the claims court and the Court of Appeals for the Federal Circuit, these specialized courts were created by Congress on the basis of the powers it exercises under Article I, rather than Article III, of the Constitution. Article III is designed to protect judges from political pressure by granting them life tenure and prohibiting reduction of their salaries while they serve. The judges of Article I courts, by contrast, are appointed by the president for fixed terms of 15 years and are not protected by the Constitution from salary reduction. As a result, these "legislative courts" are generally viewed as less independent than the Article III courts.

The appellate jurisdiction of the federal courts extends to cases originating in the state courts. In both civil and criminal cases, a decision of the highest state court can be appealed to the U.S. Supreme Court by raising a federal issue. A defendant who appeals a state court decision in federal court might assert, for example, that he was denied the right to counsel or was otherwise deprived of the **due process of law** guaranteed by the federal Constitution or that important issues of federal law were at stake in the case. The U.S. Supreme Court is not obligated to accept such appeals and will do so only if it believes that the matter has considerable national significance.

In addition, in criminal cases, defendants who have been convicted in a state court may request a **writ of habeas corpus** from a federal district court. Sometimes known as the "Great Writ," habeas corpus is a court order to the authorities to show cause for a prisoner's incarceration. The court will then evaluate whether the cause is sufficient and may order the release of a prisoner if it is found not to be. In 1867 Congress's distrust of southern courts led it to authorize federal district judges to issue such writs to prisoners who they believed had been deprived of constitutional rights in state court. Generally speaking, state defendants seeking a federal writ of habeas corpus must show that they have exhausted all available state remedies and must raise issues not previously raised in their state appeals. Federal courts of appeals and, ultimately, the U.S. Supreme Court have appellate jurisdiction for federal district court habeas decisions.

Although the federal courts hear only a small fraction of all the civil and criminal cases decided each year in the United States, their decisions are extremely important. It is in the federal courts that the Constitution and federal laws that govern all Americans are interpreted. Moreover, it is in the federal courts that the powers and limitations of the increasingly powerful national government are tested. Finally, through their power to review state court decisions, it is ultimately the federal courts that dominate the American judicial system.

Federal Courts

Describe the different levels of federal courts and the process of appointing federal judges

During the year ending in September 2019, federal district courts (the lowest federal level) received 390,555 cases. Though large, this number is less than 3 percent of the number

due process of law the right of every individual against arbitrary action by national or state governments

writ of habeas corpus a court order that the individual in custody be brought into court and shown the cause for detention; habeas corpus is guaranteed by the Constitution and can be suspended only in cases of rebellion or invasion

of cases heard by state courts (see Figure 15.3). The federal courts of appeal listened to 48,486 cases during the same period. Generally, about 15 percent of the verdicts rendered by these courts are appealed to the U.S. Supreme Court.

Most of the 6,500 or so cases filed with the Supreme Court each year are dismissed without a ruling on their merits. The Court has broad latitude to decide what cases it will hear and generally listens to only those it believes raise the most important issues. In recent years, fewer than 100 cases per year have received full-dress Supreme Court reviews.[3]

FEDERAL TRIAL COURTS

Although the Constitution gives the Supreme Court original jurisdiction in several types of cases, most cases begin in the lowest courts—the 94 federal district courts. Congress has authorized the appointment of 678 federal district judges

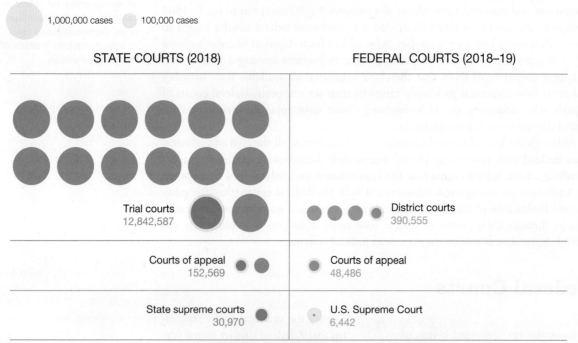

FIGURE 15.3

Caseloads of American Courts

This figure shows the total incoming caseloads of U.S. courts in 2018. More than 97 percent of the cases heard in American courts every year are heard in state courts. At both the federal and the state levels, lower-court decisions can be appealed to the appropriate court of appeals. Why do you think a larger percentage of federal district court decisions are appealed compared with state trial court decisions?

1,000,000 cases   100,000 cases

STATE COURTS (2018)   FEDERAL COURTS (2018–19)

Trial courts
12,842,587

District courts
390,555

Courts of appeal
152,569

Courts of appeal
48,486

State supreme courts
30,970

U.S. Supreme Court
6,442

SOURCES: Court Statistics Project, National Center for State Courts, www.courtstatistics.org/; Supreme Court, 2019 Year-End Report on the Federal Judiciary, www.supremecourt.gov (accessed 10/6/20).

to staff these courts, although at any given time, some of these positions may be vacant. District judges are assigned to district courts according to the workload; the busiest courts may have as many as 28 judges. Only 1 judge is assigned to each case, except where statutes provide for 3-judge courts to deal with special issues.

The routines and procedures of the federal district courts are essentially the same as those of the state trial courts except that federal procedural requirements tend to be stricter. States, for example, do not have to provide a grand jury, a 12-member trial jury, or a unanimous jury verdict. Federal courts must follow all these procedures.

FEDERAL APPELLATE COURTS

Roughly 20 percent of all lower-court cases, along with appeals from some federal agency decisions, are subsequently reviewed by federal appeals courts. As noted earlier, the country is divided geographically into 11 regional circuits and the D.C. circuit, each of which has a U.S. Court of Appeals. A thirteenth appellate court, the U.S. Court of Appeals for the Federal Circuit, has a subject-matter jurisdiction rather than a geographical one. Congress has authorized the appointment of 179 court-of-appeals judges, though, as in the case of the district courts, some spots may be vacant at any given point in time.

Except for cases selected for review by the Supreme Court, decisions by the appeals courts are final. Because of this finality, certain safeguards have been built into the system. The most important is the provision of more than one judge for every appeals case. Each court of appeals has from 6 to 28 permanent judgeships, depending on the workload of the circuit. Normally three of these judges hear each case, and in some instances a larger number sit together "en banc."

Another safeguard is provided by the assignment of a Supreme Court justice as the circuit justice for each of the 12 circuits. The circuit justice deals with requests for special action by the Supreme Court. The most frequent and best-known action of circuit justices is that of reviewing requests for stays of execution when the full Court is unable to do so—primarily during the summer, when the Court is in recess.

THE SUPREME COURT

Article III of the Constitution vests "the judicial power of the United States" in the Supreme Court, and this court is supreme in fact as well as name. The Supreme Court is the only federal court established by the Constitution. The lower federal courts were created by Congress and can be restructured or, presumably, even abolished.

The Supreme Court is made up of the chief justice of the United States and eight associate justices. The **chief justice** presides over the Court's public sessions and conferences and is always the first to speak and vote when the justices deliberate. In deliberations and decisions, however, the chief justice has no more authority than her colleagues. Each justice casts one vote. If the chief justice has voted with the majority, he decides which of the justices will write the formal opinion for the Court. The character of the opinion can be an important means of influencing the evolution of the law beyond the mere affirmation or denial of the appeal on hand.

To some extent, the influence of the chief justice is a function of her own leadership ability. Some chief justices, such as the late Earl Warren, have been able

chief justice justice on the Supreme Court who presides over the Court's public sessions and whose official title is "chief justice of the United States"

to lead the Court in a new direction. In other instances, forceful associate justices, such as the late Felix Frankfurter or William Brennan, are the dominant figures on the Court.

The Constitution does not specify the number of justices on the Supreme Court, so Congress has the authority to change its size. In the early nineteenth century, there were six justices; later there were seven. Congress set the number at nine in 1869, and the Court has remained that size ever since.

HOW JUDGES ARE APPOINTED

Federal judges are nominated by the president and must be confirmed by the Senate. They are generally selected from among the more prominent or politically active members of the legal profession, and many previously served as state court judges or state or local prosecutors. However, there are no formal qualifications for service as a federal judge. In general, presidents try to appoint judges whose partisan and ideological views are similar to their own.

Once the president has formally nominated someone, the nominee must be considered by the Senate Judiciary Committee and confirmed by a majority vote in the full Senate. In recent years, a good deal of partisan conflict has surrounded judicial appointments. Senate Democrats have sought to prevent Republican presidents from appointing conservative judges, while Senate Republicans have worked to prevent Democratic presidents from appointing liberal judges.

During the early months of the Obama administration, Republicans were able to slow the judicial appointment process through filibusters and other procedural maneuvers so that only 3 of the president's 23 nominees were confirmed by the Senate.[4] Some of Obama's allies urged the president to take a more aggressive stance because he risked allowing Republicans to block what had been considered a key Democratic priority. In 2013 the Senate voted 52 to 48 to end the use of the filibuster against all executive branch and judicial nominees except those to the Supreme Court, allowing President Obama to quickly secure the appointment of more than 300 new district court judges and 55 new appeals court judges. In 2017, as we saw earlier, Republicans turned the tables and extended these rule changes to include Supreme Court nominees, thus blocking Democratic efforts to prevent President Trump from appointing Neil Gorsuch to the Court.

Senate Republicans' strategy to not take up Obama's nomination of Merrick Garland, and to eliminate filibusters on Supreme Court nominations, paid off when President Trump nominated Neil Gorsuch in 2017. The Trump administration was able to nominate two more Supreme Court justices to the bench during Trump's presidency: judges Brett M. Kavanaugh and Amy Coney Barrett.

Comparing How States Select Judges

Judicial Selection Methods by State, 2017

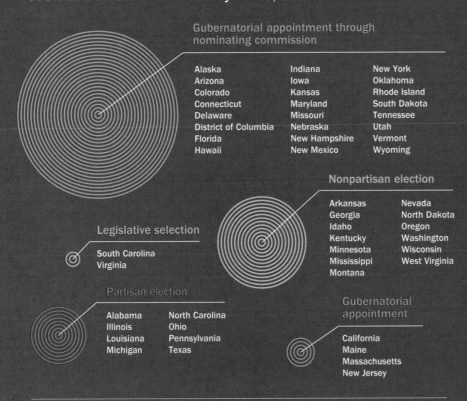

Gubernatorial appointment through nominating commission

Alaska	Indiana	New York
Arizona	Iowa	Oklahoma
Colorado	Kansas	Rhode Island
Connecticut	Maryland	South Dakota
Delaware	Missouri	Tennessee
District of Columbia	Nebraska	Utah
Florida	New Hampshire	Vermont
Hawaii	New Mexico	Wyoming

Nonpartisan election

Arkansas	Nevada
Georgia	North Dakota
Idaho	Oregon
Kentucky	Washington
Minnesota	Wisconsin
Mississippi	West Virginia
Montana	

Legislative selection

South Carolina
Virginia

Partisan election

Alabama	North Carolina
Illinois	Ohio
Louisiana	Pennsylvania
Michigan	Texas

Gubernatorial appointment

California
Maine
Massachusetts
New Jersey

States vary in their methods for selecting judges. Some elect judges through partisan election, where voters generally decide whom to vote for based on party affiliation. Most states employ a merit selection method through nominating commissions that make recommendations to the governor. Other states have judges elected by the governor without nominating commissions. Thirteen states elect their judges in nonpartisan elections, meaning that the role of political parties in judicial elections is minimized. The state legislature chooses judges in the remaining two states.

SOURCES: American Judicature Society, Judicial Selection in the States, www.judicialselection.us/; and IAALS, the Institute for the Advancement of the American Legal System at the University of Denver, "Selection and Retention of State Judges," *Texas Bar Journal* (February 2016): 92–97.

Judicial Selection Methods: A Regional View

- Gubernatorial appointment through nominating commission
- Gubernatorial appointment
- Partisan election
- Nonpartisan election
- Legislative selection

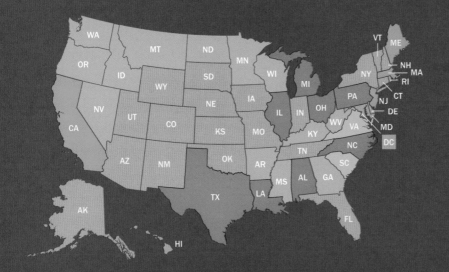

FOR CRITICAL ANALYSIS

1. What are the advantages of nonpartisan elections to select judges? Which method of selection do you think is the best, and why?

2. Are there regional patterns in how judges are selected? If so, why do you think that is?

Supreme Court Appointments While political factors play an important role in the selection of district and appellate court judges, they are decisive when it comes to Supreme Court appointments. Because the high court has so much influence over American law and politics, virtually all presidents have made an effort to select justices who share their political philosophies.

Six of the nine current justices, as of October 2020, were appointed by Republican presidents (see Table 15.1). With the exception of the months between the death of Antonin Scalia in February 2016 and the confirmation of Gorsuch in April 2017, the Court has had a conservative majority for 46 years, most recently consisting of Chief Justice Roberts and justices Samuel Alito, Clarence Thomas, Gorsuch, and Brett Kavanaugh. As we saw in earlier chapters, this majority propelled the Court in a more conservative direction in a variety of areas, including civil rights (Chapter 5) and election law (Chapter 10).

In recent decades, Supreme Court nominations have come to involve intense partisan struggle. Typically, after the president has named a nominee, interest groups opposed to the nomination mobilize opposition in the media, among the public, and in the Senate. In 1991, when President George H. W. Bush proposed the conservative judge Clarence Thomas for the Court, liberal groups launched a campaign to discredit Thomas as well. After extensive research into his background, opponents of the nomination were able to produce evidence suggesting that Thomas had sexually harassed a former subordinate, Anita Hill. Thomas denied the charge. After contentious Senate Judiciary Committee hearings, highlighted by testimony from both Thomas and Hill, Thomas narrowly won confirmation.

TABLE 15.1

Supreme Court Justices, 2020* (in Order of Seniority)

NAME	YEAR OF BIRTH	LAW SCHOOL ATTENDED	PRIOR EXPERIENCE	APPOINTED BY	YEAR OF APPOINTMENT
Clarence Thomas	1948	Yale	Federal judge	G. H. W. Bush	1991
Stephen Breyer	1938	Harvard	Federal judge	Clinton	1994
John Roberts, Jr. (Chief Justice)	1955	Harvard	Federal judge	G. W. Bush	2005
Samuel Alito	1950	Yale	Federal judge	G. W. Bush	2006
Sonia Sotomayor	1954	Yale	Federal judge	Obama	2009
Elena Kagan	1960	Harvard	Solicitor general	Obama	2010
Neil Gorsuch	1967	Harvard	Federal judge	Trump	2017
Brett Kavanaugh	1965	Yale	Federal judge	Trump	2018
Amy Coney Barrett	1972	Notre Dame	Federal judge	Trump	2020

*As of October 2020.

Republicans severely criticized Obama's nomination of Sonia Sotomayor in 2009 and Elena Kagan in 2010, though both were ultimately confirmed by the Senate. In 2016, however, as we saw in the chapter opening, Republicans refused to act on Obama's nomination of Merrick Garland. In 2017 newly elected President Trump secured the appointment of a conservative, Neil Gorsuch, and Republicans used their Senate majority to change the rules and prevent a Democratic filibuster.

In 2018, President Trump nominated the judge Brett Kavanaugh to replace retiring justice Anthony Kennedy. The Kavanaugh nomination, which promised to push the Court a bit further to the right, touched off one of the most intense political struggles in recent American history. Days before the Senate was to vote, Christine Blasey Ford, who had known Kavanaugh in high school, came forward to assert that the judge had attempted to sexually assault her 36 years earlier, when he was 17 and she was 15. Kavanaugh vehemently denied the accusation, as well as accusations of sexual impropriety by two other women who had known him in college. Televised testimony before the Senate Judiciary Committee by Kavanaugh and Ford divided the Senate and the nation, primarily along partisan lines. Democrats argued that Kavanaugh was unfit to serve on the Court, while Republicans asserted that the charges against him had been invented for political reasons. An FBI investigation failed to shed light on the allegations, and Kavanaugh was confirmed, receiving the votes of all but one Republican and only one Democrat.[5]

In September 2020, the death of Ruth Bader Ginsburg gave President Trump an opportunity to appoint a third Supreme Court justice. With only weeks remaining before the 2020 presidential election, Trump nominated former Notre Dame law professor and federal appeals court judge Amy Coney Barrett to replace Ginsburg. Barrett had served as a law clerk for the late Justice Antonin Scalia and was seen to hold conservative views similar to Scalia's. Her appointment solidified the Court's conservative majority and infuriated Democrats. Hoping that a Democratic president would be elected in 2020, Democrats demanded that the nomination be put on hold until after the election. Republicans, however, used their Senate majority to expedite the confirmation process and Justice Barrett was duly sworn in just days before the national presidential election.

The Power of the Supreme Court: Judicial Review

Explain the Supreme Court's judicial review of national law

The term *judicial review* refers to the power of the judiciary to examine actions undertaken by the legislative and executive branches and, if necessary, invalidate them if it finds them unconstitutional.

JUDICIAL REVIEW OF ACTS OF CONGRESS

The Constitution does not explicitly give the Supreme Court the power of **judicial review** over congressional enactments, although the idea was discussed at the Constitutional Convention. Some delegates expected the courts to exercise this power, while many others were "departmentalists," believing that each branch of the new government would interpret the Constitution as it applied to that branch's own actions, with the judiciary mainly ensuring that individuals did not suffer injustices.

judicial review the power of the courts to review actions of the legislative and executive branches and, if necessary, declare them invalid or unconstitutional; the Supreme Court asserted this power in *Marbury v. Madison* (1803)

Ambiguity over the framers' intentions was settled in 1803 in the case of *Marbury v. Madison*.[6] This case arose after Thomas Jefferson succeeded John Adams as president. Jefferson's secretary of state, James Madison, refused to deliver an official commission to William Marbury, who had been appointed to a minor office by Adams and approved by the Senate just before Adams left the presidency. Marbury petitioned the Supreme Court to order Madison to deliver the commission.

Jefferson and his allies did not believe that the Court had the power to issue such an order and might have resisted it. Chief Justice John Marshall was determined to assert the power of the judiciary but wanted to avoid a direct confrontation with the president. Accordingly, he turned down Marbury's petition but gave as his reason the unconstitutionality of the legislation upon which Marbury had based his claim. Thus, Marshall asserted the power of judicial review but did so in a way that would not provoke a battle with Jefferson. The Supreme Court's decision in this case established the power of judicial review:

> It is emphatically the province and duty of the Judicial Department [the judicial branch] to say what the law is. Those who apply the rule to particular cases must, of necessity, expound and interpret that rule. If two laws conflict with each other, the Courts must decide on the operation of each. . . . So, if a law [e.g., a statute or treaty] be in opposition to the Constitution, if both the law and the Constitution apply to a particular case, so that the Court must either decide that case conformably to the law, disregarding the Constitution, or conformably to the Constitution, disregarding the law, the Court must determine which of these conflicting rules governs the case. This is of the very essence of judicial duty.

The Court's legal power to review acts of Congress has not been seriously questioned since 1803. One reason for that is that the Supreme Court makes a self-conscious effort to give acts of Congress an interpretation that will make them constitutional. For example, in its 2012 decision upholding the constitutionality of the Affordable Care Act, the Court agreed with the many legal scholars who had argued that the Congress had no power under the Constitution's commerce clause to order Americans to purchase health insurance. But, rather than invalidate the act, the Court declared that the law's requirement that all Americans purchase insurance was actually a tax and, thus, represented a constitutionally acceptable use of Congress's power to levy taxes.[7]

In more than two centuries, the Court has concluded that fewer than 160 acts of Congress directly violated the Constitution.[8] These cases are often highly controversial. For example, in 2007 and 2014, the high court struck down key portions of the Bipartisan Campaign Reform Act, finding that provisions of the act limiting political advertising violated the First Amendment.[9] And as we saw in Chapter 4 with the 2017 case of *Matal v. Tam*, the Court also cited free speech concerns in striking down a federal law prohibiting trademarks that disparage people or groups. The decision was cheered by fans of the Washington Redskins football team. These cases are important but unusual in that the Court rarely overturns acts of Congress.

JUDICIAL REVIEW OF STATE ACTIONS

The power of the Supreme Court to review state legislation or other state action to determine its constitutionality is also not explicitly granted by the Constitution. But the logic of the **supremacy clause** of Article VI, which declares the Constitution itself

FOR CRITICAL ANALYSIS

During his 2005 confirmation hearings, senators asked Chief Justice Roberts why the Supreme Court was more willing to declare acts of Congress unconstitutional than it was to confront the president on the constitutionality of his actions. What reasons might you identify?

supremacy clause Article VI of the Constitution, which states that laws passed by the national government and all treaties are the supreme law of the land and superior to all laws adopted by any state or any subdivision

Who Are Federal Judges?

One factor among many that presidents may take into account when selecting judicial nominees is diversity. The number of Supreme Court justices is relatively small, so it is easy to count the number of African Americans (2), women (4), and Latinos (1). How diverse is the rest of the federal judiciary? The first section below shows the racial, ethnic, and gender composition of the lower federal courts.

Federal Judges in 2020,* by Race and Gender *As of June 2020

👤 = 10 federal judges

White men 825

African American men 90

Latino men 61

Asian American men 23

White women 288

African American women 46

Latina women 29

Asian American women 14

Appointments to Federal Courts, by Administration

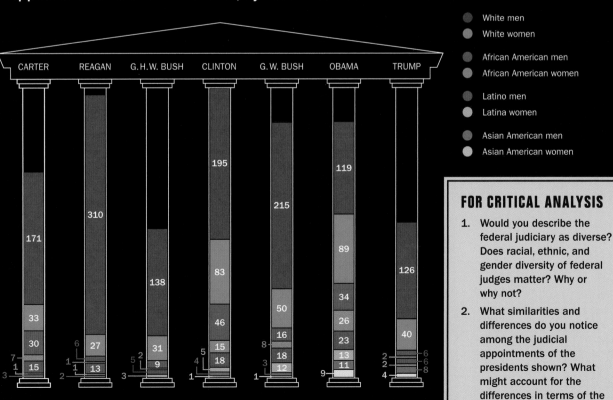

CARTER · REAGAN · G.H.W. BUSH · CLINTON · G.W. BUSH · OBAMA · TRUMP

Legend:
- White men
- White women
- African American men
- African American women
- Latino men
- Latina women
- Asian American men
- Asian American women

CARTER: 171, 33, 30, 7, 1, 15, 3

REAGAN: 310, 27, 6, 1, 1, 13, 2

G.H.W. BUSH: 138, 31, 9, 5, 2, 3

CLINTON: 195, 83, 46, 15, 18, 5, 4, 1

G.W. BUSH: 215, 50, 16, 18, 12, 8, 3, 1

OBAMA: 119, 89, 34, 26, 23, 13, 11, 9

TRUMP: 126, 40, 2, 2, 4, 6, 6, 8

FOR CRITICAL ANALYSIS

1. Would you describe the federal judiciary as diverse? Does racial, ethnic, and gender diversity of federal judges matter? Why or why not?

2. What similarities and differences do you notice among the judicial appointments of the presidents shown? What might account for the differences in terms of the diversity of their appointees?

SOURCE: Federal Judicial Center, www.fjc.gov/ (accessed 6/11/20).

The Supreme Court has the power to review state action. In *Pavan v. Smith*, the Supreme Court overturned Arkansas's law that disallowed same-sex parents to have both of their names listed on their children's birth certificates. Here, Marisa Pavan, the plaintiff in the case, holds her daughter and her birth certificate showing both parents' names.

and laws made under its authority to be the supreme law of the land, is very strong. Furthermore, in the Judiciary Act of 1789, Congress conferred on the Supreme Court the power to reverse state constitutions and laws whenever they are clearly in conflict with the U.S. Constitution, federal laws, or treaties.[10] This power gives the Supreme Court appellate jurisdiction over all the millions of cases that American courts handle each year.

The supremacy clause not only established the federal Constitution, statutes, and treaties as the "supreme Law of the Land" but also provided that "the Judges in every State shall be bound thereby, any Thing in the Constitution or Laws of the State to the Contrary notwithstanding." Under this authority, the Supreme Court has frequently overturned state constitutional provisions or statutes, state court decisions, and local ordinances it finds in violation of rights or privileges guaranteed under the federal Constitution or federal statutes.

The civil rights arena abounds with examples of state laws that the Supreme Court has overturned because they violated guarantees of due process and equal protection contained in the Fourteenth Amendment to the Constitution. For example, in the 1954 case of *Brown v. Board of Education*, the Court overturned statutes from Kansas, South Carolina, Virginia, and Delaware that either required or permitted segregated public schools, ruling that such statutes denied Black schoolchildren equal protection under the law.[11] In 2003 the Court ruled that Texas's law criminalizing sodomy violated the right to liberty protected by the due process clause.[12] In the 2017 case of *Pavan v. Smith*, the Court overturned an Arkansas law that denied same-sex couples the right to include a spouse's name on a birth certificate—a right granted to other couples. The Court said the statute denied same-sex couples equal protection of the law.[13]

State statutes in other areas of law are equally subject to challenge. Many of the Supreme Court's recent decisions overturning state law have come in cases concerning election law. In 2015, for example, the Court ruled against an Alabama legislative districting plan that opponents charged was designed to reduce the influence of Black voters.[14] The same year the Court ruled against an effort by the Arizona legislature to invalidate a districting plan drawn up by an independent commission created by a voter referendum.[15] In the 2017 case of *Cooper v. Harris*, the Court invalidated a North Carolina legislative districting plan that moved tens of thousands of Black voters into congressional districts that already had large Black majorities.[16] This tactic is known as "packing" and is designed to reduce the number of seats that might be affected by some group of voters by packing them all into as few districts as possible.

One realm in which the Court constantly monitors state conduct is that of law enforcement. As we saw in Chapter 4, over the years, the Supreme Court has developed a number of principles to ensure that police conduct does not violate constitutional liberties. These principles, however, must often be updated to keep pace with changes in technology. In a 2012 decision, the Supreme Court found that police use of a GPS tracker—a device invented more than 200 years after the adoption of the Bill of Rights—constituted a "search" as defined by the Fourth Amendment.[17] And in the 2014 case of *Riley v. California*, the Court held that the police could not undertake a warrantless search of the digital contents of a cell phone—another device hardly imagined by the framers.[18]

Courts in Comparison

Constitutional courts (courts with the power of judicial review) aim to preserve judicial independence, as they play an important role in checking executive and legislative overreach. Different countries have sought to balance the need for judicial independence with having a more responsive court. Here we see that countries have very diverse approaches to the selection and composition of their courts, including in how many justices serve, how long they serve, and who is responsible for appointing them.

1. How does the United States compare with other countries when it comes to term limits for judges? What are the benefits and drawbacks to having term limits for judges?

2. Why might some countries choose to have larger courts than others?

3. We see a variety of systems for appointing judges, including some where only one branch appoints them, others where multiple branches each appoint some judges, and still others, such as the United States, where one branch nominates judges and a second branch confirms them. Which system do you prefer, and why?

NAME	TERM LIMITS	MANDATORY RETIREMENT AGE	SIZE	HOW SELECTED?
Chilean Constitutional Court	9	—	9	Each branch appoints some
French Constitutional Council	9	—	9	Each branch appoints some
German Constitutional Court	12	68	18	Legislature
High Court of Australia	Life	70	7	Executive
Indian Supreme Court	Life	65	28	Executive
South African Constitutional Court	12	70	11	Executive
South Korean Constitutional Court	6	65	9	Each branch appoints some
Supreme Court of Canada	Life	75	9	Executive
Supreme Federal Court of Brazil	Life	75	11	Executive with Legislative confirmation
United States Supreme Court	Life	—	9	Executive with Legislative confirmation

SOURCE: CIA World Factbook, www.cia.gov/index.html (accessed 8/12/19).

JUDICIAL REVIEW OF FEDERAL AGENCY ACTIONS

Although Congress makes the law, to administer the thousands of programs it has enacted it must delegate power to the president and to a huge bureaucracy (as we saw in Chapters 12 and 14). For example, if Congress wishes to improve air quality, it cannot anticipate all the conditions that may arise with respect to that general goal. Inevitably, it must delegate to the executive substantial discretionary power to make judgments about the best ways to bring about improved air quality in the face of changing circumstances. Thus, over the years, almost any congressional program will result in thousands upon thousands of pages of administrative regulations developed by executive agencies.

Over the past two centuries, a number of court decisions have dealt with the scope of the delegation of power. Courts have also had to decide whether regulations adopted by federal agencies are consistent with Congress's express or implied intent.

Beginning in the New Deal era, many statutes gave the executive virtually unrestrained authority to address a particular concern. For example, the Emergency Price Control Act of 1942 authorized the executive to set "fair and equitable" prices without spelling out what those terms might mean.[19] Although the Supreme Court initially struck down these delegations of power, it retreated from its position when faced with a confrontation with President Franklin Delano Roosevelt.

Perhaps as a result, no congressional delegation of power to the president since then has been struck down as impermissibly broad. Particularly in recent years, the Court has found that so long as federal agencies develop rules "based upon a permissible construction" or "reasonable interpretation" of a law and use a prescribed formal rule-making process, the judiciary will defer to them.

JUDICIAL REVIEW AND PRESIDENTIAL POWER

The federal courts are also called on to review the actions of the president. On many occasions, members of Congress as well as individuals and groups have challenged presidential orders and actions in the federal courts. In recent years, the judiciary has, more often than not, upheld assertions of presidential power in such realms as foreign policy, war and emergency powers, legislative power, and administrative authority. In 2004, however, in two of three cases involving President George W. Bush's antiterrorism initiatives, the Supreme Court appeared to place some limits on presidential authority.

One important case was *Hamdi v. Rumsfeld*.[20] Yaser Esam Hamdi, apparently a Taliban soldier, was captured by American forces in Afghanistan and brought to the United States, where he was incarcerated at the Norfolk Naval Station. Hamdi was classified as an "enemy combatant" and denied civil rights, including the right to counsel, despite the fact that he had been born in Louisiana and held American citizenship. In 2004 the Supreme Court ruled that Hamdi was entitled to a lawyer and "a fair opportunity to rebut the government's factual assertions."

Thus the Court did assert that it could review and place some constraints on the president's power. But at the same time it affirmed the president's single most important claim: the unilateral power to declare individuals, including U.S. citizens, enemy combatants, who could be detained by federal authorities under adverse legal circumstances. Several of the justices implied that once designated an enemy combatant, a U.S. citizen might be tried before a military tribunal, without the normal presumption of innocence.

The courts may be called on to review the actions of the president. After President Trump's "travel ban" was implemented in early 2017, many court cases challenged this policy, and eventually one case was tried before the Supreme Court. In a 5–4 decision, the Court upheld the travel ban, sparking outrage from Democratic lawmakers like Representative Joe Kennedy III (Mass.).

Judicial review of presidential actions is not limited to presidential war powers and the realm of terrorism. In 2013 the Fourth U.S. Circuit Court of Appeals ruled that President Obama had violated the Constitution when he made so-called recess appointments to the National Labor Relations Board in order to avoid the need to secure Senate confirmation. Recess appointments are customarily used only when the Senate adjourns at the end of the year, but the president had made the appointments in question when the Senate had recessed for only 3 days. In 2014 the Supreme Court agreed that a recess of less than 10 days was "presumptively too short" to justify a recess appointment.[21]

In its 2018 decision in *Trump v. Hawaii*, however, the Court upheld the use of presidential power.[22] Through an executive order, President Trump had prohibited travel into the United States by people from several Muslim-majority countries. In a 5–4 decision, the Court held that the president had broad authority, given by statute, to determine that certain travelers might pose a risk to the security of the United States.

The Supreme Court in Action

> **Describe the process by which cases are considered and decided by the Supreme Court**

Given the millions of legal disputes that arise every year, the Supreme Court could not possibly do its job if it were not able to control the flow of cases and its own caseload. Over the years, the courts have developed specific rules that govern which cases within their jurisdiction they will and will not hear.

ACCESSING THE COURT

Article III of the Constitution and Supreme Court decisions define judicial power as extending only to "cases and controversies." This means that the case before a court must be an actual controversy, not a hypothetical one, with two truly adversarial parties. The courts have interpreted this language to mean that they do not have the power to render advisory opinions to legislatures or agencies about the constitutionality of proposed laws or regulations. Furthermore, even after a law is enacted, the courts will generally refuse to consider its constitutionality until it is actually applied.

standing the right of an individual or organization to initiate a court case, on the basis of having a substantial stake in the outcome

Parties to a case must also have **standing**—that is, they must show that they have a substantial stake in the outcome of the case. The traditional requirement for standing has been to show injury to oneself; that injury can be personal, economic, or even aesthetic, such as a neighbor's building a high fence that blocks one's view of the ocean. In order for a group or class of people to have standing (as in class-action suits), each member must show specific injury. This means that a general interest in the environment, for instance, does not provide a group with sufficient basis for standing.

mootness a criterion used by courts to screen cases that no longer require resolution

The Supreme Court also uses a third criterion in determining whether it will hear a case: that of **mootness**. In theory, this requirement disqualifies cases that are brought too late—after the relevant facts have changed or the problem has been resolved by other means. The criterion of mootness, however, is subject to the discretion of the courts, which have begun to relax it, particularly in cases where a situation that has been resolved is likely to come up again. In the abortion case *Roe v. Wade*, for example, the Supreme Court rejected the lower court's argument that because the pregnancy in question had already come to term, the case was moot. The Court agreed to hear the case because no pregnancy was likely to outlast the lengthy appeals process.[23]

Putting aside the formal criteria, the Supreme Court is most likely to accept cases that involve conflicting decisions by the federal circuit courts, important questions of civil rights or civil liberties, or appeals by the federal government. Ultimately, however, the question of which cases to accept can come down to the preferences and priorities of the justices. If a group of justices believes that the Court should intervene in a particular area of policy or politics, the justices are likely to look for a case or cases that will serve as vehicles for doing so.

writ of certiorari a decision of at least four of the nine Supreme Court justices to review a decision of a lower court; *certiorari* is Latin, meaning "to make more certain"

Writs Most cases reach the Supreme Court through a **writ of certiorari**, an order to a lower court to deliver the records of a particular case to be reviewed for legal errors. The term *certiorari* is sometimes shortened to *cert*, and cases deserving certiorari are referred to as "certworthy." An individual who loses in a lower federal court or state court and wants the Supreme Court to review the decision has 90 days to file a petition for a writ of certiorari with the clerk of the U.S. Supreme Court. Petitions for thousands of cases are filed with the Court every year (see Figure 15.4).

Since 1972 most of the justices have participated in a "certiorari pool," in which their law clerks work together to evaluate the petitions. Each petition is reviewed by one clerk, who writes a memo for all the justices participating in the pool, summarizing the facts and issues and making a recommendation. Clerks for the other justices add their comments to the memo. After the justices have reviewed the memos, any one of them may place any case on the "discuss list," which is circulated by the chief justice. If a case is not placed on the discuss list, it is automatically denied certiorari.

Cases placed on the discuss list are considered and voted on during the justices' closed-door conference. For certiorari to be granted, four justices must be convinced that the case satisfies rule 10 of the Rules of the Supreme Court of the United States, which states that certiorari is to be granted only when there are special and compelling reasons. These include conflicting decisions by two or more circuit

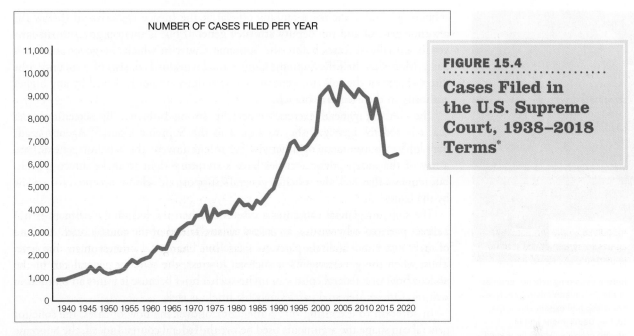

NUMBER OF CASES FILED PER YEAR

FIGURE 15.4

Cases Filed in the U.S. Supreme Court, 1938–2018 Terms*

*Number of cases filed in term starting in year indicated.
SOURCES: Years 1938–69, 1970–83, 1984–99: reprinted with permission from *The United States Law Week* (Washington, DC: Bureau of National Affairs) (copyright © Bureau of National Affairs Inc.); 2000–05: U.S. Bureau of the Census, *Statistical Abstract of the United States*; 2006–07: Office of the Clerk, Supreme Court of the United States; and Supreme Court of the United States, Cases on Docket, www.uscourts.gov/; Supreme Court, 2018 Year-End Report on the Federal Judiciary, www.supremecourt.gov/ (accessed 10/5/20).

courts, by circuit courts and state courts of last resort, or by two or more state courts of last resort; decisions by circuit courts on matters of federal law that should be settled by the Supreme Court; and a circuit court decision on an important question that conflicts with previous Supreme Court decisions.

As this list indicates, the Court will usually take action only when there are conflicts among the lower courts about what the law should be, when an important legal question has been raised in the lower courts but not definitively answered, or when a lower court deviates from the principles and precedents established by the high court. Few cases are able to gain the support of four justices needed for certiorari. In recent sessions, the Court has granted it to barely more than 80 petitioners each year—about 1 percent of those seeking a Supreme Court review.

A handful of cases reach the Supreme Court through avenues other than certiorari. One of these is the writ of certification, which can be used when a U.S. Court of Appeals asks the Supreme Court for instructions on a point of law that has never been decided. A second alternative avenue is the writ of appeal, which is used to appeal the decision of a three-judge district court.

BEYOND THE JUDGES: KEY PLAYERS IN THE FEDERAL COURT PROCESSES

In addition to the judges, other actors play important roles in how (and which) cases proceed through the federal courts: the solicitor general and federal law clerks.

The Solicitor General If any single person has greater influence than individual judges over the federal courts, it is the **solicitor general** of the United States. The

solicitor general the top government lawyer in all cases before the Supreme Court where the government is a party

Before becoming solicitor general in the Trump administration, Noel Francisco had experience in the Justice Department and in private practice, where he argued several cases in front of the Supreme Court.

amicus curiae literally, "friend of the court"; individuals or groups who are not parties to a lawsuit but who seek to assist the Supreme Court in reaching a decision by presenting additional briefs

Federal judges, including Supreme Court justices, rely on their clerks for research and help in preparing opinions. Serving as a law clerk to a Supreme Court justice is a prestigious position. Five current justices—Breyer, Kagan, Gorsuch, Barrett, and Roberts (pictured here with his clerks)—clerked for a Supreme Court justice early in their careers.

solicitor general is the third-ranking official in the Justice Department (below the attorney general and the deputy attorney general) but is the top government lawyer in virtually all cases before the Supreme Court in which the government is a party. More than half the Supreme Court's total workload consists of cases under the direct charge of the solicitor general, whose actions are not reviewed by any higher authority in the executive branch.

The solicitor general exercises especially strong influence by screening cases that any federal agency wishes to appeal to the Supreme Court.[24] Agency heads may lobby the president or otherwise try to circumvent the solicitor general, and a few of the independent agencies have a statutory right to make direct appeals, but requests that lack the solicitor general's support are seldom accepted for review by the Court.

The solicitor general can enter a case even when the federal government is not a direct party to it by writing an **amicus curiae** ("friend of the court") brief. A friend of the court is not a direct party to a case but has a vital interest in its outcome. Thus, when the government has such an interest, the solicitor general can file an amicus brief or a federal court can invite such a brief because it wants an opinion in writing. Other interested parties may file briefs as well.

In addition to exercising substantial control over the flow of cases, the solicitor general can shape the arguments used before the federal courts. Indeed, the Supreme Court tends to give special attention to the way the solicitor general characterizes the issues.

Law Clerks Every federal judge employs law clerks to research legal issues and assist with the preparation of opinions. Each Supreme Court justice is assigned four clerks, almost always honors graduates of the nation's most prestigious law schools. A clerkship with a Supreme Court justice is a great honor and generally indicates that the fortunate individual is likely to reach the very top of the legal profession. The work of the Supreme Court clerks is a closely guarded secret, but it is likely that some justices rely heavily on their clerks for advice in writing opinions and

in deciding whether the Court should hear specific cases. A former law clerk to the late justice Harry Blackmun charged that Supreme Court justices yielded "excessive power to immature, ideologically driven clerks, who in turn use that power to manipulate their bosses."[25]

LOBBYING FOR ACCESS: INTERESTS AND THE COURT

While the Court exercises discretion over which cases it will review, groups and forces in society try various ways to persuade the justices to listen to their grievances. Lawyers representing interest groups try to choose the proper client and the proper case so that the issues in question are most dramatically and appropriately portrayed. When possible, they also pick a court with a sympathetic judge in which to bring the case. Sometimes they even wait for an appropriate political climate. They must also attempt to develop a proper record at the trial court level, one that includes some constitutional arguments and even, when possible, legal errors on the part of the trial court.

One of the most effective strategies in getting cases accepted for review by the Supreme Court is to bring the same type of suit in more than one circuit (that is, to develop a "pattern of cases") in the hope that inconsistent rulings will improve the chance of a review. The two most notable users of the pattern-of-cases strategy in recent years have been the National Association for the Advancement of Colored People (NAACP) and the American Civil Liberties Union (ACLU). For many years, the NAACP (and its Defense Fund—now a separate group) has worked through local chapters and individuals to encourage litigation on issues of racial discrimination and segregation. Many pathbreaking cases on this issue and others are eventually granted certiorari because repeated refusal to review one or more of them would amount to a rule of law just as much as if the courts had handed down a written opinion. In this sense, the flow of cases, especially significant cases, influences the behavior of the appellate judiciary.

THE SUPREME COURT'S PROCEDURES

The Supreme Court's decision to accept a case is the beginning of what can be a lengthy and complex process (see Figure 15.5). After a petition is filed and certiorari is granted, the Court considers the reasoning on both sides as presented in briefs and oral argument, the justices discuss the case in conference, and opinions are carefully drafted.

Briefs First, the attorneys on both sides must prepare **briefs**, written documents in which the attorneys explain why the Court should rule in favor of their client. Briefs are filled with references to precedents chosen to show that other courts have frequently ruled in the same way the attorneys are requesting that the Supreme Court rule. The attorneys for both sides muster the most compelling precedents they can in support of their arguments.

As the attorneys prepare their briefs, they often ask sympathetic interest groups to file amicus curiae briefs that support their claims. In a case involving separation of church and state, for example, liberal groups such as the ACLU and People for the American Way are likely to be asked to file amicus briefs in support of strict separation, whereas conservative religious groups are likely to file ones

briefs written documents in which attorneys explain, using case precedents, why the court should find in favor of their client

FIGURE 15.5

Time Line of a Supreme Court Case

This calendar of events in the case of *Janus v. American Federation of State, County, and Municipal Employees* illustrates the steps of the process a case goes through as it moves through the Supreme Court. The total time from petition to the Supreme Court to the decision is just over one year, although the initial case was filed years ago in a lower court.

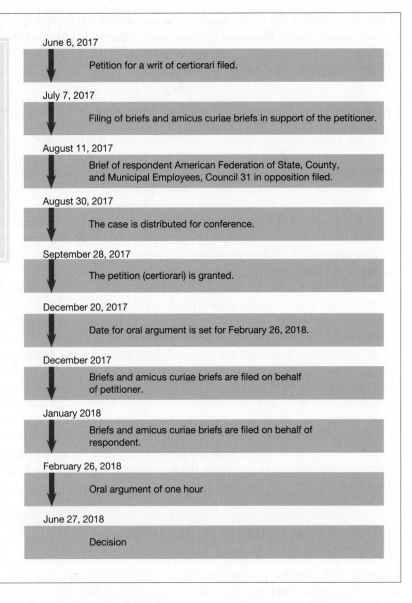

June 6, 2017
Petition for a writ of certiorari filed.

July 7, 2017
Filing of briefs and amicus curiae briefs in support of the petitioner.

August 11, 2017
Brief of respondent American Federation of State, County, and Municipal Employees, Council 31 in opposition filed.

August 30, 2017
The case is distributed for conference.

September 28, 2017
The petition (certiorari) is granted.

December 20, 2017
Date for oral argument is set for February 26, 2018.

December 2017
Briefs and amicus curiae briefs are filed on behalf of petitioner.

January 2018
Briefs and amicus curiae briefs are filed on behalf of respondent.

February 26, 2018
Oral argument of one hour

June 27, 2018
Decision

advocating increased public accommodation of religion. Often, dozens of briefs will be filed on each side of a major case. Amicus filings are one of the primary methods used by interest groups to lobby the Court. By filing these briefs, groups indicate where they stand and signal to the justices that they believe the case to be an important one.

oral argument the stage in the Supreme Court procedure in which attorneys for both sides appear before the Court to present their positions and answer questions posed by the justices

Oral Argument The next stage of a case is **oral argument**, in which an attorney for each side appears before the Court to present his position and answer the justices' questions. Each attorney has only a half hour to present a case, and this time includes interruptions for questions. Certain justices, such as the late Antonin Scalia, are known to interrupt attorneys dozens of times. Others, such as Clarence Thomas, seldom ask questions.

For an attorney, the opportunity to argue a case before the Supreme Court is an honor and a mark of professional distinction. It can also be harrowing, as when justices interrupt a carefully prepared presentation. Oral argument can be very important to the outcome of a case because it allows justices to understand better the heart of the case and to raise questions that might not have been addressed in the opposing sides' briefs. It is not uncommon for justices to go beyond the strictly legal issues and ask opposing counsel to discuss the implications of the case for the Court and the nation at large.

The Conference Following oral argument, the Court discusses the case in its Wednesday or Friday conference, a strictly private meeting that no outsiders are permitted to attend. The chief justice presides over the conference and speaks first; the other justices follow in order of seniority. The justices discuss the case and eventually reach a decision on the basis of a majority vote. If the Court is divided, a number of votes may be taken before a final decision is reached. As the case is discussed, justices may try to influence or change one another's opinions, a process that may result in compromise decisions.

Opinion Writing After a decision has been reached, one of the members of the majority is assigned to write the **opinion**. This assignment, which is made by the chief justice or by the most senior justice in the majority if the chief justice is on the losing side, can make a significant difference to the interpretation of a decision. Every opinion of the Supreme Court sets a major precedent for future cases throughout the judicial system. Lawyers and judges in the lower courts will examine it carefully to determine the Supreme Court's intent, since differences in wording and emphasis can have important implications. Thus, in assigning an opinion, the chief justice must give serious thought to the impression the case will make on lawyers and on the public and to the probability that one justice's opinion will be more widely accepted than another's.

opinion the written explanation of the Supreme Court's decision in a particular case

Julie Rikelman at lectern arguing for petitioners in June Medical Services, 3-4-20

The Supreme Court allocates just one hour to hear oral arguments, even in difficult and contentious cases. Attorneys for both sides must make their arguments succinctly and respond to the justices' questions, which are often very pointed. Here, the Court hears oral arguments for the 2020 case *June Medical Services LLC v. Russo*.

One of the more dramatic instances of this tactical consideration occurred in 1944, when Chief Justice Harlan F. Stone chose Justice Felix Frankfurter to write the opinion in the "White primary" case *Smith v. Allwright*.[26] The chief justice believed that this sensitive case, which overturned the southern practice of prohibiting Black participation in nominating primaries, required the efforts of the most brilliant and scholarly member of the Court. But the day after Stone made the assignment, Justice Robert H. Jackson wrote a letter to him urging a change of assignment on the grounds that Frankfurter, a foreign-born Jew from New England, would not win over the South with his opinion, regardless of its brilliance. Stone accepted the advice and substituted Justice Stanley Reed, an American-born Protestant from Kentucky.

Once the majority opinion is drafted, it is circulated to the other justices. Some members of the majority may wish to emphasize a particular point in the majority opinion. For that purpose, they draft a **concurring opinion**, called a *regular concurrence*. In other instances, one or more justices may agree with the majority decision but disagree with the rationale for it presented in the majority opinion. These justices may draft *special concurrences*, explaining their own rationale and how it differs from the majority's.

Dissent Justices who disagree with the majority decision may choose to publicize the character of their disagreement in the form of a **dissenting opinion**, which is generally assigned by the senior justice among the dissenters. Dissents can be used to express irritation with an outcome or to signal to the losing side that its position is supported by at least some members of the Court. Because there is no need to please a majority, dissenting opinions can be more eloquent and less guarded than majority opinions.

The current Supreme Court often produces 5–4 decisions, with dissenters writing long and detailed opinions that, they hope, will help them persuade a swing justice to join their side on the next round of cases dealing with a similar topic. During the Court's 2006–07 term, Justice Ruth Bader Ginsburg was so unhappy about the majority's decisions in a number of cases that she began to read forceful dissents aloud from the bench—a practice she continued until her death in October 2020.

Dissent plays a special role in the work and impact of the Court because it amounts to an appeal to lawyers all over the country to keep bringing similar cases. Ironically, the most dependable way an individual justice can exercise a direct and clear influence on the Court is to write an effective dissent, which influences the future flow of cases through the Court and the arguments that lawyers will use in later cases. Even more important, dissent points out that the Court's ruling is the opinion only of the majority—and one day the majority might go the other way.

Often, the division between the majority and the dissenting justices in major cases reflects deep divisions in American society. Take the 2015 same-sex marriage case of *Obergefell v. Hodges* in which the majority opinion, written by Justice Anthony Kennedy, asserted that state bans on same-sex marriage violated the Fourteenth Amendment by arbitrarily intruding upon personal choices, "central to individual dignity and autonomy," and thus denying LGBTQ persons due process and equal protection of the laws.[27] The four dissenting justices declared that the Fourteenth Amendment had never been intended or interpreted as providing a right to same-sex marriage, and they criticized the majority opinion as little more than an effort by justices to write their own views into the Constitution. In its split decision, the Court mirrored a division in American society between those who see

concurring opinion a written opinion by a judge agreeing with the majority opinion but giving different reasons for his or her decision

dissenting opinion a decision written by a justice in the minority in a particular case, in which the justice wishes to express his or her reasoning in the case

Supreme Court justices can use a dissenting opinion to express their opposing viewpoint with the hope of influencing future cases on similar questions. The late Justice Ruth Bader Ginsburg was known for her forceful dissents, such as in the 2014 Hobby Lobby case, which allowed a corporation to claim religious grounds for refusing to provide contraceptive coverage in its health insurance program.

gay rights as a natural extension of civil rights and those who are offended, often for religious reasons, by open expressions of same-sex partnership. The dissenting justices hoped to encourage further litigation in this realm, but, generally speaking, once a right is granted it is seldom revoked.

Explaining Supreme Court Decisions

> **Describe the factors that influence court decisions**

The Supreme Court makes its mark on American politics and society through the decisions it hands down. But judicial decision-making does not take place in a vacuum, of course. Like other actors in government, justices are influenced by institutional concerns, prior experience, and personal philosophy. In addition, the Court as a whole is affected by the overarching political system in which it plays a role. Over time, that role has shifted as a result of political developments both inside and outside the Court.

INFLUENCES ON SUPREME COURT DECISION-MAKING

The Supreme Court explains its decisions in terms of law and precedent. But it is the Court itself that decides what the laws actually mean and what importance the precedent will actually have. Throughout its history, the Court has shaped and reshaped the law.

In the late nineteenth and early twentieth centuries, for example, the Supreme Court held that the Constitution, law, and precedent permitted racial segregation in the United States. Beginning in the 1950s, however, the Court found that the Constitution prohibited segregation and that the use of racial categories in legislation was always suspect. By the 1970s and '80s the Court once again held that the Constitution permitted the use of racial categories—when they were needed to help members of minority groups achieve full participation in American society. Since the 1990s the Court has retreated from this position, too, indicating that governmental efforts to provide extra help to racial minorities could represent an unconstitutional infringement on the rights of the majority.

Institutional Interests The Supreme Court's justices are acutely aware of the Court's place in history, and their desire to protect its power and reputation for integrity can sometimes influence judicial thinking. During the 1935–36 term, for example, the Court struck down several of President Franklin Roosevelt's New Deal programs in a series of 5–4 votes. Furious, the president responded by proposing a reform plan that would have enlarged the Court to as many as 15 justices. Roosevelt hoped to pack the Court with his own appointees and, thus, win future cases over New Deal programs. Justice Owen Roberts, one of the five justices who had been voting against the president's initiatives, then made a sudden reversal, voting in favor of an important New Deal policy he had been expected to oppose. The media dubbed Roberts's shift "the switch in time that saved nine."

More recently, Chief Justice John Roberts seemed to have institutional concerns in mind when he surprised fellow conservatives by casting the deciding vote in favor of the constitutionality of the Affordable Care Act in 2012. The Court's conservative majority had come under increasing political fire for its positions on such matters as campaign finance and affirmative action. Roberts, according to

Since the retirement of Justice Anthony Kennedy, Chief Justice John Roberts has sometimes served as a swing vote on the Court to protect the precedents set by past decisions. In 2020, he ruled with the liberal justices to reject the Trump administration's suit against DACA, a program that protects young undocumented immigrants from deportation.

one commentator, saw himself as "uniquely entrusted with the custodianship of the Court's legitimacy, reputation, and stature" and was determined to show that the Court stood above mere political ideology.[28] As we saw on the previous page, Roberts repeated his support of the Affordable Care Act in 2015 in the case of *King v. Burwell*. In 2020, Chief Justice Roberts once again demonstrated his concern for the reputation of the institution of the Court. He angered conservatives and President Trump, in particular, when he sided with the Court's liberals in supporting LGBTQ rights, rejecting regulations on abortion, and blocking the administration's efforts to proceed quickly with the deportation of young undocumented immigrants—the so-called DREAMers. Trump responded angrily, declaring that the Supreme Court needed new justices.

Activism and Restraint Judicial philosophy also plays a role in the decisions of all judges, including those on the Supreme Court. One element of judicial philosophy is the issue of activism versus restraint. Over the years, some justices have believed that courts should interpret the Constitution according to the stated intentions of its framers and defer to the views of Congress when interpreting federal statutes. Justice Felix Frankfurter, for example, advocated judicial deference to legislative bodies and avoidance of the "political thicket" in which the Court would entangle itself by deciding questions that were essentially political rather than legal in character. Some, but not all, advocates of **judicial restraint** are also called "strict constructionists" because they look strictly to the words of the Constitution in interpreting its meaning.

The alternative to restraint is **judicial activism**. Activist judges such as Chief Justice Earl Warren believed that the Court should go beyond the words of the Constitution or a statute to consider the broader societal implications of its decisions. Such judges sometimes strike out in new directions, putting forth new interpretations or inventing new legal and constitutional concepts when they believe these to be socially desirable. For example, Justice Harry Blackmun's opinion in *Roe v. Wade* was based on a constitutional right to privacy that is not found in the words of the Constitution but was, rather, from the Court's prior decision in *Griswold v. Connecticut*.[29] Blackmun and the other members of the majority in the *Roe* case

judicial restraint judicial philosophy whose adherents refuse to go beyond the clear words of the Constitution in interpreting the document's meaning

judicial activism judicial philosophy that posits that the Court should go beyond the words of the Constitution or a statute to consider the broader societal implications of its decisions

argued that the right to privacy was implied by other constitutional provisions. In this instance of judicial activism, the Court knew the result it wanted to achieve and was not afraid to make the law conform to the desired outcome.

Activism and restraint can overlap with but are not always the same as liberalism and conservatism. For example, conservative politicians often castigate "liberal activist" judges and call for the appointment of conservative judges who will refrain from reinterpreting the law. But the Supreme Court from 1986 to 2005, dominated by conservatives under Chief Justice William Rehnquist, was among the most activist in American history, particularly in such areas as federalism and election law.

The Roberts Court is continuing along the same route. For example, in the 2014 case of *McCutcheon v. Federal Election Commission*, the Court struck down one of the major remaining elements of Congress's efforts to regulate campaign finance. The Court's five more conservative justices said that limits on how much individuals could contribute in any given election were a restraint on free speech.[30] This decision could be described as "activist" because it broadens the interpretation of "speech" and overturns congressional legislation that has significant public support. As these examples illustrate, a judge may be philosophically conservative and believe in strict construction of the Constitution but also believe that the courts must play an active and energetic role in policy making, if necessary striking down acts of Congress to ensure that the intent of the framers is fulfilled.

Political Ideology and Partisanship Nevertheless, the philosophy of activism versus restraint is indeed sometimes a smoke screen for political ideology, and justices' liberal or conservative attitudes and Democratic or Republican leanings play an important role in their decisions.[31] In the past, liberal judges have often been activists, willing to use the law to achieve social and political change, whereas conservatives have been associated with judicial restraint. Democrats who opposed the appointment of Justice Amy Coney Barrett to the Court in 2020 were suspicious of her commitment to the principle of judicial restraint. They feared that Barrett might be a conservative activist who would work to undo Obamacare as well as the Court's long-standing positions on abortion.

From the 1950s to the 1980s the Supreme Court took a liberal role in such areas as civil rights, civil liberties, abortion, voting rights, and police procedures. For example, it was more responsible than any other governmental institution for breaking down America's system of racial segregation. In the following decades, however, the conservative justices appointed by Presidents Ronald Reagan, George H. W. Bush, George W. Bush, and Donald Trump became the dominant bloc on the Court and, as we saw earlier, moved the Court to the right on a number of issues, including affirmative action and abortion.

The political struggles of recent years amply illustrate the importance of judicial ideology. Is abortion a fundamental right or a criminal activity? How much separation must there be between church and state? Does application of the Voting Rights Act to increase minority representation constitute a violation of the rights of Whites? The answers to these questions cannot be found in the words of the Constitution. They must be located, instead, in the hearts and minds of the judges who interpret that text.

Judicial philosophy, ideology, and institutional interest all influence the thinking of justices. In the end, however, the Supreme Court is a court of law and must pay heed to statutes and legal precedent. A decision that cannot be justified by law and precedent cannot be issued. To ignore the law would be to undermine the rule of law and to destroy the constitutional structure in which the Supreme Court occupies such a prominent place.

FOR CRITICAL ANALYSIS

In what ways are courts, judges, and justices shielded from politics and political pressure? In what ways are they vulnerable to political pressure? Are the courts an appropriate place for politics?

JUDICIAL POWER AND POLITICS

One of the most important institutional changes to occur in the United States over the last 75 years has been the striking transformation of the role and power of the federal courts, and of the Supreme Court in particular. Understanding how this transformation came about is the key to understanding the contemporary role of the courts in America.

Traditional Limitations on the Federal Courts For much of American history, the power of the federal courts was subject to a number of limitations.[32] First, unlike other governmental institutions, courts cannot exercise power on their own initiative. Judges must wait until a case is brought to them before they can make authoritative decisions.

Second, courts were traditionally limited in the kind of remedies they could provide to those who won cases. In general, courts acted to offer relief or assistance only to individuals and not to broad social classes.

Third, courts lacked enforcement powers and had to rely on executive or state agencies to ensure compliance with their rulings. If the executive or state agencies were unwilling to do so, judicial decisions could go unheeded, as when President Andrew Jackson declined to enforce Chief Justice John Marshall's 1832 order that the state of Georgia release two missionaries it had arrested on Cherokee lands. Marshall asserted that the state had no right to enter the lands without the Cherokees' assent.[33] Jackson is reputed to have said, "John Marshall has made his decision, now let him enforce it."

A fourth limitation on the federal courts is that because their judges are appointed by the president and require Senate confirmation, the president and Congress can shape their composition and ultimately, perhaps, the character of judicial decisions.

Finally, Congress has the power to change both the size and the jurisdiction of the Supreme Court and other federal courts. In many areas, federal courts obtain their jurisdiction not from the Constitution but from congressional statutes.

On a number of occasions, Congress has acted or threatened to take matters out of the courts' hands when it was unhappy with their decisions.[34] For example, in 1996, it enacted several laws to curb the jurisdiction of the federal courts. Among these was the Prison Litigation Reform Act, which limits the ability of federal judges to issue "consent decrees," under which the judges could take control of state prison systems. And on one memorable occasion mentioned earlier, presidential and congressional threats to expand the size of the Supreme Court—Franklin Roosevelt's "Court packing" plan—encouraged the justices to drop their opposition to New Deal programs.

As a result of these limitations on judicial power, through much of their history the federal courts' chief function was to validate acts of Congress and the executive by declaring them to be consistent with constitutional principles. Only on rare occasions did the courts dare to challenge Congress or the executive branch.[35]

Two Judicial Revolutions Since the Second World War, however, the role of the federal judiciary has been strengthened and expanded as a result of two "judicial revolutions." The first and more visible of these were the substantive innovations in judicial policy. As we saw earlier in this chapter and in Chapters 4 and 5, in many policy areas, including school desegregation, legislative apportionment, and criminal

FOR CRITICAL ANALYSIS

Are the federal courts "imperial," or are they subordinate to the elected branches of government? In what respect does the federal judiciary still play a "checks and balances" role?

procedure, and in obscenity, abortion, and voting rights, the Supreme Court was at the forefront of a series of sweeping changes in the role of the U.S. government and, ultimately, the character of American society.[36]

At the same time, the courts were also bringing about a second, less visible revolution. During the 1960s and '70s the Supreme Court and other federal courts instituted a series of changes in judicial procedures that fundamentally expanded the power of the courts in the United States.

First, the federal courts liberalized the concept of standing to permit almost any group that wishes to challenge the actions of an administrative agency to bring a federal court case. In 1971, for example, the Supreme Court ruled that public interest groups could use the National Environmental Policy Act to challenge the actions of federal agencies by claiming that the agencies' activities might have adverse environmental consequences.[37]

Congress helped to make it even easier for groups dissatisfied with government policies to bring their cases to the courts by adopting Section 1983 of the U.S. Code, which permits "fee shifting"—that is, allowing citizens who successfully sue a public official for violating their constitutional rights to collect their attorneys' fees and costs from the government. Thus, Section 1983 encourages individuals and groups to bring their grievances to the courts rather than to Congress or the executive branch. These changes have given the courts a far greater role in the administrative process than ever before.

In a second procedural expansion of judicial power, the federal courts broadened the scope of remedies they could provide by permitting suits on behalf of broad

Today, the Supreme Court is frequently at the center of major political issues. In a historic decision in 2015, the Court declared same-sex marriage a fundamental right protected by the due process and equal protection clauses of the Fourteenth Amendment to the Constitution.

class-action suit a legal action by which a group or class of individuals with common interests can file a suit on behalf of everyone who shares that interest

categories or classes of persons in "class-action" cases, rather than just on behalf of individuals.[38] A **class-action suit** permits large numbers of individuals with common interests to join together to bring or defend a lawsuit. An example is the case of *In re Agent Orange Product Liability Litigation*, in which a federal judge certified Vietnam War veterans as a class with standing to sue a manufacturer of herbicides for damages allegedly caused by exposure to the defendant's product while in Vietnam.[39] The class potentially numbered in the tens of thousands.

A third procedural expansion of the power of the federal courts came when they began to use so-called structural remedies, in effect retaining jurisdiction over a case until the court's ruling had actually been implemented to its satisfaction.[40] The best known of these remedies was the effort of federal judge W. Arthur Garrity, Jr., to operate the Boston school system from his courtroom in order to ensure its desegregation. Between 1974 and 1985, Garrity issued 14 decisions relating to different aspects of the desegregation plan that had been developed under his authority and put into effect under his supervision.[41] In another structural remedy, resulting from a suit by the NAACP, federal judge Leonard B. Sand imposed fines in 1985 that would have forced the city of Yonkers, New York, into bankruptcy if it refused to accept his plan to build public housing in White neighborhoods. Twenty-two years and $1.6 million in fines later, the city finally gave in to the judge's ruling in 2007.

Through these three procedural mechanisms, the federal courts paved the way for an unprecedented expansion of national judicial power. In essence, liberalization of the rules of standing and expansion of the scope of judicial relief drew the federal courts into alliances with important social interests and classes, such as civil rights, consumer, environmental, and feminist groups, while the introduction of structural remedies enhanced the courts' ability to serve these constituencies.

The Federal Judiciary: What Do You Think?

In their original conception, the framers intended the judiciary to be the institution that would protect individual liberty from the government. As we saw in Chapter 2, they believed that "tyranny of the majority" was a great threat to democracy, fearing that a popular majority, "united or actuated by some common impulse or passion," would "trample on the rules of justice."[42] For most of American history, the federal courts' most important decisions were those that protected the freedoms—to speak, worship, publish, vote, and attend school—of groups and individuals whose political views, religious beliefs, or racial or ethnic backgrounds made them unpopular. But today, Americans of all political persuasions seem to view the courts as useful instruments through which to pursue their policy goals. Conservatives want to ban abortion and help business maintain its profitability, whereas liberals want to enhance the power of workers in the workplace and reduce the role of private money in political campaigns.

★ These may all be noble goals, but they present a basic dilemma for students of American government. If the courts are simply one more set of policy-making institutions, who is left to protect the liberty of individuals? What would Mark Janus, featured at the start of the chapter, say about the role of the courts in American government?

★ Can you think of ways that Supreme Court decisions affect your life? For example, how might the Court's campaign-finance decisions affect who will govern the nation you inherit? How could its decisions on health care influence the type of care you receive and its cost? How will its decisions in the realm of immigration affect who will and will not be able to call themselves Americans? How might the Court's decision in Mark Janus's case against public-sector unions influence your future job and taxes?

★ Given what you know now, do you view the Court as the "least dangerous branch" or an "imperial judiciary"? What evidence do you see for each characterization?

★ STUDY GUIDE ★

The Legal System

Identify the general types of cases and types of courts in America's legal system (pp. 545–49)

Court cases in the United States proceed under two broad categories of law: criminal law and civil law. Both the federal government and the individual state governments have established systems of courts, and each system has several levels. State courts consider cases involving questions of state law, and federal courts decide cases involving federal laws, treaties with other nations, and the U.S. Constitution.

Key Terms

criminal law (p. 545)

plaintiff (p. 545)

defendant (p. 545)

civil law (p. 545)

precedent (p. 546)

trial court (p. 546)

court of appeals (p. 546)

supreme court (p. 546)

plea bargain (p. 547)

jurisdiction (p. 547)

original jurisdiction (p. 548)

due process of law (p. 549)

writ of habeas corpus (p. 549)

Practice Quiz

1. What is the name for the body of law that involves disputes between private entities such as individuals, groups, and corporations?
   a) civil law
   b) privacy law
   c) criminal law
   d) household law
   e) common law

2. The legal principle that previous court decisions should apply as precedents in similar cases is known as
   a) habeas corpus.
   b) a writ of certiorari.
   c) stare decisis.
   d) the rule of four.
   e) senatorial courtesy.

3. If a defendant decides to appeal a lower-court decision, the court of appeals will
   a) not hear witnesses or examine additional evidence.
   b) conduct an entirely new trial with new witnesses and evidence.
   c) help both parties negotiate a plea bargain.
   d) forward the case directly to the U.S. Supreme Court.
   e) assume original jurisdiction over the case.

4. Which of the following is *not* included in the original jurisdiction of the Supreme Court?
   a) cases between the United States and one of the states
   b) cases brought by one state against citizens of another state or against a foreign country
   c) cases involving challenges to the constitutionality of state laws
   d) cases between two or more states
   e) cases involving foreign ambassadors or other ministers

5. The term *writ of habeas corpus* refers to
   a) a short, unsigned decision by an appellate court, usually rejecting a petition to review the decision of a lower court.
   b) a criterion used by courts to screen cases that no longer require resolution.
   c) a decision of at least four of the nine Supreme Court justices to review a decision of a lower court.
   d) a court order to the authorities to show cause for a prisoner's incarceration.
   e) a brief filed by the solicitor general when the federal government is not a direct litigant in a Supreme Court case.

Federal Courts

. . . .

> **Describe the different levels of federal courts and the process of appointing federal judges (pp. 549–55)**

The federal judiciary is composed of 94 district courts, 12 circuit courts, several courts with specialized jurisdictions, and the U.S. Supreme Court. The federal courts hear only a very small percentage of the cases decided in the United States each year. Presidents typically nominate judges for the federal judiciary who are prominent or politically active members of the legal profession and who share their partisan and ideological views. The importance of appointments to the federal judiciary has made the confirmation process in the Senate increasingly contentious in recent years.

Key Term

chief justice (p. 551)

Practice Quiz

6. The size of the Supreme Court is determined by
   a) the president.
   b) the chief justice.
   c) the Department of Justice.
   d) Congress.
   e) the Constitution.

7. The formal requirements for service as a federal judge include
   a) experience as a state-level judge.
   b) a minimum age of 30.
   c) a minimum of 10 years' legal experience.
   d) a neutral political background.
   e) There are no formal qualifications for service as a federal judge.

The Power of the Supreme Court: Judicial Review

. . . .

> **Explain the Supreme Court's judicial review of national law (pp. 555–61)**

The Supreme Court has the power to review the constitutionality of acts of Congress, state actions, and actions of the president and the executive branch. Although the Constitution does not explicitly give the Court the power of judicial review, the Court established its duty to review acts of Congress in its 1803 *Marbury v. Madison* decision, and this power has generally been accepted since then.

Key Terms

judicial review (p. 555)

supremacy clause (p. 556)

Practice Quiz

8. The Supreme Court's decision in *Marbury v. Madison* was important because
   a) it invalidated state laws prohibiting interracial marriage.
   b) it ruled that the recitation of prayers in public schools is unconstitutional under the establishment clause of the First Amendment.
   c) it established that arrested people have the right to remain silent, the right to be informed that anything they say can be held against them, and the right to counsel before and during police interrogation.
   d) it provided an expansive definition of *commerce* under the interstate commerce clause.
   e) it established the power of judicial review.

9. The U.S. Supreme Court's power to review state actions comes from
   a) tort law.
   b) *Hamdi v. Rumsfeld* and *Hamdan v. Rumsfeld*.
   c) the supremacy clause of the Constitution and the Judiciary Act of 1789.
   d) certiorari and amicus curiae.
   e) The Supreme Court does not have the power to review state actions.

The Supreme Court in Action

Describe the process by which cases are considered and decided by the Supreme Court (pp. 561–69)

Most cases reach the Supreme Court by a writ of certiorari. The Supreme Court is most likely to grant a writ of certiorari to cases that involve conflicting decisions by the federal circuit courts, cases that present important questions of civil rights or civil liberties, and appeals by the federal government. The solicitor general, law clerks, and lawyers representing certain interests also have some influence over (or attempt to influence) which cases are ultimately heard by the Court. Once the Court agrees to hear a case, it follows what can be a lengthy and complex process—which includes reviewing briefs, hearing oral arguments, and discussing the cases at conference—before ultimately drafting opinions.

Key Terms

standing (p. 562)

mootness (p. 562)

writ of certiorari (p. 562)

solicitor general (p. 563)

amicus curiae (p. 564)

briefs (p. 565)

oral argument (p. 566)

opinion (p. 567)

concurring opinion (p. 568)

dissenting opinion (p. 568)

Practice Quiz

10. Which of the following is *not* included as a "special and compelling" reason to hear a case under rule 10 of the Rules of the Supreme Court of the United States?
    a) The president of the United States authors an amicus curiae brief on the issue in question.
    b) A circuit court decision on the issue in question conflicts with previous Supreme Court decisions.
    c) There are conflicting decisions by two or more state courts of last resort on the issue in question.
    d) There are conflicting decisions between circuit courts and state courts of last resort on the issue in question.
    e) There are conflicting decisions by two or more circuit courts on the issue in question.

11. Which of the following play an important role in shaping the flow of cases heard by the Supreme Court?
    a) the attorney general and the secretary of state
    b) the solicitor general and federal law clerks
    c) the president and Congress
    d) state legislatures
    e) the federal district and circuit courts

12. Which of the following is a brief submitted to the Supreme Court by someone other than one of the parties in the case?
    a) amicus curiae brief
    b) writ of habeas corpus
    c) writ of certiorari
    d) dissenting opinion
    e) de jure brief

Explaining Supreme Court Decisions

Describe the factors that influence court decisions (pp. 569–74)

Supreme Court justices' decisions may be influenced by their desire to protect the Court's power and reputation, their personal judicial philosophy, and their political ideology. Because of a number of limitations on the court system, for most of American history, the federal courts worked primarily to validate acts of Congress and the executive by declaring them to be consistent with constitutional principles. During the 1960s and '70s the federal courts liberalized the concept of standing, broadened the scope of relief courts could provide, and began to employ structural remedies. As a result of these changes, the power of the federal court system expanded dramatically.

Key Terms

judicial restraint (p. 570)
judicial activism (p. 570)
class-action suit (p. 574)

Practice Quiz

13. If a justice looks strictly to the words of the Constitution in interpreting its meaning, he or she would be considered an advocate of which judicial philosophy?
    a) judicial restraint
    b) judicial activism
    c) stare decisis
    d) judicial liberalism
    e) judicial conservatism

14. Which of the following is one of the limitations that federal courts have traditionally faced?
    a) Justices do not have to wait until a case is brought to them before they can make authoritative decisions.
    b) Courts were tasked with offering relief or assistance to broad social classes, not to individuals.
    c) Courts lacked enforcement powers of their own and had to rely on executive or state agencies to ensure compliance with their rulings.
    d) Courts must take the time and spend the money to recruit compelling candidates for judgeships.
    e) Courts must coordinate with the legislative and executive branches to determine their own size and jurisdiction.

15. Which of the following procedures adopted by the federal courts after 1960 fundamentally expanded the power of the judiciary in the United States?
    a) banning the practice of "fee shifting"
    b) prohibiting the courts from acting on behalf of broad categories of persons in "class-action" cases
    c) expanding the concept of standing to permit almost any group that seeks to challenge the actions of an administrative agency to bring its case before the federal bench
    d) creating a "Department of Judicial Enforcement" to independently implement the federal judiciary's decisions
    e) granting federal courts the ability to exercise power on their own initiative through the issuance of "mootness" rulings

Appendix

The Declaration of Independence

In Congress, July 4, 1776

The unanimous Declaration of the thirteen united States of America,

When in the Course of human events, it becomes necessary for one people to dissolve the political bands which have connected them with another, and to assume among the powers of the earth, the separate and equal station to which the Laws of Nature and of Nature's God entitle them, a decent respect to the opinions of mankind requires that they should declare the causes which impel them to the separation.

We hold these truths to be self-evident, that all men are created equal, that they are endowed by their Creator with certain unalienable Rights, that among these are Life, Liberty and the pursuit of Happiness.—That to secure these rights, Governments are instituted among Men, deriving their just powers from the consent of the governed.—That whenever any Form of Government becomes destructive of these ends, it is the Right of the People to alter or to abolish it, and to institute new Government, laying its foundation on such principles and organizing its powers in such form, as to them shall seem most likely to effect their Safety and Happiness. Prudence, indeed, will dictate that Governments long established should not be changed for light and transient causes; and accordingly all experience hath shewn, that mankind are more disposed to suffer, while evils are sufferable, than to right themselves by abolishing the forms to which they are accustomed. But when a long train of abuses and usurpations, pursuing invariably the same Object evinces a design to reduce them under absolute Despotism, it is their right, it is their duty, to throw off such Government, and to provide new Guards for their future security.—Such has been the patient sufferance of these Colonies; and such is now the necessity which constrains them to alter their former Systems of Government. The history of the present King of Great Britain is a history of repeated injuries and usurpations, all having in direct object the establishment of an absolute Tyranny over these States. To prove this, let Facts be submitted to a candid world.

He has refused his Assent to Laws, the most wholesome and necessary for the public good.

He has forbidden his Governors to pass Laws of immediate and pressing importance, unless suspended in their operation till his Assent should be obtained; and when so suspended, he has utterly neglected to attend to them.

He has refused to pass other Laws for the accommodation of large districts of people, unless those people would relinquish the right of Representation in the Legislature, a right inestimable to them and formidable to tyrants only.

He has called together legislative bodies at places unusual, uncomfortable, and distant from the depository of their public Records, for the sole purpose of fatiguing them into compliance with his measures.

He has dissolved Representative Houses repeatedly, for opposing with manly firmness his invasions on the rights of the people.

He has refused for a long time, after such dissolutions, to cause others to be elected; whereby the Legislative powers, incapable of Annihilation, have returned to the People at large for their exercise; the State remaining in the mean time exposed to all the dangers of invasion from without, and convulsions within.

He has endeavoured to prevent the population of these States; for that purpose obstructing the Laws for Naturalization of Foreigners; refusing to pass others to encourage their migrations hither, and raising the conditions of new Appropriations of Lands.

He has obstructed the Administration of Justice, by refusing his Assent to Laws for establishing Judiciary powers.

He has made Judges dependent on his Will alone, for the tenure of their offices, and the amount and payment of their salaries.

He has erected a multitude of New Offices, and sent hither swarms of Officers to harrass our people, and eat out their substance.

He has kept among us, in times of peace, Standing Armies without the Consent of our legislatures.

He has affected to render the Military independent of and superior to the Civil power.

He has combined with others to subject us to a jurisdiction foreign to our constitution, and unacknowledged by our laws; giving his Assent to their Acts of pretended Legislation:

For Quartering large bodies of armed troops among us:

For protecting them, by a mock Trial, from punishment for any Murders which they should commit on the Inhabitants of these States:

For cutting off our Trade with all parts of the world:

For imposing Taxes on us without our Consent:

For depriving us in many cases, of the benefits of Trial by Jury:

For transporting us beyond Seas to be tried for pretended offences:

For abolishing the free System of English Laws in a neighboring Province, establishing therein an Arbitrary government, and enlarging its Boundaries so as to render it at once an example and fit instrument for introducing the same absolute rule into these Colonies:

For taking away our Charters, abolishing our most valuable Laws, and altering fundamentally the Forms of our Governments:

For suspending our own Legislatures, and declaring themselves invested with power to legislate for us in all cases whatsoever.

He has abdicated Government here, by declaring us out of his Protection and waging War against us.

He has plundered our seas, ravaged our Coasts, burnt our towns, and destroyed the lives of our people.

He is at this time transporting large Armies of foreign Mercenaries to compleat the works of death, desolation and tyranny, already begun with circumstances of Cruelty & perfidy scarcely paralleled in the most barbarous ages, and totally unworthy the Head of a civilized nation.

He has constrained our fellow Citizens taken Captive on the high Seas to bear Arms against their Country, to become the executioners of their friends and Brethren, or to fall themselves by their Hands.

He has excited domestic insurrections amongst us, and has endeavoured to bring on the inhabitants of our frontiers, the merciless Indian Savages, whose known rule of warfare, is an undistinguished destruction of all ages, sexes and conditions.

In every stage of these Oppressions We have Petitioned for Redress in the most humble terms: Our repeated Petitions have been answered only by repeated injury. A Prince whose character is thus marked by every act which may define a Tyrant, is unfit to be the ruler of a free people.

Nor have We been wanting in attentions to our Brittish brethren. We have warned them from time to time of attempts by their legislature to extend an unwarrantable jurisdiction over us. We have reminded them of the circumstances of our emigration and settlement here. We have appealed to their native justice and magnanimity, and we have conjured them by the ties of our common kindred to disavow these usurpations, which, would inevitably interrupt our connections and correspondence. They too have been deaf to the voice of justice and of consanguinity. We must, therefore, acquiesce in the necessity, which denounces our Separation, and hold them, as we hold the rest of mankind, Enemies in War, in Peace Friends.

We, Therefore, the Representatives of the United States of America, in General Congress, Assembled, appealing to the Supreme Judge of the world for the rectitude of our intentions, do, in the Name, and by Authority of the good People of these Colonies, solemnly publish and declare, That these United Colonies are, and of Right ought to be Free and Independent States; that they are Absolved from all Allegiance to the British Crown, and that all political connection between them and the State of Great Britain, is and ought to be totally dissolved; and that as Free and Independent States, they have full Power to levy War, conclude Peace, contract Alliances, establish Commerce, and to do all other Acts and Things which Independent States may of right do. And for the support of this Declaration, with a firm reliance on the protection of divine Providence, we mutually pledge to each other our Lives, our Fortunes and our sacred Honor.

The foregoing Declaration was, by order of Congress, engrossed, and signed by the following members:

John Hancock

NEW HAMPSHIRE
Josiah Bartlett
William Whipple
Matthew Thornton

MASSACHUSETTS BAY
Samuel Adams
John Adams
Robert Treat Paine
Elbridge Gerry

RHODE ISLAND
Stephen Hopkins
William Ellery

CONNECTICUT
Roger Sherman
Samuel Huntington
William Williams
Oliver Wolcott

NEW YORK
William Floyd
Philip Livingston
Francis Lewis
Lewis Morris

NEW JERSEY
Richard Stockton
John Witherspoon
Francis Hopkinson
John Hart
Abraham Clark

PENNSYLVANIA
Robert Morris
Benjamin Rush
Benjamin Franklin
John Morton
George Clymer
James Smith
George Taylor
James Wilson
George Ross

DELAWARE
Caesar Rodney
George Read
Thomas M'Kean

MARYLAND
Samuel Chase
William Paca
Thomas Stone
Charles Carroll,
* of Carrollton*

VIRGINIA
George Wythe
Richard Henry Lee
Thomas Jefferson
Benjamin Harrison
Thomas Nelson, Jr.
Francis Lightfoot Lee
Carter Braxton

NORTH CAROLINA
William Hooper
Joseph Hewes
John Penn

SOUTH CAROLINA
Edward Rutledge
Thomas Heyward, Jr.
Thomas Lynch, Jr.
Arthur Middleton

GEORGIA
Button Gwinnett
Lyman Hall
George Walton

Resolved, That copies of the Declaration be sent to the several assemblies, conventions, and committees, or councils of safety, and to the several commanding officers of the continental troops; that it be proclaimed in each of the United States, at the head of the army.

The Articles of Confederation

Agreed to by Congress November 15, 1777;
ratified and in force March 1, 1781

To all whom these Presents shall come, we the undersigned Delegates of the States affixed to our Names, send greeting. Whereas the Delegates of the United States of America, in Congress assembled, did, on the fifteenth day of November, in the Year of Our Lord One thousand Seven Hundred and Seventy seven, and in the Second Year of the Independence of America, agree to certain articles of Confederation and perpetual Union between the States of Newhampshire, Massachusettsbay, Rhodeisland and Providence Plantations, Connecticut, New-York, New-Jersey, Pennsylvania, Delaware, Maryland, Virginia, North-Carolina, South-Carolina and Georgia in the words following, viz. "Articles of Confederation and perpetual Union between the states of Newhampshire, Massachusettsbay, Rhodeisland and Providence Plantations, Connecticut, New-York, New-Jersey, Pennsylvania, Delaware, Maryland, Virginia, North-Carolina, South-Carolina and Georgia.

Art. I. The Stile of this confederacy shall be "The United States of America."

Art. II. Each state retains its sovereignty, freedom and independence, and every Power, Jurisdiction and right, which is not by this confederation expressly delegated to the United States, in Congress assembled.

Art. III. The said states hereby severally enter into a firm league of friendship with each other, for their common defence, the security of their Liberties, and their mutual and general welfare, binding themselves to assist each other, against all force offered to, or attacks made upon them, or any of them, on account of religion, sovereignty, trade, or any other pretence whatever.

Art. IV. The better to secure and perpetuate mutual friendship and intercourse among the people of the different states in this union, the free inhabitants of each of these states, paupers, vagabonds and fugitives from Justice excepted, shall be entitled to all privileges and immunities of free citizens in the several states; and the people of each state shall have free ingress and regress to and from any other state, and shall enjoy therein all the privileges of trade and commerce, subject to the same duties, impositions and restrictions as the inhabitants thereof respectively, provided that such restriction shall not extend so far as to prevent the removal of property imported into any state, to any other state, of which the Owner is an inhabitant; provided also that no imposition, duties or restriction shall be laid by any state, on the property of the united states, or either of them.

If any Person guilty of, or charged with treason, felony, or other high misdemeanor in any state, shall flee from Justice, and be found in any of the united states, he shall, upon demand of the Governor or executive power, of the state from which he fled, be delivered up and removed to the state having jurisdiction of his offence.

Full faith and credit shall be given in each of these states to the records, acts and judicial proceedings of the courts and magistrates of every other state.

Art. V. For the more convenient management of the general interests of the united states, delegates shall be annually appointed in such manner as the legislature of each state shall direct, to meet in Congress on the first Monday in November, in every year, with a power reserved to each state, to recall its delegates, or any of them, at any time within the year, and to send others in their stead, for the remainder of the Year.

No state shall be represented in Congress by less than two, nor by more than seven Members; and no person shall be capable of being a delegate for more than three years in any term of six years; nor shall any person, being a delegate, be capable of holding any office under the united states, for which he, or another for his benefit receives any salary, fees or emolument of any kind.

Each state shall maintain its own delegates in a meeting of the states, and while they act as members of the committee of the states.

In determining questions in the united states, in Congress assembled, each state shall have one vote.

Freedom of speech and debate in Congress shall not be impeached or questioned in any Court, or place out of Congress, and the members of congress shall be protected in their persons from arrests and imprisonments, during the time of their going to and from, and attendance on congress, except for treason, felony, or breach of the peace.

Art. VI. No state without the Consent of the united states in congress assembled, shall send any embassy to, or receive any embassy from, or enter into any conference, agreement, or alliance or treaty with any King, prince or state; nor shall any person holding any office or profit or trust under the united states, or any of them, accept of any present, emolument, office or title of any kind whatever from any king, prince or foreign state; nor shall the united states in congress assembled, or any of them, grant any title of nobility.

No two or more states shall enter into any treaty, confederation or alliance whatever between them, without the consent of the united states in congress assembled, specifying accurately the purposes for which the same is to be entered into, and how long it shall continue.

No state shall lay any imposts or duties, which may interfere with any stipulations in treaties, entered into by the united states in congress assembled, with any king, prince or state, in pursuance of any treaties already proposed by congress, to the courts of France and Spain.

No vessels of war shall be kept up in time of peace by any state, except such number only, as shall be deemed necessary by the united states in congress assembled, for the defence of such state, or its trade; nor shall any body of forces be kept up by any state, in time of peace, except such number only, as in the judgment of the united states, in congress assembled, shall be deemed requisite to garrison the forts necessary for the defence of such state; but every state shall always keep up a well regulated and disciplined militia, sufficiently armed and accoutred, and shall provide and constantly have ready for use, in public stores, a due number of field pieces and tents, and a proper quantity of arms, ammunition and camp equipage.

No state shall engage in any war without the consent of the united states in congress assembled, unless such state be actually invaded by enemies, or shall have received certain advice of a resolution being formed by some nation of Indians to invade such state, and the danger is so imminent as not to admit of a delay, till the united states in congress asssembled can be consulted; nor shall any state grant commissions to any ships or vessels of war, nor letters of marque or reprisal, except it be after a declaration of war by the united states in congress assembled, and then only against the kingdom or state and the subjects thereof, against which war has been so declared, and under such regulations as shall be established by the united states in congress assembled, unless such state be infested by pirates; in which case vessels of war may be fitted out for that occasion, and kept so long as the danger shall continue, or until the united states in congress assembled shall determine otherwise.

Art. VII. When land-forces are raised by any state for the common defence, all officers of or under the rank of colonel, shall be appointed by the legislature of each state respectively, by whom such forces shall be raised, or in such manner as such state shall direct, and all vacancies shall be filled up by the state which first made the appointment.

Art. VIII. All charges of war, and all other expences that shall be incurred for the common defence or general welfare, and allowed by the united states in congress assembled, shall be defrayed out of a common treasury, which shall be supplied by the several states in proportion to the value of all land within each state, granted to or surveyed for any Person, as such land and the buildings and improvements thereon shall be estimated according to such mode as the united states in congress assembled, shall from time to time direct and appoint.

The taxes for paying that proportion shall be laid and levied by the authority and direction of the legislatures of the several states within the time agreed upon by the united states in congress assembled.

Art. IX. The united states in congress assembled, shall have the sole and exclusive right and power of determining on peace and war, except in the cases mentioned in the sixth article—of sending and receiving ambassadors—entering into treaties and alliances, provided that no treaty of commerce shall be made whereby the legislative power of the respective states shall be restrained from imposing such imposts and duties on foreigners, as their own people are subjected to, or from prohibiting the exportation of any species of goods or commodities whatsoever— of establishing rules for deciding in all cases, what captures on land or water shall be legal, and in what manner prizes taken by land or naval forces in the service of the united states shall be divided or appropriated—of granting letters of marque and reprisal in times of peace—appointing courts for the trial of piracies and felonies committed on the high seas and establishing courts for receiving and determining finally appeals in all cases of captures, provided that no member of congress shall be appointed a judge of any of the said courts.

The united states in congress assembled shall also be the last resort on appeal in all disputes and differences now subsisting or that hereafter may arise between two or more states concerning boundary, jurisdiction or any other cause whatever; which authority shall always be exercised in the manner following. Whenever the legislative or executive authority or lawful agent of any state in controversy with another shall present a petition to congress stating the matter in question and praying for a hearing, notice thereof shall be given by order of congress to the legislative or executive authority of the other state in controversy, and a day assigned for the appearance of the parties by their lawful agents, who shall then be directed to appoint by joint consent, commissioners or judges to constitute a court for hearing and determining the matter in question: but if they cannot agree, congress shall name three persons out of each of the united states, and from the list of such persons each party shall alternately strike out one, the petitioners beginning, until the number shall be reduced to thirteen; and from that number not less than seven, nor more than nine names as congress shall direct, shall in the presence of congress be drawn out by lot, and the persons whose names shall be so drawn or any five of them, shall be commissioners or judges, to hear and finally determine the controversy, so always as a major part of the judges who shall hear the cause shall agree in the determination: and if either party shall neglect to attend at the day appointed, without shewing reasons, which congress shall judge sufficient, or being present shall refuse to strike, the congress shall proceed to nominate three persons out of each state, and the secretary of congress shall strike in behalf of such party absent or refusing; and the judgment and sentence of the court to be appointed, in the manner before prescribed, shall be final and conclusive; and if any of the parties shall refuse to submit to the authority of such court, or to appear to defend their claim or cause, the court shall nevertheless proceed to pronounce sentence, or judgment, which shall in like manner be final and decisive, the judgment or sentence and other proceedings being in either case transmitted to congress, and lodged among the acts of congress for the security of the parties concerned: provided that every commissioner, before he sits in judgment, shall take an oath to be administered by one of the judges of the supreme or superior court of the state, where the cause shall be tried, "well and truly to hear and determine the matter in question, according to the best of his judgment, without favour, affection or hope of reward:" provided also, that no state shall be deprived of territory for the benefit of the united states.

All controversies concerning the private right of soil claimed under different grants of two or more states, whose jurisdictions as they may respect such lands, and the states which passed such grants are adjusted, the said grants or either of them being at the same time claimed to have originated antecedent to such settlement of jurisdiction, shall on the petition of either party to the congress of the united states, be finally determined as near as may be in the same manner as is before prescribed for deciding disputes respecting territorial jurisdiction between different states.

The united states in congress assembled shall also have the sole and exclusive right and power of regulating the alloy and value of coin struck by their own authority, or by that of the respective states—fixing the standard of weights and measures throughout the united states—regulating the trade and managing all affairs with the Indians, not members of any of the states, provided that the legislative right of any state within its own limits be not infringed or violated—establishing and regulating post-offices from one state to another, throughout all the united states, and exacting such postage on the papers passing thro' the same as may be requisite to defray the expences of the said office—appointing all officers of the land forces, in the service of the united states, excepting regimental officers—appointing all the officers of the naval forces, and commissioning all officers whatever in the service of the united states—making rules for the government and regulation of the said land and naval forces, and directing their operations.

The united states in congress assembled shall have authority to appoint a committee, to sit in the recess of congress, to be denominated "A Committee of the States," and to consist of one delegate from each state; and to appoint such other committees and civil officers as may be necessary for managing the general affairs of the united states under their direction—to appoint one of their number to preside, provided that no person be allowed to serve in the office of president more than one year in any term of three years; to ascertain the necessary sums of Money to be raised for the service of the united states, and to appropriate and apply the same for defraying the public expenses—to borrow money, or emit bills on the credit of the united states, transmitting every half year to the respective states an account of the sums of money so borrowed or emitted,—to build and equip a navy—to agree upon the number of land forces, and to make requisitions from each state for its quota, in proportion to the number of white inhabitants in such state; which requisition shall be binding, and thereupon the legislature of each state shall appoint the regimental officers, raise the men and cloath, arm and equip them in a soldier like manner, at the expense of the united states; and the officers and men so cloathed, armed and equipped shall march to the place appointed, and within the time agreed on by the united states in congress assembled: But if the united states in congress assembled shall, on consideration of circumstances judge proper that any state should not raise men, or should raise a smaller number than its quota, and that any other state should raise a greater number of men than the quota thereof, such extra number shall be raised, officered, cloathed, armed and equipped in the same manner as the quota of such state, unless the legislature of such state shall judge that such extra number cannot be safely spared out of the same, in which case they shall raise officer, cloath, arm and equip as many of such extra number as they judge can be safely spared. And the officers and men so cloathed, armed and equipped, shall march to the place appointed, and within the time agreed on by the united states in congress assembled.

The united states in congress assembled shall never engage in a war, nor grant letters of marque and reprisal in time of peace, nor enter into any treaties or alliances, nor coin money, nor regulate the value thereof, nor ascertain the sums and expenses necessary for the defence and welfare of the united states, or any of them, nor emit bills, nor borrow money on the credit of the united states, nor appropriate money, nor agree upon the number of vessels of war, to be built or purchased, or the number of land or sea forces to be raised, nor appoint a commander in chief of the army or navy, unless nine states assent to the same: nor shall a question on any other point, except for adjourning from day to day be determined, unless by the votes of a majority of the united states in congress assembled.

The congress of the united states shall have power to adjourn to any time within the year, and to any place within the united states, so that no period of adjournment be for a longer duration than the space of six Months, and shall publish the Journal of their proceedings monthly, except such parts thereof relating to treaties, alliances or military operations, as in their judgment require secrecy; and the yeas and nays of the delegates of each state on any question shall be entered on the Journal, when it is desired by any delegate; and the delegates of a state, or any of them, at his or their request shall be furnished with a transcript of the said Journal, except such parts as are above excepted, to lay before the legislatures of the several states.

Art. X. The committee of the states, or any nine of them, shall be authorised to execute, in the recess of congress, such of the powers of congress as the united states in congress assembled, by the consent of nine states, shall from time to time think expedient to vest them with; provided that no power be delegated to the said committee, for the exercise of which, by the articles of confederation, the voice of nine states in the congress of the united states assembled is requisite.

Art. XI. Canada acceding to this confederation, and joining in the measures of the united states, shall be admitted into, and entitled to all the advantages of this union: but no other colony shall be admitted into the same, unless such admission be agreed to by nine states.

Art. XII. All bills of credit emitted, monies borrowed and debts contracted by, or under the authority of congress, before the assembling of the united states, in pursuance of the present confederation, shall be deemed and considered as a charge against the united states, for payment and satisfaction whereof the said united states and the public faith are hereby solemnly pledged.

Art. XIII. Every state shall abide by the determinations of the united states in congress assembled, on all questions which by this confederation are submitted to them. And the Articles of this confederation shall be inviolably observed by every state, and the union shall be perpetual; nor shall any alteration at any time hereafter be made in any of them; unless such alteration be agreed to in a congress of the united states, and be afterwards confirmed by the legislatures of every state.

And Whereas it hath pleased the Great Governor of the World to incline the hearts of the legislatures we respectively represent in congress, to approve of, and to authorize us to ratify the said articles of confederation and perpetual union. Know Ye that we the undersigned delegates, by virtue of the power and authority to us given for that purpose, do by these presents, in the name and in behalf of our respective constituents, fully and entirely ratify and confirm each and every of the said articles of confederation and perpetual union, and all and singular the matters and things therein contained: And we do further solemnly plight and engage the faith of our respective constituents, that they shall abide by the determinations of the united states in congress assembled, on all questions, which by the said confederation are submitted to them. And that the articles thereof shall be inviolably observed by the states we respectively represent, and that the union shall be perpetual. In Witness whereof we have hereunto set our hands in Congress. Done at Philadelphia in the state of Pennsylvania the ninth day of July, in the Year of our Lord one Thousand seven Hundred and Seventy-eight, and in the third year of the independence of America.

The Constitution of the United States of America

We the People of the United States, in Order to form a more perfect Union, establish Justice, insure domestic Tranquility, provide for the common defence, promote the general Welfare, and secure the Blessings of Liberty to ourselves and our Posterity, do ordain and establish this Constitution for the United States of America.

ARTICLE I

SECTION 1
[LEGISLATIVE POWERS]

All legislative Powers herein granted shall be vested in a Congress of the United States, which shall consist of a Senate and House of Representatives.

SECTION 2
[HOUSE OF REPRESENTATIVES, HOW CONSTITUTED, POWER OF IMPEACHMENT]

The House of Representatives shall be composed of Members chosen every second Year by the People of the several States, and the Electors in each State shall have the Qualifications requisite for Electors of the most numerous Branch of the State Legislature.

No Person shall be a Representative who shall not have attained to the Age of twenty five Years, and been seven Years a Citizen of the United States, and who shall not, when elected, be an Inhabitant of that State in which he shall be chosen.

Representatives and *direct Taxes*[1] shall be apportioned among the several States which may be included within this Union, according to their respective Numbers, *which shall be determined by adding to the whole Number of free Persons, including those bound to Service for a Term of Years, and excluding Indians not taxed, three fifths of all other Persons.*[2] The actual Enumeration shall be made within three Years after the first Meeting of the Congress of the United States, and within every subsequent Term of ten Years, in such Manner as they shall by Law direct. The Number of Representatives shall not exceed one for every thirty Thousand, but each State shall have at Least one Representative; *and until such enumeration shall*

be made, the State of New Hampshire shall be entitled to chuse three, Massachusetts eight, Rhode-Island and Providence Plantations one, Connecticut five, New-York six, New Jersey four, Pennsylvania eight, Delaware one, Maryland six, Virginia ten, North Carolina five, South Carolina five, and Georgia three.[3]

When vacancies happen in the Representation from any State, the Executive Authority thereof shall issue Writs of Election to fill such Vacancies.

The House of Representatives shall chuse their Speaker and other Officers; and shall have the sole Power of Impeachment.

SECTION 3
[THE SENATE, HOW CONSTITUTED, IMPEACHMENT TRIALS]

The Senate of the United States shall be composed of two Senators from each State, *chosen by the Legislature thereof,*[4] for six Years; and each Senator shall have one Vote.

Immediately after they shall be assembled in Consequence of the first Election, they shall be divided as equally as may be into three Classes. The Seats of the Senators of the first Class shall be vacated at the Expiration of the second Year, of the second Class at the Expiration of the fourth Year, and of the third Class at the Expiration of the sixth Year, so that one third may be chosen every second Year; *and if Vacancies happen by Resignation, or otherwise, during the Recess of the Legislature of any State, the Executive thereof may make temporary Appointments until the next Meeting of the Legislature, which shall then fill such Vacancies.*[5]

No Person shall be a Senator who shall not have attained to the Age of thirty Years, and been nine Years a Citizen of the United States, and who shall not, when elected, be an Inhabitant of that State for which he shall be chosen.

The Vice President of the United States shall be President of the Senate, but shall have no Vote, unless they be equally divided.

The Senate shall chuse their other Officers, and also a President pro tempore, in the Absence of the Vice President, or when he shall exercise the Office of President of the United States.

---

[1]Modified by Sixteenth Amendment.
[2]Modified by Fourteenth Amendment.

[3]Temporary provision.
[4]Modified by Seventeenth Amendment.
[5]Modified by Seventeenth Amendment.

The Senate shall have the sole Power to try all Impeachments. When sitting for that Purpose, they shall be on Oath or Affirmation. When the President of the United States is tried, the Chief Justice shall preside: And no Person shall be convicted without the Concurrence of two thirds of the Members present.

Judgment in Cases of Impeachment shall not extend further than to removal from Office, and disqualification to hold and enjoy any Office of honor, Trust or Profit under the United States: but the Party convicted shall nevertheless be liable and subject to Indictment, Trial, Judgment and Punishment, according to Law.

SECTION 4
[ELECTION OF SENATORS AND REPRESENTATIVES]

The Times, Places and Manner of holding Elections for Senators and Representatives, shall be prescribed in each State by the Legislature thereof; but the Congress may at any time by Law make or alter such Regulations, except as to the Places of chusing Senators.

The Congress shall assemble at least once in every Year, and such Meeting shall be on the first Monday in December, unless they shall by Law appoint a different Day.[6]

SECTION 5
[QUORUM, JOURNALS, MEETINGS, ADJOURNMENTS]

Each House shall be the Judge of the Elections, Returns and Qualifications of its own Members, and a Majority of each shall constitute a Quorum to do Business; but a smaller Number may adjourn from day to day, and may be authorized to compel the Attendance of absent Members, in such Manner, and under such Penalties as each House may provide.

Each House may determine the Rules of its Proceedings, punish its Members for disorderly Behaviour, and, with the Concurrence of two thirds, expel a Member.

Each House shall keep a Journal of its Proceedings, and from time to time publish the same, excepting such Parts as may in their Judgment require Secrecy; and the Yeas and Nays of the Members of either House on any questions shall, at the Desire of one fifth of those Present, be entered on the Journal.

Neither House, during the Session of Congress, shall, without the Consent of the other, adjourn for more than three days, nor to any other Place than that in which the two Houses shall be sitting.

SECTION 6
[COMPENSATION, PRIVILEGES, DISABILITIES]

The Senators and Representatives shall receive a Compensation for their Services, to be ascertained by Law, and paid out of the Treasury of the United States. They shall in all Cases, except Treason, Felony and Breach of the Peace, be privileged from

[6]Modified by Twentieth Amendment.

Arrest during their Attendance at the Session of their respective Houses, and in going to and returning from the same; and for any Speech or Debate in either House, they shall not be questioned in any other Place.

No Senator or Representative shall, during the Time for which he was elected, be appointed to any civil Office under the Authority of the United States, which shall have been created, or the Emoluments whereof shall have been encreased during such time; and no Person holding any Office under the United States, shall be a Member of either House during his Continuance in Office.

SECTION 7
[PROCEDURE IN PASSING BILLS AND RESOLUTIONS]

All Bills for raising Revenue shall originate in the House of Representatives; but the Senate may propose or concur with Amendments as on other Bills.

Every Bill which shall have passed the House of Representatives and the Senate, shall, before it become a Law, be presented to the President of the United States: If he approve he shall sign it, but if not he shall return it, with his Objections to that House in which it shall have originated, who shall enter the Objections at large on their Journal, and proceed to reconsider it. If after such Reconsideration two thirds of that House shall agree to pass the Bill, it shall be sent, together with the Objections, to the other House, by which it shall likewise be reconsidered, and if approved by two thirds of that House, it shall become a Law. But in all such Cases the Votes of both Houses shall be determined by yeas and Nays, and the Names of the Persons voting for and against the Bill shall be entered on the Journal of each House respectively. If any Bill shall not be returned by the President within ten Days (Sundays excepted) after it shall have been presented to him, the Same shall be a Law, in like Manner as if he had signed it, unless the Congress by their Adjournment prevent its Return, in which Case it shall not be a Law.

Every Order, Resolution, or Vote to which the Concurrence of the Senate and House of Representatives may be necessary (except on a question of Adjournment) shall be presented to the President of the United States; and before the Same shall take Effect, shall be approved by him, or being disapproved by him, shall be repassed by two thirds of the Senate and House of Representatives, according to the Rules and Limitations prescribed in the Case of a Bill.

SECTION 8
[POWERS OF CONGRESS]

The Congress shall have Power

To lay and collect Taxes, Duties, Imposts and Excises, to pay the Debts and provide for the common Defence and general Welfare of the United States; but all Duties, Imposts and Excises shall be uniform throughout the United States;

To borrow Money on the credit of the United States;

To regulate Commerce with foreign Nations, and among the several States, and with the Indian Tribes;

To establish an uniform Rule of Naturalization, and uniform Laws on the subject of Bankruptcies throughout the United States;

To coin Money, regulate the Value thereof, and of foreign Coin, and fix the Standard of Weights and Measures;

To provide for the Punishment of counterfeiting the Securities and current Coin of the United States;

To establish Post Offices and post Roads;

To promote the Progress of Science and useful Arts, by securing for limited Times to Authors and Inventors the exclusive Right to their respective Writings and Discoveries;

To constitute Tribunals inferior to the supreme Court;

To define and punish Piracies and Felonies committed on the high Seas, and Offences against the Law of Nations;

To declare War, grant Letters of Marque and Reprisal, and make Rules concerning Captures on Land and Water;

To raise and support Armies, but no Appropriation of Money to that Use shall be for a longer Term than two Years;

To provide and maintain a Navy;

To make Rules for the Government and Regulation of the land and naval Forces;

To provide for calling forth the Militia to execute the Laws of the Union, suppress Insurrections and repel Invasions;

To provide for organizing, arming, and disciplining, the Militia, and for governing such Part of them as may be employed in the Service of the United States, reserving to the States respectively, the Appointment of the Officers, and the Authority of training the Militia according to the discipline prescribed by Congress;

To exercise exclusive Legislation in all Cases whatsoever, over such District (not exceeding ten Miles square) as may, by Cession of particular States, and the Acceptance of Congress, become the Seat of the Government of the United States, and to exercise like Authority over all Places purchased by the Consent of the Legislature of the State in which the Same shall be, for the Erection of Forts, Magazines, Arsenals, dock-Yards, and other needful Buildings;—And

To make all Laws which shall be necessary and proper for carrying into Execution the foregoing Powers, and all other Powers vested by this Constitution in the Government of the United States, or in any Department or Officer thereof.

SECTION 9
[SOME RESTRICTIONS ON FEDERAL POWER]

The Migration or Importation of such Persons as any of the States now existing shall think proper to admit, shall not be prohibited by the Congress prior to the Year one thousand eight hundred and eight, but a Tax or duty may be imposed on such Importation, not exceeding ten dollars for each Person.[7]

The Privilege of the Writ of Habeas Corpus shall not be suspended, unless when in Cases of Rebellion or Invasion the public Safety may require it.

No Bill of Attainder or ex post facto Law shall be passed.

No Capitation, or other direct, Tax shall be laid, unless in Proportion to the Census or Enumeration herein before directed to be taken.[8]

No Tax or Duty shall be laid on Articles exported from any State.

No Preference shall be given by any Regulation of Commerce or Revenue to the Ports of one State over those of another; nor shall Vessels bound to, or from, one State, be obliged to enter, clear, or pay Duties in another.

No Money shall be drawn from the Treasury, but in Consequence of Appropriations made by Law; and a regular Statement and Account of the Receipts and Expenditures of all public Money shall be published from time to time.

No Title of Nobility shall be granted by the United States: And no Person holding any Office of Profit or Trust under them, shall, without the Consent of the Congress, accept of any present, Emolument, Office, or Title, of any kind whatever, from any King, Prince, or foreign State.

SECTION 10
[RESTRICTIONS UPON POWERS OF STATES]

No State shall enter into any Treaty, Alliance, or Confederation; grant Letters of Marque and Reprisal; coin Money; emit Bills of Credit; make any Thing but gold and silver Coin a Tender in Payment of Debts; pass any Bill of Attainder, ex post facto Law, or Law impairing the Obligation of Contracts, or grant any Title of Nobility.

No State shall, without the Consent of the Congress, lay any Imposts or Duties on Imports or Exports, except what may be absolutely necessary for executing its inspection Laws: and the net Produce of all Duties and Imposts, laid by any State on Imports or Exports, shall be for the Use of the Treasury of the United States; and all such Laws shall be subject to the Revision and Control of the Congress.

No State shall, without the Consent of Congress, lay any Duty of Tonnage, keep Troops, or Ships of War in time of Peace, enter into any Agreement or Compact with another State, or with a foreign Power, or engage in War, unless actually invaded, or in such imminent Danger as will not admit of delay.

ARTICLE II
SECTION 1
[EXECUTIVE POWER, ELECTION, QUALIFICATIONS OF THE PRESIDENT]

The executive Power shall be vested in a President of the United States of America. *He shall hold his Office during the Term of*

---

[7]Temporary provision.

[8]Modified by Sixteenth Amendment.

four Years, and, together with the Vice President, chosen for the same Term, be elected, as follows[9]

Each State shall appoint, in such Manner as the Legislature thereof may direct, a Number of Electors, equal to the whole Number of Senators and Representatives to which the State may be entitled in the Congress: but no Senator or Representative, or Person holding an Office of Trust or Profit under the United States, shall be appointed an Elector.

The electors shall meet in their respective States, and vote by ballot for two Persons, of whom one at least shall not be an Inhabitant of the same State with themselves. And they shall make a List of all the Persons voted for, and of the Number of Votes for each; which List they shall sign and certify, and transmit sealed to the Seat of the Government of the United States, directed to the President of the Senate. The President of the Senate shall, in the Presence of the Senate and House of Representatives, open all the Certificates, and the Votes shall then be counted. The Person having the greatest Number of Votes shall be the President, if such Number be a Majority of the whole Number of Electors appointed; and if there be more than one who have such Majority, and have an equal Number of Votes, then the House of Representatives shall immediately chuse by Ballot one of them for President; and if no Person have a Majority, then from the five highest on the List the said House shall in like Manner chuse the President. But in chusing the President, the Votes shall be taken by States, the Representation from each State having one Vote; A quorum for this Purpose shall consist of a Member or Members from two thirds of the States, and a Majority of all the States shall be necessary to a Choice. In every Case, after the Choice of the President, the person having the greatest Number of Votes of the Electors shall be the Vice President. But if there should remain two or more who have equal Votes, the Senate shall chuse from them by Ballot the Vice President.[10]

The Congress may determine the Time of chusing the Electors, and the Day on which they shall give their Votes; which Day shall be the same throughout the United States.

No Person except a natural born Citizen, or a Citizen of the United States, at the time of the Adoption of this Constitution, shall be eligible to the Office of President; neither shall any Person be eligible to that Office who shall not have attained to the Age of thirty five Years, and been fourteen Years a Resident within the United States.

In Case of the Removal of the President from Office, or his Death, Resignation, or Inability to discharge the Powers and Duties of the said Office, the Same shall devolve on the Vice President, and the Congress may by Law provide for the Case of Removal, Death, Resignation or Inability, both of the President and Vice President, declaring what Officer shall then act as President, and such Officer shall act accordingly, until the Disability be removed, or a President shall be elected.

---

[9]Number of terms limited to two by Twenty-Second Amendment.

[10]Modified by Twelfth and Twentieth Amendments.

The President shall, at stated Times, receive for his Services, a Compensation, which shall neither be increased nor diminished during the Period for which he shall have been elected, and he shall not receive within that Period any other Emolument from the United States, or any of them.

Before he enter on the Execution of his Office, he shall take the following Oath or Affirmation:—"I do solemnly swear (or affirm) that I will faithfully execute the Office of President of the United States, and will to the best of my Ability, preserve, protect and defend the Constitution of the United States."

SECTION 2
[POWERS OF THE PRESIDENT]

The President shall be Commander in Chief of the Army and Navy of the United States, and of the Militia of the several States, when called into the actual Service of the United States; he may require the Opinion, in writing, of the principal Officer in each of the executive Departments, upon any Subject relating to the Duties of their respective Offices, and he shall have Power to grant Reprieves and Pardons for Offences against the United States, except in Cases of Impeachment.

He shall have Power, by and with the Advice and Consent of the Senate, to make Treaties, provided two thirds of the Senators present concur; and he shall nominate, and by and with the Advice and Consent of the Senate, shall appoint Ambassadors, other public Ministers and Consuls, Judges of the supreme Court, and all other Officers of the United States, whose Appointments are not herein otherwise provided for, and which shall be established by Law: but the Congress may by Law vest the Appointment of such inferior Officers, as they think proper, in the President alone, in the Courts of Law, or in the Heads of Departments.

The President shall have Power to fill up all Vacancies that may happen during the Recess of the Senate, by granting Commissions which shall expire at the End of their next Session.

SECTION 3
[POWERS AND DUTIES OF THE PRESIDENT]

He shall from time to time give to the Congress Information of the State of the Union, and recommend to their Consideration such Measures as he shall judge necessary and expedient; he may, on extraordinary Occasions, convene both Houses, or either of them, and in Case of Disagreement between them, with Respect to the Time of Adjournment, he may adjourn them to such Time as he shall think proper; he shall receive Ambassadors and other public Ministers; he shall take Care that the Laws be faithfully executed, and shall Commission all the Officers of the United States.

SECTION 4
[IMPEACHMENT]

The President, Vice President and all civil Officers of the United States, shall be removed from Office on Impeachment for, and Conviction of, Treason, Bribery, or other high Crimes and Misdemeanors.

ARTICLE III

SECTION 1
[JUDICIAL POWER, TENURE OF OFFICE]

The judicial Power of the United States, shall be vested in one supreme Court, and in such inferior Courts as the Congress may from time to time ordain and establish. The Judges, both of the supreme and inferior Courts, shall hold their Offices during good Behaviour, and shall, at stated Times, receive for their Services, a Compensation, which shall not be diminished during their Continuance in Office.

SECTION 2
[JURISDICTION]

The judicial Power shall extend to all Cases, in Law and Equity, arising under this Constitution, the Laws of the United States, and Treaties made, or which shall be made, under their Authority;— to all Cases affecting Ambassadors, other public Ministers and Consuls;—to all Cases of admiralty and maritime Jurisdiction;— to Controversies to which the United States shall be a Party;—to Controversies between two or more States;—*between a State and Citizens of another State;*—between Citizens of different States,— between Citizens of the same State claiming Lands under Grants of different States, *and between a State,* or the Citizens thereof, *and foreign States, Citizens or Subjects.*[11]

In all Cases affecting Ambassadors, other public Ministers and Consuls, and those in which a State shall be Party, the supreme Court shall have original Jurisdiction. In all the other Cases before mentioned, the supreme Court shall have appellate Jurisdiction, both as to Law and Fact, with such Exceptions, and under such Regulations as the Congress shall make.

The Trial of all Crimes, except in Cases of Impeachment, shall be by Jury; and such Trial shall be held in the State where the said Crimes shall have been committed; but when not committed within any State, the Trial shall be at such Place or Places as the Congress may by Law have directed.

SECTION 3
[TREASON, PROOF, AND PUNISHMENT]

Treason against the United States, shall consist only in levying War against them, or in adhering to their Enemies, giving them Aid and Comfort. No Person shall be convicted of Treason unless on the Testimony of two Witnesses to the same overt Act, or on Confession in open Court.

The Congress shall have Power to declare the Punishment of Treason, but no Attainder of Treason shall work Corruption of Blood, or Forfeiture except during the Life of the Person attainted.

ARTICLE IV

SECTION 1
[FAITH AND CREDIT AMONG STATES]

Full Faith and Credit shall be given in each State to the public Acts, Records, and judicial Proceedings of every other State. And the Congress may by general Laws prescribe the Manner in which such Acts, Records and Proceedings shall be proved, and the Effect thereof.

SECTION 2
[PRIVILEGES AND IMMUNITIES, FUGITIVES]

The Citizens of each State shall be entitled to all Privileges and Immunities of Citizens in the several States.

A Person charged in any State with Treason, Felony or other Crime, who shall flee from Justice, and be found in another State, shall on Demand of the executive Authority of the State from which he fled, be delivered up, to be removed to the State having Jurisdiction of the Crime.

No person held to Service or Labour in one State, under the Laws thereof, escaping into another, shall, in Consequence of any Law or Regulation therein, be discharged from such Service or Labour, but shall be delivered up on Claim of the Party to whom such Service or Labour may be due.[12]

SECTION 3
[ADMISSION OF NEW STATES]

New States may be admitted by the Congress into this Union; but no new State shall be formed or erected within the Jurisdiction of any other State; nor any State be formed by the Junction of two or more States, or Parts of States, without the Consent of the Legislatures of the States concerned as well as of the Congress.

The Congress shall have Power to dispose of and make all needful Rules and Regulations respecting the Territory or other Property belonging to the United States; and nothing in this Constitution shall be so construed as to Prejudice any Claims of the United States, or of any particular State.

SECTION 4
[GUARANTEE OF REPUBLICAN GOVERNMENT]

The United States shall guarantee to every State in this Union a Republican Form of Government, and shall protect each of them against Invasion; and on Application of the Legislature, or of the Executive (when the Legislature cannot be convened), against domestic Violence.

ARTICLE V
[AMENDMENT OF THE CONSTITUTION]

The Congress, whenever two thirds of both Houses shall deem it necessary, shall propose Amendments to this Constitution, or, on the Application of the Legislatures of two thirds of the

---

[11]Modified by Eleventh Amendment.

[12]Repealed by the Thirteenth Amendment.

several States, shall call a Convention for proposing Amendments, which, in either Case, shall be valid to all Intents and Purposes, as Part of this Constitution, when ratified by the Legislatures of three fourths of the several States, or by Conventions in three fourths thereof, as the one or the other Mode of Ratification may be proposed by the Congress; *Provided that no Amendment which may be made prior to the Year One thousand eight hundred and eight shall in any Manner affect the first and fourth Clauses in the Ninth Section of the first Article;*[13] and that no State, without its Consent, shall be deprived of its equal Suffrage in the Senate.

ARTICLE VI
[DEBTS, SUPREMACY, OATH]

All Debts contracted and Engagements entered into, before the Adoption of this Constitution, shall be as valid against the United States under this Constitution, as under the Confederation.

This Constitution, and the Laws of the United States which shall be made in Pursuance thereof; and all Treaties made, or which shall be made, under the Authority of the United States, shall be the supreme Law of the Land; and the Judges in every State shall be bound thereby, any Thing in the Constitution or Laws of any State to the Contrary notwithstanding.

The Senators and Representatives before mentioned, and the Members of the several State Legislatures, and all executive and judicial Officers, both of the United States and of the several States, shall be bound by Oath or Affirmation, to support this Constitution; but no religious Test shall be required as a Qualification to any Office or public Trust under the United States.

ARTICLE VII
[RATIFICATION AND ESTABLISHMENT]

The Ratification of the Conventions of nine States, shall be sufficient for the Establishment of this Constitution between the States so ratifying the Same.[14]

Done in Convention by the Unanimous Consent of the States present the Seventeenth Day of September in the Year of our Lord one thousand seven hundred and Eighty seven and of the Independence of the United States of America the Twelfth. *In Witness* whereof We have hereunto subscribed our Names,

---

[13]Temporary provision.

[14]The Constitution was submitted on September 17, 1787, by the Constitutional Convention, was ratified by the conventions of several states at various dates up to May 29, 1790, and became effective on March 4, 1789.

G:⁰ WASHINGTON—
Presidt. and deputy from Virginia

NEW HAMPSHIRE
John Langdon
Nicholas Gilman

MASSACHUSETTS
Nathaniel Gorham
Rufus King

CONNECTICUT
Wm. Saml. Johnson
Roger Sherman

NEW YORK
Alexander Hamilton

NEW JERSEY
Wil: Livingston
David Brearley
Wm. Paterson
Jona: Dayton

PENNSYLVANIA
B Franklin
Thomas Mifflin
Robt. Morris
Geo. Clymer
Thos. FitzSimons
Jared Ingersoll
James Wilson
Gouv Morris

DELAWARE
Geo: Read
Gunning Bedford jun
John Dickinson
Richard Bassett
Jaco: Broom

MARYLAND
James McHenry
Dan of St Thos. Jenifer
Danl. Carroll

VIRGINIA
John Blair—
James Madison Jr.

NORTH CAROLINA
Wm. Blount
Richd. Dobbs Spaight
Hu Williamson

SOUTH CAROLINA
J. Rutledge
Charles Cotesworth
Pinckney
Charles Pinckney
Pierce Butler

GEORGIA
William Few
Abr Baldwin

Amendments to the Constitution

Proposed by Congress and Ratified by the Legislatures of the Several States, Pursuant to Article V of the Original Constitution.

Amendments I–X, known as the Bill of Rights, were proposed by Congress on September 25, 1789, and ratified on December 15, 1791.

AMENDMENT I
[FREEDOM OF RELIGION, OF SPEECH, AND OF THE PRESS]

Congress shall make no law respecting an establishment of religion, or prohibiting the free exercise thereof; or abridging the freedom of speech, or of the press; or the right of the people peaceably to assemble, and to petition the Government for a redress of grievances.

AMENDMENT II
[RIGHT TO KEEP AND BEAR ARMS]

A well regulated Militia, being necessary to the security of a free State, the right of the people to keep and bear Arms, shall not be infringed.

AMENDMENT III
[QUARTERING OF SOLDIERS]

No Soldier shall, in time of peace be quartered in any house, without the consent of the Owner, nor in time of war, but in a manner to be prescribed by law.

AMENDMENT IV
[SECURITY FROM UNWARRANTABLE SEARCH AND SEIZURE]

The right of the people to be secure in their persons, houses, papers, and effects, against unreasonable searches and seizures, shall not be violated, and no Warrants shall issue, but upon probable cause, supported by Oath or affirmation, and particularly describing the place to be searched, and the persons or things to be seized.

AMENDMENT V
[RIGHTS OF ACCUSED PERSONS IN CRIMINAL PROCEEDINGS]

No person shall be held to answer for a capital, or otherwise infamous crime, unless on a presentment or indictment of a Grand Jury, except in cases arising in the land or naval forces, or in the Militia, when in actual service in time of War or in public danger; nor shall any person be subject for the same offence to be twice put in jeopardy of life or limb; nor shall be compelled in any criminal case to be a witness against himself, nor be deprived of life, liberty, or property, without due process of law; nor shall private property be taken for public use, without just compensation.

AMENDMENT VI
[RIGHT TO SPEEDY TRIAL, WITNESSES, ETC.]

In all criminal prosecutions, the accused shall enjoy the right to a speedy and public trial, by an impartial jury of the State and district wherein the crime shall have been committed, which district shall have been previously ascertained by law, and to be informed of the nature and cause of the accusation; to be confronted with the witnesses against him; to have compulsory process for obtaining witnesses in his favor, and to have the Assistance of Counsel for his defence.

AMENDMENT VII
[TRIAL BY JURY IN CIVIL CASES]

In suits at common law, where the value in controversy shall exceed twenty dollars, the right of trial by jury shall be preserved, and no fact tried by a jury, shall be otherwise reexamined in any Court of the United States, than according to the rules of the common law.

AMENDMENT VIII
[BAILS, FINES, PUNISHMENTS]

Excessive bail shall not be required, nor excessive fines imposed, nor cruel and unusual punishments inflicted.

AMENDMENT IX
[RESERVATION OF RIGHTS OF PEOPLE]

The enumeration in the Constitution, of certain rights, shall not be construed to deny or disparage others retained by the people.

AMENDMENT X
[POWERS RESERVED TO STATES OR PEOPLE]

The powers not delegated to the United States by the Constitution, nor prohibited by it to the States, are reserved to the States respectively, or to the people.

AMENDMENT XI

[*Proposed by Congress on March 4, 1794;
declared ratified on January 8, 1798.*]
[RESTRICTION OF JUDICIAL POWER]

The Judicial power of the United States shall not be construed to extend to any suit in law or equity, commenced or prosecuted against one of the United States by Citizens of another State, or by Citizens or Subjects of any Foreign State.

AMENDMENT XII

[*Proposed by Congress on December 9, 1803;
declared ratified on September 25, 1804.*]
[ELECTION OF PRESIDENT AND VICE PRESIDENT]

The Electors shall meet in their respective states and vote by ballot for President and Vice-President, one of whom, at least, shall not be an inhabitant of the same state with themselves; they shall name in their ballots the person voted for as President, and in distinct ballots the person voted for as Vice-President, and they shall make distinct lists of all persons voted for as President, and of all persons voted for as Vice-President, and of the number of votes for each, which lists they shall sign and certify, and transmit sealed to the seat of the government of the United States, directed to the President of the Senate;—the President of the Senate shall, in presence of the Senate and House of Representatives, open all the certificates and the votes shall then be counted;—The person having the greatest number of votes for President, shall be the President, if such number be a majority of the whole number of Electors appointed; and if no person have such majority, then from the persons having the highest numbers not exceeding three on the list of those voted for as President, the House of Representatives shall choose immediately, by ballot, the President. But in choosing the President, the votes shall be taken by states, the representation from each state having one vote; a quorum for this purpose shall consist of a member or members from two-thirds of the states, and a majority of all the states shall be necessary to a choice. And if the House of Representatives shall not choose a President whenever the right of choice shall devolve upon them, before the fourth day of March next following, then the Vice-President shall act as President, as in the case of the death or other constitutional disability of the President.—The person having the greatest number of votes as Vice-President, shall be the Vice-President, if such number be a majority of the whole number of Electors appointed, and if no person have a majority, then from the two highest numbers on the list, the Senate shall choose the Vice-President; a quorum for the purpose shall consist of two-thirds of the whole number of Senators, and a majority of the whole number shall be necessary to a choice. But no person constitutionally ineligible to the office of President shall be eligible to that of Vice-President of the United States.

AMENDMENT XIII

[*Proposed by Congress on January 31, 1865;
declared ratified on December 18, 1865.*]

SECTION 1
[ABOLITION OF SLAVERY]

Neither slavery nor involuntary servitude, except as a punishment for crime whereof the party shall have been duly convicted, shall exist within the United States, or any place subject to their jurisdiction.

SECTION 2
[POWER TO ENFORCE THIS ARTICLE]

Congress shall have power to enforce this article by appropriate legislation.

AMENDMENT XIV

[*Proposed by Congress on June 13, 1866;
declared ratified on July 28, 1868.*]

SECTION 1
[CITIZENSHIP RIGHTS NOT TO BE ABRIDGED BY STATES]

All persons born or naturalized in the United States, and subject to the jurisdiction thereof, are citizens of the United States and of the State wherein they reside. No State shall make or enforce any law which shall abridge the privileges or immunities of citizens of the United States; nor shall any State deprive any person of life, liberty, or property, without due process of law; nor deny to any person within its jurisdiction the equal protection of the laws.

SECTION 2
[APPORTIONMENT OF REPRESENTATIVES IN CONGRESS]

Representatives shall be apportioned among the several States according to their respective numbers, counting the whole number of persons in each State, excluding Indians not taxed. But when the right to vote at any election for the choice of electors for President and Vice-President of the United States, Representatives in Congress, the Executive and Judicial officers of a State, or the members of the Legislature thereof, is denied to any of the male inhabitants of such State, being twenty-one years of age, and citizens of the United States, or in any way abridged, except for participation in rebellion, or other crime, the basis of representation therein shall be reduced in the proportion which the number of such male citizens shall bear to the whole number of male citizens twenty-one years of age in such State.

SECTION 3
[PERSONS DISQUALIFIED FROM HOLDING OFFICE]

No person shall be a Senator or Representative in Congress, or elector of President and Vice-President, or hold any office, civil or military, under the United States, or under any State, who, having previously taken an oath, as a member of Congress, or as an officer of the United States, or as a member of any State legislature, or as an executive or judicial officer of any State, to support the Constitution of the United States, shall have engaged in insurrection or rebellion against the same, or given aid or comfort to the enemies thereof. But Congress may by a vote of two-thirds of each House, remove such disability.

SECTION 4
[WHAT PUBLIC DEBTS ARE VALID]

The validity of the public debt of the United States, authorized by law, including debts incurred for payment of pensions and bounties for services in suppressing insurrection or rebellion, shall not be questioned. But neither the United States nor any State shall assume or pay any debt or obligation incurred in aid of insurrection or rebellion against the United States, or any claim for the loss or emancipation of any slave; but all such debts, obligations and claims shall be held illegal and void.

SECTION 5
[POWER TO ENFORCE THIS ARTICLE]

The Congress shall have power to enforce, by appropriate legislation, the provisions of this article.

AMENDMENT XV
[*Proposed by Congress on February 26, 1869; declared ratified on March 30, 1870.*]

SECTION 1
[NEGRO SUFFRAGE]

The right of citizens of the United States to vote shall not be denied or abridged by the United States or by any State on account of race, color, or previous condition of servitude.

SECTION 2
[POWER TO ENFORCE THIS ARTICLE]

The Congress shall have power to enforce this article by appropriate legislation.

AMENDMENT XVI
[*Proposed by Congress on July 2, 1909; declared ratified on February 25, 1913.*]
[AUTHORIZING INCOME TAXES]

The Congress shall have power to lay and collect taxes on incomes, from whatever source derived, without apportionment among the several States, and without regard to any census or enumeration.

AMENDMENT XVII
[*Proposed by Congress on May 13, 1912; declared ratified on May 31, 1913.*]
[POPULAR ELECTION OF SENATORS]

The Senate of the United States shall be composed of two Senators from each State, elected by the people thereof, for six years; and each Senator shall have one vote. The electors in each State shall have the qualifications requisite for electors of the most numerous branch of the State legislatures.

When vacancies happen in the representation of any State in the Senate, the executive authority of such State shall issue writs of election to fill such vacancies: *Provided,* That the legislature of any State may empower the executive thereof to make temporary appointments until the people fill the vacancies by election as the legislature may direct.

This amendment shall not be so construed as to affect the election or term of any Senator chosen before it becomes valid as part of the Constitution.

AMENDMENT XVIII
[*Proposed by Congress December 18, 1917; declared ratified on January 29, 1919.*]

SECTION 1
[NATIONAL LIQUOR PROHIBITION]

After one year from the ratification of this article the manufacture, sale, or transportation of intoxicating liquors within, the importation thereof into, or the exportation thereof from the United States and all territory subject to the jurisdiction thereof for beverage purposes is hereby prohibited.

SECTION 2
[POWER TO ENFORCE THIS ARTICLE]

The Congress and the several States shall have concurrent power to enforce this article by appropriate legislation.

SECTION 3
[RATIFICATION WITHIN SEVEN YEARS]

This article shall be inoperative unless it shall have been ratified as an amendment to the Constitution by the legislatures of the several States, as provided in the Constitution, within seven years from the date of the submission hereof to the States by the Congress.[1]

AMENDMENT XIX
[*Proposed by Congress on June 4, 1919; declared ratified on August 26, 1920.*]
[WOMAN SUFFRAGE]

The right of citizens of the United States to vote shall not be denied or abridged by the United States or by any State on account of sex.

Congress shall have power to enforce this article by appropriate legislation.

---

[1]Repealed by the Twenty-First Amendment.

AMENDMENT XX

[Proposed by Congress on March 2, 1932;
declared ratified on February 6, 1933.]

SECTION 1
[TERMS OF OFFICE]

The terms of the President and Vice President shall end at noon on the 20th day of January, and the terms of Senators and Representatives at noon on the 3d day of January, of the years in which such terms would have ended if this article had not been ratified; and the terms of their successors shall then begin.

SECTION 2
[TIME OF CONVENING CONGRESS]

The Congress shall assemble at least once in every year, and such meeting shall begin at noon on the 3d day of January, unless they shall by law appoint a different day.

SECTION 3
[DEATH OF PRESIDENT-ELECT]

If, at the time fixed for the beginning of the term of the President, the President elect shall have died, the Vice President elect shall become President. If a President shall not have been chosen before the time fixed for the beginning of his term, or if the President elect shall have failed to qualify, then the Vice President elect shall act as President until a President shall have qualified; and the Congress may by law provide for the case wherein neither a President elect nor a Vice President elect shall have qualified, declaring who shall then act as President, or the manner in which one who is to act shall be selected, and such person shall act accordingly until a President or Vice President shall have qualified.

SECTION 4
[ELECTION OF THE PRESIDENT]

The Congress may by law provide for the case of the death of any of the persons from whom the House of Representatives may choose a President whenever the right of choice shall have devolved upon them, and for the case of the death of any of the persons from whom the Senate may choose a Vice President whenever the right of choice shall have devolved upon them.

SECTION 5
[AMENDMENT TAKES EFFECT]

Sections 1 and 2 shall take effect on the 15th day of October following the ratification of this article.

SECTION 6
[RATIFICATION WITHIN SEVEN YEARS]

This article shall be inoperative unless it shall have been ratified as an amendment to the Constitution by the legislatures of three-fourths of the several States within seven years from the date of its submission.

AMENDMENT XXI

[Proposed by Congress on February 20, 1933;
declared ratified on December 5, 1933.]

SECTION 1
[NATIONAL LIQUOR PROHIBITION REPEALED]

The eighteenth article of amendment to the Constitution of the United States is hereby repealed.

SECTION 2
[TRANSPORTATION OF LIQUOR INTO "DRY" STATES]

The transportation or importation into any State, Territory, or Possession of the United States for delivery or use therein of intoxicating liquors, in violation of the laws thereof, is hereby prohibited.

SECTION 3
[RATIFICATION WITHIN SEVEN YEARS]

This article shall be inoperative unless it shall have been ratified as an amendment to the Constitution by conventions in the several States, as provided in the Constitution, within seven years from the date of the submission hereof to the States by the Congress.

AMENDMENT XXII

[Proposed by Congress on March 21, 1947;
declared ratified on February 27, 1951.]

SECTION 1
[TENURE OF PRESIDENT LIMITED]

No person shall be elected to the office of President more than twice, and no person who has held the office of President or acted as President, for more than two years of a term to which some other person was elected President shall be elected to the office of the President more than once. But this Article shall not apply to any person holding the office of President when this Article was proposed by the Congress, and shall not prevent any person who may be holding the office of President, or acting as President, during the term within which this Article becomes operative from holding the office of President or acting as President during the remainder of such term.

SECTION 2
[RATIFICATION WITHIN SEVEN YEARS]

This article shall be inoperative unless it shall have been ratified as an amendment to the Constitution by the legislatures of three-fourths of the several States within seven years from the date of its submission to the States by the Congress.

AMENDMENT XXIII

[Proposed by Congress on June 16, 1960;
declared ratified on March 29, 1961.]

SECTION 1
[ELECTORAL COLLEGE VOTES FOR THE DISTRICT OF COLUMBIA]

The District constituting the seat of Government of the United States shall appoint in such manner as the Congress may direct:

A number of electors of President and Vice President equal to the whole number of Senators and Representatives in Congress to which the District would be entitled if it were a State, but in no event more than the least populous State; they shall be in addition to those appointed by the States, but they shall be considered, for the purposes of the election of President and Vice President, to be electors appointed by a State; and they shall meet in the District and perform such duties as provided by the twelfth article of amendment.

SECTION 2
[POWER TO ENFORCE THIS ARTICLE]

The Congress shall have power to enforce this article by appropriate legislation.

AMENDMENT XXIV

[Proposed by Congress on August 27, 1962;
declared ratified on January 23, 1964.]

SECTION 1
[ANTI-POLL TAX]

The right of citizens of the United States to vote in any primary or other election for President or Vice President, for electors for President or Vice President, or for Senator or Representative of Congress, shall not be denied or abridged by the United States or any State by reason of failure to pay any poll tax or other tax.

SECTION 2
[POWER TO ENFORCE THIS ARTICLE]

The Congress shall have power to enforce this article by appropriate legislation.

AMENDMENT XXV

[Proposed by Congress on July 6, 1965;
declared ratified on February 10, 1967.]

SECTION 1
[VICE PRESIDENT TO BECOME PRESIDENT]

In case of the removal of the President from office or his death or resignation, the Vice President shall become President.

SECTION 2
[CHOICE OF A NEW VICE PRESIDENT]

Whenever there is a vacancy in the office of the Vice President, the President shall nominate a Vice President who shall take the office upon confirmation by a majority vote of both houses of Congress.

SECTION 3
[PRESIDENT MAY DECLARE OWN DISABILITY]

Whenever the President transmits to the President pro tempore of the Senate and the Speaker of the House of Representatives his written declaration that he is unable to discharge the powers and duties of his office, and until he transmits to them a written declaration to the contrary, such powers and duties shall be discharged by the Vice President as Acting President.

SECTION 4
[ALTERNATE PROCEDURES TO DECLARE AND TO END PRESIDENTIAL DISABILITY]

Whenever the Vice President and a majority of either the principal officers of the executive departments, or of such other body as Congress may by law provide, transmit to the President pro tempore of the Senate and the Speaker of the House of Representatives their written declaration that the President is unable to discharge the powers and duties of his office, the Vice President shall immediately assume the powers and duties of the office as Acting President.

Thereafter, when the President transmits to the President pro tempore of the Senate and the Speaker of the House of Representatives his written declaration that no inability exists, he shall resume the powers and duties of his office unless the Vice President and a majority of either the principal officers of the executive department, or of such other body as Congress may by law provide, transmit within four days to the President pro tempore of the Senate and the Speaker of the House of Representatives their written declaration that the President is unable to discharge the powers and duties of his office. Thereupon Congress shall decide the issue, assembling within forty eight hours for that purpose if not in session. If the Congress, within twenty one days after receipt of the latter written declaration, or, if Congress is not in session, within twenty one days after Congress is required to assemble, determines by two-thirds vote of both Houses that the President is unable to discharge the powers and duties of his office, the Vice President shall continue to discharge the same as Acting President; otherwise, the President shall resume the powers and duties of his office.

AMENDMENT XXVI

[Proposed by Congress on March 23, 1971; declared ratified on July 1, 1971.]

SECTION 1
[EIGHTEEN-YEAR-OLD VOTE]

The right of citizens of the United States, who are eighteen years of age or older, to vote shall not be denied or abridged by the United States or by any State on account of age.

SECTION 2
[POWER TO ENFORCE THIS ARTICLE]

The Congress shall have power to enforce this article by appropriate legislation.

AMENDMENT XXVII

[Proposed by Congress on September 25, 1789; declared ratified on May 8, 1992.]
[CONGRESS CANNOT RAISE ITS OWN PAY]

No law varying the compensation for the services of the Senators and Representatives, shall take effect, until an election of representatives shall have intervened.

The Federalist Papers

NO. 10: MADISON

Among the numerous advantages promised by a well constructed Union, none deserves to be more accurately developed than its tendency to break and control the violence of faction. The friend of popular governments never finds himself so much alarmed for their character and fate, as when he contemplates their propensity to this dangerous vice. He will not fail therefore to set a due value on any plan which, without violating the principles to which he is attached, provides a proper cure for it. The instability, injustice, and confusion introduced into the public councils have, in truth, been the mortal diseases under which popular governments have everywhere perished, as they continue to be the favorite and fruitful topics from which the adversaries to liberty derive their most specious declamations. The valuable improvements made by the American constitutions on the popular models, both ancient and modern, cannot certainly be too much admired; but it would be an unwarrantable partiality to contend that they have as effectually obviated the danger on this side, as was wished and expected. Complaints are everywhere heard from our most considerate and virtuous citizens, equally the friends of public and private faith and of public and personal liberty, that our governments are too unstable, that the public good is disregarded in the conflicts of rival parties, and that measures are too often decided, not according to the rules of justice and the rights of the minor party, but by the superior force of an interested and overbearing majority. However anxiously we may wish that these complaints had no foundation, the evidence of known facts will not permit us to deny that they are in some degree true. It will be found, indeed, on a candid review of our situation, that some of the distresses under which we labor have been erroneously charged on the operation of our governments; but it will be found, at the same time, that other causes will not alone account for many of our heaviest misfortunes; and, particularly, for that prevailing and increasing distrust of public engagements and alarm for private rights which are echoed from one end of the continent to the other. These must be chiefly, if not wholly, effects of the unsteadiness and injustice with which a factious spirit has tainted our public administration.

By a faction I understand a number of citizens, whether amounting to a majority or minority of the whole, who are united and actuated by some common impulse of passion, or of interest, adverse to the rights of other citizens, or to the permanent and aggregate interests of the community.

There are two methods of curing the mischiefs of faction: the one, by removing its causes; the other, by controlling its effects.

There are again two methods of removing the causes of faction: the one, by destroying the liberty which is essential to its existence; the other, by giving to every citizen the same opinions, the same passions, and the same interests.

It could never be more truly said than of the first remedy, that it is worse than the disease. Liberty is to faction what air is to fire, an aliment without which it instantly expires. But it could not be a less folly to abolish liberty, which is essential to political life, because it nourishes faction, than it would be to wish the annihilation of air, which is essential to animal life, because it imparts to fire its destructive agency.

The second expedient is as impracticable, as the first would be unwise. As long as the reason of man continues fallible, and he is at liberty to exercise it, different opinions will be formed. As long as the connection subsists between his reason and his self-love, his opinions and his passions will have a reciprocal influence on each other; and the former will be objects to which the latter will attach themselves. The diversity in the faculties of men, from which the rights of property originate, is not less an insuperable obstacle to a uniformity of interests. The protection of these faculties is the first object of Government. From the protection of different and unequal faculties of acquiring property, the possession of different degrees and kinds of property immediately results; and from the influence of these on the sentiments and views of the respective proprietors, ensues a division of the society into different interests and parties.

The latent causes of faction are thus sown in the nature of man; and we see them everywhere brought into different degrees of activity, according to the different circumstances of civil society. A zeal for different opinions concerning religion, concerning Government, and many other points, as well of speculation as of practice; an attachment to different leaders ambitiously contending for pre-eminence and power; or to persons of other descriptions whose fortunes have been interesting to the human passions, have in turn divided mankind into parties, inflamed them with mutual animosity, and rendered them much more disposed to vex and oppress each other, than to co-operate for their common good. So strong is this propensity of mankind to fall into mutual animosities, that where no substantial occasion presents itself, the most frivolous and fanciful distinctions have been sufficient to kindle their unfriendly passions, and excite their most violent conflicts. But the most common and durable source of factions has been the various and unequal distribution of property. Those who hold and those who are without property have ever formed distinct interests in society. Those who are creditors, and those who are debtors, fall under a like discrimination. A landed interest, a manufacturing interest, a mercantile interest, a moneyed interest, with many lesser interests, grow up of necessity in civilized nations, and divide them into different classes, actuated by different sentiments and views. The regulation of these various and interfering interests forms the principal task of modern Legislation, and involves the spirit of party and faction in the necessary and ordinary operations of Government.

No man is allowed to be judge in his own cause, because his interest would certainly bias his judgment and, not improbably, corrupt his integrity. With equal, nay with greater reason, a body of men are unfit to be both judges and parties at the same time; yet what are many of the most important acts of legislation but so many judicial determinations, not indeed concerning the rights of single persons, but concerning the rights of large bodies of citizens; and what are the different classes of legislators but advocates and parties to the causes which they determine? Is a law proposed concerning private debts? It is a question to which the creditors are parties on one side and the debtors on the other. Justice ought to hold the balance between them. Yet the parties are, and must be, themselves the judges; and the most numerous party, or in other words, the most powerful faction must be expected to prevail. Shall domestic manufacturers be encouraged, and in what degree, by restrictions on foreign manufacturers? are questions which would be differently decided by the landed and the manufacturing classes, and probably by neither with a sole regard to justice and the public good. The apportionment of taxes on the various descriptions of property is an act which seems to require the most exact impartiality; yet there is, perhaps, no legislative act in which greater opportunity and temptation are given to a predominant party to trample on the rules of justice. Every shilling with which they overburden the inferior number is a shilling saved to their own pockets.

It is in vain to say that enlightened statesmen will be able to adjust these clashing interests and render them all subservient to the public good. Enlightened statesmen will not always be at the helm. Nor, in many cases, can such an adjustment be made at all without taking into view indirect and remote considerations, which will rarely prevail over the immediate interest which one party may find in disregarding the rights of another or the good of the whole.

The inference to which we are brought is that the *causes* of faction cannot be removed and that relief is only to be sought in the means of controlling its *effects*.

If a faction consists of less than a majority, relief is supplied by the republican principle, which enables the majority to defeat its sinister views by regular vote. It may clog the administration, it may convulse the society; but it will be unable to execute and mask its violence under the forms of the Constitution. When a majority is included in a faction, the form of popular government, on the other hand, enables it to sacrifice to its ruling passion or interest both the public good and the rights of other citizens. To secure the public good and private rights against the danger of such a faction, and at the same time to preserve the spirit and the form of popular government, is then the great object to which our enquiries are directed. Let me add that it is the great desideratum by which alone this form of government can be rescued from the opprobrium under which it has so long labored and be recommended to the esteem and adoption of mankind.

By what means is this object attainable? Evidently by one of two only. Either the existence of the same passion or interest in a majority at the same time must be prevented, or the majority, having such co-existent passion or interest, must be rendered, by their number and local situation, unable to concert and carry into effect schemes of oppression. If the impulse and the opportunity be suffered to coincide, we well know that neither moral nor religious motives can be relied on as an adequate control. They are not found to be such on the injustice and violence of individuals, and lose their efficacy in proportion to the number combined together, that is, in proportion as their efficacy becomes needful.

From this view of the subject it may be concluded that a pure Democracy, by which I mean a Society consisting of a small number of citizens, who assemble and administer the Government in person, can admit of no cure for the mischiefs of faction. A common passion or interest will, in almost every case, be felt by a majority of the whole; a communication and concert results from the form of Government itself; and there is nothing to check the inducements to sacrifice the weaker party or an obnoxious individual. Hence it is that such Democracies have ever been spectacles of turbulence and contention; have ever been found incompatible with personal security or the rights of property; and have in general been as short in their lives as they have been violent in their deaths. Theoretic politicians, who have patronized this species of Government, have erroneously supposed that by reducing mankind to a perfect equality in their political rights, they would at the same time be perfectly equalized and assimilated in their possessions, their opinions, and their passions.

A Republic, by which I mean a Government in which the scheme of representation takes place, opens a different prospect and promises the cure for which we are seeking. Let us examine the points in which it varies from pure Democracy, and we shall comprehend both the nature of the cure and the efficacy which it must derive from the Union.

The two great points of difference between a Democracy and a Republic are: first, the delegation of the Government, in the latter, to a small number of citizens elected by the rest; secondly, the greater number of citizens and greater sphere of country over which the latter may be extended.

The effect of the first difference is, on the one hand, to refine and enlarge the public views by passing them through the medium of a chosen body of citizens, whose wisdom may best discern the true interest of their country and whose patriotism and love of justice will be least likely to sacrifice it to temporary or partial considerations. Under such a regulation it may well happen that the public voice, pronounced by the representatives of the people, will be more consonant to the public good than if pronounced by the people themselves, convened for the purpose. On the other hand, the effect may be inverted. Men of factious tempers, of local prejudices, or of sinister designs, may, by intrigue, by corruption, or by other means, first obtain the suffrages, and then betray the interests of the people. The question resulting is, whether small or extensive Republics are most favorable to the election of proper guardians of the public weal; and it is clearly decided in favor of the latter by two obvious considerations.

In the first place it is to be remarked that however small the Republic may be, the Representatives must be raised to a certain number in order to guard against the cabals of a few; and that however large it may be they must be limited to a certain number in order to guard against the confusion of a multitude. Hence, the number of Representatives in the two cases not being in proportion to that of the Constituents, and being proportionally greatest in the small Republic, it follows that if the proportion of fit characters be not less in the large than in the small Republic, the former will present a greater option, and consequently a greater probability of a fit choice.

In the next place, as each Representative will be chosen by a greater number of citizens in the large than in the small Republic, it will be more difficult for unworthy candidates to practise with success the vicious arts by which elections are too often carried; and the suffrages of the people being more free, will be more likely to centre on men who possess the most attractive merit and the most diffusive and established characters.

It must be confessed that in this, as in most other cases, there is a mean, on both sides of which inconveniencies will be found to lie. By enlarging too much the number of electors, you render the representative too little acquainted with all their local circumstances and lesser interests; as by reducing it too much, you render him unduly attached to these, and too little fit to comprehend and pursue great and national objects. The Federal Constitution forms a happy combination in this respect; the great and aggregate interests being referred to the national, the local and particular to the State legislatures.

The other point of difference is the greater number of citizens and extent of territory which may be brought within the compass of Republican than of Democratic Government; and it is this circumstance principally which renders factious combinations less to be dreaded in the former than in the latter. The smaller the society, the fewer probably will be the distinct parties and interests composing it; the fewer the distinct parties and interests, the more frequently will a majority be found of the same party; and the smaller the number of individuals composing a majority, and the smaller the compass within which they are placed, the more easily will they concert and execute their plans of oppression. Extend the sphere and you take in a greater variety of parties and interests; you make it less probable that a majority of the whole will have a common motive to invade the rights of other citizens; or if such a common motive exists, it will be more difficult for all who feel it to discover their own strength and to act in unison with each other. Besides other impediments, it may be remarked, that where there is a consciousness of unjust or dishonorable purposes, communication is always checked by distrust in proportion to the number whose concurrence is necessary.

Hence, it clearly appears that the same advantage which a Republic has over a Democracy in controlling the effects of faction is enjoyed by a large over a small republic—is enjoyed by the Union over the States composing it. Does this advantage consist in the substitution of representatives whose enlightened views and virtuous sentiments render them superior to local prejudices and to schemes of injustice? It will not be denied that the representation of the Union will be most likely to possess these requisite endowments. Does it consist in the greater security afforded by a greater variety of parties, against the event of any one party being able to outnumber and oppress the rest? In an equal degree does the increased variety of parties comprised within the Union increase this security? Does it, in fine, consist in the greater obstacles opposed to the concert and accomplishment of the secret wishes of an unjust and interested majority? Here again the extent of the Union gives it the most palpable advantage.

The influence of factious leaders may kindle a flame within their particular States but will be unable to spread a general conflagration through the other States: a religious sect may degenerate into a political faction in a part of the Confederacy; but the variety of sects dispersed over the entire face of it must secure the national Councils against any danger from that source: a rage for paper money, for an abolition of debts, for an equal division of property, or for any other improper or wicked project, will be less apt to pervade the whole body of the Union than a particular member of it; in the same proportion as such a malady is more likely to taint a particular county or district than an entire State.

In the extent and proper structure of the Union, therefore, we behold a republican remedy for the diseases most incident to Republican Government. And according to the degree of pleasure and pride we feel in being republicans ought to be our zeal in cherishing the spirit and supporting the character of federalist.

PUBLIUS
November 22, 1787

NO. 51: MADISON

To what expedient, then, shall we finally resort, for maintaining in practice the necessary partition of power among the several departments as laid down in the constitution? The only answer that can be given is that as all these exterior provisions are found to be inadequate the defect must be supplied, by so contriving the interior structure of the government as that its several constituent parts may, by their mutual relations, be the means of keeping each other in their proper places. Without presuming to undertake a full development of this important idea I will hazard a few general observations which may perhaps place it in a clearer light, and enable us to form a more correct judgment of the principles and structure of the government planned by the convention.

In order to lay a due foundation for that separate and distinct exercise of the different powers of government, which to a certain extent is admitted on all hands to be essential to the preservation of liberty, it is evident that each department should have a will of its own; and consequently should be so constituted that the members of each should have as little agency as possible in the appointment of the members of the others. Were this principle rigorously adhered to, it would require that all the appointments for the supreme executive, legislative, and judiciary magistracies should be drawn from the same fountain of authority, the people, through channels having no communication whatever with one another. Perhaps such a plan of constructing the several departments would be less difficult in practice than it may in contemplation appear. Some difficulties, however, and some additional expense would attend the execution of it. Some deviations, therefore, from the principle must be admitted. In the constitution of the judiciary department in particular, it might be inexpedient to insist rigorously on the principle: first, because peculiar qualifications being essential in the members, the primary consideration ought to be to select that mode of choice which best secures these qualifications; second, because the permanent tenure by which the appointments are held in that department must soon destroy all sense of dependence on the authority conferring them.

It is equally evident that the members of each department should be as little dependent as possible on those of the others for the emoluments annexed to their offices. Were the executive magistrate, or the judges, not independent of the legislature in this particular, their independence in every other would be merely nominal.

But the great security against a gradual concentration of the several powers in the same department consists in giving to those who administer each department the necessary constitutional means and personal motives to resist encroachments of the others. The provision for defence must in this, as in all other cases, be made commensurate to the danger of attack. Ambition must be made to counteract ambition. The interest of the man must be connected with the constitutional rights of the place. It may be a reflection on human nature that such devices should be necessary to control the abuses of government. But what is government itself but the greatest of all reflections on human nature? If men were angels, no government would be necessary. If angels were to govern men, neither external nor internal controls on government would be necessary. In framing a government which is to be administered by men over men, the great difficulty lies in this: You must first enable the government to control the governed; and in the next place oblige it to control itself. A dependence on the people is, no doubt, the primary control on the government; but experience has taught mankind the necessity of auxiliary precautions.

This policy of supplying, by opposite and rival interests, the defect of better motives, might be traced through the whole system of human affairs, private as well as public. We see it particularly displayed in all the subordinate distributions of power, where the constant aim is to divide and arrange the several offices in such a manner as that each may be a check on the other; that the private interest of every individual may be a sentinel over the public rights. These inventions of prudence cannot be less requisite in the distribution of the supreme powers of the State.

But it is not possible to give to each department an equal power of self-defense. In republican government, the legislative authority necessarily predominates. The remedy for this inconveniency is to divide the legislature into different branches; and to render them, by different modes of election and different principles of action, as little connected with each other as the nature of their common functions and their common dependence on the society will admit. It may even be necessary to guard against dangerous encroachments by still further precautions. As the weight of the legislative authority requires that it should be thus divided, the weakness of the executive may require, on the other hand, that it should be fortified. An absolute negative on the legislature appears, at first view, to be the natural defense with which the executive magistrate should be armed. But perhaps it would be neither altogether safe nor alone sufficient. On ordinary occasions it might not be exerted with the requisite firmness, and on extraordinary occasions it might be perfidiously abused. May not this defect of an absolute negative be supplied by some qualified connection between this weaker branch of the stronger department, by which the latter may be led to support the constitutional rights of the former, without being too much detached from the rights of its own department?

If the principles on which these observations are founded be just, as I persuade myself they are, and they be applied as a criterion to the several State constitutions, and to the federal Constitution, it will be found that if the latter does not perfectly correspond with them, the former are infinitely less able to bear such a test.

There are, moreover, two considerations particularly applicable to the federal system of America, which place that system in a very interesting point of view.

First. In a single republic, all the power surrendered by the people is submitted to the administration of a single government; and usurpations are guarded against by a division of the government into distinct and separate departments. In the compound republic of America, the power surrendered by the people is first divided between two distinct governments, and then the portion allotted to each subdivided among distinct and separate departments. Hence a double security arises to the rights of the people. The different governments will control each other, at the same time that each will be controlled by itself.

Second. It is of great importance in a republic not only to guard the society against the oppression of its rulers, but to guard one part of the society against the injustice of the other part. Different interests necessarily exist in different classes of citizens. If a majority be united by a common interest, the rights of the minority will be insecure. There are but two methods of providing against this evil: The one by creating a will in the community independent of the majority—that is, of the society itself; the other, by comprehending in the society so many separate descriptions of citizens as will render an unjust combination of a majority of the whole very improbable, if not impracticable. The first method prevails in all governments possessing an hereditary or self-appointed authority. This, at best, is but a precarious security; because a power independent of the society may as well espouse the unjust views of the major as the rightful interests of the minor party, and may possibly be turned against both parties. The second method will be exemplified in the federal republic of the United States. Whilst all authority in it will be derived from and dependent on the society, the society itself will be broken into so many parts, interests and classes of citizens, that the rights of individuals, or of the minority, will be in little danger from interested combinations of the majority. In a free government the security for civil rights must be the same as that for religious rights. It consists in the one case in the multiplicity of interests, and in the other in the multiplicity of sects. The degree of security in both cases will depend on the number of interests and sects; and this may be presumed to depend on the extent of country and number of people comprehended under the same government. This view of the subject must particularly recommend a proper federal system to all the sincere and considerate friends of republican government: Since it shows that in exact proportion as the territory of the Union may be formed into more circumscribed Confederacies, or States, oppressive combinations of a majority will be facilitated; the best security, under the republican form, for the rights of every class of citizens, will be diminished; and consequently the stability and independence of some member of the government, the only other security, must be proportionally increased. Justice is the end of government. It is the end of civil society. It ever has been and ever will be pursued until it be obtained, or until liberty be lost in the pursuit. In a society under the forms of which the stronger faction can readily unite and oppress the weaker, anarchy may as truly be said to reign as in a state of nature, where the weaker individual is not secured against the violence of the stronger: And as, in the latter state, even the stronger individuals are prompted, by the uncertainty of their condition, to submit to a government which may protect the weak as well as themselves: So, in the former state, will the more powerful factions or parties be gradually induced, by a like motive, to wish for a government which will protect all parties, the weaker as well as the more powerful. It can be little doubted that if the State of Rhode Island was separated from the Confederacy and left to itself, the insecurity of rights under the popular form of government within such narrow limits would be displayed by such reiterated oppressions of factious majorities that some power altogether independent of the people would soon be called for by the voice of the very factions whose misrule had proved the necessity of it. In the extended republic of the United States, and among the great variety of interests, parties, and sects which it embraces, a coalition of a majority of the whole society could seldom take place on any other principles than those of justice and the general good; and there being thus less danger to a minor from the will of the major party, there must be less pretext, also, to provide for the security of the former, by introducing into the government a will not dependent on the latter, or, in other words, a will independent of the society itself. It is no less certain than it is important, notwithstanding the contrary opinions which have been entertained, that the larger the society, provided it lie within a practicable sphere, the more duly capable it will be of self-government. And happily for the *republican cause,* the practicable sphere may be carried to a very great extent by a judicious modification and mixture of the *federal principle.*

PUBLIUS
February 6, 1788

The Anti-Federalist Papers

Essay by Brutus in the *New York Journal*

When the public is called to investigate and decide upon a question in which not only the present members of the community are deeply interested, but upon which the happiness and misery of generations yet unborn is in great measure suspended, the benevolent mind cannot help feeling itself peculiarly interested in the result.

In this situation, I trust the feeble efforts of an individual, to lead the minds of the people to a wise and prudent determination, cannot fail of being acceptable to the candid and dispassionate part of the community. Encouraged by this consideration, I have been induced to offer my thoughts upon the present important crisis of our public affairs.

Perhaps this country never saw so critical a period in their political concerns. We have felt the feebleness of the ties by which these United-States are held together, and the want of sufficient energy in our present confederation, to manage, in some instances, our general concerns. Various expedients have been proposed to remedy these evils, but none have succeeded. At length a Convention of the states has been assembled, they have formed a constitution which will now, probably, be submitted to the people to ratify or reject, who are the fountain of all power, to whom alone it of right belongs to make or unmake constitutions, or forms of government, at their pleasure. The most important question that was ever proposed to your decision, or to the decision of any people under heaven, is before you, and you are to decide upon it by men of your own election, chosen specially for this purpose. If the constitution, offered to your acceptance, be a wise one, calculated to preserve the invaluable blessings of liberty, to secure the inestimable rights of mankind, and promote human happiness, then, if you accept it, you will lay a lasting foundation of happiness for millions yet unborn; generations to come will rise up and call you blessed. You may rejoice in the prospects of this vast extended continent becoming filled with freemen, who will assert the dignity of human nature. You may solace yourselves with the idea, that society, in this favoured land, will fast advance to the highest point of perfection; the human mind will expand in knowledge and virtue, and the golden age be, in some measure, realised. But if, on the other hand, this form of government contains principles that will lead to the subversion of liberty—if it tends to establish a despotism, or, what is worse, a tyrannic aristocracy; then, if you adopt it, this only remaining assylum for liberty will be shut up, and posterity will execrate your memory.

Momentous then is the question you have to determine, and you are called upon by every motive which should influence a noble and virtuous mind, to examine it well, and to make up a wise judgment. It is insisted, indeed, that this constitution must be received, be it ever so imperfect. If it has its defects, it is said, they can be best amended when they are experienced. But remember, when the people once part with power, they can seldom or never resume it again but by force. Many instances can be produced in which the people have voluntarily increased the powers of their rulers; but few, if any, in which rulers have willingly abridged their authority. This is a sufficient reason to induce you to be careful, in the first instance, how you deposit the powers of government.

With these few introductory remarks, I shall proceed to a consideration of this constitution:

The first question that presents itself on the subject is, whether a confederated government be the best for the United States or not? Or in other words, whether the thirteen United States should be reduced to one great republic, governed by one legislature, and under the direction of one executive and judicial; or whether they should continue thirteen confederated republics, under the direction and controul of a supreme federal head for certain defined national purposes only?

This enquiry is important, because, although the government reported by the convention does not go to a perfect and entire consolidation, yet it approaches so near to it, that it must, if executed, certainly and infallibly terminate in it.

This government is to possess absolute and uncontroulable power, legislative, executive and judicial, with respect to every object to which it extends, for by the last clause of section 8th, article 1st, it is declared "that the Congress shall have power to make all laws which shall be necessary and proper for carrying into execution the foregoing powers, and all other powers vested by this constitution, in the government of the United States; or in any department or office thereof." And by the 6th article, it is declared "that this constitution, and the laws of the United States, which shall be made in pursuance thereof, and the treaties made, or which shall be made, under the authority of the United States, shall be the supreme law of the land; and the judges in every state shall be bound thereby, any thing in the constitution, or law of any state to the contrary notwithstanding." It appears from these articles that there is no need of any intervention of the state governments, between the Congress and the people, to execute any one power vested in the general government, and that the constitution and laws of every state are nullified and declared void, so far as they are or shall be inconsistent with this constitution, or the laws made in pursuance of it, or with treaties made under the authority of the United States.—The government then, so far as it extends, is a complete one, and not a confederation. It is as much one complete government as that of New York or Massachusetts, has as absolute and perfect powers to make and execute all laws, to appoint officers, institute courts, declare offences, and annex penalties, with respect to every object to which it extends, as any other in the world. So far therefore as its powers reach, all ideas of confederation are given up and lost. It is true this government is limited to certain objects, or to speak more properly, some small degree of power is still left to the states, but a little attention to the powers vested in the general government, will convince every candid man, that if it is capable of being executed, all that is reserved for the individual states must very soon be annihilated, except so far as they are barely necessary to the organization of the general government. The powers of the general legislature extend to every case that is of the least importance—there is nothing valuable to human nature, nothing dear to freemen, but what is within its power. It has authority to make laws which will affect the lives, the liberty, and property of every man in the United States; nor can the constitution or laws of any state, in any way prevent or impede the full and complete execution of every power given. The legislative power is competent to lay taxes, duties, imposts, and excises;—there is no limitation to this power, unless it be said that the clause which directs the use to which those taxes, and duties shall be applied, may be said to be a limitation: but this is no restriction of the power at all, for by this clause they are to be applied to pay the debts and provide for the common defence and general welfare of the United States; but the legislature have authority to contract debts at their discretion; they are the sole judges of what is necessary to provide for the common defence, and they only are to determine what is for the general welfare; this power therefore is neither more nor less, than a power to lay and collect taxes, imposts, and excises, at their pleasure; not only [is] the power to lay taxes unlimited, as to the amount they may require, but it is perfect and absolute to raise them in any mode they please. No state legislature, or any power in the state governments, have any more to do in carrying this into effect, than the authority of one state has to do with that of another. In the business therefore of laying and collecting taxes, the idea of confederation is totally lost, and that of one entire republic is embraced. It is proper here to remark, that the authority to lay and collect taxes is the most important of any power that can be granted; it connects with it

almost all other powers, or at least will in process of time draw all other after it; it is the great mean of protection, security, and defence, in a good government, and the great engine of oppression and tyranny in a bad one. This cannot fail of being the case, if we consider the contracted limits which are set by this constitution, to the late [state?] governments, on this article of raising money. No state can emit paper money—lay any duties, or imposts, on imports, or exports, but by consent of the Congress; and then the net produce shall be for the benefit of the United States: the only mean therefore left, for any state to support its government and discharge its debts, is by direct taxation; and the United States have also power to lay and collect taxes, in any way they please. Every one who has thought on the subject, must be convinced that but small sums of money can be collected in any country, by direct taxe[s], when the foederal government begins to exercise the right of taxation in all its parts, the legislatures of the several states will find it impossible to raise monies to support their governments. Without money they cannot be supported, and they must dwindle away, and, as before observed, their powers absorbed in that of the general government.

It might be here shewn, that the power in the federal legislative, to raise and support armies at pleasure, as well in peace as in war, and their controul over the militia, tend, not only to a consolidation of the government, but the destruction of liberty.—I shall not, however, dwell upon these, as a few observations upon the judicial power of this government, in addition to the preceding, will fully evince the truth of the position.

The judicial power of the United States is to be vested in a supreme court, and in such inferior courts as Congress may from time to time ordain and establish. The powers of these courts are very extensive; their jurisdiction comprehends all civil causes, except such as arise between citizens of the same state; and it extends to all cases in law and equity arising under the constitution. One inferior court must be established, I presume, in each state, at least, with the necessary executive officers appendant thereto. It is easy to see, that in the common course of things, these courts will eclipse the dignity, and take away from the respectability, of the state courts. These courts will be, in themselves, totally independent of the states, deriving their authority from the United States, and receiving from them fixed salaries; and in the course of human events it is to be expected, that they will swallow up all the powers of the courts in the respective states.

How far the clause in the 8th section of the 1st article may operate to do away all idea of confederated states, and to effect an entire consolidation of the whole into one general government, it is impossible to say. The powers given by this article are very general and comprehensive, and it may receive a construction to justify the passing almost any law. A power to make all laws, which shall be *necessary and proper*, for carrying into execution, all powers vested by the constitution in the government of the United States, or any department or officer thereof, is a power very comprehensive and definite [indefinite?], and may, for ought I know, be exercised in a such manner as entirely to abolish the state legislatures. Suppose the legislature of a state should pass a law to raise money to support their government and pay the state debt, may the Congress repeal this law, because it may prevent the collection of a tax which they may think proper and necessary to lay, to provide for the general welfare of the United States? For all laws made, in pursuance of this constitution, are the supreme law of the land, and the judges in every state shall be bound thereby, any thing in the constitution or laws of the different states to the contrary notwithstanding.—By such a law, the government of a particular state might be overturned at one stroke, and thereby be deprived of every means of its support.

It is not meant, by stating this case, to insinuate that the constitution would warrant a law of this kind; or unnecessarily to alarm the fears of the people, by suggesting, that the federal legislature would be more likely to pass the limits assigned them by the constitution, than that of an individual state, further than they are less responsible to the people. But what is meant is, that the legislature of the United States are vested with the great and uncontroulable powers, of laying and collecting taxes, duties, imposts, and excises; of regulating trade, raising and supporting armies, organizing, arming, and disciplining the militia, instituting courts, and other general powers. And are by this clause invested with the power of making all laws, *proper and necessary*, for carrying all these into execution; and they may so exercise this power as entirely to annihilate all the state governments, and reduce this country to one single government. And if they may do it, it is pretty certain they will; for it will be found that the power retained by individual states, small as it is, will be a clog upon the wheels of the government of the United States; the latter therefore will be naturally inclined to remove it out of the way. Besides, it is a truth confirmed by the unerring experience of ages, that every man, and every body of men, invested with power, are ever disposed to increase it, and to acquire a superiority over every thing that stands in their way. This disposition, which is implanted in human nature, will operate in the federal legislature to lessen and ultimately to subvert the state authority, and having such advantages, will most certainly succeed, if the federal government succeeds at all. It must be very evident then, that what this constitution wants of being a complete consolidation of the several parts of the union into one complete government, possessed of perfect legislative, judicial, and executive powers, to all intents and purposes, it will necessarily acquire in its exercise and operation.

Let us now proceed to enquire, as I at first proposed, whether it be best the thirteen United States should be reduced to one great republic, or not? It is here taken for granted, that all agree in this, that whatever government we adopt, it ought to be a free one; that it should be so framed as to secure the liberty of the citizens of America, and such an one as to admit of a full, fair, and equal representation of the people. The question then will be, whether a government thus constituted, and founded on such principles, is practicable, and can be exercised over the whole United States, reduced into one state?

If respect is to be paid to the opinion of the greatest and wisest men who have ever thought or wrote on the science of government, we shall be constrained to conclude, that a free republic cannot succeed over a country of such immense extent, containing such a number of inhabitants, and these encreasing in such rapid progression as that of the whole United States. Among the many illustrious authorities which might be produced to this point, I shall content myself with quoting only two. The one is the baron de Montesquieu, spirit of laws, chap. xvi. vol. I [book VIII]. "It is natural to a republic to have only a small territory, otherwise it cannot long subsist. In a large republic there are men of large fortunes, and consequently of less moderation; there are trusts too great to be placed in any single subject; he has interest of his own; he soon begins to think that he may be happy, great and glorious, by oppressing his fellow citizens; and that he may raise himself to grandeur on the ruins of his country. In a large republic, the public good is sacrificed to a thousand views; it is subordinate to exceptions, and depends on accidents. In a small one, the interest of the public is easier perceived, better understood, and more within the reach of every citizen; abuses are of less extent, and of course are less protected." Of the same opinion is the marquis Beccarari.

History furnishes no example of a free republic, any thing like the extent of the United States. The Grecian republics were of small extent; so also was that of the Romans. Both of these, it is true, in process of time, extended their conquests over large territories of country; and the consequence was, that their governments were changed from that of free governments to those of the most tyrannical that ever existed in the world.

Not only the opinion of the greatest men, and the experience of mankind, are against the idea of an extensive republic, but a variety of reasons may be drawn from the reason and nature of things, against it. In every government, the will of the sovereign is the law. In despotic governments, the supreme authority being lodged in one, his will is law, and can be as easily expressed to a large extensive territory as to a small one. In a pure democracy the people are the sovereign, and their will is declared by themselves; for this purpose they must all come together to deliberate, and decide. This kind of government cannot be exercised, therefore, over a country of any considerable extent; it must be confined to a single city, or at least limited to such bounds as that the people can conveniently assemble, be able to debate, understand the subject submitted to them, and declare their opinion concerning it.

In a free republic, although all laws are derived from the consent of the people, yet the people do not declare their consent by themselves in person, but by representatives, chosen by them, who are supposed to know the minds of their constituents, and to be possessed of integrity to declare this mind.

In every free government, the people must give their assent to the laws by which they are governed. This is the true criterion between a free government and an arbitrary one. The former are ruled by the will of the whole, expressed in any manner they may agree upon; the latter by the will of one, or a few. If the people are to give their assent to the laws, by persons chosen and appointed by them, the manner of the choice and the number chosen, must be such, as to possess, be disposed, and consequently qualified to declare the sentiments of the people; for if they do not know, or are not disposed to speak the sentiments of the people, the people do not govern, but the sovereignty is in a few. Now, in a large extended country, it is impossible to have a representation, possessing the sentiments, and of integrity, to declare the minds of the people, without having it so numerous and unwieldly, as to be subject in great measure to the inconveniency of a democratic government.

The territory of the United States is of vast extent; it now contains near three millions of souls, and is capable of containing much more than ten times that number. Is it practicable for a country, so large and so numerous as they will soon become, to elect a representation, that will speak their sentiments, without their becoming so numerous as to be incapable of transacting public business? It certainly is not.

In a republic, the manners, sentiments, and interests of the people should be similar. If this be not the case, there will be a constant clashing of opinions; and the representatives of one part will be continually striving against those of the other. This will retard the operations of government, and prevent such conclusions as will promote the public good. If we apply this remark to the condition of the United States, we shall be convinced that it forbids that we should be one government. The United States includes a variety of climates. The productions of the different parts of the union are very variant, and their interests, of consequence, diverse. Their manners and habits differ as much as their climates and productions; and their sentiments are by no means coincident. The laws and customs of the several states are, in many respects, very diverse, and in some opposite; each would be in favor of its own interests and customs, and, of consequence, a legislature, formed of representatives from the respective parts, would not only be too numerous to act with any care or decision, but would be composed of such heterogenous and discordant principles, as would constantly be contending with each other.

The laws cannot be executed in a republic, of an extent equal to that of the United States, with promptitude.

The magistrates in every government must be supported in the execution of the laws, either by an armed force, maintained at the public expence for that purpose; or by the people turning out to aid the magistrate upon his command, in case of resistance.

In despotic governments, as well as in all the monarchies of Europe, standing armies are kept up to execute the commands of the prince or the magistrate, and are employed for this purpose when occasion requires: But they have always proved the destruction of liberty, and [are] abhorrent to the spirit of a free republic. In England, where they depend upon the parliament for their annual support, they have always been complained of as oppressive and unconstitutional, and are seldom employed in executing of the laws; never except on extraordinary occasions, and then under the direction of a civil magistrate.

A free republic will never keep a standing army to execute its laws. It must depend upon the support of its citizens. But when a government is to receive its support from the aid of the citizens, it must be so constructed as to have the confidence, respect, and affection of the people. Men who, upon the call of the magistrate, offer themselves to execute the laws, are influenced to do it either by affection to the government, or from fear; where a standing army is at hand to punish offenders, every man is actuated by the latter principle, and therefore, when the magistrate calls, will obey: but, where this is not the case, the government must rest for its support upon the confidence and respect which the people have for their government and laws. The body of the people being attached, the government will always be sufficient to support and execute its laws, and to operate upon the fears of any faction which may be opposed to it, not only to prevent an opposition to the execution of the laws themselves, but also to compel the most of them to aid the magistrate; but the people will not be likely to have such confidence in their rulers, in a republic so extensive as the United States, as necessary for these purposes. The confidence which the people have in their rulers, in a free republic, arises from their knowing them, from their being responsible to them for their conduct, and from the power they have of displacing them when they misbehave: but in a republic of the extent of this continent, the people in general would be acquainted with very few of their rulers: the people at large would know little of their proceedings, and it would be extremely difficult to change them. The people in Georgia and New-Hampshire would not know one another's mind, and therefore could not act in concert to enable them to effect a general change of representatives. The different parts of so extensive a country could not possibly be made acquainted with the conduct of their representatives, nor be informed of the reasons upon which measures were founded. The consequence will be, they will have no confidence in their legislature, suspect them of ambitious views, be jealous of every measure they adopt, and will not support the laws they pass. Hence the government will be nerveless and inefficient, and no way will be left to render it otherwise, but by establishing an armed force to execute the laws at the point of the bayonet—a government of all others the most to be dreaded.

In a republic of such vast extent as the United-States, the legislature cannot attend to the various concerns and wants of its different parts. It cannot be sufficiently numerous to be acquainted with the local condition and wants of the different districts, and if it could, it is impossible it should have sufficient time to attend to and provide for all the variety of cases of this nature, that would be continually arising.

In so extensive a republic, the great officers of government would soon become above the controul of the people, and abuse their power to the purpose of aggrandizing themselves, and oppressing them. The trust committed to the executive offices, in a country of the extent of the United-States, must be various and of magnitude. The command of all the troops and navy of the republic, the appointment of officers, the power of pardoning offences, the collecting of all the public revenues, and the power of expending them, with a number of other powers, must be lodged and exercised in every state, in the hands of a few. When these are attended with great honor and emolument, as they always will be in large states, so as greatly to interest men to pursue them, and to be proper objects for ambitious and designing men, such men will be ever restless in their pursuit after them. They will use the power, when they have acquired it, to the purposes of gratifying their own interest and ambition, and it is scarcely possible, in a very large republic, to call them to account for their misconduct, or to prevent their abuse of power.

These are some of the reasons by which it appears, that a free republic cannot long subsist over a country of the great extent of these states. If then this new constitution is calculated to consolidate the thirteen states into one, as it evidently is, it ought not to be adopted.

Though I am of opinion, that it is a sufficient objection to this government, to reject it, that it creates the whole union into one government, under the form of a republic, yet if this objection was obviated, there are exceptions to it, which are so material and fundamental, that they ought to determine every man, who is a friend to the liberty and happiness of mankind, not to adopt it. I beg the candid and dispassionate attention of my countrymen while I state these objections—they are such as have obtruded themselves upon my mind upon a careful attention to the matter, and such as I sincerely believe are well founded. There are many objections, of small moment, of which I shall take no notice—perfection is not to be expected in any thing that is the production of man—and if I did not in my conscience believe that this scheme was defective in the fundamental principles—in the foundation upon which a free and equal government must rest—I would hold my peace.

BRUTUS
October 18, 1787

Presidents and Vice Presidents

	PRESIDENT	VICE PRESIDENT		PRESIDENT	VICE PRESIDENT
1	George Washington *(Federalist 1789)*	John Adams *(Federalist 1789)*	12	Zachary Taylor *(Whig 1849)*	Millard Fillmore *(Whig 1849)*
2	John Adams *(Federalist 1797)*	Thomas Jefferson *(Dem.-Rep. 1797)*	13	Millard Fillmore *(Whig 1850)*	
3	Thomas Jefferson *(Dem.-Rep. 1801)*	Aaron Burr *(Dem.-Rep. 1801)*	14	Franklin Pierce *(Democratic 1853)*	William R. D. King *(Democratic 1853)*
		George Clinton *(Dem.-Rep. 1805)*	15	James Buchanan *(Democratic 1857)*	John C. Breckinridge *(Democratic 1857)*
4	James Madison *(Dem.-Rep. 1809)*	George Clinton *(Dem.-Rep. 1809)*	16	Abraham Lincoln *(Republican 1861)*	Hannibal Hamlin *(Republican 1861)*
		Elbridge Gerry *(Dem.-Rep. 1813)*			Andrew Johnson *(Unionist 1865)*
5	James Monroe *(Dem.-Rep. 1817)*	Daniel D. Tompkins *(Dem.-Rep. 1817)*	17	Andrew Johnson *(Unionist 1865)*	
6	John Quincy Adams *(Dem.-Rep. 1825)*	John C. Calhoun *(Dem.-Rep. 1825)*	18	Ulysses S. Grant *(Republican 1869)*	Schuyler Colfax *(Republican 1869)*
7	Andrew Jackson *(Democratic 1829)*	John C. Calhoun *(Democratic 1829)*			Henry Wilson *(Republican 1873)*
		Martin Van Buren *(Democratic 1833)*	19	Rutherford B. Hayes *(Republican 1877)*	William A. Wheeler *(Republican 1877)*
8	Martin Van Buren *(Democratic 1837)*	Richard M. Johnson *(Democratic 1837)*	20	James A. Garfield *(Republican 1881)*	Chester A. Arthur *(Republican 1881)*
9	William H. Harrison *(Whig 1841)*	John Tyler *(Whig 1841)*	21	Chester A. Arthur *(Republican 1881)*	
10	John Tyler *(Whig and Democratic 1841)*		22	Grover Cleveland *(Democratic 1885)*	Thomas A. Hendricks *(Democratic 1885)*
11	James K. Polk *(Democratic 1845)*	George M. Dallas *(Democratic 1845)*	23	Benjamin Harrison *(Republican 1889)*	Levi P. Morton *(Republican 1889)*

	PRESIDENT	VICE PRESIDENT		PRESIDENT	VICE PRESIDENT
24	Grover Cleveland *(Democratic 1893)*	Adlai E. Stevenson *(Democratic 1893)*	35	John F. Kennedy *(Democratic 1961)*	Lyndon B. Johnson *(Democratic 1961)*
25	William McKinley *(Republican 1897)*	Garret A. Hobart *(Republican 1897)*	36	Lyndon B. Johnson *(Democratic 1963)*	Hubert H. Humphrey *(Democratic 1965)*
		Theodore Roosevelt *(Republican 1901)*	37	Richard M. Nixon *(Republican 1969)*	Spiro T. Agnew *(Republican 1969)*
26	Theodore Roosevelt *(Republican 1901)*	Charles W. Fairbanks *(Republican 1905)*			Gerald R. Ford *(Republican 1973)*
27	William H. Taft *(Republican 1909)*	James S. Sherman *(Republican 1909)*	38	Gerald R. Ford *(Republican 1974)*	Nelson Rockefeller *(Republican 1974)*
28	Woodrow Wilson *(Democratic 1913)*	Thomas R. Marshall *(Democratic 1913)*	39	James E. Carter *(Democratic 1977)*	Walter Mondale *(Democratic 1977)*
29	Warren G. Harding *(Republican 1921)*	Calvin Coolidge *(Republican 1921)*	40	Ronald Reagan *(Republican 1981)*	George H. W. Bush *(Republican 1981)*
30	Calvin Coolidge *(Republican 1923)*	Charles G. Dawes *(Republican 1925)*	41	George H. W. Bush *(Republican 1989)*	J. Danforth Quayle *(Republican 1989)*
31	Herbert Hoover *(Republican 1929)*	Charles Curtis *(Republican 1929)*	42	William J. Clinton *(Democratic 1993)*	Albert Gore, Jr. *(Democratic 1993)*
32	Franklin D. Roosevelt *(Democratic 1933)*	John Nance Garner *(Democratic 1933)*	43	George W. Bush *(Republican 2001)*	Richard Cheney *(Republican 2001)*
		Henry A. Wallace *(Democratic 1941)*	44	Barack H. Obama *(Democratic 2009)*	Joseph R. Biden, Jr. *(Democratic 2009)*
		Harry S. Truman *(Democratic 1945)*	45	Donald J. Trump *(Republican 2017)*	Michael R. Pence *(Republican 2017)*
33	Harry S. Truman *(Democratic 1945)*	Alben W. Barkley *(Democratic 1949)*	46	Joseph R. Biden, Jr. *(Democratic 2021)*	Kamala Harris *(Democratic 2021)*
34	Dwight D. Eisenhower *(Republican 1953)*	Richard M. Nixon *(Republican 1953)*			

Endnotes

....

CHAPTER 1

1. Lydia DePillis, Mike Spies, Joshua Kaplan, Kyle Edwards and Caroline Chen, "Here's Why Florida Got All the Emergency Medical Supplies It Requested While Other States Did Not," *ProPublica*, March 20, 2020, www.propublica.org/article/heres-why-florida-got-all-the-emergency-medical-supplies-it-requested-while-other-states-did-not (accessed 3/23/20).

2. V-Dem Institute, "Democracy for All? V-Dem Annual Democracy Report 2018," May 2018, www.v-dem.net/media/filer_public/3f/19/3f19efc9-e25f-4356-b159-b5c0ec894115/v-dem_democracy_report_2018.pdf (accessed 1/19/20).

3. Eugen Weber, *Peasants into Frenchmen: The Modernization of Rural France, 1870–1914* (Stanford, CA: Stanford University Press, 1976), chap. 5.

4. Harold Lasswell, *Politics: Who Gets What, When, How* (New York: Meridian Books, 1958).

5. "2020 Ballot Measures," Ballotpedia, https://ballotpedia.org/2020_ballot_measures#Notable_topics_and_trends_in_2020 (accessed 10/12/20).

6. U.S. Citizenship and Immigration Services, "Citizenship Rights and Responsibilities," www.uscis.gov/citizenship/learners/citizenship-rights-and-responsibilities (accessed 6/1/19).

7. This definition is taken from Norman H. Nie, Jane Junn, and Kenneth Stehlik-Barry, *Education and Democratic Citizenship in America* (Chicago: University of Chicago Press, 1996).

8. Kyle Dropp and Brendan Nyhan, "One-Third Don't Know Obamacare and Affordable Care Act Are the Same," *New York Times*, The Upshot, February 7, 2017, www.nytimes.com/2017/02/07/upshot/one-third-dont-know-obamacare-and-affordable-care-act-are-the-same.html?_r=0 (accessed 12/28/17).

9. Pew Research, Global Attitudes & Trends, "Attitudes toward Elected Officials, Voting, and the State," February 26, 2020, www.pewresearch.org/global/2020/02/27/attitudes-toward-elected-officials-voting-and-the-state/pg_2020-02-27_global-democracy_02-1/ (accessed 3/21/20).

10. Pew Research Center, "Attitudes toward Elected Officials, Voting, and the State."

11. U.S. Census Bureau, Population Clock, April 15, 2018, www.census.gov/popclock/ (accessed 4/15/18).

12. Susan B. Carter et al., eds., *Historical Statistics of the United States: Millennial Edition Online* (New York: Cambridge University Press, 2006), Table Aa145-184, Population, by Sex and Race: 1790–1990, 23. Data from 2016 available at U.S. Census Bureau, "2016 American Community Survey 1-Year Estimates: Selected Characteristics of the Native and Foreign-Born Populations," https://factfinder.census.gov/faces/tableserVices/jsf/pages/productview.xhtml?pid=ACS_16_1YR_S0501&prodType=table (accessed 12/26/17).

13. Carter et al., *Historical Statistics of the United States*, Table Aa145-184, Population, by Sex and Race: 1790–1990, 23.

14. Carter et al., *Historical Statistics of the United States*, Table Aa145-184, Population, by Sex and Race: 1790–1990, 23; Table Aa2189-2215, Hispanic Population Estimates.

15. Campbell J. Gibson and Emily Lennon, "Historical Census Statistics on the Foreign-Born Population of the United States: 1850–1990," February 1999, www.census.gov/population/www/documentation/twps0029/twps0029.html (accessed 4/10/16).

16. Carter et al., *Historical Statistics of the United States*, Table Aa22-35, Selected Population Characteristics.

17. Michael B. Katz and Mark J. Stern, *One Nation Divisible: What America Was and What It Is Becoming* (New York: Russell Sage Foundation, 2006), 16.

18. Carter et al., *Historical Statistics of the United States*, Table Aa145-184, Population, by Sex and Race: 1790–1990, 23. Karen R. Humes, Nicholas A. Jones, and Roberto R. Ramirez, "Overview of Race and Hispanic Origin: 2010,"

2010 Census Briefs, no. C2010BR-02 (Washington, DC: U.S. Census Bureau, March 2011), 4, www.census.gov/prod/cen2010/briefs/c2010br-02.pdf (accessed 10/14/2011).

19. U.S. Census Bureau, "American Community Survey 2018, 1-year Estimates Data Profiles, Table DP05," https://data.census.gov/cedsci/table?t=Hispanic%20or%20Latino&tid=ACSDP1Y2018.DP05&hidePreview=false (accessed 3/23/2020).

20. U.S. Census Bureau, "2018 American Community Survey, Selected Social Characteristics in the United States," https://data.census.gov/cedsci/table?d=ACS%201-Year%20Estimates%20Data%20Profiles&tid=ACSDP1Y2018.DP02 (accessed 3/18/20).

21. U.S. Census Bureau, "2016 American Community Survey 1-Year Estimates: Selected Characteristics of the Foreign-Born Population by Region of Birth: Latin America," https://factfinder.census.gov/faces/tableservices/jsf/pages/productview.xhtml?pid=ACS_16_1YR_S0506&prodType=table (accessed 12/26/17).

22. U.S. Census Bureau, "2016 American Community Survey 1-Year Estimates: Selected Characteristics of the Foreign-Born Population by Region of Birth: Asia," https://factfinder.census.gov/faces/tableservices/jsf/pages/productview.xhtml?pid=ACS_16_1YR_S0505&prodType=table (accessed 12/2/17).

23. U.S. Census Bureau, "2016 American Community Survey 1-Year Estimates: Selected Characteristics of the Foreign-Born Population by Region of Birth: Europe," https://factfinder.census.gov/faces/tableservices/jsf/pages/productview.xhtml?pid=ACS_16_1YR_S0503&prodType=table (accessed 12/26/17).

24. Bryan Baker, "Estimates of the Illegal Alien Population Residing in the United States: January 2015," Department of Homeland Security, December 2018, www.dhs.gov/sites/default/files/publications/18_1214_PLCY_pops-est-report.pdf (accessed 1/17/20).

25. *Plyler v. Doe*, 457 U.S. 202 (1982).

26. National Conference of State Legislatures, "Federal Benefit Eligibility for Unauthorized Immigrants," February 24, 2014, www.ncsl.org/research/immigration/federal-benefits-to-unauthorized-immigrants.aspx (accessed 5/22/19); National Conference of State Legislatures, "Undocumented State Tuition: Overview," March 14, 2019, www.ncsl.org/research/education/undocumented-student-tuition-overview.aspx (accessed 5/22/19).

27. Gallup, "Religion," https://news.gallup.com/poll/1690/religion.aspx (accessed 10/12/20).

28. Gallup, "Religion."

29. U.S. Census Bureau, "Demographic Trends in the 20th Century, Table 5: Population by Age and Sex for the United States: 1900 to 2000," www.census.gov/prod/2002pubs/censr-4.pdf (accessed 4/11/16); U.S. Census Bureau, "Population Estimates, Age and Sex," www.census.gov/quickfacts/fact/table/US/PST045217 (accessed 12/26/17).

30. World Bank, "Population Ages 65 and Above (% of Total)," March 1, 2018, http://data.worldbank.org/indicator/SP.POP.65UP.TO.ZS (accessed 4/15/18).

31. U.S. Census Bureau, "2010 Census Urban Area Facts," www.census.gov/geo/reference/ua/uafacts.html (accessed 4/11/16); Central Intelligence Agency, "World Factbook: Urbanization," 2017, www.cia.gov/library/publications/the-world-factbook/fields/2212.html (accessed 4/15/18).

32. See, for example, David B. Grusky and Tamar Kricheli-Katz, eds., *The New Gilded Age: The Critical Inequality Debates of Our Time* (Stanford: Stanford University Press, 2012).

33. Thomas Piketty and Emmanuel Saez, "Income Inequality in the United States, 1913–1998," *Quarterly Journal of Economics* 118, no. 1 (2003) (Tables and Figures Updated to 2018), https://eml.berkeley.edu/~saez/ (accessed 1/17/20).

34. U.S. Census Bureau, "Income: Historical Income Data. Tables F-2, F-3, and F-6," www.census.gov/hhes/www/income/data/historical/index.html (accessed 4/12/16).

35. U.S. Census Bureau, "Historical Poverty Tables, Table 2: Poverty Status of People by Family Relationship, Race, and Hispanic Origin: 1959 to 2014," www.census.gov/hhes/www/poverty/data/historical/hstpov2.xls (accessed 4/11/16).

36. Jesse Sussell and James A. Thomson, "Are Changing Constituencies Driving Rising Polarization in the U.S. House of Representatives?" RAND Corporation Research Report RR-396-RC, 2015, www.rand.org/pubs/research_reports/RR896.html (accessed 1/15/18).

37. See Judith N. Shklar, *American Citizenship: The Quest for Inclusion* (Cambridge, MA: Harvard University Press, 1991).

38. Herbert McClosky and John Zaller, *The American Ethos: Public Attitudes toward Capitalism and Democracy* (Cambridge, MA: Harvard University Press, 1984), 19.

39. *Burwell v. Hobby Lobby Stores, Inc.*, 573 U.S. 682 (2014).

40. Kevin McCoy and Kevin Johnson, "U.S. Demands Apple Unlock Phone in Drug Case," April 10, 2016, www.usatoday.com/story/news/2016/04/08/justice-moving-forward-separate-apple-case/82788824 (accessed 4/10/16).

41. J. R. Pole, *The Pursuit of Equality in American History* (Berkeley: University of California Press, 1978), 3.

42. *Plessy v. Ferguson*, 163 U.S. 537 (1896).

43. *Brown v. Board of Education*, 347 U.S. 483 (1954).

44. See Rogers M. Smith, *Liberalism and American Constitutional Law* (Cambridge, MA: Harvard University Press, 1985), chap. 6.

45. Janell Fetterolf, "Many Around the World Say Women's Equality Is Very Important," Pew Research Center, January 19, 2017, www.pewresearch.org/fact-tank/2017/01/19

/many-around-the-world-say-womens-equality-is-very
-important/ (accessed 2/16/18); John Gramlich, "10
Things We Learned about Gender Issues in the U.S. in
2017," Pew Research Center, December 28, 2017, www
.pewresearch.org/fact-tank/2017/12/28/10-things-we
-learned-about-gender-issues-in-the-u-s-in-2017/
(accessed 2/16/18); "The Partisan Divide on Political
Values Grows Even Wider," Pew Research Center, October 5, 2017, www.people-press.org/2017/10/05/1-partisan
-divides-over-political-values-widen/ (accessed 2/16/18);
Pew Research Center, "Support for Same-Sex Marriage
Grows, Even among Groups That Had Been Skeptical," June 26, 2017, www.people-press.org/2017/06/26
/support-for-same-sex-marriage-grows-even-among
-groups-that-had-been-skeptical/ (accessed 2/16/18); Pew
Research Center, "Trends in American Values, 1987–
2012," June 4, 2012; Pew Research Center for the People
and the Press and for the Public, "For the Public, It's Not
about Class Warfare, but Fairness," March 2, 2012, www
.peoplepress.org/2012/03/02/for-the-public-its-not
-about-class-warfare-but-fairness (accessed 2/16/18).

46. See the discussion in Eileen McDonagh, "Gender Political
Change," in *New Perspectives on American Politics*, ed.
Lawrence C. Dodd and Calvin C. Jillson (Washington,
DC: CQ Press, 1994), 58–73. The argument for mov-
ing women's issues into the public sphere is made by Jean
Bethke Elshtain, *Public Man, Private Woman* (Princeton,
NJ: Princeton University Press, 1981).

47. Veronique de Rugy and Donald J. Boudreaux, "COVID-19
Is Not a Good Reason to Enact a Permanent Federal
Leave Entitlement," *National Review*, March 13, 2020,
www.nationalreview.com/2020/03/covid-19-is-not-a
-good-reason-to-enact-a-permanent-federal-paid-leave
-entitlement/?itm_source=parsely-api (accessed 3/23/20).

48. Richard L. Hasen, *Plutocrats United: Campaign Money,
the Supreme Court, and the Distortion of American
Elections* (New Haven, CT: Yale University Press, 2016).

49. FairVote, "Voter Turnout," www.fairvote.org/voter
_turnout#voter_turnout_101 (accessed 4/10/16).

50. Center for the Study of the American Electorate, "2008
Turnout Report: African-Americans, Anger, Fear and
Youth Propel Turnout to Highest Level since 1960,"
December 17, 2008, www.american.edu/research/news
/loader.cfm?csModule5security/getfile&pageid523907
(accessed 2/19/16); United States Election Project, "2020
November General Election Turnout Rates," November 4,
2020, www.electproject.org/2020g (accessed 11/6/20).

51. Lydia Saad, "The U.S. Remained Center-Right, Ideologically, in 2019," Gallup News, January 9, 2020, https://
news.gallup.com/poll/275792/remained-center-right
-ideologically-2019.aspx (accessed 1/19/20).

52. Gallup News, "Government," https://news.gallup.com
/poll/27286/government.aspx (accessed 1/19/20); and Pew
Research Center, "Views of Government and the Nation,"
December 17, 2019, www.people-press.org/2019/12
/17/views-of-government-and-the-nation/ (accessed
1/19/20).

53. Pew Research Center, "How Republicans and Democrats
View Federal Spending," April 24, 2017, www.people
-press.org/2017/04/24/how-republicans-and-democrats
-view-federal-spending/ (accessed 1/15/18).

54. Benjamin I. Page and Lawrence R. Jacobs, *Class War?
What Americans Really Think about Economic Inequality*
(Chicago: University of Chicago Press, 2009).

55. Pew Research Center, "Americans' Views of Government: Low Trust, but Some Positive Performance
Ratings," September 14, 2020, www.pewresearch.org
/politics/2020/09/14/americans-views-of-government-low
-trust-but-some-positive-performance-ratings/ (accessed
10/12/20).

56. Frank Newport, "10 Key Findings: Public Opinion on
Coronavirus," Gallup Polling Matters, March 20, 2020,
https://news.gallup.com/opinion/polling-matters/296681
/ten-key-findings-public-opinion-coronavirus.aspx (accessed
3/23/20).

57. Joseph S. Nye, Jr., "Introduction: The Decline of
Confidence in Government," in *Why People Don't Trust
Government*, eds. Joseph S. Nye, Jr., Philip D. Zelikow,
and David C. King (Cambridge, MA: Harvard University Press, 1997), 4.

58. Pew Research Center, "Public Trust in Government,
1958-2017."

CHAPTER 2

1. "Jim Obergefell," *Biography.com*. www.biography.com
/people/jim-obergefell (accessed 3/4/18).

2. Jim Obergefell, "Gay Activist Jim Obergefell: Love, Loss
and Steadfast Commitment Lead a Nation Forward,"
Variety, June 29, 2015, http://variety.com/2015/biz/news
/gay-activist-jim-obergefell-love-loss-commitment-lead
-nation-forward-1201529672/ (accessed 3/4/18).

3. *Obergefell v. Hodges*, 576 U.S. — (2015).

4. Richard E. Neustadt, *Presidential Power and the Modern
Presidents: The Politics of Leadership from Roosevelt to
Reagan* (New York: Simon & Schuster, 1991), 29.

5. The social makeup of colonial America and some of the
social conflicts that divided colonial society are discussed
in Jackson Turner Main, *The Social Structure of Revolutionary America* (Princeton, NJ: Princeton University
Press, 1965).

6. George B. Tindall and David E. Shi, *America: A
Narrative History*, 8th ed. (New York: W. W. Norton,
2010), 202.

7. For a discussion of events leading up to the Revolution,
see Charles M. Andrews, *The Colonial Background of the
American Revolution* (New Haven, CT: Yale University
Press, 1924).

8. See Carl Becker, *The Declaration of Independence* (New York: Knopf, 1942).

9. An excellent and readable account of the development from the Articles of Confederation to the Constitution will be found in Alfred H. Kelly, Winfred A. Harbison, and Herman Belz, *The American Constitution: Its Origins and Development*, 7th ed., vol. 1 (New York: W. W. Norton, 1991), chap. 5.

10. Reported in Samuel E. Morrison, Henry Steele Commager, and William Leuchtenburg, *The Growth of the American Republic*, vol. 1 (New York: Oxford University Press, 1969), 244.

11. Quoted in Morrison, Commager, and Leuchtenburg, *Growth of the American Republic*, 242.

12. Charles A. Beard, *An Economic Interpretation of the Constitution of the United States* (New York: Macmillan, 1913).

13. Max Farrand, ed., *The Records of the Federal Convention of 1787*, vol. 1 (New Haven, CT: Yale University Press, 1966).

14. Madison's notes, along with the somewhat less complete records kept by several other participants in the convention, are available in a four-volume set. See Max Farrand, ed., *The Records of the Federal Convention of 1787*, 4 vols., rev. ed. (New Haven, CT: Yale University Press, 1966).

15. Alexander Hamilton, James Madison, and John Jay, *The Federalist Papers*, ed. Clinton L. Rossiter (New York: New American Library, 1961), no. 71.

16. *Federalist Papers*, no. 70.

17. Melancton Smith, quoted in Herbert J. Storing, *What the Anti-Federalists Were For* (Chicago: University of Chicago Press, 1981), 17.

18. *Federalist Papers*, no. 57.

19. *Federalist Papers*, no. 10.

20. "Essays of Brutus," no. 7, in Storing, *Complete Anti-Federalist*.

21. "Essays of Brutus," no. 6, in Storing, *Complete Anti-Federalist*.

22. Storing, *What the Anti-Federalists Were For*, 28.

23. *Federalist Papers*, no. 51.

24. Quoted in Storing, *What the Anti-Federalists Were For*, 30.

CHAPTER 3

1. White House, "Remarks by President Trump after Tour of the Centers for Disease Control and Prevention," Atlanta, GA, March 6, 2020, www.whitehouse.gov/briefings -statements/remarks-president-trump-tour-centers-disease -control-prevention-atlanta-ga/ (accessed 3/27/20).

2. Robert P. Baird, "Why Widespread Coronavirus Testing Isn't Coming Anytime Soon," *New Yorker*, March 24, 2020, www.newyorker.com/news/news-desk/why-widespread -coronavirus-testing-isnt-coming-anytime-soon (accessed 3/26/20).

3. Pietro S. Nivola, "Why Federalism Matters," Brook-ings Institution Policy Brief #146, October 2005, www .brookings.edu/wp-content/uploads/2016/06/pb146.pdf (accessed 7/15/19).

4. The public policy exception stems from developments in case law tracing back to the 1930s. In Section 283 of the Restatement (Second) of Conflict of Laws (1971) a group of judges and academics codified existing case law related to marriage: "A marriage which satisfies the re-quirements of the state where the marriage was contracted will everywhere be recognized as valid unless it violates the strong public policy of another state which had the most significant relationship to the spouses and the mar-riage at the time of the marriage." However, in *Baker v. General Motors Corp*, 522 U.S. 222 (1998), the Supreme Court explicitly stated that its decision "creates no general exception to the full faith and credit command."

5. Adam Liptak, "Bans on Interracial Unions Offer Perspective on Gay Ones," *New York Times*, March 17, 2004, A22.

6. *Loving v. Virginia*, 388 U.S. 1 (1967). The Lovings were charged with violating Virginia's miscegenation laws and were sentenced to one year in jail, which would be suspended if they left the state for 25 years. Five years later, with the assistance of the American Civil Liberties Union, the Lovings filed a motion to vacate their convic-tion. The Supreme Court heard the case and overturned the Lovings' conviction, finding Virginia's miscegenation law unconstitutional under the due process clause and equal protection clause of the Fourteenth Amendment.

7. *Obergefell v. Hodges*, 576 U.S. — (2015).

8. *Hicklin v. Orbeck*, 437 U.S. 518 (1978).

9. *Sweeny v. Woodall*, 344 U.S. 86 (1952).

10. A good discussion of the constitutional position of local governments is in Richard Briffault, "Our Localism: Part I, the Structure of Local Government Law," *Colum-bia Law Review* 90, no. 1 (January 1990): 1–115. For more on the structure and theory of federalism, see Larry N. Gerston, *American Federalism: A Concise Introduc-tion* (Armonk, NY: M. E. Sharpe, 2007), and Martha Derthick, "Up-to-Date in Kansas City: Reflections on American Federalism" (1992 John Gaus Lecture), *PS: Political Science and Politics* 25 (December 1992): 671–75.

11. *McCulloch v. Maryland*, 4 Wheaton 316 (1819).

12. *Gibbons v. Ogden*, 9 Wheaton 1 (1824).

13. The Sherman Antitrust Act, adopted in 1890, for exam-ple, was enacted not to restrict commerce but rather to protect it from monopolies, or trusts, in order to prevent unfair trade practices and to enable the market again to become self-regulating. Moreover, the Supreme Court sought to uphold liberty of contract to protect businesses. For example, in *Lochner v. New York*, 198 U.S. 45 (1905), the Court invalidated a New York law regulating the sanitary conditions and hours of labor of bakers on the grounds that the law interfered with liberty of contract.

14. The key case in this process of expanding the power of the national government is generally considered to be *NLRB v. Jones & Laughlin Steel Corporation*, 301 U.S. 1 (1937), in which the Supreme Court approved federal regulation of the workplace and thereby virtually eliminated interstate commerce as a limit on the national government's power.

15. Kenneth T. Palmer, "The Evolution of Grant Policies," in *The Changing Politics of Federal Grants*, eds. Lawrence D. Brown, James W. Fossett, and Kenneth T. Palmer (Washington, DC: Brookings Institution Press, 1984), 15.

16. Palmer, "Evolution of Grant Policies," 6.

17. Morton Grodzins, *The American System*, ed. Daniel J. Elazar (Chicago: Rand McNally, 1966).

18. See Donald F. Kettl, *The Regulation of American Federalism* (Baton Rouge: Louisiana State University Press, 1983).

19. *Gonazales v. Oregon*, 546 U.S. 243 (2006).

20. Brady Dennis and Juliet Eilperin, "California and Nearly Two Dozen Other States Sue Trump Administration for the Right to Set Fuel-Efficiency Standards," *Washington Post,* November 15, 2019, www.washingtonpost.com /climate-environment/2019/11/15/california-nearly-two -dozen-other-states-sue-trump-administration-right -require-more-fuel-efficient-cars/ (accessed 1/21/20).

21. The phrase "laboratories of democracy" was coined by Supreme Court Justice Louis Brandeis in his dissenting opinion in *New State Ice Co. v. Liebmann*, 285 U.S. 262 (1932).

22. W. John Moore, "Pleading the 10th," *National Journal*, July 29, 1996.

23. *Printz v. United States*, 521 U.S. 98 (1997).

24. Timothy Conlan, *New Federalism: Intergovernmental Reform from Nixon to Reagan* (Washington, DC: Brookings Institution Press, 1988); U.S. Advisory Commission on Intergovernmental Relations, *Federal Regulation of State and Local Governments*.

25. For an assessment of the achievements of the 104th and 105th Congresses, see Timothy Conlan, *From New Federalism to Devolution: Twenty-Five Years of Intergovernmental Reform* (Washington, DC: Brookings Institution Press, 1998).

26. Centers for Medicare and Medicaid Services, "Health Adult Opportunity Fact Sheet," January 30, 2020, www .cms.gov/newsroom/fact-sheets/healthy-adult-opportunity (accessed 3/21/20).

27. Education Commission of the States, "50-State Comparison: Charter School Policies," January 2018, www.ecs.org /charter-school-policies/ (accessed 6/5/18).

28. National Council of State Legislatures, "NCSL Fiscal Brief: State Balanced Budget Requirements," October 2010, www.ncsl.org/documents/fiscal/StateBalancedBudget Provisions2010.pdf (accessed 7/26/17).

29. Robert Jay Dilger and Richard S. Beth, "Unfunded Mandates Reform Act: History, Impact, and Issues" (Washington, DC: Congressional Research Service, April 19, 2011), 40, http://digital.library.unt.edu/ark:/67531 /metadc40084/m1/1/high_res_d/R40957_2011Apr19 .pdf (accessed 11/16/13).

30. Congressional Research Service, "Unfunded Mandates Reform Act: History, Impact, and Issues, May 22, 2019, https://fas.org/sgp/crs/misc/R40957.pdf (accessed 7/16/19).

31. U.S. Committee on Federalism and National Purpose, *To Form a More Perfect Union* (Washington, DC: National Conference on Social Welfare, 1985). See also the discussion in Paul E. Peterson, *The Price of Federalism* (Washington, DC: Brookings Institution Press, 1995), esp. chap. 8.

32. Malcolm Gladwell, "Remaking Welfare: In States' Experiments, a Cutting Contest," *Washington Post*, March 10, 1995, 6.

33. Elissa Cohen, Sarah Minton, Megan Thompson, Elizabeth Crowe, and Linda Giannarelli, "Welfare Rules Databook: State TANF Policies as of July 2015," OPRE Report 2016-67 (Washington, DC: Office of Planning, Research and Evaluation, Administration for Children and Families, U.S. Department of Health and Human Services, 2016), http://wrd.urban.org/wrd/data/databooks /2015%20Welfare%20Rules%20Databook%20 (Final%2009%2026%2016).pdf (accessed 7/30/17); and Mary Jo Pitzi, "Arizona Limits Poverty Aid to 1 Year; Strictest in U.S." azcentral.com, July 1, 2016, www .azcentral.com/story/news/politics/arizona/2016/07/01 /arizona-limits-poverty-aid-1-year-strictest-us/86499262/ (accessed 7/30/17).

34. Ashley Burnside and Ife Floyd, "TANF Benefits Remain Low Despite Recent Increases in Some States," Center on Budget and Policy Priorities, October 12, 2018, www .cbpp.org/sites/default/files/atoms/files/10-30-14tanf.pdf (accessed 10/12/18).

35. Malcolm Gladwell, "Remaking Welfare."

36. Andrea Louise Campbell, *Trapped in America's Safety Net: One Family's Struggle* (Chicago: University of Chicago Press, 2014), 82.

37. Kate Linthicum, "Obama Ends Secure Communities Program as Part of Immigration Action," *Los Angeles Times*, November 21, 2014, www.latimes.com/local/california /la-me-1121-immigration-justice-20141121-story.html (accessed 8/16/15).

38. "Enhancing Public Safety in the Interior of the United States," Executive Order 13768, January 25, 2017, www .federalregister.gov/documents/2017/01/30/2017-02102 /enhancing-public-safety-in-the-interior-of-the-united -states (accessed 7/27/17).

39. Camila Domonoske, "Judge Blocks Trump Administration from Punishing 'Sanctuary Cities,'" NPR, November 21, 2017, www.npr.org/sections/ thetwo-way/2017/11/21/565678707/enter-title (accessed 2/18/18).

40. Tal Axelrod, "9th Circuit Rules in Favor of Trump Admin in 'Sanctuary City' Case," *The Hill*, July 12, 2019, https://thehill.com/regulation/court-battles/452862-9th-circuit-rules-in-favor-of-trump-admin-in-sanctuary-city-case (accessed 7/15/19).

41. *Gonzales v. Raich*, 545 U.S. 1 (2005). For more, see William Yardley, "New Federal Crackdown Confounds States That Allow Medical Marijuana," *New York Times*, May 8, 2011, A13.

42. *NFIB v. Sebelius*, 567 U.S. 519 (2012); Congressional Research Service, "Medicaid and Federal Grant Conditions after *NFIB v. Sebelius*: Constitutional Issues and Analysis," July 17, 2012, www.everycrsreport.com/files/20120717_R42367_a89885d16da5c5604c8d7900024f5f433ecb4805.pdf (accessed 7/16/19).

43. Local Solutions Support Center, "The Growing Shadow of State Interference: Preemption in the 2019 State Legislative Sessions," August 2019, https://static1.squarespace.com/static/5ce4377caeb1ce00013a02fd/t/5d66a3c36044f700019a7efd/1567007722604/LSSCSiXReportAugust2019.pdf (accessed 3/21/20).

44. Emma G. Ellis, "Guess How Much That Anti-LGBTQ Law Is Costing North Carolina," *Wired*, September 18, 2016, www.wired.com/2016/09/guess-much-anti-lgbtq-law-costing-north-carolina/ (accessed 7/27/17).

45. Lisa L. Miller, "The Representational Biases of Federalism: Scope and Bias in the Political Process, Revisited," *Perspectives on Politics* 50, no. 2 (June 2007): 305–21.

46. U.S. Department of Labor, "Consolidated Minimum Wage Table," January 1, 2020, www.dol.gov/agencies/whd/mw-consolidated (accessed 3/27/20).

CHAPTER 4

1. This account taken from April Baer, "The Slants: Trading in Stereotypes," NPR, June 11, 2008, www.npr.org/templates/story/story.php?storyId=90278746; Katy Steinmetz, "The Slants' Suit: Asian-American Band Goes to Court over Name," *Time*, October 23, 2013, http://entertainment.time.com/2013/10/23/the-slants-suit-asian-american-band-goes-to-court-over-name/; Kat Chow, "The Slants: Fighting for the Right to Rock a Racial Slur," NPR, January 19, 2017, www.npr.org/sections/codeswitch/2017/01/19/510467679/the-slants-fighting-for-the-right-to-rock-a-racial-slur; *Matal v. Tam*, 582 U.S. — (2017); Ian Shapira and Ann E. Marimow, "Washington Redskins Win Trademark Fight over the Team's Name," *Washington Post*, June 29, 2017, www.washingtonpost.com/local/public-safety/2017/06/29/a26f52f0-5cf6-11e7-9fc6 c7ef4bc58d13_story.html?utm_term=.22ed3bf39917 (accessed 2/4/18).

2. Alexander Hamilton, James Madison, and John Jay, *The Federalist Papers*, ed. Clinton Rossiter (New York: New American Library, 1961), no. 84, 513.

3. *Federalist Papers*, no. 84, 513.

4. Clinton Rossiter, *1787: The Grand Convention* (New York: W. W. Norton, 1987), 302.

5. Rossiter, *1787*, 303. Rossiter also reports that "in 1941 the States of Connecticut, Massachusetts, and Georgia celebrated the sesquicentennial of the Bill of Rights by giving their hitherto withheld and unneeded assent."

6. *Barron v. Baltimore*, 7 Peters 243, 246 (1833).

7. The Fourteenth Amendment also seems designed to introduce civil rights. The final clause of the all-important Section 1 provides that no state can "deny to any person within its jurisdiction the equal protection of the laws." It is not unreasonable to conclude that the purpose of this provision was to obligate state governments as well as the national government to take positive actions to protect citizens from arbitrary and discriminatory actions, at least those based on race. Civil rights will be explored in Chapter 5.

8. For example, *The Slaughterhouse Cases*, 16 Wallace 36 (1883).

9. *Chicago, Burlington and Quincy Railroad Company v. Chicago*, 166 U.S. 226 (1897).

10. *Gitlow v. New York*, 268 U.S. 652 (1925).

11. *Near v. Minnesota*, 283 U.S. 697 (1931); *Hague v. C.I.O.*, 307 U.S. 496 (1939).

12. *Palko v. Connecticut*, 302 U.S. 319 (1937).

13. All of these were implicitly included in the *Palko* case as "not incorporated" into the Fourteenth Amendment as limitations on the powers of the states.

14. There is one interesting exception, which involves the Sixth Amendment right to public trial. In the 1948 case *In re Oliver*, 33 U.S. 257, the right to a public trial was, in effect, incorporated as part of the Fourteenth Amendment. However, the issue in that case was put more generally as "due process," and public trial itself was not actually mentioned in so many words. Later opinions, such as *Duncan v. Louisiana*, 391 U.S. 145 (1968), cited the *Oliver* case as the precedent for more explicit incorporation of public trials as part of the Fourteenth Amendment.

15. *Abington School District v. Schempp*, 374 U.S. 203 (1963).

16. *Engel v. Vitale*, 370 U.S. 421 (1962).

17. *Wallace v. Jaffree*, 472 U.S. 38 (1985).

18. *Lemon v. Kurtzman*, 403 U.S. 602 (1971). The *Lemon* test is still good law, but as recently as the 1994 Court term, four justices have urged that the test be abandoned. Here is a settled area of law that may soon become unsettled.

19. *Van Orden v. Perry*, 545 U.S. 677 (2005).

20. *McCreary County v. American Civil Liberties Union of Kentucky*, 545 U.S. 844 (2005).

21. *West Virginia State Board of Education v. Barnette*, 319 U.S. 624 (1943). The case it reversed was *Minersville School District v. Gobitis*, 310 U.S. 586 (1940).

22. *Holt v. Hobbs*, 574 U.S. 352 (2015).

23. *Burwell v. Hobby Lobby Stores*, 573 U.S. 682 (2014).

24. *Abrams v. United States*, 250 U.S. 616 (1919).

25. *United States v. Carolene Products Company*, 304 U.S. 144 (1938), n4. This footnote is one of the Court's most important doctrines. See Alfred H. Kelly, Winfred A. Harbison, and Herman Belz, *The American Constitution: Its Origins and Development*, 7th ed. (New York: W. W. Norton, 1991), 2:519–23.

26. *Schenck v. United States*, 249 U.S. 47 (1919).

27. *Brandenburg v. Ohio*, 395 U.S. 444 (1969).

28. *Buckley v. Valeo*, 424 U.S. 1 (1976).

29. *Federal Election Commission v. Wisconsin Right to Life*, 551 U.S. 449 (2007).

30. *Citizens United v. Federal Election Commission*, 558 U.S. 310 (2010).

31. *McCutcheon v. Federal Election Commission*, 572 U.S. 185 (2014).

32. Arthur Delaney, "Supreme Court Rolls Back Campaign Finance Restrictions," Huffington Post, March 23, 2010, updated May 25, 2011, www.huffingtonpost.com/2010/01/21/supreme-court-rolls-back_n_431227.html (accessed 7/9/12).

33. *Chaplinsky v. State of New Hampshire*, 315 U.S. 568 (1942).

34. *Dennis v. United States*, 341 U.S. 494 (1951), which upheld the infamous Smith Act of 1940 that provided criminal penalties for those who "willfully and knowingly conspire to teach and advocate the forceful and violent overthrow and destruction of the government."

35. Laura Kipness, *Unwanted Advances* (New York: Harper, 2017).

36. *Capitol Broadcasting Company v. Acting Attorney General*, 405 U.S. 1000 (1972).

37. *R.A.V. v. City of St. Paul*, 505 U.S. 377 (1992).

38. *United States v. Schwimmer*, 279 U.S. 644 (1929).

39. *Bethel School District No. 403 v. Fraser*, 478 U.S. 675 (1986).

40. *Hazelwood School District v. Kuhlmeier*, 484 U.S. 260 (1988).

41. *Morse v. Frederick*, 551 U.S. 393 (2007).

42. *City Council v. Taxpayers for Vincent*, 466 U.S. 789 (1984).

43. *Bigelow v. Virginia*, 421 U.S. 809 (1975).

44. *Texas v. Johnson*, 491 U.S. 397 (1989).

45. Charles Babington, "Senate Rejects Flag Desecration Amendment," *Washington Post*, June 28, 2006, www.washingtonpost.com/wp-dyn/content/article/2006/06/27/AR2006062701056.html (accessed 11/13/13).

46. *Snyder v. Phelps*, 562 U.S. 443 (2011).

47. *Hague v. Committee for Industrial Organization*, 307 U.S. 496 (1939).

48. For a good general discussion of speech plus, see Louis Fisher, *American Constitutional Law* (New York: McGraw-Hill, 1990), 544–46. The case upholding the buffer zone against the abortion protesters is *Madsen v. Women's Health Center*, 512 U.S. 753 (1994).

49. *Near v. Minnesota*, 283 U.S. 697 (1931).

50. *New York Times Co. v. United States*, 403 U.S. 713 (1971).

51. *Branzburg v. Hayes*, 408 U.S. 665 (1972).

52. *New York Times Co. v. Sullivan*, 376 U.S. 254 (1964).

53. See *Zeran v. America Online*, 129 F3d 327 (4th Cir. 1997).

54. *Roth v. United States*, 354 U.S. 476 (1957).

55. Concurring opinion in *Jacobellis v. Ohio*, 378 U.S. 184 (1964).

56. *Reno v. American Civil Liberties Union*, 521 U.S. 844 (1997).

57. *United States v. Williams*, 553 U.S. 285 (2008).

58. *United States v. Playboy Entertainment Group*, 529 U.S. 803 (2000).

59. *Brown v. Entertainment Merchants Association*, 564 U.S. — (2011).

60. *District of Columbia v. Heller*, 554 U.S. 570 (2008).

61. *McDonald v. Chicago*, 561 U.S. 742 (2010).

62. *In re Winship*, 397 U.S. 358 (1970). An outstanding treatment of due process in issues involving the Fourth through Seventh amendments will be found in Fisher, *American Constitutional Law*, chap. 13.

63. *Horton v. California*, 496 U.S. 128 (1990).

64. *Mapp v. Ohio*, 367 U.S. 643 (1961). Although Mapp went free in this case, she was later convicted in New York on narcotics trafficking charges and served 9 years of a 20-year sentence.

65. For a good discussion of the issue, see Fisher, *American Constitutional Law*, 884–89.

66. *United States v. Grubbs*, 547 U.S. 90 (2006).

67. *National Treasury Employees Union v. Von Raab*, 489 U.S. 656 (1989).

68. *Skinner v. Railway Labor Executives' Association*, 489 U.S. 602 (1989).

69. *Vernonia School District 47J v. Acton*, 515 U.S. 646 (1995).

70. *Chandler v. Miller*, 520 U.S. 305 (1997).

71. *Florida v. Jardines*, 569 U.S. 1 (2013).

72. *United States v. Jones*, 565 U.S.400 (2012).

73. *Maryland v. King*, 569 U.S. 435 (2013).

74. *Riley v. California*, 573 U.S. 373 (2014).

75. *Terry v. Ohio*, 392 U.S. 1 (1968).

76. Edwin S. Corwin and J. W. Peltason, *Understanding the Constitution* (New York: Holt, 1967), 286.

77. *Benton v. Maryland*, 395 U.S. 784 (1969).

78. *Miranda v. Arizona*, 348 U.S. 436 (1966).

79. *Gideon v. Wainwright*, 372 U.S. 335 (1963).

80. *Wiggins v. Smith*, 539 U.S. 510 (2003).

81. *Furman v. Georgia*, 408 U.S. 238 (1972).

82. *Gregg v. Georgia*, 428 U.S. 153 (1976).

83. J. Baxter Oliphant, "Public support for the death penalty ticks up," Pew Research Center, June 11, 2018, https://www.pewresearch.org/fact-tank/2018/06/11/us-support-for-death-penalty-ticks-up-2018/ (accessed 2/3/2020).

84. Death Penalty Information Center, "Facts about the Death Penalty," October 11, 2018, https://deathpenaltyinfo.org/documents/FactSheet.pdf (accessed 10/12/18).

85. *Kennedy v. Louisiana*, 554 U.S. 407 (2008).

86. *Snyder v. Louisiana*, 552 U.S. 472 (2008).

87. *Glossip v. Gross*, 576 U.S. — (2015).

88. *Hudson v. McMillan*, 503 U.S. 1 (1992).

89. *Miller v. Alabama*, 567 U.S. — (2012).

90. *Olmstead v. United States*, 277 U.S. 438 (1928). See also David M. O'Brien, *Constitutional Law and Politics*, 6th ed. (New York: W. W. Norton, 2005), 1:76–84.

91. Thomas P. Crocker, "The Political Fourth Amendment," *Washington University Law Review* 88, no. 2 (2010): 347.

92. *Marcus v. Search Warrant*, 367 U.S. 717 (1961).

93. *Herring v. United States*, 555 U.S. 135 (2009).

94. *Berman v. Parker*, 348 U.S. 26 (1954). For a thorough analysis of the case, see Benjamin Ginsberg, "*Berman v. Parker*: Congress, the Court, and the Public Purpose," *Polity* 4 (1971): 48–75. For a later application of the case that suggests that "just compensation"—defined as something approximating market value—is about all a property owner can hope for protection against a public taking of property, see Theodore Lowi et al., *Poliscide: Big Government, Big Science, Lilliputian Politics*, 2nd ed. (Lanham, MD: University Press of America, 1990), 267–70.

95. *Kelo v. City of New London*, 545 U.S. 469 (2005).

96. *Griswold v. Connecticut*, 381 U.S. 479 (1965).

97. *Griswold*, concurring opinion. In 1972 the Court extended the privacy right to unmarried women: *Eisenstadt v. Baird*, 405 U.S. 438 (1972).

98. *Roe v. Wade*, 410 U.S. 113 (1973).

99. *Webster v. Reproductive Health Services*, 492 U.S. 490 (1989), which upheld a Missouri law that restricted the use of public medical facilities for abortion. The decision opened the way for other states to limit the availability of abortion.

100. *Planned Parenthood of Southeastern Pennsylvania v. Casey*, 505 U.S. 833 (1992).

101. *Ayotte v. Planned Parenthood*, 546 U.S. 320 (2006).

102. *Gonzales v. Carhart*, 550 U.S. 124 (2007).

103. *June Medical Services L.L.C. v. Russo*, 591 U.S. — (2020).

104. *Bowers v. Hardwick*, 478 U.S. 186 (1986).

105. *Lawrence v. Texas*, 539 U.S. 558 (2003).

106. *Lawrence* (2003). It is worth recalling here the provision of the Ninth Amendment: "The enumeration in the Constitution, of certain rights, shall not be construed to deny or disparage others retained by the people."

107. *Obergefell v. Hodges*, 576 U.S. — (2015).

108. *Bostock v. Clayton County*, 590 U.S. — (2020).

CHAPTER 5

1. Shannon Green, "Desmond Meade Helps Restore Voting Rights to Millions of Ex-felons across Florida," *Orlando Sentinel*, February 5, 2019, www.orlandosentinel.com /opinion/os-ae-desmond-meade-ex-felon-voting-rights -20190130-story.html (accessed 7/27/19).

2. Stacey Abrams, "Desmond Meade," *Time*, April 17, 2019, https://time.com/collection/100-most-influential-people -2019/5567673/desmond-meade/ (accessed 7/27/19).

3. Green, "Desmond Meade Helps Restore Voting Rights."

4. Lawrence Mower, "Ron DeSantis Signs Amendment 4 Bill, Limiting Felon Voting," *Tampa Bay Times*, June 28, 2019, www.tampabay.com/florida-politics/buzz/2019/06/28 /ron-desantis-signs-amendment-4-bill-limiting-felon -voting/ (accessed 7/27/19).

5. P. R. Lockhart, "Florida Faces an Intense Legal Battle over Restoring Former Felons' Voting Rights," Vox, July 2, 2019, www.vox.com/policy-and-politics/2019/7/2/20677955 /amendment-4-florida-felon-voting-rights-lawsuits-fines -fees (accessed 7/27/19); Patricia Mazzei, "Ex-Felons in Florida Must Pay Fines Before Voting, Appeals Court Rules," *The New York Times*, September 11, 2020, www .nytimes.com/2020/09/11/us/florida-felon-voting-rights .html (accessed 11/15/20).

6. Paula Baker, "The Domestication of Politics: Women and American Political Society, 1780–1920," *American Historical Review* 89 (June 1984): 620–47.

7. *Dred Scott v. Sandford*, 60 U.S. 393 (1857).

8. August Meier and Elliott Rudwick, *From Plantation to Ghetto* (New York: Hill and Wang, 1976), 184–88.

9. Jill Dupont, "Susan B. Anthony," New York Notes (Albany: New York State Commission on the Bicentennial of the U.S. Constitution, 1988), 3.

10. *Plessy v. Ferguson*, 163 U.S. 537 (1896).

11. Dupont, "Susan B. Anthony," 4.

12. *Missouri ex rel. Gaines v. Canada*, 305 U.S. 337 (1938).

13. *Sweatt v. Painter*, 339 U.S. 629 (1950).

14. *Shelley v. Kraemer*, 334 U.S. 1 (1948).

15. *Brown v. Board of Education of Topeka, Kansas*, 347 U.S. 483 (1954).

16. The Supreme Court first declared that race was a suspect classification requiring strict scrutiny in the decision *Korematsu v. United States*, 323 U.S. 214 (1944). In this case, the Court upheld President Roosevelt's executive order of 1941 allowing the military to exclude persons of Japanese ancestry from the West Coast and to place them in internment camps. It is one of the few cases in which classification based on race survived strict scrutiny.

17. The two most important cases were *Cooper v. Aaron*, 358 U.S. 1 (1958), which required Little Rock, Arkansas, to desegregate, and *Griffin v. Prince Edward County School Board*, 377 U.S. 218 (1964), which forced all the schools of that Virginia county to reopen after five years of being closed to avoid desegregation.

18. In *Cooper v. Aaron*, the Supreme Court ordered immediate compliance with the lower court's desegregation order and went beyond that with a stern warning that it is "emphatically the province and duty of the judicial department to say what the law is."

19. *Shuttlesworth v. Birmingham Board of Education of Jefferson City*, 358 U.S. 101 (1958) upheld a "pupil placement" plan purporting to assign pupils on various bases, with no mention of race. This case interpreted *Brown* to mean that school districts had to stop explicit racial discrimination but were under no obligation to take positive steps to desegregate. For a while black parents were doomed to a case-by-case approach.

20. For good treatments of this long stretch of the struggle of the federal courts to integrate the schools, see Paul Brest and Sanford Levinson, *Processes of Constitutional Decision-Making: Cases and Materials*, 2nd ed. (Boston: Little, Brown, 1983), 471–80; and Alfred H. Kelly, Winfred A. Harbison, and Herman Belz, *The American Constitution: Its Origins and Development*, 6th ed. (New York: W. W. Norton, 1983), 610–16.

21. Aimee Green, "Elmer's Restaurant Says It Made Black Man Prepay Because He Sat in a Bar, Ordered Alcohol," *Oregon Live*, October 29, 2015, www.oregonlive.com/clark-county/index.ssf/2015/10/elmers_told_state_investigator.html (accessed 8/2/18).

22. See Hamil Harris, "For Blacks, Cabs Can Be Hard to Get," *Washington Post*, July 21, 1994, J1.

23. For a thorough analysis of the Office for Civil Rights, see Jeremy Rabkin, "Office for Civil Rights," in *The Politics of Regulation*, ed. James Q. Wilson (New York: Basic Books, 1980).

24. This was an accepted way of using quotas or ratios to determine statistically that blacks or other minorities were being excluded from schools or jobs and then, on the basis of that statistical evidence, to authorize the Justice Department to bring suits in individual cases and class-action suits. In most segregated situations outside the South, it is virtually impossible to identify and document an intent to discriminate.

25. *Swann v. Charlotte-Mecklenberg Board of Education*, 402 U.S. 1 (1971).

26. *Milliken v. Bradley*, 418 U.S. 717 (1974).

27. *Board of Education v. Dowell*, 498 U.S. 237 (1991).

28. *Parents Involved in Community Schools v. Seattle School District No. 1*, 551 U.S. 701 (2007).

29. *Griggs v. Duke Power Company*, 401 U.S. 424 (1971). See also Allan Sindler, *Bakke, DeFunis, and Minority Admissions* (New York: Longman, 1978), 180–89.

30. For a good treatment of these issues, see Charles O. Gregory and Harold A. Katz, *Labor and the Law* (New York: W. W. Norton, 1979), chap. 17.

31. In 1970 this act was amended to outlaw for five years literacy tests as a condition for voting in all states.

32. Ford Fessenden, "Ballots Cast by Blacks and Older Voters Were Tossed in Far Greater Numbers," *New York Times*, November 12, 2001, A17.

33. Aaron Blake, "Texas Redistricting Case: Five Things You Need to Know," *Washington Post*, December 13, 2011, www.washingtonpost.com/blogs/the-fix/post/texas-redistricting-case-five-things-you-need-to-know/2011/12/13/gIQAdowHsO_blog.html; Manny Fernandez, "Federal Judges Approve Final Texas Redistricting Maps," *New York Times*, February 28, 2012, www.nytimes.com/2012/02/29/us/final-texas-redistricting-maps-approved.html (accessed 6/22/12).

34. *Shelby County v. Holder*, 570 U.S. 529 (2013).

35. *Crawford v. Marion County Election Board*, 553 U.S. 181 (2008). See also David Stout, "Supreme Court Upholds Voter Identification Law in Indiana," *New York Times*, April 29, 2008, www.nytimes.com/2008/04/29/washington/28cnd-scotus.html (accessed 1/13/14).

36. See Douglas S. Massey and Nancy A. Denton, *American Apartheid: Segregation and the Making of the Underclass* (Cambridge, MA: Harvard University Press, 1993), chap. 7.

37. *Loving v. Virginia*, 388 U.S. 1 (1967).

38. *Windsor v. United States*, 699 F.3d 169 2nd Cir. (2012).

39. *Adarand Constructors, Inc. v. Peña*, 515 U.S. 200 (1995).

40. *Fisher v. University of Texas*, 570 U.S. 297 (2013).

41. *Fisher v. University of Texas*, 579 U. S. — (2016).

42. See Jane J. Mansbridge, *Why We Lost the ERA* (Chicago: University of Chicago Press, 1986); and Gilbert Steiner, *Constitutional Inequality* (Washington, DC: Brookings Institution Press, 1985).

43. See *Frontiero v. Richardson*, 411 U.S. 677 (1973).

44. See *Craig v. Boren*, 429 U.S. 190 (1976).

45. *Franklin v. Gwinnett County Public Schools*, 503 U.S. 60 (1992).

46. Jennifer Halperin, "Women Step Up to Bat," *Illinois Issues* 21 (September 1995): 11–14.

47. Joan Biskupic and David Nakamura, "Court Won't Review Sports Equity Ruling," *Washington Post*, April 22, 1997, A1.

48. Debra DeMeis and Rosanna Hertz, "Sex, Sports, and Title IX on Campus: The Triumphs and Travails," Daily Beast, June 22, 2012, www.dailybeast.com/articles/2012/06/22/sex-sports-and-title-ix-on-campus-the-triumphs-and-travails.html (accessed 6/22/12).

49. *Meritor Savings Bank v. Vinson*, 477 U.S. 57 (1986). See also Gwendolyn Mink, *Hostile Environment: The Political Betrayal of Sexually Harassed Women* (Ithaca, NY: Cornell University Press, 2000), 28–32.

50. *Harris v. Forklift Systems, Inc.*, 510 U.S. 17 (1993).

51. *Burlington Industries v. Ellerth*, 524 U.S. 742 (1998); *Faragher v. City of Boca Raton*, 524 U.S. 775 (1998).

52. Laura Kipness, *Unwanted Advances: Sexual Paranoia Comes to Campus* (New York: Harper, 2017).

53. *Ledbetter v. Goodyear Tire and Rubber Co.*, 550 U.S. 618 (2007).

54. Sarah Kliff, "A Stunning Chart Shows the True Cause of the Gender Wage Gap," Vox, February 19, 2018, www.vox.com/2018/2/19/17018380/gender-wage-gap-childcare-penalty (accessed 10/9/18).

55. New Mexico had a different history because not many Anglos settled there initially. (*Anglo* is the term for a non-Hispanic white, generally of European background.) Mexican Americans had considerable power in territorial legislatures between 1865 and 1912. See Lawrence H. Fuchs, *The American Kaleidoscope* (Hanover, NH: University Press of New England, 1990), 239–40.

56. *Mendez v. Westminster*, 64 F. Supp. 544 (S.D. Cal. 1946), aff'd, 161 F.2d 774 (9th Cir. 1947) (en banc).

57. On the United Farm Workers and César Chávez, see Marshall Ganz, *Why David Sometimes Wins: Leadership, Organization, and Strategy in the California Farm Worker Movement* (New York: Oxford University Press, 2009); Miriam Pawel, *The Union of Their Dreams: Power, Hope and Struggle in Cesar Chavez's Farm Worker Movement* (New York: Bloomsbury Press, 2010); and Jacques E. Levy, *Cesar Chavez: Autobiography of La Causa* (Minneapolis: University of Minnesota Press, 2007).

58. *Trump v. Hawaii*, 585 U.S. ___ (2018).

59. *United States v. Wong Kim Ark*, 169 U.S. 649 (1898).

60. *Korematsu v. United States*, 323 U.S. 214 (1944).

61. Children of the Camps, "Historical Documents: Civil Liberties Act of 1988," http://pbs.org/childofcamp/history/civilact.html (accessed 2/17/08).

62. *Lau v. Nichols*, 414 U.S. 563 (1974).

63. On the resurgence of Native American political activity, see Stephen Cornell, *The Return of the Native: American Indian Political Resurgence* (New York: Oxford University Press, 1990); and Dee Brown, *Bury My Heart at Wounded Knee* (New York: Holt, Rinehart, 1971).

64. Naomi Schaefer Riley, *The New Trail of Tears* (New York: Encounter Books, 2016).

65. See the discussion in Robert A. Katzmann, *Institutional Disability: The Saga of Transportation Policy for the Disabled* (Washington, DC: Brookings Institution Press, 1986).

66. For example, after pressure from the Justice Department, one of the nation's largest rental-car companies agreed to make special hand controls available to any customer requesting them. See "Avis Agrees to Equip Cars for Disabled," *Los Angeles Times*, September 2, 1994, D1.

67. For more, see Dale Carpenter, *Flagrant Conduct: The Story of* Lawrence v. Texas (New York: W. W. Norton, 2013).

68. *Romer v. Evans*, 517 U.S. 620 (1996).

69. *Obergefell v. Hodges*, 576 U.S. — (2015).

70. Pew Research Center, "Changing Attitudes on Gay Marriage," June 26, 2017, www.pewforum.org/fact-sheet/changing-attitudes-on-gay-marriage/ (accessed 10/9/18).

71. The Department of Health, Education, and Welfare (HEW) was the cabinet department charged with administering most federal social programs. In 1980, when education programs were transferred to the newly created Department of Education, HEW was renamed the Department of Health and Human Services.

72. *Regents of the University of California v. Bakke*, 438 U.S. 265 (1978).

73. See, for example, *United Steelworkers v. Weber*, 443 U.S. 193 (1979); and *Fullilove v. Klutznick*, 448 U.S. 448 (1980).

74. *Adarand Constructors, Inc. v. Peña*.

75. *Gratz v. Bollinger*, 539 U.S. 244 (2003).

76. *Grutter v. Bollinger*, 539 U.S. 306 (2003).

CHAPTER 6

1. Suzanna Hupp, "In Their Own Words: The Gun Rights Advocate," *Texas Monthly*, March 23, 2016, www.texasmonthly.com/list/in-their-own-words/the-gun-rights-advocate/ (accessed 3/3/18).

2. Brianna Sacks, "After Florida School Shooting, Several Survivors and Victims' Parents Pan Trump's Idea to Arm Teachers," BuzzFeed News, February 24, 2018, www.buzzfeed.com/briannasacks/students-and-parents-react-to-armed-teacher-proposal?utm_term=.rtNPqM580#.xrVbnry1A (accessed 3/3/18).

3. Jeffrey M. Jones, "U.S. Preference for Stricter Gun Laws Highest since 1993," Gallup Social & Policy Issues, March 14, 2018, http://news.gallup.com/poll/229562/preference-stricter-gun-laws-highest-1993.aspx (accessed 5/30/18).

4. Alvin Chang, "Gun Sales Usually Skyrocket after Mass Shootings. But Not This Time," Vox, March 7, 2018, www.vox.com/2018/3/7/17066352/gun-sales-mass-shooting-data (accessed 5/30/18).

5. Aaron Smith, "Public Attitudes toward Technology Companies," Pew Research Center, June 28, 2018, www.pewinternet.org/2018/06/28/public-attitudes-toward-technology-companies/ (accessed 1/15/20).

6. Richard Wike and Katie Simmons, "Global Support for Principle of Free Expression, but Opposition to Some Forms of Speech: Americans Especially Likely to Embrace Individual Liberties," Pew Research Center, November 18, 2015, www.pewglobal.org/2015/11/18/global-support-for-principle-of-free-expression-but-opposition-to-some-forms-of-speech/ (accessed 11/18/15).

7. Kim Parker, "The Growing Partisan Divide in Views of Higher Education," Pew Research Center, August 19, 2019, www.pewsocialtrends.org/essay/the-growing-partisan-divide-in-views-of-higher-education/ (accessed 1/15/20).

8. Parker, "The Growing Partisan Divide."

9. Paul R. Abramson, "Political Attitudes in America: Formation and Change," *Political Science Quarterly* 98, no. 4 (April 1983): 694, https://doi.org/10.2307/2149731 (accessed 1/15/20).

10. Nicholas Riccardi, "Here's the Reality Behind Trump's Claims about Mail Voting," AP News, September 30, 2020, https://apnews.com/article/virus-outbreak-joe-biden-election-2020-donald-trump-elections-3e8170c3348ce3719d4bc7182146b582 (accessed 10/12/20).

11. Pew Research Center, "In Views of U.S. Democracy, Widening Partisan Divides Over Freedom to Peacefully Protest," September 2, 2020, www.pewresearch.org/politics/2020/09/02/in-views-of-u-s-democracy-widening-partisan-divides-over-freedom-to-peacefully-protest/ (accessed 10/12/20).

12. See Paul M. Sniderman and Edward G. Carmines, *Reaching beyond Race* (Cambridge, MA: Harvard University Press, 1997).

13. David Hopkins and Matt Grossmann, *Asymmetric Politics: Ideological Republicans and Group Interest Democrats* (New York: Oxford University Press, 2016).

14. Lydia Saad, "U.S. Still Leans Conservative, but Liberals Keep Recent Gains," Gallup News, January 8, 2019, https://news.gallup.com/poll/245813/leans-conservative-liberals-keep-recent-gains.aspx (accessed 1/15/20).

15. Steven W. Webster, *American Rage* (New York: Cambridge University Press, 2020).

16. See Angus Campbell et al., *The American Voter* (New York: Wiley, 1960), 147.

17. Betsy Sinclair, *The Social Citizen: Peer Networks and Political Behavior* (Chicago: University of Chicago Press, 2012).

18. Pew Research Center, "Support for Same-Sex Marriage Grows, Even among Groups That Had Been Skeptical," June 26, 2017, www.people-press.org/2017/06/26/support-for-same-sex-marriage-grows-even-among-groups-that-had-been-skeptical/ (accessed 5/21/18).

19. Pew Research Center, "Gun Policy Remains Divisive, but Several Proposals Still Draw Bipartisan Support," October 18, 2018, www.people-press.org/2018/10/18/gun-policy-remains-divisive-but-several-proposals-still-draw-bipartisan-support/#impact-of-changes-in-access-to-guns-on-crime-mass-shootings (accessed 1/15/20).

20. Raymond E. Wolfinger and Steven J. Rosenstone, *Who Votes?* (New Haven, CT: Yale University Press, 1980); Steven J. Rosenstone and John Mark Hansen, *Mobilization, Participation, and Democracy in America* (New York: Macmillan, 1993).

21. Katherine Tate, *Black Faces in the Mirror* (Princeton, NJ: Princeton University Press, 1993).

22. Pew Research Center. "On Views of Race and Inequality, Blacks and Whites Are Worlds Apart: About Four-in-Ten Blacks Are Doubtful That the U.S. Will Ever Achieve Racial Equality," June 27, 2016, www.pewsocialtrends.org/2016/06/27/on-views-of-race-and-inequality-blacks-and-whites-are-worlds-apart/ (accessed 4/3/18).

23. Tate, *Black Faces in the Mirror*.

24. Kim Parker, Juliana Menasce Horowitz, and Monica Anderson, "Amid Protests, Majorities Across Racial and Ethnic Groups Express Support for the Black Lives Matter Movement," Pew Research Center, June 12, 2020, www.pewsocialtrends.org/2020/06/12/amid-protests-majorities-across-racial-and-ethnic-groups-express-support-for-the-black-lives-matter-movement/ (accessed 10/15/20).

25. National Conference of State Legislatures, "Legislative Responses for Policing—State Bill Tracking Database," October 28, 2020, www.ncsl.org/research/civil-and-criminal-justice/legislative-responses-for-policing.aspx (accessed 10/28/20).

26. Jens Manuel Krogstad, "Key Facts about the Latino Vote in 2016," Pew Research Center, October 14, 2016, www.pewresearch.org/fact-tank/2016/10/14/key-facts-about-the-latino-vote-in-2016/; Antonio Flores, "2015, Hispanic Population in the United States Statistical Portrait," Pew Research Center, September 18, 2017, www.pewresearch.org/hispanic/2017/09/18/2015-statistical-information-on-hispanics-in-united-states-current-data/ (accessed 1/15/20).

27. Anna Brown and Renee Stepler, "Statistical Portrait of the Foreign-Born Population in the United States, 1960–2013," Pew Research Center, September 28, 2015, www.pewhispanic.org/2015/09/28/statistical-portrait-of-the-foreign-born-population-in-the-united-states-1960-2013-key-charts/#2013-fb-origin (accessed 12/22/15).

28. Mark Hugo Lopez, Ana Gonzalez-Barrera, and Jens Manuel Krogstad, "Views of Immigration Policy," Pew Research Center, October 25, 2018, www.pewresearch.org/hispanic/2018/10/25/views-of-immigration-policy/ (accessed 10/28/20).

29. Pew Research Center, "Latinos and the New Trump Administration," February 23, 2017, www.pewhispanic.org/2017/02/23/latinos-and-the-new-trump-administration/ (accessed 4/3/17).

30. Pew Research Center, "Shifting Public Views on Legal Immigration into the U.S.," June 28, 2018, www.people-press.org/2018/06/28/shifting-public-views-on-legal-immigration-into-the-u-s/ (accessed 1/15/20).

31. Matt Barreto and Gary M. Segura, *Latino America: How America's Most Dynamic Population Is Poised to Transform the Politics of the Nation* (New York: Public Affairs, 2014).

32. Amanda Barroso, "Key Takeaway on Americans' Views On Gender Equality a Century After U.S. Women Gained the Right to Vote," Pew Research Center, August 13, 2020, www.pewresearch.org/fact-tank/2020/08/13/key-takeaways-on-americans-views-on-gender-equality-a-century-after-u-s-women-gained-the-right-to-vote/ (accessed 10/20/20).

33. Michael Lipka, "Religious 'Nones' Are Not Only Growing, They're Becoming More Secular," Pew Research Center, Fact Tank, November 11, 2015, www.pewresearch.org/fact-tank/2015/11/11/religious-nones-are-not-only-growing-theyre-becoming-more-secular/ (accessed 11/11/15).

34. 2014 Cooperative Comparative Election Study.

35. See Richard Lau and David Redlawsk, *How Voters Decide: Information Processing during an Election Campaign* (New York: Cambridge University Press, 2006).

36. Kim Parker, Juliana Menasce Horowitz, and Monica Anderson, "Amid Protests, Majorities Across Racial and Ethnic Groups Express Support for the Black Lives Matter Movement," Pew Research Center, June 12, 2020, www.pewsocialtrends.org/2020/06/12/amid-protests-majorities-across-racial-and-ethnic-groups-express-support-for-the-black-lives-matter-movement/ (accessed 10/15/20).

37. Morris Fiorina, Samuel Abrams, and Jeremy Pope, *Culture War? The Myth of a Polarized America* (New York: Longman, 2004).

38. Caroline Tolbert, Christopher Witko, and Cary Wolbers, "Public Support for Higher Taxes on the Wealthy: California's Proposition 30," *Politics and Governance* 7, no. 2 (June 27,

2019); William Franko and Christopher Witko, *The New Economic Populism* (New York: Oxford University Press, 2017).

39. Nathan J. Kelly and Peter K. Enns, "Inequality and the Dynamics of Public Opinion: The Self-Reinforcing Link between Economic Inequality and Mass Preferences," *American Journal of Political Science* 54, no. 4 (2010): 855–70; Jacob S. Hacker and Paul Pierson, *Winner-Take-All Politics: How Washington Made the Rich Richer—and Turned Its Back on the Middle Class* (New York: Simon and Schuster, 2010).

40. Larry M. Bartels, "Homer Gets a Tax Cut: Inequality and Public Policy in the American Mind," *Perspectives on Politics* 3, no. 1 (2005): 15–31; Larry M. Bartels, *Unequal Democracy: The Political Economy of the New Gilded Age* (Princeton, NJ: Princeton University Press, 2008).

41. John Gramlich, "Young Americans Are Less Trusting of Other People—and Key Institutions—Than Their Elders," Pew Research Center, August 6, 2019, www.pewresearch.org/fact-tank/2019/08/06/young-americans-are-less-trusting-of-other-people-and-key-institutions-than-their-elders/ (accessed 1/15/20).

42. Peter Marks, "Adept in Politics and Advertising, 4 Women Shape a Campaign," *New York Times*, November 11, 2001, B6.

43. Donald J. Trump (@realDonaldTrump), "I am being investigated for firing the FBI director by the man who told me to fire the FBI director! Witch Hunt," Twitter, June 16, 2017, 6:07 a.m., https://twitter.com/realdonaldtrump/status/875701471999864833?lang=en (accessed 4/3/18).

44. Donald J. Trump (@realDonaldTrump), "You are witnessing the single greatest WITCH HUNT in American political history - led by some very bad and conflicted people! #MAGA," Twitter, June 15, 2017, 4:57 a.m., https://twitter.com/realdonaldtrump/status/875321478849363968?lang=en (accessed 4/3/18).

45. Jason Gainous and Kevin Wagner, *Tweeting to Power: The Social Media Revolution in American Politics* (New York: Oxford University Press, 2013).

46. See Shanto Iyengar, *Is Anyone Responsible? How Television Frames Political Issues* (Chicago: University of Chicago Press, 1991); Shanto Iyengar, *Do the Media Govern?* (Thousand Oaks, CA: Sage, 1997).

47. David W. Moore, "Support for Invasion of Iraq Remains Contingent on U.N. Approval," Gallup, November 12, 2002, www.gallup.com/poll/7195/support-invasion-iraq-remains-contigent-un-approval.aspx (accessed 3/2/18); Tom Rosentiel, "Public Attitudes toward the War in Iraq: 2003–2008," Pew Research Center, March 19, 2008, www.pewresearch.org/2008/03/19/public-attitudes-toward-the-war-in-iraq-20032008 (accessed 1/15/20).

48. Tom Rosentiel, "Public Attitudes toward the War in Iraq: 2003–2008," Pew Research Center, March 19, 2008, www.pewresearch.org/2008/03/19/public-attitudes-toward-the-war-in-iraq-20032008 (accessed 1/15/20).

49. J. Baxter Oliphant, "The Iraq War Continues to Divide the U.S. Public, 15 Years After It Began," Pew Research Center, March 19, 2018, www.pewresearch.org/fact-tank/2018/03/19/iraq-war-continues-to-divide-u-s-public-15-years-after-it-began/ (accessed 1/15/20).

50. John R. Zaller, *The Nature and Origins of Mass Opinion* (New York: Cambridge University Press, 1992).

51. Milton Lodge, Kathleen McGraw, and Patrick Stroh, "An Impression-Driven Model of Candidate Evaluation," *American Political Science Review* 83, no. 2 (1989): 399–419.

52. Benjamin I. Page and Robert Y. Shapiro, *The Rational Public: Fifty Years of Trends in Americans' Policy Preferences* (Chicago: University of Chicago Press, 1995); Eugene Wittkopf, *Faces of Internationalism: Public Opinion and Foreign Policy* (Durham, NC: Duke University Press, 1990).

53. *Varnum v. Brien*, 763 N.W.2d 862 (Iowa 2009).

54. Rebecca J. Kreitzer, Allison J. Hamilton, and Caroline J. Tolbert, "Does Policy Adoption Change Opinions on Minority Rights? The Effects of Legalizing Same-Sex Marriage," *Political Research Quarterly* 67, no. 4 (July 10, 2014): 795–808.

55. *Obergefell v. Hodges*, 576 U.S. — (2015).

56. Cary Funk and Brian Kennedy, "How Americans See Climate Change in 5 Charts," Pew Research Center, April 19, 2019, www.pewresearch.org/fact-tank/2019/04/19/how-americans-see-climate-change-in-5-charts/ (accessed 1/15/20).

57. Pew Research Center, "Majorities See Government Efforts to Protect the Environment as Insufficient," May 14, 2018, www.pewresearch.org/science/2018/05/14/majorities-see-government-efforts-to-protect-the-environment-as-insufficient/[0] (accessed 1/15/20).

58. Pew Research Center, "Majorities See Government Efforts."

59. John Zaller, *Nature and Origins* (Cambridge: Cambridge University Press 1992).

60. Carroll Glynn et al., *Public Opinion*, 2nd ed. (Boulder, CO: Westview, 2004), 293. See also Michael X. Delli Carpini and Scott Keeter, *What Americans Know about Politics and Why It Matters* (New Haven, CT: Yale University Press, 1996).

61. Delli Carpini and Keeter, *What Americans Know*.

62. Adam J. Berinsky, "Assuming the Costs of War: Events, Elites and American Support for Military Conflict," *Journal of Politics* 69, no. 4 (2007): 975–97; Zaller, *Nature and Origins*.

63. Richard R. Lau and David P. Redlawsk, "Advantages and Disadvantages of Cognitive Heuristics in Political Decision Making," *American Journal of Political Science* 45 (October 2001): 951–71; Lau and Redlawsk, *How Voters Decide*.

64. For a discussion of the role of information in politics, see Arthur Lupia and Matthew D. McCubbins, *The Democratic Dilemma: Can Citizens Learn What They Need to Know?* (New York: Cambridge University Press, 1998). See also Shaun Bowler and Todd Donovan, *Demanding Choices: Opinion and Voting in Direct Democracy* (Ann Arbor: University of Michigan Press, 1998). See also Samuel Popkin, *The Reasoning Voter: Communication and Persuasion in Presidential Campaigns* (Chicago: University of Chicago Press, 1991); Arthur Lupia, "Shortcuts versus Encyclopedias: Information and Voting Behavior in

California Insurance Reform Elections," *American Political Science Review* 88 (1994): 63–76; and Wendy Rahn, "The Role of Partisan Stereotypes in Information Processing about Political Candidates," *American Journal of Political Science* 37 (1993): 472–96.

65. James Druckman, Erik Petersen, and Rune Slothuus, "How Elite Partisan Polarization Affects Public Opinion Formation," *American Political Science Review* 107, no. 1 (February 2013): 57–79.

66. Lee Rainie et al., "Social Media and Political Engagement," Pew Research Center, October 19, 2012, www.pewinternet.org/2012/10/19/social-media-and-political-engagement (accessed 8/14/14).

67. Tony Dokoupil, "Is the Internet Making Us Crazy? What the New Research Says," *Newsweek*, July 9, 2012, http://mag.newsweek.com/2012/07/08/is-the-internet-making-us-crazy-what-the-new-research-says.html (accessed 3/19/14); Nicholas Carr, *The Shallows: What the Internet Is Doing to Our Brains* (New York: W. W. Norton, 2011).

68. OECD, "Income Inequality," https://data.oecd.org/inequality/income-inequality.htm (accessed 5/4/2020).

69. Kim Parker, Juliana Menasce Horowitz, and Anna Brown, "About Half of Lower-Income Americans Report Household Job or Wage Loss Due to COVID-19," Pew Research Center, April 21, 2020, www.pewsocialtrends.org/2020/04/21/about-half-of-lower-income-americans-report-household-job-or-wage-loss-due-to-covid-19/ (accessed 5/4/2020).

70. Page and Shapiro, *The Rational Public*.

71. Gerald C. Wright, Rober S. Erikson, and John P. McIver, "Public Opinion and Policy Liberalism in the American States," *American Journal of Political Science* 31, no. 4 (November 1987): 980–1001.

72. Christopher Wlezien, "The Public as Thermostat: Dynamics of Preferences for Spending," *American Journal of Political Science* 39, no. 4 (1995): 981–1000.

73. See Julianna Pacheco, "Attitudinal Policy Feedback and Public Opinion: The Impact of Smoking Bans on Attitudes toward Smokers, Secondhand Smoke, and Anti-Smoking Policies," *Political Research Quarterly* 77, no. 3 (2013): 714–34; Barbara Norrander, "The Multi-Layered Impact of Public Opinion on Capital Punishment Implementation in the American States," *Political Research Quarterly* 53, no. 4 (2000): 771–93; Suzanne Mettler and Joe Soss, "The Consequences of Public Policy for Democratic Citizenship: Bridging Policy Studies and Mass Politics," *Perspectives on Politics* 2, no. 1 (2004): 55–73; Andrea Hetling and Monika L. McDermott, "Judging a Book by Its Cover: Did Perceptions of the 1996 U.S. Welfare Reforms Affect Public Support for Spending on the Poor?" *Journal of Social Policy* 37, no. 3 (2008): 471–87; Joe Soss, "Lessons of Welfare: Policy Design, Political Learning, and Political Action," *American Political Science Review* 93, no. 2 (1999): 363–80; Joe Soss and Sanford F. Schram, "A Public Transformed? Welfare Reform as Policy

Feedback," *American Political Science Review* 101, no. 1 (2007): 111.

74. Malcolm E. Jewell, *Representation in State Legislatures* (Lexington: University Press of Kentucky, 1982).

75. Lawrence R. Jacobs and Robert Y. Shapiro, *Politicians Don't Pander: Political Manipulation and the Loss of Democratic Responsiveness* (Chicago: University of Chicago Press, 2000).

76. John Griffin and Brian Newman, "Are Voters Better Represented?," *Journal of Politics* 67 (2005): 1206–27.

77. Bartels, *Unequal Democracy*.

78. Other authors have endorsed Bartels's view that government policy exacerbates income inequality. See, for example, Hacker and Pierson, *Winner-Take-All Politics*.

79. Martin Gilens, "Inequality and Democratic Responsiveness," *Public Opinion Quarterly* 69, no. 5 (2005): 778–96; and Martin Gilens, "Preference Gaps and Inequality in Representation," *PS: Political Science and Politics* 42, no. 2 (2009): 335–41.

80. Campbell et al., *The American Voter*; Sidney Verba, Kay Lehman Schlozman, and Henry Brady, *Voice and Equality* (Cambridge, MA: Harvard University Press, 2002); Christopher Achen and Larry Bartels, *Democracy for Realists* (Princeton, NJ: Princeton University Press, 2017).

81. Robert Dahl, *A Preface to Democratic Theory* (Chicago: University of Chicago Press, 1956).

82. Herbert Asher, *Polling and the Public* (Washington, DC: CQ Press, 2001), 64.

83. Courtney Kennedy and Hannah Hartig, "Response Rates in Telephone Surveys Have Resumed Their Decline," Pew Research Center, February 27 2019, www.pewresearch.org/fact-tank/2019/02/27/response-rates-in-telephone-surveys-have-resumed-their-decline/ (accessed 1/15/20).

84. Michael Kagay and Janet Elder, "Numbers Are No Problem for Pollsters, Words Are," *New York Times*, August 9, 1992, E6.

85. Adam J. Berinsky, "The Two Faces of Public Opinion," *American Journal of Political Science* 43, no. 4 (1999): 1209–30.

86. Lynn Vavreck and Douglas Rivers, "The 2006 Cooperative Congressional Election Study," *Journal of Elections, Public Opinion and Parties* 18, no. 4 (2008): 355–66. See also Simon Jackman and Lynn Vavreck, "Primary Politics: Race, Gender, and Age in the 2008 Democratic Primary," *Journal of Elections, Public Opinion and Parties* 20, no. 2 (2010): 153–86.

87. Nate Silver, "FiveThirtyEight's Pollster Ratings," August 5, 2016, http://projects.fivethirtyeight.com/pollster-ratings/ (accessed 10/16/16).

88. Berinsky, "Two Faces of Public Opinion." See also Adam Berinsky, "Political Context and the Survey Response: The Dynamics of Racial Policy Opinion," *Journal of Politics* 64, no. 2 (2002): 567–84.

89. Nate Silver, "Which Polls Fared Best (and Worst) in the 2012 Presidential Race," *FiveThirtyEight* (blog), November 10, 2012, http://fivethirtyeight.blogs.nytimes.com/2012/11/10/which-polls-fared-best-and-worst-in-the-2012-presidential-race/ (accessed 2/24/16).

90. Ruth Igielnik et al., "Commercial Voter Files and the Study of U.S. Politics," Pew Research Center, February 15, 2018, www.pewresearch.org/methods/2018/02/15/commercial-voter-files-and-the-study-of-u-s-politics/ (accessed 1/15/20).

91. David Redlawsk, Caroline J. Tolbert, and Todd Donovan, *Why Iowa? How Caucuses and Sequential Elections Improve the Presidential Nominating Process* (Chicago: University of Chicago Press, 2010).

92. Sasha Issenberg, *The Victory Lab: The Secret Science of Winning Campaigns* (New York: Broadway Books, 2012); Sasha Issenberg, "A More Perfect Union: How President Obama's Campaign Used Big Data to Rally Individual Voters," *MIT Technology Review*, December 19, 2012, www.technologyreview.com/featuredstory/509026/how-obamas-team-used-big-data-to-rally-voters/ (accessed 11/25/15).

93. Nanette Byrnes, "Twitter May Have Predicted the Election," *Technology Review*, December 2, 2016, www.technologyreview.com/s/603010/twitter-may-have-predicted-the-election/ (accessed 8/2/18).

94. Katerina Eva Matsa, Amy Mitchell, and Galen Stocking, "Searching for News: The Flint Water Crisis," Pew Research Center, April 27, 2017, www.journalism.org/essay/searching-for-news/ (accessed 3/17/18).

95. Chris Taylor, "Triumph of the Nerds: Nate Silver Wins in 50 States," Mashable, November 7, 2012, http://mashable.com/2012/11/07/nate-silver-wins/#6aWvyWVGcaqq (accessed 2/24/16).

96. FiveThirtyEight, "How Popular/Unpopular Is Donald Trump? An Updating Calculation of the President's Approval Rating, Accounting for Each Poll's Quality, Recency, Sample Size and Partisan Lean," June 23, 2017, www.fivethirtyeight.com/features/how-were-tracking-donald-trumps-approval-ratings/ (accessed 3/17/18).

CHAPTER 7

1. A. W. Geiger, "Key Findings about the Online News Landscape in America," Pew Research Center Fact Tank, September 11, 2019, www.pewresearch.org/fact-tank/2019/09/11/key-findings-about-the-online-news-landscape-in-america/ (accessed 12/10/19).

2. This account taken from Anisa Subedar, "The Godfather of Fake News," BBC News, November 27, 2018, www.bbc.co.uk/news/resources/idt-sh/the_godfather_of_fake_news (accessed 12/10/19); and Eli Saslow, "Nothing on This Page Is Real: How Lies Become Truth in Online America," *Washington Post*, November 17, 2018, www.washingtonpost.com/national/nothing-on-this-page-is-real-how-lies-become-truth-in-online-america/2018/11/17/edd44cc8-e85a-11e8-bbdb-72fdbf9d4fed_story.html (accessed 12/10/19).

3. Subedar, "The Godfather of Fake News."

4. Pew Research Center, "Public Broadcasting Fact Sheet," July 23, 2019, www.journalism.org/fact-sheet/public-broadcasting/ (accessed 12/4/19).

5. Shanto Iyengar, *Media Politics* (New York: W. W. Norton, 2019).

6. Iyengar, *Media Politics*.

7. Quoted in Rodney Tiffen, "Journalism in the Trump Era," Inside Story, February 24, 2017, http://insidestory.org.au/journalism-in-the-trump-era (accessed 4/4/18).

8. David Folkenflik, "AT&T Deal for Time Warner Casts Renewed Attention on CNN," NPR, October 25, 2016, www.npr.org/2016/10/25/499299869/at-t-deal-for-time-warner-casts-renewed-attention-on-cnn (accessed 5/21/18).

9. Columbia Journalism Review, "Resources," https://archives.cjr.org/resources/index.php (accessed 8/2/18).

10. For a criticism of the increasing consolidation of the media, see the essays in Patricia Aufderheide et al., *Conglomerates and the Media* (New York: New Press, 1997).

11. Elisa Shearer and Elizabeth Grieco, "Americans are Wary of the Role Social Media Sites Play in Delivering the News," Pew Research Center, October 2, 2019, www.journalism.org/2019/10/02/americans-are-wary-of-the-role-social-media-sites-play-in-delivering-the-news/ (accessed 5/12/20).

12. Amy Mitchell, "Americans Still Prefer Watching to Reading the News—and Mostly Still through Television," Pew Research Center, December 13, 2018, www.journalism.org/2018/09/10/news-use-across-social-media-platforms-2018/ (accessed 12/4/2019).

13. Pew Research Center, "Amid Criticism, Support for Media's 'Watchdog' Role Stands Out," August 8, 2013, www.people-press.org/2013/08/08/amid-criticism-support-for-medias-watchdog-role-stands-out (accessed 4/27/14).

14. Pew Research Center, "Digital News Fact Sheet," www.journalism.org/fact-sheet/digital-news/ (accessed 1/15/20).

15. Clay Shirky, *Here Comes Everybody: The Power of Organizing without Organizations* (New York: Penguin Books, 2008).

16. Pew Research Center, "State of the News Media," www.pewresearch.org/topics/state-of-the-news-media/ (accessed 12/4/19).

17. Shirky, *Here Comes Everybody*; Amy Mitchell, Jesse Holcomb, and Rachel Weisel, "State of the News Media 2016," Pew Research Center, June 15, 2016, www.journalism.org/2016/06/15/state-of-the-news-media-2016 (accessed 3/19/18).

18. Elisa Shearer and Elizabeth Grieco, "Americans Are Wary of the Role Social Media Sites Play in Delivering the News," Pew Research Center, October 2, 2019, www.journalism.org/2019/10/02/americans-are-wary-of-the-role-social-media-sites-play-in-delivering-the-news/ (accessed 12/4/19).

19. Tony Romm, "Facebook CEO Mark Zuckerberg Says in Interview He Fears 'Erosion of Truth' but Defends Allowing Politicians to Lie in Ads," *Washington Post*,

October 17, 2019, www.washingtonpost.com/technology /2019/10/17/facebook-ceo-mark-zuckerberg-says-interview -he-fears-erosion-truth-defends-allowing-politicians-lie -ads/ (accessed 12/4/19).

20. Jeff Desjardins, "How the Tech Giants Made Their Billions," Visual Capitalist, March 29, 2019, www.visualcapitalist .com/how-tech-giants-make-billions/ (accessed 5/12/20).

21. "The Washington Post Records 86.6 Million Unique Visitors in March 2019," *WashPost PR* (blog), April 17, 2019, www.washingtonpost.com/pr/2019/04/17/washington -post-records-million-unique-visitors-march/ (accessed 12/4/19).

22. Robert McChesney and John Nichols, *The Death and Life of American Journalism: The Media Revolution That Will Begin the World Again* (New York: Nation Books, 2010).

23. Elizabeth Grieco, "U.S. Newspapers Have Shed Half of their Newsroom Employees since 2008," Pew Research Center, April 20, 2020, www.pewresearch.org/fact-tank /2020/04/20/u-s-newsroom-employment-has-dropped-by -a-quarter-since-2008/ (accessed 5/12/20).

24. Darrell West, *The Next Wave: Using Digital Technology to Further Social and Political Innovation* (Washington, DC: Brookings Institution Press, 2011).

25. Laura Wamsley, "Big Newspapers Are Booming: 'Washington Post' to Add 60 Newsroom Jobs," NPR, December 27, 2016, www.npr.org/sections/thetwo-way/2016/12/27/507140760 /big-newspapers-are-booming-washington-post-to-add -sixty-newsroom-jobs (accessed 1/22/18).

26. Mitchell, Holcomb, and Weisel, "State of the News Media 2016."

27. Michael Barthel, Elizabeth Grieco, and Elisa Shearer, "Older Americans, Black Adults, and Americans with Less Education More Interested in Local News," Pew Research Center, August, 14, 2019, www.journalism .org/2019/08/14/older-americans-black-adults-and -americans-with-less-education-more-interested-in-local-news/ (accessed 12/4/19).

28. Pew Research Center, "Local TV News Fact Sheet," June 25, 2019, www.journalism.org/fact-sheet/local-tv-news/ (accessed 12/4/19).

29. Elisa Shearer, "Social Media Outpaces Print Newspapers in the U.S. as News Source," Pew Research Center, December 10, 2019, www.pewresearch.org/fact-tank/2018 /12/10/social-media-outpaces-print-newspapers-in-the-u-s -as-a-news-source/ (accessed 12/4/19).

30. Pew Research Center, "The Internet's Broader Role in Campaign 2008," January 11, 2008, www.people-press .org/2008/01/11/internets-broader-role-in-campaign -2008/; and "Journalism, Satire or Just Laughs? 'The Daily Show with Jon Stewart,' Examined," May 8, 2008, www.journalism.org/2008/05/08/journalism-satire-or -just-laughs-the-daily-show-with-jon-stewart-examined/ (accessed 9/7/12).

31. Pew Research Center, "Audio and Podcasting Fact Sheet," July 9, 2019, www.journalism.org/fact-sheet/audio -and-podcasting/ (accessed 12/4/19).

32. Pew Research Center, "Audio and Podcasting Fact Sheet."

33. Pew Research Center, "Audio and Podcasting Fact Sheet."

34. West, *The Next Wave;* Edward Glaeser, *Triumph of the City: How Our Greatest Invention Makes Us Richer, Smarter, Greener, Healthier, and Happier* (New York: Penguin Press, 2011).

35. Aaron Smith and Maeve Duggan, "Online Political Videos and Campaign 2012," Pew Research Center, November 2, 2012, www.pewinternet.org/2012/11/02/online-political -videos-and-campaign-2012 (accessed 4/29/14); Galen Stocking, Patrick van Kessel, Michael Barthel, Katerina Eva Matsa, and Maya Khuzam, "Many Americans Get News on YouTube, Where News Organizations and Independent Producers Thrive Side by Side," Pew Research Center, September 28, 2020, www.journalism.org/2020/09/28 /many-americans-get-news-on-youtube-where-news -organizations-and-independent-producers-thrive-side-by -side/ (accessed 10/15/20).

36. Aaron Smith and Monica Anderson, "Social Media Use in 2018," Pew Research Center, March 1, 2018, www .pewinternet.org/2018/03/01/social-media-use-in-2018/ (accessed 3/19/18).

37. Antony Wilhelm, *Digital Nation: Toward an Inclusive Information Society* (Cambridge, MA: MIT Press, 2006); Paul DiMaggio et al., "Social Implications of the Internet," *Annual Review of Sociology* 27, no. 1 (2001): 307–36.

38. Karen Mossberger, Caroline J. Tolbert, and Mary Stansbury, *Virtual Inequality: Beyond the Digital Divide* (Washington, DC: Georgetown University Press, 2003); Pippa Norris, *Digital Divide: Civic Engagement, Information Poverty, and the Internet Worldwide* (New York: Cambridge University Press, 2001).

39. Karen Mossberger, Caroline Tolbert, and Ramona McNeal, "Digital Citizenship," MIT Press, Internet Broadband Fact Sheet, 2008; Elisa Shearer and Katerina Eva Matsa, "News Use across Social Media Platforms 2018," Pew Research Center, September 10, 2018, www .pewresearch.org/internet/fact-sheet/internet-broadband/ (accessed 12/4/19).

40. U.S. Census Bureau, "Nearly 8 in 10 Americans Have Access to High-Speed Internet," American Community Survey, November 13, 2014, www.census.gov/ newsroom/press-releases/2014/cb14-202.html (accessed 3/2/16).

41. Mossberger, Tolbert, and Stansbury, *Virtual Inequality.*

42. Pew Research Center, "Mobile Fact Sheet," June 12, 2019, www.pewresearch.org/internet/fact-sheet/mobile/ (accessed 12/4/19).

43. Amy Mitchell, Jeffrey Gottfried, and Katerina Eva Matsa, "Political Interest and Awareness Lower among Millennials," Pew Research Center, June 1, 2015, www.journalism .org/2015/06/01/political-interest-and-awareness-lower -among-millennials/ (accessed 12/7/15).

44. Jordan Misra, "Voter Turnout Rates among All Voting Age and Major Racial and Ethnic Groups Were Higher Than in 2014," U.S. Census Bureau, April 23, 2019, www

.census.gov/library/stories/2019/04/behind-2018-united-states-midterm-election-turnout.html (accessed 12/4/19).

45. Pew Research Center, "Social Media Fact Sheet," June 12, 2019, www.pewresearch.org/internet/fact-sheet/social-media/ (accessed 12/4/19).

46. Jason Gainous and Kevin Wagner, *Tweeting to Power: The Social Media Revolution in American Politics* (New York: Oxford University Press, 2013).

47. Gainous and Wagner, *Tweeting to Power*, 1.

48. Politifact, "Donald Trump's File," www.politifact.com/personalities/donald-trump/ (accessed 1/22/18).

49. Greg Sargent, "This Brutal New Poll Shows That Trump's Safe Space Is Shrinking," *Washington Post*, August 8, 2017, www.washingtonpost.com/blogs/plum-line/wp/2017/08/08/this-brutal-new-poll-shows-that-trumps-safe-space-is-shrinking/?utm_term=.744ad3651728 (accessed 3/8/18).

50. Erin McCann, "United's Apologies: A Timeline," *New York Times*, April 14, 2017, www.nytimes.com/2017/04/14/business/united-airlines-passenger-doctor.html (accessed 5/21/18).

51. Richard Davis, "Interplay: Political Blogging and Journalism," in *iPolitics: Citizens, Elections, and Governing in the New Media Era*, eds. Richard L. Fox and Jennifer M. Ramos (Cambridge: Cambridge University Press, 2012), 76–99.

52. Karen Mossberger and Caroline J. Tolbert, "Digital Democracy: How Politics Online Is Changing Electoral Participation," in *Oxford Handbook of American Elections and Political Behavior*, ed. Jan E. Leighley (New York: Oxford University Press, 2010), 200–218.

53. Caroline Tolbert and Ramona McNeal, "Unraveling the Effects of the Internet on Political Participation," *Political Research Quarterly* 56, no. 2 (2003): 175–85.

54. W. R. Neuman, M. R. Just, and A. N. Crigler, *Common Knowledge: News and the Construction of Political Meaning* (Chicago: University of Chicago Press, 1992).

55. A. Healy and D. McNamara, "Verbal Learning and Memory: Does the Modal Model Still Work?" in *Annual Review of Psychology* 47, eds. J. Spense, J. Darley, and D. Foss (Palo Alto, CA: Annual Reviews, 1996), 143–72.

56. Cass Sunstein, *Republic.com* (Princeton, NJ: Princeton University Press, 2001). See also Mossberger and Tolbert, "Digital Democracy."

57. Hannah Roberts, "This Is What Fake News Actually Looks Like—We Ranked 11 Election Stories That Went Viral on Facebook," Business Insider, November 17, 2016, www.businessinsider.com/fake-presidential-election-news-viral-facebook-trump-clinton-2016-11 (accessed 5/21/18).

58. Krysten Crawford, "Stanford Study Examines Fake News and the 2016 Presidential Election," *Stanford News*, January 18, 2017, www.news.stanford.edu/2017/01/18/stanford-study-examines-fake-news-2016-presidential-election/ (accessed 5/21/18).

59. Amy Mitchell, Jeffrey Gottfriend, Galen Stocking, Mason Walker, and Sophia Fedeli, "Many Americans Say Made-Up News Is a Critical Problem that Needs to be Fixed," Pew Research Center, June 5, 2019, www.journalism.org/2019/06/05/many-americans-say-made-up-news-is-a-critical-problem-that-needs-to-be-fixed/ (accessed 5/12/20).

60. Mitchell et al., "Many Americans Say Made-Up News."

61. Mitchell et al., "Many Americans Say Made-Up News."

62. Pew Research Center, "Public Highly Critical of State of Political Discourse in the U.S.," June 19, 2019, www.people-press.org/2019/06/19/public-highly-critical-of-state-of-political-discourse-in-the-u-s/ (accessed 12/4/19).

63. Matthew A. Baum, "Preaching to the Choir or Converting the Flock: Presidential Communication Strategies in the Age of Three Medias," in *iPolitics: Citizens, Elections, and Governing in the New Media Era*, eds. Richard L. Fox and Jennifer M. Ramos (Cambridge: Cambridge University Press, 2012), 183–205.

64. Eli Pariser, *The Filter Bubble: What the Internet Is Hiding from You* (New York: Penguin Press, 2011).

65. Michael X. Delli Carpini and Scott Keeter, *What Americans Know about Politics* (New Haven, CT: Yale University Press, 1996); Sunstein, *Republic.com*.

66. Mossberger, Tolbert, and Stansbury, *Virtual Inequality*.

67. Jeffrey Gottfried, Galen Stocking, and Elizabeth Grieco, "Partisans Remain Sharply Divided in Their Attitudes about the News Media," Pew Research Center, September 25, 2018, www.journalism.org/2018/09/25/partisans-remain-sharply-divided-in-their-attitudes-about-the-news-media/ (accessed 12/4/19).

68. Jeffrey Gottfried, Mason Walker, and Amy Mitchell, "Americans' Views of the News Media During the COVID-19 Outbreak," Pew Research Center, www.journalism.org/2020/05/08/americans-views-of-the-news-media-during-the-covid-19-outbreak/ (accessed 5/12/20).

69. Amy Wong, "'That's How Dictators Get Started': McCain Criticizes Trump for Calling Media 'the Enemy,'?" *Washington Post*, February 8, 2017, www.washingtonpost.com/news/the-fix/wp/2017/02/18/thats-how-dictators-get-started-mccain-criticizes-trump-for-calling-media-the-enemy/?noredirect=on&utm_term=.90e929b9948d (accessed 5/21/18).

70. David J. Garrow, *Protest at Selma: Martin Luther King, Jr., and the Voting Rights Act of 1965* (New Haven, CT: Yale University Press, 2001).

71. See Todd Gitlin, *The Whole World Is Watching* (Berkeley: University of California Press, 1980).

72. Tim Groseclose, *Left Turn: How Liberal Media Bias Distorts the American Mind* (New York: St. Martin's Press, 2011).

73. Pew Research Center, "How Journalists See Journalists in 2004: Views on Profits, Performance and Politics," May 2004, http://people-press.org/files/legacy-pdf/214.pdf (accessed 9/7/12).

74. "Media Bias Ratings," AllSides, www.allsides.com/media -bias/media-bias-ratings (accessed 3/25/20).

75. Doris Graber, ed., *Media Power in American Politics*, 5th ed. (Washington, DC: CQ Press, 2006).

76. Amber E. Boydstun, Stefaan Walgrave, and Anne Hardy, "Two Faces of Media Attention: Media Storms vs. General Coverage," *Political Communication* 31, no. 4 (2014): 509–31.

77. Larry M. Bartels, *Presidential Primaries and the Dynamics of Public Choice* (Princeton, NJ: Princeton University Press, 1988).

78. David P. Redlawsk, Caroline J. Tolbert, and Todd Donovan, *Why Iowa? How Caucuses and Sequential Elections Improve the Presidential Nominating Process* (Chicago: University of Chicago Press, 2011).

79. Larry M. Bartels, *Unequal Democracy: The Political Economy of the New Gilded Age* (Princeton, NJ: Princeton University Press, 2008).

80. Robert Entman, "Framing: Toward Clarification of a Fractured Paradigm," *Journal of Communication* 43, no. 4 (1993): 51–58.

81. Shanto Iyengar and Donald R. Kinder, *News That Matters: Television and American Opinion* (Chicago: University of Chicago Press, 1987), 63; John Zaller, *The Nature and Origins of Mass Opinion* (New York: Cambridge University Press, 1992).

82. Todd Donovan, Caroline J. Tolbert, and Daniel A. Smith, "Priming Presidential Votes by Direct Democracy," *Journal of Politics* 70, no. 4 (October 2008): 1217–31, www .journals.uchicago.edu/doi/abs/10.1017/S0022381608081164.

83. *New York Times v. United States*, 403 U.S. 713 (1971).

84. United Nations General Assembly, "Report of the Special Rapporteur on the Promotion and Protection of the Right to Freedom of Opinion and Expression," 2011, www.ohchr.org/EN/Issues/FreedomOpinion/Pages /OpinionIndex.aspx (accessed 3/14/16).

85. Andrew Chadwick, *Internet Politics: States, Citizens, and New Communication Technologies* (Oxford: Oxford University Press, 2006).

CHAPTER 8

1. Kaynakrit Vongkiatkajorn, Marian Liu, Rachel Hatzipanagos, and Linah Mohannad, "Voices of Protest," *Washington Post*, June 4, 2020, www.washingtonpost.com /graphics/2020/national/protesters-george-floyd/ (accessed 6/5/20).

2. Vongkiatkajorn et al., "Voices of Protest."

3. Maneesh Arora and Davin L. Phoenix, "Will the Floyd Protests Lead to Police Reform? Here's What We Know," *The Washington Post*, June 11, 2020, www.washingtonpost .com/politics/2020/06/11/will-floyd-protests-lead-police -reform-heres-what-we-know/ (accessed 10/12/20).

4. John Gramlich, "What Makes a Good Citizen? Voting, Paying Taxes, Following the Law Top List," Pew Research Center, July 2, 2019, www.pewresearch.org/fact-tank /2019/07/02/what-makes-a-good-citizen-voting-paying -taxes-following-the-law-top-list/ (accessed 12/6/19).

5. Sidney Verba, Kay Lehman Schlozman, and Henry E. Brady, *Voice and Equality: Civic Voluntarism in American Politics* (Cambridge, MA: Harvard University Press, 2005), chap. 3 for kinds of participation; 66–67 for prevalence of local activity.

6. Michael P. McDonald, "American Voter Turnout in Historical Perspective," in *The Oxford Handbook of American Elections and Political Behavior*, ed. Jan E. Leighley (New York: Oxford University Press, 2010), 125–43.

7. Todd Donovan and Shaun Bowler, *Reforming the Republic: Democratic Institutions for the New America* (Upper Saddle River, NJ: Pearson Education, 2004).

8. For a discussion of voter turnout over time, see Ruy A. Teixeira, *The Disappearing American Voter* (Washington, DC: Brookings Institution Press, 1992). See also Michael McDonald and Samuel Popkin, "The Myth of the Vanishing Voter," *American Political Science Review*, 95 (2001): 963–74; and Michael McDonald, "2012 November General Election Turnout Rates," United States Election Project, www.electproject.org/2012g (accessed 9/14/12).

9. Michael McDonald, "2016 November General Election Turnout Rates," United States Election Project, www .electproject.org/2016g (accessed 3/25/20).

10. Michael McDonald, "2020 November General Election Turnout Rates," United States Election Project, www .electproject.org/2020g (accessed 11/23/20).

11. Jordan Misra, "Voter Turnout Rates among All Voting Age and Major Racial and Ethnic Groups Were Higher Than in 2014," U.S. Census Bureau, April 23, 2019, www.census.gov/library/stories/2019/04/behind-2018 -united-states-midterm-election-turnout.html (accessed 12/6/19).

12. Elisa Shearer and Jeffrey Gottfried, "News Use across Social Media Platforms 2017," Pew Research Center, www.journalism.org/2017/09/07/news-use-across-social -media-platforms-2017/ (accessed 3/29/18).

13. Meredith Rolfe, *Voter Turnout: A Social Theory of Political Participation* (New York: Cambridge University Press, 2012).

14. Lee Rainie et al., "Social Media and Political Engagement," Internet, Science & Tech, Pew Research Center, www .pewinternet.org/2012/10/19/social-media-and-political -engagement/ (accessed 6/24/14).

15. Helen Margetts, Peter John, Scott Hale, and Taha Yasseri, *Political Turbulence: How Social Media Shape Collective Action* (New York: Oxford University Press, 2017).

16. Philip Bump, "'60 Minutes' Profiles the Genius Who Won Trump's Campaign: Facebook," *Washington Post*, October 9, 2017, www.washingtonpost.com/news/politics /wp/2017/10/09/60-minutes-profiles-the-genius-who

-won-trumps-campaign-facebook/?utm_term= .ad2bd8d8194a (accessed 3/29/18).

17. Caroline J. Tolbert and Ramona S. McNeal, "Unraveling the Effects of the Internet on Political Participation," *Political Research Quarterly* 56, no. 2 (2003): 175–85; see also Bruce Bimber, "Information and Political Engagement in America: The Search for Effects of Information Technology at the Individual Level," *Political Research Quarterly* 54 (2001): 53–67; Bimber, *Information and American Democracy: Technology and the Evolution of Political Power* (Cambridge: Cambridge University Press, 2009); J. Thomas and G. Streib, "The New Face of Government: Citizen-Initiated Contacts in the Era of E-Government," *Journal of Public Administration Theory and Research* 13, no. 1 (2003): 83–102; D. V. Shah et al., "Information and Expression in a Digital Age: Modeling Internet Effects on Civic Participation," *Communication Research* 32, no. 5 (2005): 531–65; K. Kenski and N. J. Stroud, "Connections between Internet Use and Political Efficacy, Knowledge, and Participation," *Journal of Broadcasting and Electronic Media* 50, no. 2 (2006): 173–92.

18. Sasha Issenberg, *The Victory Lab: The Secret Science of Winning Campaigns* (New York: Broadway Books, 2013); Andrew Chadwick, *The Hybrid Media System: Politics and Power* (New York: Oxford University Press, 2017).

19. OpenSecrets.org, "2020 Election to Cost $14 Billion, Blowing Away Spending Records," October 28, 2020, www .opensecrets.org/news/2020/10/cost-of-2020-election -14billion-update (accessed 11/15/20).

20. OpenSecrets, "Small Donor Donations as a Percentage of Total Fundraising, Current Candidates Only," www .opensecrets.org/2020-presidential-race/small-donors (accessed 11/23/20).

21. Jason Gainous and Kevin Wagner, *Tweeting to Power: The Social Media Revolution in American Politics* (New York: Oxford University Press, 2013).

22. Gainous and Wagner, *Tweeting to Power.*

23. Pew Research Center, "National Politics on Twitter: Small Share of U.S. Adults Produce Majority of Tweets," October 23, 2019, www.people-press.org/2019/10/23 /national-politics-on-twitter-small-share-of-u-s-adults -produce-majority-of-tweets/ (accessed 12/6/19).

24. Karen Mossberger and Caroline J. Tolbert, "Digital Democracy: How Politics Online Is Changing Electoral Participation," in *Oxford Handbook of American Elections and Political Behavior*, ed. Jan E. Leighley (New York: Oxford University Press, 2010), 200–218.

25. Philip Bump, "'60 Minutes' profiles the genius that won Trump's campaign: Facebook," *The Washington Post*, October 9, 2017, https://www.washingtonpost.com /news/politics/wp/2017/10/09/60-minutes-profiles-the -genius-who-won-trumps-campaign-facebook/ (accessed 2/13/2020).

26. W. R. Neuman, M. R. Just, and A. N. Crigler, *Common Knowledge: News and the Construction of Political Meaning* (Chicago: University of Chicago Press, 1992).

27. Bruce Bimber and Richard Davis, *Campaigning Online: The Internet in U.S. Elections* (Cambridge: Cambridge University Press, 2003).

28. Robert Putnam, *Bowling Alone: The Collapse and Revival of American Community* (New York: Simon and Schuster, 2000).

29. Russell Dalton, *The Good Citizen: How a Younger Generation Is Reshaping American Politics* (Washington, DC: CQ Press, 2008).

30. "Same-Sex Marriage Tweets Takeover the Internet," *USA Today*, June 27, 2015, www.usatoday.com/story/news /nation-now/2015/06/27/same-sex-marriage-scotus-gay -marriage-twitter-love-wins-trending/29389167/ (accessed 1/7/16).

31. Russell Dalton, "Citizenship Norms and the Expansion of Political Participation," *Public Choice* 56 (2008): 76–98.

32. Anamitra Deb, Stacy Donohue, and Tom Glaisyer, "Is Social Media a Threat to Democracy?" The Omidyar Group, October 1, 2017, www.omidyargroup.com/wp -content/uploads/2017/10/Social-Media-and-Democracy -October-5-2017.pdf (accessed 3/29/18).

33. Deb, Donohue, and Glaisyer, "Is Social Media a Threat to Democracy?"

34. David S. Cloud, "Facebook Tells Congress 126 Million Americans May Have Seen Russia-Linked Ads," *LA Times*, October 31, 2017, www.latimes.com/nation/la-na -russia-tech-20171031-story.html (accessed 3/29/18).

35. Josh Constine, "120K Instagrams by Russian Election Attackers Hit 20M Americans," Tech Crunch, November 1, 2017, techcrunch.com/2017/11/01/instagram-election -interference (accessed 3/29/18).

36. Julian Borger, Lauren Gambino, and Sabrina Siddiqui, "Tech Groups Face Congress as Showdown over Russian Election Meddling Looms," *The Guardian*, October 27, 2017, www.theguardian.com/technology/2017/oct/22 /facebook-google-twitter-congress-hearing-trump-russia -election (accessed 3/29/18); Deb, Donohue, and Glaisyer, "Is Social Media a Threat to Democracy?"

37. Brian Fung and Ahiza Garcia, "Facebook has shut down 5.4 billion fake accounts this year," *CNN Business*, November 13, 2019 (accessed 3/16/20).

38. Brian Fung, "Twitter Says It Labeled 300,000 Tweets Around the Election," *CNN Business*, November 12, 2020, www.cnn.com/2020/11/12/tech/twitter-election -labels-misinformation/index.html (accessed 11/23/20).

39. Pew Research Center, "Internet/Broadband Fact Sheet," June 12, 2019, www.pewresearch.org/internet/fact-sheet /internet-broadband/ (accessed 12/6/19).

40. Anthony Downs, *An Economic Theory of Democracy* (New York: Harper and Row, 1957); William H. Riker and Peter C. Ordeshook, "A Theory of the Calculus of

Voting," *American Political Science Review* 62, no. 1 (1968): 25–42.

41. Julianna Pacheco and Jason Fletcher, "Incorporating Health into Studies of Political Behavior: Evidence for Turnout and Partisanship," *Political Research Quarterly* 68, no. 1 (2014): 104–16; Misra, "Voter Turnout Rates."

42. Angus Campbell et al., *The American Voter* (New York: Wiley, 1960); Steven Rosenstone and John Mark Hansen, *Mobilization, Participation, and Democracy in America* (New York: Macmillan, 1993); Kay Lehman Scholzman, Sidney Verba, and Henry E. Brady, *The Unheavenly Chorus: Unequal Political Voice and the Broken Promise of American Democracy* (Princeton, NJ: Princeton University Press, 2012).

43. Raymond E. Wolfinger and Steven J. Rosenstone, "Who Votes?" *Yale University Press* vol. 22, 1980.

44. U.S. Census Bureau, "Voting and Registration in the Election of November 2016," May 2017, www.census .gov/data/tables/time-series/demo/voting-and-registration /p20-580.html (accessed 3/29/18).

45. Misra, "Voter Turnout Rates."

46. U.S. Census Bureau, "Table 7. Reported Voting and Registration of Family Members, by Age and Family Income: November 2016," Voting and Registration, www .census.gov/data/tables/time-series/demo/voting-and -registration/p20-580.html (accessed 3/29/18).

47. Sidney Verba and Norman H. Nie, *Participation in America: Political Democracy and Social Equality* (New York: Harper and Row, 1972); and U.S. Census Bureau, "Voting and Registration in the Election of November 2018," Table 7, https://www.census.gov/data/tables/time -series/demo/voting-and-registration/p20-583.html (accessed 3/8/20).

48. Shiva Maniam and Samantha Smith, "A Wider Partisan and Ideological Gap between Younger, Older Generations," Pew Research Center, March 20, 2017, www .pewresearch.org/fact-tank/2017/03/20/a-wider-partisan -and-ideological-gap-between-younger-older-generations (accessed 3/29/18); Richard Frey, "Millennials and Gen Xers Outvoted Boomers and Older Generations in 2016 Election," Pew Research Center, July 31, 2017, www .pewresearch.org/fact-tank/2017/07/31/millennials-and -gen-xers-outvoted-boomers-and-older-generations-in -2016-election/ (accessed 3/29/18).

49. Eric Plutzer, "Becoming a Habitual Voter: Inertia, Resources, and Growth in Young Adulthood," *American Political Science Review* 96, no. 1 (March 2002): 41–56.

50. Eitan D. Hersh, *Hacking the Electorate: How Campaigns Perceive Voters* (New York: Cambridge University Press, 2015).

51. Tyler Kingkade, "Youth Vote 2012 Turnout: Exit Polls Show Greater Share of Electorate Than in 2008," Huffington Post, www.huffingtonpost.com/2012/11/07/youth-vote -2012-turnout-exit-polls_n_2086092.html (accessed 5/24/14).

52. Jennifer Lawless and Richard Fox, *Running from Office: Why Young Americans Are Turned Off to Politics* (New York: Oxford University Press, 2015).

53. Rene Rocha et al., "Race and Turnout: Does Descriptive Representation in State Legislatures Increase Minority Voting?" *Political Research Quarterly* 63, no. 3 (2010): 890–907.

54. Susan Banducci, Todd Donovan, and Jeffrey Karp, "Minority Representation, Empowerment and Participation," *Journal of Politics* 66, no. 2 (2004): 534–56.

55. Mark Hugo Lopez and Paul Taylor, "Dissecting the 2008 Electorate: Most Diverse in U.S. History," Hispanic Trends, Pew Research Center, April 30, 2009, www.pewhispanic.org/2009/04/30/dissecting-the -2008-electorate-most-diverse-in-us-history/ (accessed 9/14/12).

56. Thom File, "The Diversifying Electorate—Voting Rates by Race and Hispanic Origin in 2012 (and Other Recent Elections)," Current Population Survey, U.S. Census Bureau, May 2013, www.census.gov/prod/2013pubs/p20 -568.pdf (accessed 4/11/16).

57. Jens Manuel Krogstad and Mark Hugo Lopez, "Black Voter Turnout Fell in 2016, Even as a Record Number of Americans Cast Ballots," Pew Research Center, May 12, 2017, www.pewresearch.org/fact-tank/2017/05/12/ black-voter-turnout-fell-in-2016-even-as-a-record-number -of-americans-cast-ballots/ (accessed 3/29/18).

58. Jessica Trounstine, *Segregation by Design: Local Politics and Inequality in American Cities* (New York: Cambridge University Press, 2018).

59. Jan E. Leighley and Jonathan Nagler, "Individual and Systemic Influences on Turnout: Who Votes? 1984," *Journal of Politics* 54, no. 3 (1992): 718–40.

60. Michael Dawson, *Black Visions: The Roots of Contemporary African-American Political Ideologies* (Chicago: University of Chicago Press, 2003).

61. "2016 Election Exit Polls," *Washington Post*, November 29, 2019, www.washingtonpost.com/graphics/politics/2016 -election/exit-polls/ (accessed 12/6/19).

62. Betsy Cooper et al., "How Immigration and Concerns about Cultural Change Are Shaping the 2016 Election," Public Religion Research Institute, June 23, 2016, www.prri.org/research/prri-brookings-poll -immigration-economy-trade-terrorism-presidential-race/ (accessed 12/6/19).

63. John Sides, Michael Tesler, and Lynn Vavreck, *Identity Crisis: The 2016 Presidential Campaign and the Battle for the Meaning of America* (Princeton, NJ: Princeton University Press, 2018); Brenda Major, Alison Blodorn, and Gregory Major Blascovich, "The Threat of Increasing Diversity: Why Many White Americans Support Trump in the 2016 Presidential Election," *Group Processes & Intergroup Relations* 21, no. 6 (2018), 931–40.

64. File, "The Diversifying Electorate."

65. Matt Barreto and Gary Segura, *Latino America: How America's Most Dynamic Population Is Poised to Transform the Politics of the Nation* (New York: Public Affairs, 2014).

66. Mark Hugo Lopez, Ana Gonzalez-Barrera, and Jens Manuel Krogstad, "Hispanic Voters and the 2018 Midterm Elections," Pew Research Center, October 25, 2018, www.pewresearch.org/hispanic/2018/10/25/hispanic-voters-and-the-2018-midterm-elections/ (accessed 12/6/19).

67. Matt Barreto, Gary Segura, and Nathan Woods, "The Mobilizing Effect of Majority-Minority Districts on Latino Turnout," *American Political Science Review* 98 (2004): 65–75, and authors' update.

68. Lopez, Gonzalez-Barrera, and Krogstad, "Hispanic Voters and the 2018 Midterm Elections."

69. Barreto and Segura, *Latino America*; Gary Langer et al., "Key Exit Poll Takeaways: Voters Negative on Trump, Most Interested in Health Care, Immigration," ABC News, November 7, 2018, https://abcnews.go.com/Politics/negative-trump-divided-issues-voters-reshuffle-cards-washington/story?id=59025819 (accessed 11/9/18).

70. Lopez, Gonzalez-Barrera, and Krogstad, "Hispanic Voters and the 2018 Midterm Elections."

71. John Griffin and Brian Newman, *Minority Report: Evaluating Political Equality in America* (New York: Cambridge University Press, 2008); Rodney R. Hero, *Latinos and the U.S. Political System: Two-Tiered Pluralism* (Philadelphia: Temple University Press, 1992); Daniel Bowen and Christopher Clark, "Revisiting Descriptive Representation in Congress: Assessing the Effect of Race on the Constituent–Legislator Relationship," *Political Research Quarterly* 67, no. 3 (2014): 695–707.

72. File, "The Diversifying Electorate."

73. Thom File, "Voting in America: A Look at the 2016 Presidential Election," *Census Blogs*, May 10, 2017, www.census.gov/newsroom/blogs/random-samplings/2017/05/voting_in_america.html (accessed 3/29/18).

74. "Election 2016: Exit Polls," *New York Times*, November 8, 2016, www.nytimes.com/interactive/2016/11/08/us/politics/election-exit-polls.html (accessed 11/11/16).

75. Noah Y. Kim, "How Andrew Yang Quieted the Asian American Right," *The Atlantic*, February 3, 2020 https://www.theatlantic.com/politics/archive/2020/02/yang-asian-americans-affirmative-action/605917/ (accessed 3/16/2020).

76. "The Gender Gap Fact Sheet," Center for the American Woman and Politics, January 2017, https://cawp.rutgers.edu/sites/default/files/resources/ggpresvote.pdf (accessed 3/16/2020).

77. Kira Sanbonmatsu, "Political Parties and the Recruitment of Women to State Legislatures," *Journal of Politics* 64, no. 3 (August 2002): 791–809; Jennifer L. Lawless and Richard L. Fox, *Why Are Women Still Not Running for Public Office?* (Washington, DC: Brookings Institution Press, 2008).

78. Center for American Women and Politics, *The Impact of Women in Public Office: Findings at a Glance* (New Brunswick, NJ: Rutgers University Press, 1991); Lawless and Fox, *Why Are Women Still Not Running for Public Office?*

79. David E. Campbell et al., "Putting Politics First: The Impact of Politics on American Religious and Secular Orientations," *American Journal of Political Science* 62, no. 3 (2018): 551–65.

80. See Richard A. Brody, "The Puzzle of Political Participation in America," in *The New American Political System*, ed. Anthony King (Washington, DC: American Enterprise Institute, 1978), chap. 8.

81. Rosenstone and Hansen, *Mobilization, Participation, and Democracy*, 59.

82. Alan S. Gerber and Donald P. Green, "The Effects of Canvassing, Telephone Calls, and Direct Mail on Voter Turnout: A Field Experiment," *American Political Science Review* 94, no. 3 (September 2000): 660.

83. Robert M. Bond et al., "A 61-Million-Person Experiment in Social Influence and Political Mobilization," *Nature* 489 (2012): 295–98.

84. Bond et al., "A 61-Million-Person Experiment."

85. Katerina Eva Matsa and Kristine Lu, "10 Facts about the Changing Digital News Landscape," Pew Research Center, September 14, 2016, www.pewresearch.org/fact-tank/2016/09/14/facts-about-the-changing-digital-news-landscape/ (accessed 10/16/16).

86. Michael P. McDonald and John Samples, eds., *The Marketplace of Democracy: Electoral Competition and American Politics* (Washington, DC: Brookings Institution Press, 2006).

87. Todd Donovan, "A Goal for Reform: Make Elections Worth Stealing," *PS: Political Science and Politics* 40, no. 4 (2007): 681–6; Gary W. Cox and Michael C. Munger, "Closeness, Expenditures, and Turnout in the 1982 U.S. House Elections," *American Political Science Review* 83, no. 1 (1989): 217–31; James G. Gimpel, Karen M. Kaufmann, and Shanna Pearson-Merkowitz, "Battleground States versus Blackout States: The Behavioral Implications of Modern Presidential Campaigns," *Journal of Politics* 69, no. 3 (2007): 786–97.

88. Mark N. Franklin, "Electoral Participation," in *Comparing Democracies: Elections and Voting in Global Perspective*, eds. Lawrence LeDuc, Richard G. Niemi, and Pippa Norris (Thousand Oaks, CA: Sage, 1996), 216–35; G. Bingham Powell, "American Voter Turnout in Comparative Perspective," *American Political Science Review* 80, no. 1 (1986): 17–43.

89. Gimpel, Kaufmann, and Pearson-Merkowitz, "Battleground States versus Blackout States"; Julianna Sandell Pacheco, "Political Socialization in Context: The Effect of Political Competition on Youth Voter Turnout," *Political Behavior* 30, no. 4 (2008): 415–36; Keena Lipsitz, "The Consequences of Battleground and 'Spectator' State Residency for Political Participation," *Political Behavior* 31, no. 2 (2009): 187–209.

90. Caroline J. Tolbert, Daniel C. Bowen, and Todd Donovan, "Initiative Campaigns: Direct Democracy and Voter Mobilization," *American Politics Research* 37, no. 1 (2009): 155–92.

91. Caroline J. Tolbert, John A. Grummel, and Daniel A. Smith, "The Effects of Ballot Initiatives on Voter Turnout in the American States," *American Politics Research* 29, no. 6 (2001): 625–48; Mark A. Smith, "The Contingent Effects of Ballot Initiatives and Candidate Races on Turnout," *American Journal of Political Science* 45, no. 3 (2001): 700–706; Caroline J. Tolbert and Daniel A. Smith, "The Educative Effects of Ballot Initiatives on Voter Turnout," *American Politics Research* 33, no. 2 (2005): 283–309; Frederick Boehmke and Daniel Bowen, "Direct Democracy and Individual Interest Group Membership," *Journal of Politics* 72, no. 3 (2010): 659–71.

92. Stephen Nicholson, *Voting the Agenda: Candidates, Elections, and Ballot Propositions* (Princeton, NJ: Princeton University Press, 2005).

93. John Myers, "That Blockbuster California Ballot Will Be a $452-Million Battle," *Los Angeles Times*, February 18, 2016, www.latimes.com/local/california/la-pol-sac-november-ballot-500-million-20160215-story.html (accessed 10/18/16).

94. Daniel A. Smith and Caroline J. Tolbert, *Educated by Initiative: The Effects of Direct Democracy on Citizens and Political Organizations in the American States* (Ann Arbor: University of Michigan Press, 2004).

95. Bruce E. Cain, Todd Donovan, and Caroline J. Tolbert, *Democracy in the States: Experiments in Election Reform* (Washington, DC: Brookings Institution Press, 2008).

96. U.S. Census Bureau, "Table 10. Reasons for Not Voting, by Selected Characteristics: November 2012," Voting and Registration, www.census.gov/hhes/www/socdemo/voting/publications/p20/2012/tables.html.

97. Brennan Center for Justice, "Automatic Voter Registration, a Summary," July 10, 2019, www.brennancenter.org/our-work/research-reports/automatic-voter-registration-summary (accessed 12/6/19).

98. "Automatically Registering Voters Is a Useful Reform. But We Need More," editorial, *Washington Post*, October 23, 2019, www.washingtonpost.com/opinions/automatically-registering-voters-is-a-useful-reform-but-we-need-more/2019/10/23/69594d5e-f44d-11e9-8cf0-4cc99f74d127_story.html (accessed 12/6/19).

99. Robert A. Jackson, Robert D. Brown, and Gerald C. Wright, "Registration, Turnout and the Electoral Representativeness of U.S. State Electorates," *American Politics Quarterly* 26, no. 3 (July 1998): 259–87. See also Benjamin Highton, "Easy Registration and Voter Turnout," *Journal of Politics* 59, no. 2 (April 1997): 565–87.

100. Michael Hanmer, *Discount Voting: Voting Registration Reforms and Their Effects* (New York: Cambridge University Press, 2009); Melanie Springer, *How the States Shaped the Nation: American Electoral Institutions and Voter Turnout, 1920–2000* (Chicago: University of Chicago Press, 2014); Mary Fitzgerald, "Greater Convenience but Not Greater Turnout: The Impact of Alternative Voting Methods on Electoral Participation in the United States," *American Politics Research* 33, no. 6 (2005): 842–67; Craig Leonard Brians and Bernard Grofman, "When Registration Barriers Fall, Who Votes? An Empirical Test of a Rational Choice Model," *Public Choice* 99 (1999): 161–76.

101. National Conference of State Legislatures, "Voter Identification Requirements," www.ncsl.org/research/elections-and-campaigns/voter-id.aspx (accessed 10/12/18).

102. Zoltan Hajnal, Nazita Lajevardi, and Lindsey Nielson, "Voter Identification Laws and the Suppression of Minority Votes," *Journal of Politics* 79, no. 2 (2017): 363–79.

103. National Conference of State Legislatures, "Voter Identification Requirements."

104. E. Ann Carson, "Prisoners in 2013," U.S. Department of Justice, Bureau of Justice Statistics, September 30, 2014, www.bjs.gov/content/pub/pdf/p13.pdf (accessed 4/11/16); National Conference of State Legislatures, "Felon Voting Rights," April 30, 2017, www.ncsl.org/research/elections-and-campaigns/felon-voting-rights.aspx (accessed 10/12/18).

105. Justin Wolfers, David Leonhardt, and Kevin Quealy, "1.5 Million Missing Black Men," The Upshot, *New York Times*, April 20, 2015, www.nytimes.com/interactive/2015/04/20/upshot/missing-black-men.html?_r50&abt50002&abg51 (accessed 1/6/16).

106. Jean Chung, *Felon Disenfranchisement: A Primer* (Washington, DC: The Sentencing Project, 2016), www.sentencingproject.org/wp-content/uploads/2015/08/Felony-Disenfranchisement-Primer.pdf (accessed 10/12/16).

107. National Conference of State Legislatures, "State Laws Governing Early Voting," https://www.ncsl.org/research/elections-and-campaigns/early-voting-in-state-elections.aspx (accessed 10/12/20).

108. Paul Gronke, Eva Galanes-Rosenbaum, and Peter Miller, "Early Voting and Turnout," *PS: Political Science and Politics* 40, no. 4 (October 2007): 639–45; Fitzgerald, "Greater Convenience but Not Greater Turnout"; Adam J. Berinsky, "The Perverse Consequences of Electoral Reform in the United States," *American Politics Research* 33, no. 4 (2005): 471–91.

109. Michael Ritter and Caroline J. Tolbert, *Accessible Elections: How the States Can Help Americans Vote* (New York: Oxford University Press, 2020).

110. John Griffin and Michael Keane, "Are Voters Better Represented?" *Journal of Politics* 65, no. 4 (2005): 1206–27.

CHAPTER 9

1. Taxdayteaparty.com, "Meet Keli Carender, Tea Party Organizer in Seattle, Washington," March 15, 2009, http://taxdayteaparty.com/2009/03/meet-keli-carender-tea-party-organizer-in-seattle-washington/ (accessed 1/26/18).

2. Walter Dean Burnham, *Critical Elections and the Main-springs of American Politics* (New York: W. W. Norton, 1970).

3. Larry M. Bartels, *Unequal Democracy: The Political Economy of the New Gilded Age* (Princeton, NJ: Princeton University Press, 2008).

4. Kathleen Bawn et al., "A Theory of Political Parties: Groups, Policy Demands and Nominations in American Politics," *Perspectives on Politics* 10, no. 3 (2012): 571–97.

5. Morris Fiorina, Samuel Abrams, and Jeremy Pope, *Culture War? The Myth of a Polarized America* (New York: Pearson Longman, 2004).

6. Todd Donovan and Shaun Bowler, *Reforming the Republic: Democratic Institutions for the New America* (Upper Saddle River, NJ: Prentice Hall, 2003).

7. Pew Research Center, "Partisan Antipathy: More Intense, More Personal," October 10, 2019, www.people-press.org/2019/10/10/partisan-antipathy-more-intense-more-personal/ (accessed 1/16/20); Pew Research Center, "The Public, the Political System and American Democracy," April 26, 2018, www.people-press.org/2018/04/26/the-public-the-political-system-and-american-democracy/ (accessed 1/16/20).

8. James Madison, *The Federalist Papers*, no. 10, http://thomas.loc.gov/home/histdox/fed_10.html (accessed 11/11/12).

9. John H. Aldrich, *Why Parties? A Second Look* (Chicago: University of Chicago Press, 2011).

10. For an excellent analysis of the parties' role in recruitment, see Paul Herrnson, *Congressional Elections: Campaigning at Home and in Washington* (Washington, DC: CQ Press, 1995).

11. Marty Cohen et al., *The Party Decides: Presidential Nominations before and after Reform* (Chicago: University of Chicago Press, 2008).

12. Sasha Issenberg, *Victory Lab: The Secret Science of Winning Campaigns* (New York: Crown, 2012).

13. Donald P. Green and Alan S. Gerber, *Get Out the Vote*, 4th ed. (Washington, DC: Brookings Institution Press, 2019); David Ingram, "YouTube 2020: Why Politics Have Exploded on the Video Platform," NBC News, September 16, 2020, www.nbcnews.com/tech/tech-news/youtube-2020-why-politics-have-exploded-video-platform-n1240160 (accessed 11/23/20).

14. Glen Justice, "F.E.C. Declines to Curb Independent Fund Raisers," *New York Times*, May 14, 2004, A16.

15. See Harold Gosnell, *Machine Politics: Chicago Model*, rev. ed. (Chicago: University of Chicago Press, 1968); Terry Golway, *Machine Made: Tammany Hall and the Creation of Modern American Politics* (New York: Liveright, 2014).

16. For a useful discussion, see John Bibby and Thomas Holbrook, "Parties and Elections," in *Politics in the American States*, eds. Virginia Gray and Herbert Jacob (Washington, DC: CQ Press, 1996), 78–121.

17. Katherine Schaeffer, "Far More Americans See 'Very Strong' Partisan Conflicts Now Than in the Last Two Presidential Election Years," Pew Research Center, March 4, 2020, www.pewresearch.org/fact-tank/2020/03/04/far-more-americans-see-very-strong-partisan-conflicts-now-than-in-the-last-two-presidential-election-years (accessed 4/30/20).

18. Tara Golshan, "Reckless, Outrageous, and Undignified Behavior: Sen. Flake Quits the Senate over Trump," Vox, October 24, 2017, www.vox.com/2017/10/24/16536756/flake-retirement-over-trump-announcement (accessed 5/12/18).

19. Donald Green, Bradley Palmquist, and Eric Schickler, *Partisan Hearts and Minds* (New Haven, CT: Yale University Press, 2004).

20. Samara Klar and Yanna Krupnikov, *Independent Politics: How American Disdain for Parties Leads to Political Inaction* (Cambridge: Cambridge University Press, 2016).

21. Pew Research Center, "Political Independents: Who They Are, What They Think," March 14, 2019, www.people-press.org/2019/03/14/political-independents-who-they-are-what-they-think/ (accessed 1/16/20).

22. Alan Abramowitz, *The Great Alignment: Race, Party Transformation, and the Rise of Donald Trump* (New Haven, CT: Yale University Press, 2018).

23. Lilliana Mason, *Uncivil Agreement: How Politics Became Our Identity* (Chicago: University of Chicago Press, 2018); Christopher Achen and Larry M. Bartels, *Democracy for Realists: Why Elections Do Not Produce Responsive Government* (Princeton, NJ: Princeton University Press, 2017).

24. Pew Research Center, "Amid Campaign Turmoil, Biden Holds Wide Leads on Coronvirus, Unifying the Country," October 9, 2020, www.pewresearch.org/politics/2020/10/09/the-trump-biden-presidential-contest/ (accessed 11/3/2020); *The New York Times*, "National Exit Polls: How Different Groups Voted," November 18, 2020, www.nytimes.com/interactive/2020/11/03/us/elections/exit-polls-president.html?action=click&pgtype=Article&state=default&module=styln-elections-2020&region=TOP_BANNER&context=election_recirc (accessed 11/20/20).

25. Chris Alcantara, Scott Clement, and Emily Guskin, "Battleground District Poll: What Voters in Key Districts Said on Election Day," *Washington Post*, November 7, 2018, www.washingtonpost.com/graphics/2018/politics/midterm-battleground-districts/ (accessed 1/16/20).

26. Alec Tyson, "The 2018 Midterm Vote: Divisions by Race, Gender, Education," Pew Research Center, November 8, 2018, www.pewresearch.org/fact-tank/2018/11/08/the-2018-midterm-vote-divisions-by-race-gender-education/ (accessed 1/16/20); *The New York Times*, "National Exit Polls: How Different Groups Voted," November 18, 2020, www.nytimes.com/interactive/2020/11/03/us/elections/exit-polls-president.html?action=click&pgty

pe=Article&state=default&module=styln-elections-20
20&region=TOP_BANNER&context=election_recirc
(accessed 11/20/20).

27. Alex Leary, "Hispanics Voting in Record Numbers in Florida, Other States, Boosting Hillary Clinton," *Miami Herald*, November 6, 2016, www.miamiherald.com /news/politics-government/election/article112958953 .html (accessed 11/11/16).

28. Pew Research Center, "Religious Landscape Study: Party Affiliation," 2014, www.pewforum.org/religious-landscape -study/party-affiliation/ (accessed 1/16/20).

29. Alcantara, Clement, and Guskin, "Battleground District Poll."

30. Bartels, *Unequal Democracy*.

31. Pew Research Center, "Political Typology Reveals Deep Fissures on the Right and Left: Appendix 1: Typology Group Profiles," October 24, 2017, www.people-press.org /2017/10/24/appendix-1-typology-group-profiles-2/ (accessed 1/16/20).

32. Shaun Bowler, Gary Segura, and Stephen Nicholson, "Earthquakes and Aftershocks: Race, Direct Democracy, and Partisan Change," *American Journal of Political Science* 50 (January 2006): 146–59.

33. Pew Research Center, "Amid Campaign Turmoil, Biden Holds Wide Leads on Coronavirus, Unifying the Country"; *The New York Times*, "National Exit Polls: How Different Groups Voted."

34. Pew Research Center, "Partisan Antipathy."

35. Pew Research Center, "Partisan Antipathy."

36. Nathan P. Kalmoe and Lilliana Mason, "Lethal Mass Partisanship: Prevalence, Correlates, and Electoral Contingencies," presented at APSA 2018, www.dropbox.com /s/bs618kn939gq0de/Kalmoe%20%26%20Mason% 20APSA%202018%20-%20Lethal%20Mass%20 Partisanship.pdf.

37. Bruce Drake and Jocelyn Kiley, "Americans Say the Nation's Political Debate Has Grown More Toxic and 'Heated' Rhetoric Could Lead to Violence," Pew Research Center, July 18, 2019, www.pewresearch.org/fact-tank /2019/07/18/americans-say-the-nations-political-debate -has-grown-more-toxic-and-heated-rhetoric-could-lead -to-violence/ (accessed 1/16/20).

38. "CQ Roll Call's Vote Studies—2013 in Review," February 3, 2014, http://media.cq.com/votestudies/ (accessed 7/25/16).

39. David Hawkings, "Ahead, the First Pure Party-Line Modern Tax Cut?" Roll Call, October 31, 2017, www .rollcall.com/news/hawkings/party-line-tax-cut (accessed 8/15/18).

40. Benjamin Page and Martin Gilens, *Democracy in America: What Has Gone Wrong and What We Can Do about It* (Chicago: University of Chicago Press, 2017).

41. Donovan and Bowler, *Reforming the Republic*. See also Marty Gilens, *Affluence and Influence: Economic Inequality and Political Power in America* (Princeton, NJ: Princeton University Press, 2014).

42. Mason, *Uncivil Agreement*.

43. Stephen Skowronek, *Building a New American State: The Expansion of National Administrative Capacities, 1877–1920* (Cambridge: Cambridge University Press, 1982).

44. Stephen Gruber-Miller, "Chuck Grassley Says He Tried to Remind President That Tariffs 'Brought about Adolf Hitler,'?" *Des Moines Register*, May 15, 2019, www .desmoinesregister.com/story/news/politics/2019/05/15 /chuck-grassley-tariffs-donald-trump-brought-great -depression-hitler-world-war-2-smoot-hawley-trade /3683407002/ (accessed 1/16/20).

45. Thomas Mann and Norman J. Ornstein, *It's Even Worse Than It Looks: How the American Constitutional System Collided with the New Politics of Extremism* (New York: Basic Books, 2016).

46. For a discussion of third parties in the United States, see Daniel Mazmanian, *Third Parties in Presidential Elections* (Washington, DC: Brookings Institution Press, 1974).

47. See Maurice Duverger, *Political Parties* (New York: Wiley, 1954).

48. Donovan and Bowler, *Reforming the Republic*; André Blais, ed., *To Keep or to Change First Past the Post? The Politics of Election Reform* (New York: Oxford University Press, 2008).

49. Lee Drutman, *Breaking the Two-Party Doom Loop: The Case for Multiparty Democracy in America* (New York: Oxford University Press, 2020).

50. Todd Donovan, Caroline J. Tolbert, and Kellen Gracey, "Campaign Civility under Preferential and Plurality Voting," *Electoral Studies* 42 (2016): 157–63.

51. Stanley Kelley, Jr., Richard E. Ayres, and William Bowen, "Registration and Voting: Putting First Things First," *American Political Science Review* 61 (June 1967): 359–70.

CHAPTER 10

1. Associated Press, "Seattle Is Giving Voters $100 Worth of 'Democracy Vouchers' to Donate to Politicians," June 19, 2019, www.marketwatch.com/story/seattle-is-giving -voters-100-worth-of-democracy-vouchers-to-donate-to -politicians-2019-06-19 (accessed 8/3/19).

2. Sarah Kliff and Kenny Malone, "Seattle's Voucher Test Tried to Flood Local Politics with Small Money," NPR, December 21, 2018, www.npr.org/2018/12/21/679036745 /seattle-s-voucher-test-tried-to-flood-politics-with-small -money (accessed 8/3/19).

3. Associated Press, "Seattle Is Giving Voters $100."

4. Daniel Beekman, "Washington State Supreme Court Unanimously Upholds Seattle's Pioneering Democracy Vouchers Program," *Seattle Times*, July 11, 2019, www .seattletimes.com/seattle-news/politics/washington-state -supreme-court-unanimously-upholds-seattles-pioneering -democracy-vouchers-program/ (accessed 8/3/19).

5. Associated Press, "Seattle Is Giving Voters $100"; National Conference of State Legislatures, "Same Day Voter Registration," June 28, 2019, www.ncsl.org/research/elections-and-campaigns/same-day-registration.aspx (accessed 8/3/19).

6. Amber Phillips, "Is Split-Ticket Voting Officially Dead?" *Washington Post*, November 17, 2016, www.washingtonpost.com/news/the-fix/wp/2016/11/17/is-split-ticket-voting-officially-dead/?utm_term=.ace9dff09c60 (accessed 5/14/18).

7. Sarah Zimmerman, "Illinois Protecting against Russian Election Tampering," February 28, 2018, *U.S. News and World Reports*, www.usnews.com/news/best-states/illinois/articles/2018-02-28/illinois-protecting-against-russian-election-tampering (accessed 5/14/18).

8. *Baker v. Carr*, 369 U.S. 186 (1962); *Gray v. Sanders*, 372 U.S. 368 (1963); *Wesberry v. Sanders*, 376 U.S. 1 (1964); *Reynolds v. Sims*, 377 U.S. 533 (1964).

9. *Thornburg v. Gingles*, 478 U.S. 613 (1986).

10. Christopher Ingraham, "This Is the Best Explanation of Gerrymandering You Will Ever See. How to Steal an Election: A Visual Guide," *Washington Post*, March 1, 2015, www.washingtonpost.com/news/wonk/wp/2015/03/01/this-is-the-best-explanation-of-gerrymandering-you-will-ever-see/?utm_term=.97e9bcf9a627 (accessed 7/25/18).

11. "Reelection Rates over the Years," Center for Responsive Politics, www.opensecrets.org/overview/reelect.php (accessed 11/9/18).

12. Christopher Ingraham, "'Sprawling,' 'Rorschachian,' 'Corrosive' to Democracy: Pennsylvania's Top Court Condemns State's Gerrymandered Districts," *Washington Post*, February 8, 2018, www.washingtonpost.com/news/wonk/wp/2018/02/08/sprawling-rorschachian-corrosive-to-democracy-pas-top-court-condemns-states-gerrymandered-districts/?noredirect=on&utm_term=.a009cd0645f9 (accessed 7/25/18).

13. *Shaw v. Reno*, 509 U.S. 630 (1993).

14. David Redlawsk, Caroline J. Tolbert, and Todd Donovan, *Why Iowa? How Caucuses and Sequential Elections Improve the Presidential Nomination Process* (Chicago: University of Chicago Press, 2011).

15. Redlawsk, Tolbert, and Donovan, *Why Iowa?*

16. State legislatures determine the system by which electors are selected. Almost all states use this "winner-take-all" system. Maine and Nebraska, however, provide that one electoral vote goes to the winner in each congressional district and two electoral votes go to the winner statewide.

17. Jeffrey Karp and Caroline J. Tolbert, "Polls and Elections: Support for Nationalizing Presidential Elections," *Presidential Studies Quarterly* 40, no. 4 (2010): 771–93.

18. Todd Donovan and Shaun Bowler, *Reforming the Republic: Democratic Institutions for the New America* (Upper Saddle River, NJ: Pearson Press, 2003).

19. André Blais, *To Keep or to Change First Past the Post? The Politics of Electoral Reform* (Oxford: Oxford University Press, 2008).

20. Daniel Smith and Caroline J. Tolbert, *Educated by Initiative: The Effects of Direct Democracy on Citizens and Political Organizations in the American States* (Ann Arbor: University of Michigan Press, 2004).

21. Shaun Bowler, Todd Donovan, and Caroline J. Tolbert, *Citizens as Legislators: Direct Democracy in the United States* (Columbus: Ohio State University Press, 1998).

22. Ballotpedia, "2020 Ballot Measures," https://ballotpedia.org/2020_ballot_measures (accessed 11/23/20).

23. Stephen Nicholson, *Voting the Agenda: Candidates, Elections, and Ballot Propositions* (Princeton, NJ: Princeton University Press, 2005).

24. Ryan Grim and Sabrina Siddiqui, "Call Time for Congress Shows How Fundraising Dominates Bleak Work Life," Huffington Post, January 9, 2013, www.huffingtonpost.com/2013/01/08/call-time-congressional-fundraising_n_2427291.html (accessed 8/8/16).

25. "Most Expensive Races," Center for Responsive Politics, February 19, 2020, www.opensecrets.org/overview/topraces.php?cycle=2018&display=currcands (accessed 2/19/20).

26. Stephen Ansolabehere and James Snyder, "Campaign War Chests and Congressional Elections," *Business and Politics* 2 (2000): 9–34.

27. Gary W. Cox and Eric Magar, "How Much Is Majority Status in the U.S. Congress Worth?" *American Political Science Review* 93 (1999): 299–309.

28. "Two-Thirds of Presidential Campaign Is in Just 6 States," Nationalpopularvote.com, www.nationalpopularvote.com/campaign-events-2016 (accessed 5/14/18); Daron Shaw, *The Race to 270: The Electoral College and the Campaign Strategies of 2000 and 2004* (Chicago: University of Chicago Press, 2006).

29. Anna Massoglia and Ilma Hasan, "2020 Presidential Candidates' Political Ad Spending Floods Super Bowl," Center for Responsive Politics, January 31, 2020, www.opensecrets.org/news/2020/01/2020-political-super-bowl-ads-flood/ (accessed 2/12/20).

30. John Geer, *In Defense of Negativity: Attack Ads in Presidential Campaigns* (Chicago: University of Chicago Press, 2006).

31. Nicholas Confessore and Karen Yourish, "$2 Billion of Free Media for Donald Trump," *New York Times*, March 16, 2016, www.nytimes.com/2016/03/16/upshot/measuring-donald-trumps-mammoth-advantage-in-free-media.html (accessed 7/25/18).

32. Brian Stelter, "Debate Breaks Record as Most-Watched in U.S. History," CNN Money, September 27, 2016, www.money.cnn.com/2016/09/27/media/debate-ratings-record-viewership/ (accessed 10/17/16).

33. D. Sunshine Hillygus and Todd G. Shields, *The Persuadable Voter: Wedge Issues in Political Campaigns* (Princeton, NJ: Princeton University Press, 2009).

34. Sasha Issenberg, *The Victory Lab: The Secret Science of Winning Campaigns* (New York: Crown, 2012).

35. Alan S. Gerber and Donald P. Green, "The Effects of Canvassing, Telephone Calls, and Direct Mail on Voter Turnout: A Field Experiment," *American Political Science Review* 94, no. 3 (2000): 660.

36. M. Ostrogorski, *Democracy and the Organization of Political Parties* (New York: Macmillan, 1902).

37. For discussions of the consequences of this, see Thomas Edsall, *The New Politics of Inequality* (New York: W. W. Norton, 1984). See also Thomas Edsall, "Both Parties Get the Company's Money—but the Boss Backs the GOP," *Washington Post*, National Weekly Edition, September 16, 1986, 14; and Benjamin Ginsberg, "Money and Power: The New Political Economy of American Elections," in *The Political Economy*, eds. Thomas Ferguson and Joel Rogers (Armonk, NY: M. E. Sharpe, 1984).

38. OpenSecrets.org, "2020 Election to Cost $14 Billion, Blowing Away Spending Records," October 28, 2020, www.opensecrets.org/news/2020/10/cost-of-2020-election-14billion-update (accessed 11/15/20).

39. *Buckley v. Valeo*, 424 U.S. 1 (1976).

40. *Citizens United v. Federal Election Commission*, 558 U.S. 50 (2010).

41. *Citizens United*.

42. Martin Gilens, *Affluence and Influence: Economic Inequality and Political Power in America* (Princeton, NJ: Princeton University Press; New York: Russell Sage, 2012).

43. *McCutcheon et al. v. Federal Election Commission*, 572 U.S. 185 (2014).

44. OpenSecrets.org, Sen. Bernie Sanders, www.opensecrets.org/politicians/summary.php?cid=N00000528 (accessed 6/23/16).

45. *Buckley v. Valeo*.

46. Morris Fiorina, *Unstable Majorities* (Stanford, CA: Hoover Institution Press, 2017).

47. Josh Pacewicz, *Partisans and Partners* (Chicago: University of Chicago Press, 2016).

48. Kim Hart, "Most Democrats See Republicans as Racist, Sexist," *Axios*, November 12, 2018, www.axios.com/poll-democrats-and-republicans-hate-each-other-racist-ignorant-evil-99ae7afc-5a51-42be-8ee2-3959e43ce320.html (accessed 11/13/20).

49. Pew Research Center, "Campaign Engagement and Interest," July 7, 2016, www.people-press.org/2016/07/07/1-campaign-engagement-and-interest/ (accessed 11/13/20).

50. Noah Bierman, "Tensions Flare in Fight for Key States, and Trump Cheers a Truck Caravan Swarming a Biden Bus," *Los Angeles Times*, October 31, 2020, www.latimes.com/politics/story/2020-10-31/trump-biden-campaigns-turnout (accessed 11/15/20).

51. Nate Silver, "Biden's Favored in Our Final Presidential Forecast, But It's a Fine Line between a Landslide and a Nail-Biter," FiveThirtyEight, November 3, 2020, https://fivethirtyeight.com/features/final-2020-presidential-election-forecast/; Nathaniel Rakich, "Final Forecast: Democrats Have a 3-in-4 Chance of Flipping the Senate," FiveThirtyEight, November 3, 2020, https://fivethirtyeight.com/features/final-2020-senate-forecast/?cid=referral_taboola_feed; Geoffrey Skelley, "Final Forecast: Democrats Are Clear Favorites to Maintain Control of the House," FiveThirtyEight, November 3, 2020, https://fivethirtyeight.com/features/final-2020-house-forecast/?cid=referral_taboola_feed (accessed 11/15/20).

52. Silver, "Biden's Favored in Our Final Presidential Forecast."

53. United States Election Project, "2020 November General Election: Turnout Rates," November 10, 2020, www.electproject.org/2020g (accessed 11/11/20).

54. Holly Otterbein, "Democrats Return Nearly Three Times as Many Mail-In Ballots as Republicans in Pennsylvania," *Politico*, November 3, 2020, www.politico.com/news/2020/11/03/democrats-more-mail-in-ballots-pennsylvania-433951 (accessed 11/11/20).

55. Astead W. Herndon, "Conor Lamb, House Moderate, on Biden's Win, 'the Squad' and the Future of the Democratic Party," *New York Times*, November 8, 2020, www.nytimes.com/2020/11/08/us/politics/conor-lamb-democrats-biden.html (accessed 11/15/20).

56. "National Exit Polls: How Different Groups Voted," *New York Times*, www.nytimes.com/interactive/2020/11/03/us/elections/exit-polls-president.html (accessed 11/15/20).

57. "National Exit Polls: How Different Groups Voted."

58. "Election Week 2020: The Latino Youth Vote," Center for Information and Research on Civic Learning and Engagement, November 16, 2020, https://circle.tufts.edu/latest-research/election-week-2020 (accessed 11/17/20).

59. Wyatte Grantham-Philips, "One-Term Presidents: Trump Joins the List of Commanders-in-Chief Denied a Second Term," *USA Today*, November 7, 2020, www.usatoday.com/story/news/politics/elections/2020/10/30/one-term-presidents-u-s-presidents-who-ran-reelection-but-lost/6085465002/ (accessed 11/17/20).

CHAPTER 11

1. CNN "What's in the $2 Trillion Coronavirus Stimulus Bill," March 26, 2020, www.cnn.com/2020/03/25/politics/stimulus-package-details-coronavirus/index.html (accessed 3/28/20).

2. Caitlin Emma, Jennifer Scholtes, and Theodoric Meyer, "Who Got Special Deals in the Stimulus and Why They Got Them," Politico, March 27, 2020, www.politico.com/news/2020/03/26/stimulus-coronavirus-special-deals-151108 (accessed 3/28/20).

3. Emma et al., "Who Got Special Deals"; Jeff Stein, "What's in the $2.2 Trillion Coronavirus Senate Stimulus Package," *Washington Post,* March 26, 2020, www.washingtonpost.com/business/2020/03/26/senate-stimulus-bill-coronavirus-2-trillion-list-what-is-in-it/ (accessed 3/28/20).

4. CNN, "What's in the $2 Trillion Coronavirus Stimulus Bill."

5. Richard Rubin, "Who's Left Out of Coronavirus Stimulus Payments? Many College Students, Adult Dependents," *Wall Street Journal,* March 28, 2020 (accessed 3/28/20).

6. Alexis de Tocqueville, *Democracy in America*, ed. J. P. Mayer and trans. George Lawrence (New York: Harper Collins, [1835–40] 1988), 513.

7. Lee Drutman, *The Business of America Is Lobbying: How Corporations Became Politicized and Politics Became More Corporate* (New York: Oxford University Press, 2015).

8. Kay Lehman Schlozman, Henry E. Brady, and Sidney Verba, *Unequal and Unrepresented: Political Inequality and the People's Voice in the New Gilded Age* (Princeton, NJ: Princeton University Press, 2018), Table 8.3.

9. Center for Responsive Politics, "Lobbying Database: Ranked Sectors," www.opensecrets.org/lobby/top.php?showYear=2018&indexType=c (accessed 9/10/19).

10. Drutman, *The Business of America Is Lobbying*, 13.

11. Center for Responsive Politics, "Lobbying Database: Top Industries," www.opensecrets.org/lobby/top.php?showYear=a&indexType=I; and "Lobbying Database: Top Spenders," www.opensecrets.org/lobby/top.php?indexType=s&showYear=a (accessed 9/10/19).

12. Schlozman, Brady, and Verba, *Unequal and Unrepresented*, Table 8.3.

13. G. William Domhoff, "The Rise and Fall of Labor Unions in the U.S.," Who Rules America?, February 2013, https://whorulesamerica.ucsc.edu/power/history_of_labor_unions.html (accessed 9/10/19); and Bureau of Labor Statistics, "Union Members Summary," January 18, 2019, www.bls.gov/news.release/union2.nr0.htm (accessed 9/10/19).

14. Sean McElwee, "How Unions Boost Democratic Participation," *American Prospect*, September 16, 2015, https://prospect.org/article/how-unions-boost-democratic-participation (accessed 9/10/19).

15. *The Economist*, "Democratic Smiles in Pennsylvania's Special Election," March, 14, 2018, www.economist.com/democracy-in-america/2018/03/14/democratic-smiles-in-pennsylvanias-special-election (accessed 9/10/19).

16. Schlozman, Brady, and Verba, *Unequal and Unrepresented*, Table 8.3.

17. Anthony J. Nownes, *Interest Groups in American Politics*, 2nd ed. (New York: Routledge, 2013).

18. Schlozman, Brady, and Verba, *Unequal and Unrepresented*, Table 8.3.

19. Frank R. Baumgartner et al., *Lobbying and Policy Change* (Chicago: University of Chicago Press, 2009).

20. Jeffrey M. Berry, *The New Liberalism: The Rising Power of Citizen Groups*, 1st ed. (Washington, DC: Brookings Institution Press, 1999).

21. Baumgartner et al., *Lobbying and Policy Change*.

22. Schlozman, Brady, and Verba, *Unequal and Unrepresented*, Table 8.3.

23. Nownes, *Interest Groups in American Politics*, 28–32.

24. Nownes, *Interest Groups in American Politics*, 30.

25. See, for example, the Singles Section of the New Jersey Sierra Club: www.sierraclub.org/new-jersey/sierra-singles (accessed 9/4/19).

26. Martin Gilens and Benjamin I. Page, "Testing Theories of American Politics: Elites, Interest Groups, and Average Citizens," *Perspectives on Politics* 12, no. 3 (Sept. 2014): 564–81; Martin Gilens, *Affluence and Influence: Economic Inequality and Political Power in America* (Princeton, NJ: Princeton University Press, 2012); Benjamin I. Page and Martin Gilens, *Democracy in America? What Has Gone Wrong and What We Can Do about It* (Chicago: University of Chicago Press, 2017).

27. E. E. Schattschneider, *The Semisovereign People: A Realist's View of Democracy in America* (New York: Holt, Rinehart and Winston, 1960).

28. Kay Lehman Schlozman and John T. Tierney, *Organized Interests and American Democracy* (New York: Harper and Row, 1986), 60.

29. Karlyn Bowman, "Public Opinion on the Tax Cuts and Jobs Act of 2017," American Enterprise Institute, *Tax Notes*, July 9, 2018, www.aei.org/articles/public-opinion-on-the-tax-cuts-and-jobs-act-of-2017/ (accessed 9/8/19).

30. The Tax Cuts and Jobs Act: Preliminary Economic Analysis, December 18, 2017, www.taxfoundation.org/tax-cuts-and-jobs-act-preliminary-analysis/ (accessed 4/5/18).

31. David Truman, *The Governmental Process* (New York: Knopf, 1951).

32. For an exploration of lower-class interest groups and social movements, see Frances Piven and Richard Cloward, *Poor People's Movements* (New York: Vintage, 1978).

33. Center for Responsive Politics, "Lobbying Database," www.opensecrets.org/lobby/ (accessed 6/10/20).

34. See Sean McMinn and Kate Ackley, "Lobbying Hits $3.9 Billion in Trump's First Year," Roll Call, January 23, 2018, www.rollcall.com/news/politics/lobbying-trump-first-year; and Derek Kravitz and Alex Mierjeski, "Trump's Appointees Pledged Not to Lobby After They Leave. Now They're Lobbying," ProPublica, May 3, 2018, www.propublica.org/article/trump-appointees-pledged-not-to-lobby-after-they-leave-now-lobbying (accessed 9/5/19).

35. U.S. PIRG, "Lobbyist Registrations Hit 18-Year Low," January 30, 2017, https://uspirg.org/news/usp/lobbyist-registrations-hit-18-year-low (accessed 9/5/19).

36. Tim LaPira, "How Much Lobbying Is There in Washington? It's DOUBLE What You Think," Sunlight Foundation, November 25, 2013, https://sunlightfoundation.com/2013/11/25/how-much-lobbying-is-there-in-washington-its-double-what-you-think/ (accessed 9/8/19).

37. For discussions of lobbying, see Allan J. Cigler and Burdett A. Loomis, eds., *Interest Group Politics* (Washington, DC: CQ Press, 1983). See also Jeffrey M. Berry, *Lobbying for the People* (Princeton, NJ: Princeton University Press, 1977).

38. On procedural advice from former-lawmakers-turned-lobbyists, see Timothy LaPira and Herschel F. Thomas III, *Revolving Door Lobbying: Public Service, Private Influence, and the Unequal Representation of Interests* (Lawrence: University Press of Kansas, 2017).

39. Brookings Institution, *Vital Statistics on Congress*, Table 5.1, March 4, 2019, www.brookings.edu/multi-chapter-report /vital-statistics-on-congress/ (accessed 9/5/19).

40. Drutman, *The Business of America Is Lobbying*, 33–34.

41. Christine Stapleton, "Trump's Mar-a-Lago Transitions from Society Galas to Political Hub," *Palm Beach Daily News*, May 10, 2019, www.palmbeachdailynews.com /news/20190510/trumps-mar-a-lago-transitions-from -society-galas-to-political-hub (accessed 3/28/20); Luke Darby, "Political Group Spending at Trump Hotels Rocketed Up to $19 Million," *GQ*, November 11, 2019, www.gq.com/story/trump-hotels-millions-from-politics (accessed 3/28/20).

42. For an excellent discussion of the political origins of the Administrative Procedure Act, see Martin Shapiro, "APA: Past, Present, Future," *Virginia Law Review* 72, no. 477 (March 1986): 447–92.

43. *Brown v. Board of Education of Topeka, Kansas*, 347 U.S. 483 (1954).

44. *Obergefell v. Hodges*, 576 U.S. — (2015).

45. *Webster v. Reproductive Health Services*, 492 U.S. 490 (1989).

46. Drutman, *The Business of America Is Lobbying*, 16.

47. Mike Spies and Ashley Balcerzak, "The NRA Placed Big Bets on the 2016 Election, and Won Almost All of Them," OpenSecrets News, November 9, 2016, www .opensecrets.org/news/2016/11/the-nra-placed-big-bets -on-the-2016-election-and-won-almost-all-of-them/ (accessed 9/5/19); OpenSecrets.org, "National Rifle Assn," November 5, 2020 (accessed 11/5/20).

48. Martin Gilens, *Affluence and Influence: Economic Inequality and Political Power in America* (Princeton, NJ: Princeton University Press, 2012).

49. *Citizens United v. Federal Election Commission*, 558 U.S. — (2010); Center for Responsive Politics, "Behind the Candidates: Campaign Committees and Outside Groups," www.opensecrets.org/pres16/raised-summ (accessed 4/6/18).

50. Michael J. Malbin and Brendan Glavin, "CFI's Guide to Money in Federal Elections: 2016 in Historical Context," Table 1-7, Campaign Finance Institute, 2018, www .cfinst.org/pdf/federal/2016Report/CFIGuide_Moneyin FederalElections.pdf (accessed 9/11/19).

51. Malbin and Glavin, "CFI's Guide to Money in Federal Elections," Tables 2-8 and 2-9.

52. Center for Responsive Politics, "2020 Election to Cost $14 Billion, Blowing Away Spending Records," October 28, 2020, www.opensecrets.org/news/2020/10/cost-of-2020 -election-14billion-update (accessed 11/6/20).

53. Russell Berman, "The November Surprise," *The Atlantic*, October 7, 2020; Patrick Svitek, "GOP Super PAC Focused on Voter Registration Builds Massive Organization," *Texas Tribune*, February 1, 2020, www.texastribune.org /2020/02/01/engage-texas-super-pac-voter-registration/ (accessed 11/6/20).

54. Elisabeth R. Gerber, *Populist Paradox: Interest Group Influence and the Promise of Direct Legislation* (Princeton, NJ: Princeton University Press, 1999).

55. *The Federalist Papers, no.* 10.

56. Nownes, *Interest Groups in American Politics*, 171–73.

57. Eric Lipton and Alexander Burns, "The True Source of the N.R.A.'s Clout: Mobilization, Not Donations," *New York Times*, February 24, 2016, www.nytimes .com/2018/02/24/us/politics/nra-gun-control-florida .html?searchResultPosition=1 (accessed 9/10/19).

58. Robert Maguire, "Audit Shows NRA Spending Surged $100 Million amidst Pro-Trump Push in 2016," Center for Responsive Politics, November 15, 2017, www .opensecrets.org/news/2017/11/audit-shows-nra-spending -surged-100-million-amidst-pro-trump-push-in-2016/ (accessed 7/27/18).

59. Theda Skocpol, *Diminished Democracy: From Membership to Management in American Civic Life* (Norman: University of Oklahoma Press, 2003).

60. Christine Day, *AARP: America's Largest Interest Group and Its Impact* (Westport, CT: Praeger, 2017).

61. Matt Grossman, *The Not-So-Special Interests: Interest Groups, Public Representation, and American Governance* (Stanford, CA: Stanford University Press, 2012).

62. Drutman, *The Business of America Is Lobbying*, 16.

63. Drutman, *The Business of America Is Lobbying*.

64. Nownes, *Interest Groups in American Politics*.

65. Jacob S. Hacker and Paul Pierson, *Winner-Take-All Politics: How Washington Made the Rich Richer, and Turned Its Back on the Middle Class* (New York: Simon and Schuster, 2010).

66. Richard L. Hall and Frank W. Wayman, "Buying Time: Moneyed Interests and the Mobilization of Bias in Congressional Committees," *American Political Science Review* 84 (1990): 797–820.

67. Kevin M. Esterling, *The Political Economy of Expertise: Information and Efficiency in American National Politics* (Ann Arbor: University of Michigan Press, 2004).

68. Amy McKay and Susan Webb Yackee, "Interest Group Competition on Federal Agency Rules," *American Politics Research* 35, no. 3 (May 2007): 336–57.

69. This paragraph is based on Baumgartner et al., *Lobbying and Policy Change*.

70. LaPira and Thomas, *Revolving Door Lobbying*.

71. Ida A. Brudnick, "Congressional Salaries and Allowances: In Brief," Congressional Research Service, April 11, 2018, www.senate.gov/CRSpubs/9c14ec69-c4e4-4bd8-8953 -f73daa1640e4.pdf (accessed 9/24/19).

72. David Kirkpatrick, "Congress Finds Ways of Avoiding Lobbyist Limits," *Washington Post*, February 11, 2007, 1.

73. Drutman, *The Business of America Is Lobbying*, 226–27.
74. Mancur Olson, *The Logic of Collective Action* (Cambridge, MA: Harvard University Press, 1965).

CHAPTER 12

1. Emily Flitter, "Small Businesses Will Get Help Paying Workers, If They Can Wait," *New York Times,* March 26, 2020, www.nytimes.com/2020/03/26/business/coronavirus-stimulus-small-business.html (accessed 3/26/20).
2. This account from Kate Zezima and Colby Itkowitz, "Flailing on Fentanyl," *Washington Post*, September 20, 2019, www.washingtonpost.com/graphics/2019/investigations/fentanyl-epidemic-congress/?wpisrc=nl_most&wpmm=1 (accessed 11/18/19); Sharyn Alfonsi, "Cops Bring Addiction Counselor on Drug Raids to Fight Opioid Crisis," CBS News, June 16, 2019, www.cbsnews.com/news/cops-bring-addiction-counselor-on-drug-raids-to-fight-opioid-crisis/ (accessed 11/18/19); Colby Itkowitz, "Senate Easily Passes Sweeping Opioids Legislation, Sending to President Trump," *Washington Post*, October 3, 2018, www.washingtonpost.com/politics/2018/10/03/senate-is-poised-send-sweeping-opioids-legislation-president-trump/ (accessed 11/18/19).
3. David Mayhew, *Congress: The Electoral Connection* (New Haven, CT: Yale University Press, 1974).
4. Author's calculations based on election results.
5. Jennifer E. Manning, *Membership of the 116th Congress: A Profile* (Washington, DC: Congressional Research Service, March 31, 2020), https://fas.org/sgp/crs/misc/R45583.pdf (accessed 4/8/20).
6. Jennifer E. Manning, *Membership of the 116th Congress: A Profile* (Washington, DC: Congressional Research Service, March 31, 2020), https://fas.org/sgp/crs/misc/R45583.pdf (accessed 4/8/20).
7. Manning, *Membership of the 116th Congress.*
8. For a discussion, see Benjamin Ginsberg, *The Consequences of Consent* (New York: Random House, 1982), chap. 1.
9. See Kristen D. Burnett, *Congressional Apportionment*, U.S. Census Bureau, November 2011, www.census.gov/prod/cen2010/briefs/c2010br-08.pdf (accessed 1/23/12). For some interesting empirical evidence, see Angus Campbell et al., *Elections and the Political Order* (New York: Wiley, 1966), chap. 11; for more recent considerations about the relationship between members of Congress and their constituents, see Lawrence Jacobs and Robert Y. Shapiro, *Politicians Don't Pander: Political Manipulation and the Loss of Democratic Responsiveness* (Chicago: University of Chicago Press, 2000); and Larry M. Bartels, *Unequal Democracy: The Political Economy of the New Gilded Age* (Princeton, NJ: Princeton University Press, 2008).
10. Norman J. Ornstein et al., *Vital Statistics on Congress* (Washington, DC: Brookings Institution Press, 2017), Tables 5–3 and 5–4, www.brookings.edu/,/media/Research/Files/Reports/2013/07/vital-statistics-congress-mann-ornstein/Vital-Statistics-Full-Data-Set.pdf?la5en (accessed 3/22/18); Norman J. Ornstein, Thomas E. Mann, and Michael J. Malbin, *Vital Statistics on Congress 2008* (Washington, DC: Brookings Institution Press, 2009), 111–12.
11. Ashley Parker, "Spotlighting Constituents to Buoy Congressional Candidates," *New York Times*, October 8, 2014, www.nytimes.com/2014/10/09/us/politics/out-of-the-mouths-of-constituents-candidates-find-a-message.html (accessed 9/14/15); Juana Summers, "Constituent Services Give Voters Something to Remember," NPR, www.npr.org/2014/10/28/359615965/constituent-services-give-voters-something-to-remember (accessed 9/14/15).
12. Linda Fowler and Robert McClure, *Political Ambition: Who Decides to Run for Congress* (New Haven, CT: Yale University Press, 1989); and Alan Ehrenhalt, *The United States of Ambition: Politicians, Power, and the Pursuit of Office* (New York: Three Rivers Press, 1992).
13. Center for Responsive Politics, "Incumbent Advantage," www.opensecrets.org/elections-overview/reelection-rates (accessed 11/15/20).
14. Center for Responsive Politics, "Reelection Rates over the Years," www.opensecrets.org/overview/reelect.php (accessed 2/18/20).
15. Autumn Johnson, "Union Sanitary District Dedicates New Green Energy Facility," Patch, April 6, 2015, https://patch.com/california/unioncity/union-sanitary-district-dedicates-new-green-energy-facility (accessed 2/18/20).
16. Diana Evans, *Greasing the Wheels: Using Pork Barrel Projects to Build Majority Coalitions in Congress* (New York: Cambridge University Press, 2004).
17. Mayhew, *Congress: The Electoral Connection.*
18. Mark Hugo Lopez and Paul Taylor, "The 2010 Congressional Reapportionment and Latinos," Pew Research Center, www.pewhispanic.org/2011/01/05/the-2010-congressional-reapportionment-and-latinos/ (accessed 2/24/14).
19. Eric McGhee, "Are the Democrats Still at a Disadvantage in Redistricting?" *Monkey Cage* (blog), July 9, 2013, https://themonkeycage.org/2013/07/09/are-the-democrats-still-at-a-disadvantage-in-redistricting/ (accessed 12/2/13).
20. Royce Crocker, *Congressional Redistricting: An Overview* (Washington, DC: Congressional Research Service, November 21, 2012), www.fas.org/sgp/crs/misc/R42831.pdf (accessed 12/2/13).
21. Adam Liptak, "Supreme Court Rebuffs Lawmakers over Independent Redistricting Plan," *New York Times*, June 29, 2015, www.nytimes.com/2015/06/30/us/supreme-court-upholds-creation-of-arizona-redistricting-commission.html?_r50 (accessed 9/14/15).
22. *Rucho v. Common Cause*, 588 U.S.__(2019).
23. R. E. Cohen, "Did Redistricting Sink the Democrats?" *National Journal*, December 17, 1994, 2984.
24. *Miller v. Johnson*, 515 U.S. 900 (1995).

25. *Abbott v. Perez*, 585 U.S. __ (2018).

26. Richard Fenno, Jr., *Home Style: House Members in Their Districts* (Boston: Little, Brown, 1978).

27. Derek Willis, "Republicans Mix It Up When Assigning House Chairmen for the 108th," *Congressional Quarterly Weekly*, January 11, 2003, 89.

28. Rebecca Kimitch, "CQ Guide to the Committees: Democrats Opt to Spread the Power," *Congressional Quarterly Weekly*, April 16, 2007, 1080.

29. Richard E. Cohen, "Crackup of the Committees," *National Journal*, July 31, 1999, 2210–16.

30. See, for example, the announcement of an agreement on the Agricultural Act of 2014, House Committee on Agriculture, "House–Senate Negotiators Announce Bipartisan Agreement on Final Farm Bill," press release, http://agriculture.house.gov/news/documentsingle .aspx?DocumentID51220 (accessed 9/21/15).

31. Norman J. Ornstein et al., *Vital Statistics on Congress* (Washington, DC: Brookings Institution and American Enterprise Institute, July 2013), chap. 5, www.brookings .edu/research/reports/2013/07/vital-statistics-congress -mann-ornstein (accessed 6/13/16).

32. "Statistics and Historical Comparisons: Bills by Final Status," govtrack.us, www.govtrack.us/congress/bills /statistics (accessed 9/21/15).

33. Jonathan Weisman, "House Votes 411–18 to Pass Ethics Overhaul," *Washington Post*, August 1, 2007, A1.

34. Leigh Munsil, "Graham Won't Lift Nominee-Hold Threat over Benghazi," Politico, November 11, 2013, www.politico.com/blogs/politico-live/2013/11/graham -wont-lift-nomineehold-threat-over-benghazi-177154 .html (accessed 11/30/13).

35. Sean Sullivan and Mike DeBonis, "Congress Averts Home-land Security Shutdown with One-Week Extension," *Washington Post*, February 28, 2015, www.washingtonpost.com /politics/house-gop-hopes-to-pass-stopgap-dhs-funding -before-midnight-shutdown/2015/02/27/22021530 -be88-11e4-b274-e5209a3bc9a9_story.html (accessed 9/21/15).

36. Lindsey McPherson, "Paul Ryan Talks Up Return to Regular Order," Roll Call, December 16, 2015, www .rollcall.com; see also "A Better Way: Our Vision for a Confident America," issued by Speaker Ryan's office and the Republican leadership of the House of Representatives, June 16, 2016, www.gop.gov/wp-content/uploads/2016 /07/ABetterBooklet_update.pdf.

37. Barbara Sinclair, *Unorthodox Lawmaking: New Legislative Processes in the U.S. Congress* (Washington, DC: Sage/CQ Press, 2012).

38. Walter Oleszek, *Congressional Procedures and the Policy Process* (Washington, DC: CQ Press, 2019), 170.

39. Oleszek, *Congressional Procedures,* 182.

40. CRS, 30; also see Doug Andres, "Congress and Why Process Matters" (master's thesis, Johns Hopkins University, 2015).

41. National Priorities Project, "Federal Budget Process," https://www.nationalpriorities.org/budget-basics/federal -budget-101/federal-budget-process/ (accessed 3/16/2020); see also Judy Schneider and Michael Koempel, Congressional Deskbook (Washington, DC: TheCapitol.Net, 6th ed., 2012), 322–23; and Oleszek, *Congressional Procedures*, 73–76.

42. David M. Herszenhorn, "Failed Spending Bills Pile Up in Senate as Budget Agreement Breaks Down," *New York Times*, July 12, 2016, A11.

43. John W. Kingdon, *Congressmen's Voting Decisions* (New York: Harper and Row, 1973), chap. 3; and R. Douglas Arnold, *The Logic of Congressional Action* (New Haven, CT: Yale University Press, 1990).

44. Eric Lipton and Ben Protess, "Banks' Lobbyists Help in Drafting Financial Bills," *New York Times*, May 23, 2013, dealbook.nytimes.com/2013/05/23/banks-lobbyists -help-in-drafting-financial-bills/ (accessed 9/21/15); Michael Corkery, "Citigroup Becomes the Fall Guy in the Spending Bill Battle" *New York Times*, December 12, 2014, dealbook.nytimes.com/2014/12/12/citigroup-becomes-the -fall-guy-in-the-spending-bill-battle/ (accessed 9/21/15).

45. Norman J. Ornstein and Thomas E. Mann, *Vital Statistics on Congress* (Washington, DC: Brookings Institution, 2018), Table 6-4.

46. "115th Congress (2017–2018)," www.congress.gov (accessed 11/9/18).

47. Thomas Kaplan, "Congress Approves $1.3 Trillion Spending Bill, Averting a Shutdown," *New York Times*, March 22, 2018, www.nytimes.com/2018/03/22/us/politics/house -passes-spending-bill.html?login=email&auth=login -email (accessed 7/30/18).

48. Geoffrey C. Layman, Thomas M. Carsey, and Juliana Menasce Horowitz, "Party Polarization in American Politics: Characteristics, Causes, and Consequences," *Annual Review of Political Science* 9 (2006): 83–110.

49. For example, Fredreka Schouten, "Club for Growth Plans New Push in House Races," *USA Today*, August 17, 2015, http://onpolitics.usatoday.com/2015/08/17/club-for -growth-plans-new-push-in-house-races/ (accessed 9/21/15).

50. Eric Lipton and Sheryl Gay Stolberg, "Health Law Rollout Provides Rich Target for Oversight Chief," *New York Times*, November 12, 2013, www.nytimes.com/2013/11/13/us /politics/health-law-rollout-provides-rich-target-for -oversight-chief.html?_r50 (accessed 12/12/13).

51. Michael S. Schmidt and Maggie Haberman, "Aides for Hillary Clinton and Benghazi Committee Dispute Testimony Plan," *New York Times*, July 25, 2015, www .nytimes.com/2015/07/26/us/clinton-to-testify-publicly -before-house-committee-investigating-benghazi-attacks .html (accessed 9/21/15).

52. *United States v. Pink*, 315 U.S. 203 (1942).

53. *United States v. Pink*, 315 U.S. 203 (1942). For a good discussion of the problem, see James W. Davis, *The American Presidency* (New York: Harper and Row, 1987), chap. 8.

54. U.S. House, "Impeachment," http://history.house.gov /Institution/Origins-Development/Impeachment/ (accessed 4/18/14).

1. Craig Spencer, "Utilizing the Defense Production Act Will Save Health Care Workers' Lives," *The Hill,* March 28, 2020, https://thehill.com/opinion/healthcare/489976-utilizing-the-defense-production-act-will-save-health-care-workers-lives (accessed 4/1/20).

2. Zolan Kanno-Youngs and Ana Swanson, "Wartime Law Has Been Used Routinely by Trump," *New York Times,* April 1, 2020; Li Zhou, 'How Congress Could Force Trump to Use the Defense Production Act," Vox, March 25, 2020, https://www.vox.com/2020/3/25/21191600/congress-defense-production-act-trump (accessed 4/2/20).

3. Ana Swanson, "Peter Navarro Has Antagonized Multinational Companies. Now He's in Charge," *New York Times,* April 6, 2020, www.nytimes.com/2020/04/06/business/economy/peter-navarro-coronavirus-defense-production-act.html (accessed 4/7/20).

4. These statutes are contained mainly in Title 10 of the U.S. Code, Sections 331, 332, and 333.

5. The best study covering all aspects of the domestic use of the military is that of Adam Yarmolinsky, *The Military Establishment* (New York: Harper and Row, 1971). Probably the most famous instance of a president's unilateral use of the power to protect a state "against domestic violence" was President Grover Cleveland's dealing with the Pullman strike of 1894. The famous Supreme Court case that ensued was *In re Debs,* 158 U.S. 564 (1895).

6. In *United States v. Pink,* 315 U.S. 203 (1942), the Supreme Court confirmed that an executive agreement is the legal equivalent of a treaty, despite the absence of Senate approval. This case approved the executive agreement that was used to establish diplomatic relations with the Soviet Union in 1933. An executive agreement, not a treaty, was used in 1940 to exchange "fifty over-age destroyers" for 99-year leases on some important military bases.

7. *United States v. Nixon,* 418 U.S. 683 (1974).

8. For a different perspective, see William F. Grover, *The President as Prisoner: A Structural Critique of the Carter and Reagan Years* (Albany: State University of New York Press, 1988).

9. A third source of presidential power is implied from the provision for "faithful execution of the laws." This is the president's power to impound funds—that is, to refuse to spend money Congress has appropriated for certain purposes. One author referred to this as a "retroactive veto power" (Robert E. Goostree, "The Power of the President to Impound Appropriated Funds," *American University Law Review* 11 [January 1962]: 32–47). This impoundment power has been used freely and to considerable effect by many modern presidents, and Congress has occasionally delegated such power to the president by statute. But in reaction to the Watergate scandal, Congress adopted the Congressional Budget and Impoundment Control Act of 1974, which was designed to circumscribe the president's ability to impound funds by requiring that the president spend all appropriated funds unless both houses of Congress consented to an impoundment within 45 days of a presidential request. Therefore, since 1974, the use of impoundment has declined significantly. Presidents have had either to bite their tongues and accept unwanted appropriations or to revert to the older and more dependable but politically limited method of vetoing the entire bill.

10. For more on the veto, see Robert J. Spitzer, *The Presidential Veto: Touchstone of the American Presidency* (Albany: State University of New York Press, 1989).

11. Dan Eggen, "Bush Announces Veto of Waterboarding Ban," *Washington Post,* March 8, 2008, www.washingtonpost.com/wp-dyn/content/article/2008/03/08AR2008030800304.html (accessed 6/10/10).

12. John Yoo, *The Powers of War and Peace* (Chicago: University of Chicago Press, 2003). See also Dana D. Nelson, "The 'Unitary Executive' Question," *Los Angeles Times,* October 11, 2008, www.latimes.com/opinion/la-oe-nelson11-2008oct11-story.html (accessed 4/20/18).

13. See Eric Posner and Adrian Vermeule, *The Executive Unbound: After the Madisonian Republic* (Chicago: University of Chicago Press, 2011).

14. "Unchecked Abuse," *Washington Post,* January 11, 2006, www.washingtonpost.com/wp-dyn/content/article/2006/01/10/AR2006011001536.html (accessed 3/25/18).

15. Elena Kagan, "Presidential Administration," *Harvard Law Review* 114 (June 2001): 2262.

16. Kenneth F. Warren, *Administrative Law,* 3rd ed. (Upper Saddle River, NJ: Prentice-Hall, 1996), 250.

17. Theodore J. Lowi, *The End of Liberalism,* 2nd ed. (New York: W. W. Norton, 1979), 117.

18. Louis Fisher, "The Unitary Executive and Inherent Executive Power," *Journal of Constitutional Law* 12, no. 1 (February 2010): 586.

19. 10 Annals of Cong. 613 (1800).

20. Louis Fisher, "Presidential Inherent Power: The 'Sole Organ' Doctrine," *Presidential Studies Quarterly* 37, no. 1 (March 2007): 139.

21. *United States v. Curtiss-Wright Corp.,* 299 U.S. 304 (1936).

22. Clement Fatovic, *Outside the Law: Emergency and Executive Power* (Baltimore: Johns Hopkins University Press, 2009).

23. Louis Fisher, "Invoking Inherent Powers."

24. John Gramlich, "Holder Sees Constitutional Basis for Obama's Executive Actions," Roll Call, January 29, 2014, www.rollcall.com/news/holder_sees_constitutional_basis_for_obamas_executive_actions-230528-1.html?pg=1 (accessed 4/20/18).

25. Harold C. Relyea, "National Emergency Powers," Congressional Research Service, 2007, http://fas.org/sgp/crs/natsec/98-505.pdf (accessed 3/27/18).

26. Matthew Crenson and Benjamin Ginsberg, *Presidential Power: Unchecked and Unbalanced* (New York: W. W. Norton, 2007), 341–42.

27. Andrew Reeves, "Political Disaster: Unilateral Powers, Electoral Incentives, and Presidential Disaster Declarations," *Journal of Politics* 73, no. 4 (October 2011): 1142–51.

28. A substantial portion of this section is taken from Theodore J. Lowi, *The Personal President* (Ithaca, NY: Cornell University Press, 1985), 141–50.

29. The actual number is difficult to estimate because, as with White House staff, some EOP personnel, especially in national security work, are detailed to the EOP from outside agencies.

30. Article I, Section 3, provides that "the Vice-President . . . shall be President of the Senate, but shall have no Vote, unless they be equally divided." This is the only vote the vice president is allowed.

31. White House, "Be Best," www.whitehouse.gov/bebest/ (accessed 3/17/20).

32. Samuel Kernell, *Going Public: New Strategies of Presidential Leadership*, 3rd ed. (Washington, DC: CQ Press, 1997); also Jeffrey K. Tulis, *The Rhetorical Presidency* (Princeton, NJ: Princeton University Press, 1987).

33. James MacGregor Burns, *Roosevelt: The Lion and the Fox* (New York: Harcourt, Brace, 1956), 317.

34. Kernell, *Going Public*, 79.

35. Claire Cain Miller, "How Obama's Internet Campaign Changed Politics," *New York Times*, November 7, 2008, https://bits.blogs.nytimes.com/2008/11/07/how-obamas-internet-campaign-changed-politics/ (accessed 4/7/14); David Plouffe, *The Audacity to Win: The Inside Story and Lessons of Barack Obama's Historic Victory* (New York: Viking, 2009).

36. "Presidential Job Approval Center," Gallup, www.gallup.com/poll/124922/presidential-approval-center.aspx (accessed 3/14/14).

37. Lowi, *Personal President*.

38. Lowi, *Personal President*, 11.

39. Gallup, "Trump Job Approval," October 27, 2020, https://news.gallup.com/poll/203207/trump-job-approval-weekly.aspx (accessed 10/27/20).

40. Sidney M. Milkis, *The President and the Parties* (New York: Oxford University Press, 1993), 128.

41. Milkis, *President and the Parties*, 160.

42. Kagan, "Presidential Administration," 2265.

43. John M. Broder, "Powerful Shaper of U.S. Rules Quits, with Critics in Wake," *New York Times*, August 4, 2012, A1.

44. Nadja Popovich, Livia Albeck-Ripka, and Kendra Pierre-Louis, "85 Environmental Rules Being Rolled Back under Trump," *New York Times*, September 12, 2019, www.nytimes.com/interactive/2019/climate/trump-environment-rollbacks.html (accessed 10/4/19).

45. Terry M. Moe and William G. Howell, "The Presidential Power of Unilateral Action," *Journal of Law, Economics and Organization* 15, no. 1 (January 1999): 133–34.

46. Harold C. Relyea, "Presidential Directives: Background and Overview," Congressional Research Service, November 26, 2008, http://fas.org/sgp/crs/misc/98-611.pdf (accessed 3/25/18).

47. Adam L. Warber, *Executive Orders and the Modern Presidency* (Boulder, CO: Lynne Rienner Publishers, 2006), 118–20.

48. Vivian S. Chu and Ted Garvey, "Executive Orders: Issuance, Modification, and Revocation," Congressional Research Service, April 16, 2014, http://fas.org/sgp/crs/misc/RS20846.pdf (accessed 3/25/18).

49. Chu and Garvey, "Executive Orders," 10.

50. *Dames & Moore v. Regan*, 453 U.S. 654 (1981).

51. Philip Cooper, *By Order of the President* (Lawrence: University Press of Kansas, 2002), 201.

52. Edward S. Corwin, *The President: Office and Powers*, 5th ed. (New York: NYU Press, 1984), 283.

53. Scott R. Anderson, "What to Make of Trump's NDAA Signing Statement," Lawfare, August 23, 2018, www.lawfareblog.com/what-make-trumps-ndaa-signing-statement (accessed 10/4/19).

54. Terry Moe, "The Presidency and the Bureaucracy: The Presidential Advantage," in *The Presidency and the Political System*, ed. Michael Nelson (Washington, DC: CQ Press, 2002), 416–20.

55. *National Labor Relations Board v. Noel Canning*, 573 U.S. 513 (2014).

CHAPTER 14

1. This account from Alexis C. Madrigal and Robinson Meyer, "How the Coronavirus Became an American Catastrophe," *The Atlantic*, March 21, 2020, www.theatlantic.com/health/archive/2020/03/how-many-americans-are-sick-lost-february/608521/ (accessed 4/3/20); Sheri Fink and Mike Baker, "'It's Just Everywhere Already': How Delays in Teseting Set Back the U.S. Coronavirus Response," *New York Times*, March 10, 2020, www.nytimes.com/2020/03/10/us/coronavirus-testing-delays.html (accessed 4/3/20); and Conor Friedersdorf, "The Government Is Failing by Doing Too Little, and Too Much," *The Atlantic*, March 26, 2020, www.theatlantic.com/ideas/archive/2020/03/two-kinds-pandemic-failures/608767/ (accessed 3/26/20).

2. Amy B. Zegart, *Spying Blind: The CIA, The FBI, and the Origins of 9/11* (Princeton, NJ: Princeton University Press, 2009).

3. Paul C. Light, "A Cascade of Failures: Why Government Fails, and How to Stop It," Brookings Institution, July 14, 2014, www.brookings.edu/research/a-cascade-of-failures-why-government-fails-and-how-to-stop-it/ (accessed 8/5/17).

4. OSHA National News Release, "U.S. Department of Labor's OSHA and CDC Issue Interim Guidance to Protect Workers in Meatpacking and Processing Industries," April 26, 2020, www.osha.gov/news/newsreleases/national/04262020 (accessed 5/4/20).

5. Juliet Eilperin, "EPA Needed More Data before Ruling on Greenhouse Gas Emissions, Report Says," *Washington Post*, September 28, 2011, www.washingtonpost.com /national/health-science/epa-needed-more-data-before -ruling-on-greenhouse-gas-emissions-report-says/2011 /09/28/gIQABs2X5K_story.html (accessed 1/2/12).

6. Thanks to Andy Rudalevige for this formulation.

7. Environmental Protection Agency, "Regulations and Standards: Light Duty," www3.epa.gov/otaq/climate /regs-light-duty.htm#new1 (accessed 7/9/16).

8. Nathan Rott and Jennifer Ludden, "Trump Administration Weakens Auto Emissions Standards," NPR March 31, 2020, www.npr.org/2020/03/31/824431240 /trump-administration-weakens-auto-emissions-rolling -back-key-climate-policy (accessed 4/21/20); Ella Nilsen, "Trump Just Started A Huge Legal Battle With California Over Lowering Car Emission Standards," Vox, September 18, 2019, www.vox.com/policy-and -politics/2019/9/18/20872226/trump-california-car -emission-standards (accessed 4/21/20).

9. Margaret Cronin Fisk et al., "Volkswagen Agrees to $15 Billion Diesel-Cheating Settlement," Bloomberg News, June 28, 2016, www.bloomberg.com/news/articles /2016-06-28/volkswagen-to-pay-14-7-billion-to-settle-u-s -emissions-claims (accessed 7/8/16).

10. Gary Bryner, *Bureaucratic Discretion* (New York: Pergamon Press, 1987).

11. Nicholas Bagley, "Legal Limits and the Implementation of the Affordable Care Act," *University of Pennsylvania Law Review* 164, no. 7 (2016): 1715–52.

12. Li Zhou, "Many Small Businesses Are Being Shut Out of a New Loan Program by Major Banks," *Vox*, April 7, 2020, www.vox.com/2020/4/7/21209584/paycheck-protection -program-banks-access (accessed 5/4/20).

13. Office of Management and Budget, Historical Tables, "Table 16.2, Total Executive Branch Civilian Full-Time Equivalent (FTE) Employees, 1981–2020," www.whitehouse .gov/omb/historical-tables/ (accessed 12/12/19).

14. Congressional Research Service, "Selected Homeland Security Issues in the 116th Congress," November 26, 2019, https://fas.org/sgp/crs/homesec/R45701.pdf (accessed 12/10/19).

15. For example, see Government Accountability Office, "High-Risk Series: Substantial Efforts Needed to Achieve Greater Progress on High-Risk Areas," March 2019, www.gao.gov/assets/700/697245.pdf (accessed 12/10/19).

16. Joseph A. Pika, John Anthony Maltese, and Andrew C. Rudalevige, *The Politics of the Presidency*, 9th ed. (Washington, DC: CQ Press, 2016), 315.

17. For more details and evaluations, see David Rosenbloom, *Public Administration* (New York: Random House, 1986), 186–221; Charles H. Levine and Rosslyn S. Kleeman, *The Quiet Crisis of the Civil Service: The Federal Personnel System at the Crossroads* (Washington, DC: National Academy of Public Administration, 1986).

18. Partnership for Public Service, Center for Presidential Transition, "Appointments: Incoming Administration," December 18, 2018, https://presidentialtransition.org /workstream/appointments (accessed 12/9/19).

19. Matt Ford, "An Administration Run by Temp Workers," *New Republic*, June 19, 2019, https://newrepublic.com /article/154243/trump-administration-cabinet-acting -department-secretaries (accessed 12/9/19).

20. Congressional Budget Office, "Comparing the Compensation of Federal and Private-Sector Employees, 2011–2015," April 2017, www.cbo.gov/system/files/115th-congress-2017 -2018/reports/52637-federalprivatepay.pdf (accessed 12/20/17).

21. Vice President Gore's National Partnership for Reinventing Government, "Appendix F, History of the National Partnership for Reinventing Government: Accomplishments, 1993–2000, A Summary," http://govinfo.library.unt.edu /npr/whoweare/appendixf.html (accessed 3/28/08).

22. President Barack Obama, First Inaugural Address, January 21, 2009, https://obamawhitehouse.archives.gov/blog /2009/01/21/president-barack-obamas-inaugural-address (accessed 8/5/17).

23. Kate Rogers, "USDA's Plan to Relocate Research Agencies to the Midwest Unleashes a Brain Drain," CNBC, July 22, 2019, www.cnbc.com/2019/07/22/usdas-plan-to-move -research-agencies-to-midwest-starts-a-brain-drain.html (accessed 11/14/19).

24. Office of Personnel Management, "Executive Branch Civilian Employment Since 1940," www.opm.gov/policy -data-oversight/data-analysis-documentation/federal -employment-reports/historical-tables/executive-branch -civilian-employment-since-1940/ (accessed 4/24/20); United States Postal Service, "Number of Postal Employees Since 1926," https://about.usps.com/who-we-are/postal -history/employees-since-1926.pdf (accessed 4/24/20); George M. Reynolds and Amanda Shendruk, "Demographics of the U.S. Military," Council on Foreign Relations, April 24, 2018, www.cfr.org/article/demographics-us -military (accessed 10/13/18).

25. Bureau of Labor Statistics, Current Employment Statistics, "Table B-1a, Employees on Nonfarm Payrolls by Industry Sector and Selected Industry Detail, Seasonally Adjusted," www.bls.gov/web/empsit/ceseeb1a.htm (accessed 4/21/20).

26. John J. Dilulio, Jr., *Bring Back the Bureaucrats: Why More Federal Workers Will Lead to Better (and Smaller!) Government* (West Conshohocken, PA: Templeton Press, 2014); Kimberly J. Morgan and Andrea Louise Campbell, *The Delegated Welfare State* (New York: Oxford University Press, 2011).

27. Jennifer L. Selin and David E. Lewis, *Sourcebook of United States Executive Agencies*, 2nd ed. (Washington, DC: Administrative Conference of the United States, 2018).

28. Marjorie Censer, "Five Provisions in the New Defense Policy Legislation for Contractors to Watch," *Washington Post*, January 5, 2014, www.washingtonpost.com/business /capitalbusiness/five-provisions-in-the-new-defense

-policy-legislation-for-contractors-to-watch/2014/01/0/f6dd00ec-6c10-11e3-a523-fe73f0ff6b8d_story.html (accessed 1/24/14).

29. Charlie Savage, "U.S. to Phase Out Use of Private Prisons for Federal Inmates," *New York Times*, August 18, 2016, www.nytimes.com/2016/08/19/us/us-to-phase-out-use-of-private-prisons-for-federal-inmates.html (accessed 11/8/17).

30. Peter Baker, "Obama Orders Federal Contractors to Provide Workers Paid Sick Leave," *New York Times*, September 7, 2015, www.nytimes.com/2015/09/08/us/politics/obama-to-require-federal-contractors-to-provide-paid-sick-leave.html (accessed 9/30/15).

31. Gregory Korte, "Trump Signs Four Bills to Roll Back Obama-Era Regulations," *USA Today*, March 27, 2017, www.usatoday.com/story/news/politics/2017/03/27/trump-signs-four-bills-roll-back-obama-era-regulations/99690456/ (accessed 11/8/17).

32. William G. Howell, *An American Presidency: Institutional Foundations of Executive Politics* (Boston: Pearson, 2015), 246.

33. Richard E. Neustadt, *Presidential Power and the Modern Presidents: The Politics of Leadership from Roosevelt to Reagan* (New York: Free Press, 1990), 29.

34. Daniel P. Gitterman, *Calling the Shots: The President, Executive Orders, and Public Policy* (Washington, DC: Brookings Institution Press, 2017).

35. Alan Rappeport, "Andrew Puzder Withdraws from Consideration as Labor Secretary," *New York Times*, February 15, 2017, www.nytimes.com/2017/02/15/us/politics/andrew-puzder-withdrew-labor-secretary.html (accessed 11/4/19).

36. Selin and Lewis, *Sourcebook of United States Executive Agencies*, 121.

37. Selin and Lewis, *Sourcebook of United States Executive Agencies*, 121.

38. Terry M. Moe, "The Politics of Bureaucratic Structure," in *Can the Government Govern?*, eds. John E. Chubb and Paul E. Peterson (Washington, DC: Brookings Institution Press, 1989).

39. Adam Andrzejewski, "Trump's Leaner White House 2019 Payroll Has Already Saved Taxpayers $20 Million," *Forbes*, June 28, 2019, www.forbes.com/sites/adamandrzejewski/2019/06/28/trumps-leaner-white-house-2019-payroll-has-already-saved-taxpayers-20-million/#5a991169386d (accessed 12/12/19); White House, "Statement from the Press Secretary Regarding the President's Coronavirus Task Force," January 29, 2020, hwww.whitehouse.gov/briefings-statements/statement-press-secretary-regarding-presidents-coronavirus-task-force/ (accessed 5/4/20).

40. Selin and Lewis, *Sourcebook of United States Executive Agencies*, 27.

41. David M. Cohen, "Amateur Government: When Political Appointees Manage the Federal Bureaucracy," (CPM Working Paper 96-1, Brookings Institution, 1996), www.brookings.edu/wp-content/uploads/2016/06/amateur.pdf (accessed 12/12/19).

42. Howell, *An American Presidency*.

43. Selin and Lewis, *Sourcebook of United States Executive Agencies*, 34.

44. Food and Drug Administration, "Learn about FDA Advisory Committees," June 21, 2018, www.fda.gov/patients/learn-about-patient-affairs-staff/learn-about-fda-advisory-committees (accessed 12/12/19).

45. Linette Lopez and Lydia Ramsey, "'You Asked for It'—Congress Railed on the Maker of EpiPen," Business Insider, September 21, 2016, www.businessinsider.com/mylan-ceo-heather-bresch-house-oversight-committee-hearing-epipen-2016-9 (accessed 11/9/17); see Mathew D. McCubbins and Thomas Schwartz, "Congressional Oversight Overlooked: Police Patrols versus Fire Alarms," *American Journal of Political Science* 28, no. 1 (1984): 165–79.

46. Charlie Savage and Peter Baker, "Trump Ousts Pandemic Spending Watchdog Known for Independence," *New York Times*, April 7, 2020; Peter Baker, "Trump Moves to Replace a Watchdog Who Irked Him," *New York Times*, May 2, 2020.

47. The Office of Technology Assessment was a fourth research agency serving Congress until 1995. It was one of the first agencies scheduled for elimination by the 104th Congress. Until 1983, Congress had still another tool of legislative oversight: the legislative veto. Each agency operating under such provisions was obliged to submit to Congress every proposed decision or rule, which would then lie before both chambers for 30 to 60 days. If Congress took no action by one-house or two-house resolution explicitly to veto the proposed measure during the prescribed period, the measure became law. The legislative veto was declared unconstitutional by the Supreme Court in 1983 on the grounds that it violated the separation of powers—the resolutions Congress passed to exercise its veto were not subject to presidential veto, as required by the Constitution. See *Immigration and Naturalization Service v. Chadha*, 462 U.S. 919 (1983).

48. Government Accountability Office, "About GAO," www.gao.gov/about/ (accessed 12/8/19).

49. Congressional Research Service, "About CRS," www.loc.gov/crsinfo/about/ (accessed 12/8/19).

50. Congressional Budget Office, "Introduction to CBO," www.cbo.gov/about/overview (accessed 12/8/19).

51. Consumer Financial Protection Bureau, "Creating the Consumer Bureau," www.consumerfinance.gov/about-us/the-bureau/creatingthebureau/ (accessed 12/7/19); NPR, "How the Consumer Financial Protection Bureau Came into Creation," November 28, 2017, www.npr.org/2017/11/28/567057893/how-the-consumer-financial-protection-bureau-came-into-creation (accessed 12/7/19).

52. Selin and Lewis, *Sourcebook of United States Executive Agencies*, 38.

53. Andrew Prokop, "Read: The Whistleblower Complaint about Trump and Ukraine," Vox, September 26, 2019, www.vox.com/2019/9/26/20884022/whistleblower-complaint-trump-ukraine-read (accessed 11/14/19).

54. See Aram A. Gavoor and Daniel Miktus, "Oversight of Oversight: A Proposal for More Effective FOIA Reform," *Catholic University Law Review* 66, no. 3 (Spring 2017): 528.

55. Alison Young, "Congress Demands Details of Secret CDC Lab Incidents Revealed by USA Today," *USA Today*, January 17, 2017, www.usatoday.com/story/news /2017/01/17/congress-wants-details-of-cdc-lab-accidents /96551636/ (accessed 11/14/19).

56. U.S. Department of Veterans Affairs, "Veterans Access, Choice, and Accountability Act of 2014 Fact Sheet," www .va.gov/opa/choiceact/documents/choice-act-summary .pdf (accessed 8/6/17).

57. Dominic Gates, "Flawed Analysis, Failed Oversight: How Boeing, FAA Certified the Suspect 737 MAX Flight Control System," *Seattle Times*, March 17, 2019, www .seattletimes.com/business/boeing-aerospace/failed -certification-faa-missed-safety-issues-in-the-737-max -system-implicated-in-the-lion-air-crash/ (accessed 11/4/19).

58. Selin and Lewis, *Sourcebook of United States Executive Agencies*, 85–87.

CHAPTER 15

1. This account draws from Austin Berg, "Meet the Man Who Could End Forced Union Fees for Government Workers," Illinois Policy, 2018, www.illinoispolicy.org /story/meet-the-man-who-could-end-forced-union-fees -for-government-workers/ (accessed 3/3/18); and P. R. Lockhart, "What the Latest Union Case before the Supreme Court Could Mean for Workers of Color," Vox, February 26, 2018, www.vox.com/policy-and-politics /2018/2/26/17053328/janus-afscme-supreme-court -unions-minorities (accessed 3/3/18).

2. *Abood v. Detroit Board of Education*, 431 U.S. 209 (1977).

3. U.S. Courts Statistical Tables, www.uscourts.gov/statistics -reports/analysis-reports/statistical-tables-federal-judiciary (accessed 9/19/15).

4. Michael A. Fletcher, "Obama Criticized as Too Cautious, Slow on Judicial Posts," *Washington Post*, October 16, 2009, www.washingtonpost.com/wp-dyn/content/article /2009/10/15/AR2009101504083.html (accessed 3/1/10).

5. John Bowden, "Timeline: Brett Kavanaugh's Nomination to the Supreme Court," The Hill, October 6, 2018, https://thehill.com/homenews/senate/410217-timeline -brett-kavanaughs-nomination-to-the-supreme-court (accessed 10/16/18).

6. *Marbury v. Madison*, 5 U.S. 137 (1803).

7. *National Federation of Independent Business v. Sebelius*, 567 U.S. __ (2012).

8. "Acts of Congress Held Unconstitutional in Whole or in Part by the Supreme Court of the United States," General Printing Office, www.gpo.gov/fdsys/pkg/GPO-CONAN -2013/pdf/GPO-CONAN-2013-11.pdf (accessed 4/20/14).

9. *Federal Election Commission v. Wisconsin Right to Life*, 551 U.S. 449 (2007); *McCutcheon v. Federal Election Commission*, 572 U.S. 185 (2014).

10. This review power was affirmed by the Supreme Court in *Martin v. Hunter's Lessee*, 14 U.S. 304 (1816).

11. *Brown v. Board of Education*, 347 U.S. 483 (1954).

12. *Lawrence v. Texas*, 539 U.S. 558 (2003).

13. *Pavan v. Smith*, 582 U.S. __ (2017).

14. *Alabama Legislative Black Caucus v. Alabama*, 575 U.S. __ (2015).

15. *Arizona State Legislature v. Arizona Independent Redistricting Commission*, 576 U.S. __ (2015).

16. *Cooper v. Harris*, 581 U.S. __ (2017).

17. *United States v. Jones*, 565 U.S. __ (2012).

18. *Riley v. California*, 573 U.S. 373 (2014).

19. Emergency Price Control Act, 56 Stat. 23 (1942).

20. *Hamdi v. Rumsfeld*, 542 U.S. 507 (2004).

21. *National Labor Relations Board v. Noel Canning*, 573 U.S. 513 (2014).

22. *Trump v. Hawaii*, 585 U.S. __ (2018).

23. *Roe v. Wade*, 410 U.S. 113 (1973).

24. Robert Scigliano, *The Supreme Court and the Presidency* (New York: Free Press, 1971), 162. For an interesting critique of the solicitor general's role during the Reagan administration, see Lincoln Caplan, "Annals of the Law," *New Yorker*, August 17, 1987, 30–62.

25. Edward Lazarus, *Closed Chambers* (New York: Times Books, 1998), 6.

26. *Smith v. Allwright*, 321 U.S. 649 (1944).

27. *Obergefell v. Hodges*, 576 U.S. __ (2015).

28. Charles Krauthammer, "Why Roberts Did It," *Washington Post*, June 29, 2012, www.washingtonpost.com/opinions /charles-krauthammer-why-roberts-did-it/2012/06/28 /gJQA4X0g9V_story.html (accessed 4/22/14).

29. *Griswold v. Connecticut*, 381 U.S. 479 (1965).

30. *McCutcheon v. Federal Election Commission*, 572 U.S. 185 (2014).

31. R. W. Apple, Jr., "A Divided Government Remains, and with It the Prospect of Further Combat," *New York Times*, November 7, 1996, B6.

32. For limits on judicial power, see Alexander Bickel, *The Least Dangerous Branch* (Indianapolis, IN: Bobbs-Merrill, 1962).

33. *Worcester v. Georgia*, 31 U.S. 515 (1832).

34. Walter Murphy, *Congress and the Court* (Chicago: University of Chicago Press, 1962).

35. Robert Dahl, "The Supreme Court and National Policy Making," *Journal of Public Law* 6 (1958): 279.

36. Martin Shapiro, "The Supreme Court: From Warren to Burger," in *The New American Political System*, ed. Anthony King (Washington, DC: American Enterprise Institute, 1978).

37. *Citizens to Preserve Overton Park v. Volpe*, 401 U.S. 402 (1971).

38. See "Developments in the Law—Class Actions," *Harvard Law Review* 89 (1976): 1318.

39. *In re Agent Orange Product Liability Litigation*, 100 F.R.D. 718 (E.D.N.Y. 1983).

40. Donald Horowitz, *The Courts and Social Policy* (Washington, DC: Brookings Institution Press, 1977).

41. *Morgan v. McDonough*, 540 F2d 527 (1 Cir., 1976; *cert. denied*, 429 U.S. 1042 [1977]).

42. Alexander Hamilton, James Madison, and John Jay, *The Federalist Papers*, ed. Clinton Rossiter (New York: New American Library, 1961), no. 10, 78.

Answer Key

Chapter 1
1. d
2. c
3. c
4. c
5. d
6. e
7. a
8. d
9. b
10. e
11. c
12. d
13. b

Chapter 2
1. b
2. a
3. b
4. c
5. e
6. c
7. c
8. d
9. b
10. e
11. e
12. b
13. a
14. b
15. a

Chapter 3
1. c
2. c
3. b
4. e
5. a

6. c
7. d
8. b
9. b
10. b
11. a
12. d
13. d
14. b
15. e

Chapter 4
1. a
2. c
3. b
4. e
5. b
6. a
7 e
8. b
9. b
10. d
11. a
12. e
13. c
14. a
15. d

Chapter 5
1. b
2. e
3. a
4. c
5. b
6. d
7. a
8. a

9. d
10. a
11. d
12. a
13. d
14. c
15. d

Chapter 6
1. c
2. c
3. a
4. d
5. e
6. d
7. c
8. e
9. a
10. c
11. c
12. b
13. a
14. b
15. e

Chapter 7
1. b
2. a
3. b
4. c
5. e
6. d
7. c
8. c
9. a
10. b
11. b

12. e
13. b
14. c
15. c

Chapter 8
1. a
2. b
3. d
4. d
5. e
6. e
7. a
8. d
9. d
10. d
11. c
12. d
13. b
14. c
15. d

Chapter 9
1. a
2. c
3. d
4. b
5. d
6. e
7. a
8. d
9. c
10. e
11. e
12. e
13. d
14. d
15. a

Chapter 10
1. c
2. e
3. e
4. c
5. c
6. b
7. c
8. b
9. d
10. a
11. d
12. b
13. a
14. a
15. c

Chapter 11
1. d
2. c
3. b
4. c
5. d
6. b
7. d
8. d
9. a
10. e
11. c
12. a
13. d
14. b
15. e

Chapter 12
1. b
2. a
3. d

4. c
5. c
6. a
7. a
8. d
9. b
10. b
11. d
12. e
13. a
14. b
15. a

Chapter 13
1. a
2. c
3. b
4. b
5. b
6. c
7. b
8. a
9. a
10. c
11. c
12. b
13. d
14. d
15. a

Chapter 14
1. d
2. b
3. c
4. c
5. c
6. d
7. c
8. a
9. a
10. d
11. a
12. c
13. e

Chapter 15
1. a
2. c
3. a
4. c
5. d
6. d
7. e
8. e
9. c
10. a
11. b
12. a
13. a
14. c
15. c

Credits

PHOTOGRAPHS

Front Matter: Page vi: Paul Hennessy/NurPhoto via Getty Images; p. vii (top): Alex Wong/Getty Images; p. vii (bottom): Bing Guan/Bloomberg via Getty Images; p. viii: Anthony Pidgeon/Redferns/Getty Images; p. ix (top): Scott Mcintyre/The New York Times/Redux; p. ix (bottom): Jay Mallin/ZUMAPRESS.com/Alamy Live News; p. x: Jabin Botsford/The Washington Post via Getty Images; p. xi (top): Darwin BondGraham/BerkeleySide; p. xi (bottom): Rod Lamkey /Getty Images; p. xii: AP Photo/Elaine Thompson; p. xiii (top): Stefani Reynolds/Bloomberg via Getty Images; p. xiii (bottom): Ryan Fisher/The Herald-Dispatch via AP; p. xiv: Leonard Ortiz/MediaNews Group/Orange County Register via Getty Images; p. xv (top): John Vicory; p. xv (bottom): AP Photo/Andrew Harnik; p. xvi (top): Dan Koeck/Reuters/Newscom; p. xvi (bottom): Spencer Platt/Getty Images; p. xvii: Jerry Hotl/TNS via ZUMA Wire.

Chapter 1: Page 2: Shutterstock; p. 3 (left): Paul Hennessy/NurPhoto via Getty Images; p. 3 (right): Air National Guard photo by Master Sgt. Christopher Schepers; p. 7: Bettmann/Corbis via Getty Images; p. 8: Bettmann/Corbis via Getty Images; p. 10 (left): Erik McGregor/Pacific Press/LightRocket via Getty Images; p. 10 (right): Alex Milan Tracy/Sipa via AP Images; p. 11 (left): Christopher Brown via ZUMA Press, Inc./Alamy Stock Photo; p. 11 (right): Megan Jelinger/SOPA Images/ZUMA Wire/Alamy Live News; p. 12: Library of Congress; p. 13: Courtesy of April Lawson; p. 14 (left): Rue des Archives/Granger NYC — All rights reserved; p. 14 (right): Paul Ratje/AFP via Getty Images; p. 18: Reproduced by permission of The Economist Intelligence Unit; p. 21: Bettmann/Corbis via Getty Images; p. 23 (left): Christian Hansen/The New York Times/Redux;

p. 23 (right): Scott Sommerdorf/The Salt Lake Tribune via AP; p. 24: Frederic J. Brown/AFP via Getty Images; p. 26: AP Photo/Patrick Semansky; p. 28: 2016 U.S. Department of Education Office of Federal Student Aid; p. 30 (top): Paul Hennessy/NurPhoto via Getty Images; p. 30 (bottom): Air National Guard photo by Master Sgt. Christopher Schepers.

Chapter 2: Page 34: Shutterstock; p. 35: Alex Wong/Getty Images; p. 37: Granger NYC — All rights reserved; p. 39: IanDagnall Computing/Alamy Stock Photo; p. 42: Sarin Images/Granger NYC — All rights reserved; p. 43: Howard Sun/Alamy Stock Photo; p. 44: Samuel Jennings (active 1789-1834). *Liberty Displaying the Arts and Sciences, or The Genius of America Encouraging the Emancipation of the Blacks*, 1792. Oil on canvas. 60 1/4" x 74" Library Company of Philadelphia. Gift of the artist, 1792; p. 48: Billion Photos/Shutterstock; p. 54: Library of Congress; p. 56: Paul J. Richards/AFP/Getty Images; p. 60: Alex Wong/Getty Images; p. 63: Alex Wong/Getty Images.

Chapter 3: Page 68: rehab-icons/Shutterstock; p. 69 (left): Bing Guan/Bloomberg via Getty Images; p. 69 (right): White House Photo/Alamy Stock Photo; p. 74: AP Photo/Adam Beam; p. 77 (left): Courtesy of Domingo Morel; p. 77 (right): Derek Davis/Portland Portland Press Herald via Getty Images; p. 80: Library of Congress; p. 81: Library of Congress; p. 86: AP Photo/Sue Ogroki; p. 88: Ilene MacDonald/Alamy Stock Photo; p. 89: Homeland Security Photo/Alamy Stock Photo; p. 92 (left): AP Photo/Skip Foreman; p. 92 (right): Max Faulkner/Fort Worth Star-Telegram/Tribune News Service via Getty Images; p. 94 (top): Bing Guan/Bloomberg via Getty Images; p. 94 (bottom): White House Photo/Alamy Stock Photo.

Chapter 4: Page 98: Shutterstock; p. 99: Anthony Pidgeon/Redferns/Getty Images; p. 107: Jerry Holt/Star Tribune via Getty Images; p. 108 (left): Gary Tramontina/Getty Images; p. 108 (right): Gary Tramontina/Getty Images; p. 109: Chip Somodevilla/Getty Images; p. 110: Everett Collection/Alamy Stock Photo; p. 113: Chine Nouvelle/SIPA/Newscom; p. 114: Josh Edelson/AFP via Getty Images; p. 115: Clay Good/ZUMA Press; p. 116: Michael S. Williamson/The Washington Post via Getty Images; p. 117 (left): Saul Loeb/AFP/Getty Images; p. 117 (right): Baikal/Alamy Stock Photo; p. 119: Sandy Huffaker/Getty Images; p. 124: AP Photo/Matt York; p. 125: Bettmann/Getty Images; p. 127: Tracy A. Woodward/The Washington Post via Getty Images; p. 130: Stefani Reynolds/CNP/MediaPunch/Alamy Stock Photo; p. 133: Anthony Pidgeon/Redferns/Getty Images.

Chapter 5: Page 138: Shutterstock; p. 139: Scott Mcintyre/The New York Times/Redux; p. 141 (left): Lanmas/Alamy Stock Photo; p. 141 (right): Historic Collection/Alamy Stock Photo; p. 143: World History Archive/Alamy Stock Photo; p. 144: Library of Congress; p. 145 (left): Library of Congress; p. 145 (right): Underwood Photo Archives/Superstock; p. 147: Bettmann/Getty Images; p. 150 (left): Bettmann/Getty Images; p. 150 (right): AP Photo/File; p. 151 (left): AP Photo; p. 151 (right): Octavio Jones/Tampa Bay Times/ZUMA Wire/Alamy Live News; p. 157 (top): Francis Miller/The LIFE Picture Collection via Getty Images; p. 157 (bottom): Ann Johansson/The New York Times/Redux Pictures; p. 162 (left): Dina Rudick/The Boston Globe via Getty Images; p. 162 (right): Robin Alam/Icon Sportswire via Getty Images; p. 163 (left): AP Photo/Ron Edmonds; p. 163 (right): Scott Olson/Getty Images; p. 166 (left): Kent Sievers/The World-Herald via AP; p. 166 (right): Alex Milan Tracy/Sipa via AP Images; p. 167: John Moore/Getty Images; p. 168: John Moore/Getty Images; p. 170: Eliot Elisofon/The LIFE Picture Collection via Getty Images; p. 173: Alex Wong/Getty Images; p. 176: Scott Mcintyre/The New York Times/Redux.

Chapter 6: Page 180: Shutterstock; p. 181 (left): Jay Mallin/ZUMAPRESS.com/Alamy Live News; p. 181 (right): Tom Brenner/The New York Times/Redux; p. 187: HANDOUT/MCT/Newscom; p. 188: WDC Photos/Alamy Stock Photo; p. 190: Amy Harris/Shutterstock; p. 191 (top): Gabriel Olsen/WireImage/Getty Images; p. 191 (bottom): Thomas A. Ferrara/Newsday RM via Getty Images; p. 194 (left): Alex Wong/Getty Images; p. 194 (right): Ed Lefkowicz Photography; p. 200 (left): Everett Collection Historical/Alamy Stock Photo; p. 200 (right): Twitter/@realDonaldTrump; p. 202 (left): Saul Loeb/AFP/Getty Images; p. 202 (right): Twitter/@realDonaldTrump; p. 205: Alex Wong/Getty Images; p. 206: Jaap Arriens/NurPhoto via Getty Images; p. 208: Calvin And Hobbes © 1994 Watterson. Reprinted with permission of Andrews McMeel Syndication. All rights reserved; p. 210: Bo Rader/The Wichita Eagle via AP File; p. 212: Courtesy of Neil Newhouse/Public Opinions Strategies; p. 213: Courtesy of American Broadcasting Company, Inc.; p. 217 (left): Bettmann/Getty Images; p. 217 (right): Lionel Hahn/ABACAPRESS.com/Sipa via AP Images; p. 221 (top): Jay Mallin/ZUMAPRESS.com/Alamy Live News; p. 221 (bottom): Tom Brenner/The New York Times/Redux.

Chapter 7: Page 226: Shutterstock; p. 227: Jabin Botsford/The Washington Post via Getty Images; p. 231: Drew Angerer/Getty Images; p. 232: Mario Tama/Getty Images; p. 236 (left): Mike Blake/REUTERS/Newscom; p. 236 (right): Mandel Ngan/AFP/Getty Images; p. 241: Courtesy of RealClear Politics; p. 244: Twitter/@realDonaldTrump and @JoeBiden; p. 245: Jeff Dean/AFP via Getty Images; p. 246 (left): AP Photo/David Zalubowski; p. 246 (right): Brendan Smialowski/Getty Images; p. 247 (top): dpa picture alliance/Alamy Stock Photo; p. 247 (bottom): Courtesy of Politifact/Poynter Institute; p. 249 (left): Paul Marotta/Getty Images; p. 249 (right): AP Photo/Richard Drew; p. 254: Charles Moore/Getty Images; p. 256: Paul Davey/Barcroft Images/Barcroft Media via Getty Images; p. 257: AP Photo/Nick Ut; p. 258: AP Photo/Mary Altaffer; p. 259: Jabin Botsford/The Washington Post via Getty Images.

Chapter 8: Page 264: Shutterstock; p. 265 (left): Darwin BondGraham/BerkeleySide; p. 265 (right): Neal Waters/Anadolu Agency via Getty Images; p. 268 (left): Richard Ellis/Alamy Stock Photo; p. 268 (right): Tribune Content Agency LLC/Alamy Stock Photo; p. 269 (left): Samuel Corum/Anadolu Agency/Getty Images; p. 269 (right): Crush Rush/Alamy Stock Photo; p. 270: Bettmann/Getty Images; p. 276 (top): Xinhua/Eyevine/Redux; p. 276 (bottom): The Photo Works/Alamy Stock Photo; p. 277: Inked Pixels/Shutterstock; p. 280: Logan Cyrus/AFP via Getty Images; p. 284 (left): Marco Bello/AFP via Getty Images; p. 284 (right): Jessica McGowan/Getty Images; p. 288 (left): Alex Edelman/AFP via Getty Images; p. 288 (right): Sean Rayford/Getty Images; p. 290: Michael B. Thomas/Getty Images; p. 291: Smith Collection/Gado/Getty Images; p. 294: Courtesy of

Maggie Bush; p. 295: Keith Bell/Alamy Stock Photo; p. 298: AP Photo/Elaine Thompson; p. 299 (top): Darwin BondGraham/BerkeleySide; p. 299 (bottom): Neal Waters/Anadolu Agency via Getty Images.

Chapter 9: Page 304: Shutterstock; p. 305: Rod Lamkey/Getty Images; p. 308 (left): Justin Merriman/Bloomberg via Getty Images; p. 308 (right): Chris Crook/Times Recorder via AP, Pool; p. 311: Barry Chin/The Boston Globe via Getty Images; p. 312: Bill Clark/CQ-Roll Call, Inc via Getty Images; p. 315 (left): AP Photo/Carolyn Kaster; p. 315 (right): Erin Scott/Pool via CNP/AdMedia/Newscom; p. 316: Bettmann/Getty Images; p. 317 (top): Bettmann/Getty Images; p. 317 (bottom): Paul J. Richards /AFP /Getty Images; p. 319: Mike Theiler/UPI/Alamy Live News; p. 324: Ethan Miller/Getty Images; p. 325 (left): Erin Scott/Bloomberg via Getty Images; p. 325 (right): Chandan Khanna/AFP via Getty Images; p. 332: Granger NYC — All rights reserved; p. 334: Granger NYC — All rights reserved; p. 336: AP Photo; p. 337 (left): Drew Angerer/Getty Images; p. 337 (right): Jim Thompson/The Albuquerque Journal via AP; p. 340: Rod Lamkey /Getty Images.

Chapter 10: Page 344: Shutterstock; p. 345: AP Photo/Elaine Thompson; p. 347 (left): Bettmann Archive/Getty Images; p. 347 (right): Bettmann Archive/Getty Images; p. 349 (left): Marc Serota/Reuters/Newscom; p. 349 (right): Nicholas Kamm/AFP/Getty Images; p. 351 (left): Granger NYC — All rights reserved; p. 351 (right): OpenStreetMap contributors; p. 353: Scott Olson/Getty Images; p. 355: Graeme Sloan/Sipa USA/Alamy Live News; p. 361: Saul Loeb/AFP via Getty Images; p. 365: Courtesy of Sam Lozier; p. 365: Sean Rayford/Getty Images; p. 366: Chip Somodevilla/Getty Images; p. 367 (left): Bettmann/Getty Images; p. 367 (right): Morry Gash/UPI/Alamy Live News; p. 368: Mark Makela/Getty Images; p. 370: Jay Mallin/ZUMAPRESS; p. 376: Leigh Vogel/Getty Images for MoveOn; p. 378: Xinhua/Alamy Live News; p. 380: Sam Wolfe/Bloomberg via Getty Images; p. 384: Kent Nishimura/Los Angeles Times via Getty Images; p. 386: Angela Weiss/AFP via Getty Images; p. 388: Michael Loccisano/Getty Images for Food Bank for New York City; p. 389: Andrew Harnik-Pool/Getty Images; p. 394: AP Photo/Elaine Thompson.

Chapter 11: Page 394: Shutterstock; p. 395 (left): Stefani Reynolds/Bloomberg via Getty Images; p. 395 (right): Joe Raedle/Getty Images; p. 397: AP Photo/Sue Ogrocki; p. 401: AP Photo/Robert F. Bukaty; p. 403 (left): Chris Langford Photography; p. 403 (right): Glen Stubbe/Minneapolis Star Tribune/ZUMA Wire/Alamy Live News; p. 406 (left): Matthew Busch/Bloomberg via Getty Images; p. 406 (right): Amanda Cowan/The Columbian via AP; p. 407: AP Photo/Bloomington Herald-Times/Jeremy Hogan; p. 410 (left): AP Photo/Alex Brandon; p. 410 (right): AP Photo/Jacquelyn Martin; p. 411: Chip Somodevilla/Getty Images; p. 413: U.S. Food and Drug Administration; p. 417: Theresa McCracken/www.CartoonStock.com; p. 418 (left): Steve Schapiro/Corbis via Getty Images; p. 418 (right): North County Times/ZUMAPRESS.com/Alamy Stock Photo; p. 419 (left): Tomas Abad/Alamy Stock Photo; p. 419 (right): Justin Sullivan/Getty Images; p. 420: Stefani Reynolds/Bloomberg via Getty Images; p. 424 (top): Stefani Reynolds/Bloomberg via Getty Images; p. 424 (bottom): Joe Raedle/Getty Images.

Chapter 12: Page 428: Shutterstock; p. 429: Ryan Fisher/The Herald-Dispatch via AP; p. 432: Bettmann/Getty Images; p. 433: Michael Brochstein/Sipa USA/AP Images; p. 436: Twitter/@AOC; p. 443: AP Photo/Ross D. Franklin; p. 448: Alex Wong/Getty Images; p. 452: Senate TV via AP; p. 456: ZUMA Press, Inc./Alamy Live News; p. 458: Sarah L. Voisin/The Washington Post via Getty Images; p. 459: AP Photo/David Eggert; p. 461: Bill Clark/CQ Roll Call via AP Images; p. 465 (left): Drew Angerer/Pool via Xinhua/Alamy Stock Photo; p. 465 (right): Bill Clark/CQ-Roll Call, Inc via Getty Images; p. 467 (top left): Science History Images/Alamy Stock Photo; p. 467 (top center): William Philpott/Getty Images; p. 467 (top right): Geopix/Alamy Stock Photo; p. 467 (bottom): Ryan Fisher/The Herald-Dispatch via AP.

Chapter 13: Page 472: Shutterstock; p. 473 (left): Leonard Ortiz/MediaNews Group/Orange County Register via Getty Images; p. 473 (right): Doug Mills/The New York Times/Redux Pictures; p. 476: Bettmann/Getty Images; p. 477 (left): AP Photo/File; p. 477 (right): Carolyn Cole/POOL/AFP via Getty Images; p. 478: Anthony Wallace/AFP via Getty Images; p. 479: AP Photo/File; p. 480: Leah Millis/Reuters/Bloomberg via Getty Images; p. 484: Joe Raedle/Getty Images; p. 488: Jim Watson/AFP/Getty Images; p. 491: Brian Cahn/ZUMA Wire/Alamy Live News; p. 493: Aurora Samperio/NurPhoto via Getty Images; p. 494: Bettmann/Getty Images; p. 495: Twitter/@realDonaldTrump; p. 497: Shealah Craighead/White House Photo/Alamy Live News; p. 502: 2020 Images/Alamy Stock Photo;

p. 504 (top): Leonard Ortiz/MediaNews Group/Orange County Register via Getty Images; p. 504 (bottom): Doug Mills/The New York Times/Redux Pictures.

Chapter 14: Page 508: Vectores de Lia/Shutterstock; p. 509 (left): John Vicory; p. 509 (right): CDC via AP; p. 513: Michael Williamson/The Washington Post via Getty Images; p. 514: NG Images/Alamy Stock Photo; p. 517: Storms Media Group/Alamy Live News; p. 524: Toni L. Sandys/The Washington Post via Getty Images; p. 526: Jeffrey MacMillan/For The Washington Post via Getty Images; p. 529: Alex Edelman/Bloomberg via Getty Images; p. 531: USAJobs.gov; p. 533: UPI/Alamy Stock Photo; p. 535: UPI/Alamy Stock Photo; p. 537 (top): John Vicory; p. 537 (bottom): CDC via AP.

Chapter 15: Page 542: Shutterstock; p. 543: AP Photo/Andrew Harnik; p. 545: AP Photo/Michael Tarm; p. 552 (left): Cheriss May/NurPhoto via Getty Images; p. 552 (right): Pool/Getty Images; p. 558: Michael Hibblen/KUAR News; p. 561: Mark Wilson/Getty Images; p. 564 (top): Mark Wilson/Getty Images; p. 564 (bottom): Jonathan Ernst/REUTERS/ Newscom; p. 567: Art Lien; p. 568: Bill O'Leary/The Washington Post via Getty Images; p. 570: Michael Brochstein/Sipa USA via AP Images; p. 573: Alex Wong/Getty Images; p. 574: AP Photo/Andrew Harnik.

TEXT

Figure 3.3 (p. 90): State Marijuana Laws in 2018 Map, originally published by Governing.com, March 30, 2018. Reprinted by permission of Governing.

Chapter 4, America Side by Side Map (p. 111): Global Press Freedom in Peril from Freedom and the Media 2019, Media Freedom: A Downward Spiral, by Sarah Repucci. © 2019 Freedom House. Reprinted by permission of Freedom House.

Figure 7.5 (p. 242): Figure: Profile of Social Media News Consumers in the U.S." from "Americans Are Wary of the Role Social Media Sites Play in Delivering the News," Pew Research Center, Washington, DC (October 2019) https://www.journalism.org/2019/10/02/americans-are-wary-of-the-role-social-media-sites-play-in-delivering-the-news/.

Figure 8.1 (p. 269): Figure: "More Engage with Politics Digitally than by Volunteering or Attending Rallies," from "Political Engagement, Knowledge and the Midterms," Pew Research Center, Washington, DC (April 2018) https://www.pewresearch.org/politics/2018/04/26/10-political-engagement-knowledge-and-the-midterms/.

Figure 9.5 (p. 327): Map: "2020 Presidential Election, Purple America," by Robert J. Vanderbei, Princeton University. http://www.princeton.edu/~rvdb/JAVA/election2020/. Reprinted by permission of the author.

Chapter 10, America Side by Side Map (p. 356): Map: "U.S. among few democracies that indirectly elect combined head of state/government," Pew Research Center, Washington, DC (November 2016) https://www.pewresearch.org/fact-tank/2016/11/22/among-democracies-u-s-stands-out-in-how-it-chooses-its-head-of-state/ft_16-11-21_headsofstate_map/

Table 11.1 (p. 400): Table: "Top Spending on Lobbying Activities by Industry, 1998-2018" from OpenSecrets.org. Reprinted by permission of Center for Responsive Politics.

Glossary/Index

Page numbers in *italic* refer to figures or photos.

age
See also demographics; older Americans; voter demographics; young Americans
election of 2020 and, 280, 286, 326–27, 384, 387
media and, 239, *239*, 240
political participation and, *363*
political parties and, 326–27, *333*
social media use and, *242*
trust/distrust in government and, 198
U.S. population and, *15*, 19
voter turnout and, 280–81, *280*, *283*
voting rights and, 26, 270, *347*

agenda setting (media), 250, **250**, 252, 254–55 the power of the media to bring public attention to particular issues and problems

agenda setting (presidential legislative initiative), 480–81, 496

agents of socialization, 189–91, **189**, *190* social institutions, including families and schools, that help to shape individuals' basic political beliefs and values

Agnew, Spiro, 482
agriculture, 80
Agriculture, Department of, 520–21
Alabama, 148–49, 558
Aldrich, John, 310
Alien and Sedition Acts (1791), 110
Alito, Samuel, 554, *554*
Al Jazeera, 246
Alphabet, 235
alternative-energy (green) technologies, 317
Amazon, 235

amendments, 58, 453 changes added to bills, laws, or constitutions
See also specific amendments to the U.S. Constitution, e.g. First Amendment

American Civil Liberties Union (ACLU), 413, 565
American Federation of State, County, and Municipal Employees (AFSCME), 542
American Jewish Congress, 287
American National Election Studies (ANES), 216
American people. See demographics
American Revolution, 7–8, 37–39, 183
See also Founding
Americans with Disabilities Act (ADA) (1990), *88*, 90, 172

amicus curiae, 413, **564**, 565–66 literally, "friend of the court"; individuals or groups who are not parties to a lawsuit but who seek to assist the Supreme Court in reaching a decision by presenting additional briefs

amnesty, 478
ANES (American National Election Studies), 216
Annapolis Convention (1786), 41, 42
Anthony, Susan B., 143
anticipatory warrants, 123
Anti-Defamation League, 287

Antifederalists, *53*, **53–54**, 56, 57, 73, 102, 309, 332 those who favored strong state governments and a weak national government and who were opponents of the Constitution proposed at the American Constitutional Convention of 1787

antislavery movement, *141*, 142, 309, 334
anti-terrorism
bureaucracy and, 520
drone strikes, 486
inherent powers and, 486
judicial review and, 560
liberty and, 22
mass media and, 201
unitary executive theory and, 482
veto and, 481–82
appellate courts, 546–47, 548, *548*, 551, 563
Apple, 22, *56*, 124, 235
appointments. See presidential appointments

apportionment, 19–20, 442, *442* the process, occurring after every decennial census, that allocates congressional seats among the 50 states

appropriations, 51, 440, 450, **457**, 464, 530 the amounts of money approved by Congress in statutes (bills) that each unit or agency of government can spend
See also budget process

Arizona, 156, 167, 285, 478
Arkansas, 132, *147*, 148, *152*
Arpaio, Joe, 478
ARPANET, 514

Articles of Confederation, 40–42, **40**, 46, *47*, 48, 49, 52, 71 America's first written constitution; served as the basis for America's national government until 1789

Ashcroft, John, 84
Asian/Pacific Islander Americans
civil rights and, 98–100, 168, 170
Congress and, 434, *434*

election of 2020 and, 387
immigration policy and, 16, 168, 170
political parties and, 323
in U.S. population, 14, 16
vice presidency and, 380
voter turnout, 285–86
Assange, Julian, *256*
assisted suicide, 84
Associated Press, 234
AT&T WarnerMedia (CNN), 238

attitudes (opinions), 183 specific preferences on particular issues

attorney general, 84, 152, 154, 517

authoritarian government, 7 a system of rule in which the government recognizes no formal limits but may nevertheless be restrained by the power of other social institutions

autocracy, 5 a form of government in which a single individual—a king, queen, or dictator—rules

automatic voter registration (AVR), 293
Ayotte, Kelly, 429
Ayotte v. Planned Parenthood of Northern New England, 132
Azar, Alex, *465*, 530

B
Baker v. Carr, 350
Bakke case, 174, *175*

ballot initiatives, 359 proposed laws or policy changes that are placed on the ballot by citizens or interest groups for a popular vote
See also ballot measures

Ballot Initiative Strategy Center, 417
ballot measures, 9, *291*, 292, 359–60, 417
ballots, 349–50, *349*

bandwagon effects, 219 shifts in electoral support to the candidate whom public-opinion polls report as the front-runner

Barker, Nathan, 461
Barrett, Amy Coney, 379, 453, *465*, 544, *552*, *554*, 555, 571
Bartels, Larry, 198, 207
Bartkus, Joanne, 69
battleground (swing) states and districts
campaign strategy and, 364
congressional constituencies and, 459
election of 2016 and, 278, 291–92, 337, 364
election of 2020 and, 326, 381–82

Latino/a Americans and, 285
suburban areas and, 323
third parties and, 337
voter mobilization and, 289, 290
voter turnout and, 292
BBC (British Broadcasting Company), 246, 258
Beard, Charles, 42, 43
"Be Best" campaign, 493, *493*
Benghazi investigation, 448, 453, 464–65
Benton v. Maryland, 105, 125
Better Angels, 13
Bezos, Jeff, 235, *236*, 237

bicameral, 46, **431** having a legislative assembly composed of two chambers or houses; distinguished from *unicameral*

Biden, Hunter, 467, 536
Biden, Jill, 493
Biden, Joe
battleground states and, 382, 386
campaign finance and, 274
debates and, *232*, *367*
electoral college and, 357, 386
emotional appeals and, 190
fundraising, 279
gender gap and, 324
integrity and, 375
law enforcement and, 248
media agenda setting and, 254
policy issues and, 380
primary elections and caucuses and, 354, 379–80
public health and, 380
public-opinion polls and, 216, 219, 381
social media and, *244*
third parties and, 337
Ukraine scandal and, 252, 256, 320, 467, 535–36
vice presidency and, 379, 492
victory of, 375, 381–82, *389*
voter demographics and, 280, 282, 284, *284*, 323, *324*, 325, 327, 354, 384, 388
big data, 219–20, 368

Bill of Rights, 46, 101–6, **102**, *103* the first 10 amendments to the U.S. Constitution, ratified in 1791; they ensure certain rights and liberties to the people
See also freedom of speech

civil liberties vs. civil rights and, 139–40
Constitutional limits on federal government and, 50–51, 52–53, 56, 57

due process of law in, 62, 103, 122–28, *123*, 162, 549
freedom of the press in, 103, *104*, *111*, 116–19, 184, 226, 229
history of, 101–2
on liberty, 21
majority rule, minority rights and, 25
nationalization of, 102–6
selective incorporation of, 103–6, *104–5*, 125

bills, 450 proposed laws that have been sponsored by a member of Congress and submitted to the clerk of the House or Senate
See also lawmaking

Bipartisan Campaign Reform Act (BCRA) (2002), 110, *110*, 112, 372, 416, 556
birth control, 22, 62, 108, *109*, 129–30
birthright citizenship, 106
Black Americans. *See* African Americans
Black Lives Matter, *151*, *419*
See also racial injustice protests (2020)
NFL protests and, 267, *268*
origins of, 149–50, 418, 419
social media and, *245*
Blackmun, Harry, 565, 570–71
Black Power movement, *152*
Blair, Christopher, 226–28, *227*
Bland, Sandra, 419

block grants, 87, 88 federal grants-in-aid that allow states considerable discretion in how the funds are spent

blogging. *See* social media
Bloomberg, Mike, 372
Bloomberg News, 238
Boehner, John, *410*
Boeing Corporation, 440, 537
Bolton, John, 491
Bono, Mary, 429
Booz Allen Hamilton, *526*
Boston Massacre (1770), 38
Boston Tea Party (1773), 39, *39*
Bowers v. Hardwick, 132, 172, 173
Bowling Alone (Putnam), 276
Boydstun, Amber, 252
Bradley, Neil, 473
Brady Handgun Violence Prevention Act, 86
Brandeis, Louis, 84, 128
Brandenburg, Charles, 110
Brandenburg v. Ohio, 110
Brennan, William, 118, 128, 552
Bresch, Heather, *533*
Breyer, Stephen, 107, *554*

briefs, 565–66, **565** written documents in which attorneys explain, using case precedents, why the court should find in favor of their client

British Broadcasting Company (BBC), 246, 258

broadcast media, 238 television, radio or other media that transmit audio and/or video content to the public
See also media

campaign strategy and, 364
free media and, 366
government regulation of, 118–19, 258
ownership of, 233, 234, 239, 258–59
presidency and, 200, *200*, 257
public, 232, 240
radio, 200, *200*, 232, 240, 257, 258, 494, *494*
sound bites and, 238, 246
television, 118–19, 236, 238–40, *239*, 258, 364, 366
Brooks, Rayshard, killing of, 381
Brown, Dwayne, *514*
Brown, Michael, 264
Brown, Xavier, 264–65

Brown v. Board of Education, 23, 146–47, **147**, 148, 150, *152*, 174, 413, 558 the 1954 Supreme Court decision that struck down the "separate but equal" doctrine as fundamentally unequal; this case eliminated state power to use race as a criterion of discrimination in law and provided the national government with the power to intervene by exercising strict regulatory policies against discriminatory actions

Brown v. Entertainment Merchants Association, 119
Bryan, William Jennings, 335
Buckley v. Valeo, 110, 370, 372
Budget and Accounting Act (1921), 480
budget process, 456–59, *529*
See also government spending
bureaucracy and, 521
bureaucratic control and, 529, 530, 533
congressional oversight and, 464
congressional "power of the purse" and, 450, 457
new order and, 457–59
presidency and, 480, 481, 490–91, 496

bureaucracy, 508–27 the complex structure of offices, tasks, rules, and principles of organization that is employed by all large-scale institutions to coordinate the work of their personnel

bureaucracy *(continued)*

See also bureaucratic control; Executive Office of the President; government regulation; *specific agencies, e.g. Food and Drug Administration*

administrative law and, 546
agency creation, 498, 521
agency locations, 521, 525, 529, 530
applying for federal jobs, 531
characteristics of, 514, 516
civil rights and, 151
Congress and, 496–97, 511–12, 516–17, 560
congressional staff agencies, 449–50
coronavirus pandemic and, 508–10, 511, 512
delegated powers of, 483–84, 516–17
demographics, *523*, 524
employment in, 153, 516
environmental policy and, 512, 517
executive departments, 517, 521, 528
functions of, 511–14
independent agencies, 490, 517–18, 521
innovation and, 513–14
international comparisons, *519*
judicial review and, 535, 560
law enforcement by, 513
military and, 520
organization of, 517–18, *518*, 520–21
party machines and, 316–17, 521–22
political parties and, 235
principal-agent problem, 516–17
privatization and, 526–27, *526*, *527*
public opinion on, *515*
Republican Party and, 335
rule-making, 411, 421, 483, 496–97, 512–13, 546
size of, 28, 490, 496, *519*, 524–25, *525*
solicitor general and, 564
Supreme Court and, 560, 573
trust/distrust in government and, 29
bureaucratic control, 527–37
agency location and, 529, 530
budget process and, 529, 530, 533
Cabinet status and, 529
challenges of, 527–28, 536–37
citizen oversight, 536
Congress and, 530, 532–33, *533*, 534–35
Consumer Financial Protection Board case study, 534–35
Executive Office of the President and, 529
federal courts and, 535
inspectors general and, 532–33
policy czars and, 529–30
presidency and, 528–30, 533, 534–35
reorganization and, 537
whistleblowers and, 535–36
Bureau of Indian Affairs, 171

Burger, Warren, 160
Burnham, Walter Dean, 307
Burwell v. Hobby Lobby Stores, 22, 108–9, *109*, 568
Bush, George H. W., 484, 554–55, 571
Bush, George W., and administration
ballots and, 349
business interests and, 522
economic inequality and, 198
education and, 93
election of 2000 and, 336, 337, 349, 357, 368
evangelicals and, 288
executive orders and, 498
federal government power and, 93
immigration policy and, 166
inherent powers and, 484, 486
Iraq War and, 495
judicial review and, 560
media priming and, 255
micro-targeting and, 368
policy czars and, 530
public opinion and, 200
public-opinion polls and, 219
regulatory review and, 497
Republican Party and, 336
September 11, 2001, terrorist attacks and, 480, 495
Supreme Court appointments and, 571
tax policy and, 207, 254
traditional media and, 201
unitary executive theory and, 482
veto and, 481–82
voter mobilization, 290
Bush, Maggie, 294
Bush v. Gore, 357
Business Insider, 238
business interests
See also employment; financial industry; wealthy Americans, influence of
Affordable Care Act and, 22
American Revolution and, 38
Articles of Confederation and, 41
ballot measures and, 417
bureaucracy and, 530
bureaucratic law enforcement and, 513
citizen groups and, 402
Citizens United v. Federal Election Commission and, 112
congressional decision-making and, 460
congressional elections and, 440
congressional oversight of, 464
conservatism and, 187
coronavirus stimulus legislation and, 394, *395*, 517
corporate taxes, 407
Defense Production Act and, 473

federalism and, 80
government regulation and, 80
immigration policy and, 319
influence of, 421–22
institutional advertising, 417–18
interest groups for, 399, *401*, 405–6, 421
litigation by, 413–14, *413*
lobbying by, 394, *395*, 399, *400*, 401, *411*, *423*, 460
media ownership, 231, 233–34, *233*, 235, *236*, 239, 250, 258–59
media profit motives, 231–32, *232*, 237, 254
PACs and, 371, 415
political appointees and, 522, 528
political parties and, 307, 308, 318, 334, 335, 377
regulatory review and, 497
trade associations, 371, 399
transgender discrimination and, 161
busing, 153
Buttigieg, Pete, *353*, 354
Byrd, Robert, 440

C

Cabinet, 489–90, **489** the secretaries, or chief administrators, of the major departments of the federal government; Cabinet secretaries are appointed by the president with the consent of the Senate

appointments of, 490, 522
bureaucratic control and, 529
congressional testimony, *465*
executive departments and, 517
National Security Council and, 491
presidential succession and, 492
Calhoun, John C., 86
California
ballot measures, 292
electoral laws, 298
environmental policy, 513
government regulation, 84
immigration policy, 165
Latino/a Americans, 163, 165, 285
policy diffusion and, 87
recall elections, 360
same-sex marriage and, 359
school segregation/desegregation, 163
welfare reform, 88
campaign advertising
campaign finance and, 372
campaign strategy and, 364, 366
digital, 236, 276, 279
government regulation and, 110, 416
misinformation and, 236, 277–78
negative, *110*, 311, 366, *366*

committee markup, 452 the session in which a congressional committee rewrites legislation to incorporate changes discussed during hearings on a bill

Communications Decency Act (CDA), 118
Community Oriented Policing Services (COPS), 89–90
Community Reinvestment Act (1977), 156
Compromise of 1877, 143
concentrated poverty, 282

concurrent powers, 73 authority possessed by both state and national governments{,} such as the power to levy taxes

concurring opinions, 568 written opinions by judges agreeing with the majority opinion but giving different reasons for their decisions

Confederate statue removals, 267

confederations, 40 systems of government in which states retain sovereign authority except for the powers expressly delegated to the national government

conference committees, 448–49, 448, 454, 456 joint committees created to work out a compromise on House and Senate versions of a piece of legislation

conferences, 444 gatherings of House Republicans every two years to elect their House leaders; Democrats call their gatherings "caucuses"

confidence in government. *See* trust/distrust in government
Congress
See also budget process; congressional committee system; congressional elections; congressional representation; coronavirus stimulus legislation; lawmaking; lobbying; redistricting; stimulus legislation
advice and consent powers of, 465–66
agency creation and, 521
in Articles of Confederation, 40
Benghazi investigation, 448, 453, 464–65
bicameral nature of, 46, 431
bureaucracy and, 496–97, 511–12, 516–17, 560
bureaucratic control and, 530, 532–33, 533, 534–35
Cabinet members and, 465, 490
campaign committees, 316
civil rights and, 140, 148, 150

constituency service (casework) and, 436, 438, 439, 440
Constitution on, 47, 48–49
contacting your member, 461
court system and, 548–49
decision-making in, 459–60, 462–64
earmarks, 409, 454
election of 2020 and, 376, 381, 382–83
executive agreements and, 479
executive delegated powers and, 483–84
executive power expansion and, 502, 502, 503
foreign policy and, 49, 446
House vs. Senate, 48, 431–32, 431, 462
impeachment powers, 466–67, 480, 492, 502, 503, 536
importance of, 428–30
inaction of, 429
inherent powers and, 486, 488
interest group influence strategies, 408
iron triangles and, 412–13, 412
judicial review and, 555–56
limitations on federal courts and, 572
lobbying of, 410, 421
organized labor and, 401
oversight powers of, 447, 464–65, 524, 532–33
party leadership in, 444–45, 445, 446, 455–56, 456, 459
party polarization and, 320, 329, 378, 378, 449, 462, 463–64, 463
pork barreling, 440, 454
powers of, 48
presidential decrees and, 500
presidential elections and, 354
racial discrimination and, 146
Russian election interference investigations, 448, 462, 465, 480
single-member districts, 309, 310, 338, 348
social media and, 436, 436
staff system, 449–50
symbolic legislation and, 440
unitary executive theory on, 482
war powers, 484
Congressional Budget and Impoundment Control Act (1974), 457
Congressional Budget Office (CBO), 450, 533
congressional committee system, 445–46
conference committees, 448–49, 454, 456
iron triangles and, 412, 412
joint committees, 448
lawmaking and, 450–52
lobbying and, 410
oversight and, 447, 464–65, 532
political parties and, 320

select committees, 448, 448, 464–65
standing committees, 446–47, 447
congressional elections
apportionment and, 442
campaign finance and, 361–62, 362, 416, 438, 440
candidates in, 438–39
electoral competition and, 291
incumbency and, 439–40, 439
international comparisons, 348–49
midterm elections, 271, 347
party polarization and, 329, 464
redistricting and, 442–44
symbolic legislation and, 440
third parties and, 338
voters in, 441
"winner take all" system and, 309
congressional representation, 431–38, 432
See also descriptive representation
Great Compromise, 43–44, 45
House vs. Senate, 431–32
inequality of, 208
influence of wealthy Americans and, 210, 371
ratification debates and, 54
substantive, 433, 434, 435
Three-Fifths Compromise, 44, 44, 46
trustee vs. delegate, 432
Congressional Research Service (CRS), 450, 533
Connecticut, 293
consent decrees, 572
consent of the governed, 7, 48, 143, 182
conservatism, 186–87, 188
See also political ideology; Republican Party
Americans' view of government and, 28
federalism and, 86–87, 93
media and, 240
religion and, 195–96
Supreme Court and, 378–79, 554, 571
Tea Party movement, 128, 243, 304–6, 305, 336–37, 418, 418, 419

conservatives, 186 today this term refers to those who generally support the social and economic status quo and are suspicious of efforts to introduce new political formulas and economic arrangements; conservatives believe that a large and powerful government poses a threat to citizens' freedom
See also conservatism

constituencies, 51, 431, 459, 459 the residents in the areas from which officials are elected
See also constituency service

constituency service (casework), 436, 438, 439, 440
Constitution, U.S., 40–63
 See also Bill of Rights; civil rights; federalism; *specific amendments, e.g. Fourteenth Amendment*
 amendment process, 50, 58, *58*, 60, 61–62
 amendments to, 57–62, *59*, *60*, *61*, 101–2
 on appropriations, 51, 450
 vs. Articles of Confederation, *47*, 48, 49, 52
 bureaucracy and, 528, 530
 civil liberties in original, 101–2, *102*
 comity clause, 50, 76
 economic policy and, 46
 elastic clause, 48, 56, 73
 Equal Rights Amendment and, 160
 expressed powers and, 48–49, 52–53, 71–72
 federal courts and, 546
 federal government power in, 50
 federalism in, 50, 52, 71, 73–74, 76
 framers of, 42–43, 46–47, 48, 49, 101–2
 Great Compromise, 43–44, *45*
 implied powers in, 73, 80, 482–83
 judicial review and, 555, 556, 558
 on liberty, 21
 limits on federal government in, 28, 50–53, *51*, *52*, 56, 57
 Native Americans and, 171
 necessary and proper clause, 48, **73**, 79
 political culture and, 21
 on presidency, 49, 475–76, 503
 provisions of, 46–53, *48*, *123*
 ratification of, 50, 51, 53–54, *54*, 56–57
 on state electoral laws, 357
 supremacy clause, 50, 56, 73, 556, 558
 on Supreme Court, 49–50, 551, 552
 Supreme Court interpretation of, 62, 570–71
 on Supreme Court jurisdiction, 548, 561–62
 on vice presidency, 491
Constitutional Convention (1787), 42–46, *43*, 101, 555

constitutional government, 7 a system of rule in which formal and effective limits are placed on the powers of the government

Consumer Confidence Index, 374, *375*
Consumer Financial Protection Bureau (CFPB), 534–35, *535*
Consumer Product Safety Act (1972), 484
Consumer Product Safety Commmission (CPSC), 521
consumer protection, 484, 521, 534–35, *535*

 See also Food and Drug Administration; government regulation
contraceptive care, 22
contract cases, 546

contracting, 527 the power of government to set conditions on companies seeking to sell goods or services to government agencies
 See also privatization

Coons, Chris, 277–78
Cooperative Congressional Election Study, 215

cooperative federalism, 82–83, *83* a type of federalism existing since the New Deal era in which grants-in-aid have been used strategically to encourage states and localities (without commanding them) to pursue nationally defined goals; also known as *intergovernmental cooperation*

Cooper v. Harris, 558
Cordray, Richard, 534
Coronavirus Aid, Relief, and Economic Security Act (CARES Act). *See* coronavirus stimulus legislation
coronavirus pandemic (2020), 2–4
 See also coronavirus stimulus legislation
 abortion and, 132
 bureaucracy and, 508–10, 511, 512
 Defense Production Act and, 472–74, *473*
 devolution and, 88
 economic inequality and, 24, 197, 207
 election of 2020 and, 240–41, 326, 354, *368*, 380, 382, 384, 387–88
 eminent domain and, 129
 federal government power and, 28
 federalism and, 68–69, *69*, 70, 78, 93
 federal military force and, *477*
 freedom of religion and, 108–9
 government regulation and, 22
 hoarding/price gouging and, *497*
 inherent powers and, 486, 488
 inspectors general and, 533
 lawmaking and, 453
 misinformation and, 68, 244
 political knowledge and, 207
 political parties and, 326
 public health and, 207
 racial injustice protests and, 264
 social media and, 244
 state of emergency declarations, 3–4, 478, 488
 task force for, *395*, 530
 Trump's diagnosis, 245, 380
 trust/distrust in government and, 29
 trust/distrust in media and, 249
 unemployment and, 388

 unemployment insurance and, 88, 395, 512
coronavirus stimulus legislation
 bureaucracy and, 516–17
 congressional decision-making and, 462, 463
 election of 2020 and, 380
 federal government power and, 28
 importance of Congress and, 428
 lobbying and, 394–96, *395*
corporate interests. *See* business interests
corporate taxes, 407
corruption, 231, 244, 371, 422
Cosby, Bill, 162
Coulter, Ann, 113
Council of Economic Advisers (CEA), 491
Council on Environmental Quality, 491
counsel, right to, *105*, 126
court-martial, trials by, 549
Court of Appeals for the Federal Circuit, 548
Court of Appeals for Veterans Claims, 549
Court of Federal Claims, 548
Court of International Trade, 548
Court of Military Appeals, 549

courts of appeals, 546–47, **546**, 548, *548*, 551, 563 courts that hear appeals of trial court decisions

coverture, 142
COVID-19 pandemic. *See* coronavirus pandemic
criminal justice system
 See also due process of law; federal courts
 comity clause and, 76
 due process of law, 62, 103, 122–28, *123*, 162, 549
 felon voting rights, 138–39, *139*, 157–58, 296
 Miranda rule, 62, *105*, 125–26, *125*
 political ideologies on, 187
 privatization and, 526–27
 reasonable doubt standard, 122

criminal law, *545*, **545** the branch of law that regulates the conduct of individuals, defines crimes, and specifies punishment for proscribed conduct

Croker, Richard, *316*
cruel and unusual punishment, *105*, *123*, 126–28
Cruz, Ted, *317*, 319
Cuban Americans, 323, 387
cultural identities. *See* demographics
Cunningham, Jeff, 396

D

DACA (Deferred Action for Childhood Arrivals), 166, *166*, *433*
See also DREAM Act
Daily Show, The, 240
Dalton, Russell, 276
dark money (501(c)(4) committees), 372
data mining, 219–20
Davis, Gray, 360
Davis, Kim, *74*
Dawes Act (1887), 171
Dawson, Michael, 282
death penalty, 126–28, *127*
debates, political, *232*, 314, 367–68
de Blasio, Bill, 124
Declaration of Independence, 21, 22, 39–40, 63, 182
Declaration of Sentiments and Resolutions, 142, *143*
Deepwater Horizon Gulf oil spill, 537

de facto, 147 literally, "by fact"; refers to practices that occur even when there is no legal enforcement, such as school segregation in much of the United States today

de facto segregation, 147–48, 152

defendant, 545 the one against whom a complaint is brought in a criminal or civil case

Defense, Department of (DoD), 117, 490, 513–14, 520
defense industry, 380, *412*
See also military
Defense of Marriage Act (DOMA) (1996), 34, 74, 160, 173
Defense Production Act (DPA) (1950), 472–74, *473*
Deferred Action for Childhood Arrivals (DACA), 166, *166*
DeJonge v. Oregon, 105

de jure, 147 literally, "by law"; refers to legally enforced practices, such as school segregation in the South before the 1960s

de jure segregation, 147, 153
DeLay, Tom, 422

delegate, 432 a representative who votes according to the preferences of his or her constituency

delegated powers, 483–84, **483,** 496–97 constitutional powers that are assigned to one governmental agency but are exercised by another agency with the express permission of the first

delegates (convention), 315, **354,** 355 representatives who vote according to the preferences of their constituencies
See also national conventions

democracy, 5 a system of rule that permits citizens to play a significant part in the governmental process, usually through the election of key public officials

civil liberties and, 109
civil rights movement and, 63
direct, 8, 9, *291,* 292, 359–60, 417
federalism and, 84
flawed, 18
Founders' distrust of, 8, 25, 46, 49
importance of media to, 226, 228, 229, 231, 257
interest groups and, 396
international comparisons, 55, *55*
party polarization and, 328
political culture and, 24–26
political knowledge and, 206–7
as political value, 5, 184
Democratic National Committee (DNC), 256, 314
Democratic Party
See also political ideology; political parties; *specific presidents, e.g. Obama, Barack, and administration*
absentee voting and, 352
Affordable Care Act and, 492
budget process and, 458
congressional committee system and, 449
divisions within, 319, *319*
education and, *326,* 532
EEOC and, 154
election of 2018 and, 337, 492
election of 2020 results and, 382–83
evolution of, 334, 335, 338
felon voting rights and, 157–58
filibuster and, 453, 458
House caucus, 444
national conventions, *315*
New Deal and, 335
origins of, 332, 334
party identification, 322, *322*
party rules, 315–16, 354, 355
policy issues and, 317, 318, 325, *328,* 377, 382
Populist Party and, 335
primary elections and caucuses and, 254, 290, *311,* 354, 379
progressive caucus, 319, *319,* 377, 378, 379, 382
Russian election interference investigations and, 465

social media and, 495
superdelegates, 355
Supreme Court appointments and, 555, 571
Vietnam War and, 335
voter demographics and, 281, 282, 285, 286, *288,* 323, 324–25, 326–27, *326, 327*
voter ID laws and, 155
voter mobilization and, 314
voting by mail and, 156, 382
youth vote and, 280, 286, 327
demographics, 14–17, *15,* 19–20
See also voter demographics; *specific categories, e.g. age*
bureaucracy and, *523,* 524
candidate characteristics and, 374–75, *385*
Congress and, 165, 286, 382, *432, 433–34, 434, 435, 436, 437*
digital news and, *253*
fake news and, *251*
federal judges and, *557*
history of, 12, 14, 16
immigration and, 12, 14, 16–17, *17,* 19, *169*
interest groups and, 402
party polarization and, 329–30
presidency and, *485*
social media and, 242–43, *242*
vice presidency and, 492
demonstrations. *See* protest
Dennis v. United States, 112
Department of Homeland Security (DHS). *See* Homeland Security, Department of
deregulation, 336, 380
DeSantis, Ron, 139

descriptive representation (Congress), 432–34, **433,** *435,* 436 a type of representation in which representatives have the same racial, gender, ethnic, religious, or educational backgrounds as their constituents; it is based on the principle that if two individuals are similar in background, character, interests, and perspectives, then one can correctly represent the other's views

African Americans, 282, 433, 434, *434*
defined, 432–33
international comparisons, *437*
Latino/a Americans, 165, 285, 434, *434*
political participation and, 282
ratification debates and, 54
redistricting and, 444
women, *159,* 286–87, *287,* 324, 382, *432,* 434, *437*

desegregation. *See* segregation/desegregation

Development, Relief, and Education Act for Alien Minors (DREAM Act), 165–66, 570, *570*

devolution, 86–89 policy to remove a program from one level of government by delegating it or passing it down to a lower level of government, such as from the national government to the state and local governments

DeVos, Betsy, 112, 162

Dewey, John, 229

Dewey, Thomas, *217*

Dial, Hank, 428–29

diffusion, 87 the process by which policy decisions in one political jurisdiction are influenced by choices made in another jurisdiction

digital citizens, 241–42, **241** daily internet users with broadband (high-speed) home internet access and the technology and literacy skills to go online for employment, news, politics, entertainment, commerce, and other activities

digital divide, 241–42, **242**, 279 the gap in access to the internet among demographic groups based on education, income, age, geographic location, and race/ethnicity

digital news, 240–49
    See also misinformation in media
    advertising and, 234, 235, *238*
    benefits of, 245–46
    citizen journalism and, 236, 244–45
    concerns about, 236, 246, 248–49
    consumers of, *253*
    digital political participation and, 273
    evaluating, 247, *247*
    government regulation and, 259
    growth of digital media and, 234, 235–36, *235*, 240
    internet access and, *230*, 241–42, 259
    journalism/journalists and, 234, 236, 237, 241
    media leaks and, 256
    media ownership and, 233, 234
    misinformation and, 243, 244, 246, *246*, 248
    news aggregators and, 241, *241*
    newspapers and, 237–38
    party polarization and, 248–49, *249*
    political knowledge and, 10, 206, *206*, 246, 248–49
    radio and, 240

    on social media, 234, 235–36, 241, 242–43, 248–49
    streaming video, 240–41

digital political participation, 241–42, 273–74, **273**, 276–79, 364, 495 activities designed to influence politics using the internet, including visiting a candidate's website, organizing events online, and signing an online petition

digital social networks, 243, 273, 276

diplomacy, 520 the representation of a government to other governments

direct-action politics, 9, *10*
    See also protest

direct democracy, 8, 9, *291*, 292, 359–60, 417 a system of rule that permits citizens to vote directly on laws and policies

directives, presidential, 500

Director of National Intelligence (DNI), 537

Disability Rights Education and Defense Fund, 172

disabled Americans
    civil rights, 87–88, *88*, 172
    political participation, 293, 296

discrimination, 141 the use of any unreasonable and unjust criterion of exclusion
    See also gender discrimination; racial discrimination

    sexual orientation and, 133, 172–73

Disney, 233

dissenting opinions, 568–69, **568** decisions written by justices in the minority in a particular case, in which a justice wishes to express his or her reasoning in the case

district courts, 548, *548*, 551

District of Columbia v. Heller, 120

diversity. *See* demographics

DNA testing, 123–24

Dodd-Frank Wall Street Reform and Consumer Protection Act (2010), 460, 534

DOMA (Defense of Marriage Act) (1996), 34, 74, 160, 173

Donnelly, Glynis, 428

Donovan, Todd, 290–91

"Don't Ask, Don't Tell" policy, 172

double jeopardy, 104, *105*, **125**, 162 the Fifth Amendment right providing that a person cannot be tried twice for the same crime

Douglas, William O., 129, 130

Douglass, Frederick, 142

DREAM Act (Development, Relief, and Education Act for Alien Minors), 165–66, 570, *570*
    See also DACA

Dred Scott v. Sanford, 142

Drudge Report, 238

drug testing, 123

Drutman, Lee, 421

dual federalism, 78–81, *78*, *83* the system of government that prevailed in the United States from 1789 to 1937 in which most fundamental governmental powers were shared between the federal and state governments

due process of law, 62, 103, 122–28, **122**, *123*, 162, **549** the right of every individual against arbitrary action by national or state governments

Duverger's law, 310 a law that holds that plurality rule elections where the winner has the most votes, but not necessarily a majority within single-member geographic districts, tend to result in a two-party system, whereas proportional representation tends to result in a multi-party system

E

early America
    demographics, 12
    political parties, 308–9, 332
    voter turnout, 268

early voting, 298, 382 the option in some states to cast a vote at a polling place or by mail before the election

earmarks, 409, 454

East India Company, 38

eBay, 235

echo chambers, 277

economic conditions
    See also Great Depression; Great Recession; unemployment
    media priming and, 255
    voter decisions and, 360, 374, *375*, 388

economic inequality
    See also socioeconomic status
    agreement on, 328–29
    digital divide and, 242, 279
    Founding and, 197
    growth of, 19, *20*
    minimum wage and, *24*

equal time rule, 259 the requirement that broadcasters provide candidates for the same political office equal opportunities to communicate their messages to the public

ERA (Equal Rights Amendment), 60, *60*, 160

Ernst, Joni, 383

Escobedo v. Illinois, 105

Espionage Act (1917), 110

establishment clause, 106–8, 106, *107, 108* the First Amendment clause that says "Congress shall make no law respecting an establishment of religion"; this constitutional provision means that a "wall of separation" exists between church and state

ethnicity, 194–95

    See also immigrants; Latino/a Americans; race

Europe, immigrants from, 12, 16, *169*

European Americans. *See* White Americans

evangelicals

    election of 2020 and, 387

    grassroots mobilization and, 418

    political participation, 288, *288*, 418

    Republican Party and, 195–96, 288, 324

Everson v. Board of Education, 105

Every Student Succeeds Act (2015), 93

excessive fines, *105*, 128

exclusionary rule, 122–23, 122 the ability of courts to exclude evidence obtained in violation of the Fourth Amendment

executive agreements, 465–66, **466,** 478–79, **479** agreements, made between the president and another country, that have the force of treaties but do not require the Senate's "advice and consent"

executive branch

    See also bureaucracy; executive power expansion; presidency

    congressional oversight of, 483, 524

    delegated powers of, 483–84

    iron triangles and, 412–13, *412*

    lobbying and, 411, 421

    unitary executive theory and, 482–83

executive departments, 517, 521, 528 the 15 departments in the executive branch headed by Cabinet secretaries and constituting the majority of the federal bureaucracy

Executive Office of the President (EOP), 490–91, **490,** 494–95, 496, 502, 517, 529 the permanent agencies that perform defined management tasks for the president; created in 1939, the EOP includes the OMB, the Council of Economic Advisers (CEA), the NSC, and other agencies

    See also executive branch

executive orders, 377, **498,** *499* a rule or regulation issued by the president that has the effect and formal status of legislation

    See also specific policy issues, e.g. immigration policy

executive power expansion, 493–500

    administrative strategy, 483, 496–500, 502

    bureaucracy and, 560

    checks and balances and, 502–3

    civil rights and, 151, 152

    Congress and, 502, *502,* 503

    judicial review and, 560–61

    party polarization and, 377

    political appointees and, 528–29

    public appeals and, 493–96, *494*

    unitary executive theory and, 482–83

executive privilege, 479–80, *479,* **479** the claim that confidential communications between a president and close advisers should not be revealed without the consent of the president

expressed powers, 48, 476 specific powers granted by the Constitution to Congress (Article I, Section 8) and to the president (Article II)

    Bill of Rights and, 52–53

    of federal government, 48–49, 52–53, 71–72, 73, 79

    of presidency, 476–82, 484, 486

extraordinary renditions, 486

F

Facebook

    See also social media

    advertising and, 235, 236

    congressional oversight and, *113,* 228, 464

    elections and, 236, 276, *276,* 284

    evaluating posts, *247*

    expressive politics and, 277

    hate speech and, 113, *113*

    misinformation on, 204–5, 228, 236, 248, 278

    news on, 235, 241, 242, 243

    political socialization and, 190

    public opinion and, 200

    Russian election interference and, 248, 278

    voter mobilization and, 284, 289

fact-checking, 205, 231, 243, 247, 248

FactCheck.org, 248

Fair Housing Act (1968), 156

Fair Housing Amendments Act (1988), 156

fairness doctrine, 259

fake news, 248 false stories intended to be read as factual news that are circulated to benefit one candidate or party over another or to generate ad revenue

    birther conspiracies and, *246*

    concerns about, 246, 248

    congressional oversight and, 228

    demographics and, *251*

    digital political participation and, 277

    election of 2016 and, 204–5, 226–27, 236, 248

    evaluating news and, 247, *247*

    ironic creation of, 226–28, *227*

    Russian election interference (2016) and, 205, 248, 278

    Trump's accusations, 118, 249, 377

family, political socialization by, 190, *190*

Family and Medical Leave Act (FMLA) (1993), 90

Farook, Syed, 124

Faubus, Orval, 148, 477

FBI (Federal Bureau of Investigation), 200, 465, 477

FCC (Federal Communications Commission), 258, 259

FDR. *See* Roosevelt, Franklin Delano, and administration

Federal Aviation Administration (FAA), 537

Federal Bureau of Investigation (FBI), 200, 465, 477

Federal Communications Commission (FCC), 258, 259

federal courts, 543–61

    See also Supreme Court

    bureaucratic control and, 535

    caseloads, 549–50, *550*

    civil rights and, 150, *152,* 153

    civil rights movement and, 145, 146

    demographics, *557*

    executive orders and, 498

    expanded power of, 572–74

    interest groups and, 413–14

    international comparisons, 559

    law analysis by, 158, 160

    lawmaking and, 562

    levels of scrutiny, 109, **147,** 158, 160, 174, 175, *175*

    lifetime appointments, 50

    limitations on, 572

    nominations to, 465

    political appointees, 549

FiveThirtyEight, 213, *213*, 220

527 committees (Super PACs), 279, 314–15, 366, 370, **372**, 414, **416**, 440 nonprofit independent political action committees that may raise unlimited sums of money from corporations, unions, and individuals but are not permitted to contribute to or coordinate directly with parties or candidates

flag burning, 115
flawed democracy, 18
Florida
    election of 2000 and, 349
    felon voting rights and, 138–39, *139*, 158, 296
    Latino/a Americans, 285
Florida Rights Restoration Coalition (FRRC), 138, *139*
Floyd, George, killing of, 150, 191, 192, 194, 196, 264, 265, 267, 381, 419, 477
Flynn, Michael, 465, 491
FMLA (Family and Medical Leave Act) (1993), 90
Food and Drug Administration (FDA)
    advisory committees, 532
    bureaucracy organization and, 520, 521
    coronavirus pandemic and, 69, 509, 511
    interest groups and, *413*, 530
food stamps. *See* Supplemental Nutrition Assistance Program
Ford, Christine Blasey, 555
Ford, Gerald, 478, 492
foreign policy
    See also national security policy; trade policy
    Articles of Confederation and, 41
    Congress and, 49, 446
    coronavirus pandemic and, 473–74
    Muslim ban, 168, 486, 561, *561*
    political ideologies on, 187
    presidency and, 49, 465–66, 478–79, *478*, 486
    signing statements on, 500
    Twitter and, 496
Founding, 39–46
    See also American Revolution; Constitution, U.S.
    Annapolis Convention, 41, 42
    Articles of Confederation, 40–42, 46, *47*, 48, 49, 52, 71
    Constitutional Convention, 42–46, *43*, 101, 555
    Declaration of Independence, 21, 22, 39–40, 63, 182
    distrust of democracy and, 8, 25, 46, 49
    economic inequality and, 197

influence of wealthy Americans and, 41, 42–43, 46
    limited government and, 8
    majority rule, minority rights and, 25
    political culture and, 21
    political parties and, 307
    Shays's Rebellion and, 42
    slavery and, 62–63

Fourteenth Amendment, 143 one of three Civil War amendments; it guaranteed equal protection and due process

    adoption of, 103, 141
    citizenship and, 14, 142
    double jeopardy in, 104, *105*, 125, 162
    equal protection clause, 141, 144, 146, 148, 158, 160, 165, 174
    grand juries and, 124–25
    nationality and, 165
    same-sex marriage and, 35, 74, 132, 413, 568
    selective incorporation and, 103–4, *104–5*, 106, 125
    Supreme Court interpretation of, 144–45, 146, 568
    text of, 103
Fourth Amendment, 122–24, *123*, *124*, 128–29, 558
    See also due process of law
fourth branch of government, 231
Fox Corporation, 233, *236*, 238, 250
Fox News, 239, 248, 250, 377
fracking, *92*
framers of the Constitution, 42–43, 46–47, 48, 49, 101–2
    See also Founding

framing, 254–55, **254** the power of the media to influence how events and issues are interpreted

France, 71
franchise. *See* voting rights
Francisco, Noel, *564*
Frankfurter, Felix, 552, 568, 570
Franklin, Benjamin, 39
Franklin v. Gwinnett County Public Schools, 161
Frederick, Joseph, 114
freedom. *See* liberty
freedom of assembly, *105*, 229, 402
Freedom of Information Act (FOIA) (1966), 536
freedom of religion, *104*, *105*, 106–9, *107*, *108*, *109*
freedom of speech, 109–10, 112–16
    campaign finance and, 110, 112, 346, 366, 370, 372, 571

commercial speech, 115
    education and, 112, 113–15, *114*, *115*
    hate speech, 112–14
    interest groups and, 402
    judicial review and, 556
    political speech, 110, *110*, 112, 229
    as political value, 184
    protest and, 115–16, *116*, 267
    selective incorporation and, 103, *104*
    speech-plus, 116
    strict scrutiny and, 109
    Super PACs and, 416
    symbolic speech, 115–16
    trademarks and, 99–100, 556
freedom of the press, 116–19
    international comparisons, *111*
    libel and slander and, 117–18
    media and, 226, 229
    as political value, 184
    pornography and obscenity and, 118–19
    prior restraint and, 116–17
    selective incorporation and, 103, *104*

free exercise clause, 108–9, **108** the First Amendment clause that protects a citizen's right to believe and practice whatever religion he or she chooses
    See also freedom of religion

free media, 366

free riders, 404, 405 those who enjoy the benefits of collective goods but did not participate in acquiring or providing them

Free Soil Party, 142
French and Indian War, 38
fugitive slave clause, 79

full faith and credit clause, 73–74 provision from Article IV, Section 1, of the Constitution requiring that the states normally honor the public acts and judicial decisions that take place in another state

Fulton, Robert, 79
fundraising. *See* campaign finance

G

gag rules (closed rules), 452, 455
Gainous, Jason, 243
gambling, 171
Gannett corporation, 234
Garcia, Chuy, *433*
Gardner, Cory, 383
Garland, Merrick, 543, 544, 555
Garner, Eric, 419
Garrity, W. Arthur, Jr., 574

gatekeeping, 250, **252** a process by which information and news are filtered to the public by the media; for example, a reporter choosing which sources to include in a story

Gates, Rick, 465

gay rights movement, 172, 173, 413
See also LGBTQ Americans

Geer, John, 366

Geithner, Timothy, *535*

gender
See also demographics; gender discrimination; transgender Americans
cruel and unusual punishment and, 127
federal judges and, *557*
political parties and, 287, 323, 324, *333*
presidency and, *485*
public opinion and, *194*, 195, *195*
social composition of Congress and, 433–34, *434*, *435*
social media use and, *242*
vice presidency and, 380, *491*, 492
voter demographics and, 195, *195*, 286–87, 324

gender discrimination
in education, *159*, 160, 161, *162*
in employment, 23–24, 150, *159*, 160, 161–63, *162*
international comparisons, *164*
Supreme Court on, 160–61, 163

gender gap, *195*, **195**, **286**, **324**, 387 a distinctive pattern of voting behavior reflecting the differences in views between women and men

General Agreement on Tariffs and Trade (GATT), 479

general elections, 347–48, **347** regularly scheduled elections involving most districts in the nation or state, in which voters select officeholders; in the United States, general elections for national office and most state and local offices are held on the first Tuesday after the first Monday in November in even-numbered years (every four years for presidential elections)

general revenue sharing, 87 the process by which one unit of government yields a portion of its tax income to another unit of government, according to an established formula; revenue sharing typically involves the national government providing money to state governments

generational differences, 198
See also age

Generation Z, 198

geographic sorting, 196
See also regional differences

Georgia, 132, 282, 293, 376, 382

Gerber, Alan, 289

Gerber, Elisabeth, 417

Gerry, Elbridge, 350

gerrymandering, 154, 350, 443 the apportionment of voters in districts in such a way as to give unfair advantage to one racial or ethnic group or political party

candidate recruitment and, 311
electoral competition and, 291
party polarization and, 329, 351, 464
political parties and, 350–51, 443
race and, *351*, 444
racial discrimination and, 154–55

Gibbons v. Ogden, 79–80

Gideon v. Wainwright, 105, 126

GI Forum, 165

Gilded Age, 19

Gilens, Martin, 210

Gill v. Whitford, 351

Gingrich, Newt, 449, 460, 462

Ginsburg, Ruth Bader, 128–29, 163, 379, 544, 555, 568, *568*

Gitlow v. New York, 104

Goldberg, Arthur, 130

Goldwater, Barry, 336, 364

Gonzales v. Carhart, 132

Google, 220, 235, 236, 241, 259

Google News, 241

Gore, Al, 349, 357, 525

Gorsuch, Neil, 133, 453, 543, 544, 552, *552*, 554, *554*, 555

government, 5–9, **5** institutions and procedures through which a territory and its people are ruled

Americans' views of, 4, 5, 26, 28–30
corruption, 231, 244, 371, 422
dependence on, 5, *6*, 28
forms of, 5, 7–8, *7*, 18, *18*
information websites, *28*
international comparisons, 7, 55, *55*
limited, 5, 7, 8, 21, **21**, 28, 56–57, **56**
and political participation, 8–9
trust/distrust in, 5, 29–30, *29*, 190, 198, *199*, 271

Government Accountability Office (GAO), 450, 520, 533

government corporations, 518 government agencies that perform market-oriented public services and raise revenues to fund their activities

government employment. *See* bureaucracy

government regulation
See also consumer protection; *specific laws and agencies, e.g. Occupational Safety and Health Administration*
bureaucratic rule-making and, 512–13
business interests and, 80
of campaign finance, 370, 371, 372, 414
citizen journalism and, 244–45
deregulation, 336, 380
election of 2020 and, 380
employment and, 512, 521
environmental policy and, 380, 513, *513*, 537
federalism and, 83–84
financial industry and, 460, 534
interest groups and, 411, *413*, 530, 536–37
liberty and, 22
of lobbying, 409, 422, 424
of media, 118–19, 232, 234, 248, 258–59, *258*, 278
political parties and, 317, 335, 336
regulatory review, 483, 496–98

government spending, 87, 379, 462–63
See also budget process; welfare state

GPS monitoring, 123

Graham, Lindsey, 453

grand juries, 124–25, **124** juries that determine whether sufficient evidence is available to justify a trial; grand juries do not rule on the accused's guilt or innocence

grants-in-aid, 81–82, **81**, *82*, 87, 88, 89–90, 151, 152 programs through which Congress provides money to state and local governments on the condition that the funds be employed for purposes defined by the federal government

Grassley, Chuck, *188*

grassroots campaigns, 289–90, **364** political campaigns that operate at the local level, often using face-to-face communication to generate interest and momentum by citizens

grassroots mobilization, 418 a lobbying campaign in which a group mobilizes its membership to contact government officials in support of the group's position
See also protest

Gratz v. Bollinger, 175

Gray, Freddie, killing of, 419

Great Compromise, 43–44, **44**, *45* the agreement reached at the Constitutional Convention of 1787 that gave each state an equal number of senators regardless of its population but linked representation in the House of Representatives to population

Great Depression
   See also New Deal
   federal government power and, 23, 26, 81
   federalism and, 81
   political parties and, 335, 373
   socioeconomic status and, 19
   voter decisions and, 387
Great Recession (2008)
   age differences and, 326
   bureaucracy and, 537
   Consumer Financial Protection Board and, 534
   election of 2008 and, 374
   federal government power and, 28, 78
   health care and, 88
   lobbying and, 409
   mortgage lending and, 156
   public opinion and, 203
Great Writ. *See* habeas corpus
Green, Donald, 289
green (alternative-energy) technologies, 317
Green New Deal, 377, 382
Green Party, 188, 337, 348
Green-Yates, Kimberly, 2
Griswold v. Connecticut, 129–30, 570
Grodzins, Morton, 83
group politics. *See* interest groups
Gruber, Justin, 181, *181*
Grutter v. Bollinger, 175, *175*, 176
Guardian, The, 246
Gulf War, 484
gun control
   See also gun rights
   advocacy groups, 403, *403*
   agreement on, 329
   executive orders and, 498
   grassroots mobilization and, 418
   mass shootings and, *119*, 120, 122
   political ideologies on, 187
   protest and, *194*
   public opinion on, 120, 122, 181–82, 191, *203*
   Second Amendment and, 119
   state laws, *120, 121*
   states' rights and, 86, *86*
Gun-Free School Zones Act, *86*
gun rights
   See also gun control
   interest groups and, 414, 418, 460, 464
   protest and, *11, 194*

public opinion on, 120, 122, 180–82, *203*
Second Amendment and, *105*, 119
state laws, *120, 121*
Supreme Court on, 120
gun violence, *119*, 120, *121*, 122, 181, 190–91, 418, 526

H

habeas corpus, 101, 475, 486, 488, **549** a court order demanding that an individual in custody be brought into court and shown the cause for detention

Hague v. Committee for Industrial Organization, 116
Hamdi v. Rumsfeld, 560
Hamilton, Alexander
   on Bill of Rights, 101, 102
   on Congress, 48
   on executive branch, 49
   on political parties, 309
   ratification debates and, 54, 57
Hamilton v. Regents of the University of California, 104
Hanage, William, 509
Hannity, Sean, 240
hard news, 232
Hardwick, Michael, 132
Harris, Kamala, 376, 380, *389*, 491
Harrison, Benjamin, 334, *334*, 357
Harrison, William Henry, 492
Hatch Act (1939), 516
hate speech, 112–14, *113*
Hawaii, 173
Hayes, Rutherford B., 143, 357
Health, Education, and Welfare, Department of, 2–3, 174, 521, 532
Health and Human Services, Department of (HHS), 514, 516, 520, 521, 532, 533
health care
   See also Affordable Care Act; Medicaid
   agreement on, 328
   business interests and, 399
   congressional oversight and, 532, *533*
   devolution and, 88
   election of 2020 and, 377, 382
   elections and, 374
   party polarization and, 377
   presidential agenda setting power and, 480–81
   spending on, 380
   Tea Party movement and, 419
   undocumented immigrants and, 16–17, 165
Hearst Communications, 234
Help America Vote Act (HAVA) (2003), *349*, 350

Henry, Patrick, *21*, 54
Hernandez v. Texas, 165
hidden partisans, 322
higher education
   affirmative action and, 160, 174–76
   civil rights movement and, 282
   freedom of speech and, 112, 113–14, *114*
   gender discrimination in, 161, 162
   "separate but equal" rule and, 146
Hill, Anita, 554
Hispanic Americans. *See* Latino/a Americans
Hobby Lobby case, 22, 108–9, *109*, 568
Holder, Eric, 480, 486
holds (Senate), 453
Holmes, Oliver Wendell, 109, 114
Holt v. Hobbs, 108
Homeland Security, Department of (DHS)
   bureaucracy organization and, 520, 532
   creation of, 93, 483, 537
   federalism and, 89
   immigration policy and, 166
homelessness, 21, 407
homeownership
   See also mortgage lending
   racial discrimination and, 146, 152, 156, 163

home rule, 76 power delegated by the state to a local unit of government to manage its own affairs

Honest Leadership and Open Government Act (2007), 409, 422
Hoover, Herbert, 81, 335, 387
Hopwood v. Texas, 175
House of Representatives
   See also Congress
   apportionment for, 19–20, 442, *442*
   Bill of Rights and, 102
   Constitutional amendment process and, 58
   Constitution on, 48, 450, 457
   election of 2020 and, 376, 382
   Great Compromise and, 44
   impeachment and, 378, 466, 480, 502, 536
   lawmaking and, 450, 452, 455, 456, 457
   majority rule, minority rights and, 25
   party discipline in, 462
   party leadership in, 444–45, *445, 456*
   presidential succession and, 492
   vs. Senate, 48, 431–32, *431*, 462
House Rules Committee, 446, 452
House Select Committee on Benghazi, 448
House Ways and Means Committee, 446
housing
   See also homeownership; mortgage lending
   racial discrimination and, 146, 152, 156, 163

housing *(continued)*
    segregation/desegregation and, 148, 150, 156, 163
Housing and Urban Development, Department of (HUD), 156
Howell, William, 527
Human Rights Campaign, 173
Hunt, Ward, 143
Hunter, Noelle, 438
Hupp, Suzanna, 180, *181*
Hurricane Katrina, 394, 511

I

ideological groups, 401, 415
"I Have a Dream" (King), 149
iHeartMedia, 259
immigrants
    See also demographics; immigration; immigration policy
    age and, 19
    citizenship, 14, 16, *166*, 187, 194, 285, 324
    civil rights of, 165–68, *169*
    undocumented, 16–17, 106, 165, 166, *166*, *168*, *169*, 194
    in U.S. population, 12, 14, 16–17, *17*
    voter turnout, 285
    voting rights, 269
immigration
    See also immigrants; immigration policy
    anxieties about, 14, 20
    history of, *14*
Immigration Act (1965), 168, 170
Immigration and Customs Enforcement (ICE), 89–90, *89*, 166, *168*
immigration policy
    See also Trump administration immigration policy
    DACA, 166, *166*
    DREAM Act, 165–66, 570, *570*
    election of 2016 and, 167, 318, 374
    election of 2020 and, 380
    executive orders and, 377, 498
    federalism and, 89–90
    Fourteenth Amendment and, 106
    history of, 14, 16
    political ideologies on, 187
    political parties and, 324
    protest and, *11*, *166–67*, *570*
    public opinion on, 194–95, 208
    regulatory review and, 497–98
    Secure Communities program, 89, 166
    state of emergency declarations and, 478, 482
    Supreme Court on, 16, 165, 167, 168, 570

impeachment, 466–67, **466**, *467*, 502 the formal charge by the House of Representatives that a government official has committed "Treason, Bribery, or other high Crimes and Misdemeanors"
    See also Trump impeachment

implementation, 496–97, 511–12, **512** the efforts of departments and agencies to translate laws into specific bureaucratic rules and actions

implied powers, 73, 80, 482–83, **482** powers derived from the necessary and proper clause of Article I, Section 8, of the Constitution; such powers are not specifically expressed but are implied through the expansive interpretation of delegated powers

income inequality. *See* economic inequality

incumbency, 360–61, **439** holding the political office for which one is running

    campaign finance and, 311, 362, *362*, 416, 440
    congressional elections and, 439–40, *439*
    economic conditions and, 374, *375*
    electoral competition and, 291
    gender and, 286
    gerrymandering and, 311, 350, 351
    party polarization and, 329
    presidential elections and, 387
    redistricting and, 442

incumbent, 360 a candidate running for re-election to a position that he or she already holds
    See also incumbency

independent agencies, 490, 517–18, 521

independent regulatory commissions, 518 government agencies outside the executive department usually headed by commissioners

independents, 322, *322*, 326, 384, 387
Indiana, 155–56
Indian Removal Act (1830), 171
Indian Self-Determination and Education Assistance Act, 171
industry interests. *See* business interests

informational benefits, 404 special newsletters, periodicals, training programs, conferences, and other information provided to members of groups to entice others to join

information literacy, 249
in-group bias, 330

inherent powers, 484, 486, 488 powers claimed by a president that are not expressed in the Constitution but are inferred from it

innovation, 513–14
In re Agent Orange Product Liability Litigation, 574

inspectors general (IGs), 532–33, **532** independent audit organizations located in most federal agencies

Instagram, 205, 235, 242, 278
    See also social media
instant organization, 369
instant runoff voting, 339, 348, 359

institutional advertising, 417–18, **418** advertising designed to create a positive image of an organization

institutional presidency, 489–93, *489*
intelligence agencies, 476–77, 491
Intercept, The, 235

interest groups, 397–424, **397** individuals who organize to influence the government's programs and policies

    ambivalence about, 9
    ballot measures and, 417
    bureaucracy and, 530
    congressional decision-making and, 459–60
    effectiveness of, 419–22
    elections and, 414, *415*, 416–17
    environmental policy and, 408–9
    federal courts and, 413–14
    government regulation and, 411, *413*, 530, 536–37
    grassroots mobilization, 418
    House vs. Senate and, 432
    international comparisons, *398*, 402
    iron triangles and, 411–13, *412*
    legislative scorecards, 460
    lobbying expenditures, *423*
    lobbyists for, 394
    for older Americans, 401, 420–21
    vs. political parties, 307–8, 397
    protest and, *418–19*, 419
    public opinion and, 417–18
    selective benefits, 404–6, *405*, 406, 420
    strategy overview, 408–9, *408*
    Supreme Court and, 565–66
    symbolic legislation and, 440
    types of, 399, 401–2

unions as, *397*
unique U.S. strength of, 402
unrepresented interests, 406–7, *406–7*
intergovernmental cooperation. *See* cooperative federalism
intergovernmental lobby, 402

intergovernmental relations, 71 the processes by which the three levels of American government (national, state, local) negotiate and compromise over policy responsibility

Interior, Department of the, 521, 537

intermediate scrutiny, 158, 160, 161 a test used by the Supreme Court in gender discrimination cases that places the burden of proof partially on the government and partially on the challengers to show that the law in question is unconstitutional

Internal Revenue Service (IRS), 128, 483–84, 500, 520
international comparisons
bureaucracy, *519*
cabinet, 489
campaign finance, 369–70
democracy, 55, *55*
election rules, 309, *321*, 338, 348–49
federal courts, 559
federalism, 71, *85*
forms of government, 7
freedom of the press, *111*
gender equality, *164*
interest groups, *398*, 402
internet, *230*
legislative representation, *437*
media regulation, 232, 258
political culture, 184
political parties, 309, *321*, 338
presidency, *487*, 489
presidential elections, *356*
public broadcasting, 232
trust/distrust in government, *199*
voter turnout, 271, *275*, 288
internet
See also digital news; social media
access to, *230*, 241–42, 259
Congressional representation and, 436
content regulation, 118, 258
creation of, 513–14
international comparisons, *230*
metadata surveillance, 22
net neutrality and, *258*
political participation and, 241–42, 273–74, 276–79, 364, 495
privacy and, 184, *230*
public-opinion polls on, 215–16
Tea Party movement and, 305

Internet Tax Freedom Act (ITFA) (1998), 84
interracial marriage, 74, 156–57, *157*, 174
interstate commerce, 79–80, 151, *152*
Interstate Commerce Commission (ICC), *152*
investigative hearings, 447, 464
investment, 521
Iowa, caucuses in, 352, 353
Iraq War, 201, 374, 484, 495

iron triangles, 412–13, *412*, **412** stable, cooperative relationships that often develop among a congressional committee, an administrative agency, and one or more supportive interest groups; not all of these relationships are triangular, but iron triangles are the most typical

IRS (Internal Revenue Service), 128, 483–84, 500, 520
Issenberg, Sasha, 219

issue networks, 413 loose networks of elected leaders, public officials, activists, and interest groups drawn together by specific policy issues

J
Jackson, Andrew, 86, 332, 572
Jackson, Henry M., 440
Jackson, Robert H., 568
Janus, Mark, 542–43
Janus v. AFSCME, 542–43, *566*
Japanese American internment, 170, *170*
Jay, John, 54
Jefferson, Thomas
Bill of Rights and, 102
on civil liberties, 100
Declaration of Independence and, 39, 40
on freedom of religion, 106
judicial review and, 556
on limited government, 5
political parties and, 332
slavery and, 63
Jeffersonian Republicans (Antifederalists), *53*, 53–54, 56, 57, 73, 102, 309, 332
Jewish Americans
See also religion
immigration and, 14
political participation, 287
political parties and, 324
symbolic legislation and, 440
in U.S. population, 17, 19
Jim Crow era
See also civil rights movement
civil rights movement origins and, 145
Compromise of 1877 and, 143
federalism and, 83, 86
voting restrictions, 269–70, 281, 568

Jim Crow laws, 143 laws enacted by southern states following Reconstruction that discriminated against African Americans
See also Jim Crow era; segregation/ desegregation

job discrimination. *See* employment
Johnson, Andrew, 466, *467*, 478, 503
Johnson, Gary, *337*
Johnson, Lyndon B., and administration, *152*
affirmative action and, 174
civil rights movement and, 336, 498
negative ads, 364
political parties and, 335, 336
Vietnam War and, 335
Johnson v. McIntosh, 171
Joint Chiefs of Staff, 520

joint committees, 448 legislative committees formed of members of both the House and Senate

Jones, Doug, 383
journalism/journalists
See also digital news; media
adversarial, 201, 256–57, *257*
citizen journalism, 236, 244–45
digital news and, 234, 236, 237, 241
influence of, 250
traditional media and, 231, 234

judicial activism, 570–71, **570** judicial philosophy that posits that the Court should go beyond the words of the Constitution or a statute to consider the broader societal implications of its decisions

judicial branch, 49–50, 51, 549, 572
See also federal courts; Supreme Court

judicial restraint, 570 judicial philosophy whose adherents refuse to go beyond the clear words of the Constitution in interpreting the document's meaning

judicial review, 50, 51, 62, 535, 555–56, **555**, 558–61 the power of the courts to review actions of the legislative and executive branches and, if necessary, declare them invalid or unconstitutional; the Supreme Court asserted this power in *Marbury v. Madison* (1803)

judicial revolutions, 572–74
judicial scrutiny, 109, 147, 158, 160, 161, 174, 175, *175*
Judiciary Act (1789), 558
June Medical Services LLC v. Russo, 567

jurisdiction, 547–48, **547**, 561–62 the sphere of a court's power and authority

jury trial, right to, *105*, 106
Justice, Department of, 152–53, 155, 167

K

Kagan, Elena, *554*, 555
Kavanaugh, Brett, 453, 544, *552*, 554, *554*, 555
Keating-Owen Child Labor Act (1916), *80*
Kelo v. City of New London, 129
Kennedy, Anthony, 123, 544, 555, 568
Kennedy, Joe, III, *311*
Kennedy, John F., Jr., and administration, *152*, 336, 367, *367*, 494
Keystone XL pipeline, 482
Kim Jong-un, *478*, 496
King, Martin Luther, Jr., 148, 149, *150*, *151*, *152*, *418*, 419, 440
King Caucus process, 354
King v. Burwell, 570
Kissinger, Henry, 491
Knowledge Networks, 215
Koch, Charles, *210*
Korean War, 473, 484
Ku Klux Klan, 110, 334
Kushner, Jared, 490

L

Labor, Department of, 521
labor relations. *See* organized labor

laissez-faire capitalism, 22 an economic system in which the means of production and distribution are privately owned and operated for profit with minimal or no government interference

Lamb, Conor, 401
Lambda Legal Defense and Education Fund, 173
Land Ordinance (1785), 41
Landrieu, Mary, *410*
language minorities, 154, 170–71
Lanham Act (1946), 99
Lanza, Michael, 3
La Raza Unida, 165
Lasswell, Harold, 8
Late Show, The, 240
Latino/a Americans
    See also demographics; racial discrimination; voter demographics
    apportionment and, 154–55
    civil rights of, 163, 165
    Congress and, 165, 433–34, *433*, *434*
    election of 2020 and, *284*, 285, 387, 388
    political parties and, 285, 323, 324
    public opinion and, 194–95
    redistricting and, 154–55
    Trump's racist rhetoric and, 377, 388

trust/distrust in government, 30
    in U.S. population, 12, 14, 16, 163, 165, 285, 444
    voter turnout, 284–85
    voting rights of, 154–55, 163, 165
Lau, Richard, 205
Lau v. Nichols, 170, 171
law. *See* federal courts; law enforcement; lawmaking; Supreme Court; *specific laws, e.g. Clean Air Act*
law clerks, 564–65, *564*
law enforcement
    See also criminal justice system
    aggressive tactics of, 124
    civil rights movement and, *254*
    election of 2020 and, 382
    executive orders and, 498
    Floyd murder, 150, 191, 192, 194, 196, 264, 265, 267, 381, 419, 477
    judicial review and, 558
    Miranda rights, 62, *105*, 125–26, *125*
    racial discrimination and, 124, 149–50, *191*, 192, 194, 196
    reform proposals, 194, 248
    Secure Communities program, 89, 166
lawmaking, 450–59
    See also budget process
    committee deliberation, 450–52
    conference committees and, 448–49, 454, 456
    debate, 452–53
    federal courts and, 562
    interest groups and, 460
    new order, 455–56, 457–59
    overview, *451*
    presidency and, 454, 480–81
    voting, 453–54
Lawrence v. Texas, 132, 173
Lawson, April, 13
leadership PACs, 371
League of Conservation Voters, 460
League of United Latin American Citizens (LULAC), 165
League of Women Voters, 294
Ledbetter v. Goodyear Tire and Rubber Co, 163
Lee, Barbara, *187*
Lee, Richard Henry, 54
legal system, 545–49
    See also federal courts; judicial branch
legislative branch. *See* Congress
legislative hearings, 447

legislative initiative, 480–81, *480*, 485, **495** the president's inherent power to bring a legislative agenda before Congress

legislative scorecards, 460

***Lemon* test, 107** a rule articulated in Lemon v. Kurtzman that government action toward religion is permissible if it is secular in purpose, neither promotes nor inhibits the practice of religion, and does not lead to "excessive entanglement" with religion

Lemon v. Kurtzman, 107
LePage, Paul, *401*
"Letter from Birmingham Jail" (King), *152*
Lewinsky, Monica, 466
Lewis, John, *205*
LGBTQ Americans, 190, 413
    See also same-sex marriage; sexual orientation
    civil rights, 132–33, 172–73, 558, 570
    discrimination against, 133, 172

libel, 117–18, **117** a written statement made in "reckless disregard of the truth" that is considered damaging to a victim because it is "malicious, scandalous, and defamatory"

liberal governments, 7
liberalism, 185–86, *187*, 196, 250, 377
    See also political ideology

liberals, 186 today this term refers to those who generally support social and political reform, governmental intervention in the economy, more economic equality, expansion of federal social services, and greater concern for consumers and the environment
    See also liberalism

Libertarian Party, 337, 348

libertarians, 187, 337, 348 those who emphasize freedom and believe in voluntary association with small government

liberty, 5, 9, 21–22, **21**, **183**, 184, 226 freedom from governmental control

Liberty Displaying the Arts and Sciences, 44
Liberty Party, 142
Libya, 486
    See also Benghazi investigation
Lilly Ledbetter Fair Pay Act (2009), 162, 163, *163*
Limbaugh, Rush, 240

limited government, 5, 7, 8, 21, **21**, 28, 56–57, **56** a principle of constitutional government; a government whose powers are defined and limited by a constitution

Lincoln, Abraham
    debates and, 367

electoral college and, 359
habeas corpus and, 475, *476*, 486
inherent powers and, 484
political parties and, 334
linked fate, 191, 194, 282
literacy tests, 154, 171, 269, 270, 281
Little Rock school desegregation (1957), *147*, 148, *152*, 477, *477*
Littlewolf, Nevada, 265–66
living Constitution concept, 62
Livingston, Robert, 40

lobbying, 409 a strategy by which organized interests seek to influence the passage of legislation by exerting direct pressure on government officials
 by business interests, 394, *395*, 399, *400*, 401, *411*, 460
 by citizen groups, 402
 congressional decision-making and, 460
 coronavirus stimulus legislation and, 394–96, *395*
 direct, 409–11
 government regulation of, 409, 422, 424
Lobbying Disclosure Act (LDA) (1995), 409, 422
local governments
 bureaucracy and, 526
 federalism and, 76, *76*, 92, *92*
 immigration policy and, 166
 lobbying for, 394, 402
 number of, *76*
 political participation and, *75*, 77–78
Locke, John, *7*, 40, 47
Louisiana, 132
#LoveWins, 277, *277*
Loving v. Virginia, 74, 156–57, *157*, 174
Lozier, Sam, 365, *365*
Lucy, Autherine, *152*

M
Maddow, Rachel, *249*
Madison, James
 Great Compromise and, 43
 judicial review and, 556
 on political parties, 309
 ratification debates and, 54, 57
 Three-Fifths Compromise and, 44
mail-in voting, 156, 184, 290, 296, 298, 312, 382, *383*

majority leader, 444 the elected leader of the majority party in the House of Representatives or in the Senate; in the House, the majority leader is subordinate in the party hierarchy to the Speaker of the House

majority-minority districts, 155, **352** electoral districts, such as congressional districts, in which the majority of the constituents belong to racial or ethnic minorities

majority party, 320 the party that holds the majority of legislative seats in either the House or the Senate

majority rule, minority rights, 25 the democratic principle that a government follows the preferences of the majority of voters but protects the interests of the minority

majority systems, 348 electoral systems in which, to win a seat in the parliament or other representative body, a candidate must receive a majority of all the votes cast in the relevant district

Maklin, Fern, 396
Malkin, Michelle, 305
Malloy v. Hogan, 105
Manafort, Paul, 465
Manning, Chelsea, 117, *117*
Mapp v. Ohio, 105, 122
Mar-a-Lago, 411
Marbury v. Madison, 535, 556
March on Washington (1963), 149, *150*
Marcus v. Search Warrant, 128
marijuana, 90, *90*, *291*, 329, 360

marketplace of ideas, 109, **201** the public forum in which beliefs and ideas are exchanged and compete

Markey, Edward, *311,* 429
marriage. *See* interracial marriage; same-sex marriage
Married Women's Property Act (New York), 143
Marshall, John, 48, 79, 486, 556, 572
Marshall, Thurgood, 146
Martin, Trayvon, killing of, 264, 418, 419
Marucci, Anthony, 531
Maryland v. King, 123–24
Mason, Lilliana, 196, 329–30
Massachusetts, 87
mass incarceration, 157–58, *157*
mass media. *See* media; social media
mass shootings, *119*, 120, 122, 181, 190–91, 418, 526
Matal v. Tam, 98–100, 556

material benefits, 404 special goods, services, or money provided to members of groups to entice others to join

McCain, John, 219, 249, 319, 371, 372, 482
McCain-Feingold bill (1996), 416
 See also Bipartisan Campaign Reform Act
McClatchy corporation, 234
McConnell, Mitch, 319, 320, 438, *456*
McCreary County v. American Civil Liberties Union of Kentucky, 107–8
McCulloch v. Maryland, 79
McCutcheon et al. v. Federal Election Commission, 371, 571
McDonald v. Chicago, 105, 120
McKinley, William, 335
McSally, Martha, 383
Meade, Desmond, 138–39, *139*, 158

media, 226–59, **229** print and digital forms of communication, including television, newspapers, radio, and the internet, intended to convey information to large audiences
 See also digital news; fake news; internet; misinformation in media; social media

 adversarial journalism, 201, 256–57, *257*
 advertising and, 232, 233, 234, 235, 236, 237, *238*, 364
 agenda setting by, 250, 252, 254–55
 alarm vs. patrol modes, 252
 ballot measures and, 360
 campaign strategy and, 364, 366–67
 civil rights movement and, 149, 250, *254*
 congressional elections and, 439–40
 congressional oversight and, 532
 consumer ideology, *252*
 evaluating, 247, *247*
 framing by, 254–55
 freedom of the press and, 226, 229
 government regulation of, 118–19, 232, 234, 248, 258–59, *258*, 278
 importance to democracy, 226, 228, 229, 231, 257
 influence of, 250, 252, 254–55
 journalism/journalists and, 231, 234, 236, 237, 241, 250
 leaks, 256, *256*, 257
 national conventions and, 315, *315*, 355
 net neutrality, *258*
 newspapers, 236, 237–38, *238*
 news sources, 226, 234, *253*
 ownership of, 231, 233–34, *233*, 235, 236, 239, 250, 258–59
 party identification and, 320, 322
 party polarization and, 248–49, *249*, 274, 277, 320, 322, 376
 political ideology and, *249*, 250, *252*
 political participation and, 229, 231
 politicians' use of, 250

National Aeronautics and Space Administration (NASA), *514*

National American Woman Suffrage Association (NAWSA), 145–46

National Association for the Advancement of Colored People (NAACP), 145, 146, 282, 413, 565, 574

national conventions, 315–16, *315*, **315**, 354–55, *355* convened by the Republican National Committee or the Democratic National Committee to nominate official candidates for president and vice president in the upcoming election, establish party rules, and adopt the party's platform

National Defense Authorization Act (2019), 500

National Emergencies Act (1976), 486, 488

National Environmental Policy Act (NEPA) (1969), 573

National Federation of Independent Business, 399, 460

National Federation of Independent Business v. Sebelius, 90

national government. *See* federal government; federalism

National Institutes of Health (NIH), 520

National Organization for Women (NOW), 160

National Origins quota system, 14

National Park Service, *458*, 521

National Popular Vote Interstate Compact, 357, 359

National Public Radio (NPR), 232, 240

National Review, 238

National Rifle Association (NRA), 397, 414, 418, 460, 464

National Right to Life Committee, 130, 460

national security adviser, 491

National Security Agency (NSA), 22, 117, 477, 486

National Security Council (NSC), 476–77, **491** a presidential foreign policy advisory council composed of the president, the vice president, the secretary of state, the secretary of defense, and other officials invited by the president

national security policy

See also foreign policy; military
bureaucracy and, 518, 520
federal government power and, 93
freedom of speech and, 110
intelligence agencies and, 476–77, 491
military spending and, 380
trust/distrust in government and, 29

national unity, 40, 50, 57, 71, 76, 388–89

National Voter Registration Act (NVRA), 293

National Woman's Party, 146

National Women's Political Caucus, 286–87

Native Americans

See also demographics; voter demographics
citizenship, 14, 171
colonial America and, *37*
election of 2020 and, 387
federal courts and, 572
stereotypes of, 99–100
in U.S. population, 12, *12*

native digital news, 237

natural disasters, 478, 488, *488*, 495, 511

Navarro, Peter, 473–74, *473*

NBC, 238, 239

Near v. Minnesota, 104, 116

necessary and proper clause, 48, **73**, 79 Article I, Section 8, of the Constitution, which provides Congress with the authority to make all laws "necessary and proper" to carry out its expressed powers

negative ads, *110*, 364, 366, *366*

Negotiated Rulemaking Act (1990), 411

net neutrality, *258*

Neustadt, Richard, 528

New Deal
federal government power and, 28, 76, 80–81
grants-in-aid, 81
judicial review and, 560
political parties and, 325, 335, 338, 377
socioeconomic status and, 19
Supreme Court and, 569, 572
Works Progress Administration, *81*

New Federalism, 87 attempts by Presidents Nixon and Reagan to return power to the states through block grants

New Hampshire, 352, 353, 354

Newhouse, Neil, 212–13

New Jersey, 298

New Jersey Plan, 43 a framework for the Constitution, introduced by William Paterson, that called for equal state representation in the national legislature regardless of population

news aggregators, *241*, **241** applications or feeds that collect web content such as news headlines, blogs, podcasts, online videos, and more in one location for easy viewing

News Corp, *236*

news media. *See* digital news; media

newspapers, 236, 237–38, *238*, 240

New York Times, 160, 234, 237–38, 256, 257

New York Times Co. v. Sullivan, 118

New York Times Co. v. United States (Pentagon Papers case), 117

Nexstar Media Group, 239

NextGen America, 280–81

NFL (National Football League), 267, *268*

9/11. *See* September 11, 2001, terrorist attacks

Nineteenth Amendment, 26, *59*, *145*, 146, 270

Ninth Amendment, 130

Nixon, Richard, and administration
See also Watergate scandal
civil rights and, 154
debates and, 367, *367*
devolution and, 87
environmental policy and, 517
National Security Council and, 491
pardon, 478
political parties and, 335
resignation, 492
southern strategy, 336, *336*
Vietnam War and, 250

No Child Left Behind Act (NCLB) (2001), 93

no-excuse absentee voting, 298

nomination, 311, 352–55 the process by which political parties select their candidates for election to public office

Northam, Ralph, *231*

North Carolina, 92, *92*, 161, 443, 558

North Dakota, 132

North Korea, *478*, 496

Northwest Ordinance (1787), 41

Nownes, Anthony, 402

NRA (National Rifle Association), 397, 414, 418, 460, 464

NSA (National Security Agency), 22, 117, 477, 486

NSC (National Security Council), 476–77, **491** a presidential foreign policy advisory council composed of the president, the vice president, the secretary of state, the secretary of defense, and other officials invited by the president

nuclear option (Senate), 453

nullification, 84, 86

Nwalorizi, Stephen, 258

O

OAN, 377

Obama, Barack, and administration
anti-terrorism and, 486
approval ratings, 495–96, *501*
big data and, 219, 368
birther conspiracies and, *246*
bureaucracy and, 525

Obama, Barack, and administration *(continued)*
 campaign finance and, 112, 274, 369, 372
 campaign strategy and, 364
 congressional investigations and, 464–65
 Consumer Financial Protection Board and,
  534–35, *535*
 criminal justice system and, 526–27
 debates and, 367
 Democratic Party and, 492
 economic conditions and, 374
 environmental policy and, 513, *513*
 executive orders and, 498
 executive privilege and, 479–80
 federalism and, 93
 filibuster and, 453
 on gender discrimination, 161, *162*, 163
 gun control and, 122, 182
 health care and, 255, 374, 480–81, 492
 immigration policy and, 89, 166, 167, 498
 Latino/a Americans and, 323
 lawmaking and, 453–54
 LGBTQ Americans and, 161, 172, 497
 lobbying and, 409
 mass incarceration and, 157
 media and, 200, 243, 254, 255, 274, 495
 micro-targeting and, 368
 minimum wage and, 527
 nonenforcement of laws and, 500
 policy czars and, 530
 political appointees, 522
 political parties and, 336
 primary elections and caucuses and, 353
 public-opinion polls and, 216, 217
 recess appointments and, 561
 regulatory review and, 497
 same-sex marriage and, 277
 Supreme Court appointments and, 378–79,
  543, 552, 555
 tax policy and, 254
 Tea Party movement and, 305, 336, 419
 transgender Americans and, 161, 497
 Veterans Health Administration and, 536
 veto and, 482
 voter demographics and, 26, 271, 281,
  282, 323, 336
 voter mobilization and, 290, 314
 voter turnout and, 271
Obamacare. *See* Affordable Care Act
Obergefell v. Hodges, 34–35, *35*, 36, 74, 173,
  173, 413, 568–69, *573*
obscenity, 118–19, 258
Ocasio-Cortez, Alexandria, 188, 319, *319*, *436*
Occupational Safety and Health
  Administration (OSHA), 512, 521
Occupy Wall Street movement, 418, 419, *419*
Office of Civil Rights (OCR), 112, 152, 153,
  161, 162

Office of Information and Regulatory Affairs
  (OIRA), 496–97

Office of Management and Budget (OMB),
  490–91, 496, 512, **529** the agency in
  the Executive Office of the President
  with control over the federal budget and
  regulations

Office of Personnel Management, 522
older Americans
 See also age; Medicaid; Medicare; Social
  Security
 election of 2020, 387
 interest groups for, 401, 420–21
 media and, 239
 political parties and, 326
 in U.S. population, 19
 voter turnout, 280, *280*
 voting by mail and, 156
Oleszek, Walter, 455

oligarchy, 5 a form of government in which
 a small group—landowners, military
 officers, or wealthy merchants—controls
 most of the governing decisions

Omar, Ilhan, 319, *319*
OMB (Office of Management and Budget),
  490–91, 496, 512, **529**
Omidyar, Pierre, 235

omnibus appropriations bills, 458–59, **458**
 bills that deal with a number of unrelated
 topics

online news. *See* digital news
online-processing model, 202

open primaries, 348 primary elections in
 which the voter can wait until the day
 of the primary to choose which party to
 enroll in to select candidates for the
 general election

open rule, 452 provision by the House
 Rules Committee that permits floor
 debate and the addition of new
 amendments to a bill

Operation Fast and Furious, 480
Operation Warp Speed, 380

opinions (Supreme Court), 567–68, **567**
 written explanations of the Supreme
 Court's decisions in particular cases

opioid crisis, 428–29

oral argument, 566–67, **566**, *567* the stage
 in the Supreme Court procedure in which
 attorneys for both sides appear before

the Court to present their positions and
answer questions posed by the justices

Oregon, 84, 293, 296, 298, 477
organized labor
 decline of, 543
 federal government role, 80
 as interest group, 397, *397*, 399, 401, 407
 political parties and, 323
 socioeconomic status and, 407
 Supreme Court on, 80, 542–43
 United Farm Workers, 165, 421

original jurisdiction, 548, 550 the authority
 to initially consider a case; distinguished
 from appellate jurisdiction, which is the
 authority to hear appeals from a lower
 court's decision

OSHA (Occupational Safety and Health
  Administration), 512, 521
outsourcing. *See* privatization

oversight, 447, 464–65, **464**, 532–33, **532**
 the effort by Congress, through hearings,
 investigations, and other techniques,
 to exercise control over the activities of
 executive agencies

P

PACs (political action committees), 26, 371,
  397, 414, *415*, 416, 421
Page, Benjamin, 207–8
Palko v. Connecticut, 103–4, 125
panel surveys, 215, 217–18
Papadopoulos, George, 465
pardons, 478
Parkland school shooting (2018), 120, 181, 418
Parks, Rosa, 148, *150*
partial-birth abortion ban, 132

partisan gerrymandering, 351 occurs when
 politicians from one party intentionally
 manipulate the boundaries for legislative
 election districts to disadvantage their political
 opponents' chance of winning an election and
 advantage their own political party
 See also gerrymandering

partisanship, 307 identification with or
 support of a particular party or cause
 See also party identification

Partnership for Public Service, 522, 524

party activists, 323, 377 partisans who
 contribute time, energy, and effort to
 support their party and its candidates

party discipline, 460, 462, *462*

party identification, 307, **320**, 322–23, *322, 333*, 373, *373* an individual voter's psychological ties to one party or another

party machines, 289, 316–17, *316*, **316**, 522 strong party organizations in late nineteenth and early twentieth-century American cities; these machines were led by often corrupt "bosses" who controlled party nominations and patronage

party organization, 314–17, *314*, **314** the formal structure of a political party, including its leadership, election committees, active members, and paid staff

party platforms, 315, 316, 355

party polarization, 308, 327–30, **329** the division between the two major parties on most policy issues, with members of each party unified around their party's positions with little crossover

budget process and, 457–58
Congress and, 320, 329, 378, *378*, 449, 462, 463–64, *463*
coronavirus pandemic and, 380
demographics and, 329–30
digital news and, 248–49, *249*
election of 2020 and, 376–79, *376*, 384–86, 389
executive power expansion and, 377
gerrymandering and, 329, 351, 464
increase in, 317, *318*
in-group bias and, 330
media and, 248–49, *249*, 274, 277, 320, 322, 376–77
party activists and, 377
party discipline and, 460, 462
personal nature of, 327
political knowledge and, 205–6
public opinion and, 196, 206
public policy and, 317–18, 327, *328*
respectful debate and, 13
social media and, 274, 277
Supreme Court appointments and, 543, 552, 554–55
voter ID laws and, 296
party systems, 330, *331*, 332, 334–37

party unity votes, 460, **460**, *462* roll-call votes in the House or Senate in which at least 50 percent of the members of one party take a particular position and are opposed by at least 50 percent of the members of the other party

Paterson, William, 43

Patient Protection and Affordable Care Act. *See* Affordable Care Act
Patriot Act, *452*

patronage, 316 the resources available to higher officials, usually opportunities to make partisan appointments to offices and to confer grants, licenses, or special favors to supporters

pattern-of-cases strategy, 565
Paul, Rand, 319, *452*
Pavan v. Smith, 558, *558*
Paycheck Protection Program (2020), 516–17
See also coronavirus stimulus legislation
paywalls, 238
Pelosi, Nancy, 320, 378, *378*, 434, 456, *456*
Pence, Mike, 380, 530
Pendleton Civil Service Reform Act (1883), 521–22
Pennsylvania, 382, 386

penny press, 240 cheap, tabloid-style newspaper produced in the nineteenth century, when mass production of inexpensive newspapers first became possible due to the steam-powered printing press; a penny press newspaper cost one cent compared with other papers, which cost more than five cents

Pentagon Papers, 117, 201, 256, 257

permanent absentee ballots, 298 the option in some states to have a ballot sent automatically to your home for each election, rather than having to request an absentee ballot each time

Perot, H. Ross, 337, 372
pharmaceutical industry, 380, 399, *401*, 530
ping-ponging, 448–49, 456

plaintiff, 545 the individual or organization that brings a complaint in court

Planned Parenthood of Southeastern Pennsylvania v. Casey, 132

platforms, 315, 316, **355** party documents, written at national conventions, that contain party philosophy, principles, and positions on issues

plea bargains, 547 negotiated agreements in criminal cases in which a defendant agrees to plead guilty in return for the state's agreement to reduce the severity of the criminal charge or prison sentence the defendant is facing

Plessy v. Ferguson, 23, 144–45, *144*

pluralism, 9, 406, **406** the theory that all interests are and should be free to compete for influence in the government; the outcome of this competition is compromise and moderation

plurality systems, 310, 338, **348**, 357 systems in which, to win a seat in the parliament or other representative body, a candidate need only receive the most votes in the election, not necessarily a majority of the votes cast

Plyler v. Doe, 16

pocket veto, 454, **481**, 503 a presidential veto that is automatically triggered if the president does not act on a given piece of legislation passed during the final 10 days of a legislative session

podcasting, 240
polarization. *See* party polarization
police behavior. *See* law enforcement

"police patrol" oversight, 532 regular or even preemptive congressional hearings on bureaucratic agency operations

police power, 73 power reserved to the state government to regulate the health, safety, and morals of its citizens

policy czars, 529–30

policy entrepreneurs, 317–18, **317** individuals who identify problems as political issues and bring policy proposals into the political agenda

policy feedback, 203–4, 208
policy issues. *See* public policy

political action committees (PACs), 26, **371**, 397, 414, **414**, *415*, 416, 421 private groups that raise and distribute funds for use in election campaigns

political appointees, 522, 524, 528–29 the presidentially appointed layer of the bureaucracy on top of the civil service

political culture, 21–30, **21** broadly shared values, beliefs, and attitudes about how the government should function; American political culture emphasizes the values of liberty, equality, and democracy

Americans' views of government, 4, 5, 26, 28–30
democracy and, 24–26
equality, 22–24
international comparisons, 184
liberty, 5, 9, 21–22, 183, 184, 226

political efficacy, 10–11 the belief that one can influence government and politics

political equality, 23 the right to participate in politics equally, based on the principle of "one person, one vote"
See also civil rights; voting rights

political ideology, 183 a cohesive set of beliefs that forms a general philosophy about the role of government
See also conservatism; party polarization

    media and, *249*, 250, *252*
    political parties and, 323, 325–26, 377, 462
    public opinion and, 185–88, *189*
    social groups and, 195, 196
    Supreme Court and, 571

political knowledge, 9–10 information about the formal institutions of government, political actors, and political issues

    descriptive representation and, 282
    digital news and, 10, 206, *206*, 246, 248–49
    limits of, 10, *11*
    public opinion and, 202, 204–7, *205*, *206*, 232, 249
    social media and, 204–5, 206, 226, 232, 241, 245–46, 248–49

political participation, 264–99
    See also protest; voter turnout; voting rights
    African Americans, 143, 154
    age and, *363*
    American Revolution and, 7–8
    ballot measures and, 360
    contacting your member of Congress, 461
    descriptive representation and, 282
    digital, 241–42, 273–74, 276–79, 364, 495
    elections and, 307, *363*
    expressive politics, 276–77, *277*
    extent of, *269*
    federalism and, 93
    interest groups and, 419
    internet access and, 241–42, *258*
    local governments and, *75*, 77–78
    media and, 229, 231
    organized labor and, 401
    political environment and, 289–92
    political parties and, 307
    as political value, 184
    racial injustice protests (2020) and, 264–66
    right to privacy and, 128–29
    traditional, 268, 271–72
    voting rights and, 268–72
    young Americans, *26*, *27*, 242

political parties, 304–40, **307** organized groups that attempt to influence the government by electing their members to important government offices
See also party polarization; primary elections and caucuses

    big data and, 220
    bureaucracy and, 521–22
    campaign finance and, 308, 314–15, 316, 317, 371
    caucuses and, 311, *313*, 352–54, 444
    changes in, 309
    congressional decision-making and, 460, 462, *462*
    congressional elections and, 438
    congressional leadership, 320, 444–45, *445*, *446*, 455–56, 459
    decline of local, 26
    divisions within, 318–19, *319*
    elections and, 310–14
    evolution of, *331*
    formation of, 308–9
    functions of, 304, 310
    gerrymandering and, 350–51, 443
    vs. interest groups, 307–8, 397
    international comparisons, 309, *321*, 338
    national conventions, 315–16, *315*, 354–55, *355*
    party identification, 307, 320, 322–23, *322*, *333*, 373, *373*
    party-line voting, 320
    party machines, 289, 316–17, *316*, 522
    party organization, 314–17, *314*
    party platforms, 315, 316, 355
    party systems, 330, *331*, 332, 334–37
    political ideologies and, 325–26
    presidency and, 319, *485*, 492
    public opinion and, 196, *197*
    reform proposals, 339
    social composition of Congress and, *435*
    Supreme Court and, 378–79, 571
    third parties, 337–39, 359
    two-party system, 309–10, 320, 330, 339, 349
    voter demographics and, 143, 285, 287, 308, *308*, 322, 323–27, *324*, *325*, *326*, *327*, *333*, 336
    voter registration and, 294
    voting by mail and, 382
    voting rules and, 309–10

political power, 8 influence over a government's leadership, organization, or policies

political socialization, 189–91, **189**, *190*, *191*, *192*, 322 the induction of individuals into the political culture;

learning the underlying beliefs and values on which the political system is based

political speech, 110, *110*, 112, 229
political values. *See* values
Politico, 238

politics, 5, 8–9, *10* conflict over the leadership, structure, and policies of governments

PolitiFact.com, 205, 243, 248
polling. *See* public-opinion polls
polling aggregators, 220
poll taxes, 139, 154, 269, 270, 281
poor, the. *See* poverty; socioeconomic status

popular sovereignty, 24 principle of democracy in which political authority rests ultimately in the hands of the people

population. *See* demographics; voter demographics
populism, 198, 284, 308, 309, 325, 332, 417
    See also Populist Party; Trump, Donald, and administration
Populist Party, 334–35, 337

pork barreling, 440, 454 appropriations made by legislative bodies for local projects that are often not needed but that are created so that local representatives can win reelection in their home districts

pornography, 118–19
Portman, Rob, 429
position taking, 440
potential interest groups, 407
poverty
    See also economic inequality; socioeconomic status
    cruel and unusual punishment and, 127
    interest groups and, 407
    welfare programs and, 88

precedents, 546, 565 prior cases whose principles are used by judges as the basis for their decision in a present case

predatory lending, 156

preemption, 84, 92 the principle that allows the national government to override state or local actions in certain policy areas; in foreign policy, the willingness to strike first in order to prevent an enemy attack

presidency, 472–504
    See also executive power expansion; presidential elections; *specific presidents and administrations, e.g. Obama, Barack, and administration*

agency location and, 521, 525, 529
approval ratings, 495–96, *501*
broadcast media and, 200, *200*, 257
budget process and, 480, 481, 490–91, 496
bureaucracy and, 521
bureaucratic control and, 528–30, 533, 534–35
civil rights and, 140
Constitution on, 49, 475–76, 503
death in office, 492
Defense Production Act and, 472–74
demographics of, *485*
executive agreements, 465–66, 478–79
executive orders, 377, 498, *499*
expressed powers of, 476–82, 484, 486
foreign policy and, 49, 465–66, 478–79, *478*, 486
head of state role, 475, *478*, 493
implied powers, 73, 80, 482–83
inherent powers, 484, 486, 488
inspectors general and, 533
institutional structure, 489–93, *489*
international comparisons, *487*, 489
lawmaking and, 454, 480–81
legislative initiative, 480–81, *480*, 485, 496
lobbying and, 410–11
media agenda setting and, 250
policy czars and, 529–30
political parties and, 319, *485*, 492
powers of, 49
qualifications for, *475*
social media and, 200, *202*, 243–44, *244*, 274, 319, 495, *495*
take care clause and, 475, 482, 528
term limits, 502–3
transition into office, 522, 524
unitary executive theory, 482–83
vesting clause, 475, 482
veto power, 49, 51, 454, 481–82, *481*
presidential appointments
bureaucracy and, 524
bureaucratic control and, 528–29, 530
Cabinet, 490, 522
checks and balances and, 51
expressed powers and, 479
federal judges, 549, 552, 572
filibuster and, 453
recess, 503, 534, 561
Supreme Court, 453, *465*, 543–44, 552, *552*, 554–55, *554*, 571
presidential elections, 352–59
See also elections; electoral college; *specific elections, e.g.* election of 2016
debates, 314, 367–68
international comparisons, *356*
media agenda setting and, 254

national party conventions, 315–16, *315*, 354–55, *355*
primary elections and caucuses, 311, 313, 329, 347–48, 352–55, *353*
social media and, 236, 273
steps in process, *358*
vice presidency and, 491–92
voter mobilization, 289–90
Presidential Succession Act (1947), 492
President's Commission on Civil Rights, 146
press, freedom of the, 103, *104*, *111*, 116–19, 184, 226, 229
Pressley, Ayanna, 319, *319*

primary elections, 311, 347 elections held to select a party's candidate for the general election
See also primary elections and caucuses

primary elections and caucuses, *311*, 347–48
campaign finance and, 352–53
debates and, 367–68
election of 2020, *311*, *313*, 354, 367–68, 379, *379*
media agenda setting and, 254
media and, 353–54
national conventions and, 315, 354–55
open vs. closed primaries, 348
origins of, 348
party elites and, 311, 354
party organization and, 314
political participation and, *26*
retail politics and, 352–53, *353*
voter mobilization and, 290
voter turnout, *313*

priming (media), 202, **255** the process of making some criteria more important than others when evaluating a politician, problem, or issue

principal-agent problem, 516–17, **516** a conflict in priorities between an actor and the representative authorized to act on the actor's behalf

Printz v. United States, 86

prior restraint, 116 an effort by a governmental agency to block the publication of material it deems libelous or harmful in some other way; censorship; in the United States, the courts forbid prior restraint except under the most extraordinary circumstances

Prison Litigation Reform Act, 572
privacy, right to, 62, 128–30, *131*, 132–33, 184, *230*, 570–71
private property, 21, 60, 62, 73, 129

privatization, 526–27, *526*, **526**, *527* the process by which a formerly public service becomes a service provided by a private company but paid for by the government

privileges and immunities clause, 76 provision, from Article IV, Section 2, of the Constitution, that a state cannot discriminate against someone from another state or give its own residents special privileges

probability sample (simple random sample) (polling method), 211
probable cause, *123*, 124, 125
proclamations, presidential, 500
professional associations, 401
progressive caucus (Democratic Party), 319, *319*, 377, 378, 379, 382
Progressive movement, 8, 316, 337, 338, 348, 360, 417
progressive taxation, 186
Prohibition, 60
property, private, 21, 60, 62, 73, 129

proportional representation, 309, *321*, 338, 339, 348–49, **348** a multiple-member district system that allows each political party representation in proportion to its percentage of the total vote

prospective voting, 374 voting based on the imagined future performance of a candidate or political party

PROTECT Act, 118

protest, 9, *10–11*, **267** participation that involves assembling crowds to confront a government or other official organization

See also Black Lives Matter; racial injustice protests (2020)
civil rights movement and, 148–50, *149*, *150*, *151*, *152*, *418*, 419
election of 2020 and, *376*
electoral college and, 273
environmental policy and, *10*, *92*
First Amendment and, 115–16, *116*, 267
gun rights and control and, *11*, *194*
immigration policy and, *11*, *166–67*, *570*
interest groups and, *418–19*, 419
Latino/a Americans and, 165
minimum wage and, *24*
net neutrality and, *258*
Occupy Wall Street movement, 418, 419, *419*
as political value, 184
public opinion and, *202*

numbers, with every effort made to avoid bias in the construction of the sample

ranked choice voting (RCV), 339, 348, 359, 360
Rankin, Jeanette, *432*
Rap the Vote, 281
rational basis test, 158
R.A.V. v. City of St. Paul, 113
Reagan, Ronald, and administration
    deregulation and, 336
    devolution and, 87
    evangelicals and, 288
    political socialization and, 190
    Republican Party and, *317*, 318, 336
    Supreme Court appointments and, 571
    unitary executive theory and, 483
RealClearPolitics.com, 211, 213, 241, *241*
reasonable doubt standard, 122

recall, 360 a procedure to allow voters to remove state officials from office before their terms expire by circulating petitions to call a vote

recess appointments, 503, 534, 561
Reconstruction, 8, 86, 143, 144, 466, 549
Red Cloud, *12*
Reddit, 241, 242, 273

redistributive programs, 88 economic policies designed to transfer income through taxing and spending, with the goal of benefiting the poor

redistricting, 350, 442, *443* the process of redrawing election districts and redistributing legislative representatives; this happens every 10 years, to reflect shifts in population or in response to legal challenges in existing districts

    congressional elections and, 442–44
    demographics and, 19–20
    election of 2020 and, 376
    gerrymandering and, 154–55, 291, 311, 329, 350–51, 443, 444, 464
    judicial review and, 558
    majority-minority districts, 155, 352
    party polarization and, 329
    race and, *351*, 352, 444
Redlawsk, David, 205

redlining, 152, **156** a practice in which banks refuse to make loans to people living in certain geographic locations

red mirage/blue shift, 382
Reed, Stanley, 568

referendum, 9, *291*, 292, 359–60, **359** the practice of referring a proposed law passed by a legislature to the vote of the electorate for approval or rejection

Reform Party, 337
refugees, 167
Regents of the University of California v. Bakke, 174, *175*
regional differences
    See also voter demographics
    apportionment and, 442
    electoral college and, 357
    political ideologies and, 196
    political parties and, 326, *327*
    presidency and, *485*
    U.S. population and, *15*, 19
regular concurrences, 568

regulated federalism, 83–84 a form of federalism in which Congress imposes legislation on states and localities, requiring them to meet national standards

regulation. *See* government regulation

regulatory capture, 536–37, **536** a form of government failure in which regulatory agencies become too sympathetic to interests or businesses they are supposed to regulate

regulatory review, 483, 496–97
Rehabilitation Act (1973), 172
Rehnquist, William, 571
Reid, Harry, 453
religion
    See also voter demographics
    civil rights movement and, 282, 287
    evangelicals, 195–96, 288, *288*, 324, 418
    freedom of, *104*, *105*, 106–9, *107*, *108*, *109*
    government regulation and, 22
    immigration and, 14, 17, 168
    political parties and, 195–96, *288*, 324–25
    public opinion and, 195–96
    Republican Party and, 196, *288*, 324, 336
    social composition of Congress and, *435*
    in U.S. population, 17, 19
    voter turnout and, 287–88, *288*
Religious Freedom Restoration Act (RFRA), 108
Reno v. American Civil Liberties Union, 118
reparations, 377
representation. *See* congressional representation; descriptive representation

representative democracy (republic), 8, 9 a system of government in which the populace selects representatives, who play a

significant role in governmental decision-making

Republican National Committee (RNC), 314
Republican Party
    See also conservatism; political parties; *specific presidents, e.g. Bush, George W., and administration*
    Benghazi investigation and, 448, 453, 464–65
    budget process and, 457, 458
    congressional committee system and, 449
    Consumer Financial Protection Board and, 534–35
    demographics and, 143, 196, 286, *288*, 323, 324, 325, 326, *327*, 336
    devolution and, 87
    divisions within, 318–19
    education and, 532
    election of 2020 results and, 382–83
    evangelicals and, 195–96, 288, 324
    evolution of, 334, 335, 338
    felon voting rights and, 157–58
    filibuster and, 453
    formation of, 309, 334, *334*
    gerrymandering and, 443
    government regulation and, 84
    health care and, 255, 459, 492
    House conference, 444
    interest groups and, 307
    lawmaking and, 453–54
    media framing and, 255
    national conventions, *315*
    party discipline and, 460, 462
    party identification, 322, *322*
    policy issues and, 317, *317*, 318, 325, *328*, 377, 382
    race and, 323, 324
    Reconstruction and, 8
    redistricting and, 376, 443, 444
    religion and, 196, *288*, 324, 336
    social issues and, *317*, 318, 324, 377
    southern strategy, 336, *336*
    Supreme Court appointments and, 543, 554–55
    Tea Party movement and, 305, 306, 336–37, 419
    Trump nomination and, 311
    voter ID laws and, 155
    voter mobilization and, 290
    voting by mail and, 156, 382
    White Americans and, 281, 282, 284, 336
research, 513–14
reservations, 171

reserved powers, 73, 84 powers, derived from the Tenth Amendment to the Constitution, that are not specifically

reserved powers (continued)
delegated to the national government or
denied to the states

respectful debate, 13
restrictive covenants, 146, 152, 156, 163, 451

retail politics, 352–53, **352**, *353* a style of
campaigning where candidates connect to
voters face-to-face at intimate gatherings,
rallies, town halls, and local events

retrospective voting, 374 voting based on
the past performance of a candidate or
political party

"reverse discrimination," 160
See also affirmative action
Revolutionary War. *See* American Revolution
Rice, Tamir, 419

right of rebuttal, 259 a Federal
Communications Commission regulation
giving individuals the right to have the
opportunity to respond to personal attacks
made on a radio or television broadcast

right to bear arms. *See* gun rights

right to privacy, 62, 128–33, **128**, *131*, 184,
230, 570–71 the right to be left alone,
which has been interpreted by the Supreme
Court to entail individual access to birth
control and abortions

Riley, Akil, 264–65
Riley v. California, 124, 558
Roberts, John, Jr., 114, 554, *554*, *564*,
569–70
Roberts, Owen, 569
Robinson v. California, 105
robocalls, 289
Rock the Vote, 281
Rock the Vote a lo Latino, 281
Roe v. Wade, 130, *130*, 131, 413, 562,
570–71
Rolfe, Meredith, 273

roll-call votes, 460 votes in which each
legislator's yes or no vote is recorded as
the clerk calls the names of the members
alphabetically

Romer v. Evans, 172–73
Romney, Mitt, 217, 284, 319, 467
Roosevelt, Eleanor, 493
Roosevelt, Franklin Delano, and
administration
See also New Deal
bureaucracy and, 529
fireside chats, 200, *200*, 257, 494, *494*

first spouse and, 493
inherent powers and, 484
Japanese American internment and,
170
judicial review and, 560
legislative agenda setting power and,
480
policy czars and, 530
political parties and, 335, 373
public appeals, 494, *494*
Supreme Court and, 569, 572
Roosevelt, Theodore, 257, 493
Rucho v. Common Cause, 443
rural/urban divisions. *See* urban/rural
divisions
Russian election interference (2016)
adversarial journalism and, 257
campaign advertising and, 277–78
congressional decision-making and,
462
fake news and, 205, 248, 278
hacking and, 350
investigations of, 200, 248, 257, *448*,
462, 465, 480
Trump administration and, 200, 257,
465, 480, 491
values and, 184
voter suppression and, 278
Rutledge, John, 57

S
Salwell, Eric, 439–40

same-day registration, 293 the option in
some states to register on the day of the
election, at the polling place, rather than
in advance of the election

same-sex marriage
ballot measures and, 359
Defense of Marriage Act and, 34, 74, 160,
173
elections and, 368
federalism and, 74, *74*
interest groups and, 413
judicial review and, 558
media framing and, 255
Obergefell v. Hodges, 34–35, *35*, 36, 74,
173, *173*, 413, 568–69, *573*
Pavan v. Smith, 558, *558*
public opinion on, 190, 203–4, *203*
Republican Party and, 377
social media and, 276–77, *277*

samples, 211, 213, 214, 215, 381 small
groups selected by researchers to represent
the most important characteristics of entire
populations

sampling error (margin of error), 214
polling error that arises based on the small
size of the sample

San Bernardino, California terrorism incident
(2015), 22, *56*
sanctuary cities, 89–90, 166, 167, *168*
Sand, Leonard B., 574
Sanders, Bernie
campaign finance and, 279, 371
digital media and, 273, 279
divisions within Democratic Party and, 319
primary elections and caucuses and, 353,
354, 379–80
Russian election interference and, 277
socialism and, 187–88
socioeconomic status and, 308
superdelegates and, 355
voter demographics and, 281
Santelli, Rick, 305
Sasse, Benjamin, 318
savings-and-loan crisis (1980s), 537
Scalia, Antonin, 120, 543, 554, 555, 566
Schattschneider, E. E., 307–8, 310, 406
Schenk, Maarten, 228
school prayer, *107*
schools. *See* education; school segregation/
desegregation; school shootings
school segregation/desegregation
Asian Americans and, 168
Brown v. Board of Education, 23, 146–47,
148, 150, *152*, 174, 413, 558
busing and, 153
Civil Rights Act (1964) and, 151–53
civil rights movement and, 146–48, *152*
de jure vs. de facto, 147–48
equality and, 23, 163
federal courts and, 574
federal military force and, 148, *152*, 477,
477
Justice Department efforts, 153
Latino/a Americans and, 163, 165
southern resistance to, 147–48, *147*
U.S. Congress and, 150
school shootings, 181, 418
Schwarzenegger, Arnold, 360
SCLC (Southern Christian Leadership
Conference), 149, *152*, 419
Scott, Dred, 142
Scott, Shaun, *345*
scrutiny, levels of, 109, 147, 158, 160, 161,
174, 175, *175*
searches and seizures, 104, *105*, 122–24, *124*,
128, 558
Seattle Democracy Voucher Program, 344–46
Second Amendment, *11*, *105*, 119–20, *120*,
121, 122, 180–82, *203*
Second Continental Congress, 39–40

Second Founding, 40–42
    See also Constitutional Convention
Section 1983, 573
secularism, 288
Secure Communities program, 89, 166
Securities and Exchange Commission (SEC),
    521
segregation/desegregation
    See also Jim Crow era; school segregation/
        desegregation
    de jure vs. de facto, 147–48, 152
    housing policy and, 148, 150, 156, 163
    interstate commerce and, 151, *152*
    ongoing, 282
    political values and, 184
    public accomodations and, 148–49, 150,
        151
    "separate but equal" rule and, 23, 144–45,
        144, 146

select committees, *448*, **448**, 464–65
    (usually) temporary legislative committees
    set up to highlight or investigate a
    particular issue or address an issue
    not within the jurisdiction of existing
    committees

selection bias, 211, 217–19, **217** polling
    error that arises when the sample is
    not representative of the population
    being studied, which creates errors in
    overrepresenting or underrepresenting
    some opinions

selective benefits, 404–5, *405*

selective incorporation, 103–6, *104–5*,
    104, 125 the process by which different
    protections in the Bill of Rights were
    incorporated into the Fourteenth
    Amendment, thus guaranteeing citizens
    protection from state as well as national
    governments

self-incrimination clause, 125–26
self-sorting, 329
Senate
    advice and consent powers of, 465–66
    Constitutional amendment process and, 58
    Constitution on, 48
    election of 2020 and, 376, 381, 382–83
    federal court appointments and, 572
    filibuster, 452–53, *452*, 456, 458, 465,
        552
    foreign policy and, 49, 446
    Great Compromise and, 44
    vs. House of Representatives, 48, 431–32,
        431, 462
    impeachment and, 256, 466, 480, 492

lawmaking and, 456
party leadership in, 445, *446*, *456*
presidential appointments and, 51, 490,
    503, 522, 524, 528, 530, 534
presidential succession and, 492
recess appointments and, 503, 534, 561
Supreme Court appointments and, 453,
    465, 544, 552, 554–55
vice president's role, 491
Senate Committee on Foreign Relations, 446
Senate Finance Committee, 446
Senate Intelligence Committee, 248
Seneca Falls Convention (1848), 142–43, *143*

Senior Executive Service (SES), 522 the top,
    presidentially appointed management rank
    for career civil servants

seniority, 449 the ranking given to an
    individual on the basis of length of
    continuous service on a committee in
    Congress

sensationalism in media, 232, *232*, 233, 254

"separate but equal" rule, 23, 144–45,
    144, **144**, 146 doctrine that public
    accommodations could be segregated by
    race but still be considered equal

separation of church and state, 106–8

separation of powers, 47, 50, 51, *51* the
    division of governmental power among
    several institutions that must cooperate in
    decision-making

September 11, 2001, terrorist attacks
    bureaucracy and, 510, 520, 537
    federal government power and, 78, 93
    presidential agenda setting power and, 480
    presidential approval ratings and, 495
    traditional media and, 201
    trust/distrust in government and, 29
Seventeenth Amendment, 48
sex discrimination. *See* gender discrimination
sexual harassment, 161–62, 190, *191*
sexual misconduct guidelines, 112
sexual orientation
    See also LGBTQ Americans
    discrimination based on, 133, 158, 160,
        172–73
    freedom of speech and, 116, *116*
Shapiro, Robert, 207–8
sharing economy, 92
Shaw v. Reno, 352
Shays's Rebellion (1786–87), 42, *42*
Shelby County v. Holder, 155
Shelley v. Kraemer, 146
Sherman, Roger, 39–40

"shield laws," 117
Shinseki, Eric, 536
Sides, John, 284
Sierra Club, 408–9

signing statements, 500 announcements
    made by the president when signing bills
    into law, often presenting the president's
    interpretation of the law

Silver, Nate, 220

**simple random sample (probability sample),
    211** a method used by pollsters to select
    a representative sample in which every
    individual in the population has an
    equal probability of being selected as a
    respondent

Sinclair, Betsy, 190
Sinclair Broadcast Group (SBG), 239
"sit-lie" ordinances, 21
Sixth Amendment, *123*, 126, 162

slander, 117 an oral statement made in
    "reckless disregard of the truth" that
    is considered damaging to the victim
    because it is "malicious, scandalous, and
    defamatory"

Slants, The, 98–100, *99*, 133
slavery
    abolitionist movement, *141*, 142, 309, 334
    abolition of, 79, 143
    civil rights and, 141–42
    Founding and, 62–63
    fugitive slave clause, 79
    history of, 12, 141–42
    liberty and, 21
    nullification and, 86
    political parties and, 309, 334
    political values and, 184
    Three-Fifths Compromise, 44, *44*, 46
Slotkin, Elissa, *459*
Small Business Administration (SBA),
    516–17, 520
smartphones, 242
    See also cell phones
Smith v. Allwright, 568
SNAP. *See* Supplemental Nutrition Assistance
    Program
SNCC (Student Nonviolent Coordinating
    Committee), 149, *152*
Snopes.com, 248
Snowden, Edward, 22, 117, *117*, 526
Snyder v. Phelps, 116
social capital, 276

social desirability effect, 216–17, **217** the
    effect that results when respondents

in Articles of Confederation, 40
ballot measures, 9, *291*, 292, 359–60, 417
bureaucracies of, 511, 526
capital punishment provisions, 126–27
civil liberties and, 103–6
Congressional representation, 43–46, *45*
Constitutional amendment process and, 58
coronavirus pandemic and, 380
devolution and, 86–89
electoral laws, 26, 155–56, 292–93, 296, *297*, 298, *298*
expressed powers and, 48–49
federal military force and, 477
grand juries and, 124–25
gun control and, 86, *86*, 119–20, *120*, *121*
immigration and, 167, *169*
Jim Crow era and, 83
judicial appointments, *553*
judicial review and, 556, 558
LGBTQ rights and, 132–33
lobbying for, 394–95, 402
local governments and, 76
obligations among, 73–74, 76
powers under federalism, 73, 74, 78
professional associations and, 401
recall elections, 360
reciprocity among, 50
segregation and, 147–48, 151–52
state of emergency declarations and, 488, *488*
supremacy clause and, 50, 73, 556, 558
Supreme Court and, 49, 103–6
unfunded mandates and, 87–88
voting rights and, 145, 154–56, *155*

states' rights, 84, 86 the principle that the states should oppose the increasing authority of the national government; this principle was most popular in the period before the Civil War

Steering and Policy Committee, 445
Stein, Jill, 188, *337*
Stepien, Bill, *361*
Stevens, John Paul, 118, 120
Stewart, Potter, 118
Steyer, Tom, 188, 372
stimulus legislation
See also coronavirus stimulus legislation
Great Recession and, 28
St. Mary's Honor Center v. Hicks, 175
stock market. *See* investment
Stone, Harlan F., 568
Stonewall riots (1969), 172
stop and frisk tactics, 124

straight-ticket voting, 349 selecting candidates from the same political party for all offices on the ballot

Strategic National Stockpile, 2–4, *3*, 509
streaming video, 240–41, 366–67
strict construction, 62, 571

strict scrutiny, 109, **147**, 160, 175, *175* a test used by the Supreme Court in racial discrimination cases and other cases involving civil liberties and civil rights that places the burden of proof on the government rather than on the challengers to show that the law in question is constitutional

structural remedies, 574
Student Nonviolent Coordinating Committee (SNCC), 149, *152*
student speech, 112, 114, *115*

substantive representation, 54, 433, **433** a type of representation in which a representative is held accountable to a constituency if he or she fails to represent that constituency properly; this is incentive for the representative to provide good representation when his or her personal background, views, and interests differ from those of his or her constituency

suburban areas, 156, 323, 381, 384, 387

suffrage, 268 the right to vote; also called *franchise* *See also* voting rights; women's suffrage

Sugar Act (1764), 38
superdelegates, 355

Super PACs (527 committees), 279, 314–15, 366, 370, 372, **414**, 416, 440 nonprofit independent political action committees that may raise unlimited sums of money from corporations, unions, and individuals but are not permitted to contribute to or coordinate directly with parties or candidates

supremacy clause, 50, 56, 73, **556**, 558 Article VI of the Constitution, which states that laws passed by the national government and all treaties are the supreme law of the land and superior to all laws adopted by any state or any subdivision

Supreme Court
See also specific cases, e.g. Dred Scott v. Sanford
on abortion, 130, *130*, 131, 132, 413, 562, 570–71

access to, 561–63
on affirmative action, 174–75, *175*, 569, 571
on Affordable Care Act, 90, 108, 556, 569–70
anti-terrorism and, 560
appeals to, 549
appointments to, 378–79, 453, *465*, 543–44, 552, *552*, 554–55, *554*, 571
on assisted suicide, 84
on Bill of Rights, 102–3
bureaucracy and, 560, 573
on bureaucratic control, 535
on campaign finance, 110, *110*, 112, 366, 370–71, 416
caseload, 550
cases filed in, *563*
chief justice, 551–52
Civil Rights Act (1964) and, 151
class-action suits and, 573–74
on commerce clause, 79–80, *86*
on commercial speech, 115
Constitution on, 49–50, 551, 552
on cruel and unusual punishment, 126–28
on double jeopardy, 125
on eminent domain, 103, 129
on employment discrimination, 153–54
on executive agreements, 466
on executive privilege, 479
federal government power and, 79–80, 84, 86
on freedom of religion, 106–7, 108–9, *109*
on freedom of speech, 99, 109, 110, 112, 113, 114, 115, *115*
on freedom of the press, 116–17, 256
on gender discrimination, 160–61, 163
on gerrymandering, 351
on gun rights/gun control, 120
on immigration policy, 16, 165, 167, 168
influences on, 569–71
on inherent powers, 486
interest groups and, 565–66
interpretation of the Constitution, 62, 570–71
on interracial marriage, 74, 156–57, *157*, 174
on Japanese American internment, 170
judicial restraint/activism, 570–71
judicial review and, 50, 51, 62, 535, 555–56, 558–61
jurisdiction of, 548, 550, 558, 561–62
on language minorities, 170
law clerks and, 564–65, *564*
on law enforcement, 558
on LGBTQ rights, 132–33, 172–73
on medical marijuana, 90

campaign advertising and, *366*
campaign consultants and, *361*
campaign finance and, 274, 279, 369, 372
census and, 480
Consumer Financial Protection Board
	and, 534
coronavirus stimulus legislation and,
	394–96, *395*
criminal investigations into, 378
debates and, *232*, 314, 367, *367*
Democratic Party and, 337
devolution and, 87
divisions within Republican Party and,
	318–19
election of 2020 legitimacy and, 383–84
electoral college and, 273, 357, 369,
	386
electoral laws and, 298
emotional appeals and, 190
environmental policy and, 204, 513
evangelicals and, 288, 387
executive orders and, 498
executive privilege and, 480
fake news accusations by, 118, 249, 377
filibuster and, 453
freedom of speech and, 112
free media and, 366
gender gap and, 195, *195*, 286, 324
government regulation and, 84
gun control and, 122, 182
health care and, 380, 459, 481, 492, 500
integrity and, 375
interest groups and, 414
Kamala Harris and, 492
Latino/a Americans and, 284, 323, 377,
	387, 388
lobbying and, 409, 411, *411*
media framing and, 255
media profit motive and, 233
misinformation and, 68, 205, 243, 244,
	248, *495*
nomination, 311
nonenforcement of laws and, 500
PACs and, 416
pardons and, 478
party polarization and, 327, 377, *378*
policy czars and, 530
political appointees, 522, 524, 528
political ideologies and, 188
popular vote and, 348
pork barreling and, 454
presidential diplomatic power and, *478*
primary elections and caucuses and, 348,
	353–54, 367, 379
privatization and, 527
public health and, 380
public opinion and, 200

public-opinion polls and, 217–18, *217*
racial injustice protests (2020) and, 381
Russian election interference investigations
	and, 200, 257, 465, 480, 491
sensationalism in media and, 233
social media and, 200, *202*, 205, 243–44,
	244, 274, 276, 284, 319, 495, *495*
socioeconomic status and, 308
state of emergency declarations, 478, 482,
	488
State of the Union addresses, 378, *378*,
	480
Supreme Court appointments and, 131,
	378–79, 543, 552, 555, 570, 571
Supreme Court decisions and, 570
tax policy and, 207, 407, 481
Tea Party movement and, 306
trade policy, 167, 198, 377
transgender Americans and, 161, 497, 498
Trump's coronavirus diagnosis, 245, 380
trust/distrust in government and, 29
trust/distrust in media and, 249
Ukraine scandal, 252, 256, 320, 378, 467,
	535–36
veto and, 482
voter demographics and, 280, 281, 284,
	285, 286, 288, 323, 325, 327
voter mobilization and, 284, 314
voting by mail and, 298, 382
Trump, Ivanka, 490
Trump, Melania, 245, 493, *493*
Trump administration foreign policy
	election of 2020 and, 380
	Muslim ban, 168, 486, 561, *561*
	North Korea and, *478*, 496
	signing statements and, 500
Trump administration immigration policy
	birthright citizenship and, 106
	DACA and, 166
	divisions within Republican Party and,
		318–19
	election of 2016 and, 167, 318, 374
	election of 2018 and, 285
	election of 2020 and, 380
	executive orders and, 377, 497–98
	family separation and, 166–67, *167*
	ICE raids, 194, 196
	Latino/a American voter turnout and,
		285
	Mexico border wall, 167, 318, 374
	Muslim ban and, 167–68
	protest and, *166–67*
	racial discrimination and, 377
	Republican Party and, 377
	sanctuary cities and, 89–90
	state of emergency declaration, 478
	voter demographics and, 324

Trump impeachment, *467*, 503
	congressional decision-making and, 462
	executive privilege and, 480
	Kamala Harris and, 492
	media and, 256
	party polarization and, 378
	political nature of, 467
	political parties and, 320
	Republican Party and, 492
	whistleblowers and, 536
Trump International Hotel, 411
Trump v. Hawaii, 486, 561
trust/distrust in government
	demographics and, 29–30, *29*, 198
	emotional appeals and, 190
	international comparisons, *199*
	limited government and, 5
	voter turnout and, 271

trustee, 432 a representative who votes based
	on what he or she thinks is best for his or
	her constituency

Tubman, Harriet, *141*

turnout, 271 the percentage of eligible
	individuals who actually vote
	See also voter turnout

Tweeting to Power (Gainous and Wagner), 243
Twenty-Fifth Amendment, 492
Twenty-First Amendment, 60
Twenty-Fourth Amendment, 154
Twenty-Seventh Amendment, 62
Twenty-Sixth Amendment, 26, *59*, 270, **347**
Twitter
	See also social media
	advertising and, 236
	alarm vs. patrol modes and, 252
	big data and, 219–20
	congressional use of, *436*
	foreign policy and, 496
	misinformation on, 205, 243, 244, 278,
		495
	news on, 235, 241, 242, 243
	political knowledge and, 205, 206
	political participation and, 273
	politicians' use of, 239
	public opinion and, 200
	Russian election interference and, 205, 278
	Trump's use of, 200, *202*, 205, 243–44,
		244, 319, 495, *495*
	voter mobilization and, 274, 284

two-party system, 309–10, **309**, 320, 330,
	339, 349 a political system in which only
	two parties have a realistic opportunity to
	compete effectively for control

Tyler, John, 492

tyranny, 54, 56 oppressive government that employs cruel and unjust use of power and authority

U

Ukraine scandal (2019), 252, 256, 320, 378, 467, 535–36
UN. *See* United Nations
unauthorized immigrants. *See* undocumented immigrants
Uncivil Agreement (Mason), 196, 329–30
Underground Railroad, 142
undocumented immigrants, 16–17, 106, 165, 166, *166, 168, 169,* 194
unemployment, 81, 387
See also unemployment insurance
unemployment insurance, 88, 395, 512

unfunded mandates, 87–88 laws or regulations requiring a state or local government to perform certain actions without providing funding for fulfilling the requirement

Unified Combatant Commands, 520
unions. *See* organized labor
unitary executive theory, 482–83

unitary systems, 71, *85* centralized government systems in which lower levels of government have little power independent of the national government

United Airlines, 244–45
United Farm Workers (UFW), 165, 421
United Nations (UN), 259
United States v. Curtiss-Wright Export Corp., 486
United States v. Grubbs, 123
United States v. Jones, 123
United States v. Lopez, 86
United States v. Nixon, 479
United States v. Playboy Entertainment Group, 118
United States v. Wong Kim Ark, 170
universities. *See* higher education
upper classes. *See* wealthy Americans, influence of
urbanization, 19
See also urban/rural divisions
urban/rural divisions
election of 2020 and, 384–86
party polarization and, 196
political parties and, 323, 462
redistricting and, 20, 350, 443
regional differences and, 326
USAJobs, 531
USA PATRIOT Act (2001), 93
U.S. Chamber of Commerce, 399, 420, *420,* 473

U.S. Commission on Civil Rights, 154
U.S. Patent and Trademark Office, 99

V

values (beliefs), 5, **183** basic principles that shape a person's opinions about political issues and events
See also political culture

agreement on, 183–85, *185, 186*
federalism and, 73
immigration and, 14
values lobbying, 418
Van Duyne, Beth, *312*
Van Orden v. Perry, 107–8
Vavreck, Lynn, 284
venue shopping, 93
vesting clause, 475, 482
Veteran Affairs, Department of, 511, 532, 536
Veterans Health Administration (VHA), 536

veto, 49, 51, **454,** 481–82, *481,* **481,** 500 the president's constitutional power to turn down acts of Congress; a presidential veto may be overridden by a two-thirds vote of each house of Congress

Vice, 238
vice presidency, 491–92, *492*
Vietnam War
adversarial journalism and, 201, 257, *257*
class-action suits and, 574
Democratic Party and, 335
executive agreements and, 466
freedom of the press and, 117
media and, 250
media leaks and, 256, 257
protest and, *152,* 270
voting rights and, 26, 270
Virginia, 267, *269*

Virginia Plan, 43 framework for the Constitution, introduced by Edmund Randolph, that called for representation in the national legislature based on the population of each state

Volkswagen, 513
voter demographics
economic inequality and, 281
economic policy and, 284
election of 2008, 26, 281, 282
election of 2012, 281, 282, 284, 286
election of 2016, *27,* 280, 281, 284, 285, 286, 288, 323, 326
election of 2018, *27,* 271, 280, 281, 282, 284, 285, 286, 323

election of 2020, 280, 281, 282, *284,* 285, 286, 323, *324,* 326–27, 354, 379, *379,* 384–86
political parties and, 143, 285, 287, 308, *308,* 323–27, *324, 325, 326, 327, 333,* 336
public policy and, 280–81, 284, 285, 286
turnout and, *27,* 271, 272, 279–82, *283,* 284–88
voter fraud, 155–56
voter ID laws, 26, 155–56, 293, 296
voter mobilization
campaign activism and, 416–17
digital political participation and, 274
election of 2020, 314, *368,* 388, 416–17
emotional appeals and, 190
micro-targeting and, 312
personal contact and, 289–90, *290, 312,* 314, 364, *368*
primary elections and caucuses and, 290
public-opinion polls and, 369
young Americans and, 280–81
voter registration, 292–93, 294, *295,* 312, 346, *347*
voter suppression
See also racial discrimination
current conditions, 139, 154, 296, 558
Latino/a Americans, 163
Russian election interference and, 278
voter ID laws and, 26, 155–56, 293, 296
voter turnout
See also voter mobilization; youth vote
ballot measures and, 360
campaign finance and, 345
current trends, 271, *272*
decline in, 26
demographics and, *27,* 271, 272, 279–82, *283,* 284–88
early America, 268
election of 2008, 26, *27,* 271, 307
election of 2014, *27*
election of 2016, 26, 271, 284, 307
election of 2018, *27,* 271, 416–17
election of 2020, 26, 271, 298, 307, 376, 381–82, 388, 389, 417
interest groups and, 416–17
international comparisons, 271, *275,* 288
primary elections and caucuses, *313*
state electoral laws and, 292–93, 296, *297,* 298, *298*
voting
See also voter mobilization; voter suppression; voting rights
absentee, 290, 298, 352, 365
early, 298, 382
how to register and vote, 294–95, *295*
ranked choice, 339, 348, 359, 360

state electoral laws, 26, 155–56, 292–93, 296, *297*, 298, *298*

voter decisions, 373–75

voter ID laws, 26, 155–56, 293, 296

voter registration, 292–93, 294, *295*, 312, 346, *347*

voting by mail, 156, 184, 290, 296, 298, 312, 382, *384*

voting rights, 268–72

See also African American voting rights; women's suffrage

age and, 26, 270, *347*

Constitutional amendments and, *59*

felons, 138–39, *139*, 157–58, 296

immigrants, 269

language minorities, 154, 170–71

Latino/a Americans, 154–55, 163, 165

original restrictions on, 8, 23, 25, 268

political parties and, 235

as political value, 184

young Americans, 26

Voting Rights Act (VRA) (1965), 26, 270, *347*

current voter suppression and, 154

Democratic Party and, 336

impact of, *155*

1970 and 1975 amendments, 171

on preclearance, 155

protest and, *152*

redistricting and, 352, 444

Vought, Russ, *529*

Vox, 238

VRA. *See* Voting Rights Act

W

Wagner, Kevin, 243

Walker, Scott, 360

Wallace, George, *152*

Wall Street Journal, 234, 237, 256

war, declaration of, 484

Wards Cove Packing Co., Inc. v. Atonio, 175

WarnerMedia, 238

War of 1812, 332

war on drugs, 123, 157

War on Poverty, 83, *152*

War Powers Resolution (1973), 484

Warren, Earl, 125, 551–52, 570

Warren, Elizabeth, 378, 379, 534, *535*

Washington, George, 42, 309, 517

Washington Post, 234, 235, 237–38, 256, 257

Washington Redskins football team, 99–100, 556

Washington State, 298, 440

watchdog role of the media, 231, *231*, 244

Watergate scandal (1972)

campaign finance and, 414

congressional select committees and, 448

executive privilege and, 479, *479*

media and, 201, 257

Nixon resignation and, 492, 503

right to privacy and, 128

Watson, Gregory, 62

Watts, Shannon, *403*

wealth inequality. *See* economic inequality

wealthy Americans, influence of

See also business interests

American Revolution and, 38

campaign finance and, 112, 344, *370*, 371, 416, *417*

Citizens United v. Federal Election Commission and, 112, *370*

congressional representation and, 210, 371

Founding and, 41, 42–43, 46

interest groups and, 406, 407, 417

national conventions and, 354

party polarization and, 329

tax policy and, 198, 329

voter turnout and, 271

Webster v. Reproductive Health Services, 130, 413

web surfing, 246

wedge issues, 368

Weinstein, Harvey, 162

Weld, William, *337*welfare state, 87, 88, 214, 379

See also social policy

Westboro Baptist Church, 116, *116*

West Virginia, 440

West Virginia State Board of Education v. Barnette, 108

westward expansion, 39, 41

WhatsApp, 235

Wheeler-Howard Law (1934), 171

Whig Party, 332, *332*, 334

whip, 445 a party member in the House or Senate responsible for coordinating the party's legislative strategy, building support for key issues, and counting votes

Whistleblower Protection Act (1989), 535

whistleblowers, 244, 252, 256, 535–36, **535** federal employees who report wrongdoing in federal agencies

White Americans

See also race

citizenship, 16

election of 2020 and, 387, 388

evangelicals, 195–96, 288, *288*, 387

in-group identity and, 284

party polarization and, 377

political parties and, 323, 324, 325

presidency and, *485*

public opinion and, 192, *192*

public-opinion polls and, 217, 381

redistricting and, 444

Republican Party and, 281, 282, 284, 336

trust/distrust in government, 30

in U.S. population, 12, 14, 16

voter turnout, 281, 282, 284, 286

voting rights, 23, *59*, 267

White House Communications Office, 494–95

Whitehouse.gov, 496

White House staff, 490 analysts and advisers to the president, each of whom is often given the title "special assistant"

White nationalism, 267, 377

Whitmar, Bill, 68–69

Why Parties (Aldrich), 310

WikiLeaks, 256, *256*

Wilson, James, 46

Wilson, Woodrow, and administration, 145, *145*, 146, 257, 493

Windsor v. United States, 160

"winner take all" systems, 309, 354, 357

Wisconsin, recall elections, 360

women

See also gender; gender discrimination; women's rights movement; women's suffrage

Democratic Party and, 324

economic global equality, *164*

in electoral office, *159*, 287–88, *287*, 324, 382, *432*, 434, *434*, *437*

military service, 162, *163*

sexual harassment and, 161–62, 190, *191*

vice presidency and, 380, *491*, 492

Women's Campaign Fund, 287

Women's Equity Action League (WEAL), 160

Women's March, *268*

women's rights movement, 60, *60*, 142–43, 160, 413

women's suffrage

denial of, 141, 142

Nineteenth Amendment and, 26, *59*, *145*, 146, 270

organizations for, 145–46

Progressive movement and, 8

protest and, 143–44, *145*, 270, *270*

separate sphere and, 141

workplace. *See* employment

Works Progress Administration (WPA), *81*

World Anti-Slavery Convention, 142

World War I, 110

World War II

bureaucracy and, 526

civil rights movement and, 146

immigration policy and, 16, 170

inherent powers and, 484

Japanese American internment, 170, *170*

racial discrimination during, 146

WPA (Works Progress Administration), *81*

writ of appeal, 563
writ of certification, 563

writ of certiorari, 562–63, **562**, 565 a
decision of at least four of the nine
Supreme Court justices to review a
decision of a lower court; certiorari is
Latin, meaning "to make more certain"

writs of habeas corpus. *See* habeas corpus

Y

Yang, Andrew, 286
Yiannopoulos, Milo, 113, *114*

YouGov, 215, 216
young Americans
    See also age; youth vote
    digital news and, 239, *239*, 240
    political participation, 26, *27*, 242
    political parties and, 322, 323, 326–27
    social media use, *242*
    in U.S. population, 19
    voting rights, 26, *59*
youth vote
    election of 2018, *27*
    election of 2020, 280, 286, 326–27,
        384, 387

social media and, 242
voter mobilization and, 280–81
voter registration and, 292, 293
voting by mail and, 156
YouTube, 205, 235, 236, 240, *242*, 243, 273,
    276, 281, 314

Z

Zaller, John, 201–2
Zelensky, Volodymyr, 256
    See also Ukraine scandal
Zimmerman, George, 418
Zuckerberg, Mark, *113*, 228, 236

Voter Registration Information

State	Registration Deadline before Election	Early Voting Permitted?	Identification Required to Vote?*	More Information
Alabama	15 days	No	Photo ID required	alabamavotes.gov
Alaska	30 days	Yes	ID requested; photo not required	elections.alaska.gov
Arizona	20 days**	Yes	ID required; photo not required	azsos.gov/elections
Arkansas	30 days	Yes	Photo ID required	sos.arkansas.gov
California	15 days; Election-Day registration permitted	Yes	No	sos.ca.gov
Colorado	8 days by mail or online; no in-person deadline	Yes (all voting by mail)	ID requested; photo not required	sos.state.co.us
Connecticut	7 days by mail or online; no in-person deadline	No	ID required; photo not required	portal.ct.gov/sots
Delaware	Fourth Saturday prior to election	No	ID requested; photo not required	elections.delaware.gov
District of Columbia	21 days by mail or online; no in-person deadline	Yes	No	dcboee.org
Florida	28 days**	Yes	Photo ID requested	dos.myflorida.com/elections
Georgia	28 days	Yes	Photo ID required	sos.ga.gov
Hawaii	30 days; no in-person deadline	Yes (all voting by mail)	Photo ID requested	hawaii.gov/elections
Idaho	25 days; Election-Day registration permitted	Yes	Photo ID requested	idahovotes.gov
Illinois	28 days by mail; 16 days online; no in-person deadline	Yes	No	elections.il.gov
Indiana	29 days	Yes	Photo ID required	in.gov/sos/elections
Iowa	10 days; Election-Day registration permitted	Yes	Photo ID required	sos.iowa.gov
Kansas	21 days	Yes	Photo ID required	kssos.org
Kentucky	29 days	Yes	Photo ID required	elect.ky.gov
Louisiana	30 days; 20 days online	Yes	Photo ID required	sos.la.gov
Maine	15 days by mail**; no in-person deadline	Yes	No	maine.gov/sos
Maryland	21 days	Yes	No	elections.state.md.us
Massachusetts	10 days**	No	Photo ID requested	sec.state.ma.us
Michigan	15 days online or by mail; no in-person deadline	No	Photo ID required	michigan.gov/sos
Minnesota	21 days; Election-Day registration permitted	Yes	No	mnvotes.org
Mississippi	30 days	No	Photo ID required	sos.ms.gov
Missouri	Fourth Wednesday prior to election	No	ID requested; photo not required	sos.mo.gov
Montana	37 days by mail**; no in-person deadline	Yes	ID requested; photo not required	sos.mt.gov
Nebraska	Third Friday prior to election by mail; second Friday prior to election in person; 10 days online	Yes	No	sos.nebraska.gov
Nevada	28 days by mail; 21 days in person; 19 days online	Yes	No	nvsos.gov

State	Registration Deadline before Election	Early Voting Permitted?	Identification Required to Vote?*	More Information
New Hampshire	6–13 days before the election, varies by county; Election-Day registration permitted	No	ID requested; photo not required	sos.nh.gov
New Jersey	21 days	Yes	No	njelections.org
New Mexico	28 days by mail or online; Saturday before Election Day in person	Yes	No	sos.state.nm.us
New York	25 days	Yes	No	elections.ny.gov
North Carolina	25 days	Yes	No	ncsbe.gov
North Dakota	No voter registration required	Yes	ID required; photo not required	vote.nd.gov
Ohio	30 days	Yes	ID required; photo not required	sos.state.oh.us
Oklahoma	25 days	Yes	ID requested; photo not required	ok.gov/elections
Oregon	21 days	Yes (all voting by mail)	No	sos.oregon.gov
Pennsylvania	15 days	Yes	Only for first-time PA voters	votespa.com
Rhode Island	30 days; Election-Day registration permitted	Yes	Photo ID required	elections.ri.gov
South Carolina	30 days	No	ID requested; photo not required	scvotes.org
South Dakota	15 days	Yes	Photo ID requested	sdsos.gov
Tennessee	30 days	Yes	Photo ID required	tn.gov/sos/election
Texas	30 days	Yes	Photo ID requested	votetexas.gov
Utah	30 days by mail; 11 days in person or online**; Election-Day registration permitted	Yes (all voting by mail)	ID requested; photo not required	elections.utah.gov
Vermont	No registration deadline; Election-Day registration permitted	Yes	No	sec.state.vt.us/elections
Virginia	19 days**	Yes	ID requested; photo not required	elections.virginia.gov
Washington	8 days by mail and online; Election-Day registration permitted	Yes (all voting by mail)	ID requested; photo not required	sos.wa.gov/elections/
West Virginia	21 days	Yes	ID requested; photo not required	sos.wv.gov
Wisconsin	20 days by mail or online; Election-Day registration permitted	Yes	Photo ID required	myvote.wi.gov
Wyoming	14 days; Election-Day registration permitted	Yes	No	sos.wyo.gov

Sources: Project Vote Smart, www.votesmart.org/elections/voter-registration (accessed 11/16/20); National Conference of State Legislatures, www.ncsl.org (accessed 11/16/20); Ballotpedia, "Changes to Election Dates, Procedures, and Administration in Response to the Coronavirus (COVID-19) Pandemic, 2020," https://ballotpedia.org/Changes_to_election_dates,_procedures,_and_administration_in_response_to_the_coronavirus_(COVID-19)_pandemic,_2020#Voting_procedure_modifications_for_the_general_election (accessed 12/2/20).

* In states where an ID is "requested," voters who do not bring ID to the polls may be required to sign an affidavit of identity, vote on a provisional ballot, have a poll worker vouch for their identity, or take additional steps after Election Day to make sure their vote is counted.

**Provision in place due to COVID-19.

Note: To prevent large crowds from forming during the coronavirus pandemic, many states implemented vote-by-mail or early voting rules to vote in the 2020 primaries and general election. These rules may change once the public health emergency is over. Please go to vote.org or your secretary of state's website to learn more about how to vote in your state.